The way we once learned history . . .

. . . IS NOW HISTORY

Just as a panoramic image provides a broad view, *Panorama* provides a ground-breaking, broad view of the world's history by reaching across regional boundaries and highlighting large-scale, global patterns. *Panorama's* easily understood chronology, coupled with its innovative, proven digital tools, ensures that learners are always moving forward as they study change and continuity across time, assess knowledge gaps, and mold critical thinking skills. The result is improved course performance through greater understanding of our world's past, its large-scale global trends, and its impact on and relevance to 21st-century students.

Panorama is a program for the 21st Century

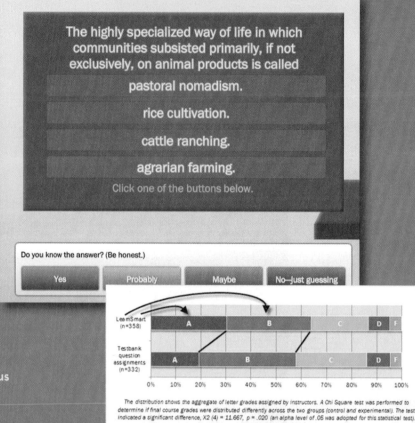

LEARNSMART®

LEARN BETTER WITH LEARNSMART

LearnSmart is the premier learning system designed to effectively assess a student's knowledge of course content through a series of adaptive questions. LearnSmart intelligently pinpoints concepts the student does not understand and maps out a personalized study plan for success. LearnSmart prepares students for class, allowing instructors to focus on higher-level learning.

THINK CRITICALLY WITH CRITICAL MISSIONS

Critical Missions immerse students as active participants in a series of transformative moments in history. As advisors to key historical figures, students read and analyze sources, interpret maps and timelines, and write recommendations. As part of each mission, students learn to think like an historian, conducting a retrospective analysis from a contemporary perspective.

CONNECT | HISTORY

SUCCEED FASTER WITH CONNECT HISTORY

Connect History strengthens the link between faculty, students and coursework. Innovative, adaptive technology aligns the goals of students and faculty, allowing them to work together to accomplish more in less time. It engages students in the course content so they are better prepared, more active in discussions, and able to excel.

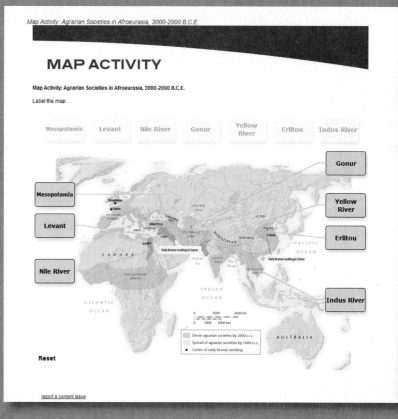

Mc Graw Hill Education | Campus

EASY ACCESS WITH MHCAMPUS

Enjoy Easy Access with MHCampus, which integrates our digital tools into your school's course management system.   This integration provides single sign-on access for students and a comprehensive grade book for instructors allowing for easy tracking of students' progress as well as remediation on challenging topics. MHCampus ensures that students will master the learning outcomes and core objectives of their world history course.

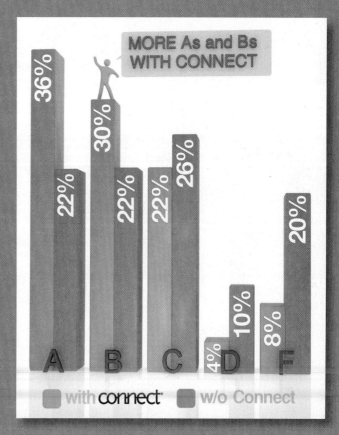

Praise for *Panorama*

"Finally, a world history text that puts human history on world time! Focused on humankind as a whole and its interactions over time, *Panorama* provides a conceptually organized and integrative approach to the human past."

Edmund Burke III, University of California, Santa Cruz

"*Panorama* demonstrates the promise of the 'new world history,' as revealed in the authors' skillful integration of far-reaching global connections with careful attention to the lives of individuals in specific places. Their discussion of peoples who are often found at the periphery of world history, such as Africans, is certain to push world historians and their students to diversify their historical perspectives."

Richard Warner, Wabash College

"This is an excellent text. Dunn and Mitchell's categories of analysis, global research, and their years of experience teaching world history are brilliantly displayed. For those of us who have been in the trenches teaching world history, we finally have a masterful global textbook by world history scholars who have extensive experience teaching such courses."

-Elaine Carey, St. John's University

"I think I've finally found a world history book that is truly 'world' in an intelligent and useful way. It's readable, its coverage is very good, and it has a clear analytical framework. I particularly like its environmental perspective."

-Phyllis Jestice, College of Charleston

"What makes *Panorama* unique is a truly comparative framework that is global in scope within successive eras. It lays a solid foundation for the development of individual societies in the Americas and the Pacific and the cooperative and competitive cultures of Afroeurasia before contact is established in the late 15th century. Then *Panorama* unfolds a gradual and impressive analysis of human interaction across the globe since that pivotal event."

-Ryan Thompson, Cleveland State Community College

"Students want to understand the order of events, but so often world history begins to look like stacked timelines. *Panorama*'s format helps to bring global issues and broad themes together in a manageable, chronological way. It also prompts students to think of other examples that they may already be aware of. "

-Erika Briesacher, Worcester State University

"This is a compelling text that makes me eager to teach World History as soon as possible! *Panorama* introduces issues of climate and geography to the human story in a truly profound and innovative way."

-Brian Black, Pennsylvania State University, Altoona

Panorama

A World History

ROSS E. DUNN

San Diego State University

LAURA J. MITCHELL

University of California, Irvine

McGraw Hill Education

PANORAMA: A WORLD HISTORY
Published by McGraw-Hill Education, 2 Penn Plaza, New York, NY 10121. Copyright © 2015 by McGraw-Hill Education. All rights reserved.
Printed in the United States of America. No part of this publication may be reproduced or distributed in any form or by any means, or
stored in a database or retrieval system, without the prior written consent of McGraw-Hill Education, including, but not limited to, in any
network or other electronic storage or transmission, or broadcast for distance learning.

Some ancillaries, including electronic and print components, may not be available to customers outside the United States.

This book is printed on acid-free paper.

1 2 3 4 5 6 7 8 9 0 DOW/DOW 1 0 9 8 7 6 5 4

ISBN 978-0-07-340704-3 (complete)
MHID   0-07-340704-6 (complete)
ISBN 978-0-07-748232-9 (volume 1)
MHID   0-07-748232-8 (volume 1)
ISBN 978-0-07-748233-6 (volume 2)
MHID   0-07-748233-6 (volume 2)

Senior Vice President, Products & Markets: *Kurt L. Strand*
Vice President, General Manager, Products & Markets:
  Michael J. Ryan
Vice President, Content Production & Technology Services:
  Kimberly Meriwether David
Managing Director: *Gina Boedeker*
Director: *Matt Busbridge*
Brand Manager: *Laura Wilk*
Director of Development: *Rhona Robbin*
Managing Development Editor: *Nancy Crochiere*
Development Editor: *Cynthia Ward*
Map Development: *Robin Mouat*

Brand Coordinator: *Kaelyn Schulz*
Digital Product Analyst: *John Brady*
Executive Marketing Manager: *Stacy Best Ruel*
Director, Content Production: *Terri Schiesl*
Content Project Manager: *Rick Hecker*
Senior Buyer: *Laura M. Fuller*
Design: *Matthew Baldwin*
Cover Image: © *2013 Michael Markieta*
Content Licensing Specialist: *Shawntel Schmitt*
Typeface: *9.75/12 Palatino LT STD*
Compositor: *Thompson Type*
Printer: *R. R. Donnelley*

All credits appearing on page or at the end of the book are considered to be an extension of the copyright page.

Library of Congress Cataloging-in-Publication Data

Dunn, Ross E.
    Panorama : a world history / Ross E. Dunn, San Diego State University, Laura J. Mitchell,
The University of California, Irvine.
      pages cm
    Includes bibliographical references and index.
    ISBN 978-0-07-340704-3 (complete : alk. paper) — ISBN 0-07-340704-6 (complete : alk. paper) —
ISBN 978-0-07-748232-9 (volume 1 : alk. paper)—ISBN 0-07-748232-8 (volume 1 : alk. paper) —
ISBN 978-0-07-748233-6 (volume 2 : alk. paper)—ISBN 0-07-748233-6 (volume 2 : alk. paper)
    1. World history—Textbooks. I. Mitchell, Laura Jane, 1963– II. Title.
  D21.D936 2015
  909—dc23

                        2013037646

The Internet addresses listed in the text were accurate at the time of publication. The inclusion of a website does not indicate
an endorsement by the authors or McGraw-Hill Education, and McGraw-Hill Education does not guarantee the accuracy
of the information presented at these sites.

www.mhhe.com

About the Authors

Ross Dunn

Ross Dunn is Professor Emeritus of History at San Diego State University, where he taught African, Islamic, and world history. In his early career he specialized in North African history, publishing *Resistance in the Desert: Moroccan Responses to French Imperialism, 1881–1912* (1977). Teaching world history inspired him to write *The Adventures of Ibn Battuta, a Muslim Traveler of the Fourteenth Century* (1987). This book is in its third edition. A leadership role in the project to write national standards for world history led to publication, with Gary B. Nash and Charlotte Crabtree, of *History on Trial: Culture Wars and the Teaching of the Past* (1997). In 2000 he edited the essay collection *The New World History: A Teacher's Companion.* He is an associate director of the National Center for History in the Schools at UCLA. In 2012 he received the annual Pioneers of World History award from the World History Association. He was the first elected president of that organization.

Laura J. Mitchell

Laura J. Mitchell is Associate Professor at the University of California, Irvine, where she teaches African and world history. She strives to make sense of early-modern societies in a digital age and to make history accessible to diverse audiences. Her research on colonial southern Africa has been supported by grants from Fulbright, the American Council of Learned Societies, the National Endowment for the Humanities, the UC Office of the President, and the Mellon Foundation. She has collaborated with a wide range of scholars and history educators, serving as president of the Forum on European Expansion and Global Interaction, as a member of the World History Association Executive Council, and as a co-chair of the AP World History Curriculum Assessment and Development Committee. Her book *Belongings: Property, Family and Identity in Colonial South Africa* (2009) won the American Historical Association's Gutenberg-e Prize.

Brief Contents

Contents

Settling the Planet
Beginnings to the First Millennium B.C.E.

part 1

Agrarian Societies and Their Interconnections   1200 B.C.E.–300 C.E.   part 2

Shifting Power, Thickening Webs
Afroeurasia, 200–1000 C.E.

part **3**

The Great World Convergence
1450–1750

part
5

The Modern World Takes Shape
1750–1914

part
6

An Interview with the Authors of *Panorama: A World History*

Ross Dunn and Laura Mitchell discuss how they came to write *Panorama* and how they believe it contributes to the study of the human past.

Q: Tell us about the unique approach you have taken in *Panorama*.

A: In *Panorama*, we have created a unified narrative of world history, assuming that the primary subject we are investigating is humankind as a whole, and the primary setting of the narrative is the globe. We have organized the chapters chronologically, by consecutive historical periods—never repeating a period from different regional or thematic angles. Our aim is to advance the mission of conceptualizing the human experience in ways that are more holistic and integrated. To do this, we have had to select the very broad developments that define particular historical periods and that we think readers ought to understand.

Q: Why did you choose this approach?

A: We wanted to contribute to the important work of making the history of humankind intelligible, to write a unified narrative that is clear and coherent and that gives readers a sturdy framework for thinking about the global past. We believe we can begin to understand big and rapid changes in the world today only if we have a mental scaffolding of ideas and words for thinking, talking, and writing about the world as a whole. Similarly, we can begin to grasp how the world got to be the way it is only if we have world-scale narratives that help us connect the histories of particular groups—nations, civilizations, religions, corporations—to patterns of change in human society writ large.

Q: How do you balance large historical generalizations with knowledge about particular peoples, places, and events?

A: We know from experience that if the presentation is too broad, abstract, or theoretical, students may have a hard time grasping the generalizations. But if the writing is too loaded with historical details (all of which may be significant at some level), then the big pictures of change tend to get lost in thickets of information about particular societies, individuals, conquests, wars, philosophies, artistic movements, and so on.

Like all writers of world history, we have made choices to leave out a great deal of perfectly useful and interesting knowledge. Only by doing this are we able to keep our sights on the panoramic view and on the unified narrative. We have also, however, aimed to write in concrete, descriptive language, recognizing that history is fundamentally about human beings, individually or in groups, thinking, working, fighting, and creating.

Q: How are you able to combine the telling of "large-scale" history with in-depth, "small-scale" knowledge of people and events?

A: In every chapter, we shift between larger- and smaller-scale narratives, but we aim consistently to relate developments at relatively small scales to those at much larger scales. We cannot understand the Industrial Revolution as the world event it was by studying just one English factory town, but historians might write about such a town as an example of how large-scale changes played out on a local level and affected people's lives.

Q: Does *Panorama* have a central theme?

A: Yes, it does. This theme is the growing complexity of human society from the early era of stone toolmaking to today. Looking over the very long term of history, we see a nearly continuous though by no means inevitable trend toward greater complexity in the relations of human groups with one another and with the earthly environment. This movement from lesser to greater complexity has been manifested across the ages in several nearly continuous trends of growth, even though the rates and dimensions of change in these areas have been uneven:

- Global population (more people and more groups interacting with one another)
- Human use of the planet's energy supply to produce food and other goods
- Human intervention to alter the natural and physical environment
- The intricacy and sophistication of technology and science
- The density and speed of systems of communication and transport

- The density of human networks of interchange, including movement of people, goods, and ideas
- The size of governments and their capacity to manage and control people
- The technical capabilities of weaponry to kill people and destroy property
- The size and elaborateness of systems of belief, including religions, ethical structures, and philosophies

Throughout the book, we pose the same question in different ways: How and why did the world move relentlessly toward greater cultural complexity, despite breaks and unevenness in that trend, for example, short-term drops in global population, periods of economic contraction, or the disappearance of particular languages and local religions?

Q: How did you decide on the topics for each chapter?

A: In aiming to write a unified narrative of history, we followed the basic principle of bringing to the fore historical developments that had (and may still have) an impact on relatively large numbers of people, that is, developments of large scale. We let these big developments generally determine the chronological frame of each chapter, and we investigate them in whatever geographical context seems appropriate for clear discussion of their importance. If most chapters focus in part on developments in a region, it is because a development of large-scale significance happened or started there in that particular period. For example, we devote a primary chapter section to developments in China under the Song dynasties of the eleventh and twelfth centuries because China in those centuries generated exuberant economic innovation and growth, a phenomenon that had effects all across the Eastern Hemisphere.

Q: What is distinctive about *Panorama*'s periodization of the past?

A: As a unified narrative, *Panorama* proposes a plan for dividing the past into specific chunks of time, with the beginnings and endings of those chunks determined by the important historical developments that occurred within them. Our periodization plan is a single chronology, or timeline moving from the remote to the recent past. One way that *Panorama*'s periodization differs from the majority of world history books is its greater attention to very early human history, that is, to the long paleolithic era that preceded the coming of agriculture. The whole paleolithic era (old stone age), which started perhaps 2.5 million years ago, constitutes about 99.6 percent of the history of humankind and its near biological ancestors. Attention to early history encourages readers to think about how and why humans made radical changes in the way they lived—taking up farming, building cities, creating mechanized industries, populating the world

with billions—when they got along without doing these things for hundreds of thousands of years.

Q: You refer to your narrative as "unified"; can you elaborate?

A: One element of our approach to a unified narrative is to conceive of Africa, Asia, and Europe together as a single land mass, a sort of "supercontinent" within which humans interacted, or at least had the physical possibility of interacting, since paleolithic times. As discussed in our Introduction, we refer to this supercontinent as Afroeurasia. For periods of world history up to 1500 c.e., we conceive of the world as divided into four primary geographical regions: Afroeurasia (where the great majority of human beings have always lived—about 86 percent today), the Americas (North and South together), Australia, and Oceania (the Island Pacific). Within these regions, human groups interacted with one another, though with greater or lesser intensity and from different chronological starting points. On the other hand, people did not interact, at least not in any sustained way, between one of these regions and another because wide expanses of ocean and to some extent contrasting climatic conditions prevented or discouraged it. For periods up to 1500 c.e., therefore, we explore developments in these regions in different chapters or sections of chapters, even though we also introduce points of historical comparison between one region and another. Starting in the late fifteenth century, the four regions began to throw out lines of communication to one another, though not all at once. The Great World Convergence, as we call it, began when sea captains established regular transport routes between Afroeurasia and the Americas. For periods after 1500, we treat the entire world as a single zone within which human interrelations became increasingly complex and large-scale developments occurred. From that chronological point to the present, all the chapters are global in scope.

Q: How does *Panorama* cover the significance of individuals—both men and women—in the course of human history?

A: *Panorama* endeavors to take full account of the historical fact that men and women share the planet. Even though much of the narrative is not explicitly gender specific, it aims to be "gender sensitive." This has meant repeatedly asking ourselves as we move from topic to topic how both men and women, whether aristocrats, city workers, peasants, or forager-hunters, acted as agents of change.

In every chapter of this book, the cast of characters is necessarily very large. We aim, however, to remind readers of the importance of individuals as agents of change by introducing a chapter feature titled "Individuals Matter." It presents a biographical sketch of an individual whose life in some way illuminates the period the chapter addresses. In most cases, this individual is a person of public importance, for example, Empress Wu of the Chinese Tang dynasty, or Diego Rivera, the twentieth-century Mexican artist. In a few chapters, however, the individual is an "ordinary" woman or man whose life or deeds illustrate some aspect of the period—for example, Ötzi, the ascribed name of a neolithic traveler in the Alps, or Olga Lisikova, a Russian combat pilot in World War II.

Q: Does *Panorama* incorporate primary sources?

A: Yes. A feature titled "Weighing the Evidence" appears in every chapter—and in the accompanying Connect History program—offering students an opportunity to critically examine a piece of historical evidence relating to the chapter content. The selection is usually a written document (for example, a nineteenth-century Moroccan diplomat's description of France), though in a few chapters a visual artifact (for example, an image of a giant stone head from ancient Mexico) is included. In some chapters, we present two pieces of evidence to compare with each other. "Weighing the Evidence" includes questions that prompt readers to analyze, interpret, and discuss the selection. This feature reminds readers that the *Panorama* narrative rests on the work of thousands of professional historians and other scholars who have examined, authenticated, and interpreted written documents, works of art, fossilized bones, and numerous other kinds of primary evidence.

Q: Is there a theme to your chapter-opening vignettes?

A: Yes. A key element of the trend toward greater complexity in world history has been the development of systems of communication that have allowed humans to move from one place to another and to create networks for exchanging ideas and things in increasingly complicated ways and at faster and faster speeds. To highlight this aspect of human complexity, we open each chapter with a brief story or vignette that has to do with some kind of communication, transport, or movement pertinent to the historical period under study. The subjects of these stories range widely from camel caravans to the profession of telephone operator.

Q: Is *Panorama* available as an e-book?

A: Even better—it is available as a SmartBook, which means not only that students can read it online, but they can quiz themselves after every section. The SmartBook then adapts to their response, highlighting areas in the narrative that they need to study more.

Q: Are any other digital resources available?

A: Absolutely. The Connect History program offers activities with *Panorama*'s maps, primary sources, key concepts and terms, as well as auto-gradable test items and essay questions.

Panorama: A New View of World History

Panorama presents the big picture: a unified chronological narrative of world history that gives students a valuable framework for thinking about the global past.

part 3

Shifting Power, Thickening Webs
Afroeurasia, 200–1000 C.E.

I f in the very long term human history has been a story of more and more people sharing the planet, while inventing increasingly complex of ways of organizing themselves, interacting with one another, and exploiting the earth's energy to their own benefit, this trend has not been entirely steady. Within the overall movement toward greater complexity, there have been cycles in which population has declined and recovered, cities have shrunk and flourished again, and economies have contracted and expanded. These cycles may be merely regional in scope, but they have also had interregional or even global dimensions, as we have seen in modern times when business recessions reverberate quickly around the world. The three chapters in Part 3 encompass approximately eight hundred years in the history of Afroeurasia, an era when the demographic and economic trends of the previous millennium temporarily slowed down or even reversed themselves, before accelerating again at an even faster pace.

The third century C.E., where Part 3 begins, represents a jarring break—in some places violent and destructive—in the prevailing pattern of population and economic growth. Between about 200 and 600, the Han, Kushana, Parthian, and western Roman empires all collapsed. These upheavals occurred partly in connection with the aggressive migrations of peoples from the Inner Eurasian steppes to neighboring agrarian lands. Western Europe, North Africa, northern India, and northern China all experienced serious economic turmoil. Disease epidemics that swept around the Mediterranean rim and across Southwest Asia in the sixth century had similar consequences. Conditions of life in several regions became harsh enough that Afroeurasia's overall population declined by several tens of millions between the third and seventh centuries, perhaps the first significant drop since the invention of agriculture.

A terra-cotta camel and rider from the era of the Tang dynasty in China.

246

Panorama's seven parts correspond to seven eras of global history. Within each part, chapters are organized chronologically by consecutive historical periods, never repeating a period from different regional or thematic angles. This organization gives students the mental scaffolding needed to think about the world as a whole. Each part-opening spread previews the major trends of the global era and includes both a time-band placing that period in the larger context of world history and a graph illustrating the era's population growth.

into deep ...sanid Per-...d invaders. ...large part ...ern China, ...y escaped ...te regional ...n the Inner ...a to South-...an suffered

...d economic ...asia:

...China ...dynasties ...f technical ...owing

...e mid-...e effect on ...iles, pep-...across

■ In western Africa, merchants who discovered the hardy qualities of the dromedary camel set up commercial operations that connected the Mediterranean lands with West Africa. This pioneering enterprise, well under way by the seventh century, lubricated the whole Afroeurasian exchange system with injections of West African gold.

■ Assaults of Eurasian nomads on China, India, and Southwest Asia tailed off. In the steppes new warrior empires arose in the sixth century, but they also stabilized political conditions and recharged silk road commerce. In the late first millennium, Europe endured an incursion of Magyar warriors from the steppes, but these intruders settled down quickly.

■ Finally, invaders from the Arabian Desert, who proclaimed Islam as a new universalist religion, politically united most of Southwest Asia, a region of agricultural and urban productivity that had been divided between rival states for nearly a thousand years. The cities of Southwest Asia had for millennia funneled commercial goods and new ideas along a corridor that connected the Mediterranean basin with the whole expanse of Asia

and eastern Africa. Following unification under Arab leadership, that corridor became more animated than ever before. From Southwest Asia, Arab soldiers, preachers, and merchants introduced Islam along the routes of conquest and trade. This new expression of monotheistic faith drew on the teachings of both Judaism and Christianity, and it put great emphasis on social cooperation and codes of proper ethical and legal behavior. Thus, Islam joined Buddhism and Christianity as a universalist faith offering the promise of community harmony and individual salvation. Together, these three religions reached just about every part of Afroeurasia in the late millennium.

Between 200 and 1000 C.E. migrant farmers, long-distance merchants, conquering armies, and wandering missionaries brought more of Afroeurasia into a single arena of human interchange. This happened without any revolutionary breakthroughs in communication and transport technology, though artisans and engineers tinkered endlessly with ship designs, navigational tools, and more efficient systems of banking and credit. By the end of the millennium, signs of new economic growth and social complexity were abundant. Afroeurasia's overall population climbed nearly back to where it had been eight hundred years earlier. Interlinked commercial networks operated across the breadth of Afroeurasia. China was moving into an era of unprecedented industrial growth. And after suffering a half-millennium of chronic disorder, western Europeans were building a new urban civilization.

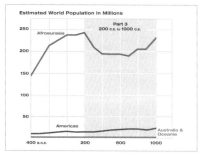

247

A Panoramic View

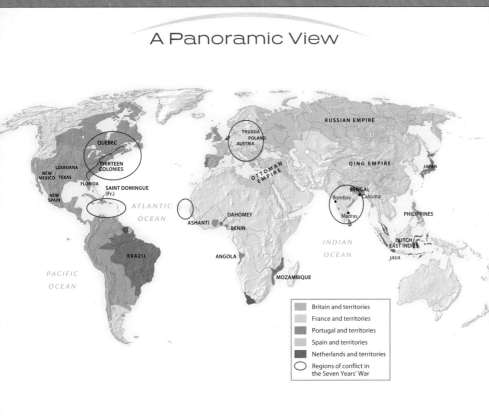

MAP 20.1 Major states and colonial territories after the Seven Years' War (1756–1763).

Empires claimed huge swaths of territory—some in contiguous stretches of land and others overseas. Desire for even more territory and wealth fueled rivalries among empires. What aspects of this political map of states after the Seven Years' War might explain the global nature of that conflict among European powers?

Panorama's maps are designed for optimal classroom projection as well as pedagogical clarity (see Map List, pp. xxvii–xxviii). Maps titled "A Panoramic View" at the beginning of each chapter provide a big-picture overview for the narrative. Within each chapter, additional maps zoom into the regional or local level or provide other views. Questions for each map engage students in thinking about geography and history.

Connect History, an online learning tool, offers 28 interactive maps that actively engage students, supporting geographical as well as historical thinking. These dynamic maps allow students to selectively focus on elements of the map. For example, they can examine the spread of specific crops one at a time, then reconstruct the full global process of agricultural diffusion. Other interactive maps enable students to analyze periodization, comparing changing political boundaries or the spread of technology over time.

MAP 13.2 Mongol states and their neighbors, 1300.

What geographical or ecological features might help account for the Chagatai khanate being the economically weakest of the four great Mongol states?

MAP 24.1 States and colonial dependencies, 1910.

On the eve of World War I, western European countries, the United States, and Japan claimed or administered large parts of Africa, Asia, and the Island Pacific. Which countries claimed the largest overseas empires?

Each chapter offers students the opportunity to examine historical evidence through a **Weighing the Evidence** selection. The primary sources in these boxed features include public and private documents, visual sources, and material artifacts; sometimes two sources are presented for comparison. A headnote puts the source in context, and a series of questions after the source challenges students to think deeply and analytically about its significance.

Weighing THE EVIDENCE

Frantz Fanon on the Shortcomings of the National Bourgeoisie

One of the most influential texts to emerge from colonial independence movements is Frantz Fanon's The Wretched of the Earth. Fanon (1925–1961) came from a middle-class family on the French Caribbean island of Martinique. During World War II he went to North Africa to join the Free French resistance against the Germans. He was wounded in battle and awarded the Croix de Guerre. After the war he studied medicine and psychiatry in France. There, he became starkly aware of the limits of social assimilation. Though he had grown up in a thoroughly French environment and fought for the country, whites never viewed him as an equal. His interest in the psychological effects of colonialism resulted in his first book, Black Skin, White Masks (1952).

In 1953 Fanon accepted a position at an Algerian psychiatric hospital and gave support to FLN revolutionaries. He became acutely aware, through experiences of his patients, of the violent foundations of French colonial rule. In 1956 the French government expelled him from Algeria. He then moved to Tunisia where he continued his work on behalf of Algerian independence.

Suffering from terminal leukemia, Fanon wrote The Wretched of the Earth in 1961. The book attracted notoriety for its apparent approval of violence as a means to end colonial rule. Fanon recognized, however, that both perpetrators and victims of violence can never escape its psychological effects. In subsequent essays he explained that revolutionary violence must be short lived, or it will destroy all whom it touches.

In the excerpt below, he discusses how the nation (here referring to a body of people with shared political goals) must negotiate the transition from colonialism to independence. Within a general Marxist framework of class struggle, Fanon argues that the indigenous colonial bourgeoisie are ill equipped to lead the nation because they have identified with the values of their capitalist colonial oppressors and lost touch with the masses.

The national middle class which takes over power at the end of the colonial regime is an under-developed middle class. It has practically no economic power, and in any case it is in no way commensurate with the bourgeoisie of the mother country which it hopes to replace. . . .

Seen through its eyes, its mission has nothing to do with transforming the nation; it consists, prosaically, of being the transmission line between the nation and a capitalism, rampant though camouflaged, which today puts on the masque of neocolonialism. The national bourgeoisie will be quite content with the role of the Western bourgeoisie's business agent, and it will play its part without any complexes in a most dignified manner. But this same lucrative role, this cheap-jack's function, this meanness of outlook and this absence of all ambition symbolize the incapability of the national middle class to fulfill its historic role of bourgeoisie. Here, the dynamic, pioneer aspect, the characteristics of the inventor and of the discoverer of new worlds which are found in all national bourgeoisies are lamentably absent. In the colonial countries, the spirit of indulgence is dominant at the core of the bourgeoisie; and this is because the national bourgeoisie identifies itself with the Western bourgeoisie, from whom it has learnt its lessons. It follows the Western bourgeoisie along its path of negation and decadence without ever having emulated it in its first stages of exploration and invention, stages which are an acquisition of that Western bourgeoisie whatever the circumstances. . . . The national bourgeoisie will be greatly helped on its way towards decadence by the Western bourgeoisies, who come to

it as tourists avid for the exotic, for big-game hunting and for casinos. . . . Because it is bereft of ideas, because it lives to itself and cuts itself off from the people, undermined by its hereditary incapacity to think in terms of all the problems of the nation as seen from the point of view of the whole of that nation, the national middle class will have nothing better to do than to take on the role of manager for Western enterprise, and it will in practice set up its country as the brothel of Europe. . . .

If you really wish your country to avoid regression, or at best halts and uncertainties, a rapid step must be taken from national consciousness to political and social consciousness. . . . The battle-line against hunger, against ignorance, against poverty and against unawareness ought to be ever present in the muscles and the intelligences of men and women. . . . There must be an economic program; there must also be a doctrine concerning the division of wealth and social relations. . . . It is only when men and women are included on a vast scale in enlightened and fruitful work that form and body are given to that consciousness. . . . The living expression of the nation is the moving consciousness of the whole of the people; it is the coherent, enlightened action of men and women. . . . No leader, however valuable he may b[e] . . . [can substitute] himself for the popular will; and the nation[al government . . . ought first to give back their] dignity to all citizens.

Source: Frantz Fanon, *The Wretched of [the Earth]* (New York: Grove Press, 1965), 149, 1[5 . . .]

Thinking Critically

Why, in Fanon's view, does the national middle class feel a stronger relationship to the coloni[zing country than to] its own country? What do you think Fanon means by saying that the middle class will turn its [country into the brothel of] Europe? What do you think he means by the term "neocolonialism"? What problems must a [nation address if it is to] ensure its viability? From this selection, what can you infer about Fanon's views of those taki[ng the lead in newly indepen-] dent countries? In what ways, if any, does the selection reveal the influence of Marxism on F[anon's thought?]

Individuals MATTER

Queen Arsinoe II: Ruler of Ptolemaic Egypt

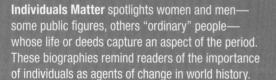

Coruler, high priestess, and goddess, Queen Arsinoe II (316–270 B.C.E.) was one of the most powerful royal women in Egypt's long dynastic history. Her father was the Macedonian general Ptolemy I, who founded the Ptolemaic dynasty following the death of Alexander the Great. About 300 B.C.E., when Arsinoe was fifteen or sixteen years old, her father arranged her marriage, an entirely political transaction, to Lysimachus, the sixty-one-year-old king who ruled territory on either side of the Bosporus Strait. The couple had three sons in rapid succession, but Agathocles, a child from Lysimachus's previous marriage, stood ahead of them in the line of royal succession. To improve her sons' political positions, as well as her own, Arsinoe accused Agathocles of plotting to kill his father. Consequently, Lysimachus ordered him executed, a vile act that triggered violent uprisings. In 281 B.C.E., less than a year after the murder, the elderly Lysimachus died in battle against Seleucus, ruler of the Seleucid empire of Persia.

When she lost her husband, Arsinoe fled to Macedonia. Once there, she soon accepted a second marriage, this time to her own half-brother Ptolemy Keraunos. Greeks generally regarded marriage between siblings as indecent, but Arsinoe and her new spouse took their cue from Egypt, where such royal unions were customary. Ptolemy Keraunos had

Arsinoe II strikes a characteristically Egyptian pose, but she sports a Greek hairstyle.

seized part of the dead Lysimachus's territories, and he assured Arsinoe that he would place her sons back in the line of succession as his adopted heirs. He deceived her, however, and fearing these sons as potential threats to his power, murdered the two younger boys, while the eldest escaped. Arsinoe fled once again, this time back to Egypt and the protection of her full brother Ptolemy II (r. 282–246 B.C.E.), who was by this time Egypt's king.

Arsinoe lost no time getting back on her feet and maneuvering for power. She persuaded Ptolemy II that his wife was plotting against him and deserved to be sent into exile. Ptolemy not only complied but also made Arsinoe his new queen. The evidence from surviving texts and images demonstrates convincingly that, although she lived only for another five or six years, she enjoyed equality with her husband-brother as coruler and may have governed more energetically than he did. Historians think she may have helped design the strategy that led to Egypt's victory in a war against the Seleucids for control of territory in Syria. She may also have supervised a major expansion of the Egyptian navy. She appears with her brother on some coins of the period but alone on others, implying her commanding status.

In the years leading to her death in 270 B.C.E. at about the age of forty-five, Arsinoe became not only priestess of her own cult, a typical practice among Egyptian rulers, but also a goddess, worshiped warmly during her own lifetime and for a long time after. A grand shrine was dedicated to her in Alexandria, and towns were named after her in Greece.

Historians, both ancient and modern, have often represented Arsinoe as conniving and power hungry, though these qualities were hardly rare among monarchs of the Hellenistic centuries. She doubtless exercised great political influence during her brief reign, and she offered a model for ambitious Ptolemaic queens that followed her. For example, Cleopatra VII (r. 51–30 B.C.E.), the last of the Ptolemaic rulers, adopted Arsinoe's crown as her own.

Thinking Critically

What political advantages might Arsinoe have gained by encouraging her subjects to worship her as a deity while she shared the throne with her brother?

families that lived there adopted an elegant part-Greek, part-Egyptian lifestyle. The city also attracted a large, multiethnic merchant population that made money supplying luxuries to the ruling class. The Hellenistic elite liked to think of the city as a kind of outpost of the Greek Aegean, not really *in* Egypt but merely *next to* it. Actually, native Egyptians made up the great majority of the population.

Public life in Hellenistic cities was as patriarchal, that is, as dominated by males, as it generally was in urban societies throughout Afroeurasia. We have some evidence, however, that in the bustling, impersonal climate of the larger cities, upper-class women had somewhat wider scope to pursue private interests than they had in fifth-century B.C.E. Athens, where a tight guard of male relatives kept them close

Individuals Matter spotlights women and men—some public figures, others "ordinary" people—whose life or deeds capture an aspect of the period. These biographies remind readers of the importance of individuals as agents of change in world history.

The Coming of Farmers: A Peculiar Event

FOCUS Why did humans in several parts of the world take up farming, given that our species had survived without it for 200,000 years?

The activity we call farming refers specifically to the technical process of *producing* food in a systematic way by planting, tending, and harvesting edible plants and by grazing domesticated animals on pasture. These new methods allowed humans to capture and consume much more of the sun's energy, the source of all plant life, than in earlier times. But coaxing food energy and surplus wealth from the soil involved more than tools and techniques. Woven into the activity are social habits, moral rules, and supernatural beliefs. Until the start of the industrial age barely more than 200 years ago, all complex societies were **agrarian societies,** based on farming as the primary way of life. And like the earlier colonization of the world, farming emerged as a consequence of human beings making countless everyday decisions century after century, though no one at the time could see where these experiments might be taking our species.

agrarian society A society in which agriculture, including both crop production and animal breeding, is the foundation of both subsistence and surplus wealth.

Change over Time

1582	Confucian scholars encounter Catholic Christian missionaries in China.
1632	Galileo Galilei offers proof of heliocentric theory of planetary motion.
1639	Russian explorers advancing across Siberia reach the Pacific.
1642–1660	The English Civil War involves temporary abolition of monarchy.
1643–1715	Louis XIV rules France, promoting absolutist principles.
1644	The Qing dynasty comes to power in China, replacing the Ming dynasty.
1648	The Peace of Westphalia proposes principles to guide international relations in Europe.
1652	Khoisan peoples of South Africa encounter Dutch East India Company (VOC) colonizers.
1654–1722	The Kangxi emperor expands China's land frontiers.
1675–1676	Native Americans unsuccessfully rebel against settlers in Massachusetts Bay Colony.
1682–1725	Peter the Great transforms Russia into a major European power.
1687	Isaac Newton publishes *The Principia*, detailing laws of gravity and motion.
1688	The Glorious Revolution in Britain limits the monarchy's power.
1689	China and Russia settle land frontier disputes with the Treaty of Nerchinsk.
1690	John Locke publishes *Two Treatises of Government*, criticizing absolutist government.
1690s	The Austrian Habsburg empire drives Ottoman forces out of Hungary.
1701–1714	The War of the Spanish Succession drains economies of western European states, especially France.
1713–1740	Frederick William I consolidates power in Prussia.
1792	Mary Wollstonecraft publishes *A Vindication of the Rights of Woman*, arguing for equal education for women.
Early 1800s	The Spanish American empire reaches its greatest territorial extent.

Instructor Resources for
Panorama: A World History

More Primary Sources in Create

The World History Document Collection in McGraw-Hill's Create (www.mcgrawhillcreate.com) allows you to choose from over 100 primary and secondary sources—each with a headnote and questions—that can be added to your print text. Create also allows you to rearrange or omit chapters, combine material from other sources, and/or upload your syllabus or any other content you have written to make the perfect resources for your students. You can search thousands of leading McGraw-Hill textbooks to find the best content for your students, then arrange it to fit your teaching style. When you order a Create book, you receive a complimentary review copy in three to five business days or an electronic copy (eComp) via e-mail in about an hour. Register today at www.mcgrawhillcreate.com and craft your course resources to match the way you teach.

Instructor Resources on the Online Learning Center

The Online Learning Center for *Panorama* at www.mhhe .com/panorama1e contains a wealth of instructor resources, including an Instructor's Manual, Test Bank, and Power-Point presentations for each chapter. All maps and most images from the print text are included. A computerized test bank powered by McGraw-Hill's EZ Test allows you to quickly create a customized exam using the publisher's supplied test questions or add your own. You decide on the number, type, and order of test questions with a few simple clicks. EZ Test runs on your computer without a connection to the Internet.

CourseSmart e-books

CourseSmart offers thousands of the most commonly adopted textbooks across hundreds of courses from a variety of higher education publishers. It is the only place for faculty to review and compare the full text of a textbook online, providing immediate access without the environmental impact of requesting a printed exam copy. At CourseSmart, students can save up to 50 percent off the cost of a printed book, and gain access to powerful web tools for learning, including full text search, notes and highlighting, and e-mail tools for sharing notes among classmates. Learn more at www.coursesmart.com.

McGraw-Hill Campus

McGraw-Hill Campus is the first-of-its-kind institutional service providing faculty with true single sign-on access to all of McGraw-Hill's course content, digital tools, and other high-quality learning resources from any learning management system (LMS). This innovative offering allows for secure and deep integration and seamless access to any of our course solutions such as McGraw-Hill Connect, McGraw-Hill Create, McGraw-Hill LearnSmart, or Tegrity. McGraw-Hill Campus includes access to our entire content library, including e-books, assessment tools, presentation slides, and multimedia content, among other resources, providing faculty open and unlimited access to prepare for class, create tests and quizzes, develop lecture material, integrate interactive content, and much more.

List of Maps

Acknowledgments

We undertook to write *Panorama* out of a conviction that we must construct holistic, integrated, earth-scale accounts of the past because they will surely help us understand how the world came to be the staggeringly complex place it is today. Such accounts may also help us imagine alternative futures for ourselves as the species that now dominates the earth but that nonetheless faces profound ecological, economic, and social challenges.

Writing a unitary history of humankind has required us to enter an enormous storehouse of historical and social scientific knowledge that other men and women have been filling over many years. We have explored this vast treasury for ideas—sorting, selecting, analyzing, and synthesizing them. A large team of reviewers, editors, designers, cartographers, educational technologists, professional colleagues, and family members have joined us in our mission to transform masses of knowledge into the twenty-eight chapters of *Panorama: A World History*. We offer warm thanks to the numerous instructors, listed separately, who critically and insightfully reviewed, and sometimes reviewed again, the draft chapters.

Our experience working with our editorial, design, and marketing team at McGraw-Hill Education has been nothing short of marvelous. We have worked day by day with a supremely talented publishing and editorial core group— Matthew Busbridge, Nancy Crochiere, Stacy Ruel, Cynthia Ward, Laura Wilk, and Robin Mouat. Their talents have continually amazed us. We would also like to thank Rick Hecker, Danny Meldung, Amy Marks, Kaelyn Schulz, Wes Hall, and Maureen West for their valuable contributions.

We owe warm thanks to the historians who contributed to the project by undertaking research, developing draft materials, and pointing out our errors. We especially thank Nicholas Bomba, Maura Cunningham, Ingrid de Haas, and Ian Kelly. Edmund "Terry" Burke III, a provocative and original world history thinker, read drafts of every chapter and demonstrated an uncanny ability to critique not just sentences and paragraphs but fundamental structures, concepts, and embedded assumptions. Elizabeth Cobbs Hoffman participated in the project for several years and contributed to early iterations of the text.

Ross Dunn writes:

I would never have attempted a project like this were it not for the enduring inspiration of Philip D. Curtin, Marshall G. S. Hodgson, and William H. McNeill, three world history pioneers who, knowingly or not, have shaped my entire teaching and scholarly career. I also thank the members of the San Diego State University history department who encouraged me to introduce a world history course in a decade when deep specialization was the prime qualification for academic success. I remember fondly the band of instructors that first team-taught world history at SDSU (Neil Heyman, William D. Philips, Charles D. Smith, Ray Smith, and Frank Stites). And I appreciate and admire the commitment several members of the department have made, notably under the leadership of Harry McDean and Joanne Ferraro, to perpetuate SDSU's reputation as a center of innovation in global, cross-cultural, and comparative history.

Then there are those colleagues and friends who have profoundly influenced the conceptual foundations of this book by simply feeding me intellectually, and often morally, as I have listened to their lectures and papers, chatted and e-mailed with them, visited their universities and homes, and shared good times. Among many others, these long-time friends and mentors include Terry Burke, David Christian, Bob Bain, Stan Burstein, Bill Cheek, Julia Clancy-Smith, the late Jerry Bentley, Susan Douglass, Tim Keirn, Paul Keeler, Howard Kushner, Craig Lockard, Patrick Manning, Gary Nash, Kevin Reilly, Linda Symcox, John Voll, and Merry Wiesner-Hanks.

The year after I started teaching at SDSU, I married Jeanne Mueller Dunn. My partnership with this remarkable, compassionate, and aesthetically gifted woman has moved into its fifth decade. I could not have written this book without her. Nor would I have undertaken it without the steadfast love and support of our daughters, Jordan and Jocelyn, and their wonderful families.

Laura Mitchell writes:

I have been lucky beyond measure to have joined two history departments that value world history as intellectual inquiry in its own right, and not just as a challenging teaching opportunity. My colleagues, first at the University of Texas in San Antonio and, since 2002, at the University of California, Irvine, have been a consistent source of support, knowledge both arcane and general, inspiration, and good humor.

The University of California Multi-Campus Research Group in World History, spearheaded by Ken Pomeranz and Terry Burke, enabled me to build on my foundation as an Africanist. The collegiality and experimentation of those MRG workshops enabled an assistant professor hired to address just one region of the world to embrace an ever-widening intellectual horizon. A New Directions Fellowship from the Mellon Foundation supported a year devoted to developing new skills working with visual sources, which profoundly shaped my subsequent teaching and research. The many graduate students engaged in world history at UCI have been central to my own development as a scholar and teacher. These pages reflect many robust conversations with them within and beyond the seminar room in Krieger Hall. My engagement with the Advanced Placement program in world history provided another community of exceptional interlocutors. I am grateful for each of these intellectual strands.

I have also been blessed with a joyous and supportive collective of family and friends who have offered encouragement, nourishment, fellowship, and love. You understood when our plans had to change and when I missed dinner. Thank you for putting up with me as I worked on this project and for realizing that a first draft isn't forever. Thank you especially to Graham and Ian, who have borne the intrusions on our family life with grace.

Reviewers and Advisors for *Panorama: A World History*

The authors and publisher would like to express their deepest gratitude to all those faculty members who read the manuscript, consulted on the digital program, did detailed fact-checking, and provided advice on content, images, maps, design, and cover concepts.

Board of Advisors

Carol Bargeron
Central State University

Brian Black
Pennsylvania State University, Altoona

Elaine Carey
St. John's University

Stephanie Field
University of Delaware

Phyllis Jestice
College of Charleston

Hallie Larebo
Morehouse College

Stephanie Musick
Bluefield State College

Ryan Schilling
Mississippi Gulf Coast Community College, Jackson

Ryan Thompson
Cleveland State Community College

Reviewers

Heather Abdelnur
Augusta State University

Jonathon Ablard
Ithaca College

Wayne Ackerson
Salisbury University

Calvin Allen, Jr.
University of Memphis

David Atwill
Pennsylvania State University, University Park

Carol Bargeron
Central State University

Michael Birdwell
Tennessee Tech University

Brian Black
Pennsylvania State University, Altoona

Beau Bowers
Central Piedmont Community College

James Brent
Arkansas State University, Beebe

Michael Brescia
SUNY, Fredonia

Erika Briesacher
Worcester State University

Michael Brose
University of Wyoming, Laramie

Gayle Brunelle
California State University, Fullerton

Edmund Burke III
University of California, Santa Cruz

Stanley Burstein
California State University, Los Angeles

Antonio Cantu
Ball State University

Elaine Carey
St. John's University

Robert Carriedo
U.S. Air Force Academy

Roger Chan
Washington State University

Dana Chandler
Tuskegee University

Mark Christensen
Assumption College

Edward Crowther
Adams State College

Edward Davies
University of Utah, Salt Lake City

Thomas Davis
Virginia Military Institute

Peter Dykema
Arkansas Tech University

David Eaton
Grand Valley State University

Gloria Emeagwali
Central Connecticut State University

David Fahey
Miami University of Ohio, Oxford

Edward Farmer
University of Minnesota, Minneapolis

Alan Fisher
Michigan State University

Nancy Fitch
California State University, Fullerton

Denis Gainty
Georgia State University

Steven Glazer
Graceland University

Steve Gosch
University of Wisconsin, Eau Claire

Gayle Greene-Aguirre
MGCCC Perkinston Campus

Christian Griggs
Dalton State College

Jeffery Hamilton
Baylor University

Casey Harison
University of Southern Indiana

John Hayden
Southwest Oklahoma State University

Linda Heil Wilke
Central Community College

Laura Hilton
Muskingum University

Stephanie Holyfield
University of Delaware

Aiqun Hu
Arkansas State University

Tamara Hunt
University of Southern Indiana

Erik Jensen
Miami University of Ohio, Oxford

Paul Jentz
North Hennepin Community College

Scott W. Jessee
Appalachian State University

Phyllis Jestice
University of Southern Mississippi

Amy Johnson
Berry College

Roger Jungmeyer
Lincoln University

Alan Karras
University of California, Berkeley

Pam Knaus
Colorado State University

Paul Kuhl
Winston-Salem State University

Brian LaPierre
University of Southern Mississippi

Hallie Larebo
Morehouse College

Jonathon Lee
San Antonio College

Anu Mande
Fullerton College

Susan Maneck
Jackson State University

Brandon Marsh
Bridgewater College

Nathan Martin
Charleston Southern University

Tim Mattimoe
Beaufort Community College

Chris Mauriello
Salem State University

Tim May
North Georgia College and State University

Tamba M'bayo
Hope College

Mark McLeod
University of Delaware

Eileen McMahon
Lewis University

Peter Mentzel
University of Utah

Garth Montgomery
Radford University

Jay Moore
University of Vermont

William Morison
Grand Valley State University

Stephanie Musick
Bluefield State College

Catherine Brid Nicholson
Kean University

Jim Overfield
University of Vermont

Alice Pate
Columbus State University

Daniel Pavese
Wor Wic Community College

Ruth Percy
University of Southern Mississippi

Matthew Perry
John Jay College of Criminal Justice

Amanda Podany
California State Poly University, Pomona

Kenneth Pomeranz
University of Chicago

Niler Pyeatt
Wayland Baptist University

Dean James Quirin
Fisk University

Dana Rabin
University of Illinois, Champaign

Stephen Rapp, Jr.
Georgia State University

Joshua Sanbron
Lafayette College

John Thomas Sanders
U.S. Naval Academy

Sharlene Sayegh
California State University, Long Beach

Pamela Sayre
Henry Ford Community College

Bill Schell
Murray State University

Ryan Schilling
MGCCC Perkinston Campus

Robert Scull
Craven Community College

Michael Seth
James Madison University

Munir Shaikh
Institute on Religion and Civic Values

Howard Shealy
Kennesaw State University

Brett Shufelt
Copiah Lincoln Community College

David Simonelli
Youngstown State University

Mary Ann Sison
Mississippi Gulf Coast Community
College, Jackson County

Corey Slumkoski
St. Francis Xavier University

Karla Smith
Mississippi Gulf Coast Community
College

Adam Stanley
University of Wisconsin, Platteville

Philip Suchma
St. John's University

Mark Tauger
West Virginia University, Morgantown

Ryan Thompson
Cleveland State Community College

Joel Tishken
Washington State University

Sarah Trebanis
Immaculata University

Michael Vann
California State University, Sacramento

Rick Warner
Wabash College

Merry Wiesner-Hanks
University of Wisconsin, Milwaukee

Richard Williams
Washington State University, Pullman

Carlton Wilson
North Carolina Central University

Panorama

A World History

Introduction

The Earth: World History's Theater

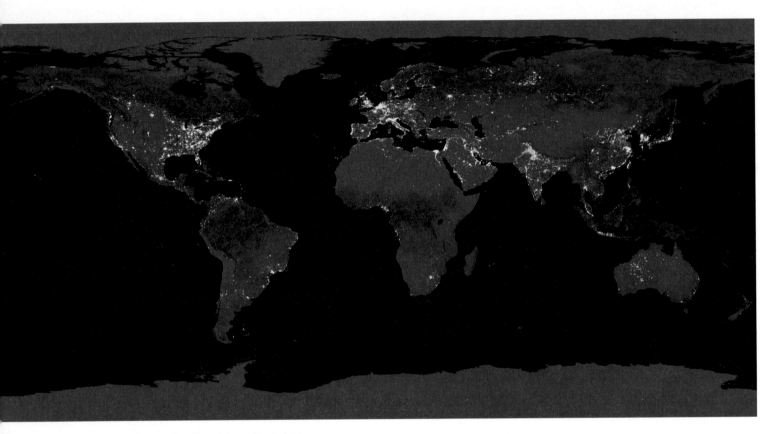

A composite satellite view of the earth at night.

ost of us spend our typical days (when not staring at cell phones or computer screens) in the company of friends, family, or work and school associates. But we are also connected, often unconsciously, to numerous other networks of human relationships that affect the course of daily life. Some of these "communities" may be fleeting (passengers sharing an airplane flying at 30,000 feet), and some may be very large (all members of the Greek Orthodox Church). No individual anywhere in the world is truly isolated from global relationships, not hunters in the Amazon rainforest, not peasants in high Himalayan valleys.

The global nature of change is not simply a matter of one event there (war in the Middle East) affecting some condition of life here (a rise in the price of gas). Nor is it just that products or ideas spread quickly from one place to another. The most striking feature of global interaction is that a significant development occurring in one place is likely to set off a complex chain reaction, disrupting and rearranging numerous relationships over an extensive area. A surge of change in one network of relationships, international trade for example, easily sparks changes in other networks, such as diplomatic negotiations or the migration of workers from one country to another.

As individuals we carry on our daily routines right in the midst of this tumultuous restructuring. We are shielded to some extent from its more jarring effects by our cultural and social bonds, some of them new, some long tested. Even so, all aspects of life are subject to disturbance and revision. The "cultures" that we like to think of as solid and enduring are themselves undergoing ceaseless change.

For how long have peoples of the world been interconnected? Since the Industrial Revolution? Since World War II? A better question might be: How far back in time would we have to go to find a world divided into a collection of separate, self-contained societies, each moving through time along its own track, and unresponsive to wider regional developments? The answer is that we could cast back hundreds of thousands of years and still not find a world of completely atomized societies. Indeed, the earliest history of humankind is a story of long-distance migrations of hunting and foraging bands to all the world's land masses, a process that involved interaction between one group and another and therefore at least small disruptions and surprises wherever such contact occurred. In a sweeping way, then, the history of humanity from remote times is a tale of how groups of men and women connected with one another and how those interactions affected and complicated the lives people lived in different parts of the earth. This challenges us to rethink humanity's history in a more holistic, interconnected way, history that is not only the stories of different nations, civilizations, and regions but also a single story of the species and its development on the spherical earth over the past few million years. Indeed, the history of humankind and the planet are inextricably connected.

We may find it easier to think about human history on a large scale and over the very long term if at the outset we have some familiarity with the planet's geographical "personality," that is, its major land masses, oceans, and large topographical and climatological features. If we consider the whole sphere as the primary "place" where history has unfolded, and keep that context in mind as we investigate the past, we may better grasp the location of particular places and peoples in relation to one another. We may also better

Chapter Outline

• • •

equip ourselves to make historical connections between one place or group of people and another, to compare historical developments in different places, and to understand large-scale developments that cut across the conventional borders between states, cultural groups, or civilizations.

The Big Land Masses: The Main Stage of History

Most of us think of the earth's surface as the two-dimensional space where ground meets sky. In fact the human drama has unfolded on a stage that has depth as well as length and width. This is the **biosphere**, the zone that shelters all life-forms, including human beings.

> **biosphere** The zone of the earth that can support life.

The biosphere may be visualized as constituting three layers, each one making up part of the whole. On top, as it were, is the atmosphere. About 78 percent of this layer of gasses is nitrogen and about 21 percent oxygen, the substance humans and other higher life-forms need to survive. Second is the hydrosphere, the watery realm, about 97 percent of which is the oceans. Third is the lithosphere, that is, the solid earth, or outer crust of sand, soil, rock, and fossilized organic matter that we recognize as coal, oil, and natural gas. Humans depend for survival on the stability of the biosphere and live in relationship to its sun-powered cycles—photosynthesis, wind, and the evaporation and condensation of water. Our species has a genetic relationship to all living organisms, sharing, for example, a significant portion of our genes with the banana. In short, the arena of history is not just Asia, England, or the Aztec empire, but the "green skin" that envelops the earth.

For thousands of years, humans have known how to move across water, which covers about 71 percent of the planet, in various types of boats. Recently, we have mastered air travel and even ventured beyond the atmosphere into space. Nevertheless, our history has played itself out mostly on the surface of the lithosphere, the rocky earth, which we see on the globe as chunks of land, some enormous and some small.

Moving Land Masses

The science of tectonics tells us that the lithosphere is an interlocking puzzle board of sections, or plates. Heat and turbulence in the softer part of the earth's mantle below the lithosphere cause these plates to move. Sometimes they drift apart, sometimes they converge. The seams between the **tectonic plates,** which for the most part lie along the floors of the oceans, are places of volcanic activity and earthquakes. The movement of the plates relative to each other changes the shape and position of the land masses. This phenomenon happens of course in geological time, at the rate of not more than a few centimeters a year.

> **tectonic plates** Irregular blocks of solid rock that make up the earth's lithosphere and that constantly shift and change shape.

About 200 million years ago, one giant land mass, the continent geologists call Pangaea, dominated the earth. Over the succeeding tens of millions of years, it slowly broke

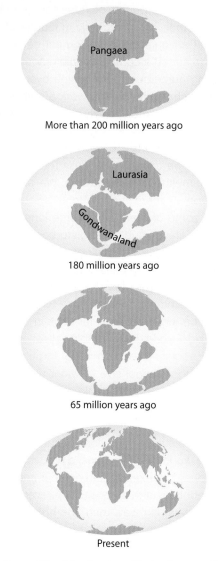

More than 200 million years ago

180 million years ago

65 million years ago

Present

Changes in the earth's plate structure. The land masses that humans inhabit sit atop tectonic plates that are continually in motion. Satellite imagery can accurately detect the tiny distances that continents move in a year's time. On the scale of hundreds of millions of years, patterns of continental drift have affected the ways living species have evolved.

into segments along several lines of seismic upheaval. First it split into two supercontinents, then into several. India, once part of the continent called Gondwanaland, broke off to glide relentlessly northward. It rammed into Eurasia about 30 million years ago, the collision buckling the earth to form the Himalaya Mountains. Because the process of continental drift continues, the land mass configuration that has endured for the past 20 million years or so is only temporary. Africa is heading toward Europe, eventually to close off the Strait of Gibraltar and transform the Mediterranean into an inland sea. Coastal California, part of the Northern Pacific Plate, pushes northward and, to the possible satisfaction of some New Yorkers, might someday separate itself from the rest of North America.

Seven Continents, or Only Five?

Schoolbooks still teach that there are seven primary land masses, or continents: Africa, Antarctica, Asia, Australia, Europe, North America, and South America. In our view this convention needs rethinking. If we accept even a loose physical definition of a continent as a distinct land mass surrounded, or nearly so, by water, Europe and Asia do not separately qualify. No significant waterway or other partition divides the eastern side of Europe from the western side of Asia. Rather, the two places constitute, and have constituted for millions of years, a single great land mass. A little more than a century ago, scholars named this land mass Eurasia. Since then, many have recognized that the standard physical definition of a continent properly applies to it. Logically, then, Europe is a long peninsula at the far western end of Eurasia, that is, a *subcontinent* roughly comparable to South Asia (Bangladesh, India, and Pakistan), a peninsula that juts south.

The precept that Europe is a continent goes back to the ancient Greeks, whose world centered on the Aegean Sea in the eastern Mediterranean basin. They conceived the planet as made up of three parts: Europe was the territory generally north and west of the Aegean Sea (including the Republic of Greece today), Asia was all land to the east and southeast, and Africa (called Libya) lay south and southwest.

In the Middle Ages, European scholars perpetuated the Greeks' three-part scheme, though recognizing that these territories were much larger than the Greeks had known them to be. Europeans came to identify their region with "Christendom," the land where most Christians lived, and they defined Asia and Africa as the continents inhabited mainly by people who were *not* Christians. Therefore, religion, not an ocean or a sea, separated Europe from Asia. This was one way to define what continents were, but this definition was based predominantly on *cultural*, not *physical* distinctions.

But where exactly did Europe leave off and Asia start? In the eighteenth century, a Swedish military officer who traveled to Siberia proposed the Ural Mountains of Russia as a suitable continental boundary.[1] Debates over the proper dividing line continued, but gradually European scholars came to accept the Urals as a "natural" partition, even though those round-topped mountains rise no higher than about six thousand feet and have no compelling significance as a topographical, cultural, or historical boundary. The same may be said of the Bosporus and Dardanelles, the two straits that connect the Mediterranean with the Black Sea and that have served conveniently to demarcate Europe from Asia. But those straits have hardly ever impeded the flow of history, and today one can drive from "Europe" to "Asia" on either of two bridges across the Bosporus. Yet despite the obvious artificiality of the markers, the doctrine of European continent-hood has persisted. European nations came to dominate much of the world militarily and economically in the later nineteenth century. To them, the idea of Europe as a primary world region seemed more natural than ever.

One standard map of the world has reinforced this idea. In 1569, Gerardus Mercator, a Flemish cartographer, devised a flat projection of the world as an aid to sea captains: A straight line drawn between any two points on the map represents a constant true compass bearing. The Mercator map of the world, which until recently served as the standard

An ancient Greek map of the world.
Hecateus of Miletus, a Greek scholar of the fifth century B.C.E., conceived of this circular map of the world. Why do you think Hecateus located the Mediterranean Sea at the center of the map?

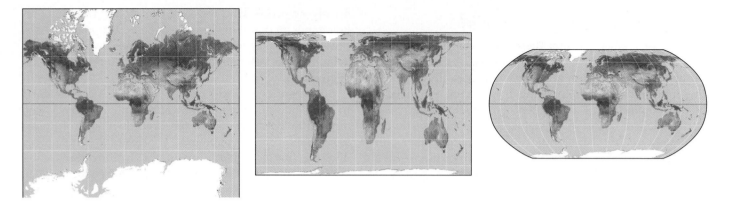

MAP I.1 From left to right: Mercator, Gall-Peters, and Robinson map projections.
The sixteenth-century Mercator world map, which severely distorts the relative size of land masses, was used in school rooms for centuries. In 1973, Arno Peters published an equal area map of the world. It represents the relative size of land areas accurately but distorts their shapes. The Robinson projection, devised in the 1960s, attempts to strike a balance between size and shape distortions. Peters aimed deliberately to correct what he regarded as the Eurocentric bias of the Mercator projection. How do you think the Gall-Peters map accomplishes that aim?

projection, makes Europe look much bigger than it actually is relative to regions that lie farther south. This is because this projection severely distorts the size of land masses toward the poles, so that territories at far northern or far southern **latitudes** appear much larger than they actually are relative to lands nearer the equator. Consequently, Europe, from the southern end of Greece to the northern tip of Norway, looks much bigger relative to South America, Africa, or the Indian subcontinent, for example, than it really is on the round globe.

latitude The imaginary east–west lines that circle the earth and that indicate distance in degrees north and south of the equator, which has the value of 0 degrees.

Mercator maps also sometimes situate Europe in the center of the flat map relative to all four of its edges. That configuration requires pushing the equator to the lower third of the map, which falsely compresses the size of lands in the Southern Hemisphere relative to Europe and the rest of the Northern Hemisphere. Looming as large and conspicuous as it does on this projection, Europe appears as though it might deserve membership in the club of continents.

All flat map projections distort size, shape, distance, or direction in *some* way because the surface of the earth is not flat but curved. Accuracy of all these elements requires a globe, an object impossible to reproduce on a book page. Since the eighteenth century, cartographers have been publishing various equal area maps that rectified Mercator's size perversions. Projections in wide use today, such as Robinson maps, make agreeable compromises between shape and volume of land areas, though they may still somewhat exaggerate size near the poles (see Map I.1).

Afroeurasia

Accepting the idea of Europe as an integral part of geophysical Eurasia, students of global history should find it easier to conceive visually of that entire land mass from the North Atlantic to the North Pacific as a continuous stretch of territory within which humans have lived, migrated, fought, and traded for many thousands of years. But what about Africa? Because it is separated from Eurasia only by the Mediterranean and the Red Seas, it qualifies as a continent by the conventional definition, though barely. Africa also rests on one of the large sections of the lithosphere known as the African Plate. Is it possible, nevertheless, to conceive of Eurasia and Africa together as constituting *one* continent? Look at Map I.2. Cover up the Mediterranean Sea with the thumb of your left hand and place the index finger of your right hand over the Red Sea. Notice that with those two seas covered, it is not hard to see Eurasia and Africa together as a single land mass, and one much bigger than Eurasia alone. Compared to the Atlantic or the Pacific Ocean, the Mediterranean and the Red Seas are merely "lakes." Humans have been shuttling routinely back and forth across them for thousands of years. And it is worth noting that one can *walk* from Africa to Eurasia by crossing the Sinai Peninsula and one of the bridges that spans the Suez Canal.

Because of regular interaction among peoples living around the rims of the Mediterranean and the Red Seas, historical developments in Africa, Asia, and Europe have been intertwined far more intensely than the conventional continental divisions would encourage us to think. In other words, an integrated approach to world history demands that we visualize not only Eurasia as a whole but Africa and Eurasia together (plus adjacent islands or island groups like Japan, the Philippines, and Britain) as a *single space* within which important historical developments have taken place from very early times.

In fact, ancient scholars had no trouble imagining Africa, Asia, and Europe together as constituting a larger interconnected whole. The Romans called it the *Orbis Terrarum,* or "the circle of the world." However, the three-continents scheme, a product of human invention to start with, has become so standardized in schoolbooks as the "right" way to

MAP I.2 Major physical and climatic features of Afroeurasia.
What physical features work to connect Afroeurasia as a single geographical unit? Which features support an understanding of this landmass as three continents?

see the world that modern geographers have never settled on a label for all of Africa and Eurasia together. In the sixteenth century the term "Old World" appeared in European languages to distinguish the land masses of the Eastern Hemisphere from the "New World," that is, the Americas. These terms, however, are vulnerable to criticism because the Americas were only "new" to the Europeans who first visited them, not to the people who had been living there for thousands of years. In this book we adopt the single word

> **Afroeurasia** The land masses of Africa and Eurasia, together with adjacent islands, as a single spatial entity.

Afroeurasia to express the continuum of lands comprising Africa and Eurasia. It will serve as a convenient geographical tool for discussing large-scale historical developments that cut across the conventionally defined continental boundaries.

Afroeurasia takes up nearly 60 percent of the surface of the earth that is not water. This land mass is not only the biggest one on the planet, it is also where the human species

first evolved (as far as we know), and it has historically been home to most of the humans who have ever lived. Today, about 86 percent of the globe's population inhabits Afroeurasia. To understand the patterns of migration, settlement, exchange, and conquest that unfolded on this land mass, it helps to know its broad physical and climatological features.

The Great Arid Zone

A large part of the Afroeurasian land mass is a belt of dry or semidry country that extends all the way from the Atlantic coast of Africa in a generally northeasterly direction to the northern interior of China. This enormous tract, which we refer to as the **Great Arid Zone,** comprises a chain of

> **Great Arid Zone** The belt of arid and semiarid land that extends across Afroeurasia from the Sahara Desert in the west to the Gobi Desert in the east. It has been home to both pastoral nomadic communities and to farming societies where sufficient water is available.

The Great Arid Zone. Climate in the long band of dry country that stretches across Afroeurasia ranges from extreme year-round aridity to semiarid conditions in which winter rains nourish spring grasses. Dromedaries, or one-humped camels, shown here (left) ambling across the western Arabian Desert, are in several respects biologically better suited to harsh environments than are horses, which for several thousand years have thrived on the grassy steppes of northeastern China.

interconnected deserts, mountains, and semiarid steppes. A steppe may be defined as flat or rolling grassland, equivalent to what Americans call "prairie" and Argentineans call "pampas." The main climatic characteristic of the Great Arid Zone is low annual rainfall, which may range from an average of less than five inches in the bleakest of deserts to twenty inches or so in better watered steppes.

The Sahara Desert, the largest area of intense aridity in the world, constitutes the western end of the Great Arid Zone. The Arabian and the Syrian Deserts, climatological extensions of the Sahara, connect on the east to the Iranian Plateau. A spur of dry country extends eastward from Iran across southern Pakistan to form the Great Indian Desert. North and northeast of Iran lie the steppes that cover a significant part of the huge interior region we call **Inner Eurasia.** Rainfall on the grasslands of western Inner Eurasia, that is, the lands roughly north of the Black Sea, is relatively abundant, as much as twenty inches a year. But further east, Inner Eurasia becomes progressively arid. The Gobi Desert, which overlaps China and Mongolia, marks the eastern end of high aridity, though much of northern China is semiarid.

> **Inner Eurasia** The interior land mass of Eurasia, whose dominant features are flat or rolling regions of grassy steppe or forest, interrupted by deserts and highland areas.

Old Hollywood stereotypes represent the Great Arid Zone as a hellish sea of sand frequented only by camel nomads and French Foreign Legionnaires. Some sections of the belt are indeed infernal and uninhabited, but the movie image is way off the mark. Densely settled farming populations have inhabited dry lands for thousands of years. In fact, the earliest farming societies arose in the Great Arid Zone or on the margins of it. Aridity does not necessarily mean infertility as long as water for crops and pasture is available from rivers or underground sources. The Tigris-Euphrates, Nile, Indus, and Yellow (Huang He) Rivers, which nourished the earliest civilizations, all flow through parts of the Great Arid Zone. Indeed, oases supporting farmers and even great cities have sprung up wherever aquifers (areas under the earth's surface containing significant amounts of water) could be tapped by springs, wells, or underground channels. Moreover, the zone includes highland regions as well as grassy plains. Rainfall and runoff in mountain valleys have nourished farmers from very ancient times.

Where farmers could not make a living in the Great Arid Zone, people found another way to survive. Beginning between four thousand and five thousand years ago, small communities adapted to low precipitation by raising domesticated animals. These stock breeders developed a specialized economy based on herds of sheep, horses, goats, cattle, or camels that could be exploited for meat, milk, blood, hide, and bone. The earliest pastoralists, that is, people whose living depends on pasture, inhabited the semiarid grassy steppes of Inner Eurasia. Stock raisers also adapted long ago to the Sahara, the Arabian Desert, and the Iranian Plateau, in places where seasonal rains and strategically placed wells could keep herds alive. Because herding communities required extensive grazing land, their population densities had to remain low compared to farming societies. Nevertheless, pastoral peoples—hardy, mobile, and often militant—have, as we will see, played a role in world history out of all proportion to their sheer numbers.

The Tropical Belt

South of the Great Arid Zone a broad belt of tropical or subtropical territory runs across Afroeurasia, straddling the equator. In basic geographical terms, the "tropics" is the region bounded by two latitudinal lines: the Tropic of Cancer on the north and the Tropic of Capricorn on the south. The sun shines from directly overhead at least once a year in all areas between these lines. In the west of Afroeurasia lie the humid grassy or wooded savannas and the equatorial rainforests of Africa south of the Sahara. To the east are the woodlands and tropical forests of southern India, the Ganges River plain, Southeast Asia, and southern China. In contrast to the Great Arid Zone, the wet tropics have a short annual dry season and rainfall as high as 430 inches a year. Both plant and animal life are luxuriant and vastly diverse. The earliest human societies made their living hunting and foraging on tropical, sometimes wooded grasslands in eastern Africa. Farming and herding peoples settled the tropical zone of both Africa and Eurasia starting about the second millennium B.C.E., though encountering great ecological challenges owing to nutrient-poor soils and a range of tropical diseases.

The Northern Latitudes of Temperate Climate

Running along the northern tier of the Afroeurasian land mass from the Atlantic to the Pacific is the wide band of temperate climate that was once covered in boreal and deciduous forests. Westerly winds, encircling the earth, blow across northern Eurasia year-round. They create alternating conditions of warm and cold, wet and dry weather, as polar air masses compete for dominance with warm, tropical air. Streaming across the North Atlantic, the westerlies bring high rainfall, mostly in winter, to ocean-facing Europe. But deeper into Eurasia, and especially east of the Ural Mountains, the climate is much drier and winters much colder. From late in the first millennium C.E., the immense hardwood forests of Europe dwindled gradually before the axe and the plow, though east of the Urals and on across Siberia, the taiga, or coniferous forestlands, remained sparsely settled right into modern times.

Sandwiched between the northern forest belt and the Great Arid Zone at the western end of Eurasia is the basin of the Mediterranean Sea, the largest of the "internal" seas of Afroeurasia. Mild, rainy winters and hot summers of almost complete drought characterize the mountains and plains of the Mediterranean basin. Open woodlands once covered much of this temperate region, but in ancient times farmers converted plains and hillsides into wheat fields, olive orchards, and vineyards.

Afroeurasia's Mountain Spine

The regularity of the broad east-to-west climatic zones of Afroeurasia is broken partially by the string of mountains that extends across the land mass. Map I.2 (inset) highlights the mountain chain, which begins in the west with the Atlas Mountains of North Africa and extends eastward to the highlands of southwestern China. Afroeurasia's mountains, where they are high and rugged enough, have frustrated communication between peoples living on either side of their ridges. The Himalaya and Kunlun ranges, for example, were formidable barriers to direct overland communication between China and India. The towering Alps also made travel difficult between the Mediterranean and the forested lands to the north. Indeed, the Alpine wall explains in some

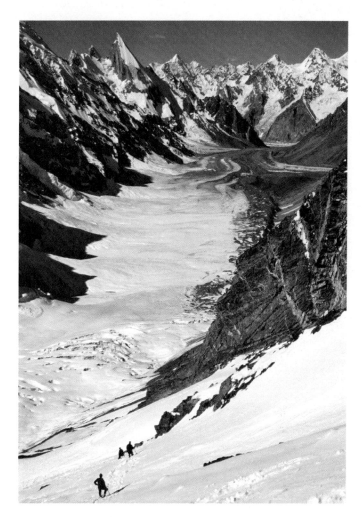

A high pass in the Himalaya Mountains. Merchants have carried goods across high Himalayan passes since ancient times. Only in 1986, however, was a route marked out for trekkers across the 19,500-foot Gondogoro Pass in northern Pakistan.

measure the cultural differences that characterized the development of the southern and northern parts of Christian Europe.

By contrast, Afroeurasia's highland valleys became home to foraging and hunting bands early in human history, later to farmers and herders. The highlands were explored and settled, and ancient trekkers mapped out trails over summer passes. Gaps in even the most foreboding of ranges became channels of slow but regular communication that linked distant peoples in trade. Nomads migrating with their herds and flocks, not to mention great armies of horsemen hell-bent on conquest, also crossed high passes of the Atlas, Carpathians, Zagros, or Hindu Kush at different times in history, appearing suddenly out of the hills and plunging down on unsuspecting villagers in the plain below.

The Eleven Seas

A chain of seas also links the extremities of Afroeurasia. Map I.3 identifies the sequence of seas, beginning with the

MAP I.3 The eleven seas of Afroeurasia.
How might sea traders sailing across the South China Sea, the Bay of Bengal, or the Arabian Sea in premodern times have benefited from knowledge of the seasonal patterns of the monsoon winds?

Sea of Japan (East Sea) at the far northeastern end of the continent and ending with the Baltic in northern Europe. Straits, more or less narrow, connect several of these seas. The Red Sea and the Persian (Arabian) Gulf are parallel water routes between the Mediterranean and the Arabian Sea. The Red Sea links to the Mediterranean by a short landward passage across the Sinai Peninsula, though the Suez Canal now serves as a human-made strait. Communication between the Mediterranean and the Persian Gulf requires a longer overland passage across Iraq and Syria.

Climate and weather on the eleven seas vary drastically owing to their differing latitudes and wind conditions. However, by the first millennium B.C.E., or in some places much earlier, humans were observing and recording seasonal regularities in weather, wind, and current all along the chain. The largest-scale Afroeurasian wind cycle is the Indian Ocean monsoons, a climatological phenomenon in which the winds over a region reverse direction at particular times of the year. Owing to differences in surface temperature between the Indian Ocean and the Eurasian land mass, winds blow from the northeast in the winter months, passing across Southeast Asia and India toward Africa. Then in the summer months they reverse themselves, blowing from the southwest. In very ancient times, peoples who lived around the rims of the South China Sea, the Bay of Bengal, and the Arabian Sea became aware of the monsoons. Early seafarers soon got the hang of sailing out of port during certain seasons of the year, then back again after the monsoons shifted.

In all the eleven seas, mariners learned how to take advantage of local wind and current to sail out of sight of land with reasonable confidence that they would get where they wanted to go. In time, traders, as well as migrants, pilgrims, and sometimes pirates and seaborne conquerors, regarded the open waters of the eleven seas, not as fearsome voids but as channels of rapid and, compared to overland transport, inexpensive communication. By the end of the first millennium C.E., the entire four-thousand-mile-long corridor of seas was developing into a single network of trade. Individual merchants, even in modern times, have hardly ever carried a cargo from one end of the chain to the other. Rather, groups of traders commonly handed off their shipments to other groups in the commercial ports that sprang up where two seas meet.

Rivers

We may also think of Afroeurasia's great rivers as extensions of oceans, narrow corridors of communication leading deep into the interior of the land mass. The mouths of some major rivers, including the Yangzi (YAHNG-zuh) in China, or the Rhine and Danube in Europe, are broad and deep enough to permit oceangoing vessels to sail directly upriver to inland ports. On other rivers, sandbars, marshes, waterfalls, or shallow deltas block entry from the sea to large craft. Beyond such barriers, however, some rivers are navigable for hundreds or even thousands of miles. For example, the lower course of the Congo River drops precipitately over a series of waterfalls between Central Africa's interior plateau and the Atlantic. Travelers must go around these cataracts by land. Above the falls, however, the river and its numerous tributaries open out to form a network of about 8,700 miles of navigable streams that reach a huge part of equatorial Africa. Many of Afroeurasia's secondary rivers are too short, shallow, or steep to permit useful navigation. The streams that flow from the interior of southern India, for example, fall into that category, and among the dozens of watercourses that empty into the Mediterranean only the Nile and the Rhône provide waterborne access to the deep interior. Rivers of course also mean valleys.

Whether navigable or not, a river may guide travelers along overland routes that parallel its banks, especially where the flow has carved broad bottom land.

Humans began communicating with one another along river valleys, whether overland or in canoes, rafts, and sailcraft, several millennia before they ventured onto the deep oceans. Rivers have partly determined the directions that migrants, merchants, and the carriers of new ideas have taken, and they have shaped the geographical distribution of languages and cultural styles. In Afroeurasia's dry lands, river valleys are typically ribbons of fertility, blessing ancient farmers and city builders with both water and rich soil. Afroeurasia's earliest civilizations all arose in river valleys, where sun, soil, and abundant water created ecological conditions where dense populations could flourish even in the most barren parts of the Great Arid Zone.

Unfortunately, rivers are also among the least stable formations on the earth's surface. Depending on the particular topographical, hydrological, or climatic conditions, rivers may flood unpredictably, change their course abruptly, fill with salts that harm crops, and accumulate alluvial silt that clogs irrigation channels, halts shipping, and creates swamps and marshes. For example, northern China's Yellow River has sustained dense populations, great cities, and boundless wheat lands, but over the centuries periodic floods and channel shifts have also caused millions of deaths and economic disasters severe enough to weaken dynasties.

We cannot, however, blame nature alone for the way rivers behave. Humans began thousands of years ago to clear forests upstream, a practice that invariably increased runoff and with it the risk of flooding and erosion. In modern times, governments have conceived more and more ambitious schemes to put rivers to economic use by rechanneling them, lining them with dikes and levees, and stopping them with mammoth dams, all to uncertain long-term effects. As we explore the past in the chapters to come, we will

Cataracts on the Congo River. This mighty river and its numerous tributaries form the largest network of navigable waterways in Africa. They have served for millennia as avenues of regional commerce. Ships cannot, however, reach this network from the Congo's Atlantic mouth owing to the presence of thirty-two cataracts, or rapids. The lower course of the river drops nearly 900 feet over a distance of about 220 miles.

notice many interconnections between human history and the ever-changing landscapes of rivers and their valleys.

Australia

Geographers continue to argue about Australia. Is it the world's smallest continent or its biggest island? Scholars also recognize "Australasia," that is, Australia plus Tasmania, New Zealand, and sometimes New Guinea, as a distinct world region. A hemispheric view that puts Australia at the center gives it the appearance of a lonely island in the midst of a large sea. But if we focus on the northwestern quadrant of this hemisphere, we can perceive the land mass as the biggest island in an archipelago (chain of islands) that stretches from New Zealand to the Philippines. Only short sea passages separate Australia's northern coast from island Indonesia. And the first humans who set foot "down under" perhaps 60,000 years ago almost certainly arrived there in small boats after a quick trip from some island to the north.

Australia is certainly the most uniform of the great land masses (see Map I.4). It lacks many deep coastal indentations or any large internal lakes or seas. It is also the flattest of all the continents. Most of it consists of boundless plateaus and depressions. Like Afroeurasia, it has a distinctive chain of highlands. The Great Dividing Range runs the length of the continent parallel to the eastern coast. These wooded hills, however, have never impeded human communication since few of the ridges rise more than five thousand feet.

The eastern coastal plains, a narrow strip between the Great Dividing Range and the South Pacific, have adequate water resources because of the southeasterly trade winds that drop Pacific rain as they rise up over the interior hills. But just west of the mountains is the Outback, the uninterrupted dry country that stretches four thousand miles to the Indian Ocean. Australia's own Great Arid Zone of deserts, steppes, and vast fields of sand dunes makes up about two-thirds of the continent. Only the east coast, the far north, and parts of the southern shore receive seasonal rainfall of more than twenty inches a year. Compared to Afroeurasia, Australia is also poor in rivers that may be navigated far inland. The major exception is the Murray River, which originates in the Snowy Mountains of the far southeast and empties into the Indian Ocean.

Australia's distinctive plant and animal life (the eucalyptus tree, the kangaroo, and the duckbilled platypus) is an evolutionary consequence of the continent's physical removal from the once biologically interconnected supercontinent of Gondwanaland (see page I-4). About 200 million years ago, the land masses that are today Australia, Antarctica, Africa, and India went their separate ways. Africa and India moved toward what became Eurasia, but Australia remained farther away. Consequently, the stock of plant and animal life inherited from Gondwanaland continued to evolve along separate lines. In more recent geological ages, however, Australia has exchanged numerous flora and fauna with what is now the Indonesian archipelago.

That exchange included Australia's early human colonization. Throughout almost all of the past 60,000 years,

MAP I.4 Physical features of Australia.

Look at the composite satellite view of the earth at night on page I-2. What geographical factors might help explain the concentration of light along the southeastern and southwestern coasts of Australia?

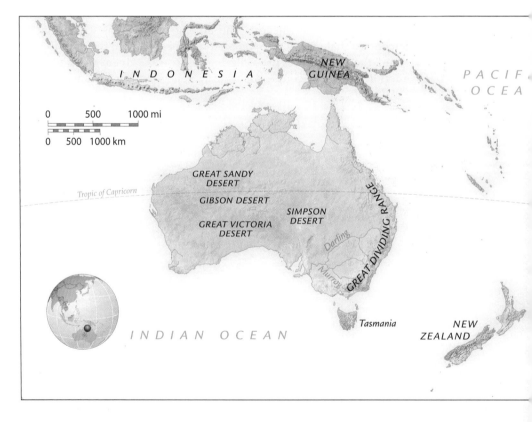

however, the continent's aboriginal societies, which remained small and scattered compared to Afroeurasia's population, lived in isolation, even from the peoples of neighboring Southeast Asia. New colonizers introduced themselves to the continent only a little more than two centuries ago. In 1788, English-speaking Europeans arrived in ships to settle the relatively well-watered eastern coast. From that moment, Australia's native population became firmly connected, whether they liked it or not, to the wider human community.

North and South America

As with any sphere, we can tilt or rotate the globe to get any hemispheric perspective that we like. In other words, we can

longitude The imaginary north–south lines that extend between the North Pole and the South Pole and that run perpendicular to lines of latitude. By international agreement the line with a value of 0 degrees, called the Prime Meridian, passes through Greenwich, England.

bisect the planet along any lines of **longitude** we care to choose. The best known bisection is the one that runs through Greenwich, England, and that we call the Prime Meridian. This line serves as the baseline both for measurement of longitude, that is, distances in degrees east or west of that line, and for marking out the world's standard time zones. The line continues around to the Pacific side of the world as the International Date Line. There is nothing "natural" about this line: A conference of nations meeting in 1884 agreed that it should run through Greenwich, a suburb of London. The vote was twenty-two to one, and France abstained.

No matter what line we choose to bisect the planet, however, schoolbook geography and cultural habit make it difficult *not* to think of Afroeurasia as one side of the world and North and South America as the other side. After all, we call them the Eastern and Western Hemispheres. If we turn a globe on its polar axis so that Afroeurasia faces us, the Americas are on the opposite side and disappear from view. But if we tilt and rotate the earth so that we face the North

The Prime Meridian. These children in their colorful sneakers are straddling a stretch of the Prime Meridian marked on the ground where it passes through Greenwich, England. The line, which marks 0° longitude and runs from North Pole to South Pole, traverses Greenwich because that is where late nineteenth-century European diplomats and scientists decided it should go. How do you think Britain's status as a major world power in that period might have influenced that decision?

Atlantic Ocean, then Europe, Greenland, and Canada all become visible as an almost continuous arc of land bridging the two conventionally defined hemispheres. If we turn the globe again to focus on the North Pacific Ocean, a crescent of nearly connected land stretches from East Asia across Siberia and Alaska to North America. From these northerly angles shown in Map I.5, it is clear that no long oceanic voyage is required for communication between the northerly reaches of Afroeurasia and North America. Vikings figured out how to sail from Europe to Canada more than a thousand years ago, though the connection did not endure. The

MAP I.5 Two northerly views of the earth, one focused on the Atlantic (far left) and one on the Pacific.

What factors do you think might have inhibited humans from traveling regularly between Afroeurasia and North America along these ocean rims for thousands of years?

first humans who crossed from Asia to the Americas thousands of years before that may have blazed a water route along the rim of the North Pacific in rafts or canoes

History, however, does lend some support to the Western Hemisphere–Eastern Hemisphere division because for thousands of years the peoples of both Afroeurasia and Australia lived in virtual isolation from societies in the Americas. No group on either side had the technological or organizational skills to set up regular communication across the Atlantic or the Pacific. From about 12,000 B.C.E. until a little more than five hundred years ago, these two particular halves of the planet were indeed separate "worlds." Only in the late fifteenth century C.E. did European sea captains make transoceanic connections between Afroeurasia and the Americas destined to last. Since that time, advancing transport technology, including air travel over the North Pole, has steadily reduced the historical significance of the physical distinction between the Eastern and Western Hemispheres. In fact, scientists and engineers have formulated plans to dig a sixty-five-mile rail line tunnel under the Bering Strait that would one day link the trans-Siberian railroad to Amtrak.

Connecting the Americas

In the past century, schoolchildren in the United States and most other countries have learned that the Western Hemisphere has two continents, North America and South America. Only the Isthmus of Panama, just thirty miles across at its narrowest stretch, prevents the complete physical separation of the two land masses. Moreover, the isthmus is an area of dense wet tropical forests and mountains that until recent times has significantly impeded overland commercial and cultural exchange between South America and **Mesoamerica.**

Mesoamerica The region comprising southern Mexico plus the seven small Central American states.

On the other hand, North and South America have never been completely disconnected historical worlds. As far as we know, human beings first migrated from North to South America 12,000 years ago or more by advancing along either the isthmus or its coastal waters. Climate, vegetation, and cultural styles in the areas surrounding the Panama neck share more similarities than differences. Also, we do not have to strain our imaginations too much to perceive the Gulf of Mexico and the Caribbean as two internal seas of a single American land mass, much the way we have considered the Mediterranean and the Red Seas as "inside" Afroeurasia. The Caribbean and the Gulf are bounded on three sides by land and on the west by a long string of closely clustered islands. We might then think of a line drawn from Florida along this island chain to the far eastern coast of Venezuela as the eastern edge of a single continent. Indeed, we know from archaeological and linguistic evidence that the peoples who settled Caribbean islands thousands of years ago continued to maintain contacts with mainland societies. This unitary continent—North America, Caribbean islands,

and South America together—could be called simply America, though in this book we also use the more conventional plural term, the Americas.

The Americas' Long *Cordillera*

We can also see on a world map that whereas the long axis of Afroeurasia runs about 8,000 miles east to west, the long axis of the Americas runs nearly 11,000 miles north to south. The northern rim of North America lies within the polar region. Tierra del Fuego at the southern tip of South America is only about 600 miles from Antarctica. In both the Eastern and Western Hemispheres, the high mountain spines extend along a long axis, east–west in Afroeurasia, north–south in the Americas. The Americas' long *cordillera*, or cord, of interconnected ranges extends virtually the entire length of the hemisphere (see Map I.6). It is geologically young and therefore rugged, and it hugs the western side of North and South America. It divides the Americas longitudinally, separating narrow coastal plains on the Pacific side from very broad plains on the eastern side that stretch off toward the Atlantic Ocean. The Appalachian Mountains and the Guyana and Brazilian Highlands of South America interrupt the sweep of the plains on the Atlantic side, but these mountains are much older and more round-topped than the Rockies, Sierra, and Andes ranges.

Most of North America lies in zones of subarctic or temperate climate and shares with Eurasia broad latitudinal bands of tundra, boreal forest, and deciduous forest. Southern Mexico, Central America, and about half of South American regions of Mesoamerica and about half of the continent of South America have tropical or subtropical humid climates similar to Afroeurasia's equatorial zone. South America bulges out to its widest extent in the equatorial latitudes. The Amazonian rainforest plateaus therefore make up a large portion of that continent's mass. This is the largest tropical forest ecosystem in the world. The southern quarter of South America lies across temperate latitudes, but the land mass narrows so much at its "southern cone" that both Atlantic and Pacific sea winds reduce the range of temperature and free the region from the extreme winter cold and summer heat that characterize much of temperate North America.

The climate of the Americas is also complicated by the north–south alignment of high mountains, which skews the flow of oceanic winds on the Pacific side and prevents uninterrupted east–west climatic zones. Neither North nor South America, for example, has a latitudinal belt of dry country comparable to Afroeurasia's Great Arid Zone. Rather, deserts and semiarid prairies lie for the most part in strips running north–south. The starkest of dry lands are found west of the *cordillera* near or bordering the Pacific: the deserts of the southwestern United States and northern Mexico in North America and the coastal deserts of Ecuador, Peru, and Chile in South America. Just east of the *cordillera* are the rain shadows that create long bands of dry or semiarid prairie, notably the Great Plains that run most of the length of North America just east of the Rockies and the Patagonian steppe of Argentina east of the Andes.

Rivers and Seas

In Afroeurasia, as we have seen, the eleven seas have for millennia eased human maritime linkage east and west across the region. The Americas have no comparable belt of usable seas to join people north and south. Though Indian mariners almost certainly paddled canoes along stretches of the Pacific and perhaps Atlantic shores thousands of years ago, the great ocean voids did not invite deep-sea exploration in small boats. On the Atlantic side, water routes give easy access to the far interiors of both continents. The Gulf of Mexico links the North American coastal plains and the Mississippi River valley with tropical Mexico. To the north, Hudson's Bay thrusts deep into North America, and just 275 miles south of it the five Great Lakes make up a complex of inland freshwater "seas" that connect extensive areas of forests and plains.

As in Afroeurasia, several great river systems open the interiors of the two Americas. Indeed, Afroeurasia has no network of navigable streams as extensive as the Mississippi and Amazon watersheds, both of which are accessible directly from the sea. From the Atlantic side, numerous other rivers connect the sea to the deep interiors of both continents. Indian migrants and traders used these rivers for long-distance internal communication, and the Europeans who first arrived at the end of the fifteenth century found them an easy way to extend waterborne colonization from the Atlantic to the Great Lakes, the North American plains, and the far interiors of Brazil and Argentina. By contrast, the Pacific side of the Americas is more like Australia in the poverty of its navigable rivers, owing mainly to the sharp drop from mountain to shore nearly the entire length of the land masses. The two major exceptions are the navigable Columbia, which forms part of the border between Oregon and Washington, and, in the far north, Alaska's Yukon.

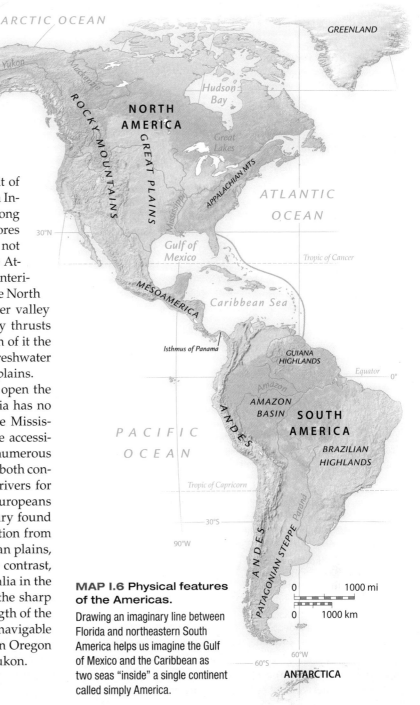

MAP I.6 Physical features of the Americas.

Drawing an imaginary line between Florida and northeastern South America helps us imagine the Gulf of Mexico and the Caribbean as two seas "inside" a single continent called simply America.

The Oceans

Our ancestors may have invented rudimentary watercraft as many as 100,000 years ago and used them to colonize Afroeurasian coastlands and some islands, but human exploration of ocean waters beyond the sight of land is a more recent development. Because of the seasonal regularity of the monsoon winds and the relative serenity of the northern Indian Ocean, valiant mariners of six thousand years ago or more may

monsoon winds
The seasonally reversing winds that governed long-distance sailing in the Indian Ocean and China seas.

have dared to steer primitive sailboats across open stretches of the Arabian Sea or Bay of Bengal. The Atlantic and the Pacific Oceans, however, are so big that they defied human attempts to make roundtrip open-ocean crossings until a little more than five hundred years ago. The Pacific covers a much greater area than the Atlantic. It is fifteen times larger than the United States, the Atlantic less than six and a half times larger. The Pacific, however, has many more islands than the Atlantic, about 25,000 of them. Between

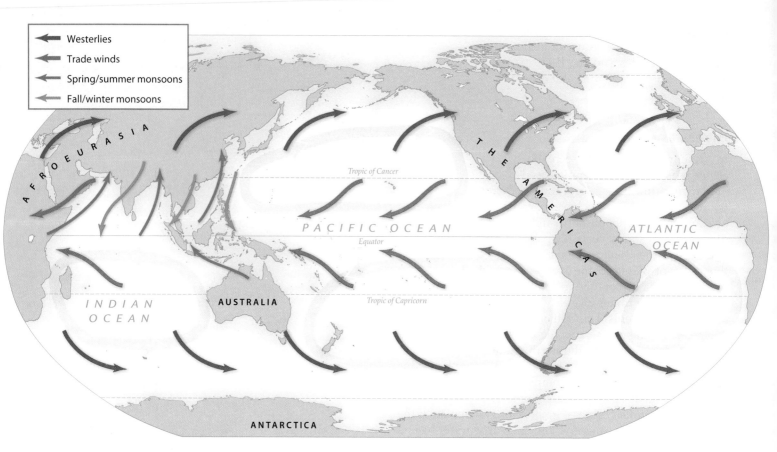

MAP I.7 Ocean wind patterns.

This simplified chart of oceanic winds highlights the giant wind wheels that circulate in the Atlantic and Pacific. Looking at the North Atlantic, what general route do you think Christopher Columbus followed in sailing successfully between Europe and the Caribbean Islands in the late fifteenth century?

about 1600 B.C.E. and 1000 C.E., Polynesian-speaking mariners, moving generally east and northeast from Afroeurasia, colonized many of these islands, collectively called the Island Pacific or **Oceania.** They reached Rapa Nui (Easter Island) in the vast emptiness of the southeastern ocean, and some Polynesians may even have made landfalls in South America. They did not, however, create a network of sea communication that linked the Pacific's western and eastern rims.

> **Oceania (also, the Island Pacific)** The enormous region centered on the tropical Pacific Ocean and its islands. This definition of the region excludes Australia though not New Zealand.

Not until the fifteenth century C.E. did deep-sea explorers gain sufficient technical skill and geographical knowledge to initiate regular travel *back and forth* across the Atlantic and the Pacific. Success came when sailors figured out that, like the Indian Ocean monsoons, the Atlantic and Pacific winds (and the surface currents driven by those winds) adhere to regular cycles (see Map I.7). Because of a combination of unequal atmospheric pressure and the influence of the earth's rotation, the winds of both the Atlantic and the Pacific flow in a circular, clockwise pattern north of the equator and in the reverse direction south of it. Only in the fifteenth and sixteenth centuries did European navigators begin to map out the Atlantic patterns accurately enough to allow routine roundtrip oceanic voyages. In fact, this four-wheel model of wind and current has numerous local variations and is much more complicated than this introduction suggests. Sea travelers gradually mastered these complexities, however, and by the end of the eighteenth century they were navigating the saltwater passages that connected all the great land masses and most of the world's islands with one another. Only Antarctica remained to be seriously explored.

• • •

Conclusion

This introduction to "big geography"—the large-scale and unifying features of the biosphere—is an important foundation for globe-girdling history. The earth is a single continuum of space, and the events that have mattered most to humankind as a whole have had a cross-cultural or interregional scope. Readers should therefore be ready to range across the whole wide world, considering the achievements, disasters, and dilemmas of the past in whatever context of *space* is most appropriate—whether that context is Afroeurasia, the Atlantic basin, or the rim lands of the Sahara Desert. It is impossible to look at a globe and see the round earth all at once. But fortunately we can encompass the whole in our minds. This is the starting point for a unified history of humankind.

• • •

Key Terms

Afroeurasia I-7	latitude I-6	Oceania (also, the Island Pacific) I-16
biosphere I-4	longitude I-13	tectonic plates I-4
Great Arid Zone I-7	Mesoamerica I-14	
Inner Eurasia I-8	monsoon winds I-15	

part 1

Settling the Planet

Beginnings to the First Millennium B.C.E.

Part 1 of this book sets *Homo sapiens* on the road to complexity. These first four chapters investigate four developments that have successively complicated human society and its relationship to the earth's environment.

The first was human colonization of all the planet's large land masses, a migration that started from eastern Africa. This was the first genuinely global event in our history, and we are the only higher primate species that accomplished it. Settling nearly the whole world required humans to adapt to starkly different ecological conditions. That meant that communities relying on wild food sources had to invent sophisticated ways to adjust to new environments and to long-term changes in world climate. These communities also built networks of exchange with

A wooden carving from the
Middle Kingdom shows an Egyptian
peasant guiding a plow pulled by two oxen.

one another. They traded not only useful material objects but also technological ideas. The spread of ideas about tools or food-gathering strategies to more communities tended to generate even more clever ways to exploit and manage the natural and physical world.

The second great jump into complexity was the invention of farming. This development got under way about 12,000 years ago, and it happened in several different parts of the world independently. Scholars have reached a broad consensus that this "agricultural revolution" was linked to the coming of the Holocene, the global warming trend that started around 14,000 years ago. Holocene conditions produced more abundant wild grain supplies in some parts of the world. In those places, communities of foragers began to experiment with new ways of nurturing and selecting grains and other edible plants they found appealing, though they had little conscious grasp of the biological causes or potential consequences of what they were doing,

Over many centuries of trial and error, communities found themselves genetically altering certain wild plants and animals to increase their size or otherwise improve their value to humans. This meant that people could settle in permanent and indeed larger communities to grow crops and raise animals. Between about 12,000 and 5,000 years ago, global population surged upward, social relations became more intricate, and networks of exchange became denser. This development happened in several parts of Afroeurasia and the Americas.

The third leap into complexity started about 5,500 years ago, when people in just a few places devised ways to produce large surpluses of food. This happened initially in river valleys where rainfall was low, but where people could generously irrigate fertile soil. These regions could sustain populations of unprecedented size, but people had to live close together to be near water and food. That meant inventing more complex tools, engineering methods, exchange webs, and social organizations. People could do this because the jump in available food energy allowed some individuals to devote full time to finding solutions to the challenges of living in larger, denser communities. Meeting these challenges led to the emergence of "complex societies," that is, societies characterized by cities, occupational specializations, social class divisions, central

governments, sophisticated record keeping, elaborate religious systems, and several other features. Not long after 5,500 years ago, complex societies emerged in both Afroeurasia and the Americas, although for several more millennia the great majority of humans lived in the countryside, not in cities.

Finally, in parts of Afroeurasia's Great Arid Zone, the belt of dry land that extends across the supercontinent, humans invented a third way of life that depended neither on foraging nor on settled farming. Starting as early as the fifth millennium B.C.E., people who raised animals for food, fiber, hides, and other useful products developed technologies and strategies that allowed them to pasture large numbers of cattle, sheep, or horses on seasonal grasslands where arid conditions severely limited farming. In a sense, wild grasses and shrubs became available to humans as food because animals biologically converted these plants into meat, milk, and blood, which humans could digest. People could colonize arid regions in larger numbers. Consequently, mobile herding societies, or pastoral nomads, began to play a much larger part in history.

We start Part 1 by investigating how and why these leaps into complexity occurred. What special endowments allowed humans, alone among animal species, not only to adapt to all but the most extreme environments, but also to transform and manage them in such elaborate ways?

Estimated World Population in Millions

1

The Peopling of the World

7,000,000–10,000 B.C.E.

The footprints of ancient ancestors, found at Laetoli.

Some time at least four million years ago our ancestors stood up on two legs and started walking, first in Africa and eventually around the world. A few ancient trekkers even left their footprints. One set is embedded in hardened earth at a site called Laetoli (lie-a-TOE-lee) in a wooded region of northern Tanzania. The scientists who have studied these prints think that one day about 3.6 million years ago three apelike creatures, the biggest of them less than five feet tall, trudged together along a riverbed. They may have been scavenging for the meat of dead or dying animals. As they walked, they pressed their feet into rain-dampened ash, which was spewing out of a nearby volcano. The tropical sun hardened the ash before it blew away, and more layers of it fell to cover the prints. Consequently, the tracks of these individuals endured across the ages. The creatures were bipedal. That is, they walked upright on two legs, one skill among others that distinguishes humans and their forebears—known collectively as hominins—from chimpanzees, gorillas, and other apes.

In 1995 a geologist working at a coastal lagoon near Cape Town, South Africa, discovered another set of ancient footprints pressed into rock. Analysis of the impressions and the surrounding geological formations showed that a small individual walked along this stretch of the Cape coast about 117,000 years ago, leaving two tracks in wet sand, which eventually hardened. The shape of the prints shows that the individual was no remote human ancestor but rather one of our own species, *Homo sapiens* ("wise human"). The individual was almost certainly anatomically "modern," that is, it exhibited the same fundamental physical characteristics that we do. In fact, these prints are the earliest tracks of *Homo sapiens* so far discovered.

Homo sapiens appeared as a distinct species about 200,000 years ago, and during the following 100,000 years or more of its career, it left evidence of itself only in Africa. Then, starting perhaps 90,000 to 70,000 years ago, it migrated beyond Africa to Eurasia, Australia, and the Americas, and to thousands of islands scattered across the oceans. Among the millions of animal life-forms that trot, crawl, and slither on the surface of the earth, human beings are among the relatively few that made their way around the world and adapted to environments ranging from Arctic to equatorial rainforest. Even our close genetic cousins in the primate family—orangutans, gorillas, bonobos, and chimpanzees—have never left their limited tropical habitats, except in the company of human beings who offered them no choice. The first big story in world history, then, is the peopling of the earth, the story of how and why human beings came to live almost everywhere, not just in eastern and southern Africa.

One of humankind's forebears, the hominin usually identified as *Homo erectus,* preceded our own species out of Africa, migrating as far as Southeast and East Asia. This early traveler, however, took perhaps a million years to get as far east as China, possessed only rudimentary tools, and like all other hominins except us, eventually went extinct. The first part of this chapter introduces briefly the story of these ancestors, whose long but finally doomed sojourn on earth throws into relief the relatively much shorter but, until now at any rate, biologically much more successful history of our own species.

When *Homo sapiens* first left its African cradle to venture north and east, it probably already possessed a biologically modern brain and a much more advanced tool kit than any other hominin species had ever possessed. It had also probably evolved the capacity for self-conscious symbolic thought, expressed through speech, gesture, ritual, and art. On this single talent rested all the astonishing cultural achievements of later millennia. The second part of the chapter surveys the exclusively African evolution of our anatomically modern and intellectually gifted species, an episode that covers something like 60 percent of our history to date.

The third section traces humankind's early colonization of the world, from all regions of Africa, across the breadth of Eurasia, and on to Australia and the far southern reaches of South America. In contrast to the slow and halting movements of *Homo erectus* across Eurasia, bands of foraging and hunting humans advanced to all of the world's major land masses in less than 100,000 years. As they moved and

Chapter Outline

HUMAN ANCESTORS IN AFRICA AND BEYOND
Early Hominin Evolution
Well-Traveled Hominins
INDIVIDUALS MATTER The Turkana Boy: A Distant Ancestor
Other Traveling Hominins

MODERN HUMANS IN AFRICA: THE FIRST 100,000 YEARS
The Debut of *Homo Sapiens*
The Power of Language

COLONIZING THE WORLD
The Roads from Africa
South to Australia
Colonizers of Europe
The American Frontier
WEIGHING THE EVIDENCE The Kennewick Man Controversy
Why Did *Homo Sapiens* People the Earth?
Homo Sapiens: The Last Surviving Hominin
Why People Look Different

GLOBAL CULTURE OF THE UPPER PALEOLITHIC
Dawn of a Multicultural World
Social and Economic Life
Technical Wonders
A World of Symbols

• • •

multiplied, they demonstrated their talents for adapting to and altering contrasting physical and natural environments on a much larger scale than any more ancient species had been able to manage.

As human groups fanned out around the world, the pace of invention in toolmaking, shelter building, social organization, symbolic imagery, and techniques for exchanging goods and ideas speeded up as well. Between about 40,000 and 10,000 B.C.E., the era that scholars call the upper paleolithic ("late stone age"), humankind emerged as a species of exquisitely complex culture. The final part of the chapter explores this explosion of technological and artistic innovation, which happened nearly simultaneously in several parts of the world.

A Panoramic View

Pakefield
700,000 ya

North
Sea

Zhoukoudian, 1 mya

ALPS

Danube

Black Sea

Caspian Sea

Volga

AFROEURASIA

HIMALAYAS

Mediterranean Sea

Ob

Yenisey

Lena

Amur

Yellow

Yangzi

Tropic of Cancer

Toumai (site of
*sahelanthropus
tchadensis* fossil)

Nile

Red Sea

Persian Gulf

Indus

Ganges

Arabian
Sea

Bay of
Bengal

Mekong

South
China
Sea

P A C I F I C

O C E A N

Dikika,
Selam,
3.3 mya

Hadar, Lucy, 3.6 mya

Middle Awash, Ardi, 4.4 mya

SUBSAHARAN
AFRICA

Niger

Nariokotome, Turkana Boy 1.5 mya

Equator

Homo ergaster/erectus
migrations out of Africa began
+/- 1.8 million years ago (mya).
Homo heidelbergensis
migrations out of Africa began
600,000 years ago.

Olduvai Gorge, *Homo habilis*, 1.8 mya
Laetoli

1.5 mya

JAVA

I N D I A N

O C E A N

ATLANTIC

OCEAN

Tropic of Capricorn

A U S T R A L I A

Malapa,
Australopithecus sediba,
2.2 mya

MAP 1.1 Early hominin finds and the spread of *Homo ergaster/erectus*.
The slow spread of *Homo ergaster* and *Homo erectus* from eastern Africa to other parts of Afroeurasia differentiates these species from other primates and from later migrations of *Homo sapiens*. What do the migratory directions of *Homo ergaster* and *Homo erectus* tell us about the success these species had adapting to contrasting climates?

Human Ancestors in Africa and Beyond

FOCUS What types of evidence have scholars used to construct histories of humankind's biological ancestors from 7 million to 200,000 years ago?

The era we investigate in this chapter is a long one, stretching from about seven million years ago, the earliest period

> **hominin** The family of species that includes *Homo sapiens* and its ancestors of the past 6–7 million years.

for which we have evidence of **hominins** as a class of primate separate from the ancestors of chimpanzees and other apes, to about 10,000 B.C.E., when people in some parts of Afroeurasia (the "supercontinent" of Africa, Eurasia, and adjacent islands as a single geographical unit) began to domesticate plants and take up farming. We can, however, tell this long story in just one chapter. One reason is that during most of those seven million years, the ways of life of hominins changed very slowly, especially compared to today, when human society is restructuring itself year-by-year. Key turning points that we can perceive in the fossil or genetic record—for example, toolmaking, control of fire, or the earliest sign of hominins traveling beyond Africa—occurred at widely spaced intervals, perhaps millions of years apart. Nor can we date any of those developments precisely.

A second reason for making a long story short is that the material evidence is scattered sparsely across time and space. The knowledge we possess for constructing hominin history down to 10,000 B.C.E. is miniscule, compared to the data we have about what happened in the world in, say, the first decade of the twenty-first century. The four main types of evidence available to us are human and animal fossil bones, surviving tools and other artifacts (mostly of stone), physical indicators of climatic change that may have affected hominin biological success, and, more recently, genetic material (DNA) from both fossil remains and living men and women. Archaeological and genetic discoveries have been adding new bits of evidence for the deep past just about every month. But as archaeologists have sometimes joked, the number of experts who work in ancient fossil sites exceeds the number of human bones they have so far discovered. Analysis of DNA promises to supply much more knowledge about human evolution and spatial migration, though this class of evidence still has limited uses. The data attesting to our early history are so restricted, and the time gaps between periods for which evidence is available are so long, that we can discern only broad developments. As much as we might like to do it, we cannot write histories about, or even identify, particular communities, leaders, or short-term events.

Early Hominin Evolution

The human species, just one of the millions of plant and animal species that occupy the globe, may be defined simply as a class of individual life-forms capable of interbreeding to perpetuate themselves but incapable of successfully breeding with individuals of other classes. Humans, for example, cannot mate with chimpanzees, and chimpanzees cannot breed with gorillas, even though all three species share between 96 and 99 percent of their genes.

Toumai: The oldest hominin remains. The story of how humans became a species begins with the biological separation of hominins from the ancestors of modern chimpanzees nearly seven million years ago. Evidence for this estimate came in 2001, when French archaeologists working in Chad in west central Africa found a skull bearing hominin characteristics. Dated to that distant time and nicknamed Toumai (TOO-meye), a word meaning "hope of life" in a local language, this individual (*Sahelanthropus tchadensis*) had a brain about the size of a chimp's but remarkably hominin-like facial features, suggesting that a new species genetically different from other primates may have arrived. Scientists are divided on the question of whether Toumai walked upright, but the way the skull appears to have connected to the spine suggests that it did. Just why hominins, in contrast to other primates, evolved a body suited for upright locomotion, including a curved lower spine, knee joints, and a two-footed sense of balance, is a subject of continuing debate among scholars. Hominins definitely had to compete with other animals for food, and perhaps in this game the advantages of full-time bipedalism came to outweigh the disadvantages. **Bipedal** animals faced the danger that large four-legged predators

> **bipedal** Walking upright on two legs, one skill among others that distinguishes hominins from apes.

could outrun them, at least over short distances. On the other hand, upright walkers may have been tall enough to see a predator far out across a grassy plain and so have time to get away from it. Like other primates, bipedal creatures had opposable thumbs for grasping things. By walking on two limbs they had their hands free not only to scurry up trees when they had to, but also to carry food quickly away from rival animals to a place where they could dine in safety. Also, two-legged walkers exposed less surface area of their body to the direct rays of the sun—not their entire back but just the top of their head. They could therefore keep their bodies and brains at efficiently cool temperatures more easily than could animals whose posture was "horizontal" and closer to the ground. That meant they could move around in the midday heat when four-legged animals had to rest in the shade.

Lucy and other australopithecines. While the origins of bipedalism remain speculative, a picture of early bipedal creatures is emerging from the fossil evidence. Until recently, the most famous early hominin was Lucy. In 1975, researchers working in northern Ethiopia found the skeletal remains of at least thirteen **australopithecines** (ah-strah-loh-PITH-uh-seens),

> **australopithecines** Several species of the earliest bipedal hominins, now extinct, whose remains have been found in eastern Africa.

"Lucy." This young, small, and presumably female representative of the species *Australopithecus afarensis* may have looked very much like this reconstruction. Paleoanthropologists and the artists who collaborate with them, however, can only make informed guesses about this species' skin color, hairiness, and nose and lip shape. Modern humans have a large braincase with a small face set beneath the front part of it. Lucy and her australopithecine cousins, by contrast, had a small braincase but a broad, protruding face. In this photo Lucy seems to peer at us with a wistful expression. Might reconstructions like this mislead us into thinking this creature was more "human" than she probably was?

the genus that included a number of early hominin species. One of them was the skeleton, or about 40 percent of it, of a young female. While they were celebrating the discovery in camp, the scientists played the famous Beatles song "Lucy in the Sky with Diamonds." Thus, this fossilized creature got her enduring nickname. Classified as *Australopithecus afarensis* and dated to about 3.2 million years ago, Lucy was only about three feet tall, but she definitely walked upright and could use her flexible thumb and fingers to gather food, perhaps carrying an infant at the same time.

In the past several years, however, Lucy has had to share some of her fame with other Ethiopian fossils. In 2000,

paleoanthropologist
A scientist concerned with the study of human evolution and the physical and behavioral characteristics of early humans and their biological ancestors.

paleoanthropologists discovered Selam, the nearly complete skeleton of a three-year-old female. This child had been buried in sand and rock for 3.6 million years; perhaps she drowned in a sudden flood. Found at a site in the Dikika region not far from where Lucy lived, Selam had gorillalike shoulders good for tree climbing but also a braincase whose size may not have reached full maturity for an australopithecine adult. This feature points to an extended dependent childhood, a biological trait peculiar to human beings. In 2009, scientists proclaimed more confidently that bipedal australopithecines lived at least 4.4 million years ago. This announcement followed the discovery of a partial skeleton of an adult female creature named *Ardipithecus ramidus,* or Ardi. Analysis of the remains indicates that this individual,

who was 1.2 million years older than Lucy, could walk upright, if in a lumbering sort of way. We know that species of australopithecines ranged all the way to the southern tip of Africa. Recently, scientists have been analyzing the skull and several other bones of a creature, named *Australopithecus sediba,* that fell into a deep cave in South Africa nearly two million years ago.

Australopithecines like Lucy, Selam, Ardi, and *Australopithecus sediba* were likely quite intelligent compared to animal competitors, and they may have formed small social bands that cooperated in collecting food and eluding ferocious predators. Even so, this species was a long way from modern humanhood. The australopithecine brain was much smaller than ours—not much larger than a softball. Moreover, we have no evidence that these creatures used even the most rudimentary stone tools. "Despite their human-like posture," one anthropologist has written, "the brain-to-body ratio of Lucy and her friends were such that it is highly probable they could have led full mental and spiritual lives in any municipal zoo."[1] It is possible that one of these varieties of australopithecines was a direct, though very distant ancestor of our own species. But we can only speculate about which one it may have been.

Homo habilis. Less than two million years ago, toolmaking hominins appear in the fossil record. The earliest ones we know of lived near a lake on the Serengeti Plain in modern Tanzania. Discovered in 1960 in Olduvai (OHL-duh-way) Gorge, a region that has yielded a treasury of ancient fossils, this 1.8-million-year-old hominin is the oldest one that scientists have classified as *Homo,* the genus to which we belong. The archaeologists who found the bones of this species named it *Homo habilis,* or "handy person." This species had special attributes, including a larger brain than the likes of Lucy and highly dexterous opposable thumbs, which allowed it to delicately manipulate small objects. It made a number of different tools, including hammers, hand axes, and flakes with sharp edges for chopping or scraping. The evidence available suggests that *Homo habilis* individuals ate plant food as well as meat scavenged from dead animals. Some researchers now argue that a different hominin species living as many as 2.5 million years ago also made tools and that more than one species may have acquired this talent. In any case, the appearance of toolmaking represents the beginning of the **paleolithic,** or "old stone age," an epoch that extended to about 10,000 B.C.E., when the human tool kit became much more sophisticated.

paleolithic Meaning "old stone age," this period dates from approximately 2.5 million years ago, when hominin species first devised stone tools, to about 12,000 years ago, when humans starting experimenting with agriculture.

Well-Traveled Hominins

Perhaps not much later than 1.9 million years ago, a hominin species perhaps to be identified as *Homo ergaster* made its way northward from Africa into Eurasia. During the ensuing million years, small bands of this species, together with its descendant *Homo erectus,* trekked to regions as far apart from one another as western Europe, eastern China, and Indonesia (see Map 1.1). They also extended their range in Africa. Equipped with more complex brains and better tool kits than their genetic ancestors, these species adapted to natural environments very different from those of tropical Africa.

Clever but not quite "us." *Homo ergaster* and *Homo erectus* were tall and full-bodied, not short and slight like australopithecines. They were too heavy to swing through trees but robust enough to stand their ground against formidable animal predators. More important, they had a larger braincase than earlier hominins, suggesting a brain size about three-quarters as large as ours. This bigger skull may have enclosed more complex neural "wiring," a biological advance that permitted more intricate mental processes than earlier hominins could handle. For example, they appear to have fashioned stone tools with some sort of "plan" in their heads for how to use them later.

After millions of years when hominin brain size did not change much, the rather sudden debut of these relatively keen-witted creatures is not easy to explain. We know that *Homo erectus* became omnivorous, eating just about everything that could be eaten, including much larger quantities of meat than its forebears had consumed. The species could never have grown such an ample brain relative to body size, if it had not built up its supply of food energy by consuming meat rich in calories, protein, and fat. *Homo ergaster* and *Homo erectus,* plus a species called *Homo heidelbergensis,* which evolved in Africa perhaps 600,000 years ago, applied their brains to developing diverse, sophisticated tools of chipped and flaked stone, including choppers, chisels, cleavers, scrapers, awls, and hammers, as well as finely fashioned, teardrop-shaped

An Acheulean hand axe. The style of stone tools called Acheulean derives its name from Saint-Acheul, a suburb of the French city of Amiens, where a paleolithic hand axe was discovered in the nineteenth century. Painstakingly worked on both sides, this tool type first appeared in East Africa more than 1.7 million years ago and was used in several parts of Afroeurasia for hundreds of thousands of years. The hand axe shown here is nearly eight inches long. What sort of useful tasks might a person perform with one of these implements?

hand axes. Females of the species, who probably spent time every day gathering vegetable foods, almost certainly invented and refined much of this equipment.

The intelligence of the species may have evolved in response to the intellectual demands of daily cooperation in small bands and natural selection favoring individuals with brains capable of complex functions useful in group living. But why would hominins need to work together in groups? A likely factor is that *Homo erectus* mothers, unlike most mammals, gave birth to biologically immature offspring. As with modern humans, the brains of newborns grew gradually in infancy and early childhood, that is, to a fully developed size that was larger than what could have passed through the birth canal. Such offspring had no ability to look after themselves for a long time. Therefore, intensive childcare, including breastfeeding, occupied females for two years or more. This required males and females to find ways to work together routinely to collect food, defend their camp, and chase after toddlers. The species may have been more than intelligent enough to organize some degree of coordination in the hunt. Bands not only killed and ate large, fierce animals from time to time, but also engaged in tactical planning. At one fossil site in Kenya dated to about 480,000 years ago, the configuration of stone hand axes and cleavers, together with the bones of sixty-three baboons, suggests that a band of *Homo ergaster* or related hominins surrounded the primates, then systematically attacked and clubbed them to death.

Homo **species on the move.** On the largest scale, the history of our close genetic ancestors must be framed within the whole of Afroeurasia. Fossil discoveries at a site near Dmanisi (duh-man-EE-see), a village in the Republic of Georgia, show that tool-using hominins whose forebears almost certainly came from Africa lived in the Caucasus Mountains about 1.8 million years ago. Experts are divided over the

The Turkana Boy: A Distant Ancestor

Samuel Muteti, a research scientist at the National Museums of Kenya, displays a replica of the 1.6 million-year-old Turkana Boy (also, Nariokotome Boy).

Human forebears of a million and a half years ago had a good chance of dying young. The Turkana Boy did, falling face down in a soggy marsh where his body decomposed and his skull and bones slowly separated from one another. He was probably between eight and eleven years old when he died. He was walking, maybe running, near a river that lay west of Lake Turkana in what is today northwestern Kenya. His remains show possible signs of spinal disease or injury, and he had inflammation in his lower jaw, which might suggest blood poisoning. He stood well over five feet tall, and he might have reached six feet or more in adulthood, if he had lived. Typical of the Turkana people who inhabit the region today, he had a long, slender body, and his shoulders and hips were narrow. This was a physical type genetically adapted to a hot, tropical environment because it maximized the surface area of the body and therefore its capacity to shed heat. He was certainly a meateater, at home on the African savanna because he could run fast and far and hunt in the midday sun.

Some scientists classify Turkana Boy, whose remains lie in boxes in Kenya's national museum, as an early representative of *Homo ergaster.* He probably looked quite like modern humans do, except for his head. He had a protruding face, strong brow, wide nose, and no chin. The small size of his vertebral canal, which encases the nerve-laden spinal cord connecting the brain to the rib cage, suggests that he could not have controlled his breathing in the precise way that we can. He could have made a range of sounds, but, lacking the physical equipment to exhale in a finely modulated way, he could not have strung together nuanced utterances carrying complex meanings. Indeed, his preteen brain was about the size of a modern one-year-old's.

The fossilized bones of a paleolithic hominin rarely give us any sense that they once belonged to a living, moving individual. But with Turkana Boy, stretched out in the mud, we have a kind of stop-action picture of someone on the point of death. The scene invites us to speculate how he died—exhausted from running, badly injured, mauled by an animal, murdered by someone of his own species?

Thinking Critically

Do you think a hominin like Turkana Boy would have been easy prey for other large animal species? Why or why not?

Biological separation of hominins from ancestors of modern chimpanzees (Toumai skull from Chad)

4.4–3 mya: australopithicines, northeastern Africa, Ardi 4.4 mya

7   6   5   4

Millions of years ago (mya)

Evolution of human ancestors.

question of whether these bones represent *Homo erectus,* but the evidence we have so far tells us that this species made its way, by about 1.5 million years ago, to the tropical island of Java in modern Indonesia and, by about 1 million years ago, to northern China. Flint tools found in eastern England reveal that a species probably descended from *Homo ergaster* lived there about 700,000 years ago, though these hunters may have ventured that far north only during relatively short periods when global temperatures rose temporarily.

Under what conditions did these distant ancestors migrate so far and wide, especially considering that chimps, gorillas, and other African primates did not explore beyond their tropical habitats. One theory has it that the brains of *Homo* species, larger than those of earlier hominins, had great food energy needs. (The brain of modern humans is ravenously hungry, consuming about 20 percent of the body's total metabolic energy.) Therefore, forager (or hunter-forager) bands tended to eat themselves out of one local ecological niche after another, especially when competing with other meat-loving animals that shared the neighborhood. When local resources dwindled relative to the size of the band, some members formed a new band, hived off, and searched for a food niche of its own beyond the next hill. One archaeologist has calculated that if subsistence bands, splitting in this way over and over again, drifted only twelve miles in a generation, they could have covered the distance from eastern Africa to China in a mere 20,000 years.[2] In fact, they likely took much longer than that.

Long-term fluctuations in global temperature may also have propelled migration. About 1.6 million years ago, the planet entered the **Pleistocene** (PLEYES-tuh-seen), an epoch of cycles of cooling and warming, each

> **ice age** Any geological epoch, most recently the **Pleistocene** era (1.6 million to 12,000 years ago), when glaciers covered a large part of the world's surface.

cycle lasting about 100,000 years over the past million years. Long periods of cooling, or **ice ages,** produced glaciers, that is, great ice sheets that extended from the north polar region southward to cover large areas of northern Eurasia and North America. Glaciers transformed so much saltwater into ice that ocean levels fell, extending coastal zones and exposing land bridges between territories once separated by water. During relatively shorter periods of warming, called **interglacials,** the ice retreated and sea levels rose again. During the past million years, warm periods

> **interglacial** A period of global warming and retreating glaciers between ice ages. Our current geological epoch, the **Holocene,** is an interglacial.

have lasted only about 10,000 years. Indeed, we have been living in an interglacial, called the **Holocene,** since about 9600 B.C.E. Bands of *Homo erectus* or related species spread across Afroeurasia during the Pleistocene, when temperature cycles produced successive northward and southward shifts in patterns of rainfall and vegetation. Migratory drift across Eurasia may have been linked to these climatic rhythms, with forager bands roving into more northerly areas during interglacials and then having to either adapt or retreat south when temperatures dropped again.

Because these creatures migrated so far and wide, they must have developed tools and social practices rich and flexible enough to adapt to widely varying environments. Learning how to control fire was a key advance. Charred ground found at fossil sites in both eastern and southern Africa suggests that *Homo ergaster* was the first hominin to build fires to keep warm, scare off predators, illuminate murky caves, and perhaps cook food. In 2004 a site in northern Israel yielded evidence of burned chips of flint rock, indicating that hominin bands built campfires some 790,000 years ago. Hominin bands certainly could not have survived in northern climates, even during interglacials,

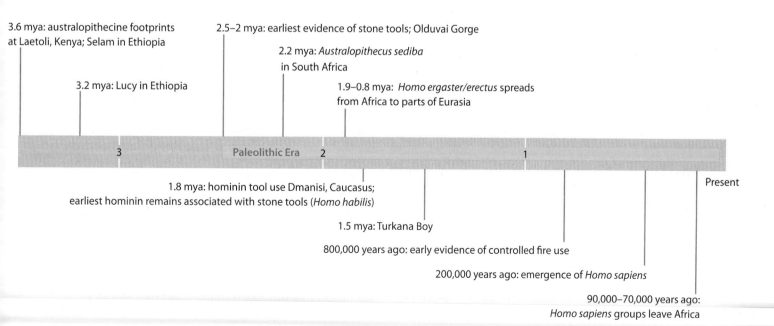

3.6 mya: australopithecine footprints at Laetoli, Kenya; Selam in Ethiopia

2.5–2 mya: earliest evidence of stone tools; Olduvai Gorge

2.2 mya: *Australopithecus sediba* in South Africa

3.2 mya: Lucy in Ethiopia

1.9–0.8 mya: *Homo ergaster/erectus* spreads from Africa to parts of Eurasia

3   Paleolithic Era   2   1

1.8 mya: hominin tool use Dmanisi, Caucasus; earliest hominin remains associated with stone tools (*Homo habilis*)

Present

1.5 mya: Turkana Boy

800,000 years ago: early evidence of controlled fire use

200,000 years ago: emergence of *Homo sapiens*

90,000–70,000 years ago: *Homo sapiens* groups leave Africa

without knowing how to use fire. The site at Zhoukoudian (joh-koh-dee-ehn), a town in northern China, reveals that *Homo erectus* individuals occupying a cave there some 300,000 to 400,000 years ago built fires, though scientists continue to dispute the evidence.

A diverse stone tool kit, elemental social organization, and knowledge of fire enabled *Homo erectus* and its like to become a "cosmopolitan" species. This means that it adapted successfully to several contrasting ecological niches. Even so, there is something alien and remote about these creatures. They did not, as far as we know, devise social rules for sharing food, resolving conflicts, or strategizing long-term survival. Fossil and tool sites have so far turned up no evidence that they knew anything of religion or art or even how to build a simple hearth. No wall paintings, no stone carvings, no burial of the dead. In fact, by comparison with the 200,000-year history of our species, the life ways of this species changed remarkably little in the nearly 2 million years that it survived.

Other Traveling Hominins

Starting 200,000 years ago or more, hominin species possessing greater intelligence and more sophisticated tool kits than *Homo erectus* begin to appear in the fossil record. So far, we have evidence of four of them. We know quite a bit about one of these species, the Neanderthals (nee-ANN-duhr-tawls), but not much about two of them, the Floresians and the Denisovans. The fourth one is *Homo sapiens,* the subject of the rest of this book. All four species may be biological descendants of *Homo erectus,* but we cannot demonstrate the lines of descent with certainty.

The Neanderthals. The hominin species known formally as *Homo neanderthalensis* occupied a large part of Europe and Southwest Asia, the region that in modern contexts we call the Middle East. Named after the Neander River valley in northern Germany, where bones were discovered in the nineteenth century, this large-brained species flourished 200,000 years ago, then went extinct about 28,000 years ago. Accumulating scientific evidence has nearly demolished the theory that the Neanderthals are our own direct biological ancestors. More likely, they represent a separate branch descended from an earlier species.

Popular culture has treated Neanderthals harshly, depicting them as ugly, dunderheaded cave-dwellers. This species did live in caves, and they had short, stocky, muscular, strong-jawed bodies. But they were not dimwits. They had brains in the same size range as ours, and they used a complex kit of specialized stone tools. They dressed themselves in warm clothing of fur and skin, controlled fire, and hunted game along the fringes of glaciers. They also buried their dead and placed material objects in the graves, suggesting that they believed the deceased might carry these goods into an afterlife. Fossil remains have also revealed individuals who survived for months or years despite having arthritic or broken bones. Here is a hint that Neanderthal

bands cared for sick or aging members of the group rather than abandoning them to die alone. Neanderthals no doubt communicated with one another using both sounds and gestures. Their throat structures, however, may have been ill-designed for stringing together complex sounds, and we have no evidence that they possessed language. Nor did they make art or build even rudimentary houses. But what we know of their behavior suggests that they may have been on the way to acquiring some of these abilities.

Neanderthals had sufficient intelligence and skill to live in a range of climates in Southwest Asia, Europe, and northwestern Africa (see Map 1.2). Within the climatic cycles of the Pleistocene epoch, they probably advanced north during warm, interglacial periods, following the tracks of reindeer and other game. When temperatures dropped and the glaciers spread, however, they retreated southward to friendlier ecological zones. Whatever their adaptive skills, however, they eventually had to face intrusive *Homo sapiens.* We come back to that confrontation later in the chapter.

The Floresians. In 2004, researchers digging in a cave on Flores, an Indonesian island east of Java, announced that they had found what appeared to be a previously unknown hominin species. Scientists reconstructed a partial skeleton, revealing an upright-walking, long-armed adult female barely three feet tall. Her braincase, however, was small, about the size of a chimpanzee's.

The specimen and the excavated materials associated with it presented several puzzles. The shape and size of the face and teeth suggested a species quite close to *Homo sapiens* on the hominin family tree. The interior of the skull indicated lobes and ridges characteristic of the high-powered *Homo sapiens* brain. Stone tools found at the site were small and fine, suggesting more advanced technological skills than *Homo erectus* probably had. Finally, scientists dated the skeleton to only about 18,000 years ago, suggesting that the species far outlived *Homo erectus* and shared tropical Southeast Asia with modern humans, possibly for thousands of years. Scientists named the creatures *Homo floresiensis,* or simply the Floresians, after their island home.

The archaeologists who discovered the fossils have argued that the Floresians are probably not descended from *Homo erectus.* Rather, they represent an entirely different branch of the hominin tree, some members of which migrated from Africa to Southeast Asia either before or after *Homo erectus* did. Other scholars have contended that the cave-dwellers are *Homo sapiens* and that the miniature skull is evidence of a developmental disease. In any case, the skull specimen has impelled scientists to think again about the relationship between intelligence and brain volume. The species that hunted in the island's mountain forests may have had much more complex neural wiring packed into its tiny cranium than other early hominins did.

The Denisovans. Applying new biochemical techniques, scientists have succeeded in the past few years in sequencing the DNA of a young female hominin who spent time in

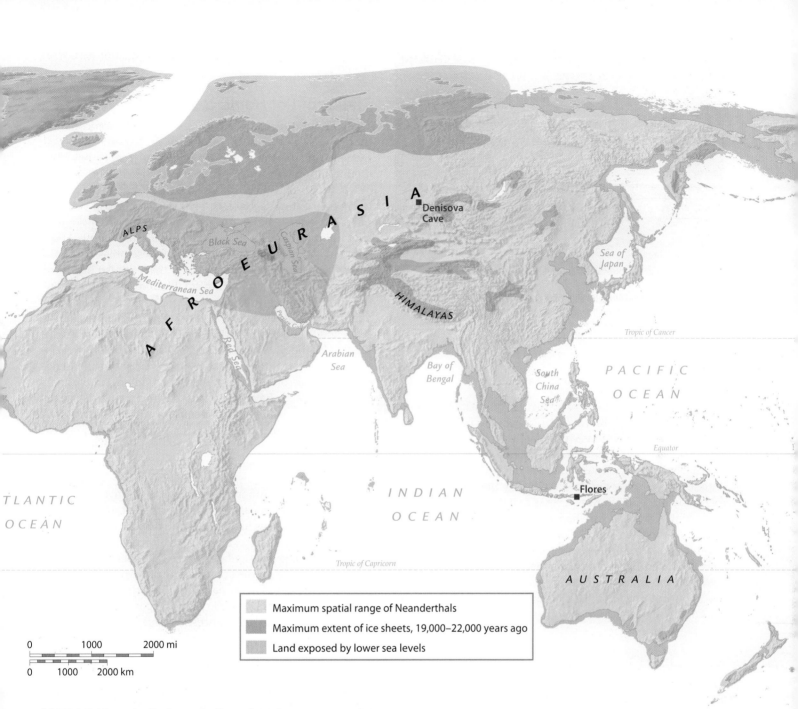

MAP 1.2 Neanderthals and other close human ancestors.

What climatic and geological relationship existed between the expansion of ice sheets and the appearance of land bridges that migrating human ancestors may have crossed?

Map legend:
- Maximum spatial range of Neanderthals
- Maximum extent of ice sheets, 19,000–22,000 years ago
- Land exposed by lower sea levels

a cave in southern Siberia as many as 80,000 years ago. Since the 1970s molecular biologists interested in human evolution have been studying the properties of DNA, the main constituent of the human chromosome and the one that carries genes. As DNA flows from one generation to the next, small alterations, or mutations, occur and at a regular rate. This means that over time the genetic differences between individuals sharing a common ancestor increase statistically. The longer two human populations have no contact with one another, the greater the genetic distance between them will be. Using complex laboratory procedures, scientists can measure the rate of change in genetic material and therefore estimate how long ago in thousands or even tens of thousands of years two hominin groups separated from one another. Analysis of the Siberian girl's genome, that is, her complete set of chromosomes, has revealed that her ancestors separated biologically from *Homo sapiens* somewhere between 170,000 and 700,000 years ago. In other words, she

Historical evidence from a pinky finger. Laboratory analysis of undamaged DNA contained in a finger bone fragment from Siberia has revealed that our species probably has a previously unknown cousin. Genetic studies can tell us many things about early human history. What aspects of the past do you think they *cannot* explain?

was not a member of our own species, but neither was she a Neanderthal or *Homo erectus*. Rather, she belonged to a hominin species previously unknown.

The Denisova Cave, as it is known, has so far revealed no treasure trove of skeletal parts but only a small bone in one pinky finger and two teeth. The bone yielded such high-quality DNA, however, that scientists have declared confidently that the girl had brown hair, eyes, and skin. They have told us that she was a closer genetic cousin of Neanderthals than of modern humans and that her species inhabited Siberia perhaps tens of thousands of years before *Homo sapiens* arrived in the region. So far, however, we know nothing of the Denisovans' territorial range or the sort of tool kit they used.

Modern Humans in Africa: The First 100,000 Years

FOCUS What physical and intellectual characteristics distinguish *Homo sapiens* from our species' hominin ancestors?

Homo erectus, Neanderthals, Floresians, and Denisovans all migrated long distances from Africa, but none of them, as far as we know, made their way to Australia, the Americas, or the far-flung islands of the Pacific. That distinction belongs to *Homo sapiens*, which, starting from eastern Africa, colonized all the world's large land masses except Antarctica. Owing to genetic research and fossil finds in recent years, most scholars have come around to the view that people like us evolved exclusively in Africa, emerging about 200,000 years ago. *Homo sapiens* then populated several parts of Africa and may not have moved out from there in significant

numbers to colonize the rest of the world until as few as 70,000 years ago.

The Debut of *Homo Sapiens*

The dominant theory of *Homo sapiens'* dispersion contends that our species evolved in eastern and southern Africa. Evidence sustaining this "Out of Africa" theory has been accumulating steadily. Archaeological digs have found the oldest *Homo sapiens* bones only in Africa. In 2005, scientists using new dating technology estimated the age of two partial *Homo sapiens* skulls discovered in southern Ethiopia at about 195,000 years. A fully modern skull from South Africa dated to about 36,000 years ago closely resembles the skulls of *Homo sapiens* individuals who by that era also inhabited far-flung parts of Eurasia, if in small numbers. This similarity suggests that our species evolved fully in Africa *before* venturing to other regions to take up permanent residence.

Genetic research has also supported the Out of Africa theory. In the past few decades, DNA studies have confirmed repeatedly that greater variety exists in the genes of individuals of African descent than among individuals whose ancestors have lived in other regions. This means that the common ancestor of people of African descent in a set of DNA samples, wherever those people live today, existed at an earlier time than the common ancestor of any non-African in the sample. In other words, individuals of African descent in the sample could trace their genetic lineage back to a common ancestor without anyone of non-African descent appearing in it. By contrast, non-Africans in the sample always had at least one African ancestor.

Theoretically then, everyone alive in the early twenty-first century possesses a family tree that goes back to forebears who lived in eastern or southern Africa 150,000 to 200,000 years ago. We all have inherited the DNA (specifically mitochondrial DNA, the type that passes only through women) of distant African ancestors, and from them the genetic branches of the human family tree began to multiply and leaf out. Eventually, humans began to explore other parts of the world, creating more genetic diversity as they drifted in different directions and lost contact with one another. Today, scientists are mapping genetic variations in full detail, a project that will eventually give us a much richer understanding of when and by what routes *Homo sapiens* occupied the world.

The Power of Language

Our fully human ancestors remained exclusively in Africa for a long time, but they made history there by expanding their territorial range over many thousands of miles—from South Africa to Morocco's Mediterranean coast. A large part of Africa lies within the tropical latitudes, but our species nonetheless penetrated a wide range of ecological zones—rainforests, mountain valleys, and semiarid plains, as well as temperate lands in the far north and south where winters required warm shelters. After about 80,000 years ago, human forager communities appear to have started multiplying along the belt of wooded and open savanna that runs the breadth of Africa from Ethiopia to the Atlantic Ocean. *Homo sapiens* thus acquired the brain power to adapt to a great variety of environmental niches.

The men and women who originally colonized many parts of Africa probably resembled us fairly closely in an anatomical sense. If a 100,000-year-old *Homo sapiens* were to walk onto a college campus today wearing conventional clothes and sporting an adequate haircut, she would probably attract no more attention than anyone else. If someone tried to speak to her, however, she might have been at a loss for words. This is because humans were only just about then acquiring the gift of language. When they did, the power of humans to work in groups and to manipulate their physical and natural environment swelled dramatically.

Possessing language, people formed social communities that could consciously share, accumulate, and transmit complicated information to offspring. *Homo sapiens* did not have to depend, as all other animals do, on genetic alterations to adapt successfully to changing physical and natural environments. Rather, they had the power to bring about change through the nuanced interaction of many minds. In a word, they acquired the capacity to create culture. And cultural change, by comparison with the sluggish pace of biological adaptation through natural selection, could take place in the blink of an eye. The historian David Christian calls this ability "**collective learning.**"[3] Among higher primates like chimps and gorillas, the young learn behaviors related to such things as finding food and avoiding predators by observing and imitating their parents. But the learning largely stops there, and no primate can pass on to its offspring the details of its life experience—"here's what I did a few years ago when this pack of hyenas saw me." In their early months, human babies learn mainly from the sounds and gestures that other family members make, but as they grow older and acquire language, they tap in to vast stores of knowledge communicated not only by their family but also by thousands of other people, as well as by books, radio, television, and the Internet. In turn, these individuals can pass arrays of information to the next generation. Over time, the process of collective learning has led to exponential growth of knowledge, and humans have used it to alter and manage their physical and natural environments in increasingly intricate and powerful ways.

collective learning The process whereby humans accumulate and share complex knowledge and transmit it from one generation to the next.

Symbolic thinkers. All animal species have ways of communicating, but language is another matter. Humans evolved an anatomical sound-making apparatus that could not only pronounce words—that is, individual sounds with meanings assigned to them—but also arrange words in complex clusters of meaning and transmit those meanings from one person to another at a fast rate. This ability to control sounds to convey elaborate, subtle meanings, which people shared with one another, separated even the earliest human language speakers from animals that communicated through grunts, barks, chirps, and screeches.

Underlying the act of speaking is the capacity for symbolic thought, a talent that, as far as we know, only *Homo sapiens* has. The human brain, unlike that of any other animal, has the capacity to transform sensory information coming from the outside world into symbols that represent, or stand for, that information. These symbols take the form of language, and it is language with which we think, that allows us to be self-aware. All animal species monitor and react to the environment outside themselves in one way or another, and they communicate with other members of their species in ways that have evolved biologically. But only humans engage in complex symbolic reasoning regarding the external environment—pondering it, constructing analogies from it, remembering it in detail, or transferring pieces of information from one context to another. Humans can give to things names that symbolically represent those things, talk about things that are not present, and explain technical procedures without having to demonstrate them. They can discuss things that happened in the past, things that are abstract, things that probably do not exist (elves, dragons, sky gods), and things that might happen in the future. Try explaining to a group of friends that you will meet them a week from Thursday at a particular address but only if it is not raining and only if they feel in the mood. Do this, however, using only gestures and sounds that a chimp might make—no speech, pictures, written notes, text messages, or props.

Equipped with language, hunters of 40,000 years ago could huddle together to plan tactics for trapping and slaughtering a herd of zebras. Mothers could explain and children understand why it would be dangerous to go near certain animals. The members of a foraging band could

Early symbols on ochre clay. About 75,000 years ago, someone made these regular marks on a piece of ochre found at the Blombos Cave paleolithic site in South Africa. The marks clearly *stand for something.* The were etched to convey meaning, though we have no idea what the engraver intended to communicate. Why might the production of symbols like this have signaled the early development of spoken language?

make rules to govern social relationships between men and women, create myths to explain how the world began, and express the feelings, desires, affections, and fears that are fundamental to human experience. Language made possible rapid innovation because knowledge of how to construct and use tools could be transmitted from group to group in symbolic form through spoken or pictorial language. For example, a more efficient type of scraping tool could be given a name and classified relative to other tools, and its usefulness could be described.

Body paint and ostrich eggshell beads. *Homo sapiens* appears to have acquired language and culture well before the peopling of the world beyond Africa got seriously under way. An archaeological site on South Africa's Cape coast called Blombos Cave has yielded material dating to between 70,000 and 110,000 years ago. The site includes fragments of human bones having modern anatomical characteristics. The cave has also revealed evidence of decidedly "modern" behavior. The people who lived there manufactured tools that suggest collective sharing of information and intense cooperation. These objects include the world's oldest known tools made of bone, including projectile points and awls (a pointed instrument for piercing holes in skins or other material).

Early jewelry? These perforated shell beads dabbed with red ochre, dated to about 82,000 years ago, come from a site in northeastern Morocco. Can we safely infer that a person strung these shells together to make a necklace or bracelet? Why else might someone have cut holes in shells? What sort of messages do people communicate when they wear jewelry?

Furthermore, the Blombos Cave dwellers made objects that appear to have carried symbolic meaning. They produced pigment of ochre, a red earth that they applied in some way, perhaps as body paint that communicated something about the individual who wore it. Inhabitants also deliberately engraved pieces of ochre with hatched markings. Archaeologists have found tiny seashells intentionally pierced with holes to fashion beads. These objects have been dated to 75,000 years ago, early evidence from southern Africa of humans creating decorative ornaments. Traces of iron oxide pigment on the beads suggest that they were painted. The job of perforating small shells took time and patience, hinting at a division of labor in which at least a few people took on special jobs part of the time rather than finding and preparing food. The owner of a collection of beads worn as a bracelet or necklace likely intended to display it to others. That is, the members of a cohabiting group may have identified themselves to a "foreign" band through distinctive visual signs, or they may have sealed friendly relations with neighbors by symbolic exchange of valuable objects.

Archaeologists have unearthed tantalizing evidence of advanced technological skill and symbolic thinking at other African sites as well. In 2007, scientists working in a limestone cave in eastern Morocco announced the discovery of perforated marine shell beads that they believe are 82,000 years old. These trinkets are covered with red ochre, and some of them show wear patterns suggesting they were suspended from a cord. Other researchers have found beads nearly as old in Algeria and Israel. A site called Twilight Cave in Kenya has revealed ostrich eggshell beads dated to about 40,000 years ago. Men and women appear to have been making and wearing beads—and perhaps talking about them—from South Africa to the shores of the Mediterranean thousands of years before our species ventured to other parts of the world. In the equatorial Congo River valley, researchers have dated finely crafted stone implements, including delicate barbed points, to as many as 80,000 years ago.

Finally, evidence in stone suggests that the world history of material and cultural exchange among human groups had its beginning in eastern and southern Africa. Several digs have revealed objects of particular stone material that does not occur naturally in the area where the items were found. Excavations have turned up many objects of obsidian, a hard volcanic glass used to fashion axes, blades, and projectile points. According to geological evidence, these objects must have been brought to the site from somewhere else, in some cases from locations two hundred miles away. This means that people either carried pieces of obsidian distances significantly greater than the range of a single forager band or, more likely, that networks were being created to relay valuable objects from one band to another. It is possible that these objects were not only practical items of trade but also gifts meant to seal relationships between cooperating bands. The archaeology shows that only a tiny percentage of artifacts found in African sites had to have originated from some distant area. But from about 50,000 years ago, just when humans were migrating to far-flung parts of the planet, material exchange among Africans shows evidence of becoming increasingly voluminous and complex.

The fossils and artifacts that researchers have found in Africa for periods before 40,000 years ago are all subject to multiple and sometimes contradictory interpretations. It seems clear, however, that when humans started leaving that land mass in significant numbers, they already had a well-packed suitcase of mental, linguistic, technical, and social abilities to help them tackle the environmental challenges of new lands.

Colonizing the World

FOCUS What factors contributed to our species' successful colonization of all the world's major land masses (except Antarctica) between about 70,000 and 10,000 years ago?

Among hominin species, only *Homo sapiens* migrated to all the continents and mastered every earthly climate short of the polar ice caps. The story of how this happened is sketchy. So far, we lack the evidence to trace with much precision the routes and timing of the long migrations across Eurasia and on to Australia and the Americas. We do know, however, that between about perhaps 70,000 and 10,000

years ago, a fleeting era in the scale of evolutionary time, humans dispersed to regions as distant from one another as northwestern Europe, southern Australia, eastern Canada, and the far end of South America (see Map 1.3).

The Roads from Africa

We have evidence that as many as 115,000 years ago at least a small number of humans crossed the Sinai Peninsula from the Nile River valley to inhabit an area that is today in Israel. That foray into Southwest Asia, however, appears to have been brief; we have no evidence of movement deeper into Eurasia at that time. Genetic evidence indicates that the pioneers who initiated the sustained colonizing of Eurasia 90,000 to 70,000 years ago may have descended from people who lived along the African coast of the Red Sea in the previous 55,000 years, subsisting partly on shellfish. We cannot demonstrate that communities along that shore had rafts or canoes, but short voyages across the southern Red Sea would have taken them to the Arabian Peninsula. Forager bands making their way eastward from Arabia could have thrived, multiplied, and advanced quite rapidly (on a scale of thousands of years) because they would not have had to face radically varying ecological conditions if they kept to the Asian coastlands. Their diet of edible plants and the fruits of the sea was likely abundant and nutritious. Traces of their

MAP 1.3 Global migrations of *Homo sapiens*.

The dates on the map are approximations. Scholars continue to debate the dates of early human movements, though the sequence and relative chronology of migrations show a fairly rapid peopling of the planet compared to the pace of previous hominin dispersals (see map 1.1). What factors might explain why humans migrating from Africa reached Australia about 20,000 years earlier than they reached Europe?

campsites and boats, however, may now lie deep under water because sea levels rose as the last ice age receded, starting about 18,000 years ago.

South to Australia

Skeletal remains discovered near Lake Mungo in southeastern Australia indicate that the earliest human colonizers reached that continent from Southeast Asia as many as 60,000 years ago. DNA research has supported this hypothesis, marking a genetic separation between Southeast Asians and the native peoples (Aborigines) of Australia 55,000 to 60,000 years ago. Pleistocene conditions in that period locked up polar ice, lowering the sea level in Southeast Asia enough to create land bridges between many of the thousands of islands that make up the Indonesian archipelago. Consequently, small migrant bands might have been able to walk west-to-east across much of the region or to island-hop short distances on log or bamboo rafts. The low sea level also conjoined Australia, New Guinea, and Tasmania into a single land mass, a bygone continent known as Sahul. If migrants reached New Guinea by making a water passage of as little as fifty miles, they could have turned south and continued "down under" on foot. Other pioneers may have followed shortly thereafter, though an initial Australian population of a few dozen men and women would have been enough to jumpstart steady population growth.

When the Pleistocene ice loosened its grip on the world, water flooded in, dividing Australia once again from New Guinea. Sahul no longer existed, but by that time humans had made Australia their own. Most scholars think that people advanced across the immense interior of the continent rather than hugging the shores. Whatever the routes taken, people colonized far southern Australia more than 35,000 years ago. Except on a stretch of the northern coast, where episodic contact between Indonesian mariners and Australians continued, the continent's forager population played out its history in isolation from the rest of the world, until Europeans came ashore in the late eighteenth century C.E.

Colonizers of Europe

Despite the brief occupation of land just east of the Mediterranean more than 100,000 years ago, modern humans did not continue into Europe or any other part of western Eurasia for another 60,000 years or so. If approximate dates now available are correct, people occupied Australia perhaps 10,000 to 20,000 years *before* they entered Europe, even though Europe is much closer to our species' African homeland. Why the long time lag? One theory is that the glacial climate of much of the Eurasian land mass between 80,000 and 40,000 years ago was biologically uninviting to *Homo sapiens*. Our relatively slim, long body type was genetically

Sophisticated tools. These five tools illustrate the remarkable technological advances that appear in the archaeological record between about 40,000 and 20,000 years ago. These implements from Europe—two hand axes, two blades, and a harpoon—are much more finely crafted than the Acheulean tools of earlier times. How might a person of the upper paleolithic equipped with language have explained to someone else the usefulness of a delicately carved barbed harpoon?

unsuited to cold climates as long as people lacked the technology to fashion warm permanent shelters or snugly fitting clothing and footwear. Neanderthals already had the run of ice age Europe, but this species had short, thick-boned bodies that more effectively retained heat.

Between 40,000 and 50,000 years ago, however, an interglacial warming trend set in. Modern humans reestablished themselves in Southwest Asia, which in that age had a greener landscape and more temperate climate than it does today. By then, moreover, their tool kit included finely crafted blades, scrapers, awls, barbed points, and other implements that helped them adapt to novel ecological conditions. In the following 20,000 years, forager bands gradually advanced northward to occupy a belt of temperate land extending from the Atlantic coast of Europe to Siberia. Although global temperatures dropped again after about 30,000 years ago, humans survived the cold with their new tools, weapons, and schemes of social cooperation. When the climate of northern Eurasia became too harsh for survival even with their new inventions, foragers simply retreated south as far as necessary. Nevertheless, *Homo sapiens* was gradually conquering winter.

The American Frontier

Like Australia, the Americas had, as far as the physical evidence shows, no hominin population until *Homo sapiens* showed up. Most experts take the view that bands of *Homo sapiens* arrived in the Americas from departure points in northeastern Asia. As material and genetic evidence has accumulated, however, questions about how and when the peopling of the Americas took place have become more puzzling, not less. For decades, paleoanthropologists conventionally argued that the earliest migrants reached North America by trekking from Siberia to Alaska. Today the Bering Strait, an oceanic passage fifty-three miles wide, separates Eurasia from America. But during the last ice age, a land bridge connected them. Named Beringia by modern geologists, this vanished isthmus supported plant and animal life, especially after global temperatures started going up around 18,000 years ago. The optimum time for forager bands to cross Beringia would have been during the following few thousand years. About 12,000 years ago (10,000 B.C.E.), Beringia surrendered to the rising sea, but by then the first Americans had established themselves and were drifting southward.

Many questions remain about the numbers and precise origins of these colonizers. From a genetic perspective, a single band of migrants including as few as four women of childbearing age could have been the founding ancestors of everyone who subsequently occupied the Americas up to 1492 C.E. However, recent fossil finds and analysis of DNA suggest that more than one wave of colonization may have taken place. Skeletal remains uncovered in Washington state, Nevada, Minnesota, Brazil, and a few other places indicate bone structures different enough from those of later American Indian populations to suggest that groups of migrants originating in different parts of Asia entered North America at different times up to about 12,000 years ago. On the other hand, recent genetic studies have linked living Native American individuals in North, Central, and South America to groups native to Siberia. This evidence suggests that a single group migrating from northeastern Asia to North America is ancestral to all Native Americans.

Peopling the Americas: Overland or by coast? Scholars conventionally have argued that humans who first arrived in Alaska subsequently migrated across the Canadian interior through a habitable corridor of green that opened up between two colossal ice sheets as global temperatures warmed. These hunters and foragers advanced south of the glaciers into thick woodlands and eventually open plains, then fanned out to eventually populate the rest of the

Kennewick Man. This skull, part of the remains of a 9,300-year-old North American male dubbed Kennewick Man, has suggested that humans having different physical characteristics migrated from Asia to the Americas in successive waves. This photo shows a plastic casting of the original skull, which is housed at the University of Washington in Seattle. The Weighing the Evidence box on page 36 addresses the public controversy that the discovery of Kennewick Man has caused.

The Kennewick Man Controversy

In 1996, scientists were startled to learn that a nearly complete human skeleton discovered on federal land in the shallows of the Columbia River near Kennewick, Washington, was about 9,300 years old. Kennewick Man, as he came to be known, exhibited physical features suggesting that American Indians who live in the Pacific Northwest today are not his biological descendants. The Native American Graves Protection and Repatriation Act (NAGPRA) stipulates that Indian remains discovered on federal land must be returned to local tribes for reburial. Paleoanthropologists argued, however, that such ancient bones should be subjected to extensive study. In 2004 a federal court ruled in favor of the scientists. Armand Minthorn, an Umatilla Indian leader, and Robson Bonnichsen, an anthropologist, expressed opposing views on Kennewick Man's appropriate fate.

DOCUMENT 1 Armand Minthorn, Umatilla Indian leader

Our religious beliefs, culture, and our adopted policies and procedures tell us that this individual must be re-buried as soon as possible. Our elders have taught us that once a body goes into the ground, it is meant to stay there until the end of time. . . . Under the Native American Graves Protection and Repatriation Act, tribes are allowed to file a claim to have ancestral human remains reburied. My tribe has filed a claim for this individual and when it is approved, we will rebury him and put him back to rest. . . . If this individual is truly over 9,000 years old, that only substantiates our belief that he is Native American. From our oral histories, we know that our people have been part of this land since the beginning of time. We do not believe that our people migrated here from another continent, as the scientists do. Some scientists say that if this individual is not studied further, we, as Indians, will be destroying evidence of our own history. We already know our history. It is passed on to us through our elders and through our religious practices.

Source: Armand Minthorn, "Human Remains Should be Reburied," Confederated Tribes of the Umatilla Indian Reservation, September 1996, http://www.umatilla.nsn.us/kman1.html. At the time of writing, the author was a member of the Board of Trustees and a religious leader of the Umatilla Confederated Tribes.

DOCUMENT 2 Robson Bonnichsen, anthropologist

A scientist's ability to teach effectively, to write publishable articles, to plan new research projects and to develop and test new theories is dependent upon access to the most up-to-date and accurate information possible. Unfortunately, First Americans researchers like myself are not blessed with an abundance of direct evidentiary data with which to work. Sites and artifacts from the earliest periods of American prehistory are not plentiful, and even less common are well-preserved skeletal remains and other human biological materials. Every new discovery of an early site or human skeleton is important, and each must be investigated as thoroughly and carefully as possible if we hope to ever unravel the mysteries of the peopling of the Americas.

The processes that led to human colonization of the Americas can never be understood without answers to two fundamental questions: who were the first Americans and where did they come from. Sites and artifacts can be informative, but they alone can never provide the definitive answers. People of different biological backgrounds can generate similar sites and artifacts, and people that are closely related biologically can produce very different material cultures. Only skeletal remains and other biological materials can answer questions about biological relationships.

Although the Kennewick skeleton does not date from the time of the first human colonists of the New World, it can provide important data that can be used to develop and test theories about the evolution and development of early New World human populations. The studies of the skeleton that were conducted for the Department of the Interior . . . in 1999 indicate that it does not resemble any of the modern human populations compared in those studies. Measurements and observations reported for the skeleton also indicate that while it is similar in many respects to some of the other early human skeletal remains found in North America, it also differs substantially from some of the others. Such findings, if true, could have important implications for understanding how the Americas were colonized by humans. Among other things, they could indicate that colonization of the New World may have involved multiple colonizing groups and that those groups may have originated in different regions of Eurasia.

Source: United States District Court, District of Oregon, *Bonnichsen, et al. v. United States of America, et al.,* Affidavit of Robson Bonnichsen, Nov, 2002. At the time of the affidavit, the author was director of the Center for the Study of the First Americans and professor of anthropology at Texas A&M University.

Thinking Critically

What underlying assumptions do you think informed these two statements, and how do those assumptions differ? Why do you think the bones of a 9,300-year-old man triggered a prolonged public controversy in the late twentieth century?

Americas. In recent years, however, experts have been paying more attention to a potentially much faster route south. Like the discoverers of Australia, the earliest American pioneers had watercraft, perhaps skin-covered boats sturdy enough to make headway along the Pacific coast. Perhaps they did not walk across Beringia at all but paddled along the northeastern coast of Asia and straight on to Alaska and the western Canadian coast. They would have made camps on islands or habitable coastal strips that the ice walls of the interior did not quite reach. Relying on coastal plants and seafood, these men and women might have had to make relatively small changes in their technology and life ways as they advanced from one latitude to the next. However, we have no physical evidence of boat-building on the Pacific coast before 6,000 years ago. Still, the coastal theory remains attractive because it offers plausible answers to perplexing questions about the timing of American colonization. A site rich in stone, bone, and ivory tools excavated in Monte Verde, Chile—10,000 miles from Beringia—has been dated to more than 14,500 years ago. How did humans make their way over such a vast distance in only a few thousand years? One possible explanation is that they migrated down the western coasts of North and South America, at least part of the way in boats.

Researchers have also speculated that humans first reached the eastern side of North America, not by migrating southward through the Canadian interior, but rather by advancing over many generations from the Pacific coast across what is now the southwestern United States to the Gulf of Mexico. From there, they could have moved into the woodlands east of the Mississippi and south of the retreating glaciers. In the last few years, archaeologists have found stone blades, choppers, and projectile points at a complex of sites called Buttermilk Creek in the hills north of Austin, Texas. A dating technique that measures light energy lodged in

minerals in the soil around the artifacts has revealed that people were making tools at Buttermilk Creek as long as 15,500 years ago. The ancestors of these early Texans may have migrated eastward from the Pacific coast. The evidence is controversial, but excavations at Meadowcroft Rockshelter in southwestern Pennsylvania suggest that people lived there as many as 16,000 years ago, cooking meat and fashioning flint blades. A site called Cactus Hill in southeastern Virginia has yielded tools and bits of charcoal hinting that people whose forebears migrated from the west reached a point only about seventy miles from the Atlantic Ocean 15,000 years ago.

Why Did *Homo Sapiens* People the Earth?

Most animal species occupy only certain parts of the world. Humans, by contrast, are biologically cosmopolitan—they live just about everywhere. Why did this happen? We would not be thinking historically if we presumed that people occupied all the continents because human beings have an inherent urge to "explore new lands." Local communities, whether foragers or farmers, historically have tended to live out their lives within a single confined territory as long as they had reasonable security and a sufficient food supply. On the other hand, they have also had to calculate continuously an acceptable balance between the resources their local environment could provide and their prospects for survival. In paleolithic times, periodic shortages, climatic fluctuations, and competition from human or animal predators must have obliged cooperating bands to be ready to move down the coast or over the next hill when they might otherwise have preferred to stay put.

Population growth was almost certainly a key factor in global colonization. Genetic studies suggest that, as recently

Archaeologists at Buttermilk Creek. Researchers working at the Buttermilk Creek complex in Texas have in recent years found a deep level of artifacts suggesting human occupation of the region nearly two and a half thousand years earlier than previously known.

as 70,000 years ago, the total *Homo sapiens* population, all of it in Africa, may have numbered as few as 10,000 individuals. Scientists have theorized that long periods of cold temperatures and arid conditions may have kept humankind on the edge of extinction. Fortunately for us, numbers started climbing again. Estimates vary widely, but total population may have risen to about 300,000 by 30,000 years ago and to perhaps 6 million by 10,000 years ago.

Population growth and human migration were closely interrelated. The very climatic conditions that taxed human ingenuity for survival may have stimulated creative responses to environmental stress, including more effective social cooperation, the invention of new tools, and language development. These improvements permitted groups searching for resources to penetrate lands where conditions were hotter, colder, higher, drier, or in some way different from what could have been tolerated in earlier ages. Also, regional climates continued to fluctuate somewhat, producing ecological alterations serious enough to force communal

bands to abandon deteriorating habitats for new ones offering a better chance of survival. A band of just twenty or thirty men, women, and children required an extensive area within which to hunt, fish, or collect plants. If the group got too big, routines of social cooperation and sharing might break down. One way to avoid social strain was to permit some members of the group to move to another neighborhood to start a new band. As groups divided over and over again, the range of human colonization expanded steadily. Cooperating bands therefore neither wandered aimlessly nor set off on long-distance explorations. Rather, they budded off from one another, advancing into new territory to fulfill very short-term goals to survive and reproduce.

Homo Sapiens:
The Last Surviving Hominin

When *Homo sapiens* started its long journey around the world, did other hominin species still exist? Certainly

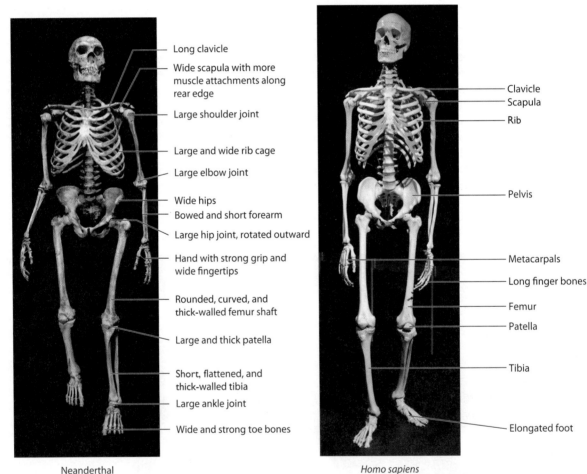

Long clavicle

Wide scapula with more muscle attachments along rear edge

Large shoulder joint

Large and wide rib cage

Large elbow joint

Wide hips
Bowed and short forearm

Large hip joint, rotated outward

Hand with strong grip and wide fingertips

Rounded, curved, and thick-walled femur shaft

Large and thick patella

Short, flattened, and thick-walled tibia

Large ankle joint

Wide and strong toe bones

Clavicle
Scapula
Rib

Pelvis

Metacarpals

Long finger bones

Femur

Patella

Tibia

Elongated foot

Neanderthal

Homo sapiens

Neanderthal and *Homo sapiens* compared. In general, Neanderthals had wider, stockier, shorter bodies than our own species. This physique would have helped them conserve body heat in northern ice age climate. Modern humans were on the whole taller and leaner than Neanderthals, but they also became more proficient at fabricating warm clothes. What factors might explain why we have remains of many more Neanderthal individuals (several hundred of them) than we have of earlier hominin species like *Homo erectus*?

Neanderthals and Denisovans did, probably Floresians, and possibly *Homo erectus.* Recent dating of bones discovered on Java in Indonesia suggests that *Homo erectus* survived, at least in that part of the world, until 50,000 years ago or later. If that is true, our species might have met *Homo erectus* bands and even lived alongside them for a time. At some point *Homo erectus* disappeared, probably because modern humans deployed their amazing mental tools to outwit, outcompete, and outpopulate it.

Scholars generally agree that *Homo sapiens* and Neanderthal groups occupied parts of Southwest Asia and Europe at the same time. The two species had similar stone tool kits for thousands of years, and archaeologists have unearthed tool sites in Europe suggesting that Neanderthals adopted, copied, and even traded for refined tools that modern humans first introduced. Scientists sequenced the Neanderthal genome in 2010, and since then evidence has accumulated showing that humans of non-African origin share as much as 4 percent of their DNA with Neanderthals. This finding indicates that the two species interbred, perhaps in Southwest Asia. These couplings may have occurred rarely, and we have no idea whether they took place in circumstances of friendly intimacy or violent aggression. Some scholars have suggested that since Neanderthals achieved biological adaption to the European disease environment long before *Homo sapiens* arrived there, they may have contributed elements to our genome that provided immunities against certain cold-climate maladies.

In any case, as *Homo sapiens* bands fanned across Europe in the millennia after 40,000 years ago, they gradually pushed surviving Neanderthals off to the margins of good foraging land. When glaciers advanced and temperatures dropped again about 30,000 years ago, humans proved technologically better equipped than Neanderthals to survive in more northerly parts of Europe. Scientists have also proposed that Neanderthal males and females hunted together and, contrary to humans, never developed a division of labor in which females spent more time gathering plants, hunting small game near camp, and nurturing children, a diversification of activities that may have allowed cooperating bands to grow in size and density. Still another theory argues that Neanderthals had "antisocial" inclinations. They formed small hunting bands that had little to do with one another, whereas human groups, endowed with wagging tongues, interacted more congenially and over longer distances, thereby accelerating the process of collective learning for the species as a whole. Recent tool finds near Gibraltar indicate that the Iberian Peninsula was the last, hopeless refuge of *Homo neanderthalensis.* The species vanishes from the record about 26,000 years ago.

As for the Denisovans, genetic analysis of the Siberian girl's pinky finger demonstrates that this species also mated

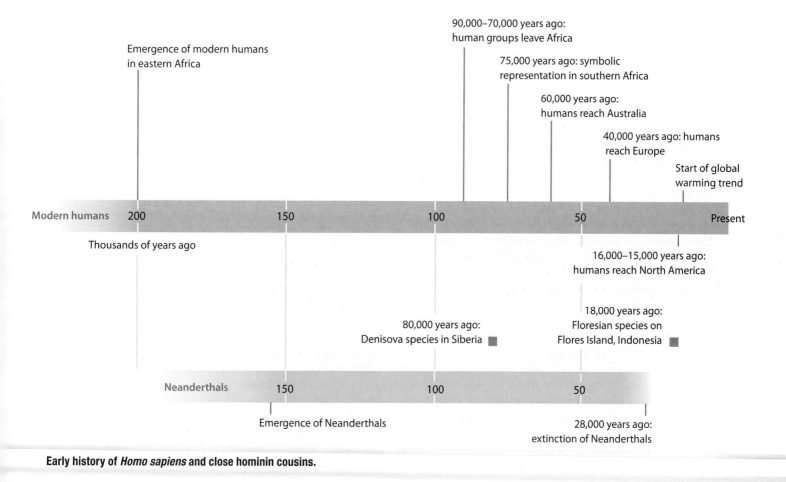

Early history of *Homo sapiens* and close hominin cousins.

with humans. About 3 percent of the genes of people living in Papua New Guinea in Southeast Asia, as well as a much smaller percentage of the DNA of living Chinese, reveal Denisovan ancestry. As in the Neanderthal case, however, scientists can only speculate about where and under what circumstances these sexual episodes took place. And like Neanderthals, the Denisovans vanished. Perhaps archaeological evidence of this species' existence, other than a finger bone and two teeth, will one day turn up.

Why People Look Different

The genes of all human beings are 99.9 percent identical; in fact we share 96–99 percent of our genetic code with chimpanzees. Because of variation within the remaining 0.1 percent, however, all individuals in the world are genetically unique. Our species has evolved in a way that has produced a few broad but observable physical differences between large aggregates of people whose ancestors have lived in different parts of the world and have tended to mate with one another much more often than they have mated with people who live far away. We particularly notice these differences between populations whose forebears lived in starkly different climatic zones. Minor differences in traits, such as skin and hair color, eye shape, nose width, and body type, are the result of either adaptations to particular physical and natural environments or simply random genetic variations. For example, humans who colonized northern Europe evolved skin color lighter than peoples of tropical lands partly because of an ancient and natural deficiency of vitamin D in the basic foods that northerners consumed. Lighter skin allowed greater penetration of the sun's ultraviolet rays, which enhanced the body's own production of vitamin D, thereby decreasing vulnerability to the crippling disease known as rickets. Similarly, the epicanthic fold, that is, an overlap of skin that covers the inner corner of the upper eyelid and is characteristic of people native to northeastern Eurasia, is likely an evolutionary adaptation to northern climate and latitude. Natural selection favored the inner eye fold because it protected people who had it against long summer light, cold, and swirling dust.

Differences like these have in no *biological* way hindered the ability of Sumatrans, Norwegians, Mongols, and Congolese to talk, live, work, and reproduce together. Although the word *race* and its variants are used today to express a variety of social and cultural meanings, respectable scientists and historians have abandoned the notion that separating humankind into a fixed number of separate "races," whether three of them or three hundred, has any useful biological significance. Genetic differences among human groups are minute compared to the total number of our genes. These tiny differences must therefore have developed, not millions of years ago, but in connection with the relatively recent peopling of the world from eastern Africa. As one scientist has put it, "We are all members of a very young species, and our genes betray this secret."[4]

Global Culture of the Upper Paleolithic

FOCUS How may we account for the acceleration of cultural and social change in human societies between about 40,000 and 12,000 years ago?

"We are what we wear," the saying goes. In other words, we send messages about ourselves by the way we drape and decorate our bodies. We paint our faces, wear trousers of a particular cut, and hang golden objects from our ears to communicate to others where we think we fit in the social universe. Humans, we have seen, may have begun to express symbolically their distinctiveness as individuals or as members of groups more than 80,000 years ago by wearing bead necklaces or painting themselves with ochre. This elaboration of human culture is likely to have happened in association with the acquisition of language. In the ensuing tens of thousands of years, human talent for symbolic expression through spoken words, gestures, and visual symbols probably developed gradually, exclusively in Africa at first, then wherever in the world *Homo sapiens* migrated.

Between 40,000 and 30,000 years ago, just when the Pleistocene was heading into its last cycle of extreme cold, the pace of cultural change began to speed up and human society moved in the direction of greater complexity. We know from an ever-growing body of fossil and other material evidence that in the upper paleolithic era (40,000–12,000 years ago) global population rose at a faster rate than ever before, tool kits became more varied and sophisticated, cooperating groups in some regions grew larger and more socially intricate, and symbolic imagery in the form of statues, cave paintings, and abstract designs multiplied. People began to adorn both themselves and the bodies of their dead with necklaces, pendants, bracelets, garment pins, and a multitude of other objects made from stone, bone, shell, or ivory. We will probably never understand much about the symbolic meaning that men and women attached to the decorative objects left to us from the upper paleolithic. But the urge to bedeck and beautify was an elemental part of the emergence of humankind as a species of exquisitely complex culture.

Dawn of a Multicultural World

Because ways of life dependent on gathering, hunting, or fishing had several common elements (limitations on the size of social groups, for example), human culture in the paleolithic had a certain uniformity. However, as global numbers inched upward and people adapted to a wider range of natural environments, cultural expression worldwide became more diverse. The archaeological record makes it clear that communities inhabiting far-flung localities gradually developed distinctively different ways of doing things—designing tools, building houses, or carving animal images in stone.

Owing to the complex collective learning that language made possible, practical ideas for improving tools, shelters, or food sources flowed more widely and rapidly from one group to another. Population growth within a region meant that strangers were likely to live closer to one another and therefore interact more intensively. There is no doubt that encounters between bands sometimes produced rock and spear fights. For example, many of the human remains found in a 14,000-year-old graveyard at Jebel Sahaba (JAH-bahl sa-HAH-bah) on the Nile River show signs of people having been stabbed or clubbed to death. It is also certain, on the other hand, that strangers met together peaceably to share technical information, news about food sources, or hunting and fishing lore.

Regional networks for bartering food, tools, or ornaments also became more elaborate than they had been in their earlier, exclusively African settings. Groups organized exchange networks to barter ivory, seashells, sharks' teeth, high-grade flint, and other practical or ornamental objects. For example, archaeologists digging in upper paleolithic sites in southern Europe have found yellow amber that originated near the Baltic Sea coast hundreds of miles to the north. Forager bands may also have exchanged exotic items as part of rituals to reinforce bonds of feeling and memory among their members, that is, to encourage enduring social relations among people who did not see one another very often. In short, as groups came face to face with new things from far away, they rejected some innovations and accepted or modified others, depending on their own needs and tastes. In these ways, localized populations became more culturally differentiated from their neighbors.

Social and Economic Life

Thirty thousand years ago, all human communities made their livings gathering, hunting, or fishing wild food. A co-operating band typically numbered twenty to thirty individuals but might run to one hundred depending on the local ecosystem. Bands might have been relatively large in western Eurasia where they hunted wild horses, cattle, or bison by driving them over cliffs or into swamps and then slaughtering them in a single operation. This strategy would not work well without a substantial force of men, women, and children to chase, kill, and dress the prey. By contrast, bands that inhabited deserts, high mountain valleys, or other marginally productive regions had to be small enough to maintain a workable balance between local resources and mouths to feed.

The members of a foraging band had to work together intently because upper paleolithic life was too dangerous and unpredictable to permit selfish, go-it-alone behavior. By that era, young men and women of childbearing age almost certainly bonded permanently to produce families. The way animal bones are distributed in some sites in Europe suggests that families within a band shared food with one another. Certainly some men and women stood out as natural group leaders. In fact, evidence dating back at least 25,000 years indicates that communities buried some corpses with especially

numerous and refined ornaments or other grave goods. This suggests that certain people had special status and that social differences based on leadership, good fortune, ritual expertise, or spiritual insight were beginning to emerge.

The division of labor within the band, that is, the distribution of economic tasks among members, was uncomplicated. Adult men probably had the job of ranging beyond the immediate neighborhood of the camp to forage or hunt. Women who were pregnant or had small children to look after collected edible plants or small animals close to home. Bands organized work this way, not because males were anatomically larger and stronger than females, but more likely because hunting large animals was hazardous. The death of a woman of childbearing age was in principle a greater threat to the survival of the group than was the death of a man. A hunter also had to move quickly and quietly, something a female carrying a small child could hardly manage. A woman, on the other hand, could gather berries, tubers, and other plants close to home with children in tow.

Certainly, the old cliché of Stone Age Man as macho hunter, killing saber-toothed tigers and dragging them home for the evening meal, is far off the mark. At sites in central Europe, for example, archaeologists have found fragments of pollen and processed vegetable matter suggesting that people ate a remarkably wide variety of plant foods. And small game such as birds, rodents, and even insects may have made up a much larger part of a band's diet than did grizzly bear or giant sloth. Excavations in Europe have also uncovered pieces of clay impressed with crisscrossed strands of fiber. These specimens, dating back more than 25,000 years, hint that women wove nets to catch small game.

The extent to which foragers relied on animal protein depended largely on ecological circumstances. In the cooler latitudes of both Eurasia and North America, for example, a relatively heavy meat diet compensated for the comparatively short plant-producing summers and for the loss of body heat in the cold months. Northern Eurasians especially prized reindeer, which provided hides and antler bone as well as meat. Nearer the end of the upper paleolithic, when temperatures rose again, some western Eurasian peoples turned increasingly to a fish-centered diet. By about 14,000 years ago, communities were forming along rivers or seacoasts where they thrived on salmon and other big fish, using specialized techniques to net, dry, and smoke their catch. This economy encouraged groups to stay in one place a long time and may have permitted relatively larger bands to thrive. On the expansive plains of North America, hunters became expert at following bison herds. By about 11,000 years ago, they were fashioning sharp, finely shaped projectile points and mounting them on long spears. This weapons technology, which is associated with an assemblage of stone tools referred to as Clovis (after a site near Clovis, New Mexico), spread remarkably fast from Canada to Central America.

Humans preyed on reindeer and bison without sending them to extinction, but they may have had a hand in the disappearance of dozens of large animal species from the face of the earth. Mammoths in Inner Eurasia, large marsupials in Australia, and mammoths, horses, camels, and giant ground sloths in the Americas all vanished during the upper paleolithic. Perhaps these doomed species failed to adapt to the globe's climatic warming trend after 18,000 years ago, though numerous temperature cycles had occurred during the previous 2 million years without such fatal consequences for big species. Could skill and social coordination in the hunt have been so ruthless and efficient that people wiped out whole classes of animals in the course of several thousand years? Even if large animals initially had no natural instincts to run away from humans, it seems improbable that hunter bands would have systematically slaughtered certain animals simply because they had the technology to do it. Nevertheless, humans evolved a much greater variety of collective skills and strategies than any other animal species. They were establishing themselves at the top of the food chain and starting to have a noticeable impact on other life-forms, particularly ones good to eat.

Technical Wonders

One of the marvels of the late ice age is that when global temperatures started dropping about 30,000 years ago, humans became more inventive than ever. In northern Eurasia the key to survival was keeping body temperature up. Many communities endured by huddling in ice-free valleys or in caves and rock shelters. In eastern Europe and Inner Eurasia, cohabiting groups built tents of skins fitted over wood or animal-bone frames. Sites uncovered near the Don River in Russia, for example, have revealed hamlets where the residents dug "pit houses," then ringed them with mammoth bones and covered these structures with hides. They kept hearth fires going continuously and preserved meat in "freezers" dug in the cold earth.

Early colonizers of northerly latitudes draped themselves in leather and fur, as their Neanderthal cousins did. Recently, archaeologists have found fibers of flax (the plant from which linen is made) in the Republic of Georgia dating to 34,000 years ago. Some of these strands were twisted and others were dyed, suggesting that the occupiers of the site were fashioning ropes, baskets, or clothing. About 20,000 years ago, some clever individual invented the needle. Made of bone or ivory, this simple device spread quickly and was used to fashion custom-fitted trousers, shirts, parkas, hoods, and boots. Lengths of fiber cord served as thread and also material for snares, nets, tethers, handles, and binders. Upper paleolithic carvings show women wearing string skirts. One scholar argues that the "string revolution" was one of the most important technical breakthroughs of the era.[5]

Keeping warm in the Ukraine.
Shelters fashioned from the bones of mammoths, and probably covered with hides, are among the earliest known built structures. A farmer enlarging the cellar of his house in the western Ukraine in 1965 found a jawbone that led to the discovery of this circular hut. It dates to about 15,000 years ago.

Another key innovation was a "core," or chunk of rock, flint, or other fine-grained stone from which a worker could strike off rough blades. These "blanks" were then fashioned into specialized tools depending on the job at hand. A particular type of carving blade, for example, might be used to fashion bone or antler into an even more specialized device such as a spearhead, fish hook, or harpoon. Hunter-gatherer bands of Inner Eurasia and northern China developed a sophisticated kit of exquisite **micro-liths,** tiny blades that could be attached to handles and used as spears, scrapers, or knives. Similarly, hunters in North America struck blades off flint cores to make their elegant Clovis spear points.

> **microlith** A small blade of flaked stone used as a tool.

In tropical latitudes, upper paleolithic remains are sparser, partly because warmer, rainier climates provided abundant wood and fiber, an "organic" technology that long ago rotted away and vanished from the historical record. In southern China and Southeast Asia, for example,

people continued to use relatively unrefined stone chopping tools for thousands of years. But they probably also invented tools of bamboo, a plant that is superbly suited for making strong, resilient objects, including spears, knives, scrapers, baskets, and even houses and boats. Bamboo may have contributed as much to the growth of human populations in East and Southeast Asia as stone blades did in regions nearer the glaciers.

A World of Symbols

We may define the art of the upper paleolithic fundamentally as the objects or images that women and men made to represent their world symbolically. Art bloomed in myriad styles and materials—paintings on cave and rock shelter walls, carved figures of humans and animals, and geometric patterns etched on bone. Even the sound of music was heard. More than thirty flutelike instruments made of long hollow bone and equipped with finger holes have been found in western Eurasia dated to roughly 37,000 years ago. Wherever people lived, they took advantage of the local materials and opportunities they had at hand. Wall painting, for example, is concentrated heavily in northern Spain and southwestern France where deep limestone caves provided "gallery space" protected from rain and wind. In eastern Europe, by contrast, cave shelters are rare, so people commonly carved small, portable figurines.

Trying to explain the meanings that paleolithic men and women attached to painting, sculpture, stone carvings, or music is always risky because so much depends on the cultural context of the work, about which we know little, and on the presumptions we ourselves bring to the interpretation. The meaning of a piece of twenty-first-century art may be problematic enough, much less the chiseling and daubing of people who lived 20,000 years ago. We can hardly do more than speculate on the aesthetic, social, or spiritual intentions of individuals who drew pictures of bison galloping across rock shelter walls, painted images of human hands, or carved mysterious spiral patterns on pieces of bone. Take, for example, the hundreds of "Venus" figurines found in sites scattered across Eurasia from western Europe to Siberia, one from Germany dating to at least 35,000 years ago. The best-known samples of these have exaggerated breasts and buttocks. Were these female statues sex objects for men? This interpretation used to be popular but has few advocates today. Were the figures symbols of female fertility, and if so, did the symbolic power appeal to men, women, or both? Were they part of a symbolic system by which women shared rituals with one another? Did their meaning vary from one region to another? This debate will continue for a long time.

A panoramic view of upper paleolithic art suggests some general trends. First, as cohabiting bands interacted over increasing distances, artistic forms and styles, as well as the material objects themselves, spread from one region to another. That is, networks of shared symbols became more

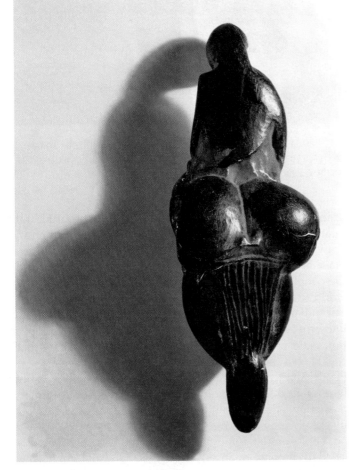

Venus of Lespugue. This female figurine dating to between 24,000 and 26,000 years ago comes from a cave in southwestern France. The back view reveals a string skirt attached to a hip belt. Since this is not a very practical piece of clothing, why might an upper paleolithic woman have worn one?

Art in the cave of Chauvet. In 1994 three spelunkers discovered marvelous art like this on the walls of chambers deep in a cave in southern France. Compared with other paleolithic cave art, the Chauvet paintings, dating to about 31,000 years ago, are unusual for their depiction of large wild animals like this rhinoceros and for the artists' use of shading and perspective. What specific artistic features do you notice in this work?

widespread. A second pattern is that art was increasingly important to ritual life, including initiation ceremonies for adolescents, mating rites, funerals, and appeals to supernatural powers to protect the community. For example, one group of nameless folk who lived in southern Europe 15,000 years ago took the trouble to crawl far back into the dark bowels of a cave to carve clay statuettes of bison that hardly anyone was ever likely to see. Surely, there was complex ritual purpose here, not just amusement or "art for art's sake." A third pattern is that people decorated their bodies more and more elaborately to express their social identity, as we do today. Cooperating bands might also have festooned themselves in special ways to signal to other groups whether they were friend or foe. That is, paleolithic decoration was an early expression of ethnic identity.

We have no material artifacts at all to help us know how spoken languages sounded. We may assume that as groups split off and moved apart from one another, the common language they once spoke became in time differentiated in vocabulary and grammatical structure. Consequently, distinct languages, that is, speech systems that were mutually unintelligible, began to multiply. By studying the structural relationships between languages and their distribution in the world today, scholars have formulated theories to explain how and when early forms of those languages, and the people who spoke them, migrated from one part of the world to another. We know, for example, that most American Indian languages may be grouped together in a family known as Amerind and that the relationships and distribution patterns among languages in this family indicate that speakers of them initially migrated from North America to South America, not the other way around. For periods before about 8000 B.C.E., however, conclusions about human movements drawn from linguistic data alone are necessarily sketchy and tentative.

People of the upper paleolithic era clearly communicated in complex, nuanced languages and visual symbols. A material discovery in Southwest Asia in the mid-1990s, however, has shaken conventional theories of just how sophisticated cultural expression had become among foragers in at least one part of the world. On a hill called Göbekli Tepe (goh-behk-LEE teh-peh), overlooking a plain in southeastern

Göbekli Tepe. The site of this astonishingly early stone monument in southeastern Turkey features massive, T-shaped pillars. Because some of the pillars have human limbs carved on them, archaeologists assume they represent human beings, perhaps deities or priests. People deliberately buried the entire complex around 2,000 years after it was built. Why might they have done that?

Turkey, archaeologists have found the site of an elaborate temple complex dating to as many as 12,000 years ago (10,000 B.C.E.). There, people whose identities we will never know constructed a series of stone circles, at least seven of them and perhaps several more, on a twenty-five-acre site. These structures feature stone walls surrounding T-shaped pillars as much as eighteen feet tall ornamented with intricately detailed carvings of animal figures—cattle, lions, leopards, foxes, ducks, snakes, ants, and spiders. Many of the pillars have humanlike shapes, including arms, shoulders, and elbows, though none have faces.

The site has astonished scholars because no construction of such size and complexity appears anywhere else in the world's archaeological record until thousands of years later. Researchers generally agree that Göbekli Tepe had a ritual function. Bones on the site suggest animal sacrifice.

The humanlike pillars indicate representation of gods or goddesses, and the carved animals may have mythic or religious significance. There is no evidence that people who frequented the stone circles practiced agriculture or permanently resided in the vicinity. Rather, foraging groups appear to have converged on the site from many miles around at particular times of the year. This suggests that as many as 12,000 years ago forager populations shared religious beliefs and practices on a regional scale. A religious elite may also have existed because someone must have organized at least several hundred people to haul giant blocks of stone from quarries at least a quarter-mile away from where they were installed. About 10,000 years ago, people abandoned the site and deliberately covered it with soil, as if to suggest that they were finished with the old gods and temples and wanted new ones.

• • •

Conclusion

The peopling of all the great land masses except Antarctica was the first world-scale event in the history of our species. Practical, short-range objectives to find food and secure the survival of the cohabiting group impelled the initial global colonization mile by mile. Humans had no long-range knowledge of where they might be going, nor any consciousness of a destiny to colonize the world. Nevertheless, they accomplished the feat, walking or paddling all the way, in as little as 40,000 years after the first migrants left Africa for points east.

Settling the planet would have taken far longer if our species had not possessed language and the multiplying opportunities for collective learning—accumulating, sharing, and transmitting knowledge—which followed from that special talent. The material record of similarities in tools, shelter construction, and artistic styles within broad regions hints at exchanges among groups on a large territorial scale.

Encounters between strangers took place when a small band split off from a larger one, when a bartering expedition traveled far from home, or when some natural calamity forced migration to uncharted territory. As a result of tens of thousands of such encounters over generations, the "cultural capital" of useful ideas, techniques, symbols, and words generally accumulated for everyone.

Human cultural life appears to have emerged gradually in the past 100,000 years. Then, from about 40,000 years ago, it started to accelerate in its complexity, as we know from the proliferation of symbolic objects and images. Perhaps the stark conditions of the last ice age, whether high-latitude cold or tropical drought, propelled communities to devise ever more ingenious ways to make a living, organize social life, and share ideas. Then the interglacial warming that followed obliged our species to confront a whole new range of environmental perils and challenges.

• • •

Key Terms

australopithecines 23	hominin 23	interglacial 27
bipedal 23	*Homo erectus* 21	microlith 43
collective learning 31	*Homo ergaster* 24	Neanderthal 28
Göbekli Tepe 44	*Homo sapiens* 21	paleoanthropologist 24
Holocene 27	ice age 27	paleolithic 24

Change over Time

7 million years ago	Biological separation occurs between hominins and the ancestors of modern chimpanzees.
4.4–3 million years ago	Evidence of australopithecine species in eastern Africa appears.
2.5–2 million years ago	Evidence of stone toolmaking in eastern Africa appears, initiating the paleolithic era.
2 million years ago	Several hominin species coexist in Africa.
1.9 million–800,000 years ago	*Homo ergaster/Homo erectus* hominin species migrate across Eurasia.
200,000–28,000 years ago	The Neanderthal species flourishes in Europe and Southwest Asia.
200,000–150,000 years ago	*Homo sapiens* (anatomically modern humans) evolves in Africa as a distinct species.
100,000–75,000 years ago	Humans in Africa show evidence of symbolic thought.
90,000–70,000 years ago	Human groups begin to move from Africa into Eurasia.
40,000–12,000 years ago	An accelerating pace of tool invention, artistic creativity, and social experimentation marks the start of the upper (or late) paleolithic period.
14,500 years ago	Human groups reach the southern third of South America.
12,000 years ago	Göbekli Tepe temple complex is constructed in Southwest Asia.

Please see end of book reference section for additional reading suggestions related to this chapter.

Farms, Cities, and the New Agrarian Age

10,000–2000 B.C.E.

Jewelry of gold, carnelian, and lapis lazuli from the Royal Cemetery of Ur, southern Iraq, about 2600 B.C.E.

apis lazuli is an opaque, intensely blue semiprecious gemstone that sparkles with tiny flecks of gold. Polished stones make elegant jewelry, and a powdered form of lapis was the basis of ultramarine, a pigment prized by artists before the advent of synthetic paints. Lapis is mined today in a number of countries, but the most beautiful stone comes from mines in the mountains of northwestern Afghanistan. Trade in lapis dates to the fourth millennium B.C.E. (3999–3000 B.C.E.), if not earlier, and the workings in Afghanistan, together with a site in southwestern Pakistan, may be the oldest continually operating gem mines in history. Lapis was likely an object of gift exchange among early farmers, and by the third millennium B.C.E., it began to appear in the households and burial chambers of the rulers of city-states and kingdoms in Mesopotamia, Egypt, and the Indus River valley. Archeologists excavating the tomb of Pu-Abi, an important woman in the ancient Mesopotamian city of Ur in the twenty-sixth century B.C.E., uncovered a stunning collection of grave goods, including jewelry studded with lapis that could only have come from mines hundreds of miles to the east. Within a few more centuries, a lapis exchange network extended 1,600 miles from the Indus to the Nile.

We saw in Chapter 1 that trade among forager bands had its origins deep in the paleolithic era. But after about 10,000 B.C.E., webs of barter and gift-giving in copper, gold, silver, shells, gemstones, and fabricated products expanded rapidly in several regions of Afroeurasia. This quickening of human exchange happened in association with a sharp upward trend in world population and, in some places, a surge in the size, number, and density of human settlements. The invention of farming made both of these developments possible.

The emergence of a world of farms, cities, and commerce is a recent episode in the history of our species. Anatomically modern humans lived exclusively by hunting and foraging for about 200,000 years, and in *biological* terms, *Homo sapiens* may be best suited to live in tiny communities, eat nutritious food found in the wild, walk a lot, and sit on the ground. During those two hundred millennia, however, our species also acquired the gift of language. With it, humans gained a talent for collective learning, the ability, which no other animal has ever had, to share, accumulate, store, and transmit complex knowledge about themselves and the world around them.

After about 10,000 B.C.E. (12,000 years ago), humans in a few parts of the world began to apply their collective learning skills to the problem of *producing* food rather than merely gathering or hunting whatever nature provided. Over a span of several thousand years, some communities shifted to a way of life that involved deliberately planting, nurturing, and harvesting food crops, as well as confining and protecting animals in order to use them for ritual sacrifice, food, fiber, and bone. This chapter introduces the early era of farming, a startling change in human history, and the spread of this radically new way of living to several regions of the world.

Farming could dramatically increase a community's food supply, offering nourishment for many more individuals than a foraging territory of the same size could provide. Consequently, between 10,000 and 4000 B.C.E., the population in certain parts of the world rose faster than it ever had before, and permanent settlements grew larger and closer together. Social relations among families and settlements became more intricate; leaders emerged who wielded serious authority over the community; technologies increased in sophistication; and trade expanded. The first section of this chapter

• • •

examines these developments, especially in the region between the Mediterranean basin in the west and South Asia in the east.

From about 4000 B.C.E., the pace of change began to accelerate even faster in farm communities of that broad region. People moved together into settlements that in some places numbered many thousands. Some individuals stopped growing or collecting food altogether in order to specialize in making useful products, supervising other people's work, keeping public order, or communicating with powerful gods to keep them happy and cooperative. The culture of equality that characterized small forager bands or small farm communities gave way to formal social divisions based on wealth, spiritual prestige, special skill, or the power to command armed followers. In the second part of the chapter, we explore the development of complex societies—a new and multifaceted way to organize human communities—which we conventionally call "civilizations." The earliest societies of this type arose between the fourth and third millennia B.C.E. in three river valleys: the Tigris-Euphrates in Mesopotamia (modern Iraq), the Nile in Egypt, and the Indus in modern Pakistan and northwestern India. We investigate these three societies in a comparative frame, focusing on the geographical and ecological conditions under which they emerged and the distinguishing

A Panoramic View

Southwest Asia
Food crops: wheat, barley, rye, lentils
Domesticated animals: sheep, goats, pigs, cattle, dogs

East Asia
Food crops: rice, millet, soybeans
Domesticated animals: pigs, water buffalo

Mesoamerica
Food crops: maize, beans, peppers, squashes, tomatoes

Amazon River Valley
Food crops: manioc

West Africa
Food crops: yams, okra, black-eyed peas

Andean South America
Food crops: potatoes, quinoa, sweet potatoes
Domesticated animals: llamas, alpacas, guinea pigs

Sudanic and Saharan Africa
Food crops: sorghum, finger millet, rice
Domesticated animals: cattle

Southeast Asia
Food crops: taro, yams, sugar cane, coconut, bananas, citrus fruits
Domesticated animals: chicken

ATLANTIC OCEAN
PACIFIC OCEAN
INDIAN OCEAN
NORTH AMERICA
SOUTH AMERICA
AFRICA
EURASIA
AUSTRALIA
Tropic of Cancer
Equator
Tropic of Capricorn
Abu Hureyra
Çatal Hüyük
Jericho
Nile Valley
Tigris-Euphrates Valley
Indus Valley
Yellow River Valley
Yangzi River Valley

Fertile Crescent
Spread of domesticated plants and animals

MAP 2.1 Early domestication and the spread of agriculture.
Humans domesticated food plants and animals independently in several parts of the world. What geographical or climatic factors may have contributed to plant or animal domestication in each of these eight regions?

cultural styles they all developed in their formative centuries. These societies also made trade and cultural connections with one another that affected the histories of them all. Finally, they achieved sufficient size and collective skill to manipulate their natural and physical environments on a much larger scale than humans had ever done before.

The Coming of Farmers: A Peculiar Event

FOCUS Why did humans in several parts of the world take up farming, given that our species had survived without it for 200,000 years?

The activity we call farming refers specifically to the technical process of *producing* food in a systematic way by planting, tending, and harvesting edible plants and by grazing domesticated animals on pasture. These new methods allowed humans to capture and consume much more of the sun's energy, the source of all plant life, than in earlier times. But coaxing food energy and surplus wealth from the soil involved more than tools and techniques. Woven into the activity are social habits, moral rules, and supernatural beliefs. Until the start of the industrial age barely more than 200 years ago, all complex societies were **agrarian societies,** based on farming as the primary way of life. And like the earlier colonization of the world, farming emerged as a consequence of human beings making countless everyday decisions century after century, though no one at the time could see where these experiments might be taking our species.

agrarian society A society in which agriculture, including both crop production and animal breeding, is the foundation of both subsistence and surplus wealth.

The current state of archeological evidence points to Southwest Asia as the site of the earliest communities that grew cereals, especially wheat, barley, and rye, as well as lentils, chickpeas (garbanzo beans), and a few other legumes. At Abu Hureyra (A-boo hoo-RAIR-a) on the Euphrates River in north central Syria, archaeologists have found large, plump seeds of domesticated rye that date to about 12,000 years ago—the oldest known trace of farming in the world. Other agrarian settlements that emerged in the following millennium or two lie along an arc of high country in Southwest Asia, the region traditionally known as the Fertile Crescent.

Early Farming and the Big Thaw

Ten thousand years ago the world had around six million people scattered across Afroeurasia, Australia, and the Americas. Paleolithic bands lived with danger and insecurity, and most people probably died before they reached forty. Nevertheless, foragers ensured themselves of a plentiful, varied food supply, at least much of the time, and they had shorter daily working hours than most humans have enjoyed since farming societies arose. They sheltered themselves adequately in a wide range of climates, and they shared in a rich social and ceremonial life. Why, then, should some groups in certain places take up a strangely different way of life, one that involved hoeing crops in the hot sun, milking animals every day, living in cramped villages, and perhaps handing part of their food supply to local chiefs? Certainly no paleolithic woman suddenly got a flash of brilliance and said to her friends, "Why don't we plant these seeds, care for the young plants, and harvest the food when it's ripe?" Rather, farming evolved as many small groups made small decisions and alterations, many of them unconscious and unintentional. An **agricultural revolution** occurred, but humankind backed into it.

agricultural revolution The transition from collecting food in the wild to domesticating and producing particular plants and animals for human consumption.

Scholars generally agree that early farming was connected in complicated ways to the onset of the Holocene, the global climatic warming cycle that fully set in after about 9600 B.C.E. and that continues today. During the transition from the Pleistocene to the Holocene era, global temperatures increased by fractions of degrees over centuries.

Global temperature change and early farming. The Pleistocene was the long geological era characterized by cycles of climatic cooling and warming. The Holocene is the recent warming, or interglacial, era. The Younger Dryas was a temporary period of colder temperatures lasting about 1,200 years. Does the chronological match between rising global temperature and evidence of agriculture necessarily mean that global warming *caused* people to take up farming?

The retreat of the great ice sheets, warmer seasons, and increased rainfall permitted small animals, marine life, and forests to multiply across the Northern Hemisphere. In some regions, the early Holocene created new ecological niches for various species of wild grass that produced edible and nutritious grains.

The earliest evidence we have of humans systematically collecting and consuming wild grain comes from northeastern Africa between the Nile and the Red Sea (today part of Sudan and Ethiopia). Discoveries of stone blades and grinding implements show that some foragers in that region began between 16,000 and 13,000 B.C.E. to subsist partly on grain, which they roasted or ground into flour to make bread. The idea of grain collecting may well have diffused from the Nile region to the Fertile Crescent around 11,000 B.C.E. Historians have associated this dispersal with an ancient movement of people, perhaps small numbers of them, from Africa to Southwest Asia.

In relatively high and well-watered elevations of the Fertile Crescent, forager bands began to identify and collect wild grains ancestral to einkorn and emmer wheat, as well as barley and rye. Cohabiting groups that found these seeds tasty, nourishing, and easy to harvest with sharp flint blades had good reason to station themselves next to large stands of grain for months at a time. Eventually, they took to husbanding cereal plants by pulling out competing weeds, bringing in water, and scaring away pesky birds and rodents. Because wild cereals contributed an increasing number of daily calories relative to other food sources, some bands settled permanently near abundant stands of the coveted plants. That is, they became sedentary. We know that sedentism was taking place in Southwest Asia from about 11,000 B.C.E. The earliest villages in the Fertile Crescent were no more than little clusters of circular "pit houses" of stone and wood. The residents of these tiny villages ate wheat, barley, or rye boiled, roasted, or ground up for bread. They did not, however, stop foraging for tubers, fruits, and nuts in the neighborhood or hunting gazelles and small game. Farming and foraging economies overlapped for thousands of years.

The Drift toward Domestication

To tend patches of wild grain was one thing. To *domesticate* plants or animals was a more complicated matter. Domestication means that humans changed the genetic makeup of plants and animals by influencing the way they reproduce, thereby making them more appealing in taste, size, and nutrition, as well as easier to grow, harvest, process, or cook. People could not invent new plant species, but they could select plants that possessed certain observable mutations, that is, unusual characteristics that made them desirable.

The marriage of plants and humans. There is no doubt that foragers of the early Holocene knew a great deal about wild plants. They could distinguish between flora that were good to eat and those that were too small, oily, or bitter—or even fatally toxic. At first, however, women and men domesticated desirable plants with no consciousness of what they were doing. They unintentionally disseminated the seeds of plants they liked to eat because waste seeds frequently sprouted near the settlement, especially around latrines and trash heaps. If people looked after desirable plants that were close to the camp, they effectively segregated them from wild plants in the wider neighborhood. Doing this over decades and generations, they unwittingly protected the plants they wanted against genetic contamination from wild ones they did not want. Probably very early in this process, people deduced a connection between seeds that lay on the ground and the later sprouting of new plants. Eventually, they got the hang of broadcasting or sticking in the ground desirable seeds, thereby increasing the yield. Thus, they improved a species further, creating a superior hybrid without knowing they were doing it. Full domestication occurred when humans and their farm products became codependent. That is, the community came to rely for an important part of its food supply on genetically altered plants. The plants, in turn, were so changed that they could no longer grow in the wild.

When we think about world history's first farmers, we should probably picture mostly girls and women. The division of labor in paleolithic bands was informal, but women who had to stay close to camp to breastfeed and look after young children became experts in the locally available food plants. While men were hunting far from camp, women were busy, whether consciously or not, genetically manipulating plants.

Domestication of animals. Humans and animals also domesticated each other unintentionally at first. In Southwest Asia, dogs, which are descended from species of wolves, partnered with humans thousands of years before the advent of farming. A likely scenario is that wolves prowled around forager camps looking for food scraps. Individual animals genetically disposed to be slightly less skittish in the presence of humans tended to stay closer to the camp. Eventually, people captured some of these relatively more placid beasts, perhaps wanting them because they would bark when strangers approached. As canines inclined to tameness interbred with one another in captivity over numerous generations, they gradually transformed themselves into hunting companions and camp guards that could no longer survive in the wild alongside their distant wolf cousins.

Pig bones associated with a human settlement in southeastern Turkey point to domestication of that mammal about 10,000 B.C.E. A recent theory contends that in the early farming era people kept tame pigs, and soon thereafter sheep, goats, and cattle, because they wanted them not for meat or milk but as objects of periodic ritual sacrifice or communal feasting.[1] In time, communities that did this came to recognize the usefulness of these animals as sources of food, hides, hair, wool, and traction (plow-pulling). Humans became more dependent on domesticates than on wild game,

A harvest ballet. The women in this scene painted on rock in the Tassili-n-Ajjer region of southeastern Algeria bend gracefully to gather grain. An artist made the painting between 5000 and 6000 B.C.E., a time when the central Sahara was significantly wetter than it is now.

and, in turn, domesticated pigs, sheep, goats, and cattle genetically acquired tameness, smaller size, and sense organs less adapted to the necessity of alertness or sudden flight. These creatures could no longer live in the wild. Eventually, humans began deliberately to cull and interbreed animals that had desirable qualities, for example, mating sheep that had softer, woolier coats but killing and eating animals that had stiffer ones before they reproduced.

Of the thousands of relatively large animal species in the world, barely a dozen of them have been domesticated as major sources of food, fiber, or traction. These domestications occurred in different parts of the world over a span of thousands of years. For example, horses, camels, water buffalo, and donkeys tied their fates to humans several millennia after the domestication of pigs, sheep, and goats. As for cattle, the world's oldest archaeological evidence of domesticated species comes from the eastern Sahara Desert. Between 9000 and 8000 B.C.E., that region had significantly higher rainfall than it does now, permitting early cattle tamers to herd animals from the banks of the Nile far into the Sahara in winter months when sufficient water was available. About a thousand years later, domesticated cattle appeared in both Southwest Asia and India.

Neolithic Innovations

Farming emerged in several parts of Afroeurasia independently during the early Holocene. Many scholars think this may have happened because the warming trend was irregular rather than steady. About 10,800 B.C.E., global temperatures dove suddenly, an event linked to the surge of cold water from melting glaciers in the North Atlantic. Scientists call this recurrence of cooler, drier weather in the

Northern Hemisphere the Younger Dryas after the name of an arctic wildflower (see temperature chart, p. 51). It lasted about 1,200 years, and it likely increased ecological stress on both foragers and early farmers in several regions nearly simultaneously, especially where population was already rising when the cold snap started. This reversal of prevailing weather patterns in turn pushed communities to experiment more urgently with domesticated crops than they would otherwise have chosen to do.

In several regions, groups that had at first shifted to farming without consciously intending to do it eventually recognized the benefits of agrarian life. Food supplies became more secure and predictable. Permanent houses were more comfortable than temporary ones. Community life became more diverse and interesting. Children, the sick, and the aged had their needs met in a more sheltered environment. A sedentary life meant that women could wean children earlier and thus resume ovulation faster. If a woman gave birth more often, more of her children were likely to survive to adulthood and contribute to the family's food needs.

As land cultivation expanded, settlements grew in size and density, obliging their inhabitants to invent clever new tools and techniques. This surge of ingenuity marks the beginning of the **neolithic era,** which we associate with the dawn of farming. Neolithic innovations included finer stone blades (microliths), curved sickles, stone containers and grinders, and houses of sun-dried mud brick. Scholars conventionally date the end of the neolithic to about 4500 B.C.E. in Southwest Asia and Europe, when copper implements came into use alongside stone.

> **neolithic era** The period from about 10,000 to 4000 B.C.E. characterized by refined stone toolmaking and the development of agriculture.

The Spread of Agrarian Societies

The earliest farm communities that we know of appeared in the Fertile Crescent. But given that farming emerged independently in several places, perhaps seven or eight of them, the question of who was first is really beside the point. Agrarian societies appeared on all the inhabited continents except Australia between about 10,000 and 3000 B.C.E. (see Map 2.1). Compared to the paleolithic's 2.4 million years or so of hunting, foraging, and unhurried stone tool development, the agricultural revolution took place practically overnight.

Agriculture from the Mediterranean to India. Several important domesticated plants and animals, and the ideas and technologies connected to them, spread from the Fertile Crescent both east to South Asia (the Indian subcontinent) and west to the lands bordering the Mediterranean Sea. This entire belt of land and sea occupies approximately the same range of latitude: Days and seasons are of a similar length; temperatures, plant populations, animal habitats, and rainfall averages (less than twenty inches a year) are fairly similar. No lofty mountain ranges or other natural obstacles impede communication and travel across the region, and the large bodies of water within it—the Mediterranean, Black, Red, and Arabian Seas, plus the Persian Gulf—link the region from one end to the other.

Most, though not quite all, of the crops and animals that became important in the diets of people along this belt appear to have been domesticated first in either Southwest Asia or northeastern Africa. The staples of the new agrarian economy were wheat (emmer and einkorn), barley, legumes (lentils, peas, chickpeas), sheep, goats, pigs, cows, and flax (for making textiles). All these "founder crops" and domesticated animals were climatically adaptable to most of the region. Indeed, they spread across it within a few thousand years. Some important crops, including cotton and eggplant, were first domesticated in India and then moved westward to Southwest Asia and the Mediterranean basin.

Agrarian ways of life spread in two principal ways. One was by cultural diffusion, that is, the dissemination of *ideas* about how to farm. People probably exchanged information about farming chiefly in connection with regional trade. For example, early peddlers carried products throughout Southwest Asia. Copper from the Sinai Peninsula, shells from Mediterranean shores, salt from the Dead Sea, and obsidian, a dark volcanic glass from mines in Anatolia (modern Turkey), all moved back and forth across the region. These traders probably also took along seeds, animals, and farm tools from one village to another, thus stimulating local farming experiments in new places. Second, farming spread in connection with the migration of people from one locality to another. For example, agriculture centered on wheat, barley, cattle, sheep, and pigs, along with a kit of knowledge and sophisticated tools, probably started moving from Southwest Asia into Europe before 7000 B.C.E. This happened almost certainly as a result of cultivators migrating westward along the Mediterranean coast or into the Balkan Peninsula and the fertile Danube River valley.

Farmers around the world. Beyond the India-to-Mediterranean zone, people took up crop growing and livestock raising in several places independently. One broad region of innovation was northern China, extending from the middle Yellow River (Huang He) southward to the Yangzi (YAHNG-zuh) River. This area of northern China was significantly less arid in the fourth millennium B.C.E. than it is today. People probably domesticated rice and millet (an important grain staple in China today) between about 7000 and 6500 B.C.E. Farmers in the Yellow River region worked light, deep soil known as loess with simple digging sticks. They built hamlets of houses with sunken floors and storage pits, used stone axes and serrated knives, raised pigs and chickens, and laid the dead to rest in cemeteries.

In Africa, the highlands of Ethiopia, the savannas (grasslands) just south of the Sahara Desert, and the wet tropical forests farther south all emerged as distinct centers

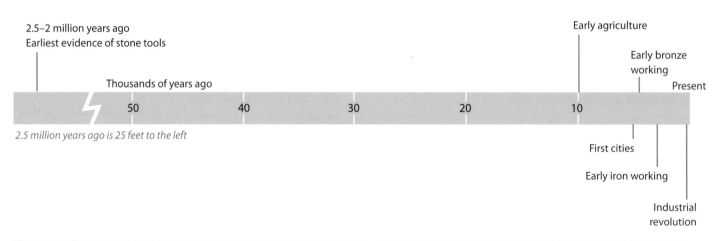

Milestones of technology. Why do you think the pace of technological change accelerated so slowly for about 2.5 million years? Why did it then speed up dramatically from about 10,000 years ago?

of independent domestication between about 10,000 and 5000 B.C.E. Food plants included sorghum, finger millet, yams, and other crops, the choice depending on soil and climate. In Asia's tropical belt, dwellers in what is today Thailand appear to have domesticated rice on their own about 7200 B.C.E. Inhabitants of New Guinea in island Southeast Asia started harvesting sugar cane, yams, and certain species of banana about 7000 B.C.E. Peoples of North and South America definitely invented farming with no stimulus from Afroeurasia. We return to that development in Chapter 4.

Sunrise over the Village

If a group of hardy travelers of 5000 B.C.E. were to tramp 2,600 miles from southeastern Europe to the northwestern frontiers of India (an unlikely journey), they could probably have found refuge almost every night in a village consisting of a few dozen round or rectangular huts of stone, brick, or wood. The resident families would have cultivated small fields of grain and legumes; raised a few pigs, sheep, or cows; and foraged in the surrounding countryside. They would have worn garments of roughly woven wool, animal hair, or plant fiber, as well as skins and furs. Their material inventory would have included an array of stone, bone, and wooden tools, as well as grain and other food.

Households would have had a variety of containers for cooking, storing, and transporting food. The ceramic pot—waterproof, fireproof, and made from readily available clay—was a key development of the neolithic era, not least because it could be used to cook nutritious plant food into soft, mushy gruel that enriched the diets of everyone, including babies and toothless old people. Unlike stone or wood, clay could easily be molded into any of a thousand useful forms and then heated to a high temperature in bonfires, later in furnaces and kilns. "Firing" the clay dried up the water content in it and made it hard. Foragers, not farmers, appear to have brought about the "pot revolution." The oldest potsherds, that is, broken pieces of ceramic, have been found in northern China and dated to as many as 18,000 years ago. Foraging people in Japan began making pots a few thousand years later. On the western side of the hemisphere, the oldest pottery comes from the eastern Sahara Desert, where people began using baked clay utensils to boil wild grain for porridge about 9000 B.C.E. Ceramic containers

An early ceramic pot. This pot from the Jomon culture in Japan is reconstructed from shards dating to about 12,000 B.C.E.

appeared in farming communities in Southwest Asia two thousand or so years later.

Firing pottery in rudimentary furnaces may have suggested the idea of heating pieces of rock enough to extract beads of molten copper, which could then be cooled, reheated, and hammered into tools or ornaments. Farmers in Anatolia seem to have initiated the era of copper metallurgy about 5000 B.C.E. Within a few centuries, and perhaps in the same region, people figured out the more complicated process of liquefying copper and pouring it into clay molds to fashion bracelets, statues, blades, and many other useful objects. Tools of pure copper, however, did not replace stone. They tended to be too soft or brittle to last very long. But within about two thousand years, societies from western Europe to China either invented copper metallurgy or learned about it from strangers.

In regions where farming became established, social relations invariably became more complicated. The division of labor remained quite simple, and adult men and women probably treated each other with near equality. Both sexes contributed skill and muscle to farming's many tasks and to weaving clothing, nets, baskets, and other essential items from wool, flax, cotton, or reed. But because villages were likely to have several extended families living closely together, leaders inevitably emerged to guide group decisions and mediate personal disputes. Chiefs stood apart because of their physical strength, good judgment, or presumed ability to communicate with the gods. At the same time, permanent settlements and success at farming meant that families had the possibility of storing up wealth. As soon as some villagers accumulated more food reserves than others, the conditions were laid for social inequality. Burial sites in Southwest Asia and other regions of early farming reveal that some people, including children, went to their graves adorned with jewelry and other valuables, while most villagers received more meager interments. These differences suggest that some families gained higher social status than others and that social hierarchy—the ranking of some families and individuals over others—was becoming part of human communal life.

Super Villages

In Southwest Asia, the remains of several agrarian settlements are conspicuous for their size and complexity. One of them is ancient

Jericho, which is also a modern city near the Jordan River. There, about 7000 B.C.E., the inhabitants enclosed their village in a stone wall more than eleven feet high and nearly five feet thick. They also dug a moat and put up a tower. They may have done these things to protect their food, water, or trade goods, though the early inhabitants continued to collect food in the surrounding wild. Building the wall took such a sophisticated level of technical skill and cooperation that the town must have had fairly complex social organization, including distinctions between an elite class of leaders and the rest of the population.

The biggest neolithic center so far discovered is Çatal Hüyük (CHAH-tahl HOO-yook). Located on a grassy plain in south central Anatolia, this site also goes back to about 7000 B.C.E. It covers nearly thirty-two acres, and may at its height have had a population close to ten thousand. The settlement was a solid block of more than a thousand mud-brick houses built so closely together that there was no room for streets. The inhabitants moved from one dwelling to another by scrambling across multilevel rooftops and descending to interiors on wooden ladders. Some dwellings had multiple rooms and upper stories. Domestic activity took place in a large space outfitted with hearth, clay oven, and platforms for sitting and sleeping. Some rooms served as shrines to local deities (about which we know little) and were richly decorated with clay statuary, relief sculptures, and painted walls depicting scenes from daily life.

Çatal Hüyük's inhabitants raised grain, legumes, sheep, and cattle along the banks of a local river. But they also foraged in nearby hills and marshes for almonds, crab apples, and gazelle meat. Material remains suggest a social life centered on clusters of families. Each family appears to have ventured out to farm or forage every morning and then returned to its own "apartment" at nightfall. We do not know why so many people chose to live together in this teeming pile of buildings, but in any case the settlement flourished for one to two thousand years, before falling into ruin around 5400 B.C.E.

About that same time, however, farmers who had planted themselves west of the Black Sea and up the Danube River

Çatal Hüyük. Historians have debated whether Çatal Hüyük was a town that might in other circumstances have become a city or simply an oversized farming village, doomed to fail because the local area could not produce enough food to sustain its large population. Why do you think the builders made no room for streets or alleys between houses?

Ötzi: A Neolithic Traveler

Farming and village living probably reached western Europe mainly overland from the southeast and was well established by 4000 B.C.E. One remarkable piece of evidence of neolithic life in that region is the body of a man who had been frozen in a glacier for 5,300 years.

In 1991 two German tourists hiking in the Italian Alps near the border with Austria came across a desiccated human corpse. Since then, painstaking analysis of the remains has revealed that this individual died sometime around 3300 B.C.E. Scientists nicknamed the body "Ötzi" after the Ötz valley where he was discovered. Because he became frozen shortly after he died, his corpse remained largely intact. Extensive testing and DNA analysis have allowed scientists to piece together a picture of his life and death. He was probably a herdsman or hunter. He may also have been a warrior or a leader in his community, because he carried a costly item, a finely constructed copper-bladed axe with a yew tree handle.

Ötzi stood about 5 feet 5 inches tall and weighed about 110 pounds. He ate a mixed diet of meat, grains, fruits, and roots. To protect himself against the harsh Alpine climate, he wore clothes made of a variety of skins, tanned and stitched together with animal sinews. The excavation turned up a bearskin hat near his head. Grass stuffed in his leather shoes kept his feet warm. About forty-five years old when he died, he suffered from intestinal parasites and degenerative joint problems. He had more than fifty tattoo marks on his body, made by rubbing charcoal into small incisions. Remarkably, these marks match acupuncture lines, suggesting an early form of this treatment to relieve joint pain.

Objects discovered near his corpse tell us that he carried a variety of weapons on the day he died: his axe, a flint-bladed knife, a bow with arrows, and some unidentified items. He also carried two baskets, which held berries, mushrooms, and a kit for starting fires.

Ötzi was not alone when he died. Researchers originally assumed that he had fallen victim to exposure during a mountain storm, but further analysis of the body has complicated this story. Unhealed cuts and bruises indicate that he was engaged in a violent struggle shortly before his death. A flint arrowhead lodged in his shoulder suggests that someone shot him. He might have died from trauma to his head, though we cannot know whether he fell or sustained a savage blow. Some scientists have speculated that he died when a raiding party he was with attacked an enemy group.

We would like to know much more about Ötzi and the community from which he came. But the information scientists have gleaned from his body and his possessions offer a rare glimpse into the life of an ordinary western European man during the late neolithic age.

Two Dutch artists fashioned this life-sized model of Ötzi based on analysis of the 5,300-year-old mummy.

Thinking Critically

Based on the evidence we have about Ötzi, what generalizations might you propose about the character of society in western Europe around 3300 B.C.E.?

---

valley started building villages of as many as two thousand houses. These settlements, whose economies were based on wheat, barley, cattle, and sheep, were enclosed in wooden palisades. Some of the dwellings of wood and plaster had multiple rooms and two stories. Archaeologists see a succession of material cultural styles known collectively as "Old Europe," extending from about 5500 to 3500 B.C.E. These related societies, which encompassed most of southeastern Europe, produced elaborately decorated pottery, gold and copper jewelry, and tools such as axes and knives cast from smelted copper. This practice almost certainly indicates the existence of social distinctions. Archaeologists have found female figurines in abundance, probably associated with particular goddesses or spirits venerated in households. Other finds indicate that a network of trade in gold and copper, as well as decorative shells from the Aegean Sea, bound southeastern Europe's farm towns and villages together.

Wherever frontiers of farming advanced in Afroeurasia, populations inevitably grew. Nevertheless, farming technology available between nine thousand and five thousand years ago almost certainly prevented populations from rising above a certain level relative to local food resources. In three parts of the Indo-Mediterranean region, however, a startling transformation began to take place from about

4000 B.C.E. In those places, agricultural production accelerated, population soared, and large, dense clusters of human habitation, that is, cities, started to appear for the first time. That phenomenon began to take place barely six thousand years ago, a time span representing only the most recent 3 percent or so of the years that humans have walked the earth.

Early Complex Societies

FOCUS How did complex societies take shape in the Tigris-Euphrates, Nile, and Indus River valleys, and in what ways did they interact with one another and alter their environments?

complex society A type of society, also called a "civilization," possessing most of the following features: dense population, agricultural economy, cities, complex social hierarchy, complex occupational specialization, centralized state, monumental building, writing, and a dominant belief system.

Complex society, the form of social organization we conventionally refer to as "civilization," first appeared in the Tigris-Euphrates, Nile, and Indus River valleys (see Map 2.2). These societies became "complex" because of the relative size and density of their populations and the intricacy and variety of their social institutions, occupations, technologies, government systems, and forms of creative expression (see Table 2.1). Like farming itself, complex societies emerged as a consequence of humans making countless everyday decisions century after century, no one capable of seeing where these experiments might take them. Village

farmers did not decide to invent complex society because they thought it was a good idea or knew somehow that it was supposed to happen next. Rather, a dynamic interplay among rising population, climate change, and human success at producing food led in a few places to a surge of innovations unlike anything paleolithic hunting bands could have imagined.

Although early complex societies represented a definable type of social organization, the societies of the Tigris-Euphrates (Mesopotamia), the Nile, and the Indus each emerged with a characteristic cultural style expressed in distinctive forms of government, religion, architecture, literature, and so on. These cultural peculiarities reflected underlying differences in the physical and natural environments, the dynamics of interaction among social groups, and simply the flow of historical events. We should not, however, think that these differing styles were innate or remained fixed. The cultural elements that made a complex society culturally identifiable were all susceptible to change because local environmental conditions inevitably changed, social tensions and conflicts occurred among groups within the society, and strangers and strange ideas arrived from outside. Civilizations have never existed as unchanging, self-enclosed cultural packages, and that fact of world history needs to be kept in mind.

Irrigation and Complex Society in Mesopotamia

The three earliest complex societies all arose within the Great Arid Zone, the band of dry country that stretches across Afroeurasia from southwest to northeast (see Map 2.2).

Harappan society

Egypt

Mesopotamia

Great Arid Zone

MAP 2.2 The earliest complex societies.
Why do you think the earliest complex agrarian societies arose in arid regions of the world rather than in places with high rainfall?

TABLE 2.1 Types of Societies Compared

Feature Category	Foraging Societies	Early Agrarian Societies	Complex Agrarian and Urban Societies
Economy	Collecting and hunting wild food at subsistence level	Production of domesticated crops and animals at subsistence level, plus collecting and hunting	Production primarily of crops and secondarily of domesticated animals at surplus levels, as well as urban and village manufactures
Settlement	Temporary or semipermanent camps or hamlets	Permanent homesteads, villages, and village clusters	Cities, towns, and villages
Occupations	All members of group forage for food	All members of group raise crops or animals; some members exercise special technical or leadership skills	The great majority engages in farming; minorities in full-time specialized occupations or in urban labor
Social structure	Group is egalitarian; no significant social class divisions; social relations based on kinship	Social class divisions are informal and fluid; certain individuals or families enjoy special status as political and religious leaders; social relations based partly on kinship	Permanent hierarchy of social classes: (a) rulers and aristocrats, (b) skilled artisans, technicians, and professionals, (c) rural farmers and urban workers, (d) in many societies, slaves; social relations based on kinship at local levels and on common obedience to the ruler at the level of the state
Gender relations	Society is egalitarian; simple division of tasks between women and men	Society is egalitarian; more complex division of tasks between women and men	Patriarchal society; most women restricted to the domestic sphere
Political organization	Egalitarian bands generally restricted in size to fewer than 100; informal, fluid leadership	Informal village leadership exercised by individuals, elders, or families with special status	States characterized by central governments, authoritarian rule, hierarchies of officials, and systematic taxation
Laws	Informal, customary rules and prohibitions	More complex customary rules and prohibitions	Complex civil and penal laws, enforced by the state and often organized in written codes
Technological change	Slow pace of technological innovation	Accelerating pace of technological innovation, especially in food production and village manufacturing	Continuous, though often uneven, technological and scientific innovation in a wide range of human activities
Built environment	Shelter in simple, sometimes mobile structures	Permanent dwellings; village construction of shrines, communal granaries, or defensive walls	Dense urban dwelling construction; monumental building of walls, temples, palaces, tombs, and public plazas
Communication	Speech and forms of symbolic expression	Speech and complex symbolic expression	Writing systems and complex symbolic expression; literacy of particular elite groups
Religion	Beliefs and practices associated with local nature spirits and divinities	Beliefs and practices associated with local, natural, and household deities and spirits	Complex systems of belief and practice often associated with central political authority, a class of religious specialists, and written scriptures; centers of development of major belief systems such as Confucianism, Buddhism, or Christianity

Climatologists have theorized that the hot, dry conditions now prevailing in the western Great Arid Zone, that is, from the Sahara to the Great Indian Desert, set in from about 4000 B.C.E., though with periodic cycles of higher or lower temperature and rainfall. Dense concentrations of population were possible in that region only because fresh water flowed from green highlands far away. The Tigris and the Euphrates Rivers originate in the mountains of eastern Anatolia, the Indus River flows from the Himalayas of Tibet, and the Nile has its source in highland Ethiopia and tropical East Africa.

As far as we know, the Tigris-Euphrates River valley is the earliest place where a complex society appeared. Lying largely within what is today Iraq and eastern Syria, the region came to be known by its Greek name, Mesopotamia, or "land between the rivers." From about 7000 B.C.E., farming

settlements flourished on well-watered slopes of the Zagros Mountains, which parallel the Tigris River to the east. As the hill population grew, farmers looking for new land migrated to lower elevations and eventually settled on the valley's alluvial plain. This is the relatively flat, gently sloping area where over the millennia the two rivers deposited layers of alluvium, that is, a mix of silt, clay, sand, and gravel. There, early farmers gradually selected food plants that grew successfully in hot, dry conditions.

In 5000 B.C.E. southern Mesopotamia was a labyrinth of creeks, lakes, and marshes. In the spring, highland runoff inundated the valley, depositing fresh layers of fertile silt. Rain rarely fell in summer, but farmers irrigated fields using simple techniques, and they built mud-brick villages along creeks and lakes. The soil was so rich and easy to work that farms yielded copious crops of wheat, barley, legumes, vegetables, and fruits. Irrigation farming, combined with hunting and fishing in the teeming marshes, gave these settled communities a secure food supply in most years.

The river valley as population trap. From about 4000 B.C.E., population density in the river valley rose dramatically, a development likely related to a climatic shift toward lower rainfall across Southwest Asia. The spring floods abated somewhat, and lagoons and swamps receded, exposing more acreage for fields, pastures, and settlements. Relatively drier conditions also encouraged people to innovate, for example, building granaries to store food and seeking wider trade relations to acquire a greater variety of products. Villages multiplied, especially along the Euphrates, and "super settlements" that economically dominated neighboring villages began to arise. At some point farmers began to yoke domesticated oxen or donkeys to light wooden plows.

In such conditions of surplus food production and rising population, social changes became a practical necessity. In earlier times forager bands that outgrew local resources had to segment and disperse over a wider territory. The Mesopotamian plain dwellers could not do that because the surrounding lands were much too dry to support the farming they had come to depend on. We might say that the peoples of the plain became "trapped" into creating bigger settlements and more complicated forms of social organization as a result of their own success at producing bounteous crops.

Occupational specialization. As more people packed into the valley, work had to be organized in more complicated ways. Production of surplus food meant that not everyone had to farm full time. Conversely, population growth raised the demand for men and women who could provide special talents and services as potters, basket weavers, brick masons, stone carvers, coppersmiths, merchants, labor supervisors, soldiers, and religious professionals. Occupational specialization also tended, as it does in modern times, to encourage specialists to experiment with new techniques and products, which generated even more jobs requiring expertise.

Environmental pressures and the first cities. Archaeology has shown that because water and fertile mud were so abundant in the formative period of Mesopotamian society, large settlements multiplied before there was any need for extensive irrigation of crop land. In time, however, water and soil management became more difficult. For one thing, the region's climatic drying trend continued into the third millennium B.C.E. Wetlands and creeks continued to recede, forcing people to dig canals and ditches to lead water to fields. For another, the spring floods were unpredictable. In some years the rivers carried too little water, in some years too much, though people settled in greater numbers along the Euphrates because its elevation drop was gentler than its twin's. Furthermore, the climate required that spring planting normally take place *before* the flood arrived. These perennial conditions motivated farmers to engineer ways to

store water in lakes and ponds and then channel it to fields as needed. As arduous as water management became, there was no going back to simpler days. The valley's population continued to climb, so agricultural productivity had to go up, too. That reality underlay herculean efforts to build dikes, dams, canals, and reservoirs to keep water flowing to fields and pastures that stretched farther and farther from the river banks.

Some settlements in the valley grew larger than others, and when they did they attracted even more people because they offered more opportunities for jobs and trade. These big settlements may be described as cities when they became multifunctional. The residents engaged in many different jobs and professions, not just farming, and they depended for their livings mainly on food imported from outside.

Mesopotamia's early cities emerged in two major clusters (see Map 2.3). The oldest centers appeared sometime after 4000 B.C.E. at the harshly arid southern end of the valley, the region called Sumer (SOO-mehr). There, the alluvial plain bulges out, offering an expanse of potentially arable land to the extent that water could be brought to it. In the early third millennium B.C.E., the southern cluster extended about 150 miles up the valley to encompass Akkad (AHK-ahd), the region near modern Baghdad. The second urban constellation developed in northern Mesopotamia, where winter rains were sufficient to support crops and herds. This region, part of it hill country, extended over a wide area of what is today northern Iraq and eastern Syria. Only in the past half-century have archaeologists discovered that small but flourishing cities began to spring up in northern Mesopotamia from about 3000 B.C.E. and that this phenomenon had little or no connection to the rise of Sumer in the south. In the third millennium B.C.E., however, a growing network of commercial and cultural exchanges knitted the two city clusters permanently together.

Complex society in Sumer and Akkad. In the centuries after 4000 B.C.E., more than a dozen major cities appeared in southern Mesopotamia. The biggest center was Uruk (OO-rook), which in 3000 B.C.E. had a population of around fifty thousand. Remarkably, the world's oldest cities thrived in a region lacking many natural resources. Other than fertile soil, clay for bricks, poplar trees for wood construction, and marsh reeds for making baskets and small river boats, the southern valley had little to offer. The cities had to trade not only with one another but also with peoples who lived along the Persian Gulf and in the highlands to the north and east. Sumer's continuing urban growth depended on steady importation of timber and stone for construction, copper and tin for bronze making, and an array of precious metals, gemstones, and other luxuries to satisfy urban tastes.

Within each of Sumer's cities, intricate social and occupational relationships, the constant flow of goods in and out, and the relentless upkeep of waterworks demanded vigorous leaders to organize and command the population. Civil peace and order required urban leaders to show a deft mix of public persuasion, group mediation, and threats of punishment. The city's wealth paid for the services of deputies and soldiers to enforce the leaders' will, a condition most city folk accepted in return for a reasonable level of calm and security.

The new forms of power that cities required gave rise to the world's first states. The early state was a type of political organization utterly different from the egalitarian forager band. Decisions became the prerogative of a ruling group and a privileged class of officials backed by armed enforcers. These bosses claimed authority to resolve social conflict, outlaw private vengeance, proclaim public laws, and monopolize the use of violence. Once they achieved enough power to pass it on to their own children, they began to make the case that it was natural and good that power reside permanently with particular families, that this practice encouraged social order and prevented disputes over leadership. Here was the origin of the **dynasty**.

dynasty A sequence of rulers from a single family.

city-state A politically sovereign urban center with adjacent agricultural land.

The early cities of Sumer were **city-states,** centrally governed territories that included a single urban complex and surrounding villages and farmland. For many centuries, the cities of Sumer competed for land and resources, sometimes viciously. Chronic tensions punctuated by intercity wars help explain why ruling elites were able to assert more central authority and why the walls and guard towers that encased cities got progressively taller and thicker.

Religion and the rise of priests. We have ample evidence of a close connection between the emerging state and organized religion. Most scholars agree that as soon as paleolithic humans acquired language, they began to try to "explain the unexplainable" to one another—why the heavenly bodies move across the sky, why rain falls or fails to, why people die and where they go after death. Ritual burials and art from the upper paleolithic tell us that early societies found persuasive explanations for many things in the workings of unseen forces and spiritual beings. There is little doubt that early Mesopotamian farmers regarded the well-being of their communities as dependent on the good will of powerful supernatural entities. People could appeal to these deities, which might be represented in human, animal, or abstract forms, to grant good harvests, help women produce children, or ensure safe passage of the dead into another world. At household shrines and village temples, women and men sought to communicate with deities through ceremonies and sacrificial offerings.

And as Sumerian cities grew, so too did their temples and the power of the gods and goddesses believed to live in them. Each city had its own major divinity, represented in stone

MAP 2.3 Early states in Mesopotamia.
What factors might explain why Sargon's empire expanded in the particular directions it did?

or wooden images. For example, the moon god Nannar (also named Sin) presided over the city of Ur. Inanna, goddess of love, and Anu, the sky god, shared the patronage of Uruk. That city's White Temple, which has remained remarkably preserved to the present, belonged to Anu. It stood atop a brick pyramidal platform that loomed above the city. The temple walls, sheathed in gypsum plaster, shone in the hot white light of the Mesopotamian sun. Temples also served as the headquarters of city-state administration, which took in tax revenues in grain and other commodities, then reallocated it for irrigation works, public construction, war making, famine relief, and other civic purposes.

Every urban temple had its religious personnel, or priests, who had the job of keeping the gods satisfied with continuous rituals, festivals, and sacrifices. The priests, proclaiming that all human labor was dedicated to the service of the deities, monopolized the right to command the city's population and economy. This small minority came to control extensive farmland and to assume powers and privileges that lowlier people did not have. The priests organized the population to work the city's farms and to produce textiles, pottery, and other goods in temple workshops. They dedicated food stores to the resident deity, and from those stores they supported temple officials, servants, and themselves. In short, religious practice came to justify the state, upholding the right of its elite guardians to accumulate property and wield power.

Sounds into symbols. One of the keys to priestly rule was the invention of writing. Foragers of the upper paleolithic had carved abstract signs that might be interpreted as early forms of writing, but the earliest fully developed system emerged, as far as we know, in Mesopotamia sometime before 3000 B.C.E. Complex societies must keep track of a great many things, as our to-do lists and bank statements continually remind us. In Uruk, temple authorities figured out how to keep precise track of the receipt and distribution of grain and animals, first by making distinctive clay tokens that stood for a fixed number of a particular item, later by incising signs on little clay tablets to represent particular goods or numbers. Scribes invented pictograms, or simple signs that looked like the thing being represented, for example, a duck, a donkey, or a house.

Early writers made signs by pushing a stalk of reed with a wedge-shaped end into a tablet of wet clay, which was then dried in the sun or, in later times, baked. From *cuneus*,

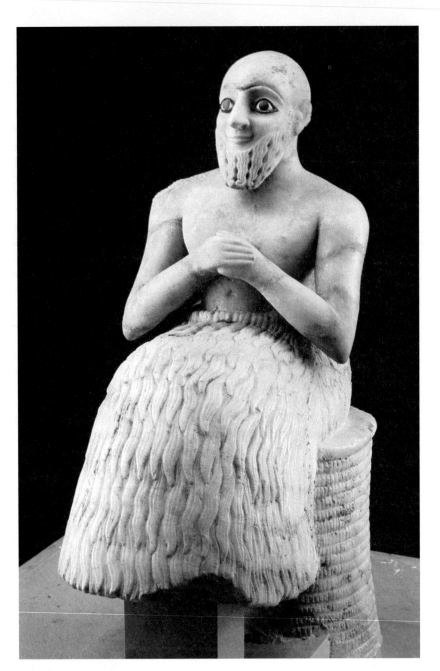

A Mesopotamian official. An inscription at the back of this alabaster statue dating to about 2400 B.C.E. identifies the figure as Ebih-II, "the superintendent dedicated to Ishtar Virile," goddess of war. The statue comes from the temple of Ishtar in the Euphrates city of Mari. This man is clearly of high social rank and appears to be at prayer. What sort of life might he have led compared to that of Ötzi, the neolithic European on page 57?

the Latin word for wedge, we get *cuneiform*, the conventional name for early Mesopotamian writing. Sumerian was the first spoken language translated into a complex sign system. The inhabitants of Akkad upriver from Sumer spoke different languages, and in the third millennium B.C.E. literate specialists transformed some of those tongues into visual symbols using cuneiform script.

Over about a thousand years, temple record keepers worked out an elaborate system of signs, some that represented the sound of syllables ("ba," "bo," "ka," etc.) and

	3200 B.C.E.	3000 B.C.E.	2400 B.C.E.	1000 B.C.E.
Water				
Bird				
Bread				

Early writing in Mesopotamia. The chart shows that the writing system invented in Sumer in the fourth millennium B.C.E. changed considerably over the centuries. Pictograms, signs that look like the things they represent, evolved into abstract logographic symbols. Straight or curved lines were transformed into short lines attached to wedges. Why do you think that Mesopotamian scribes transformed pictograms into abstract signs?

others, called logograms, that represented units of meaning, that is, whole words, or sometimes combinations of words. Logograms stand for particular objects, actions, ideas, or emotions. Modern English is written mainly in an alphabetic, not logographic system, but it still incorporates logograms. For example, we known that the "$" sign stands for the word "dollar," even though it has no sound value to help us pronounce that word. Number signs (1, 2, 3, and so on) are also logograms. They represent meaning but not sounds. The most widespread logographic system in use today is Chinese, though Chinese characters also incorporate signs representing syllables to guide pronunciation.

Most ordinary Mesopotamians remained illiterate, having neither time nor resources to master hundreds of logographic signs. The temple elite no doubt liked it that way because they controlled information other people did not have, and this monopoly contributed to their power. Gradually, however, a larger minority learned to read and write because society found more and more activities to record: royal decrees, government letters, king lists, astronomical observations, merchants' transactions, and eventually myths, hymns, and proverbs.

Monarchy in Mesopotamia. Despite writing and other tools of power, the authority of the Sumerian priesthood diminished in the mid-third millennium B.C.E. Excavations at several Sumerian and Akkadian cities have uncovered large building complexes that appear to be kingly palaces, not temples. The constant demand for materials and labor to maintain irrigation, the increasingly intricate relations among social and occupational groups, and the periodic wars between city-states combined to force a shift of power from a minority of religious professionals to military rulers.

A cuneiform tablet dating to about 2100 B.C.E. provides a long list of Sumerian kings. Mebaragesi of Kish, who lived around 2600 B.C.E., is the thirtieth name on the list but the first for which we have archaeological evidence that attests to his existence. The ruling dates of many of the early kings are the stuff of myth. The tablet reports that the first eight of them enjoyed reigns ranging from 18,600 to 36,000 years! Gilgamesh, listed among the rulers of the First Dynasty of Uruk, became the subject of legendary tales of heroism, superhuman strength, and flawed ambition that storytellers passed down through the centuries. In the second millennium B.C.E. these yarns were brought together in the Epic of Gilgamesh, the most celebrated work of ancient Mesopotamian poetry. The narrative recounts the king's battles with monsters, his defiance of the gods, and his fruitless search for the key to immortality.

We have substantial evidence from statuary and inscriptions of the reign of Sargon (2340–2284 B.C.E.), a warrior king who founded a state in Akkad. Under his command Akkadian lancers and swordsmen conquered both the city-states of Sumer and territories far up the Tigris and Euphrates valleys. Sargon and his four royal successors, ruling many cities and a linguistically diverse population, should be

Cuneiform tablet. The writing on this small clay tablet probably gives an account of grain distributed from a temple.

empire A type of state in which a single political authority, often identified with a particular kinship, linguistic, or ethnic group, rules over peoples of different ethnic or linguistic identities.

credited with having created the world's earliest **empire**. These rulers also appear to have claimed that their authority derived directly from the gods. For example, statues depicting Naram-Sin, grandson of Sargon, show him sporting a horned helmet previously reserved only for images of deities. Mesopotamian monarchs did not, as far as we know, claim to be heavenly beings, but, as we shall see, god-kings and god-queens became a standard feature of state-building across Afroeurasia in later millennia.

About 2190 B.C.E., the Akkadian empire collapsed, possibly in connection with extended periods of drought, as well as hostile incursions of hill people from the nearby Zagros Mountains. After that event, power shifted back to Sumer. There, a line of rulers in the city of Ur, called the Third Dynasty of Ur, kept southern Mesopotamia united for another two centuries and presided over a new flowering of monumental building and fine art. The kings of Ur also fought nearly continuously with small monarchies and city-states of the Zagros range and the Iranian Plateau east and southeast of Mesopotamia. The brick-walled cities of western Iran, then known as Elam, were strategic prizes because their merchants transshipped copper, tin, lapis lazuli, turquoise, and other valuable metals and gems originating in lands to the east. About 2000 B.C.E., an alliance of Elamite and other western Iranian states captured the last monarch of the Third Dynasty and for the next few centuries dominated the politics of Mesopotamia.

In their third millennium glory days, the rulers of both Sumer and Akkad took steps to build a strong command system, that is, a set of institutions and practices for centrally controlling their subjects and extracting taxes from them. For example, Sargon and his successors appointed military officials to represent royal authority in cities and villages

bureaucracy A hierarchy of officials within a government that carries out the laws, decrees, and functions of the state.

throughout the empire. This way of delegating power constitutes **bureaucracy.** Defined precisely, bureaucrats are more than simply "people who work for the government." Mesopotamian bureaucrats were officials who governed villages, cities, or provinces not in their own right but as formal representatives of the state. Whatever an official said or did publicly was to be understood, not as a personal act, but as one mirroring the ruler's will and backed by the full weight of the state's armed power. A particular official might be relieved of his duties for one reason or another, but the office itself, which usually included special regalia and rituals, remained intact as an instrument of the state. Writing was a potent tool of the bureaucratic command system. It allowed officials to exchange precise messages over many miles and to store accurate records of royal decrees, tax receipts, and military supplies.

Class divisions. The third millennium B.C.E. also witnessed the rise of an aristocracy, or land-owning class. This was a secular elite; its power and prestige rested fundamentally on wealth, not on special religious authority. A small but rich landlord minority emerged as larger areas of irrigated land fell into the hands of private families. In some cities, this elite formed assemblies, which took part in urban governance. At the same time, the economic and social status of ordinary farmers may have declined as more and more

Victory stele of Naram-Sin. This stele, or upright stone slab, commemorates this Akkadian emperor's triumph over a people of the Zagros Mountains. Wearing a horned helmet signifying divinity, Naram-Sin (r. 2260–2223 B.C.E.) marches majestically upward, crushing an enemy soldier under foot as he goes. In front of him, one foe clutches a spear embedded in his neck, another begs the conquering king for mercy. Why do you think the stonecutter included stars twinkling over Naram-Sin's head?

peasants The social and economic class of farmers or herders who hold relatively small amounts of productive land as owners, rent-paying tenants, or serfs bound to a particular estate.

slavery The social institution in which an individual is held by law, custom, or simply coercion in servitude to another individual, a group, or the state.

of them became **peasants,** renting land from affluent families or working as day laborers. Indeed, **slavery** became a significant institution in Mesopotamia. In Mesopotamia most enslaved people originated either as prisoners of war or destitute foreigners, and the great majority of them belonged to the city temple or the ruler. A slave could be bought or sold for about the price of a donkey, but social practice appears to have awarded them some rights to protest publicly if they were abused.

Gender inequality. Complex society brought not only slavery but also new constraints on women. In Mesopotamia, men came to spend much more time producing food than they had in paleolithic times. They herded sheep, fed pigs, and tilled fields using plows pulled by draft animals. Although men largely took charge of public affairs and warfare, women sometimes held high and powerful positions as priestesses, and they could own property and represent themselves in court. Ordinary women, however, spent less time farming and more time preparing food and weaving cloth, which tied them closer to their homes and villages. Gradually, the social value of female labor diminished relative to that of men. This male "takeover" of early civilization

occurred slowly. Even so, **patriarchy** was on the way to becoming the norm in all known early agrarian civilizations.

patriarchy A society in which males dominate social, political, and cultural life.

Mesopotamian science. The sheer profusion of human activities in densely populated Mesopotamia demanded more sophisticated methods of computation than any earlier society had required. Sometime before 3000 B.C.E., Sumerian scribes worked out a system of numerical notation in cuneiform script. They devised both base-10 (decimal) and base-60 (sexagesimal) systems. The base-60 method has endured in the ways we keep time (60 seconds to the minute, 60 minutes to the hour) and reckon the circumference of a circle (360°). Mesopotamians used a combination of base-10 and base-60 mathematics, together with geometric concepts for everyday government and commercial transactions as well as to survey land, chart the stars, design buildings, and build irrigation works. Other technical innovations of the age of Sumer and Akkad included the seed drill, the vaulted arch, refinements in bronze metallurgy, and, most ingenious of all, the wheel. This device was probably applied first to pottery making, later to transport and plowing.

Despite class divisions and frequent interurban wars, Mesopotamia achieved remarkable cultural unity expressed in distinctive styles of art, architecture, literature, and science. The southern valley, a productive land hedged on all sides by desert, mountain, or sea, made for a compact cultural world. Ideas and information moved easily from one

The Standard of Ur. This two-sided wooden panel inlaid with lapis lazuli and other materials comes from a tomb constructed about 2700 B.C.E. in the city of Ur. The pictures on one side of the panel, whose function is not certain, illustrate Mesopotamian class divisions: At the top the ruler and his high officials make merry. In the middle common people bring cattle and other animals to the banquet. At the bottom war prisoners or other foreigners lug various burdens. Can you spot the female companion at the ruler's feast?

city to another by donkey train, wheeled cart, or riverboat. Writing multiplied the possibilities of cultural communication, transforming oral versions of myths, epics, and customary laws that had circulated in the valley for centuries into a fairly standardized literature. In other words, writing hugely broadened the range of collective learning—knowledge that could be shared, preserved, remembered, and passed along.

Complex Society on the Nile

In the Tigris-Euphrates River valley, complex society emerged gradually over two thousand years. In Egypt it came, relatively speaking, all in a rush. The climate of northern Africa gradually dried out starting in the fifth millennium B.C.E., and as it did people who once lived in the Saharan steppes and hill country east and west of the river pushed into the valley, where water was abundant. They brought domesticated cattle from the Sahara and adapted cereals and legumes that had been introduced from the Fertile Crescent. Once farmers began to reap lush harvests twice a year by simply broadcasting wheat or barley seeds in damp Nile mud, the agrarian economy grew fast, especially from about 4000 B.C.E.

The Nile was a fairly efficient hydrological machine. The White Nile, Blue Nile, and Atbara Rivers, the three principal tributaries of the Egyptian Nile, originated in tropical highlands of East Africa and Ethiopia, thousands of miles to the south. Summer rains there produced a gentle but voluminous swelling of the waters, which rolled into Egypt in mid-August. Suspended in these waters were millions of tons of rich sediment. In early fall the river flooded out over the alluvial valley. Then it receded, leaving saturated ground and a thick layer of dark silt. Egyptian farmers needed only simple dikes and ditches to guide the Nile's waters. The black soil produced a cornucopia of wheat, barley, leeks, onions, cucumber, garlic, lettuce, dates, and grapes. Of course there were years when the flood fell short and people went hungry or when it rose too high and swept away villages. Ancient texts show that the Egyptians worried a lot about this. But on the whole the pulse of the river was more predictable than the Tigris-Euphrates.

From the first of several cataracts, or rapids, near the modern city of Aswan, the Nile traced a winding green path about six hundred miles long. Near modern Cairo the river segmented into several channels that fanned out across the coastal plain to form the marshy and immensely fertile Nile delta. Ancient Egyptians visualized their land as divided into two parts, Lower Egypt, which was the delta, and Upper Egypt, which extended upriver more than five hundred miles from the apex of the delta to the First Cataract. Increasing aridity in the fourth and third millennia B.C.E. left Egypt's burgeoning population "caged" within the river valley, as were the populations of the Tigris and Euphrates. Irrigation canals could allow for farming some distance from the river and delta, but farther out only animal herders and

scattered oasis communities could survive. Consequently, Egyptians had no choice but to organize society in drastic new ways, just as the Mesopotamians had done some centuries earlier (see Map 2.4).

The rise of the pharaohs. In contrast to the Sumerians, Egyptians did not respond to the problem of population growth within a rigidly limited space by forming clusters of independent city-states. Rather, strong leaders, known historically as pharaohs, politically unified Upper and Lower Egypt about 3100 B.C.E. This event is associated in Egyptian legend with Narmer (also called Menes), the reputed founder of Egypt's First Dynasty. During the following two millennia, a succession of twenty dynasties ruled the valley. Scholars partition this era into Old, Middle, and New Kingdoms, separated from one another by relatively short Intermediate Periods of disturbance and fragmentation.

In Mesopotamia, rulers took to proclaiming themselves agents of the gods, but the pharaohs went further. Beginning

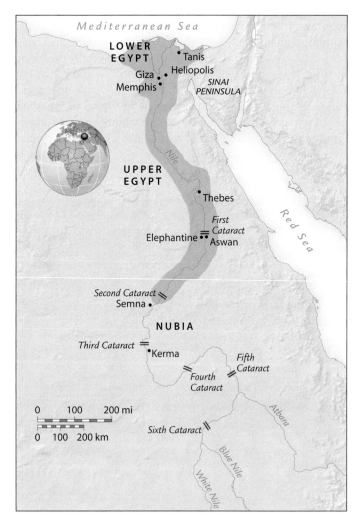

MAP 2.4 Egypt from 3000 to 1000 B.C.E.
The green area represents the maximum territorial extent of the Egyptian state during the Old Kingdom and Middle Kingdom periods. Why is this territory so much wider at the northern end than it is farther south?

TIME PERIODS OF ANCIENT EGYPT

3100–2686 B.C.E.	Early Dynastic Period	Dynasties 1–2
2686–2160 B.C.E.	Old Kingdom	Dynasties 3–8
2160–2040 B.C.E.	First Intermediate Period	Dynasties 9–11 (early)
2040–1652 B.C.E.	Middle Kingdom	Dynasties 11 (late)–13
1652–1540 B.C.E.	Second Intermediate Period	Dynasties 14–17
1540–1070 B.C.E.	New Kingdom	Dynasties 18–20

of the god-king in his palace, whereas the top official, a sort of prime minister, took charge of day-to-day affairs. Meeting the pharaoh's tax demands in grain and other commodities, the rural populace made complex society possible. Indeed, the rich surviving record of sculpture and painting vividly portrays Egyptian villagers at their daily farm routines. Individuals could hold land and sell produce privately, but the pharaoh "owned" Egypt. Ordinary people labored for his pleasure, getting back a share of the riches in famine relief in bad harvest years or in payment for labor on public works projects.

Written words and pyramids. Recent archaeological work in southern Egypt has revealed evidence of writing, including a sequence of abstract symbols and human and animal figures carved into a limestone, dating to about 3250 B.C.E. The Egyptian sign system, called hieroglyphs or "sacred carvings," was at first made up of pictograms, but, as in Mesopotamia, the signs later came to represent both words, or logograms and specific sounds. An aspiring scribe of the pharaoh's court had to master more than seven hundred distinct signs to be considered literate.

Old Kingdom pharaohs spent vast amounts of wealth on temples, monumental sculptures, and paintings, and the bureaucracy mastered the art of mobilizing the population for big civic projects. The most spectacular undertaking was construction of massive royal tombs across the Nile from modern Cairo. The three great pyramids of Giza preserved deep in their cool interiors the remains of three kings of the Fourth Dynasty (2613–2494 B.C.E.). Constructed of millions of blocks of cut limestone brought in by boat from upriver, the pyramids are only the most grandiose of the Old Kingdom's many royal burial sites. In Egyptian religious thought, death was an inevitable event, but

in the era known as the Old Kingdom (2686–2160 B.C.E.), Egyptians accepted their monarchs as incarnations of the hawk-headed sky god Horus. This deity was one of many that controlled the fate of humans and the forces of nature, chief among them Amon and Re, gods associated with the sun. According to Egyptian religious thought, cosmic power underlay the pharaoh's authority, and the prosperity of the valley depended on the ruler's well-being in both life and death. The monarch, in turn, had a moral responsibility to maintain *ma'at,* that is, the essential vitality and balance of the universe, the force that made both the sun and the summer Nile rise. The pharaohs were hardly democratic leaders, but the ideal of *ma'at,* which fundamentally meant "truth," impelled them, at least much of the time, to rule with justice and competence, rather than brutal coercion.

Pharaohs of the five dynasties that encompassed Old Kingdom Egypt maintained their main governing complex at Memphis, near modern Cairo at the apex of the delta. Subordinate centers of command arose in other parts of the valley, as did temple complexes. These places did not, however, grow into densely populated walled cities. On the contrary, most of the population inhabited a strand of hundreds of villages that ran nearly continuously from the First Cataract to the Mediterranean. In the early third millennium B.C.E., this tightly settled corridor was transformed into a highway for government officials and tax collectors.

The term *pharaoh* means "great household," and from the ruler's palace ranks of royal officials marched out to implement the royal will in the countryside. Courtiers, scribes, and servants surrounded the person

Palette of Narmer. Dating to Egypt's first dynasty, this slate ritual object narrates the political unification of the upper and lower Nile valley. The pharaoh Narmer, wearing the white crown of Upper Egypt, commands the scene. Before him, the falcon, symbol of the sky god Horus, sits atop papyrus plants signifying Lower Egypt. What similarities and differences in design and in the representation of figures do you notice on the palette of Narmer compared with the victory stele of Naram-Sin on page 64?

A Pharaoh's Warning in Stone

Pharaohs of the Old Kingdom occasionally sent exploratory missions upriver beyond the First Cataract of the Nile into Nubia, the historic region corresponding today to southern Egypt and northern Sudan. The pharaohs knew the lands at the southern edge of the Sahara Desert to be a rich source of gold, copper, ivory, ebony, cattle, and slaves. Early in the second millennium B.C.E., Sesostris I (also Senusret), a pharaoh of the Twelfth Dynasty, pursued an aggressive policy of expansion into Nubia in order to tap and control trade farther to the south. This king's great-grandson, Sesostris III (r. 1878–1839 B.C.E.), completed a series of forts near the Second Cataract to defend Egyptian territory and to launch campaigns into Nubia. The pharaoh's soldiers, however, faced potentially strong opposition from the African monarchy centered at Kerma, beyond the Third Cataract. This state dated back to the third millennium B.C.E., flourishing partly on Nile trade and partly on farming and herding on grasslands east and west of the river. At the fortress of Semna (Heh) just south of the Second Cataract, Sesostris III had stone markers erected carrying inscriptions that proclaimed Egypt's power in the region and alerting intruders to beware.

The living Horus: Divine of Form; the Two Ladies: Divine of Birth; the King of Upper and Lower Egypt: Khakaure, given life; the living Gold-Horus; Being; the Son of Re's body, his beloved, the Lord of the Two Lands: Sesostris, given life-stability-health forever. Year 16, third month of winter: the king made his southern boundary at [Semna]:

I have made my boundary further south than my fathers,
I have added to what was bequeathed me.
I am a king who speaks and acts,
What my heart plans is done by my arm.
One who attacks to conquer, who is swift to succeed,
In whose heart a plan does not slumber.
Considerate to clients, steady in mercy,
Merciless to the foe who attacks him.
One who attacks him who would attack,
Who stops when one stops,
Who replies to a matter as befits it.
To stop when attacked is to make bold the foe's heart,
Attack is valor, retreat is cowardice,
A coward is he who is driven from his border.
Since the Nubian listens to the word of mouth,
To answer him is to make him retreat.

Attack him, he will turn his back,
Retreat, he will start attacking.
They are not people one respects,
They are wretches, craven-hearted.
My majesty has seen it, it is not an untruth.
I have captured their women,
I have carried off their dependents,
Gone to their wells, killed their cattle,
Cut down their grain, set fire to it.
As my father lives for me, I speak the truth!
It is no boast that comes from my mouth.

As for any son of mine who shall maintain this border which my majesty has made, he is my son, born to my majesty. The true son is he who champions his father, who guards the border of his begetter. But he who abandons it, who fails to fight for it, he is not my son, he was not born to me.

Now my majesty has had an image made of my majesty, at this border which my majesty has made, in order that you maintain it, in order that you fight for it.

Source: Miriam Lichtheim, *Ancient Egyptian Literature, Volume I: The Old and Middle Kingdoms* (Berkeley: University of California Press, 2006), 118–120.

Thinking Critically

Who was likely Sesostris III's intended audience for this inscription? How does Sesostris III describe the Nubians, and what does his description convey about Egyptian attitudes toward them? What qualities in a ruler does Sesostris III emphasize? Based on the inscription, what knowledge might we infer about Egyptian campaigns into Nubia?

---

it might be survived. A pleasant afterlife presumably awaited individuals who had refrained from evil deeds and who made proper preparations for the transition, including the elaborate process of mummifying the body to preserve it for later revival. Almost everything we know about Egypt's culture of death relates to the experience of rich and powerful families, not common farmers. A deceased pharaoh clearly

had to be preserved and safeguarded because the corpse remained inseparable from the immortal soul.

In fact, preparations for a pharaoh's passing became a kind of national industry. Relying on engineering and geometric skill, superb tactical organization, and sheer muscle, the government mobilized thousands of artisans and peasants to build the pyramids. Since the proper entombing of

The pyramids of Giza and a protecting sphinx. This monumental creature with a man's head and a lion's body stands guard before the colossal tomb pyramid of the Fourth Dynasty pharaoh Khafre. The sandstone sculpture, which faces the rising sun, may represent the pharaoh himself. The Old Kingdom's pyramids of Giza loom near the western bank of the Nile opposite modern Cairo. How does the sphinx's pharaonic headdress enhance the visual power of the statue?

the divine ruler was a matter of profound importance to Egypt's well-being, the population went to the task more or less willingly, especially during inactive periods in the agricultural year. Eventually, however, the dynasties of the Old Kingdom scaled down royal burial projects to relatively modest dimensions. Not even the riches of the Nile could provide ruler after ruler with monuments of such stupendous volume.

Harappan Society in the Indus Valley

Complex society emerged along the Indus River just a few centuries later than in Mesopotamia and Egypt. Before British archaeologists started digging in the 1920s, however, the world did not even know that a civilization, named Harappan (huh-RAH-pan) after one of its leading cities, had ever existed. Scholars have so far identified 1,052 ancient Indus settlements, from sprawling cities to modest villages. Their total area embraces most of modern Pakistan and the northwestern corner of India.

The ecological setting. Like the Tigris-Euphrates and the Nile, the Indus transects Afroeurasia's Great Arid Zone. The direct distance between the Tigris and the lower Indus is a little more than 1,300 miles. In neolithic times, farming and herding communities gradually multiplied along this belt of territory, clustering in highland valleys of what are today Iran, Afghanistan, and Pakistan. By around 6000 B.C.E., farmers of the Sulayman Mountains just west of the Indus were raising wheat, barley, sheep, and goats, as well as producing pottery and copper tools. As the highland population grew, it spilled down the Sulayman slopes and onto the Indus River plain much as cultivators spread from Iran's Zagros Mountains to southern Mesopotamia in earlier times.

Plentiful water, rich silt, and a brilliant sun offered farmers higher productivity than the neighboring highlands could provide. Population on the plain grew denser, and as in Mesopotamia and Egypt, early Indus settlers found themselves gradually "trapped" in the valley with no place to go except in the direction of greater social complexity (see Map 2.5).

The Indus and its four major tributaries gush from the great snowy wall of the Himalaya Mountains. These channels converge as they flow across the northern region of the plain, called the Punjab. The rivers conjoin for a stretch, then divide again to form the delta, the region known as Sind, before emptying into the Arabian Sea. The valley's alluvial soil was not only rich but also extended over an area of about 250,000 square miles, twice the arable land area of Mesopotamia or Egypt. The flood season arrived in June, forming numerous natural lakes and ponds on the plain. Farmers planted crops in early fall after the waters receded. In contrast to the hydrological conditions in southern Mesopotamia, these temporary reservoirs saved Indus farmers from having to construct large-scale irrigation works. Monsoon winds flowing from the African land mass across the western Indian Ocean between late spring and early autumn bring rain in varying quantities to South Asia. Recent studies based on evidence from archaeology, geology, and satellite imagery suggest that before about 3000 B.C.E., summer monsoons were powerful, dumping so much rain on the Indus region that annual flooding prevented much human settlement. In the fourth millennium B.C.E., however, the rain-bearing winds weakened gradually over the long term, opening more land to year-round cultivation and encouraging population buildup along the Indus system as well as the Ghaggar-Hakra River and its tributaries east of the Indus.

MAP 2.5 Complex society in the Indus valley.

Would early complex society in South Asia have been possible if the Himalaya Mountains did not exist?

Cities of the Indus.

Between 2800 and 2600 B.C.E., Indus valley dwellers started building cities. As in Mesopotamia, Indus cities developed as dense, distinct settlements separated by village-dotted countryside. One of the biggest centers was Harappa, which arose on the Punjab plain along the Ravi River, an Indus tributary. The city had a circuit of about three miles and a fluctuating population that may have reached as many as eighty thousand when people gathered from near and far to trade in seasonal markets. The largest urban complex so far discovered is Mohenjo-daro, four hundred miles south of Harappa. In contrast to the jumbled maze of lanes and alleys that characterized Mesopotamian cities, the streets of both Harappa and Mohenjo-daro were laid out on a grid pattern, suggesting thoughtful urban design. Houses, stores, and shops of baked brick lined city streets. Subterranean channels brought in fresh water and flushed out sewage. Residents built private homes around a central courtyard, and most of them had toilet and bathing rooms equipped with sewer drains.

Indus city people followed a variety of occupations. Some were specialists at crafts such as masonry, coppersmithing, ivory carving, pottery making, and weaving. Textile production was probably a home industry for every family.

Cities of the Indus valley. If we cast back to the late third millennium B.C.E., we might imagine this straight street in Mohenjo-daro crowded with local residents, shopkeepers, and traders. Why do you think the cities of the Harappan civilization remained unknown to the wider world until the twentieth century?

Many city residents may have been full-time farmers, who trudged daily to the surrounding countryside to tend fields of wheat, barley, peas, dates, sesame, and cotton, or herds of sheep, buffalo, and humped zebu cattle.

Material remains of Indus settlements have so far revealed much less than we would like to know about Harappan society. Recovered treasures include superbly crafted jewelry, masks, seals, ceramics, and figurines. We may assume, therefore, that a minority of men and women were rich. But houses were relatively uniform in size, which hints at a fair degree of social equality rather than a strict division between a land-controlling aristocracy and everyone else. In archaeological sites, baked clay figurines of women often displaying fancy hair styles predominate over male figurines. And ceramic seals carry engravings of female deities. These objects suggest that women could rise to important ceremonial or social positions in Harappan cities, though the evidence is indirect.

Harappan government? The material ruins of Indus society have left no trace of kings, queens, or sprawling palaces. Nor is there any evidence that a single state or even cluster of city-states ever dominated the plain. In stark contrast to Mesopotamia and Egypt, surviving pictorial art shows no warriors capturing people or stabbing and clubbing one another. On the other hand, the rise of cities as impressive as Harappa and Mohenjo-daro suggests some kind of central management. Urban planning and engineering were precise and uniform, suggesting watchful public supervision. Bricks for construction had standard dimensions, main streets were exactly twice as wide as side streets, and artisans dug wells lined with ingenious wedge-shaped bricks that could withstand (and have withstood) centuries of earthquakes. In Mohenjo-daro a cluster of elevated buildings and towers dominated the landscape. These structures, resting on a brick platform of 600,000 square yards, may have served as a fortress or as storehouses for city grain reserves. Although Harappans made figurines and seals that represented deities, no evidence of a temple priesthood has been found. Mohenjo-daro's central complex includes a water

tank nearly forty feet long. People could descend into the tank by either of two sets of stone steps. Many scholars think that the "great bath," as it is called, was a place of ritual cleansing and regeneration, a key element of Indian religious practice as it emerged in later centuries. But no one knows for sure.

The Harappan cultural style. Archaeological work has revealed many similarities from one Indus city to another in urban planning, architecture, pottery, statuary, seals, and jewelry design. This unity of style points to intense cultural intercommunication on the plain and the maturing of a coherent cultural tradition that thrived for more than 500 years. Since we have no evidence of an empire-builder like Sargon of Akkad, we may infer that cultural interchange occurred mainly in association with regional trade, or perhaps with intercity social ties based on kinship or occupation.

Indus society had a written language. Seals, tablets, pottery, and other objects inscribed with a distinctive script have been found in nearly every part of the plain. Unfortunately, linguists have so far been unable to decipher much of the sign system, which dates to as early as 3300 B.C.E. Harappan jottings appear to represent both pictographic and sound symbols, but inscriptions are never more than two lines long. It is likely that only a small minority of the valley's population could read or write because as Indus civilization declined after 1900 B.C.E., the writing system gradually disappeared.

An early yogi? This stone seal from the ancient city of Mohenjo-daro depicts a male deity having three faces and sporting bangles on his arms. He is seated on a throne in *baddha konasana*, the name of a pose familiar to modern practitioners of yoga. He wears an extravagant headdress. On either side of it are signs in the Indus writing system. Why do you think it has been so hard for linguists to decipher the Indus script?

Interregional Communication and Commerce

We should not forget that the populations of early complex societies represented only a small percentage of the world's total in the third millennium B.C.E. Most people around the globe continued to subsist as foragers or as farmers and herders inhabiting small, dispersed settlements. Nevertheless, to the extent that country and city dwellers had knowledge of each other, strong mutual attractions existed between them. Rural people were drawn to the handcrafted goods, precious wares, tools, and technological knowledge that urban centers had to offer. Conversely, the river valley societies reached into the surrounding hinterlands for food, minerals, gems, and timber, as well as live captives to put to work as slaves. As the populations of the three valleys grew, "concentric circles" of exchange around these hubs inevitably grew as well. In time, they overlapped, which brought the valleys into sustained contact with one another. When that happened, products, skills, and knowledge originating in one of the centers began to affect life in the others. Thus, the entire India-to-Mediterranean region emerged as a single zone of communication and exchange (see Map 2.6).

The Mesopotamian network. The oldest intercity trade web emerged in Mesopotamia. In the third millennium B.C.E., canoes, barges, and small sail craft glided up and down the rivers, carrying bulk commodities like barley, hides, and cheap pottery. Donkey pack trains and ox-drawn carts lumbered from the cities to farming villages on the plain and in distant hills. In Sumer, which had few natural resources besides arable land, temple priests controlled most exchange, sending commercial agents far and wide to trade Mesopotamian farm products, as well as textiles, pottery, and other finished goods made in temple workshops for timber, copper, and other commodities. Mesopotamian agents voyaged southeastward along the rim of the Persian Gulf to acquire copper, dates, fish, pearls, and diorite (a hard decorative stone) for Sumerian and Akkadian cities. Trade in the valley grew so much that figuring out the relative value of hundreds of different goods relative to one another became very complicated. Consequently, Mesopotamians began to use units of silver, copper, barley, or other commodities both as units for determining the relative value of other goods and as mediums of exchange. For example, a shekel of silver, which weighed one-third of an ounce, or slightly more than three U.S. pennies, came to serve as a

MAP 2.6 Trade in the region from South Asia to the Mediterranean, third millennium B.C.E.

What factors explain why trade was more active between the Indus valley and Mesopotamia than between Egypt and Mesopotamia?

standard to express the value of particular items, say, the price of a slave or a basket of figs.

By about 3000 B.C.E., exchange routes knitting together cities in northern and southern Mesopotamia formed a single network extending from the sources of the Tigris and Euphrates to the Persian Gulf. As this happened, a new breed of trader joined the commercial agents who served temple and palace. These were individuals who trafficked privately and for personal profit—the world's earliest professional merchant class. City-states such as Mari and Ebla near the upper Euphrates River tapped minerals and gems found in Anatolia and northern Iran. Merchants of Assyria, that is, the region centered on the northern Tigris valley, made the city-state of Ashur an important commercial hub. Beginning around 1900 B.C.E., Assyrians penetrated deep into Anatolia, founding twenty or more satellite settlements to deal in gold, silver, and copper, which they shipped throughout Southwest Asia. At a place called Tepe Yahya in southwestern Iran, local artisans began as early as 2800 B.C.E. to manufacture stone bowls of a special style and to ship them more than five hundred miles to Mesopotamia.

Egypt's trade links. We know from archaeological evidence that Mesopotamia had significant commercial and cultural contacts with Egypt by the late fourth millennium B.C.E. For example, archaeologists excavating Egyptian sites have found specimens of lapis lazuli that Mesopotamian traders probably acquired from Afghanistan or Baluchistan (a region that overlaps modern Iran and Pakistan) and carried to the Nile. As Egypt's complex society expanded, however, direct trade with Mesopotamia appears to have remained modest or even shrank. One factor may be that increasing aridity in northern Arabia made overland pack transport directly between southern Mesopotamia and Egypt increasingly expensive and dangerous. The Old Kingdom dynasties also tried to control the movement of goods in and out of the Nile valley, and Egyptian texts of that age make no mention of merchants running private businesses or commercial expeditions.

The pharaoh's commercial agents, however, served the state's interests well. Their main link from the Nile to Southwest Asia was not the desert track to Sumer but shipping routes to ports of the Levant, the eastern Mediterranean coastal region that is today Israel, Palestine, Lebanon, and part of Syria. The Levant's most important export to Egypt was wood, especially large timbers of cedar, pine, and fir from Lebanon's highland forests. Boats could transport timber around the southeastern curve of the Mediterranean in much greater quantity than pack animals could haul it across the Sinai Peninsula.

Like the Tigris-Euphrates, the Nile was a natural highway of north–south trade, though a much longer one. Egyptian

Transport on the Nile. These figures carved from wood crowd onto a boat propelled by rowers. The model, dated to about 1900 B.C.E., comes from the tomb of an Egyptian estate manager. Note the large stern rudder. What uses might a craft like this have had?

agents operated upriver to Nubia to buy gold, slaves, and a variety of exotic products that came from the African tropical latitudes further south. Tomb inscriptions record the trade exploits of Harkhuf, an Egyptian official who held the governorship of southern Egypt between about 2290 and 2270 B.C.E. and who led four commercial expeditions into Nubia. In the inscriptions, he boasts of his success: "I came down [the Nile] bringing gifts from that country in great quantity, the likes of which had never before been brought back to this land. . . . Then his majesty sent me a third time. . . . I came down with three hundred donkeys laden with incense, ebony, . . . panther skins, elephant's tusks, throw sticks, and all sort of good products."[2] Other Egyptian missions traded to the region they identified as Punt, which was most likely the land just west of the Red Sea where the modern states of Eritrea and Ethiopia are today.

Far-flung Harappan trade. In the Indus valley, the inter-urban trade network took shape from about 2400 B.C.E. Pack trains, two-wheeled ox carts, and flat-bottomed boats transported foodstuffs and luxury wares throughout the plain and into the neighboring hills. Merchants who were probably private entrepreneurs, not state agents, traveled west into Baluchistan and southeast toward tropical India in search of metals and gemstones. Harappan colonizers also ventured a thousand miles from the valley to found a trading post in northeastern Afghanistan, probably for transshipping gold, silver, copper, and lapis lazuli.

Harappans were among the world's early sea traders, steering rudimentary watercraft from the Indus River delta along the northern edge of the Arabian Sea to the Persian Gulf. Discovery of Harappan artifacts such as weights and seals show that Indus merchants made contact with Mesopotamian counterparts in the gulf, mainly at Dilmun on the island of Bahrain. An inscription of the emperor Sargon tells of ships from Meluhha, which scholars identify with the Indus, docking at Akkad in the twenty-fourth century B.C.E.

Long-distance cultural exchange. The routes linking the three complex societies inevitably carried ideas and information as well as goods. Each of these societies developed profoundly different cultural styles in many respects, but mutual cultural influences were not negligible in the third millennium B.C.E. Mesopotamia was, as far as we know, the world birthplace of a number of key inventions and discoveries, including the wheel, the traction plow, brick-building methods, and bronze metallurgy, plus several major plant and animal domesticates. Several of these ingredients of agrarian culture almost certainly diffused from Mesopotamia to Egypt, India, and lands beyond. Materials and ideas related to food production probably diffused east and west quite rapidly, in part because the climates and seasonal latitudes were similar in all three valleys.

Mesopotamia was also the recipient of innovations. Archeological finds suggest that pottery-making technology spread initially from northeastern Africa to the Fertile Crescent. Around 2000 B.C.E., Harappan farmers began to grow sorghum and pearl millet, both domesticated plants of African origin that probably reached the Indus overland or by way of early Arabian Sea trade. Cotton and several minor food plants are likely to have spread from India westward. The idea of sacred rulership, that is, the belief that chiefs and monarchs possess supernatural powers or even fully divine natures almost certainly spread from the savanna lands surrounding the upper Nile to Egypt—and possibly from there to Mesopotamia. Finally, there is little doubt that Sumerian scribes invented the first full writing system, but Egyptian and Harappan signs have now been dated early enough to weaken the theory that the *idea* of writing necessarily originated in Mesopotamia.

Complex Societies and the Environment

The advent of food production, the crowding of people into dense settlements, and the incessant growth of human numbers worldwide represented a new variable in the continually changing global biosphere. Though neither farmers nor city dwellers were conscious of any but the short-term effects of their behavior, they began to alter the earthly landscape on a scale far beyond the capabilities of paleolithic foragers. Like global society today, they also began to experience unintended and sometimes worrying ecological consequences of settled and urban living.

Agrarian life and infectious disease. One change that accompanied the rise of complex societies, and has been with us ever since, was growing human susceptibility to a host of lethal microorganisms. Paleolithic men and women might die from any number of accidents or calamities long before their fortieth birthdays but not so frequently from infectious disease. When humans began to pack themselves into villages, and then cities, they were obliged to live much closer to their own heaps of garbage and bodily waste—havens for potentially dangerous microbes. Farm people also commonly shared living space with all sorts of animals—sheep, pigs, cows, chickens, and dogs. A number of the maladies that have tormented humankind in the past five millennia, including smallpox, measles, chickenpox, tuberculosis, and flu, started out as pathogens whose hosts were domestic animals. Contagious diseases spread easily among flocks and herds, and some microbes thrived by making genetic adaptations to human bodies. When people transmitted pathogens by coughing, sneezing, touching, defecating, or sharing sleeping mats, they might trigger a citywide epidemic. We do not have much concrete evidence of the larger social effects of these "crowd diseases" on early complex societies. There is little doubt, however, that the first cities were less healthy places to live than foraging camps and that the coming of agriculture permanently transformed the ecological relationships among humans, animals, and disease-producing germs.

Changes on the land. By its very nature, food production required that people deliberately intervene more energetically to alter the physical and natural landscape. To create arable fields, neolithic farmers felled trees or set whole forests on fire. In some regions they practiced shifting agriculture, clearing a field, growing crops on it for a few seasons until the soil became depleted, then moving on with axe and hoe to new ground. If cultivators burned an area repeatedly or permanently grazed animals on it, they might keep woodland from ever regenerating. As early as 5000 B.C.E., for example, neolithic farmers in Britain were already turning large areas of forest into treeless moorland or bogs.

Building complex societies involved more drastic environmental manipulation. In the Tigris-Euphrates, Nile, and Indus valleys, urbanization and intensive farming led to deforestation, calamitous floods, deteriorating soil, and other ecological stresses that seriously affected the directions those societies took. All three civilizations had ravenous appetites for wood for household fuel, construction, and brick making. After depleting local resources, they turned to neighboring areas, and the damage spread. Timber cutters in eastern Anatolia and the Zagros Mountains of western Iran labored to meet Mesopotamia's insatiable appetite for wood but at the cost of deforestation and increased risk of violent flooding and silt buildup downstream on the irrigated plain. In Egypt, forests and marshes receded so fast in the third millennium that by 2200 B.C.E. the populations of elephant, gazelle, giraffe, and rhinoceros that had once flourished there had all but vanished. To the east the Harappans used huge quantities of oven-baked bricks to build their splendid cities. This industry rapidly consumed most of the woodland on the Indus plain, then ate away at the highland forests to the west and north, producing the same problems of erosion and flooding that Mesopotamia faced.

Sumer's special ecological curse was salinization. Because the angle of the alluvial plain was gentle and drainage slow, salts dissolved in river water accumulated gradually in topsoil, poisoning the roots of plants. Sumerian farmers worked endlessly to flush crystallized salts from their fields. But extra irrigation eventually caused water logging, and the salt always returned. Crop yields on salt-infected land dropped slowly, and large areas of once cultivated land had to be abandoned or turned over to animal grazing. By the early second millennium B.C.E. the populations and economies of most of the Sumerian city-states were declining.

Today, wind-swept hillocks in the Iraqi desert mark their ancient locations.

A long drought cycle. Recent climatic research has provided persuasive evidence that all three of the great river valleys, and perhaps much of the Northern Hemisphere, suffered heightened aridity and volatile climatic fluctuations for three centuries beginning about 2200 B.C.E. Relationships of cause and effect between climate change and particular cases of social or economic stress are hard to pin down. But the long-term "dry event" that began in the late third millennium chronologically matches serious crises in the three valleys.

In Mesopotamia the Akkadian empire that Sargon built collapsed about 2190 B.C.E. Aside from extended drought and salinization on the river plain, low rainfall in the deserts east and west of the river valley may have provoked animal-herding peoples to invade farmland close to cities. In the north of Mesopotamia, however, new centers of production and trade sprouted in the second millennium, as we shall see.

In Egypt the Old Kingdom's central authority began to disintegrate about 2134 B.C.E. Political division and civil unrest dragged on for several decades, a time historians call the First Intermediate Period. Scientists studying ancient sediment layers on the Blue Nile in Ethiopia have hypothesized that extended drought severely reduced summer floods on the lower river about the same time that the Old Kingdom fell. This ecological crisis may have triggered famine and social upheaval. Egyptian texts from the era support the theory: "[Grain] has perished everywhere. . . . People are stripped of clothing, perfume, and oil. . . . The dead are thrown in the river. . . . Laughter has perished. Grief walks the land."[3] Nevertheless, strong new leaders united the valley about 2040 B.C.E., ushering in the new era called the Middle Kingdom (2040–1652 B.C.E.).

Harappan civilization peaked around 1900 B.C.E. and then went into permanent decline. Scholars have pointed to an array of ecological stress points, including silt buildup, deforestation in the hill country, excessive flooding, overgrazing, persistent drought, and recurring shifts in the course of the Indus and its tributaries. In the third millennium, weakening summer monsoons appear to have speeded the development of complex society. But as that climatic trend continued, so recent research proposes, farmers in the southern valley experienced increasing water shortages and had to migrate north and east. The Ghaggar-Hakra River network, which was probably fed by monsoons rather than Himalayan glaciers, dried up during part of the year, forcing people to abandon their cities. By about 1500 B.C.E., large-scale complex society no longer existed in the Indus region, though it would return eventually.

• • •

Conclusion

Much of this chapter has focused on the broad region of Afroeurasia between India and the Mediterranean because striking changes in human society occurred there between 10,000 and 2000 B.C.E. Within the fruitful Tigris-Euphrates, Nile, and Indus valleys, population growth and food production reinforced one another in a roughly upward spiral. If those societies were not to burst at the seams, novel social and technological solutions had to be found. Accelerating innovation produced bustling cities, many new occupations, access to exotic goods, grand religious festivals, and conditions of law and order. They also produced iron-fisted rulers, crowded living, infectious diseases, social inequalities, slavery, taxes, and the concentration of public power in the hands of males. Civilization, humans learned early, brought both blessings and vexations.

Meanwhile, the rest of the world by no means stood still. By 3000 B.C.E., agrarian communities were spreading across all the inhabited continents except Australia, transforming landscapes as they advanced. Estimates of total world population growth for such remote times are only educated guesses, but numbers rose from perhaps ten million in 8000 B.C.E., when the agrarian era got seriously under way, to about fifty million by 3000 B.C.E. In that same five thousand years, the number of foragers in the world declined significantly, relative to the total population. Some forager communities saw advantages in turning to farming, but others were displaced or marginalized by cultivators who arrived with their axes, hoes, chiefs, and disease pathogens. By the start of the second millennium B.C.E., where this chapter ends, a fourth complex society was emerging on the floodplains of the Yellow and Yangzi Rivers in northern China. And in temperate Europe, the savanna lands of Africa, tropical Southeast Asia, North America, and the Andes Mountains, men and women were creating more intricate technologies and institutions to meet the demands of farm life and growing populations.

• • •

Key Terms

agrarian society 51	Fertile Crescent 51	neolithic era 53
agricultural revolution 51	Gilgamesh 63	Old Kingdom Egypt 73
bureaucracy 64	Harappan society 69	patriarchy 65
Çatal Hüyük 56	hieroglyphs 67	peasants 65
city-state 61	Jericho 56	pharaoh 66
complex society 58	logogram 63	pictograph 67
cuneiform 62	Mesopotamia 63	slavery 65
dynasty 61	Middle Kingdom Egypt 75	Sumer 72
empire 64	Mohenjo-daro 70	Uruk 60

Change over Time

10,000 B.C.E.	Farming in Southwest Asia marks the onset of the neolithic age.
10,000–3000 B.C.E.	Farming and agrarian societies emerge in several regions in Afroeurasia and the Americas.
7000 B.C.E.	Neolithic settlements are founded at Jericho and Çatal Hüyük in Southwest Asia.
5000 B.C.E.	Copper metallurgy emerges.
4000 B.C.E.	Complex society founded on irrigated farming in Mesopotamia appears.
3500 B.C.E.	Cities appear in Mesopotamia, the largest of them Uruk in the region of Sumer.
3200 B.C.E.	Evidence of hieroglyphic writing in Egypt and of pictographic writing in Mesopotamia appears.
2800–2600 B.C.E.	Urbanization gets under way in the Indus River valley, with large centers at Harappa and Mohenjo-daro.
2686–2160 B.C.E.	Centralized government emerges in Egypt's Old Kingdom period.
2340–2190 B.C.E.	Sargon of Akkad founds the first empire in Mesopotamia.
2200–1900 B.C.E.	Southwest Asia experiences extended drought.
2040–1652 B.C.E.	Political stability is restored in Egypt, ushering in the Middle Kingdom.
1900 B.C.E.	Assyrian merchants establish trade settlements in Anatolia; long-distance trade networks develop from hubs in the Tigris-Euphrates, Nile, and Indus River valleys.

Please see end of book reference section for additional reading suggestions related to this chapter.

3 Afroeurasia's Moving Frontiers: Farmers, Herders, and Charioteers

3000–1000 B.C.E.

The Uluburun vessel rests on the bottom of the Mediterranean near the Turkish coast.

n the summer of 1982 a young man diving for sea sponges off the southwestern coast of Turkey reported seeing oddly shaped metal objects on the Mediterranean floor. A team of underwater archaeologists shortly identified them as part of the wreckage of an ancient ship. Examining fragments of pottery and other datable artifacts, the scientists calculated that the vessel sank sometime around 1306 B.C.E. Excavation at the site 170 feet down yielded thousands of items—commercial goods, pieces of the wooden hull, even personal belongings of crew members.

Because of its rich cargo and great antiquity, the shipwreck of Uluburun, named after a nearby point on the Turkish coast, has become world famous. Scientists have not been able to determine exactly where the ship was going, though some have speculated that it was carrying official gifts from Southwest Asian rulers to the pharaoh of Egypt. Whatever its mission, the vessel's freight came from many different lands. The metal objects the sponge diver spotted turned out to be copper ingots, probably from the island of Cyprus. The hull also contained cobalt blue glass disks manufactured in Mediterranean coastal towns as well as Greek pottery, swords, daggers, and silver jewelry. Some items came from far beyond the Mediterranean: amber from northern Europe, ebony logs from tropical Africa, and tin from as far east as Afghanistan.

Until the late third millennium B.C.E., dense agrarian societies with cities existed only in the Tigris-Euphrates, Nile, and Indus valleys, and, on a smaller scale, coastal Peru. Everywhere else, people lived in either farm villages or forager-hunter camps. The Uluburun discoveries, and the patterns of trade and urbanization they reveal, are just one illustration of how radically the human community changed in the following one thousand years. Farming and herding practices capable of supporting cities, social hierarchies, numerous occupational specializations, and centralized states spread widely in Afroeurasia (see Map 3.1). Many of the inventions and techniques that made accelerating population growth and social complexity possible diffused from the three ancient river valley civilizations to neighboring regions. But in all of the seven or eight places in the world where farming arose independently, men and women devised new ways of producing greater food surpluses, organizing larger numbers of people, and exchanging goods and ideas with strangers. The first part of this chapter explores the emergence in the second millennium B.C.E. of more complex agrarian societies in new regions of Afroeurasia: the Mediterranean basin, western Europe, Central Asia, and, finally, East Asia, where a fourth great river valley civilization arose in the Yellow and Yangzi River valleys.

In the second part of the chapter, we introduce the new and specialized way of life based on animal herding that emerged gradually in several parts of the Great Arid Zone, the wide zone of dry country that extends across Afroeurasia. Crop growing had been intertwined with domestic animal breeding since the beginnings of agriculture. But the practice of large-scale pastoralism, that is, the raising of hoofed animals as a society's *primary* source of food, developed between the fourth and second millennia B.C.E. This type of pastoralism emerged in connection with three fundamental innovations—the domestication of horses, horseback riding, and wheeled wagon transport. These inventions and discoveries allowed people to graze animals over immense stretches of grassland and brushland where crop raising was severely limited. As pastoral populations grew, they began to play an increasingly important role in world history, intruding, peacefully or not, into agrarian and urbanized regions; spreading their languages; and facilitating long-distance trade across Eurasia. Indeed, in the second millennium B.C.E., all the lands from the Mediterranean basin

Chapter Outline

• • •

to China became for the first time incorporated into a single zone of commercial and cultural interchange.

In the third section of the chapter, we shift southward to Afroeurasia's tropical latitudes, where migrations and economic innovations also stimulated population growth and introduced new social and cultural ways, including new languages. In Africa south of the Sahara Desert and in tropical Southeast Asia, peoples with warm-climate crops and in some places cattle herds impinged on lands previously inhabited only by foragers. Sometime in those two thousand years, populations that produced food probably came to

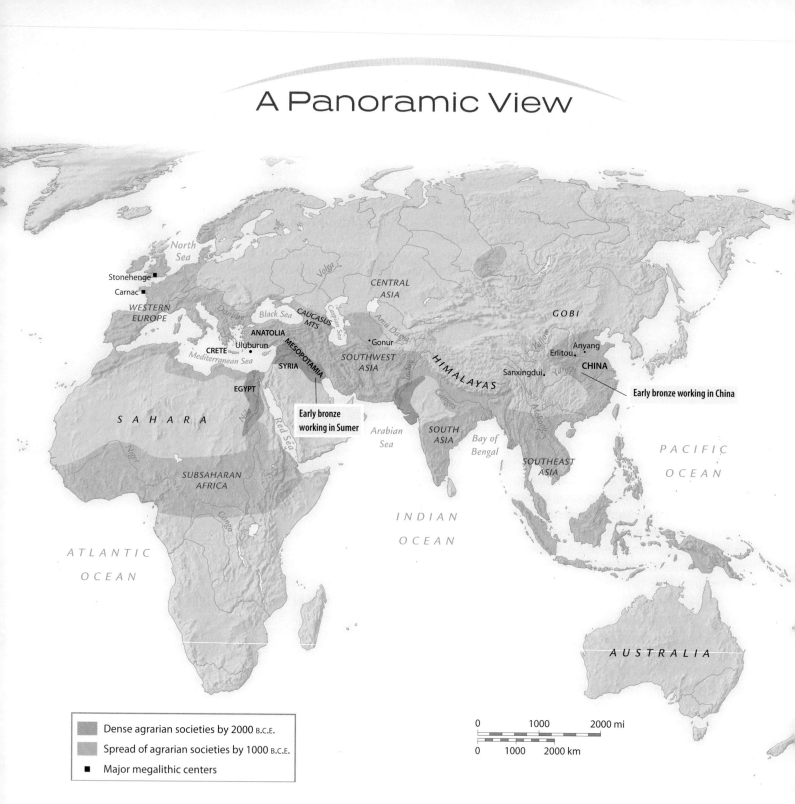

MAP 3.1 Agrarian societies in Afroeurasia, 3000–2000 B.C.E.
People in Southwest Asia and China probably invented bronze technology independently of each other. What geographical or climatic factors might help explain the *absence* of farming in extensive areas of Afroeurasia as of 1000 B.C.E.?

Legend:
- Dense agrarian societies by 2000 B.C.E.
- Spread of agrarian societies by 1000 B.C.E.
- ■ Major megalithic centers

outnumber on a hemispheric scale populations that hunted and gathered it in the wild. In other words, human efforts to alter the face of the earth in increasingly ingenious ways spread far beyond the core lands where food plants and animals were first domesticated to embrace Afroeurasian regions from equatorial rainforests to arid, windswept steppes.

Across Afroeurasia: More Farmers, More Cities

FOCUS What aspects of life during the bronze age in Afroeurasia distinguish it from earlier eras?

Scholars have estimated that the population of the entire world rose from around 6 million in 8000 B.C.E., when the agrarian age was well under way, to about 120 million by 1000 B.C.E.[1] This change in global numbers represents a dramatic upswing in the rate of growth compared to the previous 200,000 years of human history. In the second millennium B.C.E. (1999–1000 B.C.E.), population grew at the fastest rate in Afroeurasia, where farming had the earliest start and continued to expand in every direction. In the Americas, numbers inched upward also, rising fastest in the regions of Mesoamerica and the Andes where crop growing took root. (We examine these developments in Chapter 4.) Nevertheless, the total population of the Americas may have reached no more than about 4.5 million by 1000 B.C.E., less than 4 percent of the numbers in Afroeurasia at that time.[2]

In the world generally, second millennium B.C.E. growth was mostly *extensive,* that is, it took place as small farming and herding communities multiplied across the landscape. By contrast, *intensive* growth took place in areas where technological innovation and surplus farm production allowed a given area of land to support more and more people, in some places in large cities. In this section, we explore four regions that experienced both extensive and intensive growth in the second millennium B.C.E.: the eastern Mediterranean (specifically the shores and islands of the Aegean Sea), western Europe, Central Asia, and East Asia. Keep in mind, however, that as of 1000 B.C.E., city dwellers still accounted for only a small percentage of global numbers.

The Cavalcade of Inventions

Continuing technical innovation was essential to intensive growth in the three early river valley civilizations that we discussed in Chapter 2. Those societies contributed new ideas and tool kits out of all proportion to their share of global population, for example, the wheel, brick making, the closed pottery kiln, hydraulic irrigation devices, star charts, and complex writing and computation systems. In the second millennium B.C.E., much of this technology advanced into other parts of Afroeurasia, all the time undergoing numerous refinements and elaborations. New tools and methods contributed immensely to farming productivity, urban manufacturing, and long-distance communication. Many new techniques, such as glass making, stronger ship design, and lighter wheeled vehicles, spread widely as well. Bronze metallurgy and the traction plow, both invented in the third millennium, were among the most socially significant novelties.

Making bronze. So many thousands of bronze tools, weapons, containers, chariot fittings, and ornaments have been found in Eurasian and northern African archaeological sites from the third and second millennia B.C.E. that scholars have conventionally labeled that period the **bronze age.** Sometime before 3000 B.C.E., metalsmiths discovered that if they mixed copper with small amounts of arsenic or tin, they could produce a metal alloy far superior to copper alone. These alloys were easier to cast and more durable, and they could hold an edge. Tin bronze gradually became the standard as metallurgists realized that arsenic chronically poisoned anyone who worked with it.

> **bronze age** The era centered on the third and second millennia B.C.E. when bronze making was the most advanced metallurgical technology in the world.

In the Sumerian cities of Mesopotamia, artisans made ornamental and ritual objects of bronze, as well as axes, sickles, chisels, and spears. The technology probably radiated from there to the Nile and Indus valleys. Mesopotamia, however, was not the only center of diffusion. Wherever villagers built kilns to fire pottery, the idea of blending metal alloys at a high temperature in the same oven might plausibly have come to mind. In the third millennium B.C.E., innovators in northern China probably inaugurated bronze working independently. Both southeastern Europe and mainland Southeast Asia are possible candidates for independent innovation. Whatever the source, bronze metallurgy promoted farm productivity and more complex social and political organization across Eurasia and North Africa.

Because of the costs of mining, transporting, and forging, most people could not afford bronze objects. Copper ore occurs quite commonly in nature, but tin does not. The main sources of tin for Mesopotamian and Indus valley bronzesmiths may have been mines in Inner Eurasia. Merchants would therefore have shipped tin hundreds of miles, greatly elevating its cost at the point of final sale. Bronze tools, weapons, and craftwork therefore acquired great social value as symbols of high class

A warrior's bronze helmet. Made in southwestern Iran in the fourteenth century B.C.E., this bronze headgear displays three golden images: a male god in the center and females on either side of him. A bird spreads its wings over these deities. Why might a soldier, certainly one of high rank, want a helmet decorated with divine images?

status or political authority, especially for men. Expanding production of bronze swords, javelins, arrow points, helmets, and body armor made warfare, as well as the power of rulers, possible on a larger scale than ever before. The booming industry also generated a host of new occupations for laboring folk in mining, furnace making, smithing, boat building, and the master crafts.

Plowing the land. A second major innovation of the third millennium B.C.E. was the traction plow, a tilling device pulled by oxen, horses, or mules. To prepare ground for planting, a farmer had to break the soil into particles, aerate it, and kill weeds. Women and men could do this with sticks and hoes, but an animal-powered plow could do it faster with less human energy expended and more arable ground covered. After about 3000 B.C.E., the Sumerians used simple ox-drawn plows to till the light, easily worked soils of the Tigris-Euphrates valley. In the subsequent 1,500 years, farmers gradually applied the new technology to rain-dependent land where soils were sometimes heavier and deeper and therefore resistant to handheld tools.

Farmers who hitched an animal or two to a wooden plow, perhaps one with a bronze tip, often found they could increase grain harvests significantly. This encouraged tillers to drain marshes or clear forests to open more fields and build more villages. Along the belt of territory from India to the Mediterranean, this innovation supported population growth. In some regions, however, plows had little appeal. In the Yellow River valley in northern China, for example, villagers found that their hoes and digging sticks worked well to till the fine, easily aerated soil known as loess. In short, the plow was a useful farm tool only in certain ecological conditions.

Complex Society and Commerce in the Mediterranean Basin

Schoolroom geography tells us that the Mediterranean Sea divides the continents of Africa, Asia, and Europe from one another. But it is also useful to think of the Mediterranean as a sea "inside" the supercontinent of Afroeurasia, a passageway that links peoples all around its rim. Numerous islands and peninsulas within the Mediterranean divide it into several smaller seas that make it relatively easy to navigate. The Aegean Sea in the eastern Mediterranean was especially appealing to ancient mariners. In fact, recent discovery of stone tools on the Aegean island of Crete indicate that foragers crossed water to get there at least 130,000 years ago and perhaps earlier.

After about 3000 B.C.E., farm communities and maritime trade centers multiplied around the eastern Mediterranean rim, notably in the Nile delta and along the seaboard known historically as the Levant, or Levantine coast, today Israel, the Palestinian territories, Lebanon, and western Syria. The same thing happened on the shores and numerous islands of the Aegean Sea. Because that region is mostly mountainous,

farmers had to plant on slopes or small plains. By adopting animal-powered plows, however, they produced bountiful wheat harvests in good years. They also cultivated olive trees and wine grapes, two plants that thrive where terrain is uneven and summers hot and brilliant. Nutritious and calorie rich, olive oil had several uses—for cooking, heating, and lighting, and as an ingredient of fine perfumes. Wine consumption cut down on illnesses from waterborne microorganisms, and no doubt made social life more agreeable. Both commodities, preserved in large earthenware jars and transported readily by ship, became basic staples of Mediterranean trade. As Aegean farmers accumulated surpluses of wheat, oil, and wine (also sheep and goats), inequalities of wealth and social class inevitably appeared. Some individuals were buried with bronze weaponry and other precious grave goods, indicating their special social or political status. Towns began to appear where chiefs or big landowners taxed the local farmers to pay for forts, palatial houses, and artisans' workshops. One of these centers was Troy, a complex of fortifications and dwellings whose third millennium rulers possessed dazzling wealth in bronze, silver, gold, and gemstones.

Minoan society on Crete. A remarkable cluster of small cities also emerged on Crete, the mountainous, 150-mile-long island that marks the southern extremity of the Aegean Sea. Called Minoans after a legendary king named Minos, the islanders started building these centers around 2000 B.C.E. In some of them the main structure was a complex of public or private rooms, spacious courtyards, and storehouses. From these little palaces, an affluent class of aristocrats supervised the village population, which raised olives, grapes, wheat, and sheep. Knossos, the largest center, may have had a second millennium B.C.E. population of about twenty thousand.

Crete's prosperous society may have arisen where it did partly because the island was only a short sailing distance from the culturally weightier societies of the Nile and Southwest Asia. Aspects of Minoan architecture, wall decoration, and religion appear to have originated in Egypt, including adoption of the bull god as a central figure in the Cretan belief system. Cuneiform archives from Mari on the Euphrates River nine hundred miles to the east reveal that that city had contact with Crete. The Minoans also adopted a writing system, perhaps independently but more likely borrowed from one of its mainland neighbors. It is called Linear A, and the governing elite used it to keep track of goods that flowed in and out of the palaces. This script has not been deciphered, nor is anything known of Minoan speech. However, paintings and decorations on the walls of buildings suggest that the population, or at least the aristocratic class, had a remarkably benign view of social life and nature. The ruins have yielded almost no evidence of intercity warfare, nor any gargantuan statues of glowering god-kings. Minoan art abounds in images of men and women enjoying games and other public activities side by side,

A dangerous Minoan sport. These three figures appear to lack no confidence in challenging this rambunctious bull, a sacred animal in Minoan religion. This reconstructed fresco from the palace of Knossos shows Egyptian influence in the way the faces are drawn and in the rendering of the two female figures on the left and right with lighter skin than the male figure performing the somersault.

suggesting that women had more equality and influence in their communities than was true in the early river valley civilizations. Some historians challenge this interpretation, however, and the physical remains of Minoan culture are too limited to permit firm conclusions.

The expanding trade zone. From the late third millennium B.C.E. onward, towns flourished in several localities around the eastern Mediterranean partly because of sea trade, which was typically cheaper and faster than overland hauls using donkeys and ox-drawn wagons. In effect, this trade represented a widening of the ancient route network that connected the Indus valley, Southwest Asia, and Egypt. The palace centers of Crete benefited from their position as gateways to the Aegean. Minoan traders launched fleets of ships, founded commercial colonies on neighboring islands, and exported Crete's high-grade olive oil and woolen cloth far afield. On the Levantine coast, Byblos and Ugarit flourished as commercial ports. Their merchants profited as intermediaries of trade between greater Southwest Asia and the Mediterranean basin. They sold timber from the hills of Lebanon to wood-starved Mesopotamia and Egypt, and they manufactured bronze goods, cosmetics, and textiles, notably cloths of bright purple.

The Mediterranean trade rarely required heroic voyages far from land. Ships like the sunken wreck found near Uluburun typically tramped from island to island and bay to bay, the crews bartering as they went. When it went down, the Uluburun ship might have been following a counterclockwise circuit of eastern Mediterranean ports. Some daring merchants even set sail for the western horizon, probing their way to Italy or Sicily, where they introduced city wares to rustic farmers. Near the end of the second millennium B.C.E., agrarian societies of the far west, that is, the regions that are today Algeria, Morocco, Spain, and Portugal, joined actively in the trans-Mediterranean commercial system.

The material demands of ruling groups stimulated much trade. To the rising aristocracies of the Aegean region, for example, silver jewelry, fine linens, and bronze ornamental daggers were not simply comforts and amusements. They were also emblems of power and status. They spoke a symbolic language of lavish display that helped validate elite class dominance over humble cultivators. Aristocratic landowners, however, could afford luxury goods only if they collected taxes and **tribute** from ordinary people, persistently rousing them to produce more food, fabric, and handicrafts for export.

> **tribute** Wealth in money or material goods paid by one group to another, often a conquered group to its conquerors, as an obligation of submission or allegiance.

The eastern Mediterranean economy therefore continued to grow, even though driven mainly by the power interests of a small minority of the population.

Developments in Western Europe

In the third and second millennia B.C.E., Europe's climate was probably warmer and wetter than it is now. Dense hardwood forests and dismal marshes covered much of the region, presenting stern challenges to early farmers. Nonetheless, villages multiplied in parts of Europe as cultivators adopted traction plowing and cleared forests for pasture or cropping. When families thought the neighborhood was getting too crowded, they plodded off with their sheep and oxen to found new settlements in the distant reaches of northern and western Europe. The region therefore underwent social and economic changes similar to those that occurred in the Aegean. An upper class of chiefs and property holders appeared, bronze weaponry and handicrafts were traded, and larger population centers sprouted up. These nascent towns usually had walls, ramparts, or ditches, suggesting the need to protect stores of trade goods or artisan workshops. Woodland Europeans also linked themselves into the growing Mediterranean trade net. For example, merchants traded copper mined in central Europe both northward to Scandinavia and southward to the Aegean. The busiest avenue of long-distance trade was probably the Danube River valley, which flowed from the interior of Europe to the Black Sea.

Most of what we know of life in woodland Europe in the third and second millennia B.C.E. comes from scattered finds of pottery, metal ware, earthworks, and other artifacts. The most spectacular material remains are **megaliths,** structures built of massive stone slabs. Concentrated along Europe's Atlantic rim,

> **megalith** A large stone sometimes roughly carved and used to build a structure often having religious significance.

these constructions took the form of either tombs enclosing multiple burials or circles of huge standing stones that clearly had some ceremonial purpose. Megalithic building began in Europe in the fourth millennium B.C.E. and mostly ended by the second. Stonehenge in southern Britain is the most famous of the megalithic stone circles. Completed between 2400 and 2200 B.C.E., its stones were set up to be astronomical clocks, the slabs arranged to serve as sight lines for charting sun, moon, and stars. We know little about the people who frequented those centers. The erecting of a complex like Stonehenge, however, required so much labor, skill, and organization that an elite class of some sort, perhaps religious specialists, likely directed the work. The recent discovery of the remains of sick and injured individuals buried near Stonehenge in the third millennium B.C.E. suggests that people came to the site in search of supernatural healing.

Megaliths in France. This famous megalithic site at Carnac on Brittany's Atlantic coast consists of 3,000 standing stones arranged in multiple parallel rows. Dated 4500–2000 B.C.E., Carnac certainly had ritual purpose, but we know nothing of ceremonies performed there. What might we infer about the organization of society from the erection of these stones?

Megalithic sites from Spain to the Orkney Islands north of Britain share enough similarities in technique and design to suggest lively exchange of goods and knowledge all along Europe's Atlantic coast and back and forth across the English Channel. In any case, such interchange did not lead quickly to high social complexity. Thick forests, swamps, and heavy clay soils continued to put limits on productivity and population in northern Europe until well into the first millennium C.E.

The Oxus Civilization in Central Asia

From ancient times to the nineteenth century, the sector of the Great Arid Zone that runs between the Caspian Sea on the west and the snow-capped Himalaya ranges on the east was one of the most important commercial and cultural hinges of world history. Central Asia is the term geographers have given to this region of deserts and semiarid highlands interrupted by green river valleys. It corresponds roughly to the territories of four states that used to be part of the Soviet Union (Kazakhstan, Uzbekistan, Tajikistan, and Turkmenistan), plus northern areas of Iran and Afghanistan. Topographically, Central Asia was a natural corridor of relatively unobstructed communication between Inner Eurasia and the densely populated agrarian lands of the region stretching from India to the Mediterranean.

About 2100 B.C.E., people began to build walled cities in Central Asian river valleys, notably along the Amu Darya River (known to Greek geographers as the Oxus River). Until the 1990s, however, hardly anyone knew about this urban society except for Soviet archaeologists, who published their discoveries only in Russian. Since then, the physical contours and material culture of this "lost civilization" have become better known, and teams of scientists from several countries continue to advance our knowledge. The physical remains of this complex society, known formally as the Bactria-Margiana Archaeological Complex after two ancient regional names, suggest that newcomers, perhaps migrants from drought-stricken hill towns farther south, planned and built several cities quite quickly.

The residents of the Oxus cities, including the carefully excavated site known as Gonur in modern Turkmenistan, erected thick brick walls and high corner towers that commanded the surrounding countryside. In the larger towns, the ruling class, about which we know little, commanded construction of royal bastions and palaces that included temples. At Gonur, canals from a river fed water into the city. In the valley, farmers planted wheat and barley and raised sheep, goats, zebu cattle, and Bactrian (two-humped) camels. The material record of architecture, pottery, clay seals, ivory combs, and bronze work shows clearly that the cities shared a common cultural style and therefore probably intense commercial and social interchange, perhaps including marriage alliances among elite families. Geometric designs on clay seals suggest signs that carried meaning, but there is no evidence of an indigenous writing system.

Uncovering the Oxus civilization. Members of an archaeological team dig at Anau, one of several ancient towns in what is now Turkmenistan in Central Asia. In recent decades archaeologists have uncovered a treasury of information about early urbanization along trade routes that connected Persia with Inner Eurasia and China beyond. Gonur, a city east of Anau, had well-designed streets, sewers, residential neighborhoods, and fortifications. It flourished, however, for only about 300 years.

Oxus artisans and merchants almost certainly initiated Central Asia's historic role as commercial turnstile between Inner Eurasia and the agrarian societies to the south and west. Pot shards, soapstone jars, and other objects of Oxus origin have turned up across Iran, in ports along the Persian Gulf, and in the Indus valley. Oxus artisans made beads of shells that came from both the Indian Ocean and the Mediterranean Sea and also imported gemstones, silver, and gold.

Oxus city building lasted only a few centuries. After 1800 B.C.E. the major towns contracted in size and within two hundred years were abandoned. The cause of decline and collapse is unknown. Deteriorating ecological conditions or intercity warfare may be explanations. The decline also coincides with the arrival of horse-riding, chariot-driving peoples from the steppes to the north, though we do not know whether they came as city-wrecking invaders or peaceful migrants.

Complex Society in East Asia

At the start of the second millennium B.C.E., farming and village life were well established across much of East and Southeast Asia, though foraging communities were still common where food supplies were abundant. In Japan, for example, communities had such plenteous supplies of tubers, nuts, and seafood that they rejected intensive grain farming long after they knew about it, until about 1000 B.C.E. By contrast, complex societies evolved rapidly in the part of northern China extending from the Yellow River valley southward to the Yangzi River, where, as we saw in Chapter 2, people had been cultivating rice and millet since about 7000 B.C.E.

Early urban centers in China. About 2600 B.C.E., people in several localities began building settlements surrounded by walls constructed of earth rammed into wooden forms. Material evidence of walls, as well as graves in which special individuals were buried along with precious objects, indicate that elite groups were emerging in northern China to mobilize and direct the work of others, just as had happened in the Tigris-Euphrates, Indus, and Nile valleys some centuries earlier. Privileged families of warriors and ritual leaders probably appropriated the best land and largest stores of grain and began to collect tribute and labor services from everyone else. Beautifully crafted bronze goblets, cauldrons, animal figures, daggers, and spear points, which first appeared in East Asia about 2000 B.C.E., were closely associated with the needs of chiefs, who took charge of both religious rituals at home and hostile raids on neighbors.

Archaeological evidence shows that, in the Yellow-Yangzi region, fundamental characteristics of complex society appeared not in just one place but in several starting in the late third millennium B.C.E., significantly later than in the three great river valleys to the west. One important site is at Erlitou (er-lee-toh), a village on the plain just south of where the middle Yellow River flows today. Flourishing between about 1900 and 1500 B.C.E., the Erlitou site reveals evidence of a complex of compounds that archaeologists identify as a palace and therefore perhaps the capital of an early Chinese state. It is not clear whether Erlitou was a bustling town or mainly a ritual and political center, but it had large platforms of pounded earth, bronze foundries, paved roads, and richly equipped graves.

About four hundred miles to the southwest of Erlitou in China's Sichuan (seh-chwan) province, archaeological work since 1986 has uncovered a walled town known as Sanxingdui (sahn-shing-dway). It also flourished in the second millennium B.C.E., but its cultural style was dramatically different from that of Erlitou. Two excavated pits containing sacrificed animals also contained a treasure of bronze, gold, stone, and jade objects, including fifty-seven bronze heads, some with gold masks. Styles of pottery and other objects make clear that large centers in the region projected their cultural and probably political influences outward to smaller settlements. They also developed contacts with one another through trade, gift exchange among rulers, migration, or diffusion of techniques and styles from one center to the next. For example, rulers or merchants organized transport of copper, tin, gold, and jade to workshops sometimes hundreds of miles from where these materials were extracted. In short, the Yellow and Yangzi valleys comprised a single zone of human interconnection well before the first large state arose in East Asia.

The Shang state. Historians identify that first large state with the Shang, a dynasty of kings that exercised power for more than half a millennium, from about 1750 to 1045 B.C.E. Shang rulers supported by an elite warrior class likely started out as one local military state among many in northern China. Over centuries, these kings asserted growing power over their neighbors. Anyang, the largest Shang ritual and royal tomb center so far discovered, sprawled for miles across the Huan River, a tributary of the lower Yellow. The Shang state encompassed only a small part of the territory of modern China, but physical remains, ancient inscriptions, and

Bronze statue from Sanxingdui. Among numerous bronze heads and masks, archaeologists discovered this imposing six-foot-tall figure in a burial pit dating to 1300–1100 B.C.E. The figure has enormous hands that probably once gripped an object, perhaps an ivory tusk. What details of dress and adornment do you notice? Do they suggest anything about the figure's status in society?

chronicles written in later centuries qualify it as the earliest East Asian empire. At the height of their power between the thirteenth and eleventh centuries B.C.E., Shang kings resident in Anyang occupied mansions atop great platforms of compacted earth. The monarch and his officers likely wielded direct authority over a core area, dominated allied monarchs and chiefs in a wider circle, and conducted periodic war campaigns in even more distant regions. The kings organized the state along military lines and required villagers and war prisoners to build tombs, palaces, and perhaps several royal capitals. The Shang therefore initiated a pattern of centralized imperial government that characterized Chinese history down to the early twentieth century.

The kings became patrons of a bronze-centered artistic culture whose influence radiated out across much of northern China. In contrast to Mesopotamia or Egypt, they did not erect giant monuments, so far as we know, but the walls around major towns sheltered extraordinary artisanal skill, notably master work in bronze. At Anyang, archaeologists have unearthed royal tombs containing costly objects, notably from the burial site of Lady Hao, who was likely one of the wives of the Emperor Wu Ding (reigned 1250–1192 B.C.E.) and a military commander in her own right. Her tomb, the only elite Shang grave at Anyang never to have been looted, has yielded hundreds of bronze vessels, bells, and weapons, and numerous items of jade, ivory, bone, and stone. The presence of sixteen corpses in the tomb adds to the ample evidence that the state practiced human sacrifice on a significant scale. According to Shang belief, a deceased king would reside in his tomb and therefore needed to take along with him a select group of nobles, slaves, attendants, and mistresses, as well as horses and other animals. Sacrificial victims usually included even larger numbers of war prisoners, perhaps hundreds of them.

Beginning no later than the reign of Wu Ding, Shang scribes wrote inscriptions on thousands of animal bone fragments known as "oracle bones." The East Asian practice of venerating ancestors originated in neolithic times, as men and women offered grave goods and sacrifices to the spirits of the dead in hopes of receiving protection and favor in return. Shang kings who exercised both political and priestly power ritually communicated with the ancestors of their own royal lineage. These spirits were thought to have sufficient influence to pass on the king's appeals for rain, good harvests, military victories, the birth of healthy sons, and other blessings to Di, the supreme supernatural entity, who might have been associated with the dynasty's ancestor-founder. Monarchs typically made public decisions only after performing ceremonies to reveal the gods' intentions and foretell the future. In one type of divination the king, assisted by **shamans**, asked questions of either ancestors or nature spirits by heating a tortoise shell or cow's shoulder blade bone

shaman A man or woman who the community believes has access to supernatural forces or beings and who can appeal to the spirit world to discern the future, bring good fortune, or perform physical healing.

	Turtle	Horse
Oracle-bone script of the Shang dynasty (16th century– 11th century B.C.E.)		
Zhou dynasty script (11th century– 3rd century B.C.E.)		
Qin dynasty script (221–207 B.C.E.)		
Han dynasty script (207 B.C.E.–220 C.E.)		
Modern script (3rd century C.E.–the present)		
Contemporary script, People's Republic of China (1950–the present)		

Writing in China. Inscriptions on oracle bones from the Shang period reveal the earliest East Asian writing system. How do the two words represented on the chart show evolution away from pictographic forms?

in a particular way until it cracked. Then the diviners "read" the cracks to discover the response.

These oracle bones are the earliest written "documents" of Chinese history. After diviners analyzed the cracks in the heated bone or shell, scribes wrote questions, interpretations, or commentaries on them using signs that conveyed a combination of meanings and sounds. These characters, as modern scholars figured out early in the twentieth century, were the forerunners of modern Chinese script. By deciphering many oracle-bone inscriptions, linguists have learned not only the names of Shang rulers and towns but also details of such matters as religious practice, warfare, farming lore, and climate.

The northern Chinese very likely invented their own writing system independently of any influence from the civilizations to the west. But this raises a larger question: What role did communication between northern China and westerly lands in the third and second millennia B.C.E. play in the rise of complex society in East Asia? East–west contacts would most likely have occurred by way of Inner Eurasia. Trade goods, technical innovations, and the seeds of wheat or food plants may well have been relayed from one community to another. On the other hand, East Asian farmers probably domesticated pigs, chickens, and two types of millet entirely on their own. Bronze metallurgy very likely arose there independently. One advance of undoubted Chinese origin was the technology of fabricating silk from the cocoons of caterpillars that ate white mulberry leaves. Silk threads discovered on an Egyptian mummy suggest that merchants passed Chinese silk fabric as far west as the Nile as early as 1000 B.C.E.

Within East Asia, economic and cultural interchange advanced rapidly in the second millennium B.C.E. Shang political influence in the Yangzi valley was sporadic, but that region's agrarian population rose steadily owing to cultivation of tropical rice, a cereal probably first domesticated somewhere in southern China. Wheat and millet were well suited to the cool, dry north, rice to the warm, wet south. Already in Shang times traders carried sacks of these cereals between the two regions, laying the foundations for the future economic integration of north and south. Bronzes and other luxury goods of distinctive Shang design have been found all over northern China and in the Yangzi valley. The Shang state was therefore the center of an expanding zone of interaction that in time produced a characteristically Chinese style of culture.

Pastoral Peoples Ride into History

FOCUS Why did pastoral nomadism as a specialized way of life permit accelerating population growth in the steppes of Inner Eurasia between the fourth and second millennia B.C.E.?

Even before complex agrarian society first appeared in Mesopotamia and Egypt, a different way of life began to take form in some parts of the Great Arid Zone where rainfall was too low to sustain farming far from irrigation sources but high enough to support large herds of sheep, goats, cattle, camels, and horses. **Pastoral nomadism,** a highly specialized way of life in which communities subsisted primarily if not exclusively on animal products, allowed humans to reproduce in far greater numbers in arid lands than foraging bands could possibly have sustained (see Table 3.1). Starting around 2000 B.C.E., pastoral peoples of Inner Eurasia precipitated a series of complex migratory and military movements that profoundly altered cultural and political maps, both within the steppe region and eventually in the agrarian lands to the south, west, and east.

pastoral nomadism A type of economic and social organization in which livestock raising is the principal means of subsistence. Pastoral nomadic communities typically migrate seasonally in search of pasture and water.

Horses, Riders, and Wagons

Many scholars agree that an important movement of pastoral peoples from Inner Eurasia to more densely populated agrarian regions originated between the late fourth and third millennia B.C.E. in the grasslands north of the Black and Caspian Seas. Known historically as the Pontic-Caspian steppe (Pontic relates to the Greek name for the Black Sea), this region of temperate to semiarid climate encompasses a large part of what are today southern Russia, Ukraine, and Kazakhstan. Sometime after about 5200 B.C.E., sheep and cattle herding people, probably originating in Southeastern Europe, began to drift around the northwestern curve of the Black Sea and into the Pontic-Caspian grasslands. This long-term event occurred just at the high point of a climatic warming cycle in the region, which encouraged grassy pasture to expand and flourish, supporting the pastoral way of life. Animal herders, who usually also grew some crops, gradually displaced hunting and foraging communities, which either adapted to the new economy or retreated into colder forests to the north. From the fifth millennium B.C.E., pastoral communities gradually populated the Pontic-Caspian region and began spreading farther eastward across the plains in the direction of China.

Three developments particularly favored human adaptation to the steppes. The first was domestication of wild horses, which probably first occurred in the Pontic-Caspian lands around 4800 B.C.E. These animals may have looked something like the small, shaggy Przewalski's horse, the only wild breed that survives in Inner Eurasia today. Horses turned out to be good candidates for an interdependent relationship with humans. Mares, that is, female horses, instinctively bunch together and form a pecking order of leaders and followers, something cats, we can be sure, will never do. A dominant mare, along with a spirited, aggressive stallion, always led the herd, but humans learned that they could also guide and manage docile mares. They also figured out at some point how to identify relatively meek and pliable stallions, then bred mares and stallions that had similarly submissive characteristics. Domesticated horses could outrun most predators, and they acquired heavy coats as protection against frigid steppe winters. Among domesticates, horses also had instincts for finding winter pasture. Cattle and sheep use their noses to move snow out of the way to uncover grass but only if the snow yields easily. Horses, by contrast, use their hooves to plow away crusty snow and to break ice to get at water.[3]

Steppe dwellers probably first exploited horses as meat. In time, they discovered the value of what one scholar of the neolithic era famously labeled "secondary products."[4] These included mare's milk, blood, hair, hides, and bone, as well as horse power for transport and plowing. This "secondary products revolution" allowed communities to depend more on horses and other domesticated animals than on crops if ecological conditions required it.[5] Between the fifth and second millennia B.C.E., domesticated horses multiplied on the Pontic-Caspian steppes by the millions, and in this environment human societies built their mobile way of life around their animals.

A second fundamental ingredient of the pastoral nomadic way of life was mastery of riding. Probably somewhere in the Pontic-Caspian grasslands as early as 4200 B.C.E., a courageous herder climbed on the back of a horse and managed to stay there. Early riders had no saddles or stirrups but learned to control their mounts using their legs and either a nose ring or a bit and reins. From horseback, a single rider could manage a large number of docile domesticated animals. By one estimate, a shepherd on foot, plus a reliable dog, could handle about two hundred sheep. A mounted herder and a dog could control five hundred.[6] Pastoralists on horses could also accumulate larger herds because they could drive animals farther away from water sources and camps and return much faster than if they had to walk. Eventually, horseback riding spread beyond the steppes, for example, across Iran to Mesopotamia, where the earliest images of people sitting on horses appear in the later third millennium B.C.E.

A third tool of the steppe economy was the two- or four-wheeled cart pulled by cattle, oxen, horses, mules, or, eventually, camels. Wagon technology probably reached the Pontic-Caspian steppes sometime between 3500 and 3300 B.C.E., spreading there from Southwest Asia by way of either southeastern Europe or the Caucasus Mountains. Lumbering along on solid wooden wheels, wagons extended the potential range of herders even farther than horse riding allowed. Now, pastoral groups could remain more or less

An uneasy rider. This ceramic mold from Mesopotamia offers evidence of the spread of horseback riding from Inner Eurasia to Southwest Asia, probably through Persia, by the early second millennium B.C.E. The figure on this mount is no horse soldier. He is sitting too far back on the horse's rump to control the animal very well. What technical improvements can you think of that would have contributed to the later development of cavalry warfare?

permanently on the move, transporting food and tools, as well as families with nursing infants, small children, and elderly folk. Wagons equipped with frames and hide or felt covers served as reasonably comfortable mobile homes. Pastoral nomads sometimes left members of the group in camps to grow small amounts of grain; they also ate wild seeds, greens, and a version of the honey-based fermented beverage known as mead. But their main diet remained meat and dairy products.

Pastoral Nomadic Society

Ancient communities of pastoral nomads were almost certainly organized on foundations of **kinship,** the idea that people belonged together, not because they occupied a fixed territory or obeyed a particular ruler, but because they shared descent from a common ancestor. Strangers might also be assimilated into a group by customs of fictional kinship: over time the group deliberately "forgot" that the erstwhile newcomers had not always been part of the extended family. A herding community likely constituted a lineage group, a few generations of people who regarded themselves as blood relatives.

Evidence from graves shows that some individuals and lineages became richer than others and, therefore, achieved

kinship The quality or state of being related by shared genealogical descent or by marriage. Kinship may also be claimed among a group of people for social or cultural reasons even though no biological relationship exists.

TABLE 3.1 Types of Societies Compared

Feature Category	Pastoral Nomadic Societies	Complex Agrarian and Urban Societies
Economy	Production primarily of domesticated animals, sometimes at surplus levels; secondarily of crops	Production primarily of crops and secondarily of domesticated animals at surplus levels, as well as urban and village manufactures
Settlement	Mobile camps and sometimes permanent structures used part of the year	Cities, towns, and villages
Occupations	The great majority engages in herding; a small minority in specialized occupations such as blacksmithing or textile production	The great majority engages in farming; minorities in full-time specialized occupations or in urban labor
Social structure	Social class divisions informal and fluid; minority of individuals and families with special status as political and religious leaders; social relations based on kinship	Permanent hierarchy of social classes: (a) rulers and aristocrats, (b) skilled artisans, technicians, and professionals, (c) rural farmers and urban workers, (d) in many societies, slaves; social relations based on kinship at local levels and on common obedience to the ruler at the level of the state
Gender relations	Society generally patriarchal but women and men share economic tasks, especially animal management	Patriarchal society; most women restricted to the domestic sphere
Political organization	Hierarchy of kinship groups from levels of local lineages to large, and usually temporary, confederations of kin groups; leadership exercised informally by individuals, elders, or families with elite status	States characterized by central governments, authoritarian rule, hierarchies of officials, and systematic taxation
Law	Customary, usually unwritten laws enforced by the consensus of the community or by military leaders	Complex civil and penal laws, enforced by the state and often organized in written codes
Technological change	Generally slow pace of technological innovation; periodic advances, especially in the military sphere	Continuous, though often uneven, technological and scientific innovation in a wide range of human activities
Built environment	Temporary, mobile structures; sometimes fortified camps or towns under pastoral nomad control	Dense urban dwelling construction; monumental building of walls, temples, palaces, tombs, and public plazas
Communication	Most members of society nonliterate; elite use of writing systems	Writing systems and complex symbolic expression; literacy of particular elite groups
Religion	Beliefs and practices associated with local deities and other spiritual forces; local religious specialists who communicate with the supernatural realm; from the first millennium B.C.E., adherence of some pastoral nomad societies to major belief systems	Complex systems of belief and practice often associated with central political authority, a class of religious specialists, and written scriptures; centers of development of major belief systems such as Confucianism, Buddhism, or Christianity

social prestige and political influence. Many of these sites have revealed sacrifice and careful burial of horses, as well as cattle and sheep, signs that the deceased had special social or political status. Horseback riding and wagon technology together allowed especially clever, industrious, or lucky families to acquire enormous herds. The most successful owners could amass more power than ordinary people because they had more animals for exchanging gifts with other leaders, making loans to poorer herders, and hosting funeral sacrifices and public feasts, acts that produced allies and loyal followers. Rich individuals could also marry their daughters into other wealthy families by paying more in bride-wealth, that is, animals presented to the family of the bride in exchange for the loss of her labor when she went to live with her new husband.

The pastoral division of labor. The emergence of elite families, however, did not mean that distinctions between upper and lower social classes became formal and rigid, as they did in dense agrarian societies. Rather, the pastoral economy required the intense and willing cooperation of everyone in the herding community—men, women, and children. Our knowledge of pastoral societies from later eras shows that fairly egalitarian relations prevailed among adults. The community had to value the skills of women not only as domestic and child-raising experts but also as managers of livestock.

Even so, as pastoral nomadism expanded and herding groups competed more fiercely for choice pasture and water sources, adult men came to revel in a "horse culture" that prized male military skill and bravado. The Pontic-Caspian steppes are the likely birthplace of the mounted warrior and cattle rustler. Burial sites signify that the great majority of elite fighters were men, though in some places archaeologists have also found the remains of women in full military dress. This finding suggests that women sometimes led raids and distinguished themselves on the field of battle.

The horse culture of the steppes was also the likely source of the chariot, a small, two-wheeled vehicle drawn by one or more horses and designed for speed. In the steppes northeast of the Caspian Sea, an ancient site known as Sintashta has revealed graves containing the material vestiges

A Chinese chariot. Shang dynasty burials at Anyang include the remains of horses and chariots. Knowledge of chariot technology spread from Inner Eurasia to northern China by about 1200 B.C.E. Why do you think the graves of Shang rulers included these items?

of chariots and the horses that pulled them. Dated to about 2100 B.C.E., these artifacts mark the start of a period of about a thousand years during which chariotry had great importance in both warfare and political ritual across large parts of Afroeurasia.

The defining characteristics of a chariot are two spoked wheels, rather than heavy solid ones; a small enclosed platform where the driver and perhaps one or two other warriors stand; and harness gear for horses. The chariot was designed for war, intimidation, and the display of power. In combat one fighter usually controlled the animals, while a second threw bronze-tipped projectiles or fired arrows. Sometimes a third warrior held a shield to protect the other two. Well-built defensive walls and towers at Sintashta and neighboring settlements suggest that regional warfare was common, perhaps in response to growing competition for grazing land. Warrior bands may also have competed violently for control of export trade in copper and tin to the Indus and Mesopotamia. Chariots were expensive machines, requiring skilled bending and joining of wood, manufacturing bronze and leather horse gear, and training of horses, drivers, and fighters who could launch spears or arrows from the chariot platform with reasonable accuracy. Consequently, only leaders who could command substantial resources, make alliances, and amass supporters with generous gifts could afford to deploy them. In short,

chariots became weapons of choice of aristocratic warrior groups, not ordinary soldiers. Nevertheless, chariot teams could operate over relatively long distances, permitting more extended military campaigns and encouraging state building on a larger scale than had previously been possible in the steppes.

Encounters Between Agrarian Societies and Migrating Peoples

FOCUS How did the movements of peoples speaking Indo-European languages contribute to political, social, and cultural changes in several parts of Afroeurasia in the second millennium B.C.E.?

Sometime around 3300 B.C.E., pastoral bands began moving beyond the Pontic-Caspian steppes to neighboring regions of Afroeurasia. One explanation for these movements is the occurrence of a cycle of regional climatic drying at the same time that pastoral populations were getting larger and improving their ability to travel long distances. If population exceeded locally available resources, migration offered a potential alternative to chronic dearth or warfare. Whatever the primary triggering factor, the scale of these movements

MAP 3.2 Spread of Indo-European languages.
If Indo-European languages or language families spread in particular directions, can we assume that people speaking those languages migrated in those directions as well?

increased in the third and second millennia B.C.E.—southward around the Black Sea to Southwest Asia, westward into Europe, southeastward to Iran and India, and eastward into steppes that today lie within the borders of China. We can only guess at the numbers of people involved, though the process took centuries, and it was spasmodic and fragmented. There was no sudden flood of peoples or a single conquering horde.

The science of historical linguistics has shown us that most of these migrants spoke languages sharing fundamental grammatical elements and word forms. We call this family of related languages Indo-European. All of the many tongues in this family are descended from a distant parent language. Scholars have named this ancestral tongue Proto-Indo-European. Many of them believe that people spoke it in the Pontic-Caspian region between about 4500 and 2500 B.C.E. During the following several millennia, Indo-European languages spread far and wide. Today about three billion people in the world speak languages in this family, which includes English, Spanish, German, Greek, Russian, Persian, Kurdish, Hindi, and many more.

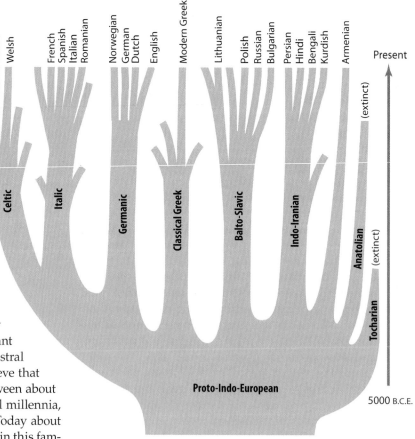

Indo-European languages tree. What are some major languages that do not appear anywhere on this tree?

All languages change over time, and when a population speaking a single language separates into groups that lose regular contact with one another, the speech of those groups invariably diverges. As Proto-Indo-European speakers spread in various directions, the parent language eventually sprouted numerous linguistic branches and twigs, that is, new subfamilies and individual tongues. Groups that spoke Indo-European languages did not *necessarily* share other basic cultural forms, such as way of life or religion, or any sense of common identity. On the other hand, by comparing modern Indo-European languages, scholars have reconstructed a basic vocabulary of ancient Proto-Indo-European. This vocabulary shows that its speakers lived in a temperate climate because the list includes words for beaver, bear, and birch tree. It also includes words for horse, sheep, wheeled vehicle, and plow, suggesting that Proto-Indo-Europeans practiced combinations of stock breeding and farming.

The movement of Indo-European pastoral groups from Inner Eurasia, together with the diffusion of chariot warfare, represented dynamic new elements in the histories of several agrarian lands from western Europe and the Mediterranean basin to South Asia and even China. Relations between densely populated agrarian and pastoral societies played themselves out in a number of different ways: Settled and pastoral groups might engage in mutually beneficial trade and cultural exchange; pastoral bands might advance gradually into agrarian regions, sometimes maintaining their herding way of life, sometimes eventually turning to farming; mounted nomad forces might intrude aggressively into settled and urbanized lands, and sometimes the rulers of agrarian states pushed them back into the steppe or desert; and from time to time pastoral cavalry invaded and overran centralized kingdoms, imposing themselves as a new ruling class.

Indo-European Speakers in Southwest Asia: The Hittite Empire

Migrants from the Inner Eurasian steppes reached Anatolia (modern Turkey) in the third millennium B.C.E. They probably arrived already possessing intimate knowledge of horses and a political culture that stressed alliance building and personal bonds between chiefs and followers. They bred horses and other animals in the grassy highlands of eastern Anatolia, intermingling with existing farming populations. In the sixteenth century B.C.E., the Anatolian group that became known as the Hittites—a word that refers to both the Indo-European language they spoke and the elite warrior culture they practiced—seized control of central Anatolia. There they founded the kingdom of Hatti. Over six centuries the Hittite aristocracy created a well-ordered empire whose monarchs established the rule of law and largely honored the local customs of diverse subject populations.

Archaeologists have excavated the remains of Hattusa, Hatti's impressive capital in north central Anatolia. The city featured a grand palace complex, numerous temples

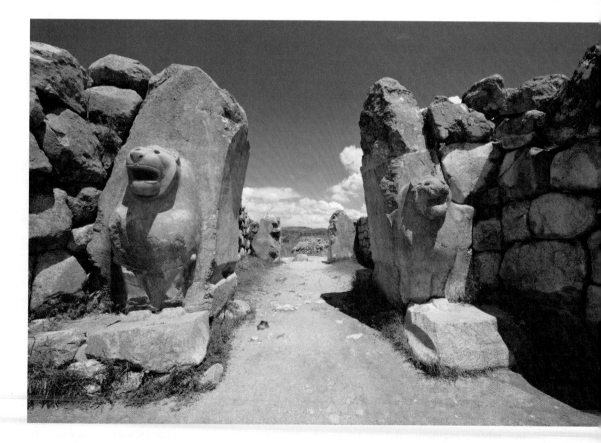

The Lion Gate at Hattusa. These two fierce beasts, symbolic sentries guarding the Hittite capital, stand seven feet tall at the entrance to the citadel. The lion as defender of royal power was a common motif in ancient Southwest Asia. The face of the lion on the left has recently been reconstructed.

MAP 3.3 Major states of the eastern Mediterranean in the second millennium B.C.E.
What factors might explain why New Kingdom Egypt expanded in a generally north–south direction?

dedicated to the Hittite pantheon of gods and goddesses, imposing fortifications, and an entry gate guarded by two enormous stone lions. Hittite scribes produced thousands of official documents on clay tablets using the Babylonian cuneiform script that originated in Mesopotamia. Surviving tablet fragments dating to about 1900 B.C.E. provide

the earliest evidence of inscriptions written in an Indo-European language.

The Hittite kings, like earlier Southwest Asian monarchs, represented themselves as agents of the gods, on whose authority they kept order and defended the land. A class of priests took charge of worship and ritual sacrifice, but the king was the chief priest of the storm-god, the principal deity. According to one cuneiform inscription, "Heaven, earth, and the people belong to the storm-god alone. He has made the . . . king his administrator and given him the entire Land of Hatti. . . . May the storm-god destroy whoever should approach the person of the . . . king, and the borders of (Hatti)!"[7] The monarch typically had several wives, but the Great Queen, or ranking wife, often exerted great influence over the state's internal affairs.

The Hittite economy rested on farmers and stock breeders, the majority of them descended from populations who spoke ancient languages other than Indo-European. Subjects of the king paid a portion of their production to the state to support the administration, army, and royal household. As the kingdom expanded, it also gained control of immensely important Anatolian sources of copper, silver, and tin. The markets for these items in the cities of Mesopotamia, Syria, and Egypt were practically limitless, and those regions reciprocated with linen and woolen textiles and manufactures of silver, lead, and bronze.

After 1400 B.C.E., Hittite armies, perhaps seeking control over a wider circle of commercial routes and cities, overran most of Anatolia and penetrated southward into Syria and the Levantine coast of the Mediterranean. The core of the army was infantry, but chariot squadrons served well to terrorize and scatter enemy forces. Horses put into chariot service required lengthy, expensive training. In the fourteenth century B.C.E., a trainer named Kikkuli dictated a detailed handbook on the proper conditioning of chariot horses. Written on clay tablets in both Hittite and Akkadian, the manual instructs the handler:

> When he lets the horses onto the meadow in the autumn, he harnesses them. He lets them trot 3 miles, but he lets them gallop over 7 fields. But on the way back he has them gallop over 10 fields. Then he unharnesses them, provides for them, and they are watered. . . . Then he gives them mixed together 1 handful of wheat, 2 handfuls of barley, and one handful of hay. They eat this up.[8]

States of Mesopotamia and Syria

In Southwest Asia, the city dwellers of the Tigris-Euphrates River valley had ambivalent relationships, ranging from peaceful commerce to violent conflict, with pastoral communities of neighboring hill country and steppes. In 2191 B.C.E., Akkad,

the world's earliest known agrarian empire (see Chapter 2), collapsed in connection with hostile incursions of people from the Zagros Mountains to the east. Early in the second millennium B.C.E., a much larger-scale pastoral movement emanated from west of Mesopotamia, perhaps from the Syrian-Arabian Desert (see Map 3.3). These steppe herders, known from ancient cuneiform tablets as Amorites, spoke Semitic languages, which were not Indo-European but belong to the large Afroasiatic family that included languages ancestral to modern Arabic and Hebrew. They raised sheep, goats, and cattle but also farmed part of the time. Perhaps because of a long-term drought cycle in Southwest Asia, which started about 2200 B.C.E., Amorite bands intruded bit-by-bit into the irrigated floodplain, competing with villagers for choice land, hiring out to city-states as mercenaries, and, when they felt strong enough, attacking towns. Over the following two centuries, some Amorite leaders gave up their old pastoral ways to become rich landlords and patrons of city culture.

In the eighteenth century B.C.E., Hammurabi (r. 1792–1750 B.C.E.), king of the Mesopotamian city-state of Babylon and descendant of an Amorite herdsman, revived the idea Sargon of Akkad had conceived five hundred years earlier to unite Mesopotamia under one authority. During forty-two years of military campaigning, Hammurabi extended Babylonian rule from the Persian Gulf to the upper Euphrates. Like Sargon before him, he aimed to tax the region's huge agricultural and manufacturing output and make sure that vital raw materials such as timber, copper, tin, and silver flowed into Mesopotamia from neighboring lands. To do this, he created a tightly centralized system of command, personally directing its business and deploying a host of officials up and down the valley to carry out his will. Also, social class distinctions appear to have sharpened because Sargon's regime encouraged private property holding and

Stele of Hammurabi. "If a man has struck a free woman with child, and has caused her to miscarry, he shall pay ten shekels for her miscarriage." This decree is just one of the 282 Mesopotamian legal traditions engraved on a black diorite slab at the orders of King Hammurabi. At the top of the stele, the seated figure of the sun god Shamash offers divine blessing on Hammurabi and his legal code. Why would Hammurabi want these legal precedents carved on a rock stele rather than simply on clay tablets?

commercial enterprise that gave large wealth-gathering opportunities to relatively few.

Cuneiform writing became more important than ever as a tool of state. About 150 of Hammurabi's official letters, written on clay tablets in Akkadian Semitic, have come down to us. The most famous document is Hammurabi's Code, a collection of 282 legal precedents preserved as engraved inscriptions on an eight-foot-high stele, or stone slab. These precedents, which range over such subjects as burglary, property disputes, irrigation management, marriage, trade practices, and personal injury, express the ruler's insistence on orderly government and fairness in dispensing justice. Babylonian judges were expected to be honest in court procedures, which involved hearing witness testimony, weighing evidence, examining contracts, and rendering verdicts.

The strong-willed Hammurabi died in 1750 B.C.E., and the Amorite empire disintegrated shortly thereafter. The various Mesopotamian city-states went their own ways for about a century and a half, though the city-state of Babylon remained the premier custodian of Sumerian and Semitic cultural traditions.

Two other important states arose in Southwest Asia in the mid-second millennium B.C.E. One was a revived Babylonia under the rule of the Kassites, another band of migrant warriors, possibly mountain people from east of the Tigris-Euphrates valley. The Kassites, who probably spoke a Semitic language, took eagerly to chariot warfare. Shortly after 1500 B.C.E., they united southern Mesopotamia, ruling from Babylon on the Euphrates.

The second state was Mittani, founded about that same time in the fertile upper Euphrates valley, territory that is today mainly in Syria. The Mittani military elite, who may have founded the kingdom as chariot-riding invaders, appear to have used an Indo-European language but soon adopted local tongues. For more than two centuries this kingdom dominated the northern Euphrates region and its corridor of trade.

From Middle Kingdom to New Kingdom in the Nile Valley

Off to the southwest, the Old Kingdom of Egypt, which endured more than nine hundred years, ended about 2160 B.C.E. when the central rule of the pharaohs disintegrated (see Chapter 2). Civil strife, known to scholars as the First Intermediate Period, lasted more than a century. About 2040 B.C.E., however, one political faction assembled sufficient military power to reunite Upper Egypt with the bountiful delta (Lower Egypt), ushering in the Middle Kingdom of the eleventh and twelfth dynasties of pharaohs (2040–1786 B.C.E.). These monarchs revived and expanded Egypt's impressive bureaucracy, and irrigation engineers added thousands of acres of cultivable land to the realm. The pharaoh's armies advanced far upriver into Nubia (today southern Egypt and the northern Sudan), pushing the kingdom's power deeper into Africa than at any earlier time. And as the eastern Mediterranean commercial system matured, the kings promoted closer seaborne ties with the Aegean basin, Minoan Crete, and the Levant.

Despite this renewed unity and prosperity, the shadow of armed violence lengthened. In the mid seventeenth century B.C.E., intruders whom the Egyptians called Hyksos, meaning "foreign chiefs," migrated into the delta and then conquered it and part of Upper Egypt. The Hyksos were probably a mix of migrating herders and chariot fighters from Syria and Anatolia, some of them Semitic speakers, others Indo-European. They also appear to have incorporated bands of military mercenaries and outlaws, a type of freelance warrior quite common in Southwest Asia in that era. The Hyksos succeeded in seizing Egypt partly because the Middle Kingdom had already corroded politically and partly because they fielded chariots and bronze weaponry more expertly than the Egyptians did. For two centuries beginning about 1648 B.C.E., Hyksos kings ruled the lower Nile valley, striving to make themselves into legitimate pharaohs and

Akhenaten and his family. The New Kingdom pharaoh Akhenaten is best known for radically departing from traditional Egyptian religion by elevating the god Aten—and Akhenaten himself as Aten's divine servant—above all other deities. The priesthood, and probably most Egyptians, despised him for it, and the new teaching died with the pharaoh. In this limestone relief we see a contented Akhenaten at home with his wife Nefertiti and three of their children. Aten, represented by the sun disk, shines down upon them. What elements do you see in this scene that give it a humane and domestic flavor?

champions of Egyptian culture, neither with very convincing results.

Further upriver in Nubia, a kingdom based at Kerma between the Third and Fourth Cataracts (river rapids) took advantage of the Hyksos invasion to shed Egyptian domination and assert itself as a regional African power. The earliest Nubian state dates to about 2400 B.C.E., and over the centuries it tended to move through successive cycles of expanding and contracting Egyptian political and cultural influence. During the Hyksos period, Kerma flourished on farming and stock raising and on the trade in gold, ivory, ebony, cattle, timber, and slaves that flowed northward toward the Mediterranean.

Then, early in the sixteenth century B.C.E., Egyptian nobles rallied an army that evicted the Hyksos from the valley. This event ushered in the New Kingdom (1540–1070 B.C.E.), an era when Egypt's sphere of power expanded beyond all earlier borders. Pharaohs of the New Kingdom's eighteenth dynasty reasserted their authority far upriver, reducing Nubian rulers to Egyptian dependency once again. To the northeast, they not only chased the Hyksos back into Southwest Asia but also conquered the Levant up to the frontier of Anatolia. Taking lessons from the Hyksos, Egyptian commanders made numerous improvements in chariot technology and tactics.

Notably under the leadership of Thutmose I, Thutmose III, Hatshepsut (coruler with Thutmose and the only female New Kingdom pharaoh), and Akhenaten (inclusive dates 1493–1335 B.C.E.), the empire remained stable and prosperous. Picking up where their Middle Kingdom forebears had left off, these rulers made Egyptian bureaucratic government more efficient than ever. Reigning as divine beings from a splendid complex of palaces and temples at Thebes, they managed the state and closely regulated the economic life of Egyptian peasants with the help of thousands of officials and a professional standing army. They also monopolized foreign trade. As the empire grew, merchants from both the Mediterranean lands and Nubia converged on Egypt, though they had to conduct all their business through the pharaoh's commercial agents. Even so, vast amounts of

Opening of the Mouth Ceremony. This painting on papyrus from the *Book of the Dead*, a collection of spells to help the departed move safely to the next world, depicts a ritual performed for a deceased scribe named Honefer. The mummy's mouth is ritually opened to restore the dead man's senses and faculties. The white stele on the right is engraved with hieroglyphics and at the top is an image of Honefer standing before a seated god. Compare this image to the one on the stele of Hammurabi on page 95. In both, if the deity were to stand up, he would be much taller than the mortal he is facing.

"Here Is the Situation":
The King of Alashiya Writes to the Pharaoh of Egypt

More than 380 clay tablets have preserved correspondence among rulers of Southwest Asia and the eastern Mediterranean in the fourteenth century B.C.E. Scholars first discovered these letters in the late nineteenth century at el-Amarna, an archaeological site in Upper Egypt that was the short-lived capital of the New Kingdom pharaoh Akhenaten (r. 1353–1335 B.C.E.). Now scattered among the collections of several of the world's major museums, the letters brightly illuminate ancient diplomatic, political, and commercial exchange.

The majority of the letters are correspondence sent to Egyptian kings over a span of about thirty years. They are written in Akkadian cuneiform, the language of international diplomacy. Authors of the texts include Southwest Asian rulers, as well as leaders of small states in Syria and the Levant. The letters' concerns range from negotiating marriages to trade relations to political alliances. The international correspondence is generally framed in the language of "brotherhood," signifying that all rulers had equal social status and that in fact royal families commonly intermarried as a way of cementing ties of mutual obligation. Monarchs and princes exchanged gifts but also demanded support from one another in times of need.

This document is part of a letter from the king of Alashiya, a state located on the island of Cyprus in the eastern Mediterranean. This monarchy carried on extensive trade with Egypt, notably copper exports. Referring to the presence of Nergal, a Mesopotamian god associated with disease, destruction, and death, in his realm, the king informs the Egyptian pharaoh of the current situation in Alashiya and seeks to resolve diplomatic and economic issues between the two states.

Say to the king of Egypt, my brother: Message of the king of Alashiya, your brother. For me all goes well. For my household, my wives, my sons, my magnates, my horses, my chariots, and in my country, all goes very well. For my brother may all go well. For your household, your wives, your sons, your magnates, your horses, your chariots, and in your country, may all go very well. My brother, I herewith send my messenger with your messenger to Egypt.

I herewith send to you 500 (*talents*) of copper. As my brother's greeting gift I send it to you. My brother, do not be concerned that the amount of copper is small. Behold, the hand of Nergal is now in my country; he has slain all the men of my country, and there is not a (single) copper-worker. So, my brother, do not be concerned.

Send your messenger with my messenger immediately, and I will send you whatever copper you, my brother, request.

You are my brother. May he send me silver in very great quantities. My brother, give me the *very best* silver, and then I will send you, my brother, whatever you, my brother, request. . . .

Moreover, my brother, men of my country keep speaking with me about my timber that the king of Egypt receives from me. My brother, give me the payment due.

Moreover, here is the situation: a man from Alashiya has died in Egypt, and his things are in your country, though his son and wife are with me. So, my brother, look to the things of the Alashiya people and hand them over, my brother, to the charge of my messenger.

My brother, do not be concerned that your messenger has stayed 3 years in my country, for the hand of Nergal is in my country and in my own house. There was a young wife of mine that now, my brother, is dead. . . .

Moreover, may my brother send to me in very great quantities the silver that I have asked you for. Send, my brother, the things that I asked you for. My brother should do quite everything, and then whatever things you say I will do.

You have not been put (on the same level) with the king of Hatti [the Hittite kingdom] or the king of Sanhar [possibly Babylonia]. Whatever greeting-gift he (my brother) sends me, I for my part send you back double.

May your messenger come to me as of old, and may my messenger go to you as of old.

Source: Letters from Mesopotamia, trans. A. Leo Oppenheim, pp. 122ff. Copyright © 1967 by The University of Chicago. Reprinted by permission of The University of Chicago Press. Diacritical marks have been removed from words in this selection.

Thinking Critically

What particular diplomatic and economic issues does the king of Alashiya want to take up with the ruler of Egypt? From the king's references to the presence of "the hand of Nergal" in his country, what sort of crisis might have been happening in Alashiya? What particular products figure in exchange between the two states? Do you think exchange of gifts between these two rulers might have been important to diplomatic and commercial relations? Why do you think the king of Alashiya mentions the kings of Hatti and Sanhar? What point might he be trying to make by telling the Egyptian king that those rulers are not "on the same level" as him?

wealth poured into the valley in the form of royal trade, tribute from conquered princes, and war booty. The plunder included large numbers of enslaved prisoners from both Nubia and Southwest Asia, who were set to work building colossal temples, among other tasks.

Rivalry and Diplomacy among Militarized Kingdoms

Despite its imperial adventure, New Kingdom Egypt was by no means the only great power in the region. The political arena also included Hatti, the Kassite kingdom of Babylonia, Mittani, and, by the fourteenth century B.C.E., Assyria, a monarchy on the northern Tigris River plain. The spectacle of five large, militarized kingdoms competing with one another for territory, trade, and political advantage was unprecedented in world history. Such grand rivalries were possible, and indeed tempting, because of the rising wealth of Southwest Asia and Egypt, the new war-making technology, and the immense value of interurban trade.

Despite their fierce competition with one another, these large states may have endured as long as they did partly because their aristocratic classes developed methods of diplomacy in order to defuse potential conflicts over territory and trade. Monarchs exchanged ambassadors, lavish gifts, and numerous letters written on clay tablets; they also negotiated treaties and married into one another's families. In 1350 B.C.E., for example, Tadu-Heba, daughter of Tushratta, the king of Mittani, traveled more than six hundred miles from the Euphrates to the Nile to marry Pharaoh Amenhotep III, thereby strengthening cordial relations. In 1284 B.C.E., Egypt signed a formal peace treaty with the Hittites, and shortly after that Ramses II (r. 1279–1213 B.C.E.) married a Hittite princess. Akkadian, the Semitic language written in cuneiform and spoken principally in Babylonia, became a diplomatic *lingua franca* (LING-gwuh FRANG-kuh), a common language that emissaries and officials used to inform and negotiate with one another. Over time, the conventions and protocols governing international relations—for example, rules for the safety of messengers or for proper use of language in letters from one monarch to another—became quite complex. In short, the ruling groups of the whole region from the eastern Mediterranean to Mesopotamia gradually created an international system for engaging in regular political dialogue that encouraged trade and in some measure restrained warfare.

lingua franca A spoken or written language that facilitates commercial or diplomatic communication across cultural frontiers.

The major states of Southwest Asia and the eastern Mediterranean not only exchanged gifts and messengers. They also periodically made war on one another. Most battles took place in Syria or the Levant because that is where frontiers of the Hittite kingdom, Mittani, and Egypt abutted one another. For example, Egypt under Ramses II and the Hittites under Mutawallis II (r. 1295–1272 B.C.E.) clashed at Kadesh in northern Syria in 1275 B.C.E. There, festering disputes over frontier territory escalated into a fight between thousands of archers firing from chariots. Both sides sustained severe losses, but neither army carried the day. The border remained largely as it was, and fifteen years later Egypt and the Hittites signed a peace treaty.

By the late thirteenth century B.C.E., however, the political geography of the region was changing radically. Both Mitanni and the Kassites were finally obliterated by their enemies, and Egypt gave up most of its Syrian territories following the reign of Ramses II. The Hittite empire fragmented amid popular revolts, civil struggles among claimants to the throne, and an extended crisis of drought and famine. In the succeeding century, Assyria became the rising star in Southwest Asia, as we see in Chapter 5.

Early Greeks

Impressive centers of power and wealth also appeared on mainland Greece from about 1700 B.C.E. The most striking material evidence are the well-stocked burial chambers, or shaft graves, that have been excavated at Mycenae in the Peloponnesus, the peninsula that forms the southern part of Greece (see Map 3.4). Carved deep into rock, these tombs contained priceless hoards of gold, silver, and bronze that only an aristocratic class could possibly have accumulated. Citadels protected by thick defensive walls also arose at several locations in the Peloponnesus. Like the Minoan palaces on Crete in an earlier period, these bastions evolved into regional centers of agrarian production and artisanry.

Historians associate the rise of the Mycenaeans (meye-seh-NEE-uhns), as this Aegean aristocracy is known, with the appearance of bands of warriors who spoke an archaic form of Greek, an Indo-European language. Most likely, the earliest Greeks, like the Hittites and Hyksos, started out as loosely organized migrant groups who raised cattle, sheep, and horses supplemented by farming. The *Iliad*, the legendary epic poem recounting a siege of the city of Troy, portrays the Mycenaeans simultaneously as god-like heroes and swaggering pillagers who prized horses, chariots, and stockpiles of bronze weapons. Most historians think that the earliest Greek-speaking people reached the Balkan Peninsula from the north, entering the Aegean Sea region around 2000 B.C.E. By no later than 1450 B.C.E., the Greek language is evident on both Crete and the Peloponnesus in the form of a written script called Linear B.

Around 1500 B.C.E., Mycenaean Greek warriors seized Crete, and Minoan civilization collapsed. Nature may have hastened that development. Sometime in the later seventeenth century B.C.E., a volcano erupted on the little island of Thera (Santorini), which lies about sixty-eight miles north of Crete. The explosion blew apart Thera and very likely caused a tsunami and massive clouds of dust and ash. Some volcanologists, scholars who study eruptions past and present, have hypothesized that the Minoans suffered not only catastrophic destruction but also long-term disruption of agriculture and sea trade.

MAP 3.4 Mycenaean centers, second millennium B.C.E.
Mycenaean society included many small settlements in addition to the main palace centers indicated here. Connect this close-up on early Greek movement into the Aegean region with the wider perspective on the spread of Indo-European languages shown in Map 3.2.

The Mycenaean warrior aristocracy that held power between about 1500 and 1200 B.C.E. participated in the larger culture and economy of the eastern Mediterranean. Palace centers around the Aegean came to share a common culture in such areas as pottery design and burial practice. The Mycenaeans also looked to Egypt, the Levant, and Crete for cultural goods and information to help transform themselves from rough-and-ready soldiers into self-assured city elites. In fact, their shaft graves present a microcosm of long-distance commercial connections. Archaeologists excavating these chambers have found ivory from Syria, ostrich eggs from Nubia, lapis lazuli from east of Mesopotamia, and amber from the Baltic Sea. The Mycenaeans exchanged olive oil, wine, and ceramics for these luxuries. Shards of characteristically Mycenaean pottery have been found in Sicily and Italy, a sign that Aegean merchants were

venturing far to the west to found settlements. In short, the rise of Mycenaean power represented an extension of complex urban life along the northern Mediterranean rim.

Indo-Europeans in Iran and South Asia

As Indo-European-speaking groups advanced west through Southwest Asia and the Aegean region, other bands migrated east of the Caspian Sea into the semiarid plains and highlands of what are today Turkmenistan, Uzbekistan, and northern Iran. Gradually, these groups diverged from one another in both space and time. So did their speech. Some migrants moved onto the Iranian Plateau, the region of uplands and mountains that encompasses most of modern Iran and parts of Afghanistan and Pakistan. The newcomers there emerged in the first millennium B.C.E. as speakers

Mycenaean dagger. Excavation of a Mycenaean shaft grave revealed this ceremonial bronze dagger with gold work depicting a lion hunt. The decoration has several elements that indicate the artistic influence of Minoan Crete on Mycenaean society. Compare the leaping lion on the dagger with the bull in the Minoan fresco on page 83.

of an ancestral version of Persian (Farsi), as well as several other languages including Kurdish and Pashto. Other groups drifted across Afghanistan into South Asia (the Indian subcontinent). The languages of those herders are classified today as Indic (or Indo-Aryan), an Indo-European subfamily that includes modern Hindi, Urdu, Bengali, and several other tongues.

When Indo-European speakers penetrated the Indus valley, probably beginning about 1700 B.C.E., they almost certainly found the once-great cities of the Harappan civilization in full decline (see Chapter 2). It is likely that a succession of Indic groups filtered through and around the already dilapidated Indus towns over a period of centuries. We have no evidence that they entered the subcontinent in massive numbers. By the later second millennium B.C.E., nevertheless, bands of Indic speakers were advancing eastward along a corridor of grassy plains just south of the Himalayan foothills. Opening before them was the Ganges (GAN-jeez) River, which flowed more than one thousand miles to the Bay of Bengal. In that era the indigenous populations of the valley were either foragers or farmers growing wheat, millet, and, later, rice. They spoke languages of the ancient Dravidian family, perhaps as the Harappan city dwellers had.

The principal source of information on the early period of interaction between Indic speakers and preexisting populations has been the Vedas (VAY-duhs). These are compilations of hymns and prayers that Indic priests presumably recited and passed orally from one generation to the next. From these texts, notably the classic work of Indian literature known as the *Rig Veda,* we may distill a portrait of Indic immigrants as proud militarists who quarreled constantly among themselves and who violently subdued the local population of "dark" demon people. The characters in the *Rig Veda* organized themselves in **clans** led by warrior heroes, and their society was divided into four main social classes: warrior-aristocrats,

priests, common people, and the inferior Dasas, or despised victims of conquest. Historians see in this system the remote origins of the more formal hierarchy of social classes, or castes, that emerged in later centuries. The Indic newcomers also possessed horses, cattle, sheep, bows, metal weapons, and chariots. They worshiped gods of heaven, earth, sun, and fire, notably Indra, ferocious god of war, who rode a celestial chariot and hurled thunderbolts at his enemies.

The *Rig Veda*'s representation of late second millennium B.C.E. India is dramatic, but it is also an idealized origins myth later incorporated into Hindu cultural and religious tradition. The Vedas did not appear in written form until about 400 B.C.E., and other types of historical evidence force us to modify their testimony. For example, the Indic languages absorbed numerous words from the older Dravidian tongue, which might suggest intermarriage and social exchange between Indic speakers and local populations, not just violent domination. The newcomers, moreover, may have had a military culture based on chariots, horses, and bronze weapons, but extremely little material evidence of these things has ever been found on the subcontinent. On the other hand, the Indic languages gradually advanced across the northern and central subcontinent, and Dravidian-speaking populations there virtually disappeared. Today, Indic languages in the Indo-European family are spoken by more than 800 million people.

Indo-Europeans and Chariots from the Far West to the Far East

Indo-European languages also spread to Europe in the second and first millennia B.C.E. in connection with migrations of groups coming from either the Pontic-Caspian steppes or southeastern Europe. With them emerged mixed economies of **pastoralism** and farming, along with horses, wheeled carts, and chariots (which served mainly as symbols of political prestige rather

clan A type of social organization in which a group of people claim shared identity as descendants of a single, usually distant ancestor. Clan organization is common among pastoral nomadic societies.

pastoralism A type of economic and social organization involving the breeding and raising of domesticated hoofed animals, or livestock.

Individuals MATTER

The Beauty of Xiaohe: A Woman of the Steppes

A close look at the "Beauty of Xiaohe" mummy reveals her eyelashes intact.

It must have been cold at the eastern edge of the Taklamakan when the woman died. Those who buried her dressed her for warmth. A fur-lined hat sat atop her long auburn hair, matching the fur-trimmed boots on her feet. She wore a string skirt, and her body was wrapped in a large woolen blanket. Scientists have named her the Beauty of Xiaohe (sh-ih-ow-h-uh) after the cemetery site where she and other human remains were excavated in 2003. She lay in her tomb for nearly four thousand years, reposing beneath a boat of wood and cowhide turned upside down.

In the twentieth century, archaeologists have discovered more than two hundred of these bodies, along with the clothing they wore when they died, in different parts of the Tarim Basin, today China's far western Xinjiang (shin-jyahng) region. Scholars commonly refer to the corpses as "mummies," though their community did not deliberately preserve them with special techniques comparable to ancient Egyptian mummification. Rather, extreme aridity and frigid winters preserved the bodies naturally. Recent DNA testing of human remains, some of which date to about 2000 B.C.E., indicates that these individuals descended from people who migrated into the region from the west and married into local populations. Their forebears may therefore have been speakers of an early Indo-European language who lived in the Pontic-Caspian steppes. If that is the case, the Beauty of Xiaohe probably spoke a Tocharian tongue, though all the languages in this family are now extinct. Many of the mummies exhibit features not typically East Asian, for example high-bridged noses, deep-set eyes, and light-colored hair. Their brightly hued clothing provides another link with peoples to the west. Some of the later mummies wear plaid twills resembling textiles woven by ancestral speakers of the Celtic branch of Indo-European languages who once lived in central Europe.

By four thousand years ago, the lands that fringed the Taklamakan had already become meeting places for people of diverse origins. In her lifetime the Beauty of Xiaohe may have seen caravans of traders moving from one oasis to another, tracing out the "silk roads" that would eventually run along the northern and southern fringes of the great desert, connecting China with Iran and the Mediterranean beyond.

Thinking Critically

Why do you think political controversy over the origins of the Beauty of Xiaohe and other mummies found in the Tarim Basin has arisen in China in recent years?

---

than as war machines). By around 1500 B.C.E., all building of megalithic tombs and ritual centers along Europe's Atlantic rim had come to an end. This suggests the rising cultural dominance of newcomers, though there is no sign that Indo-European movements produced a sudden or violent break in Europe's history. Rather, general trends continued: the population grew, large fortified settlements appeared, chiefly families accumulated great wealth in bronze and gold, and long-distance trade flourished from the Baltic Sea to the Mediterranean and along the Danube River. Gradually, branches and twigs of the Indo-European language trunk appeared all across Europe, including ancestral forms of Latin and Celtic, Slavic, and Germanic languages, including English.

On the eastern side of Inner Eurasia, inhabitants of what are today Mongolia and northwestern China took up pastoral nomadism and a full-fledged "horse culture." Groups speaking Indo-European languages associated with a linguistic branch known as Tocharian moved eastward after about 3500 B.C.E. to occupy the slopes of the Altai and Tien Shan Mountains and eventually the Tarim Basin, location of the enormous Taklamakan Desert.

It seems certain that peoples of the Inner Eurasian steppes came into contact with the Shang dynasty of northern China. Like the older complex societies to the west, the Shang army fielded squadrons of two-horse chariots from around 1200 B.C.E. Chariot technology very likely diffused from Inner Eurasia. The spoked wheels were similar in design to those used in Southwest Asia. Chinese chariotry also carried great aristocratic prestige. Physical remains of vehicles have been found in several Shang tombs along with ritually sacrificed horses.

The chariot was indeed an early example of a single development that affected peoples across Eurasia and northern Africa within the space of a few hundred years. More broadly, by the start of the second millennium B.C.E., if not earlier, the combination of horseback riding, wagon travel, chariotry, and customs and techniques to promote trade permitted the formation of a single network of commercial and cultural exchange that extended from China to Europe and the Mediterranean basin.

Looking across the entire region where militarized, chariot-riding elites took power, historians have also noticed that the mother goddesses and other female deities prevalent in the late paleolithic and neolithic eras gave way in religious worship to ascendant male gods of war and thunder. Evidence from languages, graves, and official documents supports the hypothesis that patriarchal institutions became more entrenched in the second millennium B.C.E. and that the legal and social status of women declined in general. Such correlations suggest at the very least that the migrations and state-building enterprises of male charioteers wielding bows and bronze swords had profound social and cultural effects on a large part of Afroeurasia.

Developments in the Tropical Belt

FOCUS In what circumstances did agrarian societies become more widely established in both Southeast Asia and central and southern Africa between the fourth and second millennia B.C.E.?

Large-scale migrations of a different origin reshaped human landscapes in Afroeurasia's tropical belt in the third and second millennia B.C.E. For the first time, large areas of both Subsaharan Africa and island Southeast Asia became inhabited by people who grew crops and herded animals (see Map 3.5). The fundamental consequence was a more or less steady increase of population and the complexity of society in latitudes near the equator.

MAP 3.5 Diffusion of grain farming in the Afroeurasian tropical belt.
How did the tools and skills needed to introduce cereal crops in tropical lands differ from those required in temperate or arid river valley climates?

Herders and Farmers South of the Sahara Desert

In tropical Africa, climatic fluctuation was an engine of migration. Six to seven thousand years ago the region that is today the Sahara Desert passed through a long cycle of higher rainfall. Hunters, fishers, and cattle herders flourished on lakeshores, riverbanks, and marshland. By about 2500 B.C.E., however, the wet phase ended. The Sahara, together with the adjacent Arabian Desert east of the Red Sea, moved toward the extreme levels of aridity that characterize these regions today. As that happened, humans progressively retreated from the central Sahara. Some migrated either north toward the Mediterranean or south into the semiarid and grassland zone known historically as the Sudan. Others drifted eastward to the Nile valley to participate in the young civilization blossoming there.

South of the desert, the open or wooded savannas of the Sudan stretched from the Atlantic coast to the mountains of Ethiopia. Saharan cattle-keeping peoples moved into this belt, most of them probably speaking languages belonging to a linguistic family known as Nilo-Saharan. These herding folk shared the region with farming populations already established. Perhaps in response to climatic pressures, farmers of the Sudan domesticated a particularly wide range of nutritious grains, including sorghum, pearl millet, African rice, and, in Ethiopia, the tiny grain called teff.

Migrations into East Africa. Herders who populated the savanna belt could advance only so far southward before reaching tropical forests where their cattle, as well as horses, became susceptible to trypanosomiasis, a lethal disease for most bovine species. This malady, the animal form of sleeping sickness carried by tsetse flies, flourished only where certain kinds of bushes offered cover. On the eastern side of Africa, however, people who practiced a combination of cattle herding and farming were able to move southward along a corridor of highlands inhospitable to tsetse flies. By the third millennium B.C.E., cattle breeders, who used stone tools and made pottery, were advancing toward East Africa's Great Lakes, an upland region of moderate climate and fertile soil. There, and farther south, they gradually assimilated or displaced forager populations, or pushed them deeper into the tropical forests. These older populations spoke languages belonging to the ancient Khoisan (KOI-sahn) family, whose origins may go back to the early days of *Homo sapiens*. The incoming herders and farmers, whose numerous languages belonged to either the Nilo-Saharan or the Afroasiatic families, adopted a variety of Khoisan words. But over the long run, Khoisan languages nearly

Cattle economies in tropical Africa. Long-horned Ankole cattle and related breeds have sustained numerous peoples in East and southern Africa for several millennia.

disappeared in East Africa as agrarian groups spread further and grew larger.

Bantu-speaking farmers. In another theater of migration, farmers who lived in western and central Africa just south of the Sahara also began to advance southward toward the wet forests. Climatic drying was almost certainly a factor in this movement. A second factor was that tropical farmers practiced one form or other of **shifting agriculture.** The nutrient-rich layer, or humus, in tropical soils tended to be thin and to leach away easily under pounding rain.

> **shifting agriculture** A method of crop production in which a farmer clears and cultivates a plot of land until the soil loses its nutrient value, and then moves on to clear and plant a new field, allowing the first one to lie fallow and recover.

The women and adolescent girls who did most of the cultivating therefore had to use hoes and digging sticks, not animal-powered plows. Even if delicately worked, however, humus tended to diminish within two or three years, so fields had to be left to recover over several seasons. The farm family had to move to a new spot to clear and plant again. Consequently, shifting agriculture (sometimes called swidden agriculture) often resulted in slow migratory drift of local populations.

Farmers whose major crop was the yam, a highly nutritious root plant first domesticated in West Africa perhaps about 8000 B.C.E., advanced slowly south and east from a core area of woodland centered on what is today southern Cameroon. The surviving archaeological record shows that they manufactured durable pottery and used both fire and stone axes to clear away forests, opening land to sunlight and yam plots. They also hunted, fished, and produced oil from palm trees.

Scholars have combined archaeology with comparative analysis of languages spoken in Africa today to learn much about the long-distance movements of cultivators into equatorial and southern Africa. They spoke languages classified within the Niger-Congo family and more specifically a subfamily of very closely related tongues called Bantu (BAHN-too). Just as scholars have compared basic vocabularies of living Indo-European languages to reconstruct Proto-Indo-European, linguists have analyzed numerous Bantu languages to recover Proto-Bantu. They hypothesize that it originated sometime after 4000 B.C.E. in Cameroon. The word *Bantu* comes from the root word *ntu*, which means "person," and the plural-forming prefix *ba-*. Linguistic clues tells us that early Bantu speakers built rectangular houses with palm thatch roofs; navigated rivers in boats; made sculptures of wood; and venerated both a supreme creator god, who did not intervene regularly in human affairs, and a range of more accessible deities and ancestral spirits.

In the third and second millennia B.C.E., Bantu-speaking farmers advanced along two major routes. One was southward into the equatorial forests, then upstream along the Congo River (the world's seventh longest) and its numerous tributaries. Some groups settled along the way, others kept moving through the forest belt, emerging eventually into the savannas of the Southern Hemisphere. As centuries passed, paths of migration lengthened, and pioneer farmers colonized a variety of ecological niches. Gradually, therefore, Bantu languages multiplied, and local religious and social practices became more diverse. Foragers who occupied the Congo valley forests before Bantu speakers arrived very likely traded, intermarried, and shared skills with the newcomers. Many must have taken up farming, though some, including ancestors of the Batwa (people known conventionally as Pygmies), remained in the forests to collect and hunt.

Bantu speakers also migrated across the northern savanna zone, then southward into lands around East Africa's Great Lakes. There, they planted cereal crops, notably sorghum and millet. Where the local ecosystem permitted, they also took up herding, which they learned from cattle-keeping people already there. After 1200 B.C.E. the Great Lakes area became one of the most densely populated places in the world's tropical latitudes. In the following millennia, Bantu-speaking farmers and herders occupied nearly the entire southern third of Africa. We come back to this epic story in later chapters.

Austronesian Farmers in Southeast Asia

Paralleling these developments in Africa, farming peoples also moved throughout the tropical lands of maritime Southeast Asia. In terms of sheer geographical scope, this migration was one of the greatest in world history, ultimately extending from Madagascar in the western Indian Ocean to Oceania (the Island Pacific). Both linguistic and archaeological evidence shows that, by the fifth millennium B.C.E., agrarian communities that produced rice, millet, pigs, and chickens were multiplying in the well-watered valleys and coastal plains of both southern China and mainland Southeast Asia, the region that today includes Vietnam, Thailand, and Malaysia. Around 4000 B.C.E., some adventurous farm families crossed the Formosa Strait, which separates mainland China from the large island of Taiwan. These migrants spoke ancient languages of the Austronesian family.

Subsequently, Taiwan became the major dispersal point for further movements of rice-growing farmers southward into the wet tropical islands of the Philippines and Indonesia, as well as to many of the islands that rimmed the western Pacific. (We return to the peopling of Oceania in Chapter 4.) At some point, Austronesian voyagers moving south from Taiwan invented the outrigger canoe. This type of craft has a lateral support float attached to the hull, sometimes one on each side, to add stability to the vessel. A double-outrigger could stay upright in the heaviest of seas. As colonizers sailed from one Southeast Asian island to another, they brought with them an ecological "suitcase" of rice, pigs, chickens, durable pottery, and finely ground stone tools. One factor in their demographic success was the position of maritime Southeast Asia on the "ring of fire," the zone of volcanic activity that arcs around the rim of the Pacific, encompassing both eastern Asia and the western edge of the Americas. Volcanic eruptions in Southeast Asia did (and still do) kill people, but they also deposit layers of fertile volcanic soil, which almost certainly encouraged Austronesian groups to continue to explore and colonize new territory. For example, rice-growing populations became notably dense and productive on Java, an Indonesian island well-endowed with volcanic earth.

Across much of maritime Southeast Asia, Austronesian farming communities replaced forager economies and older languages. This did not, however, happen everywhere. On the great forested island of New Guinea, the much older Papuan-speaking population held its own in the interior regions against Austronesian intruders. The main reason may be that several millennia earlier the Papuans had domesticated varieties of yam, taro, banana, and perhaps sugar cane entirely on their own. Therefore, when Austronesian explorers appeared on New Guinea's shores, they confronted not a scattering of food collectors but relatively dense agrarian societies that were not about to budge.

• • •

Conclusion

Compared to the eight thousand years of the neolithic era, the second millennium B.C.E. was a revolutionary period of population growth, agrarian expansion, and city building across the more northerly latitudes of Afroeurasia. During that millennium, two contrasting trends developed simultaneously. On one hand, as more people adopted either farming or herding (or a combination of the two) and carried those ways of life into regions where they had previously been unknown, languages and numerous other elements of culture proliferated. Also, human adaptation to new ecological conditions, from tropical rainforests to arid grasslands, required continuous cultural innovation and adjustment. In other words, the Afroeurasian map of languages and cultural beliefs and practices became much more complex. Migratory movements, sometimes involving conquest, caused long-enduring communities to split apart, producing new linguistic and cultural offshoots. Indo-European languages multiplied across a territory extending from Europe to India. Austronesian speech became dominant in Southeast Asia from the Indian Ocean to the western Pacific. In Africa, ultimately hundreds of languages in three major linguistic families spread into and beyond the tropical forest zone.

On the other hand, in the same millennium that Afroeurasia was becoming more culturally diverse, intercommunication among communities became more intense and extended over longer distances in connection with migration, trade, conquest, and state building. With the exception of Shang China, no new centers of complex society arose that had quite the cultural weight and density of Mesopotamia, Egypt, or the Indus. However, new kingdoms and ruling groups such as the Hittites, the Mycenaeans, and the builders of the Oxus cities did much to advance regional productivity and interregional commerce for several centuries running. Also, the more that agrarian towns and oases sprang up on the landscape, the faster information tended to circulate from one to the other. Relative to the pace of communication in paleolithic times, the most attractive ideas and inventions spread like wildfire. For example, societies across the breadth of Eurasia and northern Africa adopted the complicated technology of bronze metallurgy within less than a thousand years. Knowledge of chariotry galloped from society to society even faster. By the thirteenth century B.C.E., chariots of a fairly uniform design were in use in places as far from one another as western Europe, Nubian Africa, and China.

This dual process, in which human society became simultaneously more culturally diverse and more firmly interconnected, was not a development unique to Afroeurasia. It also happened, though on a much smaller scale in terms of the number of people involved, in the Americas, Australia, and the Pacific basin. In Chapter 4, we visit these regions, which together encompassed more than half the globe.

• • •

Key Terms

Bantu migrations 105	megalith 84	pastoralism 101
bronze age 81	Minoan civilization 82	shaman 87
clan 101	Mycenaean society 99	Shang dynasty 86
Hittite kingdom 93	New Kingdom 96	shifting agriculture 105
Indo-European migrations 92	Nubia 96	tribute 83
kinship 89	oracle bones 87	Vedas 101
law code of Hammurabi 94	Oxus civilization 85	
lingua franca 99	pastoral nomadism 88	

Change over Time

4200 B.C.E.	People take up horseback riding in the Pontic-Caspian steppes.
4000 B.C.E.	Austronesian-speaking farmers migrate from China to Taiwan, a dispersal point for further migrations into tropical Southeast Asia.
3300 B.C.E.	Indo-European herders begin migrating west, south, and east from Pontic-Caspian steppes.
2400 B.C.E.	Builders in Britain begin constructing Stonehenge, one of many megalithic sites along Europe's Atlantic rim.
2100–1600 B.C.E.	Walled cities emerge in the Oxus civilization in Central Asia.
2000 B.C.E.	Chariots become important vehicles in warfare and political ritual.
2000–1450 B.C.E.	Minoan civilization develops on Crete.
Third and second millennia B.C.E.	Bronze metallurgy spreads across Eurasia and northern Africa (bronze age).
Third and second millennia B.C.E.	Bantu farmers establish agrarian societies in equatorial Africa.
1792–1750 B.C.E.	King Hammurabi expands Babylonian rule in Southwest Asia.
1750–1045 B.C.E.	The Shang dynasty rules over China's first large state.
1700 B.C.E.	Indo-European-speaking herders enter South Asia, a period later mythologized in the *Rig Veda.*
1650–1180 B.C.E.	The Hittite kingdom (Hatti) thrives in Anatolia and Syria.

Please see end of book reference section for additional reading suggestions related to this chapter.

4 Early Odysseys in the Americas, Australia, and Oceania

8000–500 B.C.E.

An outrigger sailing canoe in the southern Pacific, as depicted by an eighteenth-century artist.

n 1947, the Norwegian adventurer Thor Heyerdahl sailed from the coast of Peru on a balsa wood raft named the *Kon-Tiki*. More than three months later, he and his small crew landed in the Tuamotu Archipelago in the south central Pacific 4,300 miles to the west. Heyerdahl made the voyage as part of a larger project to demonstrate that many centuries ago sailors from South America reached Rapa Nui (Easter Island) and other islands of eastern Polynesia. Heyerdahl's theory never made much headway with scholars, who have argued that the historical record points overwhelmingly to the peopling of the Pacific not from America but from Southeast Asia starting about 10,000 years ago.

Nevertheless, scientists have also generally accepted evidence that a variety of sweet potato domesticated in the tropical Americas spread to the Island Pacific centuries before European mariners first crossed that sea. Perhaps Polynesian seafarers seeking new islands to settle reached the coast of South America and returned home with sweet potatoes. Possibly, an American Indian coastal vessel carrying these tubers drifted westward, eventually to be discovered and planted by Polynesian farmers.

The sweet potato mystery is just one example of rare communication between regions that, after the initial human colonization from Africa, had almost no contact with one another for thousands of years. Peoples of the Americas and Afroeurasia did not interact in any sustained way for about 12,000 years. But we also know that Norse settlers from Iceland or southern Greenland founded a short-lived community on the coast of Newfoundland in eastern Canada around 1000 C.E. The forager (or forager-hunter) population of Australia and the inhabitants of Afroeurasia remained almost entirely isolated from each other from about 6500 B.C.E. to 1788 C.E. Nevertheless, we have evidence that people of New Guinea and some Indonesian islands made sporadic connections with northern Australians during those millennia.

Despite sporadic episodes like these, we can think of the inhabited globe as constituting four distinct macro-regions, four different "worlds" of human interchange, from the neolithic era or earlier up to the past few centuries. Three of these worlds, Afroeurasia, the Americas, and Australia, were continental land masses. Oceania, the fourth, was a universe of islands scattered across the Pacific. The huge majority of humans have always lived in Afroeurasia and its adjacent islands, and beginning in paleolithic times its societies have forged increasingly complex interrelations. Within the other three macro-regions, people also exchanged goods and ideas over long distances, though the numbers involved relative to Afroeurasia were small, even in the Americas. Even so, the early colonizers of those three worlds adapted ingeniously to a wide array of physical and natural environments, and, in the case of the Americas, they created dense agrarian societies.

This chapter explores those three regions, starting with the Americas. There, people in both Mesoamerica ("Middle" America, or the region that is today southern Mexico and Central America) and the Andean Mountain spine of western South America experimented with domesticated crop production only a few thousand years after that process started in Southwest Asia. Maize (or corn) supplemented by other plant foods gradually established itself as a large-seeded grain staple everywhere in the Americas except where summers did not last long enough to sustain it. In the late third millennia B.C.E., farming societies also appeared in the arid region that is today the southwestern United States, in the North American woodlands from the Mississippi to the Atlantic, and in Amazonia (the Amazon River basin). In several regions, such as northern Canada or the California coast, people continued the foraging and hunting way of life because

• • •

crop growing, even if the concept was known, offered no particular advantages as long as fish, game, and wild plants remained plentiful. In a few places, however, farming societies grew large and dense enough to propel more complex forms of social and economic organization, including cities. Such innovations started appearing along the Pacific coast of Peru as early as the fourth millennium B.C.E. and along the gulf coast of Mexico, the site of the Olmec urban civilization, in the second millennium B.C.E.

In the second part of the chapter we zoom across the Pacific to Australia, which our species began to colonize as early as 60,000 years ago, as much as 20,000 years earlier than *Homo sapiens* populated Europe. Despite such a long history of adaptation to a continent that is today about 70 percent arid, all Australians continued to forage and hunt, not plant and hoe, until after the first Europeans arrived barely two and a quarter centuries ago. Nevertheless, research in archaeology, linguistics, and genetic shows that Aboriginal society—Australians whose ancestors populated the continent before Europeans came—experienced long-term historical change as much as peoples of Afroeurasia or the Americas did, even if the population remained consistently tiny compared to both those regions.

A Panoramic View

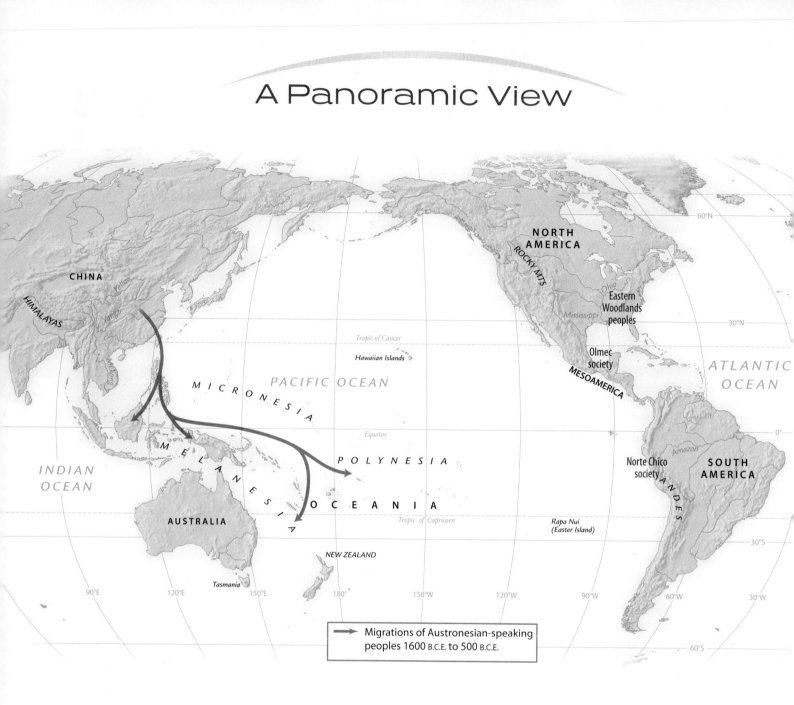

MAP 4.1 The Americas, Australia, and the Pacific Basin to 500 B.C.E.
Permanent contacts among peoples of the Americas, Australia, and Oceania were forged only in the past 250 years. Considering that narrow sea passages separated them, why were contacts between Aboriginal peoples of Australia and the inhabitants of both Southeast Asia and western Oceania so limited before the eighteenth century C.E.?

Until about 3,600 years ago, humans inhabited only far western islands of the Pacific basin. The third section of the chapter describes how, in the ensuing 2,500 years or so, voyagers undertook an astonishing fan-shaped migration far into the sea, hopping, as it were, from island to island. Among the ancient migratory movements that peopled the world, this was the only one accomplished exclusively by boat. As colonization advanced, men and women adapted successfully to contrasting ecological conditions and created different types of societies. Where islands formed archipelagos or were not more than a few hundred miles apart, seaborne trade and cultural exchange took place. But for a few thousand years, Pacific peoples had no sustained contact with the other three inhabited worlds.

Farmers and Platform Builders in the Americas

FOCUS Under what environmental and social circumstances did complex societies emerge in South America and Mesoamerica?

Between 12,000 and 7,000 years ago, people whose genetic ancestors had migrated from northeastern Asia colonized all latitudes of the Americas from tundra to tropical rainforest (see Chapter 1). As of 4000 B.C.E., a time when agrarian societies were spreading rapidly in several parts of Afroeurasia, the Americas had, as far as we know, no full-time farmers. All communities practiced some combination of hunting, foraging, and fishing. Nevertheless, experiments with plant domestication had started much earlier in a few places, as much as 10,000 years ago in southern Mexico.

Around 3500 B.C.E., people along the arid coast of what is today northern Peru planted cotton and food crops to supplement resources from the sea. They also began constructing ritual and residential centers exhibiting characteristics of complex agrarian society. In the following 1,500 years, ceremonial complexes associated with a social class system, including a ruling elite, multiplied in high Andes Mountain valleys in Peru and Ecuador. In Mesoamerica, maize came into use as a staple crop that could support larger concentrations of population. This happened in several localities, notably along the Gulf of Mexico, where the Olmec started building cities about 1350 B.C.E. In the millennium that followed, Mesoamerica and the Andes zone remained the largest centers of population growth and urbanization. A trend toward social complexity, however, also took place in semiarid northern Mexico and the Southwest of the United States, in the eastern woodlands of North America, and, on a smaller scale, in Amazonia.

Native Americans definitely invented agriculture without any cues from the Afroeurasian experience. There is no evidence that what became the principal American food crops—maize, beans, squash, potatoes, peppers, manioc— were grown anywhere in Afroeurasia until after Columbus linked the two hemispheres in the late fifteenth century (see Table 4.1). But despite the absence of sustained contact between human societies from the two hemispheres for at least 12,000 years, they developed in fundamentally similar ways. In both Afroeurasia and the Americas, overall population rose steadily after food production spread, while the proportion of foragers to farmers declined. In both regions, complex societies appeared, characterized by cities, social class divisions, centralized states, writing systems, and streams of technological and scientific innovation. In a sense, humans in Afroeurasia and the Americas provided "control groups" for each other. The two together bore out the hypothesis that wherever in the world crop-growing societies began to produce regular surpluses, greater social complexity followed, including crowded towns, teeming markets, tax collectors, high priests, accumulations of knowledge and skill, and unrelenting alteration of the natural environment.

American Farmer Power

An agricultural revolution took place in the Americas a few millennia later than in several regions of Afroeurasia, but no one in either hemisphere thought they were racing for the title of "First Farmers." As we saw in Chapter 2, forager-hunter communities in Southwest Asia and the Nile River valley experimented with plant and animal domestication, not because they thought life would be better if they became farmers (assuming they could have known what farmers *were*), but because climatic changes and accompanying social and demographic stresses slowly, and in large measure unconsciously, pushed them in that new direction. Under similar conditions of environmental stress, early Americans (a term we will use as synonymous with Native Americans or American Indians) are likely to have selected and sown food or fiber plants they thought had more desirable qualities than others. Farming developed too late in the Americas to be linked to the climatic changes that defined the last Ice Age (Pleistocene) and the onset of the warmer Holocene (see Chapter 2). But in later millennia, regional climatic fluctuations may have produced alternating periods of wet and dry conditions that impelled forager-hunter communities to experiment with crops.

Some of those fluctuations may have been associated with **El Niño Southern Oscillation (ENSO)** events that affected climate over land areas, notably the western coasts of the Americas. Even small-scale efforts to domesticate edible plants offered a potential hedge against disaster when wet and dry years followed one another unpredictably, especially in places where population was growing. Another theory relates to the extinction of several species of large mammals, including mammoths, huge bison, and ancestors of horses and camels, an event that occurred as a result of either climatic changes or relentless human hunting (see Chapter 1). Because of these extinctions, especially in North America, people may have faced more frequent food crises. This obliged them to figure out how to make plant foods more abundant and reliable. As in the Afroeurasian cases of agricultural invention, societies that reached a point where humans and domesticated crops became interdependent and population kept growing would have found it difficult, probably impossible, to return to the old foraging economy.

> **El Niño Southern Oscillation (ENSO)** A warming of ocean surface temperatures that occurs about every five years in the equatorial Pacific Ocean. An El Niño episode produces unusual, sometimes extreme weather in various parts of the world. A Pacific cooling cycle is called La Niña.

American crops and the triumph of maize. As early as 8000 B.C.E., when farming was just getting under way in Southwest Asia, people living in the tropical highland

TABLE 4.1 **Examples of Independent Plant Domestication**

Twelve Plants Domesticated in the Americas but Unknown in Afroeurasia	Twelve Plants Domesticated in Afroeurasia but Unknown in the Americas
maize (corn)	wheat
squashes	barley
potatoes	rice
manioc (cassava)	lentils
sweet potatoes	cane sugar
beans	coffee
tomatoes	bananas
peanuts	onions
avocadoes	oranges
cacao	grapes
pineapple	coconuts
tobacco	flax

valleys of Oaxaca (wah-HAH-kah) in southern Mexico appear from archaeological evidence to have selected and planted seeds of a particular species of squash. According to one interesting hypothesis, foragers watered and protected wild bottle gourds, then dried them, and used them as containers. Incidentally, some gourd cultivators, quite likely women, found that the plant's seeds toasted on the campfire tasted good. That discovery may then have suggested the food value of the seeds of similar plants, notably wild squashes. From there, people may have started selecting squashes for larger and tastier seeds.

Domestication of a long list of American plants proceeded at a leisurely pace in both North and South America over the ensuing six thousand years. There was no rush to farming because forager bands almost certainly preferred to continue their existing way of life, with its relatively short "work week" of collecting wild food, unless some natural force pressured them to change. It is also likely that in some places people at first consumed domesticated plants as "snack foods" that merely supplemented wild resources. Full-time farming may also have developed slowly because the wild ancestors of wheat, barley, rice, and other relatively large-seeded cereals that formed such productive partnerships with humans in Afroeurasia, did not grow anywhere in the Americas.

The one great exception was maize, a staple grain traded in larger quantities today than any other cereal except wheat and rice. Maize is a highly adaptable plant that flourishes in a wide range of environmental conditions. In the Americas it grows from southern Canada to the southern tip of Chile. It lends itself to endless genetic variation. At present, farmers produce about sixty varieties of maize in Mexico alone. Before the modern era, as many as 30,000 varieties may have existed.

Scholars have not pinpointed the original homeland of maize domestication with any certainty, but the process most likely began in one valley or another of southern Mexico around 7000 B.C.E. Evidence has accumulated indicating that teosinte (TEE-eh-SIN-tee), a wild mountain grass, is probably the genetic ancestor of maize. One may wonder how this could be, since teosinte is a plant with an inch-long "cob" holding about a dozen hard, tiny seeds. People could never have transformed teosinte into large-seeded maize cobs as many as two feet long without a lengthy, painstaking, conscious process of selecting for more desirable plants. Generalizing from later evidence of the division of family labor, we can imagine women in some ancient tropical valley sifting carefully through stands of wild teosinte to find plants with marginally better characteristics, then planting their seeds. They must have repeated this process over and over, perhaps across many generations, until they produced "genetically engineered" plants having kernels large and numerous enough to provide the staple food for an entire village. Early maize ears discovered in caves in southern Mexico's Tehuacán Valley were bigger than teosinte seeds but still six times smaller than the average cob of buttered corn we might eat today.

Maize, however, matures so rapidly, stores so well, and thrives in so many different conditions of soil and climate that farmers kept on experimenting with it. Families

The genetic evolution of maize. Over generations Mesoamerican farmers repeatedly selected and planted maize with desirable characteristics to improve the size of the ear and the size and number of the kernels. On the left is an ear of teosinte, the genetic ancestor of maize. Why do you think Mesoamericans developed not just a few but around sixty different varieties of maize?

also supplemented maize with beans, squash, and other foods that provided additional nutrients. Mesoamerican farmers took to growing crops in a *milpa*, producing altogether a nutritionally complete diet. *Milpa* cultivation may have spread northward across Mexico in association with farmer migrations, reaching what are today Arizona and New Mexico by about 2000 B.C.E.

milpa In Mesoamerica a farm plot created by cutting or burning forest and planted with maize, squash, beans, and other crops.

Maize and potatoes in South America. Scholars generally agree that people of the Andes Mountains and the adjacent Pacific coastal zone (Ecuador, Peru, Bolivia, and Chile) independently domesticated the white potato and at least a few other edible plants some centuries before they grew maize. Potato consumption definitely contributed to Andean population growth because it is jam-packed with essential nutrients, notably vitamin C, potassium, vitamin B_6, and fiber. Did Andeans also domesticate maize, or did the idea arrive from outside? Even today, direct overland travel between North and South America is difficult because thick marshes, swamps, and dense mountain rainforests straddle the border between Panama and Colombia. Panama's southeastern Darién Province is known as the Darién Gap because this is the one place where the intercontinental Pan-American Highway has never been completed. Nevertheless, most scholars think that maize cultivation diffused from Mesoamerica. Travelers could easily have carried kernels or young plants around the Darién Gap by boat. In any case, maize farming got under way in the northern Andes region sometime around 2200 B.C.E. The Andes diet came to include a nutritionally healthy mix of potatoes, maize, beans, and the seeds of quinoa, a protein-rich grain that in recent years has gained some popularity in the United States.

Until quite recently scholars have misconstrued Amazonia before the nineteenth century as an immense region of forest and grassland where only scattered forager bands lived before modern times. In fact, inhabitants of what is today far western Brazil domesticated the root crop manioc about 2000 B.C.E. In Amazonia, like the equatorial belt in Africa and Southeast Asia, soils tend to be low in nutrient-rich humus content. Forest-dwellers, however, began systematically to build up large tracts of *terra preta*, in which to plant manioc, fruit trees, and other warm-climate crops. They created these fields by partially burning biomass (wood and other plant material) to make charcoal, which they then mixed with soil to enrich it. In this way they improved soil by consciously engineering its chemical characteristics, without knowing the theory involved, of course. This practice had advanced far enough by the start of the Common Era to allow people to build sizable

terra preta A type of nutritionally rich soil that farmers of Amazonia produced by mixing charcoal, organic matter, and pottery shards. Literally "black earth" in Portuguese.

permanent villages. Archaeologists have found remains of some of these settlements in central Amazonia.

The absence of big animal domesticates. In contrast to Afroeurasia, few large animals presented themselves as suitable candidates for domestication anywhere in the Americas. The mass extinctions of the Ice Age–Holocene transition swept away something like 80 percent of hoofed mammal species, including the cousins of horses and camels that might have been susceptible to taming and selective breeding. Nor did the Western Hemisphere have any sheep, cattle, or pigs. Nevertheless, Native Americans domesticated at least five species: the turkey in Mesoamerica; the llama, alpaca, and guinea pig in the Andes; the Muscovy duck in the tropical latitudes; and the dog, which some people ate, just about everywhere.

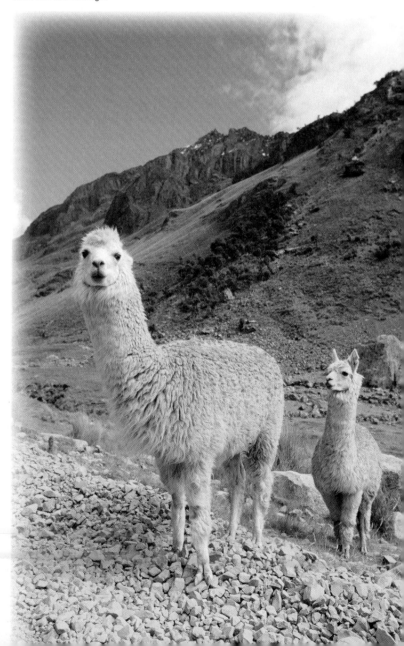

Alpacas in the Peruvian Andes. Alpacas and llamas are among the few domesticated hoofed animals native to the Americas. They are biological cousins of the camel, which disappeared in the Western Hemisphere after the last ice age.

The absence of large domesticated mammals made a difference in the capacity of Native Americans, in comparison with peoples of Afroeurasia, to adapt to and manage their environment. Wild game may have supplied abundant animal fat and protein in some regions, but people could not, for example, exploit semiarid grassland environments the way they did in Inner Eurasia. This is because they did not have animals that could be grouped, herded, and ridden and that converted grass or brush into the meat, milk, blood, and hides that humans used. Consequently, the North American prairies and the comparable South American pampas could support no more than thin populations of forager-hunters. Native Americans did not invent either heavy plows or wheels used for anything except toys, but these inventions would in any case have had limited use without horses, mules, cattle, oxen, or camels to pull them. Llamas and alpacas, which adapted to a limited range of territory in Andean South America, provided meat, hair, and hides, but they were not big enough to transport heavy packs and would have cut poor figures trying to pull plows or war chariots. In short, the expansion of agrarian societies in the Americas, which eventually included construction of cities and mammoth public structures, depended fundamentally on human muscle assisted by tools of stone, bone, and wood.

The shortage of big domesticates, however, was not entirely a bad thing. Like humans everywhere, ancient Americans were susceptible to disease. But they do not appear to have suffered the virulent infectious epidemics that raged through Afroeurasian cities. We know that in the Eastern Hemisphere both settled and pastoral populations lived in close proximity to large numbers of animals. We also know that pathogens that originally caused diseases only in animals mutated to afflict their human neighbors with smallpox, chickenpox, measles, and other lethal infections that frequently surged through dense populations (see Chapter 2). None of the few American domesticates either lived in giant herds or outnumbered humans in the confined spaces they shared. Moreover, there is no evidence of a disease microorganism moving from llamas to humans. If the absence of cows, sheep, and pigs deprived Americans of certain advantages, it may also have left them generally less exposed to infectious pathogens than their fellow humans across the oceans.

Platform Builders of Norte Chico

We noted in Chapter 2 that archaeologists first discovered the remains of early Indus valley civilization only in the 1920s. Consequently, that region's ancient history had to be revised radically. Similarly, no one knew anything about America's oldest complex society, a cluster of as many as thirty small cities on the Pacific coast of Peru, until about two decades ago. Since then, archaeological teams have uncovered urban sites whose construction started no later than about 3200 B.C.E. The earliest of these centers, located along a thirty-mile coastal strip known as Norte Chico, predates the

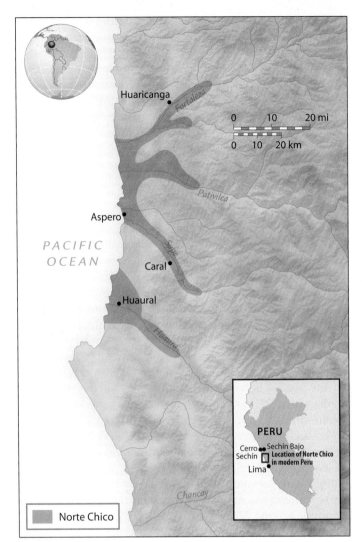

MAP 4.2 Urban centers in the Norte Chico region of Peru.

Did ancient urban societies in Norte Chico and Mesopotamia share any geographical or ecological similarities?

appearance of cities anywhere in the world except Sumer in Mesopotamia (see Map 4.2). They predate the Indus valley cities by at least four hundred years and Egypt's Great Pyramid by more than six hundred years. It would seem, then, that the time lapse between the invention of farming and emergence of the earliest complex society was about three thousand years shorter in the Americas than in Afroeurasia.

Cities of the rain shadows. The Tigris-Euphrates, Nile, and Indus civilizations all arose within Afroeurasia's Great Arid Zone. Their agrarian economies depended on river irrigation, not rainfall. Similarly, the Norte Chico centers sprang up in what might be called South America's great arid zone. In fact, "arid zone" puts it mildly. The narrow belt of contiguous deserts that run along the Pacific coast about 1,500 miles from northern Peru to central Chile are among the driest places on earth. Parts of Chile's Atacama Desert have had no rainfall in recorded history. The scant precipitation that is detectable comes mainly from perennial fog and mist. The region is nearly waterless because it lies between two rain shadows. On the Pacific side, a combination of cold sea current and atmospheric temperature causes trade winds to dump rain offshore, almost never over land. On the east the Andes Mountains, the second highest range after the Himalayas, squeeze the rain out of winds blowing from tropical Amazonia before they reach the coastal strip.

In other respects, however, ecological conditions on the Peruvian coast were quite different from those in the arid Afroeurasian river valleys. Norte Chico's four rivers do not flow across broad fertile plains but pour down out of the snowy Andes, cut across less than fifty miles of bleached desert, and empty into the sea. In Mesopotamia and the Indus valley, farmers struggled constantly against salt contamination of soil resulting from water evaporation in gently flowing irrigation canals. At Norte Chico, by contrast, water gushed along the river courses in spring, flushing out channels and ditches built to irrigate fields of vegetables, fruits, and cotton.

Though shore settlements existed, most of Norte Chico's population clustered some miles up the river valleys where crop irrigation was feasible. We know nothing about the local language or social life, but the society consumed quantities of anchovies, sardines, shellfish, and other marine life, including birds and sea mammals. These species all flourished in the cold Humboldt Current, which even today nourishes the most bountiful fishing ground on the planet. An economic synergy seems to have developed between upriver and shore settlements. Fishing communities supplied seafood to the valley centers, while irrigation farmers reciprocated with crops and, perhaps just as important, cotton string for making fishing nets. Material clues suggest that the population also produced cotton textiles for clothing and bags. Two items are conspicuous for their absence in the economic repertoire. One is maize, whose cultivation does not appear to have reached that region until around 2000 B.C.E. The other is ceramic pottery. We have evidence that foragers made pottery in eastern Amazonia as early as 6000 B.C.E. and in the Colombia-Panama region about a thousand years later. Norte Chico people no doubt used gourds, bags, and baskets for containers, but, as far as we know, they had no pots.

Faint outlines of Norte Chico society. The population must have had an extended kinship system or other form of social organization because it undertook complex communal projects to build monumental earthen platforms, sunken circular plazas, and a variety of stone buildings in all four of the narrow river valleys. The upriver urban site of Caral, for example, has six platform mounds, one of which rises sixty feet in the air. A large workforce would have been needed to pile up and shape earth for the platforms, move giant stones, and dig irrigation canals. Leaders must have directed these operations, but they may have

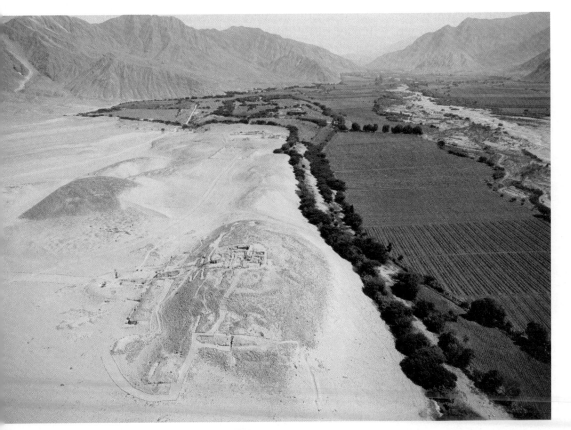

A city of Norte Chico. The Supe River, flowing from the high Andes, supported the ancient city of Caral. The ruins of its urban platforms lie near the river's left bank. Looking at this modern photo, why do you think the cultivated area stops short of the city's remains?

been religious figures who organized volunteers, perhaps in groups of kin. Men and women would thus have ratified their membership in the local society by joining work crews and by celebrating public rituals in temples that may once have gilded the tops of the platforms.

In contrast to later South American complex societies, Norte Chico has so far yielded no evidence of a social hierarchy, no class of chiefs, priests, or aristocrats who told other people what to do or collected taxes from them. For example, the sites have revealed no evidence of special tombs or grave goods signifying a privileged elite. Everyone—men, women, and children—got buried the same way. Nor is there evidence of a fighting class or even conflict among the cities. No fortifications or artistic representations of warriors, prisoners, or mutilated bodies have been found. In fact, with the exception of what may have been decorative textiles, Norte Chico has revealed almost no visual art, no stone carving, sculpture, or wall painting. The society probably had no full writing system, but archaeologists have discovered remains of *quipu* (KEE-poo). These are sets of knotted and colored strings that later Andean societies used to record and preserve collective knowledge. Their presence at Norte Chico suggests early experiments to create a system of symbols to convey meanings that at least some members of the community could jointly understand.

Material remains show that Norte Chico people traded with other settlements up and down the Pacific coast and with Andean highlanders to the east. By the third millennium B.C.E., therefore, an Andean zone of commercial and cultural exchange took shape, linking communities that lay at different altitudes and therefore had different goods to barter. Lowlanders, for example, traded salt, cotton, and shells to mountain people in exchange for such items as dyes and obsidian. Another item in demand was mind-altering snuff, which came from Amazonia. Norte Chico is likely to have shared irrigation and architectural technology, as well as cultural practices, with neighboring societies. For example, archaeologists discovered a gourd at Caral carrying the image of a hooded and fanged Staff God. This deity continued to show up in later Andean religious symbolism.

Norte Chico's status as the Americas' earliest urban society may not stand for long. Archaeologists have recently excavated a large stone plaza at Sechín Bajo, a site about two hundred miles farther up the Peruvian coast. It appears to predate Norte Chico construction by a few centuries. In any case the Norte Chico cities went into decline after about 1800 B.C.E. as new centers arose elsewhere along the Andes Mountain spine.

Andean Societies in the Second Millennium B.C.E.

From about 2200 B.C.E., both pottery and maize spread widely across South America. In the ensuing millennium, highland populations rose steadily. Farmers who tilled valley bottoms began to move outward and upward by carving erosion-resistant terraces—green steps marching up hillsides. In Andean Ecuador and Peru, people built dozens of ceremonial and administrative centers, typically focused on stone, mud-brick, and earthen platforms or pyramids. In contrast to the bare walls at Norte Chico, the interior rooms of Andes pyramids and temples displayed elaborate murals featuring deities, warriors, and animals in rich shades of red, blue, yellow, cream, rose, and black. Artisans carved similar motifs in stone. As these centers multiplied, they exhibited distinctively different local cultural styles, and they appear to have remained politically independent of one another. Large centralized Andean states still lay in the future.

Violence at Cerro Sechín. Engraved stones at this Peruvian ceremonial center tell a tale of ritual sacrifice. The warrior armed with a club and wearing plumed headgear bares his teeth. One severed head lies in front of him and a stack of twelve more appear peaceful in death. Why do you think the ruling group at Cerro Sechín would have instructed artists to carve images like this?

As at Norte Chico, leaders in the Andes must have emerged to mobilize men and women for public building, terracing, and irrigation, but practices of that era show little sign of sharp social distinctions. On the other hand, we have more evidence of intercommunal violence than at Norte Chico. Some groups stockpiled great quantities of stones for slingshots, and ominous imagery appeared in public art. For example, on the façade of the enormous U-shaped structure at Cerro Sechín (SER-oh se-CHEEN) in northern Peru, a site dating to about 1300 B.C.E., artisans carved a line of bas reliefs of severed heads, limbs, and torsos, a macabre parade supervised by stone warriors armed with ornate clubs.

Many Andean valleys run north and south rather than east and west, a geographical configuration that may have facilitated the southerly diffusion of maize, pottery, and other technological innovations toward southern Peru, Bolivia, and Chile. Around the shores of Lake Titicaca (tee-tee-kah-kah), located at 12,500 feet above sea level on the modern border between Peru and Bolivia, villagers herded llamas and alpacas and planted potatoes, quinoa, and maize. They also harvested and chewed coca leaves, whose stimulant properties relieved the symptoms of altitude sickness. In that region, communities began to construct platforms and plazas about 1000 B.C.E. As in the northern Andes, leaders having mainly religious functions may have mobilized families and kinship groups to undertake large-scale construction.

The Mesoamerican Zone of Intercommunication

By around 1500 B.C.E. (about when the Shang state was forming in China and the New Kingdom arose in Egypt), pottery-making maize farmers were to be found in nearly every part of Mesoamerica. Agriculture continued to spread *extensively*, meaning that as village populations rose, small pioneer groups trekked off to found new settlements on virgin soil somewhere down the valley or over the hills. Mesoamerica's "pot revolution," which got under way after 1800 B.C.E., enriched settled life by enlarging the technical possibilities of cooking, storage, and transport.

Agrarian society. From the Central American rainforest to the arid Southwest of what is now the United States, men and women built their village dwellings in quite similar styles, suggesting that this whole region formed a single zone of cultural interaction from very early times.

Mesoamerican ball player. This terracotta athlete from Jalisco state in west central Mexico wears a helmet and other decorative sports gear. The sculpture is dated between 200 B.C.E. and 500 C.E.

In the period from 1500 B.C.E. to 150 C.E., villagers typically founded hamlets of ten to twelve dwellings. In time, many of those settlements grew much larger. Dwellings had recessed dirt floors and walls of "wattle and daub," that is, sticks and canes woven together between vertical poles and plastered with mud. Farmers stored maize in bell-shaped underground pits covered with stone slabs. Villages appear to have had a fairly simple division of labor, with women and men working in different parts of the house. Excavations of ancient house floors have revealed needles, spindles, and cornhuskers of bone or ceramic clustered in a part of the dwelling where women presumably sat. Men very likely worked with the stone blades and drills found in different corners.

As the only large-seeded grain staple Mesoamericans had, maize presented one serious drawback. Unlike wheat, barley, or rice, it lacks niacin, an essential human nutrient also known as vitamin B^3. Prolonged niacin deficiency may trigger pellagra, a disease characterized by diarrhea, skin sores, and mental confusion. Early in the agrarian era, however, Mesoamerican women discovered the idea of soaking dried maize in water mixed with white limestone powder, then grinding this mixture into flour. Combining water with lime produced calcium hydroxide (slaked lime), a compound that restored niacin to baked tortillas. Of course no one in those times understood the biochemistry, but families that made tortillas with lime proved less susceptible to pellagra. (Notice that the corn tortillas in your local market are also made with maize, water, and lime.)

From about 1500 B.C.E., Mesoamericans began to create not only beautifully incised and painted ceramic pots but also imaginative figurines of animals and humans. These have turned up in burial remains. For example, the Tlatilco archaeological site is located in the Valley of Mexico, the highland plateau surrounded by mountains and volcanoes where Mexico City now lies. Since the 1940s, researchers at the site have discovered clever sculpted images of animals that people hunted—deer, waterfowl, frogs, turtles, and wild turkeys. Artists also painted scenes of daily life on ceramic ware: women carrying children, men wearing breechcloths, and dancers with rattles strapped to their legs. Excavations have turned up numerous female figurines. These are usually nude, shapely, and adorned with grass skirts, elegant hairdos, body paint, and jewelry. By contrast, images of men are few and comparatively plain. Did female potters wish to portray themselves? Did these figurines serve as dolls? Were they ritual objects in fertility cults? Did they have symbolic significance for communication among women? As in the case of Eurasian "Venus" figurines from the late paleolithic era, we can only guess at their cultural meaning.

At Tlatilco and many other sites, archaeologists have found miniature representations of both athletes and ball courts, an architectural form that became a signature characteristic of Mesoamerican urban society. Figurines of players, both men and women, identify themselves by their gear: a pad on one knee and wrist and a heavy leather belt around the hips to protect body organs. Rules of the game varied from region to region, but typically players tried to hit a hard rubber ball through a center ring. They could use only their hips, knees, and elbows—no hands or feet. Both individuals and teams may have competed. We know from later American Indian sources that the ball game could be both a religious ritual and a high-speed sport involving betting. But we have little knowledge of who made the rules and how they may have changed from one region to another. Ball games may also have contributed to an esprit de corps—a common purpose and identity for people who lived near one another.

The Olmec. Agriculture and the accompanying population growth stimulated greater social complexity in Mesoamerica in the later second millennium B.C.E., just as it had in Andean South America as much as two thousand years earlier. People built big settlements like Tlatilco in the Valley of Mexico, erected ritual structures and defensive walls in the Oaxaca Valley, and designed stone ball courts in southern Mexico's Chiapas (chee-AH-puhs) region. Most impressive of all before 1000 B.C.E. was the society labeled Olmec, which rose up along the Gulf of Mexico's tropical shore south of the modern city of Veracruz (see Map 4.3). In that region of hot, swampy coasts and densely forested uplands, inhabitants of the city called San Lorenzo built a ceremonial platform of nearly 2.8 million cubic yards of rock. They also created a social class system featuring a minority of aristocratic rulers, and probably Mesoamerica's earliest monarchs. We have no idea what these people called themselves. But they made rubber balls, and that suggested "Olmec," which in the Nahuatl language of the later Aztecs refers to "people from the land of rubber." In the sixteenth century C.E., Aztec sages invoked distant memories of this legendary land where

in a certain era
which no one can reckon,
which no one can remember
. . . there was a government for a long time.[1]

The Olmec heartland curved along the gulf for about 125 miles and extended inland about 50 miles. Moist winds

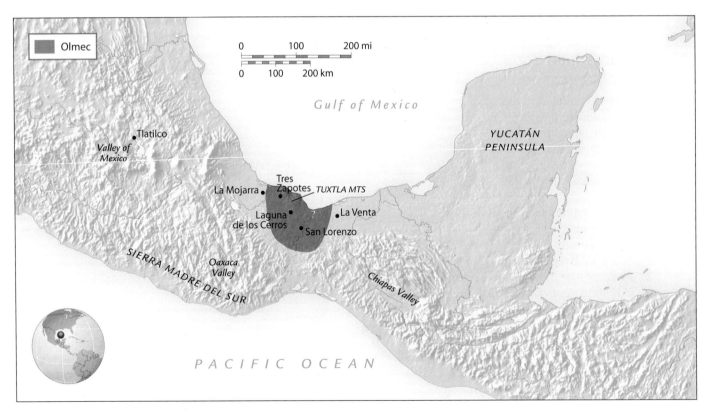

MAP 4.3 Olmec civilization in Mesoamerica.
How might similarities or differences in geography and climate have shaped particular characteristics of Olmec urban society compared to Norte Chico?

The Olmec Heads

The most dramatic Olmec art objects are the exquisitely carved stone heads that have been found in several different places along the gulf coast. Seventeen of these heads, ranging in volume from six to fifty tons, have turned up so far. All the heads, the tallest more than eleven feet high, have individualized faces, leading art historians to hypothesize that the figures represent portraits of Olmec leaders. Some appear quite grim, others benevolent. They all wear headdresses that look like old-fashioned American football helmets, each marked with distinctive insignia that likely indicate the name and identity of the person whom the head depicts.

Carved with stone tools, the volcanic basalt rock for the giant heads came from sites in the Tuxtla Mountains at least forty miles to the west. Some scholars think that workers pushed them on log rollers to a riverbank, transferred them to rafts, floated them downriver, and steered them to their destination on more rollers. Others think the workers slid them the whole distance overland. The hardness of the volcanic basalt rock, which has contributed to the survival of the heads over the millennia, also points to the technical sophistication of the Olmec, since carving the rock without the use of metal tools required considerable skill.

Thinking Critically

What similarities do these heads appear to share? In what ways are they dissimilar? Considering the size and weight of the heads and the distances they had to be moved, what might they suggest, if anything, about the character of Olmec government, the power of an elite group, and the society's artistic and engineering skills? What might the construction and placement of these heads suggest about their function and importance in Olmec society? Some of the heads have gouges and pits that suggest deliberate acts of defacement. Under what circumstances might people have mutilated the heads?

blew in from the gulf, bringing abundant rain in normal years. The earliest farmers in the region probably depended more on shellfish and other aquatic resources than on crops. But along rivers that flowed from the Tuxtla Mountains, which lie not far to the west, farmers cultivated bounteous *milpas* of maize, beans, squash, and numerous other foods.

The region's population grew large enough by about 1350 B.C.E. to support the building of San Lorenzo on a long ridge overlooking a river and an expanse of marshes that stretched forty miles to the coast. A swarm of laborers must have erected San Lorenzo's central platform, an artificial plateau 150 feet high and two-thirds of a mile on each side. They hauled rock from quarries as much as fifty miles away. Atop the big podium, supervisors directed the construction of smaller platforms, more than two hundred of them, as well as courtyards and almost certainly buildings that have long since disappeared.

Archaeologists exploring San Lorenzo and its vicinity in the past several years have gradually shed light on Olmec society. The main center may have had an average population of about 5,500 during its most flourishing period, from about 1200 to 900 B.C.E.[2] An elite class, plus the ordinary men and women who served it, resided in that center. This may indeed have been the earliest place in the Americas where a privileged minority exercised some type of permanent authority over everyone else. Other members of the elite lived in satellite centers. Researchers have found at least nineteen villages and a larger number of single, isolated households in a wide surrounding area. Farmers, artisans, and hunters would have lived in those places, perhaps sending tribute in food or other goods to the ruling group.

Both archaeologists and local residents have found a great number of stone sculptures in the Olmec heartland, including large human and animal sculptures of stone, stele (upright stone slabs bearing carved images), carved altars, and figurines.

The city of San Lorenzo, where ten of the colossal heads have been found, disintegrated about 1200 B.C.E. In fact, many stone sculptures on the site show signs of being vandalized and mutilated. Scholars do not know what happened, perhaps an invasion, a popular uprising, or a famine that forced evacuation of the city. In any case, other Olmec centers arose about that time or later, notably La Venta, Tres Zapotes (TRACE zah-POE-tace), and Laguna de los Cerros. These cities declined only after about 400 B.C.E. While it thrived, La Venta boasted a massive, cone-shaped clay mound rising 110 feet. A grand pavilion, courtyard, and more giant stone heads were associated with it. Many scholars think the clay mound represents a volcano similar to those that rumble away in the Tuxtla Mountains. The Olmec may have regarded one of these volcanoes as the site of creation. La Venta's massive constructions suggest a strong governing authority, even if people did the work voluntarily and for religious motives. San Lorenzo, La Venta, and the other cities appear, however, to have been politically autonomous. There are no signs of a centralized state exercising authority over the whole Olmec region.

It is clear, however, that the cities were part of a growing Mesoamerican zone of commercial and cultural interchange. We do not know whether people relayed trade items from one village to another or full-time merchants carried goods over long distances. In any case, pottery and other ceramic ware of distinctive Olmec style have turned up in archaeological sites from the Valley of Mexico to Guatemala. Researchers have chemically analyzed the clay composition of pots to demonstrate that communities located hundreds of miles from the gulf coast acquired objects made with clay that originated in Olmec centers. Communities across central and southern Mexico imitated Olmec stone imagery, including representations of the jaguar, the predator that became an emblem of supernatural power throughout much of Mesoamerica. Figurines of chubby infants that play with balls, suck their fingers, and tug at their hair also typify Olmec exports. In the opposite direction of trade, Olmec men and women, perhaps mainly elite families that wished to adorn themselves and their homes, acquired goods from distant parts of Mesoamerica, including obsidian, jade, greenstone, and concave mirrors made of iron oxide.

Experts continue to debate the historical significance of Olmec civilization. The more traditional view is that this complex society should be understood as the "mother culture" from which emanated the foundational elements of all later Mesoamerican urban civilizations. More recently, scholars have tended to regard the Olmec as one of several "sister cultures," including early dense farming societies in the Valley of Mexico, Oaxaca, and Chiapas. According to this theory, all these societies, the Olmec among them, both gave and received goods, ideas, and styles in a complex process of interaction over many centuries. Few doubt that between about 1500 and 400 B.C.E. the Olmec achieved social complexity on an impressive scale. Their centers almost certainly presented the earliest model of societies having a formal social hierarchy headed by a monarch or high priest. In terms of strong elite government, however, later Mesoamerican and South American societies surpassed the Olmec many times over.

North of Mexico

Starting perhaps more than 15,000 years ago, human groups migrated generally from west to east across the temperate latitudes of upper North America (the United States and Canada; see Map 4.4). These forager communities used tools and projectile points broadly associated with a style that scholars call Clovis. Most of them probably spoke ancestral languages in the huge Amerind family of languages, as did all early peoples of Mesoamerica and South America. There were two major exceptions. One was the several peoples in western Canada and Alaska, plus the Navajo in the United States Southwest, who spoke languages in

Harvester Mountain Lord: A Mesoamerican King

The archaeology of the Olmec era reveals almost nothing about individual rulers and their deeds, let alone ordinary women and men. An exception is Harvester Mountain Lord, a boy king born about 144 C.E. in the region that had once been the heartland of Olmec civilization. The knowledge we have of Harvester Mountain Lord's career is carved on a stone stele discovered in 1986 in the Acula River near a village called La Mojarra south of the modern city of Veracruz. The slab, which weighs four tons and stands nearly seven feet tall, displays a carved image of Harvester Mountain Lord wearing an elaborate headdress. It also carries a set of glyphs (graphic figures or characters carved into stone), more than five hundred of them, which scholars have partially deciphered. The text describes several key events of the king's reign, though the decipherment, translation, and interpretation of the glyphs have been fraught with linguistic difficulties.

In Harvester Mountain Lord's time, the great Olmec cities had long deteriorated, but small states still existed along the southern coast of the Gulf of Mexico. According to the writing on the stele, a political faction that supported his rulership triumphed over an opposing one. At about the age of twelve he ascended the throne, following a propitious solar eclipse. The coronation ritual may have featured the new king cutting off the head of an enemy who had challenged his royal birthright.

The engraved text describes the ruler and his aristocratic followers, named "noble war-leader ones," conducting ceremonies, probably to prove their worthiness and ensure the blessing of the gods. These rituals involved the king having his buttocks and penis cut so that drops of his royal blood might be offered to the spirits. As his blood flowed, the king shouted to those around him, "My blood is getting sprinkled for others."[3]

Like monarchs the world over, Harvester Mountain Lord appears to have faced a threat from a person close to the royal court. A sister's husband plotted to overthrow him and seize the throne. The king's supporters, however, killed the conspirator in battle, piercing him with arrows. Then, to demonstrate what happens to brothers-in-law who turn traitor, the

king had his body cut into pieces. Rebels had apparently toppled monuments to Harvester Mountain Lord's exalted reign, but now the king had them set upright again. The text also refers to the ruler's association with a priest, or shaman, and to a trance in which a supernatural animal companion appeared in the king's body. Some time after these events, artisans carved the ruler's image and the glyphs on the stele. No one knows the ultimate fate of Harvester Mountain Lord's kingdom or how long the slab rested on the bottom of the river before its modern recovery.

Harvester Mountain Lord, wearing extravagant headgear and a feathered cape, appears on the left side of La Mojarra stele.

La Mojarra Stele (la moo-hahr-UH STEE-luh) is one of the few examples of Olmec writing so far discovered. Linguists succeeded in deciphering many of the glyphs by starting with the premise that the language they recorded was ancestral to Indian languages still spoken in the region today. The text offers not only scraps of Harvester Mountain Lord's biography but also a glimpse into royal elements of culture—state politics, ceremonial regalia, ritual bloodletting, and beliefs about animal spirits—that prevailed in the gulf coastal lowlands at the start of the first millennium C.E.

Thinking Critically

Do you think La Mojarra Stele should be trusted as historical evidence of the reign of Harvester Mountain Lord? Is it more likely to have been an objective account or a piece of royal propaganda?

---

the family named Na-Dene, which some linguists have linked to tongues spoken in Asia. The other exception was speakers of Eskimo-Aleut languages, hunters who gradually spread from the Bering Strait region eastward across northern Canada, even as far as the coast of Greenland. As bands moved across upper North America, they and their languages diverged and multiplied. The Amerind family,

for example, spawned several subfamilies, including Ute-Aztecan, Siouan, Iroquoian, and Algonquin.

As of about 2500 B.C.E., all peoples living north of Mexico presumably consumed only wild foods. Foraging and hunting, however, did not necessarily mean continuous wandering. Just as forager bands in Southwest Asia made seasonal camps near stands of wild grain in the centuries before farming, North Americans set up central bases from which they exploited local wild resources for months at a time. When they moved on, they sometimes left behind tools and food, expecting to return to the same place the following year. By the second millennium B.C.E., the rich marine diets of peoples inhabiting the Pacific Northwest and southern Alaska permitted groups to settle in particular ecological niches for long periods and even to build villages with solid rectangular houses of planked timber.

Early North American mound builders.
In the lower Mississippi valley, evidence of settlement without farming extends even further back in time. At a site named Watson Brake, located near the Ouachita (WOSH-i-taw) River in northeastern Louisiana just west of the Mississippi, foragers who lived there about 3400 B.C.E. constructed eleven earthen mounds, the highest rising nearly twenty-five feet. These structures, linked by a ridge to form an oval shape, might just be older than any artificial platform so far discovered in Mesoamerica or even South America. If people settled on the Ouachita floodplain for several months, or even year-round,

they could have built the mounds as a long-term communal project that did not require a big labor force or an elite of chiefs and bosses. We have no evidence that the mounds had anything to do with burials or religious ceremonies. But they were not unique. Other earthworks dating not much later than Watson Brake may be seen in the southern Mississippi watershed.

Poverty Point.
Sometime after 1750 B.C.E., people residing about 100 miles east of Watson Brake at the site known as Poverty Point began building a center featuring several mounds and six rows of earthen ridges resembling half an octagon. One of the mounds is conical, others are platforms, and two appear, by a stretch of the imagination, to resemble birds. The Poverty Point people built perishable structures of wood, bark, and mud on top of the ridges, which face toward the Mississippi. They also produced pottery, beads, animal-like figurines, and fine microlithic tools for scraping and cutting. They made long-distance trade contacts, importing shells and copper from the Gulf of Mexico or as far away as the Great Lakes. Perhaps as many as five thousand people lived at Poverty Point some of the time, but we do not know what they did there. Men and women from the surrounding region may have congregated at the site periodically to perform religious rituals. Or, they may have gathered to exchange gifts among kinship groups, meet with distant relatives, or find marriage partners. Some scholars think the mounds and certain pottery styles hint at Mesoamerican influence, perhaps the Olmec, whose centers lay only about 1,200 miles around the curve of the gulf. The evidence is inconclusive.

Farming in the eastern woodlands.
Despite its size and complexity, Poverty Point reveals no sign of agriculture. In the eastern woodlands, that is, the lands stretching from the Great Lakes and the Mississippi valley to the Atlantic coast, wild nuts, fruits, berries, and game provided sufficient nutrition to sustain communities as long as some members of the group could break off in times of shortage to find new hunting and gathering grounds not already occupied. Large numbers of upper North Americans *never* took up farming any time before Europeans started arriving just five centuries ago.

Nevertheless, some groups living in the middle Mississippi valley and east from there toward Tennessee and Ohio began to experiment with selective planting of edible seed-producing species by around 2000 B.C.E., that is, as much as six thousand

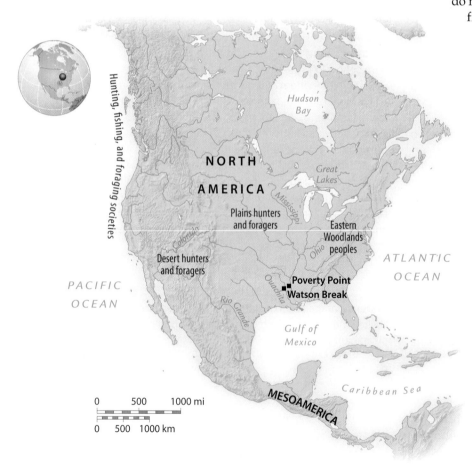

MAP 4.4 Early farming and mound-building societies in North America.
From a geographical perspective, do you think that cultural contacts in the later second millennium B.C.E. between Olmec society and settlements like Poverty Point in the lower Mississippi valley were likely or not?

The Poverty Point settlement. In this artist's rendering of ancient Poverty Point (1750–700 B.C.E.), smoke rises from houses lined up along the town's six earthen ridges. Archaeological digs on the ridges have revealed hearths, as well as postholes where wooden building posts probably once stood. The largest earthen structure on the site is Mound A, visible in the top center of the picture. Why might the residents have built this semicircle of six ridges?

years later than communities in southern Mexico started planting squash. Woodland dwellers may have tried out plant selection, not because wild resources were giving out, but as a practical hedge against cycles of good and bad years related to modest climatic fluctuations. Some of these may have been related to El Niño episodes, which could affect eastern North America.

As in Mesoamerica, gourds and squashes that yielded tasty seeds may have been the first domesticates. No large-grained plants resembling wheat or barley grew in upper North America, nor did maize, which had not yet reached that far north. Rather, woodland people, probably women and girls, experimented to select the most desirable specimens of small-seeded plants. These flora included the oily seeded sunflower but also plants like goosefoot, marsh elder, and knotweed, which we are unlikely to see in supermarkets today. The tiny seeds of these plants had hard coverings, so domestication involved selecting and nurturing specimens that were marginally more desirable generation after generation. By the second millennium B.C.E., many woodlanders already made pottery, which eased the collecting, storing, and cooking of these grains.

Woodlanders almost certainly became farmers without any stimulus from Mesoamerica. The region qualifies, therefore, as one of the seven or eight places in the world where agriculture emerged independently. For most woodland communities, however, crops like squash, sunflowers, and goosefoot continued to supplement rather than replace wild foods until the Common Era or even much later. Maize farming diffused gradually from Mesoamerica northward but did not become the dominant grain crop in upper North America (as far north as southern Canada) until about 1000 C.E.

Change in Australia

FOCUS Why did all human communities in Australia continue to forage and hunt from the initial colonization of the continent down to modern times rather than adopting farming?

The descendants of foragers who first colonized Australia 60,000 years ago or more (see Chapter 1) spent the following tens of thousands of years spreading across the continent (see Map 4.5). Archaeological evidence points to human occupation reaching as far as Tasmania more than 35,000 years ago, a time when it was attached to the continent, not the island it has been since Holocene sea levels rose. In distant millennia probably the largest forager populations lived either in southern Australia's Murray River region or along the tropical northern coasts facing the Arafura Sea and the Indonesian archipelago beyond. And until about 8,500 years ago, a land bridge connected northern Australia to New Guinea.

We sometimes hear the claim that Australian Aborigines (native peoples) really had no history because until the modern era their way of life never changed. This notion is wrong. Our knowledge of Aboriginal history before the late eighteenth century C.E. depends on archaeology, historical linguistics, Aboriginal oral traditions, and, more recently, genetic analysis. It is therefore difficult to perceive change over short runs of time but not over the long term. On long chronological timelines, scholars have found plenty of evidence of change in migratory patterns, tool making, ceramic technology, settlement construction, and art styles displayed on the walls of rock shelters and caves.

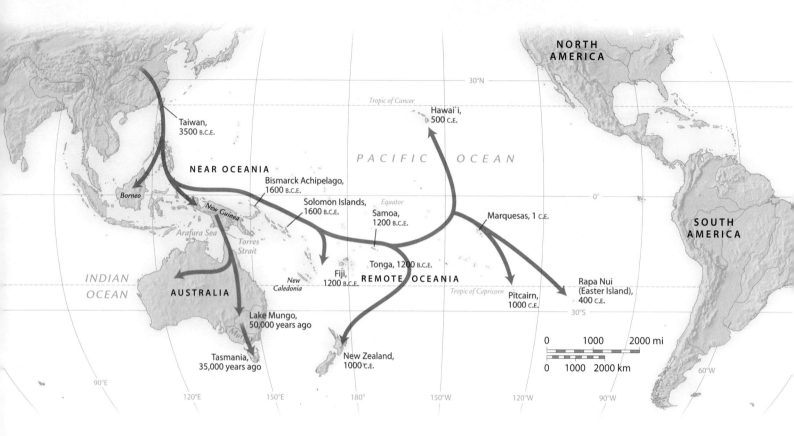

MAP 4.5 Settlement in Australia and Oceania to 1000 C.E.
Agrarian societies became established on Southeast Asian islands in the third and second millennia B.C.E. But farming did not reach Australia until modern times. What geographical factors might account for this long time difference?

The global climatic transition from the Ice Age to the warmer Holocene, which got under way about 16,000 years ago, almost certainly accelerated social change because it affected local environmental conditions for plants and animals. For example, in southwestern Tasmania during the Ice Age, cooperating bands made camps in caves and hunted wallabies (marsupial species smaller than kangaroos). But they appear to have abandoned the region as the Holocene set in because the growth of thick, tangled rainforests made the hunting economy untenable. The inhabitants therefore moved to coastal lands, where they and their descendants successfully switched to a marine diet requiring different technologies and food-gathering knowledge.

Melting glaciers and rising sea levels not only submerged the land bridges connecting both New Guinea and Tasmania to Australia but also pushed back coastlines, forcing shore-dwelling communities to repeatedly abandon their camps, whose material remains now lie under water. Regular human contacts between Australia, New Guinea, and perhaps other islands of the Indonesian archipelago diminished, leaving Australia's foragers and the vastly larger population of Afroeurasia as a whole in separate arenas of interaction. One way of thinking about this development is to note that in the millennia after 8,500 years ago, the inhabitants of the

Indonesian islands became progressively more enmeshed in a greater Afroeurasian web of exchange, while Australians did not.

The isolation between Afroeurasia and Australia was not, however, absolute. People living on the continent's northern coasts had at least sporadic contact with inhabitants of New Guinea. We know this because pottery shards of New Guinean style and certain plants native to Indonesia turned up in Australia after the land bridge disappeared. The wild Australian dog known as the dingo arrived from Southeast Asia about 1500 B.C.E. The Torres Strait separating New Guinea from Australia is only ninety miles across at its narrowest, and most scholars think that at least sporadic trade took place by way of several little islands scattered across the strait. In later millennia, traders of maritime Southeast Asia made frequent landfalls on the coast of Arnhem Land (today Australia's Northern Territory) in search of sea cucumbers, a marine animal regarded as a culinary delicacy.

Change over the Long Term

Occasional contact with Indonesia or not, Australia's history marched on. In some localities, populations continued to grow, nourished by the abundance of game and plant

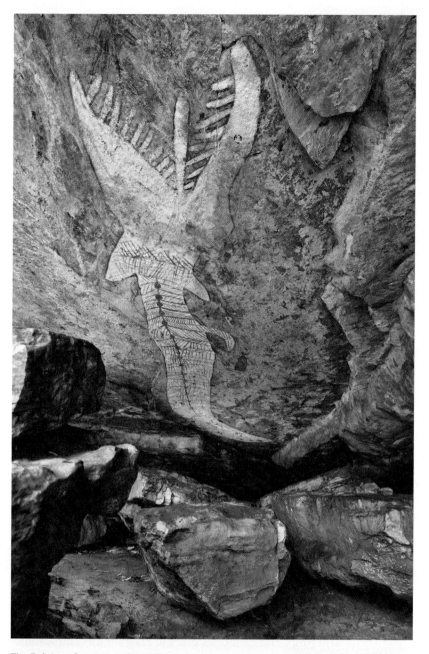

The Rainbow Serpent. In Australia's far northern Arnhem Land, images of the Rainbow Serpent, a potent mythological being linked with bright, variegated color, began to appear on rock walls from about 6000 B.C.E. In Aboriginal tradition this figure is associated with both creation and destruction and with the quest of communities for unity and peace. Some scholars associate the coming of the Rainbow Serpent with long-term social instability and conflict that accompanied coastal flooding at the end of the last ice age.

to 8000 B.C.E. in which simple grave goods such as shells, kangaroo teeth, and pieces of ochre (used for body paint) appear to have identified deceased members of a particular community. Excavations also turned up human skulls with elongated shapes possibly formed by binding or massaging the heads of infants to give newborn members of the group a characteristic "look" that people in neighboring groups would not have. Also, as bands migrated throughout the continent, which extends nearly 2,500 miles from east to west, language communities diverged. At the time of European contact, Australians may have spoken more than 250 languages.

Scholars have pieced together enough material evidence to show that, between about 5000 and 6000 B.C.E., groups distant from one another exchanged a number of new ideas for making more delicate and versatile knives, spear points, barbs, drills, adzes (a thin blade attached to a handle), chisels, and grinding stones. In parts of the continent where population densities were relatively high, trade intensified, people from different bands joined in ceremonial gatherings, communities occupied camps along rivers or seashores for longer periods of time, and leaders with special social status started to emerge. Rock and cave art took on more distinctive features from one region to another. In religious life, people across most of Australia shared stories and beliefs about the creator spirit known as the Rainbow Serpent. Some researchers have argued that Aboriginal societies had to keep innovating, at least over the long term, because of the particular instability of Australia's climate. Like the Americas along the Pacific coast, the continent is subject to El Niño cycles, which increases the range of variability between wet and dry conditions over periods of years or decades.

A Continent without Farmers

Nowhere in Australia, however, did food-collecting strategies lead to plant or animal domestication and full-on agriculture. We have made the point in earlier chapters that in both Afroeurasia and the Americas societies became dependent for survival on domesticated plants and animals, not because they foresaw that farming and village living would turn out to be a great idea, but because they faced social stress related to climatic change, pressure on wild resources, or population growth that obliged them to experiment with ways to *produce* food systematically. Apparently nowhere in Australia did such stresses reach a level critical enough to induce

foods. In those conditions, communities had to create more complex social groupings and rules in order to determine which stretches of territory and its food resources belonged to which cooperating band. As in other parts of the world in paleolithic times, this competition for resources encouraged individual groups to mark themselves out from other bands by adopting distinctive dress, adornments, and perhaps speech habits. In the Murray valley, for example, archaeologists have discovered burial sites dating from 9500 serious efforts to domesticate plants. As for animals, the very large species of marsupials (mammals with pouches for carrying their young) that once roamed Australia all vanished during the Pleistocene as most large mammals did in the Americas somewhat later. Moreover, surviving species of kangaroos and their relatives have never proven susceptible to domestication. Australians did not take to farming even though people near the northern coasts probably knew something about it through contact with New Guinea.

This does not mean, however, that Aborigines never experimented with new ways of finding and processing food. In the southeastern interior, women and men used stones to grind wild seeds into flour as much as 35,000 years ago. In later millennia, groups in the north and east collected wild millet, the sort of activity that in the Fertile Crescent, Egypt, and China eventually led to grain domestication. From very distant times, cooperating bands engaged in what some scholars have called "fire stick farming." They deliberately burned areas of bush or grass in order both to flush out game and to speed the growth of new plants, some of which might be edible. Succulent growth also encouraged herbivorous animals to return, giving hunters opportunities to lie in wait to kill them.

Over tens of thousands of years, trade, migratory wanderings, and intermarriage among bands stimulated innovation in Australia life. But as long as population and wild food resources remained on the whole in balance, change moved at a more stately pace than it did in either Afroeurasia or the Americas. When Europeans first landed down under in 1788, the entire continent may have had a population of no more than 750,000. That number represents about six times fewer people than live in the Sydney metropolitan area today.

Pioneers on the Pacific Frontier

FOCUS How did humans succeed in colonizing many of the islands of Oceania between 1600 B.C.E. and 400 C.E.?

The eastern end of Afroeurasia was the jumping-off point for human colonization of both Australia and the Americas but also of many of the 25,000 islands that dot the Pacific Ocean. Geographers refer to this region of sea and scattered bits of land as Oceania, or sometimes the Island Pacific (see Map 4.5). Australia and the Americas existed as distinct "worlds" of human history for thousands of years partly because the land bridges that connected them with Afroeurasia disappeared. Oceania became a distinct region of settlement because the earliest colonizers migrated across such immense areas of open ocean that they lost touch not only with peoples of Afroeurasia, Australia, and the Americas but also, except where islands lay relatively closely together, with one another. The Pacific Ocean is 10,400 miles wide at the equator

and constitutes nearly a third of the earth's surface. As early explorers advanced in wooden boats eastward from maritime Southeast Asia, they found that the islands they landed on got progressively smaller and the sea gaps between them wider. The most distant frontiers that these migrants reached were the Hawaiian Islands in mid-Pacific and tiny Rapa Nui (RA-pa NEW-ee) in the far southwestern ocean. That crumb of land lies only about 2,600 miles west of Chile.

As European ship captains mapped Oceania in the nineteenth century, geographers categorized the islands into three primary groups—Melanesia, Micronesia, and Polynesia (see Map 4.1). This terminology remains in use, but scholars have also conceived more recently of a two-part division. One is Near Oceania, the islands in the western ocean just south of the equator, which include New Guinea and the Melanesian islands not far east of it. This region has close ecological affinities with maritime Southeast Asia, and humans occupied it sometime between 60,000 and 10,000 years ago. The other region is Remote Oceania, which includes all the rest of the Island Pacific and which humans did not colonize until between about 1600 B.C.E. and 400 C.E.—the end date representing the approximate arrival of seaborne migrants on the Hawaiian Islands and Rapa Nui. Near Oceania, being close to tropical Southeast Asia, has historically exhibited much diversity in plant and animal species. In Remote Oceania, by contrast, that diversity decreased progressively toward the east as the sea gaps between islands widened. Consequently, distant islands offered early settlers relatively meager natural resources or, if fresh water was lacking, no chance of settlement at all.

Colonizers of Near Oceania

By 8000 B.C.E., forager bands occupied Melanesia as far east as the Solomon Islands, which are located about five hundred miles east of New Guinea. The technology of these migrants definitely included seagoing canoes or rafts, though no trace of their design remains. Early Melanesians had a limited tool kit of stone and bone. They also made beads, arm rings, and fishhooks of shell. They set up camps, sometimes under rock outcroppings, of thirty or so people. We have evidence that inhabitants of the Bismarck Archipelago between New Guinea and the Solomons traded obsidian from one island to another. The populations of both New Guinea and the neighboring islands dispersed into numerous localized groups that tended to live in isolation from one another for long periods. We know this because of the extreme diversity of languages classified broadly as Papuan. Today, people in western Melanesia speak about 750 Papuan tongues, and until modern times there were probably more. The grammatical and word relationships among many of these languages are so distant that linguists have categorized them in something like sixty different language subfamilies.

In New Guinea, tropical forest highlanders domesticated bananas, yams, and taro from about 7000 B.C.E., that is, just a little later than Mesoamericans made their first experiments. The archipelagos east of the big island shared generally the same tropical climate and volcanic soils. This may partly explain why inhabitants of those islands, in contrast to the foragers of northern Australia, took up cultivation of New Guinea crops in subsequent millennia.

The coming of the Austronesians. Then, about 1600 B.C.E., a cultural transformation began to take place in Near Oceania. In Chapter 3 we described the long and complex movements of Austronesian-speaking farmers and fishers from China to Taiwan about 4000 B.C.E. and subsequently to the Philippines and Indonesia. Some of these migrants turned east, reaching the coastal lowlands of New Guinea, as well as the nearby Bismarck Islands. They brought with them a trunk load of crops, animals, tools, and ornamental designs previously unknown in Melanesia. This kit included stone adzes, polished chisels, shell decorative styles, dogs, chickens, and pigs. Austronesian speakers settled in larger hamlets than the older Papuan population had done, and they built rectangular dwellings, sometimes erecting them on stilts along the shoreline.

The Lapita people. Most famously, Austronesian speakers introduced distinctive red gloss pottery beautifully embellished with stamped geometric shapes. For archaeologists, this pottery style, called Lapita after a site in Southeast Asia where it was first discovered, came to epitomize the entire cultural complex associated with Austronesian newcomers. On the Bismarck and Solomon Islands and perhaps New Guinea, Lapita-making women and men intermarried with Papuan speakers already there. They also assimilated Papuan tools, ornaments, and crops such as yam and taro, producing, perhaps within decades, a new cultural synthesis having elements of both Papuan and Austronesian origin.

The era of the Lapita style lasted about 1,500 years, to about the first century C.E. During that time, Lapita people migrated farther east, colonizing islands that humans had never reached before, that is, westerly islands of Remote Oceania. Lapita pot shards have been discovered as far east as Samoa and Tonga, which are more than a quarter of the way across the South Pacific.

These mariners have left no material evidence of their boats or navigational lore. Very likely, however, their Austronesian forbearers brought a maritime technology from Southeast Asia including single- and double-outrigger canoes, double canoes, and triangular sails. (See the photo at the beginning of this chapter.) These craft were sturdy enough to inspire sailors to travel out of sight of land for days or weeks in search of new islands. An outrigger, a device presumably invented in Southeast Asia, was a heavy length of wood set parallel to a canoe some feet away from it and firmly attached to it with poles. The outrigger stabilized the canoe by preventing it from tipping either to port or starboard when a wave hit. A double-outrigger provided

A Lapita pot. This piece of Lapita ware, reconstructed from shards, comes from the Pacific island of New Caledonia. How may study of the geographical distribution of a particular pottery style help historians understand the direction and timing of ancient migrations?

even greater stability. Perhaps in outrigger boats equipped with sails and paddles, explorers discovered the Fiji archipelago around 1100 B.C.E. after crossing at least 527 miles of open ocean and most of the time bucking contrary winds and currents.

Maritime historians continue to wonder how these seafarers found their way to landfalls whose existence they could not have known in advance. These voyagers became experts at navigating by sun, moon, and stars, and they also observed the flight of birds, the characteristics of plant matter floating on the sea, and subtle alterations in current, wind, and temperature. Ancient mariners might willingly have taken great risks sailing into the trackless Pacific because their own experience told them that a great sea covered the whole surface of the world and that survival from one generation to the next depended on finding new bits of land that protruded here and there out of the water.

Into Remote Oceania

As sea migrants moved east and southeast to occupy Fiji, Tonga, Samoa, and other islands, they found that local biodiversity narrowed. But they successfully colonized new places because they piled their canoes with Lapita-era cargo, not only pots but also plants and seeds to grow root crops, vegetables, fruits, and nut trees. They also crammed in numerous tools, plus live pigs, chickens, and dogs. If they did not have obsidian, they substituted volcanic basalt, modifying tool designs to make cutters and scrapers from this hard stone. Obviously, both men and women had to travel to uninhabited islands if they intended permanent settlement. Recent genetic research suggests, however, that once a group planted a colony, women mostly remained at home while some males periodically sailed out to neighboring islands to trade or explore.

As colonizers fanned out across the deep, their Austronesian languages changed and multiplied. The western edge of Remote Oceania appears to have been the homeland of the Polynesian subfamily, which evolved into at least thirty-six tongues. Polynesian languages are linguistically closely related, indicating that, similarly to the Bantu languages in Subsaharan Africa, the dispersal of migrating groups from one island to another took place over the course of hundreds, not thousands of years. Recent DNA analysis of tissue samples of living Pacific islanders reveals close genetic relationships among all Remote Oceania's founding populations.

Pacific pioneers adapted ingeniously to a great variety of geographical and ecological settings, from low-lying atolls to towering volcanic islands. They also had to adapt to jarring swings in rainfall resulting from three- to seven-year El Niño cycles of change in Pacific surface temperatures. Remote Oceania did have the advantage of a milder disease environment, with fewer dangerous microorganisms. Colonists created a variety of social and political institutions, living in egalitarian foraging bands on some islands, forming small village communities in others, and, in a few places, including Tonga and eventually Hawaii, creating social hierarchies and chieftaincies.

Wherever they landed, they radically intervened in local environments in ways they did not consciously intend. Their rapidly multiplying pig populations voraciously consumed ground cover. Settlers quickly depleted forests in search of fuel and building material, and they routinely set fires to clear land for planting and grazing. Fire, farming, and deforestation caused chronic soil erosion, and it drove to extinction native plant and animal species that had flourished for eons. When they first arrived, hunters may have swiftly reduced native animal populations to feed themselves while they got their farms established. Studies on the large island of New Caledonia, for example, show

that particular species of crocodile, land snail, and turtle disappeared long ago. Also, the search for islands very likely continued, not because people liked to explore, but because settlers faced combinations of environmental degradation and population growth that forced some families to try to find new places to live. Some succeeded, others undoubtedly perished at sea in a vain search for land. In time, some island communities devised social rules and ritual taboos to protect animal species, slow forest loss, and limit childbirths. Others did none of those things and inevitably suffered.

Colonization of Remote Oceania reached as far east as Fiji, Tonga, and Samoa by about 1100 B.C.E. but then stopped for more than a thousand years. North and east of there, islands and archipelagos were mostly small and farther from each other. Perhaps the Lapita people, who traveled no farther than Samoa, took many centuries to regroup, strengthening their technologies and devising new sailing and navigating methods before daring to push on. At the start of the Common Era, for example, potters stopped making the finely decorated Lapita ware in favor of containers that were thicker, plainer, and more durable. It was also about then that long-distance migrations resumed, leading to the colonization of islands and island clusters farther to the east and northeast. Ironically, no humans reached the two much bigger islands that today comprise New Zealand until close to 1000 C.E.

Except for the mysterious sweet potato connection with South America that we described at the start of the chapter, the inhabitants of Remote Oceania lost all regular contact with the "worlds" of Afroeurasia, the Americas, and Australia. They also became more isolated from one another. No trans-Pacific network of maritime communication took form, and cultural and commercial exchanges between groups occurred within regions where islands were no more than a few hundred miles apart. In short, Remote Oceania did not become an arena of complex interactions of people, goods, and ideas comparable to Afroeurasia, the Americas, or even Australia. Nevertheless, Polynesian-speaking peoples settled the far reaches of the Pacific basin long before any known sailors crossed the much narrower Atlantic.

• • •

Conclusion

If we think of Hawaii, Rapa Nui, and New Zealand as final frontiers of humankind's colonization of the earth, then by the late first millennium C.E., people—unlike most animal species—lived almost everywhere, Antarctica excluded. As human groups starting from the eastern side of Africa girdled the planet, their networks of contact and exchange grew longer, denser, and busier. However, until five hundred years ago or even less, those networks had significant gaps. The world was not yet encased, as it is today, in a single, thick mesh of communication.

In this chapter we described the gaps that until recent centuries separated four macro-regions, four "worlds" of human interchange, from one another for thousands of years. These long-term communication breaks existed for several reasons. One was the disappearance of land bridges as Holocene sea levels rose. A second was that the connecting points between the macro-regions were so far apart as to discourage migration. Few Afroeurasians or North Americans other than locally adapted hunters had much incentive to travel between Siberia and Alaska. The far North Atlantic passage between North America and Europe was also unpromisingly frigid, though Eskimo-Aleut speakers sailed as far east as Greenland, and Vikings later made an abortive attempt to settle Newfoundland. Southeast Asian farmers who might plausibly have colonized northern Australia would have faced tough adaptation to deserts, marshes, and swamps. A third explanation for the gaps was the deficiency of maritime technology. Since the eastern Pacific is nearly devoid of islands, even the most skilled outrigger sailors were unlikely to have reached South America except by a fluke of winds and currents. And only in the fifteenth and sixteenth centuries C.E. did European shipbuilders and navigators figure out how to traverse the Atlantic and Pacific in both directions, and do it routinely.

Because of their mutual isolation for long eras, Afroeurasia, the Americas, Australia, and Oceania offer interesting laboratories for comparing social behavior and historical change.

First of all, it is clear the inhabitants of these four worlds did not come to behave in radically alien ways from one another. They all remained *Homo sapiens,* sharing all but a minute portion of their genes. The cultural and social differences among them became broad and deep but no more so than differences among peoples *within* a single macro-region who had no direct or regular contact with one another—Indonesians and Southwest Africans, for example. In all four worlds, the first colonizers adapted to and altered their environments by hunting and foraging with tools of stone. They all developed institutions of group cooperation to ensure day-to-day survival and to resolve conflict. And in all four, similar processes of linguistic and cultural division occurred as groups split off and migrated away from one another.

In three of the four regions, some people took up farming, though not all. Afroeurasians and Americans domesticated plants and animals independently of each other, though agriculture in the Pacific islands probably diffused entirely from Southeast Asia. After learning how to produce surplus food, Afroeurasians and Americans went on, in several places where ecological conditions permitted, to create complex societies featuring cities, states, social classes, monumental building, and other characteristics of dense living. In Oceania, signs of social complexity began to appear in places like Tonga and Hawaii, though strict limits on island populations prevented innovation on a grand scale. Australians did not become either farmers or city builders because they did not face serious ecological pressures urging them in that direction.

From a bird's-eye view, the most conspicuous difference among the four macro-regions is that Afroeurasia, the physically biggest of them, supported at, say, the start of the Common Era, as much as 95 percent of the globe's population. We return therefore to Afroeurasia in the next few chapters, recognizing that because of its numbers and dense networks of exchange the pace of social, technological, and human-induced environmental change accelerated faster there than in the other three regions.

• • •

Key Terms

Aboriginal society 109
Cerro Sechín 117
Clovis 120
Eastern Woodlands peoples 111
El Niño Southern Oscillation (ENSO) 111

Lapita 127
milpa 113
Norte Chico 114
Olmec 109
Poverty Point 122

San Lorenzo 118
terra preta 113
Tlatilco 117
Watson Brake 122

Change over Time

The Americas

8000 B.C.E.	Evidence of farming in Mesoamerica appears.
7000 B.C.E.	Maize is domesticated in Mesoamerica.
3400 B.C.E.	Mound construction takes place at Watson Brake, Louisiana.
3200 B.C.E.	City building emerges in Norte Chico region of Peru.
2200 B.C.E.	Farmers in the northern Andes region of South America begin to cultivate maize.
2000 B.C.E.	Evidence of plant domestication in eastern woodlands of North America appears.
1750 B.C.E.	Native Americans construct mounds at Poverty Point, Louisiana.
1500 B.C.E.	Evidence of pottery making in Mesoamerica appears.
1500 B.C.E.–400 B.C.E.	Olmec society flourishes in Mesoamerica.

Australia

60,000–35,000 B.C.E.	Humans colonize Australia and Tasmania.
9500–8000 B.C.E.	Evidence of human burials with symbolic grave goods in southern Australia appears.

Oceania

1600 B.C.E.–400 C.E.	Humans colonize Oceania as far as Hawaii and Rapa Nui (Easter Island).
1500 B.C.E.–1 C.E.	Lapita cultural style develops in Near and Remote Oceania.

Please see end of book reference section for additional reading suggestions related to this chapter.

part 2
Agrarian Societies and Their Interconnections
1200 B.C.E.–300 C.E.

A stone mask from Teotihuacán in Mesoamerica. The color tiles were added some 700 years after the original was carved.

In the late second millennium B.C.E., where we begin Part 2, agrarian societies were well established in several parts of Afroeurasia and the Americas. During the centuries that we explore in the next four chapters, no event transformed humankind's relationship to the natural and physical environment the way farming had done starting about eight thousand years earlier. Even so, the pace of change in the world continued to speed up, and relations among human communities, as well as between humans and the environment, became much more complex. Why did this happen?

A fundamental factor is that both agrarian and pastoral nomadic peoples spread into new parts of the world. And in places where agriculture already thrived in the late second millennium B.C.E., farmers coaxed higher yields from existing fields by selecting new plant hybrids, introducing new crops, and improving irrigation systems. A given acreage of land transformed into fields or pastures could support many more people and much more complex social and economic organization than the same acreage used only for hunting or foraging.

The pace of change also accelerated because societies in much of Afroeurasia, though not until much later in the Americas and Australia, mastered iron metallurgy. This development took place first in both Southwest Asia and East Africa around 1200 B.C.E. Once early users demonstrated how hard, sharp iron tools benefited farming and many other tasks, the technology spread rapidly across Afroeurasia. Wherever iron objects—axes, hoes, wheels, plows, horse gear, boat rigging, arrow points—came into common use, they permitted societies to alter and manage their environments on a larger scale. The coming of iron metallurgy represented a key turning point in the history of

Afroeurasian peoples. Five other major developments of the first millennium B.C.E. signified not sharp breaks with the past, but dramatic boosts in the scale of human activity and organization.

■ First, world population rose by around 137 million between 1000 B.C.E. and 200 C.E., about 23 million more in those 1,200 years than in the previous 7,000. Population growth of that order, most of it in Afroeurasia rather than the Americas, inevitably required more complex social organization and systems of exchange.

■ Second, cities, which had always been arenas of experimentation with class hierarchies, job specialization, government organization, religion, and social relations between men and women, continued to multiply and expand. In 1200 B.C.E., there were probably no cities in the world with more than 50,000 inhabitants. By 100 C.E. there were about thirty-five, the top two rankings going to Rome and Luoyang (China).

■ Third, as cities proliferated, so did routes of exchange. In several regions, cities became vibrant centers of manufacturing, artistry, learning, and finance, and they sent out tentacles of exchange to one another and to their own rural hinterlands. Merchants also linked cities thousands of miles from one another, trading in exotic goods and in the process exchanging technological skills and creative ideas.

■ Fourth, the number of city-states, centralized monarchies, and multiethnic empires in the world multiplied, and some empires became enormous. Leaders who controlled abundant agricultural surpluses invested heavily in soldiers, weapons, and communication systems, deploying them against their neighbors and enriching themselves even more. Several innovations of the first millennium B.C.E., including mass-produced iron weapons and armor, improved road networks, and more tightly organized chains of command, helped rulers build bigger empires.

By definition, empires incorporated peoples of varied languages, customs, social classes, and political interests. Rulers who strove to hold diverse populations together invariably faced uprisings, frontier attacks, and problems arising from massive military and administrative expense. Some empires therefore lasted longer than others. For example, Rome ruled the Mediterranean basin for several centuries, and in Mesoamerica, Teotihuacán endured as a city-state and empire for about 950 years. By contrast, the empire of Alexander the Great lasted just eleven years. Big empires stimulated urban growth, trade, and cultural creativity. They

also provoked great violence, exploited slaves, used up forests, and reinforced the social dominance of men over women.

In addition to empires founded on agrarian wealth, pastoral nomadic groups inhabiting the prairies and mountains of Inner Eurasia, where big crop surpluses could not be grown, founded powerful states of their own. Their sources of wealth were giant animal herds, trade with agrarian neighbors, and incessant raiding. It was in late centuries B.C.E. that pastoral nomads began for the first time to field armies of mounted archers mighty enough to threaten large agrarian states of China, India, or Southwest Asia.

■ Fifth, empire building, urbanization, and denser exchange networks all contributed to the emergence of new religions that appealed to men and women across cultural and social frontiers. From the later second millennium B.C.E., monarchs, priestly groups, and merchants began to propagate certain belief systems more widely. Brahmanism, the precursor of Hinduism, advanced across South Asia. Zoroastrianism made gains in Southwest Asia with the encouragement of Persian emperors. In China, the aristocratic land-owning class disseminated Confucianist ethics. After 500 B.C.E., first Buddhism, then Christianity emerged as genuinely universalist faiths, religions that appealed to individuals no matter their language, culture, class, or political loyalties. These two systems served men and women well in a time of increasingly complex inter-regional exchange because shared standards of worship and morality facilitated cooperation, fellowship, and trust among strangers. In both Mesoamerica and South America, people of different ethnic identities shared particular deities.

Estimated World Population in Millions

Part 2 1200 B.C.E. to 300 C.E.

5 Afroeurasia: Centers of Power, Trade, and New Ideas

1200–600 B.C.E.

Assyrian scribes taking records, royal palace at Nimrud, 730 B.C.E.

Today, about three hundred of the written languages in the world use the Latin alphabet or modified versions of it. Dozens of other languages use different alphabets such as Arabic, Cyrillic, or Bengali. An alphabet is fundamentally a set of signs: characters that correspond to distinct units of sound. The human vocal cords can emit only a limited number of individual sounds. An alphabetic system, therefore, requires no more than a few dozen signs to convert speech into letters written on paper or some other surface. These signs, however, may be combined and arranged in complex ways—into words, sentences, and paragraphs—to represent the nuances of human thought.

The invention of the first alphabets between about 1400 and 1200 B.C.E. represented an immensely important cultural development in world history. Earlier writing systems were much more complicated because they variously included numerous individual signs, some representing single sounds, other standing for syllable sounds, whole words, or even groups of words with a particular meaning. Ancient cuneiform writing, for example, had hundreds of individual signs. Learning such systems involved exhaustive education and great expense. A small child, however, could learn a set of alphabetic characters in a short time. Consequently, in the first millennium B.C.E., more people who did not have wealth or leisure began to learn to write. Literate men and women, though remaining small minorities in all societies, took part in recording knowledge and everyday information and sharing it with others, sometimes over long distances. Over several hundred years, alphabetic writing spread widely from Europe and North Africa across Southwest Asia to India.

This phenomenon was just one indication of accelerating social change and thickening networks of intercommunication in Afroeurasia in the approximate period from 1200 to 600 B.C.E. In the supercontinent as a whole, human population continued to grow at an accelerating pace. This happened as farming societies advanced into new regions, notably into tropical latitudes of Southeast Asia, southern India, and Africa. By contrast, forager bands commanded an ever-shrinking share of global territory. For reasons we will see, the total number of cities in Afroeurasia probably declined in the late second millennium B.C.E., but then began to grow and multiply again, especially in China, northern India, and the Mediterranean lands. On the political landscape, some ruling groups invented new military and organizational techniques for expanding their territories and collecting revenues from larger numbers of people. Small states and self-governing cities also proliferated, and merchant-adventurers founded new seaports that served as nodes of expanding trade networks. In Afroeurasia as a whole, a single trans-hemispheric web of routes gradually took form.

Most of these developments may be connected in one way or another to iron metallurgy, a momentous technological breakthrough that began to spread across Afroeurasia starting about 1200 B.C.E. (see Map 5.1). The first section of the chapter describes early iron making and its growing impact on farming, manufacturing, commerce, and war. We also survey the unintended effects that iron metallurgy began to have on physical and natural environments.

In the second part of the chapter we zoom in on the Mediterranean Sea and the lands around it, including Southwest Asia. Relative to the rest of Afroeurasia, this was a region of particularly intense human interchange associated with several interrelated developments. We first survey the crisis that beset the eastern Mediterranean in the twelfth century B.C.E., when aggressive bands that historians identify as Sea People threw the region, including Egypt, Syria, and the Aegean basin, into turmoil, ending an era of relatively orderly relations among several states. Out of this period of upheaval emerged the Neo-Assyrian empire, the first state to politically unite, at least for a short time, the whole region from the Tigris-Euphrates to the Nile. Also in the aftermath of the Sea People tumult, Hebrew-speaking inhabitants of the southern Levant (the lands along the eastern end of the Mediterranean) put forth the idea, peculiar for that era, that they ought to worship one deity as their protector and moral lawgiver, rather than a crowded hierarchy of gods and goddesses. These Israelites, as they became known, laid the foundations of monotheistic Judaism. Finally, in this part of the chapter we make a sweep around the Mediterranean and outlying regions, exploring the growth of trade and city building in the sea basin, the development of farming societies in Europe, and the rise of a powerful state in the Nile valley south of Egypt.

Chapter Outline

THE CLANG OF IRON

The Spread of Iron:
The Southwest Asian Epicenter
The Spread of Iron:
The Tropical African Epicenter
Iron's Benefits and Costs

WARFARE, EMPIRE BUILDING, AND TRADE IN SOUTHWEST ASIA AND THE MEDITERRANEAN LANDS

Twelfth-Century Troubles
The Neo-Assyrian Empire

INDIVIDUALS MATTER Adad-Guppi:
Babylonian Priestess and Queen Mother

The Hebrews and the Origins of Judaism
Phoenicians and Greeks: Trade and Migration
Woodland Europe and the Mediterranean World
Nubia on the Nile Corridor

SOUTH ASIA: A NEW ERA OF CITY BUILDING

New Cities and Kingdoms
The Development of the South Asian
Class System
Brahmins and Brahmanism

THE EAST ASIAN SPHERE

The Era of the Western and Eastern Zhou
Destruction and Innovation
during the Later Zhou Period

WEIGHING THE EVIDENCE The Book of Songs

• • •

The third section of the chapter takes us to South Asia, where in the late second millennium B.C.E. the Ganges River valley became the most dynamic center of population growth and urbanization, a process speeded by new iron metallurgy. The 1200–600 B.C.E. period witnessed social and cultural developments fundamental to later Indian civilization. One was formation of a distinctive way of organizing social class relations, known in later times as the caste system. The other was Brahmanism, a complex cluster of religious beliefs and practices that underlay the Hindu tradition of later millennia.

In the final section, we consider developments in East Asia, where at the end of the second millennium B.C.E. the Shang state, a monarchy of unprecedented size and endurance, fell to the Zhou (JOH) dynasty. The Zhou kings then built an even larger state, ruling for more than 250 years, an

A Panoramic View

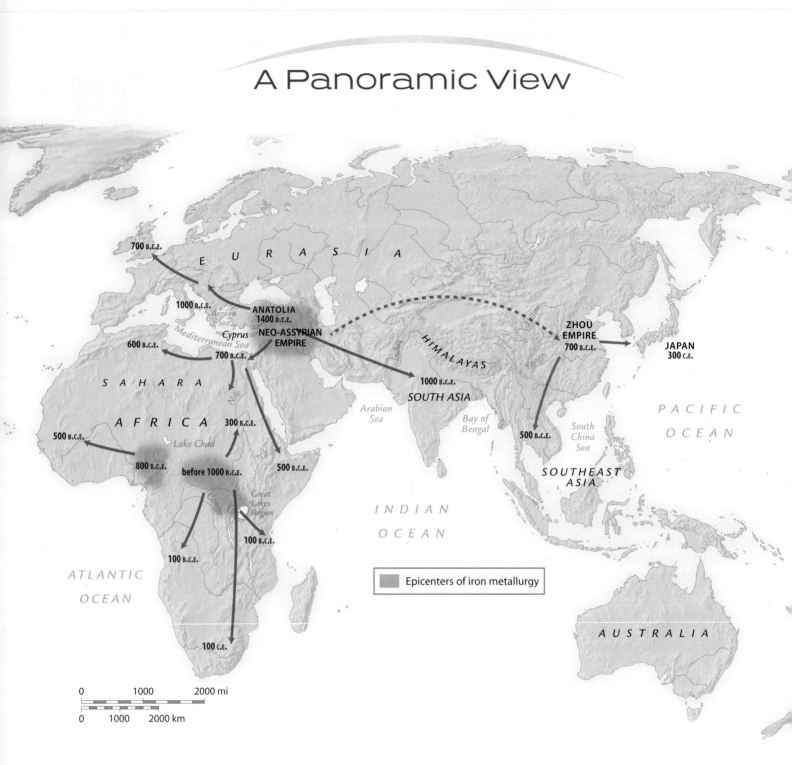

MAP 5.1 Major states and the spread of iron metallurgy, 1200–800 B.C.E.

The dotted line represents the likely route along which iron technology spread to China. What factors may have permitted the spread of iron-making across large distances in many regions of Afroeurasia?

era of population growth in the Yellow and Yangzi valleys related to agricultural innovations, including new iron tools. The trend of demographic and economic growth in China continued after 850 B.C.E., despite the Zhou royal family's loss of all but ceremonial authority over a collection of regional states, which warred with one another off and on for the next 450 years.

The Clang of Iron

FOCUS What part did iron metallurgy play in economic, environmental, or political change in Afroeurasia between 1200 and 600 B.C.E.?

History books have conventionally characterized 1200 to 600 B.C.E. as the "early iron age." This term highlights the initial effects of iron metallurgy on economy and society in Afroeurasia. On the other hand, the label may somewhat overstate iron's importance. For one thing, societies did not suddenly switch from copper and bronze to iron. Rather, both copper and bronze continued in use for a multitude of purposes, including sculpture, jewelry, armor, swords, spears, ship fittings, and numerous other handcrafted objects. Also, ironworking took several centuries to spread from region to region. Basic knowledge of iron metallurgy was one thing, but the creation of iron industries and related cultural changes took time. In every society that learned about the new technology, people had to find iron deposits, figure out ways to haul ore to smelters, tinker continuously with furnace efficiency, train young people for a new type of occupation, enlist merchants to distribute iron goods, convince rulers to buy iron armor and weapons, and persuade skeptical women and men to adopt hoes, knives, pots, pans, and other household tools made of the newfangled metal. Only from around 500 B.C.E. did iron become a primary workaday material in several parts of Afroeurasia. Finally, iron technology was not known in the Americas until the arrival of Columbus or in Australia until the late eighteenth century.

The Spread of Iron: The Southwest Asian Epicenter

The best available evidence indicates that people independently invented iron technology in as few as two places in the world. One of these founding centers was in Southwest Asia, the other in tropical Africa. The earliest evidence of iron smelting comes from eastern Anatolia (modern Turkey) about 1400 B.C.E. There, artisans who probably already possessed skills as bronze makers began to fashion iron ornaments and other objects on a small scale. Within about four hundred years, the Levant and the island of Cyprus became important centers of iron smelting. Subsequently, the new technology spread slowly into neighboring regions. Material evidence shows that both Egypt and the lands around the Aegean Sea began to make ironware on a significant scale by the seventh century B.C.E. Within about another hundred years, Chinese artisans were forging iron, and by the early centuries C.E. the technology reached Japan. Because East Asia had a long history of sophisticated bronze metallurgy, some scholars think that Chinese innovators made the leap to iron independently of developments in Anatolia. Others think the knowledge spread gradually from Southwest Asia eastward by way of routes across Inner Eurasia.

Like copper and tin, iron ore had to be transformed to make the metal useful. Early ironsmiths heated the ore with charcoal in an enclosed space, usually a pit with a facing of clay or stone and one or more pipes or tubes to allow air to reach the lower part of the smelter. The heated mixture produced a "bloom," a spongy mass of iron globules mixed with a slag of impurities. The smith then repeatedly reheated and hammered this substance to separate the iron from the slag and to shape the purified metal into an object of wrought, or "worked," iron. Because of bubbles and impurities, early iron tools cracked or shattered easily. In time, however, craftsmen adopted more exacting techniques, for example, dousing iron objects in cold water after each heating and hammering cycle to strengthen them.

Iron had definite advantages over bronze for a variety of uses. Iron ore is much more commonly available than copper and often lies close to the surface of the ground. Bronze industries also required tin, whose sources were limited and seldom anywhere near copper mines (see Chapter 2). Second, the relative abundance of iron lowered the cost of production and therefore the price of iron tools and weapons relative to bronze. Finally, iron masters learned to produce a metal that lasted longer and held a sharper edge than bronzeware. By experimenting doggedly, artisans found proportions of iron to carbon that produced steel, which had more tensile strength than wrought iron.

Around 700 B.C.E., Chinese artisans pioneered cast iron. That is, they liquefied the metal and poured it into molds to make numerous useful objects, including projectile points, pipes, and bells. Iron melts at 2800°F (1538°C), a temperature much higher than the melting point of copper. To get the desired results, Chinese inventors built larger furnaces with sealed interiors and fashioned bellows to blow air through pipes or shafts to regulate the flow and raise the internal temperature. Cast iron technology became known outside China only several centuries later.

The Spread of Iron: The Tropical African Epicenter

Scholars have firmly established that societies in one or two regions of tropical Africa invented ironworking independently of that development in Southwest Asia. Archaeological digs have revealed smelters in the Great Lakes region of east central Africa by 1000 B.C.E. or earlier and, farther west, in the area between Lake Chad and modern Cameroon by about 800 B.C.E. We do not know whether people in those regions acquired iron skills independently of each other or whether an earlier, so far undiscovered epicenter fed them both. We do know, however, that tropical Africans were making iron some centuries *before* the technology reached Egypt or other parts of northern Africa, so the technology is extremely unlikely to have come from Anatolia.

In contrast to the early metalsmiths in Southwest Asia, African furnace builders did not take any clues from bronze

Iron horse bit from central Europe. Substituting iron for bronze lowered the cost of horse harnesses in the first millennium B.C.E. This set of iron mouthpiece and bridle rings from the sixth century B.C.E. was found in the Czech Republic. Why do you think effective cavalry warfare depended on equipment like this?

making. Copper technology was already known in parts of Africa but not bronze. Tropical Africans simply skipped the bronze age, as it were. There is also evidence that iron masters of the Great Lakes region were the first in the world to design smelters hot enough to produce steel, at least in small amounts, without the additional process of heating, hammering, and quenching.

From the West African and Great Lakes epicenters, iron technology spread gradually throughout most of tropical Africa. In the course of the first millennium B.C.E., the technology advanced from the Cameroon–Lake Chad area westward to other societies of savanna and forest. The Great Lakes region was almost certainly the point from which iron and the numerous economic and social elements associated with it radiated throughout eastern, central, and southern Africa by the early centuries C.E.

The peoples inhabiting the Great Lakes neighborhood, a region that straddles the equator, presented a cultural kaleidoscope. They spoke myriad languages classified in four different major language families, and they practiced various combinations of farming, cattle raising, foraging, and hunting. Then, maybe a century or two after some villagers started experimented with ironworking, a new population arrived on the scene. These were farmers who migrated from the equatorial Congo River lands eastward to the forests rimming the Great Lakes. They spoke languages in the Bantu language group, and they had an agricultural economy based on yams (see Chapter 3).

During the centuries after 1000 B.C.E., the interaction of Bantu speakers with indigenous farming and herding peoples intensified, creating new cultural blends. Bantu farmers adopted local grain-growing methods, house styles, and iron techniques and tools. They also introduced new religious ideas centered on veneration of ancestors, a musical culture that emphasized polyrhythmic drumming, and a division of labor in which women took charge of both domestic and farm work. By about 400 B.C.E., population pressure on farm and grazing land began to force settled societies just west of the Great Lakes to consider new economic strategies. Some Bantu-speaking communities supplemented their yam crops with sorghum, finger millet, sheep, and cattle. Others, however, set out to find new land, toting their iron axes and hoes with them. These conditions signaled the start of an epic migratory drift that between about 300 B.C.E. and 300 C.E. introduced farming, cattle breeding, iron, and Bantu languages to the entire southern third of the continent. We return to the story of Bantu peoples in southern Africa in Chapter 13.

Iron's Benefits and Costs

In the first millennium B.C.E., people awoke gradually to the amazing utility of ironware—knives, spades, plowshares, swords, arrowheads, nails, wire, wagon wheel rims, keys, hooks, razors, and tubes for blowing glass. Using implements of iron rather than of stone, bone, or wood, workers found they could accomplish numerous specific tasks expending less time and energy. For example, a person could cut and shape hardwoods more economically using an iron axe, saw, and woodworking plane. These advantages also suggested many new uses for wood. Similarly, stonemasons who built temples, palaces, forts, city walls, and ordinary houses worked more efficiently and creatively once they had iron hammers, chisels, and wedges.

A barren hillside on the island of Crete. After farmers began smelting iron and adopting iron tools to expand cultivation, woodlands rapidly contracted throughout the Aegean Sea basin. Much of this deforestation remained permanent.

As smelting technology improved and production costs fell relative to bronze, iron tools came within the reach of ordinary farmers. In China, villagers started using cast iron plowshares as early as the sixth century B.C.E. In many places, rural women became prime consumers of iron pans, skillets, knives, and a host of food-preparing devices. States with armies continued to acquire various types of bronze weaponry throughout the first millennium B.C.E., but iron and steel gradually took precedence. Rulers wealthy and well organized enough to set up their own iron industries could supply their troops with spears, swords, and arrowheads at much lower prices than they had to pay for bronze. Pirates, bandits, and professional mercenaries became similarly equipped. Iron itself in the form of ore, sponge iron (directly from the furnace), bars, rods, and numerous wrought or cast wares became a major item of both local and interregional trade in most of Afroeurasia.

Iron tools permitted cultivators to alter the landscape faster and more extensively than in earlier times. As agricultural production rose in the first millennium B.C.E., so too did the rate at which farmers destroyed trees and other woody plants, the major component of the earth's **biomass.** Humans had been cutting forests since paleolithic times and witnessing the resulting flooding and soil erosion (see Chapter 2). A man or woman swinging iron, however, could fell a tree in a fraction of the time it took to do it using a stone axe. Iron power, combined with techniques of controlled burning, permitted farmers to clear land for planting or grazing more efficiently than ever before. Moreover, the iron smelters that

> **biomass** Plant matter, including wood, brush, straw, and animal waste, used especially as a source of fuel.

multiplied across Afroeurasia devoured enormous amounts of wood and its derivative charcoal. Consequently, wherever iron industries arose, local woodland disappeared in ever-widening circles. For example, in the area around Lake Victoria, the largest of East Africa's Great Lakes, pollen analysis shows that by the late first millennium B.C.E., land clearing combined with iron smelting had already consumed nearly all woodland. Based on a survey of the remains of ancient slag heaps, one scholar has estimated that from as early as the fifth millennium B.C.E., when copper was first liquefied, to the fourth century C.E., smelters in the Mediterranean region consumed fifty to seventy million acres of trees.[1] By 500 B.C.E., the lands around the eastern Mediterranean presented scenes of permanently denuded hillsides. Writing in the fifth century B.C.E., the philosopher Plato lamented the degradation of Greece's forests and soils, though he did not link it to smelting:

> There has never been any considerable accumulation of the soil coming down from the mountains, as in other places, but the earth has fallen away all round and sunk out of sight. The consequence is, that in comparison of what then was, there are remaining only the bones of the wasted body, as they may be called, . . . all the richer and softer parts of the soil having fallen away, and the mere skeleton of the land being left.[2]

The scale of biomass eradication in ancient times was small compared to the rate of global deforestation today. Nevertheless, metal technology strengthened human confidence in the idea that the earthly environment was a bountiful, limitless storehouse of resources to be extracted, managed, and transformed.

Warfare, Empire Building, and Trade in Southwest Asia and the Mediterranean Lands

FOCUS What historical developments contributed to increasing commercial and cultural interaction among peoples of Southwest Asia and the Mediterranean basin between 1200 and 600 B.C.E.?

Starting about 1200 B.C.E. and for the next six centuries, iron metallurgy spread from its creative epicenter in Anatolia westward to the Mediterranean and woodland Europe and eastward across Iran to India. The increasing complexity of human interchange that this diffusion involved was especially apparent along the belt of land and sea from the Tigris-Euphrates River valley (Mesopotamia) westward to the Atlantic shore. The peoples of this zone became more intricately meshed together in several ways. For a time in the twelfth and eleventh centuries B.C.E., a prolonged period of military upheaval around the eastern Mediterranean rim depressed trade and city growth, but this decline did not last.

Between the tenth and seventh centuries B.C.E., the rulers of Assyria in the northern Tigris River valley raised the craft of empire building to a new level. Assyrian kings subjugated and ruled more people representing greater linguistic and ethnic diversity than any earlier state had accomplished. In the lands beyond the Assyrian realm, Phoenicians, Greeks, and Etruscans built commercial networks that together extended across the Mediterranean and even reached into the Atlantic. As sea trade grew, more distant peoples of woodland Europe, North Africa, and the Nile River valley became firmly linked into the Mediterranean exchange web.

Twelfth-Century Troubles

Between the sixteenth and thirteenth centuries B.C.E., the cluster of empires and kingdoms occupying the land between the Nile and the Tigris-Euphrates worked out a reasonably practical strategy for getting along with one another. The largest of these states were New Kingdom Egypt, the northern Euphrates valley state of Mitanni, Babylonia and Assyria on the Tigris, and the Hittite empire (Hatti) of Anatolia. These monarchies periodically went to war over territory and resources, but they also invented informal rules for exchanging envoys, negotiating peace, and carrying on trade (see Chapter 3). Then, in the twelfth century B.C.E., this promising system of international relations disintegrated amid widespread violence. For more than a century, Southwest Asia, Egypt, and the Aegean basin experienced upheavals that today's historians, disadvantaged by scanty documentation from the period, continue to struggle to understand.

Mysterious Sea People. Catastrophe descended quite suddenly. In the course of half a century, assailants sacked and burned nearly fifty towns and cities from the Aegean

MAP 5.2 Sites of Sea People attacks, 1200–900 B.C.E.

Does the spatial distribution of the cities that Sea People attacked suggest where these invaders might have originated?

basin to the northern Tigris-Euphrates. We have yet to identify these city burners precisely. One theory argues that usually peaceful farmers and herders of the eastern Mediterranean and its hinterlands went on the warpath owing to drought, famine, or rulers' heavy tax demands.

Another theory highlights new weapons technology. Strong states that deployed well-disciplined infantries and chariot forces usually kept pirates, bandits, hired mercenaries, peasant rebels, and other troublemakers under control or at arm's length. In the mid-second millennium B.C.E., wealthy states had a near monopoly on chariots because vehicles, horses, weapons, and skilled fighters cost a great deal to maintain. Chariot squadrons, together with trained infantry, could usually limit threats from poorly armed brigands and insurgents.

By the thirteenth century B.C.E., however, unruly groups that lived beyond the easy reach of disciplined armies began to adopt a new technology of infantry warfare. It included several elements: tough metal or leather body armor, sturdy round shields, short javelins, and long bronze swords with sharply tapered ends designed for both thrusting and slashing. Fighters who could never afford chariots outfitted themselves as foot soldiers at reasonable cost. Not only did they carry lethal weapons; they also devised new battlefield tactics for surrounding and attacking chariots with javelins and swords. This new war kit appears to have spread around the eastern Mediterranean quite rapidly, though iron weaponry did not replace bronze until later centuries.

This new chariot-challenging weaponry appears to have intersected with another development, the gradual weakening of the established kingdoms and city-states of the region between the Aegean and the Tigris-Euphrates. These states waned under any of a number of possible pressures—food shortages linked to long-term drought, top-heavy and oppressive governments, forced transfer of land from peasants to wealthy classes, or revolts by discontented mercenary solders. Both New Kingdom Egypt and the Hittite empire, for example, had sumptuous royal courts, numerous paid officials, and expensive chariot and infantry forces. The ordinary folk who paid for this magnificence with their taxes and labor had little incentive to support their rulers against sudden intruders.

The throngs that began burning cities around 1200 B.C.E. do not appear to have come from any single direction. Sometimes they moved as large groups of male fighters, sometimes as crowds of women, children, and armored men. In the Aegean, raiding bands attacked Troy, Mycenae, and many other cities. They effectively obliterated the urban Mycenaean society that had flourished for three centuries (see Chapter 3). South of the Mediterranean, seaborne fighters sailed from Libya to Egypt to strike the Nile delta. In Anatolia and Syria, marauders sacked several Hittite cities and brought that once great monarchy to its knees.

Mass bands of swordsmen that historians have named the Sea People, a deliberately vague term reflecting the mystery over their identity and origin, attacked and destroyed at least eighteen cities in Syria and the Levant (see Map 5.2). In a surviving letter on a clay tablet, the king of Alashiya, a state on Cyprus, advised the ruler of Ugarit, one of the leading commercial cities on the Levantine coast, to prepare for an attack: "Where are your troops and chariots? Are they not with you? If not, who will deliver you from the enemy? Surround your cities with walls and bring your troops and chariots into them. Watch out for the enemy and reinforce

A sea battle at the mouth of the Nile. Egyptian forces repelled both Libyan and Sea People incursions into the Nile delta. This relief on a wall of Pharaoh Ramses III's mortuary temple in Luxor commemorates an Egyptian naval victory over Sea People in 1178 B.C.E. In this chaotic scene of shipboard combat, the warrior's horned helmet identifies him as a Sea People marauder. What do we learn from this scene about Sea People weaponry?

yourself well." In reply, Ugarit's ruler exclaimed that attacks had already started: "the ships of the enemy have been coming. They have been burning down my villages and have done evil things to the country."[3] Ugarit was subsequently demolished and not rebuilt for a thousand years.

Raiders who penetrated Southwest Asia appear to have operated in several independent groups. Some Sea People looted and burned cities and villages, then went away. One band of assailants, known from the Old Testament Bible as the Philistines, sacked and burned cities of Canaan, the ancient name for the southern part of the Levantine coast. Those invaders eventually faded from history, though they live on in the regional name "Palestine."

The aftermath. From the smoke and ash of the twelfth-century B.C.E. catastrophe came three important changes. One was a rapid if temporary economic decline in the eastern Mediterranean basin as states fell and bustling ports disappeared. Evidence of shrinking wealth comes from the remains of elite graves in the region. During and after the troubles, a single sword or spear point might accompany a dead aristocrat rather than an assortment of bronzeware and other precious objects. A second change was the decline of the chariot as anything other than a vehicle for racing and royal display. Rulers relied increasingly on well-disciplined foot soldiers equipped with long swords, javelins, and stabbing spears made of either bronze or iron.

A third consequence of the mayhem was a large power void in Southwest Asia. The Egyptian pharaohs withdrew from the Levant and Syria and fell back to the Nile. The Hittite empire gave way to a set of much weaker successor kingdoms. Similarly, Assyria had to defend its Tigris River valley cities against attacks from both mountain people and desert nomads. Assyria, however, held up better than any other Southwest Asian state.

The Neo-Assyrian Empire

Indeed, in the mid-tenth century, Assyria asserted itself as a regional power, in fact as one of the ancient world's greatest empires. One important trend of the first millennium B.C.E. in several parts of Afroeurasia was the effort of rulers to invent more effective ways to organize, integrate, and extract wealth from conquered people. In other words, kings created more powerful and efficient systems of command. Following the Sea People episode, Assyria typified this trend. The Tigris valley, an agriculturally rich and populous region encompassing both rain-watered and irrigated land, supported large military investment. Starting with King Ashurdan II in 934 B.C.E., monarchs headquartered at Ashur on the west bank of the Tigris (today in northern Iraq) dispatched armies far and wide, filling the Southwest Asian power vacuum (see Map 5.3). Assyrian forces even invaded Egypt and occupied it for about twenty years. For more than a century, it ruled Babylonia in southern Mesopotamia and generally looked to the great city of Babylon for proper standards of art, architecture, literature, and cuneiform writing. As the

Neo-Assyrian empire grew, wealth poured in from plunder, taxation, and interregional trade. These riches fueled an impressive infrastructure of military and political communication and an ever bigger, increasingly ironclad army.

The new era of the horse soldier. Neo-Assyria was also the first major state we know of to deploy horse **cavalry.** Fighters had been launching raids on horseback on the Inner Eurasian steppes since the fourth millennium B.C.E. But only after about 900 B.C.E. did rulers begin to organize units of mounted soldiers that would behave like trained infantry, that is, respond without hesitation to the commands of officers and to maneuver as a team on a field of battle.

> **cavalry** The part of a military force trained to fight mounted on horses or camels.

Cavalry combat became effective, however, only after several innovations were introduced. Charioteers had been fighting with bows and arrows for several centuries, including bows made both lighter and stronger by fusing strips of wood or bone together. Sometime after 1000 B.C.E., artisans began to shorten the length of these composite bows so that horse soldiers could more nimbly swing the weapon around and even fire to the rear of their mount. Arrows and arrowheads were also standardized and made more compact so that every rider could carry dozens of them, permitting well-trained cavalry to fire a blizzard of projectiles. The Assyrian army imported thousands of horses from Anatolia, Iran, and Inner Eurasia and taught riders how to move and fight in coordination with infantry. Even though saddles and stirrups had yet to be invented, mounted troops could travel faster and maneuver with greater alacrity than chariots. The cost of mobile warfare also decreased, and within a few hundred years, cavalry almost completely replaced massed chariots throughout Afroeurasia.

The Neo-Assyrian command system. Neo-Assyria not only grew to enormous territorial dimensions but also achieved remarkable success at politically integrating diverse peoples. Building on earlier models of centralized command in Mesopotamia, the state introduced a number of institutions to concentrate and systematize its power. For example, the kings promoted an elaborate ideology of themselves as possessors of absolute, unquestionable authority over everyone else. They represented themselves as sacred deputies of Ashur, the Assyrian high god, though they did not, in contrast to the Egyptian pharaohs, claim to be deities themselves. They typically took personal charge of planning and leading wars of conquest, extolling themselves as superheroic warriors. They meted out mercy and vengeance as they pleased, and they terrorized their enemies as a policy calculated to encourage negotiation and surrender. Assyrian conquerors treated resistance and disloyalty with all manner of cruelty, piling up decapitated heads and skinning hapless victims alive. The emperors recorded these deeds on numerous stone inscriptions. Concerning an expedition to the Euphrates and the Levant, King

MAP 5.3 States, cities, and trade routes of the Mediterranean region, 1000–600 B.C.E.
Why do you think geographers have described the Mediterranean as many seas rather than one?

Ashurnasirpal II (r. 883–859 B.C.E.) had this boast inscribed: "While I was in the city of Aribua [in Syria], I conquered the cities of the land of Luhutu. I killed many of them [i.e., the inhabitants]. I demolished; I destroyed; I burnt with fire. I captured soldiers alive by hand. I impaled [them] on stakes in front of their cities."[4]

From this authoritarian platform, the emperors organized the expanding empire. They divided it into provinces over which they appointed regional governors and military officers staunchly loyal to the throne. In this way they bypassed to some extent the established land-owning families, who might be tempted to put their own local interests ahead of those of the state. The queens and royal daughters of Assyria did not, so far as we know, hold formal offices, but they controlled immense agricultural estates and on at

least a few occasions held the government together in times of internal conflict over the royal succession.

Effective command, as always, depended on good communication. Conscripting laborers from around the empire, the government built a system of roads that unified the Tigris-Euphrates valley and connected the imperial heartland to the urban centers of Syria and the Mediterranean coast. Commodities and luxury goods passed into and through the empire from every direction: textiles and horses from Babylonia, incense and spices from the Arabian peninsula, horses and tin from Persia, silver and iron from Anatolia, timber and glass from the Levant, gold from Egypt.

The Assyrians also tried to integrate the empire by forcefully moving and resettling large numbers of people, mainly from conquered territories to the central region. The

A royal scene from the Neo-Assyrian capital. King Ashurbanipal (r. 668–630 B.C.E.) and his queen relax in a garden following his victory over Teumman, the ruler of the enemy state of Elam. On a tree at left the severed head of Teumman hangs by its nose. How does this palace carving from Nineveh communicate the idea that the king has restored peace to his realm?

state implemented this policy ruthlessly in order to place tens of thousands of military recruits, road builders, farm workers, and skilled artisans where it wanted them. As merciless as this practice was, it likely produced greater cultural mixing than occurred in any earlier large state. This does not mean, however, that the empire's numerous ethnic groups all identified culturally with their rulers. From start to finish Assyria was an **authoritarian monarchy.** Its kings collaborated with loyal lieutenants and aristocratic families to pump revenue from the farming and herding population, and then spent it to augment government power and the elite's extravagant lifestyle. Assyria generally sustained this system of domination for more than three centuries, foreshadowing even mightier empires to follow.

> **authoritarian monarchy** A state, headed by a king, a queen, or an emperor, whose ruling class demands strict authority over the rest of the population.

Under the pressures of frontier attacks and provincial revolts, however, Assyria rapidly declined in the early seventh century B.C.E. The fatal blow came from Babylonia, a state subjugated to dependence on Assyria. In 610 B.C.E., a resurgent Babylonia under the military leadership of King Nebuchadnezzar II (neb-uh-kud-NEZ-er, r. 605–562 B.C.E.) sent forces up the Tigris valley, destroyed the Assyrian capital of Nineveh, and brought down the empire. Nebuchadnezzar then organized a new Mesopotamian state and undertook vigorous conquests of his own to seize nearly all the territories that Assyria once held. This Neo-Babylonian empire, as historians call it, did not, however, last much past Nebuchadnezzar's reign.

The Hebrews and the Origins of Judaism

Two of the states the Assyrians attacked in the seventh century B.C.E. were Israel and Judea, small kingdoms located in the fertile hill country of Canaan, identified with the southern part of the Levant (see Map 5.3). In this region, speakers of Hebrew, one of the Semitic languages of Southwest Asia, laid the foundations of Judaism and the Jewish cultural identity. In contrast to other societies of Southwest Asia, the Hebrews came to worship a single god, named Yahweh (YAH-way), rather than numerous deities. That is, they professed **monotheism,** though Yahweh came to be understood only gradually as God the creator of the universe and humankind, rather than one local deity competing with others for allegiance.

> **monotheism** The doctrine or belief that there is one supreme and universal deity.

Over several hundred years, Hebrew-speaking scholars compiled numerous long books about the origin and early history of their people—chronicles, poems, and the orations of prophets all centered on the often contentious relationship between the Hebrews and Yahweh. This collection of writings, which we know as the Hebrew Bible, or in the Christian tradition as the Old Testament, constitutes a more detailed, vivid historical account than we have of probably any other ancient society. Early Hebrew history, however, remains a challenge for scholars because the Bible is the sole source of almost all we know about it. Only from about the sixth century B.C.E. does evidence independent of the Bible begin significantly to enrich the ancient history of the Jews.

The Ishtar Gate in Babylon. This is a twentieth-century artist's depiction of a ritual procession passing through the Ishtar Gate, one of the entryways to Babylon constructed in the reign of Nebuchadnezzar II. Dedicated to the goddess Ishtar, a reconstructed version of the gate may be seen today in the Pergamon Museum in Berlin. What sources of information could an artist use to render the Babylonian cityscape as it might have looked in the sixth century B.C.E.?

From Hebrews to Israelites. From the Bible, as well as inferences made from other sources, historians have hypothesized that sometime between about 1300 and 1100 B.C.E. the Hebrews emerged as a confederation of extended kinship groups, or tribes, in Canaan. There they became known as Israelites, in the Bible as the Twelve Tribes of Israel. The Hebrew emergence may well be associated with the Sea People invasions, which rid the Levant of Egyptian or Hittite domination and opened the way for local populations to form a number of alliances, small kingdoms, and city-states. However, the biblical account, which begins with the Book of Genesis and Yahweh's creation of the world, explains Hebrew origins in terms of the careers of numerous special individuals—mostly men but some women. These figures struggle to fulfill a covenant with God to obey his commandments and lead exemplary lives

of morality and virtue, though some accomplished that task more successfully than others. In fact, it is the narratives of Hebrew leaders backsliding and then redeeming themselves in the eyes of God that give the Hebrew Bible its dramatic force and moral power.

Among the larger-than-life biblical figures are Abraham, the founding patriarch, or father, of the monotheistic tradition. According to Genesis, he was born in the ancient Mesopotamian city of Ur, but Yahweh promised him possession of the Land of Canaan. As Genesis recounts, Abraham started for Canaan with his family and other companions:

> The LORD had said to Abram, "Go from your country, your people and your father's household to the land I will show you.
> I will make you into a great nation,
> —and I will bless you;
> I will make your name great,
> —and you will be a blessing."
> So Abram went, as the LORD had told him; . . . He took his wife Sarai, his nephew Lot, all the possessions they had accumulated and the people they had acquired in Harran, and they set out for the land of Canaan, and they arrived there.[5]

Other biblical luminaries include Joseph, who was sold into slavery by his brothers and taken into Egypt; Moses, who led the Hebrews out of enslavement in Egypt and received from God the Ten Commandments, a set of absolute moral laws; and Joshua, who finally guided the Hebrews into Canaan, conquering that land and dividing the territorial spoils among the Twelve Tribes, from this point known as the Israelites. According to scripture, God promised this chosen people prosperity and large families for generations to come. The Israelites, however, had to abide by God's sacred law, which in time came to include not only the Ten Commandments but also rules for eating, dress, sacrificial rituals, marriage, sex, property inheritance, crime, and other spheres of collective life. Many of these laws echoed the legal systems of early states in Mesopotamia.

Scholars transcribed and edited Hebrew scriptures from oral accounts, a process that went on for hundreds of years. Consequently, the question of who actually formulated the Jewish theology expressed in scripture and when they did it has been the subject of much learned debate. The Hebrew Bible represents God as a person, rather than as an abstract cosmic force. But it also proclaims him to be utterly transcendent, above and beyond nature. This idea of God contrasts strikingly with the religions of ancient Mesopotamia or Egypt, where different elements of nature—sun, moon, rain, lightning—are associated with particular gods or goddesses. For example, in Mesopotamian tradition the sun was the particular deity Shamash, but in Hebrew scripture the sun is merely an instrument of God. In the ancient **polytheistic** belief systems, divine beings

polytheism A belief system that incorporates multiple deities or spirits.

Adad-Guppi: Babylonian Priestess and Queen Mother

This stele is dedicated to the Neo-Babylonian ruler Nabonidus, son of Adad-Guppi. Just to the right of the king's staff is the circular symbol of the moon god Sin.

Nabonidus, the last king of Neo-Babylonia, came to power with the help of his aged mother Adad-Guppi, a priestess devoted to the moon god Sin. This woman lived for more than a hundred years, a remarkable achievement for anyone in the first millennium B.C.E. She witnessed the fall of the Assyrian empire, lived through the forty-year reign of Nebuchadnezzar, and saw her son mount the Babylonian throne when she was in her nineties.

None of the three kings who followed Nebuchadnezzar held power in Babylon for long. They all came and went within six years of his death. However, Nabonidus, the fourth king, enjoyed a longer reign—seventeen full years. When he fell, so did the short-lived empire.

Nabonidus was not a member of the Babylonian royal family. But apparently through the efforts of Adad-Guppi, who had served in the temple of Sin in the Euphrates city of Harran, he held posts in the courts of both Nebuchadnezzar and his son. This career apparently gave him the connections he needed to seize power when the opportunity came. Since the previous king had reigned for only a month, scholars have speculated that Nabonidus had him murdered.

When Nebuchadnezzar's forces seized Harran in 601 B.C.E., the temple of Sin had been destroyed and the statue of the god taken away. Adad-Guppi made it her prime mission in life to see the god restored and the temple rebuilt. Once Nabonidus ascended the throne, he fulfilled his mother's wish.

All that we know about Adad-Guppi comes from two stelae erected at the rebuilt temple, which display what are claimed to be her autobiography, plus a short postscript describing her death. We cannot be sure that she composed the autobiographical text herself, but it may nonetheless express her own experiences and opinions. She recounts her longtime devotion to the gods, particularly to Sin, and to the sacrifices she made after Sin "became angry with his city and his temple and went up to heaven," that is, when the temple was destroyed. By demonstrating her piety, she hoped to convince the deities to return to their temple: "In order to calm the heart of my god and my goddess, I would not wear a fine wool dress, gold or silver jewelry, a new garment, nor would I let perfume or sweet oil touch my body, [but] I wore a torn garment and my clothing was sackcloth."

The inscription recounts that owing to Adad-Guppi's dedication to Sin, the god had chosen her son to lead the Neo-Babylonian empire. In turn, Nabonidus showed his own reverence for Sin by rebuilding the temple in Harran and making it a major religious center. According to Adad-Guppi, "Sin, king of the gods, made me live one hundred and four good years. . . . I myself, the sight of my two eyes is sharp and my comprehension is excellent, my hands and feet are healthy and my words are well chosen, food and drink agree with me, I am in good health, my heart is full."

When Adad-Guppi died in the ninth year of Nabonidus's reign, the text's postscript explains that he led the entire Neo-Babylonian empire in mourning: "He assembled [the people] of Babylon. . . . He [had them] mourn and . . . they made lamentation. They cast [dust] on their heads for 7 days and 7 nights; they murmured; their clothes were cast off. On the seventh day, the people of the entire land cut their hair." Nabonidus ruled another eight years or so after his mother's death. But then Persians invaded Mesopotamia, deposed him, and eliminated the Neo-Babylonian dynasty.

Adad-Guppi's autobiography in stone has transmitted to modern scholars important insights into the influential roles that elite women might play in ancient imperial politics, as well as the complex interplay between political and religious life.

Thinking Critically

What do the inscriptions about Adad-Guppi's long life tell us about the influence of elite women in Neo-Babylonian royal politics?

Source: Mark W. Chavalas, ed., *Historical Sources in Translation: The Ancient Near East* (Malden, MA: Blackwell, 2006), 389–393.

behave unpredictably and indifferently toward human beings. In Hebrew scripture, God cares deeply about his creation and continually uplifts his people in body and spirit.

God's people, however, had to accept full responsibility for the divine covenant, abiding by his moral commandments not just as individuals but also collectively as a society. God governs the universe, but humans must make a choice for social order rather than chaos by upholding God's laws. In the polytheistic systems of the first millennium B.C.E. and later, humans constantly tried to persuade various deities to behave reasonably and not make human troubles worse than they were. By contrast, Hebrew scripture is suffused with the tension between God's promise of protection and prosperity and his people's often-faltering efforts to build a society that deserves God's blessings. This idea of a covenant between God and humankind was to be carried into Christianity and Islam, the other two faiths founded on Abraham's dedication to one god.

A Hebrew seal from Jerusalem. This stone seal dating to the seventh century B.C.E. may have belonged to a Hebrew military officer. He depicts himself as an archer and gives his name in Hebrew characters as Hagab. The decorative style shows strong Assyrian influence.

Phoenicians and Greeks: Trade and Migration

Between 1200 and 600 B.C.E., communication networks stretching from South Asia to the Atlantic Ocean became denser and more tightly interlocked. The Mediterranean basin was a particularly busy zone of commercial and cultural interaction. For the first time, sea travelers connected all the lands around the rims of the Mediterranean and the Black Seas. From ports on those seas, merchants exchanged goods with overland traders, who trekked into the deep hinterlands of Europe and northern Africa.

An important transition also took place in the conduct of trade, notably in the Mediterranean. Since at least the third millennium B.C.E., individuals engaged in commerce typically operated as employees, or agents, of rulers. They also took part in expeditions that rulers organized mainly to obtain luxury goods for temple priesthoods, royal palaces, or wealthy households. New Kingdom Egypt is a classic case of merchants acting as agents of the government, which dispatched and paid for commercial expeditions in the name of the pharaoh.

Unity and expansion, division and exile. From the tenth to the sixth centuries B.C.E., the story of the Israelites was in large part a history of state politics, war, and finally catastrophic defeat. About 1000 B.C.E., the Twelve Tribes united under King Saul. David and Solomon, Saul's successors, led the Israelites in capturing the small hill city of Jerusalem, naming it their capital, building a temple, fielding a chariot army, extending the state's borders, and encouraging trade with neighbors. Owing to unresolved conflicts among the tribes, however, the monarchy split into two following Solomon's death in 922 B.C.E., the kingdom of Judah in the south, which included Jerusalem, and the kingdom of Israel in the north.

In 722 B.C.E., however, the Assyrian army defeated Israel and sent much of its population to other parts of the empire. The Assyrians also invaded Judah, but the Israelite prophet Isaiah assured its ruler Hezekiah that "Jerusalem shall not be given into the hand of the king of Assyria."[6] Indeed, Assyria finally gave up its siege of the city, though Judah paid it tribute. Then, in 610 B.C.E., the reenergized kingdom of Babylonia eradicated Assyria and went on to capture Jerusalem and burn down its temple. The conquerors also exiled the entire Israelite population to Babylonia, ending the first long chapter in the history of the Hebrews, known increasingly from that time as the Jews.

In the early first millennium B.C.E., however, statemanaged trade generally declined in importance while private enterprises multiplied. More individuals and small groups of partners traded on their own accounts as entrepreneurs, investing in private ventures with the aim of making personal profit. This change was certainly linked to the rise of both farming and urban populations around the Mediterranean rim. Ordinary people could not afford lapis lazuli jewelry or ivory statues, but they went to the local market to buy imported grain, oil, wine, or cloth. Unlike state commercial agents who served exclusively the consumer needs of the rich, private merchants had potentially much bigger markets. This encouraged them to search for new sources of goods and for new populations to sell them to. In this way, the Mediterranean web of exchange grew in all directions.

Phoenicians and their trading posts. The eastern Mediterranean lands took decades to recover from the twelfth-century B.C.E. city burnings. Assyria's imperial expansion was one sign of that recovery. Another was the commercial revival of ports on the Levantine coast, the strategic interface between the Mediterranean basin and Southwest Asia. A string of towns along the central coast (mainly in what

A Phoenician war galley. This coin from a city on the Levantine coast commemorates Phoenician naval power. In what ways might a vessel powered by rowers be tactically superior to a sailing ship in Mediterranean naval warfare?

Art from Carthage. Phoenician artisans began making terra-cotta masks like this one in the seventh century B.C.E. This grimacing male figure has decorative disks on his forehead and cheeks. Participants in religious rituals or theatrical productions may have worn the masks. Archaeologists have also found them in tombs. Why do you think a person might have wanted to be buried with a mask like this one?

is now Lebanon) somehow escaped the scourge of the Sea People. Their inhabitants, known generally as Canaanites and more specifically as Phoenicians, manufactured and traded textiles, bronzework, pottery, glassware, ivory-inlaid furniture, and other fine wares. The Phoenicians, occupying notably the ports of Tyre, Sidon, and Byblos, spoke a Semitic language closely related to Hebrew (see Map 5.3).

Phoenician merchants extended their lines of trade across the Mediterranean, motivated by both economic recovery and the rise of Assyria as a voracious consumer of metals, timber, and luxury wares. In the ninth and eighth centuries B.C.E., Phoenician vessels sailed far to the west, erecting trading posts on Sicily, Sardinia, and other islands, as well as along the coasts of North Africa and Iberia (Spain). There, Carthage and Cadiz merged as the leading centers. Phoenicians even planted several colonies west of the Strait of Gibraltar, thereby becoming the first traders to link the Mediterranean with nearby Atlantic coastlands. In return for their manufactures, Phoenician merchants shipped tons of silver from mines in Iberia, much of this precious metal reaching Egypt or Assyria. They also transported iron, copper, tin, wine, olive oil, and slaves from numerous Mediterranean ports. Shipwrights in the Levantine ports, using cedar wood from the mountains of Lebanon, built seagoing vessels big enough to transport bulky, heavy commodities. Powered by large square sails and single or double banks of rowers, these vessels crisscrossed the Mediterranean in the summer months, when seas were usually calm and when the visible sun and stars aided navigation. In winter frequent storms and cloudy skies limited trade except close to shore.

Gradually, the Phoenician ports in the western Mediterranean loosened their ties with the Levant and emerged as independent city-states. By the eighth century B.C.E., Carthage, the key port in North Africa, ruled several satellite towns and a large area of backcountry in what is now Tunisia. The Berber-speaking farming and herding peoples of this hinterland appear to have adapted quickly to the Phoenician newcomers because they also benefited from growing maritime commerce.

The Phoenician expansion may best be understood as an early example of a **commercial diaspora,**

commercial diaspora
Merchants who share cultural identity but who live among alien communities to operate networks of trade.

that is, a scattering of merchants and their trading posts across a region where they made up only a small part of the population. Generally speaking, the members of a diaspora who settled among alien groups fulfilled two related functions. First, they acted as commercial agents for fellow merchants who moved back and forth along the maritime trade routes. These agents offered visiting traders lodging, places to store their goods, loans, up-to-date price information, and local commercial contacts. Second, they served as cultural go-betweens, learning the language, politics, and business etiquette of indigenous people in order to facilitate negotiations with local traders and help close deals. Briefly put, commercial diasporas lubricated exchange between people who otherwise lacked common speech, cultural expectations, or good reasons to trust one another. In time, diasporas took shape in many parts of the world where long-distance trade was important.

Greeks and their colonies. Greek-speaking merchants and migrants also moved out across the Mediterranean. At least partly because of the devastations of Sea People, the early Mycenaean Greek civilization with its mighty citadels and splendid tombs (see Chapter 3) disappeared. From about 900 B.C.E., however, the region bounced back. Its high-quality wine, olive oil, figs, and pottery enjoyed rising demand in the wider Mediterranean world, and Aegean land-owners raised more crops for export. The richest families also led reconstruction of cities, which well-disciplined, sword-wielding militias of local farmers defended. Partly owing to its rugged coasts, narrow mountain valleys, and numerous islands, the Aegean rim remained politically fragmented. Here and there, however, local kings or alliances of aristocratic families organized strong civic governments. They built walls around their towns, erected temples dedicated to the city's patron god or goddess, and taxed the wealth that farmers of the surrounding countryside generated. The Greeks called this type of state the **polis** (POH-lis), a city-centered community founded on the claim that its citizens were all kin of one another and

> **polis (plural, poleis)** The ancient Greek term for a sovereign state centered on a single city; a city-state.

mutually dedicated to self-rule. From *polis* (plural, *poleis*), we derive the words *politics, political,* and *politician.*

As population increased and farmers put more good land to wine and olive production, wheat and other staple foods had to be imported from afar. Moreover, as we have seen, intensive farming and grazing on steep hillsides gradually depleted soil. Unable to make land much more productive, many Aegean city-states organized schemes to resettle groups of citizens on new farms abroad. In the eighth century B.C.E., numerous bands of pioneers moved to eastern Sicily and southern Italy, founding colonies on coastal plains that were broader and more fertile than around the Aegean. Other migrants went farther afield, settling in northern Libya and along the southern coast of what is today France and Spain. To the northeast, Greek farmers colonized coastlands of the Black Sea, a region that from their perspective was a kind of gigantic lagoon

Ruins of a Greek colony. Greek migrants from the Aegean island of Thera (Santorini) founded the colony of Cyrene in northern Libya in the late seventh century B.C.E. It thrived as a Mediterranean commercial center for about a thousand years.

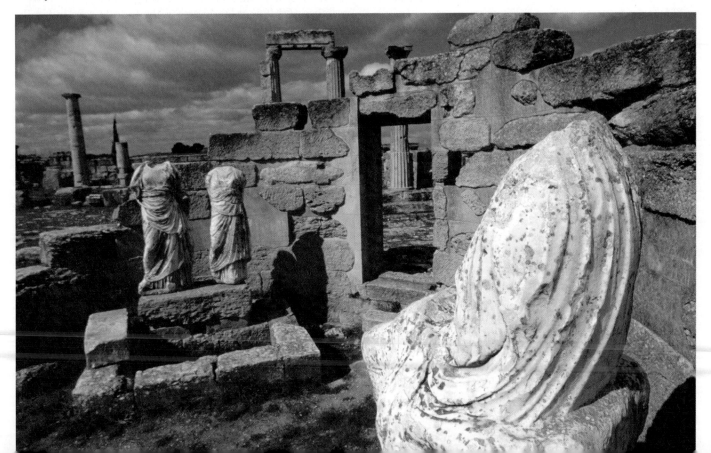

of the Mediterranean reaching deep into the plains of Inner Eurasia.

Greek colonization naturally produced merchants as well as farmers. In the poleis of the Aegean homeland, most traders were noncitizen immigrants or visitors from other regions. Called *metics*, this social class did not have rights to own land or take part in civic life. Partly because of these restrictions, *metics* flourished in trade, creating their own commercial diaspora that, like the Phoenicians, operated in distant parts of the Mediterranean and that knitted the Aegean home city-states and the colonies together.

By the sixth century B.C.E., the number of Greek speakers living and trading outside the relatively small part of southeastern Europe that is today the Republic of Greece probably significantly exceeded the number that lived within it. One important consequence of this dispersion was that a fairly uniform style of Greek urban culture emerged across a large part of the Mediterranean–Black Sea region. We look in more detail at Greek political organization and culture in Chapter 6.

Phoenicians, Greeks, and alphabetic writing. The earliest known alphabets emerged among speakers of Semitic languages in the Levant and Syria in the later second millennium B.C.E. Scribes based in Mediterranean ports experimented with several forms of writing, inventing sound-based signs that drew inspiration from symbols used in both Egyptian hieroglyphic and Mesopotamian cuneiform systems. We associate alphabetic writing especially with the Phoenicians because the particular set of signs they used from about 1200 B.C.E. attracted wide interest. Within two hundred years, the Phoenicians passed their system on to Greek scholars and eventually to the wider Mediterranean world.

As we described earlier (see Chapter 2), both Mesopotamian cuneiform writing and Egyptian hieroglyphics incorporated signs that represented logograms, which are symbols that stand for meanings (one or more whole words). They also included large numbers of signs that stood for syllables. Since humans can make hundreds of syllable sounds by combining different consonants with different vowels, this type of system, especially combined with logograms, required many signs. Modern Chinese, for example, is basically a logographic system with thousands of individual characters that represent whole words (units of meaning rather than units of sound), plus phonetic elements to aid pronunciation. Functional literacy in Chinese requires learning about three thousand distinct characters.

The Phoenician alphabetic system, by contrast, had only twenty-two signs. These were arranged in a particular order, as is our modern alphabet. But this early system included only consonants, not vowels. A reader pronounced a particular word correctly—adding the right vowels—by recognizing the word from the context of words that came before and after it, that is, by the intended meaning of a passage. For example, if the English alphabet did not have vowels, a reader could still identify the sequence of consonants "frmr" as meaning "farmer" rather than "firmer" by the context of surrounding words. (Today people routinely use text messaging shorthand that omits vowels.) The modern Arabic and Hebrew alphabets, which emerged in the same general region as Phoenician, have no letters for vowels, only special marks that may be inserted to clarify pronunciation. However, when Greek scribes appropriated the Phoenician system, they added two new consonants and six signs for vowel sounds, a system that inspired Latin.

Scribes in the Neo-Assyrian empire composed texts on clay tablets or in stone using cuneiform, but they also wrote documents in Aramaic, which used an alphabet. We have no physical remains of these early Aramaic texts because scribes used perishable writing surfaces. But we know what they were doing from cuneiform tablet descriptions and from pictures of Aramaic scholars at work. Some historians think that Aramaic inspired the alphabet that came into use in northern India to write Sanskrit, the Indo-European language that priests and teachers used. In any case, by 600 B.C.E. alphabetic writing was spreading rapidly from the Mediterranean to South Asia.

Woodland Europe and the Mediterranean World

At the start of the first millennium B.C.E., the most culturally complex societies of inland Europe lay along a belt of heavily forested territory extending from modern Switzerland eastward to Hungary. That region had no centralized states, but people built stout hill forts, buried their chiefs with costly grave goods, and worked expertly in bronze, silver, and gold. Also, farming and cattle-keeping peoples who spoke a number of different languages in the Indo-European family continued to move from western Inner Eurasia to territories west of the Black Sea (see Chapter 3).

Prominent among Indo-European migrants were the ancestral speakers of Italic languages, from which Latin later derived, as well as the Celtic-speaking peoples, who by 600 B.C.E. probably occupied most of western Europe. Celtic clans whose warriors carried bronze weaponry, rode horses and transported their families on lumbering wagons, arrived in Iberia by the seventh century B.C.E. They reached Britain and Ireland on boats or rafts not long after that. These newcomers probably came to politically dominate the earlier populations of western Europe. In time, Indo-European languages displaced all preexisting ones across central and western Europe. The only exception is Basque, an ancient tongue still spoken in the Pyrenees Mountain region between France and Spain.

Once Phoenician and Greek merchants entered the western Mediterranean, the pace of change in Europe accelerated. These sea traders wanted Europe's silver, copper, tin, iron, and lumber, exchanging them for Mediterranean wine, oil, fine ceramics, and finished ironware, which went mainly to the families of woodland clan chiefs. The

Mediterranean network linked to inland Europe along a number of passages, for example the Guadalquivir River in Iberia, the Rhône River in France, high passes across the Alps, and, from very early times, the Danube River, which connected western Europe to the Black Sea. Europe's elite groups, installed in their hill forts, aimed to control the flow of trade across their territories, thereby enriching themselves, elevating their social status, and founding modest kingdoms.

Almost no serious urbanization took place north of the Alps until after 600 B.C.E., but in the plains and river valleys of northern Italy a cluster of impressive city-states emerged as early as the ninth century B.C.E. in tandem with growing commercial activity in the central Mediterranean. Possessing rich mineral and agricultural resources, the Etruscans, a people of the region of Etruria in north central Italy, traded widely by land and sea. From the sixth to the fourth centuries B.C.E., they controlled the trade routes across the Alps. Organized in a loose confederation of city-states, they also competed with both Phoenician and Greek colonies for commercial advantage in the western Mediterranean.

Recent archaeological work suggests that Etruscan society emerged gradually from older populations of Italy. They adopted a variant of the Greek alphabet, which they passed on to the Romans. Etruscan society was remarkably innovative, building efficient iron smelters, crafting exquisite objects in gold and silver, inventing the "Roman arch" before the Romans did, and mastering engineering skills necessary to transform low-lying marshland into productive farms. We also know something about Etruscan daily life from their elite tombs, which display not only numerous grave goods but also wall paintings. These depict people eating together, priests conducting rituals, and women and men socializing casually. The general impression is that Etruscan society, in some respects like the earlier Minoan civilization on Crete (see Chapter 3), allowed greater social freedoms to women than was the case in Greek city-state culture.

Nubia on the Nile Corridor

Looking at a physical map of the Mediterranean and Black Sea regions, we might think of the Nile, like the Rhône or the Danube, as a watery arm of the sea, extending lines of exchange deep inland. The Nile in fact linked the Mediterranean to parts of Africa nearly two thousand miles upriver. Along this avenue, merchants carried an array of wares from the Mediterranean world to Nubia, the region that is today southern Egypt and northern Sudan. The return trade included gold, ivory, ebony, incense, cattle, hides, and slaves.

The Nile was also Main Street of the pharaoh's command system. As a general pattern, when the Egyptian state was strong and secure, the kings pushed their authority upriver. When it weakened or fell into crisis, they retreated closer to the Mediterranean, leaving Nubia alone. Similarly, the influence of Egyptian institutions, elite culture, and hieroglyphic writing on Nubian aristocrats waxed and waned depending on the state of things downriver. During the New Kingdom's imperial expansion between the fifteenth and thirteenth centuries B.C.E., the pharaohs dominated the Nubian state of Kush (see Chapter 3) and dispatched armed expeditions deep into the region. In the twelfth century, however, when the pharaohs were busy fighting Libyans and Sea People, Kush reasserted its independence. Nubian kings moved their capital from Kerma (in the northern part of modern Sudan) another two hundred miles up the Nile to Napata, thus distancing themselves further from meddling pharaohs.

In fact, Kush prospered so well from grain production, cattle raising, and trade that about 735 B.C.E. its armies accumulated sufficient power to turn the tables and invade Egypt. Taking advantage of political conflicts that had plagued that land since the twelfth century B.C.E., Kushite forces overpowered the pharaoh's armies and established what became known as the twenty-fifth dynasty (see

A reclining Etruscan couple. This terra-cotta sarcophagus dating to the sixth century B.C.E. takes the shape of a dining couch. It would have contained the cremated remains of this married couple. What might the representation of the two figures tell us about social relations between spouses in Etruscan society?

Map 5.3). Piye, Kush's conquering monarch (r. 747–716 B.C.E.), had his exploits inscribed on a granite stele (slab or pillar). One passage tells of his seizure of the great city of Memphis located just south of the Nile delta:

Then he sent forth his fleet and his army to assault the harbor of Memphis; they brought to him every ferry-boat, every cargo-boat, every transport, and the ships, as many as there were, which had moored in the harbor. . . . Then Memphis was taken as by a flood of water, a multitude of people were slain therein, and others were brought as living captives to the place where his majesty was. . . . Then the ships were laden with silver, gold, copper, clothing, and everything of the Northland, every product of Syria, and all sweet woods of God's-land. His majesty sailed upstream, with glad heart.[7]

For a short time after this, a huge Nile-centered state stretched all the way from southern Nubia to the Mediterranean. Political unity on such a scale must surely have intensified commercial and cultural exchange along the Nile corridor. We know, for example, that the Kushite ruling class, wishing to represent itself as the rightful heirs to New Kingdom glory, adopted Egyptian deities, court rituals, and art forms. The dynasty lasted, however, no more

A Nubian pharaoh. This sphinx in pharaonic head cloth represents Taharqo, the third member of the Nubian dynasty that ruled Egypt for seventy-seven years. Found in the ruins of a temple in Kawa, Sudan, the sphinx stands less than 30 inches high.

than half a century. When the Assyrians attacked the lower Nile valley in 671 B.C.E., Nubian forces had to withdraw. The Kushite defeat apparently taught them at least one good lesson, the effectiveness of iron weaponry. Starting in the late seventh century B.C.E., iron-making industries bloomed along the Nubian Nile, with obvious advantages to farming and trade. Kush thus survived and prospered once again, a story to which we return in Chapter 7.

South Asia: A New Era of City Building

FOCUS How were major historical developments in South Asia between 1200 and 600 B.C.E. similar to or different from developments in Southwest Asia?

In the first millennium B.C.E., iron-making technology almost certainly spread from Southeast Asia to South Asia, as did knowledge of alphabetic writing. However, the network of east–west land routes connecting the two regions remained thinner than the complex of threads integrating Southwest Asia with the Mediterranean basin. One reason for the difference is that the great urban civilization of the Indus River valley withered gradually after 1900 B.C.E. (see Chapter 2). Another was that overland travel involved crossing nearly two thousand miles of deserts, arid plateaus, and rugged mountains, regions of modern Afghanistan and Iran that were not yet heavily peopled or urbanized.

However, within South Asia, population growth, urbanization, and commercial exchange accelerated significantly in the early first millennium B.C.E. After about 1700 B.C.E., herders who spoke Indo-European languages in the Indic subgroup of tongues that includes Hindi, Punjabi, and several other modern languages moved slowly from the Indus valley eastward to the Ganges River plain (see Chapter 3). Northern India's earlier populations were probably speakers of much more ancient Dravidian languages. They were farmers, foragers, and inhabitants of a few small cities that endured following the decline of Harappan civilization. Gradually, most of the Indic-speaking newcomers turned from herding to farming, and they likely intermarried extensively with people already there. After iron-smelting technology arrived, farmers had more durable tools to clear the subtropical forests that flourished in the Ganges valley. Iron axes combined with controlled burning to clear land opened huge expanses of northern India to farming—wheat and barley in the western plains and rice in the moist country along the lower Ganges. More intensive farming and faster population growth in this region had three notable consequences: the emergence of new cities and small states, the creation of a complex social class system, and the development of Brahmanism, the belief system forming part of the foundation of the Hindu tradition.

New Cities and Kingdoms

Between the second and first millennia B.C.E. a general shift took place from the Indus valley to the Ganges as the center of population growth. From about 800 B.C.E., small cities began to spring up on the Ganges plain, a development that coincided approximately in time with the appearance of Phoenician and Greek towns in the central and western Mediterranean (see Map 5.4).

Set behind defensive mud-brick walls, some of North India's new urban centers became the capitals of small monarchies, whose ruling groups accumulated wealth by taxing landholders and collecting customs duties from merchants. With this treasure, they recruited armed forces of infantry and horse soldiers. Despite continuing assimilation between Indic language speakers and older populations, the elite families who organized these states took pride in claiming descent from Indo-European warrior groups that had penetrated the region in earlier centuries. Known as *kshatriyas* (kuh-SHAT-tree-uhs), an Indic word related to "power," these families became the dominant political class of North India. Among the sixteen or so kingdoms that emerged after 800 B.C.E., Magadha in the middle Ganges valley became the most powerful one. According to the *Mahabharata*, India's epic historical poem compiled in later

centuries in Sanskrit, the Magadha capital, located on high ground overlooking the Ganges plain, commanded the allegiance of eighty thousand villages.

The Development of the South Asian Class System

Like complex societies in other parts of the world, those that emerged in South Asia in the first millennium B.C.E. featured a hierarchy of social classes, a small privileged class occupying the top rank. In South Asia, however, class differentiations and rules evolved in particularly elaborate and formal ways. From ancient Indian texts, we learn about the mythology that explains and justifies the social system but not much about how it actually evolved.

According to the *Rig Veda*, the collection of Indic prayers and hymns that was transmitted orally for hundreds of years and first transcribed in Sanskrit about 400 B.C.E., the primal Cosmic Person (*Purusha*) generated four classes of Indians in descending order of intrinsic purity. The purest was the priestly class called Brahmins. Their principal functions were to protect and preserve fundamental cultural values, to transmit those values to the young, and to perform sacrificial rituals essential to honor and satisfy numerous deities. Second in the hierarchy were the Kshatriyas, or governing and fighting class of Indic warrior heritage. The Kshatriya class collaborated with the Brahmins, upholding their ritual and teaching authority and sharing with them much agricultural wealth. Members of the third-ranked

MAP 5.4 States of South and East Asia, 800–600 B.C.E.

Why do you think direct overland trade between China and the western side of South Asia remained less important in pre-modern centuries than exchange by the much longer maritime route between the South China Sea and the Bay of Bengal?

class were Vaishyas (VEYES-yuhs), the farmers, herders, merchants, and artisans who produced the food, fiber, manufactures, and commercial institutions that society required. The Shudras (SHOO-druhs), the fourth and least pure class, were destined to serve the other three groups as menial laborers. The Brahmins sanctioned this hierarchy, which stipulated that membership in one of the four classes was divinely ordained and determined by birth. A fifth segment of society also emerged, called Panchamas, or "fifths." It may have originated among foraging and hunting peoples that Indic-speaking newcomers regarded as hopelessly barbaric and therefore wholly unclean. Brahmin teaching declared this group to be "untouchable," its members consigned to living apart from the rest of society and to carrying out the most polluted tasks such as cleaning latrines and moving corpses.

In the course of the first millennium B.C.E. and later, Indian society established numerous social rules to ensure each of the four classes followed its dharma (DHUHR-muh), the ritual duties, occupations, privileges, and daily behavior specifically assigned to it. All formal relations among classes and the boundaries between them came to be expressed in the language of ritual purity and impurity. Depending on their class affiliations, individuals were born relatively polluted or unpolluted, but they could pollute themselves more, at least temporarily, by failing to fulfill their class duties or by physical contact with people of lower rank. For example, at some point Brahmins determined that they should not wear footwear or other clothing made of leather because leatherworking occupations involved dead animals and blood. The effort to maintain purity and avoid pollution came to determine who should have which occupations, who should marry whom, and who should be allowed to eat or socialize together. As time went on, the four major class divisions split into numerous smaller groups, or *jatis,* based mainly on occupation. Each *jati* then subscribed to its own customs and taboos relative to other groups.

caste A social class more or less rigidly separated from other classes by distinctions of heredity, occupation, wealth, or degree of ritual purity.

In the sixteenth century C.E., Europeans who visited India began to use the word *caste* to describe the social system they observed. That term came to be firmly associated with India. The Indian social structure there became increasingly rigid, but it was only relatively less flexible than social pecking orders in other premodern complex societies. In Southwest Asia or Egypt, people of high rank would likely have defended their domination of the rest of the population in similar terms: Fixed class identity promotes social order and prevents chaos in times of change, it ensures that people know what their social expectations are, all social classes are important in the eyes of the gods in terms of the functions they perform, and all members of society enjoy solidarity and support *within* their own group. In an era of expanding population, urbanization, and commerce, India's developing social system, in which all men and women knew their proper place in society and how to behave toward one another, was fundamentally rational, even though it was unbending, discriminatory, and repressive from a modern democratic perspective.

Brahmins and Brahmanism

Closely linked to the ideology of social class, Brahmanism emerged as a cluster of religious teachings and practices across northern India after 1000 B.C.E. Formulated by the Brahmin class, this belief system developed as a complex blending of Indic and ancient indigenous beliefs, some of them perhaps associated with the earlier Harappan civilization of the Indus valley (see Chapter 2). Brahmins assumed authority over religious routines, including both devotional rituals and the supervision of the duties and prohibitions for all social groups. Among thousands of gods and goddesses that South Asians venerated, certain divinities acquired

Indra, the god of rain and thunderstorms. The *Rig Veda* describes Indra as the king of the gods and courageous warrior. In this painting he is covered with all-seeing eyes. He carries weapons in three of his hands—swords and a thunderbolt. Indra is often depicted on his elephant, Airavata. How might images of Indra, Vishnu, and other gods have communicated ideas about Hindu beliefs?

multifaceted qualities and rose to prominence in the religious imagination. Vishnu (VIHSH-noo), preserver of the world, and Shiva (SHEE-vuh), creator and destroyer of the world, emerged as dominant, though they had a variety of names and manifestations. The Brahmanic religious tradition took on varying forms from one part of South Asia to another and readily incorporated numerous local religious ideas. It had neither a centralized religious organization nor a specific set of doctrines that adherents were expected to follow.

Nevertheless, this dense thicket of beliefs and devotions gradually incorporated a concrete body of teachings that gave deeper meaning to daily rituals. Early Brahmanic theology is known to us mainly from the *Upanishads* (oo-pah-NIH-shuhds), a collection of sacred texts composed in Sanskrit. These texts, which emerged between about 800 and 500 B.C.E., expounded the idea of Brahman, the infinite, sublime essence of the universe. Brahman is the divine principle of all being, the tradition proclaims, and this transcendent "all-ness" includes the soul of every individual. Brahman is god but may nonetheless appear in innumerable personal manifestations, including incarnation as Vishnu, Shiva, or any other deity.

For South Asians, performance of rituals and duties became one dimension of the supreme quest to achieve oneness with divine reality. Spiritual fulfillment, however, required obedience to the moral law of the universe, which, like class duties, was also called dharma. Success or failure at living in harmony with dharma determined how many times an individual might be subjected to death and rebirth as a being of higher or lower social rank or even as an animal. Progress was governed by karma, the principle that the right deeds done in a lifetime conditioned an individual's happiness in the next one. Reincarnation (*samsara*) became fundamental to the Brahmanic tradition. So too did the moral imperative to escape this illusory world with all its pain and disappointment by eventually attaining spiritual salvation in unification with Brahman.

Brahmanism, though extremely diverse in thought and devotional practice, was the earliest belief system to exhibit at least some characteristics of a "world religion." In contrast to the Israelite faith, that is, early Judaism, as well as to most local religions in ancient times, Brahmanic ideas attracted people across a wide spectrum of linguistic and class groups as a foundation for social relations, shared moral expectations, and spiritual hope. That is, Brahmanism was not limited to a group claiming a particular ethnic identity. We should not, however, equate the Brahmanic tradition with Hinduism (related to the word *Indus,* thus to *India*). Most historians assert that Indian religious experience linked historically to Brahmanism remained extremely diverse until the modern era.

The East Asian Sphere

FOCUS What evidence documents the expansion of complex agrarian society in China in the era of the Zhou dynasty?

The East Asian lands centered on the Yellow and Yangzi River valleys grew steadily in population and agrarian wealth during these centuries, despite great political and military commotion (see Map 5.4). The Shang dynasty emerged about 1600 B.C.E. as the first monarchy to exercise power over a large part of northern China (see Chapter 3). The Shang expired, however, between 1050 and 1045 B.C.E., when the nobles of a small vassal state called Zhou attacked and dethroned their Shang overlords. Sima Qian, the illustrious Chinese historian of the second century B.C.E., wrote about the Shang collapse nearly a thousand years after it happened. He may have worked through layers of mythology about those distant times, but he claims that the last Shang king lost all support because he oppressed his people, committed moral offenses, and had opponents roasted alive.

A jade disk from a Zhou tomb. The dragon emerged in ancient China as a symbol of royal authority.

The Era of the Western and Eastern Zhou

The Zhou dynasty (1045–256 B.C.E.), whose homeland was somewhere west of the Shang capital, proclaimed that it rightfully seized power because the emperor had lost the Mandate of Heaven. This was the concept that royal authority derived from a supreme moral force, called *tian* (TEE-ehn), or "heaven," which governed the universe. By being just and fair, a ruler demonstrated to his subjects that he possessed the Mandate of Heaven. If he was despotic and mean, he risked losing that mandate, a failing that would lead to natural disasters and social crises. In such circumstances, people were entitled to rise up in rebellion to replace an oppressive or incompetent monarch with someone more virtuous. From Zhou times onward, the idea that the monarch (the Son of Heaven) had public moral obligations sanctioned by cosmic power became part of the fabric of Chinese political culture. Whether they behaved virtuously or not, however, most rulers reigned until they died and passed on their power to a son or other male relative. Nonetheless, the Chinese ideal of moral worthiness tended to curb the worst excesses of kings and, on occasion, served as popular justification for rebellion against a despot. This ideal of the virtuous ruler was a key element of the moral and ethical doctrines of Confucianism, which we explore in Chapter 7.

In the ninth and eighth centuries B.C.E., at the same time that Assyria was expanding across Southwest Asia, Zhou infantry and charioteers built a state even larger than the Shang realm, pushing northwest to the edge of the Inner Eurasian steppes and south to the valley of the Yangzi. In contrast to the Assyrians, the Zhou adopted a decentralized governing style. The monarchs divided the empire into about fifty territories, appointing family members, loyal lieutenants, or local chiefs to govern them. These lords owed the Son of Heaven tribute and military service, but they kept their own armies and lands.

This system worked quite well for nearly three centuries. In 771 B.C.E., however, a coalition of rebellious vassals killed the king, terminating what is known as the Western Zhou state. The royal family fled from Xianyang (shan-yahng), its capital on the Wei River, about 700 miles east to a new center near the modern city of Luoyang. The dynasty survived, but the Eastern Zhou, as it was thereafter known, ruled directly only a small territory. By the fifth century B.C.E., the more powerful of regional princes no longer bothered to acknowledge even the ceremonial sovereignty of the Zhou monarch. From then until the late third century B.C.E., East Asia experienced the Warring States period (475–221 B.C.E.), when these regional rulers fought periodically with one another for territory and resources.

Destruction and Innovation during the Later Zhou Period

A general pattern noticeable in world history is that intense rivalry among several states in a region has often tended to stimulate rather than stifle technical innovation. East Asian rulers who competed with one another experimented with new tools and weapons to gain advantage over their rivals. Like the Assyrians, Chinese commanders gradually abandoned the chariot in favor of infantry and mounted archers. Cavalry troops almost certainly acquired equestrian skills from the pastoral nomads who inhabited the arid steppes northwest of the Wei and Yellow Rivers. In the seventh century B.C.E., iron-smelting industries spread across northern China, gradually supplementing bronze weaponry with iron swords and projectiles.

Along with these new destructive capabilities, which no single state could monopolize, came productive strategies for building alliances, thereby preventing endless conflict. In the aftermath of the Zhou decline, Chinese regional states created something of an "international" system similar to the one that came together in Southwest Asia in the late second millennium B.C.E. Ruling families intermarried with one another, exchanged envoys, and negotiated truces.

The tumultuous times prompted new approaches to class relationships as well. Especially after the eighth century B.C.E., rulers needed to conscript large numbers of people of the farming class, which was most of the population, to build defensive walls, fight as massed infantry, or otherwise provide military labor. One consequence was that ambitious rulers had to recognize more than in earlier times the needs and aspirations of ordinary men and women. In the Shang era, a form of **serfdom** had been common. In the Zhou period, this institution declined gradually.

> **serfdom** A system of labor in which farmers were legally bound to work for and pay fees to a particular landlord in return for protection and rights to cultivate land.

More farmers became independent land-owners or offered their labor services on the open market, a trend that surely contributed to rising productivity and improved living standards. On occasion, rulers also looked beyond the elite class for bureaucratic and military talent, recruiting at least some of their officers and administrators for their intelligence and loyalty rather than merely for their aristocratic birth.

Economic growth and innovation accompanied the constant fighting of later Zhou times. Arable land in the Yellow

ZHOU DYNASTY	
1050–1045 B.C.E.	Zhou state overthrows Shang dynasty
770 B.C.E.	Western Zhou state falls; Eastern Zhou period begins
475–221 B.C.E.	Warring States period
256 B.C.E.	End of Zhou dynasty

The Book of Songs (Shijing)

One of the most precious sources we have of the lives of ordinary women and men in the Zhou era is The Book of Songs (Shijing), *a collection of 305 poems and hymns compiled over several centuries. The earliest of the poems dates to about 1000* B.C.E. *The contents of* The Book of Songs *range from poems lauding the achievements of early Zhou rulers to folk songs outlining the daily routines of rural peasants. Many of the verses describe and celebrate farming life, in the purposeful seasonal routines that continued no matter the rise and fall of emperors. Though the origins of the poems are unclear, one traditional explanation is that the Western Zhou imperial court sent officials to newly conquered territories to record the lyrics of popular songs. When the Zhou king received these songs, he read them to try to understand the hearts and minds, as well as the daily lives, of the people he ruled.*

They clear away the grass, the trees;
Their ploughs open up the ground.
In a thousand pairs they tug at weeds and roots,
Along the low ground, along the ridges.
There is the master and his eldest son,
There the headman and overseer.
They mark out, they plough.
Deep the food-baskets that are brought;
Dainty are the wives,
The men press close to them.
And now with shares so sharp
They set to work upon the southern acre.
They sow the many sorts of grain,
The seeds that hold moist life.
How the blade shoots up,
How sleek, the grown plant;
Very sleek, the young grain!
Band on band, the weeders ply their task.

Now they reap, all in due order;
Close-packed are their stooks [piles of cut grain ready for
   threshing]—
Myriads, many myriads and millions,
To make wine, make sweet liquor,
As offering to ancestor and ancestress,
For fulfillment of all the rites.
"When sweet the fragrance of offering,
Glory shall come to the fatherland.
When pungent the scent,
The blessed elders are at rest."
Not only here is it like this,
Not only now is it so.
From long ago it has been thus.

Source: Arthur Waley, trans. and Joseph R. Allen, ed., *The Book of Songs (Shijing): The Ancient Chinese Classic of Poetry* (New York: Grove Press, 1996), pp. xxi, 304.

Thinking Critically

Who is mentioned as involved in farming in this poem? What are the relationships among those taking part in the work? What lines do you see in the poem that connect the harvest with religious belief? What religious ritual is mentioned? What sense of time and place do you think are conveyed in the final three lines? According to a traditional Chinese adage, "The sky is high and the emperor is far away." How might you link this saying to the sentiment expressed in this poem?

and Yangzi River valleys increased dramatically as a result of marsh draining, use of iron tools, and farming by **free-holders,** who had strong incentives to increase their yields of millet, wheat, or rice. By the sixth century B.C.E., Chinese farmers were turning the soil with sturdy plows tipped with cast iron and pulled by oxen. They planted crops in neat rows that could be tended more easily and weeded fields with cast iron

freeholders Farmers who own the land they cultivate.

hoes. None of these methods was known outside of East Asia until centuries later. Increasing use of bronze coins of various shapes also signaled an expanding market economy in which sellers and buyers needed a convenient medium of exchange to supplement bartering of goods. In cultural life, artisans of the Zhou era continued to make exquisite objects of bronze, jade, and ceramic. Scholars achieved new refinements of the Chinese writing system, and the earliest known works of poetry and history appeared.

• • •

Conclusion

In the period this chapter has explored, interaction among human communities across Afroeurasia grew more intense and complicated than in the previous millennium or in fact in any period before that. More complex networks of interchange followed directly from accelerating population growth. Afroeurasia's numbers grew on average 3 percent faster per century in the first millennium B.C.E. than in the previous two thousand years. The world's population, most of whom lived in Afroeurasia, may have nearly doubled during that millennium, rising to about 250 million.[8] What we call *extensive* population growth took place when people who grew crops or herded animals spread across a large region, raising its population fairly evenly across space. In the 1200–600 B.C.E. period, this phenomenon was especially noticeable in central and southern Africa, the Inner Eurasian steppes, and woodland Europe. In other places, by contrast, growth was *intensive,* meaning that numbers increasing dramatically in relatively limited areas where farming and trade could support more and more people. Population density continued to rise in the older river valley centers of Mesopotamia, Egypt, and northern China. But new clusters of intensive growth also appeared, for example, in the Ganges valley, the Aegean Sea basin, Italy, Nubia on the Nile, East Africa's Great Lakes region, and tropical Southeast Asia. In some places intensive growth involved urbanization (see Map 5.5). One compilation of estimates suggests that, in 1200 B.C.E., the world's sixteen largest cities ranged in population from 24,000 to 50,000. By 650 B.C.E., the populations of the twenty largest cities varied from 30,000 to 120,000, totaling 894,000 inhabitants.[9]

As we have seen, technical and intellectual developments of the period facilitated the growth of exchange networks. Iron metallurgy animated farming and therefore both population growth and incentives for commerce. Across Afroeurasia, smelters turned out thousands of new products of wrought or cast iron, stimulating local and long-distance trade. The invention of alphabetic scripts made it easier for scholars to share knowledge and for manufacturers and merchants to exchange business information over long distances. Diasporas of merchants who shared language, business customs, and trust lubricated the wheels of commerce, notably in the Mediterranean basin. Equestrians continually experimented with horse breeding and riding gear, which contributed to the advent of cavalry warfare and wider use of horses to move goods and transmit information.

To be sure, the Afroeurasian exchange web was in an early stage of development. Trade across the Inner Eurasian steppes was still thin and tentative. The Sahara Desert remained a forbidding deterrent to links between the Mediterranean and tropical Africa. Indian Ocean mariners continued to fear sailing too far from land. Foragers or farmers living in small communities in far southwestern Africa, the Arctic north, deep tropical forests, or high mountain valleys remained isolated from more than local routes of trade. In the following several centuries, however, people impelled by commerce, conquest, or the search for land strengthened more weak links and filled more voids.

• • •

Key Terms

authoritarian monarchy 144	Hebrew Bible 144	polis (plural, poleis) 149
biomass 139	Judaism 144	polytheism 145
Brahmanism 154	Kush 151	Sea People 140
caste 154	Magadha 153	serfdom 156
cavalry 142	Mandate of Heaven 156	*The Book of Songs* (Shijing) 157
commercial diaspora 148	*metics* 150	*Upanishads* 155
early iron age 137	monotheism 144	Warring States period 156
Etruscan city-states 151	Neo-Assyrian empire 142	Zhou dynasty 156
freeholders 157	Phoenician trading posts 147	

Change over Time

1400–1200 B.C.E.	The first alphabets are invented.
1200 B.C.E.	Iron metallurgy starts to spread across Afroeurasia (early iron age).
1200 B.C.E.	Sea People begin widespread attacks in the eastern Mediterranean.
1045–256 B.C.E.	The Zhou dynasty rules in China; its rulers claim the Mandate of Heaven.
1000 B.C.E.	An Israelite state is established in the Levant, laying the foundations of monotheistic Judaism; Brahmanism develops across northern India.
934–610 B.C.E.	The Neo-Assyrian empire unites the whole region from the Tigris-Euphrates to the Nile.
9th century B.C.E.	Etruscan city-states emerge in Italy and control trade routes across the Alps.
9th–8th centuries B.C.E.	Phoenician merchants erect trading posts along the Mediterranean coast; Carthage, among other ports, emerges as an independent city-state.
8th century B.C.E.	New cities emerge in the Ganges River valley in India; the largest is Magadha.
747–671 B.C.E.	Monarchs of Kush rule Nubia and Egypt as the Twenty-Fifth dynasty.

Please see end of book reference section for additional reading suggestions related to this chapter.

Empire Building and Cultural Exchange from India to the Mediterranean

600–200 B.C.E.

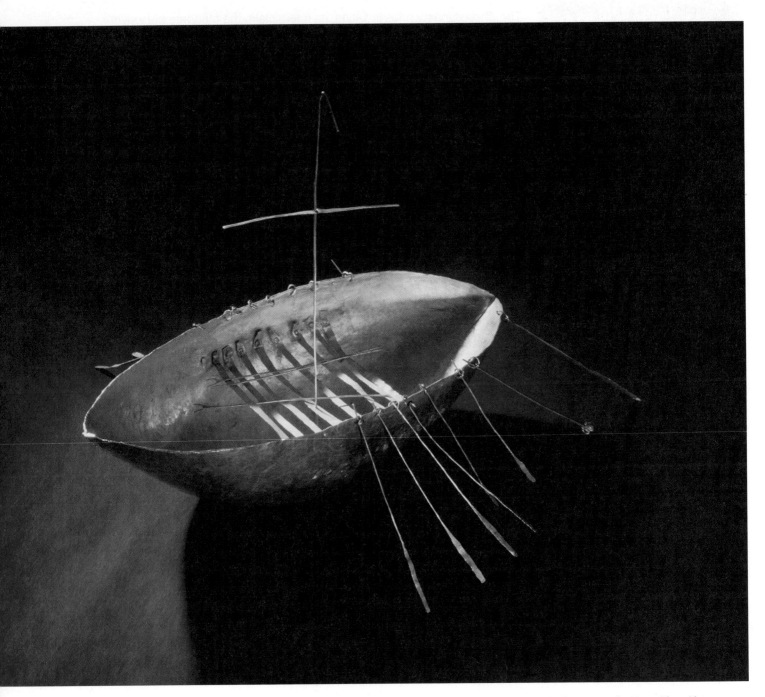

The Greek voyager Pytheas may have sailed northern European seas on a ship resembling this gold model from an ancient hoard found in northern Ireland.

Near the end of the fourth century B.C.E., a Greek-speaking official named Megasthenes traveled more than two thousand miles on a diplomatic mission from the Seleucid (sih-LOO-sid) empire in Southwest Asia to the court of the king Chandragupta in northern India. The ambassador settled for a time in the royal capital, where he carefully observed Indian society and politics. Later, he compiled his observations in a literary work titled the *Indika*. The surviving fragments of this text constitute the only eyewitness record we have of life in India during that period.

About the same time that Megasthenes traveled east, a Greek navigator named Pytheas boarded a sailing vessel at Massalia (Marseilles) on the Mediterranean coast of what is today France. He and his crew sailed west through the Strait of Gibraltar to the Atlantic, then north to Britain. Perhaps he aimed to trade with Celtic-speaking people in northern Europe. After circumnavigating Britain, he returned to Massalia to write a report of his travels. In his account he described an island called Thule Ultima, possibly Iceland, where midsummer days lasted twenty hours. He also included practical information on such subjects as the position of the North Pole and the correlation between tides and the phases of the moon.

The careers of Megasthenes and Pytheas vividly illustrate the far-flung activities of Greek-speaking people between the sixth and third centuries B.C.E. Greeks (known as "Hellenes" in the ancient world) were on the move, strengthening colonial settlements along the shores of the Mediterranean and Black Seas, plying long-distance trade, and offering their skills abroad as scholars, artisans, and soldiers. In the Aegean Sea basin, the Hellenic city-states of Athens, Sparta, and several others achieved impressive economic and military power.

The explosion of Greeks onto the world scene was one sign of intensifying human communication across Afroeurasia as a whole. Population continued to grow, more cities appeared, and migrating farmers and herders moved into new territories in Inner Eurasia and the tropical latitudes of Africa and Asia. The greatest concentrations of both cultivators and city dwellers were to be found in two regions: in the zone from the Ganges River valley to the lands rimming the eastern Mediterranean and in northern and central China. Throughout most of those four hundred years, China continued on a long trajectory of technological advancement and commercial growth but remained politically fragmented. We come back to East Asia in Chapter 7.

Chapter Outline

PERSIA ASCENDING
Empire Building on a New Scale
The Achaemenids as "Universal" Rulers
The Persian Empire as Communication Hub
The Achaemenids and the Teachings of Zoroaster
Achaemenid Multiculturalism

INVENTIVE GREEKS
Government and Society
in Greek City-States
The Flowering of Athens

ALEXANDER THE GREAT AND THE HELLENISTIC ERA
Alexander's Short, Brilliant Career
Foundations of the Hellenistic World

INDIVIDUALS MATTER Queen Arsinoe II: Ruler of Ptolemaic Egypt

Cultural Trends

BUDDHISM AND THE MAURYA EMPIRE IN INDIA
Foundations of Buddhism
The Reign of Ashoka Maurya

WEIGHING THE EVIDENCE Rock Edicts of the Emperor Ashoka

CAVALRY AND CARAVANS IN INNER EURASIA
Nomad Power
Early Times on the Silk Roads

• • •

This chapter opens on the rise of the Achaemenid (uh-KEE-muh-nid) empire of Persia, the largest state in both territory and population that the world had so far seen. On the Iranian plateau east of Mesopotamia, people speaking Persian (Farsi) founded the Achaemenid dynasty around 550 B.C.E. Persian horse troops and infantry seized the territories of the former Assyrian and Babylonian empires, and for several decades in the sixth and fifth centuries, Achaemenid governors ruled provinces stretching from northwestern India to Libya west of the Nile. For the first time in history, the three great river valleys—Tigris-Euphrates, Nile, and Indus—were incorporated into a single state, if only briefly. With this

A Panoramic View

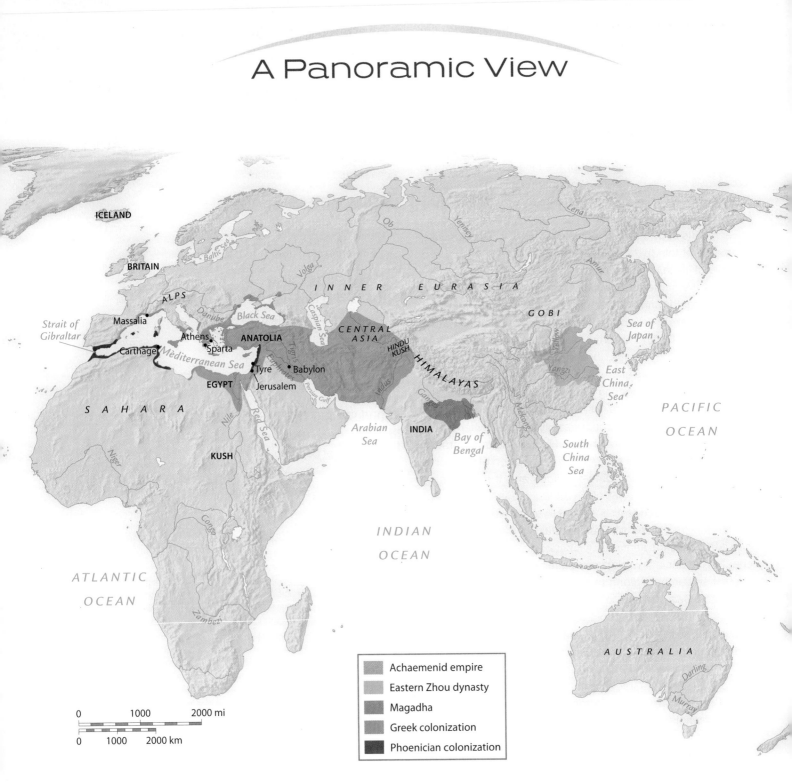

Achaemenid empire
Eastern Zhou dynasty
Magadha
Greek colonization
Phoenician colonization

0   1000   2000 mi
0   1000   2000 km

MAP 6.1 Major states in Afroeurasia, 500 B.C.E.
The voyages of Phytheas to the north Atlantic and Megasthenes to India suggest Greek speakers were interested in the world far beyond their Mediterranean homeland. Would educated Greeks of the Mediterranean in the fourth century B.C.E. likely have had more knowledge of India or of Britain?

integration, more farmers, artisans, and merchants entered into the interregional web of exchange.

Early in the fifth century B.C.E., the Achaemenids tried to bring the Greek poleis (city-states) of the Aegean into submission. In the second part of the chapter, we turn to that region in the period after the Persian threat receded, a time when several poleis participated in a remarkable flowering of science, literature, philosophy, art, and architecture. Athens shone brightest in this firmament of ideas. For about a century and a half, that city and a few others also experimented with novel institutions of government centered on the idea that a sovereign state may be founded on the collective will of a body of citizens rather than on the decrees of a monarch claiming divine authority.

In the later fourth century B.C.E., the political landscape of Southwest Asia and the eastern Mediterranean changed dramatically. In the third part of the chapter, we introduce Alexander the Great, the young ruler of the Balkan kingdom of Macedon who conquered the Aegean, Egypt, and Southwest Asia. With Alexander, both Athenian democracy and the colossal Achaemenid empire came to an end. After Alexander's death in 323 B.C.E., Greek-speaking monarchs continued to rule from the eastern Mediterranean to India as late as the first century B.C.E. During that era, Greek-inspired ideas and styles radiated far beyond the Aegean.

In the fourth part, we shift to South Asia. The monarchs of the Maurya (MORE-yuh) dynasty, the first to unite northern and central India under one authority, arose nearly simultaneously with the Hellenistic states that succeeded Alexander's empire. The Maurya established diplomatic ties with those states, a policy that also encouraged east–west trade. The empire reached its zenith under Ashoka Maurya, who warmly embraced the teachings of the Buddha, the moral sage who had lived more than two hundred years earlier. Consequently, Ashoka advanced Buddhist thought and practice in India, to some extent at the expense of the older Brahmanist (early Hindu) religion.

In the final section of the chapter, we return to Inner Eurasia, where the growing population of pastoral nomads, valley farmers, and city merchants began to have a more serious impact on developments in neighboring agrarian and urbanized lands than in any earlier time. Around 500 B.C.E., Inner Eurasian chieftains began to organize larger alliances of clans and tribes capable of attacking towns and cities to the south and east. But even as tensions grew between pastoral and settled peoples along the edges of the steppes, traders busied themselves developing Inner Eurasia's town markets, caravan trails, and commercial institutions, thereby pushing pastoral and agrarian societies into greater mutual dependence.

Persia Ascending

FOCUS In what ways did the Achaemenid empire of Persia contribute to increasing commercial and cultural exchange in Afroeurasia?

Since at least the third millennium B.C.E., trade routes have crisscrossed historic Persia, whose central regions roughly coincide with the modern Republic of Iran. As exchanges on Afroeurasia's long-distance land and sea routes became progressively busier, warrior groups with territorial conquest in mind became increasingly aware of Persia's strategic importance as an east–west funnel of trade. The region might be likened to the narrow stem of an hourglass, a conduit of routes wedged between the Caspian and Arabian Seas (see Map 6.1). Along these trails, goods, people, and ideas moved between the eastern and western expanses of Afroeurasia. No wonder that starting in the first millennium B.C.E., ambitious conquerors made Persia the core of one empire after another. Some of these rulers in fact pushed their armies beyond Persia—northward to Central Asia, eastward to India, and westward to Mesopotamia, Syria, and even Egypt—in order to absorb more routes, cities, and taxable populations.

Empire Building on a New Scale

The Achaemenid dynasty founded the first Persia-centered empire in the sixth century B.C.E. The rise of this state represented a regional power shift in Southwest Asia from the Tigris-Euphrates valley to the Iranian plateau, the arid region that stretches from the Zagros Mountains to Afghanistan. Near the end of the second millennium B.C.E., pastoral peoples speaking Indo-European languages migrated from the Inner Eurasian steppes across Central Asia to the Iranian Plateau. Two of these groups, the Persians and the Medes (meeds), took up mixed farming and herding on the western plateau. In the eighth or seventh century B.C.E., they founded modest monarchies. Compared to fertile Mesopotamia, Iran might have seemed an unlikely place to build a state that required revenue from agriculture. Much of the land is barren, including vast expanses of salt desert. Nevertheless, the slopes and valleys of the mountain ranges that nearly ring the plateau supported numerous villages and irrigated farms.

Persian conquests. In the mid-sixth century B.C.E., Persian forces, probably responding to the weakening condition of the Babylonian empire in Mesopotamia, launched an offensive. Advancing northwestward along the Zagros range, they overpowered their rivals the Medes. Under the leadership of Cyrus II (r. 559–530 B.C.E.), a brilliant strategist and head of a clan named the Achaemenids, Persian horse archers and infantry, joined by defeated Medes and other fighters, seized northern Mesopotamia, then advanced westward all the way across Anatolia to the Aegean Sea, destroying the kingdom of Lydia and converting its capital, Sardis, into an Achaemenid royal center. Other Persian troops moved northeastward across Central Asia, where they occupied the fertile Amu Darya (Oxus) River valley and the commercial towns that bordered Inner Eurasia. By the end of the century, Babylonia, the major Syrian cities, and the coastal ports of the Levant were all in Persian hands. Reaping huge agrarian revenues from Mesopotamia, the imperial government financed even wider conquests, occupying Egypt upriver to the borders of Nubia (525–523 B.C.E.) and, far to the east, a large part of the Indus valley (518 B.C.E.).

Battles in the Aegean. The Achaemenids also muscled their way into the Mediterranean, occupying Cyprus and launching warships from Levant ports in collaboration with the Phoenicians. Having gained control of the interior of Anatolia and its rich metal deposits, Persian soldiers subjugated the small, prosperous Greek poleis of Ionia, the coastland facing the Aegean Sea.

Larger and militarily stronger Hellenic poleis, however, lay across the sea on mainland Greece. When the Ionian poleis rose in rebellion against their Persian governors, Athens sent ships to support them. This provocation convinced King Darius I (r. 522–486 B.C.E.) that if Persia were to dominate the Aegean basin and its commerce, it must attack mainland Greece. In 490 B.C.E. the Athenian army fought the Persians on the plain of Marathon northeast of Athens

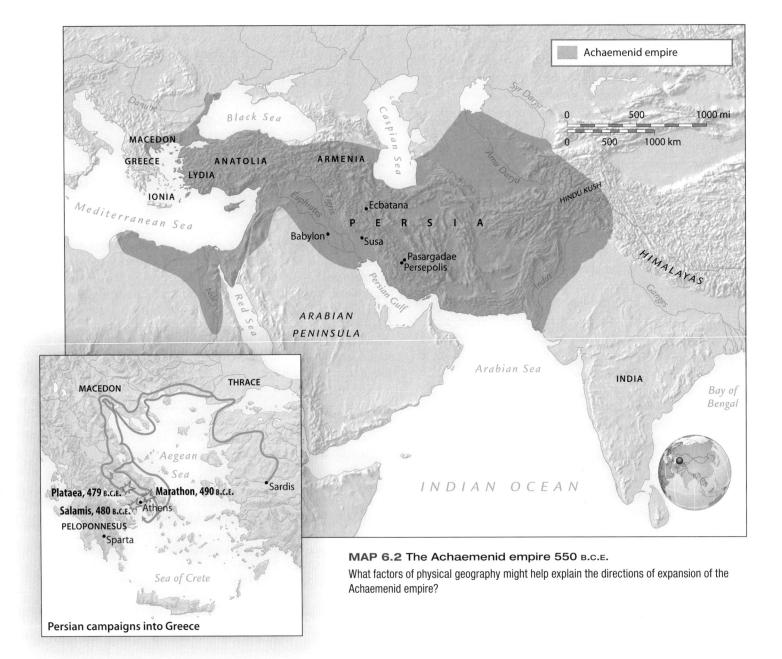

MAP 6.2 The Achaemenid empire 550 B.C.E.
What factors of physical geography might help explain the directions of expansion of the Achaemenid empire?

and turned them back. A decade later, the emperor Xerxes (r. 486–465 B.C.E.) invaded Greece, but a Hellenic navy of 370 warships defeated a larger Persian fleet off the island of Salamis. Greek victory in a land battle (Plataea) followed in 479 B.C.E. Fighting between Greeks and Persians continued for decades but sporadically and with no conclusive victory for either side.

The Achaemenids as "Universal" Rulers

The Assyrians and Babylonians provided the Achaemenids with a model of how to organize an empire in the Mesopotamian tradition of state building developed over the previous three thousand years (see Map 6.2). The Persians, however, enlarged on the possibilities of power. The emperors promoted an ideology suitable for a state of great ethnolinguistic diversity. In both royal inscriptions and architectural imagery, the emperors explicitly represented themselves as the custodians of a prosperous society whose diverse peoples happily joined together in service to the sovereign. Indeed, the Persian state claimed the right to bring all peoples into its orbit. More insistently than earlier Southwest Asian states, it proclaimed a "universal" mission to rule the world. As Darius I declared in a royal inscription, "I am Darius the Great King, King of Kings, King of countries containing all kinds of people, [king] of this great earth far and wide. . . ."[1] The sheer technological limitations of the first millennium B.C.E. made any imperial claim to global rule, or anything close to it, a practical absurdity. Since the Achaemenids, however, many regimes have claimed the mantle of **universal empire.**

universal empire A multiethnic state whose ruler claims a right to authority over all of humankind.

Persian nobles, drawn from families proud of their heritage as conquering warriors, served the emperor's government. This class of aristocrats, a tiny minority of the population, held key positions as royal court officials, provincial governors, and high army officers. Following the Assyrian model, however, the emperors systematically stripped their nobles of special powers and rights, transforming them into political servants of the state. They rewarded aristocratic families generously for loyal service with titles, gold, horses, estates, and royal daughters in marriage. But officials branded as corrupt, incompetent, or treasonous might expect to be summarily fired or even gruesomely executed. Darius I

satrapy An administrative unit of the Persian empire under the authority of a satrap, or provincial governor.

devoted much effort to bureaucratic organization, creating approximately twenty large provinces known as **satrapies** (SAY-trap-eez). Each provincial governor, or satrap, had the job of keeping order, provisioning garrisons, and, most important, collecting taxes from the population and forwarding them to the royal treasury.

The empire had no single capital. Rather, the emperors and their royal entourage moved regularly between

An Achaemenid official on state business. The figure facing backward in this model chariot of gold is probably a satrap, or Achaemenid governor. The horses represent a stout Iranian breed. The model comes from a site in the upper Amu Darya valley in Central Asia, the empire's far northeastern corner. A protective image of the Egyptian god Bes is stamped on the front of the chariot. What might that detail suggest about cultural exchange within the Achaemenid realm?

Ecbatana, Susa, Pasargadae, and Persepolis in western Iran and Babylon on the Euphrates. The palace center at Persepolis, which Darius started building about 515 B.C.E., occupied a giant platform commanding spectacular views of the countryside in three directions. The complex included military quarters, an imperial treasury, royal residences, and a vast throne room, whose seventy-two marble pillars supported a cedar wood ceiling nearly sixty-five feet high. Thirteen of those pillars still stand in the sprawling ruins that amaze visitors today.

The vast majority of the empire's subjects were farmers or herders. There were also minority classes of merchants, artisans, scribes, office holders, and priests, plus a large population of slaves, most of whom lost their freedom as prisoners of war. Many slaves labored in affluent households, craft shops, or temples. Others worked on imperial construction projects under harsh, life-shortening conditions. We do not know much about the daily lives of women, but the record of inscriptions suggests that the Achaemenid government had a more open-minded view of females in public life than earlier Southwest Asian states had. Some high-ranking women attended the emperor at court and owned their own landed estates. Moreover, because powerful families used marriage to tighten their political alliances, aristocratic mothers and wives exerted considerable public influence from within their houses.

The Achaemenid palace at Persepolis. Artisans decorated the walls and staircases of this royal center with reliefs of nobles, tribute bearers, and, in this view, imperial guards moving in stately procession.

The Persian Empire as Communication Hub

The Achaemenid communication network was essential to effective government over territories that at the imperial zenith extended east to west nearly 2,500 miles. Much of Southwest Asia already had an infrastructure of roads and trails connecting major cities and ports. The Achaemenids, however, extended this network, broadening highways and equipping them with forts and way stations. People working for the emperor had travel priority, though trade caravans certainly used the roads as long as they had government permission. Imperial officers, diplomats, and spies moved incessantly along the routes, monitoring regional political conditions, checking on the loyalty of local leaders, and suppressing any sign of rebellion.

The Achaemenids commanded the central zone of the growing India-to-Mediterranean trade web. They not only built roads but also encouraged sea trade between the Indus and the Persian Gulf, sponsoring maritime expeditions to gather information on the routes across the Arabian Sea. Persia functioned as a kind of

An Achaemenid coin. This gold Daric from fifth-century B.C.E. Persia depicts the emperor, perhaps Xerxes, carrying a bow and a spear.

economic pump, sucking in products from neighboring lands near and far, and discharging city-made luxury goods in all directions. The emperor Darius I completed construction of the first "Suez canal" linking the Mediterranean to the Red Sea, a project that an Egyptian pharaoh had started earlier. To promote commerce, Achaemenid officials introduced both gold and silver coins of standardized weight, adapting the idea of metal money, which appears to have originated in the Anatolian kingdom of Lydia.

On the periphery of this exchange system were the oasis cities that the Achaemenids dominated in Central Asia and the Greek city-states of the Aegean. Both benefited from their position, however, because they linked the Persian center to immense, mostly rural commercial hinterlands. The towns of Central Asia fronted the Inner Eurasian steppes, and the Aegean cities connected Persia with the whole Mediterranean, the Black Sea, and continental Europe. Products that flowed from those outer regions toward the Achaemenid center included iron, gold, silver, gems, grain, timber, wool, and livestock.

The Achaemenids and the Teachings of Zoroaster

The Persian emperors declared themselves to be worshipers and devout agents of the Ahura Mazda, supreme creator of the world, the Lord of Wisdom. According to an inscription from the reign of Darius I, "A great god is Ahura Mazda, who created this earth, who created yonder heaven, who created man, who created welfare for man, who made Darius king, one king of many, one lord of many."[2] In their early days on the Iranian Plateau, the Persians had very likely made ritual sacrifices to deities of sky and earth, as did other pastoral peoples. The emergence of Ahura Mazda as supreme god and guardian of all that is good, peaceful, and just in the universe is associated with the teachings of the prophet Zoroaster (the Greek version of the name Zarathustra).

The puzzle of Zoroaster. If we know less than we might like about the lives of the Buddha or Jesus, we know even less about Zoroaster. He may have been born anywhere from Iran to the Inner Eurasian steppes and lived anytime between the thirteenth and sixth centuries B.C.E. Priests preserved hymns that embodied Zoroaster's teachings by ritually transmitting them orally for many generations. In their expressive language, these hymns have much in common with the *Rig Veda*, the sacred songs and prayers of early Indo-European peoples of northern India (see Chapter 3). Only in the early centuries C.E., however, did scholars put in writing the seventeen hymns (the *Gathas*) attributed to Zoroaster plus other sacred traditions. This compilation, titled the *Avesta*, recounts that Ahura Mazda appointed Zoroaster, a member of a priestly family, to preach a divine message to a world that had become chaotic and brutal. The prophet's own society would not listen to him (a typical fate of religious reformers), so he wandered abroad and eventually attracted disciples.

Zoroastrian beliefs. Like the ancient Israelites, Zoroaster and his followers preached a monotheistic conception of deity, that is, one, universal God exclusively deserving of worship. The *Avesta* acknowledges the existence of a limited number of other divinities but conceives of them as dependent emanations of Ahura Mazda. Zoroaster also taught that evil operates in the world as Angra Mainyu, the "hostile spirit," which wars against Ahura Mazda for domination of the cosmos. At the End of Time, Ahura Mazda will defeat Angra Mainyu, and universal good will triumph. In the meantime, human beings must make moral choices between good and evil in their everyday lives. If they consistently dedicate themselves to the good, they will ascend at death to the presence of Ahura Mazda. If they behave wickedly, they risk being pitched into hell, where Angra Mainyu awaits them. Zoroaster's vision of moral living did not require renunciation of the world and its pleasures but demanded honest, just, and compassionate dealings with others. Scholars commonly characterize Zoroaster's teachings as "dualist," describing a universe in which humans have a choice of allegiance between good and evil, light and dark, the truth and the lie. This idea of a cosmic conflict in which God will inevitably prevail had a great impact in later centuries on both Christianity and Islam, monotheistic faiths that nonetheless acknowledged the stark power of evil. The Persian term *daeva*, which Zoroaster associated with malign spirits allied with Angra Mainyu, is derived from the same Indo-European root as the English *devil*.

Zoroastrian beliefs and rituals appear to have gained gradual acceptance among the Achaemenid elite class. Zoroaster commanded his followers to pray to Ahura Mazda five times a day and always in the presence of light from the sun or from fire. These were the prime agents of human purification and the focus of thanks to God. We have abundant archaeological evidence that "fire temples," where priests performed rites dedicated to Ahura Mazda, began to be built in Persia during the Achaemenid era. Only several centuries later, however, did Zoroastrian beliefs and rituals take form as the codified and coherent belief system known as Zoroastrianism (zohr-oh-ASS-tree-ahn-ism), a faith that exists today among minorities, mostly in South Asia.

Achaemenid Multiculturalism

From at least the time of Darius I, the Achaemenid emperors claimed the right to rule on the grounds that Ahura Mazda put monarchs on the earth to ensure social order and justice. Both Darius and his successor, Xerxes, had these words inscribed: "By the favor of Ahura Mazda I am of such a kind that I am a friend to what is right. . . . It is not my wish that the weak is . . . hurt because of the mighty, that the mighty is hurt because of the weak."[3] The idea that the emperor must govern all his subjects fairly shared similarities with the political ideology emerging in China about the same time (see Chapter 5). That is, the ruler's enjoyment of divine blessing, whether the Mandate of Heaven or the endorsement of Ahura Mazda, depended on his commitment to justice for all.

In this spirit the Achaemenid emperors generally encouraged their provincial officers to honor local customs and religious practices in return for loyal obedience and cooperation. King Cyrus, the Achaemenid founder, claimed to have seized the great city of Babylon in 538 B.C.E. amid "acclamation and rejoicing" and to have bowed before Marduk, the city's patron deity. "My numerous troops marched peacefully through Babylon. . . . All its cult centers I maintained in well-being."[4] Conceiving of Ahura Mazda as a boundless cosmic presence, the Achaemenids had little trouble thinking of him as the force animating all local deities, whether Marduk or the Israelite god Yahweh. Indeed, Cyrus permitted Israelites who had been deported from Judea to Mesopotamia by the Babylonian king Nebuchadnezzar a half-century earlier (see Chapter 5) to return to Jerusalem to rebuild their sacred temple. Some did go back, though by that time the prophet Jeremiah had successfully

The emperor at court. King Darius holds audience in the ceremonial complex at Persepolis. Behind him stands his son Xerxes, the royal heir. Who do you think the figures on the left and right of the relief might be?

preached that Yahweh was the god of all humankind, not just the Israelites' territorial deity, and that they could justly worship him wherever they lived. It was in the Achaemenid era that Israelites, shortly to be known as Jews (*Yuhudi,* or people of Judea), began to form communities throughout much of Southwest Asia and the Mediterranean basin, creating the Jewish diaspora.

The dispersion of Jews was just one example of the complex social and cultural cross-fertilization that took place in the Achaemenid empire. The Persian army grew into a diverse assortment of soldiers drawn from all the imperial lands. The armies that invaded Greece constituted a motley ethnic mix, including numerous Greeks who fought on the Achaemenid side. Visitors to urban marketplaces or imperial audience halls heard a cacophony of languages. The Persian warrior class originally spoke an ancient form of Farsi, the main language of Iran today. The Achaemenids, however, also promoted Aramaic, the Semitic language already widely spoken and written in Southwest Asia, as a medium of imperial administration and diplomacy. When an emperor built a new palace, his agents looked far and wide to find engineers, artisans, laborers, and construction materials. In an inscription praising the construction of a royal center at Susa in southwestern Iran, Darius captured the rich multicultural character of the Achaemenid realm:

> The silver and the ebony were brought from Egypt. The ornamentation with which the wall was adorned, that from Ionia was brought. The ivory, which was worked here, was brought from Kush (Nubia), and from India and from Arachosia [Afghanistan]. . . . The goldsmiths who worked the gold, those were Medes and Egyptians. The men who worked the wood, those were Sardians [from Anatolia] and Egyptians. The men who worked the baked brick, those were Babylonians. The men who adorned the wall, those were Medes and Egyptians. . . . At Susa a very excellent [work] was ordered.[5]

Inventive Greeks

FOCUS What factors contributed to the emergence of Greek city-states as important centers of political and cultural innovation from the sixth century B.C.E.?

As we have seen, Persian armies failed to subjugate the poleis of mainland Greece or most of the Hellenic cities and settlements of the Black Sea basin. In fact, many Greek cities enjoyed an economic boom in the sixth and fifth centuries B.C.E. Those cities took a leading part in the expanding market networks of the Mediterranean and Black Sea basins. This was economic activity in which private traders and shippers sought personal profit by looking for new products to sell and new populations to buy them. Greek farmers found that by selling olive oil, wine, pottery, and other products abroad, they could afford to import much-needed grain, timber, and iron. Greek city artisans also turned out painted ceramic vessels, silver jewelry, and other luxury merchandise that commanded markets in growing Mediterranean ports and among the affluent urban elites of Egypt and Southwest Asia. Agricultural and commercial prosperity, together with proud victories over the formidable Persians, gave the poleis a new political confidence. Wealth and independence also permitted some of the cities, especially Athens, to encourage creative citizens to devote themselves to literature, art, and philosophical speculation. For about 150 years, that single city emitted extraordinary waves of cultural energy.

Government and Society in Greek City-States

If we situate Greece in the very long term of history, we see that most of the time from the second century B.C.E. to the nineteenth century C.E., it was a colonial territory within one

A temple at Delphi. A sanctuary dedicated to the goddess Athena occupies the smaller of two shrine complexes at the spectacular site of ancient Delphi. This circular building, whose purpose is not known, dates to the fourth century B.C.E.

empire or another. In that long-term perspective, the existence of hundreds of self-governing city-states, separated from one another by mountains and rugged coastlines, was a distinctive circumstance of just a few centuries. Most poleis, which included both a city and surrounding agricultural lands and villages, had ten thousand or fewer inhabitants. These centers typically had defensive walls and an imposing temple dedicated to a patron deity in the manner of Mesopotamian cities. The poleis traded, exchanged emissaries, and fought with one another, forming political alliances that grew, changed, and fell apart from one decade to another. In the sixth and fifth centuries B.C.E., Greek identity was based on shared cultural bonds, not political unity.

Foremost among the elements that set Greeks apart from non-Greeks was a common alphabetically written language, which embraced many dialects. Greeks also generally shared the same household of gods and goddesses with numerous local variations; reverence for mythic heroes of the past, especially the military champions in the *Iliad* and the *Odyssey*, the epic narratives attributed to the eighth-century B.C.E. poet Homer; and participation in religious

ceremonies at the holy centers of Delphi, Delos, and Olympia, where, from 776 B.C.E., male Greeks from many cities took part in competitive games.

Governments in the poleis took a variety of forms. In some of them, the citizens chose a single individual to govern; in others, a small minority of aristocrats, that is, rich and influential men, ruled as an **oligarchy.** Before about 600 B.C.E., only the wealthiest land-owning males, most of them of aristocratic

> **oligarchy** A political system in which a relatively small number of individuals or families control the government.

birth, could decide who would lead and participate in government. In the following two centuries, however, several poleis gradually broadened their laws to allow nonaristocratic and less advantaged men into the political process, granting them the rights and responsibilities of full citizenship.

Militaristic Sparta. Occupying a broad plain in the Peloponnesus (pell-uh-puh-NEE-suhs), the peninsula at the southern end of mainland Greece, Sparta was one of the largest city-states. Its male citizens created a government and social system unlike that found in any other polis. The duties of citizenship included full-time army training from age seven. Men typically married at eighteen, but they lived and ate together in barracks until they were about thirty. While girls in other poleis occupied themselves with textile weaving and other domestic chores, Spartan girls undertook tough physical training, presumably to prepare them to produce strong, healthy sons. In fact, Sparta had the character of a permanent army base. When its forces conquered the neighboring state of Messenia, they reduced most of its inhabitants to the status of servile laborers (*helots*). Understandably, the oppressed classes, which came to constitute a majority of Sparta's population, periodically rose in rebellion and had to be repressed. In the sixth century B.C.E. the city-state coerced all the poleis on the Peloponnesus into submission. Consequently, the city-state's harsh military culture could never be relaxed.

Athenian democracy: direct and limited. In striking contrast to the Spartans, the inhabitants of Athens and some other city-states established governments founded on *demokratia,* meaning "rule of the people." The "people" here did not mean everyone but only adult male citizens who had rights to vote and hold office. In the sixth and fifth centuries B.C.E., Athens instituted a type of collective government in which as many as 60,000 men out of a total population of about 350,000 could legally participate. In a world of divinely anointed monarchs, this system was remarkable, though direct democracy in one form or another was not unique to the ancient Aegean. For as far back in history as we have any record, farming communities and herding bands, probably in all parts of the world, made decisions by group consensus. Like Athens, these communities defined which members of the group had the right to take part and which did not.

In Athens beginning in the late seventh century B.C.E., a succession of judicious leaders, notably Solon, Cleisthenes, and Pericles, engineered political and legal reforms that extended rights to vote and own property, as well as the privilege of speaking in the popular assembly, to all adult, native-born, free (not enslaved) males. The authority to govern was vested in this citizenry, not in a monarch. By drawing lots, citizens took turns serving on civil juries and on the Council of Five Hundred, which managed the city's day-to-day affairs. In practice, the wealthiest Athenian families continued to have great influence over daily affairs, a limitation on democracy that should not surprise us.

A Greek worshiper. This woman standing before an altar emblazons a vase from the sixth century B.C.E. Oil stored in this flask may have been used in religious rituals.

Male citizens professed equality among themselves, responsibility for the welfare of the polis, and the right to primacy over women, children, and all noncitizen residents. Free women did not have public rights, but despite their formal exclusion from government, they contributed a great deal to the city-state's economy and cultural life. The wives and daughters of free men not only managed domestic economies but also did farm work, wove textiles for market, labored in craft shops, and ran small businesses. They played important roles in religious sacrifices, processions, and festivals dedicated to one or another of the numerous deities that Greeks worshiped, including Athena, the patron goddess of the city. Some cults and festivals, which Athenians regarded as vital to the city-state's well-being, were reserved for women only.

Slavery and slave trade grew in tandem with economic expansion in the whole Mediterranean basin. In the fifth century B.C.E., slaves in Athens probably ran to the tens of thousands, though this number would have been small relative to the servile population of the Achaemenid empire. Most slaves reached Greece as prisoners of war or as captives of pirates, though impoverished or debt-ridden men and women sometimes offered themselves as slave laborers in order to survive. Slaves might serve as domestic servants, scribes, tutors, artisans, construction workers, or prostitutes. The silver and lead mines of Attica, the peninsula that was part of the Athenian state, consumed slaves at a voracious rate. According to Athenian law, an owner could physically assault slaves but not kill them wantonly.

Aside from a few restrictions, slaves had no legal rights. Rather, they were **chattels,** comparable in status to domestic animals. As the Greek philosopher Aristotle wrote, "A slave is a living possession."[6]

chattel slavery A type of slavery in which the bonded individual has the social and sometimes legal status of a unit of property and therefore no formal rights or privileges in law.

In the aftermath of the wars with Persia, Athens emerged as probably the biggest and richest polis. The farm production of Attica plus imports of grain from the Black Sea and northern Africa fed the urban population. Attica's mines swelled the city's treasury and financed a powerful navy. Foreigners (*metics*) flocked to the city, energizing craft industries, banking, and overseas trade. The fortified port of Piraeus, located five miles southwest of the city, swarmed with sailing ships that exported wine, oil, figs, pottery, and other goods and brought in grain, fish, timber, and numerous exotic wares from lands near and far.

Greek military prowess. The evolution of self-governing city-states was linked to military changes initiated in late eighth century B.C.E. In Chapter 5, we described how, after the twelfth century B.C.E., infantry progressively replaced chariot riders in Southwest Asia and the eastern Mediterranean. As Greek city-states multiplied, their inhabitants organized infantry militias. All male citizens trained and fought to defend the polis or to enlarge its territory at the expense of neighbors. Consequently, when farmers and artisans joined their city's army or navy, they had good cause to demand citizenship rights and duties equal to men who were wealthy and well born.

Except in Sparta, militia service was typically part time but also a basic duty of citizenship. Soldiers outfitted themselves with bronze helmets and body armor; they carried round wooden shields and spears designed for close-in fighting. Massing together shoulder-to-shoulder and shield-to-shield six-to-eight ranks deep, these fighters, or *hoplites* (from *hoplon*, a Greek word for shield) marched into battle in close formation. This ingenious tactical formation, called a **phalanx,** was designed to charge, smash into, and crush an enemy force. As long as a phalanx maneuvered on level ground and maintained its cohesion, it could wreak havoc on any opposing force that was deployed more loosely or that tried to stop an advancing wall of shields by firing arrows from a distance. On the political and social sides, the phalanx also fostered civic solidarity within the polis because military success depended absolutely on intense physical and psychological cooperation. Cohesion, however, did not necessarily extend beyond a city-state's frontiers. On the contrary, the more unified a polis perceived itself to be, the more it might be inclined to attack other cities.

> **phalanx** A military formation in which soldiers march and fight in closely packed, disciplined ranks.

The Flowering of Athens

Athens in fact attacked cities near and far. After the Persian threat receded, the city's leaders continued to invest lavishly in its citizen navy. The prime weapon was the trireme, a fast, quick-turning ship powered with three ranks of rowers and designed to ram enemy vessels head on. Young citizens, not slaves, powered the ships. The trireme fleet freed many poleis from Persia but then made them into tax-paying dependencies of Athens. Under the leadership of Pericles (495–429 B.C.E.), Athens reduced former military allies to the status of tribute-paying dependent states. The navy also took control of the major Aegean Sea passages, including the Bosporus, the strait leading to the Black Sea. On the Greek mainland, however, Sparta and its dependencies remained powerful rivals.

Whenever in world history a country has displayed great cultural creativity, wealth and labor have been marshaled to pay for it. In the case of Athens, riches pouring in from the seaborne empire, including slave labor, financed a period of intense intellectual and aesthetic innovation that began about 480 B.C.E. and lasted nearly a century and a half. As the Athenian empire grew, artisans, builders, and scholars converged on the teeming capital. Athenian wealth, funneled through the public treasury and the most affluent

The Acropolis. The Parthenon and the other public buildings on the fortified hill that dominates Athens display the city-state's wealth and power in the decades following Greek victory over Persian invaders. Athens obliged its allied cities to contribute generously to the lavish beautification of the Acropolis.

families, financed an ambitious building program, notably construction of a complex of temples, statues, and public spaces on the Acropolis, the hill that commanded the city. The crowning glory was the Parthenon, an exquisitely proportioned temple dedicated to the cult of Athena. The polis also patronized artists and thinkers, who dedicated themselves to painting, sculpture, architectural design, music, drama, history, philosophy, mathematics, and science.

The Athenian cultural inheritance.

This burst of ingenuity was not entirely self-generated. The inventive people who lived and worked in Athens were all heirs to the stream of ideas that had been emanating from Southwest Asia and the Nile valley during the previous three thousand years. Much of this accumulated knowledge became available to Greek thinkers, and they took great interest in it. The philosopher Aristotle, for example, contended that "it was in Egypt that the mathematical arts were first formed" thanks to the scientific work of its priestly class in earlier millennia.[7]

Despite the wars with the Achaemenids, Persia also contributed significantly to Athenian cultural achievement. Greeks spoke of the Persian elite as barbarians (mainly because they did not speak Greek) and expressed contempt for their extravagant lifestyle. Even so, the wars did not prevent Persian luxury goods—gems, jewelry, textiles, gold ware—from arriving in Greek ports. Athens sent envoys to the Achaemenid court, and Greeks in substantial numbers resided in the empire's western provinces as political exiles, mercenaries, artisans, and scribes. Herodotus (484–425 B.C.E.), the Greek historian who wrote the classic account of the Persian Wars, traveled extensively in the empire, including Egypt. Affluent Athenians took warmly to Persian finery, clothing styles, and other status symbols, for

Servants attend an affluent woman. Scenes of everyday life decorate this loutrophoros, a water container used in marriage and funeral rituals. Made in Greek style in a polis in southern Italy, the vase depicts a status symbol borrowed from Persian custom—the subordinate parasol carrier. What factors help explain the diffusion of Persian cultural practices as far west as Italy?

example, using slaves in the Achaemenid manner to carry parasols, fans, and fly-whisks.[8]

Religion and philosophy.

The citizens of Greek poleis participated in rituals and sacrifices to win favor from the gods and goddesses believed to reside on Mount Olympus in northern Greece. Religious life, however, was also diverse and jarringly incoherent. The Greeks had no sacred scripture or set of doctrines comparable to either the Hebrew Bible or the moral teachings of Zoroaster. Various cults to cure illnesses, ensure fertility, and predict the future flourished. The most influential individuals in Greek urban communities were secular, or nonreligious, civic leaders, rather than priests, who enforced codes of belief and behavior. This relatively open-minded religious climate is likely to have encouraged adventuresome thinkers to engage in wide-ranging speculation about nature, the human condition, and cosmic truth. Moreover, the civic culture of some poleis, especially Athens, stimulated remarkably open debate among free male citizens on questions of public duty, moral justice, and proper community behavior.

In the sixth century B.C.E., Greek scholars inhabiting cities of Ionia on the eastern Aegean shore led the way in formulating a method of scientific and moral inquiry that became known as **natural philosophy.** This discipline was founded on the idea that just as the polis thrived because citizens subscribed to underlying laws, so fundamental rules might also govern nature, including human action. These laws might even transcend the will of the quarreling, unreliable gods on Mount Olympus, who offered little help in making sense of the world. Natural laws, rather, might be discovered through the exercise of human logic and reason and, at least for some philosophers, careful observation of the external world.

natural philosophy A method of scientific and moral inquiry founded on the idea that fundamental laws governing nature, including human behavior, may be discovered through the exercise of logic, reason, or careful observation.

The Ionian tradition of abstract speculation bloomed in Athens in the fifth century B.C.E. Scientific work focused on mathematics and on the natural constitution of the earth and heavens. Cultural and psychological studies aimed to fathom the universal principles underlying moral and political behavior. Drama, which got its start in festivals dedicated to Dionysus, the god of wine, explored the complex relationships between individuals, society, and the gods. Sculptors and architects sought to find universal principles to represent harmonious order and symmetry, especially in the human body. Greek intellectuals heartily disagreed with one another over questions of moral truth, the proper ranking of social classes, and whether democracy was a good idea or not. They founded their speculations on the premise that humans might achieve the good life by using their reasoning power to discover natural explanations for things, rather than merely waiting helplessly while the gods bullied, seduced, and played tricks on them.

Socrates (470–399 B.C.E.), the earliest of the great philosophers, set the agenda for human action founded on reason with his celebrated declaration that "the unexamined life is not worth living." Plato (428–347 B.C.E.), who tells us almost everything we know about Socrates, and Aristotle (384–322 B.C.E.), Plato's student, wrote on a colossal range of subjects. Plato was the idealist, interested in metaphysics, that is, speculation on the "first causes" of things. He argued that the world we see with our senses is merely a flickering silhouette of perfect reality. Among many other implications, this idea led Plato to imagine the ideal political state, which in his view would not be a democracy but a system ruled by Guardians, or philosopher-kings.

In contrast to Plato, Aristotle was an empiricist, a seeker of concrete, observable knowledge about humankind and the world. Beyond that, he sought to understand the fundamental interconnectedness and coherence of all phenomena. In the process he produced a huge body of work on politics, economics, mathematics, logic, poetry, astronomy, chemistry, and biology. The ideas of Socrates, Plato, Aristotle, and numerous other Greek thinkers endured, probably less because of the theories they formulated and observations they made than because of the questions they asked. As Socrates reputedly said, "All I know is that I know nothing." This was certainly an invitation to inquiry. Greek philosophers had no monopoly on logical reasoning or high-flying speculation about the nature of reality. But the questions they posed continued to intrigue and confound thoughtful people in the succeeding centuries and indeed down to our own time.

Alexander the Great and the Hellenistic Era

FOCUS To what extent did societies within the region from northern India to the eastern Mediterranean embrace Greek-style cultural and political forms between the fourth and second centuries B.C.E.?

In the fifth century B.C.E., Greek warriors defended themselves against the Persian empire. In the last third of the fourth century, Greek and Macedonian soldiers destroyed it. The conquests of Alexander (r. 336–323 B.C.E.), the young king who led that campaign, figure among the most extraordinary military adventures in history. Marching from Greece to the Indus valley, Alexander carved out an empire even bigger than the Achaemenid state. He succeeded only fleetingly, but his conquests led to a drastic rewriting of the political map of Southwest Asia and the eastern Mediterranean (see Map 6.3). Following the conqueror's withdrawal from India, the Maurya dynasty, a third large state, united the Indus and Ganges River valleys for the first time in history. The existence of these and several smaller monarchies, most of them under the authority of Greek-speaking elites, stimulated more than two centuries of intense commercial and cultural interchange from India and Central Asia to the Mediterranean.

Alexander's Short, Brilliant Career

In the Aegean the rise of the Athenian sea-based empire sparked more than one hundred years of inter-polis conflict, starting with the Peloponnesian War (431–404 B.C.E.). Athens, Sparta, and the powerful city-state of Thebes took turns dominating the scene. Within the cities, land-owning and commercial minorities continued to accumulate wealth at the expense of ordinary people, causing bitter alienation between rich and poor. To the east, the Achaemenid empire also showed signs of stress. Imperial leadership deteriorated, rebels pushed the Achaemenids out of Egypt for fifty-seven years, and the Indus valley's subject populations reasserted their independence.

Amid these unstable circumstances, Macedon, one of a number of woodland kingdoms on the Balkan Peninsula north of Greece, arose to regional power. A small class of warrior-aristocrats who spoke Macedonian, which may have been either a dialect of Greek or a language closely related to it, ruled a population of mostly farmers and herders. Athens and the other culturally sophisticated city-states to the south tended to regard Macedon as a useful source of timber, gold, and horses but otherwise as a wild frontier. In 358 B.C.E., however, Philip II ascended the Macedonian throne and initiated a vigorous program to strengthen his kingdom, obliging the Greek poleis to take him seriously. He had no use for Athenian-style democracy, but he "Hellenized" his royal court, adopting Greek ceremonies and cultural refinements and hiring Greek artists and intellectuals to model proper standards of civilization. On the military side, he expanded his cavalry of heavily armored aristocrats, and he trained Balkan peasants to fight in a phalanx eighteen thousand strong. He armed these foot soldiers with the sarissa, a bronze-tipped pike fifteen to eighteen feet long. Macedon's enemies therefore faced a massed infantry bristling with spears.

In 339–338 B.C.E., Philip advanced south, crushing the disunited poleis, including Athens, and proclaiming himself supreme leader of a unified Macedonian and Greek federation. Within the city-states, the ideal of citizenship endured, but the brief era of Athenian democracy came to an end. Philip planned to cross the Aegean and attack western Anatolia, where thousands of Greeks still lived under Persian rule. In 336 B.C.E., however, a bodyguard, who might have been the tool of an aristocratic conspiracy, assassinated him.

Alexander's campaigns. The kingship then passed to Philip's son Alexander, who was barely twenty years old. Philip had given this bright boy a Greek education, Aristotle serving for a time as the lad's tutor. When the king was killed, Alexander moved with great speed to carry forward his father's plan. In 334 B.C.E., he invaded Anatolia at the head of an army of thirty-five thousand Macedonians and Greek allies. During the next eleven years, he blazed a trail of conquest nearly three thousand miles to the east. From 334 to 330 B.C.E., he fought his way to the heart of Persia,

MAP 6.3 Alexander's empire, 325 B.C.E.

Compare this map with Map 6.2 of the Achaemenid empire. What similarities and differences do you notice in the directions of conquest? Why do you think the conquered territories on the two maps overlap to such a great extent?

subduing Anatolia, Syria, Egypt, and Babylonia along the way. He engaged Achaemenid armies in three great battles, brilliantly deploying both cavalry and phalanx infantry, and he won every time against unfavorable odds. He forced the emperor Darius III (r. 336–300 B.C.E.) to flee for his life, occupied the great Persian capitals, and seized the imperial treasuries.

Marching onward to the northeastern Achaemenid provinces, Alexander led his army over an eleven-thousand-foot pass of the Hindu Kush mountains to Central Asia and the populous Amu Darya River valley. As if destruction of the Persian empire were not enough, he then pushed his exhausted troops back over the Hindu Kush and across Afghanistan to the Indus valley, where in 326 B.C.E. he routed the army of a local king. At this point even Alexander's toughest warriors refused to go farther. Relenting, he returned west, crossing the deserts of southern Iran to reach

Babylon in 325 B.C.E. In the final period of his career, from 325 to 323 B.C.E., he applied himself to organizing his empire. But before he could do much, he died suddenly after falling ill in the extreme heat of a Mesopotamia summer—and possibly after a night of heavy drinking with his officers. With no provision for a successor, his leading generals gave him a glorious funeral, then set quickly to fighting one another for his throne.

In thirteen years, Alexander created an empire larger than any state in history. He was personally charismatic and a phenomenal military tactician. Like most warlords of that era, he was also ruthless—terrorizing, killing, and enslaving countless numbers of people from Greece to India. For example, when the leaders of the Greek city of Thebes challenged his authority, he assaulted the city and razed every building except the temples and the house of a famous poet. He then sent most of the population into slavery. In Alexander's attack on the Mediterranean port of Tyre, his forces killed six thousand defenders, then had two thousand more crucified on the beach.

What did Alexander want? Alexander almost certainly aimed to create a state centered on Mesopotamia and Persia, not on Greece. He conceived of himself as ruler of a transformed Persian empire that would one day incorporate the entire Mediterranean and Black Sea basins. He introduced elaborate Persian rituals to his royal court and held audience there dressed in the flowing robe and sash of an Achaemenid potentate. Moreover, he linked his authority to Egyptian and Mesopotamian notions of divine monarchy, which were foreign to Greek tradition. After occupying Egypt, for example, he accepted the pharaoh's crown, in effect making himself a god.

Yet Alexander also assumed that the members of his governing class, whatever their ethnic origin, would accept the Greek model of culture, the only one he knew. He ordered new cities built in the Greek style, twenty-five or more of them in eastern Persia alone. These towns were to serve as military and administrative colonies and as regional economic centers. Army veterans, as well as civilian settlers drawn partly from crowded Aegean cities, formed a privileged elite over local non-Greeks, though Alexander permitted the new towns varying degrees of local self-government. Thousands of Greeks settled across the empire, facilitating Greek cultural diffusion into parts of Afroeurasia where such influences had previously been unknown.

Alexander at war. This detail from a mosaic that decorated a house in Pompeii, Italy, in the first century C.E. illustrates Alexander in combat. The mosaic commemorates his victory over the Persian emperor Darius III at the Issus River in Anatolia in 333 B.C.E. What sort of impression of Alexander do you think the artist might be trying to make?

Foundations of the Hellenistic World

The term *Hellenistic* refers to the political and cultural developments that occurred across much of the India-to-Mediterranean region in the three centuries following Alexander's death. The Hellenistic Age describes the period when Alexander's successors ruled much of this region and when Greek speakers interacted with peoples of diverse ethnolinguistic identity—Persians, Mesopotamians, Syrians, Arabs, Egyptians, Central Asians, North Indians—creating novel cultural amalgamations.

> **Hellenistic** Relating to the interaction between Greek language and culture and the languages and cultural forms of peoples of Southwest Asia, the Nile valley, the western Mediterranean, and the Black Sea region.

For about fifty years after Alexander's death, Macedonian commanders competed brutally for domination of the conquered lands. The unitary empire broke up but did not simply disintegrate. Rather, three of Alexander's former generals founded regional monarchies and established governments whose highest officials had Macedonian or Greek backgrounds, forming a Greco-Macedonian ruling class. The largest and richest of these new states was the Seleucid empire (312–64 B.C.E.), named after the former Macedonian officer Seleucus I (r. 305–281 B.C.E.). This monarchy embraced the greatest cities of Southwest Asia and the overland routes from the Mediterranean to Central Asia and India. Roughly speaking, it overlay the defunct Achaemenid domain. A second Hellenistic state emerged in Egypt under Ptolemy I, another of Alexander's generals. The Ptolemaic (TAWL-oh-may-ihk) dynasty (305–30 B.C.E.) endured for 275 years, dominating at the height of its power the Nile valley plus the island of Cyprus and parts of Libya, Anatolia, and Syria. The Macedonian officer Antigonus the One-Eyed took control of Philip's original Balkan kingdom, but this third state (the Antigonid dynasty) lost control of the Greek poleis, which once again formed their own alliance leagues. Far to the northeast in Central Asia, Greek commanders broke away from the Seleucid empire about 240 B.C.E. and founded the kingdom of Bactria. In short, Greek-speaking ruling groups continued to dominate an immense range of territory long after Alexander's empire had broken apart (see Map 6.4).

Hellenistic governments. Like the Achaemenids before them, the Seleucid and Ptolemaic monarchs regarded their authority as theoretically absolute. To them, monarchy existed chiefly to pump revenue from ordinary people to enrich the ruling elite, defend the imperial territories, and, when the opportunity arose, extend them by war. Hellenistic rulers also took responsibility for rituals that had to

MAP 6.4 The Hellenistic world and the Maurya empire, ca. 300–200 B.C.E.
Which of the states on this map is likely to have had the greatest volume of trade passing through its cities?

be performed to appease the gods in order to avert bad harvests and other disasters. The statecraft of the Seleucids and Ptolemies centered on massive displays of military might and quick repression of any outbreak of popular opposition.

Hellenistic monarchs ruled in association with an intimate circle of friends, advisors, and high officers, most of them from Greek or Macedonian families. The Seleucid realm numbered about thirty million people, and the road network the Achaemenids had built enabled state officials to collect taxes and administer justice with remarkable efficiency. The Ptolemaic government was even better organized. It had the advantage of ruling a core population

(about seven million) tightly concentrated in the Nile valley and fully accustomed to taking orders from the top. Hellenistic rulers collaborated with local village elders, nomad chiefs, and religious leaders, relying on them to help keep order in return for political and economic privileges. Both the Seleucids and the Ptolemies went to great lengths to inspire awe in their subjects, ordering construction of giant statues and temples in their honor.

In the Ptolemaic state, which became particularly good at managing economic life, a hierarchy of Egyptian officials, clerks, and secretaries supervised by Greco-Macedonian bosses regulated farming, irrigation, artisanry, commerce, and prices. They also monopolized the manufacture and trade of numerous products, including papyrus, linen, oil, and beer. This centralized economic management generally inhibited private economic initiative. The rulers expended revenue mainly on military procurement, payments to officials, regal pomp, and self-aggrandizing monuments. Conversely, the living standards of ordinary men and women appear to have declined steadily during the third century B.C.E.

Like the pharaohs before them, the Ptolemies sponsored commercial expeditions up the Nile to Nubia. In the third century B.C.E., they also sent seaborne trade missions to the southern end of the Red Sea, partly to purchase Indian goods coming across the Arabian Sea. Egyptian agents cultivated relations with local African traders and hunters as far south along the East African coast as modern Somalia. The commodity they most wanted was elephants, which they transported back to Egypt on ships specially designed to carry them. When Alexander invaded northwestern India, he learned the value of tamed elephants as weapons of war—ancient tanks, as it were. Subsequently, both the Seleucids and the Ptolemies traded in battle elephants, incorporating them into their armies.

Hellenistic society. Because of the ambitious building program started by Alexander, the number of cities in the lands his empire encompassed rose dramatically in the fourth and third centuries B.C.E. (see Map 6.4). Some of these cities, including Alexandria in Egypt, Antioch in Syria, Seleucia on the Tigris, and Pergamum in Anatolia, became large sprawling hubs of manufacture, trade, and cultural interchange. Others were no more than modest military colonies. Like Alexander, the Hellenistic rulers wanted their cities to conform to Greek cultural ideals in layout, architecture, and ornamentation. A new center should have a temple, theater, marketplace, gymnasium for athletic training and education, and comfortable villas on a neat grid of streets. New towns as far from Greece as Ai Khanum in northwestern Afghanistan resembled the cityscapes of Athens and Thebes.

The populations of these cities varied greatly from one region to another. Though thousands of Greek migrants and visitors poured into Seleucid cities, the majority of inhabitants were local people. In the bigger towns, a floating, polyglot populace of soldiers, merchants, artisans, and scholars came and went incessantly. We know little about everyday society in these places. Ethnic neighborhoods may have been a feature of some of them, but recent archaeology has turned up no general evidence that different language communities lived in isolation from one another. Excavations at Susa east of the Tigris show that houses inhabited by Greeks and other groups stood side by side, suggesting that men and women of different origins mingled freely in daily life.

The Ptolemies built few new cities, but they transformed Alexandria on the Nile delta into the greatest metropolis anywhere in Afroeurasia in the third century B.C.E. The city surpassed all other Hellenistic centers in population, wealth, and concentrated intellectual achievement. The Greek and Macedonian elite

A war elephant. The baby trailing its parent softens this image of an African elephant carrying soldiers into battle. The fighting tower may have been a Greek invention. This terra-cotta plate, dated to the third century B.C.E., comes from southern Italy.

Queen Arsinoe II: Ruler of Ptolemaic Egypt

Coruler, high priestess, and goddess, Queen Arsinoe II (316–270 B.C.E.) was one of the most powerful royal women in Egypt's long dynastic history. Her father was the Macedonian general Ptolemy I, who founded the Ptolemaic dynasty following the death of Alexander the Great. About 300 B.C.E., when Arsinoe was fifteen or sixteen years old, her father arranged her marriage, an entirely political transaction, to Lysimachus, the sixty-one-year-old king who ruled territory on either side of the Bosporus Strait. The couple had three sons in rapid succession, but Agathocles, a child from Lysimachus's previous marriage, stood ahead of them in the line of royal succession. To improve her sons' political positions, as well as her own, Arsinoe accused Agathocles of plotting to kill his father. Consequently, Lysimachus ordered him executed, a vile act that triggered violent uprisings. In 281 B.C.E., less than a year after the murder, the elderly Lysimachus died in battle against Seleucus, ruler of the Seleucid empire of Persia.

When she lost her husband, Arsinoe fled to Macedonia. Once there, she soon accepted a second marriage, this time to her own half-brother Ptolemy Keraunos. Greeks generally regarded marriage between siblings as indecent, but Arsinoe and her new spouse took their cue from Egypt, where such royal unions were customary. Ptolemy Keraunos had

Arsinoe II strikes a characteristically Egyptian pose, but she sports a Greek hairstyle.

seized part of the dead Lysimachus's territories, and he assured Arsinoe that he would place her sons back in the line of succession as his adopted heirs. He deceived her, however, and fearing these sons as potential threats to his power, murdered the two younger boys, while the eldest escaped. Arsinoe fled once again, this time back to Egypt and the protection of her full brother Ptolemy II (r. 282–246 B.C.E.), who was by this time Egypt's king.

Arsinoe lost no time getting back on her feet and maneuvering for power. She persuaded Ptolemy II that his wife was plotting against him and deserved to be sent into exile. Ptolemy not only complied but also made Arsinoe his new queen. The evidence from surviving texts and images demonstrates convincingly that, although she lived only for another five or six years, she enjoyed equality with her husband-brother as coruler and may have governed more energetically than he did. Historians think she may have helped design the strategy that led to Egypt's victory in a war against the Seleucids for control of territory in Syria. She may also have supervised a major expansion of the Egyptian navy. She appears with her brother on some coins of the period but alone on others, implying her commanding status.

In the years leading to her death in 270 B.C.E. at about the age of forty-five, Arsinoe became not only priestess of her own cult, a typical practice among Egyptian rulers, but also a goddess, worshiped warmly during her own lifetime and for a long time after. A grand shrine was dedicated to her in Alexandria, and towns were named after her in Greece.

Historians, both ancient and modern, have often represented Arsinoe as conniving and power hungry, though these qualities were hardly rare among monarchs of the Hellenistic centuries. She doubtless exercised great political influence during her brief reign, and she offered a model for ambitious Ptolemaic queens that followed her. For example, Cleopatra VII (r. 51–30 B.C.E.), the last of the Ptolemaic rulers, adopted Arsinoe's crown as her own.

Thinking Critically

What political advantages might Arsinoe have gained by encouraging her subjects to worship her as a deity while she shared the throne with her brother?

families that lived there adopted an elegant part-Greek, part-Egyptian lifestyle. The city also attracted a large, multiethnic merchant population that made money supplying luxuries to the ruling class. The Hellenistic elite liked to think of the city as a kind of outpost of the Greek Aegean, not really *in* Egypt but merely *next to* it. Actually, native Egyptians made up the great majority of the population.

Public life in Hellenistic cities was as patriarchal, that is, as dominated by males, as it generally was in urban societies throughout Afroeurasia. We have some evidence, however, that in the bustling, impersonal climate of the larger cities, upper-class women had somewhat wider scope to pursue private interests than they had in fifth-century B.C.E. Athens, where a tight guard of male relatives kept them close to home. Elite Hellenistic women engaged more openly in commercial and financial affairs, sought more education, and in some cases took up careers as poets or artists. In Egypt, the Ptolemaic monarchs sometimes married their sisters in order to keep the Macedonian dynasty free of foreign blood. Queen Arsinoe II (316–270 B.C.E.), for example, married her brother Ptolemy II (r. 282–246 B.C.E.) and shared the throne with him for five or six years.

Cultural Trends

The power of the Hellenistic states, the multiplying of cities, and expansion of long-distance trade all worked together to intensify cultural interchange among peoples of different languages and ethnic identities from the Mediterranean to India. By the sixth century B.C.E., the Greek language, as well as Greek religious, political, literary, and artistic ideas, had become known in Southwest Asia. But following Alexander's campaigns, these ideas and styles imposed themselves quite suddenly on the consciousness of numerous other peoples who had previously heard nothing about them. The conqueror and his successors built numerous cities as islands of Hellenistic culture, projects that required Greek merchants, artisans, architects, scholars, poets, and musicians to move to these new centers to implant civilized standards.

In the early third century B.C.E., a person could journey across Southwest Asia without ever losing the company of Greek speakers. Koine (common tongue), a dialect of Greek that developed in the Hellenistic world and incorporated vocabulary from other, mostly Semitic languages, became the premier medium of trade, business, and intellectual conversation wherever Greco-Macedonians dominated society. Like Aramaic in the Persian empire, Koine served as a *lingua franca*, facilitating diplomacy and business across

cultural and linguistic frontiers. A traveler in Southwest Asia would also see temples and homes reminiscent of Athens, painted pottery made in the Aegean, Greek statuary, Greek plays performed in Greek-style amphitheaters, and silver and gold coins bearing Greek inscriptions and the likenesses of Greek rulers and gods.

It is hard to know to what extent local people who lived under Greco-Macedonian rule accepted Hellenistic culture. Certainly only a small minority became fully converted to Greek ways. This group included local elites, notably political climbers who voluntarily cloaked themselves in Greek habits and styles to improve their chances of entering the charmed circles of influential men and women. Also, Greco-Macedonian army veterans and male civilian settlers typically severed personal attachments when they migrated to distant cities. Instead, they wedded local women, and the children of these mixed marriages usually had Greek names, spoke Greek, and grew up in a Hellenistic cultural milieu.

Philosophers and scientists. Literate residents of Hellenistic cities were likely familiar with the utterances of Socrates, Plato, Aristotle, and other Greek thinkers. For example, archaeologists have found faint physical traces of a treatise on Aristotle's philosophy as far from Athens as Ai Khanum in Afghanistan. On the other hand, the Hellenistic centuries also inspired new philosophical movements concerned with the practical problems of living a calm and stable life in cities characterized by social flux, commercial hubbub, and authoritarian governments. Cynicism, Epicureanism, and Stoicism were three of these movements. All of them focused on ethical choices individuals must make to find peace in an unpredictable and perplexing world. All of them extolled human reason as the proper guide to the

Hellenistic Philosophies

Philosophical School	A Key Idea	Key Thinkers	Quotation	Modern Use of Related Words
Cynicism (Cynics)	Individuals should seek freedom and self-reliance to the point of repudiating material possessions, social ties, and yearnings for pleasure.	Antisthenes (d. 350 B.C.E.) Diogenes of Sinope (d. 323 B.C.E.)	"I would rather go mad than enjoy myself." —Antisthenes	*Cynical:* distrustful of human motivations, sincerity, or honesty
Epicureanism (Epicureans)	Reality has no ultimate sense or structure, so the individual should strive to avoid pain by pursuing pleasure grounded in tranquility, self-control, and moderation practiced in the company of loyal friends.	Epicurus (d. 271 B.C.E.)	"Pleasure is the beginning and end of a happy life" —Epicurus	*Epicurean:* an individual fond of sensual enjoyment, especially in eating and drinking
Stoicism (Stoics)	Individuals have a fundamental duty to accept the role nature has assigned them. Neither pleasure nor pain is of any account, only the practice of virtue, which comes naturally by living in accordance with nature.	Zeno of Citium (d. 262 B.C.E.)	"Our individual natures are part of universal nature. Hence the chief good is life according to nature." —Zeno, after Diogenes Laertius (third-century C.E. biographer)	*Stoic:* an individual who is able to suffer pain or misfortune without complaining or revealing personal feelings

art of living. Though their founders all lived and worked in Athens, these schools attracted followers in the wider Hellenistic world.

Hellenistic intellectuals who studied mathematics, physics, and astronomy worked from the premise that general theories could be formulated to explain how the universe worked. Like Aristotle, they observed, measured, and classified rather than simply speculated. Some of their findings were way ahead of their time. For example, Aristarchus (d. ca. 230 B.C.E.) proposed a heliocentric solar system in which the earth turned on its axis and revolved around the sun, a theory that gained general world acceptance only two thousand years later. Eratosthenes (d. ca. 195 B.C.E.) used an ingenious geometric procedure to measure the circumference of the earth, coming up with a figure only fifteen miles off the mark. Euclid (d. ca. 270 B.C.E.) synthesized geometric knowledge whose axioms and theorems schools teach

today. Archimedes (d. 212 B.C.E.) pioneered the geometry of cylinders and spheres and calculated the value of pi more precisely than any earlier scholar had done. He is also said to have invented a screw device for raising irrigation water from one level to another.

Athens remained intellectually lively in the fourth and third centuries B.C.E., and new centers of learning blossomed in Pergamum and on the Mediterranean island of Rhodes. Alexandria in Egypt attracted intellectuals from near and far. The leading institution was the Museum, a kind of government-sponsored think tank for scientific, literary, and philosophical research. Next to it, the Ptolemies built a library that came to house nearly half a million books, probably the largest concentration of accumulated knowledge anywhere in the world. Among Hellenistic cities, Alexandria was undoubtedly the most cosmopolitan, a "world city" that had both a diverse population and an educated class

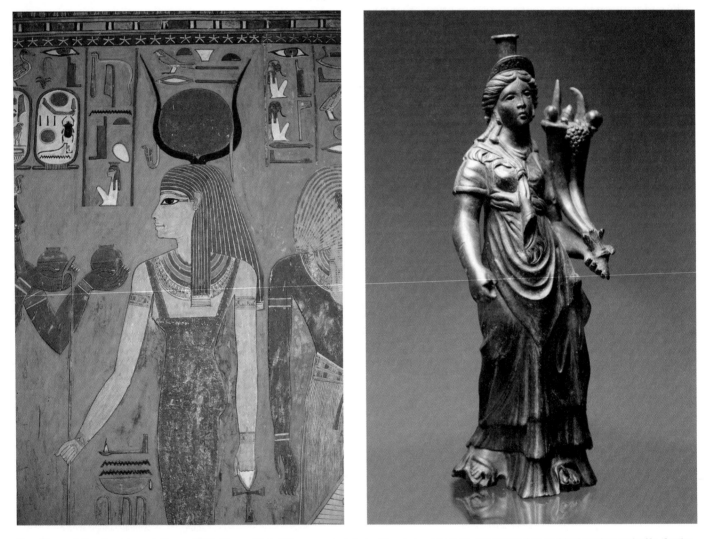

Egyptian and Greek representations of Isis. The goddess Isis was associated with nature and magic and revered as an ideal mother and wife. On the left, an Egyptian tomb mural from the fourth century B.C.E. shows Isis carrying an ankh, a symbol of eternal life, in one hand and a scepter, an emblem of dominion, in the other. On the right, the statue of a Hellenistic Isis dated to the second or first century B.C.E. holds a cornucopia, a Greek symbol of fertility. What other artistic elements in the two images would you characterize as distinctively Egyptian or Greek?

that shared philosophical, scientific, and aesthetic ideas with similarly minded people scattered in other cities.

Cultural cross-currents. Despite the influence of Greek language and cultural forms thousands of miles from Athens, the immense region exposed to them remained a complex cultural stew. Koine Greek gradually became the dominant language in Anatolia, but this did not happen in Syria or Egypt. In the Seleucid domain, Aramaic appears to have remained as important as Greek for government and commerce. Cultural forms not of Greek origin also gained importance within the Hellenistic zone. For example, Greco-Macedonians abroad adopted Egyptian or Persian gods into their pantheon by associating them symbolically with Hellenic divinities having similar character traits. The Egyptian goddess Isis took on a quasi-Greek identity and became popular in the Seleucid lands. Worship of deities like Isis sometimes metamorphosed into religious cults devoted to secret rituals, spiritual fellowship, and exercises to achieve union with the divine. Several of these mystery religions, as they are known, spread widely in the Hellenistic world and became popular among people of all classes. Among cultural fashions, rich Hellenistic families acquired tastes for female slaves of South Asian origin. These women fetched attractive prices because their exotic origins and looks elevated their value as servants in the households and bedchambers of the wealthy.

Jewish communities continued to multiply across Southwest Asia and the eastern Mediterranean between the fourth and second centuries B.C.E. The Jewish population in Alexandria rose to around 180,000, as much as a third of the city's total. Thousands learned to speak Greek, rather than Hebrew or Aramaic, as their first language. Jewish intellectuals produced a substantial body of religious, philosophical, and dramatic literature in that language. In the third century B.C.E., Ptolemy II sponsored translation of the Hebrew scriptures into Greek, a work known as the Septuagint. Greek-speaking Jews who were losing their knowledge of Hebrew needed this new edition, and non-Jews now had greater opportunity to become familiar with Jewish belief and practice. On the other hand, many Jews either resisted Hellenistic culture or had little contact with it, notably in Jerusalem and its vicinity. Some educated Jews studied Greek philosophical ideas but as worshipers of one God had nothing to do with the deities on Mount Olympus.

Buddhism and the Maurya Empire in India

FOCUS In what circumstances did Buddhist beliefs and practices achieve success among growing numbers in South Asia between the fifth and third centuries B.C.E.?

The first state to unify much of South Asia arose nearly simultaneously with the Seleucid and Ptolemaic empires. In 321 B.C.E., two years after Alexander died, the young warlord Chandragupta seized Magadha, the most powerful of a cluster of kingdoms along the Ganges River. He subdued several neighboring states and then advanced to the Indus River, where about 303 B.C.E. he defeated Greco-Macedonian occupiers, forcing them out of most of northwestern India. Ashoka, Chandragupta's grandson and the third ruler in the Maurya dynastic line, conquered more of India (see Map 6.4) and tried to create more efficient and orderly centralized government founded on a set of moral principles. He derived these precepts from the teachings of Buddhism, which was just then emerging in India as a popular religious movement.

Foundations of Buddhism

We saw in Chapter 5 that Brahmanism took root in northern and central India in the later second millennium B.C.E. Brahmanism was an intricate lacework of metaphysical ideas, sacred sacrifices, and social rules. In its spiritual dimension, it offered the individual hope of eventual release from earthly tribulation and endless cycles of rebirth. It involved worship of numerous gods and goddesses (Shiva and Vishnu chief among them), all of these deities manifestations of Brahman, the transcendent essence of the universe. This multisided religion gave the individual a spiritual anchor through the medium of daily rituals, whose performance varied from one locality to another.

The Brahmins, or male members of the privileged priestly class, aspired to define and regulate the religious and social conduct of all social groups, including the ruling warrior families. As their ritual power grew, Brahmins tended to neglect the longings of ordinary people for spiritual salvation. Instead, they devoted themselves to elaborate animal sacrifices and magical practices on which, they insisted, the well-being of the universe depended. Salvation was possible to those of low station, but only if they worked their way up the ladder of ritual purity to the Brahmin level, a process likely to require multiple rebirths, perhaps thousands of them. The sign of advancement was purer karma, the principle that good deeds done in a previous lifetime determined an individual's status in the present one. The Brahmins, however, defined good deeds mainly as scrupulous attention to ceremony and unquestioning acceptance of the rules that ritually separated the social classes, known in modern times as castes, from one another in matters of occupation, social relations, marriage, and physical contact.

The Buddha's message. Whereas Brahmins collaborated with aristocratic warriors (the Kshatriya class) to maintain the hierarchy of social inequality, teachers and preachers began to offer alternative paths to moral living and divine salvation, sometimes denouncing Brahmin dogmatism. One of these sages was Siddhartha Gautama, known to his followers as the Buddha, or Enlightened One (ca. 563–ca. 483 B.C.E.). He was born into a Kshatriya family in what is

The great stupa at Sanchi. According to tradition, when the Buddha died, his cremated remains were placed in eight earthen burial mounds, or stupas. The emperor Ashoka later redistributed the ashes among more than 60,000 stupas. To house some of the ashes and other relics of the Buddha, Ashoka also built monumental stupas, including an early form of this celebrated shrine at Sanchi in central India. Pilgrims replicate the Buddha's exodus from the world by entering the stupa's stone enclosure through one of four gates. Then they walk clockwise around the spherical structure, whose vault represents the dome of the cosmos.

today Nepal. He gave up family wealth and power to become an ascetic, an individual who renounced worldly cares and pleasures for a life of self-denial and spiritual reflection. Accompanied by a growing body of followers, he preached a message of moral renewal and the possibility of freedom from suffering.

All men and women, the Buddha taught, are responsible for right living, not mainly by acting out rituals but by giving up material desire, greed, and all conduct that kept them enslaved to pain and distress. In his best-known sermon, he expounded the Four Noble Truths: first, that earthly life is inevitably unfulfilling; second, that this suffering is a consequence of our cravings for transient things and experiences; third, that the way out of suffering is renunciation of craving; and fourth, that the only course of action is to walk the Eightfold Path, a plan for attentive, decent, meditative living. This commitment included *ahimsa* (uh-HIM-suh), or the practice of nonviolence, on the principle that all life-forms are sacred and cosmically interrelated. At the end of the Eightfold Path lies nirvana, a limitless, indescribable

state where the self is extinguished and thereby released from the cycle of rebirth and suffering. Many historians have noticed similarities between Buddhist thought as it evolved from the fifth century B.C.E. and Hellenistic philosophical movements that offered moral designs for living in harmony with the cosmos.

The Buddha's words and acts, first put in writing long after his death, originated from the Brahmanist tradition, not in opposition to it. He accepted the validity of rebirth and karma, and he did not preach social revolution against the rigid class hierarchy. He associated karma, however, with day-to-day righteousness, not ritual conformity. People of all social ranks could escape from suffering if they fulfilled the demands of the Eightfold Path. The quest, however, required great dedication.

In the centuries following the Buddha's passing, the new religion germinated mainly in self-contained communities, or monasteries. There, early devotees gathered to work, meditate, and perform charitable works. Laypeople, those who stayed "in the world" and did not become monks, also flocked to Buddhism by frequenting the monasteries or materially supporting them. Brahmanism categorized women as having essential roles in society but nonetheless as innately inferior and a source of ritual pollution to men. The Buddha, however, admitted after much consideration that both women and men could achieve nirvana and that women should be admitted to monasteries. He did not, however, preach equality between the sexes, and except in Tibet female monasteries never took root. The archaeological record shows that between the fifth and third centuries B.C.E., Buddhist *stupas,* structures in which holy relics associated with the Buddha or other saintly individuals were placed, multiplied across northern India. By the time of the Maurya empire, Buddhist practice was well established among urban mercantile and professional classes in much of the subcontinent.

Jainism. Numerous schools of philosophical thought flourished in India in the Buddha's time, but among these only Jainism (JEYEN-ism, from a Sanskrit word meaning "saint") endured as a significant religious movement into the modern era. The founding teacher, Mahavira (the "Great Hero," ca. 540–468 B.C.E.), left his warrior class family to seek enlightenment, just as the Buddha had done. Both of those worthies taught that self-centered material desires obstructed the individual's path to salvation—the attainment of a state of pure bliss. But, in contrast to the Buddha, Mahavira recommended a life of self-denial so strict that only the most zealous monk could hope to meet its demands. The members of Jain monasteries were prohibited from owning property, having sexual relations, or killing any life-form. Monks often carried brooms to brush away insects before sitting down, and they hired people outside the monastery to harvest their crops since no devotee could do that without murdering, as it were, tiny animals. Mahavira himself is reputed to have set the highest standard by going naked and eventually starving himself to death. In contrast to the Buddhist way, Jainism did not spread beyond South Asia before modern times. But there it grew into a significant religious minority, categorized by some as a sect within Hinduism.

The Reign of Ashoka Maurya

Buddhist teachings had wide impact in India during the reign of Ashoka (273–232 B.C.E.), who commanded an empire of about fifty million people employing many of the bureaucratic methods of the earlier Achaemenids of Persia. Pataliputra, Ashoka's capital in the middle Ganges valley, was reportedly nine and a half miles long and defended by mammoth timber walls. Here, the emperor received diplomatic missions, dispensed justice, and coordinated the work of his ministries, which regulated taxation, commerce, and agriculture. He launched his reign as an autocratic conqueror, but in a moment of regret over a particularly bloody military campaign, he repudiated repression and cruelty and formulated a philosophy of moral government. The key concept in his ideology, which drew heavily from Buddhist teachings, was *dhamma* (or dharma). For the emperor this meant commitment to nonviolence, political moderation, family

Pillar with a lion capital. The emperor Ashoka had this pillar erected at the town of Vaishali north of the Ganges River to commemorate the day the Buddha preached his last sermon. The use of the lion icon as an emblem of royalty points to Persian cultural influence on Ashoka's India.

Rock Edicts of the Emperor Ashoka

Most of Emperor Ashoka's rock edicts were written in a South Asian script that later fell out of use. While later generations knew about the inscriptions, they were unable to read the texts. Instead, people passed on oral legends about what the stone markers were thought to say. These legends claimed that Ashoka had erected the rocks at important Buddhist sites to commemorate people or events, so that pilgrims passing by would be aware of the locations' significance. As Buddhism waned in India over several centuries, people forgot the connection between Ashoka and the rock inscriptions altogether.

It was not until 1837 that the British scholar James Prinsep deciphered the ancient script and read the edicts. Only then did their subject matter become known. Prinsep did not realize that Ashoka was the author of the texts because the emperor referred to himself on the known inscriptions only as the Beloved of the Gods. Although other scholars suspected that the edicts were Ashoka's, they confirmed this only in 1915, when an inscription with the emperor's name in it was finally discovered.

The texts here are short selections from rock edicts in which Ashoka sought to explain how to rule justly and to spread Buddhist values in the empire.

ROCK EDICT 1

Formerly, in the kitchen of Beloved-of-the-Gods, . . . hundreds of thousands of animals were killed every day to make curry. But now with the writing of this Dhamma edict only three creatures, two peacocks and a deer are killed, and the deer not always. And in time, not even these three creatures will be killed.

ROCK EDICT 5

In the past there were no Dhamma Mahamatras [officials who looked after the spiritual and material needs of people], but such officers were appointed by me thirteen years after my coronation. Now they work among all religions for the establishment of Dhamma, for the promotion of Dhamma, and for the welfare and happiness of all who are devoted to Dhamma. They work among the Greeks, the Kambojas, the Gandharas, the Rastrikas, the Pitinikas and other peoples on the western borders. They work among soldiers, chiefs, Brahmins, householders, the poor, the aged and those devoted to Dhamma—for their welfare and happiness—so that they may be free from harassment. They (Dhamma Mahamatras) work for the proper treatment of prisoners, towards their unfettering, and if the Mahamatras think, "This one has a family to support," "That one has been bewitched," "This one is old," then they work for the release of such prisoners. They work here, in outlying towns, in the women's quarters belonging to my brothers and sisters, and among my other relatives. They are occupied everywhere.

ROCK EDICT 6

Beloved-of-the-Gods . . . speaks thus: In the past, state business was not transacted nor were reports delivered to the king at all hours. But now I have given this order, that at any time, whether I am eating, in the women's quarters, the bed chamber, the chariot, the palanquin, in the park or wherever, reporters are to be posted with instructions to report to me the affairs of the people so that I might attend to these affairs wherever I am. And whatever I orally order in connection with donations or proclamations, or when urgent business presses itself on the Mahamatras, if disagreement or debate arises in the Council, then it must be reported to me immediately. This is what I have ordered. I am never content with exerting myself or with dispatching business. Truly, I consider the welfare of all to be my duty, and the root of this is exertion and the prompt dispatch of business. There is no better work than promoting the welfare of all the people and whatever efforts I am making is to repay the debt I owe to all beings to assure their happiness in this life, and attain heaven in the next.

Sources: "The Edicts of King Ashoka," an English rendering by Ven. S. Dhammika (Kandy, Sri Lanka: Buddhist Publication Society, 1993).

Thinking Critically

What does the passage from Edict 1 infer regarding Ashoka's conversion to Buddhism and the effect it had on his actions? According to Edict 5, how did the Dhamma Mahamatras spread the value of compassion in their work? How did their efforts transcend social class barriers? Why do you think Ashoka was inclined to publish an edict about the importance of conducting imperial business promptly? What particular moral qualities does Ashoka think a good Buddhist monarch should have? How would you compare Ashoka's approach to kingship with that of Alexander the Great and other Greco-Macedonian rulers?

harmony, toleration among social groups, and dedication to the well-being and prosperity of all imperial subjects. Ashoka did not aim to reform the Indian social hierarchy, but he encouraged his subjects to accept social responsibilities for one another beyond the boundaries of class and ethnicity. We know quite a bit about his conception of *dhamma* because he had proclamations inscribed on rocks and pillars near population centers and along well-traveled roads. In one of his rock edicts, he described the event that set him on a new path, referring to himself in the third person as the Beloved of the Gods:

> Beloved-of-the-Gods, . . . conquered the Kalingas eight years after his coronation. One hundred and fifty thousand were deported, one hundred thousand were killed and many more died (from other causes). After the Kalingas had been conquered, Beloved-of-the-Gods came to feel a strong inclination towards the Dhamma, a love for the Dhamma and for instruction in Dhamma. Now Beloved-of-the-Gods feels deep remorse for having conquered the Kalingas.[9]

As "Beloved of the Gods," Ashoka, like monarchs to the west, claimed universal authority over humankind and vowed to rule justly. However, he seems to have differed from the Greco-Macedonian rulers of his era in his explicit appeal to his subjects to behave toward one another in a spirit of toleration and generosity. He appointed special officials to travel the provinces, spreading Buddhist teachings on moral behavior. Putting into practice the Buddhist precept of *ahimsa,* he also preached against the killing of animals, promoted vegetarianism, and admonished the Brahmins to halt bloody animal sacrifices.

Ashoka's philosophy was almost certainly calculated to address real problems of social conflict in a time of rapid economic change. Agricultural production in the two great river valleys was rising. Cities were mushrooming, and artisans were forming guilds to organize an array of urban industries such as metalworking, textile manufacturing, and banking. This commercialization no doubt aggravated social tensions. Although merchants and crafts workers were becoming more prosperous, the Brahmin and warrior classes generally treated them as inferiors. Consequently, many productive members of society patronized Buddhist monasteries, which practiced social egalitarianism and offered brighter hopes of salvation. Buddhism also appealed to farmers and laborers (Shudras) for the same reasons.

Dhamma as a philosophy of government did not outlast Ashoka, but it nonetheless had important long-term consequences. The emperor tried to achieve his aims of social integration partly by developing South Asia's infrastructure of communication and transport. He improved the great trunk road that ran from the city of Taxila in the upper Indus valley to Pataliputra on the Ganges, accommodating travelers with shade trees, wells, and rest houses. Other tracks stimulated exchange of foodstuffs and manufactures between the northern grain-growing plains and the tropical forests of the

far south. Long after the Maurya dynasty vanished, the road network expedited trade and cultural interchange across South Asia. Ashoka also appears to have had his edicts carved into rocks and pillars as a way of building social consensus across class lines regarding the aims of *dhamma.* We have no idea how well these messages worked as mass communication, but edicts that survive represent precious historical evidence of developments in India 2,300 years ago.

A second major consequence of Ashoka's reign was that Buddhism became for several centuries the most dynamic religious force in India. The tenets embodied in *dhamma,* extensive conversions among merchants and artisans, and the improved communication network all facilitated the spread of this faith. For several centuries Buddhism competed vigorously with Brahmanism as an alternative vision of cosmic truth and righteous living. Ashoka himself propagated Buddhist teachings by sending missionaries far and wide. Ancient sources report that he dispatched one of his sons to broadcast *dhamma* on the island of Ceylon, where Buddhism became firmly established. To the northwest his messengers carried *dhamma* into Afghanistan. A rock edict located near the Afghan city of Kandahar is inscribed, not in Prakrit, the Indic language of the Maurya state, but in both Greek and Aramaic, as if Ashoka were deliberately reaching out to peoples of the west.[10] Yet despite Buddhist success in South Asia and beyond, the Brahmin class continued to dominate the yearly cycle of sacrifices and festivals in the rural villages. And after a few centuries, Buddhism gradually declined in the land of its birth, though flowering elsewhere in Eurasia, as we see in later chapters.

When Ashoka died after a forty-two-year reign, the *dhamma* experiment ended abruptly. Succeeding Maurya kings possessed little of his energy and none of his moral vision. Revolts broke out on the edges of the empire, and the imperial bureaucracy decayed. Within a few decades South Asia's first universal empire collapsed. The next great enterprise to unify India would not appear for another six hundred years.

Cavalry and Caravans in Inner Eurasia

> FOCUS How did dense agrarian societies from the Mediterranean to China change as a result of developments in Inner Eurasia in the 600–200 B.C.E. period?

Monarchs from India to the Mediterranean, as well as rulers in China, kept a watchful eye on peoples of Inner Eurasia, the northerly land of steppes, forests, mountains, and deserts that stretches nearly five thousand miles across Afroeurasia. As their numbers grew, Inner Eurasia's pastoral nomadic groups began to organize politically on a larger scale than merely local chieftaincies. At the same time, trade across the region grew busier. Dusty trails connected

Inner Eurasian societies both with one another and with the densely populated, urbanized lands to the south and east.

Nomad Power

On the Inner Eurasia steppes, pastoral communities organized themselves in extended kinship groups, a social system suited to societies that moved from pasture to pasture as the seasons changed rather than inhabiting a fixed territory year round. That is, people expressed their social identity not primarily in terms of *where* they lived but in terms of *who* their shared paternal ancestors were, their grandfathers, great grandfathers, and so on. A group that interacted regularly in daily life and that claimed descent from a forebear who lived a few generations back constituted a lineage (see Chapter 3). Lineages were typically embedded in larger social groups, numbering hundreds or even thousands of living men and women, that we may call "clans." All the lineages constituting a clan claimed descent from a common ancestor that lived in the more distant past. On an even larger scale, several clans might regard themselves

tribe The largest social group in a region whose members claim shared descent.

as genealogically related, constituting a **tribe.** Clan and tribal identities did not have much significance in daily life. Rather, leaders called on loyalties at those levels mainly when large numbers of people had to be mobilized for defense or war.

From about the eighth century B.C.E., we have some evidence of clans and tribes forming large military coalitions led by elite families. These allied bands of mounted archers took advantage of technological innovations, including improved leather and metal horse harness, the riding saddle (though without stirrups), iron as well as bronze weaponry, and, perhaps most important, the light but powerful composite bow (see Chapter 5). Pastoral and agricultural communities regularly traded with one another, but some herding societies built up enough destructive potential to entertain ideas of attacking farm settlements, cities, or even densely populated agrarian regions. In the first millennium B.C.E., therefore, a recurring theme in world history appears: persistent political tensions and periodic warfare between mounted nomads and their settled neighbors.

Ancient texts identify Inner Eurasian warrior alliances under a variety of names—Scythians, Cimmerians, Sakas, Sarmatians, and several others. From the eighth century B.C.E., mounted bands harried the northwestern frontiers of China, and in the following century a throng of Cimmerian archers attacked the Assyrian empire in northern Mesopotamia. Of all these marauders, we know most about the Scythians. Herodotus, the Greek historian of the fifth century B.C.E., described them in detail, and archaeologists have uncovered elite Scythian tombs

littered with worked gold and other precious grave goods. Scythians inhabited the Pontic-Caspian steppes north of the Black Sea, and they spoke one or more Indo-European languages. From the sixth century B.C.E., Scythians established commercial links with Greek settlements around the rim of the Black Sea, trading grain, furs, livestock, honey, and slaves for Mediterranean commodities and manufactures. Affluent Scythian families acquired tastes for Greek wine and olive oil. Some groups added Greek gods and goddesses to their own collection of deities and displayed Greek ceramic ware in their tents.

Near the end of the seventh century B.C.E., Scythian cavalry crossed the Caucasus Mountains to pillage farms and towns from Syria to Iran. According to Herodotus, Scythian archers took part in the final destruction of the Assyrian state. These warriors, Herodotus reports, were particularly disposed to headhunting:

> As for the actual skulls—the skulls of their enemies, that is, not all skulls—they saw off the bottom part of the skull at

Scythian warriors. The two hardy-looking men on this vessel of Greek workmanship hold long spears.

the level of the eyebrows and clean out the top bit. A poor Scythian then wraps a piece of untanned cowhide tightly around the outside of the skull and puts it to use like that, while a rich Scythian goes further: after wrapping it in cowhide he gilds the inside and then uses it as a cup. Also, if a Scythian falls out with one of his relatives, they fight to the death in the presence of their king, and the winner treats the loser's skull in the way I have just described. When he has important visitors, he produces these skulls and tells how they had once been his relatives, and how they made war on him, but he defeated them.[11]

Ancient legends about Amazons, or ferocious women fighters, probably originated with the Scythians. According to one Greek text, "Their women ride horses and shoot arrows and hurl javelins from horseback and they fight in campaigns as long as they are virgins."[12] A significant number of graves excavated on the Pontic-Caspian steppe have revealed the skeletons of women in full battle gear.

The rulers of agrarian states eventually understood they had to push back at pastoral intruders. For example, in both Central Asia and on the plains west of the Black Sea, Achaemenid armies campaigned aggressively against the Scythians and other nomads. The Persians demonstrated that a strong centralized state with ample agrarian resources, many soldiers, and the skills to build walls and forts could turn the tables, challenging militarized herders on their own territory. But by the late first millennium B.C.E., pastoralists were discovering ways to organize even larger military alliances and hold them together longer.

Early Times on the Silk Roads

Trade across Inner Eurasia became significant from at least the late third millennium B.C.E., when a cluster of small walled cities sprang up in Central Asia (see Chapter 3). These cities became key centers for transshipping goods of high value and low bulk—silk, gems, furs, metalwork, ceramics—overland between East Asia and westerly lands. An unbroken chain of Inner Eurasian trails, known by the modern term "silk roads," gradually formed. There were several alternate routes not just one, and their locations tended to shift over time. Some goods might have been relayed very long distances. For example, archaeologists have discovered strands of East Asian silk on the mummy of a woman who lived in Egypt about 1000 B.C.E.

We know little about commercial organization in the early silk road centuries. Associations of merchants, guides, packers, and armed guards likely banded together temporarily to share costs and risks and, if they reached their destination safely, to sell their merchandise at a profit. If we can infer from later times how this trade worked, merchants who shared common language, culture, and business customs likely set up their own associations to facilitate trade, much as the Phoenicians and Greeks established diasporas, or scatterings of merchants and commercial agents across the Mediterranean. The silk roads therefore became regular channels of human interchange, not only for material goods but also for "cultural capital" of all kinds—new technologies, religious teachings, and artistic styles.

Why did the silk roads become busier in the first millennium B.C.E.? One factor is certainly the continuing agrarian and urban expansion taking place in the agrarian lands from China to the Mediterranean, a growth that generated rising demand for products that could not be produced locally. Inner Eurasia's population also grew steadily in that millennium. This happened mainly because the specialized economy of pastoral nomadism, together with farming in river valleys here and there, allowed relatively more people to inhabit these dry latitudes. Most herding societies wanted to encourage ties with the villages and cities that lay along the edges of the steppes in order to trade grain, livestock products, metals, and furs for goods they could not make themselves. Moreover trade moved not only east and west on the silk roads but also north and south across contrasting climatic and ecological zones. To the north, foragers and hunters of the temperate Siberian forests joined the commercial web, trading furs to pastoral peoples for wares that in some cases originated in distant cities to the south. In short, Inner Eurasia was by no means a vacant land that caravans scurried across to get from one civilization to another. Rather, it became a locus of both military and economic power, exerting a huge impact on neighboring regions of much denser population.

•   •   •

Conclusion

The political ascendancy of Alexander the Great and his Greco-Macedonian successors over a large piece of Afroeurasia lasted less than two hundred years in some places and no more than three hundred anywhere. Even so, we can only marvel that the young son of the king of a modest Balkan state instigated a run of conquests that reached from the Nile to the Indus. Alexander, together with the Achaemenid emperors who came before him, demonstrated that by the later first millennium B.C.E. the technology of overland transport, road building, army supply, and weaponry reached a level of sophistication that permitted a determined conqueror to subjugate populations numbering in the tens of millions. The Greco-Macedonian and Indian rulers who came after Alexander also showed that many millions of subjects could actually be organized, made answerable to royal laws, and taxed. In the era of the Hellenistic kings and the Maurya emperors, authoritarian governments supported construction of dozens of new cities and the expansion of farming and trade. Wealth piled up in splendid capitals as never before, and class divisions between rich minorities and ordinary people remained rigid or became more so, and long-distance communication intensified not only across the India-to-Mediterranean lands but also in lesser measure between that region and China by way of the emerging silk roads.

By the late third century B.C.E., the Afroeurasian political map was changing in significant ways. To the east the Maurya dynasty disintegrated and for the next six centuries smaller states competed for power in South Asia while also battling invaders from the steppes. The Greco-Macedonian rulers of Persia progressively lost territory, some of it to Inner Eurasian horse archers. The Athenians' lively experiment with direct democracy proved to be, not a new trend, but a political oddity. In the far west, Rome, a modest city-state on the west side of Italy, gradually rose to regional dominance. Far to the east, the leaders of the Qin and Han dynasties united much of northern and central China after several centuries of rivalry among several regional kingdoms. A new era of grand empire building was about to begin.

. . .

Key Terms

Achaemenid empire of Persia 161
Alexander the Great's empire 173
Athenian empire 171
Buddhism 181
chattel slavery 170
dhamma (dharma) 183
Hellenistic 175
Iliad and *Odyssey* 169

Jainism 182
Maurya empire 181
natural philosophy 172
oligarchy 169
Peloponnesian War 173
phalanx 171
Ptolemaic dynasty 178
satrapy 165

Scythians 185
Seleucid empire 175
silk roads 187
Sparta 169
tribe 185
universal empire 165
Zoroastrianism 167

Change over Time

9th–4th centuries B.C.E.	Scythian pastoral society flourishes north of the Black Sea.
8th–4th centuries B.C.E.	Self-governing Greek poleis dominate the Aegean Sea region.
ca. 563–483 B.C.E.	Siddhartha Gautama, the Buddha, lives.
550–330 B.C.E.	The Achaemenid empire centered on Persia proclaims a universal mission to rule the world.
6th century B.C.E.	Achaemenid rulers adopt Zoroastrian beliefs and rituals.
ca. 540–468 B.C.E.	Mahavira, founding teacher of Jainism, lives in India.
480 B.C.E.	The Greek naval victory over Persia at the Battle of Salamis thwarts Persian expansion farther west.
470–399 B.C.E.	Greek philosopher Socrates teaches in Athens.
ca. 461–429 B.C.E.	Pericles leads in Athens and the Athenian maritime empire rises.
431–404 B.C.E.	Greek city-states engage in Peloponnesian War.
336–323 B.C.E.	Alexander the Great conquers and rules the largest state in world history to this point.
321–185 B.C.E.	Northern and central India are united under the Maurya empire, which reaches its zenith during the reign of Ashoka Maurya.
312–64 B.C.E.	The Seleucid empire, the largest and richest of the Hellenistic states, dominates Southwest Asia.
305–30 B.C.E.	The Ptolemaic dynasty rules a Hellenistic state in Egypt.

Please see end of book reference section for additional reading suggestions related to this chapter.

7 An Age of Giant Empires

300 B.C.E.–300 C.E.

Bactrian camels in the Gobi Desert, Mongolia.

amel raising is a demanding occupation. The species will breed only once a year, and during this short time it may behave badly—biting, kicking, or spitting at anyone who comes near. Males find copulation an awkward business and sometimes require assistance from their human handlers to make a go of it. When mating is successful, a camel's pregnancy lasts thirteen months. A female gives birth rarely more often than once every two years. Despite these vexations, patient camel breeders of the third millennium B.C.E. gave the ancient world one of its most versatile domesticates.

Camels, along with cattle, sheep, goats, and horses, allowed humans to build herding economies in arid regions of Afroeurasia where intensive farming was not possible. Camels provided pastoral societies with meat, milk, hides, and bone. And because they have wide-spreading feet for easy walking on sand or snow, double rows of eyelashes for protection against blowing sand, and a biological constitution that allows them to forego water for more than two weeks, camels were well suited to moving people and cargo across arid terrain. In the first millennium B.C.E., pastoral nomads and merchants rode Bactrian (two-humped) camels or hitched them to wagons to cross the steppes, deserts, and mountains of Inner Eurasia. From northern India to the Sahara Desert, the dromedary (one-humped species) became the animal of choice for transport across dry country. The harnessing of camels was one of the developments that contributed to intensified exchange across Afroeurasia in the period from 300 B.C.E. to 300 C.E.

This chapter investigates how and why Afroeurasia's regional zones of intercommunication not only grew larger but also joined more firmly to one another. The chapter explores this phenomenon in connection with the rise of several new states—a few of them gigantic—that formed a nearly continuous chain of polities stretching across Afroeurasia. Each of these states provided a political framework for channeling revenue from their populations to their treasuries, while also refining the communication systems that tightened cultural and economic bonds. And because each state bordered, or nearly bordered, one or more of the others, tentacles of exchange reached out to connect one network with another. This process could be interrupted by wars. Nevertheless, it was in these centuries that a system of land and sea routes running continuously, if still somewhat tentatively, across Afroeurasia first took shape.

Human interchange became particularly intense around the Mediterranean Sea. In the first part of the chapter, we focus on the rise of Rome, which grew to encompass the entire Mediterranean rim, all of its islands, and deep hinterlands in western and central Europe. The spatial core of the empire was the sea itself, an expanse crossed easily by sailing ships and oar-powered galleys except in stormy winter months. Rome's seaborne thoroughfares conducted troops and officials thousands of miles from Italy and made possible the diffusion of a distinctively Hellenistic style of intellectual, religious, and artistic culture to cities as far apart from one another as northern England and the edge of the Sahara Desert.

In the second part of the chapter, we zoom to the opposite end of Afroeurasia, where the Qin (chin) and Han dynasties successively ruled a state that mirrored Rome in its size, population, and military might. The heart of the empire was not a central sea but the Yellow and Yangzi River valleys, which sustained the millions of farmers whose taxes largely paid for the imperial bureaucracy and army. In the Han centuries, from 206 B.C.E. to 220 C.E., Confucianism and Daoism

Chapter Outline

• • •

(DOW-ism), two belief systems originating in the fifth century B.C.E., became major shapers of Chinese society and culture.

The third part of the chapter surveys five of the most important states that occupied Afroeurasian lands between Rome and Han China: the Xiongnu (SHEE-OON-noo), Parthian, and Kushana empires of Asia, and the Kush and Axum kingdoms of Africa. Like the two giants, these monarchies embodied the hemispheric trend toward centralized states capable of amassing great wealth and military power.

In the chapter's final section, we turn to developments made possible by this new chain of states in Afroeurasia. First, we investigate the marked intensification of long-distance commerce, especially exchange on the Inner Eurasian silk roads and on the tropical southern seas. Second, we survey the growth of Buddhism and Christianity, two belief systems that transcended identification with any particular region or ethnolinguistic group and that spread far beyond their natal lands.

A Panoramic View

MAP 7.1 Major states and empires in Afroeurasia, 100 B.C.E.

A string of large states stretched across Afroeurasia in 100 B.C.E. What geographic and climatic features did these seven states share?

Rome and Mediterranean Unification

FOCUS How did the Romans, whose history began as the inhabitants of a modest city-state, succeed in subjecting peoples all around the Mediterranean rim to their rule?

In long-term historical perspective, it is useful to view the Mediterranean Sea, not as a watery barrier separating three continents from one another, but as an internal sea of Afroeurasia, binding together people all around its rim from very ancient times (see Map 7.1). This domain of intercommunication also included the Black Sea, the Mediterranean's big "lagoon" to the northeast. The agricultural, mineral, and marine wealth of the sea basin was potentially immense. Prospects of exploiting that wealth impelled Phoenicians, Greeks, Etruscans, Egyptians, and Persians to try at different times in the first millennium B.C.E. to dominate parts of the basin by controlling strategic points—islands, ports, and narrow sea passages.

republic A type of government in which supreme power rests with a body of citizens possessing rights to vote to approve laws and to select public officials and representatives.

In the third century B.C.E., Rome, a **republic** and the dominant state on the Italian peninsula, emerged as a new Mediterranean power. Unlike its predecessors, however, Rome kept expanding until it encircled the sea. At its zenith around 100 C.E., the empire embraced a population of fifty to sixty million and land area more than half the size of the continental United States. Like Achaemenid Persia and other earlier empires, it aspired to universal rule, that is, to sovereignty over the whole world.

This section of the chapter encompasses two major periods of Roman history. The first was the Republic (509–27 B.C.E.), when the Romans conquered Italy and most of the Mediterranean basin. In that period, republican government meant, as it generally did in the Greek city-states, that all adult males possessing citizenship had rights and obligations in public life. The second period was the Principate (27 B.C.E. to the later third century C.E.), when individual rulers achieved autocratic command of an enormous multiethnic state. In both periods, episodes of political instability, social upheaval, and provincial revolt disturbed the long-term pattern of imperial unity.

Rome the Republic

When Rome emerged as a republican city-state in the late sixth century B.C.E., the peoples of Italy were mostly farmers. The early Romans spoke an ancient form of Latin, a tongue in the Indo-European subfamily known as Italic. Their modest city on the lower Tiber River lay between two more sophisticated spheres of urban life. To the north were the Etruscan city-states (see Chapter 5). Kings of Etruscan origin ruled Rome throughout much of the seventh and sixth centuries B.C.E. To the southeast were numerous cities that Greek-speaking colonists had established on Sicily and along the southern Italian coast.

The Romans borrowed elements of culture from both of these neighbors. The Etruscans contributed ideas of city planning, gold and bronze metallurgy, particular gods and goddesses, arch-building technology, the Greek alphabet in modified Etruscan form, and, we should add, the toga. Greek influences on Rome were even greater. When the Romans threw off Etruscan domination about 509 B.C.E., they set up a government patterned basically on Greek-style republicanism. Rome's aristocratic land-owners fell under the spell of Greek philosophy, medicine, drama, and art. The Romans also adopted many Greek deities. These Hellenistic influences washed over Rome in successive waves: in the fourth century B.C.E., when Romans admired the Greek cities of southern Italy from afar; in the third century, when they conquered those cities and made them junior allies; and in the second century, when Rome's legions invaded Greece itself. Thereafter, Rome became the major center from which Hellenistic culture radiated out across the western Mediterranean and Europe.

Republican government and society.

When Rome became a republic, that is, a state founded on the collective authority of all land-owning male citizens, social tension no doubt already existed between the society's two principal classes. One was the aristocratic minority known as the patricians. The wealthy and privileged families who constituted this class sat in the Senate, an elective and advisory body. The other group, making up the great majority of the citizen population, was known collectively as the plebs. In early republican days, the patrician families tried to keep a tight hold on power. But plebeian leaders gradually won legal equality for all citizens, a written set of laws (the Twelve Tables), and the privilege of forming an assembly

A patrician of Rome. Like aristocratic classes in all ancient agrarian societies, the Roman elite put great value on quality of their family pedigree. This gentleman displays the busts of two of his venerable ancestors.

called the Plebeian Council. This body had authority to enact laws, hold trials, and elect officials called tribunes to look after plebeian interests. Between the fifth and second centuries B.C.E., the plebs gained additional rights and responsibilities. In the long term, this trend helped defuse social class conflict.

Elected officials, or magistrates, managed Rome's internal and foreign affairs. At first the Republic had only two magistrates, called consuls, who were elected to one-year terms and who supervised civil affairs and military campaigns. As Rome grew, however, several new public offices had to be created to oversee such affairs as public works, commerce, and military supply. Eventually, plebeians gained the right to hold high offices, including the consulship, and to take seats in the Senate, a governing body of about three hundred males who served for life. Senators managed the Republic's finances, wars, diplomacy, and provincial administration. Male citizens could vote in one of the popular assemblies that passed laws to regulate property, commerce, slavery, duties of officials, and other spheres of social life. These bodies were the Plebeian Council, plus the Curiate and Centuriate Assemblies, which included both plebeians and patricians. Roman leaders generally honored the rule of law, the precept that legislation represented the will of the citizenry and should be enforced equitably and consistently.

As in the Greek city-states, the majority of the Republic's population was excluded from the major rights and responsibilities of citizenship. Foreign immigrants and slaves (many of them captured as war prisoners) had no citizenship rights, though freed slaves could become citizens with certain restrictions. Rome usually offered generous political terms to peoples that it conquered on the Italian peninsula but granted them citizenship only incrementally over several centuries. Free women could attain citizenship but with serious restrictions. They could not attend assemblies or serve as either elected or appointed officials. On the other hand, free women could make wills, sue for divorce, circulate in public quite freely, and hold certain priestly offices. Wives and mothers in wealthy families might exert great informal influence on public decisions. Upper-class women gradually achieved rights to buy and sell property, though they remained legally subordinated to fathers, husbands, or other guardians.

The Republic's political institutions operated to perpetuate the collective government of the Roman people and to prevent any single individual from accumulating too much power. Citizens voted frequently in their assemblies, but the system was only narrowly democratic. In contrast to the assembly in Athens in the fifth century B.C.E., for example, the Roman assemblies had no provision for citizens to debate proposals. Rather, they simply voted yes or no. Citizens gathered in the forum at the center of the city or on the nearby Field of Mars to vote as members of either "centuries" (divisions of the population based on wealth) or "tribes" (territorial divisions). Each century or tribe had just one collective vote. Moreover, the richest families effectively stage managed the popular assemblies most of the time to get the decisions they wanted. Plebeians who took advantage of the Republic's prosperity to accumulate wealth tended to ally themselves not with poorer plebeians but with patrician families. In its politics, Rome remained an oligarchy, a state dominated by a small minority with power founded fundamentally on wealth.

Rome did almost all its public business through networks of patrons and clients. That is, rich and powerful individuals (patrons) sought loyal supporters from among the relatively poorer and weaker classes (clients), offering them jobs, money, physical protection, favors, or marriage alliances. In return, they expected favorable votes in the assemblies, public demonstrations of support, and a variety of personal services. **Patron–client systems** formed into hierarchical webs, with the clients of the richest and most powerful patrons acquiring clients of their own. This process replicated itself down the line to the level of people so poor and politically weak they could become no one's patron. Put another way, until quite late in its history the Roman empire did not have a strong bureaucracy, that is, a system in which officeholders were entrusted to carry out their duties as impersonal agents of the state, rather than as personal dependents or allies of someone higher up the chain of command.

> **patron–client system** A vertical social and political system in which individuals possessing relative degrees of power, wealth, or social status offer protection or economic benefits to other individuals in return for personal loyalty and services.

Rome's early imperial conquests. The Republic deployed a formidable army of citizen-soldiers. As in the fifth-century Greek city-states, property-owning farmers who paid for their own swords and other weapons constituted the core of the army. At first, infantrymen grouped in large Greek-style phalanxes, but eventually commanders cut the size of combat units to improve their speed and maneuverability. The army also formed cavalry divisions, armed auxiliaries from conquered peoples, and a corps of engineers who built roads, bridges, walls, and forts. Citizen-soldiers were expected to embody the Republic's military culture of steadfast service and manly virtue, though the promise of loot and land also motivated war service. Military campaigns provided a safety valve for social class tensions over land and income because the state awarded farm plots in conquered territories to both soldiers and poor citizens. At the same time, rich landlords got war prisoners for slave labor on their giant estates.

Rome's nearly continuous drive to expand got under way in the fourth century B.C.E. when the Republic's legions (military divisions) conquered central Italy. In the following century, the army subjugated the rest of the peninsula plus Sicily (see Map 7.2). In 264 B.C.E., Rome went to war against the Phoenician maritime empire that from Carthage, its

MAP 7.2 Roman imperial expansion, to 300 C.E.
What factors of physical geography may have shaped the directions of Roman conquest?

capital on the coast of what is today Tunisia, dominated the ports, trading posts, and routes of the western and central Mediterranean. Rome constructed a powerful navy, and over the span of 119 years the two states fought three wars, known as the Punic Wars (from the Latin word *Punicus*, meaning Phoenician). The second war (218–202 B.C.E.) featured the Carthaginian general Hannibal leading an army that included brightly painted African war elephants from Spain over high Alpine passes to Italy—though most of the beasts soon died in Italy. The invaders came close to attacking the city of Rome, but after supply and reinforcement lines dried up, Hannibal had no choice but to withdraw. In the long run, the Republic could mobilize people and resources that Carthage could not match. In 146 B.C.E., Roman troops obliterated the city of Carthage, thereby securing full control of Sicily, southern Iberia (Spain), and a long stretch of North African coast. Consequently, the empire gained thousands of square miles of wheat land in those regions, as well as a windfall of silver from Iberian mines.

After Rome's victory over Carthage, the Senate adopted a more aggressive strategy of empire building around the Mediterranean. Macedonia and Greece were absorbed, and from there, soldiers crossed the Aegean Sea to Anatolia, as Alexander the Great had done two hundred years earlier. In the first century B.C.E., a large part of both Anatolia and Syria, territories that had been part of the Hellenistic Seleucid empire, fell to Rome. In 30 B.C.E., Egypt, the other major Greek-ruled kingdom in the eastern Mediterranean, surrendered to Rome following a naval victory over Queen Cleopatra, the last monarch of the Ptolemaic dynasty.

In Iberia and Gaul (the ancient name for the region centered on modern France), legions pushed back Celtic warriors. Within another century the imperial frontiers reached to the Danube River and central Britain. On the southern shores of the Mediterranean, Romans advanced westward from Carthage across North Africa, progressively annexing the Berber-speaking peoples that inhabited what are today Tunisia, northern Algeria, and Morocco. In the first century C.E., Rome had about 250,000 troops under arms, including a navy of galleys and sailing ships that plied the Mediterranean transporting soldiers and supplies and clearing out pirates. The state drafted a large percentage of Roman males into the army at age seventeen, typically keeping them in service for seven years.

The Republic falters. Ironically, the republican institutions that propelled the empire to greatness did not survive its success. In the first century B.C.E., the regime of collective, elected government teetered slowly, then collapsed under the colossal weight of imperial might and wealth. The wars of conquest generated vast riches in tribute, plunder, trade profits, and slaves, which poured into Rome. As this happened, the Senate became increasingly fixated on internal struggles for choice military commands, governorships, and commercial deals. To fight distant wars, citizen-soldiers had to leave their farms for longer periods, putting women, children, and slaves in charge of much of Italy's agrarian economy. Meanwhile, wealthy citizens bought up the lands of absentee farmers and consolidated them into estates, called *latifundia*, which exploited huge slave gangs to produce grain and other commodities for commercial markets. Somewhat like African slave labor in the Americas in early modern times, large concentrations of chattel slaves on Roman plantations increased the likelihood of rebellion. Slave uprisings in Sicily in 135 B.C.E. and in Italy under the slave gladiator Spartacus from 73 to 70 B.C.E. forced the state to expend large sums to keep enslaved workers under control. As the empire grew, cities mushroomed but also became

THE RISE OF ROME	
509 B.C.E.	Romans oust Etruscan kings and found republican city-state
272 B.C.E.	Armies complete conquest of Italy
146 B.C.E.	End of the Punic Wars and destruction of Carthage
146 B.C.E.	Conquest of Greece
83–82 B.C.E.	Civil war in Rome
73–70 B.C.E.	Slave rebellion led by Spartacus
63 B.C.E.	Capture of Jerusalem
51 B.C.E.	Conquest of Gaul completed
49–31 B.C.E.	Civil war in Rome
30 B.C.E.	Egypt annexed to Rome
27 B.C.E.	Start of Principate under Augustus Caesar
27–180 C.E.	*Pax Romana*, when empire reaches greatest extent
43 C.E.	Emperor Claudius invades Britain
44 C.E.	Mauretania (Algeria and Morocco) annexed to Rome
106 C.E.	Conquest of Dacia (Romania)

socially less stable. Ex-farmers and their families migrated to the city of Rome and other centers by the tens of thousands. The state had to support this underemployed population with free grain distribution, while the gulf between urban rich and poor stretched wider.

Continuous military expansion coupled with the shrinking availability of citizen-farmers, convinced the Senate to eliminate property qualifications for service in the legions. Ambitious commanders such as Julius Caesar exploited this new policy to recruit virtually private armies, offering pay, war booty, and free farms to landless men in return for personal allegiance. Thus, professional fighters replaced citizen-soldiers, and imperial wars became occasions for commanders to beef up their personal political influence.

Rome the Empire

In the first century B.C.E., Rome's problems reached a tipping point. Italian groups that had been denied citizenship rebelled, and factional fighting and intrigue periodically paralyzed the capital. From 49 to 31 B.C.E., a ferocious civil war pitted the mightiest generals—Julius Caesar, Pompey, Mark Anthony, and Octavian—in a deadly competition for power that might have spelled the breakup of the empire. However, Octavian, a gifted politician, emerged triumphant and restored public order against overwhelming odds. Under the name Augustus ("the August One"), he ruled single-handedly, though with Senate compliance, from 27 B.C.E. to 14 C.E. He named himself First Citizen, or *Princeps,* inaugurating the era of the Principate, which lasted until the end of the third century C.E.

Pax Romana, **or not.** From then on, Rome had the typical characteristics of an authoritarian monarchy and virtually

A Roman slave tag. The message in Latin on this iron slave collar offers a reward of gold to anyone who returns the wearer to his master. What might you infer about slavery in Rome from the use of tags like this one?

Extinguishing rebellion. The emperor Titus celebrated his army's suppression of the Jewish rebellion in Palestine (66–70 C.E.) by erecting a triumphal arch in Rome. In this relief on one of the arch's walls, Roman troops parade through the streets of the capital carrying plunder from the temple in Jerusalem. The soldiers exult in their victory by holding aloft the temple's menorah, or candelabrum, a sacred symbol of Jewish faith.

no resemblance to a republican city-state. The citizen population, war-weary and disenchanted, accepted the new autocracy without much complaint. The empire's high period of order and prosperity, known as the *Pax Romana,* or Roman peace, extended until nearly the end of the second century C.E.

The imperial frontiers reached their greatest extent in the reign of Trajan (98–117 C.E.). He conquered more territory in eastern Europe (Dacia, or modern Romania), the northwestern fringe of the Arabian Peninsula, Armenia to the slopes of the Caucasus Mountains, and both the upper and lower Tigris-Euphrates valleys. However, his successor Hadrian (r. 117–138 C.E.) retreated from the last three of these distant Southwest Asian territories (the Tigris River was more than two thousand miles from Rome). Rather, he gave his attention to stabilizing the remaining and still enormous empire, deploying an army of 300,000 soldiers to defend the frontiers (including Hadrian's Wall across north central Britain) and to suppress rebellions.

Despite the advantages of Roman security, millions of people around the Mediterranean did not want to be absorbed into the empire as tax-paying subjects. Numerous peoples first resisted imperial invasion and later rose against military occupation. The army forged the empire amid great violence and held it together by coercion. Resistance fighters and rebels sometimes won battles though usually lost their struggles in the end. In Palestine, for example, much of the Jewish population, provoked by tensions between Jews and Greeks, Roman misrule, and onerous taxation, rose up in 66 C.E. The rebellion spread across Palestine,

but in the year 70, Roman forces led by a son of the Emperor Vespasian besieged and captured Jerusalem, sacking it and burning down the holy temple. Flavius Josephus, the first-century Jewish historian, described the seizure of the city, already in a desperate state owing to lack of food:

> When [the Roman soldiers] went in numbers into the lanes of the city with their swords drawn, they slew those whom they overtook without and set fire to the houses whither the Jews were fled, and burnt every soul in them, and laid waste a great many of the rest; . . . they ran every one through whom they met with, and obstructed the very lanes with their dead bodies, and made the whole city run down with blood.[1]

The imperial political system. Rome retained some of the forms and symbols of republican government, such as the Senate, long after its emperors centralized their power. But in a shift away from republican symbolism, rulers beginning with Augustus willingly associated themselves with an imperial cult. He allowed Romans to venerate his "life force"—the word is *genius* in Latin. And after Augustus's reign, the Senate began to issue decrees awarding divine honors, that is, deification, to deceased rulers. People revered the ruler by dedicating temples and altars to him and by displaying his image in processions and festivals. Imperial cult worship first became popular in the eastern empire, where rulers had long cultivated this tradition. The practice spread west, though in Rome itself, memories of the Republic provoked some private skepticism about making dead monarchs into gods. Moreover, despite imperial

Individuals MATTER

Boudica: British Rebel Leader

A bronze statue of Boudica stands near Westminster Bridge in London.

In 43 C.E. the Emperor Claudius, mainly to overcome a perception in Roman political and military circles that he was weak and dim-witted, ordered an army of forty thousand troops to invade Britain. The island was then a patchwork of Celtic-speaking British kingdoms and clans. The Romans suppressed initial resistance, made dependent clients of several British kings, and started building new towns, including London (Londinium). Just seventeen years into the occupation, however, the government faced a massive revolt under the leadership of Boudica, queen of the British people called the Iceni.

Little is known about Boudica prior to her rebellion, though she was the wife of Prasutagus, the Icenian king. The Roman chronicler Cassius Dio, writing more than a century after Boudica's death, offers a description of her: "In stature she was very tall, in appearance most terrifying, in the glance of her eye most fierce, and her voice was harsh; a great mass of the tawniest [sandy-colored] hair fell to her hips."[2] Dio's depiction may be a figment of his imagination, but this description has persisted down through history, probably because it nicely conjures up the image of how a "warrior queen" might appear.

The Iceni avoided direct Roman control by allying themselves voluntarily with the invaders as soon as they arrived. Prasutagus believed he had an agreement with the Romans to pass his authority as a client king to Boudica and the couple's two young daughters after his death. The Iceni elite, however, had grown wealthy mining and selling salt, and the Romans wanted that revenue. The historian Tacitus described what happened to the Iceni about 60 C.E., when Prasutagus died:

> Kingdom and household alike were plundered like prizes of war, the one by Roman officers, the other by Roman slaves. As a beginning, his widow Boudica was flogged and their daughters raped. The Icenian chiefs were deprived of their hereditary estates as if the Romans had been given the whole country. The king's own relatives were treated like slaves.[3]

In response to this treatment, Boudica vowed to avenge her family's humiliation. She assembled a rebel army in league with neighboring people also frustrated by Rome's oppressive rule. Boudica led her troops to three decisive victories over Roman units, sacking and burning the southern British cities of Colchester, London, and St. Albans, which the imperial army had left poorly defended. In a fourth battle, however, Boudica's rebels lost to a much smaller but better disciplined Roman force. The insurgents scattered, and both Boudica and her two daughters shortly died, perhaps from either illness or suicide. Nevertheless, Roman officials feared more outbreaks. To pacify the country, the occupiers changed their tactics, seeking to conciliate and compromise with local leaders rather than repress them harshly.

Cassius Dio and Tacitus, both men born long after the uprising took place, composed the only accounts we have of Boudica's revolt. Their narratives leave many gaps, and we have no archaeological evidence of the queen's short reign. Like the Egyptian monarch Cleopatra, Boudica remains a historically intriguing figure as much for the legend she generated as for her actual exploits. In the nineteenth century, when British global power was at its height, Boudica served as a symbol of national strength and determination. Queen Victoria (r. 1837–1901) invoked the memory of Boudica the warrior queen as an example of a female determined to defend the rights of her ancient British people. She remains today one of Britain's semimythical folk heroes.

Thinking Critically

Since Britain was itself an imperial power in the nineteenth century, conquering peoples in Africa and Asia, why would British citizens wish to honor as a folk hero an ancient woman who resisted a foreign invasion?

---

autocracy, the Roman legal system, which grew increasingly complex, remained vital. The worthiest emperors collaborated with jurists and legal scholars to enforce laws fairly.

The Republic's style of governing through networks of patrons and clients carried over to the empire. In many regions, emperors preferred to collaborate personally with dependent kings and princes rather than annex territory outright. Provincial governors appointed to office often brought along their own male family members, friends, and other clients to help them with their duties. Since governors typically held office for only one year, even the most dedicated appointees moved quickly to enrich themselves and their entourage by skimming revenue or trading gifts and favors with local people of means.

Cities of the empire.

Rome ruled its provinces mainly from cities, which grew in size and number along with conquered territory. From a collection of villages on a cluster of hills near the Tiber River, Rome burgeoned into a metropolis of nearly a million people by the second century C.E. Augustus and his immediate successors expanded and beautified it, constructing new public forums, temples, theaters, arches, and statues. The great amphitheater called the Coliseum, which opened in 80 C.E. in the reign of Titus, could hold about fifty thousand spectators for games and dramatic performances. The elite minority lived in magnificent houses built around grand open-air courtyards, while hundreds of thousands of ordinary folk crowded into multistory apartment buildings, about a fifth of the population surviving on public handouts of grain.

The eastern Mediterranean rim had long been urbanized. But many eastern cities grew bigger because of the presence of Roman garrisons and demand throughout the empire for the fine wares their artisans manufactured. Alexandria in Egypt and Antioch in Syria, for example, reached populations of more than 100,000. In the western provinces, that is, in North Africa and in western Europe beyond Italy, pre-empire towns were scattered and typically small. Roman rule, however, stimulated urbanization to meet the need for garrisons, administration, and trade. In frontier regions, the state often awarded free land to immigrant settlers.

One remarkable example is the city of Timgad, which lies in modern Algeria nearly one hundred miles inland from the Mediterranean. The Timgad region was home to Berber-speaking herders and farmers who had mostly lived beyond the reach of Roman legions until the first century C.E. The emperor Trajan had Timgad built from the ground up to serve as a military colony on the southern imperial frontier. As it became a grain- and cattle-producing center, architects adorned it with Hellenistic temples, theaters, baths, palatial homes, and a triumphal arch.

Cultural Romanization.

Timgad's urban refinement illustrates the spread of a distinctly imperial style of culture around the Mediterranean rim. In all ancient empires, cultural standardization took place in some measure, especially among elite classes. Rulers usually expected local aristocrats and chieftains to imitate the tastes, fashions, and refined ways practiced at the royal court. Contrariwise, local elite families in conquered territories often rushed to mimic imperial culture in order to display their allegiance and enhance their social prestige.

Romanization involved a complex intermeshing of imperial Roman and local ethnic and linguistic ideas and customs. Hellenistic influences were paramount, displayed notably in public architecture and naturalistic sculpture and painting. Greek

> **Romanization** The spread within the Roman empire, especially among elite classes, of a style of social and cultural life founded on practice in Roman Italy.

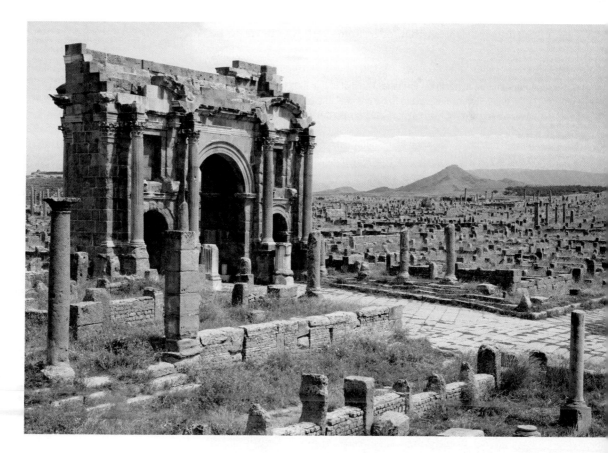

Rome's far southern frontier. The sprawling ruins of Timgad, a city built in the early second century C.E., protected imperial territory in North Africa from the incursions of Berbers who inhabited the nearby Aurès Mountains. In what other ways might a distant frontier town like this one have served the empire?

remained the most prestigious language in the eastern provinces, and throughout the empire affluent Roman families obliged their children to learn it. Latin, however, became the language of imperial administration and the primary medium of literature, law, rhetoric, and science in the western regions.

Generally speaking, Romanization transformed the western empire more than the eastern, the cities more than the countryside, and affluent elites more than ordinary people. In western Europe and North Africa, local kings and clan leaders who spoke Berber, Celtic, Germanic, and other local languages often worked hard to transform themselves into bona fide Romans by learning Latin, donning togas, and building Italian-style villas decorated with ceramics and statuary. Cities in Gaul, Iberia, and other western lands arose as much smaller versions of Rome, complete with temples, amphitheaters, baths, and arenas for chariot races.

Ordinary men and women, especially in rural areas, tended to cling steadfastly to their local customs. Romanization reached them in some measure, however, because they visited provincial towns, had contact with Roman colonists, and used imperial coinage, which circulated widely as the empire grew. Numerous and varied religious ideas also circulated, and new ones tended to attract followers among all social classes. For example, worshipers of Isis, the Hellenistic spirit derived from the Egyptian fertility goddess, built temples for her in Rome. The cult of Mithras, a god of Persian origin linked to the sun, gained popularity among Roman soldiers, who bore it to all corners of the empire. Romanization never came close to homogenizing the empire, but the Mediterranean basin attained a level of cultural integration that, once Rome fell, was never to be seen again.

A Persian god in northern England. The ruin of this little temple dedicated to the deity Mithras lies next to Hadrian's Wall, the complex of walls, forts, towers, and gates Roman soldiers built across the width of England in the second century C.E. to defend imperial towns against Celtic marauders. The cult of Mithras, imported from Southwest Asia, gave spiritual solace to soldiers posted on the empire's far northern edge.

The Era of the Han Empire in East Asia

FOCUS As the Han and Roman empires developed between about 200 B.C.E. and 200 C.E., what similarities and differences emerged in their political, social, religious, and economic systems?

For several hundred years, political developments in the Mediterranean basin and East Asia followed a fairly similar trajectory. At both ends of Afroeurasia, population, urbanization, and economic production accelerated in the late first millennium B.C.E. In both regions a single state gained ascendancy over several states between the fourth and third centuries B.C.E. In East Asia the forces of Shi Huangdi, founder of the Qin dynasty (221–207 B.C.E.), united a large part of China at approximately the same time that Rome fought and won its second war against Carthage (218–210 B.C.E.). The Qin state had only two rulers, but the Han dynasty that immediately followed it lasted for nearly 450 years (206 B.C.E.–202 C.E.), a period corresponding to Rome's most vigorous centuries. The Qin and Han dynasties together mark the beginning of a Chinese tradition of centralized, bureaucratic government that lasted with only one interruption down to the early twentieth century. Stretching about three thousand miles east to west, the Han empire at its zenith exceeded Rome in territory. Both empires encompassed peoples of diverse languages and ethnicity, but both also facilitated commercial integration and cultural interchange over large regions (see Map 7.3).

The Qin Dynasty and the First Emperor

The Qin state appeared in the fourth century B.C.E. as a minor agrarian kingdom located in the upper Wei River valley. Gradually, it gained dominance over its neighbors, emerging victorious from the Warring States period, two and a half centuries (475–221 B.C.E.) of political fragmentation and conflict in northern China. Shi Huangdi, or First Illustrious Emperor, managed during a reign of eleven short years (221–210 B.C.E.) to set up a centralized government more elaborate than that of any earlier Chinese state. He organized the empire into forty provinces, each headed by an appointed governor and army commander, who replaced

QIN AND HAN DYNASTIES	
475–221 B.C.E.	Warring States period
221–206 B.C.E.	Qin dynasty, founded by Shi Huangdi, First Illustrious Emperor
206 B.C.E. –220 C.E.	Han dynasty, founded by Liu Bang
188–180 B.C.E.	Reign of Empress Lu
141–87 B.C.E.	Reign of Han Wudi; empire reaches greatest extent

MAP 7.3 The Qin and Han empires.
Why do you think the Han state incorporated the long tongue of land that extends to the northwest?

once powerful regional lords. He then subdivided these provinces into numerous local administrative districts. He conscripted young men into his army, encouraging enthusiastic service by allowing common soldiers who killed many enemies to rise in the ranks. He also drafted peasant men and women to build roads, dikes, canals, and palaces. Earlier rulers had erected barriers of pounded earth to defend China's northwestern land frontiers against attack. Shi Huangdi ordered labor gangs to extend and connect these barricades. In this way the Great Wall first took shape, though later rulers added most of the stone wall construction that survives today.

The First Emperor's vision of an efficient authoritarian state rested on a Chinese school of thought known as Legalism. This austere philosophy asserted that human nature was fundamentally corrupt, obliging the state to closely regulate people's lives. Legalist scholars argued that laws and punishments should apply equally to everyone, whether aristocrats or peasants. State officials, furthermore, should be appointed for their ability to get the job done, not for their moral character or high social status.

Because Legalist ideology demanded standard regulations and procedures, Shi Huangdi aimed to rationalize not only politics but also economic and cultural life. He standardized weights and measures and reduced the several different coinages circulating in China to one. Perhaps most important for China's later cultural development, he instructed scholars to standardize and simplify Chinese writing, an evolving logographic system that included thousands of individual signs, not a simple alphabet. Policies that promoted uniformity meant that even though East Asian peoples continued to speak many different languages and Chinese dialects, officials, scholars, and merchants throughout the empire could now better understand one another in writing.

Since the First Emperor's time, scholars have been ambivalent about his record. In accord with Legalist principles, he and his officials praised farmers and artisans, not the aristocratic class, as the moral backbone of the state. Peasants may generally have honored him because he kept order and insisted on equality before the law. On the other hand, he severely punished all who defied him, encouraged his subjects to spy on one another, and ordered burning of books that he did not think served the interests of the state. According to one tradition, he took vengeance on several hundred disobedient scholars by burying them alive. He spent colossal sums on his own tomb near Chang'an (modern Xian) in north central China. Undergoing excavation

An army of clay. Rank upon rank of soldiers equipped with crossbows, swords, and spears and accompanied by horses and chariots guard the excavated burial chamber of the First Emperor Shi Huangdi. Artisans made the terra-cotta warriors from molds but added distinctive features to each face. The twenty-one-square-mile complex near modern Xian contains close to 8,000 life-sized figures. What sentiments might have motivated the emperor to order such a grandiose project?

since the 1970s, this astonishing mausoleum, with its army of life-sized terra-cotta soldiers and horses, each one unique, is regarded as both a marvel of the ancient world and a testament to the efforts of the ordinary folk who were obliged to construct and embellish it.

The Han State and the Ascendance of Confucianism

When the First Emperor died, his empire nearly collapsed. Within a few years, Liu Bang (r. 206–195 B.C.E.), a man of peasant origins who built up a military following, pulled the state back together under the dynastic name Han, a word that also came to refer to Chinese-speaking people in general. Liu Bang and the monarchs who followed him succeeded partly by retaining many of the Legalist laws and regulations of the Qin dynasty and by developing a hierarchy of officials reaching from the royal palace down to the village. At its height, the Han government may have employed twenty times more officials than Rome ever did.[4] The period of greatest stability and prosperity extended from the rule of the Empress Lu (188–180 B.C.E.) through the long reign of Han Wudi (141–87 B.C.E.).

Confucian ethics and the Han empire. Under Han Wudi, the set of moral and ethical ideas associated with

the sage Confucius, who had died nearly 340 years earlier, were incorporated into Han imperial ideology. Confucius (551–479 B.C.E.) was born into a minor noble family known as Kong. The name the world knows him by is derived from the Chinese *Kong Fuzi*, meaning "Master Kong." He served at a princely court for a time but then took to wandering from one kingdom to another, gathering disciples eager to discover ways to improve Chinese society and government. Like other moral teachers of that era, he sought a path out of the violence and disorder that afflicted China in the era of the Eastern Zhou (770–256 B.C.E.), a dynasty that lost almost all real authority over violently competing regional lords.

In the two and a half centuries after Confucius died, political mayhem in northern China became worse—the tumultuous Warring States period. Nevertheless, scholars and reformers continued to gain inspiration from his *Analects*, the collection of his sayings transmitted orally from one generation of students to another. Scholars such as Mencius (ca. 370–300 B.C.E.) elaborated on Confucian ideas and continued to appeal to kings and princes to exchange their greed and power-hunger for righteous and responsible government. The Qin First Emperor appears to have publicly represented himself as a righteous ruler of the sort Confucians would have admired. But it was only after 140 B.C.E., when Han Wudi came to the Han throne, that Confucianism became closely identified with the Chinese state and its governing class.

Many scholars characterize Confucianism as a path of moral and ethical enlightenment rather than as a religion. Confucius and his disciples affirmed the existence of the supernatural universe, but they had little to say about gods, the afterlife, or the workings of the divine. In the Han era, Confucian thinkers espoused four central ideas. The first was that all people share a common bond of humanity and should behave respectfully toward one another, displaying charity, courtesy, and sympathetic understanding. Second, the ideal individual was the gentleman or gentlewoman who embodied maturity, confidence, and refinement, never rudeness, vanity, or cruelty. Third, ethical principles should uplift the state. Rulers should govern righteously and prudently because when they do, they enjoy the trust and loyalty of their subjects. By acting with benevolence and compassion, the monarch demonstrates that he possesses divine approval, or the Mandate of Heaven, the moral concept that first emerged in the Zhou period several centuries earlier.

Fourth, peace in society requires propriety, that is, dedication to thinking and doing the right thing as mapped out by custom and tradition. Harmony in the family is the key to harmony in the world, and the greatest expression of propriety within the family is **filial piety.** "In serving your father and mother, you may gently admonish them," Confucius declared in one of the *Analects*. "But if you see they have no intention of listening to you, then be respectful as before and do not disobey them. You might feel distressed but should never feel resentful."[5] Decorous behavior should guide all relationships, parent to child, friend to friend, subject to sovereign, and sovereign to subject. Rules of conduct expressed in proper ritual should shape all social and political relations. Confucian ideology categorized women as appendages of their husbands, brothers, and fathers. As in Rome, however, women of wealthy families had some latitude to realize talent and exercise power. Empresses and wives of officials exerted political influence, and some educated women produced Confucian literary works.

Founding an academy of Confucian studies, the Emperor Wudi established the model of the scholar-bureaucrat—the literate, humane official who devotes his life to gentlemanly, evenhanded management of the empire. The Han state continued the First Emperor's strategy of centralizing power by shifting local authority from aristocratic landlords to imperial appointees organized in a pyramid of authority

filial piety The quality in children of showing respect and care for their parents and all ancestors.

Lady Dai's funeral banner. Modern scholars have learned an astonishing amount about Lady Dai, a Han noblewoman who died about 168 B.C.E. In 1972 archaeologists working in Hunan province discovered Lady Dai's tomb, her wondrously preserved body encased in four nested coffins and twenty layers of cloth. A t-shaped silk banner covered the innermost coffin. The painting on the silk illustrates ancient Chinese conceptions of heaven, earth, and the underworld. In the lower half of the banner, Lady Dai herself stands before two kneeling attendants. The figure at the top of the banner seated on a snake may represent Lady Dai's ascendance into the heavenly realm.

extending from the imperial palace to local districts. Wudi appointed intelligent commoners to office, not just aristocrats, and wrapped official activity in layers of ceremony. Generally, Han government relied more on the moral character and talent of officials and on their loyalty to the bureaucratic system than on personal ties between powerful officeholders and their clients and retainers, which turned the wheels of government in Rome.

Daoism: a different way. Probably all of the world's major cultural traditions have displayed two parallel tendencies in their moral and religious systems. One has been to exhort individuals to commit themselves to firm rules of moral conduct in their relations with one another as the foundation of community order. The other has been to urge detachment from the world's social complexities and to seek meaning and fulfillment in private meditation, study, or simple living.

Early Confucian philosophers argued for public moral commitment and activism to ensure stability at all levels of society. In the same centuries, however, other truth-seekers contended that individuals should not try to confront the world's greed, disorder, and violence but to disengage from society and to live quietly and privately in harmony with the cosmos. This philosophy had similarities to Stoicism in the Hellenistic world. People should seek oneness with the Dao, or Way—the invisible, indefinable, transcendent principle underlying all reality. All phenomena in the universe exist in relationship to one another, including forces that seem to be opposites (*yin yang*). Human efforts to organize, regulate, or change the world, rather than accepting the eternal flow of the Dao, lead ultimately to mayhem and confusion.

The complex set of beliefs and practices that came to be known as Daoism probably had roots in ancient Chinese ideas about ancestral and nature spirits. The earliest Daoist scripture dates from at least the fourth century B.C.E. and is associated with the sage named Laozi. This five thousand word collection of sayings, the *Daodejing* (DOW-DAY-JIHNG), or the *Classic Text of the Way and Virtue,* expresses the concept of *wuwei* (woo-WAY), the achievement of harmonious being through the paradox of "actionless action." As the *Daodejing* instructs:

> Whoever mean to take this realm and rule it—
> I see them failing to attain that end.
> For this realm below, a sacred vessel,
> Never may be subject to such rule.
> They ruin it who try,
> Lose it who hold on.[6]

Skepticism about all absolutes, that is, anything claiming to be unconditionally good or bad, beautiful or ugly, encouraged Daoist thinkers to meander along many different philosophical and spiritual byways. In time these included speculative explorations of medicine, diet, magic, martial arts, alchemy, quests for immortality, and *feng shui,* the art of living in harmony with one's physical and natural environment.

Daoist masters criticized Confucians for their vain struggles to organize and manage society. Confucians reproached Daoists for passively ignoring social responsibility. In fact, however, no titanic clash of belief systems occurred. Rather, in the Han era these multifaceted modes of thought emerged as two general tendencies in Chinese cultural life, overlapping and blending in many ways, for example, in their commitment to individual moral behavior and use of ritual. The most dedicated Confucian magistrate might, as it were, engage in Daoist meditation and study at home over the weekend.

Han economy and society. From the cosmopolitan capitals of Chang'an and, later, Luoyang, Han officers ruled a population that in the first century C.E. numbered about sixty million, probably slightly more than in the Roman empire. The productivity of Chinese farmers was clearly on the rise. Because many peasants owned land, people bought and sold it freely. Because sons inherited property in equal shares, individual holdings were likely to get smaller with each new generation. Peasants therefore had good reason to farm more efficiently and open new land to cultivation where opportunity presented itself.

Wheat, millet, and rice farmers, who increasingly used iron tools, made several important technological advances. These included the wheelbarrow, the seed drill, and the animal breast strap. Until the third century B.C.E., horses and oxen were harnessed with a throat-and-girth device that choked them if the load they had to pull was too heavy. The new breast strap, later perfected as the cushioned collar harness, transferred the load pressure from the horse's throat to its chest, allowing it to haul several times more weight. Another Chinese invention was the cast iron plow, which

Papermaking. A Han artisan raises a mesh screen from a vat of pulp. The thin layer of pulp remaining on the screen will be left to dry, forming a sheet of paper. What advantages might paper have had over silk, wooden tablets, or bamboo strips as a writing surface?

had a curved plate that pushed overturned soil to one side, burying cut weeds and forming furrows that drained excess water from the field. Iron plow technology extended the range of intensive agriculture in China, especially in the rainy, rice-growing south. The silk industry grew rapidly when farm women learned how to produce long, strong strands of fiber from the boiled cocoons of silkworms fed exclusively on mulberry leaves. Finally, paper made from rags, hemp, flax, or mulberry bark first appeared in the Han era, eventually replacing bamboo strips as a writing surface.

The Confucian conception of social hierarchy placed scholars and educated officials on top, farmers and artisans in the middle, and merchants on the bottom. Members of the commercial class, scholars argued, deserved this low station because they made their living buying and selling rather than producing anything useful. Even so, trade flourished in the Han era, and many new towns sprang up. Luoyang, the dynasty's second capital, reached a population of something like 500,000 at the start of the Common Era, making it probably the largest city in the world after Rome.

Han expansion. The territorial growth of the Han state, which got seriously under way in the second century B.C.E. under Han Wudi, had military, demographic, and cultural dimensions. The huge Chinese army, wielding swords, axes, and powerful crossbows, moved out in all directions, pushing the empire's borders south of the Yangzi River as far as the northern reaches of Vietnam and northeastward to Manchuria and the Korean peninsula. Most of the conquered peoples spoke languages other than Chinese. As the state expanded, merchants and land-hungry Chinese peasants followed voluntarily. In the first two centuries C.E., somewhere between five and ten million farmers migrated to the Yangzi valley and further south. As these cultivators penetrated the subtropical latitudes, they switched from northern grain crops, especially wheat and millet, to wet-field rice. Once southern lands came under the Han military umbrella, Chinese officials moved in to organize society and transmit tax revenue to the capital.

Sinification The spread within East Asia, especially among elite classes, of a style of social and cultural life founded on practice in China.

Han expansion and Chinese migration encouraged a process of cultural **Sinification** (from the Greek word *sino,* meaning "Chinese") comparable to the Romanization that occurred about the same time in the Mediterranean basin. Standardization of the writing system, the spread of Confucian values, the trade in Han luxury goods, and the installation of bureaucrats in new provinces combined to promote a relatively more uniform style of Chinese cultural life over a much larger part of East Asia, at least at elite social levels.

Starting in 129 B.C.E., Han Wudi also ordered campaigns of conquest deep into Inner Eurasia, the habitat of oasis dwellers and pastoral nomads. Deteriorating relations and chronic fighting between Chinese forces and the powerful pastoral nomadic state known as the Xiongnu partially motivated this expansion. We come back to the Xiongnu in the next part of the chapter. Han Wudi also saw financial benefit to the state in pushing imperial control out along the silk roads leading to Central Asia, South Asia, and Iran. Chinese infantry and cavalry seized key oasis towns on the trade routes on both the northern and southern edges of the arid Tarim Basin. To acquire superior mounts for his army, he sent expeditions all the way to the well-watered Ferghana valley, which overlaps modern Kyrgyzstan (kuhr-gi-STAHN), Tajikistan, and Uzbekistan. Chinese officials already knew of this region's reputation for "heavenly horses," a breed larger and stronger than the animals raised on arid steppe grasses. The advance into this valley meant that for a short time only about 1,600 miles separated the far western arm of the Chinese empire from the most eastern territories of Rome. Emperors who succeeded Han Wudi attempted to maintain control of these western lands, but in the first two centuries C.E., troubles multiplied in the very heart of the empire, a story we pick up in Chapter 9.

States Between Rome and China

FOCUS What part did wealth from commerce play in the growth of the Xiongnu state, Parthian Persia, Kushana, Kush, and Axum?

At the start of the Common Era, the chain of states that ran across the temperate and northern tropical latitudes of Afroeurasia numbered in the hundreds—from city-states and small kingdoms to empires almost as large, if not nearly as populous, as Rome and Han China. States next to one another or more distant typically engaged in diplomatic and mercantile relations, which stimulated exchanges of ideas and technological novelties that might in particular cases have a significant effect on society and economy. Here, we highlight five of these states—the Xiongnu, the Parthian and Kushana empires, and the African states of Kush and Axum. All five affected, in one way or another, broad patterns of change in Afroeurasia in the period 300 B.C.E.–300 C.E. All five were monarchies, though the power of the central government over local aristocrats or tribal groups varied considerably from one case and period to another.

The Xiongnu and Their Relations with Han China

In the first millennium B.C.E., pastoral nomadic groups that inhabited the Inner Eurasian steppes typically supplemented their wealth in livestock by trading with neighboring farmers and town dwellers. They also learned, however, that violent raiding of settled societies might be more profitable than peaceful commerce whenever they had sufficient armed strength and good opportunity to make war. As early as the eighth century B.C.E., peoples that circulated with their herds on the eastern steppes adjacent to China began to organize alliances of otherwise independent clan and tribal groups and to launch cavalry attacks on villages and towns in the upper Yellow River region to amass loot and prisoners. Or, they might simply threaten to attack if their settled neighbors refused to pay tribute—nomad blackmail, as it were. As Inner Eurasian pastoral societies continued to grow, talented leaders had increasing success assembling larger and longer lasting tribal coalitions. The earliest known steppe alliance to transform itself into a durable state lasting several decades was the Xiongnu confederation.

The horse-breeding people who became the core of the Xiongnu steppe empire inhabited the region where the Yellow River makes a great loop across China's northwestern frontier. They may have spoken a language ancestral to Mongolian. In the late third century B.C.E., Maodun (r. 210–174 B.C.E.), a charismatic and ruthless warrior, rallied a following of mounted archers owing personal loyalty to him, rather than to their families and clans. After murdering his own father to seize leadership, he led his cavalry, ranked in a disciplined hierarchy of military units, to victory over several other steppe peoples. As Xiongnu power grew, it drew on the riches of several ecological zones: the fur-rich forests of Siberia to the north, the metals-producing Altai Mountains, the grasslands of Mongolia, and numerous oasis towns. Xiongnu fighters, like other nomads before them, also enriched themselves raiding into China.

Early in the second century B.C.E., a Xiongnu host defeated a Chinese army on the northwestern frontier. Following this debacle for the Han, the imperial government decided prudently to recognize the Xiongnu state as a political equal and to send bountiful annual "presents" of grain, wine, and silk. They also firmed up relations by negotiating marriages between nomad aristocrats and young women of the Han royal family, who had, in effect, to live on the steppe as hostages. Chinese bureaucrats calculated that paying off the Xiongnu was cheaper than fighting them, and ceremonial gift exchanges strengthened Maodun's prestige. That made it easier for him and his successors to redistribute wealth to other warrior chiefs who in return dispatched archers to the Xiongnu army. The Xiongnu promised not to invade China and instead subjugated both pastoral and oasis communities far to the west, forging a territorially huge state in the second century B.C.E. Maodun also created a Chinese-like government hierarchy, the top rung occupied by him as supreme commander, or khan.

The negotiated agreements between China and the Xiongnu, however, did not permanently stabilize relations. Persuaded that the empire remained under threat, Emperor Han Wudi ordered a massive and costly offensive in 129 B.C.E., not only to propel Han authority out along the silk roads but also to bring the Xiongnu to heel. Several campaigns forced the nomads to accept Chinese overlordship, and the weakened Xiongnu state fell into civil war, then broke into southern and northern federations, one subordinated to the Han, the other confined to the steppes beyond the Chinese horizon.

The Parthian and Kushana Empires

Like the Xiongnu, the founders of the Parthian and Kushana states originated as Inner Eurasian steppe warriors. Unlike the Xiongnu, they conquered and ruled dense agrarian populations and large cities.

Parthian conquests. The Seleucid dynasty, founded in the late fourth century B.C.E. by Greco-Macedonian successors of Alexander the Great, ruled the Iranian Plateau, Mesopotamia, and neighboring regions in the late fourth and the third centuries B.C.E. But from about 240 B.C.E. it suffered a string of reversals. The Greek-speaking governor of Bactria threw off Seleucid authority and formed a Bactrian monarchy. To the west, a huge Seleucid army attempted to invade Greece, but Roman legions expanding eastward defeated it in 191 B.C.E. and forced the Seleucids to abandon Anatolia. Finally, the Parni, a band of nomad fighters from somewhere in Inner Eurasia, seized the Seleucid province of Parthia east of the Caspian Sea. In the mid-second century B.C.E., Mithridates I (r. 171–138 B.C.E.), the Parthian king, captured Babylon, the Seleucid capital on the Euphrates. Within another thirteen years, the Seleucid empire was all but gone and the Parthians on the ascendant from Mesopotamia to Central Asia.

Remains of Ctesiphon. Parthian rulers founded Ctesiphon on the northeast bank of the Tigris River as a winter capital. The city fell into ruin after a Roman army sacked it in 165 C.E. But the great arch, called the Taq-i-Kisra, somehow survived.

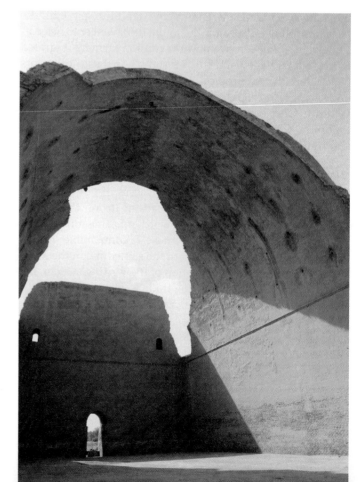

An empire loosely organized. Following the model of the Seleucids and the Persian Achaemenid dynasty before them, the Parthian conquerors expected the farmers and herders of Mesopotamia and the highlands around the Iranian Plateau to support the empire, especially its large mounted army. Boasting the title "King of Kings" to evoke past Achaemenid glory, the Parthians dominated Iran and Mesopotamia for more than four hundred years. This was a remarkable feat because in contrast to the Han in China they showed little talent for centralized bureaucratic government. Rather, they orchestrated with varying success a fluid federation of tribal groups and small kingdoms, depending on local aristocrats to send taxes and tribute to the capital and to supply troops when needed. Using horses bred specially for size and endurance, their heavy cavalry—both rider and horse swathed in bronze, iron, and leather—overpowered enemy foot soldiers or more lightly armed riders.

Like the Seleucids, the Parthians ruled over an ethnically diverse population. And much like affluent Romans, the Parthian elite class adopted Hellenistic models of refined art and court ceremony. Parthian kings built a series of Greek-looking royal cities, including Ctesiphon on the Tigris River. All that remains of that city today is a 121-foot-high vaulted arch, part of an ancient palace. Literate Parthians wrote Pahlavi, an Indo-European language, but Aramaic and Greek remained popular languages of learning and commerce. The government appears to have taken a tolerant view of their subjects' religious practices. The royal household and aristocratic families tended to favor the supreme god Ahura Mazda and beliefs and rituals of Zoroastrianism.

Parthians and Romans. Parthian cavalry advanced to the Tigris-Euphrates valley about the same time that Roman legions first crossed the Aegean to campaign in Southwest Asia. The gap between the two imperial frontiers narrowed steadily, and in 53 B.C.E. a Parthian army routed a larger Roman force in Southeastern Anatolia. (The victors severed the head of the Roman general Crassus and, according to the historian Plutarch, presented it to the Parthian royal court while they were watching a Greek play!) For the next 250 years, Parthians and Romans fought repeatedly along a fluctuating Tigris-Euphrates frontier without decisive victory for either side. The Parthians lacked sufficient armed force to drive the Romans out of Southwest Asia, but Rome found campaigning far to the east logistically difficult and too expensive to sustain permanently.

The Kushana empire. East of Parthian territory, the Kushana (or Kushan) state arose after 45 C.E. to dominate an immense area extending from Inner Eurasia to northern India. Knowledge of Kushana has come hard because few texts have survived, and the state left behind few inscriptions, sculptures, or architectural remains. So far, their history is best illuminated by their skillfully made silver and gold coins stamped with texts and images that tell us something about their rulers, their religious beliefs, and their cultural relations with their neighbors.

Kushana coin. King Vima Kadphises (r. ca. 75–100 C.E.) appears on this gold coin holding a club in his right hand. Flames, a symbol of royal legitimacy, leap from his right shoulder. Oesho, the Kushana god of the wind and of high places, appears on the reverse side. Why do you think coins are often important sources of historical evidence?

Like the Parthians, the founders of Kushana started out as Inner Eurasian nomads, a tribal group known as the Yuezhi. In the mid-second century B.C.E., the Xiongnu, then at their peak of power on the eastern steppes, forced the Yuezhi to migrate westward. They settled in Bactria and about 80 B.C.E. extinguished the Greco-Macedonian state that had ruled there. Shortly after that, leaders of the Kushana, a group within the larger Yuezhi, organized a military confederation that began conquering in every direction. In addition to their great livestock herds, Kushana warriors tapped farm and artisan wealth from the Amu Darya and Syr Darya River valleys of Central Asia, as well as collecting duties on trade that flowed through the region's urban hubs. At the start of the reign of King Kanishka (ca. 129–152 C.E.), Kushana embraced not only Central Asia and Afghanistan but also much of northern India, which had been politically fragmented since the fall of the Maurya empire in the third century B.C.E. At the farther reaches of its vast territory, Kushana kings, like the Parthians, lacked the personnel and communication technology to do more than monitor an often unruly collection of tribal groups and independent-minded cities, relying mainly on local princes to keep order and ensure revenue flow. A succession of four talented kings held the state together into the third century C.E., when, as we shall see, new empire builders arose to supplant it.

The Kushana ruling class adapted remarkably to the empire's great cultural diversity, taking a many-sided view of religion, art, and royal symbolism. Drawing nearly equally on Indian, Persian, and Hellenistic styles, Kushana coins depicted the gods and the royal titles and insignia from all those civilizations without discrimination. King Kanishka even took as one of his titles the Roman title *kaisara,* or Caesar.

The African Kingdoms of Kush and Axum

In northeastern Africa, the monarchy of Kush (whose name has no connection to Kushana) first emerged in the second millennium B.C.E. along the stretch of the Nile River that encompasses Nubia, the region corresponding today to the Republic of the Sudan. Kush thus formed a bridge of exchange between the Roman Mediterranean and tropical Africa. Trade also flowed from Kush eastward to the Red Sea, where in the first century C.E. the kingdom of Axum arose as a powerful commercial state linking the Mediterranean world to the Arabian Sea (see Map 7.4).

Kush shifts upriver. Following several decades of rule over both Nubia and Egypt in the eighth and seventh centuries B.C.E., Kush's royal court moved from the Nile city of Napata to a new capital farther upriver at Meroë (MER-oh-ee), near where the great river divides into its Blue and White branches. This location was far enough south of the Sahara Desert to sustain grain and cotton farming from rainfall. And the savannas, or grassy plains, that stretched west and east of the two Niles supported plentiful herds of cattle and wild game. Sometime in the seventh century B.C.E.,

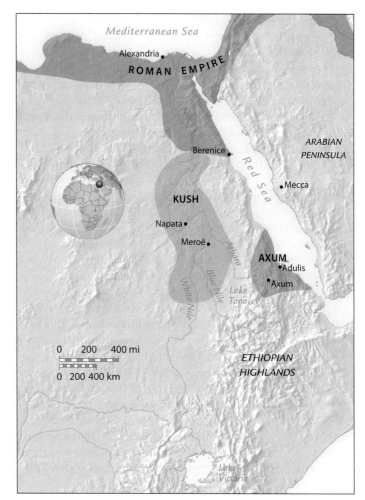

MAP 7.4 The states of Kush and Axum.
How did the geographical locations of Kush and Axum contribute to their commercial prosperity?

knowledge of iron making reached Nubia, probably having spread from East Africa's Great Lakes region to the south, one of the early centers of iron metallurgical invention. A flourishing smelting industry later developed around Meroë, where both iron ore and timber resources were apparently abundant. Giant slag heaps that have survived to today are dramatic proof of this ancient enterprise.

Meroë's distinctive culture. When Kush's center of gravity shifted upriver from Napata to Meroë, cultural interchange with Egypt weakened. Egyptian influences faded somewhat, and art, architecture, religion, and other aspects of elite culture took on more distinctively local features. In earlier times Nubians had connected their supreme god associated with the sky to the Egyptian deity Amun. In Meroë, however, the focus of worship turned to Apedemak, a Nubian god depicted in stone as a lion. Kings of Meroë had themselves buried under small pyramids, keeping alive an architectural form that the Egyptians had given up centuries earlier. In state politics both the senior wife and mother of the king played prominent political roles, much more so than in Egypt. Residents of Meroë and its region probably spoke a number of different languages. Around 300 B.C.E., officials and religious specialists developed a writing system for Meroitic, probably a language in the Nilo-Saharan family. This system was alphabetic, made up of twenty-three signs. Derived from Egyptian hieroglyphs, the alphabet had both consonants and vowels and, as far as we know, no relationship to the Phoenician system that inspired Greek and Latin. Unfortunately, linguists have not so far deciphered much of it.

Kush and Rome. Kush's prosperity after 300 B.C.E. was almost certainly connected to its brisk trade with Hellenistic Egypt and later Rome. Nubian merchants shipped ironware, cotton textiles, war elephants, gold, ivory, ebony, and slaves downriver, importing Mediterranean wine, olive oil, ceramics, and precious metalwork. Following occupation of Egypt in 30 B.C.E., Rome sent forces upriver to control a longer stretch of the Nile trade and force Kush into dependency. The Nubians, however, fought back, finally convincing Rome to agree to mutually profitable relations. Consequently, stronger Mediterranean cultural winds reached Nubia. For example, the ruins of temples and palaces in Meroë and other towns dating from the early centuries C.E. reveal an eclectic mix of local, Egyptian, and Hellenistic influences.

By the fourth century C.E., Kush went into full decline. Rome's mounting political troubles hurt the Nile-to-Mediterranean trade. Prolonged drought in Nubia may have driven pastoral nomads in the region to attack Nile towns. Finally, the kingdom of Axum dealt a lethal blow in the 340s C.E., sacking Meroë and bringing Kush's long history to a close.

Axum between Kush and the Red Sea. The kingdom of Axum (also Aksum) first appears in the historical record at the start of the Common Era, when trade was growing busier on the Red Sea corridor. Sometime in the late first millennium B.C.E., merchants founded a cluster of ports at the southern end of the Red Sea on both the Arabian and the African shores. From these ports, they shipped products that included frankincense and myrrh, both locally grown aromatic tree resins of immense value for incense, perfume, and medicine. Dromedary camel caravans also carried goods on the south–north land route that paralleled the Red Sea, connecting southern Arabia to Syria.

A temple of Kush. This small structure in the ruins of Naqa, a city east of the Nile, testifies to the flow of cultural influences along the valley. The temple, probably dedicated to the popular goddess Hathor, displays a blend of Egyptian, Hellenistic, and Roman influences. The Egyptian lintel over the entranceway is inscribed with cobras. The Corinthian capitals on the columns are of Greek inspiration, and the side arches are Roman. How might knowledge of Corinthian column design have reached Nubia?

Trade in the African Port of Adulis

Traders in the ancient world who sailed between Roman Egypt and India might have either compiled or consulted a document called a periplus. This is a type of report that helped ships' crews navigate by listing ports in the order that sailors encountered them, describing important landmarks, and estimating distances between one port and another. Sometime between 40 and 70 c.e., a Greek merchant composed the Periplus of the Erythraean Sea. *Although "Erythraean Sea" could be taken narrowly to mean the Red Sea, traders of the Roman era used it as a general term that encompassed the Red Sea, the Persian Gulf, the Arabian Sea, and the wider Indian Ocean. In this selection from the* Periplus, *the author lists commodities found in and around Adulis (or Adouli), the major port of the Axumite kingdom on the Red Sea. This account offers information on the range of products traded and the distances they were transported before reaching Adulis. Other sections of the* Periplus *offer comments on the characteristics of the people that mariners were likely to encounter in different ports. Rather than an explicitly personal account of one trader's journey between Egypt and India, the* Periplus *is a sort of instructional manual or guidebook for sailors wanting knowledge of the Indian Ocean trade network.*

Adulis [is] a port established by law, lying at the inner end of a bay that runs in toward the south. Before the harbor lies the so-called Mountain Island, about two hundred stadia [an ancient Greek unit of length] seaward from the very head of the bay, with the shores of the mainland close to it on both sides. Ships bound for this port now anchor here because of attacks from the land. . . . Opposite Mountain Island, on the mainland twenty stadia from the shore, lies Adulis, a fair-sized village, from which there is a three days' journey to Coloe, an inland town and the first market for ivory. From that place to the city [Axum] of the people called Auxumites [sic] there is a five days' journey more; to that place all the ivory is brought from the country beyond the Nile through the district called Cyeneum [probably in the modern Republic of the Sudan], and thence to Adulis. Practically the whole number of elephants and rhinoceros that are killed live in the places inland, although at rare intervals they are hunted on the sea-coast even near Adulis. . . .

There are imported into these places, undressed cloth made in Egypt for the Berbers; robes from Arsinoë [modern Suez]; cloaks of poor quality dyed in colors; double-fringed linen mantles; many articles of flint glass, and others of murrhine [probably agate or carnelian], made in Diospolis [probably Thebes]; and brass, which is used for ornament and in cut pieces instead of coin; sheets of soft copper, used for cooking utensils and cut up for bracelets and anklets for the women; iron, which is made into spears used against the elephants and other wild beasts, and in their wars. Besides these, small axes are imported, and adzes and swords; copper drinking-cups, round and large; a little coin for those coming to the market; wine of Laodicea [on the Syrian coast] and Italy, not much; olive oil, not much; for the King, gold and silver plate made after the fashion of the country, and for clothing, military cloaks, and thin coats of skin, of no great value. Likewise from the district of Ariaca [on the northwest coast of India around the Gulf of Cambay] across this sea, there are imported Indian cloth called *monaché* [fine quality cotton] and that called *sagmotogene* [probably tree cotton], and girdles, and coats of skin and mallow-colored cloth, and a few muslins, and colored lac [a resinous insect secretion used to make shellac]. There are exported from these places ivory, and tortoise-shell and rhinoceros-horn. The most from Egypt is brought to this market [Adulis] from the month of January to September.

Source: Wilfred H. Schoff, ed. and trans., *The Periplus of the Erythraean Sea: Travel and Trade in the Indian Ocean by a Merchant of the First Century* (New York: Longmans, Green, 1912), 22–24.

Thinking Critically

Create a list of broad categories into which you might divide the goods listed in this selection. Does the trade focus on practical objects, luxury items, or a mixture of the two? Which source of imports listed in the selection is farthest away from Adulis? Why do you think people in Axum wanted to buy the imports mentioned? What goods could Axumites offer that Romans did not have? What are some conditions that sailors and merchants had to take into account as they planned a voyage to or from Adulis?

The rise of Axum, situated in what are today Eritrea and northern Ethiopia, represented a consolidation of political power on the African side of the Red Sea. The early Axumite monarchs established a capital, also called Axum, in the Ethiopian highlands, which stretched west and south from the coast. Farmers herded livestock or grew millet, sorghum, wheat, and teff (a tiny grain characteristic of Ethiopian cuisine today) on mountain slopes and ridges. Axum's rulers also developed the port of Adulis to serve as an exclusive **entrepôt** (ON-truh-poh). In the process, they paid customs duties to the Axumite authorities.

> **entrepôt** A port or other urban center where merchants of different origins exchange goods and ship them onward.

We know little about the identity of the kings of Axum or the sort of government they organized. Their capital blossomed into a thriving city, the rulers adorning it with temples, a palace, and stone pillars (obelisks, or stelae) that marked the burial chambers of rulers or aristocrats. Some of these monuments, the tallest of which rose more than one hundred feet, were elaborately carved with false doors and windows. There is some evidence that the monarchs appointed provincial governors and other officials, though they may have done little more than collect tribute from rural village and clan leaders. The principal language of town dwellers, governors, and merchants was Ge'ez, a Semitic language related to Arabic and Hebrew and written with an alphabetic script.

Flourishing trade through Adulis encouraged Axum's rulers to launch campaigns to corral more routes, ports, and market towns within their sphere of influence. From the second to the sixth centuries C.E., Axumite forces advanced north along the Red Sea shore and periodically invaded South Arabia in order to control ports on both coasts. To the west, Axum may well have speeded Kush's decline by seizing territory and diverting trade in ivory and other tropical goods from the Nile route to the Red Sea. The glory of Kush had long since faded when Axum's King Ezana dispatched an army against Meroë in the mid-fourth century C.E. Fragments of stone inscriptions found at Meroë boast of Ezana's triumph over his enemies:

I fought with them on the Takkaze [River east of the Nile]. . . . Thereupon they took flight and would not make a stand. And I followed after the fugitives for twenty-three days, killing some and making prisoners of others, and capturing spoil wherever I stopped. . . . My soldiers carried off [the country's] food, and its copper, and its iron, and its brass, and they destroyed the statues in their houses, and the treasuries of food, and the cotton trees, and cast them into the River Seda [probably the Nile]. Many people died in the water; I do not know their number.[7]

After Ezana despoiled Kush, the Axumite state reached its greatest territorial extent, though control as far west as the Nile may not have lasted long. Between the fourth and sixth centuries C.E. Axum remained a wealthy and powerful state, and, as we see in Chapter 9, it became a Christian one.

Bridges Across Afroeurasia

> **FOCUS** What similarities and differences were there in the way that Buddhism, Christianity, and Confucianism emerged as large-scale belief systems in the period 300 B.C.E.–300 C.E.?

In the first and second centuries C.E., Rome, Kush, Axum, Parthia, Kushana, and Han China were all prosperous and reasonably stable states. Not accidentally, this was also a period in which long-distance commerce and cultural exchange across Afroeurasia grew significantly. In this period, private merchants handled an ever-increasing volume of interregional trade. Instead of sponsoring their own commercial expeditions, governments put more effort into ensuring conditions of security and opportunity in which private merchant operations might flourish. They did this, for example, by investing in roads, canals, and harbors, combating pirates and bandits, and granting hub cities varying degrees of self-government. High-cost luxury goods flowing to affluent classes or as gifts from one ruler to another continued to be the bread and butter of long-distance trade. By the start of the Common Era, however, merchants added to their shipments bulky, relatively cheaper wares, such as cotton textiles, everyday pottery, and glass beads.

Afroeurasia's commercial cities traded in ideas as well as merchandise, including ideas about god, compassion, salvation, ritual, and righteous behavior. In the six hundred years that this chapter addresses, Buddhism and Christianity, religions that broadcast their message universally, that is, to anyone who would listen, spread widely from their place of origin to other parts of Afroeurasia and attracted millions of adherents of diverse identity. Except for the Hellenistic tradition, which included a complex jumble of religious and philosophical ideas, Buddhism and Christianity were the first belief systems to achieve interregional scope.

East–West Interregional Trade

Ancient states invested in communication networks primarily to move armies, officials, and vital information where they were needed. State builders also understood that allowing private merchants, local farmers, slave dealers, and traveling scholars to use roads, trails, and navigable rivers helped integrate the state and increase its wealth. When the Roman empire arose, Mediterranean sea trade was already extensive. The Romans, learning from both Greeks and Etruscans, also began constructing a system of roads and bridges early in the republican centuries. This system in effect extended communication from Mediterranean shores into deep hinterlands. Engineers devised new techniques for building hard surface roads that would hold up under the weight of horses, wagons, and massed infantry. At its maximum extent in the second century C.E., the Roman empire may have had about 55,000 miles of

A road made to last. A stretch of the Appian Way near Itri in central Italy was part of a highway that connected Rome to Brindisi, a port on the Adriatic Sea coast.

highways. At the other end of the hemisphere, the Qin and Han rulers also built a highway system that radiated out from Chang'an and Luoyang, the successive royal capitals. The Qin emperor Shi Huangdi started the work, ordering that both road beds and wagon axles have standard widths to increase transport efficiency.

The Inner Eurasian silk routes. The silk roads that threaded across the steppes and mountains of Inner Eurasia, ultimately connecting the Han Chinese and Roman networks, were trails and paths, not stone-paved roads (see Map 7.5). Merchants sometimes hitched oxen or Bactrian camels to wagons, but pack trains of donkeys, horses, or camels were more suitable for crossing deserts and mountain passes. On routes in Southwest Asia, North Africa, and the Sahara, traders came to prefer dromedary camel and other animal pack trains almost exclusively. In the early centuries C.E., wheeled vehicles virtually disappeared from those regions.

Goods moved along the silk roads between China and the western lands in relay fashion. That is, groups of merchants, usually united by shared language and customs, operated along a particular segment of trails, towns, and oases. Then they sold their goods to other traders who carried them on the next stretch. In the late first century C.E., Gan Ying, a commercial envoy commissioned by the governor of a western Han province, traveled from China to somewhere in Southwest Asia, possibly Mesopotamia, on a not-quite-successful mission to make contact with the Roman empire. He was a notable exception because individual merchants rarely made such long trips. In the Han era, Chinese merchants set up operations along the silk roads both north and south of the Tarim Basin and as far west as the Ferghana valley. Conversely, the Han government encouraged caravaners from Kushana territory to visit western China.

Silk routes of the sea. Despite the growing importance of the silk roads, probably a much greater volume of long-distance trade flowed along the chain of interlinked seas that extended from East Asia to the Mediterranean (see this book's Introduction). From a commercial standpoint, merchants could move goods in larger quantities and at lower unit cost by ship than by caravan. In the tropical **southern seas,** seasonal winds, or monsoons, drove sailing ships forward. Differences in atmospheric temperatures between the Eurasian land mass and the Indian Ocean cause winds to blow generally from eastern Eurasia toward tropical Africa in the winter months. This is the northeast monsoon. In the warm months the winds reverse course, blowing from Africa toward Eurasia.

> **southern seas** The China seas and the Indian Ocean, including the Arabian Sea and the Bay of Bengal.

We know that sailors took advantage of the monsoon cycle from ancient times, but they introduced new ship and sail designs in the first millennium C.E. that more efficiently capitalized on the alternating breezes. Malay mariners who traded among the islands of Southeast Asia may have been the first to develop a sail that could be set in a fore-and-aft position, meaning that the sail was aligned parallel with the sides of the ship rather than perpendicular to them. This design allowed a vessel to "tack," that is, to sail at a fairly sharp angle to the direction from which the wind was blowing and to zigzag back and forth against the wind to stay on course. Several types of fore-and-aft sails came into use in the southern seas, notably a triangular rig called the lateen sail. Maneuverability in monsoon conditions gave captains greater confidence to sail out of sight of land and allowed them to calculate with rough accuracy the time it might take to sail from one port to another.

Malay mariners appear to have carried much of the Indian Ocean exchange. A cluster of ports associated with Funan, a rice-growing state (or federation of small states) on the Gulf of Thailand in what is today southwestern Vietnam and Cambodia, served as key entrepôts linking the South China Sea to the Bay of Bengal. A remarkable example of long distance relay trade was the westward movement of cloves, nutmeg, and mace. Inhabitants of islands in the Moluccas group, part of the Indonesian archipelago, harvested cloves from one tree and nutmeg and mace (the kernel and covering of a single fruit) from another. In the late centuries B.C.E., Malay merchants began to sell these aromatic spices at high markups in Indian and Chinese ports. By the first century C.E., small quantities of them periodically reached the spice market in Rome, nine thousand miles from where they were harvested.

Tropical African products also entered the southern seas market. Ivory, tortoise shells, leopard skins, rhinoceros horn, ebony wood, and other goods found ready buyers in India and the Roman and Parthian empires. No later than the first century C.E., a port known as Rhapta arose on the East African coast, probably in what is today Tanzania. Rhapta's residents included local Bantu-speaking farmers, artisans, and traders, as well as maritime merchants from South Arabia and Axum. Although Rhapta appears to have declined from the fourth century C.E., other East African ports later took its place, playing a strategic part in the trans-hemispheric commercial system.

Roman merchants in the southern seas. It was a measure of Roman power that its rulers could supply affluent men and women with exotic goods from distant lands, including much prized gemstones, spices, incense, ivory, aromatics, and silk originating far to the east. In that age, Chinese farmers were the only people in the world who practiced sericulture, that is, the production of silk thread and yarn from silkworm cocoons. Chinese weavers also made most of the silk cloths sent to other parts of Afroeurasia. The enormous influx of gold and silver into Rome from conquests and mining inspired wealthy Romans to invest in expensive trade ventures between the Mediterranean and the southern seas. Moreover, Rome's conquest of

Egypt and part of Southwest Asia beginning in the late first century B.C.E. opened the way to the Red Sea and the Indian Ocean beyond. Some Asian products also reached Rome overland through territory of the Parthian empire.

Roman subjects of Greek, Arab, Hebrew, Aramaean, or Egyptian origin handled most of the southern seas trade, and Greek served as a commercial *lingua franca* around the Arabian Sea rim. In that era, South Asian ports were emerging rapidly as the turnstiles of trans-hemispheric commerce. Consequently, Roman merchants had great incentive to reach ports on both the western and the eastern shores of India and on the island of Ceylon (Sri Lanka) in order to traffic with Asian merchants established there. In ports in northwestern India, merchants from the Kushana-ruled lands of the Indus valley, Afghanistan, and Central Asia met their Roman counterparts. According to the *Periplus of the Erythraean Sea*, the Greek shipping manual written in the first century C.E. (see "Weighing the Evidence"), Roman ships arriving at the port of Barbaricum near the Indus River unloaded "a great deal of thin clothing . . .; figured linens, topaz, coral, storax (an aromatic resin), frankincense, vessels of glass, silver and gold plate, and a little wine." In exchange, Kushana merchants offered such products as lapis lazuli, turquoise, silk yarn, and indigo (a blue dye).[8] In southern India, Romans bought Indian cotton textiles, black pepper, cinnamon, pearls, and Southeast Asian spices. Chinese documents record that in 166 C.E. a group of Romans, probably merchants, reached Luoyang, the Han Chinese royal capital. Nothing came of this initiative, however, and Romans had no stake that we know of in trade east of India.

Since Rome seems to have had a much greater hunger for Asian products than Asians had for Mediterranean manufactures, Roman merchants carried quantities of gold and silver coins to pay for purchases. Archaeologists have found several large hordes of Roman money in India, where natural deposits of these metals were scarce. Some Roman leaders worried about a drain of the empire's bullion supply to the east, but in fact the value of coin exports remained modest relative to the commercial wealth circulating *within* the empire.[9]

The First Missionary Religions

Why, we may ask, did Buddhism and Christianity, among a few other religions, grow into interregional, ultimately worldwide movements, when such a phenomenon had never occurred earlier? Like all religions in varying ways, these faiths answered to the individual's search for consolation, hope, and spiritual meaning in a world fraught with inexplicable events and everyday troubles. But why "big" religions? One possibility is that by the late centuries B.C.E. continuing world population growth, coupled with intensified interaction among communities, required spiritual and moral codes that might strengthen bonds among people otherwise divided by language, culture, and class. As these religions attracted followers beyond the confines of a single region, they became foundations for cultural communication and

MAP 7.5 The growth of Buddhism and Christianity, 200 B.C.E.–300 C.E.
What geographic factors might help explain why Christianity and Buddhism spread in the particular directions they did from their founding areas?

mutual trust among strangers who met to exchange information, do business, or, in any of countless ways, cooperate with one another. Buddhism and Christianity each offered a distinctive moral and spiritual path. But both religions transcended association with any particular state, ruling class, or ethnolinguistic group, thereby uniting people in shared belief and practice whoever they were and wherever they lived (see Map 7.5).

Buddhism beyond India. In the two hundred years after the death of the Buddha (ca. 483 B.C.E.), his message of hope and compassion to suffering humanity spread across South Asia (see Chapter 6). Around 250 B.C.E., a council of monks, meeting at the behest of Ashoka, king of the Maurya state, proclaimed that the Buddha's followers should actively broadcast his teachings to the world. In the following centuries, Buddhist missionaries advanced northwestward to Persia, Bactria, and Inner Eurasia, east to Burma, and south to Ceylon. Buddhist scholars also generated sacred texts (*sutras*) that introduced both teachings

attributed to the Buddha and enlightened commentaries on those doctrines.

Many Buddhist converts became monks, joining monasteries and taking up lives of self-denial, meditation, and study. Wherever clerics founded new monastic communities, they worked to copy, translate, and disseminate religious writings. Other Buddhist converts, both men and women, remained "in the world," supporting the work of the monasteries but living in their village and town communities. Buddhism's message of freedom from suffering for people of all social ranks, combined with its emphasis on personal moral responsibility, attracted large numbers of artisans and traders. Buddhist merchants who carried goods long distances helped spread the new faith beyond India.

Buddhism had an early flowering in Gandhara, the region of the upper Indus valley that is today northern Pakistan. Greek-speaking kings of Bactria ruled that region in the second century C.E. from the thriving commercial city of Taxila. After Buddhist monks and merchants started arriving, Gandhara became a lively cultural meeting ground.

One striking consequence was the flowering of a Buddhist art style that gracefully combined Greek and Indian elements. In the second and third centuries C.E., Kushana kings, noted for their cultural tolerance and cosmopolitanism, welcomed Buddhists. From Kushana territory, missionaries introduced the faith to Iran under Parthian rule and to the oasis towns strung out along the silk roads north and south of the Tarim Basin. The first Buddhist missionaries reached China as early as the first century B.C.E. We come back to that story in later chapters.

As Buddhist belief and practice took hold beyond India, several schools of thought emerged, each offering somewhat different approaches to belief and practice. The Mahayana school attracted the largest following. Its early disciples favored incorporating new scriptural ideas into the Buddhist canon of texts, notably the idea that individuals might seek total enlightenment (nirvana) without committing themselves to monastic life. Probably originating in silk road towns rather than in India, the Mahayana way taught that beings who possessed power to bestow grace on sincere seekers might help them gain spiritual illumination. These divines were of two sorts. First were saints, or *bodhisattvas* (BOH-dih-SAT-vuhs), holy individuals believed to have postponed their own enlightenment in order to aid others along the sacred path. Second was the Buddha himself, whom Mahayana viewed not only as the great teacher but also as a personal savior. Mahayana Buddhists celebrated compassion as the cardinal virtue and introduced new doctrines, rituals, and expressions of sacred art.

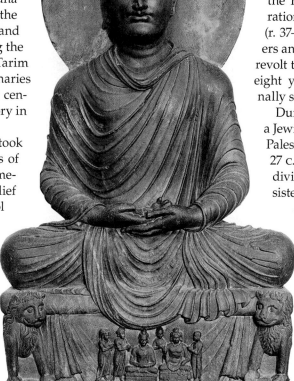

A seated Buddha. In Gandhara, a region today part of northern Pakistan, South Asian and Hellenistic cultural tides lapped against each other. This stone Buddha meditates in the simple robe of an Indian monk. But the deeply carved, naturalistic folds of the garment tell us that local or immigrant artisans also appreciated Hellenistic styles.

Jesus and the beginnings of Christianity. Roman rulers generally tolerated the welter of religious and philosophical ideas that circulated in their empire, for example, recognizing Judaism as a "legal religion." Large numbers of Jews lived in Palestine (the southern Levant), but communities of the diaspora inhabited many cities in the Mediterranean basin, Mesopotamia, Iran, and Central Asia (see Chapter 5). Jews did not proclaim a universalist mission to convert others but rather sought to preserve and vitalize Jewish law and worship.

After Roman forces seized Jerusalem in 63 B.C.E., their relations with the Jewish population deteriorated steadily. As monotheists, many Jews expressed their abhorrence for both foreign rule and Rome's plethora of gods and goddesses. In return, the Romans, notably with the collaboration of their local client king Herod (r. 37–4 B.C.E.), ferreted out Jewish resisters and imposed heavy taxes. The Jewish revolt that broke out in 65 C.E. festered for eight years before Roman authorities finally stamped it out.

During those decades of tension, Jesus, a Jewish carpenter who lived in the small Palestinian city of Nazareth, began about 27 C.E. to preach a message of peace and divine salvation through brotherly and sisterly love. He attracted a following and eventually traveled to Jerusalem, where he taught in the temple. Nearly everything he said had deep roots in the spiritual and moral teachings of Hebrew scripture. He seriously disagreed with Jewish leaders, however, over the practice of distinguishing between people who were holy, righteous, and ritually pure, and those who were not. Jesus taught that God loved all his creation, regardless of their status or circumstance, and that humans should reflect that love in their relations with one another. Like Mahayana Buddhists, he preached compassion as the key human virtue. Unlike them, he proclaimed one God, the Father of all, as the sole source of compassion. He taught that by God's grace humans receive his love, share it with others, and prepare themselves for eternal salvation. To the alarm of some pious Jews, Jesus associated freely with criminals, outcasts, and prostitutes, and he went about healing people without presuming who was worthy and who was not.

Jesus preached for just three years before the Roman authorities, advised by some Jewish leaders that he was a troublemaker and potential rebel, had him crucified for treason. The earliest records we have of this event, and everything else about Jesus' life and teachings, are found in the Gospels, the books attributed to the disciples Matthew, Mark, Luke, and John. These texts, written a generation after Jesus' time, form the first part of the Biblical New Testament. According to the Gospels, God raised Jesus from the dead; shortly thereafter, he ascended into heaven. Precisely how he perceived his own relationship to God became a matter of great dispute among the Christian congregations that arose in succeeding generations. Nevertheless, the authors of the Gospels and the other books of the New Testament clearly regarded him as the Christ, a word of Greek origin meaning the "anointed one" or messiah. Jewish doctrine already embraced the idea that a messiah would one day appear. This redeemer would serve as the instrument of God's judgment of all humankind and lead the Jews to freedom. Early Christians declared that the spirit of Christ continued to live among them and that Jesus would shortly return to proclaim the kingdom of God on earth.

For a short time, Christians formed a small group within the Jewish fold. But owing primarily to the initiative of Paul, a Jewish scholar from Anatolia who lived in Jesus' time but did not know him, Christian groups began to share their message of the resurrected Christ with Gentiles, that is, non-Jews. Paul and other preachers argued that Christians had no obligation to observe Jewish law, such as dietary restrictions that would have prevented Christians of Jewish and Gentile background from eating together. By about 100 C.E., Gentiles took over leadership of the movement, and Christianity emerged as a **universalist religion** in its mission to evangelize, that is, to bring the "good news" of the Gospel, to the world at large.

universalist religion A religion whose doctrines and practices aim to appeal to all people irrespective of their language, ethnicity, social class, or political affiliation.

Christ as shepherd. This is an early depiction of Jesus Christ (second or third century C.E.) on the wall of a catacomb, or underground cemetery in Rome. Jesus supports a goat on his shoulders. What do you think the animals (two birds, two goats, and a sheep) in this fresco collectively signify?

Christianity beyond Palestine. Paul, who had the privileged status of a Roman citizen, took advantage of the imperial roads and sea lanes to travel widely in the eastern Mediterranean, preaching to both Jews and Gentiles, helping Christian groups found churches, and finally settling in Rome. In the two and a half centuries after Jesus preached, the same centuries when Buddhism was spreading along the silk roads to China, Christians founded communities in many eastern Mediterranean cities and in a few large centers in the west, including Rome. Leaders also created an increasingly sophisticated organization of churches with a hierarchy of officers headed by bishops based in different cities.

Several factors help explain the success of Christianity in those 250 years. One was the fierce devotion of Christians impelled by expectations of eternal life and of Jesus' imminent return to earth. Another was the warm welcome early Christians gave newcomers without regard to their social or political status, including the urban poor and women. Early Christian converts of elite Roman origin appear to have been predominantly women, and some took energetic roles in missionary and organizational work. A third factor was persecution, which Christians experienced episodically in different parts of the empire. Roman authorities prosecuted and executed Christians, including Paul, not so much for what they believed about Jesus but for refusing to take part in public cult rituals that invoked Rome's numerous deities. The martyrdom of Christians had the principal effect of strengthening faith and resolve within communities and attracting the admiration and sympathy of potential converts.

At the end of the third century C.E., a period when official persecution became more systematic and severe, Christian groups formed not only in the Mediterranean basin but also in Mesopotamia, Iran, and the western coast of India. At that time, Christians may have numbered no more than about 10 percent of the Roman empire's population. But that percentage soared in the following centuries, and Christianity became the imperial religion.

• • •

Conclusion

In the six centuries we have considered in this chapter, men and women had a variety of motives for traveling long distances and encountering strangers. One was trade. On the local level, people bought and sold basic commodities such as grain, fish, coarse textiles, and ironware. Merchants hauled bulk goods from one neighboring region to another but seldom on long interregional routes. Long-distance traders, by contrast, carried mainly goods of high value and low bulk, that is, costly merchandise such as silk cloth, glassware, fine ceramics, gemstones, and spices. The profits merchants could amass moving such wares across seas and mountains provided motive enough to cooperate with one another across ethnolinguistic borders.

The process of state building also impelled people to spin more complex webs of communication. We have seen that imperial transport networks built in the first instance to move soldiers and officials also carried merchants, artisans, scholars, and missionaries—people who introduced products, skills, and ideas from one place to another. The Han road and river networks, for example, facilitated the spread of Confucian morals and ethics in China. Roman roads and ships carried Christian proselytizers. Buddhists trekked along trails that Kushana authorities made secure. Literate scholars introduced new societies to Greek, Latin, Aramaic, Sanskrit, and Chinese writing systems, all of them associated with powerful states or new religions.

Some corners of Afroeurasia still had only tenuous links to interregional networks because rugged topography isolated them, their populations were sparse, or their locations were geographical cul-de-sacs—on the way to nowhere. This was the situation for hunting communities living in far northern parts of Europe, Russia, and Siberia. Japan had been inhabited for thousands of years, but human contacts with the East Asian mainland remained weak throughout most of the first millennium B.C.E. Only in the Han period did exchange, mainly by way of the Korean Peninsula, start to quicken. In far southwestern Africa, iron-using farmers were just beginning to advance to regions that faced the empty Atlantic.

Peoples of Afroeurasia had no sustained contact with the other three "worlds" of human habitation. Except intermittently along Australia's northern edge, the foragers of that continent had no connections to Afroeurasia. The same was true of the communities scattered out across the Island Pacific. The Americas was also a separate realm, but in contrast to Australians and Pacific Islanders, ancient Americans built cities and empires of their own. In Chapter 8 we turn to developments there.

• • •

Key Terms

Analects 202	Han empire 200	Qin dynasty 200
Axum 205	Kush 205	republic 193
Christianity 211	Kushana empire 205	Roman empire 194
Confucianism 202	*latifundia* 196	Romanization 199
Daodejing 204	Legalism 201	Sinification 204
Daoism 204	Parthian dynasty 205	southern seas 212
entrepôt 211	patron-client system 194	universalist religion 216
filial piety 203	*Pax Romana* 196	Xiongnu empire 205

Change over Time

6th–4th centuries B.C.E.	The kingdom of Kush prospers, with its center at Meroë.
ca. 563–ca. 483 B.C.E.	Siddhartha Gautama, the Buddha, preaches in northern India.
551–479 B.C.E.	The Chinese philosopher Confucius lives.
509–27 B.C.E.	The Roman Republic expands Mediterranean power with a republican form of government.
ca. 250 B.C.E.	Buddhism begins to spread beyond South Asia.
247 B.C.E.**–224** C.E.	The Parthian dynasty, founded by steppe warriors, succeeds the Seleucids in Persia and battles Rome along the Tigris-Euphrates frontier.
221–207 B.C.E.	The Qin dynasty in China establishes an efficient authoritarian state based on Legalism.
210–174 B.C.E.	The Xiongnu steppe alliance becomes an empire under Maodun as khan.
206 B.C.E.**–220** C.E.	The Han dynasty in China establishes the Chinese tradition of centralized bureaucratic government.
2nd century B.C.E.	Trade on Inner Eurasian silk roads intensifies.
141–87 B.C.E.	Han Wudi incorporates Confucian ideas into the Han imperial ideology.

Please see end of book reference section for additional reading suggestions related to this chapter.

American Complexities

900 B.C.E.–900 C.E.

Numbers on this inscription give the accession date of a ruler of Palenque, an ancient Maya city-state in Chiapas, Mexico.

hen we do everyday arithmetic, we may never think about the fact that we are using a numerical system based on the ingenious concept of positional notation, also called place-value notation. In the long run of history, humans have tried a variety of systems for counting, calculating, and measuring. Positional notation is just one of them, though it is used nearly universally today. In the past three thousand years, only three societies appear to have invented a positional system independently. In Afroeurasia, Babylonians did it in Mesopotamia about 2000 B.C.E. and South Asians in the Ganges valley around 500 C.E. In the Western Hemisphere, sages somewhere in southern Mexico or Guatemala invented it in the late centuries B.C.E.

Our modern system, which the South Asian scholars passed on to us, is a base-ten counting method that uses only ten integer (whole number) signs, that is, 1 through 9 plus 0. The value of a number is determined by its position relative to other numbers in a row. Each number, reading from right to left, represents a higher power of ten. Thus, when we write 999, the 9 in the far right position signifies the value of 9. The 9 in the next position means 90, and the 9 on the left means 900. Thus we get 900 + 90 + 9, but all we have to write is 999.

In ancient Mesoamerica, Maya scholars fully developed a positional notation system, though it looked different from our modern one. The Maya used a base-twenty rather than base-ten counting method, with certain exceptions. They showed the value of numbers, not by arranging them in a positional sequence on a line from right to left but on a column of rows from bottom to top. The bottom row represented a number between 1 and 19, the next one up a multiple of 20, the third a multiple of 400 (20 × 20), and so on. The Maya used combinations of dots and bars to signify numbers, one dot representing "1" and one bar representing "5." The number 999 would therefore be expressed like this:

$$2 \left\{ \begin{array}{c} \bullet \ \bullet \end{array} \right\} \text{meaning } 2 \times 400 = 800$$

$$9 \left\{ \begin{array}{c} \bullet\ \bullet\ \bullet\ \bullet \\ \rule{1cm}{0.5mm} \end{array} \right\} \text{meaning } 9 \times 20 = 180$$

$$19 \left\{ \begin{array}{c} \bullet\ \bullet\ \bullet\ \bullet \\ \rule{1cm}{0.5mm} \\ \rule{1cm}{0.5mm} \\ \rule{1cm}{0.5mm} \end{array} \right\} \text{meaning } 19 \times 1 = 19$$

The very existence of the Maya number system speaks of a society of great complexity. The Maya and several other agrarian civilizations that emerged in the Americas after about 900 B.C.E. had no known contact with peoples of Afroeurasia (see Map 8.1). But two generalizations about long-term change appear to apply to both Afroeurasia and the Americas before modern times. First, human groups that succeeded well enough at farming to produce significant surpluses of food were likely to grow in numbers at accelerating rates. That growth in turn required new forms of social organization, usually manifested in social class divisions, occupational specializations, centralized states, city building, and indeed elaborate methods for keeping accounts and calendars. Such complexity developed in both Afroeurasia and the Americas, even though neither hemisphere borrowed or adapted any ideas or technologies from the other.

Second, in no premodern complex society anywhere in the world did a particular state, empire, or ruling class last indefinitely. All of them eventually collapsed or withered away, though the reasons for decline varied from one case to another. The American societies that we investigate in

• • •

this chapter all proved finite, their governing classes failing at some point to solve mounting ecological, political, or social problems. They abandoned once dazzling cities, leaving them to crumble. In both the Americas and Afroeurasia, however, the general trajectory toward greater complexity continued on. For every political and cultural system that faltered and fell, another one arose to take its place, in some cases on top of the old ruins.

The first part of this chapter explores developments in North America, chiefly in the region that geographers call Mesoamerica, or Middle America. (We extend the chronological range of this chapter about six hundred years longer than the other chapters in Part 2 in order to respect political and cultural continuities.) This area corresponds generally to the tropical southern half of Mexico and the Central American states of Guatemala, Belize, Honduras, and El Salvador. It is the region in which a number of complex urban societies developed starting in the late second millennium B.C.E. (see Chapter 4). Several Olmec cities from that period flourished far into the first millennium B.C.E., and they may finally have declined mainly because new centers in other parts of Mesoamerica attracted more people, skilled artisans, and commerce. In this section of the chapter, we highlight peoples who achieved social complexity on relatively large physical scales: the state centered on the city of Teotihuacán (tay-oh-tee-wa-KAHN) in the Valley of Mexico, the Zapotec city

A Panoramic View

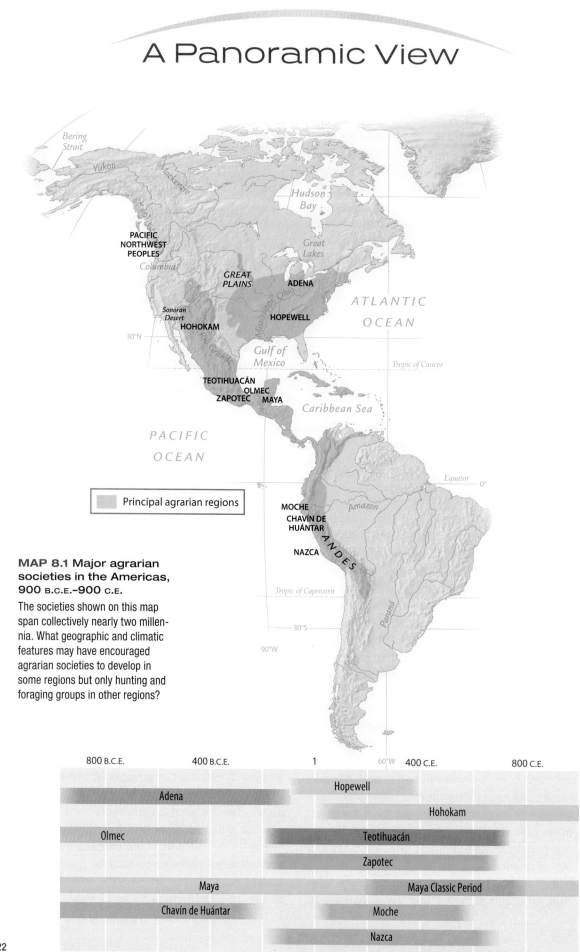

MAP 8.1 Major agrarian societies in the Americas, 900 B.C.E.–900 C.E.

The societies shown on this map span collectively nearly two millennia. What geographic and climatic features may have encouraged agrarian societies to develop in some regions but only hunting and foraging groups in other regions?

builders in the Oaxaca valley, and the Maya of southern Mexico and Central America. We then move to upper North America (northern Mexico to the Arctic), where in several places agrarian societies became more complex, though on a much smaller material scale than in Mesoamerica. These North Americans included peoples of the Pacific coast, the Sonoran Desert of northwestern Mexico and the southwestern United States, and the temperate woodlands that stretch from the Mississippi River to the Atlantic.

In the second part of the chapter we turn to South America, where societies scattered along the Pacific coastal plain and the Andean highlands began to construct remarkable ceremonial centers as early as the fourth millennium B.C.E. (see Chapter 4). Here, we focus on the large-scale building and numerous technical innovations associated with the ceremonial center of Chavín de Huántar in the northern Peruvian highlands, the Pacific coastal states of Moche (moh-CHEE), and the relatively small but artistically spectacular center known as Nazca.

The Spread of Complex Societies in North America

FOCUS What factors may explain differences in the development of political, social, and economic systems in agrarian societies in Mesoamerica and upper North America between 200 B.C.E. and the late first millennium C.E.?

All of Mesoamerica lies within the earth's northern tropical latitudes. But its ecological profile is extremely complex, owing to dramatic gradations of altitude, temperature, and rainfall, from the slopes of Pico de Orizaba, the third highest mountain in North America, to the lowland marshes of the Yucatán Peninsula. The Olmec built Mesoamerica's earliest urban society, starting about 1350 B.C.E., in the wet tropical plains and river valleys that parallel Mexico's southern Gulf coast. But even as Olmec civilization ascended, several other centers of dense agrarian settlement began to take shape in different regions and ecological conditions (see Map 8.2).

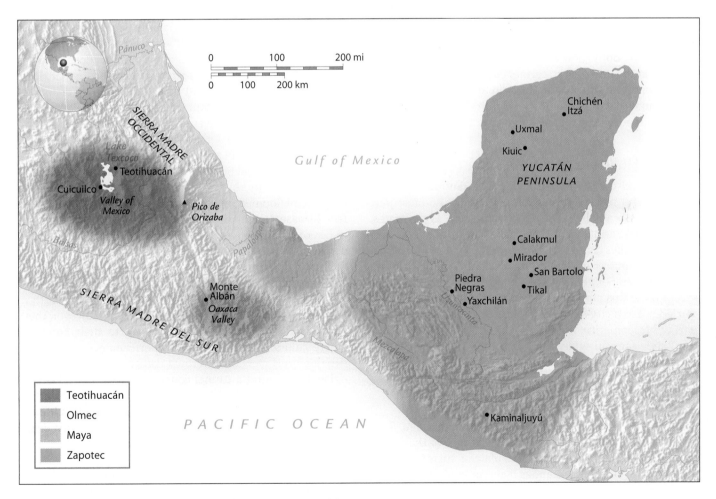

MAP 8.2 Major states in Mesoamerica, 500 B.C.E.–800 C.E.

What geographic features would likely have either facilitated or impeded travel among the states of Mesoamerica?

One of these centers arose in the Valley of Mexico, the highland basin that includes modern Mexico City. A second appeared in the fertile Oaxaca valley in the rugged mountains of southern Mexico. A third emerged in the low-lying Yucatán Peninsula and adjacent upland areas of modern Mexico, Guatemala, Belize, and Honduras, where the population spoke mainly languages in the Maya family. Archaeologists have uncovered ample material evidence to show that in the first millennium B.C.E. and thereafter all of these centers regularly exchanged goods, ideas, and techniques with one another and with neighboring rural peoples of mountain, forest, and desert. In other words, Mesoamerica as a whole became a zone of dynamic intercommunication. Despite great variety in language and cultural style, this interaction is evident in similarities in such aspects of life as architecture and religious practice.

The intensity of exchange gradually tapered off to the north (northern Mexico and the southwestern United States), where rainfall was generally much lower and farming populations smaller and more widely dispersed. On the southern frontier of Mesoamerica, cultural contact between Mayan-speaking societies and peoples of the Isthmus of Panama or South America beyond appear to have been irregular. In the 1,800 years or so that this chapter addresses, people did not, as far as we know, migrate in significant numbers or conduct long-distance trade between Mesoamerica and South America by way of Panama or its coastal waters. On the other hand, certain cultural innovations, notably knowledge of how to work gold and silver into useful objects, may have diffused from South America, reaching the Maya lands in the first millennium C.E.

Empire Builders of Teotihuacán

In the period this chapter explores, the centralized states that rose and fell in Mesoamerica were for the most part geographically small. We might think of them as city-states, that is, temple and civic centers from which monarchs and aristocratic elites controlled surrounding agricultural lands. They were similar in scale to the ancient Greek city-states in the Aegean Sea region. In Mesoamerica the single great exception to this pattern was Teotihuacán, a monarchy that started out as a city-state but later came to dominate a large part of Mesoamerica. In the process it disseminated its cultural style far and wide. Teotihuacán endured as a sovereign state from about 200 B.C.E. to 750 C.E., rising like Rome from city-state to empire and lasting about as long, approximately 950 years.

City of the gods. Twenty-two hundred years ago, Teotihuacán was a small city occupying a corner of the Valley of Mexico, an extensive highland plateau surrounded by mountains and active volcanoes that rise to 16,000 feet. The ancient basin, now the site of greater Mexico City and its more than twenty-two million people, had a mild climate, several large lakes, and a blanket of fertile volcanic soil.

Farmers drew on lake and spring water to irrigate fields of maize, squash, beans, nopal cactus (prickly pear), and numerous other crops. By 400 B.C.E., some people lived in large villages and towns. The biggest of these in the early period may have been Cuicuilco, a temple center of perhaps five thousand inhabitants. But about 50 B.C.E., a nearby volcano erupted in a spectacular display of fire and ash, spewing molten lava across Cuicuilco's fields, canals, and ceremonial buildings. The explosion buried the city and no doubt part of its population under thick debris. With Cuicuilco destroyed, people streamed into neighboring Teotihuacán. By 100 C.E., that town may have sheltered about 60,000 people, and by 600 C.E., more than 150,000. At that time it was probably one of the top ten largest cities on the planet.

Urban planning and the Pyramid of the Sun. Teotihuacán's rulers erected a magnificent capital whose sprawling ruin near Mexico City continues to amaze visitors. We do not know what the inhabitants called the city or even what language they spoke. In later centuries local people who spoke Nahuatl (the language of the Aztecs) named it Teotihuacán, meaning "Abode of the Gods," or "Where Men Became Gods." It is easy to understand why. Laid out on a grid with formal streets, the city occupied about eight square miles. It enclosed temples, palaces, a government center, single-story apartment blocks, workshops, plazas, markets, canals, lakes, and outlying neighborhoods of cheap housing. In the early centuries C.E., architects divided the city core into four quarters. A central thoroughfare, now called the Avenue of the Dead, ran four miles north to south. A second major road crossed the avenue at a right angle. Using astronomical measurements, the builders aligned this grid with particular stars and nearby sacred mountain peaks.

Teotihuacán functioned primarily as a center of religious worship and ritual. The Pyramid of the Sun, its largest monument, loomed over the city to a height of two hundred feet. Its base dimensions rivaled the largest pyramid at Giza in Egypt, though it rose less than half as high. The Egyptian pyramids served as tombs, and once they were built no one had special reasons to climb to the top of them. Excavations at Teotihuacán have uncovered burials in both the Pyramid of the Sun and the smaller Pyramid of the Moon north of it. Like pyramids throughout Mesoamerica, however, these structures also had staircases leading to their summits, where rulers erected shrines for performance of religious rituals in full view of the crowd gathered below. Archaeologists have found a tunnel connecting to a natural cavern within the Pyramid of the Sun. Some have suggested that the city's population believed this cluster of chambers to be the "house" of the storm god, an important deity, or the place where the gods created the sun and moon.

Teotihuacán society. The great majority of people who lived in Teotihuacán and surrounding villages cultivated the land. Farmers who resided in the city "commuted" to outlying fields during the day. Artisans and their apprentices

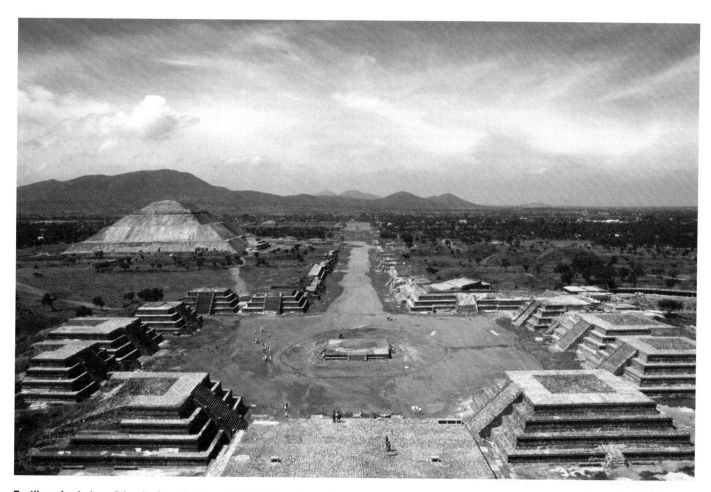

Teotihuacán. A view of the city from the Pyramid of the Moon. The Avenue of the Dead extends south. The Pyramid of the Sun, the highest structure in the city, is on the left.

made up perhaps 5 to 10 percent of the urban population. Stone carvers fashioned blades, spear tips, and fine objects of obsidian. Potters made both exquisitely decorated ceramics and everyday vessels. Other craftspeople produced sandals, baskets, building stone, and wall plaster from burnt limestone. Material objects or artistic styles that originated in other parts of Mesoamerica point to distinct urban quarters where foreigners lived, probably traveling merchants, commercial agents, or immigrant artisans. For example, archaeologists have discovered pottery, obsidian tools, and architectural forms in these neighborhoods, which suggest that people originating in the Maya region hundreds of miles to the southeast lived there. Direct evidence is scant, but there must also have been a class of officials who worked as administrators, clerks, and police. An elite minority of aristocrats, military officers, and religious specialists surely supervised these civil servants, though we know very little about Teotihuacán's urban government. There is no doubt, however, that the splendid city could not have been built without mobilizing and directing many thousands of workers.

Dwellings in the city likely fit the social status of their inhabitants. The structure called the Citadel, a complex of buildings surrounding a square 1,300 feet long on each side, almost certainly served as a center where aristocratic families lived. Other palace-like structures along the Avenue of the Dead presumably also housed elite families. One typical villa had forty-five enclosed rooms, a central courtyard with an altar in the center, and seven smaller courts and patios.

After about 250 C.E., builders knocked down plain adobe huts in the central part of the city and replaced them with more than two thousand flat-roofed apartment complexes of varying sizes. Most of the city's inhabitants apparently lived in these well-designed flats, made chiefly of a type of concrete of volcanic rock, gravel, clay, and mortar. Excavations of some of these compounds have revealed kitchens, clay braziers, sleeping quarters, wells, floor drains, and polished plaster walls. Domestic trash dumps show that families dined on maize, beans, squash, pumpkin, tomatoes, and avocados. Deer, dog, cottontail rabbit, and turkey meat added fat and protein to the diet. Apartments had no windows, but courtyards and patios allowed in light and air. Artisans painted colorful murals on the interior walls of almost all houses, as well as temples and palaces. These works portrayed gods, religious ceremonies, warriors, and jaguars but also images of men and women playing, singing, and chasing butterflies through irrigated fields. The repetition of patterns suggests that some artists may have used stencils, a type of mass-produced art that would have allowed people of ordinary means to have their walls decorated. Some wall painting also includes signs, or **glyphs** that indicate the names or titles of individuals whose images are shown. Scholarly efforts to decipher these glyphs continue, though so far we have

glyph A graphic figure or character that conveys information, often a symbol carved or incised in relief.

no evidence that the Teotihuacanos created a full writing system.

The city appears to have been the fount of religious ideas that eventually permeated much of Mesoamerica. The personalities and functions attached to particular gods and goddesses changed from one society to another, but deities whose influence spread far beyond Teotihuacán included the storm god (or rain god), whose ancestry as an image may stretch back to the were-jaguar spirit (part man, part animal) that the Olmec had worshiped in earlier times. Other Teotihuacán deities of lasting importance were Quetzalcoatl (keht-zahl-koh-AHTL), or feathered serpent deity, and the female divinity sometimes called the Great Goddess. We have no archaeological evidence that Teotihuacán's rulers and priests practiced human sacrifice on a large scale. But it did apparently happen. For example, digs at the city's Pyramid of Quetzalcoatl have revealed that, around 200 C.E., priests consecrated this monument by killing and ritually burying about two hundred young men.

What sort of empire? Starting around 150 C.E., Teotihuacán began to expand its political sway beyond the Valley of Mexico. It is difficult to determine the precise form this influence took in different localities, because the historical record is limited mostly to material artifacts. Teotihuacano armies appear to have conquered or at least intimidated many of their neighbors, ruling some groups directly and others through submissive local clients, just as the contemporaneous Romans did. Merchants and perhaps migrating colonists also disseminated Teotihuacán's religious ideas and artistic styles, introducing them to distant rulers eager to boost their own prestige by associating themselves with the great city's culture. We should remember, however, that in contrast to Afroeurasian empires of the same era, no Mesoamerican state had large transport animals or cavalry. Moving big armies long distances and regularly supplying garrisons far from the capital had to rely entirely on the walking or running speed of troops and porters. This limited direct imperial rule on the scale of the Romans, Persians, or Han Chinese.

Nevertheless, archaeological finds shows that warriors from Teotihuacán intruded into the affairs of cities hundreds of miles away. One example is Kaminaljuyú, a ceremonial center in highland Guatemala nearly 650 straight-line miles southeast of the Valley of Mexico. Kaminaljuyú's ruins have revealed so much Teotihuacáno influence in urban layout, temple

A mural in Teotihuacán. Frescos decorated the walls of Tepantitla, an apartment compound in the great city. This detail is part of a larger mural portraying a deity interpreted by some scholars as the Great Goddess. These tiny figures in the mural appear to be going about their daily business. How might you interpret the curved shapes extending upward from the faces of the two figures on the far left?

construction, and manufactured objects that some scholars have argued for a full armed takeover, which would have happened about 300 C.E. Archaeologists have discovered tombs full of luxury wares of Teotihuacán origin, indicating sustained contact. A second example of Teotihuacán's long reach is its relations with Tikal (Mutal), one of the largest cities in the Yucatán Peninsula. In 378 C.E., Teotihuacáno soldiers appear to have engineered the overthrow of the Maya ruler of Tikal. They replaced him with a man whose name glyph identifies him as Curl Nose. Tikal subsequently became a more powerful city-state, perhaps because it was an ally, if not a colonial dependency, of Teotihuacán.

We do not know exactly *why* Teotihuacán embarked on three and a half centuries of expansion, but if its population climbed to 150,000 or more, the demand for food, textile fiber, stone, and luxury wares must have far exceeded local resources. The need to make sure the flow of goods into the city never stopped may have motivated an aggressive foreign policy. Some of these goods probably arrived as tribute from subordinate towns and cities.

Uninterrupted long-distance exchange required a growing network of communication radiating out from Teotihuacán. This trade and tribute web was no doubt thicker toward the densely populated south and southeast than toward the drier lands to the north. The busiest route, named by modern scholars the Teotihuacán Corridor, connected the Valley of Mexico with the Olmec and Maya lowland regions. From there traders brought cacao beans, rubber, salt, honey, tropical bird feathers, pottery, and jade. Other merchants carried Teotihuacán's fine manufactures far and wide, including green obsidian blades, clay figurines, and ceramic ware. It is possible that Teotihuacán seized Kaminaljuyú in order to control distribution of the cacao that farmers grew in quantity along Guatemala's Pacific coast. Cane sugar was unknown in the Americas before 1492, but Mesoamericans blended cacao with water, honey, chilies, and other spices to make a chocolate drink used in rituals or for the pleasure of men and women who could afford an expensive brew.

The empire's decline. In the late fifth century C.E., Teotihuacán's commercial and cultural influence on southern Mesoamerica began to fade, and in about 650 C.E., assailants ravaged the city, plundering and burning the great temples and pyramids along the Avenue of the Dead. By this time Teotihuacán must have been so weakened that it could no longer effectively defend itself, something it had not had to do for centuries. Most scholars agree that several forces contributed to the city's fall. One factor may be that the ruling class became increasingly rigid and oppressive, inciting popular discontent and perhaps insurgency from within the city. A second may be that Teotihuacán's success at stimulating Mesoamerican trade had the unintended consequence of advancing the prosperity and power of other cities, which then refused to pay tribute to their former imperial master, or even attacked it. Third, there is little

A soldier far from home. This figure wears the costume and carries the shield of a Teotihuacano warrior, but he appears on the side of a stele in Tikal, a Maya city more than 600 miles to the southeast. The precise nature of the political relationship between the two cities is not known.

doubt that Teotihuacán voraciously consumed local forests for construction, household fuel, and production of plaster, which required burning large quantities of limestone. Deforestation would have caused erosion and leeching of arable soil on the slopes of the surrounding hills, eventually reducing the urban food supply. Climatological research shows that a drying cycle occurred in Mesoamerica in the mid-first millennium C.E. Extended droughts would have put even greater pressure on the city's elite to prevent chronic hunger, which, if it could do little to respond, might have led to insurgency and war. As many as forty thousand people continued to live in Teotihuacán for another century or so after 650 C.E., but its high civilization never recovered. Rather, the City of the Gods deteriorated into the splendid ghost town it is today.

Zapotec Civilization in the Oaxaca Valley

Teotihuacán was the largest urban center in Mesoamerica in the first millennium C.E., but the city of Monte Albán in the Oaxaca valley two hundred miles to the southwest rivaled it in architectural grandeur. Oaxacan farmers harnessed water from numerous rivers and streams to irrigate fields of maize, beans, and squash in the valley bottom and up the slopes of the surrounding mountains. At some point cultivators invented an irrigation method that involved digging shallow wells at regular intervals along the borders of long rectangular fields, then pouring pots of water from these boreholes onto individual plants. Oaxacans still use this technique today.

Around 500 B.C.E. the pace of change in the valley began to speed up. Population growth accelerated, villages multiplied, artisans took up new specializations, and several small states emerged. Within another four hundred years, the region's elite class began to use a writing system, though it has not been deciphered fully. People probably spoke languages ancestral to modern Zapotec, the name of a set of closely related Mesoamerican tongues.

Monte Albán. One of the valley's states founded a ceremonial center on a ridge in the valley, and from around 200 B.C.E., its rulers either defeated the other states or formed a federation with them. In the following centuries, this city, whose site is known as Monte Albán, expanded across two other ridges and became the capital of a much larger, centralized Zapotec state. Ruins of fortifications and stone depictions of prisoners, some of them bound and looking dejected, others mutilated and dead, suggest long periods of fighting among Zapotec groups in the valley and campaigns of conquest some distance beyond it.

Monte Albán's ruling class consisted of aristocratic families whose lords claimed both hereditary authority and descent from the gods. We know little about the Zapotec government, but the ruling elite, like the leaders in Teotihuacán, clearly had power to mobilize huge labor gangs. Amazingly, these crews sheared off the tops of Monte Albán's ridges and reshaped them into broad, flat plazas. Mammoth platforms, temples, palaces, and an astronomical observatory line the most expansive of these civic and ceremonial squares, which occupies fifty-five acres. The aristocracy no doubt lived on the great plaza, but, as in Teotihuacán, thousands of farmers and artisans

Ball court and players. This court with sloping sides is located on Monte Albán near the great temple plaza. The two ball players portrayed on a stone altar from the late eighth century C.E. are Maya rulers. Does the shape of the court or the action of the two figures suggest what the rules of the ball game might have been?

occupied apartment compounds. These residential areas were divided into wards, or urban neighborhoods, each with its own temples and other civic buildings. At its zenith in the sixth century C.E., the center had a population of about 24,000.

In earlier centuries, the Olmec of the Gulf coast had established the tradition of playing a ritual ball game on specially designed courts. Teotihuacán has revealed no evidence of a ball court, but Monte Albán had one of the earliest so far discovered. It was a rectangular space flanked on two sides by high sloping walls covered in plaster and painted red.

Oaxaca's external links. The material evidence of art, architecture, and everyday goods shows that the Zapotec took part in the trade and cultural exchange of greater Mesoamerica. As early as the second millennium B.C.E., obsidian blades and other objects of Olmec origin reached the Oaxaca valley; conversely, mirrors made from pieces of iron ore mined in Oaxaca turned up on the Gulf coast. The Zapotecs shared various gods and goddesses with Teotihuacán and other Mesoamerican peoples, including the storm god, the maize god, and Quetzalcoatl. We have no evidence that in its centuries of imperial expansion Teotihuacán ever attacked Oaxaca. In fact, beginning about 300 C.E., people from Oaxaca settled in Teotihuacán and founded a neighborhood

community. Material remains of what archaeologists call the Oaxacan Barrio indicate that these residents adapted to Teotihuacán's culture in everyday life. But they also designed tombs in Oaxacan fashion and equipped them with pottery, incense burners, and other objects either imported from Oaxaca or made by Teotihuacán's Zapotec community. We have pictorial evidence that ambassadors or other visitors traveled from Teotihuacán to Oaxaca. Carved stones in one of the great platforms at Monte Albán tell a tale of eight individuals in Teotihuacano headdresses (but carrying no weapons) leaving a place with temples in that city's style and then arriving at another location where an aristocrat in Zapotec headdress greets them. Another stone slab depicts two men, one from each city, in jaguar costumes. Accompanying glyphs seem to indicate that the two were engaging in some sort of diplomatic meeting, perhaps to keep relations between the two states running smoothly.

Monte Albán started to lose population and decay materially around 700 C.E., just a little later than Teotihuacán did. A process of political decentralization appears to have taken place in the Oaxaca valley as aristocratic groups built several new but also smaller centers in other parts of the valley. Monte Albán may have waned partly because Teotihuacán's earlier decline had a negative commercial impact on other Mesoamerican cities. Or, perhaps Oaxaca no longer needed a big government and large army once all threat from Teotihuacán had evaporated. Food production might also have suffered, as it did in the Valley of Mexico, from relentless deforestation and cycles of drought.

The Innovative Maya

The ancient Maya may be characterized fundamentally as people who spoke a number of closely related Mesoamerican languages. The most widely spoken language may have been Yucatecan, a forerunner of one of the thirty or so Mayan languages heard today. In the first millennium C.E., Classic Mayan emerged as a written medium of religious, political, and intellectual communication among priests, aristocrats, and other literate individuals, much as Sanskrit, Greek, and Latin did in Afroeurasia. The Maya writing system, combined with numerous other refined ideas and practices, infused the region, and especially its aristocratic and priestly class, with a distinctive cultural style in buildings, art, literature, and ritual.

This style, however, never coincided with a single Maya state. Rather, between 200 to 800 C.E., the era scholars call the Classic Period of Maya civilization, more than fifty independent city-states competed for territory and resources. These states variously flourished and declined, their size, wealth, and longevity

A meeting of two strangers? This drawing replicates a carved stone slab known as the Lápida de Bazán. The artist has added a hypothetical rendering of the slab's missing upper left corner. The figure at center right represents an individual of Oaxaca. The one on the left is wearing clothing characteristic of Teotihuacán.

1100 B.C.E.–200 C.E.	Preclassic Period
200–800 C.E.	Classic Period
800–1200 C.E.	Maya collapse

depending in large part on their resources in water and soil and their access to strategic goods such as salt or obsidian. As in the ancient Greek Mediterranean, Maya city-states joined in political and military alliances, which formed and reformed with changing circumstances. In some periods, particularly powerful states, for example, Tikal and Calakmul, forged regional alliance blocs and reduced weaker neighbors to political dependency. Some states lasted only a few hundred years before falling into ruin, others longer. Tikal experienced political ups and downs but carried on for as many as eight centuries.

Farmers and cities of the Maya heartland. The ancient Mayan-speaking region extended across three broadly defined geographical zones: the Pacific coastal plain in the far south, the interior highlands that include active and extinct volcanoes, and the lowlands of northern Guatemala, Belize, and the Yucatán Peninsula. The Maya built most of their cities in the lowlands, where the natural cover is tropical forest and the soil rests on a monolithic plate of white limestone. Rain falls mainly between April and October, with more of it in the southern half of the lowlands than in the northern half. Farmers began to settle the region around 1100 B.C.E. These cultivators built villages, made pottery, and planted *milpas,* or fields where maize, beans, manioc, avocadoes, and other crops grew side by side. The lowland population continued to grow, and large-scale urban building got under way about 500 B.C.E. Mirador, whose ruins lie near Guatemala's northern border with Mexico, arose sometime after 150 B.C.E. as one of the largest early cities. In the following eight hundred years, the populations of Tikal and Calakmul reached perhaps fifty thousand each.

As numbers multiplied, the ecology of water became increasingly critical. Farmers had to find ways to access and store water during the dry season from November to March. Nor could the summer rains always be expected because extended drought cycles were both inevitable and unpredictable. The Usumacinta River flows six hundred miles across the southern lowlands to the Gulf of Mexico, but the wider region has few rivers. The water in lowland swamps, lakes, and natural sinkholes (where the limestone collapsed) tends to be too saline to drink or even to use for irrigation. In the face of these challenges, ancient farmers innovated cleverly. They excavated cisterns to collect water during the rainy season, fashioning aprons of plaster around them to catch and direct the water. They dug canals to drain excess water and used the excavated mud to build raised fields. On steep hillsides they constructed stonewalled terraces to hold water and prevent erosion. In the land around some

of the cities, people built complex irrigation webs of canals and ditches. The tourist photos we see today of ruined Maya temples cloaked in wild vegetation may give the impression of remote jungle outposts. In fact, many of these structures formed the cores of densely populated cities surrounded by extensive food-growing suburbs.

Rulers, aristocrats, and rituals. The social and political class structure of Maya city-states was similar to the hierarchy in Teotihuacán, the Oaxaca valley, and indeed most Afroeurasian states of that era. A minority of aristocratic families stood at the social summit. They enjoyed greater wealth, status, and prestige than other groups and busied themselves keeping civic order and making political and economic decisions. As in other Mesoamerican centers, the Maya elite and their servants and retainers monopolized living space in temple complexes. In some states, a second tier of the elite class also existed, including temple priests, rich merchants, highly skilled artisans, and the managers of lordly estates. Not surprisingly, analysis of skeletal remains indicates that, on the whole, members of elite families lived longer and healthier lives than ordinary folk.

Like monarchs in Afroeurasia, Maya rulers had the tasks of ensuring the security and well-being of their subjects, fighting and winning wars, and negotiating with neighboring states, constantly appealing to the gods to favor those aims. Maya ruling dynasties practiced **primogeniture,** thereby avoiding bloody rivalries among siblings, children, or other relatives for the right to ascend the throne after a monarch's death. Some city-state dynasties endured for several generations. But they could end abruptly if a ruler lost a war or had to yield to a rebel challenger. Most Maya monarchs were men, though the record of ancient inscriptions shows that women occasionally succeeded to power or acted temporarily as regents for child-kings.

> **primogeniture** The legal or customary right of the firstborn child, usually the firstborn male, to inherit a family's entire estate, sometimes including a noble title or office, to the exclusion of younger children.

Rulers and the officials and priests who served them strove continually through ritual supplication to maintain the harmony of the universe and its three realms: the celestial domain where the sun, moon, and numerous other gods and goddesses dwelt; the earth, which was the back of a giant reptile, sometimes depicted as a turtle; and the soggy underworld, where other deities lurked. The political authorities made sure everyone understood that public disobedience risked not only civil punishment but, worse, the anger of the gods. Contrariwise, flood, drought, military defeat, or other social misfortune signified that the ruler might be failing in his ritual duties and alienating the cosmic powers. Somewhat like the Chinese principle of the Mandate of Heaven, Maya ideology approved withdrawal of support for such a ruler, even violent rebellion. Stone carvings and paintings depict extravagant festivals and intricate ceremonies held to distribute food and gifts to the populace, magnify the glory of the ruler, and please the

Lady Xoc: An Aristocratic Woman in Maya Politics

The royal wife known as Lady Xoc played a key part in the affairs of the Maya city-state of Yaxchilán, which lay along a stretch of the Usumacinta River that today demarcates the border between Mexico and Guatemala. In her youth, Lady Xoc, the daughter of two noble families, married Shield Jaguar, Yaxchilán's crown prince. She was also her husband's cousin. The marriage gave Shield Jaguar the support of powerful elite families within the realm, when in October 681 C.E. he took the throne at the age of thirty-four.

On that day, Lady Xoc celebrated the coronation by performing a blood sacrifice. Clothed in aristocratic robes, she pierced her own tongue with a sharp instrument. Her blood ran downward onto a pile of clean bark paper in a bowl she held before her. The bloodletting induced a hallucinatory state in which she conjured up an ancestral spirit, which emerged from the mouth of a serpent. This spirit was likely the founder of her husband's dynasty, materializing to witness and sanctify the new reign. Years later, Maya artists recorded that day's ritual event in an exquisite image carved into a stone lintel above a doorway in the building identified in Yaxchilán's ruins as Temple 23.

In 709 C.E., more than a quarter-century later, Lady Xoc again shed blood, this time to commemorate a celestial alignment between Saturn and Jupiter. A second image in Temple 23 shows her running a thorn-studded cord through her tongue as Shield Jaguar stands before her holding a long torch. About two months before this ceremony, Shield Jaguar had welcomed a new son, to be named Bird Jaguar. The mother of the child, however, was not Lady Xoc but rather Lady Evening Star, a younger royal wife from an elite family of the city of Calakmul. By marrying Lady Evening Star, Shield Jaguar appears to have sealed an alliance with that powerful city-state. Already sixty-one years old when Bird Jaguar was born, the king groomed the lad to succeed him. When the boy was thirteen, Shield Jaguar dedicated Temple 23, an event that once again featured Lady Xoc taking part in a blood ritual.

Modern scholars have interpreted the visual and textual evidence of Shield Jaguar's reign to suggest that he played an astute political game. He honored his Calakmul allies by choosing the offspring of Lady Evening Star, one of its daughters, as his royal heir. But he also consistently favored Lady Xoc with prestigious ceremonial roles, thereby firming up the support of her influential Yaxchilán family. It seems likely that she had special political status because depictions of women participating in Maya public rituals are extremely rare. Lady Evening Star, by contrast, drops out of the historical record. Shield Jaguar appears to have been such a skilled political dealmaker that he ruled Yaxchilán for sixty-two years, dying in 742 C.E. at the age of ninety-four. Bird Jaguar succeeded him.

Lady Xoc. The queen, represented in stone in the ruins of Temple 23 in Yaxchilán, sheds sacrificial blood from her tongue.

Lady Xoc occupied a place at the center of Yaxchilán's political life for about sixty-five years. But we will never know whether the king's failure to choose a son of hers as heir caused her bitterness or regret.

Thinking Critically

How would you argue for or against the reliability of biographical information about Lady Xoc based on carved images in a Maya temple?

---

gods with offerings and sacrifices. Carvings show aristocratic personages honoring or appeasing the celestial lords with their own blood, women cutting their tongues and men their tongues or penises with sharp obsidian blades or stingray spines. Elaborate public occasions such as the accession of a new ruler called for equally spectacular religious offerings, including ritual murder. The most prized victims were war prisoners of high standing, even defeated and captured kings. Captives of ordinary social class were often enslaved or adopted into families.

The Maya masses. Farmers, artisans, and laborers made up most of the population of Maya states, the majority living in neighborhoods around the city's ceremonial center. Common folk built houses of vertical poles, interlaced sticks, thatched roofs, and sometimes plastered walls. These dwellings sheltered extended families of three generations. Households maintained "kitchen gardens," and family members, very likely women, ground maize to make tortilla flour, wove and embroidered cotton cloth, and fashioned everyday pottery. Commoners paid tribute in food or textiles to both

corvée labor Unpaid labor required by a ruler, an estate lord, or another authority, usually for road work or other construction.

the rulers and the local aristocratic families, and the government typically demanded **corvée labor** to build temples, palaces, canals, or other public structures. Families offered prayers and conducted rituals as part of their everyday routine. Planting a field, harvesting a crop, building a house, or making a ceramic pot were all occasions to supplicate the gods with offerings.

Slaves occupied the bottom rung of the social ladder. Men, women, and children lost their freedom mainly in the heat of war. But criminals could also be enslaved, and destitute people sometimes sold themselves into bondage. As in Egypt and some other Afroeurasian societies, slaves who served aristocrats might be ritually killed when their master died, thus accompanying their owner into the afterlife. People enslaved for theft could regain their liberty after they made restitution to their victim, and the children of slaves typically had free status.

Words, numbers, and calendars. The Maya created a sophisticated writing system, though the deep origins of writing in Mesoamerica remain murky. In the late 1990s a crew building a road near Veracruz in southeastern Mexico discovered a stone block inscribed with sixty-two glyphs. Researchers were astonished when they dated the slab to about 900 B.C.E., pushing the dawn of writing in the ancient Olmec zone along the Gulf coast back several hundred years. The glyphs have not been deciphered, however, and material evidence of writing in Mesoamerica in the following 1,200 years has been tantalizing but meager and scattered. The locations of inscriptions dating mostly to the late centuries B.C.E. suggest that people were simultaneously experimenting with writing in the Olmec zone, the Oaxaca valley, the Valley of Mexico, and the Maya lowlands. The earliest evidence of a developed Maya writing system are glyphs painted on walls in a pyramidal building at San Bartolo in Guatemala. These inscriptions date to as early as 300 B.C.E., but for the following six centuries the evidence of Maya writing remains fragmentary.

The complex system that emerged in the Maya Classic Period represents one of just three cases in world history in which people invented writing independently, that is, without knowing about any external model that would help them go about it. The other two cases were the scripts invented earlier in Mesopotamia and China. The Maya system combined logographic signs, which corresponded to whole words (units of meaning), with phonetic signs, which indicated syllables (units of sound). To this extent the system was similar to ancient Mesopotamian cuneiform writing. Approximately 850 glyphs have been discovered so far, most of them logographs. Maya scholars carved and painted texts on stone monuments, on the walls of buildings, and even on pots and strips of bone. More than 15,000 texts have survived, and linguists have patiently deciphered many of

them. Communicating knowledge about religion, mythology, astronomy, royal reigns, wars, the histories of cities, and calendrical computations, the decoded inscriptions have opened wider windows on the Maya past.

Beginning around 200 C.E., Maya writers also produced thousands of books, or codices (singular, *codex*). Scribes painted Maya characters on long strips of bark paper or deerskin, then folded the pages together like an accordion. Probably every city-state had a chief scribe, or "keeper of the royal library." Surviving paintings show him (and sometimes her) as a busy official consulting with the monarch, writing tool in hand. Unfortunately, only four Maya codices have survived from before the sixteenth century C.E. The ravages of time destroyed most of them. In 1562, Diego de Landa, the Spanish bishop of Yucatán, burned more than two dozen Maya books, reporting with satisfaction: "We found a large number of books in these characters and, as they contained nothing in which there were not to be seen superstition and lies of the devil, we burned them all."[1] Ironically, this same priest wrote an extensive account of the Maya as he observed them, including valuable information about their writing system!

Mesopotamians first used writing to keep accounts of goods, Mesoamericans to record dates. Like most ancient societies, Mesoamericans believed that the celestial movements of sun, moon, and stars affected all aspects of life. Heavenly bodies were deities, and sages who recorded their trajectories and cycles also created calendars to indicate when important ceremonies should be held, when the rainy season was likely to start, and what the future might hold.

Several Mesoamerican societies used two intersecting calendars, usually citing dates in both of them. One was an almanac calendar of 260 days that recorded important festivals and religious observances. We do not know the rationale for 260 days, though it might relate to the period of human gestation, or about nine months. The other was a solar calendar of

A Maya scribe. This figure appears on a vase from the Late Classic Maya Period in Guatemala. The scribe holds a paint stylus in his right hand. What different sorts of functions might scribes have performed in Maya society?

365 days. Since the almanac calendar made a complete revolution in a shorter time than the solar calendar, the named dates on the two calendars were not synchronized. So, for example, the two dates that appear on today's calendar would not appear together again for 18,980 days, or approximately fifty-two years. This Calendar Round, as modern scholars call it, permitted precise dating only within a cycle that started over again every fifty-two years. It would be as if 2001 C.E. were recorded as year 1 and 2052 as year 52, but 2053 as year 1 again.

Sometime in the second century C.E., if not earlier, Maya savants rectified the deficiencies of the Calendar Round by inventing the Long Count calendar. This method was based on a much longer cycle of 1,872,000 days, or about 5,128 years. The Maya believed that the world in which human beings lived was a manifestation of one of several Great Cycles of time. They may have reckoned, though on what basis we do not know, that this world came into being on a date equivalent to 3114 B.C.E. On the Long Count calendar, days were counted from that starting date, just as the Christian calendar counts days elapsed from the birth of Jesus. To express dates precisely using the Long Count calendar, Maya scholars broke it down into smaller units of time starting with days, then "months" of 20 days, years of 360 days, and on up to the *bak'tun,* a unit of 144,000 days. The Maya carved or painted Long Count dates on many inscriptions that recorded significant events. Because scholars can now read these dates, they have produced a much more detailed chronology of Maya history than would otherwise have been possible.

Calculating dates using three different calendars (and there were others, as well) almost certainly drove all elements of Maya mathematics, including astronomical calculations, measurement of distances, business accounts, and perhaps performance of higher mathematical operations about which we have no surviving record. As the introduction to this chapter explained, the Maya based their counting system on units of twenty, rather than ten, as our modern system does. They also invented and used several symbols, for example, a picture of a seashell, to represent "zero." This was a major scientific achievement because until the Common Era no other people except the ancient Babylonians incorporated a zero into their numbering system. The Maya appear to have had some concept of zero as a whole number, that is, an integer like 1, 2, or 3. However, they used it mainly in their positional notation scheme to designate a place in a number that has no value, just as we do in our modern system. For example, when we write 900, we show that only the 9 has value. But because we place it in the third position from the right, it must mean 900. We could write this number as 9 , leaving two empty spaces. But that may cause confusion. Inserting one or more zeros shows the exact position each number occupies. The Maya used their zero signs the same way, except that they wrote numbers of vertical columns rather than in horizontal lines.

Maya cultural and commercial connections. We have some idea that Maya merchants kept track of business by writing down numbers. We also know that they engaged in complex trade operations and traveled long distances. In the Classic Period the whole Mayan-speaking region came to constitute a single zone of intense intercommunication, the larger cities serving as the main hubs. In some lowland areas, urbanization sprawled so far from the ceremonial center that the suburbs of one city ran up against those of a neighboring one. City-states fought one another, but diplomats, artisans, and merchants also moved incessantly between them, traveling over roads, trails, and lowland causeways. Aristocratic families of different states intermarried to stabilize regional political relations and seal alliances. Particular cities specialized in certain manufactures, whether painted pottery, obsidian blades, woven baskets, or jade jewelry, encouraging the growth of a sort of Maya common market within which goods circulated. Large-scale urbanization would likely have been impossible if each city had been obliged to rely entirely on its own production rather than trading numerous products with other centers near and far.

The whole Maya zone was also a commercial center of gravity that attracted trade from distant parts of Mesoamerica. Routes that connected Central America with the Valley of Mexico and other northerly population centers all passed through Maya cities and markets. Along the routes in and out of Maya country, merchants carried raw cotton, cotton textiles, dyes, ceramics, obsidian, flint, granite, shell, tobacco, cacao, honey, bark paper, tropical bird feathers, copal resin (for ritual incense), jaguar pelts, and shark teeth. Salt beds on the north coast of the Yucatán provided essential sodium for human consumption throughout Mesoamerica. In the late centuries of Maya prosperity, urban craftspeople began to work gold, silver, and copper, whose ores came mainly from mines north or southeast of the Maya region. Copper bells, cacao beans, and greenstone beads all served as mediums of exchange, that is, as money. Near the end of the first millennium C.E., artisans began to build large canoes carved from hardwood trunks to ship goods around the Yucatán Peninsula between the Gulf of Mexico and the western Caribbean Sea. The cost of moving a particular quantity of salt, cacao beans, or honey by sea from one side of the peninsula to the other was probably significantly less than the cost of transporting the same quantity overland on the backs of porters.

The end of the Maya states. The world is littered with the physical remains of ancient kingdoms, but the disintegration of the Maya urban civilization between 800 and 1200 C.E. is especially intriguing. For one thing, the biggest and most flourishing city-states of the southern lowlands deteriorated first. Some smaller cities of northern Yucatán lasted another two or three centuries. Second, the breakdown happened astonishingly fast in the southern region. The states there all crumbled within a span of about one hundred years. Archaeologists excavating the ruins of the city of Kiuic have found evidence that about 880 C.E. workers suddenly abandoned half-completed public building

A Maya Bible: An Account of Creation in the *Popol Vuh*

Maya societies no doubt produced numerous works of literature, passing them from one generation to the next both orally and in the form of codices, or painted books. Among the few texts to survive the Spanish conquest in the sixteenth century is the renowned Popol Vuh (paw-pawl vuh), or Book of Counsel, a long poetic narrative illuminating the cosmology, mythology, and history of the Quiché-speaking Maya of the Guatemala highlands. The version we have is the achievement of Maya scribes who sometime in the 1550s C.E. wrote out a text in Quiché using a modified Latin script. This work is probably a compilation of stories based on a variety of oral traditions and written sources. This text remained largely unknown until the early eighteenth century, when a Spanish monk named Francisco Ximénez acquired it in Guatemala. He transcribed the Quiché text and added a Spanish translation. Although the sixteenth century work was subsequently lost, the Ximénez text rests today in the Newberry Library in Chicago.

The Popol Vuh recounts the creation of the world and the early history of the Quiché Maya in more than nine thousand lines of verse. In the creation story, the gods mourn the fact that there was no one to honor or praise them. So they decided to create animals, only to discover that animals merely "squawked and chattered and roared" and could not speak. So the gods tried to fashion humans out of clay but found that the dolls they created could not turn their heads and tended to dissolve in the rain. Next, the gods carved men and women out of wood, but these were expressionless automatons who had "nothing in their hearts and nothing in their minds." Eventually, the creators tried molding humans out of cornmeal. Corn turned out to be the perfect substance for making animate people who thought and felt. The selection below tells of the final and successful attempt to fashion human beings.

And here is the beginning of the conception of humans, and of the search for the ingredients for the human body. So they spoke, the Bearer, Begetter, the Makers, Modelers named Sovereign Plumed Serpent [the gods of creation]:

"The dawn has approached, preparations have been made, and morning has come for the provider, nurturer, born in the light, begotten in the light. Morning has come for humankind, for the people of the face of the earth," they said. It all came together as they went on thinking in the darkness, in the night, as they searched and they sifted, they thought and they wondered.

And here their thoughts came out in clear light. They sought and discovered what was needed for human flesh. It was only a short while before the sun, moon, and stars were to appear above the Makers and Modelers. Split Place, Bitter Water Place is the name: the yellow corn [maize], white corn came from there.

And these are the names of the animals who brought the food: fox, coyote, parrot, crow. There were four animals who brought the news of the ears of yellow corn and white corn. They were coming from over there at Split Place [a mountain in modern Guatemala near the border with Mexico], they showed the way to the split.

And this was when they found the staple foods.

And these were the ingredients for the flesh of the human work, the human design, and the water was for the blood. It became human blood, and corn was also used by the Bearer, Begetter.

And so they were happy over the provisions of the good mountain, filled with sweet things, thick with yellow corn, white corn, and thick with . . . cacao, countless zapotes, anonas, jocotes, nances, matasanos [types of tropical fruit], sweets—the rich foods filling up the citadel named Split Place, Bitter Water Place. All the edible fruits were there: small staples, great staples, small plants, great plants. The way was shown by the animals.

And then the yellow corn and the white corn were ground, and Xmucane [the divine grandmother] did the grinding nine times. Food was used, along with the water she rinsed her hands with, for the creation of grease; it became human fat when it was worked by the Bearer, the Begetter, Sovereign Plumed Serpent, as they are called.

After that, they put it into words:

the making, the modeling of our first mother-father,
with yellow corn, white corn alone for the flesh,
food alone for the human legs and arms,
for our first fathers, the four human works.

It was staples alone that made up their flesh. . . . And when they came to fruition, they came out human. They talked and they made words. . . . And then they saw everything under the sky perfectly. After that, they thanked the Maker, Modeler.

Source: Dennis Tedlock, ed. and trans., *Popol Vuh: The Definitive Edition of the Mayan Book of the Dawn of Life and the Glories of Gods and Kings* (New York: Simon & Schuster, 1996).

Thinking Critically

What does this reading suggest about ancient Maya attitudes about both corn and animals? What do you think the *Popol Vuh* implies about the meaning and purpose of human life? Scholars agree that the *Popol Vuh* has characteristics of a myth. What do you think some of those characteristics are? Why do you think that since ancient times societies around the world have told stories of the creation of the earth, animals, and human beings? What creation stories are best known in the United States today?

projects and that families left pots and stone tools in their houses as if they expected to return for dinner. Third, not only states disintegrated but the entire social order. The lowland population, both elites and common folk, fell precipitately after 800 C.E., plunging from as many as 14 million in the Classic Period to 1.8 million within a mere century and a half.[2] The population appears to have been much lower when the Spanish arrived in the early sixteenth century than it had been seven hundred years earlier. Finally, the Maya collapse fascinates us because, as far as the archaeological record shows, no terrible invader put the lowland cities to the torch. Rather people abandoned those centers, and in time tropical forests closed in over the massive temples.

The precise combination of factors that brought on this calamity remains puzzling and controversial. As in the case of the fall of Teotihuacán centuries earlier, we can only consider a range of factors, recognizing that some cities endured longer than others and the causes of collapse almost certainly varied from one place to another. There is no doubt that much of Maya lowland society lived in conditions of serious environmental stress in the eighth and ninth centuries C.E. In both numbers and density, population had followed a general upward trend since the late centuries B.C.E. Farmers worked continuously to increase the productivity of the land, not only to feed their own families but to support the ruling elite and its soldiers, palaces, and temples.

The agricultural possibilities of the Maya region, however, were limited. The water table in the southern lowlands, the most densely populated region, was generally lower than in the north. Whenever a drought cycle arrived, as it inevitably did, problems of finding and storing water became acute. Researchers have discovered from skeletal remains that in densely populated areas malnutrition became widespread, an affliction likely related both to food shortages and to a diet too dependent on maize. This staple has less protein value than wheat, barley, or the meat of large animal domesticates, none of which Mesoamericans had. The absence of cattle, sheep, or chickens meant that people were spared certain animal-related infectious diseases such as measles, smallpox, or influenza. This does not mean, however, that Maya lowlanders seldom got sick. Energy-draining illnesses such as yellow fever and malaria, as well as syphilis and certain types of heart disease, were endemic. Protein deficiency would have made people generally more susceptible to these maladies.

Farmers in the Yucatán who could not coax higher crop yields from their existing fields tried to open new land. Unfortunately, this meant clearing forests in ever-widening circles around the central city. Because fertile tropical soils tended also to be thin, deforestation aggravated erosion, aggravating soil loss. That in turn caused rivers, reservoirs, and drainage systems to silt up, compounding the problems of both soil and water management.

In the Maya Classic era, intercity conflicts appear to have become more frequent and violent. Maya rulers typically responded to military crises, not by investing heavily in projects to preserve and develop resources, but by concentrating more power at the top of the social pyramid, conscripting larger armies, and building more ostentatious shrines to appease the gods. Projects to save the state by exalting it encouraged megalomania within the lordly class, which pulled more farmers away from their fields to put up grander temples. In Tikal, workers continued to erect splendorous temples even as the government was collapsing. There must have been wise officials in some states who had practical ideas for improving water management or food shortages. But the long-term economic problems resulting from simultaneous population growth and ecological degradation were probably too complex for them to solve.

For hundreds of years, Maya farmers had faced recurring droughts and survived. But climatologists have shown that starting about 760 C.E. and for a century thereafter calamitous droughts occurred every few decades, affecting particular cities at different times but eventually wearing them all down. More frequent droughts on top of chronic ecological problems may have pushed some big cities over the brink, resulting in breakdown of trade, social confusion, and mass flight, which inevitably affected smaller centers in the same region.

Archaeologists have presented evidence that by the ninth century C.E. several southern lowland cities became more vulnerable to both local rebellion and foreign attack. In Piedras Negras, a city west of Tikal, vandals mutilated stone images of rulers, suggesting that people rose up against lords who appeared to have lost the blessing of the gods. Some northern lowlands cities, which generally survived the ninth century in reasonable shape, apparently

Ruins of Kiuic. Archaeologists have been working at Kiuic in recent years to understand why the city was rapidly abandoned in the late ninth century.

took advantage of troubles in the south to launch raids or invasions. Like candles sputtering and finally burning out, Long Count date inscriptions appear less and less frequently in one southern Maya city after another after 800 c.e., finally ceasing altogether in 910 c.e. In the northern lowlands, some cities, for example, Chichén Itzá and Uxmal, endured a century or two longer. Urban centers were smaller there than in the south, which may have eased pressure on land and water. Also, attacks on weakened southern centers may have brought a short-term bonanza of loot and captive labor.

The northern cities, however, soon disintegrated as well, and between about 900 and 1200 c.e. the whole lowland population plummeted. What, then, happened to all the people? This phenomenon remains a subject of debate among scholars. Certainly war, starvation, disease, and flight to other regions played a part; over a longer term, falling birth rates coupled with rising death rates, especially among malnourished young children, could have produced rapid population fall-off. Once farmers abandoned their fields and the elites their fine homes and temples, water systems would have deteriorated quickly and tropical vegetation closed in. Large-scale recovery would have been impossible except over decades, and the much smaller farm communities that remained in the lowlands may have been quite content with village-level independence if it meant freedom from high-handed aristocrats, public bloodlettings, and heavy taxes.

Developments in Upper North America

The North American land mass has the shape of a curved funnel, and a demographic map dated, say, 100 c.e. would show the heaviest clusters of human population at the bottom end of it, that is, in Mesoamerica. Moving up the funnel from the Valley of Mexico, urban centers would have appeared smaller and fewer between and population generally thinner, correlating to progressively drier climate, especially at low elevations. No cities on the scale of Teotihuacán, Monte Albán, or Tikal would be seen anywhere on the map between Mesoamerica and the Arctic Circle (see Map 8.3). Even so, some regions of upper North America had much larger populations than others. On our hypothetical map, the largest concentrations of people who grew crops and lived in villages would have appeared along the Pacific coast of what is today the United States and Canada, in the Eastern Woodlands stretching from the Mississippi River to the Atlantic, and, on a smaller scale, in the Sonoran Desert. They spoke hundreds of languages, and they practiced various combinations of hunting, foraging, fishing, and farming depending on local ecological conditions. In the second millennium b.c.e., people of the Eastern Woodlands began to domesticate and cultivate goosefoot, may grass, and other indigenous plants yielding tiny but nutritious seeds (see Chapter 4). By the end of that millennium, maize cultivation had spread from central Mexico northward to the Sonoran Desert.

The Pacific coast. People who lived along North America's western rim from California to British Columbia did not adopt maize farming on an important scale before the arrival of Europeans, but economies based on acorn and buckeye nut meal, edible grasses, fish, shellfish, and wild game sustained village life. The archaeological record shows that, in the first millennium c.e., some villages along the coast and interior valleys sheltered hundreds of people, and lineages of privileged elites and craft specialists distinguished themselves from ordinary men and women. In the forested coast lands north of California, villagers who consumed salmon and other sea and river life built houses of split timbers, and they carved giant cedar-trunk canoes for coastal fishing and trade. In the same millennium, coastal peoples also began to adopt the bow and arrow. This weapon, which probably diffused from Canada, augmented wild animal protein in the diet but also tended to make intervillage raiding more lethal. Near the end of the millennium, communities along the north coast began to build log-walled forts on high ground, suggesting fiercer warfare over food resources and trade.

The Hohokam of the Sonoran Desert. The U.S. Southwest and far northwestern Mexico represent another area where village societies emerged in the early first millennium c.e. Communities there, known collectively as the Hohokam, a local Indian name for ancestral people, grew maize, squash, cotton, and other crops on river floodplains, constructing canals as much as ten miles long to divert water into fields. Scholars think the people who became the Hohokam migrated into the northern Sonoran Desert from Mexico, perhaps bringing maize technology with them. Their taste for platform mounds, distinctive textile designs, and ball courts attest to material, if indirect connections with Mesoamerica. Discoveries of copper bells and stone figurines at Hohokam suggest trade connections leading south. In contrast to Pacific coast societies, which preferred tar-sealed baskets to pottery, the Hohokam acquired skill at making brown, red-painted ceramic ware. At the site known as Snaketown, south of Phoenix, Hohokam inhabitants built a cluster of villages, which might have formed a local political confederation. The site includes a central plaza, platform mounds, and ball courts where some scholars think village teams competed against one another. The Hohokam were pioneer farmers whose successful adaptation to harsh land prefigured the larger-scale societies that emerged in that region in later centuries.

The Adena and Hopewell societies. A tradition of mound building in the lower Mississippi valley goes back to the mid-fourth millennium b.c.e. (see Chapter 4), but the first sustained wave of it occurred in the Eastern Woodlands starting about 800 b.c.e. The builders known as the Adena flourished in a wide area around the Ohio River valley until about 100 b.c.e. The Hopewell culture, also centered on the

MAP 8.3 Major settlements and societies in upper North America, before 400 C.E.

What geographical factors might help explain why relatively dense societies developed in the areas indicated on the map?

Ohio, existed from then until around 400 C.E. Sites identified as Adena have been discovered as far from Ohio as New England. The Hopewell tradition extends to the Mississippi valley and New York State. We do not know whether the second culture was derived directly from the first, *culture* here meaning a set of distinctive material artifacts and structures discovered on a number of sites. But the two traditions shared several characteristics. Both Adena and Hopewell people practiced a mix of hunting; foraging; and farming of squash, goosefoot, sump weed, and other regional domesticates. Climatic research indicates that Hopewell communities thrived and spread during a prolonged period of relatively mild winters. Farmers knew about maize but did not make it a staple crop. Both cultures include large earthen mounds that in some cases concealed burial chambers richly stocked with goods. The most impressive Hopewell structures take the form of embankments laid out in precisely measured squares and circles. Among the most dramatic is the Serpent Mound, an earthwork in rural southern Ohio that slithers nearly a quarter of a mile along a ridge.

The head of the snake is aligned with the summer solstice. The dating of this mound, however, remains uncertain.

Both traditions suggest a trend toward social complexity. Ordinary families cremated deceased members, but some individuals received privileged treatment. The community buried these special people under mounds in rooms constructed of stout timbers. Others were obliged to accompany them into the afterlife, probably wives, children, servants, or slaves. Goods excavated from elite tombs have included fabrics, copper jewelry, flint blades, freshwater pearl beads, gold nuggets, fine pottery, and tobacco pipes in the shape of birds, otters, and fish. The honored corpses in these tombs were doubtless leaders, but we do not know whether Adena or Hopewell ever organized themselves politically outside the level of the village or village cluster. Nor do we know any details of the religious significance of earthen mounds.

Hopewell burial sites that include copper from the Great Lakes region, carved mica figures from North Carolina, obsidian from Wyoming, and turtle shells from the Atlantic coast dramatically testify to an active network of trade

Serpent Mound. This earthwork in Adams County, Ohio, is an example of an effigy mound, a structure having the shape of a bird or animal. People of the Adena tradition may have built a mound here before 100 B.C.E., though carbon dating of charcoal in the structure suggests that it acquired its present form only in the twelfth century C.E. The mound extends more than 1,300 feet, though no burials or artifacts have been found in it. Does the Serpent Mound deserve listing as a Unesco World Heritage Site along with places like Stonehenge, the Taj Mahal, and the Great Wall of China?

stretching nearly across temperate North America. Oddly, this trade appears to have moved mostly one way, since archaeologists have rarely found Eastern Woodland products beyond the Hopewell cultural zone. Scholars have naturally wondered whether large-scale mound construction means that Eastern Woodlanders made contact with temple-building Mesoamericans, imitating or learning from them. Archaeology, however, has revealed no significant evidence of such interconnection. In any case, communities at the center of the Hopewell cultural zone gave up big mounds and sumptuous burials after about 400 C.E., a decline perhaps linked to the return of colder climate in the Ohio and upper Mississippi valleys.

South America: Complex Societies along the Andean Spine

FOCUS In what ways did changing environmental and ecological conditions in Andean South America influence the development of agrarian societies and states?

At the start of the first millennium B.C.E., the densest agricultural societies in South America clustered on the slopes and interior valleys of the Andes Mountains (see Map 8.4), growing potatoes, maize, beans, squash, peppers, and many

MAP 8.4 Major states in South America, 900 B.C.E.–800 C.E.
Routes of trade running east and west were as important as north–south routes. Why do you think that was the case?

other plant foods. Numerous rivers that plummeted from the highlands also permitted farm communities, even small cities, to flourish in the harsh deserts that paralleled the Pacific shore (see Chapter 4). By the first millennium B.C.E., an elaborate system of trade routes linked together societies up and down this "vertical" sequence of habitation, with traders, for example, carrying sea salt and dried fish far up mountain trails, then returning with sharp obsidian blades from highland mines. On the eastern Andes slopes, routes connected Andean farmers with peoples of the tropical Amazon basin. Only in the far southern cone of South America did communities continue to organize themselves exclusively in small bands of foragers and hunters, generally paralleling the way of life of societies in Canada and Alaska at the opposite end of the Western Hemisphere.

If South Americans had no sustained contact with Mesoamericans across Panama during these millennia, they

played an important part in human colonization of the Caribbean islands. The earliest humans to reach the islands probably arrived from southern Mesoamerica about six thousand years ago. But later waves of migrants paddling seaworthy canoes departed from the northern South American coasts to settle Caribbean islands one after another. About 200 B.C.E., South American immigrants introduced farming. These people were almost certainly linguistic ancestors of the Arawak-speaking communities that Columbus encountered at the end of the fifteenth century. Archaeological evidence shows that in the first millennium C.E., some islanders kept up trade links with South America, at least much more so than with the Mesoamerican coasts.

Andes Urbanization: The Example of Chavín de Huántar

In the Andes valleys and Pacific coastal plains from Ecuador to southern Peru, steady population growth compelled local societies to organize themselves on larger scales and to compete with neighbors for resources. In the second millennium B.C.E., highland communities built dozens of U-shaped temples around which small urban centers bloomed. These cities may not have had central governments, but shared worship of particular deities expressed in rituals provided a foundation of common identity. Such social glue was necessary because people had to work together to dig canals, transform steep hill slopes into terraced fields, and defend farms against intruders. However, as these centers continued to expand and as the stakes rose to protect generations of investment in complex terraces and irrigation works, elite families that at first provided war leaders, economic managers, and priests began to exert firmer authority over ordinary men and women. A similar process was taking place simultaneously in densely populated regions of Mesoamerica.

Chavín society. Among the ceremonial temple complexes erected in the central highlands, Chavín de Huántar (cha-VEEN deh wan-tar), whose construction started about 900 B.C.E., surpassed them all in size and splendor. At its greatest extent, Chavín's buildings, courtyards, and plazas occupied nearly 125 acres of land. The U-shaped central platform, which archaeologists call the Old Temple, had a cut stone façade that masqueraded as solid rock. But unlike any other platform in the central Andes, the facing concealed an interior labyrinth of passageways, galleries, chambers, and drains kept cool by hundreds of air shafts. Chavín has revealed more than two hundred stone sculptures representing supernatural beings. The center flourished for about seven hundred years, and during the last three hundred of them (500–200 B.C.E.), a huge New Temple was added to the old one. In this later period, at least a few thousand people lived at the site, transforming it from a place of ritual and worship into a lively city.

Chavín occupied a strategic midpoint between the arid north Peruvian coast and high Andes passes leading to

Amazonia. Trade routes descended along two mountain river valleys that converged at Chavín, then continued to the coast. Merchants used llama pack trains to move goods from one altitude and ecological zone to another. The center's position as a cultural and commercial node linking the Pacific shore with Amazonia is evident in its buildings and decorations. The temple's U-shaped ground plan, sunken plaza, and bas-relief wall sculptures all relate to coastal architecture of an earlier time. On the other hand, some stone carvings represent animals such as jaguars, monkeys, harpy eagles, and caymans (large reptiles related to alligators) whose natural habitat was the Amazonian forests hundreds of miles to the east.

The residents of Chavín revered an array of deities represented in sculpture as part animal and part human. In the interior of the Old Temple is a free-standing, knife-shaped stone obelisk whose blade sticks into the floor below, the handle into the ceiling overhead. Called the Lanzón, this stele depicts an elegantly robed human whose face is catlike and whose hands and feet have claws. Its thick lips are drawn back into either a smile or a snarl, exposing two large fangs. Archaeologists hypothesize that this divine being was Chavín's chief deity, responsible for keeping all the contradictory forces of the universe in balance. It also may have served as an oracle, that is, a medium that gave responses to the inquiries of worshipers. Material remains of spoons and mortars suggest that priests and ordinary worshipers ingested hallucinogenic snuff or other psychotropic drugs, temporarily leaving their mundane cares behind or transforming themselves into jaguars or birds.

Chavín's later centuries reveal signs of a widening gap between the elite class and the rest of the population. In one part of the site, researchers have found rich collections of expensive and exotic artifacts, such as gold jewelry, fine pottery, imported shells, and cinnabar (a reddish mineral and source of mercury). Families who lived in this zone enjoyed stone houses and augmented their protein diet by consuming the tender meat of young llamas. In other neighborhoods, women and men possessed fewer luxuries, inhabited adobe dwellings, and dined on older, tougher llama meat, when they had meat at all, to supplement their diets of maize, potatoes, and other plant foods.

Chavín's radiating influence. As the center grew in size and population, so did its cultural impact on neighbors near and far. We have no evidence that Chavín had a royal

Lanzón stele at Chavín. The Old Temple houses this carved, fifteen-foot pillar of white granite. Why do you suppose the temple builders placed this image of a supernatural being deep in the building's interior?

dynasty, a regular army, or a hierarchy of administrators governing distant districts. It is possible that warriors from the city raided or overran neighboring groups. For example, people in a valley not far from Chavín built twenty-one hilltop forts. Why would they do that if not to defend themselves from external threat? It seems likely, however, that Chavín evolved into a city-state with a governing elite but never into the capital of a military empire to the extent that Teotihuacán did in Mesoamerica.

Chavín's *cultural* power, however, is indisputable. The temple complex may have been the destination of pilgrims who trekked long distances to consult the oracle god, take part in rituals that might invite divine favor, or seek healing from illness. Remains of offerings or residential refuse include objects that originated hundreds of miles from the city, including pieces of pottery and other vessels in styles associated with a number of different coastal and highland societies. From about 500 B.C.E. the evidence grows of a "Chavín cult," a set of religious ideas and practice, gaining popularity across the central Andes. Chavín influence on sculpture, pottery, metalworking, fabric design, and architectural planning has also turned up in the archaeological record of sites far to the north and south. A full explanation of Chavín's cultural brilliance and long reach is beyond the skills of modern archaeology, but it appears to have happened in ways that involved little or no coercion.

Sometime around 200 B.C.E., Chavín was abandoned and partially destroyed. Why this happened is not clear, but the city had never been the only impressive ceremonial center in the Peruvian highlands. Other cities may have competed with it culturally and militarily so that its prestige contracted and pilgrims stopped coming. The soils around Chavín had never yielded bounteous crops, and the reduced population that continued to live near the great temple complex could no longer keep the place up, as it were. It is not that the central Andes suffered an absolute decline of cultural accomplishment. Rather, the scene shifted to other, newer centers, perhaps several of them, though in subsequent centuries no single city quite displayed Chavín's level of grandeur.

Back to the Coast: The Moche Society

Starting in the fourth millennium B.C.E., human communities adapted ingeniously to Peru's intensely arid Pacific coastal plain by damming and diverting the waters of narrow rivers that tumbled down Andes slopes to the sea.

People of the coastal zone called Norte Chico, an area not far north of Peru's modern capital of Lima, built the earliest known urban centers anywhere in the Americas (see Chapter 4). The Norte Chico towns crumbled after about 1800 B.C.E. But other coastal groups improved on that society's irrigated farming technology, and stretches of rainless land continued to bloom.

Farther up the Peruvian coast from Norte Chico, people we call the Moche (or Mochicas) began sometime in the late centuries B.C.E. to build sophisticated dam and canal networks along the valleys of nearly a dozen rivers in order to irrigate fields and support dense populations. Moche urban civilization flourished between about 250 and 800 C.E. Just as the Norte Chico people had done, these riverine societies also exploited the cold, northwestward-flowing Humboldt Current (or Peruvian Current) for fish, shellfish, birds, and sea mammals. Surviving pottery and other objects made in Ecuador to the north, Chile to the south, and Andes valleys to the east show that the Moche conducted a thriving long-distance trade. Fish meal, shells, dried seaweed, and cotton all commanded markets in the Andean highlands. Moche artisans built stout canoes capable of navigating Pacific coastal waters, and we know that crews regularly paddled southward to the tiny Chincha Islands, where they collected heaps of dry seabird droppings, known as guano, to use as fertilizer. (Because almost no rain falls on Peru's coastal islands, the nitrates in bird excrement that accumulated over hundreds of thousands of years did not evaporate or wash away. The ancient Moche could not have understood the fertilizing properties of nitrates, but they knew that guano helped increase crop yields. So did nineteenth-century farmers around the world. Between 1840 and 1880, Peru exported over 20 million tons of bird guano.)

The Moche style. Because of irrigated farming, the Moche valleys, which from north to south bracketed a stretch of coastal plain and Andean foothills about two hundred miles long, could support dense populations. As in Chavín and the Mesoamerican complex societies, families and clans that somehow accumulated and controlled more food resources than others made themselves into a privileged aristocratic class. These elite groups proclaimed that their special status was part of the divine nature of things, and they built great earthen platforms, plazas, and temples to make their own ideology of social class distinction visible to all. Elite families of different valleys appear to have allied and intermarried with one another, evolving a shared culture based on ritual performance, elaborate costumes, and routine cooperation in exercising authority over everyone else. As we know happened in Maya city-states, common people may have paid taxes to

valley lords in the form of corvées on elite farm estates or on irrigation and building projects.

What modern scholars call Moche culture was largely the way of life of the elite minority, including its preferred designs for public buildings and its acquisitions of fine pottery, jewelry, precious metalwork, stone carvings, and mural paintings. Altogether, these material objects revealed a distinct cultural style common to all the Moche valleys. Pots and other vessels depicted animals and vegetables, as well as every conceivable human activity—fighting, working, sleeping, giving birth, and dying. The personalities of Moche individuals seem to reach us across the centuries on pots made in the shape of male or female heads. Sex is a frequent theme in Moche material culture. Drinking from a ceramic vessel's spout, for example, might require enclosing one's lips around a ridiculously large penis. Artisans also used molds to produce everyday pots and other objects, simplifying production and reducing costs. Consequently, distinctive Moche elite styles became more readily available to working families in their small adobe houses. On the other hand, Moche architecture and art tell us much less than we would like to know about the lives of ordinary women and men. Neither the Moche nor any other South American society invented a full writing system. Government officials or couriers carried dried lima beans encoded with glyphs that

Power of the lima bean. This ceramic pot dated to between 100 and 800 C.E. probably represents a woman. She wears a necklace of fruit, and two lima beans adorn her chest. The Moche inserted this vegetable into much of their art and endowed it with spiritual potency.

signaled important information or news, though the meaning of these signs remains unknown.

The cities and their lords. In the early centuries C.E., Moche elites built numerous ceremonial centers, the biggest sheltering 10,000 to 15,000 residents. Physical remains suggest that the grandest of these centers lay in the southerly desert where the Moche River empties into the Pacific. This site displays the remains of two massive adobe brick temple platforms named the Pyramids of the Sun and the Moon (Huaca del Sol and Huaca de la Luna). Archaeologists have estimated that the builders of the Pyramid of the Sun, which covers some thirteen acres, used about 143 million bricks. Extending between the platforms was an urban zone of plazas, residences, and craft shops. The city's governing lords looked out upon their realm from an elaborate building complex perched on the pyramid's summit.

In the northern Moche zone, Sipán was an important center. There, in 1987, looters discovered gold in a burial chamber. In the nick of time a Peruvian archaeologist managed to prevent wholesale pillaging of the tomb, which turned out to be the resting place of a man of the highest social rank, probably the city's chief priest and ruler. The burial dramatically confirmed both the exclusive wealth of the local lordly class and the exquisite quality of objects produced to show off its high status and power. Ornamentation of silver, gold, copper, and semiprecious stones adorned the lord's mummified corpse, and numerous other costly items lay around him. His funeral, which took place about 300 C.E., featured human sacrifices, including his wife, two other women, a military officer, a watchman, a child, and a dog.

The Moche cultural region as a whole probably never constituted a unitary state with a single monarch and government. During Moche's seven-century history, periods of political integration in particular parts of the region alternated with years of greater fragmentation and intervalley wars. The city clustered around the Pyramid of the Sun emerged as the center of a sizable state. Laborers built a network of roads to move both warriors and goods between valleys that paid tribute to the capital. Moche painted pottery garishly depicts warriors triumphing over their enemies. Stripped naked in defeat, hapless captives ascend temple steps to pay homage to a warrior-priest, who then decides their fate. Rulers practiced human sacrifice to some extent. Ceramic objects show priests slitting prisoners' throats and consuming their blood in a gruesome ritual of thanksgiving to the gods. But periods of fighting aside, Moche elites also found it in their long-term interest to work together to preserve and enforce their shared elite status.

The Nazca

A complex society contemporary to Moche emerged about six hundred miles to the south, where the coastal plain was equally dry. Known as Nazca, this society was small in territory and population compared to Moche but nonetheless culturally rich. Eight westward-flowing rivers converge to form the Nazca River, which flows to the sea. In three of these tributary rivers, the water descended underground for some miles, then resurfaced. Nazca farmers initially settled where the streams rose to the surface. Later, they began to construct a diversionary system of subterranean tunnels, surface water tanks, and irrigation canals to elevate the water relative to the descending terrain, then stored it and directed it to land otherwise too dry to cultivate. Irrigated crops and ocean resources supported growing numbers of farmers and construction of the ceremonial center of Cahuachi, which got under way about 200 B.C.E. In contrast to the capital city in the Moche River valley, Cahuachi's remains show little evidence of residential settlement. Rather it appears to have been a place of ritual performance and feasts at special times of the year. People also came from surrounding villages to bury their dead in Cahuachi's cemetery. If an organized Nazca state existed, it was likely a loose federation of clans. The center has more than forty temple platforms, not a big central one, suggesting that various descent groups may have administered many of their own affairs within some type of cooperative framework.

Like the Moche, the Nazca amaze us today with astonishing art. Pots display farmers shooing birds from maize fields, fishermen launching canoes, and a one-man band busily playing a horn, rattle, drum, and pipes. Even more famous are the spectacular animal, plant, and geometric forms that the Nazca cut into local hillsides and plains. Whereas the Moche etched tiny symbols on lima beans, the Nazca created **geoglyphs,** enormous line drawings engraved on more than four hundred square miles of landscape. Some of these geoglyphs, forming outlines of birds, monkeys, whales, and other animals, are plainly visible today on hillsides. The Nazca people also scraped designs on flat terrain, and these are so big that no one can see them whole from the ground. In fact, archaeologists first discovered many of these pictures by studying aerial photographs. Some flat geoglyphs depict trapezoids, triangles, zigzags, and spirals. They also include many miles of straight lines that radiate outward from hills. Workers made these patterns by moving away surface stone to expose lighter colored soil beneath. Centuries of extreme aridity helped preserve images that would otherwise have washed away long ago. Modern observers have speculated that long straight lines represent ritual pathways or maps of fault lines where underground water sources might be found. People also walked along the lines that formed animals, plants, and geometric shapes, perhaps to perform ceremonies. Executing these patterns was perfectly feasible because the artists could figure out ways to keep track of the curves and angles they wanted their lines to trace. Some geoglyphs could be seen clearly from nearby hills. But we discount the several popular books arguing that the formations served as landing beacons for ancient space aliens!

> **geoglyph** An image, character, or set of lines imprinted on a landscape, usually on a large scale, by moving rocks or soil or by cutting into the ground surface.

Geoglyph of a hummingbird. Some scholars argue that the geoglyphs served as offerings to the gods of rain and fertility. Others suggest that the Nazca wished to communicate with the heavens above. The dark area in the deep Ingenio River valley on the left side is farmland.

Troubles in the Sixth Century

The Moche and the Nazca complex societies went into decline in the sixth century C.E., the first gradually, the second quite abruptly. Important archaeological clues to this deterioration are the disappearance of particular ceramic and other artistic styles, the abandonment of temple centers, and in the case of the Moche a weakening of the aristocratic culture that had manifested itself in opulent ritual objects and burial practices. By 800 C.E. the Moche no longer gave any ruler the magnificent funeral that had marked the death of the lord of Sipán.

During the sixth and seventh centuries, the western Andes and coastal plains experienced severe climatic instability.

Scholars have related this condition to the El Niño Southern Oscillation (ENSO), alternating periods when the surface temperature of the equatorial Pacific rises above normal, then falls below normal (the phase called La Niña). Extreme ENSO swings could be associated both with drought and torrential rain and with significant reduction of sea life off the South American coast. Glacial core samples from the Andes have revealed wet and dry cycles in the region in the sixth and seventh centuries, including extended periods of drought. An extreme dry period lasted from 563 to 594 C.E. and coincides with archaeological evidence of Moche's weakening and Nazca's full collapse. A drought lasting more than three decades would have radically reduced river water levels in the Andes foothills and coastal plains. As drought dragged on from one year to the next, farmers would have had to abandon fields, irrigation ditches would have clogged with sand, and toxic salt deposits would have built up in soils because mountain runoff was too weak to flush them out. Chronically diminishing harvests would have led to famine, early death, lower birth rates, and greater social tension among clans, social classes, and neighboring populations.

Priests, aristocrats, and farmers must all have prayed fervently to their rain god for relief, but ENSO shifts could suddenly bring such heavy rain and flooding that conditions got far worse. In the Moche valleys, deluges and river torrents very likely ripped apart dams, dikes, and canals and washed away adobe dwellings. Great volumes of soil washed out to sea, but then ocean waves and winds redeposited it on the coast as sand, which buried houses, fields, and canals. People who had built up the irrigation infrastructure and the civic centers over many generations had no hope of restoring them quickly after the rain stopped, perhaps to be succeeded by more drought. When people abandoned the Pyramids of the Sun and Moon about 600 C.E., they were already partially buried.

Weather extremes alone almost certainly do not explain the fall of the Moche and the Nazca political and cultural systems. Scholars have argued that, similarly to the situation in the Maya lands a few centuries later, the ecological possibilities of the Peruvian valleys had by the sixth century nearly reached their limit. In the Moche zone, however, the ruling elites appear to have lived in splendid isolation from the common population and to have insisted on controlling greater and greater shares of wealth from field, sea, and human labor to pay for bigger public structures and larger quantities of precious goods. Social dissension over gross differences in income between lordly families and everyone else may already have been simmering when the first signs of climatic instability appeared. When it grew worse, the population may have suspected that the gods had stopped responding favorably to priestly offerings and performances, signaling that the leaders in the high temples had lost their legitimacy. As in the Maya case, even the best intentioned Moche lords probably found recurring damage to the agricultural infrastructure beyond their technical and managerial powers to fix.

Political and social breakdown affected different Moche regions at different times, and the temples carried on longer in the far northern valleys than in the south. Even though all the big centers collapsed eventually, farming and fishing population did not disappear. Archaeological analysis shows that as the extreme weather alternations tapered off, people set to work rebuilding irrigation works. In some valleys, elite clans simply retreated farther up the valleys, where farmland was more restricted but water more reliable. They built new temples in some places, but the distinctive Moche cultural style was not restored.

• • • •

Conclusion

This chapter has accentuated developments in the most populous regions of the Americas, where complex societies rose, and fell, during a span of nearly two thousand years. The final quarter of that period, that is, from about 500 to 900 C.E., appears to have been a time of calamity for all the big societies we have highlighted in both Mesoamerica (Teotihuacán, the Oaxaca valley, the Maya lowlands) and South America (Chavín de Huántar, Moche, and Nazca). All of those societies moved along an arc of change that started with exuberant agricultural production, city building, and artisanship and ended in material ruin—at least the ruin of the splendid public structures that symbolized great imagination and skill. Different factors surely contributed to decline in each case. ENSO-related droughts that went on for years may have weakened all these societies. Similarly, social strains resulted from elites accumulating too large a share of wealth and then, when times got tough, failing to dissuade common people that the gods might be happier if jewel-bedecked aristocrats went away.

In any case the story of collapse in the late first millennium C.E. should not be overstated. First, and as we will see in Chapter 14, new city-states, empires, and brilliant artistic traditions arose to replace those that had crumbled, though not necessarily in exactly the same places. In both the Valley of Mexico and the Andes highlands, new empires came to display more power than any that had come before, but the Maya lowlands remained depleted of population and large temple centers until the coming of Europeans in the sixteenth century. Second, the regions where the most impressive societies arose between 900 B.C.E. and 900 C.E. covered only a small part of the two American continents. In those centuries, humans occupied just about every latitude and ecological niche from the Arctic to the tip of South America. We have no evidence that peoples who practiced village-level farming, foraging, fishing, or hunting on Alaskan tundra, Amazon forest, or Argentine plains experienced any general crisis in the later first millennium C.E. We saw that, in upper North America, the Hopewell people stopped building finely engineered earthen mounds about 400 C.E., but other groups continued to do it in other woodland regions, in a few places on a grander scale than ever before. Trends toward greater social complexity also continued in the Sonoran Desert and the Pacific Northwest.

Finally, on a global scale, the Mesoamerican and South American civilizations had no monopoly on decline and collapse in the first millennium C.E. In Chapter 9 we return to Afroeurasia, where mighty empires had deep troubles of their own.

• • • •

Key Terms

Adena society 236	Hopewell society 236	primogeniture 230
Chavín de Huántar 239	Maya city-states 224	Serpent Mound 237
corvée labor 232	Moche society 240	Snaketown 236
geoglyph 242	Monte Albán 228	Teotihuacán 224
glyph 226	Nazca society 242	Zapotec society 228
Hohokam society 236	*Popol Vuh* 234	

Change over Time

ca. 1350 B.C.E.–400 B.C.E.	The Olmecs build Mesoamerica's earliest urban society.
ca. 900–200 B.C.E.	Chavín de Huántar in Andean South America becomes a cultural and commercial node connecting the Pacific shore with Amazonia.
ca. 800 B.C.E.–400 C.E.	Adena and then Hopewell societies flourish in Woodland North America
ca. 500 B.C.E.	Early Maya urban building appears in Mesoamerica.
ca. 200 B.C.E.–750 C.E.	Teotihuacán rises from city-state to empire in Mesoamerica, then falls.
ca. 200 B.C.E.–700 C.E.	Monte Albán becomes the center of a Zapotec state in Mesoamerica.
ca. 200 B.C.E.–550 C.E.	A Nazca cultural style, including giant geoglyphs, develops among the communities along the arid coast of Andean South America.
ca. 1–1450 C.E.	The Hohokam people inhabit the Sonoran Desert of North America.
ca. 200–800 C.E.	Maya city-state construction reaches its peak (Maya Classic Period); the *Popol Vuh* and other codices are written.
ca. 250–800 C.E.	Moche urban society flourishes in Andean South America.
ca. 563–594 C.E.	Extended droughts disrupt life in Andean South America.
ca. 800–1200 C.E.	Maya city-states decline.

Please see end of book reference section for additional reading suggestions related to this chapter.

part 3

Shifting Power, Thickening Webs
Afroeurasia, 200–1000 C.E.

I f in the very long term human history has been a story of more and more people sharing the planet, while inventing increasingly complex of ways of organizing themselves, interacting with one another, and exploiting the earth's energy to their own benefit, this trend has not been entirely steady. Within the overall movement toward greater complexity, there have been cycles in which population has declined and recovered, cities have shrunk and flourished again, and economies have contracted and expanded. These cycles may be merely regional in scope, but they have also had interregional or even global dimensions, as we have seen in modern times when business recessions reverberate quickly around the world. The three chapters in Part 3 encompass approximately eight hundred years in the history of Afroeurasia, an era when the demographic and economic trends of the previous millennium temporarily slowed down or even reversed themselves, before accelerating again at an even faster pace.

The third century C.E., where Part 3 begins, represents a jarring break—in some places violent and destructive—in the prevailing pattern of population and economic growth. Between about 200 and 600, the Han, Kushana, Parthian, and western Roman empires all collapsed. These upheavals occurred partly in connection with the aggressive migrations of peoples from the Inner Eurasian steppes into neighboring agrarian lands. Western Europe, North Africa, northern India, and northern China all experienced serious economic turmoil. Disease epidemics that swept around the Mediterranean rim and across Southwest Asia in the sixth century had similar consequences. Conditions of life in several regions became harsh enough that Afroeurasia's overall population declined by several tens of millions between the third and seventh centuries, perhaps the first significant drop since the invention of agriculture.

A terra-cotta camel and rider from the era of the Tang dynasty in China.

Not all empires fell and not all economies went into deep recession during these centuries. The armies of Sasanid Persia and the eastern Roman empire held back nomad invaders. In South Asia, the kings of the Gupta state united a large part of the subcontinent. Several regions, including southern China, Southeast Asia, and tropical West Africa, generally escaped dismal depressions and continued to prosper, despite regional wars and dynastic changes. Long-distance trade on the Inner Eurasian silk roads and the chain of seas from China to Southwest Asia fell off, but only the western Mediterranean suffered an extended commercial slump.

In the sixth century, the engines of population and economic growth began to rev up nearly everywhere in Afroeurasia:

■ After three and a half centuries of fragmentation, China achieved political unification under the Sui and Tang dynasties (581–907). This development sparked a new round of technical innovation and rapid population growth in the rice-growing south.

■ In South Asia the Gupta empire disintegrated in the mid-sixth century, but this crisis appears to have had little effect on the subcontinent's swelling production of cotton textiles, pepper, and cinnamon, goods that found eager markets across Afroeurasia.

■ In western Africa, merchants who discovered the hardy qualities of the dromedary camel set up commercial operations that connected the Mediterranean lands with West Africa. This pioneering enterprise, well under way by the seventh century, lubricated the whole Afroeurasian exchange system with injections of West African gold.

■ Assaults of Eurasian nomads on China, India, and Southwest Asia tailed off. In the steppes new warrior empires arose in the sixth century, but they also stabilized political conditions and recharged silk road commerce. In the late first millennium, Europe endured an incursion of Magyar warriors from the steppes, but these intruders settled down quickly.

■ Finally, invaders from the Arabian Desert, who proclaimed Islam as a new universalist religion, politically united most of Southwest Asia, a region of agricultural and urban productivity that had been divided between rival states for nearly a thousand years. The cities of Southwest Asia had for millennia funneled commercial goods and new ideas along a corridor that connected the Mediterranean basin with the whole expanse of Asia

and eastern Africa. Following unification under Arab leadership, that corridor became more animated than ever before. From Southwest Asia, Arab soldiers, preachers, and merchants introduced Islam along the routes of conquest and trade. This new expression of monotheistic faith drew on the teachings of both Judaism and Christianity, and it put great emphasis on social cooperation and codes of proper ethical and legal behavior. Thus, Islam joined Buddhism and Christianity as a universalist faith offering the promise of community harmony and individual salvation. Together, these three religions reached just about every part of Afroeurasia in the late millennium.

Between 200 and 1000 C.E. migrant farmers, long-distance merchants, conquering armies, and wandering missionaries brought more of Afroeurasia into a single arena of human interchange. This happened without any revolutionary breakthroughs in communication and transport technology, though artisans and engineers tinkered endlessly with ship designs, navigational tools, and more efficient systems of banking and credit. By the end of the millennium, signs of new economic growth and social complexity were abundant. Afroeurasia's overall population climbed nearly back to where it had been eight hundred years earlier. Interlinked commercial networks operated across the breadth of Afroeurasia. China was moving into an era of unprecedented industrial growth. And after suffering a half-millennium of chronic disorder, western Europeans were building a new urban civilization.

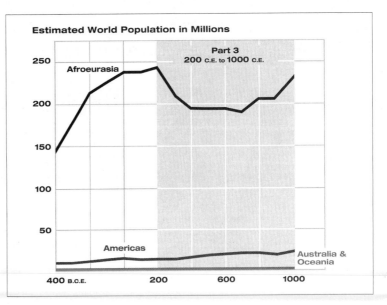

Estimated World Population in Millions

9 Turbulent Centuries
200-600 C.E.

A reminder of mortality in mosaic from the Byzantine cathedral of Santa Maria Assunta in Venice.

hen people come down with flu after flying on an airplane, they often blame the conditions of air travel—the confined space, full flight, and stale air that encourage the spread of infectious germs from one passenger to another. Infected passengers then get off the plane, and before they even know they are sick they may transmit their malady to others at home or work. In this way viral and bacterial ailments may spread from Madrid to Bangkok or Kansas City to Kinshasa in a matter of hours. In today's globalized world, we fear not only annoying contagions but also raging epidemics. Microorganisms mutate constantly into new and possibly deadly forms, and travelers may quickly carry dangerous pathogens to places where people have weak immunological defenses against them. The consequences may be a local disease outbreak or, far worse, a pandemic—an infection that moves quickly from one region to another, possibly affecting millions.

Ancient empires, which made it their business to build good transport networks, were inevitably susceptible to epidemics. Major eruptions of what might have been smallpox, measles, or anthrax spread through parts of the Roman empire in the second and third centuries C.E. A deadlier outbreak, probably bubonic plague, occurred in 541, a time when the emperor Justinian ruled in Constantinople. This infection may have originated somewhere in the upper reaches of the Nile valley, advanced downriver to the Mediterranean, then spread in every direction. Scholars have estimated that within just a few years this pandemic killed one-third to one-half of the population of the Mediterranean region, northern Europe, and perhaps Persia.

The Plague of Justinian, as it was called, caused a demographic and social shock. But it was only one of several disruptions that affected the course of events in Afroeurasia between the third and seventh centuries. In addition to recurring epidemics, the most conspicuous of these disturbances were the movements of armed migrants from Inner Eurasia into densely populated agrarian lands. Persistent political and social tumult connected to these migrations characterized much of Eurasia and northern Africa. Compared to the previous four centuries, when the Roman and Han empires reached their apogees of power, the growth of population, food production, long-distance trade, and urbanization appear to have slowed, though by no means everywhere in Afroeurasia and not all at once.

The first section of this chapter explores major political and economic changes between about 200 and 600 C.E. Here, we emphasize the dramatic interplay between the Inner Eurasian population movements and the critical shifts that took place in the configuration of large states and major centers of economic wealth (see Map 9.1). In this period, the Han, Kushana, and Parthian empires collapsed, and the Roman empire shrank to about half its former size. Powerful new states, however, arose in Persia and South Asia.

In the second section we connect political and economic change to the remarkable growth of Christianity and Buddhism, two multifaceted belief systems that proclaimed a universal message of moral and spiritual deliverance and

Chapter Outline

• • •

that attracted millions of new converts. Both religions became vehicles for the interregional exchange of ideas, people, and goods. We also consider connections between the growth of these two missionary faiths and the fates of other belief systems in that era: Zoroastrianism, Roman polytheism, the South Asian devotional religion that took shape as the Hindu tradition, and Manichaeism.

In the final section, we shift our focus to Africa south of the Sahara Desert. There, the most prominent patterns of change in the early centuries C.E. were the continuing movement of farmers and herders into the continent's southern third and in several places the rise of denser farming populations, bigger towns, and more complex systems of trade. These developments had significant connections to the shifts and disturbances taking place simultaneously in northern Africa and Eurasia.

A Panoramic View

MAP 9.1 Major states of Afroeurasia, 250 C.E.

This map represents Afroeurasia at a moment of impending transformation across the region. Comparing it to Map 7.1, what geopolitical differences do you see?

The Shifting Map
of Empires

FOCUS What impact did the armed migrations of pastoral nomads have on political and economic changes in China, Persia, the Mediterranean region, and South Asia?

Empires never last forever, but in the space of little more than two centuries, four enormous states, the largest in world history to that time, either collapsed or splintered: the Han empire in China, the Parthians in Persia, and the Kushanas in Central and South Asia, all in the third century C.E. The western half of the Roman empire fragmented in the fifth century. These crises, however, offered opportunities to new groups to found states or transform old ones. In 224 C.E., the Sasanids (suh-SAH-nids), an Iranian warrior group, eradicated the Parthian dynasty and shortly erected an even bigger Persian empire over its grave. In South Asia the Gupta (GOOP-tah) dynasty, expanding from a base in the Ganges River valley, reunited much of the subcontinent as the Maurya emperors had done five hundred years earlier. The eastern part of the Roman empire, under the new name of Byzantium (BIHZ-ann-tee-um), held firm until after 600 C.E. None of these power shifts took place without upheaval, in large part because of the violent interventions of mounted archers from the Inner Eurasia steppes.

Turbulence in Inner Eurasia

The giant states that existed at the start of the third century formed a curving arc of territories that extended across Eurasia and northern Africa. These territories, rich in food production, supported something like 200 million farmers and city dwellers. Extending north from this arc was Inner Eurasia, whose much sparser population included both cultivators and pastoral nomads. Earlier chapters described the general historical patterns of interaction, whether peaceful or violent, between nomads and densely settled societies. Since the second millennium B.C.E., nomads periodically surged into agrarian lands, sometimes as raiding expeditions and sometimes as migrations of horse archers along with their families, wagons, and livestock.

One of these pulsations started in the third century C.E. and lasted into the sixth. It involved not only attacks on farms and cities but also prolonged disruptions *within* Inner Eurasia, as mounted groups of unequal numbers and power pursued or fled from one another across mountains, deserts, and steppes. Historians have not so far explained with much confidence why this surge took place. They have associated it with various factors: climatic cooling that cut food production in Eurasia's northern latitudes, population growth that put severe pressure on grazing land, steppe wars that forced fleeing groups to push against agrarian neighbors, and weaknesses in big states that left their frontiers vulnerable to nomad attack.

Both the rise and collapse of the Xiongnu, the pastoral nomadic empire that ruled the eastern steppes between the third century B.C.E. and the second century C.E. (see Chapter 7), affected the movements of other herding peoples. In their expansionary phase, Xiongnu warriors attacked not only China but also nomad rivals to the west, provoking peoples that did not wish to be conquered to flee even farther west. The Han campaign that shattered the Xiongnu state sent more tribes westward. In the third and fourth centuries C.E., the Pontic-Caspian region became a vortex of restless herding folk of diverse origins, some of them speaking Mongolian, others Turkic, Iranian, and Germanic languages. The climatic pattern in Inner Eurasia also figured in the tendency for pastoral peoples to push west, since average seasonal rainfall increases progressively in that direction. Migrating herders discovered that the farther west they went, the greener the grazing land was likely to be, especially west of the Black Sea.

China after the Han Empire: Growth without Unity

The Han dynasty (see Chapter 7) endured for nearly four hundred years, with one short interruption. At its height, garrisons secured the borders from northern Korea and Vietnam to oasis towns far out along the Inner Eurasian silk roads. But in the second century, the Han emperors ran into increasing political and financial trouble. Steppe nomads contributed to the dynasty's misfortunes. It collapsed in 220 C.E., and from the third to the sixth centuries, China remained politically fragmented, a time known as the Age of Division.

The end of the Han. The Chinese government faced a particular structural problem that dogged almost all premodern empires. Territorial expansion filled state coffers with booty and new tax revenue. Maintaining control over conquered lands and peoples required large expenditures to pay for garrisons and administration, to suppress uprisings, and to offer lavish gifts in silk and gold to Inner Eurasian nomad leaders, a policy that allowed those chiefs to share in the wealth of China without being tempted to attack it. The great costs of empire, however, strained government resources and aggravated competition for them among China's elite. In the second century C.E., state bureaucrats, military commanders, relatives of the emperor's wife, and royal **eunuchs** all banded into rival political factions and tried to influence state decisions. The imperial corps of eunuchs

> **eunuch** A castrated male who typically served as a functionary in a royal court, especially as an attendant in the female quarters (harem).

moved freely within the palace and were expected to give the emperor unconditional service. Their numbers, however, grew into the thousands, and they increasingly meddled in political affairs to advance their own interests. A string of ineffectual or youthful monarchs made matters worse. More

Han defenses on the northwestern frontier. This remnant of a Han army watchtower stands on the edge of the Tarim Basin near the silk road town of Dunhuang.

than once in the second century, eunuch factions took control of the throne by engineering the succession of a young child and killing or banishing thousands of officials.

Growing disorder at the center inevitably weakened imperial authority throughout the empire. Han generals in distant provinces discovered they could ignore imperial commands and even recruit private armies. The property of landowning (freehold) peasants declined steadily, which meant they paid fewer taxes. This happened partly because of the tradition of families passing land in equal portions to all sons, which forced each man to make a living from a fraction of the father's legacy. But weakening government oversight in the provinces also made it easier for aristocratic estate lords to wheedle land away from peasants, whether legally or not, thereby transforming freeholders into rent-paying tenants or day workers with less taxable wealth. At the same time, rich and influential families found creative ways to escape paying taxes the central government desperately needed.

The Han dynasty's final crisis began in 184 c.e. when the Yellow Turbans, a movement inspired by Daoist ideas of mystical worship, spiritual healing, and social aid to poor people, launched an explosive rebellion against government incompetence and aristocratic land-grabbing. Han forces suppressed the revolt at great cost, but in its aftermath an assortment of warlords and generals competed violently for local power; one private army burned Luoyang, the Han capital. The imperial regime never reestablished order and finally collapsed in 220.

The Age of Division and its trends. During the following 370 years, China remained segmented into several

regional kingdoms whose boundaries and relative power shifted. While Chinese elites continued to believe that the country should be unified under a monarch possessing the Mandate of Heaven, none of those states accumulated sufficient resources to dominate all the others. Two trends of this era stand out.

First, large numbers of Chinese migrated from north to south, notably to the Yangzi River valley, which in later centuries emerged as China's economic center. Even before Han times, Chinese farmers had started drifting from the semiarid Yellow River region to the warmer, rainier south. In the process they exchanged wheat and millet fields for wet-rice farming. To escape the upsurge of fighting that characterized the Age of Division, numerous aristocratic families fled toward the Yangzi, often bringing thousands of peasants with them. Those transplanted elites created new regional states and sped up the south's agricultural development. Landowners set their laborers to building the dams, canals, and dikes required to flood and drain wet-rice fields. More commercial and manufacturing towns sprang up. Landowners also invested heavily in sericulture, the cultivation of mulberry trees to feed silkworms. Peasant women specialized in the meticulous task of unwinding silkworm cocoons, twisting the filaments into thread, and weaving cloth.

Second, the silk trade within China helped revive the commercial economy despite the political disunion. Demand for Chinese silk thread and finished textiles continued to grow in India, Persia, and the Mediterranean lands. The Han collapse coupled with pastoral nomadic wars and migrations almost certainly disrupted the flow of silk on the overland routes west. But those very disturbances coupled with economic growth in southern China stimulated more foreign trade by sea. By the third century, for example, the city of Guangzhou (Canton) on China's southern coast emerged as a window on Afroeurasia, exporting silk, bronzework, and other manufactures as far as East Africa and the eastern Mediterranean. In short, China's political fracturing resulted, not in general economic decline, but rather in an accelerating shift of the territorial center of population and economic activity from north to south.

The Sasanids: A New Power in Persia

The chain of empires that stretched from China to the Mediterranean in the early centuries C.E. included Parthia, whose monarchs ruled Persia and parts of Mesopotamia (see Chapter 7). Somewhat like Han China, the Parthian government weakened in the third century under the strain of incessant struggles among military and aristocratic factions. Whereas Han rulers had to keep Inner Eurasian nomads at bay, the Parthians spent their resources fighting Roman legions for control of Mesopotamian cities. In 224 the Parthian regime collapsed, but in contrast to China, its territories did not fragment. Rather, Ardashir I, a member of a prestigious family of Zoroastrian priests, led a victorious rebellion in southwestern Iran. He had himself proclaimed *Shahanshah*, the King of Kings, and a new imperial dynasty known as the Sasanids quickly replaced the old one.

The Parthian kings, who favored Greek-style art and literature over ancient Persian traditions, had never fully united Iranian aristocratic families in common purpose. The Sasanids, by contrast, zealously boasted their Persian heritage. They represented themselves as the direct heirs of the powerful Persian Achaemenids, the dynasty that had ruled from the sixth to the fourth centuries B.C.E. (see Chapter 6). This strategy brought them aristocratic support. For example, the early Sasanid rulers erected great palaces, temples, tombs, and stone carvings using motifs and images designed to link them historically to the Achaemenid imperial tradition. Ardashir and his son Shapur I, who ruled in succession for nearly half a century (224–272 C.E.), created a more tightly centralized system of government than the Parthians had managed, drawing somewhat on Roman ideas to set up ministries of justice, finance, and military affairs.

Zoroastrian resurgence. The Sasanids also emulated the Achaemenids by patronizing the Zoroastrian religion. Founded on the teachings of the ancient prophet Zoroaster, this faith proclaimed that the long earthly struggle between the supernatural forces of good and evil would inevitably climax in the total triumph of good at the End of Time (see Chapter 6). The Sasanids depicted themselves as servants of Ahura Mazda, the supreme creator god. They sponsored construction of Zoroastrian ritual fire temples throughout the empire, created a hierarchy of temple priests paralleling the political bureaucracy, and permitted particular clerics to exercise great power as political advisers and judges. Periodically, this priesthood moved to suppress rival religions. A third-century inscription at a Sasanid archaeological site declares that, under orders from the high priest Kartir, "Jews, Sramans (Buddhists), Brahmins, Nasoreans (Christians), . . . and Zandiks (Manichaeans) in the empire were smitten."[1] In the sixth century the government oversaw the codification of the *Avesta*, the compilation of Zoroaster's prophecies and other sacred works. In that period Zoroastrianism achieved its greatest influence as an Asian religion.

Sasanid conquests and wars with Rome. The Parthians had held off nomad intruders and even beat Roman armies a few times by fielding armies of mounted Persian nobles. These aristocratic warriors, called cataphracts, carried lances, and they encased themselves, as well as their large horses, in metal armor. Income from their estates paid the huge expense of raising specially bred horses and manufacturing military gear. Also adopting this style of warfare, the Sasanids persuaded their nobles to fight under central command. They also conscripted infantry and lightly armored horse archers from the wider population. They even took advantage of trade connections with India to import war elephants. This army, combined with talented imperial leadership, transformed the young state into a Southwest Asian power of greater threat to its neighbors than the Parthians had ever been.

Early in his reign, King Ardashir led forces eastward against the Kushana empire, which had been a power in its own right in Central Asia and northern India since the first century B.C.E. (see Chapter 7). He drove the Kushana

King Khosrow II (r. 590–628) ready for battle. The king was among the *cataphracts*, or aristocratic warriors, whose cavalry skills helped make the Sasanid army a powerful force in Southwest Asia. Notice the cylindrical helmet, the shield, and the heavy armor on the horse. This is a detail from a huge relief carved into a rock face along a caravan route in Iran's Zagros Mountains. Why might a long lance be a mounted fighter's preferred weapon?

forces out of all their territories west of the Indus River and seized several important Central Asian commercial cities. Kushana survived into the fourth century C.E. but as a much diminished monarchy.

Starting in 237 Ardashir and Shapur dispatched armies deep into northern Mesopotamia and Syria, catching Roman legions off guard and seizing several cities. They even killed one Roman ruler and captured another, delivering the emperor Valerian to the King of Kings in 257. Shapur kept this hapless potentate in chains, dragging him around with the royal entourage. According to a third-century Christian text, "The king of the Persians, who had made him [Valerian] prisoner, whenever he chose to get into his carriage or to mount on horseback, commanded the Roman to stoop and present his back. . . . Afterward, when [Valerian] had finished this shameful life under so great dishonor, he was flayed, and his skin, stripped from the flesh, was dyed with vermilion, and placed in the temple of the gods of the barbarians."[2]

These defeats and outrages caused shock waves in Rome. By the end of the third century its legions checkmated Sasanid westward expansion; for the next three hundred years, relations between the two powers in Southwest Asia oscillated between peace and war. Both poured immense resources into their chronic struggles, without either side making large territorial gains against the other.

The Sasanid economy. Persia's well-being depended overwhelmingly on agriculture, and in the large areas of Mesopotamia that the Sasanids controlled, imperial officials launched big projects to expand irrigated farming. Between the third and sixth centuries, they built canals, dams, and levees, as well as several whole cities, in the Tigris-Euphrates valley. Enslaved war prisoners and forcibly resettled peasants from other parts of the empire did the work. In the Sasanid period, if not somewhat earlier, rice, cotton, and cane sugar spread westward from South or Southeast Asia to become important irrigated crops in Southwest Asia.

The Sasanid conquests, especially to the east, meant that the dynasty controlled more cities and longer trade lines than the Parthians had (see Map 9.1). Persian caravans set out from Mesopotamia and western Iran across the deserts north of the Arabian Sea to deliver textiles, perfumes, fine woolen carpets, and Persian Gulf pearls to India. Persian merchants also helped extend imperial influence to port towns on the Arabian side of the gulf. These traders competed with Roman and other shippers on the Arabian Sea routes, founding commercial settlements as far east as Ceylon.

Crisis and Recovery in the Roman Empire

The Persian military threat was just one of the political crises that afflicted Rome in the third century C.E. A variety of troubles compelled the imperial elite to restructure both the government and the army, a challenge that exposed the colossal problems of governing a state that stretched 2,400 miles from Britain to Mesopotamia.

Third-century emergencies. The absence of clear rules of royal succession, other than the total ineligibility of women, had plagued Rome on and off since the first century C.E. Forceful sovereigns might name the successor they wanted, but if they failed to do that several rival candidates might present themselves for the job, including frontier generals or other ambitious men who could rally support from their troops. Also, a new emperor with only shaky support could provoke civil war among elite factions determined to replace him with their own man. In the half-century between 235 and 284, at least eighteen men occupied the throne with the formal endorsement of the Roman Senate, which by that period had no independent power and generally followed the political wind. Many of those rulers died after short reigns, either in battle or by assassination. This chronic turmoil at the center inevitably disrupted imperial business, especially frontier security, court decisions, and tax-gathering operations.[2]

Third-century emperors also confronted a bundle of economic and social problems. To meet growing expenses, the government allowed mints to cut the silver content in coins, which inevitably reduced their value and caused consumer prices to soar. This inflation mainly affected ordinary men and women, who depended on stable prices for wheat and other basic commodities. Like Chinese peasants in the late Han era, Roman farmers suffered as landowning elites accumulated larger estates at the expense of small freeholders and employed large numbers of renters, day laborers, armed henchmen, and slaves. By the fourth century, a Roman senator, who was almost always a big landowner, could expect to reap an annual income of 120,000 gold pieces or more; a peasant might earn 5. Nevertheless, officials pressured common citizens to pay taxes.

Germanic intruders. Violent incursions along the empire's frontiers caused serious financial drain, as it did in late Han China. Northeastern Europe, which we may think of as Inner Eurasia's far western edge, was the domain of tribally organized groups that spoke a number of Germanic languages, a branch of the Indo-European language family that also includes ancestral English. In the first and second centuries C.E., when Roman legions advanced into central Europe, Germanic tribes were drifting west toward the Rhine River and south toward the Danube. Germanic peoples raised cattle, sheep, and horses, but they were predominantly farmers, not pastoral nomads. And those tribes living nearest to Roman territory attained a level of social complexity that included village building, iron making, skilled artisanry, and a dominant class of warrior chiefs.

The worlds of Romans and Germanic populations became elaborately intertwined. Trade between them went on nearly all the time. Germanic traders supplied timber, wool, furs, and other raw products to Romans in exchange for textiles, pottery, gold or silver coins, and numerous other items. Roman governors periodically allowed Germanic groups to migrate peacefully into the empire to settle. Germanic

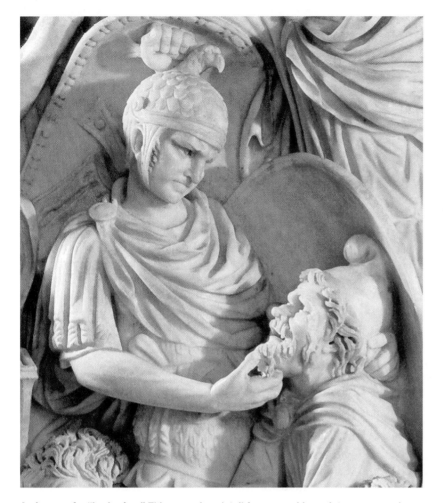

An image of a "barbarian." This scene is a detail from a marble sculpture engraved on the side of a Roman coffin known as the Ludovisi Battle Sarcophagus. The work dates to about 250 C.E., when Germanic and other armed migrants were already assailing the empire's northern frontiers. The artist depicts the captured enemy as a scruffy looking fellow with bulbous nose, long hair, and ragged beard. By contrast, the clean-shaven Roman infantryman projects calm command. What might the Roman soldier intend to do next?

Black Sea, advanced into the Roman-ruled Balkan Peninsula. In 251, Goth intruders killed the emperor Decius in battle and sixteen years later swept far south to pillage Athens and several other venerable Greek cities. Consequently, the Roman government had to spend more than ever on its European legions to defend the empire.

Reforming emperors. Rome's political and economic fortunes recovered under the energetic leadership of Diocletian (reigned 284–305 C.E.) and Constantine I (r. 306–337 C.E.). Both men vowed to address the empire's structural problems. To strengthen the army, Diocletian reorganized its hierarchy of command, increased the number of legions (incorporating more Germanic soldiers), and built up cavalry forces, including Persian-style armored cataphracts. On the eastern frontier, Roman forces halted Sasanid expansion in 298 C.E. Diocletian and Constantine achieved victories over Germanic enemies in Europe and Berber insurgents in North Africa that helped stabilize the empire's western half well into the fourth century.

Diocletian tried to strengthen regional government and reduce imperial succession disputes by dividing the empire into western and eastern sectors, each zone ruled by one of two coemperors. Each of these men had a deputy emperor and designated successor. This system of four collaborating leaders, called the Tetrarchy, worked quite well under Diocletian, but it fell apart in factional quarreling soon after he retired from office. Nevertheless, a tradition of having two corulers, if not four, continued into the fifth century, and the system probably helped prevent civil wars from breaking out more often than they did.

Rome also became more bureaucratic. In earlier centuries the government had operated largely through personal relations between individuals of status, wealth, and power and subordinate clients who did what they were told in return for money, jobs, and protection (see Chapter 7). The third-century troubles, however, persuaded Diocletian and his successors to create a larger, more formal hierarchy of salaried officers accountable to the state. Between the mid-third and fifth centuries, the number of senior functionaries handling the empire's business grew from about 250 to 6,000.[3] This bureaucracy collected new taxes, curtailed the financial independence of cities, and forced peasants to stay on the land rather than seek urban jobs no matter how impoverished these men and women were. Diocletian also tried to control inflation by fixing prices of essential commodities, though with only partial success. Finally,

warriors also routinely hired themselves out as Roman soldiers. Like the Han government, the Romans paid large sums to keep the frontier quiet, sending Germanic chiefs gifts in coin or goods. At the same time, most Romans regarded Germanic and all other transfrontier peoples as the cultural opposites of imperial citizens, as "barbarians" of inherently crude, ignorant, and hostile disposition.

Germanic leaders knew what Romans thought of them, and during the third century, some of them played their assigned role eagerly, crossing the frontier to attack settlements and raid farms. Archaeological research has shown that in this period Germanic populations were rising in number, partly owing to improving farming technology: iron plows, manure fertilizing, and crop rotation. Consequently, population pressures may have urged Germanic war bands to push into the rich Roman farmlands beyond the Rhine and Danube. The Germanic group known as Goths, whose territorial base was north and west of the

Constantine I. The emperor, radiating majestic authority, appears removed from the world of ordinary men and women. This bronze head was once part of a colossal statue. What specific features of the sculpture give it emotional power?

Diocletian, Constantine, and several of their successors altered the ideology and style of authoritarian rule. The idea of the emperor as First Citizen, a relic of the old Republic, gave way to a part-Persian, part-Egyptian model of the monarch as absolute, remote, and mysterious, a potentate governing from within multiple protective circles of officials, servants, and bodyguards.

Constantine, Constantinople, and the Christian church. In the fourth and fifth centuries, cities located quite close to the empire's turbulent frontiers served as the nerve centers of imperial government, for example, Milan in Italy, Carthage in North Africa, and Antioch in Syria. Most emperors did not govern from the city of Rome, and some rarely went there. In 313, Constantine established an imperial center on the foundations of Byzantium, an ancient Greek town on a promontory overlooking the western side of the Bosporus, the strait connecting the Black Sea with the Sea of Marmara and the Mediterranean beyond. He renamed the place Constantinople after himself. Protected on three sides by water and on the fourth by walls, the city became the headquarters of imperial security in the eastern and Balkan provinces. Constantine and his successors lavished great sums on public monuments, palaces, libraries, arenas, and waterworks. The population rapidly grew, reaching about half a million in the sixth century. The city of Rome continued to loom large in the historical imagination of all citizens, but its importance to the imperial economy and administration faded gradually, along with its former status as largest city in the world.

The cityscape of fourth-century Constantinople also included churches. Despite periodic persecutions, Christian communities had been sprouting up in towns around the Mediterranean since the first century C.E. (see Chapter 7) In the troubled third century, ordinary people turned to a variety of cults and sects for aid and solace, among them Christianity, a faith whose missionaries preached compassion, generosity, communal love, and the hope of eternal life. Jesus's promise that "the meek shall inherit the earth" appealed deeply to women and men weary of ritual sacrifices to distant and unresponsive gods. The early church devoted itself to charitable giving. When local government authorities failed to distribute food to the poor or care for epidemic victims, church communities rallied round. In the mid-third century, the church in the city of Rome had about 1,500 widows and other poor folk under its care.

Diocletian launched a brutal campaign to harass and jail Christians in 303, but this was the last major Roman persecution. Just a decade later, Constantine decreed free worship for all religions and, according to tradition, accepted Christian baptism when he was near death. In the Edict of Milan of 313, he and Licinius, who was then his coemperor, proclaimed: "We thought it fit to commend these things most fully to your care that you may know that we have given to those Christians free and unrestricted opportunity of religious worship. . . . We have also conceded to other religions the right of open and free observance of their worship for the sake of the peace of our times, that each one may have the free opportunity to worship as he pleases."[4] This act quickly reduced long festering social and political tensions between the growing Christian minority and the adherents of traditional Roman polytheism.

Constantine's edict produced no great outcry from polytheists. Romans believed that divine power sanctified the empire, and now the Christian god might substitute for the old ones as a spiritual source of imperial authority. It did not hurt that both Christianity and Roman legal ideals affirmed the equality of all before the law. Growing numbers of aristocrats and senior bureaucrats converted to Christianity, though some did, no doubt, because they thought that Christians would get choicer government posts. Constantine and his successors also asserted leadership over Christian affairs, arbitrating disputes among bishops (the heads of church administrative units), presiding over church councils, and enacting laws regarding Christian faith and practice. Then, in 380 C.E., the Emperor Theodosius made Christianity the official state religion.

Thereafter, the empire became gradually Christianized, though, as one scholar has put it, Christianity was also Romanized.[5] The emperor headed both the state and the church, appointing the Bishop of Rome as one of five **patriarchs.** The other four served in Constantinople, Antioch, Jerusalem, and Alexandria. The structure of the church was set up to mirror the empire's administrative organization.

> **patriarch** In the early Christian centuries, the title of the bishops of Rome, Constantinople, Jerusalem, Antioch, and Alexandria; in later centuries, the title of the highest official of the Greek Orthodox Church, as well as other Asian or African Christian churches.

A Christian woman. In this example of Christian art from about 300 C.E., a woman raises her arms and opens her hands in a gesture of prayer known as the *orans* position, from the Latin word for prayer. The woman appears on a fresco in the Catacomb of Priscilla near Rome. Christian clergy today assume this pose in particular church service rituals.

The church diocese, or seat of a bishop, corresponded to a late Roman political unit of the same name. Rich Roman landowners also got themselves appointed as bishops and, in that office, mimicked the royal court with displays of wealth and pageantry.

The Huns and the Collapse of the Western Empire

The western half of the empire disintegrated in the fifth century C.E., though not mainly because of economic crisis and exhaustion. Rather, most Roman provinces remained economically quite healthy well into the 400s C.E. Archaeological investigation of material consumption and of the size and number of villages has strengthened this argument. Italy and parts of Gaul gradually weakened compared to earlier levels of prosperity, but the inhabitants of eastern North Africa (the area that is today modern Tunisia and part of Algeria and Libya) remained busy producers of wheat, oil, wine, and high-quality pottery for export. The eastern Mediterranean provinces generally enjoyed significant economic growth into the sixth century. Growth, however, did not mean better lives for all. Elite families representing no more than 5 percent of the population owned about 80 percent of the productive land. Diocletian imposed higher taxes on ordinary farmers but exempted senators (whose support he wanted for his reforms) from paying anything. As in China in the post-Han era, freehold peasants continued to decrease in number relative to tenant farmers, low-wage workers, and slaves.

Huns in the saddle. "The Huns fell upon the Alans, the Alans upon the Goths and Taifali, the Goths and Taifali upon the Romans, and this is not yet the end."[6] In this single sentence, Ambrose, the Christian bishop of Milan writing about 378, nicely captured the sequence of events in Europe in the hundred years after he made this observation. In the fourth century, Roman troops were continually forced to defend the Danube and Rhine frontiers not only because of Germanic population buildup but also because of the "bumper-car effect" of wars and migrations in faraway Inner Eurasia. One of the pastoral nomadic groups that spun off from the collapse of the Xiongnu empire was a loose assemblage of migrants that became known as the Huns. This crowd of men, women, children, and animals advanced as far west as the Pontic-Caspian steppes around 360. There Hunnic warriors fought and defeated Iranian-speaking Alan herders, some of whom fled farther west, attacking Goth farmers in southeastern Europe. Bands of Huns followed the Alans, causing even more trouble for Goths. In the summer of 376, thousands of Goths arrived on the north bank of the Danube demanding Roman permission to cross to safety in the Balkan Peninsula. Roman authorities complied, but within a few months the immigrants, running short of food and winter shelter, rose in revolt. This disorder lasted for seven years, the key event taking place in 378, when Goth warriors, joined by freelance bands of Alans and Huns, defeated a Roman army at Hadrianople (Edirne). This town was less than 130 miles from Constantinople. From the Roman perspective the "barbarians" were getting too close for comfort.

Historians have long debated the identity of the Huns, agreeing only that they probably spoke either a Mongolian or a Turkic language. In any case, this horde picked up people of diverse ethnolinguistic origins as they moved west. Romans who wrote about the Huns usually betrayed deep negative prejudice, but the fifth-century scholar Ammianus probably captured their way of life quite accurately:

> Roaming at large amid the mountains and woods, they learn from the cradle to endure cold, hunger, and thirst. When away from their homes they never enter a house unless compelled by extreme necessity; for they think they are not safe when staying under a roof. . . . They are almost glued to their horses, which are hardy, it is true, but ugly, and sometimes they sit on them woman-fashion and thus perform their ordinary tasks. From their horses by night or day every one of that nation buys and sells, eats and

drinks, and bowed over the narrow neck of the animal relaxes into a sleep. . . . They are subject to no royal restraint, but they are content with the disorderly government of their important men, and led by them they force their way through every obstacle. . . . No one in their country ever plows a field or touches a plow-handle.[7]

Armed with bow and sword, one large company of Hunnic cavalry advanced from the Pontic-Caspian region southward toward the Caucasus Mountains (see Map 9.2). From there they organized giant raiding expeditions into Mesopotamia and Syria in the 390s, threatening both Roman and Persian cities. Other Huns advanced west, arriving on the grassy plains of Hungary sometime before 420. They set up permanent camps there, pasturing their herds while collecting tribute from local Germanic and the partially Romanized population. They also traded with Roman merchants, and some joined the imperial army as auxiliary cavalry.

The Germanic breakout. When the Huns penetrated central Europe, they triggered more bumper-car migrations.

MAP 9.2 Armed migrations, fifth and sixth centuries.
What geographical factors might help explain why Germanic and other invaders advanced westward all the way across Europe?

The skull of a Hunnic woman. Huns were among a number of peoples in world history, including Maya, to practice cranial manipulation. This woman's head was probably tightly wrapped in cloth when she was an infant. What social purpose do you think cranial manipulation of some members of the group might have had?

Several Germanic groups, including Visigoths, Vandals, Suevi, and Burgundians, fled the Hunnic approach in the early fifth century. Some headed toward Italy, while others crossed the Rhine into Roman Gaul without invitation. This provocative advance, which also included Iranian-speaking Alans, may have involved 100,000 people or more. In the following several decades, the citizenry of both western Europe and North Africa witnessed growing political disarray, though some Roman commanders made valiant efforts to restore order. The Germanic advance was not a single, methodical invasion but rather involved episodic movements of several separate bands who continued to trade and negotiate with Romans— and to fight one other—as they advanced across Gaul and Iberia. And as territory fell from imperial control, the revenues needed to pay the imperial army to defend cities and provinces steadily shriveled.

In northern Europe, Germanic Saxons and Angles built ships and crossed the North Sea to attack Britain in successive waves. By about 410 C.E. the island effectively dropped out of the Roman empire, though Romanized populations remained. That same year Goth warriors sacked Rome itself, though they avoided wrecking churches because many of the invaders had converted to Christianity. In 429, Vandals and Alans crossed the Strait of Gibraltar into North Africa. The Christian writer Possidius described this event, perhaps with only a little overstatement: "And everywhere through the regions of Mauretania [Morocco and Algeria], . . . raging with cruelty and barbarity, they completely devastated everything they could by their pillage, murder and varied tortures, conflagrations and other innumerable and unspeakable crimes, sparing neither sex nor age, nor even the priests or ministers of God."[8] The invaders advanced rapidly eastward nearly a thousand miles to Carthage, using good Roman roads most of the way. The fall of North Africa represented a terrible blow to the empire because that region's agriculture was a critical source of military supply.

Attila the Hun. The Huns had at first a mainly indirect impact on fighting in the empire. But shortly before 440, leadership passed to Attila. A Roman envoy described this warrior as "short, with a broad chest and large head; his eyes were small, his beard sparse and flecked with gray, his nose flat and his complexion dark."[9] Coruling with a brother until deciding to murder him, Attila appears to have wanted to found a permanent Hunnic state and to make it a base for extracting gold, goods, and slaves from Roman territory, just as his Xiongnu ancestors had milked Han China's frontiers. Between 442 and 453 he led several major forays into the empire, attacking not only Romans but also Germanic groups that stood in his way. His forces also demonstrated skills at besieging and capturing Roman cities. In 447 an army that included both Huns and Germanic recruits overran the Balkans, crushing two Roman armies and coming close to assaulting the triple line of walls that defended the landward approaches to Constantinople. In 451–452, Attila launched two invasions of what was left of the western empire, first into Gaul and then into Italy. Romans and Germanic Visigoths joined together to turn back the first invasion, and an epidemic helped cut short the second. A Christian chronicler reported that the Hunnic intruders "were victims of divine punishment, being visited with heaven sent disasters: famine and some kind of disease."[10] The following year Attila died suddenly, and in the absence of decisive leadership from any of his sons, his fledgling empire crumbled quickly. Nevertheless, his campaigns seriously damaged Gaul and Italy, aborted Roman plans to take back North Africa, and, once he was gone, freed Germanic tribes, including Franks, Burgundians, Lombards, and Visigoths, to seize the western empire's remaining pieces. In 476, Odoacer, a leader of Ostrogoth and other Germanic troops, deposed Romulus,

Skill of the Ostrogoths. Germanic artisans demonstrated extraordinary skill working in gold, enamel, and gemstones. This brooch comes from the Ostrogothic kingdom of Italy. The image of the eagle suggests Roman inspiration.

the last coemperor in Italy, and packed him off to a country estate. Thus, western Rome came rather quietly to an end.

The Mediterranean Fractured

In the next several decades, the western empire fragmented into a number of regional states ruled by kings identified with one Germanic group or another. This particular political division, however, lasted only a few decades because in the sixth century the Roman emperor Justinian (r. 527–565) went on the offensive. The rulers in Constantinople insisted that the loss of the west was temporary, though the eastern empire took on the new name of Byzantium, or the Byzantine empire. Justinian formed a particularly potent partnership with his queen, the strong-minded Theodora, to rule the Roman state with great energy. Together they supervised a new codification of Roman law, the Body of Civil Law (*Corpus Juris Civilis*), which profoundly influenced legal theory and practice in Europe in later centuries. They built lavishly in Constantinople, including the Hagia Sophia (HAH-ya SOH-fee-uh), the city's magnificent Christian cathedral. They made temporary peace with Sasanid Persia and in 533 evicted the Vandal regime from North Africa. In the next few years, Byzantine forces occupied Sicily,

seized a large part of Italy from the Ostrogoths, and refortified western Mediterranean coastal points as far west as the Strait of Gibraltar. Byzantine rulers continued to hold on to some of these territories until the eleventh century.

A great depression. Roman reconquests, however, did little for the economies of those lands that Germanic and Hun campaigns had ravaged. Archaeological work has documented the spiraling decline of agrarian production in the western Roman territories. Rural settlements disappeared over wide areas; wood and thatch replaced stone, brick, and roof tiles as building materials, even for the rich; the quality and trade of pottery declined; and the use of money, including copper coins, fell dramatically. A general if gradual process of **deurbanization** took place, as public buildings, including temples, churches, baths, theaters,

> **deurbanization** A social process in which cities in a particular region decline or disappear.

and elaborate sewer systems fell to pieces. Excavations at the Roman city of Luna on Italy's northwestern coast record that from the fifth-century grand villas were abandoned to ruin, paved roads sank beneath the soil, the major aqueduct dried up, and in time the whole city disappeared. This precipitous drop in material consumption and comfort did not

The Empress Theodora. Justinian's queen holds out a symbolic offering to Christ in this mosaic from the sixth-century church of San Vitale in Ravenna, the Byzantine provincial capital on the Adriatic coast of Italy. The mosaic largely rejects the naturalistic portrayal of figures and objects characteristic of earlier Roman art. What evidence of that rejection do you see in this picture?

take place everywhere in the west at the same time. Roughly speaking, it started in the northern European provinces, including Britain, and then advanced gradually south.

Volcanic dust and pandemic disease.
In the sixth century a set of natural calamities jolted the wider Mediterranean region. Evidence from sulfate layers in Greenland and Antarctic ice cores, tree rings measurements, and statements by ancient writers indicate that a massive volcanic eruption in 535, probably somewhere near the equator, spewed out sufficient material to cause a world-encircling "dust veil." This layer was probably thick enough to obscure the sun's rays, resulting in a decade of climatic cooling, especially in the northern hemisphere. The sixth-century Byzantine historian Procopius wrote: "The sun gave forth its light without brightness, . . . and it seemed exceedingly like the sun in eclipse, for the beams it shed were not clear nor such as it is accustomed to shed."[11] If this phenomenon lasted more than a year, it could have had serious effects on food production and therefore population levels. Tree-ring and textual evidence also suggest widespread drought in northern China, Inner Eurasia, and northern Europe in the late 530s.

> **pandemic** An infectious disease that moves quickly from one region to another, affecting large numbers of people.

Second, the plague **pandemic** we described in this chapter's introduction struck the Mediterranean in 541. By strict definition, plague refers to a particular ailment having a range of symptoms associated with a type of bacterium, called *Yersinia pestis*, or simply *Y. pestis*. This pathogen, as it is known in modern times, causes bubonic plague, named for the buboes, or dark swellings that typically appear on the victim's body. The principal carriers of this bacterium are fleas that inhabit the fur and feed off the blood of ground-burrowing rodents, including prairie dogs, squirrels, and rats. In certain environmental conditions, *Y. pestis* may accumulate in these animals. When an infected rodent dies, its fleas look for another host. If humans are at hand, bugs may jump to them to get blood meals, transmitting the infection. If the plague entered the Mediterranean from Egypt, which some evidence suggests, human contact with the pathogen may have first occurred far up the Nile River, perhaps in Ethiopia, where plague among rodent populations has been historically endemic.

From Egyptian cities, vessels that sailed relatively short distances from one Mediterranean port to another could easily have transported infected people, along with stowaway rats and fleas, around the rim of the sea in no more than a few years, causing a major pandemic. Plague struck Constantinople in 543 and killed perhaps a third of its population. Then Justinian's troops may have carried it to the western Mediterranean. The disease appears to have reached as far into Europe as Ireland. To the east, it easily crossed the military frontier between Byzantium and Sasanid Mesopotamia, where up to half the population died within a few years.[12] The first epidemic shock wave was likely the worst, but recurrences every several years continued to take lives in one region or another for another two centuries.

In regions where many people died of plague, labor shortages inevitably caused state revenues to shrink, prices to rise, and the economy generally to weaken. But if a region was prosperous when the plague arrived, which was probably the case in many of the Byzantine and Sasanid provinces, recovery may not have taken long. In the western Mediterranean and Europe, however, the pandemic likely sped up the long-term deterioration that had already set in.

More tempests from the steppes.
Besides plague, the Byzantine and Sasanid empires faced new threats from Inner Eurasia. In the mid-fifth century, a pastoral group probably related in origin to the Huns seized Central Asia's major silk road towns and proclaimed a new dynasty known as the White Huns (or Hephthalites). This ruling group formed a loosely organized empire, and during the following century, White Hun archers invaded northern India. They also repeatedly attacked Persian territory, creating enough trouble to convince Sasanid emperors to pay them off in gold. In the 560s, Khosrow I (r. 531–579), one of the most energetic Sasanid monarchs, allied with other Central Asian nomads to defeat the White Huns, finally ending their depredations.

About the same time that the Sasanids defeated that enemy, the Byzantine emperors faced a dual invasion of Slavs and Avars. Perhaps originating near the Baltic Sea, Slavic migrants (the linguistic ancestors of Russians, Poles, Czechs, Serbians, and other European peoples) advanced south across Europe to the Danube in the sixth century. By contrast, the Avars were Inner Eurasian nomads, probably a motley horde speaking Mongolian, Turkic, and Iranian tongues. Moving west of the Black Sea, Avar bands attacked and subjugated Slavs, pushing some fleeing groups into Byzantine territory. Avar kings founded a state on Attila's old territory, alternately assaulting Byzantine land and collecting large tribute payments in gold. In 626, Avars attacked Constantinople, but when that operation failed, their empire faded quickly.

A New Empire in South Asia

Since the second century B.C.E., when the Maurya empire fell, small regional monarchies shared South Asia. The political map, however, changed dramatically in the early fourth century, when Chandra Gupta I (r. 320–330) founded a powerful new kingdom in the Ganges River valley. Chandra Gupta's son and grandson, Samudra Gupta (r. 330–375) and Chandra Gupta II (r. 375–415), mounted military campaigns that brought most of the northern two-thirds of South Asia under Gupta overlordship (see Map 9.3).

Taking the title Great King of Kings, the Gupta monarchs established firm control over a core territory in the rice-producing middle Ganges. In more distant lands they conquered, they allowed regional kings and aristocratic elites

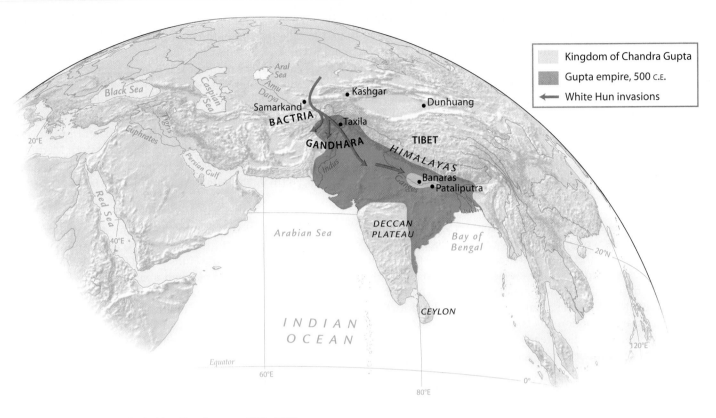

MAP 9.3 South Asia in the Gupta era, 320–550 C.E.
What geographic features may have influenced the expansion and the boundaries of the Gupta empire?

to retain their authority, as long as they paid regular tribute to Pataliputra, the Gupta capital. The emperors kept a close eye on towns and occupational guilds but mostly let them manage their own affairs. In their religious practice, the Gupta monarchs identified with the rituals of the brahmin priests and with a variety of devotions that modern scholars associate with the emerging Hindu tradition.

Textiles and sugar. Fa Xian, a Chinese Buddhist who traveled to South Asia in the fourth century in search of sacred texts, declared that the inhabitants of the towns and cities of the Ganges valley "are rich and prosperous." This characterization probably accurately describes the South Asian economy in that period. Gupta emperors regularly made large grants of land to brahmins, instructing them to organize peasants to work in the fields surrounding temples and monasteries. Spinners and weavers in homes and workshops supplied cotton, silk, linen, and woolen textiles to a large and growing South Asian market. Indeed, India emerged during this era as the single most important supplier of cotton goods to other parts of Afroeurasia.

Indian artisans also figured out how to press out and boil down the juice of sugar cane, a plant introduced from Southeast Asia, to produce crystallized sugar. South Asians were probably the first people in the world to consume sugary foods in quantity. Because this commodity was easy to

store and transport, it quickly commanded markets abroad. Indian merchants traveled the overland roads to Persia and Central Asia, as well as the shipping lanes across the Bay of Bengal to Southeast Asia. Other Indian exports included cotton and silk cloths, pepper and other spices, pearls, indigo, and perfumes. The collapse of the western Roman empire may have cut the Mediterranean market for South Asian luxuries for several centuries, but this had no severe effect, as far as we know, on India's booming commercial ports.

Gupta science and math. Both Buddhist monks and Hindu brahmins founded advanced academic schools linked to monasteries and temples. The Indic language Sanskrit was the principal medium of learning, and scholarly subjects included grammar, logic, composition, poetry, medicine, astronomy, and mathematics, in addition to deep study of religious texts. The brahmin scholar Aryabhata (476–560) accurately calculated *pi* as 3.1416 and the length of the solar year at 365.358 days. He also reasoned correctly that the earth is a sphere rotating on its axis while circling the sun. As described in Chapter 8, Maya thinkers in Mesoamerica in the late centuries B.C.E. invented a positional notation, or place-value system to express numbers, as well as a symbol to represent "zero." Although ancient Mesopotamians had come up with these ideas even earlier, they did not endure in Afroeurasia. Gupta scholars, however, came

Buddhist painting. The artistic achievements of the Gupta period are exemplified in this fresco from the Buddhist monastic caves at Ajanta in central India. Rendered with more naturalism than the Byzantine Christian art of the same era (page 260), this scene portrays a prince piously distributing alms to the poor.

up with a base-10 system for positioning numbers relative to one another, as in 777 meaning 700 + 70 + 7. That system permitted any numerical calculation using just ten signs. Like Maya scholars, Indian sages also elaborated the idea that zero, which they first signified as a dot, worked not only as a filler for an absent value, as in the sequence 707 (700 + nothing + 7), but as a number having the mathematical value of nil. The seventh-century scholar Brahmagupta published a work in 628 C.E. that instructed: "A debt minus zero is a debt; a fortune minus zero is a fortune; zero minus zero is zero."[13] After the seventh century, the Indian numerical system spread both west and east and became the foundation of modern mathematics.

South Asian society. The social system founded on four fundamental varnas, or social castes, distinguished from one another by their relative position on a scale of ritual purity (see Chapter 6), became fully rooted in South Asia in the Gupta era. Sub-castes, or *jatis*, defined by kinship, custom, place, and occupation, also proliferated. Starting in the third century B.C.E., brahmin scholars wrote numerous texts that set forth in exquisite detail the ritual duties and social

obligations of particular castes, as well as the proper behavior of members of different castes toward one another. These codes (*dharma-shastras*) underlay social relations in South Asia until the twentieth century. In the Gupta period the system was fluid enough that some groups, for example, merchants and scribes, managed to pull themselves up the caste ladder, though other groups, such as indigenous forest dwellers, tumbled down. On the whole, women gradually lost social status. The brahmins who set the rules of social rank and behavior, however, had ambivalent views regarding women, urging in some texts that husbands honor their wives and make them happy.

South Asian literature and art generally idealized women as elegant, beautiful, and virtuous. The third-century B.C.E. scholar Manu, on the other hand, declared that "in childhood a female must be subject to her father, in youth to her husband, and when her lord is dead to her sons; a woman must never be independent."[14] Only high caste women had access to any formal education, women had restricted rights to property and inheritance, and families commonly arranged the marriage of girls at very early ages. Some Buddhist women achieved a measure of autonomy by joining monasteries. Simply put, South Asian women occupied all caste ranks but within each one constituted a socially and economically subordinate group.

Gupta decline. In the second half of the fifth century, Gupta territories in northwestern India came under persistent attack from the same White Huns that attacked Sasanid Persia. These raiders never overran the Gupta heartland the way Germanic tribes swarmed across Europe, but they disrupted the Gupta economy and gradually exhausted its defense forces. The Gupta state did not collapse so much as shrink down under the growing burden of rising military costs, rebellious tributary kings, and court intrigues. By the time the Sasanids routed the White Huns in the mid-sixth century, the Gupta empire was already gone. But the framework of Hindu social relations endured.

Religions for Troubled Times

FOCUS What features of Buddhism, Christianity, and Manichaeism made those religions appealing to large numbers of people?

By the third century c.e., Buddhism and Christianity were both attracting millions of people across multiple frontiers of culture, social class, and political rule. Manichaeism (man-ih-KEE-ism), which first appeared in that century, also gained in appeal across its original borders for several centuries. In Chapter 7 we argued that, by the first millennium b.c.e., human interrelations across Afroeurasia reached a level of complexity that demanded new ideas and institutions through which people might bond together and cooperate in greater numbers and over longer distances. Buddhism, Christianity, and Manichaeism served that purpose.

The fundamental characteristic of these universalist religions is that they invited men and women, as human beings rather than as members of particular ethnolinguistic groups, tribes, cities, or kingdoms, to join together in shared morality, devotion, and trust. Moreover, the faithful were encouraged to spread the teachings and bring new followers into the fold. These religions shared several other characteristics as well. All three originated in the public teachings of a single individual—the Buddha, Jesus, Mani—who preached human subordination to divine, transcendent power and devotion to principles of moral behavior, selflessness, and social cooperation. These religions were also salvationist: They assured righteous believers of eventual freedom from care and suffering, whether through release into nonbeing or elevation into heaven. All of them accommodated special individuals, that is, saints in various manifestations, who possessed powers to mediate between believers and transcendent power and to help them along a path to well-being and salvation. All of them offered guiding scriptures, not only core texts, but eventually vast libraries of moral

and spiritual writings. Finally, they all addressed both the individual's quest for self-realization through meditation, prayer, study, or self-denial, and the community's need for moral and ethical rules by which people might work together in society, find common meaning in daily events and rituals, and take responsibility for one another's welfare.

As they grew, universalist religions embraced people of differing language, culture, and social status (see Map 9.4). And as distances of time and space widened between communities of believers professing a single tradition, particular beliefs and practices diverged and multiplied. Consequently, each religion also bloomed with distinctive, sometimes conflicting doctrines, devotions, institutions, schools, sects, and denominations.

The Buddhist Web

Starting in the first century c.e., merchants and monks carried the Buddha's moral and salvationist message across Inner Eurasia to China and by sea to Southeast Asia. Missionaries also ventured west into Persia and Syria. The staging area for the Buddhist penetration of Inner Eurasia was the Kushana empire of northern India. In that setting the Mahayana school of Buddhism, called the Greater Vehicle because it held out the promise of salvation to all, differentiated itself from Theravada Buddhism, or the Lesser Vehicle (Hinayana), which esteemed full-time devotion to monastic life. Theravadists believed that to attain nirvana, or escape from the cycle of suffering and reincarnation, meant gaining freedom from all consciousness. Individuals must strive on their own to reach that ultimate release. By contrast, Mahayana thinkers taught that nirvana is a state of total awareness and that people who led ordinary lives might achieve salvation with the assistance of *bodhisattvas*, saintly individuals who stopped short of nirvana to go back and help others along the path. Mahayana teaching also elevated the Buddha from the status of a moral teacher to a god and savior. In that tradition, deified buddhas existed in many different manifestations to encourage and assist the spiritual journeyer. Men and women who lived "in the world" but gave silver, gold, silk, or other gifts to monasteries in dedication to a *bodhisattva* or Buddha might expect to receive spiritual blessings that sped their way to salvation. Consequently, monasteries attracted wealth, and they often contributed to local production and trade.

The Mahayana way transformed Buddhism from a South Asian moral system for the hardiest seekers into a universalist religion available to anyone receptive to its message. It therefore traveled well. Kushana merchants trekked to China to buy silk, and Buddhists among them settled in Luoyang and other Han cities starting in the first century c.e. Monks also came along to found urban monasteries. Initially, Han courtiers and bureaucrats showed little interest in this new religion. Their Confucian values centered on harmonious social and political relations in this life, not on other-worldly desires and monastic privacy. However, the downfall of both

MAP 9.4 Religious diffusion, 200–600 C.E.
Looking at the arrows on the map, in what regions do you think adherents of Buddhism, Christianity, and Manichaeism might all have been found about 600 C.E.?

the Kushana and the Han empires in the early third century presented nothing but opportunity to Buddhist missionaries offering individual salvation.

Buddhists on the road to China. In China millions more people became receptive to Buddhism during the long Age of Division. Confucian ideals of wise civil government dimmed somewhat as regional states battled one another, refugees took to the road, and peasants lost their land. For poor rural folk, uprooted city artisans, and slaves, the new religion showed the way out of suffering. Imitating the Buddha's spontaneous compassion, monasteries offered food, shelter, and medical care. Even Confucian aristocrats,

many of whom lost their estates or fled south to the Yangzi valley, took up Buddhist studies to find solace and peace. In northwestern China and out on the steppes, many pastoral nomadic chiefs welcomed Buddhist monks, scribes, and merchants and benefited from the spiritual guidance, literacy, and craft skills these newcomers brought from the west. The ex-nomad leaders who founded the Northern Wei kingdom in northwestern China in the fifth century declared themselves to be incarnations of the Buddha and handsomely patronized monasteries that supported this claim. Monarchs of other regional states also identified with Buddhism and patronized monasteries and stupas (structures housing relics of the Buddha). By the early sixth

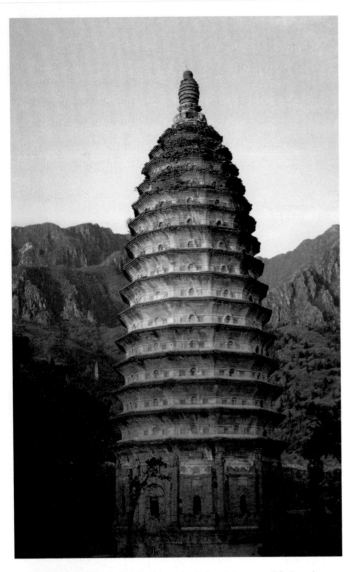

A Buddhist pagoda. Dating to the early sixth century C.E., this temple located east of Luoyang is the oldest known Buddhist structure in China. There, builders transformed the dome-shaped South Asian stupa into a multilevel tower. This basic form inspired religious architecture across East and Southeast Asia and in fact influenced Hindu temple construction back in India. Why do you think this architectural form had such wide appeal?

century, Luoyang, the Northern Wei capital, had more than a thousand monasteries.

Buddhists and brahmins in Southeast Asia. About the same time that Buddhists traveling on the silk roads reached China, others crossed the Bay of Bengal on the monsoon winds to introduce their faith in Southeast Asia. Buddhist traders and monks probably first established themselves in Funan, a kingdom, or group of small kingdoms, centered on the Mekong River delta in southern Cambodia and Vietnam (see Chapter 7).

Buddhist travelers discovered in Funan and other Southeast Asian states that local populations expected their rulers to demonstrate the rightfulness of their authority less through family descent or force of arms than by displays of both moral leadership and protective supernatural powers. Mahayana Buddhists therefore found ready listeners among aspiring monarchs, offering people stories of the great Buddhist emperor Ashoka (see Chapter 6) as a model of moral virtue and showing how *Bodhisattvas* and buddhas could assist individual progress toward enlightenment. In the first millennium C.E., Buddhist communities multiplied along the Malay Peninsula and on Sumatra and other Indonesian islands, though at first appealing more to princely courts and town dwellers than to rural people. In the seventh century, a Chinese monk named Yijing stopped off in Sumatra after traveling in India. He later wrote:

> Many kings and chieftains in the islands of the Southern Ocean admire and believe (Buddhism), and their hearts are set on accumulating good actions. In the fortified city of Bhoga Buddhist priests number more than 1,000 whose minds are bent on learning and good practices. . . . If a Chinese priest [monk] wishes to go to the West in order to hear (lectures) and read (the original), he had better stay here one or two years and practice the proper rules and then proceed to Central India.[15]

Hindu brahmins engaged in trade also traveled from South to Southeast Asia. Many of these high-caste individuals practiced *bhakti*, a devotional faith in the Hindu tradition that, like Buddhism, offered not dry and exhausting ritual sacrifices but intense experience of godly power and love. Originating in southern India, *bhakti* encouraged veneration of the deities Vishnu and Shiva. Southeast Asian elites welcomed *bhakti*'s transcendent worship as well as the possibility that through passionate devotion a ruler might achieve the spiritual rank of *cakravartin,* a king of cosmic moral authority. Buddhist and Hindu ideas and devotions spread through Southeast Asia together, and many new believers did not much care whether they distinguished between them. Historians of religion sometimes refer to the development of a Hindu-Buddhist tradition in that region. For example, temples, stupas, and monasteries that rulers sponsored often blended together symbols and images from both traditions.

One of the historical ironies of the later first millennium C.E. is that as universalist Buddhism continued to spread east of India, it faded gradually as a popular faith in the land of its birth. This happened mainly from the sixth century, when the *bhakti* movement offered spiritual seekers enlightenment through devotion to Vishnu, Shiva, and other gods long worshiped in South Asia. In fact the Hindu tradition absorbed various aspects of Buddhism. For example, by the ninth century the Hindu monastery emerged as a variation on the older Buddhist institution. Numerous Theravada Buddhist monasteries remained in South Asia, though popular Mahayana worship waned, excepting notably on Ceylon.

An image of Vishnu. This stone relief decorates a celebrated Gupta temple in the village of Deogarh in central India. The temple is dedicated to the god Vishnu, who in this image reclines gracefully on the serpent deity Ananta Shesha.

The Christian Web

Not long after Jesus preached in Palestine, Christians carried their gospels—the "good news" of his ministry, death, and resurrection—in all directions. As Christian communities sprang up in new social and cultural environments, doctrines, worship, and communal organization took on different hues, just as occurred in Buddhism. Both Buddhists and Christians believed it was critical to their faith to understand the essential nature of their founding teacher. Was he human, was he divine, or was he both? As these religions spread, leading thinkers disagreed over the answers to these questions. In the first four centuries of the Christian era, theologians argued about numerous points of doctrine but especially about the question of who Jesus really was.

Starting in the reign of Constantine, Christian patriarchs and bishops gathered periodically in councils to try to hammer out consensus on this and other questions. Several major schools of thought contended for acceptance. The Byzantine empire officially endorsed the idea of Jesus as God the Son in an equal and indivisible Holy Trinity with God the Father and God the Holy Spirit. A second school, called Arianism, asserted that God created Jesus as a divine being but remained spiritually superior to him. A third school, called Nestorianism after the patriarch Nestorius (386–451 C.E.), declared that Jesus had two distinct natures, one human and one divine, arguing that elemental unity between Jesus the man (who suffered, died, and was resurrected) and God (who could not have had such an experience) was not possible. At the polar opposite of Nestorianism was the Monophysite or Coptic doctrine, which affirmed that Jesus's human nature was fully absorbed into God and therefore disappeared. Finally, Christians known as Gnostics had a mystical view, contending that Jesus possessed a Divine Spark that gave him the power to unite with God, the Divine Spirit. As savior, Jesus showed that all humans have the possibility through spiritual knowledge of an "inner resurrection" and unity with God.

When the Emperor Theodosius made Christianity the official imperial religion, church leaders had the police power of the Byzantine government behind them to successfully outlaw doctrines they regarded as incorrect. Furthermore, they could excommunicate, imprison, or execute individuals charged with **heresy.** In the fourth and fifth centuries, Roman bishops ruled that the Arian, Nestorian, Monophysite, and Gnostic variants were all heretical. But beyond the borders of Byzantine authority, these proclamations could not be enforced.

> **heresy** In Christianity, beliefs or practices that contradict the church's official doctrine.

Working together, state and church also outlawed traditional Roman practices, such as ritual animal sacrifice. Christian communities were permitted to close down pagan temples and destroy statues of the old deities, now regarded as vile demons. Roman polytheism slowly faded out, first in the towns, more slowly in the countryside. Theodosius also abolished legal protections for Jews and refused to punish violent attacks on synagogues.

Monastic Christianity. Some scholars have argued that Buddhist monks who found their way to Persia and Syria inspired the growth of a monastic movement in Christianity. Not only Buddhism and Christianity but the Jewish, Hindu, and, later, Islamic traditions all accommodated men and women who believed that full spiritual devotion requires "leaving the world" to join a secluded spiritual

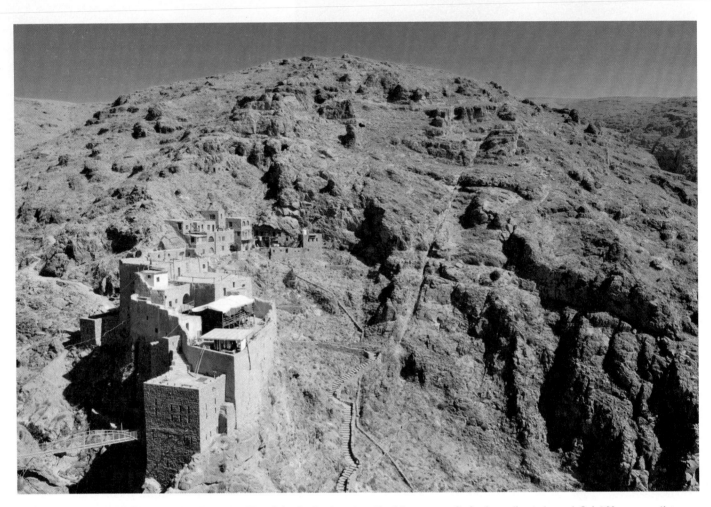

The sixth-century monastery of Saint Moses the Abyssinian in the desert north of Damascus, Syria. According to legend, Saint Moses was the son of a ruler of Abyssinia (Ethiopia) who renounced wealth and power for the life of a Christian hermit. Why do you think Christians built monasteries in such harsh environments?

community, wander the highways, or take up solitary residence in a forest or desert cave. Those believers adopted **asceticism,** that is, they renounced the needs of the flesh to one extreme or another and spent their time meditating, praying, begging, worshiping with others, doing useful work, or performing charitable acts. They believed this way of life advanced them toward spiritual enlightenment or eternal life.

> **asceticism** The principle and practice of renouncing material comforts and pleasures in pursuit of an elevated moral or spiritual state.

Many early Christian ascetics became spiritual hermits in the Egyptian desert. St. Pachomius (d. 346 C.E.) started the first communal home for monks, founding eleven monasteries housing seven thousand monks and nuns who took vows of poverty. Syria was another center of ascetic practice. St. Simeon (d. 459) took bodily renunciation to new heights, as the story goes, by ascending a pillar and refusing to budge from this perch for forty years. Most Christian ascetics renounced material pleasures, and St. Augustine (354–430), the celebrated North African theologian, counseled that if

believers felt compelled to marry, they should try to remain virgins nonetheless. Some male Christian writers claimed that men had a hard time resisting physical temptations because women, having insatiable sexual appetites, would not leave them alone. In this climate Christian theology incorporated the idea that Eve was responsible for Adam's expulsion from the Garden of Eden. Mary, the virgin mother of Jesus, became the model of female virtue.

As in Buddhism, Christian monasteries not only served the needy but also helped advance literacy and learning. In remote rural regions, monks improved farm productivity by clearing land and experimenting with new food crops. The ascetic life did not attract the majority of believers, who preferred to practice their religion while living "in the world." These "lay Christians," however, also needed **clergy** to perform essential rituals in community churches and look after the moral and physical needs of the members. In the Byzantine church, therefore, the *secular clergy* resided

> **clergy** In Christianity, people ordained for religious vocations, as distinguished from ordinary worshipers.

St. Augustine of Hippo: Christian Theologian

Born to a pagan father and Christian mother in the North African town of Thagaste in present-day Algeria, Augustine of Hippo (354–430 C.E.) grew up in a family that had Berber ancestry but was culturally Romanized. Patrick, Augustine's father, sat on Thagaste's town council, but the family was not wealthy, owning only a few acres of land. Nevertheless, Patrick and his wife Monica wanted to see their clever son educated. They sent him to local schools, and when he was seventeen years old, they secured the patronage of a wealthy landowner to finance his continuing studies in Carthage. There, Augustine became intimate with a servant woman. By law he could not marry her, but the two had a son. Though his mother hoped he would become a Christian, Augustine instead devoted himself to Manichaeism, the religion founded in the previous century that blended Christian beliefs with elements of Zoroastrianism and Buddhism.

After completing his schooling, Augustine became a teacher of rhetoric, first in Carthage and then in Rome. By that time his interest in Manichaeism had cooled, and he turned to Skepticism, a philosophical movement founded on new readings of the ancient Greek texts of Plato. Though Augustine might have been in a state of spiritual flux, his scholarly career continued to advance. When he was thirty, he won the most prominent academic position in the Latin world, the professorship of rhetoric at the Roman imperial court in Milan.

While he lived in that city, however, Augustine began to explore Christian teachings by attending the stirring lectures of Ambrose, the Bishop of Milan. Augustine continued to struggle for a clear spiritual path, when one day he heard a "childlike voice" instructing him, "Take up and read, take up and read." Opening a Bible, his eyes fell on a passage in one of St. Paul's letters that offered him a solution to his spiritual quandary: "Not in revelings and drunkenness, not in sexual indulgence and indecencies, not in contention and rivalry; but put on the Lord Jesus Christ and make no provision for the flesh in lusts."

Shortly after that, Ambrose baptized Augustine. Leaving his professorship in 387, he returned to Thagaste. There, he founded a monastery and gathered together a small community of monks. He wished to lead a life of quiet contemplation and religious writing, but this was not to be. In 391 he traveled to the North African port city of Hippo Regius, where the Christian community persuaded him to join the priesthood. Within five years, he became Bishop of Hippo, an office he held for thirty-four years. Just as Vandal invaders sacked Hippo in 430, he died of an illness, leaving behind a corpus of writings that would inspire Christian thinkers for centuries.

In his numerous letters, sermons, and theological treatises, Augustine emphasized a philosophy of inclusion and sincerity, judging actions more important than words as evidence of Christian faith and virtue. He strove to eliminate pagan elements that had seeped into North African Christianity, but he also welcomed pagan converts. His classic writings include his *Confessions,* which recounted the hedonism of his youth and his conversion to Christianity. In *The City of God,* his monumental work, he explored the relationship between the secular state and the Christian church. In a key doctrine, he declared that all humans are tainted by the original sin of Adam and Eve. Therefore, eternal salvation depends not on individual effort but on God's gift of grace.

A seventh-century fresco of St. Augustine from the Lateran Palace in Rome.

Thinking Critically

In what ways might political and economic conditions in the Mediterranean world in the late fourth and early fifth centuries have affected the course of St. Augustine's life?

---

among the mass of worshipers, whereas the *regular clergy* lived the monastic life, following a "rule," or special code of conduct for monks and nuns.

Christians beyond the Mediterranean. By the fifth century C.E. the Roman church was well established all around the Mediterranean. In the tumult that attended the collapse of the western empire, bishops and their priests often stepped in to provide local authority and services to the needy. Some Germanic groups had converted to Arian Christianity, partly because they first received Christian teaching from Arian missionaries and partly because they liked the idea of accepting the new faith without having to identify fully with the religion of imperial Rome. As

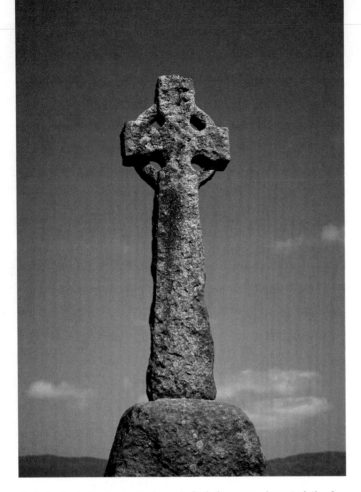

Christianity in the far north. An early Christian cross characteristic of Celtic society, notably in Ireland.

the dust of migration and war settled, however, Germanic kings seeking legitimacy transferred their allegiance to the Roman church. Arianism gradually died away.

In the fifth and sixth centuries, monks carried Christianity throughout northwestern Europe and into Britain and Ireland. Missionaries often condemned and destroyed polytheistic beliefs and images, but some found ways to Christianize indigenous religious culture. Locally worshiped gods and goddesses might, for example, be transformed in time into saints. In Celtic Ireland an annual festival to celebrate the goddess Brigid became an occasion to venerate the pious Christian St. Brigit. The sacred rocks, groves, and ponds where spirits dwelled sometimes became Christian holy sites.

Christian communities arose in Mesopotamia and Persia no later than they did in Europe. The kingdom of Armenia in far eastern Anatolia appears to have been the world's first state to adopt Christianity as its official church, about eighty years before Byzantium did. The earliest followers of Jesus to reach the Tigris-Euphrates valley were likely Jewish-Christians, that is, believers who wished to continue to live according to Jewish law. These newcomers made easy contact with the large Jewish communities already established there.

In the fourth and fifth centuries, Nestorian Christians founded communities in the Sasanid empire, facing persecution if they remained in Roman territory. One distinguishing feature of the Nestorian church was its use of Syriac rather than Greek as the language of its **liturgy,** or formal church worship. Syriac, a written language from the first century C.E., was a dialect of Aramaic, the Semitic language Jesus almost certainly spoke. Operating principally from the city of Ctesiphon on the Tigris, the Nestorian church placed bishops in cities across Persia, and its monasteries multiplied. By the early fifth century, Merv, a major city in northeastern Persia and a gateway to the silk roads, had a Christian community. From Merv, Nestorian monks and merchants traveled to Central Asia and the oasis towns beyond, building their monasteries alongside Buddhist ones. The first Christians reached China early in the seventh century, and the Nestorian church continued to attract congregations in both Inner Eurasia and China for another eight hundred years.

> **liturgy** The established forms of public worship, especially the order of services, including rituals, prayers, readings, and hymns.

According to the Acts of Thomas, a gospel associated with the Gnostic tradition but not included in the Bible of the Roman church, Jesus's apostle Thomas introduced Christianity to South Asia. By the mid-fourth century, communities existed in towns along India's western coast. Cosmas, a fifth-century Egyptian geographer, reports that there were Gnostic churches not only in India but also on Ceylon, including at least one bishop.[16] South Asia had a way of welcoming and then absorbing foreign immigrants and their beliefs into both devotional religion and the Indian social system. Consequently, the Christian community did not grow much, but it maintained its distinct identity as a particular caste within which its families intermarried. Christians subscribed to Indian dietary laws and other customs and represented Jesus Christ as an object of devotional faith parallel to Vishnu and Shiva.

Probably well before the gospels reached western Europe, caravans and ships transported Christian merchants and missionaries along the busy trade corridors of both the Nile River and the Red Sea. In the fifth and sixth centuries, Christians traveled up the Nile to Nubia, the region that corresponds roughly to the modern Republic of the Sudan. By that time the great Nubian kingdom of Kush had disintegrated (see Chapter 7), but rulers of smaller successor states, and eventually most of their populations, converted to either Monophysite (Coptic) or Orthodox Christianity, replacing older polytheistic religions. Archaeological digs in Nubia have uncovered numerous churches, monasteries, and works of Christian art dating to the fifth century and later.

Monophysite Christianity also took root in Axum, the African kingdom and commercial crossroads located in what are today Eritrea and northern Ethiopia (see Chapter 7). Around 350, Ezana, the Axumite king, became a Christian.

One ancient writer associates this act with Aedesius and Fromentius, two Christian boys who got stranded in a Red Sea port. The queen of Axum recruited these boys, especially the quick-witted Fromentius, to help her govern. He not only did that but also aided Christian merchants in Axum by "providing them with whatever was needed, supplying sites for buildings and other necessaries, and in every way promoting the growth of the seed of Christianity in the country."[17] Missionaries in Axum and eventually a bishop answered to the patriarch of the Monophysite Coptic church in Egypt. Christian scholars translated the Bible from Greek into Ge'ez, a Semitic language that became the medium of the Ethiopian church liturgy. Jewish communities already established in Axum may have also had considerable influence on Ethiopian Christianity. The church emphasized the narratives of the Hebrew Bible (Old Testament), the holiness of the biblical Ark of the Covenant, and the descent of the Axumite royal family from Solomon, the ancient Israelite king.

Manichaeans on the silk road. These Manichaean priests are writing at their desks. The image is from a book dating to the eighth or ninth centuries found at Gaochang, a town on the silk road that skirts the northern edge of the Tarim Basin. What other religions do you think residents of Gaochang practiced in that period?

The Manichean Way

Manichaeism emerged as a third universalist religion in the third century, though after about 1000 C.E., it no longer endured except as scattered sects and communities. Mani (216–272 C.E.), the prophet and founder of this movement, grew up in the Tigris-Euphrates valley. His father may have been a member of a Jewish-Christian sect, and Mani probably came in contact with other faiths as well. He also lived for a time in the Kushana empire, where he may have learned something of both Buddhist and Hindu tradition. The Zoroastrian principle of eternal struggle between the forces of Light and Darkness had already influenced the dualist tendency in Christianity—the struggle of God versus Satan. Mani associated light and goodness with spirit, darkness and evil with matter. He conceived of a universe in which particles of light are ensnared in matter but continually struggle to escape. He also taught that believers devoted to the light should live a rigorously ascetic life, including celibacy. Mani revered Zoroaster, the Buddha, and especially Jesus as prophets but declared himself to be the last and greatest bearer of truth to humankind. If the basis of Mani's teaching was, as some scholars believe, fundamentally Christian, this Christianity incorporated elements of several traditions, including monasticism, vegetarianism, veneration of images, and belief in reincarnation.

At the urging of Zoroastrian priests, the Sasanid regime put Mani in prison, where he died. In the following century, however, his followers carried his message west into the Roman empire and northeast into Central Asia. Manichean communities became well established in many Roman cities about the same time that the western empire was beginning to crack. To the east, white-robed Manichean monks and nuns followed Buddhists and Nestorians along the silk roads. There, Manichean monasteries thrived and converts multiplied, especially among merchants. Manicheans reached China along with Nestorians in the seventh century, though Han Chinese tended to regard them as advocates of one more Buddhist sect. In the following three centuries, the religion attracted many followers among Turkic steppe peoples but after 1000 no longer competed well with the other universalist traditions.

Tropical Africa: Farmers, Towns, and Iron

FOCUS In what ways did interactions with peoples in other parts of Afroeurasia affect patterns of social, cultural, and economic change in tropical Africa?

Africa south of the Saharan Desert makes up nearly 30 percent of the land area of Afroeurasia, but at the start of the Common Era it had only about 5 percent of the supercontinent's population. The fundamental explanation is that farmers began to settle Africa's tropical latitudes in significant numbers only about four thousand years ago, later than dense agricultural populations developed in the irrigated river valleys of Afroeurasia. As farming spread through wet tropical forests and savannas from the second millennium B.C.E., the general pattern was *extensive* agriculture, meaning that when the population of farming or herding communities in an area reached a level that put excessive pressure on land, some groups would move off to open new land where not many people already lived. Consequently, population densities in many areas remained low, especially relative to places like the Nile or Tigris-Euphrates River valleys.

In the early centuries C.E., tropical Africa's population grew gradually as pioneer farmers moved into and through the rainforests of the equatorial zone and out onto the savannas of southern Africa. In some regions, however, more intensive farming and population growth reinforced each other, and this greater density encouraged larger settlements, more occupational specialties, and greater reliance on trade with neighbors.

In the Sudanic belt, the zone of semiarid land (Sahel) and savannas that runs west to east across Africa just south of the Sahara desert, farming and cattle-breeding populations showed signs of increasing social complexity in the first millennium B.C.E. Villages multiplied in the western Sudan, notably among peoples speaking languages in the Mande family. Some villagers specialized in particular crafts, for example, iron smelting, pot making, cotton weaving, or leather working. These artisans formed associations that came to have the characteristics of social castes. Members not only shared religious beliefs and secret rituals but also married exclusively into one another's families. Villages with different specialties grew up in clusters around large settlements where artisans could sell their wares to local farmers and herders or perhaps to merchants from other regions.

Archaeological research has revealed quite a bit about one of these commercial centers, the city of Jenne-Jeno (Old Jenne), a site in the modern Republic of Mali. The town was located in the Niger River's inland delta, a region where in the summer months the river fans out to form a broad alluvial plain of creeks and marshes. The delta teemed with fish, game, and fertile rice-growing land. Settlers founded Jenne-Jeno about 300 B.C.E., and its population may have reached about fifty thousand in the following seven hundred years. Its artisans produced copper ware, gold jewelry, and fine painted ceramics. Iron deposits lay not far from the city, but smelted copper had to be imported from mines in the Sahara about nine hundred miles away. The town became an entrepôt, or transit center, for a variety of metals and manufactures exchanged up and down the Niger or by donkeys to overland destinations. The city and its hinterland may have formed a small state, but we have no evidence of a central government or hierarchy of social classes. Historians have found material remains of comparable towns in Sudanic West Africa, a record showing that urbanization was well under way in this region in the early centuries C.E.

The Nok Culture

Large farming settlements also began to appear near the southern rim of the Sudanic belt, where wooded savannas met tropical forests. In south central Nigeria east of the Niger River, a site named after a village called Nok has yielded iron tools, slag heaps from iron smelting furnaces, fired clay bowls and utensils, and stone carvings of animals and humans. Most remarkable of all are the remains of terra-cotta (ceramic) sculptures of human heads that are life-sized or nearly so and whose features, including triangular-shaped eyes, are naturalistically defined. Historians have speculated that these images, with wooden or ceramic bodies attached, served in rituals linked to the fertility of the land. The material record at Nok, where iron production probably started well before 500 B.C.E., tells us little about the social or political organization of the society. Might the terra-cotta heads be representations of local kings? Or might they be deities? If we can speculate from knowledge of later centuries, Nok people believed in a supreme creator god who did not intervene much in human affairs and in ancestral spirits who communicated more intimately with their living descendants. In any case the sophistication of their art suggests that Nok society had economic resources rich enough to support the work of highly skilled artisans. We also know that the Nok style of sculpture spread widely in the region, indicating the rise of many other iron-working centers.

Change was also taking place rapidly in West Africa's wet forest zone. There, immigrant farmers from the north arrived with iron axes and hoes, but they also had to switch their whole economy from grains, which did not thrive in the wet tropics, to yams and other root crops that did. These cultivators gradually displaced or assimilated small-scale foraging and hunting communities that had lived in the forests for millennia.

The African East and South

In terms of climate and vegetation, the regions of eastern and southern Africa present a more complicated scene. Owing to a north–south belt of highlands on the eastern side of the continent, ecological zones do not form neat east–west bands as they do in West Africa. Grain farmers, forest crop cultivators, cattle herders, and hunter-gatherers therefore shared eastern and southern Africa in an extremely complex mosaic of distinct ecological regions. In the early centuries C.E. Indicopleustes Cosmas, both farmers and cattle herders who spoke a variety of languages, including numerous tongues in the Bantu language family, continued to drift generally southward. Farmers practiced shifting agriculture, working relatively thin tropical soils with both iron and stone tools until nutrients gave out, then moving on to new land. Wherever farm families settled for a time, homesteads, hamlets, or villages sprang up, settlements distinctive for their round, conical-roofed houses of wood and dried mud.

The Sculptures of Nok

In 1928, tin miners working in Nigeria's Jos Plateau region uncovered an unusual object. About four inches high and made of terra cotta, the spherical artifact appeared to be a head. Colonel John Dent-Young, the British co-owner of the mine, donated the find to a nearby museum, unaware that his workers had discovered the first material evidence of an ancient West African cultural tradition.

Fifteen years passed without any more objects surfacing. Then, in 1943, tin miners came across a second terra-cotta head, this one more than twice the size of the first. Bernard Fagg, an archaeologist working in the British colonial administration of Jos Province, began investigating both of these mysterious objects. As he talked with local farmers and miners, he realized that they had been collecting heads and other sculpture fragments for years. Since the first head had been found near the village of Nok, Fagg associated the sculptures with what he called the "Nok culture."

Since Fagg's day, thousands of pieces of Nok sculpture have been excavated on the Jos Plateau. Over half of the objects recovered are terra-cotta heads. Radiocarbon dating and other tests place the earliest sculptures at around 500 B.C.E. and the latest at about 200 C.E. Many of the pieces were sculpted out of blocks of clay, an unusual approach that suggests a wood-carving tradition might also have existed in the Nok culture.

Political conditions in Nigeria have prevented professional archaeologists from conducting systematic excavations in the Jos region. Instead, commercial excavators have taken the initiative to uncover or acquire Nok artifacts, lured by the prices that these pieces fetch from collectors of African art. Because of this trade, forgeries also abound, as does the practice of improperly restoring sculptures by combining many smaller fragments to form a full human figurine. From the pieces that scholars have studied, however, we can surmise that the skilled creators of Nok sculpture worked in an economically and politically complex society that had been developing for centuries. This suggests that similar societies and artistic traditions may yet be discovered in West Africa.

Thinking Critically

What features of the figures stand out to you? Do you see stylistic elements common to both figures? What purpose might these objects have played in Nok society? Formulate hypotheses about the social status or position of the people depicted in these sculptures and about the society in which they lived.

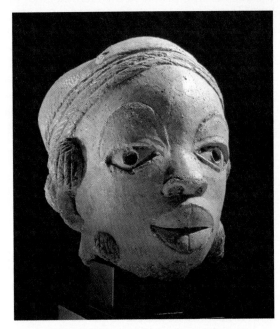

A terracotta head of a whiskered male, Nok Culture, 900 B.C.E.–200 C.E.

A terracotta head and torso of a female, Nok Culture, 500 B.C.E.

In the far south, iron-using, Bantu-speaking immigrants, first arriving sometime before 400 C.E., came in contact with both cattle-herding people known as Khoikhoi (COY-coy) and forager-hunters identified generally as San. These three groups all traded their specialized products with one another, and Khoikhoi animal-breeders taught Bantu farmers much about herding. Over many centuries, however, Bantu peoples came to vastly outnumber the earlier societies, so that Khoikhoi and San survived mainly in drier and more marginal regions, such as along the margins of Namibia's Kalahari Desert.

Southeast Asian Contributions to African Society

Sometime between the first and third centuries C.E., sea-borne travelers arrived on the East African coast. Some of these immigrants, whose numbers might have been no more than a few hundred, probably married into existing coastal societies and eventually disappeared as a distinct ethnolinguistic group. Others, however, moved southward along the coast and in the third or fourth centuries crossed the Mozambique Channel to the big island of Madagascar. That land may have been completely uninhabited at the time, and so the newcomers retained the language and some elements of the culture they brought with them. Madagascar's colonizers spoke an early version of Malagasy, which remains the island's principal language today. Malagasy belongs to the Austronesian language family; its closest cousin is a tongue spoken on the island of Borneo in Indonesia.

Just how Austronesian mariners reached East Africa, more than four thousand miles across the Indian Ocean from places like Borneo, remains something of a mystery. We know, however, that Malay merchants and shippers originating in Indonesia and the Malay Peninsula took a large part in the ancient Bay of Bengal and Arabian Sea trade. Malay voyagers founded at least one commercial settlement on the coast of southern Arabia in the late first century B.C.E. Since traders from Axum and the Arabian Peninsula visited the tropical East African coast, Malay venturers may have gone along as well, and perhaps enticed others to follow.

Even though Austronesian speakers who resided on the East African coast disappeared from the historical record, they left a sizable economic footprint. Food plant genetics tell us that these sailors almost certainly introduced Asian yams, taro root, sugar cane, and particular varieties of bananas to Africa. These plants, which thrived in the equatorial climate of Southeast Asia, flourished similarly in equatorial Africa. Farmers there had depended heavily on native varieties of yams and perhaps plantains (a starchy food related to the banana). A highly nutritious staple (cooked in a variety of ways), bananas almost certainly contributed to the growth of agrarian population in the wet tropics. They reached the West African forest sometime before 1000 C.E.

• • •

Conclusion

On the very large scale of history, the long-term trend of rising population, greater social complexity, and expanding economic production and exchange across Afroeurasia leveled off somewhat between the second and seventh centuries. Scholars have estimated that after moving consistently upward for three thousand years, Afroeurasia's overall population dropped from about 245 million to 188 million between 200 and 700 C.E. before starting to climb again.[18] According to another estimate, the number of Afroeurasian cities with populations in the approximate range of 30,000 to 450,000 shrank from seventy-five to forty-seven between 100 and 500 C.E.[19] In western Europe and North Africa, many cities withered or disappeared altogether. Justinian's Plague and recurring epidemics may also have accounted for significant population losses in Europe, North Africa, and Southeast Asia in the sixth and seventh centuries.

Population loss, deurbanization, and economic contraction, however, occurred unevenly in those centuries. The most dramatic negative change almost certainly occurred in Europe and the Mediterranean in connection with Germanic and Hunnic depredations and the breakup of the western Roman empire. Northern China, which was heavily populated and urbanized in the Han era, also appears to have suffered severe depression in the aftermath of that empire's collapse. If silk road trade did not suffer chronic decline after 200, its routes were almost certainly disrupted periodically as power relations among Inner Eurasian pastoral groups became more agitated and unstable.

On the other hand, economic expansion characterized the eastern Roman empire, South Asia in the Gupta era, and especially southern China during the Age of Division.

Tropical Africa had a much lower starting base for demographic and economic growth in 200, compared, say, to India or China. But the *rate* of growth in the following five centuries almost certainly accelerated. Even in the most prosperous Afroeurasian societies in these centuries, agrarian technology did not change much, despite incremental improvements here and there in toolkits and farming methods. Humans continued to rely overwhelmingly on biomass (wood and other vegetation), domestic animal power, human labor, and in some measure wind and water to harness productive energy.

No startling technological breakthroughs occurred in the centuries after 600 either, but the growth trend in Afroeurasia as a whole generally resumed. Several factors contributed to this, among them a new surge of interregional commercial and cultural exchange. This phenomenon was associated with Arabic-speaking peoples, who led the emergence of a zone of political and cultural energy extending from the Mediterranean to India.

• • •

Key Terms

Arianism 267	deurbanization 260	Manichaeism 264
asceticism 268	eunuch 251	Nestorianism 267
Austronesian migrations 274	Gnosticism 267	Nok culture 272
Bantu migrations 274	Gupta empire 251	pandemic 261
bhakti 266	heresy 267	patriarch 257
Byzantine empire (Byzantium) 260	Huns 257	Sasanid empire 251
clergy 268	Jenne-Jeno 272	Theravada Buddhism 264
Coptic (Monophysite) Christianity 267	liturgy 270	White Huns 261
	Mahayana Buddhism 264	

Change over Time

1st century c.e.	Buddhists first arrive in China.
200	Nok culture flourishes in the West African Sudanic region.
216–272	Mani, founder of Manichaeism, teaches in Southwest Asia.
220–581	The Age of Division in China follows the collapse of the Han dynasty.
224–651	The Sasanid empire prospers in Persia.
3rd–4th centuries	Austronesian-speaking migrants colonize Madagascar.
4th century	Bantu-speaking farmers settle in southern Africa.
313	Roman emperor Constantine establishes capital of Constantinople.
320–550	The Gupta empire dominates South Asia.
350	King Ezana of Axum in East Africa converts to Christianity.
378	Germanic Goths defeat the Roman army at Hadrianople.
380	Emperor Theodosius declares Christianity to be Rome's state religion.
400	Germanic groups push into western Roman empire. Population of Jenne-Jeno, a West African entrepôt, reaches around 50,000.
434–453	Attila the Hun leads several major raids into the Roman empire.
527–565	Justinian reigns over the eastern Roman (Byzantine) empire.
541	Bubonic plague breaks out in the eastern Mediterranean region.
7th century	Christians first reach China.

Please see end of book reference section for additional reading suggestions related to this chapter.

A page from the Quran in Kufic script, Tunisia, tenth century.

Fourteen hundred years ago, Arabic was a relatively minor language spoken in the Arabian Peninsula and parts of Syria and Iraq. Today, it is spoken by somewhere between 200 and 300 million people and is number four on the list of the most widely spoken languages, following Mandarin Chinese, Spanish, and English. It is an official language in twenty-four countries in Southwest Asia and northern Africa. Minority populations speak it in many other countries. Arabic has been a written language since about the fourth century C.E., and today its alphabetic system is used more widely than any other except the Latin alphabet, the one you are reading here.

Like English, Arabic emerged as a major world language because of historical events, in this case the rise of a new empire and the establishment of Islam as a new world religion. In the early seventh century in the desert town of Mecca in western Arabia, Muhammad ibn Abdallah, an Arabic-speaking merchant, began publicly to preach lessons of spiritual and moral reform. According to Muslim tradition, Muhammad received revelations from God in the Arabic language, and his followers eventually set these messages in a body of writings that constituted the Quran (koo-RAHN), Islam's fundamental scripture. Muhammad attracted a group of religious followers, and he also founded a political community to ensure their safety. Following his death in 632, Arab warriors enlarged this state in all directions. Wherever Arabs established their rule, they introduced Arabic, not only as the tongue of a conquering elite, but also as the sacred language of Islam.

The Arab empire grew so large and so fast in the seventh and eighth centuries that it commands attention as a startling world event. In fact, though, this was only one of several large state-building ventures in this period that originated in Afroeurasia's Great Arid Zone, the belt of dry country extending from the African Sahara to East Asia (see Map I-2). The first part of this chapter investigates the rise of these empires and the impact they had on agrarian, densely populated parts of Afroeurasia. We give most detailed attention to the creation of the Arab state. Within a century of its founding in Arabia, it incorporated most of Southwest Asia, northern Africa, and Europe's Iberian Peninsula (Spain and Portugal). The Arabs were also the only empire builders in that era to broadcast a new religious message

Arab-led armies occupied a large part of the Mediterranean rim but not all of it. In the second part of the chapter,

• • •

we investigate the Christian societies that endured both north and south of the Mediterranean. The Byzantine state, heir of the Roman empire, faced an acute crisis in the seventh century as Arab forces took over some of its richest territories and even threatened Constantinople, its great capital. But Byzantium survived as the sanctuary of a distinctive Greek Christian culture. In western and central Europe, the end of the long period of aggressive Germanic and Hunnic migrations left the population seeking a new basis for political stability and economic recovery. There the Christian church played a vital integrating role. South of the Mediterranean, Christian communities continued to flourish in the Nile River valley.

In the final part of the chapter, we turn to China, where the Sui and Tang dynasties ended the region's long Age of Division and reestablished central authority at about the same time that the Arab empire arose. A new period of population and economic growth followed China's reunification. As urbanization, manufacturing, and business surged in both East and Southwest Asia, commercial exchange across Afroeurasia by land and sea accelerated as well.

A Panoramic View

MAP 10.1 Major states of Afroeurasia, 500 C.E.

This map represents Afroeurasia in the aftermath of armed migrations into Europe and North Africa. How has the geopolitical map of the lands around the Mediterranean Sea changed since 250 C.E.? See Map 9.1.

New Empires of Steppe and Desert

FOCUS How were the development of Inner Eurasian empires and the Arab empire similar, and how were they different?

In Chapter 9, we described how several waves of pastoral nomads organized in warrior confederations surged out of the steppes of Inner Eurasia between the third and sixth centuries to disrupt neighboring agrarian societies from India to western Europe and North Africa. These movements, involving Germanic migrants, as well as Alans, Huns, White Huns, Avars, and other bands of mounted archers, precipitated the collapse of the western Roman empire and put eastern Rome, or the Byzantine empire, under prolonged threat. Invaders from the steppes also menaced Persia and northern India. To the east, nomad bands kept up pressure on the northwestern frontiers of China, as they had done off and on for many hundreds of years.

In the seventh and eight centuries, herding peoples continued to factor prominently in Afroeurasia's history, though with two new twists. First, cavalry armies organized large states *within* Inner Eurasia. These groups were not migrating hordes comparable to the Huns. Rather, they aimed to create stable, efficiently organized governments capable of controlling and exploiting large shares of Inner Eurasia's resources in pasture, oasis agriculture, and long-distance trade. Second, the arid Arabian Peninsula emerged for the first time, and quite suddenly, as a new center of political power. In the seventh century, Arabic-speaking nomads and oasis dwellers not only founded a new state but, like the Germanic tribes and the Huns in Europe two centuries earlier, attacked neighboring agrarian lands, overrunning and extinguishing the Sasanid empire of Persia and seizing several of the richest provinces of Byzantium.

Empires along the Silk Roads

After about three hundred years of disturbances and interruptions on the Inner Eurasian caravan routes, traffic picked up again in the later sixth century. This happened in association with the rise of a succession of steppe and mountain empires (see Map 10.2). The principal state-builders were Türks, Tibetans, Uighurs (WEE-goors), and Khazars.

The Türk empires. Warriors known as the Türk (spelled with the letter "ü" as distinct from "u") founded the earliest of the new states to take advantage of silk road recovery and help stimulate it further. The name Türk originally referred to a particular pastoral nomadic tribe that spoke a Turkic languages (spelled without the "ü"). Under talented leaders, Türk cavalry armed with composite bows and steel swords defeated neighboring groups and incorporated their surviving adult males into the Türk ranks to form a larger

confederation of fighters. This more powerful army then conquered more distant tribes, and the Türk war machine snowballed, as it were, across the steppes. As it grew, the state enveloped peoples speaking a number of Inner Eurasian languages, both pastoral nomads and oasis farmers. In addition to tribal and clan organization based on kinship relations, the Türk created a central governing hierarchy. From the top, the supreme leader, or *khagan,* transmitted orders to appointed provincial governors who in turn supervised local tribal and town leaders. The government accumulated wealth to sustain the army and administration by collecting tributes from subject populations and taxing trade.

Two Türk empires rose to power in succession. The first, known as the Eastern Türk, flourished from 552 to 630, then disintegrated in intertribal wars. The Tang imperial government in China played a hand in this violence, using promises of silk cargos and military support to play Türk leaders against one another. The second, or Western Türk empire lasted from 682 to 744. Between them, these states dominated a huge stretch of Inner Eurasia between northwestern China and the Pontic-Caspian steppes north of the Black Sea. In 628, Xuanzang (SHWEN-ZAHNG), a Chinese monk who traveled overland to India to collect Buddhist texts and relics, presented himself before the Türk emperor Tong Yabghu at a western silk road town. Xuanzang confirmed reports of the sumptuousness of the Türk imperial court. The king, he later wrote,

> was covered with a robe of green satin, and his hair was loose, only it was bound round with a silken band some ten feet in length, which was twisted around his head and fell down behind. He was surrounded by about 200 officers, who were all clothed in brocade stuff, with their hair braided. On the right and left he was attended by independent troops, all clothed in fur and fine-spun garments; they carried lances and bows and standards, and were mounted on camels and horses. The eye could not estimate their numbers.[1]

To gather trade revenue, the Türk formed a close collaboration with merchants of Sogdiana (SUGG-dee-an-uh), the region of Central Asia that lay between the Amu Darya and Syr Darya Rivers, today Uzbekistan and southern Kazakhstan. Speakers of a language related to Persian (Farsi), the Sogdians became distinguished for their literacy and commercial expertise. Sometime before the Common Era, they began to build a diaspora of trade settlements that radiated out along the silk roads from Samarkand in Sogdiana to cities in China. Under Türk protection, Sogdians shipped silk, linen, wine, jade, and numerous other Chinese luxuries westward in exchange for horses, camels, hides, and the manufactures of Southwest Asia. Many Sogdian merchants practiced Zoroastrianism, others Buddhism, Manichaeism, and Nestorian Christianity. They contributed to the advancement of these religions in China and Inner Eurasia, and Sogdian scholars translated sacred scripture of these faiths into a number of languages, including Chinese.

MAP 10.2 Empires of steppe and desert, seventh and eighth centuries.

How would you explain the rise of large and powerful empires in relatively arid regions of Afroeurasia where agriculture was limited?

The Uighur empire. The second Türk empire buckled in the mid-eighth century amid fierce tribal infighting for leadership. However, the Uighurs, a new confederation of Turkic-speaking fighters, quickly expanded their own domain. The Uighur state, which lasted nearly a century (744–840), commanded the eastern end of the silk roads. Uighur cavalry invaded China's Yellow River region several times, seizing urban booty, and withdrawing only when

Chinese officials bought off the intruders with thousands of bolts of silk. Like the Türk, Uighurs were familiar with Buddhism, Zoroastrianism, and Nestorian Christianity, religions that spread along the silk roads. Influenced by monks and merchants from Iran, the Uighur elite converted to Manichaeism, the rigorously ascetic faith preached by the Prophet Mani in the third century (see Chapter 9). Manichean temples and monasteries thrived in both the eastern steppes and China in the later eighth and the ninth centuries. But this religion lost ground to both Buddhism and Nestorian Christianity after the Uighur state disintegrated in 840. That reversal effectively ended Manichaeism's prospects as a major universalist religion.

Tibet. A fourth Inner Eurasian empire arose, not in the steppes, but on the rugged Tibetan plateau, which lies between the Tarim Basin and the great wall of the Himalaya Mountains. Tibetans spoke a language in the family that also includes Chinese, and they practiced a mixed economy of farming and herding. About 618 the Tibetan leader Songtsan Gampo (d. 649) organized local lords under his exclusive command. Accumulating sufficient power to field large armies of horse soldiers outfitted in chain mail armor, Tibetan warriors swooped down from the plateau to the Tarim Basin, capturing many eastern silk road towns and for a time controlling their commercial traffic. All the kings in the Tibetan dynasty patronized Buddhist monks and monasteries. This policy gave the state an aura of religious prestige and laid the foundations for popular conversion to the distinctive set of beliefs and rituals characterized as Tibetan Buddhism. The empire collapsed rather suddenly in 842, but for more than two centuries it played a major part in Inner Eurasian politics, alternately fighting and negotiating with imperial China, Türks, and Uighurs for dominance over cities and trade routes.

The Khazars. The longest lasting Turkic-speaking state of the era was Khazaria (630–965). Arising in the Pontic-Caspian steppes north of the Black and Caspian Seas, the Khazar empire at its height embraced the rich farming valleys of the Volga, Don, and Dnieper Rivers. This state originated as a coalition of disparate Turkic-speaking groups, many of whom had migrated westward in flight from Inner Eurasian wars or droughts. Founding several administrative cities, the Khazar monarchs ruled a diverse population of Indo-European and Turkic farmers, herders, and town dwellers. Khazaria also accumulated wealth by taxing trade on two major commercial arteries, the western silk road that terminated at ports on the Black Sea and the north–south routes that connected the fur-rich temperate forests of Russia with Persia and Syria.

In the eighth century, Judaism spread among the Khazar ruling and commercial classes. We know little of how that happened, though we have evidence that Jewish communities occupied the Caucasus and Black Sea regions long before the arrival of Turkic speakers. Though never converting most of the population, the Khazar kings made Judaism their official religion, inspired mainly by the ancient books of the Hebrew Bible (Old Testament). The political and commercial elite also used the Hebrew alphabet in religious practice, as well as for administrative and commercial communication. When Khazaria broke up in the tenth century, Judaism lost its special position in the region and subsequently declined. Part of the Jewish population, however, may have migrated into eastern and central Europe to form new communities there.

Taken together, the Inner Eurasian empires of the seventh and eighth centuries left an important cultural legacy. Distinctive Turkic styles of artisanry, dress, and cuisine, and especially Turkic languages, spread widely in the region. Today, Turkic tongues are dominant in six Eurasian countries and spoken widely in several others, including China, Russia, and Germany. From this period, moreover, Turkic-speaking peoples came to play an increasingly important part in world history, as we shall see in later chapters.

The Arab State and the Emergence of Islam

The sixth and by far the largest steppe empire of the later first millennium C.E. arose, not in Inner Eurasia, but in the arid country of the Arabian Peninsula. Starting in 622, Arabic-speaking town dwellers and herding tribes cooperated to found a religious and political community under the leadership of Muhammad ibn Abdallah. From its capital at Madina (Medina), the young Arab state first expanded in the peninsula, a territory nearly twice the size of modern France, Germany, and Spain combined. In contrast to Inner Eurasian empire builders of the same period, however, Arab forces invaded and conquered densely populated and urbanized lands. Within little more than a hundred years, Arab-led armies pushed far to the east and west, carving out a state that stretched from the Indus River valley to Spain.

Also in contrast to the Inner Eurasian imperial ventures, a new religion—a fresh vision

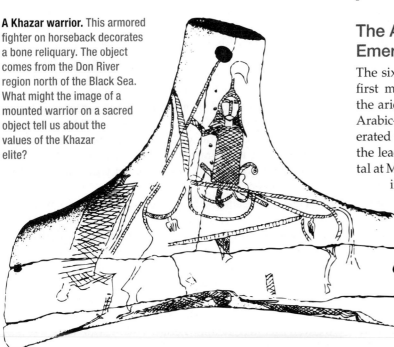

A Khazar warrior. This armored fighter on horseback decorates a bone reliquary. The object comes from the Don River region north of the Black Sea. What might the image of a mounted warrior on a sacred object tell us about the values of the Khazar elite?

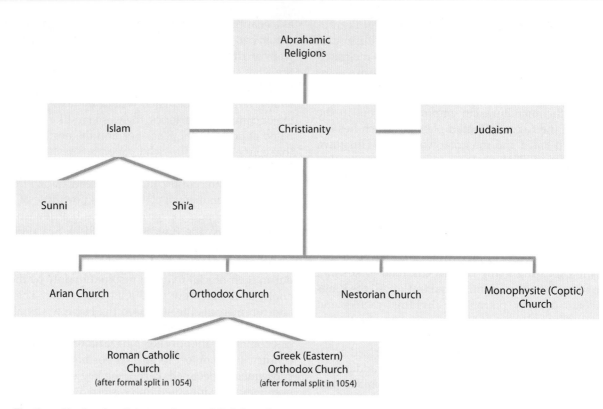

The three Abrahamic religions and some of their branches.

of monotheistic faith based in the tradition of the biblical prophet Abraham, whom Jews and Christians also venerated as an early witness to one, all-powerful god—emerged along with the Arab conquests and founding of the multiethnic Arab state. Although the Arab empire lasted only about a century as a huge unitary state, Islam gradually took root across Southwest Asia and North Africa. Islam thus joined Buddhism and Christianity as a universalist creed directed to all who were prepared to listen to its message. It also offered the religious foundations for a distinctive style of urban civilization.

The Southwest Asian scene in the sixth and seventh centuries. Evidence from ancient texts tell us that Arabic-speaking people, organized in either small states or tribes had participated in greater Southwest Asia's political and cultural life since at least the early first millennium B.C.E. Arab groups that occupied the Arabian Peninsula, Syria, and western Mesopotamia had been allies, political dependents, and trading partners of Rome and of successive Persian empires. The southwestern fringe of the Arabian Peninsula, centered on today's Republic of Yemen, also had a long history of small monarchies drawing wealth from irrigated agriculture and from export trade in incense and other exotic commodities. The peninsula's largest farming population was concentrated in Yemen, whose highlands receive summer monsoon rains.

The Arabian Desert, however, occupies most of the peninsula. Its climate is about the same as that of the eastern Sahara, the two deserts separated only by the Red Sea, a narrow waterway easily crossed in small vessels. Since the domestication of the dromedary, or one-humped camel as early as 2500 B.C.E., pastoral nomads gradually adapted to the harsh Arabian steppes, raising animals wherever oases, wells, and seasonal rainfall provided sufficient grassland and fodder. Like Inner Eurasian herders, Arabia's pastoral tribes lived a mobile way of life, competing with one another for resources and fighting with sword and bow from the backs of both horses and camels. They adopted weaponry and iron armor from Roman and Persian models. From the late centuries B.C.E., they also used the North Arabian saddle, an invention that permitted a rider to sit comfortably astride a dromedary, at the same time toting heavy baggage that hung on the animal's sides. From the fourth century C.E., Arabic-speaking groups advanced more insistently into the agrarian fringes of Syria and Mesopotamia, bringing them into closer contact with the Byzantine and Sasanid empires.

Those two giant states periodically went to war over control of the cities, farmlands, and trade of Syria, Anatolia, and western Mesopotamia (see Chapter 9). Both made pragmatic alliances with Arabs to avoid conflict with them. Both also coveted opportunities to dominate Yemen and the Red Sea commercial entrepôts linking Southwest Asia to the Indian Ocean. By the late sixth century, Byzantium abandoned hopes of restoring Roman authority over the western Mediterranean, where Germanic warrior kings prevailed. Though Byzantium still held scattered territories in

Italy and North Africa, the emperor Heraclius (reigned 610–641) shifted the weight of imperial power to the defense of Egypt, Syria, and Anatolia against the Persians and of the Balkan provinces against encroaching Avar, Slav, or Turkic cavalry. In the early seventh century, fighting between Byzantium and Persia intensified, and for a short time Sasanid forces even occupied northern Egypt. The costs of these wars, plus continuous investment in frontier garrisons and fortifications, strained the treasuries of both states and left them ill prepared to face any new enemies. Moreover, the cycle of plague epidemics that had first struck the eastern Mediterranean in 541 continued throughout the seventh century, causing recurring high mortality and economic setbacks in one region or another.

Muhammad and the preaching of Islam.

The setting for the emergence of both Islam and the new Arab state was western Arabia, or the Hijaz, a region of dry highlands that supported small cities where seasonal rivers or underground water sources could be tapped. These centers included Mecca and Madina. Since Arabia belonged to the same world of commercial and cultural interaction as Byzantium and Persia, it is no surprise that significant numbers of Arabs in Syria and northern Arabia practiced Christianity and that both Christian and Jewish communities were to be found in some Hijaz towns. However, many town dwellers and most pastoral nomads were pagans, that is, polytheists who venerated multiple deities identified with the sun, moon, stars, or sacred trees and rocks. Mecca, a parched Hijaz town nestled among treeless hills, hosted an important pagan shrine centered on a cubic structure called the Ka'ba (KAH-buh). The Meccan gods attracted pilgrim worshipers from across western Arabia.

Muhammad standing before the Ka'ba. This miniature painting is one of 814 in the Siyer-i-Nebi, a multivolume work on the life of the prophet written in the fourteenth century. The painting comes from a sixteenth-century illustrated edition. A tradition developed in Islam of respecting the prophet by veiling his face in visual representations of him. Muhammad is also surrounded by flames. What do you think the flames might signify?

Hijaz towns may have enjoyed rising commercial prosperity in the seventh century in connection with a general upswing in trade across Afroeurasia. Although Mecca's particular importance as a trade center remains historically controversial, historians have argued that growing commercialization encouraged a money-making culture that aggravated social strains among tribes, religious communities, and economic classes.

In these circumstances, Muhammad, a forty-two-year-old man without great social standing, began publicly to preach the power, mercy, and justice of one omnipotent God. Numerous biographies, chronicles, and sacred texts recount the events of his life. As is the case with both Jesus and the Buddha, however, no documents describing his career

and achievements can be dated to his own lifetime. Consequently, historians persistently argue over the reliability and authenticity of early texts that attest to his deeds, utterances, and social milieu. According to Muslim tradition, Muhammad was born into a family of the Quraysh clan in 570. He was orphaned as an infant, raised by an uncle, took up trade, and married Khadija, a successful Meccan businesswoman. In 610 he began to experience visions and hear sounds that he came to acknowledge as messages from God (*Allah* in Arabic). The Angel Gabriel imparted these revelations and instructed Muhammad to share them courageously with his fellow Meccans.

The monotheism of his message was rigorous but compatible with the existing Jewish and Christian traditions.

Human beings, God's supreme creation, must surrender themselves wholeheartedly to his will, bringing him to the center of their consciousness. God is merciful, but he is also just. A day of divine judgment will come when the righteous shall enter heaven, but those who deny God will suffer eternal damnation. Human salvation depends on unconditional devotion to him and to his holy commandments. These laws require all men and women to be pious, compassionate, generous, and respectful of all of divine creation. The willful, egocentric self must be forsaken for the one Self that is God. The Arabic word *Islam* may be translated as "surrender," "submission," or "commitment." An individual who professes Islam is a Muslim, one who surrenders to God's will.

Because Jewish and Christian communities already inhabited western Arabia, Muhammad's preaching was by no means alien. Like Jesus seven centuries earlier, he spoke to popular yearnings for moral assurance, social justice, and divine salvation in an increasingly commercialized and cosmopolitan world. Also like Jesus, he had to struggle to be taken seriously. Only a small part of the Meccan population, including his wife Khadija, listened to him. Most sympathizers were probably poor and downtrodden people, including many women. The majority, and especially the most influential families, did not wish to be told to change their social behavior, share their wealth with the poor, or repudiate the idols that brought the city profitable business.

The Muslim tradition relates that in 622, after eleven years of confronting mostly indifference and persecution, Muhammad and a small band of believers left Mecca, traveling 250 miles north to the city of Yathrib, known from that time forward as Madina. This town had a rich irrigated farming economy, but it suffered from chronic interclan feuding. Consequently, the city accepted Muhammad's moral and political leadership. He demanded only that all the Madinan clans renounce their quarrels and join together in a unified, God-directed community, called in Arabic the *umma*. For Muslims, the prophet's migration to Madina, known as the *hijra*, or flight, is the key event in history. He now had a safe base from which to preach God's word and organize his religious and political society. The year 622 C.E. is year 1 on the Muslim calendar.

In Islamic belief, Muhammad continued to receive divine directives from 610 until 632, when he died. The full body of those revelations formed the Quran (Koran), the "recitation" of God's message to the world. Muhammad transmitted that message orally, and sometime after his death Muslim scribes set it in Arabic script. For Muslims, the Quran is a work of resounding spiritual authority. They affirmed that Muhammad, more faithfully than any other human, thought and lived in accord with God's will. In addition to the Quran, therefore, Muslims also draw inspiration, guidance, and legal precedents from the Traditions of the Prophet (*Hadith*). These sacred texts are reports of Muhammad's exemplary words and deeds, which later scholars corroborated by persuasive testimony. To Muslims, Muhammad was the "perfect man," though not the Son of God, as the majority of early Christians came to regard Jesus.

The Quran also sets forth the ethical rights and responsibilities that individuals must exercise as God's favored creation. As a guide to moral living, it has much in common with the Hebrew and Christian Bibles. It specifies a body of rules, norms, and rituals, which are anchored in the five "pillars" of the faith: daily prayers, regular donations to the poor, pilgrimage to Mecca, annual fasting, and affirmation of God's oneness and Muhammad's place as His final prophet on earth.

Like the Hebrew Bible, the Quran specifies ethical standards that should govern property transactions, inheritance, commerce, kin relations, slavery, and almost any sphere of social and economic life in seventh-century Arabia. Marriage and the family were particularly important subjects. As in most of the world in the first millennium C.E., Arabian social groups were patriarchal, that is, dominated by adult men. Tribal ideology defined women and children essentially as family property and esteemed honor and loyalty among males above stable marriage relations. Muhammad did not propose radical social equality any more than Christian teachings did. But he deplored Arabian values as antagonistic to God and destructive of social harmony. Rather, all humans are deserving of moral respect, and women and men have identical responsibilities to their creator. The Quran extols stable marriage, discourages divorce, prohibits incest, condemns female infanticide, permits polygamy only under strict conditions, and awards women property and inheritance rights. Slavery was part of Afroeurasia's social fabric almost everywhere, and Muhammad did not oppose its legality. Like the Christian New Testament, the Quran instructs believers to treat slaves with compassion and encourages masters to grant them freedom.

A new Southwest Asian state. In contrast to either Jesus or the Buddha, both of whom rejected worldly leadership, Muhammad built a community that was simultaneously religious, social, and political. After moving to Madina, he organized a federation of oasis-dwelling and pastoral clans primarily to defend the young community and ensure the way of life that he believed God prescribed. He faced stern hostility from both Meccans and other western Arabian groups. Part of Madina's large Jewish minority population accepted his prophecy and political leadership. But political factions that opposed the Muslim community or violated agreements with it, including some Jews, were subjected to exile or execution. Muhammad also organized an armed force, and following a series of clashes with opponents between 622 and 628, he and his troops entered Mecca in 630. After this success, much of Arabia, including both Yemen and northern areas extending into the Syrian Desert, declared their allegiance to the Muslim state. Muhammad cleansed the Ka'ba in Mecca of its idols and, reaffirming the tradition that Abraham had built the structure as a monument to monotheistic faith, he rededicated it to the one God. He also declared that God commanded him to retain the Ka'ba's status as a pilgrimage site and to instruct Muslims to travel there at least once in their lives, if they are able, as one of their five fundamental devotional duties. This journey is named the *hajj*.

From an Afroeurasian perspective, the rise of the Arab Muslim state generally paralleled the trajectory of the Türk, Uighur, and Khazar empires in that it coalesced as an alliance among arid-zone pastoral clans and commercially minded town dwellers. The early success of the Muslim community against all odds, however, appears to have inspired Arabs with a sense of common identity and mission never known before. Scholars generally agree that Muhammad did not intend to found a new religion. He hoped, rather, to persuade Jews, Christians, and all other monotheists to join together in shared faith. Indeed, before Muhammad returned to Mecca in 630, he instructed his followers to pray facing Jerusalem, the holiest of cities for both Jews and Christians. But just as early Christians gradually separated themselves from Judaism, so Muslims, in the years following the prophet's death, increasingly defined themselves as distinct from both of those faiths.

The Arab Muslim Empire

Because Muhammad designated no successor, his death in 632 brought on a crisis of leadership. However, Abu Bakr, one of the prophet's early companions, secured a consensus among Muslim clan leaders that he should take command as **caliph** (KAL-ihf), or "deputy" of Muhammad. During his two years as leader (632–634), Abu Bakr suppressed rebellions and made political contacts with Arab groups in the Syrian Desert to the north. In alliance with them, he launched raids on the Byzantine and Persian frontiers. In these ways, he preserved and energized the young state.

> **caliph** In Sunni Islam, the deputy or successor of the Prophet Muhammad as leader of the Muslim community.

The Arab military triumph. Under the leadership of Abu Bakr and his two successors, Caliph Umar (r. 634–644) and Caliph Uthman (r. 644–656), Arab frontier incursions expanded into all-out invasion of Southwest Asia. Byzantine and Sasanid armies fought back, but militarily off balance, fiscally strained, and still hostile toward each other, they suffered defeat. The Byzantine emperor was forced to abandon Syria, Palestine, and Egypt. To the northeast, Arab forces invaded Iraq (ancient Mesopotamia). In 637 they chased the Persian king from Ctesiphon, his splendid capital on the banks of the Tigris River, and during the following twelve years overran Iraq and much of Iran. In barely more than a decade, Arab armies decisively changed the Southwest Asian political landscape. They eliminated the Persian empire, which had endured under one dynasty of rulers or another for 1,300 years. And they deprived the Byzantines of their rich Syrian and Egyptian provinces. These conquests erased the frontier that for about seven centuries had separated Southwest Asia into two great spheres of power.

Mecca's sacred sanctuary. Twilight descends on Mecca as Muslims gather in the grand mosque to pray facing the Ka'ba. That cubical structure is draped in black fabric. Compare the modern Ka'ba with the one pictured on page 285.

How did they do it? One factor was simply effective use of horse cavalry, supported by camel trains for logistical transport, against the larger but slower Byzantine and Persian armies. Another factor was that neither of those empires commanded the wholehearted loyalty of its subjects. The Byzantine state was largely Christian, but the official, or orthodox church had to compete with, and sometimes persecuted, the Monophysite and Nestorian churches, which were popular in Egypt, Syria, and Mesopotamia. Neither those two communities nor the Jewish minority of Southwest Asia felt much inclined to fight for the Byzantine emperor and his bishops. Also, the Arab conquerors let Christians and Jews continue to practice their own monotheistic faiths. On the Persian side, Christian, Jewish, and Manichean minorities in Mesopotamia and Iran had little cause to defend the Sasanid ruling class, which identified closely with Zoroastrian worship, a religion that most farmers and herders under Persian rule did not follow.

The conquests had two important short-term consequences. One was that an Arab military elite quite suddenly took the place of Byzantine and Persian officials from Egypt to northeastern Iran. Headquartered in Madina, the early caliphs appointed Arab governors in the major cities. They also kept soldiers who were not on campaign confined to military camps, reducing opportunities for ambitious officers to build local power centers of their own.

Rapid conquest also set off a violent struggle among Arab leaders. Though Muhammad would no doubt have lamented it, factional strife may have been inevitable owing to the high political stakes involved in controlling the immense agrarian wealth of Southwest Asia and Egypt. The early caliphs, clan chiefs, imperial governors, and members of Muhammad's family all emerged at one moment or another as poles around which opposing political blocs formed. Major players in the first civil struggle, which lasted from 656 to 661, included Uthman, the third caliph; Ali ibn Abu Talib, the fourth caliph and cousin and son-in-law of the prophet; Aisha, one of the prophet's widows; and Muawiya, the Arab governor of Syria. In the struggle, Uthman and Ali were both assassinated, and Muawiya, whose Meccan family was known as the Umayyads (oo-MEYE-ahds), achieved victory. Supported by a majority of Muslims, he took the title of caliph and moved the imperial capital from Madina to Damascus, an important Syrian city that was much closer to the center of the new empire.

The shift from Madina to Damascus. The new Arab leaders lost little time in transforming themselves from desert cavaliers living in tents or mud-brick houses into an urban, palace-dwelling elite. The leaders of the Umayyad Caliphate spoke Arabic rather than Greek or Persian, but they governed local populations largely as the Byzantines and Sasanids had done, employing armed officials to keep order and collect taxes. The new state maintained roads and irrigation works, founded a professional army, and, to demonstrate its piety, built religious monuments such as the

The Caliph Ali and his forces in battle. From a thirteenth-century manuscript.

beautiful Dome of the Rock in Jerusalem. The Umayyads also recruited accountants and secretaries from among educated Greek, Syrian, Egyptian, and, eventually, Persian families. Muawiya maintained the fiction that he governed with the consent of the community of believers, the Arabian model of leadership that Abu Bakr, the first caliph, had kept intact. In fact, Muawiya put forward his own son to succeed him and by that stroke founded a hereditary monarchy. Indeed, authoritarian monarchy had been the standard form of government in most of the region for the previous three thousand years.

The Great Mosque of Damascus. The Umayyad caliphs supported major public construction after they established their capital in Damascus. The mosque site is one of the oldest known places of continuous religious worship in the world. As early as 3000 B.C.E. there was an Aramean temple to the god Hadad here. The site was later a Roman temple, then a Christian church dedicated to St. John the Baptist. Why might successive states have used the same religious site?

Under the Umayyad dynasty, which ruled from 661 to 750, Islam began to spread to non-Arab peoples, though this happened slowly at first. The first generation of Arab conquerors, who saw themselves as exclusively chosen by God to fulfill divine prophecy in the world, did not encourage conversion. They largely left Christians, Jews, and other believers to their own worship. One estimate suggests that by 750 (118 years after the prophet's death), fewer than 10 percent of the non-Arab population of the Umayyad empire had become Muslims.[2] Also, diffusion of basic knowledge of Islam took time, partly because the great majority of the people who lived under Arab rule did not speak or read Arabic. In the later eighth century, however, the conversion rate began to accelerate. Zoroastrianism, whose adherents were concentrated in Iran and Central Asia, lost ground to Islam much faster than did Christianity or Judaism. From about 1000 C.E., it faded as a potential world faith, though some communities survive today, notably the Parsis of western India.

Sunni and Shi'a. A second key development in the Umayyad period was continuing debate over the organization and leadership of the Muslim state. According to Muslim tradition, Muhammad and the early caliphs regarded the growth of the political community as inseparable from the mission to establish a God-approved society on earth. That is, Muhammad founded the community to fulfill moral and spiritual ideals and to prepare humans for God's judgment, not just to set up a power hierarchy and send out tax collectors. But opposing factions disputed the proper structure of government during the first civil war (656–661) and on through a second one (683–692).

The Umayyad government in Damascus had majority support for the view that the first four caliphs set Islam on its proper path. According to this model, the caliph was the community's "chief executive" and had the task of defending the state, promoting social justice, and enforcing God's laws—for as long as he had the community's consent. Believers who accepted this ideal came to be known as Sunni (SOON-nee) Muslims, from the Arabic word *sunna*, which refers to the norms established by the prophet and the first four caliphs.

The main challengers of the Sunni view were the Shi'a (SHEE-ah), a name that in Arabic means "party" or "faction," specifically the faction loyal to Ali, the fourth caliph and kinsman of Muhammad. (An alternate version of the name is Shiite.) Shi'a adherents argued that God intended the leader of the community to be chosen exclusively from the family of Ali, who, they said, inherited some of the prophet's extraordinary moral and spiritual qualities. Although political enemies killed both Ali and one of his two sons in the civil conflicts, Muhammad had other blood descendants in Ali's line. Only they, the Shi'a claimed, had the right to rule. Furthermore, those men, who were given the title of **imam**, understood disguised meanings in the Quran that were essential to human salvation.

> **imam** In Islam in general, the individual who leads congregational worship and carries out other duties such as officiating at marriages.

The largest Shi'a group teaches that in the ninth century the twelfth Imam in the family line of Ali went into a hidden state. Since then, he has continued to live concealed from the world but guides the most devoted Shi'a leaders through inspiration. One day he will return to initiate a final era of justice on earth. This doctrine has given the Shi'a tradition a messianic quality, meaning expectation of the coming of a holy savior, or messiah, an idea comparable to the Christian doctrine of the second coming of Christ. In time, Shi'a

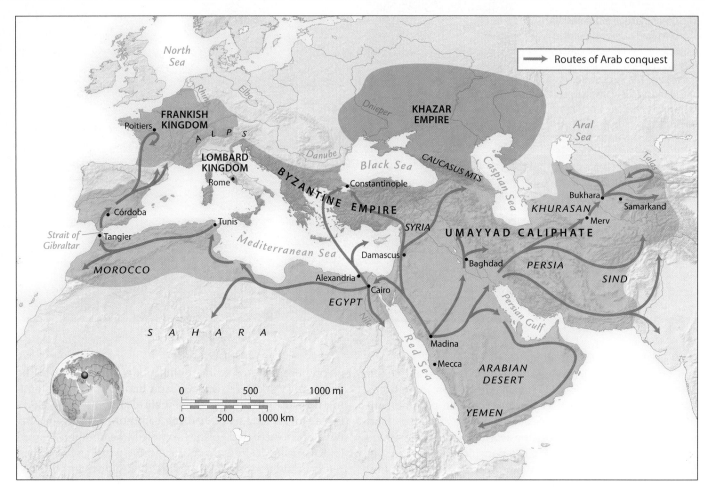

MAP 10.3 The Arab empire at its height, 750.

What geographical factors might help explain the direction of expansion of the Arab empire?

adherents split into a number of branches, each with somewhat different beliefs and practices. Nevertheless, Shi'a doctrines later inspired both religious and political movements, including the founding of a number of Muslim states. Today, upward of 20 percent of the world's Muslim population adhere to one Shi'a group or another, the greatest numbers in Iraq and Iran.

The empire at its zenith. A third development under Umayyad rule was the spectacular territorial expansion of the Arab state (see Map 10.3). Because of big victories over the Byzantines and Sasanids, no major power stood in the way of Arab advance eastward across Iran and westward across North Africa. The Umayyads wanted the revenue that more conquests would bring. They also regarded fresh military operations as a way to direct the energies of Arab soldiers who would otherwise be confined to tedious garrison duty and might become rebellious. Campaigning farther afield also promised booty, including opportunities for soldiers to sell war captives in urban slave markets.

To the west, Arab forces moved along the North African coast, seizing all remaining Byzantine coastal possessions and suppressing local Berber resistance as far as Morocco. As the armies advanced, defeated Berber warriors often joined the cause, some, though not all, converting to Islam. In 711 a large force of Arabs and Berbers crossed the Strait of Gibraltar into Spain. It quickly routed the Germanic kingdom of the Visigoths and occupied most of the Iberian Peninsula, establishing a new Umayyad province that was more than two thousand miles from Damascus.

To the northeast, Arab forces established a major base in Khurasan, previously Sasanid territory that today overlaps northeastern Iran and Turkmenistan. Following conquests there, thousands of Arab families migrated to the region to take advantage of its rich agriculture and urban commercial resources. Operating from Merv and other cities, Arab contingents advanced into Central Asia, crossing the Amu Darya and seizing one western silk road town after another. Numerous Turkic horse soldiers joined the Arab ranks. In 751, Muslim forces confronted a Chinese army at the Talas River in today's Kyrgyzstan Republic. The Muslims were victorious, and in the aftermath of the battle Chinese imperial armies pulled back from Central Asia.

To the east, Arab commanders led troops into Sind, the land neighboring the lower Indus valley, between 711 and 713. That arid region did not have abundant agricultural resources, but it was a hinge of trade between South Asia and Persia. Arab governors appointed from Damascus devoted themselves mainly to controlling and taxing that commerce. In the early eighth century, South Asia was a patchwork of regional monarchies. But states located east of the Indus were strong enough to stop Arab forces from advancing to the Ganges valley or down the western Indian coast.

Back in Southwest Asia, Arab cavalry penetrated Byzantine territory in eastern Anatolia and reached the foothills of the Caucasus Mountains. The Umayyads ordered construction of a Mediterranean navy, using the maritime skills of Christian crews and shipbuilders from Egypt and Syria. As eastern European Avars had done in 626, Arab forces laid siege to Constantinople, the massively defended Byzantine capital. Assaults in 668 and 717 both failed, however, barring Arab advance into the Balkan Peninsula and leaving the Greek emperor a weakened but still important political player in the eastern Mediterranean.

Despite their political and military successes, the Umayyad rulers did not resolve the deep religious and political conflicts that had triggered the first two civil conflicts. Following a third civil war between 747 and 750, the Umayyad government fell to the leaders of a branch of Muhammad's family known as the Abbasids. This new dynasty, the Abbasid Caliphate, solidified its authority over the central lands of the empire and moved the imperial capital from Syria eastward to the Tigris-Euphrates valley. We will return to the Abbasid empire (750–1258) in Chapter 11.

Christian Societies in Europe and Africa

FOCUS In what ways did Christian society change in Europe and the Mediterranean region between the sixth and eighth centuries?

When the Arabs first introduced their alternative monotheistic faith to Southwest Asia, Christianity was well established as the dominant religion throughout the Mediterranean basin. Two centuries later, Christian numbers were declining along the sea's southern rim as more and more people converted to Islam or were born into it. Where Arab invaders did not succeed, however, Christian societies continued to thrive and grow, though specific doctrines and practices varied considerably from one region to another. This does not mean that the Mediterranean basin was rigidly partitioned into religious compartments, each with its own bloc of territory. Christians, Jews, and Muslims shared the region as much as they divided it. They sometimes persecuted and killed one another, but they also lived together in many cities, traded with one another, and exchanged customs and

ideas. It is worth pointing out again that Judaism, Christianity, and Islam were all variants of a common monotheistic tradition that collectively distinguished these three religions from Buddhism or Hinduism.

The Byzantine Empire Holds Its Own

In the first three decades of the seventh century, the Greek-speaking rulers of Byzantium, heirs of the eastern half of the Roman Empire, managed to defend Constantinople and at least part of their Balkan territories against the onslaughts of Slavs from northeastern Europe and Avar and Bulgar archers from the Inner Eurasia steppes. In the following two decades, however, Byzantium lost about half its territory and perhaps three-fourths of its agrarian and commercial resources, notably the grain harvests of the Nile valley, to Arab conquerors. In that century, Byzantine land and sea trade contracted, church building nearly ceased, and cities shrank or even disappeared as fighting and hard times persuaded Greek Christians to huddle behind urban walls or flee to fortified country villages. For example, the once-sprawling city of Athens in Greece dwindled to the area of the Acropolis, the town's central hill fort. On the other hand, Arab forces failed to break through Constantinople's stout landward walls, and in western Anatolia local militias of Greek soldier-farmers stood firm against all attacks.

The Byzantine response to these military crises was to restructure the much-reduced empire into an even more tightly centralized state than it already was. The emperors concentrated all bureaucratic power in Constantinople, built more frontier fortifications, closely regulated commerce and manufacturing, and raised taxes on the peasantry. Under Emperor Leo III (717–741), political and economic conditions became more stable. Byzantine gold coins circulated widely again, and Constantinople's population started to grow from a low in the later eighth century of around 300,000. Except for Baghdad after 800 C.E., Constantinople remained probably the biggest Afroeurasian city west of China.

Defensive action against invaders made Byzantine society culturally more uniform and self-contained. After the loss of its Syrian and Egyptian territories, most Christians remaining within the empire practiced Greek Orthodoxy. They believed that the church and its priesthood offered Christians the exclusive path to eternal salvation. They revered Constantinople as a sacred city, venerated the emperor as God's representative on earth, and regarded the security of church and empire as identical. One consequence of this was a deep cultural and religious conservatism that produced superb churches and decorative art but not much intellectual innovation.

The Greek emperors, who were expected to live up to Christian standards in their public moral behavior, exercised tight control over religious officials and institutions. They appointed all bishops, including the patriarch of Constantinople, who was the highest ranking priest. They also closely monitored Byzantium's numerous monasteries,

Constantinople. This map of the great city dates to the early fifteenth century, but it is the earliest one in existence. Set on hills above the Bosporus and the Sea of Marmara and surrounded by thick walls, the Byzantine capital repelled attacks by Avar, Bulgar, and Ummayad Muslim armies in the seventh and eighth centuries. Can you identify on the map the domed cathedral of Hagia Sophia?

whose pious monks safeguarded the accumulated learning of the Roman empire.

In the early ninth century, the Byzantine state had little resemblance to the Rome of old, but it was still an important regional power. It possessed productive farmlands and controlled the strategic maritime route that ran beneath the walls of Constantinople to connect the Black Sea with the Mediterranean. Moreover, periodic wars between the Byzantines and their Muslim neighbors by no means precluded commercial and diplomatic exchanges. We will see in later chapters that Byzantium's day was far from over.

Christian Society in Europe

In the later seventh century, when Arab Muslim forces were advancing westward across North Africa toward the Atlantic, peoples on the northern side of the Mediterranean were still working through the consequences of the armed invasions they had experienced more than two hundred years earlier. The Germanic migrants who overran western Europe in the fifth and sixth centuries finished off all that remained of Roman government, except for the relatively small territories where Byzantine authority held on for a few more hundred years. Once the Germanic populations settled down, they divided the region into several kingdoms. Extensive intermarriage and cultural mixing occurred between Germanic newcomers and previously Romanized populations, many of them descended from more ancient Celtic-speaking peoples. The major exception to this pattern was Spain, where Arab conquerors extinguished the Germanic kingdom of the Visigoths. The Muslim state that succeeded it embraced a diverse population of Germanic, Romanized, and Celtic people, plus Berber immigrants from North Africa and Arabs from as far away as Syria.

Western Europe in pieces. When the Roman imperial administration crumbled in western Europe under Germanic and Hunnic attack, the region's population plummeted, cities shrank or disappeared, and trade withered (see Chapter 9). Imperial coins no longer circulated much in Europe, except in Italy. Even there, the population of the city of Rome declined from as many as a million people in the first century c.e. to about fifty thousand in the seventh. The flow of pottery, spices, and other luxury goods from the eastern Mediterranean contracted, and most trade took place along local networks connecting villages and towns.

The process of cultural Romanization that had characterized western Europe for about four centuries shifted into reverse. For example, Latin remained vital as the language of the church, scholarship, and diplomacy, but it faded as a commonly spoken language. Moreover, Latin gradually spawned several regional variants that eventually evolved into the Romance, or "Roman" languages, including the ancestors of modern Italian, French, Spanish, Portuguese, and Romanian. In northern Europe, Germanic-speaking newcomers became numerous and politically powerful enough to tilt the linguistic balance in their favor, though with wide regional differentiation. English, German, Dutch, and the Scandinavian languages (except for Finnish) all evolved from Germanic grammatical structure and core vocabulary, though they also borrowed thousands of words from Latin or its Romance descendants. In eastern Europe, Slavic languages came to predominate. Today, Europeans speak about forty-five different languages. By stark contrast, the southern and eastern shores of the Mediterranean moved toward greater linguistic homogeneity. The early Arab Muslim empire embraced many tongues, but over several centuries Arabic gradually won out as the premier written and spoken language all the way from Iraq to Morocco.

As Europe's languages multiplied in the post-Roman era, so too did institutions of government and social order. Among the Slavic and Scandinavian populations of eastern Europe, kinship-based clan groups, rather than states, continued for a few more centuries as the basic political and social units. In central and western Europe, including Britain, around two hundred petty kingdoms emerged. These largely Germanic monarchies, however, were all small and weak compared to Byzantium or the Muslim Caliphate.

Germanic kings wore their royal titles proudly, but their authority depended on the sworn oaths and personal loyalties of kinsmen, warrior companions, and local chiefs, not on professional armies and bureaucrats. They had little direct control over local noble families, who carved new estates, or **manors** from Europe's forests, marshes, and abandoned Roman farmlands. Wars among noble families were common. Fighting often involved long sieges against enemies who holed up in hill forts and old Roman bastions.

> **manor** In medieval Europe, a landed estate; also the main house or castle on the estate.

Social inequality and the rise of serfdom.
Between the sixth and eighth centuries, European women and men of peasant status became generally less free. Population decline meant that farm workers were in shorter supply than they had been in Roman times. Needing to secure laborers, landlords coerced local people to work on estates or provide other services for so many days a year. In return, lords offered these men and women physical protection and rights to grow food on private plots. Though social and legal relations varied widely across Europe, many peasants became bound in a tangle of labor obligations that prohibited them from abandoning the estate to look for unoccupied land (of which there was plenty) to farm on their own. The term *serf*, a word derived from the Latin *servus*, originally meaning slave, described their unfree status. Serfdom differed from slavery mainly because serfs could not legally be bought and sold as chattels, that is, mere property. Slavery in fact declined in western Europe, not because kings and estate lords morally disapproved of it but because they lacked the military and administrative resources that the Romans had marshaled to control slaves. The institution remained more prominent in the Byzantine and Arab-ruled lands partly because those states had stronger military and police power. Nevertheless, European merchants continued to acquire and export slaves, many of them non-Christians from northern and eastern Europe, to markets in the Mediterranean.

The social flux that followed the breakup of western Rome did nothing to improve the status of European women. Slavery appears to have declined at a significantly slower rate for women than for men, and peasant women became serfs alongside fathers and husbands. Male members of rich families commonly married women "informally" or kept concubines, depriving these women of the wifely legal status that would otherwise assure them of rights to property. As in most premodern agrarian societies, aristocratic men routinely used marriageable young women as instruments of negotiation and alliance with other powerful families.

The Labors of the Months. Because so much medieval European art is concerned with the spiritual realm, historians prize imagery that reveals aspects of daily rural life. This painting from the era of Charlemagne is one example of a recurring artistic subject—the intimate relationship between earthly life and the changing seasons. How would you identify and interpret the activities depicted in each of the twelve scenes?

On the other hand, the favored wives of kings and nobles might exert significant political influence. Also, because the mortality rate among warrior nobles was high, widows frequently found themselves managing estates and inheriting extensive lands.

The Christian church as unifying force.
From the fifth to the eight centuries, the only social institution in Europe that became larger and more integrated rather than smaller and more fragmented was the Christian church. To establish its predominance in western Europe, it had to prevail over alternative versions of Christian faith. It achieved an important victory in the fifth and sixth centuries when most European kings and nobles renounced Arianism, the Christian variant that many Germanic chiefs had accepted earlier. A second success, which became apparent only gradually in the later first millennium C.E., was the emergence of the Patriarch of Rome as church leader effectively independent of both the Byzantine emperor and the patriarch of Constantinople. Claiming supremacy in the west,

pope The title used from about the ninth century to designate the head of the Christian church in western and central Europe.

this cleric came to assume the title of **pope** (from the Latin *papa*, or "father"). One important factor here was the Arab conquests, which further weakened Byzantine cultural influence in the western Mediterranean.

Like the Greek Christian organization, the Roman church had a hierarchical structure of authority extending from the pope down through regional bishops to village priests. Between the fifth and seventh centuries, bishops frequently provided the only government available in the shrinking towns of western Europe. From **cathedrals,** church officials exercised political as well as religious authority over neighboring areas, often collaborating with regional monarchs. Cathedral towns also became centers where Latin education and preservation of ancient texts continued and from which priests were trained and assigned to minister to local parishes (church districts).

cathedral A church that serves as the seat, or headquarters, of a Christian bishop; typically, a large church that attracts worshipers and pilgrims from a wide surrounding region.

Monasteries numbered in the hundreds in western Europe by 800. Founded as enclosed religious communities whose members devoted themselves to prayer, study, scholarship, and agricultural labor, monasteries were vital to the spread of Christian faith and learning. Popes, bishops, and kings typically allowed monasteries to govern their own affairs. Pious monks and nuns sometimes attained great prestige for their holiness, wisdom, and learning. These communities brought at least a smattering of literate culture to areas where there might be no towns at all. In far northern Europe and east of the Rhine River, the monasteries were the main instruments of Christian conversion. Because these houses aimed to be self-sufficient, monks and nuns not only grew their own food but sometimes cleared great tracts of woodland and planted large estates that rivaled those of local aristocrats. Like the cathedrals, monasteries served as centers of Latin education, text copying, and artistic creativity, sometimes deep in the forest-bound wilderness. At first, many European monastic communities allowed both men and women, though sexual segregation later became standard.

The monk and missionary Benedict of Nursia (480–550) contributed to Christian expansion by founding a "rule," that is a set of regulations for how monks and nuns should live and worship. The Benedictine rule emphasized, not monkish isolation, but vigorous communal life, scholarship, and missionary enterprise. The Benedictines, headquartered in Italy, established an intercommunicating network of monasteries that extended to the British Isles and eastward into Germany. In the later first millennium C.E., monks and nuns, many of them Benedictines, served as key agents of cultural integration and exchange across Europe. People in Ireland and northern Britain first embraced Christianity owing entirely to the work of monks (there is little early evidence of nuns in those places). The monks built thriving communities and produced gospel manuscripts whose stunning illuminations (elaborate calligraphy, designs, and images) appeared to bear almost no influence of Mediterranean Christian artistic traditions. Some Irish and English monks left their cloisters to become perpetual pilgrims, returning to continental Europe, bringing books with them and founding new communities. In effect, Europe was partially Christianized from north to south.

The rise and fall of the Frankish empire. In the eighth century, Charles the Great, or Charlemagne, made an energetic though short-lived attempt to reunify Europe, drawing on the agricultural resources and warrior power of the kingdom of the Franks centered on the Rhine River valley. A succession of three

Plan for the monastery of St. Gall. This model of a Swiss monastery is based on a building plan that monks drew up under Charlemagne's direction. This self-contained religious community includes a church, library, dormitories, guesthouse, orchard, garden, stables, bakery, brewery, and school. No one knows whether a monastery that looked exactly like this model was ever built.

The Book of Kells. One of the most celebrated works of Celtic Christian art, the wondrously decorated Book of Kells contains the four New Testament gospels in Latin. Created by Irish monks around 800 c.e., the intricate interlaced designs reveal pre-Christian artistic influences. This illustration portrays Christ enthroned.

the rule of Pepin's son Charlemagne (r. 768–814). These two men founded the new Carolingian dynasty (from the Latin name Carolus, or Charles). From their core territory in the Rhine River valley, Frankish armies conquered almost all of what are today France and Germany, pushing farther east than Roman legions had ever done. Charlemagne's forces also marched across the Alps to take northern Italy, and he extended Carolingian authority beyond the Pyrenees into northern Spain. Advancing into Hungary, Charlemagne destroyed the Turkic Avar state, which had long harassed Byzantium. In these campaigns, Frankish aristocrats weighted both themselves and their horses with iron armor, successfully adopting heavy cavalry, or cataphract techniques introduced from Sasanid Persia by way of Byzantium. The stirrup, an Inner Eurasian invention, also came into wide use in western Europe as a device that gave a rider more stability on horseback, though Carolingian fighters typically galloped into battle, then dismounted to fight with sword and axe.

Pepin and Charlemagne regarded themselves as champions of the church. Their close alliance with it had two important consequences. One was to advance the Christianizing of central Europe. By conquering the pagan Saxons in northeastern Germany, Charlemagne opened that region to rapid conversion, and he encouraged the founding of more monasteries east of the Rhine. He also aimed to raise society's standards of moral behavior and expectation by systematizing church teachings, educating priests, and eliminating such pagan practices as polygamy and "informal marriage" for men. In 800, Pope Leo III crowned Charlemagne Emperor of the Romans, a move that symbolized both revived hopes for a new Christian Roman empire and the growing gap between the Latin and Greek churches. Irene, the Byzantine empress at the time, vigorously objected to the pope's act, but she could do nothing about it.

The second consequence of Carolingian piety was a surge of creative activity in western Europe, especially in the later decades of Charlemagne's reign. In 794 he founded a new capital at Aachen (Aix-la-Chapelle) west of the Rhine and there presided over what scholars have named the "Carolingian renaissance." Though he supported fine architecture and art (and tried without much success to start building a western version of Constantinople), he was interested primarily in the written word. He founded a royal library to collect and preserve Greek, Roman, and Christian texts. He assembled a kind of medieval "think tank" of scholars from around Europe to copy texts accurately and to educate priests, monks, nuns, and young children,

rulers led this imperial venture, beginning with Charlemagne's grandfather, Charles Martel (r. 714–741). This Germanic aristocrat was not king but rather "mayor of the palace," a position he used to direct state affairs under the Merovingian dynasty, a feeble line of rulers that proved incapable of active governance. After Muslim forces invaded Spain, numerous Arab-led raiding bands crossed the Pyrenees Mountains into Frankish territory. Martel repelled a large Arab force near the city of Tours in France's Loire Valley in 732. Historians have traditionally celebrated Martel for saving European Christendom from Arab Muslim invasion. More recently, historians have questioned whether the Arab forays, including the one against Tours, would ever have escalated into a determined invasion north of the Pyrenees.

In 741 the pope anointed Martel's son Pepin king of the Franks, but the drive for empire accelerated rapidly under

Two Views of the Battle of Tours

Not long after the Battle of Tours (sometimes called the Battle of Poitiers), both European and Arab chroniclers began to record accounts of this contest. These narratives describe the event from different, sometimes contradictory, perspectives. Modern historians have not been able to reconcile all these accounts, but they can analyze them comparatively and make informed judgments about their relative reliability. The first selection below comes from the Chronicle of 754, a narrative of Spanish history in the seventh and eighth centuries. The author, an anonymous Christian who lived under Muslim rule somewhere in Spain, composed the text in Latin, probably not long after 754. The author of the second selection was an Arabic-speaking Muslim. This individual's identity is also unknown. An early-nineteenth-century Spanish historian quoted this writer anonymously in a work on Muslim Spain based largely on early Arabic documents in Spanish archives.

Abd al-Rahman Al-Ghafiki, an officer of the Umayyad Caliphate, led the Arab and Berber soldiers that approached Tours in 732. Charles Martel is identified as leader of Franks from Austrasia, a territory that was part of the kingdom of the Franks.

DOCUMENT 1 A Christian View

Then Abd al-Rahman, seeing the land filled with the multitude of his army, crossed the Pyrenees, and traversed the defiles [in the mountains] and the plains, so that he penetrated ravaging and slaying clear into the lands of the Franks. . . . Whereupon Abd al-Rahman . . . destroyed palaces, burned churches, and imagined he could pillage the basilica of St. Martin of Tours. It is then that he found himself face to face with the lord of Austrasia, Charles [Martel], a mighty warrior from his youth, and trained in all the occasions of arms.

For almost seven days the two armies watched one another, waiting anxiously the moment for joining the struggle. Finally they made ready for combat. And in the shock of the battle the men of the North seemed like a sea that cannot be moved. Firmly they stood, one close to another, forming as it were a bulwark of ice; and with great blows of their swords they hewed down the Arabs. . . . At last night sundered the combatants. The Franks with misgivings lowered their blades, and beholding the numberless tents of the Arabs, prepared themselves for another battle the next day. Very early, . . . the men of Europe saw the Arab tents ranged still in order, in the same place where they had set up their camp. . . . In fact, during the night they had fled with the greatest silence, seeking with all speed their home land.

DOCUMENT 2 A Muslim View

The Muslims smote their enemies, and passed the river Garonne, and laid waste the country, and took captives without number. And that army went through all places like a desolating storm. . . . All the nations of the Franks trembled at that terrible army, and they betook them to [Charles Martel], and told him of the havoc made by the Muslim horsemen, and how they rode at their will through all the land of Narbonne, Toulouse, and Bordeaux. . . . Then the king bade them be of good cheer, and offered to aid them. . . . He mounted his horse, and he took with him a host that could not be numbered, and went against the Muslims. And he came upon them at the great city of Tours. . . .

Near the river [Loire], the two great hosts of the two languages and the two creeds were set in array against each other. The hearts of Abd al-Rahman, his captains and his men were filled with wrath and pride, and they were the first to begin to fight. The Muslim horsemen dashed . . . forward against the battalions of the Franks, who resisted manfully, and many fell dead on either side, until the going down of the sun. Night parted the two armies: but in the grey of the morning the Muslims returned to the battle. Their cavaliers had soon hewn their way into the center of the Christian host. But many of the Muslims were fearful for the safety of the spoil which they had stored in their tents; . . . whereupon several squadrons of the Muslim horsemen rode off to protect their tents. . . . And while Abd al-Rahman strove to check their tumult, and to lead them back to battle, the warriors of the Franks came around him, and he was pierced through with many spears, so that he died. Then all the host fled before the enemy, and many died in the flight.

Sources: Chronicle of 754, "Isidore of Beja's Chronicle" (Chronicle of 754), English translation from Internet Medieval Sourcebook, http://www.fordham.edu/halsall/sbook2.asp. The principal edition of the *Chronicle of 754* is J. E. Lopez Perreira, *Estudio critico sobre la Cronica Mozarabe de 754* (Zaragoza: Anubar, 1980). Anonymous Arab chronicler quoted in Jose Antonio Condé, *History of the Dominion of the Arabs in Spain,* trans. Mrs. Jonathan Foster, vol. 1 (London: Henry G. Bohn, 1854), 108–111.

Thinking Critically

What do the selections tell you about why and where the two adversaries fought the Battle of Tours? Which passages in these two selections appear to corroborate each other? Which passages appear to be inconsistent? Which words or phrases suggest religious or political bias on the part of one author or the other? How do the two authors appear to regard the courage and fighting qualities of both armies?

mainly boys and girls from aristocratic families. He even learned to read Latin and a little Greek (though he never got the hang of how to write). Finally, Carolingian scribes, working partly from experiments undertaken in women's monasteries, perfected a clearer, simpler alphabetic system called Caroline script (or Carolingian minuscule), which stimulated written communication in western Europe. This script is close to the "Roman" alphabet we use today.

In the political sphere, Charlemagne made a start at organizing the existing jumble of Roman and Germanic customary law and creating a rudimentary central bureaucracy to collect taxes and enforce royal decrees. As a ruler on the northern periphery of urban civilization, he made a large enough impression on the Abbasid Caliphate that the two states exchanged a number of diplomatic missions, one of them including an albino elephant—a gift from Caliph Harun al-Rashid to the Carolingian court. (The elephant, no doubt miserable in cold Europe, died within a few years.) Recent historical research has shown that in the Carolingian period both regional European and trans-Mediterranean trade began to liven, and it involved growing commercial exchange between Europeans and the subjects of Muslim states. Also, larger numbers of Christians made long pilgrimages to Palestine to visit the holy sites in Jerusalem, which was under Muslim rule. One of the busiest commercial and pilgrimage routes ran from central Europe down the Danube River to the Black Sea and from there to Constantinople and Palestine beyond.

Charlemagne's death in 814 signaled the empire's rapid decline. Whatever grand title the pope gave the monarch, his authority ultimately rested mainly on the personal loyalty of the Frankish nobility. Louis, Charlemagne's son and heir, showed himself to be a much less effective leader. Because he could not perpetuate territorial expansion, he could not ensure aristocratic allegiance by promising booty and new estates. The reunification of Europe was aborted, and the region entered a new period of political and social turbulence.

Dwindling Christian Society in North Africa

Between the fourth and early seventh centuries, Mediterranean Africa may have been on the way to becoming as thoroughly Christian as Europe did. Owing to quarrels over church organization and leadership, however, Christian practice among North Africans tended to be divisive. The Arab invasion in the seventh century further split Christian communities from one another. Islamic conversion accelerated, and within a few centuries Christianity mostly

Pope Leo III crowns Charlemagne Emperor of the Romans. This ceremony, illustrated in an early medieval manuscript, worked to the advantage of both parties. Charlemagne acquired an elevated title, and the pope cast himself as a maker of emperors. How would you identify the other figures in the picture?

disappeared in the regions that are today Tunisia, Algeria, and Morocco. Judaism, on the other hand, did not decline. In fact, the Jewish minority in those regions grew larger, perhaps because Arab unification stimulated Jewish merchants, artisans, and farmers to settle there, as well as in Spain.

Only in Egypt did a sizable Christian population survive on the southern Mediterranean rim. When Arab forces invaded the Nile valley in the mid-seventh century, they expelled the priestly representatives of the Greek Orthodox Church, but they allowed Monophysite Christians, of which there were many, to worship as a protected group. Monophysite doctrine, contrary to Greek Orthodoxy, gave primacy to Christ's spiritual nature over his humanity (see Chapter 9). Under Muslim rule the Egyptian church took on a distinctive identity, anointing its own patriarch and using Coptic, a late version of ancient Egyptian written in a modified Greek alphabet, as its language of worship. In the ensuing centuries, the Coptic community continued to flourish, though shrinking slowly relative to the number of Muslims. Today, Egypt's Christian population is about 9 percent of the total.

Up the Nile valley in Nubia (southern Egypt and northern Sudan), the Christian communities that flourished between

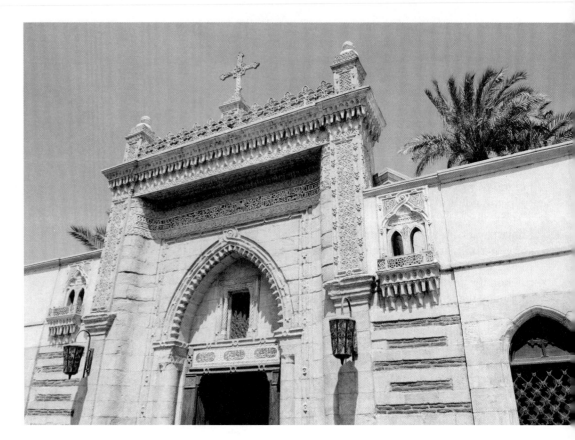

St. Mary's church in Cairo. Built originally in the seventh century, this sanctuary became the residence of the patriarch, or head of the Monophysite Coptic church, in the eleventh century. The building is also called the Hanging Church because it was erected above the gatehouse of a Roman fort.

the fifth and seventh centuries gradually faded away. After the Arabs conquered Egypt, Orthodox Christians in Nubia managed to stay in communication with Constantinople and the Greek church. Muslim traders, preachers, and pastoral nomadic groups, however, entered the region in ever-growing numbers. In the early second millennium C.E., Islam replaced Christianity in Nubia as the faith of the great majority. Southeast of the Nile, however, the Monophysite church in Ethiopia continued to thrive.

East Asia: Return to Unity in China

FOCUS What consequences did the unification of China under the Sui and Tang dynasties have for the region's economic and cultural development?

Paralleling the political unification of Southwest Asia under Muslim rulers, two successive dynasties, the Sui (SWAY) and the Tang, restored strong central government in China, absent since the collapse of the Han empire in the early third century (see Map 10.4). In 581 a military coalition whose leaders were a mix of Chinese and Turkic aristocrats conquered northern China, proclaimed the Sui dynasty (581–618), and then advanced south to the Yangzi valley. Within a decade, northern and southern China were united

once again. The two emperors of the Sui appealed to Chinese Buddhists for support and attempted to extend their authority along the Inner Eurasian frontier, as well as in southwestern China, Vietnam, and the Korean peninsula. When the Sui armies became overextended, however, civil war allowed Li Yuan, an insurgent military officer of both Chinese and Turkic descent, to seize the imperial throne in 618 and proclaim the Tang dynasty. In the more than three centuries of Sui and Tang rule, China experienced periods of both internal struggle and foreign invasion. But the Confucian model of the emperor and his hierarchy of scholar-bureaucrats as the "natural" leaders of a unified China became reality once again.

The Tang State

Up to about 750, the Tang state advanced China's political, economic, and cultural integration. This consolidation occurred mainly under four emperors: Taizong (r. 626–649), Gaozong (r. 649–683), the Empress Wu (r. 690–705), and Xuanzong (r. 712–756). As Gaozong's wife and then ruler in her own right, Wu dominated state affairs for about half a century. Though all these rulers patronized Buddhism to one degree or another, they managed state affairs according to Confucian principles of centralized command exercised through public ministries that reached down to the local level. Ideally, bureaucratic officers were sworn to

MAP 10.4 Sui and Tang empires, 589–907.
Why do you think the Tang empire narrows to a long neck of territory between northern China and Inner Eurasia?

reasonable, sympathetic administration and selfless service to the state. The government examination system, initiated in the era of the Han dynasty, was expanded greatly to educate prospective officials in the Confucian classics. Students who performed well on the exhausting tests received assignments to imperial administrative posts. The exam takers were mostly sons of wealthy landowning families, but because intelligence, diligence, and ambition were requisite qualifications for service, not simply circumstances of birth, young men who had financial sponsorship might rise from the peasantry to positions of responsibility.

Like the Emperor Justinian in sixth-century Byzantium, the Tang rulers sought to unify the empire by implementing a rational, uniform, and efficient legal system. The Tang Code followed Confucian principles in envisioning society as constituting a hierarchy of three groups: (1) the privileged class of ranking officials and imperial courtiers; (2) commoners, who made up the vast majority of peasants and town folk; and (3) "inferior people," such as slaves and others in a condition of personal bondage. The code also had numerous statutes that perpetuated legal and social inequality between men and women. A man, for example, was legally entitled to beat his wife, but a woman who killed her husband was subject to severe penalty.

Stabilizing the peasantry. The early Tang emperors aimed to put as much arable land as possible to the plow, alleviate insecurity and poverty that might ignite rural protests, and make the huge peasant class productive enough to pay regular taxes. To this end, they adopted an institution known as the **equal-field system,** an idea initiated by an earlier regional dynasty. By this policy, the state allocated arable land to individual peasant families to farm for their lifetime, the amount of acreage depending mainly on the family's size and wealth. In some cases, a family could pass on its property to the next generation, especially if the farm produced silk and therefore had to have mulberry trees that took more than a generation to mature. As for aristocratic families, the state (with varying success) put limits on the amount of land they could own in order to reduce the number of peasants who served as tenants or day workers on giant estates.

Through the equal-field system, the Tang also aimed to build a militia of farmer-soldiers who worked their acreage part of the year and gave military service the rest. Here,

> **equal-field system** The Chinese system for state distribution of land; the state assigned fixed acreages of crop land to families on the basis of labor, both adult males and animals, available to work it.

The Empress Wu: Patron of Buddhism

An eighteenth-century Chinese artist's imagining of the Empress Wu Zetian.

Empress Wu Zetian (625–705), the only woman ever to rule China in her own right, was one of the Tang era's most enthusiastic patrons of Buddhist devotion and art. She entered the Tang imperial court as a concubine of Emperor Taizong. At the time, she was between thirteen and sixteen years old. The young girl's command of literature and history soon earned her the emperor's favor. But his death a decade later left her facing a future as a Buddhist nun, the expected path for a concubine of a deceased monarch.

Instead of retiring to a monastery, however, Wu attracted the attention of Taizong's son, the new Emperor Gaozong. She eventually rose to the position of primary consort, or companion of the emperor, by giving birth to sons. She also bore a daughter, then accused Gaozong's wife, Empress Wang, of murdering the baby. Empress Wang was disgraced and killed, and in 655 Wu became Gaozong's new wife.

Within five years, however, Gaozong suffered a crippling stroke. This crisis offered Wu the opportunity to serve as ruler, first in the name of the incapacitated Gaozong and after his death in 683 as regent for her docile and submissive sons. In 690 she proclaimed herself the legitimate monarch and declared a new dynasty, the Zhou, a name that invoked the long-enduring Zhou dynasty of the first millennium B.C.E.

Traditional Confucian doctrines did not allow for the possibility of a female ruler. But Empress Wu sought to counter that ideology by patronizing Buddhism, which embodied a somewhat less constricted view of women's social roles. She promoted the cult of the Bodhisattva Maitreya, a figure prophesied to return in the body of a woman to rule over a golden age. She supported Buddhist temples and translations of important religious texts into Chinese. Reversing the policy of earlier Tang emperors, she gave Buddhists precedence over Daoists in imperial court rituals. She is best remembered for sponsoring the carving of spectacular statues of the Buddha and other divines in the Longmen Grottoes. These are niches and shallow caves excavated from the limestone cliffs above the Yishui River near Luoyang, where Wu spent her entire reign.

Besides shoring up support for her reign through these cultural avenues, Wu engaged in apparently ruthless palace politics, including possible assassination of a son and recruitment of a secret police force that ferreted out and brutally punished anyone who challenged her authority. It is difficult, however, to accurately assess her actions, since conservative Confucian scholars who wrote about her reign consistently portrayed her as a dangerous woman occupying the imperial throne in opposition to the natural order of the universe. Around 700, in any case, her health deteriorated, and she relied increasingly on the advice of two men who were not only counselors but also lovers. In 705 Wu's son Zhongzong joined a group of court officials who conspired to kill these advisers. Zhongzong then seized the emperorship, declaring the end of the short-lived Zhou dynasty and the restoration of the Tang. Empress Wu gave no resistance and moved to a residence outside the palace, where she died later that year.

Thinking Critically

What strategies were available to Empress Wu to advance her political ambitions?

---

the state wished to fashion an army whose core units were hardy, well-trained, loyal peasants, not nomad mercenaries from the steppe. Many of these soldiers, who clad themselves in iron armor and specialized in archery, did duty on the northern and western frontiers facing Inner Eurasia.

Integrating north and south. The task of militarily and politically integrating the East Asian land mass and its seventh-century population of about 60 million demanded strategic and technical innovation. The unified Roman

empire had had the advantage of the Mediterranean Sea, a giant central "lake" for moving soldiers, supplies, messages, and commercial goods long distances at costs much lower than overland transport allowed. The Tang emperors, by contrast, had no "middle sea" to speed communication. The Yellow and Yangzi Rivers, the two most important transport corridors, flowed generally west to east. The principal grain staple in the north was wheat; in the south it was rice. To encourage greater commercial integration between the two great river valleys, the Tang government undertook construction of the Grand Canal, an enormous, centrally directed engineering project to link the two great river basins by a series of north–south waterways. The state conscripted tens of thousands of laborers to do the digging, and evidence suggests that a majority of those workers were peasant women. The canal functioned primarily to supply the Chinese administration and army, which was concentrated heavily in the north, with the rice and other food products of the warmer, wetter south. Imperial roads ran alongside the canal, and numerous subsidiary channels, rivers, and tracks connected the central line to provincial cities and rural hinterlands.

Tang engineers also built a canal that extended westward to the Tang capital of Chang'an (modern Xian) near the Wei River, a tributary of the Yellow. From this imperial city, whose outer walls of brick and pounded earth extended more than five miles on each side, the royal palace and six major ministries managed affairs of state. The emperor obliged independent-minded aristocrats, especially from the south, to establish residences in Chang'an in order to keep them under close watch. The presence of this elite meant that tens of thousands of farmers, artisans, soldiers, merchants, entertainers, and servants also had to be on hand to meet aristocratic needs. Chang'an also accommodated thousands of non-Chinese residents. Until the later eighth century, the Tang government took a broadminded view of foreigners who came to trade, preach their faith, or enlist in the army or civil service. The estate-owning classes also wanted the luxury imports that merchants brought in on the silk roads or through southern China's seaports, especially Guangzhou (Canton). Consequently, Turks, Sogdians, Persians, Tibetans, Koreans, Japanese, Nestorian Christians, Manicheans, and Jews all circulated in Chang'an's streets and bazaars.

Urban Chinese also acquired enthusiastic tastes for the arts of Inner Eurasia, Persia, and India. Musicians and entertainers traveled the silk roads to seek work in Chang'an and other cities. Distant kingdoms paid tribute to the Tang royal court by sending orchestras and dance troops. These visitors brought with them musical instruments, compositional styles, and dances that influenced more traditional Chinese musical arts. Both noble households and popular urban crowds enjoyed Inner Eurasian lute players, drummers, acrobats, magicians, puppeteers, and fire eaters, as well as a company of girls who danced and twirled on top of large rolling balls. Not all educated Chinese, however, approved of so many foreigners from the "west" crowding into their cities. One Tang poet wrote:

> Ever since the alien horsemen began raising smut and dust,
> Fur and fleece, rank and rancid, have filled Hsien
> [Chang'an] and Luo [Luoyang, another Tang capital]
> Women make themselves western matrons by the study
>   of western makeup,
> Entertainers present western tunes, in their devotion to
>   western music.[3]

Counting both Chinese and expatriate residents, the population of Chang'an in the seventh and eighth centuries may have reached between one and two million, making it the largest city in the world, bigger than either Constantinople or Baghdad.

The Tang imperial thrust. Military campaigns of the first Tang century pushed Chinese imperial power from the Yangzi valley to both the subtropical coastlands of the far south and into Vietnam. For a time, the Tang also dominated part of Korea. The most spectacular campaigns, however, took place to the northwest. Emperor Taizong and the Empress Wu after him triumphed over pastoral nomads on the eastern steppes. Deftly combining military might with aggressive diplomacy, the Tang government helped engineer the collapse of the Eastern Türk empire and forced numerous war chiefs to accept Chinese suzerainty. Like the Han expansion seven hundred years earlier, these offensives aimed to expand the state's control of commerce as far across Inner Eurasia as logistically possible. The army also had an insatiable demand for horses, which the Ferghana valley in modern Tajikistan could steadily supply. Only after

Musicians of the Tang era.
These terra-cotta figures from the seventh century represent female entertainers playing a drum and a Chinese lute.

Arab forces vanquished a Chinese army northwest of Ferghana in 751 and after numerous internal problems arose within the empire did the Tang rulers pull back from their extended Inner Eurasian frontiers.

Migrations to the South

In the sphere of demographic and social change, the Tang era witnessed a steady shift of the geographical center of China's population from the Yellow River valley to the Yangzi. Chinese farmers equipped with iron hoes, axes, and plows had already been moving southward for several centuries. Their reasons for migrating included overcrowding on northern grain land, the perennial threat of nomad attack, and the north's fickle climate, which periodically brought drought and famine. As more Han Chinese farmers headed south, ancient local peoples of non-Chinese ethnicity either assimilated to the growing Chinese population through intermarriage and cultural conversion or retreated to inaccessible highlands.

The pioneering Chinese who settled the south had an enormous impact on East Asia's economic development and integration. They drained river valleys and marshes, leveled fields, and constructed dams, dykes, and canals. The draining projects also improved human prospects by reducing mortality from malaria and waterborne diseases. Transforming southern China into the urban, commercialized dynamo it became required generations of peasant labor. From the economic and social perspective, the long-term payoff was rapid population growth in the south and greatly intensified exchange of commodities and manufactures with China.

Cultural Integration

Culturally, China remained a jumble of languages and ethnic groups, but Chinese speakers, generally called Han Chinese, became progressively dominant in the south. There, literate Chinese introduced the written language, and Confucian scholars and officials exercised growing influence. Consequently, at the level of elite culture and manners, north and south fused gradually. In this respect, the Chinese script, purged by this time of most of its regional variants, served the same intellectually unifying purpose as Latin did in western Europe and Arabic in Southwest Asia and North Africa. Chinese poetry, for example, matured as a major form of literary expression throughout the Tang empire.

Tang patronage of Buddhism. Buddhism, which silk road monks and merchants introduced to China in the first century C.E., also became an important unifying force in the Tang era. Recognizing Buddhism's surging popularity and the value of identifying themselves with a universalist

Vairochana Buddha. Chinese Buddhists adopted the Indian tradition of carving images of the Buddha in rock. Caves and niches cut from sandstone cliffs at Longmen, a site on the Yi River near Luoyang, contain more than 100,000 statues of the Buddha of varying sizes. Empress Wu sponsored creation of the cave containing the Vairochana, or Resplendent Buddha, which is about forty-nine feet high. What qualities of character do you think this Buddha displays?

system of morality and worship, the early Tang emperors patronized Buddhist monasteries and convents enthusiastically. They sponsored thousands of new monastic communities, libraries, and stupas (shrines to house relics of the Buddha), as well as rock carvings and cave paintings of the Buddha, Buddhist saints (*bodhisattvas*), and other aesthetic imagery. The emperors liked to represent themselves as models of sacred Buddhist kingship, the Emperor Taizong even identifying himself vaguely with Ashoka, the great monarch and Buddhist patron of India in the third century B.C.E. (see Chapter 6). Chinese monks traveled to India in increasing numbers to visit shrines and collect religious texts. The Chinese cleric Xuanzang (596–664), whose description of the Türk monarch we quoted earlier in this chapter, crossed Inner Eurasia to reach India, returned home after sixteen years to the acclaim of the imperial court, and became a skilled translator of Sanskrit writings into Chinese.

Buddhists meet the Confucian and Daoist traditions. As much as Buddhist statuary and painting impressed ordinary Chinese, monks and scholars still had their work cut out for them putting scriptures in South Asian languages into words that made sense in East Asia. They had to express their religious concepts and moral values in ways that might resonate with Chinese people whose framework of thought and action had a Confucian orientation. Confucians stressed responsibility to family members, so Buddhists argued that *bodhisattvas* would help entire families along the road to salvation. Buddhists linked the Confucian concept of respect for authority to the Indian idea of *karuma,* or all-encompassing compassion. Confucian scholars valued quiet study and contemplation, which Buddhist teachings endorsed warmly.

Daoism, the other major Chinese belief system, shared with Buddhism the yearnings women and men had for health, inner peace, salvation, and immortality. Buddhists found they could connect quite easily with Daoist thought, which encouraged individuals to extricate themselves from worldly affairs and strive for spiritual oneness with cosmic reality. The Daoist tradition offered a private, meditative counterpoint to the incessant Confucian demand to manage and improve society. Buddhists represented themselves as offering Chinese seekers even richer inner experience, complementing more than competing with Daoist beliefs and practices. The Buddhist concept of *dharma,* which means at one level to behave righteously and at another to live in harmony with deepest reality, was linked to the *dao,* the divine principle of being. The state of *nirvana* was associated with *wuwei,* the Daoist concept of "non-action," or utter peace. In the later first millennium C.E., the Buddhist and Daoist traditions became so deeply intermingled that few Chinese thought about the precise differences between them.

Buddhism succeeded brilliantly in demonstrating its universalist appeal in China. Distinctly Chinese schools of Buddhist thought began to emerge. Chinese devotees, both aristocratic families and rural villagers, donated wealth to monasteries, and Chinese styles of Buddhist art and architecture evolved. In the first flush of Buddhist success, Confucian scholarship went into partial eclipse. But neither Buddhism nor Daoism aimed deliberately to contradict or compete with Confucian ideals that promoted harmonious family relations, social order, and good government.

A Chinese traveler. A fourteenth-century portrait of the Chinese monk Xuangzang returning from his journey to India depicts him carrying a bamboo backpack filled with scrolls. He holds a flywhisk to drive away evil spirits in one hand and a prayer scroll in the other.

• • •

Conclusion

A military strategist with a bird's-eye view of Afroeurasia in the mid-eighth century might have predicted that Arab Muslim armies were about to conquer the entire hemisphere north of the tropics. Arab forces reached Chinese-occupied territory on the northern silk route, and according to Muslim tradition, an early caliph offered the governorship of China to whichever of his generals got there first. In the west, military operations in the early eighth century might have looked like a grand pincer operation against Europe, as Arab commanders advanced simultaneously on Constantinople and Spain. As we have seen, however, the Arab Muslim juggernaut faltered, if only because invasions of China and all of Europe were beyond the technological and logistical powers of the new Muslim governments based in Southwest Asia. Nevertheless, for the first time in history, a powerful state and an emerging new religious and cultural tradition encompassed most of Southeast Asia and the eastern Mediterranean. With the Byzantine frontiers pushed back and the Sasanid empire destroyed, the land between Syria and Mesopotamia was no longer a "shatter zone" of chronic conflict between competing empires but the heart of a new and creative civilization.

The political and cultural integration of Southwest Asia under Muslim leadership helped fuel a new surge of urbanization, production, and commerce that stimulated long-distance trade linking that region to the rest of Afroeurasia. Probably even more important for trans-hemispheric exchange, China moved into a new era of economic growth in connection with the Sui and Tang unification. Given its dense population and rich resources, China's agricultural and manufacturing potential far exceeded all other Afroeurasian regions with the exception of India.

In the far west, temperate Europe began, starting in the seventh century, to recover from the wreckage of the western Roman empire and to restructure itself along new economic and political lines. In Spain, Arab conquerors, with help from engineers, architects, and irrigation experts who arrived from Southwest Asia, laid the foundations of a small but flourishing Muslim civilization. To the northeast, the Frankish conqueror Charlemagne tried to pull together a new pan-European state founded on Roman Christian culture. This experiment, however, did not outlast him. Most of Europe remained an aggregate of competing political entities, though this did not stop population and production from starting to rise.

Other forces also helped set the stage for a new era of economic growth and commercial exchange from the Mediterranean to East Asia. South Asia, though divided into a number of states, continued to churn out great quantities of cotton textiles and other products for export. The maritime network of merchants and shippers plying the southern seas from China to East Africa had been growing for centuries and was primed for more traffic. Tang and Arab expansion in Inner Eurasia, plus successful pastoral nomadic state-building there, kept the silk roads in business with few interruptions. Western and central Europe had to face serious new external threats in the ninth century, but within less than two hundred years that region was also poised for a burst of economic activity that would in time far surpass the achievement of western Rome. Finally, after two hundred years of microbial assaults, recurrences of plague faded out about 705 in the Mediterranean and Southwest Asian lands.

In short, Afroeurasia as a whole moved in the sixth century and (in some places somewhat later) into a new growth phase. From a millennial low of less than 190 million in 700 C.E., Afroeurasia's population rose to about 235 million by 1000, an increase correlated broadly with a revival of agrarian production, more vigorous trade, and proliferation in the size and number of cities.[4] This trend would continue with only modest dips for another three centuries.

● ● ●

Key Terms

Arab empire 281
Benedictines 294
caliph 287
Carolingian renaissance 295
cathedral 294
Eastern and Western Türk empires 301
equal-field system 299

Franks 294
hijra 286
imam 289
Islam 283
Khazar empire 281
manor 293
pope 294
Quran (Koran) 279

serf 293
Shi'a Muslims 289
Sui dynasty 298
Sunni Muslims 289
Tang dynasty 281
Tibetan empire 281
Uighur empire 281
Umayyad dynasty 288

Change over Time

552–744	Eastern and then Western Türk empires dominate steppes of Inner Eurasia.
570–632	The Prophet Muhammad preaches one God and founds a state in Arabia.
581–618	The Sui dynasty restores strong central government to China.
618–842	The Tibetan empire of the Tibetan plateau is a major player in Inner Eurasian politics.
618–907	The Tang dynasty integrates and expands Chinese territory.
622	Muhammad and his followers flee from Mecca to Madina (*hijra*); the Muslim calendar begins.
630–965	The Khazar empire, the longest-lasting Turkic-speaking state of the era, dominates Inner Eurasia.
632–661	The Muslim community is led by the first four caliphs.
661–750	The Umayyad Caliphate centered in Damascus leads a major expansion of the Arab state.
744–840	The Uighur empire in Inner Eurasia commands the eastern end of the silk roads.
750	The Umayyad government falls to Abbasids; the Abbasid Caliphate begins.
768–814	Charlemagne reigns over the kingdom of the Franks; "Carolingian renaissance."

Please see end of book reference section for additional reading suggestions related to this chapter.

11 State Power and Expanding Networks of Exchange

750–1000 C.E.

ot many years ago, some technology experts predicted that the computer revolution would spell the end of paper. So far, that has not happened. The human race continues to consume vast and increasing quantities of paper as a cheap, smooth-surfaced material for inscribing messages. Annual production of paper and paperboard worldwide exceeds 400 million metric tons. In the period we investigate in this chapter, people began to use paper across Afroeurasia on a significant scale. In the second century B.C.E., or perhaps earlier, Chinese artisans invented a way to fabricate paper by suspending pieces of flax, hemp, textile rags, or mulberry tree bark in a mixture of water and lye. This concoction was then cooked and pounded to break up the fibers, leaving a mushy pulp of cellulose. The next steps were to dip a framed fabric screen into a pan of the cellulose, spread the pulp over the surface, and set it out to dry. Finally, the artisan peeled the dried sheet off the screen and cut it into pieces of required size.

The secret of papermaking spread eastward to Korea and Japan in the early centuries C.E. and westward along the Inner Eurasian silk roads a few hundred years later. According to a traditional story, Arab soldiers advancing into Inner Eurasia in the eighth century took several Chinese paper experts prisoner and marched them to Baghdad in Iraq to build a mill. More likely, artisans were already manufacturing paper in Central Asian cities far west of China, and they passed the technology to the Arabs. In any case, paper became

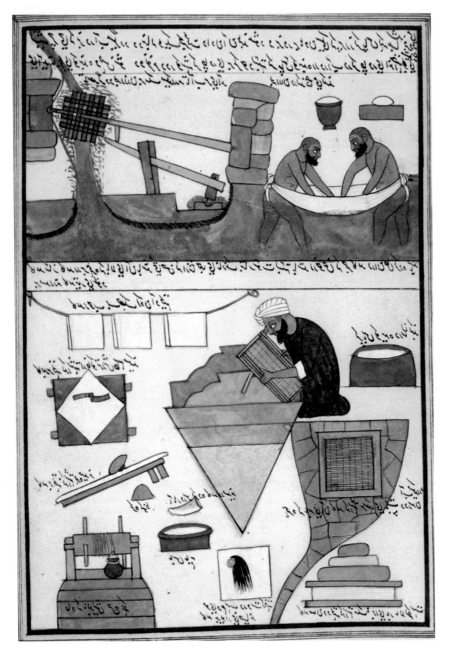

Traditional Muslim paper manufacturing is illustrated in the *Album of Kashmiri Trades,* a text of the mid-nineteenth century.

common in India, the Mediterranean basin, and Europe in the following three hundred years. Its use began to revolutionize human ability to record, transmit, and store information of all kinds.

The diffusion of paper technology is one example of the upward trend of social, cultural, and economic complexity that characterized Afroeurasia as a whole in these centuries. Around 600 C.E., long-distance commercial and cultural exchange began to pick up across the hemisphere, and this trend continued, with some fluctuations, for the next seven hundred years. Merchants, missionaries, pilgrims, and scholars moved in unprecedented numbers along land and sea routes. By rough estimates, Afroeurasia's overall population appears to have declined slightly between 400 and 700 C.E. but then jumped by nearly 50 percent in the next three hundred years. Demographic growth reflected and in turn stimulated expansion and greater complexity in farming, manufacturing, and technical knowledge, including, for example, the diffusion of paper.

This chapter starts by surveying developments in the central region of Afroeurasia, where Arabic-speaking rulers professing Islam, the youngest of the major religions, united most of Southwest Asia. The first Arab empire, created in the later seventh century under the Umayyad dynasty, extended far beyond that region, but it lasted less than a century. After 750 C.E., the Abbasid Caliphate, the second Muslim royal dynasty, continued to rule Southwest Asia but lost direct control of more distant lands, where new kingdoms multiplied. From Spain to northwestern India, however, these kingdoms were all Muslim.

Following the rise of the Abbasid state, commercial exchange along the chain of seas from the Persian Gulf to the South China Sea intensified dramatically. Farmers and artisans produced commodities that could be sold far and wide, and merchants became more sophisticated, forming larger trading diasporas to connect ports over long distances and inventing better methods for transporting goods and exchanging money. In the second part of the chapter, we take a tour along the chain of seas, stopping to investigate developments in the Arabian Sea basin, maritime Southeast Asia, China, and finally Japan and Korea.

The third section of the chapter introduces a new arena of human interchange, the rim of the Sahara Desert. Merchants who learned how to guide dromedary camels from one side of that wilderness to another without dying along the way blazed the first caravan trails, permanently joining the Mediterranean with tropical West Africa. Agrarian states already existed in West Africa when the trans-Saharan trade got under way, but exchange of gold, slaves, copper, salt, and other commodities inspired larger state-building projects, notably

Chapter Outline

MUSLIM POWER AND PROSPERITY

From Damascus to Baghdad:
The Abbasid Empire
Rival Centers of Muslim Power
The Byzantine Resurgence
Islam on New Frontiers
A "Green Revolution" in Muslim Lands
Muslim Urban Society
The Stream of Ideas

INDIVIDUALS MATTER Abu Bakr al-Razi: Muslim Physician

CITIES, MERCHANTS, AND KINGDOMS ALONG THE CHAIN OF SEAS

Trade of the Arabian Sea
The Maritime Empire of Srivijaya
Chinese Trade and the Fate
of the Tang Dynasty
Japan and Korea at the Eastern End
of the Chain of Seas

THE SAHARA RIM: A NEW ZONE OF INTERCOMMUNICATION

Gold and Slaves, Copper and Salt
The Empire of Ghana

EUROPE'S STRUGGLE FOR STABILITY

Muslims and Magyars
The Viking Adventure

WEIGHING THE EVIDENCE Bjarni Herjolfsson and the Viking Discovery of America

The Changing Shape of Western Europe

• • •

Ghana, which in the later first millennium C.E. achieved imperial proportions.

The final part of the chapter shifts northward to Europe, where in the eighth century the future looked brighter for ordinary people after three centuries of trouble and decline. However, in the ninth century the Christian empire that King Charlemagne built (see Chapter 10) broke apart. Soon afterward, military bands intruded aggressively into the heart of Europe once again, this time from North Africa, the Inner Eurasia steppes, and the Scandinavian north. These incursions interrupted Europe's return to stability but also obliged its aristocratic leaders to work out new strategies for defending their lands and ensuring social order.

A Panoramic View

MAP 11.1 Major states in Afroeurasia, 800.

Large empires continued to claim significant portions of Afroeurasia's temperate zones. What geographic features might help account for the frontiers between some of these states?

Muslim Power and Prosperity

FOCUS How did the rise of the Abbasid Caliphate and other Muslim states between the eighth and tenth centuries contribute to the emergence of a new Afroeurasian cultural tradition centered on Islam?

As the eighth century C.E. neared its midpoint, the Arab caliphs (rulers) of the Umayyad dynasty claimed sovereignty over an enormous territory extending from Damascus, the imperial capital in Syria, about 3,000 miles to the west and nearly 2,500 miles to the east. As astonishing as they were, these conquests cost the Muslim Umayyad rulers much treasure. In the 740s, Arab garrisons in the empire's outlying provinces faced a surge of local rebellions, which left the caliphate financially exhausted and militarily enfeebled. In 747 the leaders of the Abbasids, an Arab clan descended from an uncle of the Prophet Muhammad, rose up against the Umayyads and three years later drove them out of Damascus. The Abbasids declared themselves the rightful and universal caliphs, or supreme leaders of Muslims everywhere, though they did not manage to keep the whole Arab empire together. After 750, other new Muslim states appeared from Spain to Central Asia, and the Christian Byzantine monarchy fought persistently to keep control of Anatolia (modern Turkey). But for more than two centuries, the Abbasids taxed the immense agrarian and urban wealth of both Southwest Asia and Egypt, and they witnessed the continuing spread of Islam in all directions.

From Damascus to Baghdad: The Abbasid Empire

As ancient empire builders had often done, the Abbasid rulers advertised their triumph by forsaking the capital of their opponents and founding a new one. They chose Baghdad, a site on the Tigris River in Iraq not far from the former Persian capital of Ctesiphon. This change meant that the center of gravity of the Muslim state in Southwest Asia shifted from Syria eastward to Iraq (see Map 11.1). The Tigris-Euphrates valley and its tens of thousands of irrigated fields became the heartland of the Arab Muslim empire. It also meant that the people of Iran just to the east began to loom larger in Muslim state and cultural affairs.

Abbasid might. Extracting great wealth not only from Iraq but also from Egypt, Syria, and Iran, the early Abbasid caliphs supported

Abbasid artisanship. The refined skill of Abbasid artisans is evident in this exquisitely designed water pitcher. It was among the gifts that Harun al-Rashid sent to the Frankish king Charlemagne.

large armies, a complex and educated bureaucracy, and an imperial household that basked in stupendous luxury. The organization of the caliphate was not radically different from that of earlier Southwest Asian and Mediterranean empires. The Abbasids incorporated various governing methods modeled on Sasanid Persia. In fact their success as Muslim state builders depended on preserving continuity with the former Persian, and to some extent Byzantine, imperial systems. The Abbasids organized a hierarchy of provinces and districts, set up specialized ministries, employed thousands of secretaries and accountants, and appointed a Persian-style vizier, or chief counselor, to direct daily affairs in the caliph's name. The government relied increasingly on the support of Persian aristocratic families and recruited numerous literate Persians to take official jobs.

As in the former Persian and Byzantine empires, Abbasid government rested on collaboration between the royal household and the elite landowning families of the realm to control and tax the men and women who worked the land. The caliphs had no choice except to negotiate political arrangements with wealthy families, tribal groups, and ethnic communities to ensure their allegiance and cooperation.

To the general population, however, the Abbasids projected themselves as the personification of absolute authority and magical, semidivine power. In stark contrast to the first four caliphs after Muhammad, the Abbasids ruled in a distinctly Persian style, cloaking themselves in pomp and secret wonder. The caliph referred to himself as the "Shadow of God on Earth," outfitted himself in the robes and tall conical hat of a Persian potentate, and spoke to petitioners while hidden from view behind a screen. History remembers Caliph Harun al-Rashid (reigned 786–809) less as an able ruler, which he generally was, than as an exalted monarch whose magnificent palaces dazzled all who saw them.

Government communication between Baghdad and distant provinces depended initially on the system of roads and trails built earlier by Persians and Romans. The Abbasid public works ministry gradually improved this network, constructing more highways, bridges, and way stations. The government also built on the old infrastructures to create the *barid*, an elaborate postal and intelligence web. Lacing the empire together along nearly four hundred different routes, the dispatch riders of the *barid*, a sort of pony express, kept the imperial palace closely informed about provincial governors, local notables, and potential troublemakers.

Islam and the caliphate: an uncertain relationship. The Abbasids' fondness for concentrated power and semidivine monarchy had little to do with the ideals of Islam. Most of the rulers tried therefore to project a public image of spiritual humility and worthiness as the "commander of the believers." They took special care to display respect for the Muslim community's religious and legal scholars. This learned class, known in Arabic as the *ulama,* emerged as the guardians and interpreters of Islamic law, or *shari'a* (shah-REE-ah). The caliphs encouraged legal experts among the *ulama* to shape the body of laws into a unified code to regulate religious, social, and economic life throughout the empire.

ulama Muslim religious scholars, judges, teachers, and mosque officials.

shari'a The body of Islamic laws and moral precepts based on the Quran and the sayings and actions of the Prophet Muhammad.

The *ulama,* however, never fully accepted the Abbasids as legitimate successors of the revered caliphs who followed Muhammad. They contended that in the sight of God the caliph was no better than ordinary men and women. The community should therefore accept him only in so far as he was devoted and responsible, not simply powerful. The contradictions between the ideal of a community of equal, decision-making believers and the reality of an authoritarian monarchy were consequently not resolved. On one side was the principle of an egalitarian society in which the caliph, chosen by the leading religious figures, carried out the community's will. On the other was the reality of a Persian-style absolute monarchy that perpetuated itself in alliance with a wealthy class that consumed lavishly and, in the eyes of the righteous, often behaved wickedly. For example, Islamic law specified that an adult male was permitted a maximum of four wives as long as he treated them all equally. The law did not, however, authorize caliphs to keep harems of thousands of women as slaves and concubines. A further complication was that the *ulama* also wanted the social order and military defense that effective monarchs could provide. Consequently, pragmatic cooperation combined with ideological tension between the ruler and the spiritual leaders became part of the fabric of Muslim political life. In times of social distress, popular protesters or rebels could justify their actions on the grounds that the caliph had lost his moral legitimacy.

Political and ecological troubles. Provincial rebellions were just one sort of problem that the Abbasids faced within less than a century of taking power. The monarchy had no clear rules of succession. Despite the fiction that the *ulama,* representing the will of the community, chose each new caliph, various males in the royal family (with the participation of wives, mothers, and sisters) typically plotted against one another following a ruler's death until one of them got the better of the rest. The death of Caliph Harun al-Rashid in 809, for example, triggered civil strife that went on for several years. Rulers also found it increasingly difficult to prevent governors in far-off provinces from withholding tax revenues owed to the state and building their

A Muslim judge hears a case. Members of the educated class trained in jurisprudence settled civil disputes and set penalties according to Islamic law. How does the picture express the elite social status that judges enjoyed in the Abbasid Caliphate?

own power bases. The government in Baghdad could not rule any further than horses, camels, or boats could transport troops. For example, the caliphs spent heavily on summer campaigns to seize land in Anatolia from Christian Byzantium, but they made little headway. Without revenues from fresh conquests, the cost of keeping order in the existing empire increased steadily. Against good economic judgment, the Abbasids also minted huge numbers of gold and silver coins, which caused serious price inflation.

Beneath the visible surface of political and fiscal trouble lay a deeper problem, the accelerating degradation of productive farmland in the southern Tigris-Euphrates valley. Agriculture there was entirely dependent on irrigation, which in turn required a steady workforce to maintain canals, dikes, and dams. Unfortunately, a plague epidemic swept through Iraq in 749, just before the Abbasids came to power. The population of the lower valley fell, producing a serious shortage of labor to control floods and channel water to farmers. In addition, buildup of salt deposits in the soil remained a perennial and worsening problem. The wealth and glitter of Baghdad masked the fact that lower Iraq's resources were shrinking and with them wealth that the state desperately needed.

In the later ninth century, Arab and Persian landlords tried to revitalize agriculture in the valley by draining salt marshes and planting commercial crops, notably sugar cane. To meet the colossal demand for labor that this task required, they brought in thousands of slaves, mostly men and women captured in East Africa and sold to slave merchants who transported them up the Persian Gulf. Imitating the Roman model of slave labor, the landowners worked these captives in large gangs under appalling conditions. The consequence was a massive slave revolt. The Zanj Rebellion, as it was known from the Arab name for the East African coast, took the Abbasid army fifteen years to put down (869–883), cost thousands of lives, and further depleted the Abbasid treasury.

Military slavery. The Abbasids also found another way to use slaves. From the 830s, caliphs tried to strengthen their military forces by recruiting special soldiers, known in Arabic as *mamluks,* who would have no ties either to the regular army or to local families and factions. Many of these recruits were Turkic war prisoners and other captives from Inner Eurasia. Skilled as riders and archers, these "slaves on horses" were converted to Islam and in many cases given their freedom with the understanding that they remained permanently in the caliph's service.[1] As a result of this experiment, **military slavery** became a key political and social institution in the central Muslim lands.

> **mamluk** In Muslim states, a slave or freedman having primarily military or administrative duties.

> **military slavery** The personal bondage of an individual to a ruler or other authority with an obligation to provide military service.

This innovation, however, did not go according to plan. The urbane Persian scholar Jahiz (d. 869) pronounced Turks to be a people "uninterested in craftsmanship or commerce, . . . they care only about raiding, hunting, horsemanship, skirmishing with rival chieftains, taking booty, and invading other countries."[2] Jahiz exaggerated out of his own cultured bias. Nevertheless, as the slave soldiers acquired weapons, armor, horses, and an expanding sense of their own importance, they split into competing factions of their own, joined palace plots, and increasingly manipulated imperial affairs.

Rival Centers of Muslim Power

The Abbasids took power after first starting a rebellion in the northeastern region of Khurasan. But almost as soon as they succeeded, they had to face their own rebels and usurpers, some of whom managed to found independent Muslim monarchies.

The Umayyad state in Spain. The first important region to go its own way was the distant Iberian Peninsula. When in 750 the Abbasids seized Damascus and toppled the Umayyads, a member of that royal family escaped to Spain, gathered an army, and defeated the Abbasid-appointed governor there. In 756 he declared a new Umayyad dynasty with its capital at Córdoba (Cordova).

The fertile alluvial valleys of central and southern Spain, plus a Roman legacy of complex irrigation farming, offered the new Umayyad rulers a sound base for state building. The Christian population (whose rulers had been the Visigoths before the Arab invasion of 711), together with Berber newcomers from North Africa and immigrants from Syria

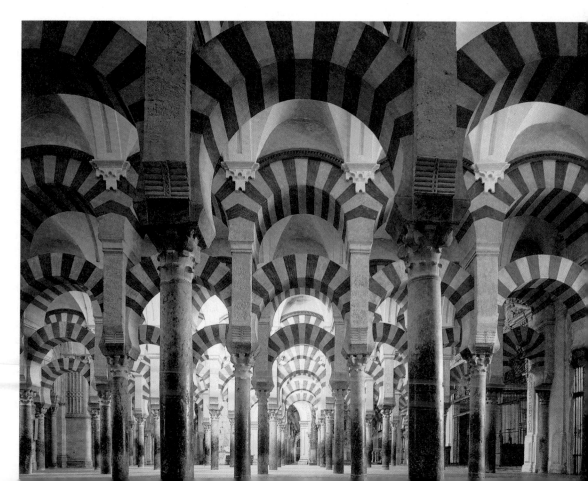

The Umayyad mosque at Córdoba. Abd al-Rahman I, the prince who founded the Umayyad dynasty of Spain, started constructing a grand mosque for his capital in 784. In the following two centuries, the structure was enlarged three times to produce one of the wonders of Muslim architecture. After capturing the city in the thirteenth century, Christian rulers built a cathedral inside the mosque but retained many of its columns and colorful, double-tiered arches.

and Iraq (some of them skilled in the science and technology of farming), created a prosperous economy. By the ninth century, Córdoba, once a Roman town, emerged as the largest city in the Mediterranean region after Constantinople.

Like the early Abbasid empire, Umayyad Spain benefited from a string of able rulers. No doubt the greatest was Abd al-Rahman III (r. 912–961). From his splendid palace complex near Córdoba, he patronized art and literature and engaged diplomatically with both the Abbasids and the Byzantines. He was far enough away from Baghdad, however, that in 929 he declared himself the rightful, universal leader of the Muslim community in opposition to the Abbasid king, thereby creating a rival caliphate in the western Mediterranean.

The Fatimids: a Shi'a empire. New Muslim power groups also established several states in North Africa in defiance of Abbasid authority. In the region that is now Tunisia and eastern Algeria, a rebellious governor founded an independent dynasty that lasted nearly two hundred years. In 909, however, it fell to revolutionaries who championed Shi'a Islam. This minority sect taught that the Abbasids had no right to rule because God approved only blood descendants of Ali, the fourth of the revered early caliphs, as legitimate leaders of the Muslim community (see Chapter 10). The new Shi'a regime, called the Fatimid dynasty (969–1171), built up its North African power base and then in 969 dispatched an army of Arab and Berber warriors to invade Egypt. This force expelled the Abbasid governor and declared Fatimid rule.

The Fatimids patronized the particular Shi'a branch of Islam known as Ismailism. Like other Shi'a groups, Ismailis believed that a descendant of Muhammad through Ali must be Islam's universal leader (Imam). Ismailis, however, identified that leadership with a different line of descent from what the majority of Shi'a accepted. They also claimed Fatima, the daughter of Muhammad and wife of Ali, as a revered ancestral figure, thus the dynastic name Fatimid. (In modern times the largest Ismaili communities have been in Pakistan and India.)

From its capital at Cairo at the apex of the Nile delta, the Fatimid regime declared itself to be Islam's true caliphate. For two hundred years they ruled a territory that at its zenith extended from Algeria and Sicily to Syria. They tried to overthrow the Abbasids, though without success. In addition to revenue from the Nile valley estates that millions of Egyptian peasants cultivated, the Fatimids benefited from a boost in commercial traffic. Indian Ocean merchants, uneasy about political and economic instability in Abbasid Iraq, increasingly sailed past the Persian Gulf and made for ports near the southern entrance to the Red Sea. This shift directed more Asian cargo up that sea and west to the Nile valley.

The Samanids and the silk roads. More than 1,100 miles northeast of Baghdad, an aristocratic Persian family known as the Samanids dominated both Khurasan and part of Central Asia in the ninth and tenth centuries (819–999). Founding their capital at the commercial city of Bukhara (today in Uzbekistan), these princes built their state on wealth from stock breeding and oasis farming. Also, the region's

Fatimid peacocks. Artists of the Fatimid dynasty created a distinctive Egyptian style of Muslim art. The peacock, perhaps symbolizing long life and good fortune, is a recurring theme. These birds appear on a limestone window screen.

major towns had long served as commercial swinging doors between the Inner Eurasian silk routes and Southwest Asia. As Islam grew in that region, Muslim merchant networks took over most of the long-distance trade through those entrepôts, and Samanid monarchs promoted Muslim missionary activity along the trails to China.

The Abbasid empire fades. In the later ninth century the Abbasid Caliphate deteriorated gradually from a sprawling empire to a patchwork of territories controlled variously by the caliph, provincial governors who professed allegiance but did what they pleased, local dynasties, and independent pastoral nomadic tribes. In 945 an aristocratic Iranian family known as the Buyids seized Baghdad and ruled there for more than a hundred years. Though they were Shi'a Muslims, they passed themselves off as the "protectors" of the caliphate. The Sunni caliph stayed on the job to make the Buyids appear legitimate, but in fact he was no longer more than one influential political figure among many.

The Byzantine Resurgence

The Byzantine state was Christian, but its political and cultural affairs were deeply intertwined with its Muslim neighbors. Despite its loss of critical territories to Arab conquerors in the seventh century, the empire remained a significant power in the eastern Mediterranean and Balkan Peninsula between the eighth and eleventh centuries. After Arab forces failed to capture Constantinople in either

Basil II, the Bulgar Slayer. Angels bestow the imperial crown on Basil II, who appears ready for combat in this depiction from a tenth-century Byzantine manuscript. How might you interpret the figures at the bottom of the image?

the islands of Cyprus and Crete from Muslim governors. That success allowed Byzantine warships to dominate the Aegean Sea as they had three centuries earlier. In the Balkan Peninsula, Basil faced the kingdom of Bulgaria, a loosely organized warrior state of Turkic horse archers that lorded over the majority of Slavic-speaking peasants. Later in history, he acquired the tag "the Bulgar Slayer" because he annexed Bulgaria and pushed the Byzantine frontier all the way to the Danube River. (According to legend, he also blinded nearly 15,000 Bulgarian captives, leaving 150 one-eyed soldiers to lead them home.) This Balkan campaign opened more of southeastern Europe to Greek Orthodox missionary activity. At Basil's death in 1025, Byzantium was a strong member of the club of mostly Muslim Mediterranean states. The rulers that followed him, however, were as inept as he was capable, so imperial expansion came to an end.

Islam on New Frontiers

Even though the unified Arab empire lasted less than a century, societies from Morocco and Spain to Central Asia and the lower Indus valley advanced toward a new cultural integration in which Islam provided an overarching framework of worship, moral ideals, and law. Islam joined Christianity and Buddhism as a universalist religion, that is, a belief system whose message was directed to all human beings, not only people of a particular ethnic or regional identity. The Islam of the Quran and the Traditions of the Prophet urged cooperative, compassionate, and egalitarian behavior among members of the community of believers. Such social collaboration rested on moral trust—between husbands and wives, parents and children, rulers and subjects, buyers and sellers. Devout Christians cherished fundamentally the same values, though with somewhat less emphasis on social cooperation and community behavior and more on individual expression of brotherly and sisterly love.

The Islamic insistence on social trust may have heightened the religion's appeal in the highly urbanized, socially fluid, and **cosmopolitan** environment of Southwest Asia, where individuals and cooperating groups sought opportunities to bind themselves to one another through agreements and contracts for doing business. This set of ethics attracted members of the commercial class and therefore oiled the wheels of exchange across Southwest Asia and far beyond. In short, Islam, like both Christianity and Buddhism in somewhat different ways, answered

> **cosmopolitan** Characteristic of a place where people of diverse origins come together or of an individual who travels widely.

668 or 717, Byzantium and the Abbasids settled into a routine of nearly continuous raid and counter-raid along a fluctuating frontier running across Anatolia. At the same time, however, Christian, Muslim, and Jewish merchants continued to do business in eastern Mediterranean ports.

Then, in the 860s, the rulers in Constantinople launched an extraordinary political comeback. A new line of capable emperors, known collectively as the Macedonian dynasty (867–1056), reorganized the imperial army and sent it on offensive campaigns against Abbasid frontier forts and cities in Anatolia. Under Basil II (r. 976–1025), the empire achieved its political high point. Smart and ruthless, he first suppressed Greek aristocratic families that tried to dodge Constantinople's authority. He then awarded greater power to the capital's salaried, educated bureaucrats, who had always been crucial to Byzantine political stability. He shrewdly avoided attacks against solidly Muslim territories. Instead, he shifted his imperial thrust to the west and north.

In the Mediterranean, Byzantine troops recaptured a substantial part of southern Italy, and Basil's navy took popular needs for coherent systems of trust and honest conduct among peoples of different regions, languages, and ethnicities who nonetheless found themselves thrown together in complex relationships.

In the two centuries following Muhammad's preaching, people in all Muslim-ruled states, including millions who did not speak Arabic or know anything of Arab traditions, accepted Islam at an accelerating rate. According to one scholarly estimate, inhabitants of Iran, who were already familiar with several religions, converted to Islam in large numbers in the late eighth and ninth centuries. By the 860s the Muslim population reached about 80 percent of the total.[3] A similar trajectory may have occurred in other areas where Muslims ruled.

proselytize To convert or attempt to convert an individual or group to one's religion.

Proselytizing for Islam was a highly informal and diffuse process. In contrast to the Christian churches, Islam had no formal religious organization, no hierarchy of appointed officials like patriarchs and bishops who helped direct the work of conversion. In contrast to the Christian patriarch in Constantinople or the pope in Rome, the caliph was not the chief administrator of a formal religious organization. Moreover, the *ulama*, the Muslim community's religious scholars, served as spiritual guides, moral counselors, and legal experts. They were not ordained priests who offered prospective converts a path to salvation through baptism or other holy sacraments. In Islam the ultimate spiritual authority was not the church but the Quran, which all believers could hear, study, and recite.

Also by the ninth century many more Muslims undertook the sort of missionary activity that had already succeeded for Christians and Buddhists. From that time, Muslim merchants, scholars, and preachers, more and more of them Persians, Turks, and Berbers, as well as Arabs, shared their religious faith with men and women in regions where Muslims did not rule (or at least not yet). Simultaneously, an interregional Muslim cultural network based on shared faith, law, moral expectations, literature, art, and architecture began to fuse together. This "style" of culture was derived in some measure from Arabia—especially the Arabic language—but mainly from Persian, Byzantine, Egyptian, and other older civilized traditions. The centers of this literate cultural life were the cities where Muslim communities became established. Christians and Jews who learned Arabic and to some extent adopted Muslim styles and manners also took part in this network.

A "Green Revolution" in Muslim Lands

Archaeological and written evidence suggests that between 750 and 1000 the Muslim-ruled lands generally experienced population, urban, and economic growth, despite serious environmental problems in the Tigris-Euphrates valley. Scholars have linked these upswings to the spread of new crops and farming technologies. Centuries or millennia earlier, farmers had domesticated rice, sugar cane, citrus fruits,

Water management in an arid climate. Dating to the ancient Achaemenid Persian empire or earlier, *qanats* are gently angled underground channels that lead water from highland slopes to arid areas. This irrigation technology spread from Iran eastward to Afghanistan and westward to North Africa. Vertical shafts to the tunnels provide ventilation and access for upkeep. Why do you think that farmers needed to maintain *qanats* diligently?

melon, mango, sweet peppers, eggplant, spinach, and cotton in the tropical and subtropical climates of southern India and Southeast Asia. Some of these crops reached Southwest Asia before the Arab Muslim conquests; others arrived during the period of expanding Muslim power (see Map 11.2). In any case, Southwest Asian farmers experimented with new crops and irrigation technologies, and Muslim governments and big estate owners encouraged these innovations. As a result, agricultural production intensified.

Farmers successfully cultivated new tropical plants in arid regions by efficiently managing water from rivers, underground sources, or moderate winter rainfall. In earlier centuries they had planted mainly winter crops such as wheat, barley, lentils, and oil seeds, leaving fields to lie fallow in the hot, rainless summers. But now they began to grow abundant quantities of crops that thrived in summer weather as long as water could be supplied. From the Abbasid lands, a veritable seed catalog of crops—oranges, lemons, watermelon, artichokes, bananas, rice, cotton—diffused northeastward into Central Asia, southward to Yemen, and westward across North Africa to Spain. Arabic became a medium for detailed agricultural manuals, and irrigation experts carried new ideas for lifting water, tapping it from underground channels, and building reservoirs. For example, ancient Iranians invented the *qanat*, an underground tunnel that led water from higher to lower elevations. In the early Muslim centuries, *qanat* technology spread from Iran to North Africa and Spain—and after 1500 to Mexico and the American Southwest.

Muslim Urban Society

Bounty from irrigated land and busy long-distance trade supported the proliferation and growth of cities in the Muslim

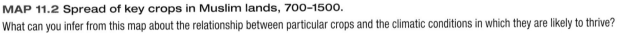

MAP 11.2 Spread of key crops in Muslim lands, 700–1500.

What can you infer from this map about the relationship between particular crops and the climatic conditions in which they are likely to thrive?

lands. The grandest of them was Baghdad. Iraq (Mesopotamia) had supported many magnificent capitals since the third millennium B.C.E., but Baghdad probably grew to metropolitan size faster than any of them. The Abbasid caliph Al-Mansur (r. 754–775) commissioned the city's construction in 762, and by the ninth century it had a population of between 200,000 and 500,000, surpassing that of Constantinople and every other city west of China. It attracted thousands of artisans, merchants, laborers, soldiers, and scholars to serve the royal household, the army, and the homes of the elite. Al-Mansur, the second Abbasid ruler, had his engineers design the city in the shape of a wheel. The royal palace was the hub, and four avenues radiated out from it, symbolically carrying goods and ideas to numerous other cities across Afroeurasia.

Islamic principles obliged Muslims who lived together in cities to worship as equals, obey the same laws, and refrain from publicly flaunting material wealth. Nevertheless, social class distinctions were as evident in Muslim towns as in any other part of Afroeurasia. Indeed, yawning

canyons of wealth and prestige separated the governing, estate-owning, and large merchant families from the laboring masses. As cities accumulated wealth from manufacturing and trade, these social divisions only widened.

Urban women of all classes made decisions in their family spheres and probably had great influence on the urban economy by choosing what foods and other goods the family would consume. Adult men dominated public spaces—places of worship, government buildings, plazas, and markets—as they had in ancient times. Research in biographies of notable Muslims compiled by Arab or Persian scholars in the early Islamic period suggests that the number of women recognized for their achievement as writers and legal specialists declined significantly after the first century or two. The cities of Umayyad Spain may have been the exception. There, an unusual number of literate women gained distinction as teachers, jurists, librarians, and copyists.

Slavery was also a part of urban life. Leaving aside the growing numbers of male slaves or ex-slaves in military service, the majority of unfree city residents were probably women, working as domestics, attendants, entertainers, and concubines. From the perspective of the enslaved, there was one slightly encouraging trend. Following the long Zanj Rebellion in southern Iraq in the later ninth century, Muslim landowners mostly abandoned the idea of using slaves in large, unwilling gangs to produce commercial crops. The potential for violent rebellion was too great.

Many Muslim-ruled cities had populations of non-Muslims, especially Jews and Christians. Those groups usually resided in distinct quarters of the city and most of the time lived in peace with their Muslim neighbors. In fact, Muslim governments encouraged such physical separation, not to enforce social segregation, but to give minority groups, who chose their own leaders, official recognition and protection. Multifaith harmony perhaps worked best in Córdoba and other cities of Spain, where, despite occasional outbreaks of conflict or persecution, daily business and intellectual exchange was common among religious communities. There, Jews, Christians, and Muslims all spoke Arabic.

The Stream of Ideas

Big Muslim cities harbored intellectuals and artists, while Islam and the Arabic language provided a matrix for lively cultural interaction among cities from Spain to northern India. Muslims traveled to acquire knowledge, do business, or perform the pilgrimage to Mecca. In the process they developed a cosmopolitan consciousness that they inhabited the Dar al-Islam (House of Islam), the amalgam of lands where Muslim populations predominated or Muslim elites ruled. Christian, Jewish, Hindu, and Buddhist sages traveled the interurban networks as well. For inquisitive men and women, the Dar al-Islam was not so much a mosaic of kingdoms as an interlinked web of cities. The people who moved throughout this web tended to pay as little attention as possible to the frontiers between the territories of one ruler and another.

The Arabic language, both written and spoken, inevitably accompanied Islam wherever it went, because in Muslim belief Arabic was the very medium of God's divine revelation to Muhammad. In much the same way that ancient Han linguists standardized Chinese writing, Muslim academicians in Iraqi cities labored in the eighth and ninth centuries to systematize Arabic script, spelling, and grammar. As a language of both statecraft and scholarship, Arabic gradually displaced Greek, Aramaic, and Latin in the Muslim lands. Persian, or Farsi, a major language of the earlier Persian empires, fared better. So many Persian speakers flocked to Islam that the language emerged in the eastern Muslim lands as the dominant medium of religious and intellectual culture.

Translating ancient texts. The first great intellectual task for scholars in Baghdad and other Southwest Asian cities was to translate scientific, technical, philosophical, and historical documents from Greek, Persian, Syriac, and Sanskrit (the main literary language of India) into Arabic. Texts were scattered in many lands, and Muslims, Christians, and Jews frequently collaborated to assemble them, learning one another's languages and arguing over the meaning and interpretation of documents. With the support of the early Abbasid caliphs, scholars set up translation projects in Baghdad. Caliph al-Ma'mun (r. 813–833) established a research center called the House of Wisdom. Its residents, including some South Asian scholars, investigated mathematical and astronomical ideas that had been formulated in the Gupta empire three hundred years earlier (see Chapter 9). Between the ninth and eleventh centuries, Cairo and Córdoba, as well as Bukhara in Central Asia, also emerged as leading centers of learning.

Producing new knowledge. Translation, however, was only the start. Scholars wanted not only to preserve ancient learning but to correct, reinterpret, and add to it. Among the numerous spheres of knowledge—and none were closed to inquiry—the Muslim religious sciences commanded the highest prestige. They included studies of the Quran,

Model of an automaton. The Egyptian mathematician, engineer, and inventor al-Jaziri (1136–1206) wrote the *Book of Knowledge of Mechanical Devices*, a study of different types of machines, including water clocks and water raising machines. Some of these devices were automata, or self-operating contrivances, made only for amusement.

Abu Bakr al-Razi: Muslim Physician

The Persian polymath Abu Bakr al-Razi (ca. 865–925 C.E.) wrote almost one hundred texts on topics such as astronomy, chemistry, alchemy, philosophy, and Islamic theology. But he gained his greatest fame as a physician and author of medical treatises. Born in Rey, a bustling Iranian commercial center that is today a suburb of Tehran, al-Razi had an early interest in music and achieved a reputation as a master of the stringed instrument called the *ud*. He also received an education in philosophy, metaphysics, logic, and mathematics before deciding to train as a doctor. In addition to practicing medicine and teaching students, he served as director of hospitals in both Rey and Baghdad in the early tenth century.

Al-Razi's most enduring legacy is his dozens of medical books. A careful observer and meticulous note-taker, he pioneered the systematic approach to experimentation that we now call the "scientific method." Working in busy hospitals with large numbers of patients enabled al-Razi to study and write on a variety of medical conditions. In one influential work, he explained how to distinguish clinically between smallpox, chicken pox, and measles. In another book he described why roses cause certain people to suffer from swelled heads, runny noses, and weepy eyes—the first identification of hay fever. He also made important contributions to ophthalmology and pediatrics. Dedicated to improving public health, he composed a home medical manual designed to enable anyone to treat a range of diseases with simple medicines prepared from common ingredients. Like Hippocrates, the ancient Greek medical authority, al-Razi argued that physicians should receive extensive training and hold licenses to practice.

Al-Razi was well versed in classical Greek medical scholarship, though he declared certain of its propositions to be incorrect or incomplete. He respected the work of his Greek

An imaginative woodcut depicts al-Razi studying a learned text.

predecessors, the physician Galen in particular, but he critiqued their findings and encouraged other scholars to do the same in the interest of medical practice. After al-Razi's death, his notebooks were compiled and published as a massive twenty-volume work titled *The Comprehensive Book on Medicine*. These tomes represented an encyclopedia of knowledge about diseases. For each ailment, al-Razi cited the views of Greek, Syrian, Indian, Persian, and Arab writers before adding his own clinical thoughts and observations. Translated into Latin during the thirteenth century and published in Europe, al-Razi's work became a fundamental text for European medical students to the end of the seventeenth century.

Thinking Critically

In what ways did al-Razi both make use of and advance beyond ancient Greek scientific and medical learning?

theology, law, grammar, and the methodology of verifying the Traditions of the Prophet. Then there were the "philosophical sciences," which in that era included logic (derived principally from the Greek philosopher Aristotle), cosmology, astrology, physics, chemistry, biology, medicine, agronomy, geography, and mathematics. Thinkers in those fields engaged not only in theoretical reasoning, but also in systematic observation and recording of natural phenomena, describing and classifying plants, for example, or compiling astronomical tables. To accomplish these things, they used an array of improved or newly invented scientific instruments, such as balances, water clocks, and astrolabes (for plotting the movement of heavenly bodies).

The progress of mathematics illustrates the importance of intellectual collaboration across cultural and political frontiers. In cooperation with Christian and Jewish

academicians, Muslims refined and expanded the mathematical knowledge of ancient Mesopotamia, Egypt, and Greece, solving, for example, geometrical problems that Euclid, the renowned Hellenistic Greek mathematician, had not cracked. Drawing also on Indian mathematics, ninth-century scholars formulated the sciences of algebra and trigonometry largely as they are taught in high schools today.

The single most conspicuous scientific development in Abbasid times was the transfer from India of the base-ten positional numerical system that incorporates a sign to indicate "zero." This system was an achievement associated with the Gupta empire. As communication picked up between South Asia and the central Muslim lands, Indian scientific ideas reached scholars in Baghdad and other cities. Among these sages was Muhammad ibn Musa al-Khwarizmi (ca. 780–850), a Persian mathematician who lived and worked in Bukhara in the ninth century. He propagated the Indian system of reckoning and brought it to bear on the study of algebra. In fact, the word *algebra* comes from the Arabic *al-jabr*, meaning "restoration." After his death about 850, other scholars gradually switched from the cumbersome Greek or Roman to the efficient Indian system. Latin Christian scholars who traveled to Muslim Toledo or Córdoba in Spain introduced what came to be called "Arabic numerals" into western Europe, where the new system caught on widely in the thirteenth century. Today, these ten simple signs represent the closest thing the world has to a universal language.

Tension between science and faith. Like ancient Greek and Roman thinkers, scholars of the Abbasid era made no formal distinction between science as we understand it today and philosophy or theology. Their work included both scientific study and speculation on matters of the spirit, that is, the relation between divine revelation and the evidence of reality gathered through the exercise of reason, logic, and observation. Muslim scholars meticulously explored the ancient Greek masters such as Aristotle and Pythagoras and wrote numerous philosophical works.

Other Muslims, however, especially religious leaders more attuned to daily ritual, law, and doctrine, became wary of theoretical speculation about nature and the universe. The early Islamic centuries witnessed much disputation among literate Muslims about faith and reason. For example, does God predetermine the life experience of every individual, or are individuals morally responsible for their own experience? A question like that often pitted theologians who accepted the totality of God's will against rationally oriented believers, who argued for free inquiry and human responsibility. The general trend from about the eleventh century was for leaders who emphasized divine revelation and obedience to sacred law to gain ascendancy in the mosques and colleges where the religious sciences were taught. Theological and philosophical musings on the nature of reality continued, but mainly in private and informal settings.

Cities, Merchants, and Kingdoms along the Chain of Seas

FOCUS What part did maritime commerce play in the development of states and cities along the chain of seas extending from the Arabian Sea to the Sea of Japan between 750 and 1000 C.E.?

Between the seventh and eleventh centuries, impressive economic growth took place not only in Muslim-ruled lands but also in several kingdoms bordering the chain of seas that extended from the Arabian Sea to the Sea of Japan (see Map 11.3). Hungry for revenue from trade, the rulers of these states cooperated readily with shippers and traders. Sea merchants also contributed to commercial expansion by organizing large networks of mercantile buyers and sellers and by employing increasingly sophisticated commercial tools, such as partnerships, loans, and letters of credit to finance enterprise and speed merchandise on its way.

Trade of the Arabian Sea

Between the sixth and eleventh centuries C.E., shipbuilders, captains, and merchants employed in Arabian Sea trade made incremental improvements in sail and hull design and learned more about the seasonal intricacies of the Indian Ocean monsoon winds. For example, they acquired more precise information about the best times of year to leave a particular port in order to reach a destination in reasonably predictable time. Consequently, mariners gained confidence sailing across open seas, notably between the Red Sea, Persian Gulf, or East Africa and the ports of southern India and Ceylon.

Maritime trade also rose in volume owing to the development of southern India's commercial economy. Because India juts southward into the Indian Ocean and narrows to a point, the inhabitants of the southern third of the subcontinent all lived close to either the Bay of Bengal or the Arabian Sea. Southern India had functioned as a commercial pivot point between the two seas for a thousand years or more. But from the seventh century, the volume of merchandise that passed through these ports increased in tandem with economic growth in the South Asian interior. Among the several monarchies that shared India, the Pallava dynasty dominated much of the south between the sixth and tenth centuries. The Pallavas patronized Hindu devotional religion, or *bhakti*, as well as Sanskrit learning. The great majority of southern India's peasants spoke Tamil, a language of the ancient Dravidian family. Most of them raised rice, a crop that the Pallava kings encouraged by constructing irrigation works and great reservoirs to conserve and distribute water during the dry winter and spring months. Farmers also increased cotton textile production and grew black pepper, both commodities exported throughout South Asia and across the seas. Burgeoning towns and merchant networks linked to coastal ports accompanied this economic prosperity. Further to the northwest, the region of Gujarat also continued to grow as a center of cloth making. Gujarati merchants were to be seen in ports all around the rim of the Arabian Sea.

Commercial towns also multiplied along the African coast south of the Red Sea, in what are now Somalia, Kenya, and Tanzania. Farming populations that lived on those shores and spoke Bantu languages emerged as Swahili, a name derived from the Arabic term for "people of the coast." The Swahili language was fundamentally Bantu in structure and vocabulary, though it absorbed many Arabic and some Persian words. The early Swahili communities were thoroughly sea oriented, selling ivory, gold, animal skins, rock crystal (transparent quartz), and other commodities to Arabian Sea traders. New towns sprang up along the coast,

MAP 11.3 Connections along the chain of seas, tenth century.

How might geographical factors have contributed differently to the commercial prosperity of the Abbasid Caliphate and the kingdom of Srivijaya?

including Shanga and Manda, which had populations of 15,000 to 18,000. Swahili merchants also traded in slaves, buying captive men and women from dealers who operated in the deep East African interior and then selling them for transport to Southwest Asia or India.

Arabs and Persians had been Arabian Sea rovers long before the advent of Islam, but the rise of the Umayyad and Abbasid empires and their new urban markets encouraged longer profit-making voyages. Between the eighth and tenth centuries, Muslim traders founded settlements on the coasts of East Africa, India, Ceylon, Sumatra, and even southern China. These outposts formed a trans-hemispheric Muslim commercial diaspora. Arab geographers of that era labeled the Indian Ocean the "Sea of China," a name suggesting the feasibility of voyaging from the Persian Gulf all the way to China and back by timing port departures with the alternating monsoon winds. For nearly two centuries, Muslim

merchants made this eighteen-month round trip regularly. They established a little colony in the Chinese port of Guangzhou (Canton), and some merchants resided there at least temporarily to act as hosts for arriving sailors and as agents for Chinese buyers. If fortune smiled on shippers, they returned to Iraq with cargos of silks, cottons, porcelain, sandalwood, jade, and spices, which Abbasid consumers purchased at huge markups.

The Maritime Empire of Srivijaya

Commercial traffic across the Bay of Bengal between India and Southeast Asia enjoyed a boost from about 700, when the kingdom of Srivijaya (SREE-vih-JAI-yuh) arose on the island of Sumatra at the western end of the Indonesian archipelago. Srivijaya's success as a maritime power for about six hundred years resulted mainly from its domination of

The Temple Mountain. Constructed of about two million stone blocks and rising more than 100 feet above the central Java landscape, the principal temple at Borobudur symbolically represents the three prime elements of the universe: the spheres of desire, form, and formlessness. A pyramid-shaped base of five square terraces constitutes the first and lowest sphere. The second is three circular platforms supporting stupas that house statues of the Buddha. The third is a mammoth stupa, which is empty.

the strategic Malacca and Sunda Straits, the two narrow sea passages that connected the South China Sea with the Bay of Bengal and all points west. Srivijaya arose as a maritime state controlling ports, agricultural hinterlands (inland areas), and sea lanes, rather than extensive territories. In the later first millennium C.E., wet-rice farmers expanded their operations in lowlands and river valleys across Southeast Asia, transforming tropical forests into paddy fields and paying taxes to Srivijayan monarchs or local lords. Centered in the fertile rice-growing Musi River valley near the modern city of Palembang, Srivijaya accumulated sufficient wealth and naval power to collect tribute from smaller states along the northern coasts of Sumatra and Java. The royal court watched over these local princes in a kind of political federation.

Like other Southeast Asian monarchs, Srivijayan kings and aristocrats became eager patrons of Buddhism. They built monasteries, employed Buddhist monks as officials, adopted Sanskrit from India as the region's main written language, and patronized Buddhist learning. Increasing numbers of Malay sailors also took up Mahayana, or popular Buddhism, and carried it from port to port. Srivijaya benefited from a close alliance with the Buddhist Sailendra dynasty, which ruled the interior of Java, where wet-rice cultivation in rich volcanic soils produced bountiful surpluses.

The Sailendra kings accumulated sufficient wealth by the eighth century to build Borobudur, a colossal Buddhist monument and one of the architectural marvels of the world. The Sailendra monarchy unfortunately enmeshed itself in a fatal civil war in the ninth century, though Srivijaya continued to dominate the straits trade for another three hundred years.

Chinese Trade and the Fate of the Tang Dynasty

Malay, Indian, Arab, and Persian merchants all gravitated to China's southern coast owing to that country's remarkable demographic and economic growth following its political unification under the Sui (581–618) and Tang (618–907) dynasties (see Chapter 10). Between 750 and 1100, China's population grew from about 50 to 100 million, and the geographical center of both population and economic production continued to shift toward the rice-growing south. Market towns and ports multiplied, especially from the Yangzi River valley to the southern coasts, where several busy ports, including Guangzhou and Quanzhou flourished handling maritime trade.

Farming, manufacturing, and foreign commerce all prospered in China even as the Tang government progressively lost control over its own imperial administration and finally collapsed. Serious trouble began in 755 when An Lushan, a disaffected general of Turkic origin, built up a personal military force of more than 100,000 soldiers and marched on Chang'an, forcing emperor Xuanzong (r. 712–756), the last of the great Tang monarchs, first to flee his capital and then to abandon his throne to a son.

In the aftermath of the rebellion, which Turkic Uighur cavalry helped put down at the price of huge payments of silk, the weakened regime had to appoint military men, rather than loyal civil bureaucrats, to top provincial posts. These officers, many of whom had supported the An Lushan revolt, set themselves up as virtually independent warlords in several parts of China and refused to send taxes to Chang'an. Buddhist monasteries, of which there may have been thirty thousand in China in the eighth century, enjoyed exemption from taxation. Many of them accumulated large agricultural estates, conducted their own commercial businesses, and even created their own militias. For nearly a century after the An Lushan rebellion, furthermore, forces of the Tibetan and Uighur empires threatened China's northwestern frontiers, ending earlier Tang campaigns to extend imperial power deep into Inner Eurasia. In the late eighth century, emperors tried to recapture the military advantage by organizing eunuchs, castrated males who served the imperial court, into a personally loyal armed force. But palace eunuchs split into feuding factions, took over palace affairs, and in the ninth century started murdering and replacing emperors.

In the later eighth century, the Tang government lost its grip on the Chinese economy; estate owners and entrepreneurs took the opportunity to engage in more freewheeling commercial activity. The Tang equal-field system, whereby the government allotted land to peasants and kept close track of both production and tax payments, gradually fell apart for lack of government funds to manage it. Consequently, big landowners put increasing pressure on peasants to sell their land to get out of debt and then employed tenants and day laborers to produce grain, silk, cotton, and other commodities for the commercial market. Poor men and women continued to stream to the south, many of them finding only low-wage jobs on farm estates. As the Tang government deteriorated, local power holders willingly promoted private business and trade because they could then tax its profits. The Tang dynasty collapsed in 907, and from then until 960 China was once again divided into a number of competing regional states. In the same period, however, exports of silk and other wares from the southern ports continued to grow.

Japan and Korea at the Eastern End of the Chain of Seas

The last links in Afroeurasia's chain of seas were the East China Sea and the Sea of Japan (or East Sea), which extend northeastward into the temperate latitudes. In the first millennium C.E., the lands around those two seas—northern China, the Korean peninsula, and the Japanese archipelago—emerged gradually as a distinct zone of seaborne intercommunication.

Ships had to cross five hundred miles of cyclone-prone waters to reach southern Japan from the Chinese coast, but only one hundred miles of the Korea Strait separated Japan from the southern tip of Korea. That passage became Japan's main link to China and indeed to the whole Afroeurasian world. Between about 400 B.C.E. and 600 C.E., rice farming, weaving technology, iron metallurgy, writing, central governing techniques, and Buddhism all apparently entered Japan by way of Korea.

Both Japan and Korea are lands with mountainous interiors. Only about 16 percent of Japan is suitable for farming, 20 percent of Korea. Japan's mountains include sixty active volcanoes, but the archipelago's volcanic soils are rich and summer rains typically ample. After knowledge of wet-rice cultivation arrived, farm hamlets spread across Japan's coastal plains and inland valleys. In the first six centuries C.E., its population rose from about one million to five million, a huge acceleration of growth. On Honshu, the big, central island, farmer power was sufficient to support a tribute-collecting class of aristocratic families. Some of them recruited enough armed retainers to found small states, which from about the third century warred against one another for control of good land and peasant labor.

In contrast to island Japan, Korea lay within the shadow of successive Chinese empires. The ancient Han dynasty occupied much of the peninsula, and the Tang made it a tributary region. In 668, however, a line of Korean rulers known as the Silla (SHEE-lah) took control of most of the peninsula and kept it unified until after 900.

Commanders of Japan. Between the sixth and eighth centuries, regional chiefs centered on Honshu gradually built up an effective system of central command. Combining cavalry troops with claims of sacred authority, these lords began to refer to themselves as "heavenly sovereigns," or emperors. Known as the Yamato dynasty (from the name of a river), these monarchs, whose line included several female heavenly sovereigns, founded the town of Nara in 710 as a palace and an administrative center. This was Japan's first true city and clear evidence of the dynasty's success at gathering surplus wealth from rice-growing peasants. In 794 the dynasty moved its capital to the even grander imperial center of Heian (pronounced HAY-ahn, later known as Kyoto).

The Yamato kings and queens associated themselves closely with beliefs and rituals that rural Japanese relied on to appease and manipulate the world of spirits. These beings, including the spirits of recent ancestors, pervaded the natural world and had power to ensure health, safety, and rich harvests. This belief system, known as Shinto, included an important role for the Yamato rulers, whose ceremonial offerings aimed to stave off natural or human-induced calamities. Beginning about 850, however, an important power shift occurred. The reigning emperors lost their grip on political affairs to aristocratic families. Nevertheless, these powerful nobles legitimized themselves by governing in the name of the emperor, who retained only ritual duties.

Silla royal tombs. Gyeongju, the city in South Korea that served as the capital of the Silla dynasty, is the site of several tumuli, or burial mounds, containing the remains of Silla rulers. Can you think of other societies in the world where important people were entombed in this way?

Currents of exchange between China and Japan. About the third century c.e., traffic between Japan and the Asian mainland began to intensify. After the Han empire (206 b.c.e.–220 c.e.) broke up, Chinese and Korean exiles and adventurers headed to Japan, a sort of East Asian "land of opportunity." The Japanese elite class, knowing it lacked the refined civilization of its Korean and Chinese neighbors, warmly received educated and skilled immigrants. These newcomers offered the Japanese much new knowledge: advanced metallurgy, writing, sericulture (silk production), textile manufacture, paper making, and techniques of government and warfare. When the Sui and Tang emperors reunified China in the late sixth century, and Silla kings mastered most of Korea, migration to Japan diminished. China's immense power, however, only stimulated Japanese appetites for its culture. Palace aristocrats invited Chinese literary scholars and experienced officials to their courts, as well as boatload after boatload of Buddhist monks and nuns, who offered the Yamato emperors spiritual learning and protection. Ships returning to China carried Japanese intellectuals, who sought out knowledge of Confucian statecraft and sacred Buddhist texts.

Japan did not, however, become a mere cultural satellite of either China or Korea. Rather, a distinctive Japanese style of culture developed out of the complex interplay between, for example, Buddhism and Shinto, Tang city design and traditional Japanese building materials, or Chinese orchestral music and Japanese instruments. Another example was the Japanese system of civil and penal codes (*ritsuryō*

seido). This governmental scheme of administrative ranks, offices, and duties was clearly derived from Chinese Confucian models of political organization, but Japanese rulers tailored it for their much smaller territory and population.

Up to the tenth century, Japanese scholars simply learned Chinese and used it to write government documents and religious texts. A few experimenters, however, devised ways to represent Japanese sounds using Chinese logographic characters. This was a tough job because Japanese had no structural relationship to Chinese. Since aristocratic males regarded Chinese as the language of social prestige, the work of creating an indigenous writing system fell largely to refined and learned women, who did not consider the task beneath them. Buddhist monks and nuns also contributed. By the tenth century these scholars collectively produced a workable script called *wabun*, which was based on simplified forms of Chinese characters.

Several schools of Mahayana Buddhism spread from China and Korea to Japan after about 600. Shrines, temples, and monasteries multiplied on the islands, and in the eighth century Nara became famous for its Buddhist teachers and soaring temples. The Great Buddha Hall (Daibutsu) in Nara remains today the largest wooden building in the world. Buddhist clerics offered common folk hope, health, and salvation, as well as supernatural defense against crop failures. Buddhist and Shinto ideas also mingled much as Buddhist and Daoist beliefs did in China. For example, Shinto nature gods became associated with Buddhist spirits and *bodhisattvas*.

Japan's population and economy continued to grow, with some interruptions, throughout the later first millennium C.E. The islands had about five million people in 700, rising to about seven million by 1200. (China's population in 1200 was about 120 million.)[4] In the 730s, however, waves of smallpox hit the islands, killing both children and adults and reducing the total population by as much as 25 percent.[5] Korean and Chinese visitors appear to have introduced this and other infectious maladies, which had long been endemic in most of Afroeurasia. Later in the eighth century, adult Japanese began to develop partial immunities to these diseases, though recurring epidemics kept the upward demographic trend modest.

Japan's emergence as a complex society owes far more to its agrarian economy, population growth, and contacts

The Great Buddha. Rulers of the Yamato dynasty avidly promoted Buddhist temple construction. The Great Buddha Hall in Nara houses the world's largest bronze statue, an image of the Vairochana Buddha originally cast in the mid-eighth century. The statue is nearly fifty feet tall. The Buddha raises his right hand in the classic gesture of assurance and protection. Compare this image to the limestone Vairochana Buddha carved in China several decades earlier (Chapter 10, page 302).

with China and Korea than to exchanges with more distant lands along the chain of seas. The islands remained culturally bonded to Korea and China, though the eastward flow of ideas diminished after 1000. By that time, however, the Japanese aristocracy was effectively creating a distinctive Japanese form of literate civilization.

The Sahara Rim: A New Zone of Intercommunication

FOCUS How did agrarian peoples living in the Mediterranean region and West Africa become linked together in a network of commercial and cultural exchange between the seventh and tenth centuries?

Japan's connection to the rest of East Asia filled in one of the significant gaps in the networks of exchange that connected peoples of Afroeurasia with one another. Another and much larger gap existing in the early centuries C.E. was the Sahara Desert (see Map 11.4). In that period pastoral peoples introduced the dromedary, or one-humped camel, from the Arabian Peninsula, probably to the semiarid country bordering the southern edge of the Sahara. The dromedary, with its wide feet and tolerance for going without water longer than most mammals, provided the "technological" solution to the problem of crossing the great desert north to south (see Chapter 7). But only later in the millennium did north–south crossings became regular.

Gold and Slaves, Copper and Salt

For merchants, the primary incentive to cross the Sahara was the simple fact that productive agrarian societies existed on both sides of it. Along the northern rim from Egypt to Morocco were young Muslim states, all of them increasingly urbanized after the eighth century and all linked into the trade of the Mediterranean and Southwest Asia. South of the desert were three broad climatic and vegetational zones. The Sahel, a belt of semiarid scrubland, bordered the Sahara. Further south lay open or wooded savannas (grasslands) where farming populations raised rice, millet, sorghum, and cattle, channeling surpluses into a network of trade that connected market towns. This web extended into the wet tropical forests, the third zone, where growing populations harvested yams and other root crops and where small states were beginning to emerge. Arab geographers of North Africa referred to the savanna belt as the *Bilad al-Sudan* ("land of black-skinned people"), or simply the Sudan, a historic region to be distinguished from the modern republics of Sudan and South Sudan.

Sudanic states. By the later first millennium C.E., enough people were producing crop and livestock surpluses in the Sudan to support significant kingdom-building ventures.

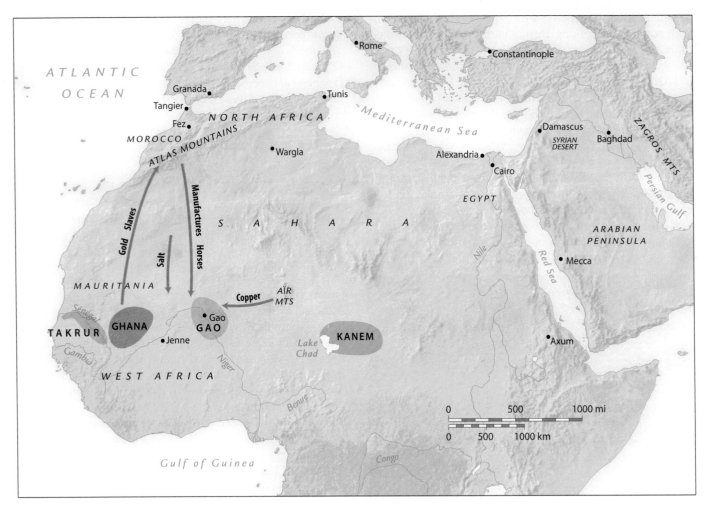

MAP 11.4 The Sahara rim, 1000.
What geographic features and natural resources help account for the location of the Takrur, Ghana, and Gao states?

From Arabic geographical texts and archaeological data, we know a fair amount about a few of the states that flourished between the eighth and eleventh centuries in West Africa—the Subsaharan zones on the western side of the continent. In the far west was Takrur, a monarchy whose economy was based on rice growing and trade in the floodplain of the middle and lower Senegal River valley. A second polity was Gao, a small state whose main city of the same name occupied a commercially strategic spot where the Niger River begins flowing south across all three climatic zones to the Atlantic Ocean. A third state was Kanem, whose founders were probably Saharan pastoral warriors. That kingdom emerged in the eighth century in the grasslands bordering Lake Chad, then a vast wetland and the sixth largest lake in the world (a status it has more recently lost owing to recurring drought).

Modern analysis of long-term climatic cycles in West Africa shows that in the period from approximately 300 to 1100 rainfall was generally higher than in the previous several centuries. During those eight hundred years, farmers were able to plant crops and herders graze cattle in more northerly parts of the Sahel. That permitted population growth and town building in areas that are today bleak deserts. In the later centuries of this "wet phase," Berber merchants in towns located along the northern rim of the Sahara began to organize camel caravans that with growing regularity crossed the desert to the Sudan.

The flow of gold. Sudanic peoples had long been involved in long-distance trade, but the trans-Saharan connection further stimulated their economies. Muslim rulers in both the Mediterranean region and Southwest Asia had an ever-growing appetite for gold, and the richest reachable deposits were in West Africa. They wanted gold mainly to display their authority and encourage commerce by minting gold coins. The chief West African mining centers lay along the upper Senegal and Niger Rivers in the transition zone between woodland and tropical rainforest. West African gold merchants typically spoke Soninke, one language among many in the Niger-Congo family of languages. We

A modern-day caravan. People of the Sahara continue to mine salt in a few places and transport it southward to West African towns. Laborers cut the salt into large slabs and tie them to the sides of camels. Why do you think camels continue to be used in this business?

have no evidence that large states controlled the mines. Rather, Soninke buyers did business with local chiefs independently, then shipped bags of dust and nuggets to the Sudanic caravan centers, where camel merchants shipped some of it northward across the desert. This trade expanded even faster after the turn of the millennium, when merchants from an economically reviving Europe began to frequent North African ports to buy gold. In the ensuing centuries, African bullion moved both northward into Europe and eastward to the central Muslim lands, even to India.

The trans-Saharan slave trade. A second important item in the trade was slaves. Caravan merchants bought slaves in Sudanic markets and force-marched them across the desert, many no doubt dying along the way. We know little of how the slave trade operated in those early centuries. Captives were the unfortunate victims of local wars, famines, social ostracism, or deliberate raiding and kidnapping. Women very likely outnumbered men in the slave caravans. They were taken to serve as domestics, entertainers, and concubines in the households of rulers or affluent families in the Mediterranean and Southwest Asia. As we have seen, Muslim monarchs began in the ninth century to recruit growing numbers of military slaves. They acquired captives from any source they could, though Muslim ethics (not always honored) prohibited enslavement of fellow believers. The majority of the slaves brought into

the central Muslim lands came from Inner Eurasia, India, and Europe. Only a minority came from Africa south of the desert.

Southbound trade. The trans-Saharan trade ran in both directions, of course. To markets in the Sudan, Berber and Arab merchants from North Africa carried products such as textiles, jewelry, ironware, and horses (which did not breed well in the Sudan owing to animal sleeping sickness). They also transported slabs of salt, a commodity with limited West African sources, from mines in the west central desert. From the Sahara's Aïr Mountains they brought copper, a mineral in great demand for making tools, ritual objects, and jewelry. In the towns of the Sahel, the camel merchants transferred their shipments to Sudanic traders and then returned north hauling not only gold and slaves but also ivory, ostrich feathers, animal skins, and grain. The desert journey, barring disastrous experiences with sand storms, bandit pillagers, missed trails, or dried-up wells, took something short of three months.

The Empire of Ghana

Among the early known West African states, Ghana was surely the largest before the turn of the first millennium C.E. Known also as Wagadu, it may have begun to take form as early as the fourth century. At its height in the tenth century,

Ghana dominated a territory extending from the Senegal valley to the great bend of the Niger River. Its heartland lay in the Sahel and its political capital almost certainly in modern Mauritania, though we do not know exactly where. The king, known in Arabic sources as "the Ghana," commanded a large royal household, a hierarchy of officials, and an army made up mainly of infantry archers. Thanks to southbound Saharan trade in horses, cavalry became possible after about 1000 C.E. The ruler did not control gold mines but may have held a monopoly over the trade, thereby enriching the state. Royal succession was **matrilineal**; that is, a king was succeeded not by his son but by a son of one of his sisters. The ruler enjoyed sacred status, which meant that he possessed special supernatural powers to mediate between humans and supernatural beings and to perform religious rituals necessary to the people's welfare. Like the Abbasid Caliph, he held public audiences from behind a screen and permitted only a privileged few ever to see him. The central administration was loosely organized. As in the case of many ancient empires, territories distant from the capital remained under the authority of local leaders, who periodically paid tribute to royal officers on pain of armed reprisals. The eleventh-century Arab geographer Al-Bakri, who lived in Spain and collected testimony from trans-Saharan travelers, described the royal household as a place festooned with gold:

matrilineal succession The practice of tracing descent or the transmission of property or authority primarily through female relatives.

> The king adorns himself like a woman (wearing necklaces) round his neck and (bracelets) on his forearms, and he puts on a high cap decorated with gold and wrapped in a turban of fine cotton. He sits in audience . . . in a domed pavilion around which stand ten horses covered with gold-embroidered materials. Behind the king stand ten pages holding shields and swords decorated with gold, and on his right are the sons of the (vassal) kings of his country wearing splendid garments and their hair plaited with gold. . . . When the people who profess the same religion as the king approach him they fall on their knees and sprinkle dust on their head, for this is their way of greeting him.[6]

Islam in West Africa. Muslim merchants and other visitors of Saharan or North African origin almost certainly first introduced Islam to West Africa. According to Al-Bakri, the royal capital of Ghana, whose location is not known, was divided into two areas. "One of these towns, which is inhabited by Muslims, is large and possesses twelve mosques, in which they assemble for the Friday prayer. There are salaried imams [prayer leaders] and muezzins [criers who call Muslims to prayer] as well as jurists and scholars. . . . The king's town is six miles distant from this one."[7] In time the Muslim residents of Ghana's capital converted Sudanic merchants, notably people who spoke Soninke. The converts subsequently carried knowledge of the faith deeper into the savanna. Islam's cultural package inevitably included

Arabic, which established itself quickly as the Sudan's alphabetic language for religion, scholarship, and administration. According to Al-Bakri, many of Ghana's royal officials were literate Muslims.

West African kings tended to walk a narrow religious line, encouraging Muslim commercial enterprise and Arabic literacy but serving their non-Muslim majorities as well by performing traditional sacred rituals. Nevertheless, the ruler of Gao converted to Islam about 1000 C.E., and the kings of Ghana and other states not much later. Thus, West Africa became enmeshed in the larger Afroeurasian network of trade and cultural exchange.

Europe's Struggle for Stability

FOCUS How did invasions and migrations between the seventh and ninth centuries affect Europe's struggle for political and economic stability?

With the exception of the Muslim Umayyad state in Spain, Europe west of the Byzantine empire in the ninth and tenth centuries was a scene of small monarchies and dukedoms, despite the effort the Frankish king Charlemagne had made between 768 and 814 to forge a new Christian empire (see Chapter 10). Within a few decades of Charlemagne's death, his kingdom fragmented amid civil struggles among his three grandsons and the subsequent dividing and subdividing of its former territory among numerous aristocratic families. None of them had sufficient military resources to reverse this trend.

Scholars used to write off the whole era of western European history from the fifth to the eleventh centuries as a "dark age" of economic stagnation nearly everywhere except Spain. More recently, historians using both written texts and archaeological data have redrawn this picture. New evidence suggests that in the eighth and early decades of the ninth centuries, including the decades when Charlemagne ruled, Europe was inching along a track of demographic and economic recovery. Evidence of this upward trend includes the movements of travelers such as diplomatic envoys, pilgrims, and merchants; the number of ships plying the Mediterranean; the flow of gold and silver coins from Muslim states and Byzantium into western Europe; the production and distribution of pottery; and amounts of expenditures on church and monastic buildings.

This growth trend used to go unnoticed partly because it faltered temporarily in the later ninth and tenth centuries as new bands of raiders and invaders stormed into western Europe: Arabs from across the Mediterranean, Magyars (MAH-jahrs) from the Inner Eurasian steppes, and Vikings (Norse) from Scandinavia. These aggressions interrupted, if only temporarily, Europe's agrarian recovery as well as its reintegration into the expanding Mediterranean exchange network.

Muslims and Magyars

Muslim states, including the Umayyad kingdom in Spain, dominated the southern and western shores of the Mediterranean. Using their agrarian wealth to build a fleet of warships, the dynasty known as the Aghlabids (800–909), whose center was modern Tunisia, seized the island of Sicily from its Byzantine Greek governors and took command of the crucial sea passages that connected the eastern and western halves of the Mediterranean. Aghlabid forces, plus bands of Muslim pirates, raided the coasts of Italy and France, advanced up the Rhône and other navigable rivers, and built a scattering of forts and trading posts. In 846, for example, the people of Rome watched in dismay as Arab-led raiders sailed up the Tiber River and sacked the city's outer neighborhoods.

The Aghlabid offensive had two important consequences for Europe. First, Muslim soldiers became major players in the politics of southern Italy, competing with Byzantine forces, troops commanded by the Christian pope, and, at times, Frankish armies for control of towns and trade. Consequently, Italy remained in a general state of turmoil and economic uncertainty until the end of the first millennium. Second, because Muslims dominated the central Mediterranean sea lanes, Italian and other Christian European merchants had a hard time breaking into the maritime trade, and therefore into the wider trans-hemispheric system, until the late tenth century.

European traders knew that they could avoid Muslim sea rovers by exporting goods to Byzantium or other points down the Danube River. In the late ninth century, however, the Magyars, a new horde of pastoral nomads, nearly shut down that route. In the typical pattern of Inner Eurasian population movements, the Magyars appear to have moved westward from the steppes north of the Black Sea into central Europe because other aggressive migrants pushed them from behind. Magyar horse culture was similar to that of Turkic pastoralists. However, the Magyar language, which was ancestral to modern Hungarian, belongs along with modern Finnish and Estonian to the Finno-Ugric family, whose origins lie in the eastern steppes.

Putting down a base on the grassy plains of Hungary west of the Carpathian Mountains, Magyar cavalry raided deep into Germany, France, and northern Italy, avoiding well-defended towns but plundering villages, disrupting harvests, and carrying off large numbers of peasant men and women to sell to eastern Mediterranean slave dealers. Fortunately for settled folk, the Magyar whirlwind blew itself out within about fifty years. Defeated by armored German cavalry in the mid-tenth century, surviving Magyar warriors and their families settled on the Hungarian plain, turned to farming, and eventually converted to Christianity.

The Viking Adventure

Arab and Magyar raids disrupted western Europe, but the Vikings, predatory migrants from Scandinavia (Denmark, Norway, and Sweden), changed it profoundly. Ranging over an astonishingly large expanse between the ninth and eleventh centuries, Vikings pillagers, conquerors, merchants, and colonizers operated from the Black Sea in the east to Newfoundland in far-off North America (see Map 11.5).

The ancestors of the Vikings, or Norse, were speakers of North Germanic languages who occupied Scandinavia as part of the westward movement of Indo-European-speaking peoples that also included the Saxons, Franks, Vandals, and other Germanic groups. Viking men and women made their livings as farmers, fishers, and traders on the coastal plains, valley floors, and islands of the Baltic Sea region. In the post-Roman centuries, when Christian culture was implanting itself in Ireland and Britain, Vikings, largely oblivious to the Holy Gospel, worshiped a household of powerful gods and goddesses.

Motives for expansion. Why did Vikings sail forth to plunder distant neighbors, set up trading posts, and found colonial settlements? One factor may have been a climatic warming trend in northern Europe starting around 800 C.E. and lasting until about 1300. Climatologists call this warming cycle the North Atlantic Warm Period (or Medieval Warm Period). This change permitted Scandinavian farmers to grow oats, barley, and wheat at higher elevations and more northerly latitudes than they previously could. Population subsequently grew, eventually outstripping available farmland and forcing some people to seek livings abroad. A second possibility is that as the Scandinavian farming and fishing economy expanded, local leaders tried to create centralized states. This may have happened in Denmark as early as the eighth century. These ventures involved political struggles, prompting independent warrior-farmers who rejected kingly rule to head off on their own. Third, Scandinavians had taken part in European commercial networks in Roman times, exchanging amber, furs, walrus ivory, and other products of the north for urban manufactures. Vikings therefore became practiced sailors and shipbuilders. When their migrations began, they already had seaworthy vessels. These relatively light ships had broad-bottomed hulls of overlapping planks that permitted both easy beaching and movement along shallow coasts and rivers. From the eighth century, oarsmen powered these ships with help from great square sails that Viking women wove from wool. Shipwrights constructed war vessels long and narrow for speed; they built cargo ships shorter and wider for ample carrying capacity. Both types were stout enough to sail on rough northern seas and out of sight of land for many days.

Viking offensives. The Norse assaults on other parts of Europe involved numerous independent campaigns. From what is today Norway, bands attacked northern Britain, Scotland, and Ireland, deliberately targeting churches and monasteries for brutal destruction because these places often had stores of gold. In 793, for example, Viking sea raiders hit the northeastern coast of England, completely demolishing Lindisfarne, the richest center of Christian

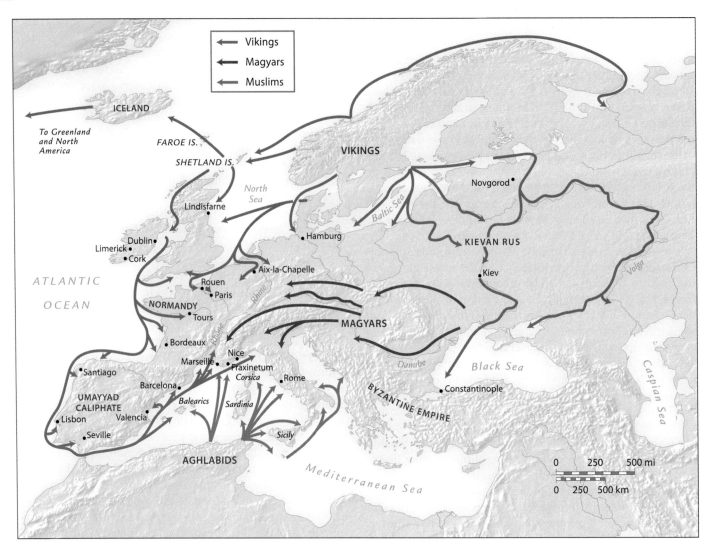

MAP 11.5 Invasion, migration, and settlement in Europe, ninth to eleventh centuries.
Did Vikings, Magyars, and North African Muslims have any similar motivations for attacking or migrating into western Europe?

learning in the British Isles. In some places, Vikings arrived as looters and killers but then stayed on to settle and colonize, founding, for example, the towns of Dublin, Cork, and Limerick in Ireland. From those centers, Norse warriors launched further expeditions, while women, children, and slaves stayed behind to grow crops and expand settlements.

Norwegian Vikings also contributed to the initial human colonization of some places. Seaborne bands very likely founded the earliest settlements on both the Faroe Islands (north of Scotland) and Iceland. Near the end of the tenth century, Viking ships reached the southern edge of ice-capped Greenland—a huge island already frequented by Inuit sea hunters from North America. A few thousand Viking men and women settled fjords along the Greenland coast. There, they scratched out grain fields, though they remained dependent for food on sea links with Iceland and Europe.

Archaeologists have verified that Viking mariners reached North America and lived for part of the eleventh century at L'Anse aux Meadows on the northeastern coast of Newfoundland. We know nothing of their interaction with local American Indians, and after a few decades they abandoned their settlement. Six hundred miles of open North Atlantic water separated L'Anse aux Meadows from Greenland, a distance that even the hardiest Viking sailors could not bridge for long.

While Norwegians prowled the far north, Danish Vikings moved out from Jutland (the peninsula that today is part of Denmark) to assail France and England, skimming along coasts and far up rivers, including the Seine and the Thames. In the ninth century, Danish forces, leaving their ships to fight on foot and horseback, conquered much of England. Anglo-Saxon warriors, whose own Germanic ancestors had

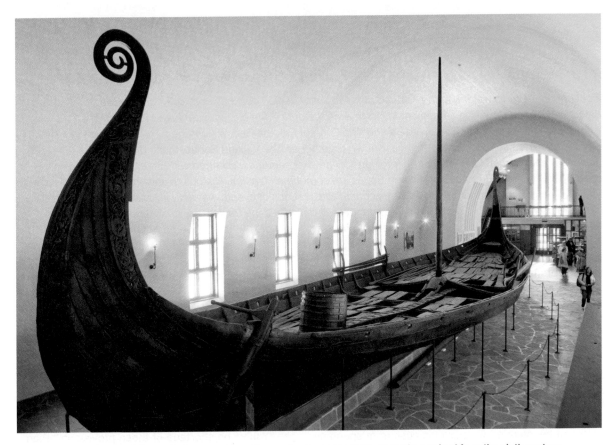

A Viking ship. This graceful vessel, discovered by a Norwegian farmer in 1903, no doubt survived from the ninth century because it was pulled from the water and transformed into a burial structure for two women, probably members of elite families. An array of grave goods accompanied the women, including the corpses of sacrificed horses, dogs, and cows. The mast supported a square sail, and the ship could accommodate thirty rowers. The ship resides in the Viking Ship Museum in Oslo. Why do you think Vikings used vessels as burial chambers?

invaded the island only a few centuries earlier, held on to the southwest and gradually pushed the Danes northward. Many Vikings settled in England, married Anglo-Saxon women, took up farming, and converted to Christianity. Eventually, the Danes of England disappeared as a distinct ethnic and linguistic group.

Viking raiders took full advantage of the disintegration of the Carolingian empire to step up attacks on northern France. They plundered and then colonized the fertile Seine valley. At the end of the tenth century, the king of the Franks, who was then simply a regional lord, ratified Norse control of a large area of northern France, henceforth known as the Duchy of Normandy. These immigrants married into local families and in time became known as the Normans.

Vikings and the rise of Kiev. Swedish-speaking Norse, more merchants than swordsmen at first, pioneered southeastward expansion from Scandinavia. Crossing the Baltic, they voyaged up several northern continental rivers, then down the Dnieper to the Black Sea. With them went furs, honey, amber, wax, and slaves for Abbasid and Byzantine markets. This "northern arc" of sea, river, and overland forest routes joined northeastern Europe with Southwest Asia. Swedish traders strengthened the northern routes by founding settlements at Novgorod, Kiev, and other strategic points already inhabited by Slavic or Turkic peoples. Archaeologists have uncovered hoards of Arab silver coins (more than 50,000 of them) in Scandinavian sites, and even a bronze Buddha dating to the sixth or seventh centuries. These finds testify to the success and long reach of the northern arc trade.

In the ninth century, Kiev, today the capital of Ukraine, emerged as the center of a Viking warrior state that supplanted the power of the Khazar kingdom (see Chapter 10) north of the Black Sea. Viking sea raiders even approached Constantinople three times between 860 and 941, though they probably hoped only to win political and commercial recognition from the Greek emperor. In the Kiev region, as in western Europe, Viking men married local women and gradually took up the ways and speech of the predominantly Slavic population. Arab geographers adopted the name "Rus" to describe this cultural merger of Swedes, Slavs, and Turks.

Bjarni Herjolfsson and the Viking Discovery of America

The discovery of a spindle weight, a ring-headed pin, and a Norwegian coin have provided conclusive archeological evidence for Viking settlement in North America during the eleventh century. In addition, two textual sources, The Saga of the Greenlanders *and* The Saga of Erik the Red, *offer thirteenth-century accounts of Viking expeditions to North America. Known together as* The Vinland Sagas, *these documents set down tales that had circulated in Viking oral traditions for several centuries. Blended with other legends and influenced by stories from Europe,* The Vinland Sagas *are sometimes fanciful. Historians have questioned their veracity and generally regard them as semifictional elaborations of events that actually took place. The selection here comes from* The Saga of the Greenlanders. *It describes the travels of Bjarni Herjolfsson, a Norwegian explorer who in 985 or 986 C.E. appears to have sighted North America but did not anchor his ships there.*

[Bjarni] was a promising young man. While still a youthful age he longed to sail abroad. He soon earned for himself both a good deal of wealth and a good name, and spent his winters alternately abroad and with his father. Soon Bjarni had his own ship making trading voyages. During the last winter Bjarni spent in Norway, [his father] Herjolf decided to accompany Erik the Red to Greenland and left his farm. . . .

Bjarni steered his ship into Eyrar [in Iceland] in the summer of the year that his father had sailed from Iceland. Bjarni was greatly moved by the news and would not have his cargo unloaded. His crew then asked what he was waiting for, and he answered that he intended to follow his custom of spending the winter with his father—"and I want to set sail for Greenland, if you will join me."

All of them said they would follow his counsel.

Bjarni then spoke: "Our journey will be thought an ill-considered one, since none of us has sailed the Greenland Sea."

Despite this they set sail once they had made ready and sailed for three days, until the land had disappeared below the horizon. Then the wind dropped and they were beset by winds from the north and fog; for many days they did not know where they were sailing.

After that they saw the sun and could take their bearings. Hoisting the sail, they sailed for the rest of the day before sighting land. They speculated among themselves as to what land this would be, for Bjarni said he suspected this was not Greenland.

They asked whether he wanted to sail up close into the shore of this country or not. "My advice is that we sail in close to the land."

They did so, and soon saw that the land was not mountainous but did have small hills, and was covered with forests. Keeping it on their port side, they turned their sail-end landwards and angled away from the shore.

They sailed for another two days before sighting the land once again.

They asked Bjarni whether he now thought this to be Greenland.

He said he thought this no more likely to be Greenland than the previous land—"since there are said to be very large glaciers in Greenland."

They soon approached the land and saw that it was flat and wooded. The wind died and the crew members said they thought it advisable to put ashore, but Bjarni was against it. They claimed they needed both timber and water.

"You've no shortage of those provisions," Bjarni said, but he was criticized somewhat by his crew for this.

[Bjarni and his crew then sighted a third land. But they did not land there and sailed back out to sea.]

Upon seeing a fourth land they asked Bjarni whether he thought this was Greenland or not.

Bjarni answered, "This land is most like what I have been told of Greenland, and we'll head for shore here."

This they did and made land along a headland in the evening of the day, finding a boat there. On this point Herjolf, Bjarni's father, lived [. . .] Bjarni now joined his father and ceased his merchant voyages. He remained on his father's farm as long as Herjolf lived and took over the farm after his death.

Following this, Bjarni Herjolfsson sailed from Greenland to Earl Erik, who received him well. . . .

Bjarni became one of the earl's followers and sailed to Greenland the following summer. There was now much talk of looking for new lands.

Source: The Vinland Sagas: The Icelandic Sagas about the First Documented Voyages across the North Atlantic, *trans. Keneva Kunz, intro. and notes by Gisli Sigurdsson (London and New York: Penguin, 2008), pp. 3–5.*

Thinking Critically

What sort of information did Bjarni rely on to guide him to Greenland? Why do you think he refused to stop and explore the first three lands his crew spotted? Should Bjarni be credited with "discovering" America? Why or why not?

The Rus thus became Russians, builders of a state of increasing size and power. Negotiation and trade, as much as conflict, characterized relations between the Rus state and Byzantium. Around 1000 the Russian prince Vladimir (r. 980–1015) converted to Greek Orthodox Christianity. Thereafter, the Russian state and the Christian church became close collaborators. One consequence was a surge of Greek artistic and architectural influence into western Inner Eurasia. In the eleventh and twelfth centuries, towns from Kiev in the south to Novgorod in the cold, forested north acquired stone churches, bishops, and church laws that regulated social and ritual life. The Russian church, however, made itself distinct from its Byzantine parent, adopting, for example, East Slavic, not Greek, as the language of religious literacy and worship.

Kiev may be counted among the most prosperous and beautifully adorned capitals in western Eurasia in those centuries. Even so, the plains and woodlands stretching north of Kiev had relatively poor soils and a short growing season. This limited agrarian base obliged the Russian rulers to press down hard on the farming population, risking local revolt. They also had to compete with other princely families, who had their own provincial power centers beyond Kiev's controlling radius. Consequently, the princes of Kiev never accumulated vast wealth or fully subordinated rival Russian noble families to their authority.

The Changing Shape of Western Europe

In western Europe, local societies experimented with new forms of defense and government in response to Arab, Magyar, and Viking raiders. In the region that is now Belgium and northern France, the crumbling of Charlemagne's empire convinced Frankish aristocratic families, none of whom had much concentrated military power, to fall back on relatively small core territories. There, they built castles and manors (fortified houses) to protect fields, grazing land, and the hamlets where their tenants and serfs lived. From these local bastions, estate holders tried to defend themselves against alien intruders and, much of the time, against one another. The individual who held the title of king in the tenth century was one of these barons and not always the most powerful. Aristocratic men did most of the fighting, adopting a war technology that had antecedents in Byzantium and, before that, Sasanid Persia. Frankish knights heavily armored both themselves and their big horses and did battle with lance and sword, sometimes mounted, sometimes on foot. A relatively small group of knights armed in this way could effectively protect a manor house and the estate around it, though aristocrats generally lacked the resources to transport arms, servants, and horses over long distances. Thus, warfare was mostly defensive and local.

An eleventh-century castle. In that era, northern European nobles and their families needed stout defenses. This replica image of a fortified residence has both a moat and a bailey, or outer wall. Behind the inner wall is the castle proper, called the keep.

Origins of European feudalism. Historians describe the style of political relations among these numerous western

> **fief** An estate of land an individual holds on condition of allegiance and service to the grantor.

European warlords as feudal, which comes from the Latin word *feudum*, meaning landed estate, or **fief.** The key element in relations among aristocratic warriors was personal obligations of military service and responsibility cemented by rituals that all parties were to take very seriously. This system of power was based not on bureaucrats serving a central authority but on associations for mutual benefit between patrons and clients, that is, between militarily strong individuals and

> **vassal** An individual who is subordinate to or dependent on another individual; in feudalism an individual who holds land given by a lord in return for loyal service.

relatively weaker ones. Feudal relations were hierarchical in the sense that one warrior, called the **vassal,** offered service, recognition, and loyalty to a more powerful warrior, the lord. In return, the lord granted protection, rewards, and privileges to his vassals.

In western Europe's still fragile economic conditions, aristocratic lords had little to offer their vassals except agriculturally productive fiefs. Moreover, the most powerful lords—the dukes and barons—needed fighting knights so badly that they granted vassals not only fiefs but also rights to transfer their property to their heirs, thereby creating multigenerational feudal relations. Some vassals became rich enough to recruit vassals of their own, awarding these lesser knights land in return for military service. This practice expanded the hierarchy of obligation and service to three or more levels.

Aristocratic men specialized in fighting, but well-born women fully involved themselves in feudal relations. To operate effectively from one generation to the next, the system required male heirs and family alliances, which meant marriage agreements over which mothers, sisters, and prospective brides exerted great influence. Also, women frequently managed estates, large and small, when sons and husbands went off to battle.

In a strict sense, feudal bonds involved only men and women of the landowning elite, a small minority of western Europe's population. Other forms of patron-client relationship, especially serfdom (see Chapter 10), bound landlords and peasants to one another, the latter farming the lands that provided revenue for war horses, manors, fortifications, and the elite's relatively comfortable lifestyle. At their master's command, peasants also went to war as infantry soldiers, servants, and laborers.

Northern state builders. The struggle for political and social order took significantly different turns in both England and northern Germany.

> **feudalism** A hierarchical system of social and political organization in which an individual gives grants of land to other individuals in return for allegiance and service.

Those regions also adopted the rituals and institutions of **feudalism,** but state building there was successful earlier than it was in France. In the later ninth century, Alfred the Great (r. 871–899), king of the small Anglo-Saxon state of Wessex in southern England, pushed back Danish invaders and even revived in some measure Latin literacy and scholarship. Dukes and barons continued to exert great power, but in the interests of political stability they more readily accepted the king as paramount than did aristocrats in northern France.

At the end of the tenth century, however, Vikings briefly triumphed once again. This time the militarily gifted and thoroughly Christian king Canute, operating from Jutland, conquered not only England but also Norway and Estonia. From about 1015 to 1035, he ruled a unified state that spanned the Baltic and North Seas. The most important stake in this project was the maritime trade of the two seas, which began to grow dramatically near the end of the first millennium. When Canute died, however, his northern sea empire disintegrated quickly, leaving England to an independent fate.

Central monarchy also succeeded, at least loosely, in northern Germany in the tenth century. There, Otto I (r. 936–973), the ruler of Saxony, managed to subdue the dukes of four other powerful German territories and in 955 crushed the Magyars. He then invaded Italy, and in 962 the pope named him Holy Roman Emperor, the same majestic but exaggerated title Charlemagne had held. Otto allied closely with the church, handing out estates and offices to bishops and the men and women who headed monasteries. He therefore commanded the loyalty of administrators who could not marry and build family power because they were members of the clergy. Otto's successors worked to perpetuate this fledgling central bureaucracy, but aristocratic families continued to press for regional autonomy, exposing the political fragility of the Holy Roman Empire.

Italian city-states. In Italy the southern region remained a land of contention among Byzantine Greeks, Muslims, and Catholic Christians. In the center and north, feudal relations had little relevance. Rather, individuals commonly identified with a particular town or city and the surrounding land it controlled. These city-states were in no way democracies, and many of them were ruled by bishops and their appointed officers. The pope governed Rome and extensive lands around it. Nevertheless, as the economy of the peninsula revived gradually, the landowning and commercial class exerted increasing influence. By the early eleventh century, Europe both north and south of the Alps was set for a burst of economic growth and cultural creativity.

• • •

Conclusion

The world historian Lynda Shaffer has characterized many of the developments discussed in this chapter as part of a larger process that she calls "southernization."[8] The term refers to a historical process whereby a number of ideas, techniques, and products of great importance in human history developed in India and Southeast Asia and then spread to other parts of Afroeurasia. Southernization got under way in the early centuries C.E. and continued as a significant pattern into the modern era. Among the elements of southernization were the thickening of trade routes and networks across the southern seas, growing production and exchange of tropical spices such as pepper, the wide diffusion of South Asian crops such as cotton and sugar, the spread of improved sailing and navigation technologies, and the dissemination of ingenious mathematical concepts. As a result of influences from India and Southeast Asia, other regions, including East Asia, the central Muslim lands, Europe, and tropical Africa, all became in some measure "southernized" in economy and culture.

Not all important ideas of the later first millennium C.E., however, spread outward from southern Asia. We may point to Christianity, Islam, the silk industry, and the invention of paper, among many innovations, that originated in other parts of the hemisphere. In any case, southernization occurred on such a large scale only because available communication and transport technologies allowed it. In the centuries this chapter has addressed, networks of interchange advanced far beyond their range and complexity as of, say, 500 C.E. The hubs in these networks were the ports and inland cities where routes converged and branched out. The era witnessed a remarkable multiplication of these hubs, notably in the lands rimming the southern seas. Traffic moved faster and more efficiently along the trans-hemispheric routes because of ideas and institutions that served the communication system itself. These included the moral and ethical codes of the major religions, which provided standards of right behavior among people who spoke different languages and had mutually unfamiliar customs; the standardizing of written languages and accompanying spread of literacy; the simplifying of commercial accounting with base-ten "Indian" numerals; the production of documents using paper; the organizing of larger, more complex diasporas of professional merchants; and an array of financial techniques for speeding market exchange. In Chapter 12, which focuses on Afroeurasia between 1000 and 1250, we will see that these trends continued, though the centers of most dynamic growth and innovation shifted significantly.

• • •

Key Terms

Abbasid empire 309	Kiev, Rus 329	shari'a 310
cosmopolitan 313	Magyars 326	Silla dynasty 321
Fatimid dynasty 312	mamluk 311	Srivijaya 319
feudalism 332	matrilineal succession 326	ulama 310
fief 332	military slavery 311	vassal 332
Ghana 325	Pallava dynasty 318	Vikings 336
Holy Roman Empire 332	proselytize 314	Yamato dynasty 321
Kanem 324	Samanid dynasty 312	Zanj Rebellion 311

Change over Time

7th–13th centuries	The kingdom of Srivijaya becomes a maritime empire in Southeast Asia.
668–935	The Silla dynasty rules in Korea.
710	The Yamato dynasty founds the town of Nara as a royal center.
750–1258	The Abbasid Caliphate rules from Baghdad, reaching its zenith of power during the reign of Harun al-Rashid (786–809).
756–1031	The Umayyad dynasty, ruling from Córdoba, presides over a prosperous urban economy in Spain.
819–999	Persian aristocrats establish the Samanid dynasty with its capital at Bukhara; the dynasty promotes Muslim missionary activity along silk roads.
869–883	The Abbasids face the Zanj Rebellion in Iraq.
9th century	Vikings assault northern Europe; Magyars invade central Europe; Muslim Aghlabids take control of Mediterranean sea lanes and raid Italy.
10th century	The kingdom of Ghana, the largest state in West Africa, reaches its height of prosperity.
936–973	Otto I reigns over the Holy Roman empire in western Europe.
969–1171	The Shi'a Fatimid dynasty in Egypt declares itself Islam's true caliphate.
976–1025	Byzantine territorial expansion resumes during the reign of Basil II.
ca. 1000	The ruler of Gao in West Africa converts to Islam.
980–1035	Prince Vladimir of Kiev establishes the Russian Orthodox Church.
11th century	Vikings settle in Newfoundland.

Please see end of book reference section for additional reading suggestions related to this chapter.

part 4

Interconnections and Their Consequences

900-1500

A blue-green porcelain vase from China's Song Dynasty.

ooking at the human past through a very wide-angle lens, we might say that the world did not change much between the era we explored in Part 3 and the six centuries we now investigate in Part 4. Between 900 and 1500, the agrarian age continued as before. In other words, agriculture, including both crop and domestic animal raising, remained the economic foundation of both rural villagers and the builders of complex societies with their cities, centralized governments, and grand buildings. The ability of humans to produce food, fiber, and fuel remained as strictly dependent on the soil as it had throughout the agrarian age. Even though people continued to invent practical new tools—better plows, horse harnesses, sails, water-lifting machines—the number of daily calories of useful energy an individual could control barely doubled from the dawn of agriculture to 1000.[1] And that number did not begin to accelerate at a much faster rate until the nineteenth century, when our species devised ways to exploit immense underground stores of energy from coal, oil, and gas.

If we view history through a somewhat narrower lens, we see that several large-scale patterns of change under way in the first millennium C.E. continued into the second. World population, economic output, and interregional trade all continued to increase, while societies fashioned more complex social and economic institutions and accumulated more scientific and technical knowledge. We saw in Part 3 that these trends, all generally characteristic of the agrarian age, could be interrupted by unforeseen slumps in population and economy accompanied by more intense social and political turmoil. This happened between the third and sixth centuries. As we shall see in Part 4, it happened again in the 1300s, a depressive period marked by the great

Afroeurasian disease pandemic we call the Black Death. But as in the first millennium, the downturn was temporary. Recovery took hold in the fifteenth century, and between 900 and 1500, the population of Afroeurasia managed to double.

If we focus even more closely on hemispheric and regional landscapes, we see that the 900–1500 period looks very different from the previous millennium. In Part 4 we explore changes that had broad regional or hemispheric effects in those six hundred years:

■ In China under the Song (960–1276) and Jin (1115–1234) dynasties, manufacturing, commerce, urbanization, and technical innovation all surged forward. China's economic growth outpaced that of all other regions. And because China both exported and imported larger quantities of goods, its prosperity affected the livelihoods and business activities of peoples as far distant as East Africa and western Europe.

■ Pastoral nomads of Inner Eurasia had a greater impact on Afroeurasia's history between 900 and 1500 than in any period before or after. Beginning in the late tenth century, Turkic-speaking nomads migrated in large numbers into densely settled lands of Southwest Asia, and they raided and conquered along an even wider arc of territory. By the twelfth century, Turkic populations, or at least military elites, dominated societies from Egypt to South Asia's Ganges valley. These movements caused social and political upheavals, but the great cities of Southwest Asia and Egypt continued to prosper as centers of manufacturing and commerce.

■ Among Afroeurasia's major belief systems, Islam spread more widely than any other during these centuries. Because Turkic migrants and conquerors were Muslims, they introduced their faith to new regions. Merchants, scholars, and wandering preachers also founded new Muslim communities from West Africa to China.

■ In Europe, improving political stability and new agricultural inventions fueled more towns and trade, a development that paralleled events in Song China on a smaller scale. By the eleventh century, a new center of urban civilization under the moral and cultural guidance of the Catholic Christian church was taking shape. Europeans linked themselves more firmly to the web of hemispheric exchange, a process interrupted but not halted by climatic change and the Black Death.

■ In Africa south of the Sahara Desert, population levels remained lower than in the agrarian lands of Eurasia and northern Africa. Nevertheless, farming and cattle-herding societies continued to grow and with them more inter-regional trade, cities, and large states. In the thirteenth and fourteenth centuries, for example, the West African empire of Mali stimulated Afroeurasian trade by exporting large quantities of gold.

■ Pastoral nomadic conquests resumed on a spectacular scale in the early thirteenth century, when Mongol and Turkic horse cavalry stormed across Eurasia, forging the largest land empire the world had ever seen. The Mongol conquests from China to Hungary were terrifying, but once the victors founded new governments, they rebuilt cities and patronized art and learning. For more than a century, Mongol rulers encouraged the flow of goods, technologies, and religious ideas across Afroeurasia.

■ In the Americas, total population may have been only a fifth of China's as of 1200, but numbers grew as farmers experimented with irrigation and land-reclaiming techniques and as maize cultivation spread more widely. Several new monument-building states appeared, culminating in the fifteenth century with the rise of the Aztec and Inca empires. Those two states demonstrated that human labor and creativity could be mobilized on an enormous scale despite the absence of iron technology or wheeled transport.

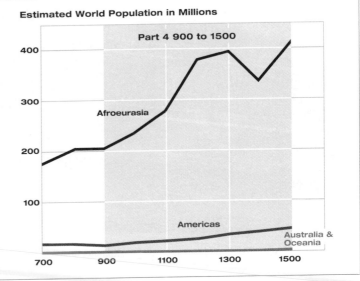

Estimated World Population in Millions

Part 4 900 to 1500

12 Dynamic Centuries across Afroeurasia

1000–1250

Scroll painting of commercial life in Kaifeng, China, in the twelfth century.

Every year more than 3,200 state and county fairs are held in North America. Some people go to fairs to compete for blue ribbons for the finest products of farm and home—the best cows, rabbits, quilts, applesauce, and dill pickles. Other people go for the Ferris wheels, Belgian waffles, and country singers. The agricultural fair, where local farmers and artisans sell goods and demonstrate crafts, has been a distinctive American institution since the early nineteenth century. It has its deep origins in the rural or small-town market, an institution that in premodern centuries usually appeared wherever settled populations, workshops, and trade flourished. Rural markets typically sprang up on the borders between different ecological regions or where geography, political conditions, and transport routes encouraged people to meet together in an open space to exchange wares. Sometimes several markets in a region were linked together in a rotation, each one taking place on a particular day of the week or season of the year. To attract merchants and customers, rural markets usually organized some kind of authority to police the grounds, set rules of public behavior, and penalize troublemakers, cheaters, and thieves. If the market also offered food and amusements, it had most of the features of a modern fair.

We have good evidence that both country and town markets were growing in number and size in several parts of Afroeurasia between the eleventh and thirteenth centuries. We know this was happening, for example, in China, the Ganges River valley, southern India, western Europe, and tropical West Africa. Historians generally agree that in most of Afroeurasia's agrarian regions, population, economic production, and commerce started trending upward about the sixth century and that this trend accelerated between 1000 and 1250. Quantitative data to demonstrate this development are very limited. Some societies preserved commercial and financial information more carefully than others did, and in no case has more than a small part of everyday economic records survived to the present. Nevertheless, historians see patterns of growth, not only in the proliferation of local markets, but also in the opening of new trade routes, the numbers of ships plying seas and inland waterways, the circulation of currencies, the invention of new credit and banking techniques, and the size of textile and other manufacturing operations.

China had possessed the largest regional economy in the world throughout most of the first millennium c.e. In the eleventh and twelfth centuries, that economy grew even bigger relative to other Afroeurasian regions, even to India. We begin this chapter with a focus on East Asia because China's Song dynasty (960–1276) presided over an unprecedented rush of industrial and commercial activity, a development

Chapter Outline

THE EAST ASIAN POWERHOUSE IN THE SONG ERA
The Elements of China's Prosperity
Governing China in an Era of Change
China and Its Near Neighbors
Japan within and without the Chinese Sphere
China in the Hemisphere

CONQUERORS AND MIGRANTS IN THE MUSLIM LANDS
Turkic Horse Power
Muslim Ships on the Mediterranean
WEIGHING THE EVIDENCE A Jewish Merchant Writes to His Wife
New Empires in the Western Mediterranean
Cultural Trends in the Muslim Lands

FOUNDATIONS OF URBAN CIVILIZATION IN EUROPE
Warm Weather, Better Plows
New Order in Political Life
INDIVIDUALS MATTER King Philip II: French State-Builder
The Expansion of Western Christendom
European Commercial Power in the Mediterranean
Western Europe's Cultural Style

• • •

that helped stimulate economic growth across Afroeurasia. This section of the chapter also addresses China's close neighbors, especially Japan, an island society that made its own economic gains in the 1000–1250 period and that emerged as a distinctive city-based civilization.

The second part of the chapter highlights the important historical transition that took place in Afroeurasia's middle regions (see Map 12.1). Repeating in some ways the tumultuous pastoral movements of the fourth to seventh centuries, migrants who spoke Turkic languages swept from Central Asia across both Southwest Asia and northern India, replacing old states with new ones and changing the ethnolinguistic identity of wide areas. Despite these political disturbances, however, the numerous cities of Southwest Asia continued to play their accustomed role as centers of manufacturing and commercial exchange. Muslim merchants sailed the Mediterranean as they had done for 350 years, though they faced increasing competition from western European newcomers. Turkic state-builders, already Muslims when they initiated their conquests, became sponsors of Muslim literature and

A Panoramic View

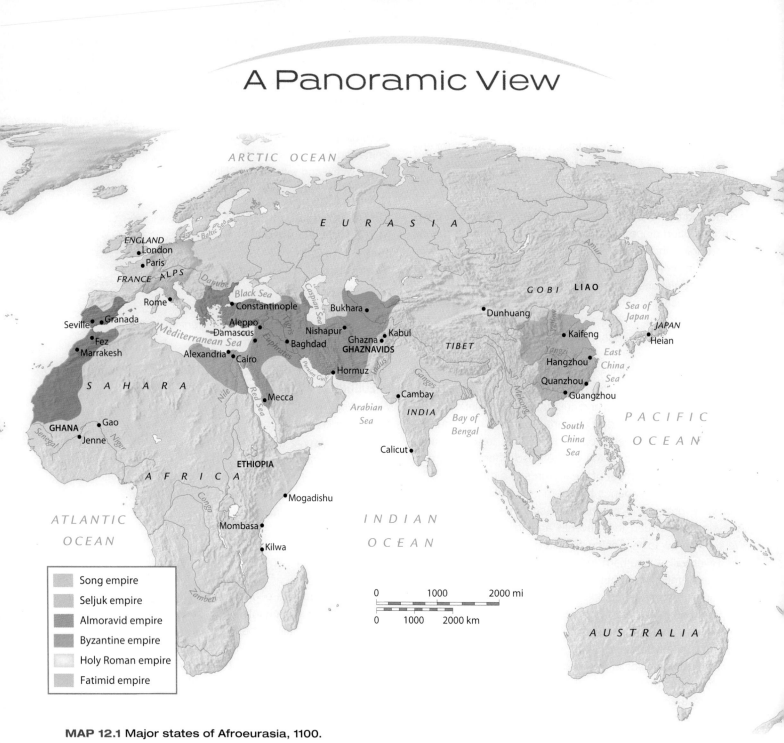

MAP 12.1 Major states of Afroeurasia, 1100.

At the start of the twelfth century, China's Song dynasty presided over Afroeurasia's largest regional economy, while the boundaries of western Christendom expanded. In what regions might you predict pastoral nomadic peoples to emerge as a potent political force?

art, and they energized the continuing spread of Islam. In the far west of the Muslim world, migrating Berber armies mirrored the Turkic invasions by conquering North Africa (modern Morocco, Algeria, and Tunisia) and a large part of Spain.

Western Europe, reduced in population between the fifth and ninth centuries, achieved greater political stability after 900 and entered an era of remarkable economic and cultural renewal. Exploiting the region's agricultural resources with greater efficiency, Europe's farmers and artisans augmented production to the point where towns and the trade routes between them began to multiply. Under the religious and cultural guidance of the Catholic Church, Europeans laid the base of a new urban civilization, pushed out the frontiers of western Christendom east and west, and entered Mediterranean trade on a much larger scale, linking themselves more firmly to the entire trans-hemispheric network.

The East Asian Powerhouse in the Song Era

FOCUS In what ways did China's economy change between the eleventh and thirteenth centuries, and what effects did these economic changes have on other parts of Afroeurasia?

Most world historians agree that China's economic surge in the era of the Song dynasty triggered large commercial and cultural changes in Afroeurasia as a whole. This expansion, centered in the warm, rice-growing latitudes of southern China, involved swelling food production and a stunning acceleration of technical innovation, urbanization, population growth, and both internal and foreign trade. A transhemispheric exchange system already existed at the start of the new millennium. China's boom reverberated all across it.

The Elements of China's Prosperity

Economic and demographic growth got seriously under way in China when the Sui and Tang dynasties unified north and south in the sixth and seventh centuries. That growth continued even after 907, when the Tang regime collapsed and China broke into several rival regional states. Then, starting in 960, Zhao Kuangyin, a military commander from a northern monarchy, consolidated his power in most of the north, conquered the south, and founded the Song dynasty (960–1127). Zhao established his capital at Kaifeng, an interior city not far from the Yellow River.

The Song government accumulated great wealth from taxes on China's prosperity, but it did not, in contrast to its Tang predecessors, push the imperial frontiers deep into the Inner Eurasian steppe. In fact, it faced powerful new states along its grassland frontiers. For example, the farming and pastoral people known as the Kitans (also Qitans), created the Liao (lee-OW) state (916–1125), which stretched across the prairies and forests of Mongolia and Manchuria. The Song government bought decades of reasonable calm with the Liao and other Inner Eurasia kingdoms by sending them annual cargos of silk and silver, as earlier dynasties had done.

A third northern kingdom proved far more dangerous to the Song. Beginning in 1115, the Jurchens, a group native to the forests of Manchuria, destroyed the Liao state and proclaimed the Jin dynasty (1115–1234). The Jurchens made their living more as farmers and hunters than as animal herders, but they were nonetheless masters of cavalry. In 1127 they overran the Yellow River valley and all of northern China. They drove the Song out of their capital of Kaifeng and ascended to power over about forty million Chinese. Meanwhile, the Song governing elite fled south, successfully regrouping in the Yangzi valley and establishing a capital at Hangzhou (hahng-jo). The later Song, or Southern Song, dynasty (1127–1276) was a large regional state more than an empire.

Despite the new political fault line between northern and southern China, both the Jin and the Song thrived. The Jin harvested the huge farm revenues of the Yellow River valley and also took annual payments from the Song in return for peace. Cut off from the immense agricultural revenues of the north, the Song compensated for the loss in part by encouraging farmers in the Yangzi valley and lands farther south to expand production. Some of the same crops that diffused from India and Southeast Asia westward to the Mediterranean also spread to China. These included cotton, sugar cane, and, most important, varieties of quick-ripening, drought-resistant rice. The new rice strains, probably introduced about the tenth century from Vietnam, delivered good harvests not only in wet lowlands but also on terraced hillsides and in relatively dry climates. Farmers could produce two or even three crops a year. Consequently, southern rice production soared. Some scholars have suggested that the North Atlantic Warm Period, the slight rise in Northern Hemispheric temperatures that extended from about 800 to 1300, contributed to larger and more stable food production in China (see Chapter 11). Researchers have linked Song economic growth to higher average temperatures in the southern regions between the ninth and eleventh centuries. There is also evidence that farmers and herders in northern China suffered fewer droughts, floods, and locust infestations than in the immediate earlier or later periods.[1]

Markets, money, and canals. Displaying an unprecedented capitalist mentality, Song economic reformers argued successfully that the state should promote private market activity and tax trade as a major source of revenue. Traditional Confucian economic ideology regarded commerce as a lowly occupation because merchants did not actually *produce* anything. And it idealized peasants as reliable creators of taxable wealth from the land. By contrast, Song policymakers contended that farmers should be encouraged to sell surplus crops, textiles, and handicrafts in local markets for money to further stimulate the commercial economy. These reformers contended that the government could push rural men and women into the market by making them pay taxes in money rather than in grain or other produce. To get money, peasants had to trade. Bronze coins had lubricated the Chinese economy for centuries, but the swelling market, in which individuals, extended families, and private partnerships did business for profit, enhanced the importance of money. The government authorized production of billions of bronze and iron coins and, near the end of the eleventh century, paper money. China's papermaking and printing industries were more than advanced enough to produce large quantities of bills. Eventually, the government backed the value of these bills with reserves of silver.

Also to encourage commerce, the Song extended China's network of canals and deep river channels, already the longest in the world, to more than 30,000 miles of navigable waterways. The north–south Grand Canal linking the Yellow and Yangzi valleys carried tons of grain, iron, copper, pottery, and a thousand other commodities. On narrow

Bronze and paper money. In Song China's prospering economy, the demand for currency, like these two bronze coins, became so great that hundreds of millions, and eventually billions, of coins were minted every year. To ease the problems of making transactions with large quantities of coins, the government began in the eleventh century to issue paper bills. The note shown here would have represented a particular quantity of coins by weight. Why do you think Chinese merchants and consumers had faith in the value of paper money?

fairs were especially popular. A thirteenth-century poet described his arrival at a market in western China:

> Coming in a palanquin [a box-shaped conveyance carried on poles] to visit the Medicine Fair.
> Our bearers' knees are caught in the press of the crowd,
> Little by little we inch our way up to the gate
> Already surrounded by a diversity of goods . . .
> Merchants have buffeted the sea-winds and the waves,
> And foreign merchants crossed over towering crags,
> Drawn onwards by the profits to be made.[2]

Commercialization encouraged new economic habits. Millions of farmers began to produce not only marketable rice and cotton but also new crops such as wine grapes, sugar cane, tea, tangerines, and oil seeds. Rural families manufactured silk thread and cloth, baskets, paper, and charcoal at home. Mounting food production in the countryside meant that cities could support more people engaged full time in industry and commerce. A specialized artisan's best customers were landowners, merchants, and high officials, who had money to spend on silks, lacquered furniture, bronze statuary, and fragile white porcelain.

Wherever metals could be exploited, private mining enterprises flourished. Under the Song and later the Jin rulers, blast furnaces concentrated in great numbers around Kaifeng produced large quantities of iron and steel, a production unmatched anywhere in the world until the nineteenth century. Chinese inventors made several advances in metals technology, notably using coke (made by baking coal to remove impurities) to heat blast furnaces to higher temperatures. The Song army purchased huge quantities of iron arrowheads, swords, and armor, and canal barges shipped iron farm tools, chains for suspension bridges, and millions of nails for the shipbuilding industry in the south.

Technical ingenuity. In the eleventh and twelfth centuries, Chinese inventors and engineers showed remarkable creative spark, a surge related to the pressures of economic growth and opportunities for specialization. Technicians stuffed gunpowder into crude rockets, bombs, and mortars, which Song forces deployed in frontier wars to create noise and confusion, if not great destruction. Woodblock printing became a standard industry, and printed books, including technical and agricultural manuals, circulated widely. Other inventions of the era included the magnetic compass, new techniques for firing porcelain, water-powered bellows for blast furnaces, and spinning wheels for making silk thread. Many of these inventions spread across Afroeurasia in the ensuing centuries.

The period also saw advances in astronomy, chemistry, mathematics, and other scientific fields. Like their counterparts in the central Muslim lands, Chinese mathematicians adopted the Indian place-value system with nine numerals, as well as the zero written as "0." Mathematicians and engineers applied their knowledge mainly to practical problems such as land surveys and construction projects.

canals, rivers, and irrigation channels—the capillaries of the system—farmers and traders transported crops to local markets on boats pushed along with poles.

Local markets and fairs multiplied in the Song period. These gatherings were commonly known as "temple markets" because local people held them in connection with Buddhist or other sacred festivals. Merchants offered the gathered crowd not only candles and other religious paraphernalia but also an array of commercial goods. Medicine

The government encouraged the founding of academies for study of Confucian philosophical and literary texts, though science was pursued outside of those colleges. Scientists, working privately, communicated with one another through letters and printed texts.

The population climb. The elements of economic growth we have described operated against a background of mushrooming population, a phenomenon related to expanding food supplies. Between about 750 and 1300, China's population doubled to around 120 million, representing about a third of the world's total population. Within China, north and south switched places as the center of demographic growth. In 750, about 60 percent of the population lived in the north. By 1200, about 75 percent lived in the Yangzi valley or farther south.

In major cities, populations spilled out beyond defensive walls to make room for shops, fairs, warehouses, and floods of job-seeking rural immigrants. The population of Kaifeng grew to about one million in 1100, making it almost certainly the largest city in the world. Hangzhou, the Southern Song capital in the Yangzi delta, moved toward the million mark in the following century. Southern coastal ports similarly thrived. Quanzhou and its suburbs reached a population of about 500,000.

Rich and poor, powerful and weak. Generally speaking, standards of living rose in the Song era for all of China's traditionally defined social classes—scholars, artisans, farmers, and merchants. The majority of farm families owned land. In contrast, for example, to European serfs, they could sell their property, pass it to their children, and take surplus crops to market. Independent farmers, however, easily slid into debt to money-lenders, and big cities teemed with underemployed rural immigrants. Enterprising merchants

of nonelite origin might accumulate great wealth. Even so, Confucian bureaucrats and landed families took full precedence over merchants in prestige and power.

The speed of economic change significantly altered social relations between men and women. On family farms and in small businesses, mothers, wives, and daughters worked alongside men. Women peddled goods in local markets, and Song laws extended their rights to property. Owing partly to wider availability of printed books, more women in educated families became literate. On the other hand, cities offered a booming market for young women to serve as concubines, entertainers, prostitutes, and domestic laborers. Though legally free, women were commonly bought and sold to do these jobs. Commercialization meant opportunity for some women but drudgery, danger, and despair for many others. Moreover, Confucian leaders tended to confront rapid social change with demands that respectable women belonged at home. Affluent men conceived the idea that small feet and a swaying walk were attractive and stylish in women. Families got the desired effect in their young girls by both binding their toes under and breaking them as they grew. This extreme form of patriarchal domination became all the fashion. Only young women crippled by foot binding could hope to make a good marriage. The practice spread from the upper classes down the social scale. Only at low social levels might girls expect to grow up with normal feet.

Governing China in an Era of Change

In the waning decades of the Tang dynasty, regional army commanders had built up considerable independent power. Zhao Kuangyin, the founder of the Song regime, was himself a military man, but perhaps for that very reason he understood the value of putting the government in civilian

West Lake in Hangzhou. In the Southern Song period, urbanites enjoyed summer boating on the city's picturesque lake.

MAP 12.2 East Asia, 1200.
Considering their relative geographical locations, how might the agricultural economies of the Jin and Southern Song states have differed?

hands and keeping the army out of it. Consequently, the traditional elite class of scholar-bureaucrats, championing Confucian ideals of public morality and enlightened state-craft, strongly supported him. They subscribed to an old Chinese saying: "The best iron is not to be used for nails, and the best men are not to be used for soldiers."[3] Both the Northern and Southern Song dynasties fielded large armies to defend their land frontiers (see Map 12.2), but civilian leaders kept a tight rein on potentially unruly or defiant military officers.

Passing the test. The Song made academic success on state civil service examinations, rather than mere member-ship in an aristocratic family, the entryway to civilian office. The exams assessed knowledge of Confucian classics and literary texts, not accounting or management skills, but they ensured that men who could read, write, and think handled imperial affairs. Thus the Chinese state became more than ever a **meritocracy.** Preparing for the tests, however, required such long and expensive training that al-most all examinees had the support of affluent families. Furthermore, male relatives of individuals who already

> **meritocracy** A government or other institution in which indi-viduals are awarded office and responsibility based on their merit—intelligence, talents, or education—rather than merely on their social status or circum-stances of birth.

held bureaucratic posts could be given the privilege of tak-ing a somewhat easier exam to qualify for at least a low-level government job. The civil service system contributed to a shared culture and worldview among the thousands of bu-reaucrats who managed the imperial state, though *within* that bureaucracy factional debates often raged over economic and political policy.

Neo-Confucianism. Song intellectuals also gave fresh thought to China's major belief systems. Daoism, a religion native to China, and Buddhism, one imported from India but thoroughly adapted to Chinese life (see Chapter 7), per-meated society from top to bottom. Buddhist monasteries and temples often had large landholdings and political in-fluence, accumulating wealth from agriculture and trade but exempted from taxes. Among the masses, Buddhist and Daoist traditions tended to blur into each other, and both incorporated veneration of local gods, goddesses, and family ancestors. In Song society, both traditions also ac-commodated themselves quite well to Confucian teachings. Confucian intellectuals had over several centuries absorbed Buddhist and Daoist ideas into their own moral and ethi-cal systems, including meditation, reverence for animal life, and metaphysical inquiry into the meaning of life.

In the twelfth and thirteenth centuries, innovative think-ers wove together several strands of Confucian, Buddhist, and Daoist thought to shape what became known as Neo-Confucianism. The worries and uncertainties that inevitably accompanied life in a commercializing society, together with the loss of northern China to "barbarian" invaders, contributed to a fresh look at Confucian ideals. Intellectual luminaries, notably the brilliant philosopher Zhu Xi (ZHOO-SHEE; 1130–1200), called for a return to the fundamental teachings of Confucius and his early disciples. To him, that meant moral living, disciplined daily ritual, respect for hierarchy, and dedication to families and local communities. A stable social order, he argued, must be built on a base of moral self-improvement. Ethical education and performance of communal service must take priority over the pursuit of imperial office and wealth. "Every day," Zhu wrote, "we must seek some amount of improvement, learning what we do not yet know and changing for the better whatever is not good; thus, we shall improve our virtuous natures. . . . If we pass our days in this fashion, then in three years we might have made a bit of progress."[4] Neo-Confucianism also made wide room for Buddhist-style theorizing on metaphysics and the cosmos, and by the end of the Song era, the Chinese educated class had thoroughly assimilated Neo-Confucian ideas.

China and Its Near Neighbors

Between the eleventh and thirteenth centuries, the Song monarchy occupied the center of a constellation of East Asian states, including island Japan. All these neighbors traded regularly with China and benefited from its economic upswing. In the Korean peninsula, the Silla monarchy (668–935) ruled for 250 years as a tribute-paying junior partner of the Tang dynasty. But the Koryo ruling family that succeeded the Silla in 918 moved out from under China's political shadow. Far to the southwest in Vietnam, local commanders founded the new state of Dai Viet in 938, ending several centuries of Chinese big brotherhood. In the eleventh and twelfth centuries, Dai Viet monarchs built roads, improved rice irrigation in the fertile Red River valley, and otherwise laid the economic foundations of a strong state that remained independent (except for a brief Chinese invasion in the early 1400s) until the late nineteenth century.

Technological and intellectual exchanges prospered between Song China and all its near neighbors. Despite official bans on arms trade, both the Liao and Jin states acquired the catapults, steel weapons, and gunpowder rockets that Chinese masterminds had invented. The Jin elite largely converted to Chinese styles of refined living, embracing Confucian literature and classical learning. In Korea, the Koryo rulers imported the Song civil service exams and used the written Chinese for administration and diplomacy. Korean artisans appear to have been the world's earliest inventors of both woodblock printing and movable type, and these technologies spread quickly to China. In Vietnam, the ruling class continued to revere the Confucian classics, and they imitated Song bureaucratic government. Finally,

Early printing. The Pure Light Dharani Sutra, a Buddhist scroll, is the world's earliest known printed text. Discovered in a temple in Korea in 1966, the scroll was printed from a woodblock. It dates to the mid-eighth century.

among all of these neighbors, variants of Buddhism, filtered largely through China, became the main popular religion.

Japan within and without the Chinese Sphere

In the later first millennium c.e., Chinese ideas and goods spilled across the Korea Strait and the East China Sea to Japan (see Chapter 11). The Japanese political and intellectual classes sorted through these new things, discarding what they did not like and adapting or modifying what they did. By the eleventh century, a distinctive style of urban civilization was emerging in the archipelago.

Japan's emperor, reigning from Heian (Kyoto) on the island of Honshu, imitated Chinese imperial court ceremony, and he had great religious prestige. But in the later ninth century real power shifted to alliances of aristocratic families, who lived in luxurious Heian mansions and owned great rice-growing estates. Between 850 and 1050, a single aristocratic clan, the Fujiwara, dominated the royal palace, effectively ruling in the name of the emperor. In the twelfth and thirteenth centuries, power shifted again, this time to a much larger elite of rural magnates, who expanded their control over rice land. They gradually supplanted the Heian aristocrats, acquiring title to large rural estates, hiring retinues of armored warriors, and coaxing their tenant farmers to adopt innovative farming techniques. Throughout much of the twelfth century, political disorder reigned across Japan, as rival landlords and coastal pirates competed for territory and loot.

The Kamakura shogunate. In the 1180s the Minamoto, one of the most powerful military clans, founded a new center at Kamakura in the rice-rich Kanto plain. Securing control over central and southern Japan, the clan leader

The *Tale of Genji*. Lady Murasaki's eleventh-century novel of romance and intrigue in the Heian imperial court has numerous characters. This illustration from the story depicts Genji's son Yugiri and his wife Kumoinokari, who leaves him when he brings home a second bride.

Minamoto no Yoritomo instituted a new government. The emperor, having no real choice in the matter, awarded him the title of shogun, or "great general." The Kamakura shogunate (1185–1333) allowed the emperor and his entourage to reign in Heian. But from this period Japan parted with the Chinese model of central rule by civilian scholar-bureaucrats. Instead, a class of professional fighters of elite status rose to prominence. Some of these warriors, known as samurai, became wealthy landowners. The great majority, however, served powerful families as cavalry soldiers dedicated to a code of courage, honor, solidarity, and military hardihood. In return for their homage and loyalty, samurai fighters typically received food allotments and rights over peasant labor. From Kamakura the shoguns orchestrated the politics of these competing families and their samurai retainers as best they could.

Economic and cultural trends. Japan's population and economy also continued to grow. In the 1100s, farmers began to harvest double crops of rice by adopting quick-ripening varieties from China. From about 1200, population growth accelerated and market towns multiplied, both inland and along the southern and central coasts. The Japanese military elite also coveted fine Chinese manufactures, and cargo vessels carried Japanese silver, copper, steel swords, and timber across the Yellow and East China Seas to the mainland. Chinese coins flooded into the islands, which also helped fuel internal commercialization.

Continuing contact with China stimulated new cultural trends. Buddhism spread more widely among nonelite men and women, and Buddhist practices became thoroughly intertwined with those of Shinto, the ancient indigenous belief system, to form a specifically Japanese religious synthesis. The Buddhist school known as Zen, which emphasized intuitive enlightenment, mental discipline, and meditation, took root in the islands. Toiling rural folk responded warmly to Buddhist teachings that promised personal salvation. Meanwhile, the elegant ladies and gentlemen who lived inside Heian's elite bubble sifted Chinese ideas of fine art and literature through a filter of Japanese language and polished manners. Aristocratic women were more willing than men to write in Japanese rather than the more prestigious Chinese, and they enjoyed greater intellectual freedom than their Song counterparts. Several women blazed creative paths. Sometime between 990 and 1012, Lady Murasaki Shikibu wrote *Tale of Genji*, a complex story of a courtier's life and loves. Some scholars classify this work as the first genuine novel ever created.

China in the Hemisphere

In the Song era, the material impact of China's agricultural and manufacturing economy extended far beyond its near neighbors. China acted as a sort of giant respirator in this period, blowing numerous goods—silks, cottons, porcelain, tea, iron tools, lacquer ware, paper—out across the hemisphere and sucking in foreign products—spices, herbs, resins, aromatic woods, medicines, silver, timber, horses—that growing numbers of Chinese could afford to buy.

The volume and value of foreign trade increased much more rapidly by sea routes than along the overland silk roads. This shift occurred for a number of reasons. First, overland caravan transport was not only more expensive than water shipment but simply inadequate for moving goods in the bulk loads that Chinese merchants wished to handle. The government encouraged private overseas trade, and it built a formidable navy to patrol the coasts and the major inland waterways. Also, goods produced in China's southern provinces had handy access by canal and road to seaports. Finally, the country's commercial expansion attracted growing numbers of foreign merchants—Malays, South Asians, Persians, Arabs, and Jews—to the southern ports. The Song government set up a Seafaring Trade Office to collect customs duties and regulate commerce as closely as it could.

Song naval architects made technical breakthroughs that produced the largest known seagoing ships, or junks, in that era. A medium-sized vessel could carry about 120 tons of cargo and a crew of sixty. The biggest ones accommodated crews of four or five hundred. Shipwrights equipped these craft with as many as six masts, giant sails of bamboo matting, multiple decks, and watertight compartments to contain flooding if the vessel hit an obstruction. They also invented the stern-post rudder, a swinging blade to steer the ship from the stern (the back end). This was an efficient advance over two side rudders. In the twelfth century or earlier, Chinese mariners began to carry compasses, usually a magnetized needle floated on a bowl of water, to help determine the position of a ship relative to the magnetic north or south pole. Indian Ocean sailors adopted this device, and it spread quickly to the Mediterranean. Chinese merchants and landowners with capital banded together to invest in ships. Private traders ventured as far west as the Arabian Sea, though in the Song period Chinese junks typically went no farther than India.

The market for porcelain illustrates the long reach of Chinese commerce. Skilled potters invented the technology to produce white porcelain, what we commonly call "china." It was harder, stronger, and thinner than both earthenware and stoneware because it was made of special clay available in southern China and fired at very high temperatures. Manufacturing centers multiplied to meet rising demand, both internal and overseas, for translucent, snowy-colored porcelain, a much-coveted luxury. Some kilns could fire fifty thousand pieces of porcelain at once, and large seagoing junks could haul tons of it. According to a twelfth-century merchant, vessels left Guangzhou crammed with porcelain, "the small pieces packed in the larger, till there is not a crevice left."[5] In Vietnam, Korea, and Japan, potters eventually learned to imitate Chinese technology and decorative styles. The beauty of East Asian ware also inspired artisans in Persia, Syria, and Egypt to invent new manufacturing, glazing, and painting techniques of their own, often substituting bright colors and bold geometric designs for more muted Chinese decoration. From the Song period, porcelain also began to appear on the tables of wealthy families in Europe.

Conquerors and Migrants in the Muslim Lands

FOCUS What impact did pastoral peoples from both Inner Eurasia and the Sahara Desert have on Afroeurasian agrarian societies between the eleventh and thirteenth centuries?

In the eleventh and twelfth centuries, armed migrants from out of the Great Arid Zone, the band of dry and semiarid lands that extends across Afroeurasia, dramatically altered the course of events in densely populated agrarian lands from China to southwestern Europe. The Jurchen invasion of northern China already described may be counted among these movements. On a larger scale, however, Turkic warriors originating in Inner Eurasia advanced on South and Southwest Asia, founding new military states that within two hundred years ruled from northern India to Egypt. In the same period, confederations of mounted fighters from the Sahara Desert and the mountains of Morocco forged empires that encompassed the western Mediterranean rim. The most potent weapon of these groups was massed cavalry and skill with bows, lances, and swords.

A Song river craft. Chinese naval architects built large seagoing ships, but the smaller vessels that plied the inland waterways powered internal commerce. This replica of a small sailing ship is on display in Millennium City Park in Kaifeng, the Song dynasty's northern capital. Why were rivers and canals so important to the Song economy?

A robe of honor. Muslim rulers wishing to seal bonds of allegiance and loyalty with one another typically exchanged richly designed ceremonial robes. In this illustration from the fourteenth century, the artist depicts the Turkic monarch Mahmud of Ghazni donning a robe sent to him by the Abbasid Caliph. Who might the other figures in the painting be?

raiding parties into South Asia to plunder the Indus River valley, loot Hindu temples, and overthrow regional Hindu monarchs. In the early thirteenth century, more Turkic fighters rode into South Asia, founding the sultanate (kingdom) of Delhi (1206–1526). They settled in as an elite military minority and expanded their reach into the subcontinent, ruling tens of millions of Hindu farmers and city dwellers.

Seljuk empire builders. In the mid-eleventh century, great throngs of Turkic horse archers pushed from Central Asia across Iran and into the densely populated Tigris-Euphrates River valley. These people were not slave soldiers but migrating pastoral nomads, and their numbers included women, children, and enormous herds of horses and

All these movements disrupted interregional trade at certain times and places, but the leaders of new kingdoms, once in control, invariably encouraged commerce and urban industry. Turkic migrants and rulers also contributed to the continuing spread of Islam. In the lands that Turks conquered, Islam became either the majority faith of the population, as in Anatolia, or the religion of a governing minority, as in Afghanistan and northern India.

Turkic Horse Power

The Turkic migrants of the eleventh century originated in Central Asia east of the Caspian Sea. They spoke languages at least distantly related to those of Huns, Uighurs, and Khazars, Inner Eurasian peoples that we encountered in earlier chapters. As Chapter 11 pointed out, Turkic soldiers began in the ninth century to serve the Abbasid Caliphate

> **mamluk** In Muslim states, a slave or freedman having primarily military or administrative duties.

(Abbasid empire) as military slaves, or *mamluks.* Unfortunately, however, for the Abbasid government in Baghdad, this corps splintered into rival factions and began to meddle in political affairs, helping to destabilize rather than strengthen the state to which they had pledged their allegiance.

In northern Iran and Afghanistan a band of Turkic *mamluk* officers rebelled against Baghdad's authority and succeeded to form their own state with its capital at Ghazna (today Ghazni in Afghanistan). The Ghaznavids, as the new dynasty was called (977–1186), gave theoretical allegiance to the caliph but otherwise ignored him. Ghaznavid cavalry fanned out to conquer both east and west. The ruler Mahmud of Ghazni (reigned 997–1030) dispatched massive

sheep. Because of the earlier missionary efforts of Muslim merchants and clerics, these Turks had largely converted to Islam before the invasion of Southwest Asia began. We do not fully understand the conditions that mobilized this movement, but population may have been growing rapidly enough on the Inner Eurasian steppes to cause serious pasture and animal shortages, triggering movements to find better land. The leaders of this migration mass belonged to a clan called the Seljuks, part of a tribal confederation whose members spoke Oghuz Turkish, one of several Turkic languages. In 1055, forces under the command of the Seljuk general Tughril Beg seized Baghdad. In the next twenty-eight years they overran Iraq, northern Syria, and eastern Anatolia. The Great Seljuks, as they became known, assumed power over millions of Arabs and Persians. In the 1080s, their empire sprawled across most of Southwest Asia. Tughril Beg offered fidelity to the caliph, who retained his status as moral and spiritual head of the Muslim community. But Tughril Beg and his successors took the title "sultan" and moved to set up a new military government. They did this with the vital cooperation of numerous educated Persians and Arabs who were skilled administrators, lawyers, and clerks.

Turks also began to alter the ethnic and linguistic profile of Southwest Asia. Simultaneously with the Seljuk conquests, pastoral groups migrated across northern Iran to the high green valleys of Armenia and eastern Anatolia. The very shape of Anatolia, a long finger of fertile land between the Black and the Mediterranean Seas, channeled the migration westward. At that time, western and central Anatolia were part of the Greek Byzantine state centered on the great city of Constantinople. But at the Battle of Malazgirt (Manzikert) in 1071, Seljuk archers trounced a Greek army. Once the Byzantines lost control of their mountainous eastern frontier, Muslim herders surged across central Anatolia's high plateau. Within a century, the Greek emperors held only their far western area. In the following centuries, Anatolia was transformed gradually into the predominantly Muslim land we now call Turkey. This process involved Turkic newcomers settling in villages, taking up agriculture, and competing with both Greek and Armenian Christian farmers for land. Most Christians who did not leave the region eventually converted to Islam; the Oghuz language, the ancestor of modern Turkish, spread widely. Turkic-speaking peoples also became an important element in the populations of Iraq, Iran, and Afghanistan.

Multiple states in Southwest Asia. Despite the Turkic influx into Southwest Asia, the unified Seljuk empire lasted less than four decades. The irrigation system of the Tigris-Euphrates valley had deteriorated badly in the late Abbasid period, reducing agricultural revenues to much less than the new rulers might have expected. In the Turkic nomad tradition, the most powerful warriors were entitled to compete with one another for top leadership. Consequently, the deaths of the first three sultans ignited feuding among members of the Seljuk clan. Army commanders, who were Sunni Muslims, also had to prepare defenses against the Fatimids, the hostile Shi'a Muslim rulers of Egypt and part of Syria (see Chapter 11). Shi'a revolutionaries repeatedly plotted to assassinate Seljuk officers and otherwise disrupt the Turkic state.

The sultans could hope to stabilize their rule only by giving their sons and officers rights to collect revenues from agricultural lands, but these estates soon became territorial bases for defiance and revolt. By the late eleventh century, the unified Seljuk state splintered into competing local kingdoms ruled by various clan leaders and former governors. By 1200 there were more than a half-dozen Turkic states in Southwest Asia.

The political map became even more complicated following the appearance of Christian crusaders from western Europe. Beginning in 1097, they attacked several points on the coasts of Syria, Palestine, and southern Anatolia. Within about a decade these armored knights and the military retainers, peasant farmers, and Catholic Christian clergy who accompanied them managed to set up four small kingdoms, known as the crusader states, along the eastern Mediterranean coast, including the holy city of Jerusalem. We will come back to the origins of this European initiative later in the chapter. From the Southwest Asian perspective, the crusaders had the good fortune to launch their adventure just when the Great Seljuk empire was breaking up and incapable of mounting a united defense. At first, Muslim leaders tended to regard the crusader states as an unfortunate development, though not a disastrous one. The fact that the intruders were Christians did not in itself cause great alarm. After all, Byzantine Christians continued to dominate part of Anatolia, and

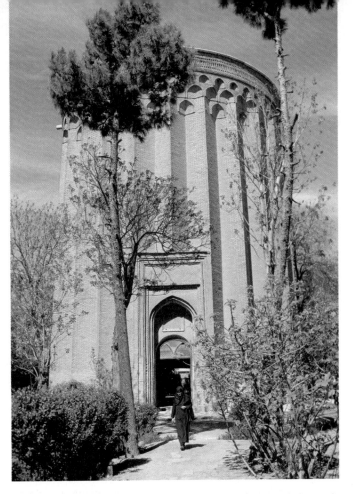

The Tughril Tower. Tughril Beg, founder of the Seljuk empire, is interred in this monumental tomb in the northern Iranian city of Rey.

both Southwest Asia and Egypt had large, long-established Christian minorities.

In the middle decades of the twelfth century, the Turkic rulers of a state centered on the Syrian city of Aleppo consolidated their authority over a wider territory. This kingdom amassed a large enough army to invade Egypt in 1169, defeating the Shi'a Fatimids and ending their two-century rule there. Salah al-Din, or Saladin (r. 1171–1193), a commander of Kurdish ethnic origin and a Sunni Muslim, emerged supreme from this war. He founded the Ayyubid dynasty (1171–1250), which united Egypt with Syria and Iraq (see Map 12.3). From this position of strength, his forces expelled the European knights from Jerusalem in 1187, though crusaders clung to small coastal zones until the late thirteenth century.

The Muslim military kingdoms that ruled most of the region from Egypt to northwestern India generally shared three elements. First, Turkic sultans continued to rely on mounted slave soldiers to defend frontiers and keep order. A ruler typically rewarded worthy officers with rights to rents and taxes from state-owned farmlands worked by local peasant families. Most of these peasants remained legally free, but they suffered poverty and sometimes brutal oppression at the hands of their lords. Also, at the low end of the social scale, nonmilitary slavery continued to be

The citadel of Aleppo.
Commanding the old city of Aleppo in northern Syria, this fortified palace is one of the largest castles in the world. Sultans of the Ayyubid dynasty completed major construction in the thirteenth century. The citadel served as a headquarters for war against the Christian crusader states on the eastern Mediterranean coast.

common, especially the use of bonded women as domestic workers, concubines, and entertainers.

A second feature of Turkic military regimes was their pragmatic alliances with the *ulama*, the city-based class of esteemed scholars and lawyers who supervised and regulated Muslim religious life and public behavior. In Southwest Asia and Egypt, Turkic commanders generally left Arab or Persian *ulama* in charge of civic affairs and employed them as judges, professors, secretaries, administrators, and accountants. In turn, the *ulama* accepted the authority of Turkic horse soldiers as preferable to political disorder. Military officers and respectable *ulama* families often sealed their working relationship through marriage. Women in educated families never got to hold public office, but they usually had great influence over marriage arrangements, which determined how the city's network of power took shape.

A third feature was the general prosperity of commerce and urban manufacturing even though little agrarian growth took place, especially compared to Song China. The Turkic movements coincided with the early phase of the North Atlantic Warm Period. This climatic event, which, as we have seen, may have improved crop yields in China, triggered extended droughts in Southwest Asia. Nevertheless, wealth continued to accumulate in the region's great cities, which served as key nodes in the busy exchange networks that linked the land and sea routes running across the hemisphere.

The cities where sultans and governors established their citadels and palaces—Cairo, Damascus, Aleppo, Nishapur, Bukhara, Ghazna (see Map 12.3)—invariably attracted voluminous trade in food, horses, military gear, and luxury wares. The urban artisans in those cities also exported woven textiles, carpets, glassware, ceramics, metalwork, and books. In the twelfth century, Cairo emerged as the greatest Muslim metropolis, owing partly to growing commercial traffic on the Red Sea route between the Indian Ocean and the Mediterranean. By 1300, Cairo's population may have neared 500,000, making it the biggest Afroeurasian city anywhere west of China.

Muslim Ships on the Mediterranean

As of about 1000 C.E., Muslim captains piloted the majority of ships plying the Mediterranean and the Black Seas. Muslim monarchs controlled all the ports of the southern and far eastern Mediterranean as well as the island of Sicily and most of Spain. The Fatimid dynasty built a fleet of war galleys, that is, ships powered by combinations of rowers and sails. These vessels patrolled the eastern Mediterranean and communicated between Fatimid Egypt and Syria. The Byzantine state had a navy as well, though it deteriorated steadily from the eleventh century owing partly to shrinking resources in the face of Turkic military pressures on its territory.

The main artery of Muslim commercial shipping ran along the Mediterranean's African shores, connecting numerous ports from Syria and Egypt to Morocco and Spain. Merchants carried a variety of products—wool, hides, leather goods, grain, and olive oil, as well as gold and slaves from Subsaharan Africa. Muslim and Jewish merchant groups, often working together, controlled trade operations that connected the Mediterranean to the Indian Ocean by way of the Nile valley and the Red Sea. In the eleventh and twelfth centuries, for example, Jewish merchants based in Cairo and as far west as Tunis engaged in both commercial and mining businesses as far away as the western coast of India.

MAP 12.3 Major states in western Afroeurasia, 1200.
What does this map suggest about the historical significance of the Strait of Gibraltar and the Bosporus Strait as dividing lines between Europe and both Africa and Asia?

New Empires in the Western Mediterranean

The first major pastoral nomadic movement to emerge from the Sahara Desert, the western third of Afroeurasia's Great Arid Zone, occurred in the mid-eleventh century. During the previous millennium, Sahara-dwelling people who spoke mainly Berber languages adapted to extremely arid conditions by herding one-humped camels. These beasts fed on seasonal grasses that sprouted in the desert and along its semidry rims. Camels provided caravan transport, as well as meat, milk, and hides. And along with horses, they gave Saharan pastoralists the means of long-range military operations.

The Almoravid empire-builders. The first great military adventure from out of the Sahara started in the far western desert just north of the Senegal River in modern Mauritania. In the ninth and tenth centuries, the region's pastoral peoples began to convert to Islam at the urging of merchants and preachers from North Africa. In the mid-eleventh century, Abdallah ibn Yasin (d. 1059), a passionate Sunni theologian from Morocco, journeyed to the western desert to exhort camel-herding Muslims to raise their standards of worship and moral behavior—regular prayer, no alcoholic drinks, no music, and strict separation of men and women in public. Ibn Yasin also organized a confederation of desert clans and tribes known collectively as the Almoravids (referring loosely in Arabic to "religious warriors").

This coalition seized major trading towns on both the southern and the northern edges of the Sahara. Mounted fighters also raided deep into the West African empire of Ghana (see Chapter 11), seriously weakening it. Bolstered by commercial profits and taxes, an Almoravid army advanced northward, crossing the High Atlas Mountains and capturing the major cities of Morocco and western Algeria. In 1086, shiploads of warriors crossed the Strait of Gibraltar into Spain. They did this at the invitation of local Muslim princes, who faced mounting pressure from Christian crusaders along their northern frontiers. Quickly defeating a Christian force from the kingdoms of León and Castile, the Almoravids united all of Muslim Spain under their authority.

At their zenith, the Almoravids could claim sovereignty over an astonishing realm extending from the Senegal River in West Africa to central Spain. However, Moroccan and Spanish Muslim leaders who at first welcomed these austere Berber reformers soon thought better of it. The Almoravid religious elite not only proved morally rigid and intolerant but also were occupied less with Islamic revival than with power, privilege, and wealth. Almoravid rulers who abandoned their desert tents for magnificent palaces also lost interest in vigorous counter-crusades against the Spanish Christian states.

The Almohads and the oneness of God. Not long into the twelfth century, discontent boiled up. An anti-Almoravid rebellion arose among Berber farmers and herders in the valleys of the High Atlas. Muhammad ibn Tumert

A Jewish Merchant Writes to His Wife

Long-distance marital relationships have never been easy. This is true today, even with our modern communications technology. It was certainly true in the thirteenth century, when couples that had to be apart kept in touch through letters The selection here is an excerpt from a letter that a Jewish merchant residing temporarily in South Asia wrote to his wife in Egypt around the year 1204. The round-trip sea voyage between Egypt and ports on the western coast of India took two years to complete, often longer if merchants encountered bad weather, financial problems, or roving pirates.

In his letter, the merchant reveals that his wife has asked for a divorce. According to Jewish law, this act had to be initiated by the husband. He has decided, however, to place the decision in her hands. He tells her that he knows his time away has placed undue burdens on her but that the separation has been no easier for him. His longing for her has driven him to drink excessively, but he assures her that he has remained faithful, declaring that he has conducted himself "in an exemplary way." Nevertheless, if a divorce is what his wife wants, he writes, he will "set [her] free."

As it turned out, the trader never sent this letter, and the couple did not divorce. He eventually returned to Egypt still in possession of the letter. He placed it in the Cairo Geniza, a special room attached to a synagogue. In the Jewish tradition, papers on which the name of God is written should not be discarded. Synagogues therefore established genizas, or storerooms, to preserve such documents. Typically, a synagogue would periodically bury the papers in the geniza, but in this case the castoff papers were left in storage. In the late nineteenth century, British scholars began exploring the contents of the Cairo Geniza. They carried texts, often just fragments of writing, back to libraries in Britain for careful study. These documents have provided a rich source of knowledge of medieval Jewish life. Though many of the papers are concerned with religious questions, a large portion, like the letter excerpted here, discuss secular issues such as trade, business, legal disputes, and personal affairs. Today, Cairo Geniza documents are to be found in major libraries around the world.

The Dedicated Husband

In your letters you alternately rebuke and offend me or put me to shame and use harsh words all the time. I have not deserved any of this. I swear by God, I do not believe that the heart of anyone traveling away from his wife has remained like mine, all the time and during all the years—from the moment of our separation to the very hour of writing this letter—so constantly thinking of you and yearning after you. . . . And you write about me as if I had forgotten you and would not remember you had it not been for your rebukes, and as if, had you not warned me that the public would reprove me, I would not have thought of you. Put this out of your mind and do not impute such things to me. . . .

Drunk but Pious

Day and night I was constantly drinking, not of my free will, but I conducted myself in an exemplary way and if anyone poked fun in foul speech in my presence, I became furious with him, until he became silent, he and others. I constantly fulfilled what God knows, and cured my soul by fasting during the days and praying during the nights. The congregations in Aden and in India often asked me to lead them in prayer, and I am regarded by them and regard myself as a pious man. . . .

As to Divorce—the Choice Is Left to the Wife

Now in one of your letters you adjure me to set you free. . . . Now, if this is your wish, I cannot blame you. For the waiting has been long. And I do not know whether the Creator will grant relief immediately so that I can come home, or whether matters will take time, for I cannot come home with nothing. Therefore I resolved to issue a writ which sets you free. Now the matter is in your hand. If you wish separation from me, accept the bill of repudiation and you are free. But if this is not your decision and not your desire, do not lose these long years of waiting: perhaps relief is at hand and you will regret at a time when regret will be of no avail.

And please do not blame me, for I never neglected you from the time when those things happened and made an effort to save you and me from people talking and impairing my honor. . . . All day long I have a lonely heart and am pained by our separation. I feel that pain while writing these lines. But the choice is with you; the decision is in your hand: if you wish to carry the matter through, do so; if you wish to leave things as they are, do so. But do not act after the first impulse. Ask the advice of good people and act as you think will be the best for you. May God inspire you with the right decision.

Source: S. D. Goitein, *Letters of Medieval Jewish Traders* (Princeton, NJ: Princeton University Press, 1973), pp. 222–225.

Thinking Critically

What do you think this letter tells us about the relationship between the trader and his wife? How would you characterize the merchant's attitude toward her? Why might the wife have wanted a divorce, and why is her husband sympathetic to her request? Why do you think the husband never sent the letter? Where is Aden in relation to India, and why would the merchant have been there? What merchandise might the merchant have shipped home from India?

(1080–1130), a Moroccan legal scholar as religiously fervent and charismatic as Ibn Yasin, declared himself to be the Mahdi, or "rightly guided one." The Mahdi, according to popular belief among both Shi'a and Sunni Muslims, was an enlightened, God-chosen individual who would lead the world to a time of peace and justice culminating in the final divine judgment of humankind. Ibn Tumert taught strict piety, and he condemned the Almoravids for betraying their own ideals. In contrast to them, however, he introduced a doctrine that emphasized the absolute spiritual unity of God. That unity prohibited any description of God in terms of human attributes or qualities. Ibn Tumert's disciples thus became known as the Almohads, a term that means "believers in the oneness of God."

In 1147 armed Almohad Berbers swept down from the mountains and within a few years crossed into Spain, overthrowing the already shaky Almoravid government. In 1151 they advanced across Algeria to Tunisia (see Map 12.3). This Berber empire incorporated the entire western Mediterranean basin. But it lasted only a little longer than its predecessor. Like the Almoravids, the second generation of Almohad leaders lost their religious zeal, and their theologians became reactionary. In contrast to earlier Spanish Muslim rulers, who generally encouraged cooperation among religious groups, the later Almohads harassed and persecuted Jews, obliging many to flee from Spain. In the early thirteenth century, Christian armies from León and Castile, deploying armored knights from several parts of Europe, broke into Almohad territory. Within several decades they overran all of Muslim-ruled Spain with the exception of the mountain-bound kingdom of Granada in the far south and a few strongholds along the Strait of Gibraltar. Later in the century, Almohad authority collapsed in North Africa as well.

The Almoravid and Almohad states, like the Great Seljuk empire, were short-lived. But between them they stimulated intense cultural interchange between Spain and North Africa for nearly two centuries. More urbanized than Morocco, southern Spain (Andalusia) set refined standards for art, craft, cuisine, and refined taste. Muslim and Jewish scholars and artisans moved easily across the strait, diffusing a Spanish cultural style more widely across North Africa. The Christian conquest of southern Spain also persuaded

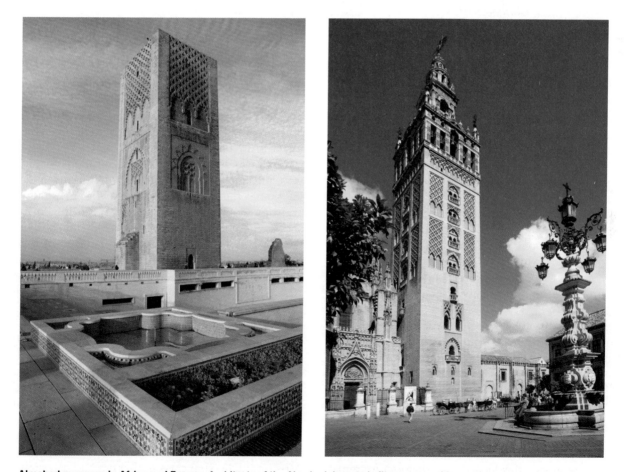

Almohad mosques in Africa and Europe. Architects of the Almohad dynasty built mosques with massive square minarets in both Morocco and Spain in the late twelfth century. The Hassan Tower (left) in Rabat, Morocco's modern capital, was originally designed to rise even taller but was never completed. The Giralda mosque and minaret in Seville (right) was converted to a church when Christian armies took the city in 1248. In the sixteenth century, Spanish builders added the ornate bell tower above the former minaret. Both structures are austere in form but incorporate finely proportioned carved arches and geometric patterning. Put your hand over the Giralda's bell tower to better see the resemblance between the two buildings.

The Twin Minaret Madrasa. Sunni Muslim scholars and students occupied this college of higher learning in the eastern Anatolian city of Erzurun to study religious and legal subjects. The madrasa dates to the 1260s.

thousands of Muslims and Jews to migrate to North African cities, which subsequently benefited from their talents and skills.

Cultural Trends in the Muslim Lands

The Muslim cavalry captains who took charge from Spain to northern India in the eleventh and twelfth centuries were the sons and grandsons of animal herders. Nevertheless, they adapted quickly to sophisticated city life, and they rivaled one another to patronize creative work in literature, architecture, science, and theology.

College education. One key innovation was the founding of many new Muslim educational institutions dedicated to advanced studies in religion, law, and medicine. In these colleges, called **madrasas** (MAH-drahs-uhs) in Arabic, scholars and students lived and worked together to pursue knowledge. The curriculum centered on the Quran, the traditions of the Prophet Muhammad, theology, logic, rhetoric, grammar, and Sunni Islamic law. Madrasa education, in which white-turbaned professors guided students through religious and legal texts, aimed primarily to preserve and transmit the spiritual and moral truths of the Islamic past. Most madrasas

madrasa A center of higher learning dedicated mainly to the study of Islamic religious and legal subjects.

operated under pious endowments, that is, gifts of rulers or other wealthy individuals. Some colleges were grand monuments to architectural and artistic skill.

Madrasas served as training institutions for judges, lawyers, mosque officials, professors, librarians, and secretaries, that is, the *ulama* class charged with maintaining social and moral stability. Colleges were also intellectual workshops where legal experts interpreted and codified Islamic law (*shari'a*). Finally, the Turkic sultans, all of them Sunni Muslims, conceived the madrasas as centers for combating Shi'a doctrines. Indeed, after the Shi'a Fatimids were driven from Egypt, Cairo emerged as the premier Sunni "university town" in the western Muslim lands.

Science and philosophy. Madrasas did not typically offer humanistic study or inquiries into nature and the cosmos. Many scholars, however, continued to pursue those areas of knowledge informally and privately. In the eleventh through the thirteenth centuries, scholars produced numerous texts in both Arabic and Persian that synthesized and extended knowledge in astronomy, mathematics, optics, medicine, botany, pharmacology, and geography. The Muslim intellectual class of that era had especially cosmopolitan outlooks. They traveled widely, seeking knowledge, books, wealthy patrons, and salaried jobs in governments, legal courts, and religious institutions. Educated Jews and Christians took part in this network as well.

The lives of three great scholars illustrate the intersection of learning and public service. Abu Rayhan al-Biruni (973–1048), born in what is now Uzbekistan, served the sultan Mahmud, the most talented of the Ghaznavid rulers of Afghanistan and northwestern India. Al-Biruni accompanied his sovereign on raiding expeditions into South Asia and from this experience wrote *The Book of India*, an illuminating description of Hindu culture and society. He spoke several languages and published altogether about 150 works on mathematics, astronomy, metallurgy, medicine, history, and philosophy. In the Muslim west, Ibn Rushd (Averroës, 1126–1198) pursued philosophical inquiry in both Spain and Morocco under the patronage of Almohad monarchs. He expanded on a dimension of earlier Islamic thought according to which natural laws, that is, rational and timeless principles, govern the workings of nature and the universe. Moreover, these laws are evidence of God's plan for his creation. Most Muslim theologians in the madrasas opposed this view, arguing that God creates all phenomena, from birds in flight to shining stars, moment by moment according to his will. Ibn Rushd's commentaries on Plato and Aristotle, translated into Latin, had great influence on the development of natural philosophy in Christian Europe. The Jewish thinker Maimonides (Moses ben Maimon, 1135–1204), a contemporary of Ibn Rushd and also a native of Spain, became royal court physician to Salah al-Din in Cairo. He codified Jewish law and wrote theological and philosophical texts that influenced all subsequent Jewish thought.

Sufism and the continuing spread of Islam. Conquerors, scholars, and merchants all contributed to the wider spread of Islam, and so did Sufi saints and devotees. Sufism is the mystical dimension of Islam important to both Sunni and Shi'a believers. Increasingly popular from the eleventh century, Sufi teachings endeavored to guide men and women toward direct experience of God and intuitive understanding of spiritual truths. Christianity and Judaism, the other two monotheistic religions, also incorporated doctrines and practices of **mysticism**. Generally speaking, mystical teachings have less to do with ritual, duty, and public morality than with individual yearnings to transcend the personal self in order to know and merge with ultimate reality, in whatever way the particular religion describes that reality. The historical record suggests that practices such as meditating, joining a monastic community, or living as a hermit in the wilderness were in some measure Islamic adaptations of both Christian and Buddhist traditions that encouraged pursuit of spiritual enlightenment through self-denial and deep devotion.

Two ideas were at the heart of Sufism, a term derived from the Arabic word for the patched woolen garment that spiritual seekers often wore. First, the individual is capable

mysticism The individual pursuit of knowledge or consciousness of spiritual truth or divine reality, through meditation, prayer, study, or ecstatic experience; also, mystical religion, teaching, or practice.

of knowing God in heart as well as mind. Second, the believer walking a path to the divine might benefit from the help of a saintly master, or "friend of God," who radiated divine grace and could transmit it to others. Guided by such holy individuals, Muslims immersed themselves in mystical texts, ecstatic rituals, or special prayers, in order to feel and express God's love.

By the twelfth century, informal associations of saintly teachers and disciples were coalescing into more formal organizations, or religious orders, whose members followed a particular mystical "way" to experience God. Sufi devotional centers—somewhat like monasteries—offered not only congregational devotions but also religious education, charity, and refuge for travelers. By the thirteenth century, Sufi orders and lodges were found across the Muslim lands, and Sufi masters came to exert moral and political influence

Sufi teacher and poet. The spiritual poetry of the thirteenth-century Muslim mystic Jalal al-Din Rumi is still read widely today. In this miniature painting from the late 1500s, Rumi, kneeling at top left, gathers with his disciples.

over rulers. For women, Sufism offered an arena for religious expression and spiritual leadership in a patriarchal world that largely denied them public office or intellectual recognition.

Among Sufi thinkers of the era, the Iranian scholar Abu Hamid al-Ghazali (1058–1111) achieved towering status. He held a law professorship in Baghdad under the Great Seljuks but devoted himself to the Sufi life and to writing theological works. In *The Revival of the Religious Sciences* he offered a guide for pious living. Prayers and rituals were not meant to be sterile, mechanical acts, he wrote, but vehicles for achieving perpetual consciousness of God. In his autobiography, he describes his journey from worldliness to spiritual illumination: "It had already become clear to me that I had no hope of the bliss of the world to come save through a God-fearing life and the withdrawal of myself from vain desire. It was clear to me . . . that this was only to be achieved by turning away from wealth and position and fleeing from all time-consuming entanglements."[6] Al-Ghazali recognized the value of philosophical and scientific inquiry, but he denied that it could help men and women feel the presence of God. He convincingly reconciled mystical practice with public worship and opened the way for Sufism to merge into the mainstream of Muslim life.

Owing to a combination of Sufi energy, new conquests, and the spreading web of Muslim commerce, Islam continued to make headway in the eleventh to thirteenth centuries in Sudanic West Africa, Anatolia, Inner Eurasia, South Asia, and around the Indian Ocean rim. Only in Spain and some Mediterranean islands did Christian soldiers and churchmen force Muslims and their religion to retreat.

Foundations of Urban Civilization in Europe

FOCUS What factors accounted for accelerating economic growth, urbanization, and military power in Europe in the 1000–1250 period?

MAP 12.4 Europe and the Mediterranean, 1200.
What factors might account for the proliferation of small states in western Europe compared to relatively larger ones in eastern Europe?

In the mid-eleventh century, Sa'id al-Andalusi, an eminent Muslim scholar of Toledo in central Spain, wrote the *Book of the Categories of Nations* in which he describes the peoples who inhabited northerly parts of Europe. Because they have to endure a cold and cloudy climate, al-Andalusi explained, "their temperament is cool and their behavior is rude. Consequently, their bodies became enormous, their color turned white, and their hair drooped down. . . . They were overcome by ignorance and laziness, and infested by fatigue and stupidity."[7] This unsparing portrait reveals the prejudices of a highly educated urban gentlemen who no doubt received reports of northern Europe as a place of tiny towns and little learning where bands of armored men mostly feuded with one another.

A moldboard plow. In this picture from the twelfth century, a European peasant couple cooperate in plowing a field with two oxen. The parts of the wheeled plow include an iron coulter, or blade that cuts vertically into the soil, an iron share that cuts horizontally to release a strip of soil, and an attached moldboard that forces the soil to lift and turn over. Can you identify these three parts of the plow in the illustration?

To be sure, Europe in 1000 C.E. had a total population of about thirty million, which was around fourteen million *fewer* people than had lived there eight hundred years earlier, when much of the region was part of the Roman empire. There were few cities or strong centralized states. Even so, al-Andalusi's bleak description was not only overstated but out of date. By the later tenth century, western Europeans were experiencing an uneven but hopeful trend toward greater social and political order. The Muslim, Magyar, and Viking marauders who had disrupted Europe in the previous two hundred years had either settled down or gone away, and feudal lords restored relative calm to hundreds of localities (see Chapter 11). Between 1000 and 1300, Europe's population rose from thirty to nearly fifty million. Market towns sprouted up, and some blossomed into cities (see Map 12.4). In those three hundred years, for example, the population of Paris increased tenfold to 200,000.

Warm Weather, Better Plows

Europe's population growth was made possible by a boost in agricultural production having several sources. Greater political stability on the local level meant fewer disruptions to the cycle of planting and harvesting. Several new farming techniques, some of them coming from other parts of Afroeurasia, spread widely in western Europe. These included four-wheeled wagons, improved designs for water-powered mills, iron horseshoes, and an efficient collar-harness that allowed horses to pull heavy loads without being choked. As early as the eighth century, farmers started using a type of plow, perhaps invented in eastern Europe, that could cut into heavy soil and channel the earth into furrows for more efficient seeding and drainage. This tool helped unlock the agricultural potential of parts of Europe where older plows suited to the relatively thin soils of the Mediterranean region had no use. Farmers also took to three-field crop rotation, sowing one plot in the spring and a second in the fall, leaving

a third fallow for a year to recover its nutrients. This technique slowed soil exhaustion and permitted planting of a greater variety of crops. Similar to its likely effects in China, the North Atlantic Warm Period brought longer growing seasons and drier summers to northern Europe, allowing farmers to increase production on land already in use. Grain farmers prospered in Scandinavia, and vintners produced drinkable wines in Britain and Poland. Between 800 and 1200, crop yields in western Europe may have doubled, and in good years farmers produced surplus food for market.

As production mounted, so did manufacturing and trade. Europe had neither the labor power nor the engineering knowledge to build a canal network anything like China's. But numerous navigable rivers penetrated far inland from the sea, permitting boat transport of bulk commodities like grain, fish, timber, iron, and stone at low cost. In the ports of the Baltic Sea, the North Sea, and the Atlantic coast, mariners improved ship designs, building vessels with high, rounded hulls that could carry cargos safely across gale-prone waters. Money came into much wider use across Europe. Numerous monarchs and lords minted their own coins, and both Byzantine and Muslim currency circulated as well, especially in Italy.

Two regions in western Europe became thriving centers of urban industry. One was Flanders, where a cluster of towns, including Bruges and Ghent (in modern Belgium) produced woolen cloth for export. London across the North Sea became closely associated with these Flemish towns, its merchants supplying raw English wool to their spinners and weavers. A second cluster of cities sprouted in northern Italy. Venice, Genoa, and Pisa all flourished in the eleventh century as ports linking northern Europe with the Mediterranean sea lanes. The success of these coastal towns stimulated the growth of Florence, Milan, and other interior cities, which developed their own woolen, armor, and other industries for export markets.

In the twelfth and thirteenth centuries, markets held in the Champagne region of north central France became key meeting points of merchants from Italy and northern Europe. The aristocratic rulers of Champagne sponsored six commercial fairs a year, held in rotation in four different towns. These nobles guaranteed market peace, appointed officials to ensure honest dealings, and provided safe conduct along the routes that led to the fairgrounds. In return for these services, they collected tolls, rents, and fees from traders. Flemish merchants brought woolen cloths, tapestries, and furs. From Italy came Mediterranean goods as well as exotic wares from more distant lands. Buyers especially coveted Asian silks, spices, porcelains, and medicines. From a hemispheric perspective, the fairs of Champagne and Song China became linked into a single commercial trade web.

New Order in Political Life

The story of European politics between the eleventh and thirteenth centuries is complicated, partly because numerous power holders competed fiercely for land and resources in a time of economic growth, and partly because kings, queens, princes, barons, popes, and bishops had varying and often conflicting ideas of how western Christendom should be governed.

The limits of the Holy Roman Empire. Three major political experiments were put in play simultaneously. One was the vision of all Christendom united under the leadership of a single devout monarch. King Charlemagne, who ruled the Frankish empire back in the eighth and ninth centuries, had dreamed of such unity (see Chapter 10). It was also the hope of the German king Otto I, on whom the pope bestowed the title Holy Roman Emperor (see Chapter 11). His successors, Otto II and III, held that title but their authority did not extend beyond central Europe and northern Italy. In the generations that followed, German nobles reasserted their independence and central Europe broke into several competing **principalities.** Also, military campaigns to control Italy and Sicily exhausted the emperor's resources and ultimately failed. By 1300 the emperors, elected by German nobles, had little independent power, though the Holy Roman Empire, as it later came to be called, lasted in name to the nineteenth century.

principality A sovereign state or dependent territory, usually relatively small, ruled by a person with a noble title of high rank, for example, prince, princess, duke, or duchess.

The power of the church. Christian popes led the second experiment in European government. The Catholic Church had traditionally argued that it rightly possessed not only spiritual and moral authority but also political preeminence over the emperor and all other monarchs and princes. In the late first millennium c.e., however, the church institution, a pyramidal structure with the pope in Rome at the top and thousands of parish priests at the bottom, had been weakly organized. Priests were often illiterate and morally lax. Europe's **secular rulers** and powerful aristocratic families had succeeded in exerting much influence over church decisions such as the appointment of bishops and the heads of monasteries.

secular ruler In the Christian tradition a monarch or other ruler who is not an ordained priest and does not formally represent the authority of the church; a temporal, as opposed to spiritual, leader.

Between the eleventh and thirteenth centuries, however, a series of intelligent, strong-willed popes, notably Gregory VII (1073–1085), Urban II (1088–1099), and Innocent III (1198–1216), strove to strengthen the church's decision-making hierarchy and to press the claim that God empowered them to *delegate* authority to secular rulers. In other words, the church sought to collaborate with monarchs and princes, not replace them, but nevertheless asserted that princes held their authority because the pope granted it. The reforming popes strove to recover full power to appoint church officials without kings or nobles interfering. They reorganized the church to ensure greater central control from Rome. They standardized church doctrines and rituals, and they systematized **canon law,** which governed Christian faith, practice, and church administration. They insisted that priests and nuns have good moral and intellectual qualifications. In the twelfth century, priestly councils established the rule that members of the clergy remain celibate (unmarried) and therefore fully dedicated to the service of God and the church.

canon law A code of laws and regulations governing a Christian church or denomination, especially in matters of faith, worship, moral behavior, and church administration.

Centralized monarchies. The third major experiment in government was the emergence of France and England as strong centralized states. Like the German sovereigns, the rulers of these two countries had recurring disputes with Rome. They showed less interest in leading all of Christendom, however, than in building well-organized regional monarchies. These kings (and, in England, one queen) aimed to expand the territories under their direct control and to limit the power of local aristocratic families.

In northern France in the eleventh century, the kings of the Capetian dynasty occupied the top rung in the hierarchy of Frankish lords and vassals but governed only the region around Paris and a few other scattered territories. After 1100, however, they gradually extended their realm through a combination of military action and astute political maneuvering. Because of healthy economic growth in the royal lands, the king's treasury filled up. This permitted recruitment of more armored knights, as well as foot soldiers skilled with iron-piercing crossbows. By 1300 the Capetian monarchy controlled much of what is today France. The kings financed a central administration that depended

The medieval social order in chess pieces. These nine figures carved from walrus ivory are among seventy-eight chess pieces dating to the twelfth century. They were discovered on the Isle of Lewis in northwestern Scotland. The two rooks take the form of soldiers or guards. The two pawns are simple geometric shapes. What characteristics of the other five figures help identify them as king, queen, bishop, and knight?

less on old aristocratic families, who had local political interests that might conflict with royal policy, and more on literate commoners eager to serve the state in return for regular salaries. The king recruited many of these officers from the rising urban, money-making class, or **bourgeoisie.** Somewhat as in Song China, this bureaucracy embraced an ideology of full devotion to the strength and defense of the central state. Beginning in the fourteenth century, the rulers periodically called a council of lords, clergy, and town citizens to Paris to listen to their political and fiscal advice. This body, known as the Estates-General, was no democratic legislature, but it strengthened social and political bonds between the royal palace and the most influential voices in society.

> **bourgeoisie** The social category of town-dwelling artisans, merchants, and bankers who occupied a position between rural peasants and the aristocratic class; in modern usage, the "middle class."

A second strong monarchy arose in England. In 1066 Duke William, ruler of Normandy (northwestern France) and a French-speaking descendant of earlier Viking conquerors, overthrew and replaced the Anglo-Saxon king of England. Subsequently, William awarded his fighting vassals extensive lands on the conquered island. In the next few centuries, this warrior class—which wielded local authority and built great stone castles—intermarried with Anglo-Saxon families and learned to speak English, spawning a distinctive Anglo-Norman elite.

Several twelfth- and thirteenth-century sovereigns, notably Henry II (r. 1154–1189), worked to strengthen central authority partly by building a system of royal law courts and encouraging development of a uniform body of law, or common law, to govern the entire realm. Like the most capable French kings, skillful Anglo-Norman rulers collaborated pragmatically with the great landowning families, the Christian clergy, and the prospering bourgeoisie of growing towns. Even so, kings and nobles had chronically tense relations. In 1215 the great barons of England forced King John, whom they rightly blamed for territorial losses in France, to sign the Magna Carta, or Great Charter. This document ratified the customary rights of the aristocracy against royal power and stipulated that the monarch could levy taxes only with aristocratic consent. The nobles regarded this event as a reaffirmation of the status quo, not a major political change.

As in France, the king periodically convened a council of lords, knights, bishops, and royal officers. In contrast

King Philip II: French State-Builder

King Philip II of France chases Henry II of England out of Le Mans.

Royal authority in France achieved a new level of consolidation during the long reign of Philip II (1180–1223), or Philip Augustus. He ascended the throne at the age of fourteen after his father Louis VII suffered a debilitating stroke. Philip stoutly resisted attempts by royal relatives and powerful nobles to take charge of his kingship, and he ruled in his own right from the start. He continued his father's mission to centralize royal power and improve the efficiency of government over the lands under royal control.

Philip also extended French territory, partly by incorporating neighboring dukedoms through negotiation and manipulation of noble marriages and partly by attacking territories that the English crown held on the European continent. He warred with England intermittently for two decades, and eventually expelled its troops from all but the region of Aquitaine in southwestern France. He suspended hostilities in 1190–1191 to join England's Richard the Lionheart on the Third Crusade to Syria. A combined force of European knights captured the port of Acre (Ako) from its Muslim rulers, but the two kings soon quarreled. Philip, a more calculating and sober personality than Richard, returned home to advance the interests of the French state.

Philip's personal character—ruthless ambition combined with keen intelligence and diplomatic cunning—served him well. He encouraged agriculture, manufacturing, and trade, and he strengthened royal defenses. He placed his kingdom on a sound financial footing by keeping the royal treasury in the black rather than accumulating debt. Under his direction, the French government took shape as a bureaucratic hierarchy with fixed rules and regulations, standards for record keeping, and professional posts staffed by literate and skilled members of the bourgeois and noble classes rather than by aristocrats with family prestige but little talent. He sought to transform Paris into a worthy capital city, paving a few of its streets and continuing construction of the magnificent Notre Dame cathedral begun during his father's reign. He also granted a **charter** to the University of Paris and established the central market of Les Halles, an institution that operated well into the twentieth century.

> **charter** A document in which a state or other political authority granted specific rights or privileges to an individual, town, guild, or other organization to carry out particular functions.

Like most medieval kings and nobles, Philip married to cement political alliances. But his domestic affairs proved troublesome. After his first wife, Isabelle, died in 1190, he agreed to wed Ingeborg, daughter of the king of Denmark. The two got married on the same day they were introduced to each other, but Philip, for reasons unknown, immediately arranged a divorce with the support of the French Catholic church. He then married the noblewoman Agnes de Méran, with whom he had two children. Pope Innocent II, however, refused to accept the divorce from Ingeborg and placed the kingdom of France under an interdict, which meant that French churches could not legitimately celebrate the mass. Agnes died in 1201, however, and Philip made the pragmatic decision to take Ingeborg back.

Many of Philip's accomplishments can be attributed to his skills as an administrator, diplomat, and military commander. In 1214 he won the Battle of Bouvines in northeastern France, defeating a much larger coalition of British, Flemish, and German troops and confirming French sovereignty over Normandy. He doubled the size of the monarchy and collected far more revenue than his predecessors had ever been able to do, eliminating any doubts of French political dominance in western continental Europe.

Thinking Critically

Taking the example of Philip, what do you think are some of the things that a premodern monarch had to do to create a strong centralized state?

---

to the Estates-General, however, the English Parliament, as it was called, gained authority to approve taxes. In the later thirteenth century, Parliament also began to make new laws. The idea of the monarch ruling in alliance with a permanent assembly of influential males had no precise counterpart anywhere else in the world, even though ruler and Parliament continued to contest the proper balance of power between them for another five hundred years.

The Expansion of Western Christendom

In the same centuries that men and women in the heart of Europe started building a new urban civilization, other Europeans—knights, farmers, artisans, merchants, priests, monks, and nuns—busied themselves doubling the size of the Catholic Christian world. This expansion took place as European conquerors and settlers, operating in different groups, extended Christian frontiers in three major directions: eastward across Germany's Elbe River and around the Baltic Sea, southwestward into Muslim Spain, and southeastward into the Mediterranean basin. In these movements, Christian knights—warrior bands using the technology of heavy cavalry, archery, and the crossbow—seized territory mainly from non-Christian peoples. To secure and develop their holdings, conquering knights typically encouraged peasants and skilled artisans, as well as merchants and Christian clergy, to come in behind them to convert unbelievers and exploit the resources of the land.

Land hunger was indeed the driving motive in all three theaters of expansion. In northwestern Europe, population was growing steadily and unclaimed land vanishing. For young male aristocrats and would-be knights, military adventure abroad offered the chance to seize land that could no longer be had where they were born. The spreading custom of primogeniture, in which an individual's estate passed exclusively to the eldest son—a custom that kept lands from being subdivided and perhaps sold off—whetted the appetites of younger sons for making war far from home and getting lands of their own. For peasant farmers, migration to new territory offered the possibility of escaping serfdom and acquiring larger farms. Business-minded lords encouraged economic growth in conquered territories by granting new towns charters that ensured residents of firm legal rights and a measure of self-government.

Expansion beyond the Elbe. The Elbe River runs generally northwestward 724 miles across today's Czech Republic and Germany, emptying into the North Sea. It marked a kind of eleventh-century starting line for the advance of German, Flemish, and Frankish heavy cavalry across the plains of central and eastern Europe. Local populations that spoke Slavic or Finno-Ugric languages (Finnish, Estonian, and Hungarian) generally lacked the organization and weaponry needed to prevent this advance. The conquerors built castles, planned new towns, and invited German farmers to move in. In the twelfth century, according to one estimate, about 200,000 German peasants settled east of the Elbe, clearing land and turning fertile soil with heavy plows.[8] The Catholic clergy arrived, too, setting up **bishoprics**, building churches and monasteries, and gradually convincing local peoples to renounce their pagan gods and goddesses.

> **bishopric** In the Catholic Church organization, a district (diocese) under the authority of a bishop.

To the southeast, the once ferocious Magyars, who had earlier invaded Europe from the Inner Eurasian steppes (see Chapter 10), gradually accepted Christ and founded a Hungarian Christian monarchy. Farther south, spiritual agents representing both the Greek Orthodox and Catholic Churches competed for the souls of Slavic princes and their subjects. Before the eleventh century, these missionaries sometimes worked together, despite chronic strains between Constantinople and Rome over authority and doctrine. In 1054, however, a dispute over Catholic claims to the pope's spiritual supremacy independent of the Orthodox Church triggered a formal divorce. Thereafter, rivalry became more intense. Eventually, a religious frontier emerged in eastern Europe that today mainly follows national borders. The populations of Greece, Bulgaria, Romania, Macedonia, and Serbia adhere chiefly to the Orthodox tradition. Croatia, Slovenia, and Hungary are predominantly Roman Catholic.

Crusades in the Iberian Peninsula. In the early eleventh century, Muslims ruled a large part of Iberia (Spain and Portugal), though the once unified Umayyad state (see Chapter 11) fragmented into several competing kingdoms. In the far northeast of the peninsula, fighting between Muslim armies and the lords of small Christian states had been chronic for three hundred years. We saw earlier in the chapter that the Almoravids and the Almohads, both African Berber powers that preached Islamic reform, successively invaded Spain and reunified the southern region for about 130 years. After 1000, landless knights who recognized the Umayyad breakup for the opportunity it was, formed cavalry bands that, with the blessing of the church, pushed southward. This Iberian crusade paralleled in both chronology and motive the Christian advances into eastern Europe, and both attracted a motley crowd of fighters—Frankish, Flemish, German, English, Italian, and Spanish knights all eager to test their military skills and seize land. Many warriors signed on to serve León-Castile, Aragon, or Portugal, the three most rapidly growing Christian kingdoms on the peninsula.

The conquests took place in two major phases. The first ran from 1080 to 1150, when Christian knights drove Muslim rulers out of central Spain. The second extended from 1212 to 1265, when combined forces of the three large kingdoms made rapid headway against Almohad armies, seizing Córdoba, Valencia, Seville, and other major cities. Only a few Muslim enclaves on the Strait of Gibraltar and the little kingdom of Granada held out longer.

As in the eastern European campaigns, knights who captured Muslim territory in Spain urged Christian farmers to migrate to the new frontier. Rulers rewarded their officers for founding villages and populating them with Christians, and they gave new towns royal charters. Unlike either northern Spain or eastern Europe, however, the southern peninsula was already urbanized when Christian conquerors arrived. In some cities the new overlords expelled Muslim residents, distributing vacated property to nobles, monasteries, and retired foot soldiers. Nevertheless, millions of Muslims and Jews remained in Spain throughout the conquest period. We have abundant evidence of peaceful everyday dealings across religious lines and of Christians learning Arabic and taking up Muslim ways of dress, etiquette, and cuisine. Even after the armies of León-Castile seized central Spain, Toledo and other formerly Muslim cities continued to serve for a time as places where Muslim, Jewish, and Christian scholars sat down together to discuss Greek and Arabic scientific and philosophical texts and translate them into Latin. Nevertheless, Spain's cultural Christianization advanced gradually, marked by Muslims and Jews either converting (or pretending to convert) to Christianity under varying degrees of pressure or else fleeing Spain. This exodus accelerated in the fourteenth century, when Christian rulers adopted harsher religious and political policies toward those minorities.

Crusades in the eastern Mediterranean. Western European crusaders advanced into the eastern Mediterranean basin in 1030, when landless Norman warriors, that is, knights from Normandy in northern France, began arriving in southern Italy. From there, they launched an invasion of Sicily, evicting its Muslim government. Then, in 1095, the reformist Pope Urban II agreed to help the Byzantine emperor resist the Muslim Turks who were just then advancing westward across Anatolia toward Constantinople. In fact, Urban II was interested primarily in capturing Jerusalem, which loomed large in the European imagination as the city where Jesus was crucified and resurrected. An armed crusade to the Holy Land was an opportunity to protect Catholic pilgrims bound for Jerusalem and to firm up Europe's political stability by encouraging landless and unruly knights to seek their fortunes on a new military frontier. Furthermore, despite the pope's show of support for the Byzantines, the Catholic and Greek Orthodox Churches had already split formally. By sponsoring a crusade, the pope saw an opportunity not only to propagate the faith in the core lands of Islam but also to make inroads against the Greek church.

In 1096, between 50,000 and 60,000 people from all over western Christendom, perhaps 6,000 to 7,000 of them mounted knights, marched across southeastern Europe to Constantinople, then on to Syria. In 1099, they took Jerusalem and killed most of its Muslim and Jewish inhabitants. This campaign was the first of seven major crusades that stretched over two hundred years. All of them declared their mission to win and hold the Holy Land, but in reality European knights were eager to capture any Mediterranean territory that offered land and wealth. As we saw earlier, the breakup of the Turkic Seljuk empire allowed Christian forces to implant small crusader states on the coasts of Syria and Palestine. The aristocratic leaders of these European colonies handed out large farm estates to loyal knights. Western European peasants, however, went to Syria or Palestine in small numbers relative to their migrations into eastern Europe or Spain. Southwest Asia was already densely populated, and its semiarid environment and intensely irrigated farming held little attraction for French or German plow farmers.

In the twelfth century, Italian sea merchants operating mainly from Venice, Genoa, and Pisa ferried a steady stream of fighters, pilgrims, war horses, and weaponry to the crusader states. As time went on, the religious fervor that motivated the First Crusade served increasingly as an ideological rationale for straightforward territorial acquisition. In 1191 King Richard I of England seized Cyprus, a Greek Christian island. The Knights Templar and the Knights Hospitaller (Knights of St. John), newly formed religious orders of fighting monks, seized other Greek islands, while European fleets attacked coastal cities in Egypt and North Africa. In 1204 the army of the Fourth Crusade bypassed the Holy Land altogether and assailed Christian Constantinople,

Krak des Chevaliers. The European Knights Hospitaller constructed this mammoth fortress in northwestern Syria in the twelfth century. The castle helped defend the borders of the County of Tripoli, one of the coastal crusader states. The Hospitallers held this citadel from 1142 to 1271, when a Muslim army drove them out.

forcing the Byzantine emperor to flee to Anatolia. A coalition of Christian aristocrats founded a new crusader state there and ruled for about half a century. Byzantine forces regrouped, however, and in 1261 took back the city.

In contrast to the Spanish campaign, the eastern crusades did not fulfill their initial aims. The Europeans did not have sufficient resources to push deep into Southwest Asia, and after 1187, when Muslim cavalry under Salah al-Din retook Jerusalem, the crusader states went on the defensive. In 1291, Muslim forces captured Acre, the last European stronghold on the Syrian coast. Nevertheless, the eastern crusades had long-term political and economic significance. Cyprus, Crete, and other Aegean territories remained in western European hands for hundreds of years. Moreover, the crusader states, like southern Spain, served as conduits for the transmission of knowledge from Muslim lands to western Europe. For example, Italian entrepreneurs learned from Muslims how to grow and process sugar cane for commercial markets, an industry that required building technically sophisticated mills. Europeans first experimented with sugar-making technology in the crusader states. From there, the industry spread westward across the Mediterranean islands to Spain.

European Commercial Power in the Mediterranean

Northern Europe's economic growth and the good business generated by the crusades encouraged Italian merchants to advance aggressively into the Mediterranean, a commercial zone that in the previous several centuries had been a preserve of Muslim and Greek Byzantine shipping. Venice, Genoa, and Pisa, all independent Italian city-states, took the lead. Italian shipwrights built both round-hulled cargo ships and sleek galleys. These port cities became clearinghouses for shipments of Syrian glassware, Indian pepper, Chinese porcelain, and West African gold to northern Europe. The twelfth-century Persian geographer Zakariya al-Qazwini, writing about a city, perhaps Mainz, on northern Europe's Rhine River, observed: "It is astonishing that, although this place is in the Far West, there are spices there which are to be found only in the Far East—pepper, ginger, cloves, spikenard, costus, and galingale [varieties of aromatics], all in enormous quantities."[9] European exports to Mediterranean markets included grain, timber, salt, metals, furs, silver and gold coinage, and, increasingly from the twelfth century, fine woolen cloths manufactured in Flanders or northern Italy.

Genoese and Venetian merchants also led the way in founding communities in both Muslim and Christian ports to serve as hosts and agents for shippers from the home city. A Genoese diaspora, or scattering of trade settlements, spread around the western Mediterranean rim, while Venetian merchants settled in eastern Mediterranean ports. These Italians, however, changed the rules of the game, combining trade with military power in ways largely unfamiliar to Muslims and Greeks. The Venetian government financed commercial enterprises, supported them with military force, seized foreign ports and islands, and pressured Muslim or Byzantine authorities to grant foreign merchants commercial privileges. Venice did not have enough armed might to conquer extensive Mediterranean territories, but it did create an empire of trading posts, protecting them with naval patrols. In Genoa, private entrepreneurs, not the government, organized most mercantile ventures, but the state furnished ships and financial incentives to expand operations. Beginning in the thirteenth century, the two city-states became increasingly violent rivals for Mediterranean trade. Meanwhile, Muslim and Greek merchants had to settle mostly for piracy or local coastal shipping.

Memento of a pilgrimage. Christian pilgrims commemorated their journeys to holy shrines by purchasing badges, which served as inexpensive souvenirs. This pewter badge shows St. Thomas Becket, Archbishop of Canterbury, returning from France to England shortly before his assassination in 1170. Canterbury Cathedral subsequently became a popular pilgrimage site.

Western Europe's Cultural Style

Europe in the eleventh century was a complex jumble of monarchies, principalities, city-states, languages, and ethnic groups. Nevertheless, in the ensuing three hundred years a distinctive European cultural style, indeed a new Afroeurasian civilization, began to take shape. The invigorated Catholic Church drove western Christendom's early cultural integration. Reform clerics not only encouraged standardized doctrine and canon law but also promoted particular styles of art and architecture. New movements to encourage Christian piety and devotion spread among ordinary women and men. These included pilgrimages to holy shrines within Europe, emotional veneration of Jesus and his mother Mary, and sponsorship of charities. Though Europeans spoke many different tongues, Latin served as the common language of priests, bureaucrats, lawyers, and scholars from Ireland to Hungary.

Efforts to unify Christian life did not, however, bode well for Europe's Jews. The popes formally accepted responsibility for protecting them, but as pious reforms progressed and crusading fervor took hold, social toleration of Jews deteriorated. Under Pope Innocent III, clerics attending the Fourth Lateran Council held in 1215 imposed new discriminatory laws on Jews, obliging them to wear distinctive dress and barring them from public office. Jewish trade diasporas had played an early part in linking Europe to the wider Afroeurasian world. But as economic growth accelerated, Jews steadily retreated from the commercial sphere, except as money lenders.

Another aspect of cultural integration was the founding of more monasteries as centers of vibrant economic and cultural activity. In the twelfth century, for example, the Cistercian monastic order specialized in opening holy houses in rural and remote corners of Europe and devoting themselves to clearing forests and cultivating the land. The Cistercians created a remarkably integrated network of monasteries that by the early thirteenth century numbered in the hundreds and extended from Spain to Norway and the frontiers of Russia. Like the reforming popes, the Cistercian founders aimed to cleanse Christian society of worldliness and spiritual complacency. Life in a monastic house was austere and rigorous—a simple diet, little heat in winter, and a ban on almost all conversation. Even so, Cistercian communities became large-scale producers of food and wool and made significant advances in animal breeding and farm technology.

Monasteries for women also multiplied but much more slowly. The Cisterians and most other male-dominated orders often obstructed their growth, arguing that nuns could pull less economic weight than male members of the community and that pious donors were less inclined to give money to support cloistered women. The male leaders of orders also justified their resistance by reciting, as priests had for centuries, tired truisms about the dangers of women's company. As one abbot pronounced, "We unanimously decree for the safety of our souls no less than that of our bodies and goods, that we will on no account receive any more sisters [into the monastery]."[10]

Christian Europe's cultural integration, especially at elite levels, proceeded hand in hand with population growth, urbanization, and expanding trade. In the thirteenth century the young civilization achieved full bloom manifested in the continuing spread of literacy, the triumph of Gothic architecture, and a remarkable synthesis of Christian, Greek, and Muslim learning. We return to these achievements in Chapter 13.

· · ·

Conclusion

Several interrelated developments mark the approximate year 1000 as an important turning point in Afroeurasian history. The weightiest of these was the extraordinary expansion of the Chinese economy under the Song and Jin dynasties. China produced so many goods that other societies wanted, and its internal market expanded so much, that its economy, more than any other single factor, stimulated trans-hemispheric commercial exchange to unprecedented levels.

A second development, paralleling China's economic surge but on a smaller scale, was the political stabilizing and economic revival of Europe. For the first time since the fall of the western Roman empire, the Mediterranean zone of inter-communication expanded outward to the north and north-west to fully incorporate western Europe. Indeed, Europeans not only pressed into the Mediterranean trade networks but in the ensuing two and a half centuries came to dominate them. Moreover, European civilization, shaped primarily by the Catholic Church and the Latin language, expanded territorially, as mounted knights and migrating peasants advanced into eastern Europe, the Iberian Peninsula, and, with limited success, the eastern Mediterranean.

Third, the central Muslim lands experienced much political turbulence in the eleventh and twelfth centuries as Turkic horse archers with their families, herds, and flocks streamed in. Turkic cavalry captains attempted to found a unitary state on the scale of the great Abbasid empire of the ninth century. But this project failed, and by the end of the twelfth century the whole region from Egypt to northern India was a collage of states, most of them ruled by Turkic military elites. In contrast to Inner Eurasia, the Sahara Desert had never spawned large pastoral confederations capable of overrunning neighboring agrarian lands. But parallel to the Turkic movements, Berber-speaking warriors burst out of the western Sahara in the eleventh century to conquer not only North Africa but also Muslim Spain. The Strait of Gibraltar as a boundary between the African and European land masses had little political or cultural meaning for the next two centuries.

The complex commercial and cultural exchanges of the eleventh and twelfth centuries clearly did not depend on the existence of several giant empires. Across Afroeurasia, in fact, there were a greater number of relatively small states than during the previous several centuries. China became divided, and South Asia already was. Turkic commanders divvied up the central Muslim lands, and no monarch or pope managed to politically unify all of Christian Europe. In West Africa the Ghana empire faded, owing partly to the assaults of the Saharan Almoravids. In the early thirteenth century, however, the largest territorial empire the world has ever known arose abruptly. The Mongolian founder of this state became known as Chingis Khan, the Universal Lord.

• • •

Key Terms

Almohads 353	Jin dynasty 341	principality 358
Almoravids 351	Kamakura shogunate 345	samurai 346
bishopric 361	madrasa 354	secular ruler 358
bourgeoisie 359	Magna Carta 359	Seljuks 349
canon law 358	*mamluk* 348	Song dynasty 350
charter 360	meritocracy 344	Sufism 355
crusades 361	mysticism 355	*Tale of Genji* 346
Dai Viet 345	Neo-Confucian 344	
Ghaznavids 348	North Atlantic Warm Period 341	

Change over Time

9th–13th centuries	The North Atlantic Warm Period is associated with more stable food production in China and Europe.
960–1276	The Song dynasty in China (960–1127, Southern Song, 1127–1276) presides over an unprecedented rush of industrial and commercial activity, stimulating economic growth across Afroeurasia.
977–1186	The Ghaznavid dynasty, founded by Turkic *mamluk* officers, rules in Afghanistan and South Asia.
1054	The Greek Orthodox and Catholic Churches split formally (Great Schism).
1055–1092	The Great Seljuk empire, founded by Turkic migrants from Inner Eurasia, encompasses much of Southwest Asia.
1058–1111	The theologian and mystic al-Ghazali integrates Sufism into Muslim belief and practice.
1062–1147	The Almoravid dynasty, founded by Berber reformers in North Africa, rules in the western Mediterranean.
1066	Normans led by William I invade and conquer England.
1088–1099	Pope Urban II champions armed Christian crusade to the Holy Land.
1099–1291	European crusader states in Syria and Palestine become conduits for the transmission of new knowledge to western Europe.
1115–1234	The Jin dynasty replaces the Song dynasty in northern China.
1120–1269	The Almohad dynasty replaces the Almoravids in the western Mediterranean.
1130–1200	The Chinese philosopher Zhu Xi teaches Neo-Confucianism.
1138–1204	The Jewish philosopher and theologian Maimonides codifies Jewish law.
1169–1250	The Ayyubid dynasty rules in Southwest Asia and Egypt; its founder, Salah al-Din, expels European knights from Jerusalem in 1187.
1185–1333	During the Kamakura shogunate in Japan, the samurai class rises to prominence.
1204–1261	Constantinople becomes a western European crusader state.
1206–1526	The Delhi sultanate, founded by Turkic fighters, rules much of South Asia.
1215	The Magna Carta is signed in England, ratifying the customary rights of the aristocracy against royal power.
1236	Muslim Córdoba falls to Christian crusaders.

Please see end of book reference section for additional reading suggestions related to this chapter.

13 Afroeurasia in the Era of Mongol Power

1200–1350

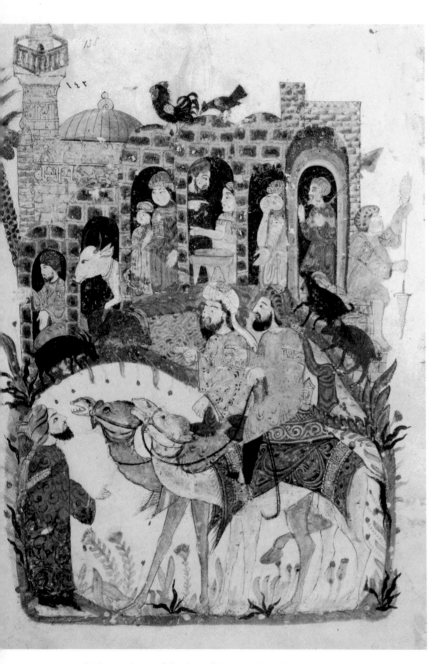

Arab travelers arriving in a village, depicted in a miniature painting from a short story collection of Abu Muhammad al-Hariri.

Many people have stories to tell of running into someone they know in an unexpected place far from home. Even though more than seven billion people share the planet, the high-speed mobility of our era means that sudden encounters between acquaintances on airplanes or in restaurants happen all the time. Before the age of fast global transport, most men and women stayed close to home and never had such experiences. But people who did travel long distances by caravan or sailing ship kept to the well-known roads, trails, and shipping lanes. Therefore, chance meetings between acquaintances thousands of miles from their hometown probably occurred more often than we might imagine.

Take the case of Abu Abdallah ibn Battuta, a Muslim legal scholar from Morocco who traveled back and forth across Afroeurasia between 1325 to 1354 and then produced a book about his experience (see Map 13.2). He made several pilgrimages to Mecca, studied with renowned scholars in Southwest Asian cities, and worked for the sultan of Delhi in India. In his narrative he tells us that during his journeys he repeatedly bumped into people he already knew. When he visited China's southern coast in 1346, he encountered a man named al-Bushri. This scholar and merchant came originally from Ceuta, a Moroccan town only forty miles from Tangier, Ibn Battuta's native city. Conversing together, the two men realized that in fact they had already met some years earlier in northern India. Shortly after that happy encounter, Ibn Battuta returned to Morocco. But more than five years later, while visiting a caravan city on the edge of the Sahara Desert (at the opposite end of the hemisphere from China), he met and lodged with a lawyer who turned out to be al-Bushri's brother!

Ibn Battuta was just one of thousands of merchants, scholars, soldiers, pilgrims, and missionaries who traveled widely in Afroeurasia in the 1200–1350 period. During much of that era, wide areas of the supercontinent experienced remarkable political stability, as well as long-distance commercial activity that exceeded in volume and complexity the already expansive scale of interchange that characterized the previous two centuries.

This upsurge in the movement of goods, as well as people and ideas, can be attributed partly to the spectacular state-building venture of the Mongol conqueror Chingis Khan (also, Genghis Khan) in the early thirteenth century. The Mongol era began as a violent military onslaught of Inner Eurasian pastoral nomads, campaigns that engulfed and subjugated the entire region from China to Iran. Chingis (CHEEN-gihs) erected an empire that after the mid-thirteenth century devolved into four major Mongol-ruled states. The combined territories of these states extended from Korea to eastern Europe, and they affected the lives, directly or indirectly, of hundreds of millions of people. Moreover, the Mongol khans, or monarchs, became protectors of trade, builders of cities, and patrons of cultural achievement.

This chapter begins with an account of the Mongol irruption—its beginnings in Mongolia, its extraordinary military triumphs, and the consequences it had for the populations it overpowered. We also describe developments in the four Mongol successor states and their continuing campaigns to bring more territory under the authority of the descendants of Chingis Khan.

The second part of the chapter investigates the period from about 1250 to 1350, when the four big Mongol states, as well as other successful monarchies, encouraged trade and cultural interchange across Afroeurasia. Historians have labeled that century the Mongol Peace (*Pax Mongolica* in Latin). It was hardly free of warfare, but relative political calm over large areas stimulated the movement of goods, ideas, and inventions to distant places where they had previously been unknown. Religious teachings and practices also moved along the busy trade routes, a phenomenon that especially benefited Islam.

Mongol khans presided over a sort of golden age of trade on the ancient silk roads across Inner Eurasia. Nevertheless, maritime commerce on the Afroeurasian seas continued, as it had in the preceding centuries, to far outweigh caravan traffic in volume and value. In the third part of the chapter we focus on the Indian Ocean basin from Southeast Asia to East Africa, a region that largely escaped Mongol attacks and where new and prospering ports, city-states, and monarchies continued to appear.

The fourth section takes us back to Europe, a region that from the tenth century enjoyed rising population, steady

Chapter Outline

THE ASCENDANCE OF THE MONGOL EMPIRES
Chingis Khan's Path of Conquest
Explaining Mongol Power
Mongol Expansion after Chingis

INDIVIDUALS MATTER Sorghaghtani Beki: A Woman of Influence

Mongol Murderers: A Deserved Reputation?

THE AMBIGUOUS MONGOL PEACE
Silk Road Traffic
Slaves, Diplomats, and Career Seekers
Cross-Fertilization in Science and Technology
The Changing Religious Map

PROFIT AND POWER IN THE SOUTHERN SEAS
Trade and State Building in Southeast Asia
The South Asian Pivot
East and Southern Africa in the Indian Ocean World

URBAN SOCIETY IN EUROPE
Many Governments and Languages
Private Groups and Charters
The Flow of Ideas

TRANS-SAHARAN CONNECTIONS
North Africa between the Mediterranean and the Sahara
The Mali Empire

WEIGHING THE EVIDENCE Ibn Battuta Assesses the Mali Empire

Other West African Kingdoms

• • •

urbanization, and a rush of cultural innovation. In the Mongol age Europe also played a more energetic part in transhemispheric exchange. For the first time since the days of the Roman empire, European merchants were to be seen in at least small numbers in the lands east of the Mediterranean, even in China. And in contrast to both China and Southwest Asia, Europe's western lands did not have to endure Mongol invasions.

In the final part of the chapter, we shift southward to the lands rimming the Sahara Desert. Though Mongol armies never penetrated any part of Africa, the trans-Saharan

A Panoramic View

MAP 13.1 Afroeurasia at the death of Chingis Khan, 1227.
Over the course of two decades, Chingis Khan forged the largest empire in world history to that point. What geographic factors contributed to the success of his conquests?

trade network became tied more firmly than ever to Eurasian routes. Several West African states benefited from long-distance trade connections, especially Mali, a Muslim empire of agrarian wealth and sources of gold, which flowed in greater abundance through trans-hemispheric pipelines, further energizing production and commerce.

The Ascendance of the Mongol Empires

FOCUS How did Chingis Khan and his armies succeed in forging a state that extended from Iran to China?

In 1206 Chingis Khan (1167?–1227) united the tribes of Mongolia and in less than two decades forged the largest empire the world had ever seen (see Map 13.1). The conquests were still going strong when Chingis Khan died, and by 1260 the Mongol imperium encompassed an area nearly four times that of the Roman empire at its zenith.[1] This gigantic state lasted less than fifty years. After 1260, it fractured into four competing Mongol kingdoms, or **khanates.** All of them, however, remained under the authority of the great conqueror's descendants—members of the House of Chingis—well into the fourteenth century or later. These four states—centered east-to-west on China, Inner Eurasia, Southwest Asia, and the lands north of the Black and Caspian Seas, including Russia—had the dimensions of empires in their own right, embracing peoples of many languages and cultural traditions.

khanate A state ruled by a khan; a Turkic or Mongol monarchy.

Chingis Khan's Path of Conquest

On the eve of Chingis's rise to power, Mongolia was home to herding peoples numbering somewhere between 700,000 and 1,000,000.[2] Like pastoral societies across Inner Eurasia, the Mongols organized themselves in tribes, that is, groups whose social cohesion was based, not on primary allegiance to a government, but on a claim of shared descent from a single male ancestor who had lived sometime in the distant past. Some Mongol families had noble status, owning large herds, assigning pasture to other groups, and leading mounted fighters into battle. Shamans, or local religious specialists, also wielded great influence. Acting as intermediaries between mortals and numerous deities and nature spirits, these men and women performed purification rituals, read omens, and blessed herds. Mongols generally believed that the highest supernatural authority resided in Blue Heaven, though, much like the Chinese Confucian idea of a supreme power called Heaven, this cosmic force took no concrete form and remained aloof from daily human affairs. Some Mongols also identified with Buddhism, Nestorian Christianity, or Manichaeism, religions that had been present in Inner Eurasia for centuries.

Mongol life revolved around the seasonal movement of herds of horses, sheep, cattle, and camels between highland valley pastures in summer and lowland plateaus in winter.

Mongol sport. This sixteenth-century Chinese painting depicts Mongol horsemen playing a type of polo.

Humble sheep had the greatest value as a source of food and fiber, but only horses, the engines of war, gave their owners social and political prestige. In the division of labor, men took charge of hunting, as well as feuding with enemies and raiding their herds and encampments. Women managed children and the domestic hearth, but they also spent long hours in the saddle, overseeing the care of animal stock. A thirteenth-century European visitor wrote:

> The men do not make anything at all, with the exception of arrows, and they also sometimes tend the flocks, but they hunt and practice archery. . . . Their women make everything, leather garments, tunics, shoes, leggings, and everything made of leather; they also drive the carts and repair them, they load the camels, and in all their tasks they are very swift and energetic. All the women wear breeches and some of them shoot like the men.[3]

The conqueror's early career. We have a version of the early life of Temujin (teh-MU-jihn), the birth name of Chingis Khan, in the *Secret History of the Mongols*, a book written in the Mongolian language sometime in the thirteenth century. Temujin belonged to a noble lineage, but at a young age he lost his father to a political assassination, leaving him and his family without herds or protection. At one point, a group of his rival kinsmen captured and imprisoned him, fastening a cangue, or heavy wooden restraining device around his neck and arms. According to the *Secret History*, he waited until his captors had dispersed after a feast, hit his guard on the head, then slipped away to the nearby Onan River: "Then, telling himself that if he lay down in the forest by the Onan, he would be seen, he reclined on his back in the water's stream and, letting his cangue float with the current, he lay with only his face clear."[4] By this ruse he made his escape.

Feats like this, the *Secret History* declares, revealed Temujin's bravery and cunning. Once free, he attracted a personal following among other young warriors, and he eventually won the allegiance of nearly all the tribes of Mongolia. In 1206 a meeting of clan leaders proclaimed him Chingis Khan, or Universal Ruler. He won this title by overawing his enemies with brilliant battle tactics and sheer ruthlessness, including executions of war prisoners. He also, however, assimilated thousands of defeated warriors into his own ranks, offering them his protection and fair shares of the horses and other booty taken on campaign.

In steppe society, the leader of a large coalition of herding tribes could hope to hold power only as long as he produced opportunities for seizing grazing land, horses, and captives. To keep the Mongol confederation together, Chingis had to find new targets for conquest. In 1209 he led his archers southward against Xi Xia (shi shyah), a pastoral nomadic state of Tibetan origin that dominated the eastern end of the silk roads and the prosperous oases scattered along them. The rulers of Xi Xia were forced to pay tribute, and Chingis incorporated thousands of their fighters into his own cavalry. Two years later, he led his growing army across the

Chingis Khan. The artist who painted this portrait lived a century or more after the conqueror died. Is any particular personality trait of the conqueror evident in this picture?

Gobi Desert to northern China, attracted, as Inner Eurasian nomads long had been, by the prospect of plundering the towns and farms of the Yellow River valley. In 1215 Chingis captured the northern capital of the Jin, the ruling group that had overthrown the Northern Song dynasty back in 1127 (see Chapter 12). Seizure of this city near modern Beijing impelled further campaigns. The Jin had a huge army, but because they themselves had risen to power in northern China as foreign invaders, they inspired little loyalty among the Chinese villagers they dominated. Consequently, the Mongols lured many Chinese to their side, recruiting archers and skilled military engineers. Even with these advantages, the fight for northern China raged on for nearly two decades.

Campaigns to the west. The Mongols were the first steppe conquerors to wage campaigns in both northern China and central Inner Eurasia simultaneously. At the same time that Chingis was fighting the Jin, other Mongol bands advanced west across the steppes to the territory of the Qara Khitai empire, which dominated the Inner Eurasian heartland. Qara Khitai had been founded in 1124 by military refugees who had fled westward in the turmoil surrounding the rise of the Jin. In 1218, Mongol forces eradicated the Qara Khitai state, handing Chingis long stretches of the silk roads and immense expanses of horse pasture. He also absorbed thousands more mounted archers, most of them speakers of Turkic languages, into his western army. In fact, these fighters came to far outnumber ethnic Mongols in the invading forces. We might therefore more accurately refer to the Turko-Mongol invasions, though most of the top commanderships went to Chingis's relatives and close companions.

Victory over Qara Khitai put Chingis on a collision course with the empire of Khwarizm. This state, founded by Turkic military men, dominated the fertile lower valley of the Amu Darya (Amu River) east of the Caspian Sea (modern Turkmenistan and Uzbekistan). In the first two decades of the thirteenth century, the rulers of Khwarizm expanded their territory spectacularly, sending cavalry into Afghanistan and Iran and capturing the Central Asian silk road center of Samarkand.

When Chingis sent three ambassadors to Khwarizm to resolve a dispute, the Turkic ruler Ala al-Din Muhammad (reigned 1200–1220) murdered one of them and humiliated the others by shaving off their beards. To answer this insult, the conqueror led his mounted army against Ala al-Din in 1219, unleashing hellfire on the peoples of Central Asia, Afghanistan, and Khurasan (northeastern Iran). The campaign, which continued for four years, earned the Mongols their enduring reputation for horrific killing. They sacked, plundered, or burned most of the great commercial and manufacturing cities of those regions, including Samarkand, Herat, Merv, and Nishapur. They massacred whole populations, though sparing skilled artisans, young women, and others fit for forced labor or sexual service. They killed or evicted tens of thousands of peasants, converting farm lands into pasture for their countless herds. In a few towns they even killed the dogs and cats. "With one stroke," lamented the Persian scholar Ata Malik Juvaini of the invasion of Khurasan, "a world which billowed with fertility was laid desolate, and the region thereof became a desert, and the greater part of the living dead, and their skin and bones crumbling dust."[5] As for the mighty Ala al-Din, he died a fugitive on an island in the Caspian Sea.

The passing of Chingis. Leaving Central Asia and northern Iran a smoldering ruin, Chingis returned to Mongolia in 1223. In his final campaign he destroyed the Xi Xia state to punish its rulers for failing to pay tribute. He died four years later, at the age of about sixty, and was buried in a secret grave in western Mongolia. Modern explorers have mounted several expeditions to find the tomb, so far without success.

Explaining Mongol Power

Chingis Khan created a gigantic state in less than twenty years, but he did it by relying on many of the same military and political methods that the Seljuk Turks and other Inner Eurasian empire-builders had employed in previous centuries. That is, the Mongol army consisted mostly of horse archers equipped with powerful compound bows, lances, and swords. Some mounted units, called heavy cavalry, outfitted themselves in many pounds of defensive armor. Light cavalry wore less armor to enhance their speed and mobility. And like earlier steppe conquerors, the Mongols financed their army and administration by extracting wealth from herders, farmers, and merchants and, whenever they had sufficient power to do it, from the citizens of the commercial cities that rimmed Inner Eurasia on the east and south.

In other respects, the Mongol empire arose out of the particular circumstances that prevailed in the early thirteenth century. First, the Mongol tribes produced a leader of extraordinary talent. In his path to power, the young Temujin brilliantly combined hard discipline with fulsome generosity, mercilessly punishing failure or betrayal but rewarding even the lowliest soldier for showing loyalty and pluck. He also exploited the fact that the Xi Xia, Qara Khitai, and Khwarizm states all had relatively fragile military governments and shallow reserves of popular support. As for the Jin, a century of chronic warfare between them and the Southern Song dynasty made them vulnerable to attack from the steppes.

Mongol success depended more than anything else on horses. Early victories allowed Chingis and his commanders to corral hundreds of thousands of them, potentially several for every warrior. One historian has estimated from later data that in the 1200s Inner Eurasia had half the horses in the world and that Turko-Mongol fighters came to own most of them.[6] With so much spare horse power, Mongol cavalry could advance thirty miles a day and launch ferocious attacks even when their adversaries outnumbered them.

Chingis also adopted some of the military technology of agrarian states. Owing to silk road connections, knowledge of war machines and tactics used in China, India, and the central Muslim lands had been spreading to Inner Eurasian peoples for centuries. Perhaps more eagerly than any earlier steppe warrior, Chingis borrowed weapons and military know-how from more technologically complex societies. These devices included Chinese battering rams and catapults used for breeching walls that cavalry could not penetrate. Chingis also recruited skilled Chinese and Persian engineers to set up and operate these complicated engines. He almost certainly employed Chinese technicians to set off gunpowder bombs and rockets, though only in the following century did gunpowder weaponry become a significant factor in warfare west of China.

Adapting another Chinese idea, Chingis organized his army in nested units of ten, one hundred, one thousand, and ten thousand fighters in order to create a tight chain of mobilization and command. In Mongol and Turkic societies, political allegiance and economic interests centered on extended families and the clans into which they were grouped. Chingis, however, placed warriors from different kinship groups into each unit at every level, thereby

Mongol assault. In this Persian miniature painting, Hulagu, a grandson of Chingis Khan, lays siege to Baghdad in 1258. The two pyramid-shaped structures in the foreground are catapults.

neutralizing kinship loyalties and ensuring that all soldiers would depend absolutely on their military comrades and devote themselves exclusively to the Mongol imperial cause.

Mongol Expansion after Chingis

In the half-century after Chingis Khan died, the Mongol empire went through two successive transformations. First, his immediate successors invested their inherited wealth and cavalry power in even more conquests, nearly doubling the size of the empire. Chingis chose his third son Ogedei (ERG-uh-day, r. 1229–1241) to succeed him as supreme commander, or Great Khan. According to custom, however, any member of the Chingis lineage could lay claim to that office. Consequently, succession disputes and family feuds became chronic. Nevertheless, Ogedei, who established the Mongol capital at Karakorum in central Mongolia, and Mongke (r. 1251–1259), one of Chingis's grandsons, had the political skill necessary to keep the empire together and to push out its frontiers for another three decades. Toregene, the wife of Ogedei, also played a key role by stepping in as de facto ruler between 1241 and 1246, when family intrigues delayed the election of a Great Khan to succeed her husband.

The second important transformation was the fracturing of the unified empire. By the 1260s, conflict within the House of Chingis over both succession to power and control of particular territories led to the rise of four separate and competing Mongol power centers. These were the Yuan (yoo-AHN) empire (the khanate of China, 1271–1368); the khanate of Chagatai in Central Asia and the eastern steppes (1225–1687); the khanate of Kipchak (the Golden Horde, 1241–1502); and the Ilkhanate of Iran and Iraq (1258–1335). All four states remained under the authority of members of the House of Chingis, and Mongol-ruled territory continued to grow until the late thirteenth century (see Map 13.2). The ideology that Mongols had an unstoppable mission to rule the whole world drove this continuing expansion.

The Yuan empire: Mongol triumph in China. The struggle between the Mongols and the Jin for dominance of northern China continued until 1234. Once the Jin fell, the victors then faced the Song state in the south. Owing to that region's spectacular economic growth in the previous three centuries, the Song monarchs had formidable resources for resisting Mongol invasion. In fact, Mongke, together with his brother and successor Kubilai Khan (r. 1271–1294), spent another forty years bringing all of China under Mongol

MAP 13.2 Mongol states and their neighbors, 1300.
What geographical or ecological features might help account for the Chagatai khanate being the economically weakest of the four great Mongol states?

authority. Horse archers had to advance into the subtropical south, where open pasture gave way to densely populated rice-growing lands and warm-climate diseases took many Mongol lives. One by one, however, the invaders captured the Song's stout-walled cities, while defecting Chinese sailors helped the Mongols win naval battles on the southern rivers and coasts. The great capital of Hangzhou fell in 1276, and the last Song emperor died three years later.

Kubilai Khan, adopting the dynastic name Yuan, meaning "the origin," united northern and southern China for the first time in a century and a half. But partly to keep up military momentum and to protect his position against family rivals, he campaigned furiously throughout his reign, incorporating the far southwestern region of Yunnan into the Yuan state, attacking Burma, and sending naval expeditions against Vietnam and Java. He also asserted Mongol domination over mountainous Korea, where the rulers of the Koryo dynasty agreed humbly to pay tribute.

Once Korea was subdued, Kubilai looked east across the Korea Strait to Japan, which he and his commanders knew to have a prosperous rice economy, numerous towns, and busy trade with Chinese ports. In the later thirteenth

Sorghaghtani Beki: A Woman of Influence

Sorghaghtani Beki and Tolui.
Some of the most historically informative images of the Mongol era, including this one of Sorghaghtani Beki and Tolui, are to be found in Persian physician and historian Rashid al-Din Hamadani's *Compendium of Chronicles*.

Ever since Chingis Khan's rise to power, women linked to the royal household by birth or marriage had taken a strong and visible part in politics. Sorghaghtani Beki was perhaps the most gifted of these women. The niece of a nomad chief that Chingis had defeated, she was given in marriage to Tolui, the youngest of the conqueror's four sons. Tolui spent most of his life fighting for his father and probably seldom went home to his young wife, who very likely managed his lands and herds in his absence.

Tolui died in 1229, just two years after Chingis, leaving Sorghaghtani a widow with four strapping sons. No doubt, she already had political influence because Ogedei, Tolui's older brother and successor to Chingis as Great Khan, awarded her the governorship of a sizable territory in northern China. Ogedei urged Sorghaghtani to marry Guyuk, his own son. She declined politely, arguing that the education and training of her four boys required all her time. According to the fourteenth-century Persian historian Rashid al-Din, she told Ogedei, "[M]y thought is only to bring up these children until they reach the stage of manhood and independence, and to try to make them well mannered and not liable to go apart and hate each other so that, perhaps, some great thing may come of their unity."[7]

Before great things could happen, however, Sorghaghtani had to build her own power base against her rivals. Her toughest foe was Toregene, Ogedei's wife and Guyuk's mother. After Ogedei died, Toregene dominated palace affairs for several years, even during her son's short tenure as Great Khan (1246–1248). Meanwhile, Sorghaghtani bided her time, forging alliances with Mongol generals and the enemies of Guyuk's family.

Her political skills paid off in 1251, when the assembly of Mongol notables made her eldest son, Mongke, the Great Khan. According to Rashid al-Din, "she had always conciliated her kinsfolk and relations by the bestowing of gifts and presents, . . . so that after the death of Guyuk Khan most men were of one mind as to the entrusting of the khanate to her eldest son, Mongke Khan."[8] Unfortunately, she died the following year, never knowing how much three of her sons would achieve. Mongke led the empire effectively for eight years and extended its borders. Her second son, Kubilai, became Great Khan in 1260, completed the conquest of China, and ruled it for three decades. Her third son, Hulagu, founded the Mongol khanate of Iran and Iraq.

Rashid al-Din testified that Sorghaghtani "was extremely intelligent and able and towered above all the women in the world."[9] As an administrator and politician she modeled two policies that her sons, as well as later Mongol monarchs, were well advised to follow. In governing part of northern China, she discouraged conversion of arable land to animal pasture, recognizing that in the long run Chinese farms would generate far more tax revenue than would horse and sheep herding. When he assumed power, Kubilai Khan generally followed her example. Second, she took a broad view of religious practice. Like some other prominent women of the House of Chingis, she was a Nestorian Christian. But she also gave money and moral support to Daoist, Buddhist, and Muslim institutions, winning the goodwill of conquered peoples. She may well deserve credit for initiating the celebrated Mongol strategy of allowing merchants and missionaries of all faiths to travel the silk roads.

Thinking Critically

How would you characterize the skills that Sorghaghtani Beki displayed as a woman involved in Mongol politics?

Sorghahtani Beki in the House of Chingis Genealogy.

century, the shoguns (supreme commanders) of the Kamakura family (1185–1333) claimed to rule Japan, but in fact they progressively lost power to a host of regional land barons and their private armies of samurai warriors. This combination of agrarian wealth and political vulnerability appears to have convinced the restless Kubilai to seize at least part of Japan, rallying Korean forces to help him do the job. He made two seaborne assaults on the islands, the first in 1274, the second in 1281, in each case marshaling thousands of Chinese ships. Both campaigns ended in disaster, however, owing partly to the skill of Japanese archers and partly to storms at sea. In the second offensive, a Pacific typhoon that the Japanese declared a kamikaze, or "divine wind," wrecked much of the invading fleet. Thereafter Japan remained free of Mongol intrusions, though the heavy cost of repelling the invasions contributed to further political disorder in the islands in the next century.

Far western conquests and the founding of the Golden Horde.
Mongol destruction of the Jin dynasty in the mid-1230s freed up troops for a new western offensive into the relatively well-watered steppes west of the Volga River, an invasion route that Huns, Magyars, and other nomads had traced in earlier centuries. The kingdom of Rus (see Chapter 11) offered the invaders an attractive target. Centered in the river valleys north of the Black Sea, this Viking-founded state had flourished in the eleventh and twelfth centuries, transforming the little trading post of Kiev into a splendid Orthodox Christian capital. By 1200, however, Kiev no longer had much authority over regional Russian princes, who competed with one another for territory and the tax revenues extracted from Slavic farmers. Turkic-speaking nomads known as the Kipchaks pastured on the western grasslands, but they had no strong tribal confederation. Taking advantage of these conditions, Batu, a grandson of Chingis, led a huge force across Russia in 1237, sacking towns, burning churches, and murdering peasants. The Russian princes, fatally underestimating the Mongol threat, put up no coordinated resistance. Kiev fell in 1240, and the Kipchak Turks either fled or, hedging their bets, joined the Mongol side.

In 1241, Mongol pursuit of Kipchak enemies escaping into Hungary turned into a full-scale invasion of eastern Europe. One army dashed into Poland, while a second force advanced south of the Carpathian Mountains into the Kingdom of Hungary, at that time a large Catholic Christian monarchy. The region's mounted knights united in defense, but the Mongols annihilated twenty-five thousand Polish fighters while their other cavalry wing destroyed a Hungarian

Bronze seal of a Mongol commander. This relic from Kubilai Khan's lost fleet was retrieved by a Japanese fisherman in the late twentieth century. It is engraved in Chinese and in Phagspa, a written form of Mongolian. Why might an item such as this have been brought onboard a Mongol warship headed for Japan?

force under King Bela IV (r. 1235–1270). In the following weeks, Mongol raiding bands advanced as far west as the Adriatic Sea. News of the Mongol storm caused panicky speculation in Rome and other European capitals. Matthew Paris, an English monk, described the invaders, whom Europeans called Tartars, from reports he received: "Swarming like locusts over the face of the earth . . . , they have razed cities, cut down forests, overthrown fortresses, pulled up vines, destroyed gardens, killed townspeople and peasants. . . . They come with the swiftness of lightning to the confines of Christendom, ravaging and slaughtering, striking everyone with terror and incomparable horror."[10]

Having smashed eastern Europe's best armored knights, the Mongols might then have pushed into Germany and Italy. In 1241, however, the Great Khan Ogedei died, prompting Batu to suspend the campaign and return to Mongolia to deal with the royal succession. Historians have also suggested an ecological reason for the withdrawal: Hungary and Poland had insufficient pasture to support hundreds of thousands of Mongol horses for very long. And far western Europe, wet and forested, offered no ecological base at all for pastoralists and their huge herds.

The Mongols never returned to Hungary and Poland, but they did remain in Russia. There, Batu and his descendants founded the khanate of Kipchak, or, as Russians later called it, the Golden Horde (perhaps a reference to the ruler's camp and his yellow tent). The khans left the Russian Christian principalities intact but considered them political dependencies, sending cavalry to collect annual tributes, intervening in their dynastic affairs, and requiring the princes to make regular appearances at the Mongol court. (Russian nobles were known to write their wills before they went.) After the conquest, however, the Mongol regime left the Russian Orthodox Church and its institutions largely alone.

The Ilkhanate of Iran and Iraq.
Between 1256 and 1260, forces under Hulagu, another grandson of Chingis, swept across Southwest Asia nearly to the shores of the Mediterranean. In this campaign the Mongols faced no great empire but only a cluster of relatively small states ruled by descendants of the Turkic warriors who had invaded the region two centuries earlier. The Sunni Muslim caliph reigned in Baghdad, but soldiers at his disposal controlled very little territory. First crossing Iran's grassy corridors, Turko-Mongol archers swarmed into the Tigris-Euphrates valley, capturing Baghdad in 1258 and killing tens of thousands.[11] According to one Muslim legend, Hulagu arrested the caliph, had him rolled in a carpet, and laid him on a

A relaxed Hulagu. The Mongol conqueror of Iran and Iraq sips from a bowl as he reclines on the ground. He might be drinking *qumizz*, or fermented mare's milk, the Mongols' favorite beverage. This imagined portrayal of Hulagu dates to the sixteenth century. What other objects besides the bowl do you see in the picture?

field for his cavalry to trample. This event marked the end of the Abbasid Caliphate (750–1258).

The Mongols also invaded Syria, but there they met their match. Just a few years earlier, a group of Turkic *mamluks,* or slave soldiers (see Chapter 11) had taken power in Egypt and Syria and proclaimed the Mamluk sultanate (1250–1517). Because they controlled the fertile Nile valley and ruled from Cairo, the biggest city in western Afroeurasia, this regime had deep resources for waging war. In 1260, Mamluk cavalry soundly defeated Mongol intruders at a battlefield in what is today northern Israel, thus limiting their influence in Syria and preventing them from entering Egypt. Mongol forces, however, remained in control of Iran, Iraq, and part of Anatolia. There, Hulagu founded the state known formally as the Ilkhanate (1258–1335), a term referring to the ruler's formally subordinate status to the Great Khan in China. This regime ruled a large part of Southwest Asia assisted by local Muslim scholars and officials literate in Persian or Arabic.

The khanate of Chagatai. The khans of Chagatai, the fourth of the Mongol successor kingdoms, ruled a large part of Central Asia and eastern steppe lands. Revenues from silk road cities, notably Samarkand, accounted for much of the khanate's wealth, as it had a weaker agricultural base than did the other three Mongol states. Chagatai

forces operating from Afghanistan tried several times to add northern India to their realm, but the Turkic-led armies of the sultanate of Delhi (see Chapter 12) forced them out of the Indus valley.

Mongol Murderers: A Deserved Reputation?

Matthew Paris, the English monk quoted earlier, almost certainly never saw a Mongol, but that did not stop him from drawing a lurid picture of them as "inhuman and beastly, rather monsters than men."[12] This frightful image of the Tartar conquerors has endured through the ages. There is no doubt that the Mongols wantonly killed men, women, and children by the hundreds of thousands, severely disrupted economic life in several regions, and destroyed what today would be priceless artworks, buildings, and libraries. But the ravagers also used terror as a deliberate tactic. For example, the Mongol forces that invaded Central Asia in 1219 did not want to besiege walled cities for prolonged periods because they knew local pasture for their tens of thousands of horses would not last long. Therefore, by butchering everyone not useful as workers or slaves in a newly captured city, commanders sometimes convinced the terrified citizens of the next town along the invasion route to open the gates without a fight. If a town surrendered fast enough, the army avoided a siege, horses could be driven to new pasture, and the defeated inhabitants got to live, unless, as sometimes happened, the aggressors decided to kill them anyway. Also, Mongol generals usually called a halt to mass killing and destruction once they achieved control of a region. And later rulers, including Kubilai Khan in China, grasped the fact that long-term political success depended on a steady flow of revenue to the state. This would not happen if most tax-producing farmers and artisans were either dead or hiding in the hills. Therefore, in some places life returned to something like normal fairly quickly.

In northern China, where the invaders demolished more than ninety cities, the economic wounds cut deep. After three centuries of accelerating growth, China's overall population, especially in the north, dropped from as much as 120 million in 1200 to about 85 million a century later.[13] No doubt, warfare, urban destruction, and interruptions of the agricultural cycle all contributed to this precipitous decline. On the other hand, Kubilai ordered his armies to show some restraint in southern China by leaving most cities intact. He permitted cooperative Chinese landlords to keep their estates and peasants to cultivate their rice fields. Therefore, the southern economy survived the conquest fairly intact. In the north, by contrast, the once-flourishing and highly advanced iron industry never recovered from the damage to property and trade.

In Russia, where urbanization, commerce, and Orthodox Christian culture had been advancing, Batu's ferocious assault of 1237–1240 sent the region spiraling into depression. For a century after the conquest, the khans of the Golden Horde continued to pump wealth from Russian princes. These landowning Christian nobles had to pay tribute, but they suffered little themselves, passing most of the financial burden to Slavic peasants who eked out meager livings from the cold northern soil.

In Central and Southwest Asia, the invasions of 1219–1223 and 1256–1260 severely damaged farming. In northern Iran the Mongols killed or scared off so many rural folk that fragile irrigation canals and underground channels silted up, dams collapsed, and salt deposits accumulated. The onslaught transformed a peasantry that had been large and free into one that was for a long time reduced in population and bound to the land by estate lords. In Iraq the Tigris-Euphrates valley's irrigation systems had been deteriorating quite steadily since the ninth century. The Mongol devastation gave it another severe jolt. Nearly a half-century after the conquest, the Persian historian Hamd-Allah Mustawfi predicted "that even if for a thousand years to come no evil befalls the country, yet will it not be possible completely to repair the damage, and bring back the land to the state in which it was formerly."[14]

In short, the Mongol assaults across Eurasia caused immense and long-term damage, but it was also geographically uneven. Some regions that came under Mongol rule suffered much more keenly than others, and all of them recovered at least partially in the following centuries.

The Ambiguous Mongol Peace

FOCUS What consequences did Mongol conquests and state building have for peoples of Eurasia in the thirteenth and fourteenth centuries?

After 1260, when the unified empire splintered, wars among the four successor states became chronic. The khanates of the Golden Horde and Iran-Iraq had consistently bad relations, especially rivalry for control of the trade routes and rich pastures of the Caucasus Mountains. In East Asia, Kubilai Khan spent much of his long reign battling his cousins in neighboring Chagatai. At the same time, however, he formed a close alliance with the Ilkhanate, also an enemy of Chagatai. Therefore, a shaky power balance among the Mongol empires helped keep warfare intermittent and local, and this allowed merchants, missionaries, and scholars to take to the trans-Eurasian highways in much greater numbers than in the time of Chingis. This partial and often fragile Mongol Peace endured well into the fourteenth century.

Silk Road Traffic

Long-distance trade across Inner Eurasia flourished once again. Once in control, Mongol rulers encouraged this commercial renewal in two major ways. First, they and the local elites who agreed to collaborate with them consumed large quantities of luxury goods, some of them transported long distances. Affluent families in Iran and Iraq wanted top-quality ceramics and silks from China. Their counterparts in China coveted carpets, ornamental glass, and other wares from Southwest Asia. Much of the trade that crossed Inner Eurasia in the Mongol era was "official," that is, valuable and exotic goods destined as diplomatic gifts, tribute payments, and political rewards from high-ranking officers to underlings. Moreover, the overland trade reached far beyond the Mongol domains, extending into Southeast Asia, India, North Africa, and western Europe.

Second, the Mongol regimes promoted commerce by creating an effective system of military and political communications. Ogedei Khan probably initiated the military network known as the *yam*, a system of routes, way stations, horses, and supplies used by the army to speed orders, information, and envoys from one part of the empire to another. Mongol governors permitted merchants and other civilians to use this network as long as those travelers had official authorization. This type of passport was often inscribed on a metal or wooden tablet called a *paiza*. Mongol officers also had the cavalry power to help safeguard commercial caravans, deterring local chiefs or bandits from robbing merchants or collecting illicit tolls.

As long as silk-road journeyers carried their *paizas*, commanders paid little attention to their religious or ethnic affiliations. Therefore, after the Mongols withdrew from Poland and Hungary in 1242, Catholic Christian merchants gradually worked up the courage to travel farther east than they ever had before. In the mid-thirteenth century, western Europe was nearing the peak of a three-century curve of strong economic growth. Consequently, aristocratic families and rich town burghers (businesspeople) craved foreign luxuries. Italian shippers, who already dominated the eastern Mediterranean routes, began sailing through the Bosporus strait to the Black Sea. This took them to the very edge of Inner Eurasia to meet and barter with Muslim silk-road traders at northern Black Sea ports such as Kaffa (modern Feodosiya). Small numbers of Italians journeyed as far as China in the later thirteenth and early fourteenth centuries. The Venetian merchant Marco Polo, along with his father and uncle, lived in China from 1275 to 1292. According to his own testimony, he served for a time in the Mongol administration. These Christian visitors, however, numbered far fewer than the thousands of Muslim and Buddhist traders who plied the silk routes.

Slaves, Diplomats, and Career Seekers

People as well as goods were on the move in Mongol times. The four Mongol governments that wielded authority over millions of people depended on tax and accounting skills, diplomatic protocols, and farm and engineering technologies about which Mongolian or Turkic herders knew little. To get the labor and expertise they needed, Mongol officials offered salaries and honors to educated people to serve as clerks, artisans, technicians, and spiritual advisers. The khans of the Golden Horde employed numerous Russian Orthodox Christians as scribes and consultants, while the rulers of the Ilkhanate depended heavily on educated Persians and Arabs to staff state ministries. Across Inner Eurasia, Mongol commanders relied on literate Uighur-speaking Turks, most of them Buddhists or Christians, who lived in the oasis towns. Where the carrots of salary and reward did not work, the stick almost always did. Mongol captains had no more hesitation about forcing people to resettle in some distant land than they had about driving their herds to new pastures. When he invaded Khwarizm, Chingis took along hundreds of Chinese military engineers, whether they wanted to go or not. He also enslaved thousands of Muslim artisans, scholars, and young women and marched them to Mongolia to labor for the army, the royal court, or elite households.

A Mongol safe conduct pass. The silver inscription on this iron passport from Mongol-ruled China reads: "By the strength of Eternal Heaven, an edict of the khan. He who has not respect shall be guilty." The script is Phakpa, named for a Tibetan monk who invented it to write Mongolian. What do you think the phrase "he who has not respect shall be guilty" might mean?

China under the Mongol Yuan dynasty became a powerful magnet for career-seeking migrants. Once on his throne in Daidu (as modern Beijing was then known), Kubilai Khan endeavored to represent himself as the rightful successor of past Chinese emperors. Nevertheless, he distrusted the traditional governing class of Confucian scholar-bureaucrats. They had, he suspected, local economic interests and family loyalties that might conflict with allegiance to the Mongol state. Convinced that only Mongols and officers of other origins personally devoted to Yuan authority should govern, he organized China into a social ranking system that favored, first, Mongols and their Turkic allies and, second, foreigners from outside China in Mongol service. Eager to benefit from this arrangement, Turks, Tibetans, and Persians traveled to China by the thousands to take up jobs as soldiers, scribes, officials, and tax collectors. For example, Christian Alans, an ethnic group from the faraway Caucasus Mountains, traveled to China to take charge of Yuan heavy cavalry.

This influx did not, however, significantly alter China's cultural landscape. The Mongols continued to depend on Chinese clerks, judges, and officials to staff lower levels of government. And as long as civil order prevailed, Kubilai and his hirelings interfered little with Chinese social and cultural life. In fact, he became a patron of Chinese art and literature, and his reign witnessed a flowering of Chinese drama, poetry, painting, and Neo-Confucian philosophy. Moreover, because the Mongols reunified northern and southern China, artists and scholars exchanged ideas more intensively than they had during the previous century and a half.

Cross-Fertilization in Science and Technology

The Mongol regimes in China and Iran-Iraq maintained a particularly firm political alliance. Partly because of that friendship, the links of intellectual communication connecting those two urbanized regions were sophisticated and lively. When Chingis's grandson Hulagu invaded Iraq in 1258, he let his soldiers sack Baghdad and burn its libraries. Within two years, however, he began to rebuild, patronizing scholars and founding an astronomical observatory at Maragheh in northwestern Iran. There, Chinese and Muslim astronomers worked together under Nasir al-Din al-Tusi (1201–1274), a celebrated Persian mathematician, to produce complex astronomical tables, which continued in use for centuries. Paralleling this development, Kubilai Khan set up the Institute for Muslim Astronomy in Beijing. There, Muslim visiting scholars collaborated with Chinese scientists. Like all premodern rulers who sponsored astronomy, the Mongol khans wanted useful information, especially precise readings of the heavens for signs and omens of the future. They also needed accurate calendars to keep track of the agricultural cycle and to predict lunar and solar eclipses—a good way to impress their subjects. Owing to the size of the Mongol domains, rulers commanded scholars to work out complex conversion tables for matching up several different calendar systems in use across Eurasia.

The China–Iran connection also produced key advances in geography, agronomy, and medicine. Chinese maps made in the fourteenth and fifteenth centuries reveal detailed knowledge of India, eastern Africa, and Europe. A Korean chart of 1402 showed identifiable outlines of Europe and the Mediterranean. Owing to plant diffusion from Iran to China, East Asians added carrots, watermelons, and a new variety of lemon to their diet. Conversely, westbound travelers introduced Chinese rhubarb, which people consumed as a digestive aid and purgative, to Southwest Asia and Europe, where the sick swore by its healing properties. Ghazan, the most enlightened Mongol khan of Iran and Iraq (r. 1295–1304), planted a royal garden in the city of Tabriz to experiment with Chinese plants and seeds. According to the Persian scholar Rashid al-Din, the khan gave an order "to bring from all countries seeds of various fruit-bearing trees, aromatic plants, and cereals which were not in Tabriz and which no one there had ever seen before, and to graft these shoots and branches."[15]

The Changing Religious Map

Chingis Khan and his early successors consulted Mongolian shamans on matters of the supernatural. But they also took a cosmopolitan view of celestial truth, believing that Nestorian monks, Tibetan Buddhists, Muslim mystics, and Catholic missionaries might all possess the keys to some part of it. Just as they employed Chinese shipbuilders or Persian siege engineers, Mongol rulers enlisted the spiritual services of any cleric who might bring good fortune to the House of Chingis. It is not that the Mongol khans had a moral ideology of tolerance but that they encouraged whatever devices might work to advance their power, including beneficial rituals and prayers of whatever religion might be at hand.

In the first few generations, no Mongol khan adopted any of the major religions, though Kubilai sponsored palace debates among clerics of different faiths. Tibetan monks attracted the attention of the royal court with their vivid rituals and willingness to declare Kubilai an incarnation of the Buddha. Their influence rose in China in the later thirteenth century, but after 1368, when Mongol power ended, the various Buddhist sects and schools in China retained about the same

Astronomers at work. In this miniature painting from the fifteenth century, Nasir al-Din al-Tusi, the figure on the right, sits at his writing desk in the astronomical observatory at Maragheh. The circular brass objects in this image are astrolabes, instruments used to make astronomical measurements. Al-Tusi persuaded the Mongol khan Hulagu to found this institution.

strength they had had before the invasion. In Mongolia itself, however, Tibetan Buddhism became the dominant faith.

Once the Mongol threat to western Europe receded, Catholic Christian missionaries joined Italian traders on journeys to the territories of the khans. As of the mid-thirteenth century, the Christian crusader states still clung to pieces of the Syrian coast, holding out Catholic hopes of progress against Islam in Southwest Asia. Some Roman leaders speculated that a concerted missionary effort, perhaps in alliance with Nestorian Christians in Asia, might bring pagan Mongols and Turks over to Christ and even facilitate an alliance between European and Mongol states against Muslim kingdoms.

The Qutb Minar. The Muslim Turkic founder of the Delhi sultanate started building this mosque in the late thirteenth century, making use of demolished Hindu temples as building material. The Qutb Minar, the mosque's minaret, rises nearly 238 feet above the Delhi landscape. It is one of the gems of Indo-Muslim architecture, melding Arab, Persian, Afghan, and South Asian elements of design and ornamentation.

The church sponsored several missions to Asia, and European monarchs exchanged diplomatic letters with Mongol khans. In 1245, for example, Pope Innocent IV sent a small mission to Mongolia under the leadership of the Franciscan monk John of Plano Carpini. Far from converting the Mongol leadership, however, John returned home with a letter from the Great Khan Guyuk commanding both the pope and all Christian kings to come to the khan's court to offer their submission. Marco Polo, his father, and his uncle went overland to Beijing in 1271 not only as Venetian merchants but also as representatives of the pope. Beginning in the 1290s, larger parties of Catholic priests and monks went east to convert souls and minister to Christians living in China.

Mongol rulers also made a few initiatives of their own. In 1287, Rabban Sauma, a Nestorian Christian, led a delegation to Europe as representative of the Mongol Ilkhanate. He traveled to Constantinople, then to Rome, Genoa, and France, where he met both the French king Philip IV and the English monarch Edward I. He tried to persuade the Catholic Church to make common cause with the Mongols against the Egyptian Mamluks, though to no avail. He left Europe carrying little more than papal letters, which lectured Nestorian Christian leaders on proper Catholic doctrine.

None of these long-distance contacts between Europeans and Mongols yielded firm results. No khans converted to Catholic Christianity, no anti-Muslim alliance materialized, and in 1291 the Mamluks of Egypt evicted the Christian crusaders from their last stronghold in Syria. When the shaky Mongol Peace disintegrated in the later fourteenth century, the church lost all contact with its missionaries in China.

Among the major religions, Islam achieved the greatest gains during the Mongol era. Between the late thirteenth and early fourteenth centuries, the khans of Iran-Iraq, the Golden Horde, and Chagatai all converted to Sunni Islam, thereby identifying religiously with the majority of their subjects. Turkic-speaking Muslims continued to migrate across Anatolia, some in flight from Mongol armies, others in their ranks. Consequently, Anatolia's Greek Christian population declined steadily. In India, the Delhi sultanate encouraged Muslims of Persian and Arab origin to migrate to India to take official jobs, introduce Islam to Hindu villagers, and settle as farmers in the Indus and Ganges valleys. The Turkic elite promoted mosque building and Muslim education, and Sufi preachers, that is, missionaries of mystical Islam, fanned out across the Hindu countryside performing righteous devotions and showing the way to unity with the divine. Consequently, Islam became established in the fourteenth century as a significant and growing minority faith in South Asia.

Profit and Power in the Southern Seas

FOCUS What factors accounted for the continuing expansion of long-distance exchange in the Indian Ocean and China Seas in the thirteenth and fourteenth centuries?

Historians have sometimes referred to the shipping routes that ran east and west across the Eastern Hemisphere as the "silk roads of the sea." China supplied much of the merchandise that camel caravans carried across Inner Eurasia, but it also pumped great quantities of goods into the sea lanes (see Map 13.3). Marco Polo reported on the trade that passed through the port of Quanzhou in southern China in the late thirteenth century: "I can tell you further that the

MAP 13.3 Maritime trade in the southern seas, 1200–1350.

Slight annual variations in the shift from one seasonal monsoon wind cycle to the other could affect the price of goods in ports of the southern seas. How would you account for that phenomenon?

revenue accruing to the Great Khan from this city and port is something colossal."[16]

Trade and State Building in Southeast Asia

In the same era that huge Mongol and Turkic states sprawled across Eurasia, many small monarchies, independent city-states, and self-governing merchant organizations rimmed the seas of Southeast Asia. A few states had enough ships and sailors to dominate an entire maritime region for a few decades, and well-organized pirate bands prowled the coasts. Despite the immense value of seaborne trade, however, no state had the fiscal resources to control long sea passages or large numbers of ports.

In Indochina, the long tropical peninsula that separates the South China Sea from the Bay of Bengal, the monarchies of Champa (7th century–1471), Khmer (889–1434), and Pagan (1044–1287) all prospered contemporaneously with Song and Mongol China. Champa had the busiest international waterborne trade because it faced the South China Sea and the routes that ran from East Asia to the Indian Ocean. All three of these rice-growing states had royal palace cultures that blended Hindu and Buddhist ceremony. Theravada Buddhism, the variant of Buddhist teaching that emphasized meditation, self-denial, and spiritual insight, emerged gradually as the dominant faith in the region, and remains so today. The Khmer state reached its peak of prosperity in the twelfth and thirteenth centuries, when its farmers expanded wet-rice irrigated farming to new areas and its merchants exported cardamom, tropical woods, ivory, and vividly colored feathers to the Chinese market. Farm taxes and tens of thousands of slaves permitted the Khmer rulers to build stupendous Hindu and Buddhist temples modeled on Indian architectural forms. The temple complex at Angkor Wat, reclaimed from the rainforest in the nineteenth century, is the largest religious structure in the world, though it represents only a fraction of a complex of temples that covered about 135 square miles.

In the Indonesian archipelago, commercial power in the thirteenth century centered on the island of Java. There, a succession of small naval states amassed revenues trans-shipping nutmeg, mace, and cloves from the Moluccas Islands to China and through the Malacca and Sunda straits to the Indian Ocean. Indeed, Java occupied such a key strategic position in the southern seas trade that in 1292 Kubilai Khan launched a Mongol war fleet southward 2,200 miles to try to seize the island. The force numbered 1,000 ships, but the campaign on land went badly, and the Mongols pulled out. In the aftermath of the war, the kingdom of Majapahit (1295–1527) arose as the pivotal Javanese emporium for the spice trade.

The South Asian Pivot

In southern India, commercialization and town building after 1000 C.E. paralleled, if on a somewhat smaller scale, China's economic florescence. As Indian Ocean traffic grew, southern Indian ports became vital turntables in the trans-hemispheric network. Arabian Sea dhows, Malay ships, and gigantic Chinese junks all dropped anchor in these ports, relaying goods from one group of international merchants to another. Marco Polo, who visited the Malabar Coast on his way home from

Angkor Wat. The twelfth-century Khmer monarch Suryavarman II oversaw construction of this central temple complex in Angkor, his capital. Dedicated to the Hindu deity Vishnu, the temple symbolizes the cosmos. The central tower represents Mt. Meru, the hub of the universe and the home of the gods. By the late thirteenth century, however, Angkor Wat became identified more with Buddhist than Hindu worship, reflecting the religious fluidity that characterized Southeast Asia in the late premodern centuries.

China, observed that visiting ships took on not only Indian products like pepper and cinnamon but also goods that were in transit from other regions:

> When merchants come here from overseas, they load their ships with brass, which they use as ballast, cloth of gold and silk, sendal [sandalwood], gold, silver, cloves, spikenard [an aromatic oil], and other such spices that are not produced here. You must know that ships come here from very many parts, notably from the great province of Manzi [China], and goods are exported to many parts. Those that go [westward] to Aden are carried thence to Alexandria.[17]

A thirteenth-century visitor to crowded southern Indian ports might hear traders speaking Tamil and several other Indian languages, plus Arabic, Persian, Malay, Chinese, and Swahili. The port populations rose and fell in rhythm with the seasonal shifts in the monsoon winds, which dictated the arrival and departure of ships and the prices of goods. In the eleventh and twelfth centuries, merchants of Egyptian and North African origin, including Muslims, Jews, and Coptic Christians, settled in the southern Indian ports. They used Arabic as a common language of trade, but many of them married local Indian women, enriching the ethnic complexity of those towns. Gradually, most coastal rulers converted to Islam, and well-organized Muslim firms pushed the Jewish and Christian merchants to the margins of the commercial economy. By the thirteenth century, the Arabian Sea basin was in commercial terms an almost exclusively Muslim "lake."

In southern India a variety of coastal states, self-governing ports, and agrarian kingdoms competed for territory and resources. In the southeast, the Hindu dynasty of Chola ruled between about 850 and 1279, extracting revenues from peasants who farmed rice in interior river valleys and from Tamil-speaking merchants who sold Indian textiles around the Bay of Bengal. Devotees of the Hindu deity Shiva, the Chola monarchs became rich enough to build numbers of soaring stone temples, whose communities of priests, servants, students, and slaves engaged in artisanry, trade, and banking, contributing significantly to the southern Indian commercial economy. The Chola monarchy, however, had continually to fend off rival states, and in the early thirteenth century it slipped into the lower ranks of South Asian regional powers.

East and Southern Africa in the Indian Ocean World

The Indian Ocean trade network extended far down the East African seaboard, and in the thirteenth century peoples of both the coasts and the deep interior linked themselves to the maritime web on a larger scale. As we have seen in earlier chapters, seaports had been multiplying along East African shores since the early first millennium C.E. As in southern India, merchant princes dominated these towns and collaborated with the leading business families. Most of the coastal town inhabitants were descendants of people who had arrived from East African interior regions many centuries earlier. By the thirteenth century these populations had largely embraced Islam. In addition, Muslim merchants, scholars, and Sufi divines from Arabia and other parts of Southwest Asia constituted significant and influential minorities in the larger towns. At the heart of the region's distinctive cultural identity was Swahili (or Kiswahili), a language of the Bantu family whose vocabulary includes many words of Arabic origin. Swahili emerged from about 1000 C.E., not only as the principal language of the coastal city-states, but also as the primary medium of commercial communication.

In the thirteenth and fourteenth centuries, Mogadishu, today the capital of Somalia, was probably the largest and busiest East African port. The Moroccan traveler Ibn Battuta, who spent a week or two in the city as a guest of its Somali Muslim ruler (see Map 13.2), reports on the business customs that facilitated trade between foreign sea merchants and Somali wholesalers:

> When a ship arrives at the anchorage, the *sumbuqs* (these are small boats) come out to it. In every *sumbuq* is a group of young people of the town, and every one of them brings a covered dish with food in it. He offers it to one of the merchants of the ships and says, "This is my guest." Each one of them does similarly. When the merchant disembarks from the ship he goes nowhere but to the house of his host from among these young people. . . . When he lodges with his host, he [the host] sells his goods for him and buys on his behalf.[18]

Kilwa, a second port of great commercial importance, lay farther down the coast on an island off modern Tanzania. The mercantile families of Kilwa prayed in expansive mosques of coral rock, entertained guests in stone houses with sunken courtyards, and dined off Chinese porcelain. Shipwrights, masons, fishers, and artisans led more frugal lives. Male and female slaves brought from the African interior occupied the bottom of the social scale.

The prosperity of the Swahili coast depended not only on seaborne trade but also on traffic with people of the region's interior. Agricultural and herding populations with economies based on grain, bananas, or cattle were growing steadily in the highland region around East Africa's Great Lakes, in the wet forests of the Congo River system, and in the temperate savanna lands of the far south. More towns appeared, and monarchs began to organize political life in more complicated ways. These developments raised the stakes for commercial links with the Indian Ocean coast. In the twelfth century, for example, Mapungubwe, a kingdom of farmers who spoke Bantu languages and the earliest state we know of in southern Africa, amassed wealth partly from exports of ivory and gold. These commodities were carried down the Limpopo River to the shore of what is today Mozambique. There, Swahili merchants bought goods, presumably in return for textiles and other products from the wider world.

The stone enclosure at Great Zimbabwe. Europeans who first saw the ruins of Great Zimbabwe in the late nineteenth century, educated as they were in that era's ideology of white racial superiority, refused to believe that local Africans had constructed this urban complex. They attributed the buildings, rather, to ancient Phoenician or Arab visitors. Archaeological work in the twentieth century proved otherwise, and in fact skilled African artisans built in stone in many places on the Zimbabwe Plateau. The construction at Great Zimbabwe suggests the presence of a strong political authority. How does the site indicate that?

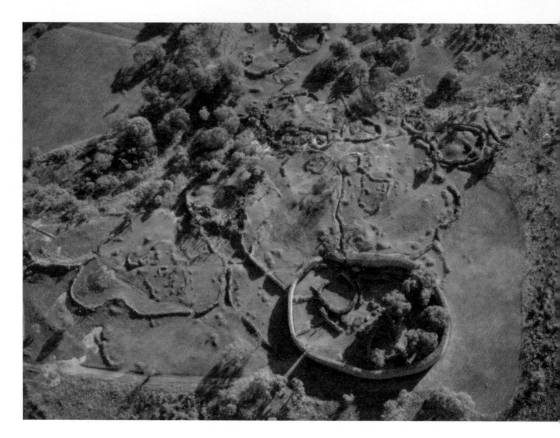

In the thirteenth century a larger stream of gold began to flow from southern Africa into the trans-hemispheric web. The main gold sources were on the Zimbabwe Plateau, a savanna region favorable to grain farming and cattle breeding. The population spoke a Bantu language ancestral to modern Shona, the majority language of modern Zimbabwe. We know that an important state flourished on the plateau from the existing evidence of stone buildings and enclosures that constituted the core of a large town that archaeologists have named Great Zimbabwe. This center, which prospered between the thirteenth and fifteenth centuries, attained a population of perhaps eighteen thousand. Finds of Chinese porcelain reveal Great Zimbabwe's Indian Ocean connection and the affluence of its population, or at least its chiefly families. After about 1430, the city declined, perhaps because an excessive buildup of people and cattle in the region led to ecological crisis. The gold trade, however, simply shifted to new centers somewhat farther north, and the Swahili city-states continued to profit from it into the fifteenth century.

Urban Society in Europe

FOCUS In what ways did Europe manifest the characteristics of a plural society in the thirteenth and fourteenth centuries?

Like Japan and Egypt, western Europe escaped Mongol devastation, if only by the skin of its teeth. Consequently, that region experienced no severe disruption of economic life comparable to what happened in China, Russia, and Southwest Asia. For example, in contrast to China, whose population declined significantly in the thirteenth century, Europe's numbers rose from about thirty-five to seventy million between 1100 and 1300. This growth was concentrated mainly in the temperate northwest from England to Germany. Farming production, commerce, and town building also continued to thrive, as they had been since the late tenth century.

Western Europe's continuing economic expansion took place in conditions of great political variety and flux. In the same era that Mongol khans built giant empires, Europe remained divided into numerous states, both large and small. The Catholic Church arched over them as the preeminent pan-European organization, but by the thirteenth century its authority over kings and princes was limited. In the absence of any single governing power, Europeans achieved remarkable skill at forming private associations devoted to various social, economic, and intellectual enterprises.

The laws, rituals, literature, and art of Catholic Christianity gave Europe its characteristic cultural style as an emerging civilization. In several respects, however, Europe remained remarkably pluralistic, characterized by considerable variety and diversity in politics, language, and social organization.

Many Governments and Languages

As of around 1200 the numerous states of Europe fell into three general categories: independent city-states, whose two principal clusters were in northern Italy and along the rim of the Baltic Sea; small regional kingdoms and principalities, notably the several German states in central Europe; and larger monarchies whose subject populations typically included peoples of varying language and ethnicity (see Map 13.4). Rivalries among these polities made Europe a place of persistent violence, but states also formed alliances, made treaties, and linked themselves to one another through a web of royal marriages.

Despite the political pluralism, several monarchies developed into strong regional states, which reined in the power of local noble families and penetrated remote areas to tax more people. The kings of France built the most efficient power base. Philip IV the Fair (r. 1285–1314) displayed great talent for enlisting loyal, well-educated administrators, who collected revenues on the king's behalf and executed royal commands over wider areas of what is today France. He strengthened ties between the royal court and the prosperous burghers of the growing towns, negotiating shrewdly with them for loans and taxes to advance royal centralization.

The English monarchy paralleled France in fortifying both royal bureaucracy and central legal institutions. King Edward I (r. 1272–1307) conquered mountainous Wales, and he crafted numerous new royal laws, replacing a hodgepodge of local customs. He consulted frequently with Parliament on state affairs, inviting the participation of lower-ranking knights and town leaders, as well as the great barons and bishops. The king had his personal council and secretariat, however, and Parliament remained one of several advisory bodies whose agendas the ruler largely set.

In the Iberian Peninsula, the monarchies of Aragon, Portugal, and Castile (Léon and Castile until they merged in 1230), all gained in centralization and wealth in the thirteenth century following the victory of Christian crusaders over the armies of the Muslim Almohad empire (see Chapter 12). In eastern Europe the kings of Hungary, which had become Catholic Christian in the eleventh century, showed special aptitude for expanding their borders and erecting strong

MAP 13.4 Major states in Europe, 1300.

What geographic features may help account for the borders of European states in 1300?

central institutions. The Mongol onslaught of 1241–1242, however, destroyed the Hungarian army and sent the region into several decades of depression.

Western Christendom also became more ethnically and linguistically diverse between the twelfth and fourteenth centuries because frontier expansion brought speakers of Hungarian, Finnish, Estonian, and several Slavic and Germanic languages into the Catholic fold. At the same time that the Roman church embraced a more diverse array of peoples, however, certain **vernacular languages** became dominant. This happened mainly because of the association of these languages with strong monarchies and because poets and essayists began to write in them. English, German, French, Italian, and Castilian Spanish were among the leading vernaculars. Latin, however, remained the premier medium of religion, law, and learning.

vernacular language The native language of a region used by ordinary people.

Carpenters in stained glass. In Europe craft guilds often donated church windows. In this window in Chartres Cathedral in France, two carpenters work on a board resting on three sawhorses. Why do you think guilds wished to depict their professional activities in church windows?

Private Groups and Charters

No single monarch in Europe had the power to monitor or restrict private economic and social activity beyond the regional level. This gave individuals fairly wide latitude to band together privately to start businesses, organize trading ventures, engage in charitable work, or set up learning institutions. Indeed, European rulers, in competition with one another for financial resources, commonly sought alliances with private groups, offering them protections and liberties in return for political loyalty and regular payment of fees and taxes. Increasingly, private groups negotiated with political leaders for corporate status, forming associations of individuals that existed as entities under the law. Legally recognized corporate groups possessed rights and obligations, often spelled out in a charter granted by the king or other political authority. As new towns sprang up and urban businesspeople accumulated wealth, rulers saw advantages in awarding charters of rights and privileges to towns in return for allegiance and promises of revenue. Chartered towns multiplied in Spain and eastern Europe, as conquering knights enticed immigrant farmers and artisans to clear land and build market and manufacturing centers in return for legal incorporation.

Other private groups might seek a charter licensing them to mine silver, build ships, open a bank, or sell woolen cloth. Urban craft guilds—for merchants, goldsmiths, weavers, carpenters, and numerous other professions—secured charters authorizing them to manage their own affairs and to regulate standards. The principal type of corporate association for women was the religious convent. Urban women, however, sometimes participated in guilds and other chartered civic groups. In a few towns women who spun silk or embroidered cloth formed their own chartered guilds but always under some measure of male supervision.

To put Europe's medieval corporatism in comparative perspective, private activity in China took a rather different form. There, business enterprise typically centered on extended families (not just parents and children but also uncles, aunts, and cousins). This tended to restrict the size and resources of those groups, whereas in Europe a corporate venture might invite anyone who could offer talent or money to participate. Moreover, China's imperial government, including the Mongol Yuan dynasty, traditionally initiated and managed commercial, industrial, and cultural projects. A thirteenth-century Confucian civil servant would have been puzzled at the idea of private groups possessing rights in law that inhibited the emperor's officials from regulating their activities.

The Flow of Ideas

Europe's urban wealth, pluralistic politics, and growing access to the accumulated knowledge of the rest of Afroeurasia encouraged technological and intellectual innovation. When the Mongol conquests began, Europe already had strong links to the big Muslim and Greek Christian cities of the eastern Mediterranean, thanks to the initiatives of merchants, pilgrims, and crusaders. Those connections enlarged the stream of useful ideas from Southwest Asia, including new textile weaving methods, papermaking technology, and Syrian secrets for producing glass. Between about 1250 and 1350, western Christendom also benefited from the long-distance technological exchanges of the Mongol age. The magnetic compass, gunpowder, and block printing, all East Asian inventions as far as we know, reached western Europe sometime between the late twelfth and fourteenth centuries. European artisans lost no time tinkering with those novelties to improve them and put them to practical use.

At the same time, European artisans, backed by chartered guilds and affluent patrons, including monarchs, invented numerous new devices and techniques in the spheres of farm technology, cloth manufacture, shipbuilding, weaponry, and the design of churches and fortifications. The grandest innovation of the twelfth century was the Gothic church. Sophisticated mathematical calculations and engineering designs permitted master masons to construct sanctuaries whose stone walls soared as high as forty modern stories. The use of pointed arches, external supports called flying buttresses, and other new devices permitted builders to leave open spaces high up the walls. These were then fitted with colorful stained-glass windows that directed light onto the lofty vaulted ceilings.

Universities. Institutions of advanced learning bloomed across Europe from Spain to Poland in the thirteenth and fourteenth centuries. Universities arose out of western Christendom's expanding need for educated professionals to take jobs in governments, private firms, and the church as administrators, clerks, accountants, secretaries, teachers, lawyers, and priests. The earliest universities were modeled on schools associated with urban cathedrals, where priests offered Latin education to the sons of both aristocrats and townsfolk. The movement that started in Muslim lands a few centuries earlier to found colleges for advanced religious and legal study influenced European ideas of the university as a central place where scholars and students gathered, and often resided, to teach and learn.

Chartres Cathedral. The church of Saint-Denis north of Paris, together with the cathedral at Chartres, a small city forty miles southwest of the capital, provided the primary models for the Gothic style of church building across western Europe. The exterior half arches, or flying buttresses, shown in this view of the cathedral from the south, helped make the construction of high walls and large windows possible.

Class in session. This fourteenth-century painting shows the German monk Henry of Friemar lecturing at the University of Bologna in Italy. He appears to struggle to hold the attention of all of his students. The student third from the near end in the first row appears to be a women. Do you think a female student's presence would have been likely in a medieval European university?

The professors in early European universities, invariably members of the Catholic clergy, organized themselves in guilds and, like urban merchants and artisans, negotiated with political authorities for charters of self-regulation. In 1200, for example, France's King Philip Augustus awarded a "diploma" to the University of Paris by which its teachers and students could largely govern their own affairs subject to the authority of the pope rather than to the local bishop or the king's officers. By 1300 Europe had as many as twenty-three universities. Properly chartered, these institutions brought prestige to rulers but also enjoyed some safeguards against lords or bishops who might be tempted to meddle in the university's finances or curriculum. A university's course of study centered on grammar, rhetoric, and dialectic (logical reasoning and argumentation), and, depending on the particular institution's orientation, on theology, law, astronomy, mathematics, music, and natural philosophy (what we would call "science"). Universities also both stimulated and benefited from other intellectual developments in Europe. These included the spread of literacy beyond the aristocratic and clerical classes, the growing availability of books, and the emergence of new literary forms such as lyric poetry, romance narratives, and travel accounts. For example, Marco Polo's *The Description of the World*, published at the end of the thirteenth century, became a "best seller" among literate Europeans hungry for knowledge of foreign lands.

Scientific awakening. The organization of education in universities, combined with growing awareness of the world beyond Europe, set off intense debates in learned circles over the nature of reason, faith, and free will. The scholars who posed new philosophical and scientific questions started by consulting the existing knowledge available to them. Those sources included the Bible and the classics of Christian theology but also the great stores of learning housed in the cities around the Mediterranean rim. As European merchants and crusaders sent out new communication lines to the cities of Southwest Asia, North Africa, and Spain, Catholic Christian intellectuals gained more access to that knowledge.

Starting in the eighth century, Muslim scholars translated numerous Greek, Persian, and Sanskrit scientific and philosophical texts into Arabic, then corrected, synthesized, and expanded that knowledge. In the twelfth century, European academicians began to acquire linguistic skills to translate this library of manuscripts from Arabic, Greek, or Hebrew into Latin. They did much of this work in Toledo, Córdoba, Palermo (Sicily), and Constantinople, cities that lay along the frontiers between western Christendom and the Byzantine and Muslim spheres. Between about 1140 and 1280, linguists translated all of the surviving texts of the ancient Greek philosopher Aristotle, along with the extensive Arabic commentaries that clarified and expanded on his work.

Translations of scientific treatises gave European thinkers raw material for further innovation. Leonardo Fibonacci (1170–1240), for example, grew up in a port city in North Africa because his father served as an Italian commercial consul. Fibonacci took up the study of mathematics, subsequently traveling far and wide in the Muslim and Greek Mediterranean in search of knowledge. Returning to Italy, he authored several important treatises on geometry and numbers theory, including the first major work explaining the base-ten "Arabic" numerical system. Thanks to him and other scientists, Europe gradually exchanged Roman numerals for the system invented earlier in India that incorporated positional notation and the zero. This shift made possible more advanced mathematical studies.

Another European sage was the English monk Roger Bacon (1214–1294), who lived and worked in both Oxford and Paris and wrote on astronomy, mathematics, optics, alchemy, and numerous other subjects, drawing on Muslim and ancient classical learning. He argued that the key to understanding the universe was not deductive reasoning from general principles but rather inductive reasoning and experimentation, employing useful instruments to observe and measure natural phenomena. "If a man who has never seen fire should prove by adequate reasoning that fire burns and injures things and destroys them," Bacon wrote, "his mind would not be satisfied thereby until he place his hand on some combustible substance in the fire, so that he might prove by experience that which reasoning taught."[19] Bacon was also the first known European to describe the properties of gunpowder.

Scholastic theology. Despite his plea for practical experimentation, Bacon fully accepted the Christian teaching that nature and the cosmos is knowable to us through divine revelation. Muslim scholars had for several centuries been pondering Aristotle's claim that a First Mover (immortal, unchanging being) existed but that humans might also apprehend reality through systematic observation, analysis, and logic. Some Muslim thinkers identified Aristotle's First Mover with the One God and contended that we can understand his creation by exercising the intellectual powers he has given us. Armed with Christian theology, Aristotle's works, and Muslim commentaries, European scholars embarked on fresh philosophical inquiry. The new methodology, called **scholastic theology,** rested on the confidence that the universe might ultimately be understood through systematic questioning. Europe's great thirteenth-century synthesizer was Thomas Aquinas (1225–1274). A lecturer for many years at the University of Paris, he produced about one hundred scholarly works that aimed to harmonize Christian revelation with Aristotle's logic. The writings of Aquinas became the touchstone of all theological and philosophical debate in Europe in the ensuing centuries.

scholastic theology In medieval Europe, systematic investigation of the relations between the authority of spiritual revelation and the claims of human reason; a method of disputation drawing on philosophy, particularly the works of the ancient Greek thinker Aristotle; also, scholasticism.

Trans-Saharan Connections

FOCUS How did trans-Saharan exchange contribute to political, economic, and religious change in societies of North and West Africa in the thirteenth and fourteenth centuries?

Like the silk roads and the routes of the southern seas, the camel trails of the Sahara Desert crossed boundless open spaces to link regions of agrarian population. Those tracks joined ports on the African shores of the Mediterranean with the dense farming societies that inhabited the grassy savannas south of the desert, the region known historically as the West African Sudan. By extension, trails ran farther south to reach states and peoples of the tropical forest zone (see Map 13.5).

The steady development of trans-Saharan camel trade contributed after about 800 C.E. to the rise of Ghana, a West African monarchy that dominated the western Sahel, the semiarid belt wedged between the Sahara proper and the better-watered savannas to the south (see Chapter 11). Ghana weakened slowly in the eleventh and twelfth centuries, but in the mid-thirteenth the kingdom of Mali, a larger and more effectively centralized state than Ghana, emerged to rule over the savanna trade, including the southern desert ports. In the thirteenth and fourteenth centuries, West African miners and merchants supplied a substantial part of the gold that circulated across Afroeurasia.

MAP 13.5 Trans-Saharan connections, 1200–1350.

The map icons locate the sources of important items in the trans-Saharan trade. Why do you think the greatest concentration of routes is in the western part of the Sahara?

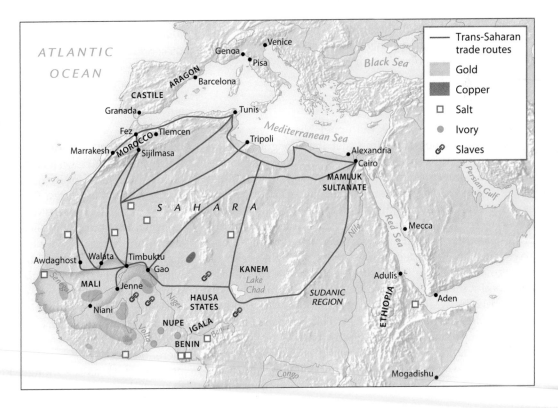

North Africa between the Mediterranean and the Sahara

The Muslim Almohad dynasty, which had unified the lands around the western Mediterranean in the twelfth century, disintegrated in the mid-thirteenth under assault from Christian crusaders (see Chapter 12). Four Muslim states took its place in different parts of the region: the mountain-bound kingdom of Granada in far southern Spain and three kingdoms in North Africa whose territories corresponded roughly to modern Morocco, Algeria, and Tunisia. Also, North Africa's long-established cities continued, despite the Almohad collapse, to prosper as centers of industry and Islamic learning. Tunis, Tlemcen, and Fez were among the most important centers.

North Africa, however, had a much smaller population than Europe did, and its Muslim states lacked the material resources to challenge European domination of western Mediterranean sea trade. Seafaring merchants from Genoa, Venice, Pisa, and the kingdom of Catalonia in Spain appeared in increasing numbers on the North African coast. Their vessels took on cargos of North African wool, leatherwork, grain, and dried fruits, as well as the ivory, ostrich feathers, slaves, and gold that arrived from across the Sahara. In return for these goods, the Europeans sold woolen and cotton textiles, ironware, wine, spices, and weaponry. One product on offer illustrates the hemispheric dimensions of trade. In the waters southwest of India, inhabitants of the Maldive Islands gathered cowrie shells. The harvesters sold the shells by the thousands to Arabian Sea merchants, who relayed them to the Red Sea. Italian shippers acquired them in eastern Mediterranean ports, carried them to North Africa, and sold them to Arab and Berber traders who transported them by camel to West Africa. There, they had scarcity value as both jewelry and a popular form of currency.

The Mali Empire

Mali, whose core area was the upper Niger River valley, emerged about the same time that the Mongol imperial army subjugated Russia and started the conquest of southern China. Mali's rise had no direct connection to Mongol power, but we know that merchants in that era coveted gold as a commodity and medium of exchange. West African mines were rich enough to supply substantial quantities of the metal to Afroeurasian markets. The flow of bullion across the Sahara started growing after the eighth century, in large part because Muslim rulers in the Mediterranean and Southwest Asia preferred to mint gold coins. Then, in the mid-1200s, western European rulers began to produce gold coinage to supplement silver. This happened first in the Italian city-state of Florence, which made the gold coin known as the florin. Since Europe did not have abundant gold resources, demand for African metal shot up. In the fourteenth and fifteenth centuries, West African mines may

have produced about two-thirds of Afroeurasia's gold supply.[20] In return for that precious metal, plus ivory, slaves, and other West African items, southbound caravans brought Mali salt and copper from Saharan deposits and a wide range of commodities from North Africa and the wider Mediterranean region.

Mali's ascendancy. The rise of Mali to primacy among Sudanic states is associated with Sunjata (Sundiata), a heroic figure still celebrated in West Africa today. Like Chingis Khan, Sunjata lost his father as a young boy but rose from adversity—in his case, crippled legs—to lead his people to military triumph. Building a powerful state among the savanna people who spoke Malinke, one of West Africa's major languages, Sunjata and his immediate successors forced all rival states to pay tribute. Deploying both infantry and cavalry troops, the Mali kings, or *mansas*, carved out an empire that extended from the semiarid Sahel to the southern savanna woodlands and from the middle Niger to the Atlantic coast.

Environmental historians have hypothesized that Mali's imperial success may have been linked to the end of an eight-hundred-year wet phase in West Africa's climate. Beginning around 1000 C.E., annual rainfall in the Sahel and northern savanna declined gradually, shrinking resources in crops and herds and perhaps contributing to Ghana's disintegration. The region from which Mali expanded, however, was located farther south in better-watered savannas. Also, Mali's military might relied on horses, which were vulnerable to the bite of the tropical tsetse fly. As drier climate set it, the tsetse fly's habitat retreated toward the rainforest, allowing Mali's horse archers to operate over a wider range of savanna than Ghana's army had been able to do. Even without tsetse flies, however, horses did not breed well in tropical West Africa. Mali's emperors had continually to import fresh mounts from the Sahara or North Africa.

The Mali state. Mali belongs in the club of big monarchies that imposed an unusual measure of political order on much of Afroeurasia during the later thirteenth and early fourteenth centuries. The royal court of the *mansa* consisted of his extended family, numerous wives, trusted officers, bodyguards, and slaves. By about 1300 the king also employed a cadre of literate Muslims, some born in Mali, some from North Africa, who served as secretaries, accountants, and administrators and who made Arabic the written language of government and diplomacy. Because of the great wealth the *mansas* accumulated from taxing farming and trans-Saharan trade, some of them exchanged diplomatic missions with the sultans of Morocco and other Muslim states north of the desert. Royal officers directly ruled the upper Niger and Senegal valleys, the empire's core. Beyond there, they collected periodic tribute from local chiefs and princes, much as the Mongol khans of the Golden Horde harvested wealth from Russian nobles. The *mansas* did not

The central mosque in Jenne, Mali. The style of this mosque, originally built in the thirteenth century but reconstructed in 1907, points to architectural influences from southern Morocco on the other side of the Sahara Desert. The structure is constructed of sun-baked mud bricks and mud plaster, the local building material readily at hand in the Niger River's inland delta.

directly control West Africa's two major gold-producing regions, but they closely monitored the Sudanic merchants who transported the metal to the desert ports, and they took for themselves a healthy share of dust and nuggets to embellish the palace and beautify members of the royal family.

Islam in West Africa. At the start of the thirteenth century, some Sudanic rulers, chiefs, and merchant groups practiced Islam, especially those who did business with the Muslim traders who operated the trans-Saharan caravans. Sunjata, Mali's founder, may or may not have been a Muslim, but later rulers practiced the basic rituals and duties of the faith. The political legitimacy of the *mansas*, however, rested on the allegiance of hundreds of local chiefs who did not practice Islam. Rather, those leaders honored the king through beliefs and symbols associated with the idea that he possessed a sacred character linked to the population's health and well-being. Consequently, the *mansas* had to perform a delicate cultural balancing act, upholding traditional standards of royal ceremony—for example, obliging subjects to approach the royal person by prostrating themselves and throwing dust over their heads—and at the same time nurturing their ties to the wider Islamic universe by attending Friday prayer and in some measure adopting Muslim legal and moral standards.

Mansa Musa (r. 1312–1337) showed particular devotion to Islam by making a pilgrimage to Mecca in 1324–1325, along with an enormous train of notables, soldiers, slaves, camels, and horses. The trip was 3,500 miles each way. He passed through Cairo and while there distributed so much gold that, according to Egyptian chroniclers, the bottom temporarily fell out of the gold market. At home he spent large sums advancing legal and religious education, building mosques, and inviting scholars and architects from abroad. Despite these developments, however, the great majority of people in Sudanic West Africa did not convert to Islam until centuries later.

Mali reached its zenith of power in the mid-fourteenth century. After that, succession disputes within the royal family and revolts in distant tributary kingdoms led to its gradual decline.

Other West African Kingdoms

We know quite a bit about Mali's history, owing in no small measure to Ibn Battuta's first-person account. This state,

Ibn Battuta Assesses the Mali Empire

In 1355, the Muslim lawyer Ibn Battuta, having returned to his Moroccan homeland after twenty-nine years of traveling through much of Afroeurasia, completed preparation of the Rihla, *or "Book of Travels," a lengthy account of his adventures. In collaboration with a young literary scholar proficient in the niceties of Arabic prose, Ibn Battuta composed the* Rihla *in the capital city of Fez at the command of Morocco's ruler. The book circulated in manuscript copies in the western Muslim world, and in the mid-nineteenth century two European scholars translated all of it into French, the first of many translations into Western and Asian languages. The* Rihla *has come down to us as a precious historical document because Ibn Battuta was an eyewitness to events and ways of life in dozens of societies in the second quarter of the fourteenth century, the twilight of the Mongol era.*

When Ibn Battuta set to work on the Rihla, *he had only just returned from the last of his heroic journeys, a trip by camel caravan across the fearsome Sahara to Mali in West Africa (see Map 13.2). Numerous Arab, Mongol, and Turkic potentates had welcomed and rewarded him during his travels, and he makes clear in the* Rihla *that he was seriously annoyed by Mansa Sulayman, the king of Mali, for failing to treat him as a scholar of high distinction. This tepid reception may have influenced his report on Mali, because he gives Mansa Sulayman and his empire a decidedly mixed review. Ibn Battuta's own upbringing in the cosmopolitan city of Tangier as a pious Arab gentleman colors his descriptions of all the Muslim kingdoms he visited in his travels. In the case of Mali, his morally conservative ideas about religious devotion and righteous conduct come through loud and clear.*

In this selection Ibn Battuta sums up what he thinks are the good and not-so-good qualities of the kingdom and its people:

Amongst their good qualities is the small amount of injustice amongst them, for of all people they are the furthest from it. Their sultan does not forgive anyone in any matter to do with injustice. Among these qualities there is also the prevalence of peace in their country, the traveler is not afraid in it nor is he who lives there in fear of the thief or of the robber by violence. They do not interfere with the property of the white man [resident of Saharan or North African background] who dies in their country even though it may consist of great wealth, but rather they entrust it to the hand of someone dependable among the white men until it is taken by the rightful claimant.

Another of the good habits amongst them is the way they meticulously observe the times of the prayers and attendance at them, so also it is with regard to their congregational services and their beating of their children to instill these things in them.

When it is Friday, if a man does not come early to the mosque he will not find a place to pray because of the numbers of the crowd. . . .

Amongst their good qualities is the putting on of good white clothes on Friday. If a man among them has nothing except a tattered shirt, he washes and cleans it and attends the Friday prayer in it. Another of their good qualities is their concern for learning the sublime Quran by heart. They make fetters for their children when they appear on their part to be falling short in their learning of it by heart, and they are not taken off from them till they do learn by heart. . . . One day I passed by a handsome youth from them dressed in fine clothes and on his feet was a heavy chain. I said to the man who was with me, "What has this youth done—has he killed someone?" The youth heard my remark and laughed. It was told me, "He has been chained so that he will learn the Quran by heart."

Among the bad things which they do—their serving women, slave women and little daughters appear before people naked, exposing their private parts. I used to see many of them in this state in Ramadan. . . . Also among their bad customs is the way women will go into the presence of the sultan naked, without any covering; and the nakedness of the sultan's daughters—on the night of the twenty-seventh of Ramadan, I saw about a hundred slave girls coming out of his palace with food, with them were two of his daughters, they had full breasts and no clothes on. Another of their bad customs is their putting dust and ashes on their heads as a sign of respect. And another is the laughing matter I mentioned of their poetic recitals. And another is that many of them eat animals not ritually slaughtered, and dogs and donkeys.

Source: Said Hamdun and Noël King, *Ibn Battuta in Black Africa* (Princeton, NJ: Markus Wiener Publishers, 2005), 58–59.

Thinking Critically

What aspects of Mali's government and society does Ibn Battuta commend? Why do you think he points out these particular conditions and customs for favorable comment? Why do you think he is particularly critical of customs of female dress in Mali's royal court? Do you think he is unjustifiably intolerant, or does he have good reasons for his criticisms? What kind of person, in terms of background and status, do you think Ibn Battuta imagined would read the *Rihla*?

however, was only one of several in West Africa. In the savanna belt east of the Niger River a cluster of city-states arose in the region generally corresponding to the northern half of modern Nigeria. The people of those towns, who spoke a language ancestral to Hausa (the native language of nearly forty-five million people today), prospered from cotton textile manufacture and trans-Saharan exchange of copper, kola nuts, slaves, and numerous products from the rainforests to the south. Further east in the vicinity of Lake Chad, the Kanem empire paralleled Mali as a large tribute-collecting state. Indeed, its ruling dynasty endured much longer than Mali's did, lasting from the eleventh to the nineteenth century.

In West Africa's wooded savannas and rainforests, numerous kingdoms and city-states began to appear from about 800 C.E. By the thirteenth century, small states whose chiefs had mainly ritual functions gave way in some regions to more powerful rulers whose authority rested on the number of troops and retainers they could muster and on the tribute they could collect. Igala, Nupe, and Benin were all states of this type that emerged in the thirteenth or fourteenth centuries in the wooded savannas or rainforests of what is today Nigeria. All of them exchanged kola nuts and other forest products for the grain, horses, and textiles that arrived from the north. The archaeological record shows that Benin, together with several city-states that emerged among the Yoruba-speaking peoples of the forest belt, developed in this period a sophisticated tradition of naturalistic brass sculpture. This work is evidence of long-distance trade links, because the copper used in brass manufacture had to be shipped in from mines located in the south central Sahara.

A Yoruba ruler. A naturalistic brass head of the monarch of a Yoruba state in what is today south central Nigeria. The sculpture dates to between the twelfth and fifteenth centuries.

• • •

Conclusion

In the era of the Mongol empires, nearly every part of Afroeurasia established contact, whether direct or indirect, with every other part, either overland or by sea. People in one region who had money to spend sought the goods of other regions, which might be thousands of miles away. More people traveled longer distances to seek knowledge or share their religion than at any earlier time. And Mongol cavalry operated in a far larger hemispheric arena than an ancient Roman legion could have imagined. Only a small part of the inhabited supercontinent—the frozen Arctic, some deep interior forests or mountain valleys, the arid lands of far southwestern Africa—remained disconnected from the hemispheric communication web.

The existence of elaborate trade networks, however, does not mean that Afroeurasian peoples were moving toward cultural unification. The number of languages spoken ran to the tens of thousands, and interchange among societies could breed suspicion, rivalry, and violence as well as toleration and understanding. On the other hand, cultural homogenizing processes were at work, at least on the regional level. Some languages and cultural styles gained numerous converts while others shrank. In this era, for example, additional millions converted to Buddhism, Christianity, and Islam and in the process learned new languages and accepted new, more uniform life ways. Languages that spread impressively in the Mongol era, along with cultural forms that invariably accompany language, included Chinese, Persian, Arabic, Oghuz Turkish, Swahili, Malinke, German, French, and English. Ironically, Mongolian never caught on much outside its homeland.

Because ship captains of the thirteenth and fourteenth centuries were masters of Afroeurasia's chain of seas, we may imagine that probes into Atlantic waters and Christopher Columbus's landfall on a Caribbean island were events waiting to happen. But even though 1492 was fast approaching, peoples of North and South America continued to explore entirely separate paths of empire building, trade, and cultural creativity. In Chapter 14 we return to the Western Hemisphere to explore developments between 900 and 1500 C.E.

• • •

Key Terms

Angkor Wat 384	guild 388	Mongol Peace (*Pax Mongolica*) 369
Benin 395	Ilkhanate 374	Mongols 371
charter 388	Kanem empire 395	scholastic theology 391
Chola dynasty 385	khanate 371	Swahili coast 385
Golden Horde 374	Khmer kingdom 384	vernacular language 388
Gothic architecture 389	Mali empire 392	Xi Xia 372
Great Zimbabwe 386	Mamluk kingdom 378	Yuan dynasty 374

Change over Time

850–1279	The Chola dynasty rules in southern India; commercial exchange and temple construction intensifies.
889–1434	The Khmer kingdom rules in Southeast Asia and sponsors construction of the Angkor Wat temple complex.
1167?–1227	Chingis Khan conquers far and wide, founding the Mongol empire.
Mid-13th–late 15th centuries	The Mali empire dominates much of West Africa.
1241–1502	The Mongol khanate of Kipchak (the Golden Horde) rules in Inner Eurasia and Russia.
1258–1335	The Mongol Ilkhanate of Iran and Iraq rules in Southwest Asia.
1260	The Mamluk sultanate of Egypt and Syria (1250–1517) repels Mongol forces.
1271–1295	Marco Polo travels from Venice to China and back.
1271–1368	The Mongol Yuan empire, founded by Kubilai Khan (r. 1271–1294), unites northern and southern China.
1272–1307	England becomes a strong regional European state under Edward I.
1274 and 1281	Japan under the Kamakura dynasty (1185–1333) repels two Mongol invasions.
1285–1314	France becomes a strong regional European state under Philip IV the Fair.
1287–1288	The Mongol envoy Rabban Sauma travels in Southwest Asia and Europe.
1291	The last of the European crusader states in Syria falls to the Mamluks of Egypt.
1324–1325	Mansa Musa, emperor of Mali, undertakes pilgrimage to Mecca.
1325–1354	Ibn Battuta travels throughout Afroeurasia.

Please see end of book reference section for additional reading suggestions related to this chapter.

14 Cities and Empires in the Americas

900–1500

In 1978, power company employees working on the Mexico City subway system made a startling discovery. As they were digging a trench for an electrical cable, they unearthed a giant stone disk showing the dismembered body of a woman. Historians identified the woman as Coyolxauhqui, an Aztec goddess who, according to legend, had conspired with her brothers and sisters to murder Huitzilopochtli, their youngest sibling, out of jealousy. When Huitzilopochtli discovered the plot, he took hold of a scepter and stabbed his sister in the heart, then cut off her head. Coyolxauhqui's body fell to the ground and broke into pieces. Huitzilopochtli promptly defeated the rest of his enemies and established himself as the preeminent god.

Recognizing the disk as an Aztec ceremonial object that might signal a major find, archaeologists extended the trench. They found a series of steps—the lower portions of a much larger staircase ascending the steep side of a pyramid. The structure appeared to have been built in five stages during the fifteenth and early sixteenth centuries. Artifacts

The dismembered body of the goddess on the Coyolxauhqui stone disk.

filled the niches under floors and between walls: masks, stone sculptures, and ceramic containers from central and northern Mexico; coral, seashells, and even alligator bones from the coast. Archaeologists theorized that subject peoples of the Aztecs presented many of these items as tribute.

These discoveries confirmed researchers' hunches that the ruins were the foundations of the Great Temple of Tenochtitlán (teh-noach-teet-LAWN), which Spanish conquistadors had destroyed in the sixteenth century. For more than a century before the arrival of Europeans, this sanctuary had been the spiritual and political heart of the largest empire in Mesoamerica. Modeled partially on the older pyramids of Teotihuacán (see Chapter 8), the Great Temple reflected the Aztecs' view of themselves as heirs of earlier Mesoamerican civilizations, divinely destined to surpass their predecessors in wealth and power. Every year, priests sacrificed thousands of human victims to Huitzilopochtli, their patron, who was said to have dismembered his treacherous sister on this very site.

At about the same time that the Aztecs were building their empire in Mesoamerica, the Incas established control over much of the Andes. While both the Inca and Aztec states surpassed earlier civilizations in size, population, and military prowess, they relied heavily on cultural foundations their predecessors had laid. The Aztecs were influenced by the earlier Mesoamerican societies of Toltec, Maya, and Teotihuacán. The Incas extended and improved on the road networks, irrigation technologies, record systems, and fine crafts developed by earlier states and temple centers in the Andean highlands and along the Pacific coast. Meanwhile, complex agrarian societies also emerged in other parts of North and South America and in the Caribbean basin. Although some of these societies built mounds, ball courts, stone temples, and palaces, they left behind more fragmented archaeological records and virtually no oral traditions, making it difficult for us to reconstruct their histories.

This chapter explores the development of large urban centers and imperial states in the Americas over a six-hundred-year period, emphasizing the influence of changing environmental conditions (see Map 14.1). The first part of the chapter surveys a variety of complex societies, moving roughly from north to south along the Western Hemisphere's long axis. Starting in the North American woodlands, we describe the continuing development of the Mississippian mound-building tradition (see Chapter 8), brought to a cultural summit in the urban complex of Cahokia (kuh-HOH-kee-uh). We then shift to the Colorado Plateau region of the southwestern United States. There, Ancestral Puebloans (Anasazi) carried on the irrigated farming technologies of earlier peoples, building remarkable multistory settlements

• • •

in semiarid canyons. Farther south in central Mexico, Toltec migrants rebuilt the city of Tula and presided over a far-reaching trade network extending to the Yucatán Peninsula and Central America. We also investigate the migration of Nahuatl-speaking peoples, ancestors of the Aztecs, into the central Mexican highlands. Finally, we turn to South America, where the Tiwanaku, Wari, and Chimu states came to dominate the central Andes and the arid Pacific coast.

Conflict for control of water, land, and labor led to the emergence of new imperial powers in the early fifteenth century. In the second part of the chapter, we explore the rise of the Aztec and Inca empires. When Spanish soldiers and missionaries arrived after 1500, they encountered complex political societies at the height of their power. The Spanish tore down many of the buildings in the Aztec and Inca capitals, destroying what would have been part of the archaeological record. They also wrote about the people they encountered, however, handing down to us striking if incomplete descriptions of American societies at the moment of European invasions. Perhaps the most enduring legacy of the Aztecs and the Incas is the oral histories they passed from one generation to the next. In the sixteenth and seventeenth centuries, Spanish Catholic missionaries transcribed these stories and taught Native American boys to write their native languages in Latin script. These sources, along with modern archaeological studies, inform our narrative.

A Panoramic View

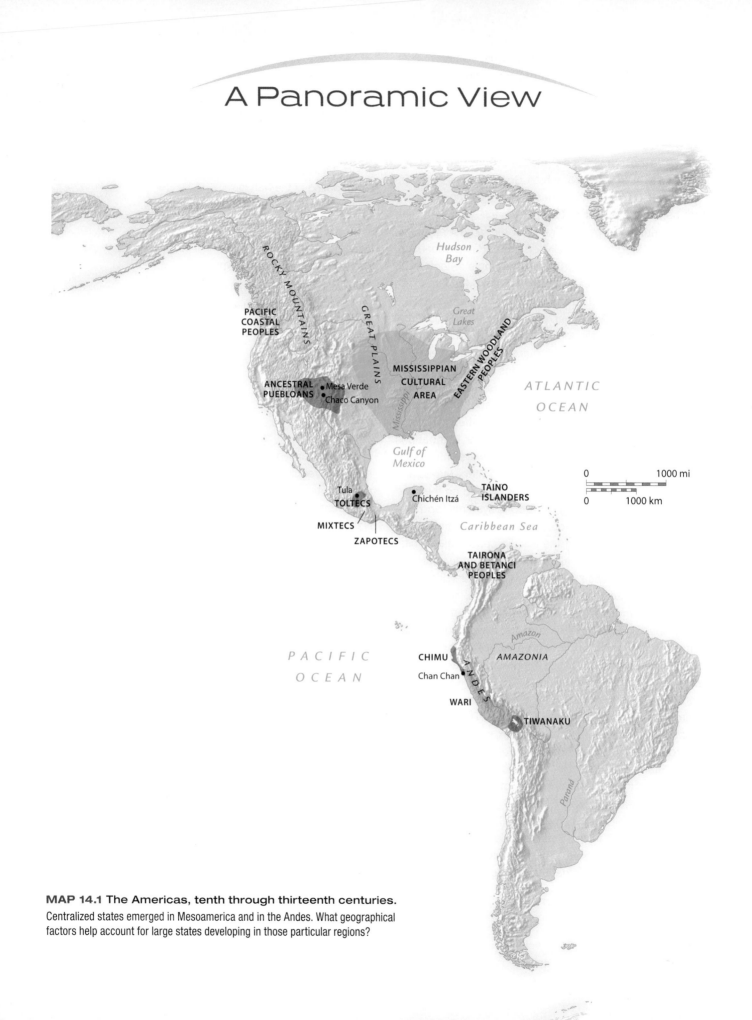

MAP 14.1 The Americas, tenth through thirteenth centuries.
Centralized states emerged in Mesoamerica and in the Andes. What geographical factors help account for large states developing in those particular regions?

American Societies in an Age of Environmental Change

FOCUS In what ways did large-scale environmental change affect historical developments in the Americas between the tenth and fifteenth centuries?

Several interconnected environmental and ecological trends affected peoples of much of the Western Hemisphere between the ninth and thirteenth centuries. The North Atlantic Warm Period, the slight rise in global temperature that occurred during those four hundred years, affected North America as well as the northern regions of Afroeurasia (see Chapter 11). In Andean South America, the climatic wet and dry cycles associated with El Niño Southern Oscillation had a large impact on ecological conditions and therefore on social change. In North America the warming trend appears to have encouraged the spread of farming, especially maize cultivation, to new regions. In western parts of both North and South America, drier conditions limited population growth, encouraging people to move into larger, denser communities with more reliable access to scarce resources. New states emerged in central Mexico and the Andes, only to fall victim to ecological changes similar to those that weakened the Teotihuacán and Moche civilizations of earlier centuries (see Chapter 8).

The uptick in global temperature boosted agricultural production, notably in humid forested areas along rivers, a type of ecological zone common in what is now the United States from the Mississippi River valley to the Atlantic. Peoples of the Eastern Woodlands farmed more productively, extended their fields, and introduced new varieties of beans, squash, and other foodstuffs. Maize production became widespread by 1000 C.E., owing in large part to the introduction of eastern flint corn, a variety of Mesoamerican origin that grew well in relatively cool and moist climatic conditions. Having a higher caloric value than other local staples, maize supported larger numbers of people, especially in the Mississippi and numerous other river valleys. As population grew, more complex social and political systems evolved. Individual leaders and chiefly families accumulated more power to regulate water consumption and protect the food supply.

Between the ninth and thirteenth centuries, the plateaus and desert valleys of what is now the southwestern United States experienced unpredictable cycles of rainfall and drought. In response to those uncertainties, local societies invented ingenious ways to irrigate land, diversify crops, and plant maize in several different places to cut risk, maximize yield, and conserve water. Despite these efforts, delicate **ecosystems**

ecosystem A biological system in which living organisms—plants, animals, microorganisms, humans—interact with one another and with nonliving elements such as air, sunlight, soil, and water.

could support only so many hungry humans. Sudden dry spells could wipe out all the farms in an area in a matter of months. Two major droughts, the first in the middle of the twelfth century and the second in the last quarter of the thirteenth, forced thousands of people to abandon communities in the Sonoran Desert (which overlaps Arizona, California, and northwestern Mexico). Some displaced groups migrated south to the comparatively temperate valleys of central Mexico. Among them were forerunners of the Toltecs and Aztecs.

Like western North America, the Andean highlands experienced fluctuations between wet and dry periods that could determine the fate of human settlements. In addition, the narrow, arid plains separating the mountains from the Pacific shore were subject to occasional yet unpredictable weather events related to El Niño cycles. Torrential rains could destroy crucial irrigation systems, inundate farmland, and disrupt fisheries. Nevertheless, between 900 and 1300, several cities in the region reached population levels in the tens of thousands by expanding the amount of farmland under their control, developing techniques to increase soil fertility, and conquering neighbors. The ability of societies to expand in this fashion depended on their skill at anticipating changing weather conditions and adapting to both deluges and water shortages.

The Mound Builders of Cahokia

Some of the most densely populated areas of North America lay in the valleys of the Mississippi, Missouri, Tennessee, Ohio, and other eastern and midwestern valleys. These rivers and their tributaries were natural conduits of trade. Dense forests provided timber for construction and firewood, as well as wild game for food, fur, hides, and bone. This environment had nurtured farming societies and large settlements since the second millennium B.C.E. (see Chapters 4 and 8).

The confluence of the Mississippi and Missouri Rivers created an eighty-mile floodplain ideal for maize and bean cultivation. Here, sometime between 800 and 1000 C.E., Mississippian peoples established the settlement of Cahokia. Its remains in Illinois eight miles east of St. Louis are listed as a UNESCO World Heritage Site. At its zenith between about 1050 and 1200, Cahokia had perhaps ten to twenty thousand inhabitants. It was probably the largest urban center north of Mexico before the arrival of Europeans. The city was a natural hub of commerce, situated at the meeting point of arteries that connected the Gulf of Mexico to the Great Lakes and the central plains to the Eastern Woodlands. Cahokian pottery and stone tools have been found in Minnesota, Kansas, Arkansas, and Mississippi, along with locally produced imitations of Cahokian wares. The city exported salt and chert (a kind of rock used to make arrowheads and blades) in exchange for copper from Lake Superior, mica from Appalachia, and seashells from the Gulf and Atlantic seaboards.

The most prominent vestiges of Cahokia are earthen mounds, the continuation of a Mississippian tradition going back to the fourth millennium B.C.E. At its height, Cahokia may have had over 120 of these structures, but owing to centuries of erosion and urban development, fewer than 80 are visible. Most of the mounds had flat summits where workers erected wooden structures that functioned as temples, administrative buildings, and residences for elite families. The largest surviving earthwork, called Monks Mound, is located near the center of the archaeological site and has a base width of fourteen acres. It has four ascending terraces, and the modern remains rise to a height of one hundred feet. Built in stages between 900 and 1200, this mound is the largest known earthen structure in North America built before European contact (see Map 14.2). It was probably the residence of Cahokia's ruling family, as well as a ceremonial and administrative center.

A Mississippian town. The earthwork known as Monks Mound dominates Cahokia as it looked about 1150 (artist's reconstruction below). The Mississippi River is visible at upper left. Monks Mound looks very different today (photograph at right) but still impresses visitors. When the American congressman Henry M. Brackenridge saw the mound in the early 1800s, he declared: "It is certainly a most stupendous pile of earth, and were it not for the strongest proof, no one would believe it the works of hands."

Mound 72, half a mile away, is aligned with the sunrise on the winter solstice and the sunset on the summer solstice. This earthwork was an important burial site, enclosing the remains of 272 individuals dating between 1000 and 1050. Some corpses were buried on litters (platforms) or wrapped in blankets, while others were merely tossed into pits, a difference in treatment that suggests social class divisions. One tomb holds the corpse of a forty-year-old man who rests on a platform made of twenty thousand seashell beads. He may have been an early Cahokian ruler. Several other bodies were buried around him. Nearby, archaeologists have uncovered several mass graves containing more than one hundred females buried in rows along with more than thirty-six thousand shell beads, arrowheads, and broken ceramic containers. Another gravesite contains four men with severed heads and hands. These burials suggest that the Cahokians practiced human sacrifice, as societies did in Mesoamerica. Servants or relatives may have been killed, presumably to accompany their deceased leader into the afterlife.

Around 1150 C.E., the rulers enclosed the city center in a log stockade. From platforms erected against the interior wall, warriors could shoot arrows at attackers and defend gates. The stockade suggests that war menaced Cahokia during the twelfth and thirteenth centuries. Neighboring communities may have challenged its regional hegemony.

Warfare and environmental degradation probably led to the depopulation of Cahokia and its eventual abandonment by about 1400. A city of its size required constant supplies of timber from nearby woodlands. Logging meant

deforestation, which may have ruined the natural habitat of certain plants and animals, depleting part of the local food supply. Deforestation may also have contributed to erosion of farmland and silt buildup in local streams, which increased the risk of flooding. The end of the North Atlantic Warm Period in the 1200s probably caused earlier seasonal frosts and smaller crop yields, especially of maize. Population declined along with the grain supply, while internal feuding over scarce resources may have intensified. Sometime during the thirteenth century, a major earthquake shook the region, liquefying the soft earth near riverbanks and rendering it useless for farming. Gradually, people left Cahokia and migrated to other areas, establishing new, though smaller settlements or assimilating into other Native American groups.

Ancestral Puebloans on the Colorado Plateau

Like the Cahokians, the Pueblo people built spectacular structures between the tenth and twelfth centuries. Most

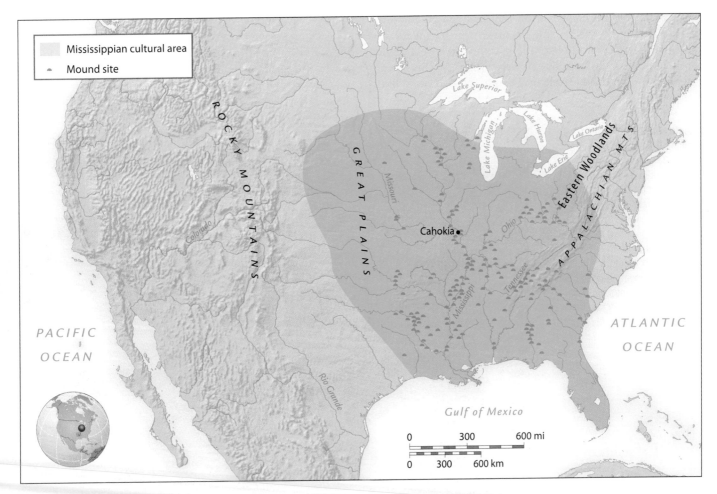

MAP 14.2 Major mounds and earthworks in North America to the fifteenth century.
The region of Mississippian cultural influence encompassed a large part of what is now the United States. What geographical factors might have facilitated trade among communities within the Mississippian area?

of the settlements of this Native American people lay on the Colorado Plateau, a semiarid region that overlaps Utah, Colorado, Arizona, and New Mexico. Initially, Ancestral Puebloans lived in small villages consisting of pit houses similar to those built by the earlier Hohokam people (see Chapter 8). Over time, some of these communities evolved into towns, or **pueblos,** each with five or six stone buildings and a kiva, a large, round, covered pit that served as a meeting place and ceremonial center. Around 900, many communities adopted maize agriculture, and the population began to grow. As pueblos expanded, residents added stories to their structures to accommodate more families.

pueblo A Spanish word meaning "village" or "small town." Spanish colonizers used this term to describe multistory stone or brick compounds that the Ancestral Puebloans (Anasazi) built in the American Southwest.

Chaco Canyon in New Mexico sheltered the densest settlements. The first villages probably appeared around the year 500, as farmers took advantage of increased rainfall to plant corn in the southern part of the canyon. Over several centuries, some of these villages evolved in size and complexity. The largest, Pueblo Bonito, set a general pattern. It began as a small cluster of pit houses and some above-ground storage rooms. During the ninth century the inhabitants constructed stone and adobe rooms in a semicircle. Around 1000, two large kivas were built. At this point, Pueblo Bonito reached five stories high and had more than six hundred rooms, which accommodated between five hundred and one thousand residents.

Inhabitants of Pueblo Bonito belonged to two main groups: the "winter people," who specialized in hunting and gathering, and the "summer people," who farmed. This division of labor shows that the Puebloans could not rely exclusively on agriculture for sustenance in an area prone to droughts and floods. The winter and the summer groups were organized in smaller kinship-based households, each of which had a series of rooms within the pueblo, bound together by a common outer wall. Each kin group had its own small kiva, workshops, storerooms, and communal spaces.

Both trade and migration connected Chaco Canyon to a wide surrounding region. During the late tenth and early eleventh centuries, the population grew faster than the valley's ecosystem could sustain. Probably as a consequence of that, some Ancestral Puebloan kin groups migrated to distant areas on or beyond the Colorado Plateau to found new villages and small pueblos. At the same time, Chaco Canyon became a major center of regional commerce, especially in precious stones and jewelry. Outsiders brought turquoise to the pueblos, where local artisans made ornaments for re-export. Archaeologists have found more than sixty thousand such artifacts.

An impressive yet enigmatic system of roads, still visible today, radiated out from Chaco Canyon like spokes of a wheel (see Map 14.3). Some of these roads are forty feet wide inside the canyon and ten feet wide beyond it. Notably,

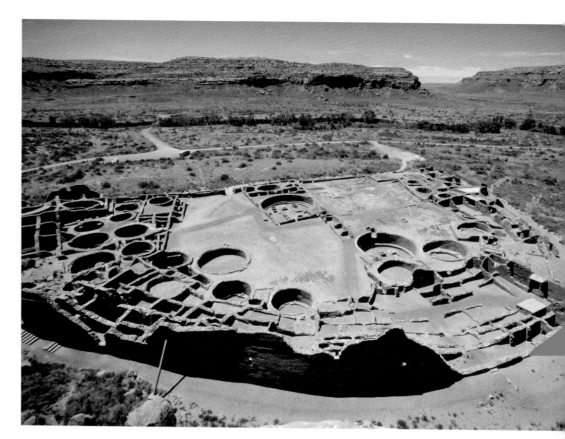

Pueblo Bonito. The largest settlement in Chaco Canyon, Pueblo Bonito's buildings rose as many as five stories high. The circular pits are the ruins of kivas, or places of ritual activity. Construction of the town began in 851 and continued for more than two hundred fifty years. The more than six hundred rooms could have accommodated many more than one thousand people. Why do you think the resident population was probably less than it could have been?

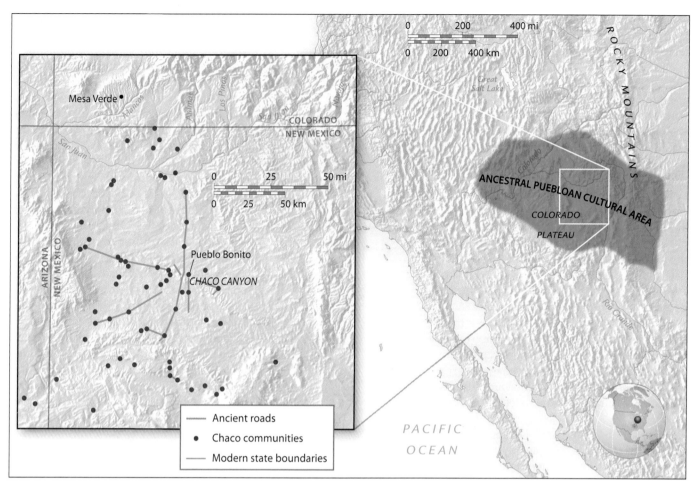

MAP 14.3 The roads from Chaco Canyon.
Ground surveys have marked out some of Chaco Canyon's highways, but other roads are visible only from the air. Referring to the scale on the inset map, estimate the approximate distance from the northernmost to the southernmost Chaco community.

they run straight even over hills and rugged terrain, rather like ancient Roman roads. Scholars have long debated the significance of these highways. One theory suggests that at special times of the year, such as the summer and winter solstices, thousands of pilgrims walked to Chaco Canyon on the roads to participate in ceremonies and to exchange goods. Another theory suggests that the roads were purely symbolic. They may have formed a representation of Puebloan cosmology, wherein Chaco Canyon was the "navel" of the world. A major causeway that heads due north was like an "umbilical cord," connecting the center to a supernatural world beyond civilization. The spirits of the dead traveled along this path to their final resting place in the middle of an uninhabited canyon.

The pueblos of Chaco Canyon declined precipitously after the middle of the twelfth century, not long before Cahokia did. Drought was almost certainly the main reason. A fifty-year dry period between 1130 and 1180 destroyed much of the canyon's farmland and wiped out the previous two centuries of urban development. As the water supply dwindled, inhabitants who survived famine and malnutrition left

to search for fertile land. Refugees migrated from the canyon in different directions, taking with them their techniques of building dams, terraces, and reservoirs. New pueblos sprang up, some of them, notably Mesa Verde in southwestern Colorado, reaching sizes that rivaled the Chaco Canyon settlements. These communities prospered during the thirteenth century but in the end met the same fate as their ancestral home. Another major drought between 1275 and 1299 destroyed the agricultural base of this area, forcing many Puebloan communities once again to disperse.

Maya, Mixtec, and Toltec

The roughly contemporaneous collapse of the Teotihuacán, Zapotec, and Maya states (see Chapter 8) created a power vacuum across much of Mesoamerica. In the Yucatán Peninsula the largest centers of Maya population shifted from the southern highlands to the low-lying north, where freshwater aquifers sustained hundreds of villages and a few large cities. After the collapse of the southern city-states, overland trade routes declined, while seaborne canoe commerce along the rim of the Gulf of Mexico prospered. During the tenth century a Maya group called the Itzá moved into the northern peninsula, where they endeavored to dominate both the canoe trade and coastal production of salt, a valuable export commodity. They established a capital at the lowland Maya city of Chichén Itzá and gradually subordinated nearby communities.

West of Yucatán in the highland valley of Oaxaca, the large Zapotec monarchies that flourished before 700 broke into smaller states (see Chapter 8), which built new fortified centers and warred with one another. After about 800, bands of warriors who spoke the Mixtec language began to invade ancestral Zapotec lands, causing more instability. A ruler named Eight Deer Jaguar Claw (1063–1115) created something close to a Mixtec empire, bringing a number of towns under his control by a combination of military conquest, intermarriage with local noble families, and tribute collection. This state endured until the sixteenth century.

The Toltec ascendancy. During the ninth and tenth centuries, people fleeing drought-ravaged deserts of northern Mexico and the American Southwest traveled long distances to the greener highland regions of central Mexico. The Toltecs were one of the groups that migrated during the ninth century. They settled in Tula, a center in the Valley of Mexico where Mexico City now sprawls. Tula had been a dependency of the great city of Teotihuacán up to the sixth or seventh century. It revived again under Toltec rule, expanding by 1100 C.E. to embrace an area of ten square miles and a population of around thirty-five thousand, plus as many as ninety thousand living in suburban communities.[1] Like Teotihuacán in its time, Tula had two large pyramidal temples surrounded by palaces, priests' residences, and government buildings. The city also had at least five ball courts. We do not understand much about the games played there, but they also certainly had ritual functions, just as these arenas did in other ancient Mesoamerican societies. Toltec monumental building, however, never reached Teotihuacán's grandeur, and the artisanry was noticeably poorer.

Tula never became a large imperial state, but its commercial influence ranged far to the north and south. Local traditions tell us that many different languages could be heard in the city, suggesting that travelers came from all over Mesoamerica to buy and sell. Archaeologists have uncovered ceramics originating in modern Costa Rica, 1,200 miles to the southeast. The Tula region had rich deposits of black and

A Toltec warrior. A stone figure from the city of Tula. What material do you think was used to make Toltec body armor, represented here in stone?

green obsidian, the volcanic glass used to make sharp blades and other wares. Toltec artisans made religious ornaments and jewelry from gold, silver, and copper, selling them for export to other parts of Mesoamerica. Demand for precious minerals like jade and turquoise led Toltec miners into the Sierra Madre Mountains to the north. Merchants ventured as far north as the Sonoran Desert to acquire rare stones, slaves, and salt, founding small villages and trading posts along the way. Evidence of Toltec influence in architectural styles and other elements of culture have been identified as far north as Chaco Canyon. After about 900, the Toltecs developed regular trade relations with the Maya state of Chichén Itzá, which was more than eight hundred overland miles east of Tula. Toltec merchants carried obsidian, among other products, and returned home with loads of salt from the Yucatán coast. The relationship between the two cities became so close that temple architecture and relief carvings at Chichén Itzá show profound Toltec influence, for example, reliefs of eagles and jaguars eating human hearts—common themes in Toltec mythology. Historians used to interpret these artistic similarities as evidence that Toltec warriors invaded Chichén Itzá and even made it a colonial dependency. But intensive and prolonged commercial and cultural exchange may have produced the same results.

The end of Toltec power. Droughts in northern Mexico in the twelfth century set off more southward migratory movements into the central highlands, including Tula-controlled areas. Some of these wanderers were Toltecs who abandoned mining and trading colonies. Others were mobile bands, both hunter-foragers and farmers. Tula suffered both water shortages and an influx of desperate and sometimes hostile intruders. Archaeologists have found evidence that invaders sacked the city, looting and defacing temples, burning palaces, and massacring both adults and children. The Toltecs abandoned their capital in the mid-twelfth century and never established another city to call their own.

Chichén Itzá may have suffered a similar fate just a few decades later. The demise of Tula deprived northern Yucatán of valuable trade items, including obsidian weapons. The city lost its regional military supremacy, and, according to traditional Maya histories, a lord from a neighboring city pillaged it. Both the Toltecs and the Itzá deserted the city by the late twelfth century, though several Maya towns regrouped to form a northern confederation that lasted for several generations. This alliance disintegrated in the mid-fifteenth century, and when the Spanish conqueror Hernán Cortés arrived on the Yucatán coast in 1518, he found the peninsula politically splintered.

The Coming of the Nahuas

The collapse of Toltec defenses in the Valley of Mexico encouraged more people from the arid north to infiltrate the region. Many of these newcomers spoke Nahuatl (NAH-watt), a language in the Uto-Aztecan language family that also includes Hopi, Shoshoni, Comanche, and other languages spoken in the central and southwestern United States. These linguistic relationships suggest that Nahuatl speakers, or Nahuas, originated in the Sonoran Desert or a neighboring region and perhaps migrated south in response to the same drought cycle that compelled the Anasazi to disperse from Chaco Canyon.

In the two centuries following the Toltec fall, dozens of city-states inhabited by Nahua and other incoming groups shared the Valley of Mexico and surrounding areas. Each city-state had a defined territory, a patron deity, and a ruler, who served as military commander and high priest to the community's god. In the typical city, a temple, a palace, and other stone buildings were clustered around a central plaza that also functioned as a marketplace. Cities were divided further into wards, neighborhoods, and households of multiple families. Within the households, men and women performed distinct tasks. Men spent most of the day farming or making crafts. When intercity wars broke out, they had to fight. Young boys typically went to school to learn combat. Women, by contrast, spent most of their time at home, raising children, preparing food, and weaving cloth.

A rigid social hierarchy characterized Nahua communities. Commoners did most of the farming, household labor, artisanry, and fighting. Free commoners produced food for their own households and gave the surplus to the leader of their ward. In turn, the wards and the noble families gave tribute to the ruler of the city. Many nobles owned slaves, and during times of drought and resulting famine, people often sold themselves into slavery in order to survive. Debtors and criminals could also be enslaved. The majority of slaves, though, were war captives, who faced either lifelong labor or death as sacrificial victims.

Fertile volcanic soils in the Valley of Mexico supported abundant agriculture. Lakes teemed with fish and waterfowl and supplied salt; rivers brought water from the surrounding mountains. Nahua farmers built and cultivated terraces in the foothills and laid out networks of canals to irrigate fields of maize, beans, and numerous other crops. Perhaps as a result of recurring droughts, farmers adopted a technique, perhaps borrowed from the Maya, of constructing *chinampas* (chee-NAHM-pahs), or "floating gardens" to extend areas of well-water cropland. Farmers built

Two pyramid temples. The architectural influence of Toltec artisans on distant Chichén Itzá is evident in this comparative view of Pyramid B at Tula (top) and the Temple of the Warriors at Chichén Itzá. The stelas at the summit of Pyramid B and the columns at the base of the Temple of Warriors both portray soldiers. What differences between the two structures do you notice?

up rectangular layers of water plants and soil dredged from shallow or marshy areas along the edges of lakes. In this way they created arable plots. Repeating the process over and over, farmers eventually reclaimed thousands of acres of wetland. Families set up residences on their *chinampas* and canoed from one to another along networks of canals.

Daily commerce took place in both local and central markets. Ward leaders oversaw local markets where farmers exchanged goods and where women did much of the trading.

Modern *chinampas*. A farmer tends a *chinampa* garden next to a canal in the Valley of Mexico. Why do you think this farming technique has survived to the present in some parts of Mexico?

The city-state ruler regulated the central market, where more valuable exchanges took place. Merchants from surrounding regions hauled in products like cotton, obsidian, feathers, gemstones, and jewelry. Merchants called *pochteca* managed long-distance trade. Forming guild-like organizations within their city, they could become politically powerful, accumulating great wealth and currying favor with the ruler. Some *pochteca* also worked clandestinely as spies, collecting information on rival cities during their travels and using their business contacts as informants.

Trade and agriculture made central Mexico one of the most densely populated regions in the world. By the late fifteenth century, the Valley of Mexico had between 1 and 2.5 million inhabitants; the population of the surrounding areas may have exceeded 6 million. Economic success, however, did not necessarily translate into prosperity for all. During the thirteenth century, population in the valley began to surpass food supplies. Periodic droughts worsened shortages. In bad times many people barely survived. Chronic imbalance between population and productivity also provoked intercity wars over farmland and labor. Sometimes military victors enslaved their neighbors and annexed their lands. More often, they forced defeated city-states to pay tribute, turning them into political satellites. In this way confederations of large and victorious city-states increasingly dominated weaker ones, while smaller cities formed their own alliances to try to preserve their independence. These conditions of violent competition set the stage for the rise of the Aztec empire.

The Caribbean and Amazonia

Maize cultivation spread throughout the Caribbean region and into Amazonia, the vast Amazon River basin, during the North Atlantic Warm Period. Complex societies emerged along the sea's southern rim after about 1000. In the lower Magdalena River valley in modern Colombia, Betanci people constructed mounds that reached up twenty-six feet. These artificial hills supported temples or entire villages. Archaeologists have excavated gold artifacts, painted pottery, and seashells at some Betanci sites. East of the Magdalena valley, the Tairona population grew rapidly from the eleventh century. They created probably the largest and most sophisticated civilization in South America outside the Andes. Archaeologists have excavated stone temples and palaces, as well as large shaft tombs with side chambers filled with gold ornaments. The largest Tairona site has over three thousand structures, including stone bridges.

The Taino, an agricultural, hunting, and fishing people, came to dominate several Caribbean islands after about 1000, moving out from Hispaniola (today Haiti and the Dominican Republic) to populate Cuba, Puerto Rico, Jamaica, and the Virgin Islands. Archaeologists have excavated sites that look like ancient ball courts. Since these ruins resemble structures in Mesoamerica, some scholars have proposed that trade links existed between at least some Caribbean peoples and the continental mainland. The most likely carriers of this trade were Maya canoe merchants who traveled the gulf waterways between Mexico and Panama. Aside from the presumed ball courts, however, there is no evidence that Maya ever journeyed to any Caribbean islands, and the ball courts may have been local inventions.

The population of the Caribbean region probably reached its peak during the thirteenth century, two hundred years before Europeans arrived. After that point, the quality of ceramics and other artifacts diminished noticeably, people built few new stone structures, and settlements shrank. When Christopher Columbus encountered Taino Indians on Hispaniola, he learned that a predatory people from neighboring islands, known as Caribes, had repeatedly raided Taino settlements and forced residents to flee. Little is known about these warrior bands, though by the fifteenth century they were launching attacks on settlements in Puerto Rico and along mainland coasts.

A Tairona pendant. A Tairona artisan living near the Caribbean coast of Colombia displayed extraordinary skill in creating this gold and copper alloy figure. What features of this object suggest that it represents a noble or chief?

A chair with supernatural properties. The Taino of the Caribbean islands used ritual seats like this one to consult with the spirit world. The seat signifies the presence of an ancestor. A supplicant would crouch on top of the chair while under the influence of a mind-altering snuff. The ancestral spirit would offer answers to questions: Will the harvest be good? Whom should my daughter marry?

In Amazonia, farmers adopted maize, as Caribbean peoples did, to supplement long-established crops like manioc, beans, squash, and potatoes. In the 900–1500 period, Amazonians extended trade links with Andes communities to the west, offering gold, coca, medicinal plants, dyes, and slaves in exchange for raw cotton, textiles, sea salt, and dogs. The Amazonian trade network ultimately connected the Andes with both the Caribbean and the Atlantic coast. Amazonian social organization ranged from small hunting and foraging bands to large farming communities with distinct social hierarchies and hereditary rulers. Spanish and Portuguese explorers reported densely settled towns in the region as late as the seventeenth century.

States of the Andes

Cycles of state building along the Pacific coastal plains and Andean slopes of what are today Ecuador, Peru, Bolivia, and Chile continued without interruption from the fourth millennium B.C.E. to the sixteenth century (see Map 14.1). In Chapter 8 we described the rise and fall of the Chavín de Huántar, Moche, and Nazca societies up to the 600s. The latter two peoples succumbed in conditions of severe drought and flooding associated with El Niño oscillations. In the sixth century, however, two new states began to emerge. One was Tiwanaku (Tihuanaco), a kingdom based in the highlands of modern Bolivia; the second was Wari (Huari), in what is now central Peru. In the eighth century, a group known as the Chimu restored part of the old Moche irrigation network along the Pacific coast and built the splendid capital city of Chan Chan.

Tiwanaku. Farming and herding people had been building central plazas and platforms around the shores of Lake Titicaca in modern Bolivia since about 1000 B.C.E. The lake lies at an elevation of 12,500 feet, so farming depended on crops like potatoes and quinoa that would grow at high altitude. Llama and alpaca herds also provided food, wool, and transport. The Tiwanaku state emerged partly in response to climate change. During the drought conditions of the later sixth century, crop production shrank and Lake Titicaca's water level dropped by a third. Consequently, rural villagers had to gather in larger settlements. Tiwanaku city at the southern end of the lake outpaced all other centers in population growth. The aristocratic elite there acquired great religious prestige and appear to have continually erected new and spectacular temples and other public monuments to attract pilgrims. This elite collected tribute from numerous smaller towns and from distant rural areas, even from peoples on the far side of the Andes crest. We do not know how much of Tiwanaku's imperial expansion depended on military conquest and how much on its talent for inspiring religious fear and wonder.

At its peak in the tenth century, the city may have had about forty thousand residents, while another seventy-five thousand lived in neighboring towns. Two great platforms faced with stone and accessible through massive gateways dominated the Tiwanaku cityscape. The empire's ruling class had residences and administrative offices atop these platforms, but most of the population lived in meager houses. The city appears to have served mainly as a ceremonial and pilgrimage center. There is no evidence at all of marketplaces.

Tiwanaku declined in the tenth century, probably as a result of deteriorating environmental conditions. The water level of Lake Titicaca rose suddenly, inundating farmland. Buildup of salt deposits in irrigated fields may have hindered crop growth. A major drought around 1150 devastated what remained of Tiwanaku civilization. The capital city and its surrounding area were both abandoned, and local populations once under imperial rule reasserted their independence and dispersed into smaller settlements.

Sailing in the Andes. This reed boat with mast and sail was used for transporting people and goods on Lake Titicaca, the largest lake in South America and one of the highest navigable waterways in the world.

A terraced landscape. Farmers who were the subjects of Wari kings carved terraces out of hillsides in southern Peru's magnificent Colca Canyon. In what ways was terracing likely to improve agricultural productivity in the Andes?

The Wari empire. Like Tiwanaku, the Wari state in the central highlands of Peru emerged in response to the extreme weather events of the sixth century. In Wari's case, successive droughts and downpours impelled small-scale farming communities to shift their most intensive agricultural activities from valley floors to high, steep mountain slopes. There, they undertook stupendous labor to construct numerous stepped terraces, laying out irrigation channels to bring water from Andean snowmelt, and planting potatoes, maize, and other crops that would grow in high, cold places. In this way farmers escaped dearth and flood. However, stronger, more centralized government appears to have been needed to organize and manage this complex infrastructure and to prevent local communities from fighting one another over water and terraced land. Consequently, a minority of noble families rose to political dominance, proclaiming a religious ideology centered on the Staff God, an ancient Andean deity, commonly depicted as a figure having clawed feet and fanged teeth and carrying a staff in each hand.

From the city of Wari, a warren of two- or three-story compounds separated from one another by high walls, the ruling elite dispatched military forces both north and south, colonizing populations and collecting revenue. Wari cultural influences, including terracing technology and pottery styles, followed the armies. At its height in the eighth century, this influence extended along the Andean range about 580 miles, a little more than the distance from Washington, D.C., to Atlanta. To ensure a constant food supply in always unpredictable weather conditions, the rulers founded towns throughout the empire as centers of food collection and storage. They built a network of roads to connect these towns with the capital, and they used *quipus*, or knotted, colored strings as a system for keeping records and sending state messages. Finally, they organized labor drafts, requiring men from communities under their control to give service every year on irrigation, building, and other public projects.

Wari declined about the same time as Tiwanaku, and by 1250 the capital and other imperial towns were abandoned. We cannot explain its demise with any certainty. More drought may be too easy an answer, since Wari had succeeded in the first place by inventing ingenious farming methods that protected it against such disaster.

Chimu. Farmers of Peru's starkly arid coastal plains suffered less from dry cycles than from El Niño events that brought rainfall and flooding severe enough to destroy crops, wipe out irrigation works, and change the course of rivers. Earthquakes also shook canals and reservoirs into ruin from time to time. If anything, urban civilization came harder on the Pacific coast than it did in the cold and rarefied air of the high Andes. Even so, coastal peoples had been building cities for thousands of years, sustaining themselves along the rivers that flowed from the mountains. In the eleventh century the kingdom of Chimu emerged along the northern Peruvian shore.

Chan Chan, the Chimu capital, rose up in the Moche River valley amid the ruins and derelict irrigation works of the older Moche civilization (see Chapter 8). By 1200 the city covered nearly eight square miles and had a population of about thirty-five thousand. The territory under Chimu domination extended along nearly seven hundred miles of coastal plain and inland valleys, embracing a population of at least 250,000. A network of roads connected Chan Chan to numerous vassal cities in neighboring valleys.

The Chimu governing class clearly anticipated extreme weather events and planned for them. To ensure adequate food supplies in all conditions, officials inspected individual households and inventoried the foodstuffs owed to the state as tribute. They were thus prepared to distribute stockpiled food in times of want to prevent mass starvation. The state also resurrected at least part of the old Moche water management system, including canals, reservoirs, hillside terraces, and aqueducts running from one river valley to another. Some canals carried no water to crops but served only as flood channels when they were needed. To collect rainwater and runoff from mountain streams, the Chimu built reservoirs and terraces on steep hills, as well as aqueducts to carry water between cities. To keep up the irrigation network, they implemented a labor draft, similar to the system the rulers of Wari had imposed. Having a ready supply of workers enabled the government to respond quickly to crises. For example, around 1100, a major El Niño storm altered the course of the Moche River, rendering the existing canal network useless. Laborers immediately went to work to build a new one.

Chan Chan consisted of ten large precincts fully enclosed by large adobe walls, some thirty feet high. These enclosures served as the residences, administrative offices, and burial sites of rulers and the governing elite that carried out their commands. Here, Chimu monarchs held public audiences and received tribute in the form of food, wool, cotton textiles, and manufactures. Each precinct had storerooms interspersed among the homes of nobles, officials, and artisans.

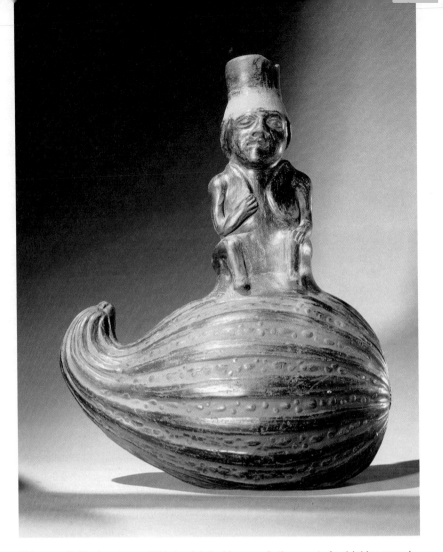

Chimu craft. The headgear of this impish-looking man is the spout of a drinking vessel perhaps used for ritual libations. What do you think the man is sitting on?

The city had several royal compounds, not just one, a phenomenon that had to do with a peculiar feature of Chimu kingship. When a ruler died, a single heir assumed the royal title and the powers associated with it. The rest of the royal family, however, took the property of the deceased monarch, including his palace and storerooms and rights to collect tribute. In fact the dead king, regarded as a divine being, was mummified and placed in a special room adjacent to the palace. Archaeologists have found fine textiles, pottery, jewelry, carved wood, and other luxuries in the chambers of these preserved corpses. Several hundred young men might also be sacrificed to accompany the ruler into the afterlife. The royal mummy continued to live on, as it were, in his own palace, and his family and retainers continued to enjoy his wealth. People visited the mummy, rendered homage to it, and asked for favors. Meanwhile, the new king had to build his own compound, establish his own imperial court, and acquire new sources of tribute because he could not touch the income that belonged to his predecessors. He therefore had no choice except to increase the tax burden on his subjects and acquire new tributaries split inheritance The practice of dividing the estate of a person among different heirs.

by conquest. This tradition of **split inheritance,** along with the need to feed growing river valley populations, helps explain Chimu's militaristic expansion.

The empire continued to grow well into the fifteenth century, but its warriors did not push far into mountain valleys. Confined largely to the dry coastal plain, the state had no control over distant sources of its water. When the rising Inca empire seized the highlands, they immediately threatened Chimu's survival.

American Empires in the Fifteenth Century

FOCUS In what ways were the historical development and political and economic institutions of the Aztec and Inca empires similar or different?

During the fifteenth century the Aztec and Inca empires achieved greater size, cohesion, and military success than any earlier states in the Americas. The armies of both empires exercised control over their multiethnic populations from strategically placed fortresses linked together by road networks that speeded messengers and state officials from one locality to another. Wealth generated from conquest, tribute, and trade supported thriving capitals: Tenochtitlán in the Valley of Mexico and Cuzco (Cusco) in southeastern Peru. As the ancient Romans had done, the ruling classes of both empires credited their success to the favor of the gods.

The Aztecs and Incas also displayed some notable differences. The Aztec rulers allowed subjugated groups to retain self-government as long as they paid tribute, which was collected mainly in material goods rather than labor service. The empire resembled a confederation of city-states with one dominant member, the Aztec army, functioning primarily as a deterrent to disorder and rebellion, not as an occupying force. The Inca state, by contrast, evolved a more centralized, bureaucratic government. Subordinate communities could preserve their cultural identities and some local autonomy, but they answered directly to Inca officials, who represented the authority of the divine king. Also in contrast to the Aztecs, the Inca state extracted tribute primarily in labor, mobilizing thousands of men and women for public works projects.

The Aztec Empire

The founding of the Aztec state was the work of the Mexica, one of the numerous Nahuatl-speaking bands that filtered into central Mexico in the twelfth and thirteenth centuries as the Toltec state declined and fell. Many Nahua groups traced their histories to a common origin, a mythic place called Aztlán that lay somewhere to the north. At some

point, Nahuas left Aztlán and migrated to the Valley of Mexico. In their origin story, the Mexica claimed to be the last of the Aztlán tribes to enter the valley. The origin of the name *Aztec* in Nahuatl is obscure, and the Mexica who built the empire did not call themselves Aztecs.

According to chronicles compiled in later centuries, the Mexica arrived in the valley around 1250 to find other Nahua groups in possession of cities and most of the fertile land. Consequently, they had to disperse into several different towns and offer their labor in exchange for permission to settle. Nevertheless, Mexica men made a reputation for themselves as skilled and ferocious mercenary fighters. Around 1325 they managed to find a home of their own on two rocky islets in Lake Texcoco in the middle of the valley. Adopting the *chinampa*, or floating garden techniques of their Nahua neighbors, they reclaimed land from the lake and made their little islands much bigger. They also built an aqueduct that brought fresh water from the surrounding mountains, as well as a causeway, or land bridge, connecting their islands to the lake shore. After that, the islands soon became important market centers. In the fourteenth century, the Mexica settlements, once on the margins of Nahua society, blossomed into the thriving cities Tlatelolco (tlah-teh-LOLE-coe) and Tenochtitlán on two ends of a single built-up island.

As the populations of these twin cities grew, they faced the same food insecurities that had troubled other Nahua city-states for two centuries. The two towns could not easily expand their resources because they paid tribute to a larger city named Azcapotzalco. Its rulers prevented them from constructing more *chinampas* and aqueducts. Their survival threatened, the Mexica formed an alliance with the nearby cities of Texcoco and Tlacopan and declared war on Azcapotzalco. They achieved victory around 1428 but then went on to more campaigns of imperial expansion. Over the next six generations, the Triple Alliance (the twin cities and their two collaborators) subjugated the entire Valley of Mexico and most of the surrounding valleys, eventually forging an empire of tribute-paying societies that stretched from the Gulf of Mexico to the Pacific (see Map 14.4). By the early sixteenth century the Triple Alliance, or the Aztecs as they came to be known in modern times, dominated somewhere between 3.3 and 6.4 million people.[2]

Tribute and governance. As a tributary empire, the Triple Alliance permitted the city-states subordinated to it to keep their lands and native rulers, but it collected annual tribute in textiles, clothing, tools, jewels, foodstuffs, animal skins, timber, and slaves. Usually, the city, rather than private households or individuals, surrendered these goods. Special tax collectors toured the empire to enforce tribute obligations. In many parts of the empire, these officials were the only representatives of the Triple Alliance that ordinary people ever saw because there was no centrally directed system of provincial administration or judicial courts. As

MAP 14.4 Growth of the Aztec empire.
At its height the Aztec empire stretched from the Pacific to the Gulf of Mexico. What geographic factors may help explain why the Aztec state expanded in the directions it did?

a general rule, the degree of communal self-government increased in proportion to the distance from the Valley of Mexico. Communities on the far frontiers paid no tribute at all but simply allied themselves with the Aztecs, serving as a first line of defense against any group that dared to make war on the empire.

The Aztecs ruled by a combination of diplomacy and war. Before sending an army to conquer a city, they dispatched emissaries to offer gifts and other inducements to surrender. In many cases, the targeted community yielded quickly, perhaps after negotiating with the ambassadors for a lower annual tribute. Only if a foreign ruler refused to comply did the Triple Alliance attack. Even then, the conquerors did not aim to annex territory but fought only until the enemy gave in, then ruled by instilling fear of military retaliation. The Triple Alliance built forts and planted garrisons throughout the empire. These posts watched for local rebellions, guarded borders against invasion, and protected long-distance trade routes. An elaborate communication system connected outlying regions with the central cities. Runners stationed at regular intervals along the major routes carried information pony-express-style between the capitals and army commanders in the field.

The twin cities. The influx of tribute and trade brought prosperity to the cities of the Triple Alliance, especially Tenochtitlán and Tlatelolco, the twin capitals of the Mexica. Tlatelolco became the leading commercial center. When the Spanish conquistador Hernán Cortés entered the Valley of Mexico in the early sixteenth century, the two cities were conjoined. In a letter to the king of Spain he described the great Tlatelolco market:

> This city has many public squares, in which are situated the markets and other places for buying and selling. There is one square twice as large as that of the city of Salamanca [a Spanish city], surrounded by porticoes, where are daily assembled more than sixty thousand souls, engaged in buying and selling; and where are found all kinds of merchandise that the world affords, embracing the necessaries of life, as for instance articles of food, as well as jewels of gold and silver, lead, brass, copper, tin, precious stones, bones, shells, snails, and feathers."[3]

Tenochtitlán and Tlatelolco grew rapidly during the fifteenth century, and together their population may have reached as much as 250,000 by the time the Spanish arrived. Mexica rulers sponsored ambitious building projects, adding an aqueduct, increasing the number of causeways, and constructing an elaborate temple complex. Two perpendicular avenues intersected at the central square, dividing Tenochtitlán into four quarters, each with its own sacred precinct. The city's layout reflected Aztec cosmology.

Nezahualcoyotl ("Fasting Coyote"): Political Strategist, Survivor, and Poet

The Aztec empire arose as an alliance of city-states representing distinct Nahua groups. The Mexica were the dominant partner, but their allies were indispensable to imperial success. Texcoco, a Nahua city east of Tenochtitlán and a member of the Triple Alliance, was an especially valuable collaborator under the leadership of Nezahualcoyotl, or Fasting Coyote (1402–1472).

Nezahualcoyotl, whose biography has been pieced together from Spanish chronicles and Nahua codices (singular, **codex**), came of age during a time of food scarcity and regional warfare. When he was fifteen, he marched into battle alongside his father, the king of Texcoco, to defend the city-state from the Tepaneca, a powerful Nahua people. The Texcoco army was annihilated. Nezahualcoyotl, the heir to the Texcoco throne, watched from a tree as enemy soldiers slaughtered his father. The invaders saw the boy, captured him, and made ready to sacrifice him to the Tepaneca patron god. A faithful Texcoco servant, however, slipped into the prison where Nezahualcoyotl was being held, exchanged clothes with him, and volunteered to die in his place. The young prince escaped to Tenochtitlán, where his mother had been born as a member of the ruling family. The Mexica welcomed the fugitive as one of their own.

> **codex** A set of pages of parchment or other material stacked together and bound along one edge or, alternatively, a continuous strip of material folded accordion-style to form pages; a codex is to be distinguished from a scroll.

After eight years in Tenochtitlán, where he was educated, Nezahualcoyotl decided to return to his native city. But Maxtla, the Tepaneca ruler who had conquered Texcoco, put an extravagant price on his head. Once again, the prince had to cheat death. He fled to the mountains where, like a hungry coyote, he hid in ravines and caves. Peasants loyal to his family kept him alive.

Nezahualcoyotl's gritty resistance inspired a larger revolt. Texcoco nobles and mountain villagers formed an army to drive out the hated Tepaneca. The prince led an assault on the city, liberated it, and in the following months joined the rulers of Tenochtitlán and the city-state of Tlacopan in the Triple Alliance. This potent confederation vanquished the Tepaneca and took control of the entire Valley of Mexico.

Nezahualcoyotl became king of Texcoco through violent revolution, but he also excelled at the art of peace. He ordered that laws be codified concerning the sale and inheritance of property. His surveyors measured the plots of both nobles and villagers to settle disputes, and he championed the rights of peasants to stay on their farms no matter which lord owned them. Like all Nahua rulers, he accepted the practice of human sacrifice. The custom, however, appears to have troubled him. As king, he refused to attend the ritual killings.

Nezahualcoyotl embarked on a massive building campaign to improve the lives of his people, constructing new temples, roads, and public gardens. His royal palace compound sprawled across two hundred acres and contained a ball court, a zoo, and a market. He reformed the government, establishing separate councils for war, finance, justice, and the arts. Painters, artisans, and writers flocked to Texcoco. Modern scholars regard poetry attributed to Nezahualcoyotl to be among the finest examples of Nahuatl literature. About a dozen philosophical poems survive thanks to the sixteenth-century historian Juan Bautista de Pomar, the ruler's half-Spanish great grandson. These verses reveal a deep love of nature, an appreciation for life's fragility, and a philosophy best described as *carpe diem*—seize the day. In "The Flower Tree," Nezahualcoyotl writes joyfully about human creativity:

An entirely imagined representation of Nezahualcoyotl on a government building in Mexico City.

> Live here on earth, blossom!
> As you move and shake, flowers fall.
> My flowers are eternal, my songs are forever.
> I raise them,
> I, a singer.
> I scatter them,
> I spill them,
> The flowers become gold,
> They are carried inside the golden place.

Thinking Critically

In terms of his actions, attitudes, and ruling policies, would you say that Nezahualcoyotl is typical or not typical of premodern monarchs?

Residents imagined the world divided into four parts. A large mountain stood at the center. From there a great tree rose into the sky, supporting the ceiling that enveloped the planet. Like medieval Christians, the Aztecs envisaged a multilayered heaven and an underworld. Archaeologists believe that the four quarters of Tenochtitlán symbolized the parts of the earth and that the Great Temple represented the central mountain. The shrine's cavernous interior, which contained numerous artifacts and human bones, stood for the underworld—the residence of the dead.

The lives of Aztec children. Antonio de Mendoza, the first Spanish governor of Mexico in the sixteenth century, may have commissioned local scholars to produce a pictorial account of Aztec history and life. The explanatory text accompanying the pictures is in Spanish. This page of the Codex Mendoza depicts chores and punishments. At the top an adult is punishing a boy (left) and a girl (right) for some infraction by forcing them to breathe the smoke of burning chili peppers. At the bottom a boy is dutifully fishing and a girl is learning to weave cloth. What do you think the children in the middle two scenes might be doing?

The Great Temple had a pyramidal shape and a steep staircase leading up to a platform and two stone huts. Each of these structures was the home of a god. From one of them Tlaloc, the god of rain, presided over the city in summer and fall—the wet months, when crops were planted and harvested. From the other house, Huitzilopochtli, the patron deity of the Mexica, ruled during winter and spring, when the farmers left their fields and went to war. According to tradition, Huitzilopochtli led the Mexica from Aztlán to the Valley of Mexico and later instructed them to found Tenochtitlán.

From their homes atop the Great Temple, the two gods oversaw the central market. It was no coincidence that the market and the temple were in the same place. Like other Mesoamerican peoples, the Mexica believed that the gods, just like human rulers, wanted to be fed, clothed, and indulged with all the material comforts their subjects could offer. The market therefore served as both a bazaar and a sacred place of making offerings to the gods. Commerce and religion were inseparable.

Religion and human sacrifice. Like the Maya of earlier centuries (see Chapter 8), the Mexica believed that blood was the most valuable gift a person could offer the gods, especially human blood and preferably one's own. According to Nahua mythology, the gods created the world and the human race by sacrificing themselves. In one story, the god Nanahuatzin threw himself into a fire and became the sun. When the other deities asked him why he stayed still and refused to move across the sky, he replied, "Because I am asking for their blood, their color, their precious substance."[4] The feathered serpent god Quetzalcoatl promptly cut open the chests of the other gods and held those deities up to Nanahuatzin as an offering. To fulfill their debt to the gods, humans were also expected to offer sacrificial blood, usually by piercing their skin. Slaves, criminals, and especially war captives gave blood by sacrificing their lives. The Mexica ritually killed thousands of people in front of the Great Temple. Most of these victims died under protest, but some perished voluntarily, apparently regarding self-sacrifice as a great honor. In one of the more infamous rituals, the condemned were made to file up the steps of the pyramid. At the top the chief priest brandished a sharp obsidian blade to slice through each victim's rib cage, removing the heart and holding it up to the sky. Other priests then hurled the dead bodies down the steps, covering the side of the temple with trails of blood.

At the bottom, priests cut off the heads of the corpses and put them on display. A rack of skulls from previous victims ringed the base of the pyramid.

Nahua beliefs about sacrifice motivated imperial conquest. Every major event, including childbirth, a battle, the movement of the sun, and the coming of rain and harvest, required some form of sacrifice. Furthermore, tribute had to be collected from as many groups as possible, both to feed urban populations and to satisfy the insatiable hunger of the gods. The armies of the Triple Alliance went to war in part to acquire victims, as did the Aztecs' enemies. In fact, cities sometimes fought prearranged battles in which each side agreed to take a fixed number of captives for ritual killing later on. Sacrifice may also have functioned as a tool of political intimidation. The Mexica were known to invite dependent rulers from distant cities to the Great Temple to watch as warriors from those cities had their hearts ripped out—a reminder that the Triple Alliance wielded the real power.

Some historians have argued that later Spanish conquerors greatly exaggerated Aztec human sacrifice to morally justify their own seizure of Mexico. There might be truth in that claim, though the visual and documentary evidence of the practice is abundant. On the other hand, we can also point to numerous societies in Africa, Asia, and Europe that at one time or another either slaughtered innocents to appease the powers of the universe or performed gruesome public executions on an appalling scale.

Through their religious ceremonies, the Triple Alliance projected confidence in its destiny to rule the earth as the gods' chosen people. Their cosmology also told them, however, that their power would not last forever. They believed that humankind lived in the Fifth Age of the Sun. Like the previous four ages, that one was due to end. In one popular tale, the king sent a group of soldiers north to Aztlán to pay respect to the mother of their patron god. They returned with ominous news. One day, the goddess informed them, the Mexica would lose all their lands to unnamed invaders from out of the eastern sea—the Gulf of Mexico. Another prophecy warned that the god Quetzalcoatl, whose beard was "extremely long and tangled," had long ago set sail in that sea. But he promised to return one day to rule the world."[5] These traditions played nicely into the hands of Cortés, the bearded Spaniard who came ashore in 1519.

A lethal instrument. This Aztec sacrificial stone knife has an ornately carved wooden handle.

The Incas

In the central Andean highlands, a period of political decentralization followed the collapse of the Wari empire in the mid-thirteenth century. Local communities of farmers and llama herders fought intermittently over land, water, and food stores, especially during drought years. These village-dwelling peoples spoke a variety of languages, including dialects of Quechua. The Incas, one small Quechua group, inhabited a number of dispersed villages in the highland area southeast of the old Wari capital. In the 1430s they began to make war on their neighbors, and over the next century they created a bigger and more politically sophisticated empire than South America had ever seen.

Inca beginnings. The Incas traced their origins to an island in Lake Titicaca, not far from where the Tiwanaku civilization had risen and fallen. According to their mythology, a god named Wira Qucha gave birth to the sun, moon, stars, clouds, and lightning—each a god in its own right. Inti the sun god gave birth to human ancestors of the *Incas,* a word that means "children of the sun." Eight of those children—four brothers and four sisters—wandered out of a cave named Pakariq Tampu in search of water and land. During their journey, three of the brothers were turned into stones. The fourth, named Manqu Qhapaq, entered the Cuzco Valley, drove out the inhabitants, and founded the city of Cuzco.

Archaeologists believe that the Incas first occupied that region around 1200 C.E. and over the next two centuries took control of kinship groups already living there. Though subordinating themselves to the Incas, these groups, called *ayllu* in Quechua, managed to preserve their identity and much of their political and social autonomy. Each *ayllu* consisted of extended families that traced descent from a common ancestor, who was often linked to a specific natural object such as a cave, a stream, a rock, or a mountain. Each *ayllu* venerated a particular sacred place, known as a *wak'a*, by making frequent pilgrimages there and offering gold, cloth, seashells, or food. In periods of famine or war, the *ayllu* sometimes also sacrificed animals or even young children, believing that the *wak'a* could bring good or bad fortune depending on how well it was fed. Devotion to the *wak'a* was a major source of the *ayllu*'s common identity.

A ruling family that carried the name Inca presided over hundreds of *ayllu* in the Cuzco Valley. Members of the royal lineage distinguished themselves from the rest of the population by wearing large earrings, a habit that prompted later Spanish colonizers to call them *orejones*, or "big ears." The head of the lineage called Sapa Inca ("Unique Child"), or simply the Inca, ruled as king alongside his wife, who was also his sister. The practice of sibling marriage aimed to uphold the purity of the royal blood line. As a direct descendant of the sun, the king was revered as a living god. According to a Spanish chronicler,

> No one was allowed to appear before him with shoes on, no matter how important a lord he might be, not even his brothers; rather, they came barefooted and with their heads bowed all the time they were speaking before him or bringing him a message. He always ate alone, without anyone daring to touch the food he was eating. Lords carried him in a litter on their shoulders. If he went out to the square, he sat on a golden seat under a parasol made of ostrich feathers dyed red. He drank from golden tumblers, and all the other service dishes of his household were of gold. He had a great many women."[6]

Artisans fashioned statues of the king in gold, silver, and other precious materials, and royal servants placed them in specially built houses throughout Cuzco, eventually throughout the empire. The king performed religious rituals vital to the health and well-being of the society. But owing to his divine status, he did not take much part in worldly affairs. Rather, he typically designated brothers or other close relatives to command armies, run state administration, and conduct less important ceremonies.

Like the Chimu, Inca society practiced split inheritance long before they became conquerors. Consequently, by the fifteenth century, Inca society included several dozen royal clans, each venerating the mummified remains of a past ruler and each possessing its own stone compound in Cuzco and its own agricultural lands and tribute rights. When a new Inca came to power, he had to gather his own wealth and find his own tribute payers. As in the Chimu case, split inheritance created a powerful motive for imperial expansion (see Map 14.5).

An empire three thousand miles long. According to oral histories, Inca imperial expansion began around 1425, when a foreign group threatened Cuzco. Out of fear, the reigning Inca and his heir apparent fled the city, while a younger son remained to fight. This lad defeated the invaders and proclaimed himself the new ruler, claiming that his father and elder brother had forfeited the throne on account of their cowardice. Taking the royal name Pachakuti, or World Shaker, the new monarch conquered neighboring peoples north and south along the highland ridges. After his death around 1471, his son Tupac Yupanqui continued the expansion. By the start of the sixteenth century, the Inca empire stretched from the mountains of modern Ecuador to the middle of modern Chile and embraced somewhere between six and thirteen million people.

Like the Mexica, the Incas founded their dominion on skillful combinations of diplomacy and violence. Initially, they lavished local lords with gifts, aiming to get them to submit without a fight. During his victorious war with the Chanka, Pachakuti accumulated rich spoils, including food stores of maize, potatoes, chilies, beans, quinoa, and meat. He hoarded these goods, knowing that harsh

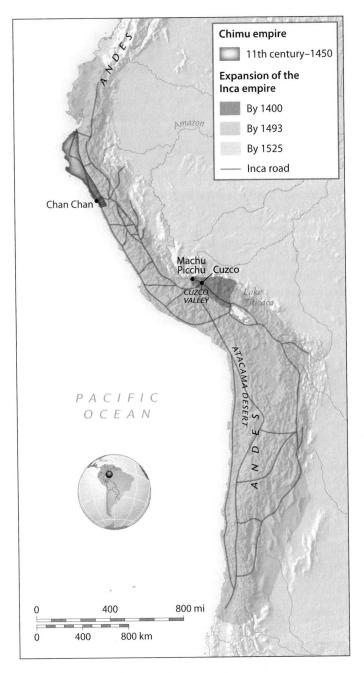

MAP 14.5 Growth of the Inca empire.
The Inca state incorporated a range of altitude from sea level to more than 20,000 feet and therefore a great variety of ecological zones. Why do you think the Inca empire took the territorial shape it did?

and unpredictable Andean weather made them valuable commodities to barter for other goods, favors, and political allegiance. He invited the rulers of neighboring groups to Cuzco, plying them with elaborate feasts and presents of gold, jewels, and other luxuries. These visiting lords brought their own gifts, and both sides exchanged women to serve as concubines, servants, and wives, in that way strengthening bonds of friendship between elite families. Through these strategies, many Andean peoples slipped into dependency on the Incas as weak allies.

Chastity and Marriage in Inca Society

Since Incas did not have a written language, most of our knowledge of their society comes from texts written by Spanish conquistadors. Such books often emphasized the "pagan" and "barbarian" natures of the Incas as justification for Spanish domination. For this reason, Garcilaso de la Vega's Royal Commentaries of the Incas and General History of Peru *stands apart from other early Spanish writings. Garcilaso (1539–1616), son of a conquistador and an Inca noblewoman, was the first* mestizo, *that is, a person of mixed European and indigenous heritage, to write about Andean peoples for a European audience.*

Garcilaso was raised in Cuzco and moved fluidly between Spanish and Inca societies. When he was twenty-one, he used an inheritance from his deceased father to travel to Spain. While there, he under-took to write the Commentaries, *a two-volume history of the Inca state and the Spanish conquest. Part One, published in 1609, is a detailed description of indigenous history, society, and culture, emphasizing the benevolence of the Inca's rule and portraying preconquest Peru as a society of noble and law-abiding pagans, similar to classical Greece or Rome. In Part Two, published the year after he died, he recounted the Spanish conquest. Although Garcilaso approved Spanish rule in Peru, he also tried to persuade readers that Inca civilization was more advanced than Spanish conquistadors wished to admit. In the excerpts below, he describes Inca attitudes toward chastity and some customs surrounding marriage.*

Other women who preserved their virginity, and widows

Besides the virgins who entered monasteries to profess perpetual virginity withdrawn from the world, there were many women of the royal blood who led a similar life in their own homes, having taken a vow of chastity, though not of reclusion. They did not fail to visit their closer relatives in case of sickness or childbirth. . . . Such women were greatly respected for their chastity and high-mindedness, and as a mark of their excellence and divinity they were called *ocllo,* a name held sacred in their idolatry. Their chastity was not feigned, but sincerely preserved, on pain of their being burnt alive as traitors and counterfeiters of their false religion or thrown into the lake of lions, if they were shown to have defiled it. . . .

Nor should one omit to mention the chastity of widows, who usually remained in complete retirement of the whole of the first year of their widowhood. Of those who were childless very few married again. Those who had children never remarried, but lived in continence [abstinence]. This virtue was greatly commended in their laws and ordinances, which prescribed that the fields of widows should be tilled before those of the *curaca* [a class of official] or those of the Inca, apart from many similar privileges.

How they usually married and set up house

It must be explained that every year or every two years, at a certain season, the king ordered all the marriageable maidens and youths of his lineage to gather together in Cuzco. The girls were between eighteen and twenty years old and the youths from twenty-four upwards. They were not allowed to marry earlier, for they said that it was necessary to be old enough and wise enough to rule their houses and estates, and for them to marry earlier would be childish.

The Inca placed himself in the midst of the contracting parties, who were near to one another, and having looked at them, called a youth and a girl, took each by the hand, united them in the bond of matrimony and delivered them to their parents. They then went to the bridegroom's house and solemnized the wedding in the presence of the nearer relatives. The celebrations lasted two, four, or six days, or longer if they wished. These were legitimate wives, and as a mark of greater honor and favor to them they were said in their language to be "given by the Inca's hand." . . .

The houses for the dwellings of bridegrooms who were Incas [members of the royal lineage] . . . were made by Indians from the provinces entrusted with the task according to the division of labor that was set down for everything. The household requirements were provided by the relatives, each bringing a piece. There were no other ceremonies or sacrifices. . . .

For the marriages of the common people the councils of each village were obliged to have houses built for those who were married, and the relatives provided the furniture. It was not lawful for those of different provinces to intermarry, or even those of different towns. All were to marry within their own towns and their own families like the tribes of Israel. . . . All those of one village regarded themselves as relatives, like the sheep of one fold. Even those of the same province did so, if they were all of one tribe and the same language. It was not permitted for them to go from one province and live in another, or from one town to another, or one quarter to another. . . .

Source: Garcilaso de la Vega, *Royal Commentaries of the Incas and General History of Peru,* Part One, trans. Harold V. Livermore (Austin: University of Texas Press, 1966), 204–206.

Thinking Critically

According to Garcilaso, what behavior was expected of widows? What role did the Inca king play in marriage transactions among elites? Why do you think it was unlawful for ordinary people to marry outside their own villages? Why do you think Garcilaso makes reference to the "tribes of Israel"? How does this text challenge sixteenth-century European perceptions of the Incas as primitive or savage?

Groups that resisted Inca entreaties could pay a devastating price, as the Guarco people did. Living in an isolated valley and encasing their city in a stone wall, they thought they could repel an Inca invasion. They threw back four Inca attempts to capture the city but finally gave way. The conquerors proceeded to kill the Guarco warriors, hanging their bodies from the city walls. The Inca ruler confiscated most of the Guarcos' land and redistributed it to colonists brought in from other parts of the empire.

After gaining control of many Andean mountain valleys that channeled snowmelt to the Pacific, the Incas set their sights on the Chimu state and its great capital of Chan Chan. Around 1470, an Inca army moved into the Moche River valley upstream from the city and threatened to obstruct the river and therefore irrigation of the coastal plain. This menace was enough to compel Chan Chan's surrender. The Inca army captured the Chimu king and forced thousands of artisans to relocate to Cuzco. The Chimu state disappeared abruptly, though its art had significant influence on Inca craft and style.

The Inca state. Incas created a more hierarchical and centralized state than the Aztecs did, though they did not stamp out local self-government. They organized the empire into four administrative sectors divided from one another by royal roads that ran outward from Awkaypata, the great public plaza at the center of Cuzco. The four imperial sectors were partitioned further into provinces and smaller districts, each under the authority of a governor drawn from the Cuzco elite. That official supervised tribute collection and presided over state religious ceremonies. The traditional rulers of subject communities kept their titles and local authority unless they resisted or rebelled. They had to recognize Inca sovereignty and surrender a third of their lands to the state. They had to set aside another third to provide tribute to the sun god and other deities, including offerings made at sacred *wak'as* and maintenance of priests and servants who safeguarded those shrines. That left a final third, often the least productive and accessible land, for the farms and pasture of the local population.

Conquered societies paid tribute mainly in labor. Men and women could be drafted into the army or into work gangs that built temples, storehouses, dams, irrigation works, and roads. This labor draft, modeled on those of Wari and Chimu, was called the *mit'a*. The state could also command people to serve in the households of the noble class. Women drafted into service wove garments, cooked, and brewed maize beer, some of which was used in religious rituals. Officials traveling around the empire handpicked girls between the ages of eight and twelve for prestigious service in Cuzco's main temple. When it suited their production and labor needs, the government also forcibly transplanted entire communities from one part of the empire to another. In fact, the state appears to have aimed to homogenize imperial society and culture. When a new area was conquered, officials compelled settlers from other regions to migrate in

An Inca *quipu*. The colors of the strings, the way they were tied together, the placement of the knots, and the type of wool used all carried specific meanings to those Inca officials who could "read" *quipus*. Only a few hundred *quipus* survive, and modern scholars have never cracked the code to this communication system. Should the *quipu* system be considered a form of writing, or not?

but discouraged them from adopting local speech and customs and obliged the noble families on both the indigenous and the immigrant sides to speak Quechua, the imperial language. If the empire had lasted longer than it did, this grand if fundamentally violent experiment might in time have yielded the most culturally integrated large empire in premodern world history.

Communication and transport. The Incas maintained control over the empire by means of a communication system more tightly organized than the Aztecs had and that rivaled those of the most technically sophisticated Afroeurasian empires. This system had three main components: record keeping, roads, and relay runners.

The Incas recorded messages on *quipus*, a device used in the earlier Wari empire. These were pieces of rope to which secondary cords were attached. Other knotted and colored string fastened to these cords represented names of groups, places, material items, or numerical values. As far as we know, *quipus* were used primarily to keep inventories of storehouses and to verify tribute payments and labor quotas. Every division of Inca society, from the province to the individual household, had a *quipu* that recorded goods and services. Historians speculate that this system of strings, knots, and colors that transmitted messages may also have preserved oral histories and cultural lore. Unfortunately, modern scholars have so far failed precisely to "read" any set of *quipus*.

A second component of Inca communication was the network of roads and bridges that connected all major cities and outposts to the capital. In the empire's early decades, the state extended and improved a road system the Wari and Chimu had built earlier. In time the Inca network ran to more than 25,000 miles. Two main roads, each about thirty-five feet wide, stretched the length of the empire. One of them bordered the Pacific coast, the other ran along highland valleys and crossed mountain passes. Numerous intersecting trails linked the coastal and mountain arteries to each other like rungs on a ladder. Where a road had to ascend a steep mountain slope, workers installed rugged staircases. In swampy areas, causeways and drainage ditches kept travelers' feet dry. Swaying suspension bridges, typically four to five feet wide and equipped with a wooden walking surface and parallel hand ropes, got people across deep ravines. These bridges were as many as 150 feet long, much longer, for example, than stone bridges found in fifteenth-century Europe.

The communication system's third element was a corps of relay runners who carried messages from one town or post to another twenty-four hours a day, every day of the year. Way stations were spaced at regular intervals along the major roads, and specially trained couriers waited at them to receive messages and parcels and carry them to the next post. Typically, a single courier ran four to six miles. Despite dauntingly rugged terrain, a relay team could carry a message about 155 miles in a day. The highway stations also served as warehouses and inns for all travelers.

The capital city. According to Inca tradition, King Pachakuti lavishly redesigned and renovated the previously modest town of Cuzco. He had clay models made to display his urban vision, and he presided over the new construction, a project that took about twenty years and thirty thousand *mit'a* labor conscripts. The few urban walls that survive today reveal extraordinary masonry craft. Workers placed enormous blocks of stone together so precisely that a straw would not fit between them, even though no adhesive mortar was used. A great temple dedicated to the sun god Inti rose up in the heart of the city. According to a Spanish chronicler, this Golden Enclosure was "one of the richest temples in the whole world. . . . There was an image of the sun, of great size, made of gold, beautifully wrought and set with many precious stones." Below the temple "was a garden in which the earth was lumps of fine gold, and it

was cunningly planted with stalks of corn that were made of gold . . . there were many tubs of gold and silver and emeralds, and goblets, pots, and every kind of vessel all of fine gold."[7]

The temple of the sun stood on one side of the grand Awkaypata plaza, where the four imperial highways came together. The residence of the Inca and the compounds of the royal clans, along with their deceased and mummified kings, flanked the plaza. Nearby were dormitory-like residences for girls who served the temple. Beyond the main precinct were private homes, inns, schools, storage facilities, and gardens. At the height of Inca power, Cuzco may have had as many as 100,000 residents, a population that included subjects forced to relocate to the capital to work on behalf of the state. Provincial aristocrats also had to live in Cuzco several months every year. These nobles built their own compounds on the outskirts of the city and brought along hundreds of family members, clients, and servants. Their sons attended state-run schools and learned Quechua if they did not already know it. Like various Afroeurasian monarchies, Inca rulers used this strategy to flatter and indulge provincial elites while making sure they had no power independent of the central state.

Inca cosmology and religion. Cuzco's design, like that of Tenochtitlán in Mexico, reflected Inca cosmology. Awkaypata, where the four arterial highways intersected, represented the hub not only of the empire but of the whole universe. The ruler performed vital rituals and sacrifices in front of an altar located in the temple of the sun. Forty-two marked lines radiated outward from it to various points in

Efficient travel in the Andes. These remains of a highway cut through the mountains near the Inca fortress city of Machu Picchu.

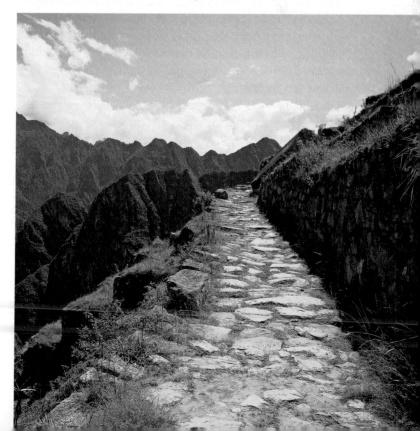

Cuzco and its suburban villages. Interspersed along these lines were some 328 *wak'a* shrines. Some of them signified important events or figures in Inca mythology.

By connecting all of these holy sites to Cuzco's central temple, the Inca rulers turned religion into a source of power. While asserting the supremacy of the sun cult, they encouraged the worship of ancestors and provincial deities, even going so far as to co-opt local cults into the state religion. In a ceremony attended by nobles from all over the empire, the monarch performed sacrifices to appease these local deities. While securing the favor of subject peoples, he reinforced his position as the chief intermediary between gods and humans.

Zenith and decline. By the start of the sixteenth century, the Inca empire was a remarkably integrated state. Regional governors and civil servants reported to Cuzco. Local farmers and herders preserved their varied languages and customs, but aristocratic families had to learn Quechua. The state tolerated local religious beliefs and worship but promoted the cult of the sun god. Provincial nobles received

honor and respect but had no authority independent of the state. The government stored food and distributed it to the population in time of dearth but required peasants to grow crops to feed *mit'a* labor crews.

Nevertheless, political and social tensions pervaded the empire. In the provinces, indigenous communities and relocated settlers often resented each other's presence. Inca armies continued to meet fierce local resistance along the northern and southern frontiers. When the empire neared the practical limits of expansion, the state pressed populations within its borders for more tribute, causing conflict between local farmers and their governors. The powerful families that venerated dead kings competed ruthlessly with one another for wealth and influence as if their mummified rulers were still leading them. If the living Inca appeared weak, these rivalries could deteriorate into civil strife. That happened in 1528, when King Wayna Qhapaq died and two competing sons set off a civil war to replace him. One of these sons emerged victorious, but political tensions were still festering when Francisco Pizarro and a band of armed Spaniards suddenly appeared from out of the sea.

• • •

Conclusion

At the start of the sixteenth century, large areas of Mesoamerica and South America were united under sophisticated political and economic systems. The Aztec and Inca empires displayed many of the attributes of Afroeurasian states of that time. They had mastered advanced engineering, urban planning, tax collection, and professional military organization. They had developed belief systems fully as complex as those of Christianity, Buddhism, and Islam. Though lacking full writing systems, they orally preserved and transmitted historical and mythological traditions that undergirded their identities and justified their imperial ventures. Though they lacked iron technology, large domesticated animals, or any transport or tools that made use of wheels, they excelled at mobilizing and organizing human labor on large scales. These giant empires, however, were no more typical of the population of the Americas as a whole than they were of fifteenth-century Afroeurasia. Rather, the majority of Native Americans grouped themselves, as they did in Afroeurasia, in hunter-forager bands, farm villages, or relatively small urban centers like those of the North American woodlands, the Colorado Plateau, or the Amazon basin.

After about 900, the general trend of history in the Americas, especially in the Northern Hemisphere, appears to have been toward faster expansion of maize-based agriculture,

rising population growth rates, more city building, and intensified long-distance trade. Cyclical climate change associated with the North Atlantic Warm Period may partly account for this trend. It was in these centuries that cities like Cahokia, Pueblo Bonito, and Tula flourished. The end of the warming cycle in the thirteenth or fourteenth century may have slowed or even arrested these developments in several regions, though certainly not everywhere, as the enormous cities of Tenochtitlán and Cuzco attest.

Those cities were the capitals of larger and more intricate political systems than the Americas had seen in any earlier time. Their sheer scale suggests that, at least in densely populated regions, Native American societies were moving along a path of increasing social complexity, perhaps toward much larger scales of political organization and urbanization in regions such as the Mississippi or Amazon valleys. The sudden arrival of people from Afroeurasia, who brought with them not only guns and horses but a diverse load of new foods, weeds, hungry domestic animals, and dangerous microorganisms, abruptly interrupted prevailing American trends. We can only imagine how societies of the Western Hemisphere might have looked in the seventeenth or eighteenth centuries if those Afroeurasians had remained on the far side of the Atlantic.

• • •

Key Terms

Amazonian trade network 410
Ancestral Puebloans (Anasazi) 404
ayllu 417
Aztecs (Triple Alliance) 413
Cahokia 401
Chichén Itzá 405
Chimu 410

chinampas 407
codex 415
ecosystem 401
Incas 417
Nahuas 407
pueblo 404
quipus 411

split inheritance 413
Taino 408
Tiwanaku 410
Toltecs 405
Wari 410

Change over Time

500–1200	Ancestral Puebloans establish settlements in Chaco Canyon on the Colorado Plateau.
800–1400	Cahokia culture flourishes in the Mississippi valley, continuing the region's mound-building tradition.
8th century	The Wari empire reaches the peak of power in the central highlands of Peru.
9th–13th centuries	The North Atlantic Warm Period is associated with greater agricultural productivity in the Eastern Woodlands and cycles of rainfall and drought in the Southwest; Tainos dominate several Caribbean islands; Amazonians extend trade links with Andean communities; Toltecs rule a central Mexican state with wider commercial influence.
10th century	The Andean state of Tiwanaku, centered around Lake Titicaca, reaches its peak of power.
11th century–1470	The Chimu empire, with its capital at Chan Chan, dominates the Moche River valley.
ca. 1150–1250	Nahuas move into the Valley of Mexico.
1200	The Inca establish a settlement in Cuzco; the Maya state of Chichén Itzá collapses.
1250	Mexicas settle in the Valley of Mexico.
1425–1532	The Inca empire dominates Andean South America.
1428–1521	The Aztec empire (Triple Alliance) dominates Mesoamerica.

Please see end of book reference section for additional reading suggestions related to this chapter.

15 Calamities and Recoveries across Afroeurasia

1300–1500

In *The Holy Trinity*, the Florentine painter Masaccio applied new principles of linear perspective to achieve an illusion of three-dimensional space.

I

f you drive a car along a straight, flat stretch of country highway, your eyes will tell you that the road ahead narrows. The two edges gradually converge to a point, and the road disappears altogether. If you should see a line of ten school buses coming toward you, you will perceive that the closest bus is bigger than the most distant one. You will *see* these things, but at the same time your brain, reasoning logically and drawing on stored knowledge, will tell you that neither perception is accurate. The road will almost certainly not vanish, and the buses will turn out to be all the same size.

No doubt, humans figured out tens of thousands of years ago that the way objects look to us depends on where we position ourselves in relation to those objects. Throughout most of our history, artists who tried to make pictures that represent objects and spaces just as they appear to the eye relied mostly on trial and error, using their powers of imagination. Early in the fifteenth century, however, architects and painters working in the Italian city of Florence formulated rules of linear perspective. These were a set of optical and mathematical principles for depicting how the eye views a particular scene from a given stationary position. In achieving this breakthrough, these artists drew on knowledge about optics found in translations of Greek and Arabic texts.

Masaccio (MUH-sah-chee-oo), a young Florentine artist (1401–1428), created one of the earliest known works that clearly shows the principles of linear perspective in action. Titled *The Holy Trinity* (1425), this fresco, a picture made by applying paint to a moist plaster surface, occupies a wall in the church of Santa Maria Novella in Florence. It depicts the crucified Jesus Christ and three other figures as though they were inside a room with an arched ceiling. The illusion of spatial depth is convincing because, in accord with the rules of perspective, all the diagonal lines in the pattern of the ceiling converge at a single point in the picture. Other artists in Florence adopted the new technique, and it subsequently spread throughout Europe. For the next few centuries, the idea that painters should apply rules of perspective so that their canvases appear as "windows" on the natural world became fundamental to European art.

Linear perspective was one of the remarkable innovations in art and architecture that Florentines achieved in the period of European history conventionally called the late Middle Ages. Ironically, the city's cultural flowering, the period that later became known as the Italian Renaissance, took place, not in a time of political and social calm, but when Europe was just beginning to recover from several decades of severe social and economic upheaval. The young Masaccio and numerous other talented Florentines went about their creative labor in a city troubled by disease, war, and poverty.

In fact, Florence was representative of several Afroeurasian cities that sparkled as points of artistic and scholarly light despite repeated episodes of epidemic, violence, and economic disruption. Beginning early in the fourteenth century, the expansionary trend of population, economic output, and long-distance trade that had characterized much of Afroeurasia for about seven hundred years went into reverse. This general downturn, recalling the prolonged economic contraction of the fourth to sixth centuries C.E., involved several crises. One was a serious decline in food production and consequent famine in the Northern Hemisphere linked to climatic change. A second was the outbreak of infectious disease in several parts of Afroeurasia, a pestilence whose initial assault became known in history as the Black Death. A third was a swell of regional wars that reconfigured Afroeurasia's political map. Finally, commercial and cultural exchange along the trans-Eurasian silk roads declined following a century of unprecedented activity. The first part of this chapter explores the environmental catastrophes of the fourteenth century. The second part investigates the economic, political, and social consequences that attended those calamities, focusing here on China, the central Muslim lands, and Europe.

In the third section, we explore how and why demographic and economic motors began to rev up again in the 1400s

• • •

in much of Afroeurasia. Several vigorous new monarchies appeared, some of them eventually to become imperial giants. Silk road traffic picked up again, the shipping lanes along Afroeurasia's chain of seas flourished as never before. The technology of mechanical printing spread along the exchange routes from East Asia to Europe, allowing knowledge to be produced and circulated on a vastly larger scale. The secrets of gunpowder weaponry also spread across the hemisphere, amplifying human capacity to kill and destroy but also enhancing the power of centralized states.

The multiple troubles of the 1300–1500 period, like earlier cycles of retrenchment, revealed humankind's extraordinary talent for adapting to jarring change. Moreover, in the very long term of history, the era represented a short and only partial interruption of the human tendency to devise ever more complex systems of economy, social organization, and cultural exchange.

A Panoramic View

MAP 15.1 Spread of the plague pandemic (Black Death), 1330–1355.

The Black Death was one of several human catastrophes to strike Afroeurasian lands during the fourteenth century. What geographical factors might help explain why the plague pandemic spread in the general directions it did?

Environmental Crises of the Fourteenth Century

FOCUS What historical developments may account for significant population decline in parts of Afroeurasia in the fourteenth century?

After about seven hundred years of steady growth, the population of Afroeurasia as a whole plunged suddenly in the mid-fourteenth century, dropping about 16 percent between 1300 and 1400. This demographic slump did not take place everywhere, nor did it occur all at once. It did not, as far as we know, happen in Subsaharan Africa. In China, Inner Eurasia, and parts of Southwest Asia, on the other hand, numbers started sinking in the 1200s in connection with Mongol destruction, then kept on sinking straight through the 1300s. After three centuries of vigorous growth, Europe's numbers leveled off in about 1300 and then nose-dived between 1340 and 1400. Afroeurasia's overall demographic recovery did not get under way until the second half of the fifteenth century.

The economies of China, Inner Eurasia, the central Muslim lands, and Europe all appear to have slowed significantly in the fourteenth century, especially set against the dramatic growth that had occurred between 1000 and 1200. Subsaharan Africa was almost certainly an exception to this trend. There, towns and trade routes multiplied throughout the crisis decades, though from a lower starting base compared, say, to China.

Monumental changes also took place in the political sphere. Two of the great Mongol states—the Yuan dynasty in China and the khanate of Iran-Iraq (Ilkhanate)—disintegrated before 1370. The other two major Mongol empires—the khanate of Chagatai in the eastern steppes and Central Asia and the Golden Horde in the western steppes and Russia—started imploding before the end of the century as a result of dynastic wars and rebellions. In the Mediterranean basin, the Turkic Mamluk empire of Egypt and Syria had increasing trouble maintaining its economic and financial health, and the three Muslim sultanates that shared North Africa all experienced serious internal troubles after 1350. In West Africa, the Mali empire, the world's most important gold-supplying state as of 1300, also shrank in the later decades of the fourteenth century amid royal succession disputes and provincial revolts.

These economic and political traumas had no single cause, and explanations for stagnancy or upheaval in one region do not necessarily apply in others. We have no index of wars and revolts to prove that the fourteenth century was more violent than any of several previous ages in world history. Russia, for example, certainly suffered more material destruction from the Mongol invasion of 1237–1240 than from any stresses that occurred in the following two hundred years. Nevertheless, we can identify, at least in

northerly parts of Afroeurasia, environmental crises that profoundly disrupted the lives and livelihoods of tens of millions of people in the fourteenth century.

Downpour and Drought

As we saw in earlier chapters, the Northern Hemisphere experienced a small but ecologically significant warming trend, known as the North Atlantic Warm Period, between the ninth and thirteenth centuries. This trend ended sometime after 1200. Temperatures in Arctic and northern temperate latitudes dropped, and this cooling cycle continued erratically to the mid-1800s. Climatologists have labeled this temperature decline the **Little Ice Age** because of the advance of polar and alpine glaciers that accompanied it. Drawing on evidence from Europe and the North Atlantic, researchers have also suggested three general types of environmental change and accompanying social upheavals centered on the fourteenth century. First, in the Baltic Sea and the North Atlantic, sea ice and colder water temperatures extended farther south, reducing fish stocks and making voyages between Europe and the Norse communities of Iceland and Greenland more dangerous. Second, annual weather patterns became more erratic. Beginning in the 1200s, brutal wind storms and sea floods periodically smashed into the North Atlantic, North Sea, and Baltic Sea coasts, inundating low-lying farmland and in some years killing tens of thousands of people. Third,

> **Little Ice Age** A trend of climatic cooling that affected weather conditions chiefly in the Northern Hemisphere approximately from the late thirteenth to the mid-nineteenth century.

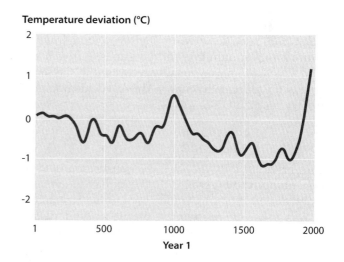

Global temperature changes, 1–2000 c.e. In what one-hundred-year period did the temperature peak of the North Atlantic Warm Period occur? In what one-hundred-year period did the lowest temperature point of the Little Ice Age occur?

summers became generally cooler and wetter all across northern Europe. In northern Britain and Scandinavia, grain farmers had to retreat south, leaving behind hundreds of deserted villages. English vintners found they could no longer produce decent wine.

Between 1315 and 1322 a succession of cool, rainy summers in northern Europe shortened the growing season, hampered crop harvesting, and made sheep and cattle more susceptible to epidemic diseases. Massive famine ensued, disrupting all economic life, expanding the ranks of the destitute, and killing perhaps 5–10 percent of the population. A modern historian, drawing on fourteenth-century chronicles, describes the sufferings of people in the region that is today Belgium during rains that started in May 1315 and continued nearly uninterrupted for a year: "The local harvest was wholly insufficient and the customary imports ceased almost entirely. In Antwerp the moans of the famishing could almost move a stone to pity. . . . They died in large numbers and great pits were dug outside the town into which were cast as many as sixty bodies."[1] Better weather returned after 1322, but climatic conditions remained highly volatile. Regional famines continued to occur throughout the century in both northern and Mediterranean Europe.

The Little Ice Age hit western Europe just when economic growth was leveling off following several centuries of robust expansion. By the later 1200s, farm production could no longer keep pace with population growth. Good cropland in the more densely populated regions of western and central Europe filled up, and the migration of German and other western European farmers to conquered frontier territories in eastern Europe and Spain slowed down (see Chapter 12). Consequently, food prices increased, living standards shrank for all but the very rich, and at the low end of the social scale many serfs and tenant farmers descended into extreme poverty. The famines of 1315 to 1322 made all these problems worse. But even though hunger and disease killed hundreds of thousands, Europe's population appears to have generally recovered in the second quarter of the fourteenth century. The real demographic catastrophe struck in midcentury.

The Great Pestilence

Writing in the late 1370s the North African historian and philosopher Ibn Khaldun recalled the horror he had witnessed two decades earlier: "Civilization both in the East and the West was visited by a destructive plague which devastated nations and caused populations to vanish. It swallowed up many of the good things of civilization and wiped them out. . . . Cities and building were laid waste, roads and way signs were obliterated, settlements and mansions became empty, dynasties and tribes grew weak. The entire inhabited world changed."[2] The infectious disease that Ibn Khaldun described did not in fact affect "the entire inhabited world." But it no doubt seemed that way to him, because

it killed a substantial percentage of North Africa's population and triggered years of economic and political disorder. Next to the massive die-off that American Indians endured when they first came in contact with Afroeurasian pathogens in the sixteenth century, the **Black Death** of 1346 to 1352 stands as the most deadly known disease crisis up to modern times. It broke upon populations from Inner Eurasia, and perhaps China, to as far west as Greenland (see Map 15.1). Everywhere that it struck, immune systems failed to defend human bodies against the invading microorganism. Millions died after days, or even just hours, of acute suffering from raging fevers, vomiting, and dark painful swellings called buboes. Though as many as 40 percent of infected victims recovered, depending on the locality, people who contracted pneumonic plague, that is, infection of the lungs, almost always died. And before they expired, they often transmitted the pathogen to others by coughing, sneezing, or just breathing. In Afroeurasia the Black Death reached the proportions of a pandemic, a contagion that spread from one region to another, in this case nearly across the hemisphere.

Black Death An infectious disease, probably plague, that caused significant population decline in parts of Afroeurasia in the mid-fourteenth century.

Origins of the Black Death. Since the late nineteenth century, epidemiologists and historians have argued that plague was the infection associated with the Black Death. We sometimes use the word *plague* to characterize any serious epidemic or, metaphorically, any sudden calamity, such as a "plague of locusts." By a stricter definition, however, plague refers to a particular disease having a range of symptoms and biological strains associated with the disease-producing bacterium, or bacillus, called *Yersinia pestis* (*Y. pestis*). For longer than anyone knows, plague has thrived among ground-burrowing rodents that live in certain parts of the world, notably in Inner Eurasia, the Himalayan Mountain foothills, East Africa, and the American Southwest. The principal vector, or carrier, of *Y. pestis* is a type of flea that inhabits the fur of living animals and feeds on their blood. In certain environmental conditions, the bacillus may spread through a large rodent population. Animals infected with *Y. pestis* soon die, forcing equally infected fleas to jump to a living animal to feed, thereby spreading the disease further. If infected animals come into sustained contact with humans, fleas that can find no other hosts may look for blood meals on human bodies, thereby passing *Y. pestis* to them. According to recent research, *Y. pestis* infections caused the first plague pandemic, the Plague of Justinian, which occurred in the mid-sixth century (see Chapter 9).[3]

Some researchers have argued recently that the Black Death had nothing to do with *Y. pestis*, pointing to differences in symptoms and other factors between the fourteenth-century pandemic and modern plague. Nevertheless, current genetic studies, including analysis of DNA from the bones of plague victims buried between 1348 and

1350 in a cemetery in London, have confirmed the presence of *Y. pestis*.[4] This research contends that the Black Death was more virulent than modern plague because infected people were already suffering from malnutrition associated with food shortages linked to the Little Ice Age.

The precise region where the Black Death originated is also debated, but the dominant theory contends that humans mingled with infected rodent communities somewhere in Inner Eurasia in the late thirteenth or early fourteenth century (see Map 15.1). Turkic and Mongol horse soldiers may have been the first to spread the disease widely. Infected rodents and fleas could have infiltrated grain stores in saddlebags and wagons, thus traveling far and wide to contaminate both humans and more rodents. Some scholars have also hypothesized that Little Ice Age conditions helped propel the disease because drier weather on the Inner Eurasian steppes forced rodents to migrate in search of water. As infected creatures moved east or west from areas of sparse to denser human habitation, they set off epidemics.

According to contemporary Chinese reports, a terrible pestilence struck the Hebei region of northern China in 1331, killing nine-tenths of the population. Though we lack a description of symptoms, it is possible that the Black Death enacted its first scene in East Asia. To the west, epidemics occurred in Inner Eurasia in the late 1330s and in the Golden Horde territories north of the Black Sea in the following decade. About 1345, disease erupted in Kaffa (Theodosia) on the Black Sea coast, infecting the resident community of Genoese Italian merchants. Ships leaving the port carried sailors, merchants, and black rats, all infected or soon to be, to other ports around the Black Sea rim. From there the pathogen spread on the sailing ships that linked the Black Sea to the Mediterranean. A ghastly epidemic hit Constantinople in 1347. That same year the contagion spread to Sicily and Egypt, almost certainly carried by Italian seafarers. The Muslim historian al-Maqrizi tells of a ship limping into the port of Alexandria. Out of a company of 332 souls, all had perished of disease at sea except for forty sailors, four merchants, and one slave, and all of those unfortunates died a short time later.[5]

In the grim year of 1348, ships coursing through the Mediterranean deposited their lethal cargo in one port after another. From those towns, caravans and wagon trains distributed the ailment to inland regions of Europe, North Africa, and Southwest Asia. In the spring and summer, epidemics hit dozens of cities—Genoa and Venice, Barcelona and Paris, Damascus and Tunis. An epidemic struck the holy city of Mecca in Arabia in 1348–1349, no doubt carried there by Muslim pilgrims. Florence, already weakened by a succession of famines, may have lost as much as 75 percent of its population of about eighty thousand. Cairo, capital of the Mamluk empire and probably the largest Afroeurasian city west of China, may have lost 300,000 of its estimated 500,000 residents. In his famous collection of stories titled *The Decameron*, the fourteenth-century Florentine writer Boccaccio describes the terrors of the pestilence in both city and countryside:

Fleas in search of blood meals bite rodents infected with plague bacillus.

Bacilli multiply in fleas' gut, causing starvation.

Starving fleas jump from rodent to rodent to try to feed.

Fleas infect healthy rodents with plague bacillus and disease spreads.

When sick rodents die, fleas look for new living hosts.

If infected rats and fleas live near humans, hungry fleas may infect them.

Infected humans become sick; 50 percent or more may die.

If lungs are infected, sick people may transmit bacillus to others through respiration; pneumonic plague is almost always fatal.

How plague spread in the fourteenth century. What are some ways in which humans may have unintentionally transported plague-infected fleas or rats from one village or city to another?

The condition of the common people (and also, in great part, of the middle class) was yet more pitiable to behold, because these . . . fell sick by the thousand daily and being altogether untended and unsuccored, died well-nigh all without recourse. Many breathed their last in the open street, by day and by night, while many others, though they died in their homes, made it known to the neighbors that they were dead rather by the stench of their rotting bodies than otherwise. . . . Throughout the scattered villages and in the fields, the poor miserable peasants and their families without succor of physician or aid of servant, died not like men, but well-nigh like beasts.[6]

In 1349 the pandemic spread like wildfire, advancing simultaneously up the Nile River valley, along the North African coast, and across the English Channel to Britain. It advanced northwestward to Ireland, Iceland, and even Greenland, where it appears to have obliterated one of the

Perspectives on the Black Death

The Black Death spawned innumerable treatises on causes and treatments. Although writers proposed theories and made recommendations that today seem illogical, and perhaps dangerous, these texts help us understand the medical and religious debates that circulated as the epidemic raged. The two selections below discuss the issue of contagion. Document 1 is from a plague tract that a French court physician wrote around 1364. A Swedish bishop republished the text in the mid-fifteenth century under the name Bengt Knutsson. Document 2 is from a work by Lisan al-Din Ibn al-Khatib, a celebrated poet, philosopher, and physician who lived in Granada, Spain, when it was a Muslim-ruled city. Ibn al-Khatib wrote "A Very Useful Inquiry into the Horrible Sickness" about 1349–1352, just when the Black Death was spreading around the Mediterranean rim.

DOCUMENT 1 Bengt Knutsson

I say that pestilence sores are contagious because of infectious humors, and the reek or smoke of such sores is venomous and corrupts the air. And therefore one should flee such persons as are infected. In pestilence time nobody should stand in a great press of people because some man among them may be infected. Therefore wise physicians visiting sick folk stand far from the patient, holding their face towards the door or window, and so should the servants of sick folk stand. . . .

Now it is to be known by what remedies a man may preserve himself from the pestilence. First see the writings of Jeremiah the prophet that a man ought to forsake evil things and do good deeds and meekly confess his sins, for it is the highest remedy in time of pestilence: penance and confession to be preferred to all other medicines. Nevertheless I promise you verily it is a good remedy to void and change the infected place. But some may not profitably change their places. Therefore as much as

they can they should eschew every cause of putrefaction and stinking, and namely every fleshly lust with women is to be eschewed. Also the southern wind, which is naturally infective. Therefore spar the windows against the south . . . until the first hour after the middle of the day then open the windows against the north. Of the same cause every foul stench is to be eschewed, of stable, stinking fields, ways or streets, and namely of stinking dead carrion and most of stinking waters where in many places water is kept two days or two nights. . . .

Also let your house be sprinkled especially in summer with vinegar and roses and with the leaves of the vine. Also it is good to wash your hands oft times in the day with water and vinegar and wipe your face with your hands.

Source: Rosemary Horrox, ed. and trans., *The Black Death* (Manchester: Manchester University Press, 1994), 175–177.

DOCUMENT 2 Ibn al-Khatib

If it were asked, how do we submit to the theory of contagion, when already the divine law has refuted the notion of contagion, we will answer: The existence of contagion has been proved by experience, deduction, the senses, observation, and by unanimous reports, and these aforementioned categories are the demonstrations of proof. And it is not a secret to whoever has looked into this matter or has come to be aware of it that those who come into contact with [plague] patients mostly die, while those who do not come into contact survive. Moreover, disease occurs in a household or neighborhood because of the mere presence of a contagious dress or utensil; even a [contaminated] earring has been known to kill whoever wears it and his whole household. And when it happens in a city, it starts in one house and then affects the visitors of the house, then the neighbors, the relatives, and other visitors until it spreads throughout the city. And coastal cities are free of the disease until it comes from the sea through a visitor from another city that has the disease, and thus the appearance of the disease in the safe city coincides with the arrival of this

man from the contagious city. And the safety of those who have gone into isolation is demonstrated by the example of the ascetic, Ibn Abu Madyan, who lived in the city of Salé [on the coast of Morocco]. He believed in the contagion, and so he hoarded food and bricked up the door on his family (and his family was large!), and the city was obliterated by the plague and not one soul [except Ibn Abu Madyan] was left in that whole town. And reports were unanimous that isolated places that have no roads to them and are not frequented by people have escaped unscathed from the plague. . . . And it has been confirmed that nomads and tent dwellers in Africa and other nomadic places have escaped unscathed because their air is not enclosed and it is improbable that it can be corrupted.

Source: M. J. Müller, "Ibnulkhatib's Bericht über die Pest," Sitzungsberichte der Königl. Bayerischen Akademie der Wissenschaften, 2 (1863): 2–12. Translated from the Arabic with assistance from Dr. Walid Saleh. In John Aberth, *The First Horseman: Disease in Human History,* 1st Edition, 44–46, © 2007. Reprinted by permission of Pearson Education, Inc., Upper Saddle River, New Jersey.

Thinking Critically

What did Knutsson think caused the deadly disease to spread? How could people avoid contracting it? How does religion figure in Knutsson's list of treatments for the disease? How is Ibn al-Khatib's understanding of contagion similar to or different from Knutsson's? How do the two authors compare in their discussion of "corrupt air" as a cause of epidemic? If fourteenth-century city officials were to consult these two texts, what public health measures might they have taken to combat the spread of the malady?Perspectives on the Black Death

A dying plague victim. In this illustration from a Czech codex (1376), Death, depicted here as a ghoulish demon, strangles a plague sufferer. Why might strangulation be an appropriate image if the victim were suffering from pneumonic plague?

two remaining Viking settlements there. To the east, it assaulted Germany, Scandinavia, and the eastern Baltic lands, reaching Moscow, though with declining virulence, in 1352.

Coping with the calamity. Fourteenth-century societies had no effective remedy for either the Black Death or the terrible epidemics that recurred every several years in different localities for another century or more. People suffered not only physical pain but also terror, helplessness, and despair. In both Europe and the Muslim Mediterranean lands, groups who lived in tight communities or administered to the sick endured particularly high mortality rates. Priests, nuns, religious scholars, university faculties, urban artisans, and soldiers living in barracks all proved highly vulnerable. Epidemics swept through armies in Germany and Italy. In southern Spain in 1349–1350, both Muslim and Christian troops battling for control of the city of Gibraltar lost large numbers to the contagion, the Black Death favoring neither side. The pestilence devastated not only crowded cities but also rural hamlets. Peasants who fled their homes to escape the scourge unwittingly passed it on to neighboring villages. A Muslim chronicler who witnessed scenes of flight in Egypt wrote of "those dead who are laid out on the highway like an ambush for others."[7]

No one understood the biology of contagion, nor was there much agreement about treatment. In both Europe and the Muslim world, learned observers blamed the high mortality on a polluted wind coming from the east, a foul corruption of the air, or a bad alignment of stars. Preventive and curative advice abounded: flee your home, do not flee your home, burn clothes, get fresh air, eat pickled onions, pray, and gather in houses of worship. Christians, Jews, and Muslims all struggled to give the catastrophe divine meaning. Christian doctrine invited the conclusion that the sins of humankind obliged God to teach his creation a lesson it would never forget. In Germany and other European countries, penance-doers, called **flagellants,** tried to expiate the sins of the world by parading through towns while beating themselves savagely with iron-studded leather thongs. Other terrified believers blamed the pandemic on Jews rumored to have "poisoned the wells." In Switzerland and Germany, **pogroms** wiped out Jewish communities in many towns. Thousands of Jews consequently fled eastward to Poland and Russia, where they established new communities that thrived in the following centuries. Despite great social trauma, Muslims interpreted the disaster mostly as a manifestation of the Creator's unknowable plan for his creation. Terror and despair abounded, but this particular catastrophe did not incite significant Muslim maltreatment of Christian or Jewish minorities.

> **flagellants** In Christian Europe in the thirteenth and fourteenth centuries, individuals who whipped, or flagellated, themselves as an act of public penance for sin.

> **pogrom** A violent attack on a minority community characterized by massacre and destruction of property; most commonly refers to assaults on Jews.

Wherever the pandemic hit hard, economic disruption immediately followed. In western Europe, Egypt, and Syria, peasant farmers died or fled their homes in such large numbers that crops rotted in the fields. In hundreds of cities, manufacturing industries temporarily ground to a halt as entire neighborhoods of skilled artisans perished. People who performed vital services—priests, doctors, teachers, lawyers, mule drivers, riverboat crews, even gravediggers—became scarce and expensive. On the brighter side, the plague completely skipped some parts of Europe and Southwest Asia altogether, though the reasons are not clear. We have no sound evidence that the pandemic spread to West Africa, South Asia, or Southeast Asia. We know that severe epidemics occurred in China in 1331, 1333, and 1353–1354, though they could have been outbreaks of diseases other than plague.

Crises in the Political and Social Realms

> **FOCUS** What evidence indicates that the fourteenth century was a period of unusual crises and instability in several parts of Afroeurasia?

A surge of political and social instability rocked large parts of Afroeurasia in the later fourteenth century. By comparison with the previous hundred years, when the great Mongol empires kept order over much of Eurasia, the century after 1350 looks troubled indeed. Several large states either shrank or collapsed, and in some regions warfare took a particularly vicious turn. We cannot conclude that famine or infectious disease were the primary causes of those upheavals because other known historical factors came into play. Nevertheless, the occurrence of a number of wars, rebellions, and regime changes corresponded with times of food shortage and pestilence, which disrupted the social order.

China: The Collapse of Mongol Rule

The Mongols first invaded China under the great conqueror Chingis Khan in 1211. By 1276 they dominated all of it (see Chapter 13). Kubilai Khan, the grandson of Chingis, founded the Yuan dynasty and ruled China to 1294. Under him and his first few successors, the empire remained unified and generally stable. By the 1320s, however, political factions within the imperial palace at Beijing (known then as Khanbaliq) descended into chronic factional infighting. The Mongol court paid less and less attention to firm administration of the provinces, and emperors lacking Kubilai's backbone became pawns of one power group or another. Togon Temur, the last Mongol emperor, reigned as little more than a figurehead for thirty-six years (1333–1368).

Below the turbulent surface of palace politics, deeper structural shifts helped undermine the Mongol state. The government had allowed military and administrative costs to swell, so that taxes ate up a burdensome portion of people's income. Worse than that, revenues dropped in the fourteenth century, partly because the population kept declining amid successive regional famines and epidemics. An extended cold snap in the second quarter of the century, almost certainly linked to the general global cooling trend, cut both food supplies and tax receipts in the northern provinces. Struggling to finance the regime, Mongol officials churned out more paper money, which accelerated price inflation and pushed down standards of living.

As chains of command broke down, discontented peasants, soldiers, and local warlords felt emboldened to protest poverty and government neglect. In 1351 an uprising flared among tens of thousands of abused and underpaid peasants whom the Mongol regime had drafted to rechannel a section of the Yellow River. Several more insurgencies broke out in the following years, especially in the south. Bandits, smugglers, peasant marauders, and fervent new religious sects all contributed to spreading turmoil. By the 1360s the beleaguered central government had to compete for authority with a dozen or so local rebel groups. Zhu Yuanzhang (JOO yuwen-JAHNG), the leader of one of these insurgent bands, built up a power base in the Yangzi River valley and then sent his army against Beijing. In 1368 he forced the emperor and his entourage to flee to Mongolia. Once in control of the capital, Zhu Yuanzhang moved vigorously to restore China's unity, this time under Chinese, not foreign, leadership. Suppressing all competing rebel movements, he proclaimed the new Ming dynasty. We return to it later in this chapter.

Political and Economic Troubles in the Central Muslim Lands

The Mongol khanate of Iran-Iraq crumbled in 1335, twelve years before the Black Death even appeared in Southwest Asia. This realm was not economically healthy. Farming in the Tigris-Euphrates valley had been shrinking gradually for several centuries. The Mongol conquest in the previous century did more damage to the economic infrastructure there, as well

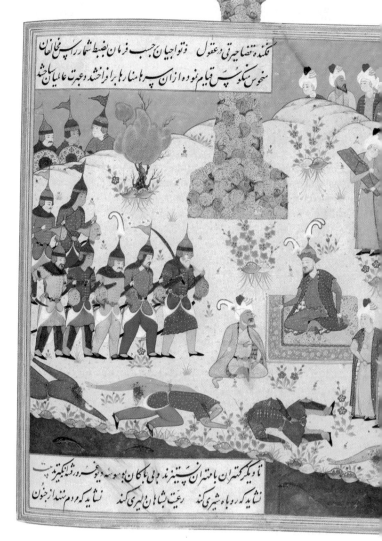

Harvest of Victory. Timur, seated on a throne, receives soldiers carrying severed heads. Decapitated enemies lie sprawling in the foreground. The painting comes from a fifteenth century Persian history of the Timurid dynasty. What do you think the structure in the upper center of the picture represents?

as to Iran's irrigated agricultural lands. A few of the khanate's rulers experimented with reforms to improve farm production but made only modest headway. The regime fell, not amid popular revolt as in China, but as a consequence of internal feuding among Mongol and Turkic princes for supreme command. The regime's collapse left the region splintered into several, relatively weak military states.

The Mamluk sultanate of Egypt and Syria, a Turkic state that had defended itself successfully against Mongol assaults, remained intact. But the population plunged in the aftermath of the Black Death and recurring epidemics. As the skilled workforce dwindled, manufacturing became depressed. To take the example of Egypt's once-thriving textile industry, the city of Alexandria had 12,000–14,000 skilled cotton and linen weavers in 1394, but only 800 by 1434.[8] The rural peasant economy suffered as well. Reduced urban populations cut demand for grain; therefore, prices fell. To compensate for their income losses, Turkic and Arab estate lords tightened the screws on peasants, demanding higher rents and taxes. Thus, millions of men and women who farmed the Nile valley and the Syrian plains fell into deeper poverty in the later fourteenth century. On the other hand, the scarcity of labor in the aftermath of the pandemic meant that urban workers who managed to survive, especially those with skills, could command higher wages, at least for a time.

As if the peoples of Southwest Asia did not suffer enough from disease and economic troubles, they also had to endure another episode of massacres and city burnings, a dismal sequel to the Mongol invasions of the previous century.

This time the perpetrator was Timur, also known later in European history as Timur the Lame, or Tamerlane. Born in Central Asia, the young Timur began his career as a local Turkic war captain. Like his role model, Chingis Khan, he bested opposing tribal lords and amassed a large following of mounted archers. He began his ascent to power in Central Asia in the 1360s. His core state embraced vast grazing lands and the fertile valley of the Amu Darya (Amu River), plus Samarkand, Bukhara, and several other silk roads cities. Taxation of these resources paid for his expanding army, and, like Chingis, he ensured the allegiance of fractious warrior clans by continually leading them on huge plundering expeditions. From 1370 to 1405 he kept on the move, incorporating fighters of many origins into his forces as they advanced. Sacking one city after another, he outdid the Mongols in cruelty, raping and enslaving women by the tens of thousands and burying prisoners alive or starving them to death.

Timur led his forces north, east, and west (see Map 15.2). In the early 1390s he advanced north of the Caspian Sea to assault the Mongol khanate of the Golden Horde, destroying several cities in the Volga River valley and seriously weakening Mongol domination of Russia. In 1399 his cavalry rode from Afghanistan to the Indus River valley, where the invaders wrecked the great city of Delhi and permanently crippled the Delhi sultanate, which had once ruled all of northern India. In 1400–1401 he took Damascus, the Mamluk capital in Syria, but then withdrew. Apparently convinced that all great steppe lords should conquer China, he set off in that direction in 1405. But he died just when the expedition was getting under way.

MAP 15.2 The empire of Timur in 1404.
When Timur died in 1405, he was planning to lead an army against China. From a geographical and political perspective, how difficult a task might that have been?

Timur had a genealogy worked up to show, without compelling evidence, that he descended from Chingis Khan and was therefore the right man to fulfill the Mongol ambition to rule the whole world. Though we know little of his thoughts on religion, he professed Islam and appears to have regarded himself as a special agent of God destined to punish both unbelievers and apathetic Muslims. He twice laid waste to the Christian kingdom of Georgia in the Caucasus Mountains and nearly extinguished the Nestorian Christian communities of Inner Eurasia. Muslims who displeased him for one reason or another got no better treatment.

Timur did not, however, match Chingis in the art of empire building. He did little to set up a firm chain of command or administration in conquered cities. He sent thousands of captured artisans and engineers to Samarkand to create a magnificent capital, but he rarely went there himself. He encouraged caravan traffic and thereby won the support of merchants, but his devastating campaigns hampered agriculture and trade. When he died suddenly, power struggles immediately erupted among his four sons and various tribal warlords. The empire soon fell apart, though the most vigorous of his descendants held Central Asia and part of Afghanistan together as a regional state. Timur deserves recognition as the last of the great Inner Eurasian steppe conquerors, but his predations only aggravated Southwest Asia's long-term economic problems.

Europe in the Aftermath of the Black Death

Like the Muslim Mediterranean, western Europe continued to lose population for about a century after 1350. In turn, labor shortages in nearly every occupation slowed economic recovery. As in Egypt and Syria, the demographic plunge reduced the market for grain and simultaneously raised the cost of labor. Land became cheap as people abandoned farms and villages or fell to the pestilence. Like the Mamluk military elite, European aristocrats who owned great manors had a harder time keeping up farm production and generating new wealth.

Population decline and the end of serfdom in western Europe. Peasants lucky enough to escape lethal contagion found that the population fall-off increased the value of their labor, giving them a measure of leverage over their landlords. Especially in northwestern Europe, farmers had some success negotiating with estate owners to lower rents, eliminate customary payments, and ease restrictions on their mobility. In other words, men and women whose labor enjoyed strong demand might bargain their way out of serfdom, the condition of legal bondage that forced them to live and work on a particular estate. Many thousands of serfs simply abandoned their lords and fled to towns, which needed their labor as well. Aristocrats desperate to preserve

their agricultural incomes retaliated by joining with royal governments, notably in France and England, to fight the rising cost of labor and the deterioration of serfdom. These regimes legislated ceilings on wages, imposed new rural taxes, and insisted that peasants meet their manorial obligations, though to little long-term avail.

In some places farmers and landless workers who thought the increased value of their labor deserved more just compensation took up knives and pitchforks in revolt. Rural rebellions flared from England to Hungary in the later fourteenth century. Indeed, these movements paralleled the uprisings that broke out in China in the 1350s and 1360s in similarly unsettled economic conditions. The Jacquerie rebellion in northern France in 1358 and the Peasants' Revolt in England in 1381 were among the most violent insurgencies. Describing the Jacquerie, a disapproving chronicler lamented that "these mischievous people thus assembled without captain or armor, robbed, burnt, and slew all gentlemen that they could lay hands on, and forced and ravished ladies and damosels, and did such shameful deeds that no human creature ought to think on any such."[9] Commanding far better fighters and weapons than the rebels did, landowning elites soon snuffed out these insurgencies. In contrast to what happened in China, none of the rebel groups came close to removing a dynasty.

Nevertheless, serfdom virtually disappeared in western Europe in the fifteenth century. Landowners discovered economic sense in paying wages to workers, collecting money rents from them, or selling them land outright, rather than trying to force labor from aggrieved serfs. Peasants became "free" in the sense that they could legally move from one place to another and to sell their labor for cash. In some Mediterranean cities, however, slaves imported from eastern Europe or Africa continued to perform domestic labor.

Long wars. Warfare among Europe's several competing states may have been no more ferocious in the fourteenth century than in earlier times. But the leveling off of economic growth, followed by famine, disease, and mass die-off, intensified political stresses and raised the stakes for control of resources. The prolonged conflict between England and France known as the Hundred Years' War (1337–1453) merely extended three centuries of hostility between the two monarchies over territories that are today part of France but were then under English rule. At first, English cavalry, as well as infantry troops armed with longbows, won most of the battles, but in the end England had to cede nearly all its continental territory to France, which emerged in the later fifteenth century as western Europe's most powerful state.

The war was marked by episodes of terrible violence alternating with extended lulls, sometimes made necessary by wet summers or epidemics. Fought mostly in France, the conflict involved long urban sieges, scorched earth tactics that destroyed cropland, and deployment on both sides of great bands of hired mercenaries, who sometimes

Ibn Khaldun: A Thinker for Troubled Times

Many scholars from China to Europe wrote narrative descriptions of the tumultuous events of the later fourteenth century. Abd al-Rahman ibn Khaldun (1332–1404) went much further, creating an elegant political theory to explain those wrenching changes. Born of a long line of Muslim scholars who made their mark in both Spain and Tunisia, Ibn Khaldun wrote on subjects as diverse as philosophy, theology, history, law, ethnology, and mathematics.

In his most celebrated work, titled *The Muqaddima* (Introduction to History), Ibn Khaldun theorized that change in human political affairs is not haphazard but follows a pattern of cycles. New dynasties arise when an energetic leader organizes a band of warriors into a sturdy, cohesive military force, which then seizes power. This conquering elite founds a state, but it soon starts to deteriorate because its members become caught up in urban luxury, political squabbling, and selfish oppression of their subject population. Eventually, the dynasty collapses under pressure from a new band of hardy warriors, and a fresh cycle begins. In formulating this theory of change, Ibn Khaldun contended that history has an identifiable shape to it and that finding the underlying pattern depends on close scrutiny of human events. Because he built his theory on concrete observation and research, not simply philosophical conjecture, he foreshadowed the methods of the modern social sciences.

Ibn Khaldun saw enough political and economic instability in the later fourteenth century to hypothesize that Muslim civilization was in jeopardy. In his view the Black Death, which struck his native city of Tunis in 1348, hastened the process of decay, overtaking "the dynasties at the time of their senility." Only a teenager at the time, he lost both of his parents to the pestilence. This personal tragedy, however, drove him to try to explain rationally why social calamities recur.

His learned family provided him with a strong education, and after his parents died he entered a career of public service. Ambitious, a bit snobbish, and sometimes politically meddlesome, he moved in and out of princely favor, holding government posts under several rulers in Tunisia, Morocco, Algeria, and Granada and even going to jail in Morocco for two years for taking part in a court conspiracy. In 1382 he traveled to Egypt, where he accepted posts as judge and law professor in the Mamluk sultanate. His wife and daughters sailed from Tunis to join him in Cairo, but they all died in a shipwreck. He gave brilliant lectures in Cairo's colleges, but he also made enemies. He got fired from every prestigious position he held.

In 1400, after making a pilgrimage to Mecca, Ibn Khaldun traveled to Damascus in Syria in the entourage of the Mamluk sultan. Later, he helped negotiate the city's surrender to Timur. He even got an interview with the conqueror and seems to have regarded Timur as the leader who might restore political unity to the Muslim world. Ibn Khaldun later returned to Cairo, where he continued his academic and legal career until his death in 1406.

Ibn Khaldun is represented as a member of the scholarly class in this modern statue on display in his native city of Tunis.

Ibn Khaldun typified the cosmopolitan spirit among educated Muslims, traveling widely to seek knowledge, serving numerous rulers without giving any of them permanent allegiance, and finding time to observe and write about the human condition. Modern scholars stand in wonder at his immense project to synthesize human history and to discover meaning in the directions it takes.

Thinking Critically

How would you argue that Ibn Khaldun's life and thought might help us better understand the era in which he lived?

---

abandoned the fighting to terrorize country peasants. In short, the brutality of the struggle only aggravated the economic problems that came in the wake of the Black Death.

The Church divided. In the fourteenth century the political authority and moral prestige of the Catholic Church plummeted along with Europe's population. The church had developed into a highly centralized and wealthy organization with its own law courts, diplomatic service, businesses, and vast properties. However, the people who managed these enterprises were generally more interested in worldly affairs than in spiritual ministry. In the political sphere, the pope directly ruled a large part of central Italy from his seat in Rome. But he also continued to press his claim, as divinely appointed shepherd of western Christendom, to supreme authority over all monarchs and princes. In fact, as powerful centralized states arose in western Europe, this assertion no longer had much force. The kings of France and England had particularly strong convictions about their independent authority to tax members of the Christian clergy, require their political allegiance, and prosecute them in royal courts of law, all practices that the pope tried to oppose.

In the fourteenth century the old ideal of Europe as a moral empire under the guiding hand of a benevolent pope perished once and for all. In 1309 the French king Philip IV pressured a newly chosen pope to move his throne from Rome, where it had always been, to Avignon in southern France. There, Philip's officials could make sure that the Holy Father led the church in ways favorable to the French crown. Palace extravagance and financial corruption thrived in Avignon, a state of affairs that appalled ordinary Christians. Moreover, thousands of nuns, monks, and priests died in the Black Death, including many of the best-educated clerics. This led to a chronic shortage of spiritual caregivers, local church leaders, and teachers. In 1378 the church hierarchy fell into near chaos when two popes, one in Avignon and one in Rome, competed for legitimacy. At one point, three men claimed the papal throne. The schism ended finally in 1417 with some church theologians and legal experts leading a reform effort, known as the Conciliar Movement, to transfer supreme church authority from the person of the pope to councils of high clergy. Since the majority of Catholics preferred a strong and morally righteous pope to fractious gatherings of clerics, the movement faded. Nevertheless, the church's prestige continued to suffer, encouraging a new generation of moral critics and reformers to come forward.

Peasants killing nobles. This miniature illustration from the *Chronicles of France* depicts the outbreak of the Jacquerie uprising in France in 1358. Peasants with daggers and swords are making short work of four unarmed aristocrats. Do you think the artist reveals a particular political bias? In favor of which side?

Fifteenth-Century Recuperation

FOCUS What factors may account for a trend of demographic and economic recovery in several parts of Afroeurasia in the fifteenth century?

The population crisis that affected so much of Afroeurasia in the fourteenth century proved to be a short-lived cyclical phenomenon, just as the downturn of the fourth to sixth centuries c.e. had been. By 1500 the supercontinent's overall population reached about 416 million—about 8 million more than the 1340 level. Long-distance trade almost certainly slowed on both land and sea routes in the immediate aftermath of the Black Death. But demand for luxury goods and exotic imports swelled among city dwellers who survived the pandemic and therefore commanded higher incomes. Ironically, cities made smaller by epidemic, famine, and war frequently entered the fifteenth century more important than ever as storehouses of wealth, knowledge, and skill. Several cities emerged as vibrant capitals of new states and dynasties, and in some regions those centers blazed with artistic and literary light.

Technologies for the Future

Both the sources of useful energy—human muscle, animal traction, wind, and water—and the technologies for moving people and goods from place to place remained largely unchanged in most of Afroeurasia between 1300 and 1500. To be sure, entrepreneurs and technicians across Afroeurasia continued to refine mechanical devices and undertake great building projects. In China, for example, engineers expanded the already immense inland waterway system, and shipwrights built ever-larger oceangoing vessels. In Europe, labor shortages and declining land values prompted estate lords and urban manufacturers to improve the technologies of textile production, mining, and wind and water mills. Medical scholars did not learn much about infectious diseases from the Black Death, but European and Muslim physicians gained a little more understanding of the mechanisms of contagion. Two technical advances that spread widely in the fifteenth century were gunpowder weaponry and printing.

Guns. Back in the thirteenth century, Mongol conquerors adopted Chinese techniques for making bombs, rockets, and incendiary weapons by mixing salt peter (potassium nitrate), sulfur, and charcoal to make gunpowder. Mongol and Mamluk armies used explosive devices in the late thirteenth century. About the same time, the gun made its world debut. In elemental form a gun is simply a tube of durable material. A charge of gunpowder is inserted into the tube's base and then ignited to propel a missile out the front end, presumably with destructive, or at least loud, effect. The earliest physical evidence of gun making is a bronze tube that archeologists found in Manchuria (northeastern China) at the site of a 1288 battle. No doubt, military commanders regarded the earliest firearms merely as new-fangled devices to supplement other types of machines for hurling objects against enemy soldiers or fortifications.

Gunpowder and recipes for making it almost certainly became known in Europe as a result of diffusion westward across Inner Eurasia during the Mongol era. By the 1320s, European soldiers were using gunpowder to propel arrows or stones from pot-shaped metal tubes, though with little force or accuracy. In the following decades, artisans in the employ of princes or towns experimented widely with barrel castings, firing mechanisms, and gunpowder blends. By the end of the century, rulers began using firearms on the battlefield. Some European monarchs had sufficient wealth to cast and deploy rudimentary cannons, which launched stone or iron balls against castle or city walls. In the late phase of the Hundred Years' War, French kings organized Europe's first artillery corps to transport and maintain guns. They used these weapons to help blow the English out of

Early artillery. Near the end of the Hundred Years' War, a French army dislodged the English from the fortress of Cherbourg on the northern coast of France. This fifteenth-century illustration documents French deployment of cannons that fired stone balls. The horse in the foreground is wearing a caparison, or fabric covering, decorated with fleurs-de-lis (lily flowers), a symbol of the French monarchy. How effective do you think artillery of this type might have been in siege warfare compared to the longbows that both sides used?

their remaining continental strongholds. In the same period, rulers in China, India, Southwest Asia, and North Africa all fielded increasing numbers of cannons and handguns. Until the sixteenth century, these weapons had limited military value. Mounted archers with composite bows, as well as infantry carrying crossbows or longbows, could load and fire their weapons much faster than could either hand gunners or artillery crews. Nevertheless, world history's age of gunpowder was well under way by 1450.

Printing. Books printed on paper circulated widely in China during the Song and Yuan (Mongol) dynasties (eleventh to fourteenth centuries) and contributed much to the spread of knowledge across East Asia. The idea of printing words or pictures by pressing sheets of paper onto carved wooden blocks brushed with ink reached Southwest Asia in the later thirteenth century. There, the government of the Mongol khanate of Iran-Iraq tried, and failed, to introduce the Chinese idea of printed paper money. Local merchants wanted no part of it. Neither in India nor in the central Muslim lands did printing for any purpose take hold in the fourteenth or fifteenth century. We should be careful, however, not to equate printing with the hand production of books on paper. In the Muslim world, for example, rulers, religious institutions, colleges, and wealthy families possessed libraries that might contain thousands of hand-copied books, mainly in Arabic or Persian.

Libraries in fifteenth-century Europe were far smaller than in the Muslim lands or China, but Europeans warmed quickly to the idea of printing. By the 1200s, western Europe had a thriving papermaking industry, another technology that originated in China and spread to Europe by way of the Muslim Mediterranean. Italian artisans knew something about block printing images, such as stamping illustrations on playing cards. But the idea of mechanically reproducing books probably reached Europe directly from China, perhaps when Christian travelers returned from Mongol lands carrying Chinese volumes in their packs.

movable type printing A technology in which characters, especially alphabetic letters and punctuation, are individually carved or cast on pieces of wood, ceramic, or metal and then assembled into a text, inked, and printed on paper or other material.

European artisans used block printing for many purposes, but in the fifteenth century they also adopted the technology of **movable type.** Metalsmiths fashioned individual characters; printers arranged them as needed in a frame, inked the frame, and printed a sheet on a press. These individual pieces of type could be used over and over. Chinese printers had invented movable type made of wood or ceramic in the eleventh century, and as early as the thirteenth century Korean artisans discovered the superior durability of metal type produced in molds. In East Asia, however, this technology proved less efficient than block printing because the particular Chinese writing system, which is logographic, not alphabetic, required production of thousands of distinct characters rather than multiple copies of the thirty or fewer signs that make up an alphabet. Nevertheless, East Asia's book industry using block technology continued to expand.

In Europe in the 1440s a team of German craftsmen led by the goldsmith Johannes Gutenberg invented movable metal type for the Latin alphabet, almost certainly independently of the Korean invention a century or more earlier. Gutenberg printed a Latin Bible in 1455 and from that date printing presses multiplied across Europe. Scribes who hunched over desks to copy books could not come close to matching the speed with which a movable type press could produce multiple copies of an absolutely uniform text. In the 1460s, printing presses opened in several cities in Italy, which already led Europe in papermaking technology. In the following decade, printers began to ply their trade in France, the Netherlands, Hungary, Poland, England, and Spain.

A screw press in Hungary. This press, shown here in a woodcut, operated for a short time in the city of Buda (modern Budapest). The man in front on the left is turning the screw to lower the flat surface of the metal platen to press a sheet of paper firmly against a set of inked type. The man in back on the left is holding inking pads. What do you think the worker on the right might be doing?

Ming China: New Prosperity and a Maritime Thrust

After the rebel leader Zhu Yuanzhang expelled the Mongols in 1368, he founded the Ming dynasty (Dynasty of Light), a thoroughly Chinese regime. Ruling for thirty-one years (1368–1398) under the imperial name Taizu, he ordered a torrent of reforms to transform China into a more centralized and efficient monarchy than the Mongols had ever imagined. Under Taizu and his early successors, China's huge economy maintained steady growth. After nearly two centuries of decline, the population recovered as well, rising from about 85 million in 1393 to about 155 million by 1500. By the mid-seventeenth century, when the Ming era ended, about one-third of the world's people lived in China.[10]

The style of early Ming government.
As the son of a poor farmer, in fact the first Chinese ruler to come from such humble origins, the emperor Taizu extolled the toiling peasant as the pillar of China's agricultural economy. He aimed to model his imperial government not on the Song dynasties (960–1276), which had given loose rein to business enterprise and technical innovation, but on the more agrarian-oriented Tang empire of the seventh and eighth centuries. He even discouraged the use of paper money, which went largely out of circulation by the mid-fifteenth century. In contrast to what some European kings did in the aftermath of the Black Death, Taizu lowered taxes on ordinary farmers and raised them on the rich. Early in his reign he decreed a comprehensive census of people, occupations, and landholdings to systematize revenue collection. To encourage social stability he prescribed laws that impeded rural people from changing occupations or migrating from village to city—again, contrary to the trend in western Europe. He also encouraged conformity to standards of Neo-Confucian morality, including restrictions on women's social and legal liberties.

Because he improved the state bureaucracy's efficiency and raised living conditions for millions of peasants, Taizu enjoyed broad popular support. Distrusting the landed aristocratic families that had traditionally dominated government offices, he reformed the Neo-Confucian school and examination system to allow talented young men from a wider range of social backgrounds to take up government careers. Also a master of political fear tactics, he created an elaborate apparatus of spies and secret police, and he periodically purged officials who he thought had failed him in one way or another.

The Ming government's policies, which favored a state-regulated, stable agrarian society, ran counter to the interests of private entrepreneurs and merchants, who yearned to pick up where the Song dynasty had left off. Yet despite the state's close supervision of commerce, China became more economically and geographically integrated than ever before. It already had the world's most complex canal and road system, but the Ming extended the Grand Canal so that it ran about a thousand miles from the Yangzi River to Beijing, which after Taizu's death became the imperial capital. The waterway had forty-seven locks, fifteen of them to move barges through hill country. Because Beijing could receive 400 million pounds of grain a year by canal, its population soared in the fifteenth century to over two million.

The Ming and its neighbors.
Like the Mongols before them, Taizu and his fifteenth-century successors insisted on government supervision of external trade. Commercial exchange with foreign states had to conform to a protocol that imagined neighboring rulers not as trading partners but as payers of tribute in the form of material goods. In turn, the sublime emperor offered these presumably dependent princes comparable "gifts." China's neighbors often played this ritual game on Ming terms in the interests of profitable commerce. And although the Ming outlawed private overseas trade, Chinese merchants routinely defied this prohibition.

The Ming never tried to conquer deep into Inner Eurasia, as the Tang dynasty had done seven centuries earlier. Even so, early emperors pursued a forceful foreign policy. In Korea the monarchs of the Choson dynasty (1392–1910) accepted a formal tributary relationship with China, while in fact governing independently. They also energetically advanced Chinese Neo-Confucian teachings. Sejong (SAY-johng, reigned 1418–1450), the strongest Korean king of the fifteenth century, patronized Neo-Confucian culture and also inspired the invention of Hangul. This remarkable Korean alphabet used a system of phonetic signs that complemented Chinese logographic writing. In relations with Japan, which was then politically fragmented, the early Ming emperors encouraged diplomatic and cultural exchanges. These initiatives did not last, but private sea trade between the islands and the mainland continued to flourish.

In the subtropical hill country of the far southwest, today Guizhou and Yunnan provinces, landless peasants and discharged soldiers opened a new frontier of Chinese settlement. These lands were by no means empty, however, and non-Chinese ethnic peoples put up stiff though finally unsuccessful resistance. In the longer term, Chinese immigrants and local peoples interacted in complex ways, including marriage. This gave the region a distinct cultural flavor. Further south, a Chinese army invaded the Vietnamese kingdom of Annam in 1407 and occupied it for two decades. Annam's ruling class had already embraced Chinese Confucianism, but it tenaciously fought the intruders. Finally deciding to cut its losses, the Chinese force withdrew in 1427, leaving little to show for the adventure. Similarly to Korea, however, Annam pragmatically accepted the formal role of Chinese tributary by sending annual "gifts" to Beijing.

The Ming government kept a close eye on the northwestern frontiers facing Inner Eurasia, putting three million soldiers under arms to defend the imperial borders. Though the Mongols had retreated to their homeland, they could still command tens of thousands of mounted archers. At

The Great Wall of China. This section of the restored wall near Beijing crosses extremely rugged country. Why do you think historians have characterized the wall as a physical barrier rather than as a series of frontier fortifications?

first, the Ming combined diplomacy and gift giving with military thrusts into pastoral nomad territory. This forward strategy, however, did not go well, and in 1449 Mongol cavalry defeated a huge Chinese army and even captured the reigning emperor. After that humiliation, the state pulled the military frontier further back. It also spent huge sums to extend and connect frontier defensive fortifications, creating most of the 1,500-mile-long Great Wall. Masons reinforced long sections of the barrier to an average height and width of twenty-five feet, and they built guard towers at close intervals to permit soldiers to send signals along the wall at great speed. The project was a stupendous engineering feat, though the northwestern frontier remained turbulent into the next century, causing Ming bureaucrats no end of worry and debate.

The Ming maritime voyages. The Yongle (YAWNG-leh) emperor (r. 1403–1424), Taizu's son and successor, shared his father's grand vision of China as the world's Middle Kingdom surrounded by satellite states. Not only did Yongle attack Mongolia and Vietnam, but he also sought to gather rulers far west of China into the tributary net. In 1405 he placed Zheng He (JUNG-huh), a talented naval officer, in charge of a new seaborne mission to make a show of Ming imperial power and glory in the Indian Ocean (see Map 15.3).

Zheng He was an interesting choice for this project. His life reflected a creative, yet sometimes violent mix of cultural influences. He came from a Muslim family, and his

father had made the four-thousand-mile holy pilgrimage to Mecca. Given the name Ma He at birth, he grew up in Yunnan in the southwest, where Ming forces expelled the Mongols when he was about ten years old. Chinese soldiers seized him and other local boys and made him a eunuch to serve in the army as an orderly. The lad, however, distinguished himself as a warrior. He made influential friends in the imperial court and became a trusted member of the corps of eunuchs, which did duty in the palace as bodyguards and administrators, as they had for many centuries. Yongle gave him the new name of Zheng, the name of a battlefield where the young eunuch distinguished himself.

At the emperor's request, Zheng He assembled a massive fleet of 287 junks—62 enormous "treasure ships" and 225 smaller ones. They carried a total crew of about 27,000. The largest vessel may have been more than twice the length of the Santa Maria, the little flagship that Christopher Columbus sailed to America almost a century later.[11] Between 1405 and 1433, Admiral Zheng He commanded seven major expeditions westward, leading his ships into the Indian Ocean and ultimately to the Persian Gulf, the Red Sea, and the East African coast. Many of the common sailors on these ships were recruited from the criminal classes, but the fleets also carried soldiers, doctors, herbalists, astrologers, diplomatic protocol experts, and Arabic and Persian translators.

Zheng He and the ship captains serving under him navigated with compasses, star charts, and coastline maps, as well as ready advice from local Muslim mariners who knew

MAP 15.3 The Zheng He expeditions, 1405–1433.
In the fifteenth century, sailors of many Asian and African lands sailed the routes that Zheng He navigated. How would Zheng He and his crews have taken advantage of their knowledge of seasonal monsoon winds in making these long-distance voyages?

the Indian Ocean intimately. He would also have been able to draw on a store of Chinese knowledge. Since the eleventh century or earlier, private traders had been sailing junks from Chinese ports to the coasts of India and possibly farther, accumulating from these journeys a rich fund of navigational and geographic information. About sixty-five years before Zheng He's first expedition, Ibn Battuta, the Moroccan traveler, saw thirteen large Chinese vessels in the port of Calicut on the southwestern Indian coast, ships of four decks, he reports, outfitted with "cabins, suites, and salons for merchants," as well as in-room latrines.[12]

Zheng He's fleet did a good deal of ordinary trading during the expeditions, but their larger mission was to magnify the influence and splendor of the Yongle emperor. The admiral returned from his second voyage with envoys from thirty South and Southeast Asian kingdoms to pay homage to the emperor. On several occasions, violent encounters took place between Chinese visitors and local populations. But Zheng He seized no ports nor founded any imperial colonies.

Not all factions in the royal court supported Yongle's initiative, and when he died in 1424, the chorus of opposition grew louder. Many of the government's scholar-bureaucrats despised palace eunuchs like Zheng He as political opportunists

Zheng He's treasure fleet sets sail. This modern bronze relief depicts the size of the admiral's ships relative to other vessels and to buildings on land. Why might Ming emperors have funded the construction of such enormous vessels? What does their size suggest about the state of Chinese shipbuilding technology in the fifteenth century?

with too much power. These officials reasoned that they might undermine eunuch influence by scuttling any more voyages. Imperial accountants fretted that the expeditions cost far too much and that public money would be better spent on northwestern frontier defenses and internal economic projects. Another factor may have been long-term deforestation in southern China, which made the cost of building more oceangoing ships prohibitive. Yongle's successor permitted a final expedition in 1433, but Zheng He died that same year, perhaps on shipboard. Thereafter, the government dismantled the yards that built the big ships, which eventually rotted away in dry dock. Ming officialdom took no further interest in long sea voyages. As East Asia's population and economy grew, however, Chinese merchants continued to traffic in the China seas at least as far west as the Strait of Malacca.

South Asia: A Steadier Course of Change

Though the international ports of South Asia remained busy throughout the fourteenth and fifteenth centuries, the region appears to have experienced a significant population decline. Evidence is lacking for a massive pandemic in India in the years of the Black Death. It is more likely that people died in larger numbers as a consequence of regional famines or epidemics having no connection to the disease that ravaged Southwest Asia or Europe.

Like Europe, India was a region of many states of varying sizes that competed for territory and resources. In the fourteenth century the Muslim Turkic military lords who ruled the North Indian sultanate of Delhi made a bid to unify the entire subcontinent. Expansion sputtered, however, and after Timur's army pillaged Delhi in 1399, the sultanate carried on as merely one of several monarchies sharing northern and central India. Islam, however, became the dominant faith in both the upper Indus valley and the Ganges watershed, as the sultans encouraged Muslim farmers to move in to clear land and build towns. The Muslim population of Bengal, the region of the Ganges delta, grew steadily, laying the religious foundation of the modern state of Bangladesh. Sufi Muslim clerics and preachers fanned out across central India, converting Hindu villagers in some places.

By contrast, the southern part of the subcontinent became more politically consolidated and remained largely Hindu. In the 1340s a victorious warrior band founded the Vijayanagar (vizh-ah-na-ya-GAR-ah) monarchy in semiarid south central India. In the ensuing decades, this upstart Hindu kingdom conquered or put under tribute several other southern states, recruiting Muslim mercenaries from the north and deploying gunpowder artillery against enemy strongholds. Revenues subsequently poured into Vijayanagar city from both the lush rice-growing valleys of the southeast and the great trade entrepôts along the southern coasts. Gold and silver coins circulated widely, market

Royal elephant stables. Fifteenth-century monarchs of Vijayanagar housed war elephants in the large arched rooms in this grand structure. The open space in front of the stables probably served as a parade ground. Why do you think a ruler would construct such an elaborate and expensive building to keep his elephants?

towns multiplied, and the farming population appears to have enjoyed prosperity.

The Hindu elite also spent great sums building magnificent temples in the capital and other cities. These buildings ingeniously combined southern Indian techniques and styles with architectural elements, including domes and arches, imported from northern India and, more broadly, from Iran. The empire remained quite loosely organized, however, held together on the strength of alliances with local potentates and frequent campaigns against rebels. Nevertheless, Vijayanagar continued to dominate southern India until the mid-1500s.

Astronomy and Empire Building in the Central Muslim Lands

Shortly after his death in 1405, the conqueror Timur's huge but fragile empire broke apart, leaving Central and Southwest Asia in the hands of several competing princes and military lords, as it had been before his rise. Political divisions and economic doldrums persisted across Southwest Asia. Against this background, however, two dynamic developments stand out, one of them artistic and intellectual, the other political.

The Timurids. In the core region of Timur's empire, his offspring managed to preserve a much smaller but nevertheless prosperous state for about a century after 1405. The main urban poles of the Timurid sultanate, as this dynasty was called, were Samarkand in what is now Uzbekistan and Herat in western Afghanistan. Through much of the fifteenth century, these two cities functioned as capitals of largely self-governing northern and southern sections of the kingdom. In both places Timurid princes erected splendid palaces using tax revenues from irrigated farming and trade. In contrast to Timur, most of these rulers cared more about knowledge and literature than military glory, and their capitals attracted scholars from throughout the Muslim world.

In the first half of the fifteenth century, Ulugh Beg (r. 1447–1449) oversaw the transformation of Samarkand into a center of art and intellect. Timur had started to beautify Samarkand with mosques and palaces, and Ulugh Beg added a grand college of advanced learning (madrasa), whose walls inside and out sparkled with the reflected light of millions of multicolored tiles. This institution expanded the traditional Muslim college curriculum from law and the religious sciences to mathematics, astronomy, history, and several other subjects. Ulugh Beg sponsored scientific research and built an imposing observatory. Indeed, Timurid scholars made important advances in algebra, trigonometry, and astronomy. Most

notably, they produced a comprehensive star catalog in the form of astronomical tables, the most advanced gazetteer of the heavens produced anywhere in the world to that point. In the following centuries, scientists in Europe used the catalog as a key research tool.

In the second half of the fifteenth century, Herat took over as the leading cosmopolitan center. Combining Persian with Chinese elements of art and design, Herat's intellectual elite excelled in painting and calligraphy, especially the art of the illustrated book. In both Herat and Samarkand, poets and prose writers composed in Persian and Arabic, as well as Chagatai, a Turkic language. The reputations of Jami and Navai, fifteenth-century Herat's most famous poets, remain very much alive today. Early in the sixteenth century, political troubles and a shift of wealth and power to other capitals sent Samarkand and Herat into cultural eclipse, though they remained important emporia on the trade routes between Southwest Asia and India.

The Ottoman Turkish state. In 1300, Anatolia (modern Turkey) was among the most politically fragmented regions of Southwest Asia. The Mongols based in Iran and Iraq ruled the eastern half of Anatolia with declining competence. Several Turkic principalities shared western Anatolia, and the Christian Byzantine monarchy clung to a chip of territory across the Bosporus from Constantinople, the Greek capital. During the fourteenth century, however, this landscape changed radically. The House of Osman, a line of Muslim warrior sultans later known as the Ottoman dynasty, rose to dominate not only much of Anatolia but also Europe's Balkan Peninsula. The transformation of Anatolia from a Greek-speaking Christian land to a Turkish-speaking

The Observatory in Samarkand. Like many of the other buildings constructed during the rule of Ulugh Beg, the observatory was beautiful as well as functional. The building is now in ruins, but this nineteenth-century watercolor offers a representation of how it might have looked to the leading astronomers of the fifteenth century. Why might this building have been important in the eyes of a European artist four centuries later?

Muslim land, a process that had started with Turkic migrations in the eleventh century (see Chapter 12), accelerated along with the Ottoman expansion.

The Turkish warlord Osman (r. 1281–1324) founded the new state, but his successors Orkhan (r. 1324–1360) and Murad I (r. 1360–1389) made it a regional power by defeating rival sultanates in Anatolia and sending cavalry across the Dardanelles, first to raid, then to occupy Christian territory deep in the Balkans. As Ottoman forces amassed booty and slaves, more warriors joined in, including many from conquered states. As in the case of the early Mongol empire, every military success bred more of the same. By the end of the century, the empire had absorbed Christian Bulgaria and reduced the kingdom of Serbia to dependency. Writing in the later fifteenth century, the Greek chronicler Kritovoulos described the Ottoman advance in Europe: "Thus they came down into the plain, and there nothing was any obstacle to them any more. They occupied the level country, sacked the villages, and captured the cities, overthrew castles, defeated armies, and subdued many peoples."[13]

Boisterous and loosely organized, the young empire kept growing, though more as a result of the sultans' skills negotiating with local chiefs than owing to any well-organized central administration. The Turkic warrior tradition of *ghaza,* a code of military honor having to do with the accumulation and division of plunder, imposed some order on the wars of conquest. Moreover, Greek Christian aristocrats and their mounted knights joined the Ottoman offensive in significant numbers. Turkic warriors, or *ghazis,* coalesced around personal loyalty to the ruler, who promised land and loot. However, *ghazi* frontier fighters tended also to be unruly and opportunistic, too undisciplined for single-minded empire building.

In the late fourteenth century, Murad I addressed this problem by creating a professional standing army. To do this, he adopted a system of drafting healthy boys from Christian families in the Balkans every three to seven years as the need arose. These recruits, called **janissaries,** had the legal status of slaves of the sultan. As sons of Christian peasants, conscripts had, in contrast to members of Turkic warrior families, no stake in Ottoman politics or factional feuding and could be expected to give absolute personal allegiance to the ruler. Moreover, Christian families did not necessarily lament the loss of these children, since at least some lads rose to positions of responsibility and influence within the Ottoman

janissaries An elite infantry corps in the Ottoman Turkish state whose members were conscripted as boys from Christian families in southeastern Europe.

The Ottoman capture of Constantinople. This illustration from a fifteenth-century French chronicle conveys the intensity of the battle to control the city. We see evidence of Ottoman naval power and the infantry using ladders to scale the city walls built by Emperor Theodosius ten centuries earlier. What features communicate the artist's impressions of this battle? Does the painting convey sympathy for the conquering Ottomans or the besieged Byzantines?

state. Young janissaries had to convert to Islam and undergo rigorous training before taking military or administrative posts. About the same time, the Ottoman state began to build powerful cavalry regiments (*sipahis*). These units ensured order in rural provinces, and their commanders received in return rights to collect taxes on their own account from an assigned number of villages.

The capture of Constantinople. For more than a century after crossing the Bosporus and Dardanelles straits to penetrate the Balkans, Ottoman forces either bypassed or failed to penetrate the great Byzantine bastion of Constantinople. They absorbed nearly all other Greek-ruled territories, and by the early fifteenth century, the Byzantine emperor found himself effectively surrounded. Finally, in 1453, Sultan Mehmed II, known as the Conqueror (r. 1451–1481), breached the city's triple walls, deploying gunpowder artillery and handguns. The Greek historian Kritovoulos described the hours preceding the victory:

The day was declining and near evening, and the sun was at the Ottomans' back but shining in the faces of their enemies. . . . First they exchanged fire with the heavier weapons, with arrows from the archers, stones from the slingers, and iron and leaden balls from the cannon and muskets. Then, as they closed with battleaxes and javelins, and spears, hurling them at each other and being hurled at pitilessly in rage and fierce anger. . . . Many on each side were wounded, and not a few died.[14]

Mehmed gave his troops free rein to plunder the city for three days, and they murdered or enslaved much of the Christian population. In imitation of Mongol conquerors before him, however, Mehmed called a halt to the carnage and immediately set to work to restore and repopulate the city as the Ottoman capital. For example, the sultan recruited a diverse team of architects, including Italians, to build his magnificent palace of Topkapi Saray, an architectural complex that blended Muslim, Greek, Roman, and Italian elements. Western European rulers reacted to the fall of the greatest of Christian cities with shock and dismay, but they soon established diplomatic contacts with the new regime. The Ottoman empire would play a key part in the politics of Europe, the Mediterranean basin, and Southwest Asia for the next 450 years.

The Meaning of Recovery in Europe

Although Europe's population began to climb again after about 1450, many of its cities showed new vigor well before that date. Urban dwellers who survived epidemics found they could command higher prices for their labor, products, and professional services. They had more money to spend on food, luxuries, and capital investment in business and property. Consumers demanded a wide range of high-quality goods, stimulating both European industry and import trade. Europe's banking industry, which nearly collapsed during the Black Death, thrived once again. Florence emerged as the leading financial hub. From there, the Medici family and other rich firms built up pan-European commercial and banking empires. In Florence, Venice, Cologne, Paris, Bruges, London, and other cities, socially well-placed families piled up great wealth.

The bourgeoisie, that is, the nonaristocratic propertied

class, took advantage of business success to build bigger houses, purchase better educations for their children, and carve out solid social positions between the privileged nobility above and the working masses below. Urban women also gained a measure of social and cultural status following the plague era. Scarce labor meant that male heads of households felt obliged, if grudgingly, to concede more value to women's homemaking and artisanry. In the fifteenth century, both urban and rural women enjoyed somewhat greater freedom to earn money as spinners, weavers, teachers, and business owners. Literary works of the fifteenth century showed a new regard for the cultural worth of motherhood and wifery. As the all-male priesthood lost prestige (especially after the pope decamped to Avignon) and as the psychological gloom of the Black Death persisted, more women emerged as spiritual guides and reformers. Christian practice in the fifteenth century paralleled in some ways Sufi tendencies in Islam, as men and women turned to personal, inward worship centered on adoration of God, Jesus, and the Virgin Mary and on acts of communal service and humble living. Among female mystics, Catherine of Siena (1347–1380) achieved renown across Europe, urging both spiritual renewal and church reform in her writings. A radical ascetic, she practiced self-denial to the point of sleeping and eating as little as possible, a habit that may have cost Catherine her life at the age of thirty-three.

Catherine of Siena. A lay member of a society associated with the Dominican monastic order, Catherine reported numerous mystical experiences, including a spiritual marriage to Christ. She also had political influence, working to end war between Florence and Rome and successfully urging Pope Gregory XI to move the papal court from Avignon, where it had been under French domination for sixty-eight years, back to the Vatican in Rome. How would you describe the way the Italian artist represents Catherine in this painting made around 1462?

Royal power. Several of Europe's numerous states achieved new strength between 1350 and 1500 (see Map 15.4). The troubles of the church, the declining incomes of local aristocrats, and the renewed economic growth of the fifteenth century offered able and ambitious rulers opportunities to assert their authority in creative ways. Out of Italy's crazy-quilt of princedoms and city-states, five polities emerged in the 1300s to tower over the peninsula: the kingdom of Naples in the south, the papal states centered on Rome, and the northern

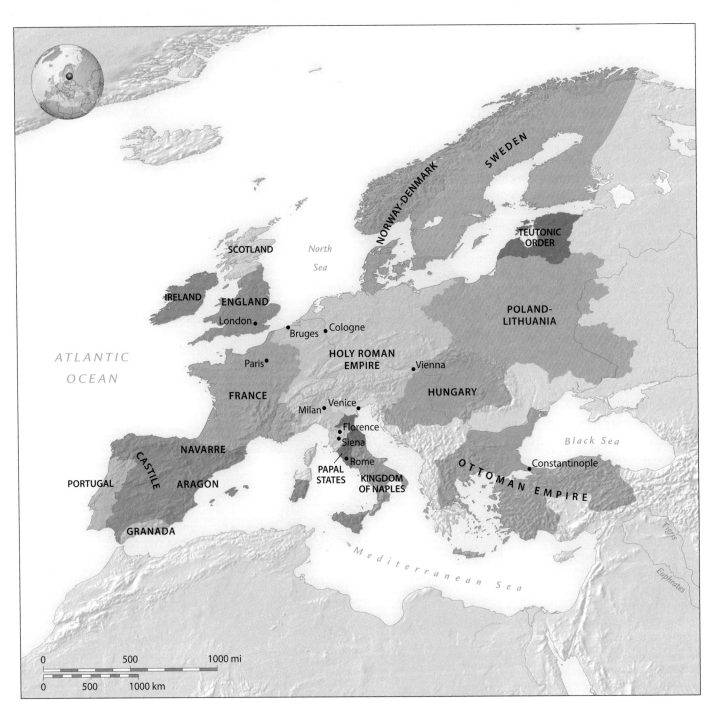

MAP 15.4 Europe in 1455.
The mid-fifteenth century was a time of prosperity in many European states. What geographical factors might help account for lavish financial patronage of the visual arts in cities of the Italian Peninsula in the fifteenth century?

city-states of Milan, Florence, and Venice. Together, these five dominated or absorbed weaker cities and small states.

The kingdoms of France, England, Spain, and Portugal all consolidated royal power. The French and English monarchs invented new taxes to impose on their subjects to pay for larger armies and more officials. Sometimes using cannons to smash castle walls, they subdued local estate lords and put royal bureaucrats directly in charge. France devoted

large sums to a standing professional army, equipping it with artillery units that no unruly duke or rebel leader could hope to afford. England endured a bitter civil war near the end of the fifteenth century (the Wars of the Roses), but Henry VII (r. 1485–1509), the first king of the Tudor dynasty, took the state to new levels of bureaucratic efficiency. In Iberia, Queen Isabella of Castile (r. 1474–1504) and King Ferdinand of Aragon (r. 1479–1516) formed a powerful alliance in 1469, unifying their two kingdoms at the dynastic level through marriage. Along the Atlantic, the kingdom of Portugal also built a sturdy central administration. In all of these states, rulers claimed supreme authority but nonetheless governed in consultation with various advisory bodies made up of aristocrats and bishops, and sometimes town leaders and rich commoners. Only in England, however, did the head of state formally share power with a representative body. In the fourteenth century, Parliament's House of Commons (see Chapter 12) evolved into a genuine legislative body, making many laws and obliging the monarch to get its approval before imposing new taxes.

Poland-Lithuania emerged as Europe's territorially largest monarchy, when in 1385 Queen Jadwiga of Poland married the Grand Duke of Lithuania to merge the two kingdoms. This state claimed sovereignty over a huge area stretching from the Baltic to the grassland frontier of the Mongol Golden Horde. Formerly pagan, Lithuanians moved steadily into the Catholic Christian fold. Especially in Poland, urbanization, commercialization, and higher education developed rapidly, bolstered by a continuing inflow of German migrants, as well as thousands of Jewish families who fled persecution in western Europe during the Black Death. In contrast to the trend in western Europe, however, local

Polish, Lithuanian, and German aristocrats retained much power within the empire. Royal governance in rural areas remained relatively weak, despite the empire's impressive size. Similarly in central Europe, the Holy Roman Empire continued to exist under the sovereignty of the Habsburg dynasty, but the emperor had limited power and functioned mainly to legitimize the regional authority of several German dukes.

The Italian Renaissance. At particular historical moments starting in ancient times, certain cities have shone more brightly than any others. Athens in the fifth century B.C.E., Baghdad in the ninth century C.E., and Hangzhou in the twelfth century produced innovations in art, literature, and science that have endured in the world's imagination. In the fourteenth and fifteenth centuries, Beijing, Vijayanagar, Delhi, Samarkand, and Cairo numbered among Afroeurasia's most creative centers of intellect and skill. In the decades following the Black Death, Florence in north central Italy emerged as Europe's liveliest hub of cultural genius. The movement that began there in the 1300s and that historians later labeled the Renaissance, or "rebirth," spread rapidly to other Italian cities and, in a variety of expressions, to the rest of Europe.

Florence in the late fifteenth century. The Arno River divides the walled city. Locate the Duomo, the cathedral that Filippo Brunelleschi completed.

Located in the Arno River valley amid the rolling hills of Tuscany, Florence had, despite its severe population loss in the later fourteenth century, the right mix of ingredients to achieve cultural distinction. It possessed sufficient wealth from manufacturing, trade, and banking to support ambitious artistic and literary projects. In that era, no city could excel in the arts or sciences without the backing of elite men and women who possessed both surplus wealth and urban cultural refinement. Often, the ruler of a city or state stepped forward as the most generous cultural patron, as in the case of Ulugh Beg in Samarkand. In Florence the eight hundred or so wealthiest families, including the Medici banking family, patronized the arts by offering stipends, commissioning projects, and purchasing sculptures, paintings, and numerous other art objects.

In Florence rich aristocrats and merchants competed with one another to spend money on art and buildings, confident that some of the glory would reflect back on them. As the city's reputation grew, artists and writers flocked there from around Europe. Other important Italian towns, some of them political enemies of Florence, vied for attention. Poets, painters, and fine metalsmiths traveled from one city to another—Milan, Siena, Rome, Venice—to look for books, find patrons, and exchange ideas with like-minded individuals. By the later fifteenth century a network of cultural exchange inspired by Italian ideas spread across Europe to embrace educated men and women from Portugal to Poland.

humanism European movement of the fourteenth to sixteenth centuries dedicated to rediscovering, investigating, and reinterpreting ancient Greek and Roman civilization.

The cultural movement centered on Florence took shape around the multifaceted philosophy called **humanism.** Today, that word is commonly associated with secularism, a human-oriented, nonreligious attitude or way of life. Six hundred years ago, however, humanism was fundamentally a project to search out and retrieve the surviving literary and aesthetic achievements of ancient Rome and, by extension, Greece. Inquisitive Italians could see Rome's physical ruins everywhere, and they knew that more of the record of classical civilization lay moldering in churches, monasteries, and palace cellars. Humanists argued that anyone wishing to restore, analyze, or interpret ancient knowledge should master the *studia humanitatis,* that is, the study of the "humanistic" disciplines of grammar, rhetoric, poetry, moral philosophy, and history. These disciplines, they said, must form the core of young people's education and should be dedicated to recovering ancient wisdom, which humanists regarded as intellectually and morally superior to anything Europe had produced in the intervening centuries. Three of the most important pioneers of this rebirth of classical culture came from Tuscany. The epic poet Dante Alighieri (1265–1321), the lyric poet Petrarch (1304–1374), and the classical scholar and storyteller Boccaccio (1313–1375) all devoted their careers to finding and elucidating ancient literary and philosophical texts and to reviving classical arts.

Humanists put forth numerous ideas. They considered Greek and Roman achievements to be the proper point of reference for moral thought and behavior. Human beings, they argued, had responsibilities not only to perform religious duties but to better themselves as individuals through education and constructive thought. Taking the early Roman republic as their model, humanists also encouraged public service as a moral obligation, though no genuinely democratic republic existed anywhere in Europe. Indeed, the classicist and diplomat Niccolò Machiavelli (1469–1527) argued in his book *The Prince* that rulers who wished to strengthen Italy against foreign invaders should be guided by ruthless pragmatism, not Christian morality. Machiavelli's humanism emphasized political activism, even violent or deceitful measures, to defend the freedom and integrity of the republican city-state.

Renaissance men and women found much to criticize about the dogmatism and corruption they witnessed in the Roman church. Somewhat like Muslim scientists and philosophers in the same era, humanist scholars gravitated mainly to princely courts and aristocratic households for support, not to established centers of learning. They tended to consider Europe's universities as preserves of narrow-minded theologians and lawyers. Eventually though, humanist ideas penetrated the universities.

The Italian Renaissance embraced all expressions of art and craft. Gifted sculptors of the era, such as Donatello (1386–1466) and the relentlessly creative and long-lived Michelangelo (1475–1564), studied classical models to create sublime naturalist images in marble and bronze. As we saw at the beginning of the chapter, early Renaissance painters, such as Masaccio, strove to recreate the "real," three-dimensional world using new techniques of perspective. Artists also depicted not only Christian subjects but also historical, mythological, and everyday secular themes. Architects such as Filippo Brunelleschi (1377–1446) built churches and other monumental structures that combined Roman engineering with clever new techniques. For example, in building a great dome for Florence's cathedral (known as the Duomo), he constructed in effect two domes, one inside the other and connected together, in order to reduce the weight of the structure on the supporting walls.

Brilliant achievements like these gave rise to the modern phrase "Renaissance man" to describe someone of wide-ranging interests and skills. It was indeed a man's world. Humanist ideology made little room for urban women to express themselves except in perfecting the arts of household management and social adornment. However, a few women achieved fame in the arts, several applying their aesthetic talents as painters, calligraphers, and book illuminators. Other upper-class women patronized male artists and scholars from behind the scenes. Among the early humanists, Christine de Pizan (1364–1431) stands out.

Daughter of an Italian astrologer who lived at the court of King Charles V of France, she made a living after the death of her husband writing poetry, biography, and political treatises under the patronage of various aristocrats. Modern historians have paid special attention to her because of her spirited writings challenging medieval male stereotypes of women as slow witted and wanton.

The Renaissance beyond Italy. The movement of Renaissance art and ideas from Italy to the rest of Europe in the later fifteenth century occurred in tandem with the spread of printing technology. The early presses of the fifteenth century put out Bibles, catechisms, and sermons, but literate Europeans soon demanded poetry, stories, histories, classical texts, scientific works, and advertising broadsheets. By 1500, just a half-century after the invention of metal movable type, presses had already turned out somewhere between six and fifteen million books. Many of these volumes appeared in regional vernacular languages, not Latin. By the sixteenth century, therefore, mechanically produced books added a revolutionary new dimension to the collective sharing of wisdom and information.

The early Renaissance evolved from an Italian into a European phenomenon, but we should also think of it as taking place within the larger Mediterranean world. Although the humanists tapped much ancient knowledge that Europeans had forgotten, they also used numerous philosophical and scientific texts that reached Europe owing to contacts with Muslim and Byzantine cities. The works of Plato, Aristotle, the Jewish philosopher Maimonides, and numerous Muslim savants were already part of Europe's intellectual library when humanism appeared. Books in Arabic—as well as Muslim textiles, art objects, and numerous ideas about design, architecture, and fine cuisine—continued to stream into Italy. When Byzantine travelers and Greek Orthodox Church envoys visited Rome, they often brought copies of ancient texts. It is no surprise that images of Muslim philosophers, Egyptian landscapes, decorative Arabic inscriptions, and Syrian textile designs turned up in early Renaissance paintings.

Although Latin Christians bemoaned the fall of Constantinople to the Turks in 1453, the new Ottoman capital quickly became a participant in Renaissance exchange. Sultan Mehmed II collected printed books from Europe to add to existing stores of Arabic and Persian literature, and

An Italian portrait of Sultan Mehmed II. The Venetian painter Gentile Bellini spent a year in Constantinople, where he painted the Ottoman ruler in royal robe and voluminous turban. Can you identify elements of Muslim art in the painting?

he took keen interest in Greek and Roman philosophy. In 1479 the Italian artist Gentile Bellini (1429–1507) painted a Renaissance-style portrait of Mehmed. Sultan Bayezid II (r. 1481–1512) invited both Michelangelo and Leonardo da Vinci (1452–1519) to Istanbul (Constantinople) to undertake commissions, though neither went. The early designs for St. Peter's Basilica in Rome, begun in 1506, emulated Constantinople's Hagia Sophia, even though Mehmed II had turned this great Byzantine church into a mosque. Lively cultural exchange between the Ottoman empire and Renaissance Europe continued into the sixteenth century, even as Turkish and Christian armies fought fiercely for control of southeastern Europe.

• • •

Conclusion

If we take a very long historical perspective, Afroeurasia's fourteenth-century population crisis and all the suffering that attended bad weather, epidemics, and war looks slightly less gloomy. In the past 200,000 years, the world's population increased fairly steadily until about three centuries ago, when it began to grow at a much faster rate. Thus, the demographic and economic decline that started around 1330 fits into the longer trend as just one of many recurring but short-lived downturns.

The fourteenth-century plunge *looks* calamitous partly because we have a richer documentation of it than of any earlier slump. It *was* calamitous because by that century human society in Afroeurasia had become so intermeshed that a demographic shift of that scope inevitably caused great upheaval. In fact, the trans-hemispheric pandemic likely occurred only because the dense exchange network strengthened by Mongol rulers was still in place to transmit infectious microbes from one person to another across steppe, mountain, and sea.

In the fifteenth century, economic growth began to accelerate again in many parts of Afroeurasia. The Zheng He voyages demonstrated spectacularly the prosperity of commerce in the southern seas. The larger classes of Chinese junks were probably seaworthy enough to brave any of the world's oceans, but Chinese officialdom decided after 1433 that it could no longer spend great sums on overseas power displays. Meanwhile, economic conditions in western Europe were improving, and shipbuilders were making incremental changes to small but buoyant sailing craft in order to explore Atlantic fishing grounds, look for new islands, and probe commercial possibilities along the North African and Saharan coast. These Italian, Portuguese, and Spanish mariners, like the crowd of Asian and African merchants who crisscrossed the Indian Ocean, no doubt anticipated that seaborne trade would continue to grow, though within networks already known. Well-traveled, cosmopolitan Afroeurasians thought the world was theirs. They had no inkling of America.

• • •

Key Terms

Black Death 428	janissaries 444	Renaissance 447
Choson dynasty 439	Little Ice Age 427	Timur (Tamerlane) 433
flagellants 431	Ming dynasty 432	Timurid sultanate 443
Great Wall 440	movable type printing 438	Vijayanagar kingdom 442
Gutenberg Bible 438	Ottoman Turks 443	Zheng He expeditions 440
humanism 448	papal schism 436	
Hundred Years' War 434	pogrom 431	

Change over Time

Late 13th–mid-19th century	Temperatures in the Arctic and northern latitudes drop (Little Ice Age), contributing to environmental changes and social upheavals of the 14th century.
1280–1324	Osman rules over the newly created Ottoman Turkish state.
1315–1322	Massive famines hit northern Europe.
1340s–early 17th century	The Vijayanagar state in southern India prospers from agriculture and trade links.
1337–1453	France and England wage the Hundred Years' War over territorial dispute.
1346–1352	The Black Death pandemic hits Inner Eurasia, Southwest Asia, North Africa, and Europe.
1350s and 1360s	Rural rebellions erupt in China and western Europe.
1368–1644	Mongols are expelled from China, ushering in several centuries of rule under the Ming dynasty.
1370–1405	From a Central Asian base, Timur leads conquests to the north, east, and west.
1378–1417	Papal schism disrupts the Catholic Church.
1392–1910	The Choson dynasty rules in Korea; Hangul, a Korean alphabet, is invented under Sejong.
1394–1449	Ulugh Beg rules the Timurid state in Central Asia and Afghanistan.
1405–1433	Zheng He leads Chinese maritime expeditions.
1453	Ottomans capture Constantinople.
1455	Johannes Gutenberg produces a printed Bible.
1474–1516	Queen Isabella of Castile) and King Ferdinand of Aragon create a powerful Christian state in the Iberian Peninsula.

Please see end of book reference section for additional reading suggestions related to this chapter.

part 5
The Great World Convergence
1450-1750

From about 1450 C.E. the pace of change in human society quickened markedly. Regional economies and populations grew again across much of Afroeurasia, after a century of economic and political troubles associated most conspicuously with recurring epidemics. In the Americas, farming based on maize continued to spread to new areas, encouraging population growth, social innovation, and larger state-building projects. On the whole, humankind was moving toward greater social complexity at a moderately accelerating speed.

We can only wonder how this trend might have played out if not for the spectacular "accident" that occurred near the end of the fifteenth century. In 1492 the Genoese sea captain Christopher Columbus, sailing into the Atlantic in search of Japan or China, stumbled onto an island off the coast of North America. Other mariners followed, and in the next few decades, trans-Atlantic voyages became commonplace. After about 12,000 years of no significant human migration between them and 250 million years of limited biological exchange of any kind, this sudden convergence of Afroeurasia and the Americas had enormous consequences for our species. The opening of Atlantic passages, as well as Pacific crossings soon thereafter, added multiple complexities to relations among human groups and between all peoples and their natural environments.

In Part 5 we investigate global and regional developments in the period just before and for about two and a half centuries after this great world convergence began. Historians conventionally call this period the early modern era. We use this term to signal the magnitude of changes taking place between 1450 and 1750 and to distinguish that period from the modern age, which emerged fully in the mid-eighteenth century.

Among world-scale developments of the early modern period, we highlight these eight:

Brass figure of a Portuguese soldier holding a musket, from Benin, Nigeria, seventeenth century.

■ The entire era lay within the cycle of slight global temperature decline that climatologists call the Little Ice Age (thirteenth to nineteenth century). Within this cyclical downturn, temperatures oscillated from one year and decade to the next. This produced erratic and unpredictable weather changes in the Northern Hemisphere, including shorter growing seasons in some regions and torrential rains, floods, or extended droughts in others. Historians associate famines, population displacements, and political upheavals with the unstable conditions this cycle generated.

■ Infectious diseases that were common in human populations in Afroeurasia but not in the Americas took a catastrophic toll among Native American societies when people carried microbes westward across the Atlantic. Horrendous epidemics extending into the seventeenth century threw Indian societies into disarray, rapidly depleted their numbers, and hobbled their capacity to control the terms of their encounters with intrusive Europeans interested in conquest, economic exploitation, and settlement.

■ The opening of transoceanic passages also permitted the transfer of a multitude of plants and animals to regions where no one had ever seen them before. This Columbian exchange profoundly affected ecological and economic conditions in most of the world. It allowed Europeans to grow Afroeurasian commercial crops on vast acreages of American land. It also introduced a variety of nutritious American plants to Afroeurasia, contributing to faster population growth in both Eurasia and Africa.

■ The great world convergence involved the interlinking of nearly all regions of the world, including Australia and Oceania, by the late eighteenth century. Consequently, mariners and merchants carried material goods over long distances in all directions. A mesh of trade routes soon encircled the globe, and economic life changed in some measure in every locality connected to this expanding network.

■ The densely populated regions of Asia remained the world's richest centers of production and commerce. Western Europe, which until the sixteenth century was perched on the edge of the Afroeurasian exchange system, suddenly became a crossroads of seaborne trade. New wealth stimulated more investment in agriculture, manufacturing, and intercity trade.

■ Firearms came into worldwide use in this era. Artillery and handguns not only transformed warfare—making it much deadlier—but also permitted rulers who could finance expensive gunpowder armies to tighten their authority, seize more territory, and coerce their subjects to pay the taxes that permitted even greater military buildup. A relatively small number of states consolidated power on an unprecedented scale. Some of them founded transoceanic empires.

■ Empire building and the emerging world economy animated migration on a growing scale—from countryside to town and from one region to another. The largest seaborne movement between 1500 and 1750 was the forced migration of more than 3.6 million enslaved Africans to the Americas to perform hard labor, mainly on commercial plantations.

■ Maritime communication, empire building, and migration contributed to the spread of major religious traditions, especially Islam and Christianity, into regions where they had previously been unknown. At the same time, educated thinkers in Europe began working out a new way of making sense of nature and the universe. It was founded, not primarily on ancient philosophical and religious writings, but on systematic observation and analysis of phenomena to arrive at general principles—in other words, the modern scientific method.

Though no one could have guessed it at the time, these three hundred years represent the last phase of the agrarian age, the 10,000 years or so when humans met their energy needs mainly by growing crops, raising animals, and burning biomass. An assortment of technical advances—more powerful ships, new farming methods, the invention of firearms—permitted our species to harness larger amounts of energy, but still at the incremental rates of increase that had characterized the whole agrarian era. The revolutionary breakthroughs in humankind's ability to exploit energy were yet to come.

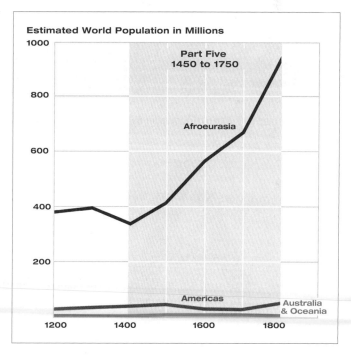

Estimated World Population in Millions

Part Five
1450 to 1750

Afroeurasia

Americas

Australia
& Oceania

16 Oceans Crossed, Worlds Connected

1450–1550

This 1532 map by German cartographer Sebastian Münster demonstrates a new but still incomplete knowledge of world geography.

According to al-Umari, a renowned Muslim geographer of the fourteenth century, a fleet of ships set forth from the West African empire of Mali early in that century to explore the Atlantic Ocean. As al-Umari tells the story, Mansa Muhammad, the king of Mali, believed the ocean could be crossed. "He wished to reach the other side and was passionately interested in doing so. He fitted out 200 vessels and filled them with men and as many again with gold, water, and food supplies for several years." These watercraft would almost certainly have been canoes carved from single logs, though big enough to carry several dozen paddlers. According to al-Umari, the king told the officers in charge of the embarkation, "Do not return until you have reached the other side of the ocean or if you have exhausted your food or water." The ships set sail, and after a long time just one vessel returned, reporting that a mighty current had gripped the rest of the fleet and carried it away. Mansa Muhammad then organized a much bigger expedition, leading it himself. This second flotilla ventured into the deep but was never heard from again.[1]

West Africans, North Africans, and Europeans—inhabitants of the eastern rim of the Atlantic—had all learned well before the fourteenth century how to build boats that could negotiate ocean waters, at least close to shore. No doubt, mariners in all three regions wondered what rich lands they might find if they dared to push west. From as early as the sixth century, Europeans told stories of Irish monks or other adventurers sailing into the setting North Atlantic sun. Vikings, we know, occupied a trading base on the coast of Newfoundland in Canada for a decade or two in the eleventh century. But medieval sailors had little knowledge of how the Atlantic's winds and currents worked, limiting their ability and inclination to venture far out to sea.

During the fifteenth century, however, mariners gained knowledge essential for attempting a roundtrip trans-Atlantic voyage. They began to understand that the North Atlantic's wind system forms a gigantic clockwise wheel. Once they realized that this pattern was relatively dependable, they became more confident about sailing out of sight of land for long stretches of time, as Christopher Columbus did in 1492. About that time, other European skippers discovered that a twin, though counterclockwise wind wheel ruled the South Atlantic.

The permanent opening of passages across the Atlantic, and shortly thereafter the Pacific, produced the "great global convergence." By this we mean not only that Europe and the Americas became permanently conjoined, but also that nearly all regions of the world became connected to one another. The convergence had revolutionary consequences because it involved a sudden, vast, and unprecedented exchange of living organisms—people, animals, plants, and microbes. To one extent or another, this exchange disturbed existing ecological and economic systems, especially because Afroeurasia and the Americas had been virtually sealed off from each other for at least 12,000 years. It enabled some people to exploit new resources in land, minerals, and human labor, whereas others became victims of that exploitation. Also for the first time, maritime routes spanned and connected all the world's big oceans. By the mid-sixteenth century, a genuinely globe-girdling economy was taking shape.

The first part of this chapter surveys the global scene in the mid-fifteenth century, just before the great world convergence got under way (see Map 16.1). This was a time of demographic, economic, and commercial recovery in Afroeurasia. It was in this context that western European sailors stepped up the tentative probes they had been making

Chapter Outline

• • •

into the Atlantic to try to tap the trade of uncharted islands, tropical Africa, or even Asia. On the other side of the globe, the Americas had only 10 to 15 percent of the world's population before Columbus, but it displayed a somewhat similar pattern of population and economic growth, as maize farming continued to spread and as empires of unprecedented size arose in Mexico and the Andes Mountains.

In the second part of the chapter, we consider the conditions in which the opening of new oceanic passages took place. First we investigate Portugal and Spain, exploring the geographical knowledge and technical innovations that made back-and-forth ocean crossings possible, as well as the motives and aims of the Europeans who took part in seaborne adventures. The section describes early encounters between Portuguese newcomers and peoples on the Atlantic side of tropical Africa. We also trace Columbus's transatlantic voyages and describe the early impact of the sudden arrival of Europeans on Caribbean societies.

A Panoramic View

MAP 16.1 Major states in the mid-fifteenth century.
On the eve of the great global convergence, several large territorial states shared Afroeurasia with small monarchies, city-states, and nomadic societies. Two large empires and many smaller polities occupied the Americas. What basic technologies did most Afroeurasian states have in the mid-fifteenth century that American states lacked?

In the third section, we describe developments in the Americas from 1492 to about 1550. This period was catastrophic for Native Americans, especially in the Caribbean and densely populated regions of Mesoamerica and the Andes. American Indians died off in massive numbers, chiefly because they lacked immunities to infectious microorganisms introduced from Afroeurasia. At the same time, Spanish and Portuguese soldiers and colonists undertook to subjugate American societies and to exploit land and labor for commercial profit. Disease, warfare, and rampant social dislocation led in short order to the collapse of the Aztec and Inca empires. In the sixteenth century, Spain and

Portugal expanded their conquests beyond those states to found territorial empires of their own.

Beginning in 1498–1499, Portuguese captains started sailing around Africa to the Indian Ocean. In stark contrast to the empty Atlantic, the chain of waterways extending from the Arabian Sea to the East China Sea teemed with maritime activity. The final part of the chapter addresses patterns of change that occurred in the southern seas in the half-century after Portuguese ships arrived there. We describe early encounters between Indian Ocean peoples and the Portuguese, and the initial effects of the European armed incursions on prevailing patterns of power and trade.

On the Eve of the Great World Convergence

FOCUS What important changes were taking place in economic and political life in both Afroeurasia and the Americas as of about 1450?

The European mariners who crossed the Atlantic, Pacific, and Indian Oceans in the late fifteenth and early sixteenth centuries had primarily, though not exclusively, economic aims—the desire to trade, raid, and find treasure. An understanding of when and how those sailors set forth, unwittingly starting the great world convergence, requires a global context, particularly regarding political and commercial aspects of change. Here, we look at developments in two geographical arenas. The first is Afroeurasia and its long-distance exchange system as it existed about 1450. The second is the Atlantic rim. As of 1450, the European, tropical African, and American societies that faced the Atlantic knew absolutely nothing or, in the case of Europeans and Africans, very little about one another. Those societies were playing out their own histories with no expectation of the transformations that encounters among them would set in motion.

Changes in the Afroeurasian Trade Network

After a century and a half of contraction associated with the Black Death and recurring infectious plague epidemics in Eurasia and northern Africa, Afroeurasia's population swung upward again from about 1450. Regional plague outbreaks diminished, and Eurasia's northerly latitudes experienced a moderate (and temporary) warming trend that brought longer growing seasons. These improving environmental conditions encouraged greater food production and accelerating population growth, notably in China, South Asia, and Europe. Although about 90 percent of Afroeurasia's population lived rural lives, cities grew and multiplied. The center of gravity for economic production, trade, population, and urbanization was in Asia. By one estimate, Asia had seventeen of Afroeurasia's twenty-five largest cities in 1450. Four were in northern Africa or Muslim-ruled parts of Europe. Christian Europe claimed the remaining four.[2]

Caravan traffic on the overland silk routes of Inner Eurasia prospered in the later fifteenth century, but maritime shipping routes carried goods in much greater volume. The busiest trade circuits connected the South China Sea, the Bay of Bengal, and the Arabian Sea. In addition to luxury wares, including silks, spices, drugs, aromatic woods, gemstones, and fine ceramic ware, ships carried everyday commodities such as lumber, rice, salt, and cheap textiles. Men dominated trading operations in the southern seas, but in many regions production of food, fiber, and cloth depended heavily on the labor of women and girls, who planted and harvested rice and other foods, spun and wove silk and cotton, and traded goods in local markets.

Antonio Galvão, a Portuguese official who lived in the spice-producing Molucca Islands of Indonesia in the early sixteenth century, observed that "the more daughters a man has, the richer he is."[3]

The Chinese trade pump. In the fifteenth century, significant changes took place in the ports, routes, and people involved in the southern seas trade. In 1433 China's imperial Ming government stopped sponsoring large naval expeditions, which in the previous three decades had sailed as far west as the Red Sea and the East African coast (see Chapter 15). Nevertheless, the Chinese economy, the largest regional one in the world, continued throughout the century to power maritime commerce. China's internal network of roads, rivers, and canals was highly developed; urban incomes were rising; and production of silk, porcelain, and numerous other wares flourished. Some of these goods were mass produced for export. At the same time, rich elites and prosperous city-dwellers craved luxury imports. This meant that economic activity in China reverberated across the hemisphere. Chinese merchants and artisans continued to visit or migrate to foreign cities, mainly in Southeast Asia, and to ship goods at least as far west as the Strait of Melaka, which connects the South China Sea with the Bay of Bengal. Conversely, traders from many lands called at southern Chinese ports.

Southern seas entrepôts: Melaka. Numerous cosmopolitan seaports faced the southern seas, though the fortunes of particular entrepôts (OH-truh-poh) rose and fell with changes in political conditions or factors of supply and demand. Early in the fifteenth century, for example, the city of Melaka (also, Malacca) emerged as a magnet of seaborne commerce. In 1403 the ruler of Singapore founded this port after being expelled from his home city by a rival prince. Melaka enjoyed a protected harbor along the narrowest stretch of the Strait of Melaka. The streets of the port soon thronged with traders of different ethnic groups, languages, religions, customs, and cuisines. According to Tomé Pires, a Portuguese druggist who lived there between 1512 and 1515, this was "a city that was made for merchandise, fitter than any other in the world; . . . the trade and commerce between different nations for a thousand leagues on every hand must come to Melaka."[4]

Merchants of Gujarat. Another fifteenth-century development was the commercial expansion of Gujarat, a Muslim state on the northwestern coast of India. In 1401 Gujarat's rulers successfully broke away from the sultanate of Delhi, South Asia's largest land empire. On its own, the region prospered by exporting cotton, as well as goods that arrived overland from greater South and Central Asia. From Cambay and other ports, Gujarati merchants fanned out across the Arabian Sea and eastward to Melaka. When Tomé Pires visited Gujarat early in the sixteenth century, he observed: "They are men who understand merchandise. . . . They are diligent, quick men in trade. . . . Those of our people who want to be clerks or factors ought to go there and learn, because the business of trade is a science in itself which does not hinder any other noble exercise, but helps a great deal."[5]

Gujarati merchants helped animate the trade of the Arabian Sea, which connected South Asia to East Africa, the Persian Gulf, and the Red Sea. Duarte Barbosa, a Portuguese official who sailed to the Indian Ocean early in the sixteenth century, wrote about Muslim merchants who shipped goods westward from India. In the southern Indian port of Calicut, he observed, the traders "took on board goods for every place, and every monsoon [the seasonal wind shifts] ten or fifteen of these ships sailed for the Red Sea, Aden, and Meca [Mecca], where they sold their goods at a profit. . . . These goods were pepper (great store), ginger, cinnamon, cardamoms, . . . precious stones of every kind, seed pearls, musk, ambergris, rhubarb, aloes-wood, great store of cotton cloths, porcelains."[6] This immensely valuable merchandise, he reported, went "to Cairo, and from Cairo to Alexandria, and thence to Venice whence they came to our regions."

Europeans looking east. In the early fifteenth century, the western European and North African societies located at the far western end of the trans-hemispheric trade system had generally smaller populations, fewer cities, and more modest manufacturing economies than did India, China, or the central Muslim lands. A much greater volume of goods flowed into the far west than out of it. Wealthy Europeans had access to gold from West Africa, silks from East Asia, and spices, drugs, and dyes from Indonesia. But the merchants who relayed these items along the exchange network practiced the usual profit-seeking rule: buy cheap and sell dear. Consequently, people in the west usually paid prices marked up many times over the cost of production. In the 1400s, for example, Indian pepper sold in England for about £200 per ton, whereas construction of a seagoing ship there cost only £2 or £3 per ton. Europe's workshops turned out a variety of products, for example, fine woolens, ironware, and weaponry, which commanded respectable markets in Mediterranean ports. But the balance of trade remained heavily tipped toward Asia, requiring European importers to buy Asian products with gold or silver coins. That exchange worked quite well because neither South Asia nor China had large endowments of those metals. Europeans mined silver in Germany, Bohemia, and other regions, though gold reached Europe principally by camel caravan trade from Sudanic West Africa.

Indians harvesting pepper. This illustration comes from a fifteenth-century edition of Marco Polo's travels, *Book of Wonders of the World*. Look for the artist's depiction of three phases of the global pepper trade: harvesting, transporting to market, and commercial exchange. Why might the artist have shown these three phases happening simultaneously?

For about a century and a half before 1350, bands of Italian and other European merchants traveled overland in small numbers to Iraq, Iran, India, and even China. Marco Polo (1254–1324) was among the Venetians who journeyed to East Asia and back. These traders found opportunities to the east because the rulers of the Mongol states that existed at the time, as well as some Muslim and Hindu princes who controlled Indian Ocean ports, allowed foreigners of just about any origin to pass through to conduct business. Western Europeans therefore acquired greater knowledge of the trans-hemispheric web as well as keen aspirations to penetrate it on a larger scale.

Unfortunately for them, the political situation changed. The Mongol state that ruled Persia collapsed in 1335, and the rulers that succeeded it regarded the presence of Franks, as Muslims called western Europeans, as a potential threat to local mercantile groups. In Egypt the Muslim military state known as the Mamluk sultanate allowed Venetian ships to enter the port of Alexandria but not to sail on the Nile or the Red Sea. Then, in 1453, Ottoman Turkish armies captured Constantinople, eradicated the Christian Byzantine empire, and took control of the sea passage between the Black Sea and the Mediterranean (see Chapter 15). The Ottoman emperor Mehmed II (reigned 1451–1481) at first encouraged European merchants to visit Aegean ports. But as the sixteenth century approached, commercial relations soured. Ottoman forces warred intermittently with Venice for control of eastern Mediterranean islands, and the merchants of Genoa lost access to ports they had frequented in the Black Sea. Thereafter, Italian traffic in the eastern Mediterranean ports fell off. In addition to that, Turkish armies seized both southern Iraq and Egypt early in the sixteenth century, positioning themselves to send naval vessels into the Indian Ocean.

The Eastern Atlantic Rim

In the fifteenth century, three major clusters of relatively dense agrarian population faced the Atlantic Ocean. Along the eastern rim of the Atlantic (see Map 16.2), one cluster extended from the British Isles southward to the northern edge of the Sahara Desert. The second cluster, also along the eastern Atlantic rim, was tropical West and Central Africa. The third was the American lands rimming the western Atlantic, around the Caribbean Sea and the Gulf of Mexico. In the late century, these three regions quite suddenly found their previously separate histories coming together.

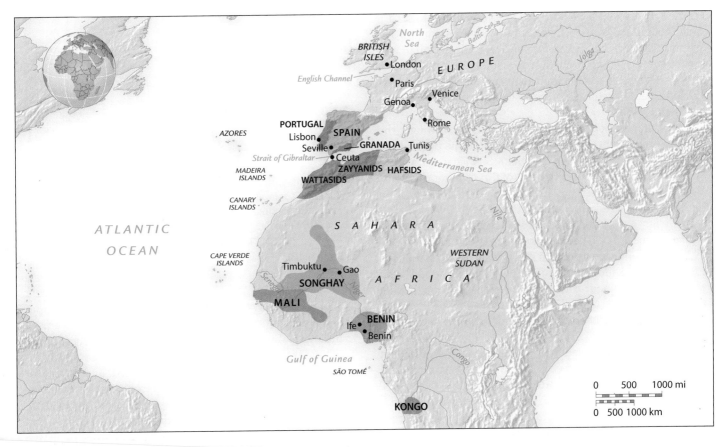

MAP 16.2 The eastern Atlantic rim, 1470.
The Sahara Desert separated the relatively densely populated regions of western Europe and North Africa from the agrarian lands of West Africa. What factors help explain increased maritime activity in the eastern Atlantic in the late fifteenth century?

Focus on the Strait of Gibraltar. In the fourteenth and fifteenth centuries, the Atlantic presented an alluring challenge to the monarchs, merchants, and navigators inhabiting the European and African lands on either side of the Strait of Gibraltar. Since ancient times, the Iberian Peninsula (modern Spain and Portugal) and western North Africa (modern Morocco and Algeria) had constituted a single zone of human interaction, especially from the eighth century, when Arab Muslim forces crossed the strait to unite the two regions in a single religious, cultural, and political sphere. By the mid-thirteenth century, three Christian monarchies—Castile, Aragon, and Portugal—wrested most of Iberia from Muslim control. Nevertheless, merchants, pilgrims, and diplomats continued to move back and forth across the strait. In the fourteenth century, the Christian states, the Muslim kingdom of Granada, and three Muslim monarchies in North Africa competed in peace and war, forming and breaking alliances and exchanging one another's goods without much regard to religious differences.

By the late thirteenth century, the Strait of Gibraltar was becoming a "river" of commerce connecting the Mediterranean world with the eastern Atlantic. Italian and other European vessels frequented the strait and the ports along its shores. Some of those ships probed Morocco's Atlantic coast to buy grain, horses, and gold. In 1291 the Genoese Vivaldi brothers conceived a much more ambitious plan to lead a small fleet of galleys southward until they found a passage around Africa to the Indian Ocean. The hulls of Italian galleys, however, were too shallow to withstand high Atlantic seas. The Vivaldis disappeared without a trace, and another 197 years passed before a Portuguese captain reached Africa's southern extremity.

Other Italian sea merchants who passed through the strait turned north, sailing around Iberia to the ports of the English Channel, North Sea, and Baltic Sea. That route could be highly profitable, since the costs of direct water transport from southern to northern Europe were much lower than hauling goods overland. From the fourteenth century, in effect, the Strait of Gibraltar fused the Mediterranean and the whole northeastern Atlantic into one network.

In those conditions, ports in southwestern Spain and Portugal attracted sailors, shipbuilders, and cartographers, who talked together about routes, hull designs, and navigation techniques. Portuguese shippers and fishermen began to grope their way farther into the Atlantic to see what landfalls they might discover. Iberians, Italians, and French-speaking Normans visited the Madeira and Canary Island groups in the first half of the fourteenth century and began to plant trading stations and small settlements.

The Madeira Islands had no native inhabitants, but sometime early in the Common Era people who spoke a Berber language voyaged across open water from Morocco to the Canaries. These small bands of migrants survived as farmers, stock breeders, or foragers on the archipelago of seven mountainous islands, though they apparently lost all contact

A Guanche man. This sixteenth-century Spanish engraving, originally published in a book about styles of dress around the world, shows a muscular, well-armed man representing the hunting and herding inhabitants of the Canary Islands. Why might the artist have portrayed the figure in this particular way?

with North Africa. When the islanders, known collectively as Guanches (HWAN-chehs), began to encounter Europeans, the consequences ranged from wars and enslavement to alliances, intermarriage, and conversion to Christianity. The long-isolated population lacked immunities to infectious diseases that Europeans introduced and therefore died in large numbers in the fifteenth century as epidemics, perhaps of typhus or pneumonia, swept across the islands. As more Europeans arrived to trade, farm, and set up sugar plantations, the Guanches gradually lost all distinctive physical or cultural identity.

The Canaries became a base for deeper Atlantic probes. Portuguese seafarers found the uninhabited Azores by 1331, an archipelago located nearly a third of the way to America. Advancing southward along the Atlantic coast, European sailors reached the Senegal River south of the Sahara Desert in 1444 and the uninhabited Cape Verde Islands twelve years later. By the mid-fifteenth century, in short, the communication network that spanned Afroeurasia east to west extended a significant distance into the eastern Atlantic and to the northern edge of tropical West Africa (see Map 16.2). But what, experienced sea dogs asked, might lie even farther south and west?

Meanwhile, the political climate around the Strait of Gibraltar became increasingly hostile. Portugal, a small, mostly rural kingdom that nonetheless became an effectively centralized monarchy, launched seaborne assaults on Morocco, a land of around seven million Arabic- and Berber-speaking Muslims. In 1415 Portugal took advantage of instability within Morocco's ruling Marinid dynasty to seize the port of Ceuta (SYOO-tah) on the African side of the strait. Throughout the following century, Portuguese marauders continued to raid Moroccan coastlands for loot and slaves and, despite local resistance, captured several more ports. Both Portugal and the other Iberian kingdoms coveted Morocco's grain and cane sugar, as well as the gold that camel trains brought from West Africa. In 1469 Ferdinand II of Aragon married Isabella of Castile, laying the political foundations of the Spanish monarchy. Shortly thereafter, the king and queen turned their combined forces against mountain-bound Granada. Victory and annexation of Granada in 1492 allowed Spain to commit more resources to two other military projects. One was war against the Ottoman Turkish navy, which presented a growing threat in the western Mediterranean. The other was further expansion into Atlantic waters in search of new territories to seize and exploit.

Tropical Africa facing the Atlantic. In the fifteenth century, most populations on the Atlantic side of tropical Africa formed either stateless societies or small monarchies supported by agriculture or cattle herding. Nevertheless, growing wealth from agriculture, mining, and trade supported a number of large state-building projects in both savanna lands and tropical forests. Moreover, the savanna region just south of the Sahara known historically as the Western Sudan had a long tradition of monarchy, including the empires of Ghana and Mali.

Along the rainforested coasts of West and Central Africa, farming societies grew rice, yams, bananas, oil palms, and other tropical crops. Forest populations rose steadily in the first millennium C.E., and state building got under way around 700 C.E. In fifteenth-century West Africa, several kingdoms occupied the lands facing the Gulf of Guinea. Those states founded their economies on forest agriculture and on trade—in palm oil, kola nuts, salt, and gold—with savanna societies to the north.

Among forest kingdoms of the region bordering the lower Niger River (modern Nigeria), Benin had probably the largest population. We know that this monarchy had sufficient resources to support state-sponsored building and creative arts. Ewuare, one of Benin's fifteenth-century *obas,* or kings, built massive walls and a moat to protect his palace, a project that testifies to skilled workmanship and the state's ability to mobilize labor. Archaeologists have recovered some of Benin's intricate, naturalistic ivory and brass sculptures depicting humans and animals.

Southeast of the Gulf of Guinea, the Kongo kingdom emerged in the late fourteenth century along the lower reaches of the Congo River. Within another hundred years, the kings of Kongo ruled a 250-mile stretch of coastline and territory stretching deep into the forested interior just south of the equator. Agriculture and mining of both copper and iron sustained the state's economy, along with trade on long stretches of the Congo and several of its tributaries. This commerce included ivory, copperware, iron goods, and pottery. Kongolese weavers produced large

Ivory hip mask from Benin. The kings of Benin wore masks like this seventeenth-century example tied to their left hip during ceremonial occasions. The figures across the top of the head represent Portuguese traders. Why do you think the kings incorporated Portuguese figures into their regalia?

quantities of textiles for regional markets. These cloths were made from fibers extracted from tree bark and the fronds (leaves) of certain palm species. According to the Portuguese captain Pacheco Pereira, writing in the early sixteenth century, "In this Kingdom of Conguo [Kongo] they make cloths of palm-leaf as soft as velvet, some of them embroidered with velvet satin, as beautiful as any made in Italy."[7] At its fifteenth-century peak, Kongo may have had a population of about 500,000. From his capital on an inland plateau, the Mwene Kongo, or king, commanded an army and a growing urban population.

States in the Americas

Even though peoples of Afroeurasia and the Americas developed entirely separately from each other for thousands of years, fundamental interactions with local environments were not so different. In some parts of the Americas, mobile bands of foragers and hunters discovered efficient ways to share land, extract wild resources, and govern small communities, as they did in Afroeurasia. In others, farming peoples created complex societies, built cities, and formed states of varying organization and size. Maize farming spread steadily across the Americas in the first millennium C.E., and by the fifteenth century, maize was the basic staple that sustained growing populations and complex settlements from Canada to the southern Andes.

The Aztec empire. Especially large agrarian populations arose in Mesoamerica, where state and city building started in the second millennium B.C.E. In the fifteenth century, the Aztec empire, centered in the Valley of Mexico (where Mexico City is today), expanded territorially and enclosed a growing circle of subject peoples (see Chapter 14). The Nahuatl-speaking Mexica, the core imperial population, incorporated numerous neighboring groups into the empire by armed conquest or the mere threat of it. Like some premodern empire builders in Afroeurasia, the Aztecs ruled their subjects largely indirectly, allowing conquered groups to retain their own leaders, as long as they pledged loyalty and sent regular tribute in food and cotton to Tenochtitlan, the capital city located on an island in Lake Texcoco.

In the early sixteenth century, the Aztec state, whose core was a "triple alliance" of Tenochtitlan and two other city-states, commanded tens of thousands of warriors and a population of about twenty-five million. Trade in gold, silver, jade, feathers, fine textiles, and an array of foodstuffs circulated throughout the empire and far beyond it. Under the emperor Motecuzoma II (also, Moctezuma or Montezuma), who

reigned from 1502 to 1520, stability and prosperity generally prevailed. On the other hand, the social distance between the noble class and commoners was widening, growing numbers of ordinary men and women occupied low rungs of society as landless laborers or tenants of rich estate lords, and slaves abounded. This was cause for chronic social tension. The Aztecs' dependent allies and tributaries also resented their subordination, and the Tenochtitlan elite imposed order by taking violent reprisals at any sign of rebellion.

The Inca empire. Along South America's Andean Mountain spine and the coastal deserts running parallel to it, a history of urbanization and state formation extends back even earlier than in Mesoamerica. The Inca state, founded in the Valley of Cuzco in what is now southern Peru, emerged as an expansive empire about 1438. Its power was based on the irrigated agriculture of highland valleys. A century later it constituted the largest territorial state the Americas had ever seen, embracing fewer people than the Aztec empire but extending along the Andean chain about 2,400 miles. In contrast to the Aztecs, Inca armies broke up the smaller Andean states they conquered and integrated local chiefs into a large centralized bureaucracy. Inca rulers also ordered involuntary population exchanges. They brought recently

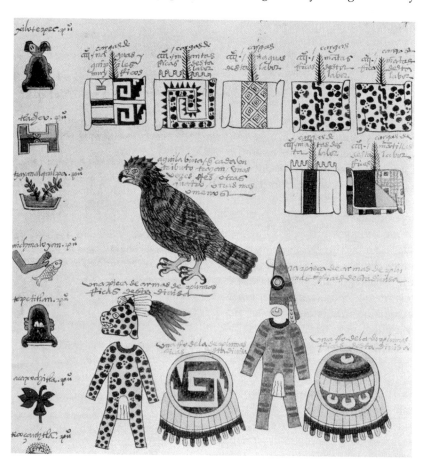

Aztec tribute list. This sixteenth-century document records the tribute that Aztec rulers collected from a single city. Why would both Aztec rulers and Spanish conquerors have kept these tribute lists?

Machu Picchu. The Inca built this citadel, perched at 7,900 feet in the Andes, in the mid-fifteenth century. It was apparently abandoned after the Spanish conquest of Peru. Probably constructed as a retreat for Inca rulers, the site has distinct residential, agricultural, and religious sectors. Why might the Inca ruler have wished to build a residence on a mountainside fifty miles from Cuzco, his capital city?

conquered people—especially rebellious groups—to live close to the capital and moved loyal peasants to the frontiers. Only at the village level did local kinship groups manage daily affairs with little government interference.

Like all other American societies, the Inca lacked wheeled vehicles or iron tools. But they drew on a long Andean state tradition of mobilizing labor on a large scale to build mountain roads and bridges, erect grain storehouses, field a large army, and meticulously collect information about social and economic conditions using a system of knotted and variously colored strings, or *quipus*. An early Spanish observer wrote that at the start of a new year village chiefs brought *quipus* to the capital city of Cuzco to report births, deaths, and other social facts. "In this way the Inca and the governors knew which of the Indians were poor, the women who had been widowed, whether they were able to pay their taxes, and how many men they could count on in the event of war, and many other things they considered highly important."[8] Just as in the Aztec and several Afroeurasian empires of the same era, the government gathered this information to support its own interests rather than that of the people, counting on tax revenues to maintain the army,

feed peasant workers drafted for public works, and support the lavish lifestyle of the royal court, noble families, and high religious and political officials.

Under a succession of three capable rulers, Inca armies incorporated more than 772,000 square miles of Andean and Pacific coastal territory into the empire between the 1430s and about 1520. By that date, the state was nearly three and a half times the size of Spain and Portugal together. Emperor Huayna Capac died about 1527, and that event set off an internal power struggle between two of his sons. This civil war was just coming to an end in 1532, when a band of pale, long-haired strangers in metal armor appeared suddenly on the Peruvian coast.

The Birth of the Atlantic World

FOCUS What factors contributed to the establishment of regular seaborne communication across the Atlantic Ocean in the late fifteenth century?

When European sailors explored the eastern Atlantic in the fourteenth and fifteenth centuries, they had limited, profit-seeking objectives, not grand plans to find direct sea routes to Asia. These mariners looked for islands or African coastal points where they might trade, raid, fish, or even settle. They also reasoned that they might not have to sail too many hundreds of miles to reach the sources of West African gold, a commodity they had always had to buy from North African merchants at elevated prices. But they had no firm knowledge that they could ever reach the Indian Ocean by going south, and America was still *terra incognita*—unknown territory.

Even so, scholars and merchants of Mediterranean Europe had for centuries theorized about a southern sea passage to Asia. The Vivaldi brothers, as we have seen, tried to test that theory in 1291, but they never came back to report. The rise of Ottoman power in the eastern Mediterranean, which dashed European hopes of traveling freely across Southwest Asia to Indian Ocean ports, ignited new interest in a South Atlantic route. Some Europeans—gallant nobles and pious churchmen more than hard-headed merchants—dreamed of carrying the successful Christian crusade for control of Iberia southward into tropical Africa. There, they imagined, monarchs might be found willing to accept the Christian gospel. Better yet, contact might be made with Prester John, a mythical ruler almost certainly associated with the very real Christian kingdom of Ethiopia. Once formed, this Christian alliance would move to encircle the Ottomans and other Muslim states and eventually squeeze them into oblivion.

European rulers who dreamed of such a crusade, however, had little urge to pay for it. For example, Prince Henry of Portugal (1394–1460), later known as Henry the Navigator, saw himself as a chivalrous warrior for Christ, and he enthusiastically supported maritime expeditions, technical improvements, and cartography. But he had little money. He dedicated much of his career to the strategically short-range goals of conquering the Canary Islands for Portugal, which he failed to do, and encouraging expeditions that might divert West African gold to Portuguese ships. The kings of Portugal awarded charters to private groups to explore southward but did not directly finance such expeditions until the 1480s.

Changing Maritime Technology

The shipwrights, pilots, cartographers, and astronomers who frequented Iberian ports in the fifteenth century made up a diverse crowd. They came not only from various parts of Portugal and Spain but also from Italy, North Africa, France, England, Germany, and Poland. The Iberian region of Catalonia and the Mediterranean island of Mallorca (Majorca), both part of the kingdom of Aragon after 1344, emerged as creative centers for making maps, navigational charts, and nautical instruments. Jewish scholars and artisans specialized in this profession. They collected information from sailors who braved gale-prone Atlantic waters. They also drew on a large fund of technical and maritime knowledge that filtered to them from northern Europe, the Muslim lands, and the Indian Ocean rim.

Shipbuilding. European traditions of shipbuilding definitely needed improvement if captains were going to venture far into the Atlantic. As of the early fifteenth century, Chinese seagoing junks, with their massive hulls, multiple masts, and watertight compartments, were probably technically capable of braving Atlantic or Pacific waters. Chinese captains, however, never tested these craft, so far as we know, beyond the China seas or the Indian Ocean. The ships that plied the Baltic and North Seas in the medieval centuries were not strong enough to carry large loads of cargo long distances. High-sided, broad-beamed vessels called round ships used in northern waters usually had only one mast. It supported a square sail that worked most efficiently when the wind blew generally from behind the vessel to push it forward. In the Mediterranean Sea, galley ships that supplemented sail power with dozens of rowers were more common. Human muscle allowed galleys to make progress in any wind condition, but they had to carry food and water for the rowers. That increased costs and restricted space for paying cargo.

Starting in the fourteenth century, western European shipwrights gradually revolutionized ship design. In earlier times, carpenters built hulls by attaching wooden planks to each other, then constructing a frame around them. In the fifteenth century they reversed this process, assembling the hard "skeleton" of the hull first, then attaching the planks to this frame. This method reduced construction time and labor; it also yielded sturdier hulls that withstood Atlantic seas and could bear heavier cargos. This innovation coincided with the introduction of gunpowder artillery in warfare. Stronger hulls made it possible to mount heavy cannons on the decks of oceangoing vessels without destabilizing them.

Stronger ships could also support multiple masts and a combination of types of sails, which provided more propulsion power and greater maneuverability. If a vessel had three masts, the two farthest forward typically carried square sails for moving downwind. The mast at the stern (the back end) held a lateen, or triangular sail. This type had been in use in the Mediterranean for many centuries and perhaps in the Indian Ocean before that. Its particular shape and construction allowed a vessel to make progress even when it was heading nearly straight into the wind. This power and flexibility gave sailors more confidence to buck contrary winds and helped reduce travel times between ports.

In the later fifteenth century, two generic models of sailing ships were in use in the Atlantic. The Portuguese-designed **caravel** was a stout fireplug of a ship equipped with two or three lateen sails. It measured only sixty-five to eighty feet long but had

> **caravel** A type of light, highly maneuverable sailing vessel used by Iberian sailors in the Atlantic in the fifteenth and sixteenth centuries.

room for crew supplies, small cannons, and cargo. It became the preferred vehicle of early exploration, well suited to sail along coasts and up rivers and estuaries. Near the end of the century, builders modified caravels to combine square and lateen sails. The **carrack,** the second general vessel type, evolved into a much larger craft designed to make long sea voyages and mount heavier cannons for defense against pirates and rival naval powers. Carracks had multiple decks for storing different types of cargo and for crew quarters. High "castles," or platforms were constructed at each end of the ship. These gave cannoniers and soldiers armed with handguns or crossbows commanding positions from which to repel seaborne attacks. In the sixteenth century, carracks became the workhorses of transoceanic trade.

carrack An oceangoing ship, larger than a caravel, used extensively by Iberian mariners in the Atlantic and Indian Oceans in the fifteenth and sixteenth centuries.

Navigation.

Open-ocean sailing required not only better ships, but also new navigation techniques to plot location on a map, plan routes, calculate a ship's speed, follow a course, and avoid hazards. Before the fifteenth century, navigation depended on landmarks. Pilots determined their ship's position at sea by estimating its distance from known coastal points. This required them to sail within sight of land as much as possible. A captain could maintain a constant heading by looking at the Pole Star (North Star) or other heavenly bodies. From the thirteenth century, he could also use a compass, a device that Chinese mariners invented and that Indian Ocean mariners passed to the Mediterranean.

Deep sea navigators could not rely on landmarks, but they knew how to estimate their latitude, that is, their location between the earth's poles and the equator. They did this by sighting the distance from the Pole Star to the horizon to reveal their approximate distance south of the North Pole. Abraham Zacuto, a Portuguese Jew, drew on the earlier work of Muslim scholars to come up with another way to measure latitude. He compiled tables indicating the sun's declination, that is, its distance north or south of the equator at noon on any given day of the year. Captains could observe the sun to verify when it was at its highest point in the sky, then use the tables to determine the ship's latitude. European sailors also used astrolabes and quadrants, devices perfected in earlier centuries by Muslim artisans, to calculate the height of heavenly bodies. Determining longitude, a vessel's position east or west of a particular point, was a much greater challenge. It required knowing the difference between the time on shipboard at a given moment and the time at a place from which the

ship had embarked. That calculation could not be made precisely until the late eighteenth century, when clocks were invented that could keep accurate time on a rolling vessel.

Charting Atlantic winds and currents.

Ship captains who ventured into the Atlantic recorded latitudes, compass directions, and landforms from day to day, thereby building up a body of geographical knowledge for sailors who wished to follow the same routes later and perhaps push deeper into unknown waters. The most useful maps displayed the swirling patterns of wind and current. Sailors embarking from Iberian ports learned in the fourteenth century that they could easily sail southwestward along the African coast or to the Canary Islands because the strong Canary Current and associated trade winds sucked them in that direction. On the return voyage, however, they usually faced contrary winds. Crews discovered, however, that they could make headway slowly by sailing diagonally across a head wind, then turning sharply to sail on the opposite diagonal, in other words, tacking (zigzagging) across the wind and current. Caravel pilots took advantage of their lateen sails to perform these maneuvers. Even more important for venturing far into the Atlantic, Portuguese mariners who frequented the Azores after 1431 discovered that those northerly islands, located eight hundred miles due west of Portugal, lay in the path of winds that blew from the west and toward Europe. If ships returning from the African coast sailed northwestward and farther out to sea, they

A Portuguese caravel. This mosaic adorns a fountain at the home of Vasco da Gama's brother, Paulo, a noted ship builder. Two of the masts carry square sails for running before the wind. The third carries a lateen sail for sailing close to the wind—close to the direction from which the wind is blowing. Sturdy decks could support artillery. What do you think the two symbols on the sails represent?

could catch the westerlies in the vicinity of the Azores and return at good speed to the Iberian coast. Soon thereafter, navigators began to understand that the trade and westerly winds formed a single clockwise wind wheel that circulated above the entire North Atlantic.

How big is the world? Fifteen-century scholars generally agreed on the roundness of the world but not on its circumference. The Italian Renaissance, the fifteenth-century intellectual and artistic movement that sought to rediscover and emulate the cultural achievements of ancient Rome and Greece (see Chapter 15), involved study of Latin and Greek geographical texts. One key document was the *Geography* (*Geographia*) of Ptolemy, a scholar who lived in Roman Egypt in the second century C.E. In 1406 Renaissance sages translated the *Geography* from Greek into Latin, triggering debate about the size of the earth. Ptolemy conceived of a round globe about 18,000 miles in circumference. In 1410 Pierre d'Ailly, a Catholic cardinal, published *Imago Mundi,* a treatise that drew on both ancient and Muslim writings to argue that European sailors could reach Asia by heading west. In 1474 Paolo Toscanelli, a Florentine businessman and geographer, wrote to the king of Portugal, arguing that Europe and China lay on opposite sides of the Atlantic a mere five thousand miles apart. Those fifteenth-century hypotheses were wrong, but they nevertheless motivated adventurous sailors, including Christopher Columbus, to test them.

Europeans and West Africans: Early Encounters

Portuguese mariners began to explore the African coast south of the Senegal River in the second half of the fifteenth century. There, they came into contact with much denser populations than they had seen in the arid Saharan latitudes. Interaction between agrarian West Africa and the rest of Afroeurasia had until then depended entirely on overland communication either across the desert or, much more irregularly, eastward across equatorial Africa to the Indian Ocean. Now, however, European sailors pioneered a new sea route that connected West Africans to the Mediterranean world. This route had much greater commercial potential than the trans-Saharan camel trails because it could carry goods and people faster, cheaper, and at much greater capacity.

Portuguese sea venturers aimed to profit from gold and other products that African agrarian societies had to sell. They also believed they could combine peaceful exchange with violent raiding and seizure of territory, just as Europeans were doing in the Canary Islands. They soon discovered, however, that such tactics would not work well in the long term. Africans were eager for trade, but they had the means to resist landward assaults, just as Moroccans had in North Africa. West Africans could usually mobilize much larger military forces than the Portuguese could, including fighters who put to sea in giant canoes to shower arrows on hostile ships and landing parties. In contrast to Canary Islanders, mainland Africans and Europeans had not been

biologically isolated from one another during the preceding millennia and therefore shared partial immunities to the same infectious diseases. Consequently, Portuguese visitors to West Africa did not often leave socially disruptive epidemics in their wake. On the contrary, Europeans who resided in tropical West Africa for even a short period frequently contracted tropical diseases, especially malaria or yellow fever. Somewhere between 25 and 50 percent of Europeans who went to tropical Africa in the fifteenth century died within a year. Thus, Africans had effective biological allies against seaborne invaders.

Portuguese expeditions continued to sail to Africa year after year, first advancing eastward along the Gulf of Guinea, then turning south toward the Cape of Good Hope. These visitors realized that they could profit handsomely from trade as long as they understood that African rulers and merchants largely controlled its terms. In 1471, for example, the Portuguese merchant Fernão Gomes reached the area known later as the Gold Coast. The local Fante-speaking rulers offered gold and other commodities and permitted Gomes to establish a trading station and later to build a coastal fort named Elmina. The Fante collected duties on cargo moving in and out, and they required European captains to seek royal permission to dock. Ships from Europe brought iron bars and tools, woolen cloth, copper, brass, alcohol, Moroccan horses, and various other products to trade for gold, pepper, ivory, African textiles, and slaves. The Portuguese shipped some of those items to Europe, but they found they could also make money by purchasing slaves or goods at one port on the African coast and selling them at another. In effect, Europeans engaged in this "carrying trade" became participants in African exchange networks.

Benin and Kongo meet the Portuguese. Before the end of the century, the Portuguese entered into relations with both Benin and Kongo, two of the most populous Atlantic-facing states. These relations, however, moved in two very different directions. Portuguese merchants obtained authorization from the king of Benin to buy pepper for export to Europe and cloth for shipment to other parts of the coast. They also bought slaves. In that period, Benin was engaged in wars to conquer and colonize neighbors and therefore generated numerous war prisoners. The king agreed to send a diplomatic mission to Lisbon and to accept Christian missionaries, but these initiatives went nowhere. In the 1550s, with the wars of expansion at an end, the king decided to stop selling slaves, a policy that continued to the late seventeenth century. Benin continued to trade with Europeans, but it strictly controlled foreign activities.

In the Kongo kingdom, by contrast, the arrival of Europeans led to severe political and social disruption. Relations between the Portuguese and the Kongolese monarchy started out as they had in Benin—amicable diplomatic formalities and plans for commercial and cultural exchanges. Portuguese priests evangelized some members of the royal family, and in 1506 a young prince who had already converted

Pompe & magnificence du Roi de Congo en donnant audience aux Etrangers.

to Christianity mounted the throne under the name Afonso I (r. 1506–1543). In the following years, the Portuguese sent him technicians, mercenary soldiers with guns, more missionaries, and a printing press. In turn, the king dispatched young Kongolese to Lisbon for education, and he opened correspondence with both the Portuguese crown and the Vatican in Rome. He also used Portuguese support to expand his territories and gain more central control over provincial noble families.

Even before Afonso came to power, however, Portuguese entrepreneurs began to set up sugar plantations on the uninhabited island of São Tomé in the Gulf of Guinea. Even though it was far south of the Madeira and Canary Islands, São Tomé was in a sense the last of the eastern Atlantic islands that Europeans colonized before 1500. Plantation owners on Madeira and the Canaries enslaved Guanches, Moroccans, and West Africans to work in fields and mills. Similarly, European planters who arrived on São Tomé in the 1490s (and who had no interest in cultural exchanges with Kongo) met their labor needs by purchasing slaves from anyone on the neighboring mainland willing to supply them in exchange for European goods. Afonso had great difficulty throughout his reign controlling the disruptive effects of slave trading. In 1526 he wrote to the Portuguese king João III:

Sir, in our Kingdoms there is another great inconvenience which is of little service to God, and this is that many of our people, keenly desirous as they are of the wares and things of your Kingdoms, which are brought here by your people, and in order to satisfy their voracious appetite, seize many of our people, freed and exempt men, and very often it happens that they kidnap even noblemen and the sons of noblemen, and our relatives, and take them to be sold to the white men who are in our Kingdoms.[9]

Nevertheless, the slave trade continued to grow, especially after 1530 when São Tomé became an important assembly point for captives destined to be shipped to new sugar plantations in Brazil. Afonso grew increasingly dependent on Portuguese advisors and mercenaries to keep the kingdom stable. A quarter-century after he died, his kingdom nearly collapsed. Meanwhile, Portuguese slavers expanded their regional operations. In 1576 they carved out a permanent if initially small territorial base at Luanda, the future colony of Angola. Afonso's hopes of his kingdom's technical development, Christianization, and diplomatic standing in the world came to almost nothing.

Rounding the Cape. In 1479, after five years of maritime war, Portugal and Spain resolved festering territorial and trade disputes by signing the Treaty of Alcáçovas. By

Martin Behaim's Fifteenth-Century Globe

In 1492, merchant and mariner Martin Behaim presented a globe to the city of Nuremberg, Germany. He called his gift "der Erdapfel," or "the Earth apple." Such a plain name, however, hardly does justice to the ornately decorated globe, its map sprinkled with miniature paintings of animals, saints, kings, and ships. Today, the globe's vibrant colors are faded, but the map still commands great interest. It is one of the oldest terrestrial globes in existence and presents a window on western European geographical knowledge on the eve of Columbus's first trans-Atlantic voyage.

Though we associate the globe with Behaim, many other people contributed to its construction. Craftsmen built the papier-mâché-like form at the center, then strengthened it with wooden hoops. A blacksmith crafted two iron rings to stabilize the sphere. In drawing the globe's map, Behaim gleaned knowledge from the ancient Greek geographer Ptolemy, the Venetian traveler Marco Polo, and Sir John Mandeville, the pseudonym of a fourteenth-century French author. After Behaim compiled the map, artist Georg Glockendon spent fifteen weeks painting it on the sphere and adding decorative elements.

The globe stood in the Nuremberg town hall for over a century. In the early 1700s, Behaim's descendants asked to have it back, and the city complied. It remained in a Behaim family home until 1907, when its owners transferred it to Nuremberg's Germanic Museum. Der Erdapfel has remained in remarkably good shape, permitting modern scholars to have some idea of how fifteenth-century sailors envisioned the world they set out to explore.

Thinking Critically

How is the relationship between western Europe and East Asia depicted on the globe? What landforms are missing from the map? How accurate do you think the map's land and sea features are? Why do you think Behaim put in the Atlantic so many islands that had never been identified? If a sailor were working from this map, why would a western route from Europe to Asia seem preferable to an eastern one?

its terms, Spain acquired sovereignty over the Canary Islands and Portugal over the Azores and Madeira. Portugal also secured rights to African trade south of the Canaries. This provision deflected Spanish interest from seeking an African route to the Indian Ocean, leaving that field to its smaller neighbor. Portuguese captains who explored the Central African coast south of Kongo gradually accumulated knowledge of South Atlantic winds and currents. Bartholomew Dias was investigating what is today the coast of Namibia in 1488 when his two small caravels were blown far southwest in a storm. When he tried to return to shore, he found himself sailing past the Cape of Good Hope and into the Indian Ocean. Deferring to his crew, who threatened mutiny if he tried to push farther, he made for Lisbon. Drawing on Dias's experience ten years later, however, Vasco da Gama led five ships into the South Atlantic, sailing southwest until he caught westerly winds that brought him back to the coast just north of the Cape. By accomplishing that maneuver, he demonstrated the existence of a South Atlantic wind wheel that revolved counterclockwise—the opposite direction of the North Atlantic one. Continuing around the Cape of Good Hope, he continued up the East African shore and on to South Asia. The Atlantic and the Indian Oceans were now connected directly by sea.

Columbus's Atlantic Crossing

While Dias confirmed an eastward sea passage to Asia in 1488, the possibility of a westward route remained a matter of debate among Iberian sailors and cartographers. Christopher Columbus (1451–1506) was consumed by the question. Born in Genoa, he sailed extensively in the Mediterranean and along the Atlantic coast during his adolescence. When he was not at sea, he pursued occupations as a weaver, bookseller, and mapmaker. Sometime in his early twenties, he settled in Portugal, where he married the daughter of a nobleman who had served Prince Henry in the Madeira Islands. As a wedding present, Columbus's father-in-law gave him his maps and navigational papers—a rare treasure in that era. In 1482 Columbus made a voyage to the Gulf of Guinea.

Though he had a flawed conception of the size of the world, he became convinced that an ocean voyage between Iberia and East Asia was possible. An enthusiastic risk-taker, he spent more than seven years trying to persuade first the Portuguese king and then Ferdinand and Isabella of Spain to finance a westward voyage. The possibility of finding a lucrative trade route to Asia not blocked by Muslim navies finally persuaded the Spanish monarchs. At the least, Columbus might discover new Atlantic islands before the Portuguese did.

Ferdinand and Isabella elevated Columbus to the rank of admiral and gave him funds to acquire ships and engage a crew. He chose two caravels, the *Niña* and the *Pinta,* and a flagship carrack, the *Santa Maria.* He and his little fleet first sailed south to the Canaries, then continued into the deep, sighting land thirty-six days later. We know that he reached the Bahamas or Turks and Caicos archipelago on the western edge of the Caribbean, but the location of his initial landfall has never been confirmed. Taino (TEYE-noh) Indians, who would have spoken an Arawakan language, greeted the strangers on the beach and graciously offered parrots and cotton thread for red Spanish caps and glass beads. Columbus had read Marco Polo's description of China, but nothing he discovered looked like that—no gold-roofed temples, no cities, no bustling wharfs. In his own account of the voyage, Columbus emphasized the nakedness of the locals he encountered, but he also declared them fully rational and human, thus disposed to Christian conversion. The islanders were no doubt equally amazed by the hairy-faced visitor.

For two months Columbus continued to search the eastern Caribbean, including the coast of Cuba. He encountered numerous settlements but not much in the way of commercial opportunity. In December 1492 the fleet began the homeward voyage, minus the *Santa Maria,* which ran aground. The returning company, which reached Portugal in March 1493, included ten Tainos, the first American Indians, as far as we know, to cross the Atlantic west to east. Columbus made three more trips to the Caribbean, many other Europeans followed, and within barely three decades round trips were becoming nearly routine.

In time Europeans came to understand that they had found, not some islands close to China, but two enormous land masses, a New World, as they came to call the Western Hemisphere, teeming with exotic people and other life forms. At the start of the sixteenth century, however, neither Tainos nor Iberians had any idea of the historic significance of Columbus's voyages. Spain and Portugal, still in competition with each other for overseas possessions, scrambled to make geographical sense of his discoveries. In 1494 Pope Alexander VI mediated the Treaty of Tordesillas, an agreement between the two monarchies that imagined a longitudinal line in the Atlantic approximately midway between the Cape Verde Islands, a Portuguese possession, and the islands that Columbus claimed for Spain. By the terms of the treaty, a breathtaking exercise in royal self-importance, the Portuguese crown could lay claim to any territory east of the line, which included the Indian Ocean basin. Spain could claim land to the west. Neither power intended to ask the inhabitants of newly discovered territories whether they *wished* to be claimed by a European monarch. The treaty did, however, give the two states assurance of continuing their maritime adventures without immediate risk of war.

American Catastrophes

FOCUS In what circumstances did large states in North and South America fall to European invaders between 1492 and 1550?

Early encounters between Europeans and American Indians took a very different course than between Europeans and Subsaharan Africans. Europeans developed increasingly complex relations with African societies in the fifteenth and sixteenth centuries. With just a few exceptions those relations involved no significant colonial subjugation of one group by another. African political leaders and merchants often squabbled and sometimes skirmished with Europeans along the coasts, but interactions involved mainly trade, including slave trade, and in some places intermarriage and cultural interchange. In startling contrast, Europeans who ventured to America took just a few decades to overrun the Caribbean, bring down the mighty Aztec empire, seize large areas of Mesoamerica, and destroy the highly centralized Inca state in the central Andes (see Map 16.3). Spain went on to lay the foundations of a mammoth American empire, and Portugal took control of coasts and hinterlands of Brazil. The Netherlands, Britain, and France arrived early in the following century to carve out territories of their own.

Cartier 1534
Cabot 1497–98
ENGLAND
Nuren
FRAN
Ge
PORTUGAL SPAIN
Lisbon
MADEIRA ISLANDS
(PORTUGUESE)
CANARY ISLANDS
(PORTUGUESE)
ATLANTIC
OCEAN
Columbus 1492
Drake 1577–80
Cortés 1519
Tenochtitlan
Havana
AZTEC
EMPIRE
CARIBBEAN
Columbus 1493–94
Drake 1577–80
Magellan 1519–21
Cabral 1500
Da Gama 1497–98
GOLD COAST
Elmina
Gulf of Guinea
SÃO TOME
(PORTUGUESE)
Pizarro 1531
Cuzco
INCA
EMPIRE
Drake 1577–80
Magellan 1519–21
Cabral 1500
Del Cano 1521–22
(after Magellan's death)
CAPE OF
GOOD HOPE
Line of
Treaty of
Tordesillas,
1494
Strait of Magellan

← Portuguese exploration
← Spanish exploration
← English exploration
← French exploration

Why such contrasting histories in Africa and the Americas? At least in general terms, the explanation is uncomplicated. Both Europeans and Africans had iron weaponry; Americans did not. Tropical African states started acquiring firearms soon after their first commercial contacts with the Portuguese. Both Europeans and some African kingdoms deployed horse cavalry in their wars; Americans had no horses. Europeans who went to Africa died at alarming rates because they lacked immunities to malaria, yellow fever, and other tropical diseases; in America, it was the indigenous people who fell in great numbers when exposed to the pathogens introduced from Afroeurasia.

American Death and the Columbian Exchange

Europeans moved as quickly to colonize Caribbean islands as they had the Canaries and Azores. On his second voyage, Columbus founded a settlement on Hispaniola (today Haiti and the Dominican Republic). Ferdinand and Isabella

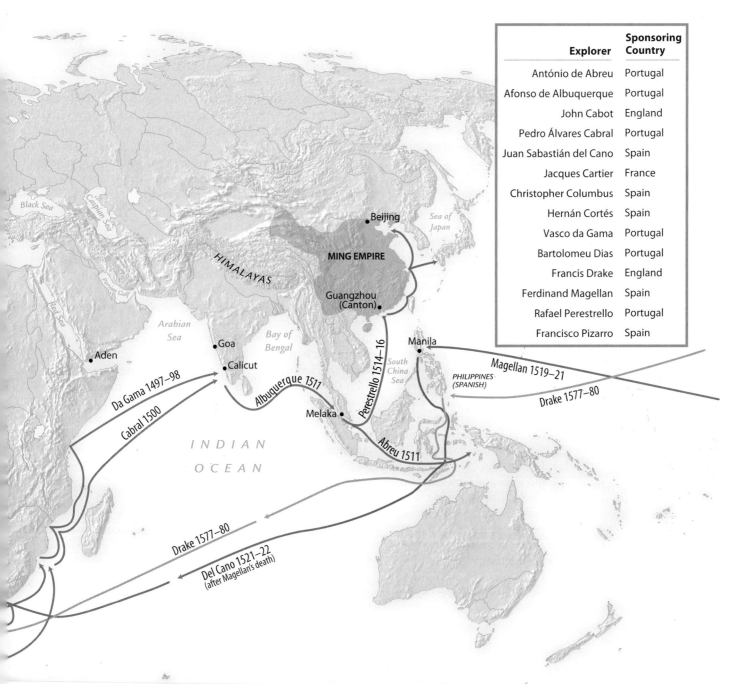

Explorer	Sponsoring Country
António de Abreu	Portugal
Afonso de Albuquerque	Portugal
John Cabot	England
Pedro Álvares Cabral	Portugal
Juan Sabastián del Cano	Spain
Jacques Cartier	France
Christopher Columbus	Spain
Hernán Cortés	Spain
Vasco da Gama	Portugal
Bartolomeu Dias	Portugal
Francis Drake	England
Ferdinand Magellan	Spain
Rafael Perestrello	Portugal
Francisco Pizarro	Spain

MAP 16.3 Major European maritime voyages, fifteenth and sixteenth centuries.
Within just a few decades, European mariners transformed the Atlantic, the Pacific, and the southern Indian Ocean into channels of intercontinental communication. How did the Treaty of Tordesillas influence Spanish and Portuguese maritime voyages after 1494?

granted him the title "Viceroy of the Indies," sharing his anticipation that "India" lay nearby. Columbus led a fleet of seventeen ships and 1,500 settlers, all of them men. These colonists, however, quickly bonded with local Taino women, and the resulting *mestizo,* or mixed-race children, contributed to the colony's growth. The Spanish crown awarded land grants to loyal subjects, including minor nobles with limited prospects in Spain, as well as farmers and artisans who hoped to strike it rich across the sea. As more Europeans arrived, they looked for additional places to colonize. In 1508 Juan Ponce de León founded a colony on Puerto Rico, where he became governor. Two years later, Vasco Núñez de Balboa started the first permanent mainland colony on the coast of present-day Colombia. Both men continued to explore: Ponce de León reached Florida, and Balboa discovered a route across the Isthmus of Panama to the Pacific.

European accounts of early colonization report that islanders identified as Taino or Caribe sometimes resisted the newcomers and, once conquered, repeatedly rose in revolt. Nevertheless, Europeans found progress easier than they might have expected from earlier African experience. Cavalry mounts, vicious attack dogs, guns, and steel swords gave them military advantages. Brutal tactics, including massacres and creative forms of torture, terrified some populations into flight or submission. The colonizers also noticed that islanders seemed to die of their own accord in large numbers from disease. Europeans died, too, both from shipboard infectious and tropical American illnesses such as dysentery or intestinal worms. Indians, however, suffered and died in raging epidemics.

A biological revolution gets under way. An Italian gentleman who accompanied Columbus on his second voyage recorded that "we brought pigs, chickens, dogs, and cats, they reproduce there in a superlative manner, especially the pigs."[10] He could not have known that these animals, along with various plants that Columbus introduced, were about to initiate what historians call the **Columbian Exchange**—a monumental transfer of foods, fibers, weeds, animals, microorganisms, and people across the Atlantic in both directions. These were living organisms that had not spanned either the Atlantic or the Pacific for, in many cases, 180 million years or more. Consequently, on each side of the oceans, biological evolution followed different paths. Humans migrated in recent geological time from Eurasia to North America by way of the northern Pacific coast or a land bridge linking Siberia with Alaska. That migration stopped, however, about 12,000 years ago. Columbus and the mariners who followed him made the trans-Atlantic linkup permanent, and as traffic grew, numerous life-forms, indeed thousands of them, moved back and forth between Afroeurasia and the Western Hemisphere for the first time.

Columbian Exchange The transfer of living organisms, including plants, animals, microorganisms, and humans, between Afroeurasia and the Americas starting in 1492.

These transfers had growing social, economic, and cultural consequences, not only for Native Americans and Europeans, but also for peoples around the world.

In its effects on human societies and their environments, the Columbian Exchange played itself out over several centuries. As of 1550, human societies were in many respects just beginning to experience ecological and social consequences of the great biological swap. We return to the long-term, global consequences of the Columbian Exchange in Chapter 18.

In one respect, however, the Atlantic linkup had immediate, shocking, and socially transforming effects. In addition to pigs, cows, and food plants, Columbus and his companions introduced a zoological garden of living pathogens resident in human and animal bodies. Sailors who reached America infected with a communicable disease could quickly pass on their malady to biologically vulnerable Caribbean islanders. Smallpox appears to have first arrived on Hispaniola in 1518. According to two Spanish Catholic friars, a smallpox epidemic among the islanders "does not cease. From it have died and continue to die to the present almost a third of the said Indians."[11] The same two friars reported that the epidemic apparently spread to nearby Puerto Rico. Additional illnesses arrived from either Europe or Africa (carried by African slaves) as the sixteenth century proceeded. And as foreign sailors, soldiers, and traders penetrated the North and South American mainlands, they introduced new ailments to Indians in ever-widening arcs.

In that era no one understood why Native Americans suffered and died in such great numbers. From modern science, however, we know that Indians lacked immunities to many diseases that were endemic, or permanently present, in much of Afroeurasia but previously unknown in the Western Hemisphere. For example, in Europe, small children often died after exposure to infectious maladies such as smallpox or measles, but if they survived they carried lifelong immunities. When the pathogens that caused these diseases, as well as tuberculosis, typhus, chickenpox, dengue fever, and other pestilences, infected Indians, neither children nor adults could biologically cope with these invaders, and mortality soared.

Afroeurasian illnesses could be transmitted through many kinds of contact. Outbreaks of disease could be set off by something as innocent as a sneeze, cough, or touch. The smallpox virus, for example, could move from one human host to another through the air or by a contaminated object. Once a pathogen became established in an Indian community, it spread easily to neighboring ones as people traveled to trade or visit relatives. Epidemics could reach areas hundreds of miles beyond the frontiers of any European settlement.

A few disease organisms endemic in America traveled eastward across the Atlantic to afflict unsuspecting Afroeurasians. Members of the crew that returned to Spain with Columbus after his first voyage introduced the bacteria that causes syphilis. Scholars think this sexually transmitted

The Seminole Indians of Florida treat the effects of Afroeurasian diseases. French artist Jacques le Moyne de Morgues accompanied an early expedition to North America. His images are an important source of information about the period. This engraving made in 1565 was widely reproduced in the sixteenth century. One man lies on his back while a woman sucks blood from a slit made in his forehead. Another lies on his stomach and inhales smoke from burning seeds. The man in the background smokes a tobacco pipe, believing the leaves have medicinal properties.

pathogen (*Treponema pallidum*) mutated quickly after the first encounter between Native Americans and Europeans and adapted readily to Afroeurasian environmental conditions. It appeared in different forms and produced a variety of symptoms. Syphilis began to spread across Europe in 1495, moving along roads and rivers in the company of soldiers, merchants, and pilgrims. It arrived in the Low Countries and England as early as 1496. It also accompanied Portuguese sailors to Africa and the Indian Ocean, reaching the port of Canton in China by 1505. Syphilis caused much suffering in Afroeurasian societies but nowhere near the mortality and upheaval that Old World diseases triggered among Americans after 1492.

The European "labor problem." The two Spanish friars who bemoaned the terrible smallpox epidemic on Hispaniola in 1518 also worried that too many Taino deaths would cause a labor shortage and hold up gold-seeking operations.[12] Wherever Europeans founded settlements in the Caribbean and mainland coasts, they aimed to exploit any economic opportunity that promised quick wealth,

whether trade, farming, or mining. To set up any commercial operation, they needed workers. Local labor supplies, however, declined as Indians died not only from disease and Spanish violence but also from starvation as fields were abandoned and trade networks were disrupted. European conquistadors (conquerors) and hopeful entrepreneurs knew well that slave labor on eastern Atlantic island plantations cut production costs and raised profits. As a result, colonizers began to enslave Caribbean Indians shortly after Columbus's first voyage. They could never get as many as they wanted, however, and local people could also flee to islands or hinterlands beyond European reach.

Another approach to the labor problem was the **encomienda** (ehn-koh-mee-EHN-dah). This was a Spanish system of labor regulation that rewarded conquerors by giving them control of groups of people and their labor. In principle, an encomendero, or holder of an

> **encomienda** A grant from the Spanish crown to its conquistadors or other Spanish settlers in the Americas, giving them the rights to the labor services and tribute payments of the indigenous people in a particular area.

encomienda, was entrusted to protect his people and give them Christian instruction in exchange for work and taxes. During the first half of the sixteenth century, the Spanish government and church debated the biological and moral nature of American Indians. Should they be regarded as human savages or even as less-than-human brutes naturally suited for lifelong slavery? Or were they fully human "brothers" capable of assimilation into civilized Christian society? The Spanish state ultimately pronounced that Indians were indeed "brothers." They were to be ranked below Europeans in the colonial social hierarchy but nonetheless were entitled to legal freedom, property ownership, and wages for labor. In America, however, encomenderos seeking profits and sumptuous lifestyles often treated their Indian workers harshly and ignored their rights under Spanish law.

As more Europeans crossed the ocean to invest in mines, lumbering, and plantations, the greater the labor demand became, especially in regions where the Native American population declined sharply. Few Spanish or Portuguese peasants felt motivated to migrate to tropical America to take jobs as field hands or mine diggers, and Europeans had no legal or moral basis to enslave other Europeans. Shackling Africans, however, was another matter. Europeans had already started putting bonded Africans to work on the Atlantic islands. There were no serious legal or logistical obstacles to bringing Africans to America to help make up for shortages of Indian labor. For European agricultural entrepreneurs in tropical America, African slave labor was the answer to their prayers (see Chapter 18).

The End of the Aztec Empire

In 1502, the year Columbus made his fourth and last voyage to the Caribbean, Motecuzoma II became monarch of the Aztec empire, or Triple Alliance. This sprawling state loomed over central Mesoamerica, but ill will festered between the elite class and the mass of the population, as well as between the dominant Mexica rulers and other Mesoamericans who had been subjugated to them. Some groups, notably Tarascans in the northwest and Tlaxcalans in the east, continued to resist Aztec conquest.

In 1517, as Spanish colonizers completed the occupation of Cuba, European explorers crossed the Gulf of Mexico to the Yucatán Peninsula, site of the once-flourishing Maya civilization. There, they discovered gold objects and impressive stone buildings, finds that encouraged the search for more riches. Hernán Cortés was the son of a minor Castilian noble who, like other Spanish aristocrats lacking strong political connections at home, regarded the Caribbean as a frontier of opportunity. The king granted him an encomienda in Cuba, and he subsequently achieved wealth, respectability, and an administrative office there. In 1519, however, he sailed for the Mesoamerican mainland with a force of eleven ships, sixteen war horses, about six hundred men, many of whom were former artisans or farmers also seeking their fortunes.

He reached the western gulf shore near the modern city of Veracruz, then marched inland.

Motecuzoma had already received reports of large, fantastically shaped boats and strange bands of pale and bearded men. Aztec envoys visited Cortés and his motley army shortly after they landed. The Spaniards had cannons and handguns, though, given the state of firearms technology in the early sixteenth century, they were likely to cause more fright than casualties. According to Aztec traditions later recorded, the emissaries described the artillery they saw: "A thing like a ball of stone comes out of its entrails; it comes out shooting sparks and raining fire. . . . If the cannon is aimed against a mountain, the mountain splits and cracks open. If it is aimed against a tree, it shatters the tree into splinters."[13]

It was not an Aztec army but Tlaxcalan warriors who first clashed with the strangers, trying to push them back to the coast. Failing that, the Tlaxcalans decided the outlanders might be militarily useful and negotiated an alliance with Cortés against the dominant Mexica. The Spaniards and as many as three thousand Indian fighters then marched on Tenochtitlan, the great Aztec capital. Other groups, weary of Aztec oppression, joined them. In effect, Cortés rode the crest of an explosive local rebellion against Mexica oppression. The attackers quickly captured Motecuzoma in his own palace, much to his surprise. But Cuitláhuac, the emperor's younger brother, soon drove the assailants out of the city. Motecuzoma was killed in the melée. Cuitláhuac reigned for three months, then contracted smallpox, which raged along

Aztecs acknowledge defeat. Ritual weeping was part of Aztec political culture, a public sign of deference or humility. This drawing comes from the Florentine Codex, a sixteenth-century study of Mesoamericans compiled by the Spanish friar Bernardino de Sahagún with the collaboration of many indigenous artists and informants. Both men (on the left) and women lament defeat at the hands of Cortés. How might people in Europe who read the codex have explained or interpreted this image?

Malinche: Translator, Diplomat, and Slave

In modern times, Mexican nationalists have twisted her name into an insult, calling those suspected of betraying their heritage "malinchistas," meaning traitors. At birth, around 1505, she was named Malinal and later known as Malinche or Doña Marina. She was the daughter of a wealthy *cacique,* or chief, on the Yucatán Peninsula, but when her father died, her mother remarried and bore a son. To erase any claim to property that the girl might make, Malinche's mother and stepfather sold her to Maya merchants.

Since slavery was practiced in Maya society, Malinche's fate was not uncommon. She lived in the region of Tabasco when Cortés arrived there in the months before his march into the Aztec empire. As tribute payment from local rulers, Cortés claimed her and nineteen other young women to serve the conquistadors. Bernal Diaz del Castillo's firsthand account of the Spanish invasion describes Malinche as a pretty woman with a "warm-hearted manner" and quick wit. He reports that she rapidly became "a person of great importance." Because enslavement had taken her to several different regions, she could communicate in both Mayan and Tabascan, as well as in Nahuatl, the principal language of the Aztec empire. She learned Spanish quickly, and as a talented translator, she helped the strangers understand how local people might interpret their gestures and behavior, how best to impress important *caciques,* and how to avoid hostile ambushes.

Cortés promised Malinche her liberty if she served the Spanish cause. He consulted her about strategy as his small army made its way toward Tenochtitlan. She mingled with local villagers, made friends, gained confidences, and collected intelligence. She persuasively conveyed Cortés's declaration that if subjugated peoples united they could throw off Aztec rule. She also assisted him in alliance negotiations with the Tlaxcalans.

Foot soldiers like Bernal Diaz developed affection for Malinche, whose forewarnings of ambush saved them more than once. He reported that she went on every expedition and "although she heard every day how the Indians were going to kill us and eat our flesh with chili, . . . [she] never allowed us to see

any sign of fear in her, only a courage exceeding that of woman."[15] When the expedition finally reached Tenochtitlan, it was Malinche who explained to Motecuzoma that he would have to submit to capture or be killed.

She bore Cortés his first son, and later she married another Spaniard with whom she had a daughter. The conquistador awarded her two estates, including land at Chapultepec that previously belonged to the Aztec emperor.

Judging her according to what historians call a "presentist" perspective—analyzing the past by the standards of the present—she betrayed the Mexican people by joining with the invaders. But in fact thousands of other Mesoamericans collaborated with the Spanish to end Aztec domination. Malinche was not Mexica, nor even a free woman. She was given as a slave to the Spanish and served them competently, managing in the process to secure her own survival.

This drawing from the Florentine Codex depicts Malinche as a translator during a meeting between Hernán Cortés and Motecuzoma II.

Thinking Critically

How do you think Malinche's status as a woman and a slave might have contributed to her success serving as an intermediary between Spanish conquistadors and Native Americans?

---

the capital's densely inhabited streets and canals. Within another few months, perhaps a third of the population of central Mexico succumbed to this and perhaps other imported diseases. Meanwhile, Cortés regrouped, raised reinforcements, and laid siege to Tenochtitlan, where according to one Spaniard's report, "the streets were so filled with dead and sick people that our men walked over nothing but bodies."[14]

Cortés took the city and made the Tlaxcalans privileged allies of Spain. More armed Europeans arrived to extend Spanish control across Mexico and Central America in the

following decades. As this conquest proceeded, Mesoamericans continued to die. The population of the Aztec realm alone may have dropped from 25.2 million on the eve of European contact to 0.7 million by 1623. As for the Caribbean, its native population had nearly gone extinct by 1550.

Assault on the Inca Empire

The conquest scenario that Cortés enacted in central Mexico was repeated elsewhere in the Americas, with local variations: Small numbers of Europeans with horses, steel weapons, metal armor, and earsplitting cannons suddenly appeared, sowing confusion among local leaders. Deadly diseases accompanied the trespassers or even preceded them, quickly producing economic and social disorder. Certain groups joined the invaders, believing they could use them to advance their own interests against political rivals or oppressors. This alliance, in which local warriors far outnumbered the Europeans, then attacked and defeated the common enemy. But initial victory produced more political disarray, and amid epidemics and much violence, the Europeans, through some combination of military skill, doggedness, and dumb luck, seized control of the strategic centers of power. Subjugation of large regions, however, typically required more years of fighting owing to tenacious local resistance.

This was certainly the general pattern of events in the central Andes, where the Spanish conquistador Francisco Pizarro, an illiterate adventurer of petty noble origin and a veteran of campaigns in Mexico and coastal South America, displaced the ruler of the Inca empire with amazing speed. About 1527, five years before Pizarro arrived on the coast of Peru with fewer than two hundred men, the emperor Huayna Capac died suddenly of smallpox, along with the son he had designated as his successor. The king appears to have caught the disease during a campaign to extend the empire further north. By this time, smallpox had already infected Indian populations on the Isthmus of Panama, and it subsequently spread southward along the Pacific coast. The death of Huayna Capac and his son left two other offspring competing for the throne. Atahualpa, a son who controlled the northern provinces, captured and killed his rival in 1532 and was on the verge of ending the war when Pizarro suddenly arrived at the town of Cajamarca. Like Motecuzoma in Mexico, Atahualpa unwisely agreed to meet the stranger and got himself taken prisoner in a Spanish ambush. The invaders fired cannons and charged on horseback, throwing Atahualpa's escort of three thousand

The Battle of Cajamarca. This engraving depicts Pizarro's capture of Atahualpa in 1532. It was made by Theodore de Bry, a Belgian artist known for his images of the Americas, though he never crossed the Atlantic. It was published over a half-century after the event. How does de Bry portray Spanish military power? Does his image seem realistic to you?

soldiers into panic. According to Francisco de Xeres, Pizarro's secretary, "It was a very wonderful thing to see so great a lord taken prisoner in so short a time, who came in such power."[16]

To try to save himself, Atahualpa ordered his loyalists to present Pizarro with numerous llama loads of gold and silver objects, which the Spaniards melted into ingots. Despite the ransom, Pizarro had his captive executed. Then, with the help of some of Atahualpa's former enemies, he marched on the capital city of Cuzco, where he placed himself and his lieutenants at the top of the Inca political hierarchy and administrative system. European soldiers, officials, priests, and merchants began arriving in force, and the empire was transformed into a dependency of Spain. In remote Andean valleys, however, popular resistance continued for another forty years or more.

Spanish Empire-Building

The quick destruction of both the Aztec and Inca empires launched the Spanish domination of the Americas from California to the tip of South America (see Map 16.4). This process demanded different strategies from settlement in the Caribbean, where mortality among Taino and Caribe Indians virtually wiped out indigenous communities. Colonization on the mainland required effective control over huge territories and large numbers of people of diverse languages and life ways—the same challenges Aztec and Inca state builders had faced earlier. Dense agrarian societies in Mesoamerica and the Andes, though reduced and weakened by Afroeurasian diseases, fighting, and labor exploitation, nonetheless survived initial contact. The Native American population continued to drop for about a century and a half, but the rate of decline slowed and recovery set in about 1650.

In zones of conquest, the Spanish crown moved early in the sixteenth century to impose its authority over both Native American political leaders and freebooting conquistadors, who operated largely as they pleased in the early decades. Like the rulers of Portugal, France, and England, the Spanish monarchy aimed to strengthen and centralize state power at home. Its high officials also intended to impose that model on the American colonies, which meant reining in the likes of Cortés and Pizarro. The crown instituted the Council of the Indies to serve as the supreme legislative, financial, judicial, and executive authority for the new colonies. It authorized creation of a complex set of civic, legal, and religious institutions to run local colonial affairs. The monarchy also founded the House of Trade (*Casa de Contratación*) to closely regulate and tax the flow of commerce in and out of American ports. During most of the colonial

Previous territory of Aztec empire
Previous territory of Inca empire
Viceroyalty of New Spain
Viceroyalty of Peru
Brazil

MAP 16.4 Iberian colonization in the Americas to 1550
The territory of the two Spanish viceroyalties incorporated the lands of the former Aztec and Inca empires. Might the argument be made that the Spanish did not destroy these empires but rather replaced the former imperial governments with their own?

era, Spanish territory was organized into two huge jurisdictions, each headed by a crown-appointed **viceroy.** One viceroyalty was New Spain, governed from the former Aztec capital

viceroy An official appointed by a monarch to govern a colonial dependency as the sovereign's representative. *Vice* is a Latin prefix meaning "in place of" and *roy* means king. The territory administered by a viceroy is called a viceroyalty.

of Tenochtitlan, renamed Mexico City. The other was Peru, with its capital at the new colonial town of Lima. Both cities became thriving administrative and commercial centers by the middle of the sixteenth century. Royal judicial courts, called *audiencias,* had jurisdictions within each of the vice-royalties. They heard civil and criminal cases involving colonists, Native Americans, and slaves. Local chiefs retained authority over Indian settlements, whereas councils, usually comprised of wealthy European landowners, governed colonial towns.

The Catholic Church, including religious orders such as Franciscans, Dominicans, and later Jesuits, set about converting Indians. By 1560 there were over eight hundred priests, monks, and nuns in New Spain serving in more than 160 churches, missions, or monasteries. Many Catholic clerics had amicable relations with Indians. Their documented observations tell us much about the devastating changes the conquest imposed on Native Americans. Bartolomé de las Casas (1484–1566), a Dominican friar and bishop of Chiapas in southern Mexico, served as the first Protector of the Indians, a royal post created to speak for indigenous interests. His book, *A Short Account of the Destruction of the Indies,* documented atrocities that colonizers committed against native peoples. He influenced the enactment of the "New Laws" of 1542, which provided greater protection for Indians, including a ban on enslavement. He also spoke out against the encomienda system, arguing that holders of rights to Indian labor had too much latitude to abuse their workers. Under his influence, Spain gradually phased out the encomiendas, replacing them with direct bureaucratic rule from Mexico City or Lima.

Portuguese Stakes in Brazil

In 1500, after Vasco da Gama returned to Portugal from the Indian Ocean, Pedro Álvares Cabral set out for the same destination. After crossing the equator, however, he sailed so far on the southeast trade winds that he bumped into the coast of Brazil. This unexpected landfall opened another theater of encounter between Europeans and Native Americans. Like Columbus, Cabral was not sure where he had landed. He found no large agrarian states comparable to Benin or Kongo, and he reported that the "island" he thought he had found offered little wealth compared to the silks and spices of India. Nevertheless, more expeditions headed for the Brazilian coast, and forest-dwelling Tupi people offered trade in timber, which they floated down rivers to coastal points, in exchange for steel axes and other useful items. Europeans also initiated a profitable trade in tropical woods from which textile dyes could be extracted.

European activity on the Brazilian coast remained limited until the 1530s, when the Portuguese monarchy, fearing French explorations in the region, encouraged crown subjects to claim land in northeastern Brazil. Indian populations there may have been quite dense when the Portuguese first arrived. But as in the Caribbean, large numbers succumbed to new diseases. Europeans found cane sugar cultivation profitable, and planters quickly adopted the economic model that had worked well on the Atlantic islands: labor-intensive harvesting, milling, and shipping of sugar on plantations using gangs of laborers. It became apparent by the later sixteenth century that Indians could not supply the demand and that economic success required large importations of African slaves (see Chapter 18). Meanwhile, Portuguese pathfinders continued to lead expeditions to Brazil's southern coasts and up river valleys to the deep interior.

New Power Relations in the Southern Seas

FOCUS In what ways did political and commercial systems change in the Indian Ocean region in the first half of the sixteenth century?

In the last quarter of the fifteenth century, merchants of the Indian Ocean and the China seas carried on flourishing trade from one busy port to another with no idea that their entire commercial network was about to be shaken. No single maritime power dominated or monopolized the southern seas trade or, as far as we know, had ever tried to do so. In the early part of the century, Ming Chinese emperors had dispatched seven mammoth expeditions to the Indian Ocean under the command of Admiral Zheng He (see Chapter 15). But their purpose, so far as we understand it, was primarily to expand the number of states that paid formal tribute to the Ming ruler, not to seize territory or drive local merchants out of business. In any case the Ming government terminated those voyages in 1433 owing to other political priorities, and Indian Ocean trade continued much as before. Merchants of diverse origin sailed lightly armed vessels, selling and buying in accord with local customs, prevailing political conditions, and fluctuating prices. The greatest dangers they faced were pirates and storms at sea.

This system came under threat in the new century when armed Portuguese carracks entered the region. The captains of these vessels attempted from the outset to control as much as they could of the trade in spices and other commodities, an aggressive strategy not previously witnessed in those waters. A Portuguese nobleman captured the spirit of this grand mission when he remarked that immensely valuable South Asian black pepper was no mere commodity. Rather, "pepper should be a sacred thing."[17] The level of seaborne violence rose markedly in the Indian Ocean between 1500 and 1550. Portuguese intruders attacked both ports and the ships of competing traders, and those traders fought back. The Ottoman imperial navy also joined the fray.

To Capture the Spice Trade

Vasco da Gama rounded Africa's Cape of Good Hope in 1498 on ships armed with artillery, and he used it in the Indian

Ocean to display his military clout and to force favorable terms of trade. He returned to Lisbon with a cargo of Indian pepper and other goods that paid huge profits. Dom Manuel, the king of Portugal, was delighted: "With the help of God, that the great trade which now enriches the Moors [Muslims] of those parts, through whose hands it passes." might now "be diverted to the natives and ships of our own kingdom."[18] New expeditions were soon on their way around the Cape. The fleet sent in 1505 returned with 1,100 tons of pepper.

Afonso de Albuquerque, who first sailed to South Asia in 1503 and subsequently commanded Portugal's coastal territories there, well understood that Asians had little demand for European goods other than gold and silver. If, therefore, the Portuguese were to acquire all the products they wished either to carry back to Europe or to sell in various Asian ports, they would have to force their way into the commercial system. Albuquerque's fleet seized several key ports in quick succession: Mombasa in East Africa (1505), Hormuz in the Persian Gulf (1507), Goa in South Asia (1510), and Melaka on the strait of the same name (1511). The threat of this new and heavily armed trading power was not lost on local rulers. According to one chronicle, Portuguese invaders sacked the port of Mombasa in what is today Kenya. Afterward the local Swahili-speaking ruler wrote a warning letter to his fellow sultan in a neighboring port: "May God's blessing be upon you, Sayyid Ali! This is to inform you that a great lord has passed through the town, burning it and laying it waste. . . . He not only killed and burnt men but even the birds of the heavens were shot down. . . . I give you these sad news for your own safety."[19]

Trading post empire. By the 1530s Portugal had several fortified enclaves facing the Indian Ocean, as well as one on Macau, an island off southern China (see Map 16.5). They

MAP 16.5 The southern seas in 1550.

The Portuguese concentrated their seaborne conquests on ports of South Asia, the pivot points of the southern seas trade. How would you compare the territorial claims of the Portuguese in Asia with those of the Ottoman or Ming empires?

bought spices for gold and silver but also began quickly to buy and sell numerous Asian commodities. They threatened naval action when necessary to require local shippers to buy trade permits and put in at Portuguese-controlled harbors to pay taxes on cargo. Similarly to their policy in Atlantic Africa, Portugal did not try to control more than coastal enclaves around the Indian Ocean rim. The one notable exception was the Zambezi River valley in southeastern Africa, where Portuguese traders pushed into the interior to found a number of small settlements. Portugal could not hope to command enough soldiers or weapons to seize densely populated interior regions or confront strong Asian or African states on land. Instead, it created a **trading post empire** aimed at controlling key ports, strategic points, and sea lanes. "I would like . . . to affirm," observed one Portuguese official in Goa, "that in no circumstances should the Portuguese enter as much as a hand-span into the interior . . . of India, because nothing keeps the peace and conserves our friendship with the kings and lords of India except that they believe and consider it most certain that we are content with the sea."[20]

In 1505 King Manuel I formalized Portugal's claims in the Indian Ocean and China seas by establishing the Estado da India (State of India), a governing body paralleling Spain's Council of the Indies. The Estado had charge of colonial administration, finance, and military operations over Portuguese coastal colonies from southeastern Africa to China. Though Lisbon was the imperial capital, Goa became the Estado's actual headquarters under the authority of a crown-appointed viceroy. Asian rulers did not necessarily respond to this development with hostility. Some of them either tolerated the Europeans or actively partnered with them to advance their own commercial interests. Ming imperial officials, for example, strictly limited foreign merchant activity in China's ports, but they allowed Portuguese venturers to establish a trading post on Macau as long as they paid tribute.

Challenges to Portuguese monopoly.
Asian rulers and merchants also realized by the mid-sixteenth century that Portugal's monopolistic ambitions were fading. Voyages around southern Africa remained expensive and dangerous. No more than seven ships a year went out from Lisbon, and in the sixteenth century nearly a third of them foundered in rough seas or were lost in Indian Ocean naval battles. The Portuguese hoped to monopolize India's pepper trade, but they could buy and transport only 10 percent of production. Many Asian sea merchants—Arabs, Chinese, Gujaratis, Malays—eluded Portuguese patrols, and they far outnumbered Europeans. As the century progressed, the Portuguese looked less like a maritime superpower and more like one more Asian commercial firm competing for business. Nevertheless, Portugal's spice trade profits were more than enough to entice the Netherlands, England, and France to send their own naval vessels around the Cape to plant their own trading posts. As the global economy emerged, so too did a new age of armed commerce.

Ottoman naval expansion.
Part of Portugal's early Indian Ocean strategy was to intercept the flow of trade from the Arabian Sea to both the Red Sea and the Persian Gulf by seizing ports at the southern approaches to those waterways. Initially, this strategy worked well enough to hurt

Fort Jesus commands the port of Mombasa, Kenya. Built on the orders of King Philip I of Portugal in 1591, this bastion was the first one the Portuguese designed in the Indian Ocean region to withstand artillery attacks from non-European powers. How might the construction of this type of fort reflect changes in the nature of warfare in the Indian Ocean during the previous century?

the commercial economies of Muslim Egypt and Southwest Asia as well as the Italian merchants who had for centuries visited Alexandria and other eastern Mediterranean ports. The Mamluk sultanate of Egypt, which had a small naval force in the Red Sea, allied with Gujarat in South Asia to expel the European interlopers from the region. This Muslim alliance defeated a small Portuguese fleet off the coast of India in 1507 but two years later lost a battle in which shipboard artillery proved decisive. Portuguese victory gave them freer run of the Arabian Sea for several years.

In 1517, however, the Ottoman Turkish army occupied Egypt and thereafter sent its own fleet down the Red Sea to confront the Portuguese and restore lost Asian trade. From then until the 1550s, Ottoman envoys and merchants cultivated relations with Muslim Asian powers, and Turkish squadrons periodically clashed with Portuguese carracks. Ottoman captains also mounted artillery on board in imitation of their adversary. Turkish expeditions sailed as far east as Aceh in Indonesia to provide its sultan with cannons. Ottoman forces expelled the Portuguese from Aden at the entrance to the Red Sea, but warfare between the two powers remained indecisive. As the ships of other European powers began to enter the Indian Ocean, however, the Ottomans abandoned their aggressive but expensive southern seas strategy.

A Portuguese ship in a Japanese port. A sixteenth-century Japanese depiction of "Southern Barbarians" repairing their ship and offloading luxury goods conveys the curiosity and wonder that early maritime encounters with Europeans elicited. This is a detail from a large screen that served as a room divider in an elite household. What might the picture tells us about Japanese perspectives on trade with foreigners?

The Trans-Pacific Link

While Portugal exploited the Cape route to Asia, mariners in the service of Spain continued to search for a way to get there by going west, despite the troublesome geographical complications that the discovery of America presented. Balboa's crossing of the Isthmus of Panama in 1513 raised new hope of a sea passage to Asia. A Spanish-funded expedition headed by Ferdinand Magellan, a Portuguese subject, finally found the westward route and demonstrated just how large the spherical earth really was. Magellan had already visited Southeast Asia as part of a Portuguese expedition, and he persuaded the Spanish crown in 1519 to sponsor a westward voyage. Commanding a fleet of five caravels, he sailed across the Atlantic and down the eastern coast of South America, then made his way through the strait that now bears his name and into the Pacific. Continuing northwestward on an interminable voyage that reduced the crew to eating leather and rats, he got as far as the Philippines. There he died in a fight with local warriors, though not before claiming the islands for Spain. It was Sebastián del Cano, Magellan's navigator, who actually circumnavigated the globe by piloting a single vessel westward across the Indian Ocean and back to Spain. Despite the expedition's success, few Europeans showed interest in the long and arduous voyage around the tip of South America as an oceanic trade route. Forty years after Magellan's journey, rather, Spain initiated colonization of the Philippines, a strategic pivot point, as we shall see, for immensely valuable trade across the northern Pacific between Mexico and China.

• • •

Conclusion

Magellan's crossing of the Pacific in 1520 filled the last gap in transoceanic communication and made genuinely globe-encircling interchange among human communities a reality. Afroeurasia and the Americas became connected from both east and west. Only Australia, as well as numerous islands here and there, remained for the time being in worlds of their own.

In the fifteenth century the world's densest and economically richest systems of production, trade, and finance were in Asia. Because Europeans understood this and because their own economies were expanding in that period, they searched for strategies to reach Asian markets without having to undertake long, immensely expensive, and probably futile wars against Muslim states to gain full access to the most direct routes to the Indian Ocean through Egypt or Southwest Asia. European mariners were well aware of educated speculation about the possibility of reaching Asia by sailing either around Africa or by heading west to the other side of the spherical earth. The Iberian countries, however, pursued exploration, trade, war, and settlement in the eastern Atlantic and along the African coast for more than a century and a quarter before they confirmed both theories and began to act on them.

Within a half-century of Columbus's voyages, the Atlantic Ocean became known territory—a "basin" of intercommunication like the Mediterranean or Arabian Sea, only much bigger. But as the sixteenth century progressed, the Atlantic also became smaller in the sense that marine technologists continually invented new ways to make ocean crossings faster, safer, and more cost-efficient. The regions of Europe and Africa that bordered the Atlantic no longer lay at the western edge of the intercommunicating world but suddenly became hubs for the movement of goods, people, and ideas in every direction. An Atlantic-centered economy began to take shape, though only very gradually did it compete with the Indian Ocean system in size, complexity, and wealth.

The way the Atlantic economy emerged is inseparable from the cataclysmic loss of Native American life. The population of the Americas in 1492 dropped by as much as 90 percent in the ensuing 150 years, a disaster that allowed Europeans to take control of the Western Hemisphere with a speed and depth that would otherwise have been impossible. Ironically, the population of Afroeurasia grew at an accelerating rate during the same time period. In Chapter 17 we return to Afroeurasia, to survey developments there in the sixteenth century, when societies were just beginning to experience the effects of the great world convergence.

• • •

Key Terms

Aztec empire 462	encomienda 473	Portuguese trading post empire 479
caravel 464	Guanches 460	sultanate 457
carrack 465	Kongo kingdom 461	Treaty of Tordesillas 469
Columbian Exchange 472	Melaka 457	viceroy 477
conquistadors 473	New World 469	

Please see end of book reference section for additional reading suggestions related to this chapter.

Change over Time

1290s–early 14th century	European sailors begin sailing deeper into the Atlantic, encountering the Guanches of the Canary Islands.
1394–1460	Henry the Navigator, a prince of Portugal, supports maritime technical improvements and expeditions along the Atlantic coast of Africa.
1403	Singapore's ruler founds the port of Melaka in Southeast Asia, which becomes a magnet for southern sea merchants.
1415	Portugal seizes the port of Ceuta on the coast of Morocco.
1433	China's imperial Ming government ceases its large naval expeditions ("Ming voyages") in the Indian Ocean.
1444	Portuguese mariners reach the Senegal River in West Africa.
1453	Ottoman Turks capture Constantinople, terminating the Byzantine state and taking control of sea trade between the Black Sea and the Mediterranean.
1469	The crowns of Castile and Aragon unite, laying the political foundation of the Spanish monarchy.
1492	Christopher Columbus sails from Spain across the Atlantic to the Caribbean Sea.
1494	Spain and Portugal settle claims to overseas possessions with the Treaty of Tordesillas, drawing an imaginary dividing line in the Atlantic.
1498	Vasco da Gama rounds the Cape of Good Hope to the Indian Ocean.
1502–1520	Motecuzoma II begins his reign over the Aztec empire, or Triple Alliance, in Mesoamerica.
1506–1543	Afonso I reigns in the Kongo kingdom and promotes political and cultural relations with Portugal.
1510	Afonso de Albuquerque's fleet captures Goa, which becomes the capital of Portugal's Asian trading post empire.
1517	The Ottoman empire's naval reach into the Indian Ocean expands following the conquest of Egypt.
1518	The first smallpox epidemic to result from the Columbian Exchange strikes Hispaniola in the Caribbean Sea.
1520	A Spanish expedition initially led by Ferdinand Magellan circumnavigates the globe.
1521	Spanish conquistadors led by Hernán Cortés defeat the Aztec Triple Alliance.
1527	The death of Inca emperor Huayna Capac and his son from smallpox leads to a battle for succession.
1532	Francisco Pizarro initiates the Spanish conquest of the Inca empire and Andean Peru.

17

Afroeurasia and Its Powerful States

1500–1600

Camel caravan merchants who crossed the western Sahara Desert in the sixteenth century may have thought that Ahmad al-Mansur, the sultan of Morocco, had taken leave of his senses. He proclaimed that he planned to send a large military expedition equipped with muskets, mortars, and cannons across a thousand miles of arid waste to launch a surprise attack on the West African empire of Songhay. A monarch of the Sa'adian dynasty, al-Mansur (reigned 1578–1603) commanded the northern terminals of the trans-Saharan camel routes, but the southern entrepôts were under the authority of Songhay. The sultan calculated that if he invaded Songhay and seized its desert ports, especially Timbuktu, he would control the entire western Saharan network and its immensely valuable trade in gold, salt, and slaves. Intelligence reports had informed him that factional struggles had weakened the Songhay state and that, despite its large cavalry, it had no guns. He scolded his advisors who opposed his scheme as too risky: "Our predecessors would have found great difficulty if they had tried to do what I now propose; . . . gunpowder was unknown to them, and so were firearms and their terrifying effect. Today, the Sudanese [people of Songhay] have only spears and swords, weapons which will be useless against modern arms."[1]

Al-Mansur won over his counselors, and in October 1590 a force of about five thousand infantry, horse cavalry, and support personnel departed from Marrakech, crossed the High Atlas Mountains, and advanced into the wilderness. The commanding officer

The Ottoman army, like Al-Mansur's Moroccan forces, used artillery to capture new territory in the sixteenth century.

was Judar Pasha, a Christian convert to Islam who had made a name for himself in the Moroccan army. He had never led such an ambitious expedition, however, and about half of his soldiers died along the route from exhaustion, sunstroke, or illness. In February 1591 the column reached the banks of the Niger River, where it skirts the southern edge of the desert.

Askiya Ishaq II, the emperor of Songhay, either did not know or failed to believe that a hostile army was about to materialize from the desert. Nevertheless, he managed to assemble a large force of cavalry and foot soldiers. Somewhere near the Niger the adversaries met. Though the emperor's army was by far the larger, Judar Pasha's disciplined gunners killed many defending troops and probably terrified many more. The emperor left the field of battle, and his remaining troops fled. Disorder and rebellion then spread through the Songhay realm, and within a few years it collapsed. Al-Mansur, however, did not get the trans-Saharan empire he wanted. The distances were simply too great. Rather, his officers settled in as lords of a small West African state and within a few decades lost political contact with Morocco.

Al-Mansur's desert adventure, as anticlimactic as it turned out to be, illustrates a major world-scale development in the sixteenth century. Morocco was just one of several Afroeurasian states that amassed formidable political power based on firearms technology. The rulers of these states created large, disciplined armies, which they deployed to conquer weaker neighbors and to tighten their authority within their own domain. On the whole, sixteenth-century rulers, in contrast to their predecessors, relied less on the cooperation of local chiefs and estate-owning aristocrats to maintain their power and more on loyal, centrally appointed civil and military bureaucrats. The first section of this chapter surveys the changing political map of Afroeurasia, focusing on regions where rulers consolidated authority over their subjects and pushed their borders outward.

The second section examines the significance of firearms technology and its spread across Afroeurasia. As this happened, armies became more lethal than they had ever been. Rulers, however, had to finance expensive armies and administrations, and this raised the stakes for control of agrarian resources, commercial routes, and subject populations that could be made to pay taxes. The immense cost of equipping land and naval forces with the new weaponry produced a revolution in political organization and finance, and it strictly limited the number of states that could compete for power on a large scale.

• • •

The third section investigates some of Afroeurasia's key sixteenth-century cultural developments, changes closely related to the rise of more powerful states and the expanding global economy. In the sphere of religious and moral systems, intense controversies took place over matters of belief and practice, notably in neo-Confucian China, the central Muslim states, and Christian Europe. A second important development was the ascendancy of particular regional languages and the distinctive cultural styles associated with them. In the sixteenth century, more local tongues gave way to languages associated with expanding states, universalist religions, and international merchant groups.

A Panoramic View

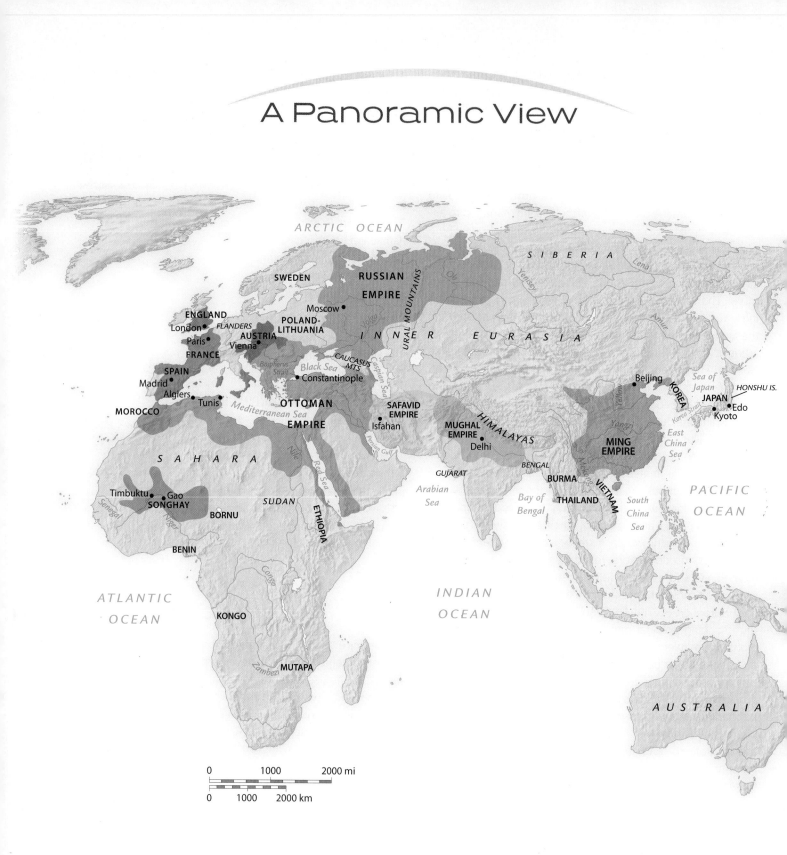

MAP 17.1 Major states of Afroeurasia, late sixteenth century.

The sixteenth century is notable for the growing number of relatively large, politically centralized states. What factors might help explain why most of these states were located in Afroeurasia's north temperate latitudes?

Afroeurasia's Political Panorama

FOCUS What developments in Afroeurasia in the sixteenth century account for the rise of more powerful centralized states?

In the sixteenth century, almost all major states in Afroeurasia had access to roughly equivalent technologies for farming, mining, communications, and war making. And most of those states shared in the population surge and accompanying economic expansion that generally characterized the period. With a few exceptions, states were organized as monarchies. Their kings, queens, emperors, sultans, or shahs occupied the apex of a hierarchy of officials, and they claimed to rule as agents of divine power. Beyond those common features, states varied widely in population, political institutions, and cultural diversity, and in the strategies they adopted to assert power and accumulate wealth (see Map 17.1).

By capitalizing on some combination of firearms technology and more efficient political organization, several states achieved remarkable success in the sixteenth century in at least one of two respects. First, those states became more efficient at controlling, regulating, keeping track of, and taxing their own populations; that is, they achieved greater political and economic centralization. Second, a number of them also used a large part of their financial resources to undertake campaigns of imperial expansion. Conquered states, which had previously been sovereign and perhaps powerful in their own right, either became tribute-paying dependents of bigger states or disappeared altogether. The number of political units in the world dropped steadily in the sixteenth century as powerful, expansionary states absorbed relatively weaker kingdoms, city-states, and self-governing clans and tribes.

The parallel trends toward greater state centralization and territorial expansion, the themes we highlight in this part of the chapter, were, however, not conspicuous in China, at least not in the sixteenth century. The Ming dynasty (1368–1644) reigned over the most populous and in many respects the most economically developed society in the world, and the state had achieved more effective central bureaucratic organization in the previous 130 years. The imperial palace generated laws and policies in consultation with commissions of administrative officials ideally guided by Confucian moral and political values. The dynasty's line of sixteen potentates ranged in leadership ability from brilliant to inept, but the bureaucrats that formed a chain of authority reaching from the capital to the most distant provinces continued for the most part to do their jobs whether the emperor was effective or not.

Nevertheless, China experienced growing political troubles after 1500. Both Confucian officials and imperial eunuchs (who served the emperor as bodyguards and palace administrators) became increasingly factionalized and hostile to one another. Local estate lords found new ways to avoid taxes and make the rural peasantry pay more. In the later century an influx of silver from American mines caused serious economic and financial turbulence. (We return to that issue in Chapter 18.) The later emperors largely rejected imperial expansion and adopted defensive strategies to protect their Inner Eurasian borderlands from Mongol or other nomad assaults. The government extended the Great Wall across western China. As Chinese emperors had long done, the Ming represented the empire as the world's "middle kingdom," deserving of the formal allegiance of all neighbors. Missions from Korea, Vietnam, and various Inner Eurasian power groups traveled periodically to Beijing to offer tribute. But these relationships served more to stimulate trade between China and societies that in fact ran their own political affairs.

The Ottoman Empire's Dramatic Expansion

The Ottoman Turkish sultanate, founded in Anatolia (modern Turkey) in the late 1200s, achieved the most spectacular territorial and seaborne expansion of any sixteenth-century state, with the exception of Spain and its American conquests. The Ottoman sultanate emerged as a major Afroeurasian empire after 1453, when its army seized Constantinople (modern Istanbul) and eradicated the Greek Byzantine empire (see Chapter 15). From that city, which overlooked the Bosporus Strait, the sultans commanded the immensely valuable shipping that passed between the Mediterranean and the Black Seas. By the start of the sixteenth century, the empire embraced the agrarian lands of Anatolia and a large part of the Balkan Peninsula in southeastern Europe. The central government evolved as a system in which the sultan reigned over a hierarchy of advisors and administrators, all of whom had the formal status of imperial slaves. This meant that the sultan commanded the absolute personal loyalty of this ruling elite and could appoint, dismiss, or execute any of its members at will. Starting with the reign of Selim I (1512–1520), the government marshaled its rich farm and commercial resources to undertake a new round of territorial conquests in almost every direction.

Ottoman army and state. All departments of the Ottoman government, except for the system of judicial courts run by Sunni Muslim legal scholars, had a strong military character. In one way or another, those ministries devoted themselves to imperial defense and relentless frontier expansion. In the sixteenth century, Ottoman forces consisted of three major elements. First were cavalry regiments, either Turkish frontier fighters (*ghazis*) or mounted units whose officers (*sipahis*) raised imperial troops in return for the right to tax peasants. The second element were the janissaries, the corps of slave infantry that in the sixteenth century numbered up to about thirty-seven thousand combatants and

Topkapi Palace. The center of Ottoman imperial administration for over 400 years, the palace buildings overlook the Bosporus —then as now a vital commercial waterway. Note the palace's location within a dense urban landscape.

that could match any land force in the world in martial skill and discipline (see Chapter 15). The third arm of Ottoman might was the navy, which in the early century supplanted Venice and Genoa as the preeminent maritime power in the eastern Mediterranean and Black Seas and which advanced into the Arabian Sea nearly simultaneously with the arrival there of Portuguese warships.

Like all early modern monarchs, the Ottoman sultans claimed to rule with divine consent. Their authority was limited only by the requirements of the *shari'a,* or Muslim law. The political nucleus of the empire from the later fifteenth century was the Topkapi Palace, resplendently situated on a site in Istanbul above the Bosporus. A continually growing complex of elaborate pavilions, chambers, and courtyards, Topkapi eventually had room for some five thousand residents, including members of the imperial family, state officials, soldiers, concubines, and a host of servants. From within the palace, the sultan's high council (*divan*) and a sort of prime minister holding the title of *vizir* gave advice and directed the various offices. Government in the provinces was less centralized than, for example, in Ming China. Cavalry officers, not civil bureaucrats, administered local affairs, and they forwarded to the capital fixed proportions of the revenue they collected from peasants.

Sixteenth-century conquests. The most aggressive Ottoman expansion took place in the reigns of Selim and his successor Suleyman I, called "the Magnificent" (r. 1520–1566). Selim extended Ottoman power to the south by conquering the populous Arabic-speaking lands of Syria and Egypt. To the east, he warred repeatedly with the Safavid (SAH-fah-vihd) empire of Persia, mainly for control of the cities and agricultural resources of Iraq. Ottoman forces invaded Egypt

in 1517, overthrowing the Sunni Muslim Mamluk dynasty that had ruled there for two and a half centuries. Shortly after that, Turkish privateers sailing under the Ottoman flag seized Tunis, Algiers, and other Mediterranean ports, thereby controlling North Africa's coastline as far west as the frontier of Morocco. Ottoman successes in the Mediterranean, plus persistent threats to invade Italy, set off several decades of warfare with Habsburg Spain and Venice on both land and sea. The tide of battle shifted repeatedly during Suleyman's reign, though in 1580 the adversaries agreed to an extended maritime peace, recognizing that neither of them was going to achieve complete dominance in the Mediterranean.

On the European front, Ottoman land armies invaded Romania in 1504 and subjugated the kingdom of Hungary in 1526. Three years later Suleyman's forces advanced up the Danube River valley and surrounded Vienna, the capital of Habsburg Austria. Though this siege alarmed western Europe, an early winter forced the attackers to retreat. Some historians have referred to the prolonged conflict between the Ottomans and several European powers as the "sixteenth-century world war" because the contending forces fought battles from the western Mediterranean to the coasts of India. The struggle was not, however, a straightforward clash between Muslims and Christians. Both France and several independent German princes allied with the Turks out of shared hostility to the Habsburgs.

The sprawling Ottoman state embraced many ethnolinguistic groups and a total population of about twenty-two million by the later seventeenth century. The ruling class proudly identified with the Turkic-speaking people that in earlier centuries had migrated from the Inner Eurasian steppes and after 1000 C.E. achieved dominance over Anatolia. As the empire grew, however, the Turkic population

A European Ambassador Compares Armies

In 1554 Ogier Ghiselin de Busbecq (1522–1592) traveled to Constantinople as the Habsburg or Holy Roman empire's ambassador to the Ottoman court. Raised in Flanders and educated in western European universities, Busbecq entered diplomatic service only months before receiving this important mission. During his eight years in Constantinople, he wrote numerous letters to his friend and fellow diplomat Nicholas Michault. In this correspondence he recounted travel stories and his observations of Ottoman life. Busbecq was especially interested in comparing the Holy Roman and Turkish empires. He was worried that Ottoman forces might defeat western European states because they seemed to him much hardier and better disciplined. Busbecq compiled his Turkish Letters *for publication in 1589, long after he left Constantinople. They remain a precious source of knowledge of the Ottoman state.*

The Turkish monarch going to war takes with him over 40,000 camels and nearly as many baggage mules, of which a great part, when he is invading Persia, are loaded with rice and other kinds of grain. These mules and camels also serve to carry tents and armor, and likewise tools and munitions for the campaign. . . . The invading army carefully abstains from encroaching on its magazines [stored supplies] at the outset; as they are well aware that when the season for campaigning draws to a close, they will have to retreat over districts wasted by the enemy, or scraped bare by countless hordes of men and droves of baggage animals. . . . Then the Sultan's magazines are opened, and a ration just sufficient to sustain life is daily weighed out to the Janissaries [imperial slave soldiers] and other troops of the royal household. The rest of the army is badly off, unless they have provided some supplies at their own expense. And this is generally the case, for the greater number, and especially the cavalry, having from their long experience in war already felt such inconveniences, lead with them a sumpter horse [packhorse] by a halter, on which they carry many of the necessities of life; namely, a small piece of canvas which they use as a tent, for protection against sun and rain, with the addition of some clothes and bedding; and as provisions for their private use, a leathern bag or two of the finest flour, with a small pot of butter, and some spices and salt, on which they sustain life when they are hard pressed. . . .

From this you will see that it is the patience, self-denial and thrift of the Turkish soldier that enable him to face the most trying circumstances and come safely out of the dangers that surround him. What a contrast to our men! Christian soldiers on a campaign refuse to put up with their ordinary food, and call for thrushes, beccaficos [a small bird], and suchlike dainty dishes! If these are not supplied, they grow mutinous and work their own ruin; and, if they are supplied, they are ruined all the same. For each man is his own worst enemy, and has no foe more deadly than his own intemperance. . . . It makes me shudder to think of what the result of a struggle between such different systems must be; one of us must prevail and the other be destroyed, at any rate we cannot both exist in safety. On their side is the vast wealth of their empire, unimpaired resources, experience and practice in arms, a veteran soldiery, an uninterrupted series of victories, readiness to endure hardships, union, order, discipline, thrift, and watchfulness. On ours are found an empty exchequer, luxurious habits, exhausted resources, broken spirits, a raw and insubordinate soldiery, and greedy quarrels; there is no regard for discipline, license runs riot, the men indulge in drunkenness and debauchery, and worst of all, the enemy are accustomed to victory, we, to defeat. Can we doubt what the result must be?

Source: Charles Thornton Forster and F. H. Blackburne Daniell, *The Life and Letters of Ogier Ghiselin de Busbecq*, vol. 1 (London: Kegan Paul, 1881), 219–222.

Thinking Critically

What particular traits does Busbecq believe that Ottoman soldiers possess, compared to European Christian troops? Why does he consider Turks a threat to the Holy Roman empire? How do you think a European reading this letter might react to Busbecq's characterization of the Ottoman army? Do you think that Busbecq might be exaggerating differences between Ottoman and Christian European armies? If so, what attitude or feelings might lead him to exaggerate?

came to be outnumbered by conquered peoples speaking Arabic, Persian (Farsi), Greek, Armenian, several Slavic languages, and a variety of other tongues. In its religious complexion, Muslims accounted for only a slight majority of the empire's total population. Christians in eastern Anatolia, Syria, Egypt, and especially southeastern Europe comprised more than 30 percent of the sultan's subjects. Jews accounted for another 10 percent in the sixteenth century. Indeed, the sultans welcomed thousands of Jews following their expulsion from Christian Spain in 1492. The state organized Greek and Armenian Christian groups, plus Jews, into *millets,* or legally constituted religious communities that were permitted to run their own internal affairs, including courts, schools, and tax collection. But Christians and Jews did not enjoy legal and social equality with Muslims. Members of these communities could not serve in the government or army, and they paid a tax (the *jizya*) that did not apply to Muslims.

An empire of trade. As it expanded, the Ottoman state spilled across the east–west trade arteries running between the Mediterranean and both Inner Eurasia and the Indian Ocean. In the later sixteenth century, after Portuguese commercial aggression in the Arabian Sea quieted down, Muslim sea traders returned in large numbers, enjoying Ottoman naval protection on the routes through the Red Sea and Persian Gulf. Muslim, Jewish, and Armenian merchants moved goods from one part of the empire to another. Egypt exported rice and sugar, Syria supplied dates and pistachios, Anatolia shipped dried fruit and silk, and the Balkans traded wheat, timber, and wine. To encourage Italian and other European shippers to visit Ottoman ports to buy textiles, carpets, and other products, the government offered them special commercial privileges, beginning with a treaty with France in 1536. Under these **capitulations,** European merchants enjoyed reduced tariffs, freedom from Ottoman taxes, and if they became involved in civil or criminal cases the right to try them in their own consular courts rather than before Muslim judges.

> **capitulations** International agreements in which one state awarded special privileges within its borders to subjects or citizens of another state.

Shah Isma'il and the Red Heads. This miniature painting depicts the Safavid ruler and his elite warriors, identified by their red hats. Compare this picture to the chapter's opening image. What differences do you notice between Safavid and Ottoman visual representations of military action?

The Safavid Empire of Persia

After more than a century and a half of political division, a new political force arose in the early sixteenth century to unify Persia, the region centered on the Iranian plateau. Like the Ottoman governing elite, the new Safavid dynasty traced its ancestry to Turkic horse archers who had entered Southwest Asia in the tenth and eleventh centuries. Isma'il, the first Safavid king, began his political career in the late fifteenth century and at the tender age of seven as chief of a Turkic military state located in the hill country that is today Azerbaijan and northwestern Iran. He also headed a Muslim Sufi association, which gave its name to the Safavid political movement. This mystical brotherhood, dedicated to individual spiritual enlightenment, attracted Turkic pastoral groups that inhabited the grassy valleys south of the Caucasus Mountains.

The Safavid state and the ascendance of Shi'a Islam. Beginning in 1501, Isma'il's cavalry vanquished one after another of the several small Turkic states that dominated Iran and Iraq. Isma'il's fighters were known as the Qizilbash, or Red Heads, because of the red Sufi headgear they wore. Advancing down the Tigris-Euphrates River in 1508, warrior bands seized Baghdad in 1508 and in a short time most of the commercial and manufacturing cities of Persia.

Isma'il also declared his devotion to Shi'ism, the wing of Islamic belief and practice that was taking militant forms in Southwest Asia in the fifteenth century. Sunni Islam, the faith of the great majority of Muslims, affirmed that supreme spiritual authority belonged with the Muslim community as a whole. The caliphs, or "deputies," who had succeeded the Prophet Muhammad since the seventh century, were obligated to implement and defend the community's will. Shi'ism proclaimed to the contrary that authority rested with the blood descendants of Ali, who was the fourth caliph and a kinsman of the Prophet. Ali's successors, called imams, were, according to Shi'a teaching, the rightful leaders of all Muslims. Isma'il came to profess the particular variant of Shi'ism that venerates the twelfth imam in the line of succession after Ali. According to Shi'a belief, this imam had gone into an occult, or hidden, state

Imam Mosque in Isfahan, Iran.
Shah Abbas commissioned this mosque as part of the reconstruction of Isfahan as his new capital city in the early seventeenth century. The walls and domes are covered with inscriptions from the Quran and floral patterns formed from hundreds of thousands of glistening tiles. This type of ornamentation is a distinctive feature of Persian architecture. What architectural elements let you know this building was intended to communicate the power and splendor of a Muslim ruler?

but would one day return to reign over the world with divine authority. Claiming leadership as earthly representative of the Hidden Imam, Isma'il and his warriors strove to impose Shi'a doctrines on subjugated Sunni populations. Shi'a scholars and theologians, many from Iraq and Syria, formed a new religious elite. Gradually, Shi'ism became, by armed pressure or willing conversion, Iran's majority religion, though in many respects Sunni and Shi'a teachings and devotions are identical. In southern Iraq, a province of the Safavid state, Arabic-speaking populations converted to Shi'ism in large numbers. In this period, therefore, Iran and Iraq took on the religious profiles they largely have today.

The reign of Shah Abbas. After Isma'il's death in 1524, his early successors, who claimed the ancient Persian royal title of "shah," had a hard time holding the state together. It survived, however, by balancing the power of Red Head cavalry officers, who had rights to extract taxes from the mass of population, against the influence of urban, educated Iranian and Iraqi families, who ran the central government and enforced Shi'ism as the state religion.

The Safavid empire came to full flower under Shah Abbas, a ruler of unusual talents. Ascending the throne in 1587, he reigned for forty-three years (r. 1587–1629). To check the power of rural tribal commanders, he created a standing professional army. This force of as many as thirty-seven thousand troops included artillery and musket units advised by a group of English mercenaries. Healthy male prisoners seized in wars against the Christian kingdoms of Georgia and Armenia in the Caucasus Mountains were trained to serve in elite military units. These soldiers had the legal status of slaves of the shah, as the janissaries did in the Ottoman state. The shah's gunpowder army showed its mettle in victories over Ottoman forces in Iraq and over the Mughal

(MOO-guhl) empire of India in Afghanistan. The Safavids had no navy, but in 1622 Abbas evicted the Portuguese from their fortress at Hormuz on the Persian Gulf with the aid of gunships supplied by friendly English trading partners.

The Persian empire had more limited resources than the Ottomans did. About 70 percent of Iran is extremely arid, and most farming required intensive irrigation. Shah Abbas, however, strengthened the economy by investing in water management, improving the trans-Iranian road and trail system, encouraging silk textile and carpet exports, and striking trade deals with European merchant firms. To boost overland traffic, he appointed Armenian Christian merchants as his special agents. They operated a commercial network linking the Volga River valley in Russia with both Europe and Southwest Asia. The shah's capital at Isfahan, a city built around an expansive central square flanked by spectacular domed mosques and an enormous covered bazaar, attracted a population of about 400,000. The government invited both Armenian and Roman Catholic clerics to build churches in Isfahan, no doubt finding friendly contacts with Christian powers a useful counterweight to the Ottoman empire, its enduring enemy.

Mughal Power in South Asia

Like Persia, South Asia experienced a long period of political fragmentation before achieving unification in the sixteenth century under a new and militarily aggressive dynasty. From the thirteenth to the early sixteenth centuries, several Muslim dynasties in succession dominated the river plains of northern India and the majority population of Hindu farmers and town dwellers. These regimes also fought, and sometimes allied with, local Hindu kingdoms. In 1526, however, Babur, ruler of a minor state in Afghanistan, led an assault on northern India, seizing most of it by fielding an army that included both traditional horse archers and gunpowder cannons. A descendant of the thirteenth-century Mongol conqueror Chingis Khan and a lover of Persian art and poetry, Babur (r. 1526–1530) founded a dynasty that became known as Mughal, a corruption of the word *Mongol*. As in both the Ottoman and Safavid empires, the ruling military elite boasted descent from Inner Eurasian warriors.

The reign of Akbar the Great. Babur governed for only four years, and his son Humayun failed to gain firm control of northern India until just before his death in 1556. It was Babur's grandson Akbar (r. 1556–1605) who put the Mughal state on a firm footing and transformed it into a powerful regional empire. He organized an elaborate system of administration and taxation and during his half-century rule sent armies in all directions—south into the subcontinent's central plateau (the Deccan), north into Himalayan Kashmir, southwest into the cloth-producing region of Gujarat, and east into Bengal, the rice-rich lower Ganges River valley. He made no investment in a navy but relied on Indian Ocean merchants, including Portuguese and other Europeans, to export South Asian cotton textiles and other goods to the wider world.

Akbar had the same ambitions as many other monarchs of that era: to make war on neighboring states, confiscate their treasuries, tax his subjects, ensure public order, and display imperial power on a magnificent scale. To pursue these aims, he organized the upper level of officialdom into thirty-three ranks of imperial commanders, or *amirs*. These officers, including both Muslims and Hindus, raised cavalry troops—the higher the rank, the greater the number of horsemen required—to defend or extend imperial territory. The state paid them salaries or gave them rights to income from farm land. In this way Akbar created a **service nobility.** This was a governing class that enjoyed imperial income and privilege but did not constitute a land-owning aristocracy. It could not pass on property to heirs or build a power base independent of the state. Akbar also bolstered central authority by appointing agents to conduct surveys to determine the value of agricultural land. He then named local princes, landlords, or simply profit-minded entrepreneurs, who used survey information to collect taxes from Hindu and Muslim peasants. These intermediaries transferred a predetermined portion of revenue to the state but kept the balance for themselves to help maintain local order and pay for their own luxurious households.

Akbar founded the Mughal dynasty's authority on absolute loyalty and service to the monarch—the Royal Person. In this spirit, he and his successors demanded continuous, breathtaking displays of power, including intricate court rituals and lavish consumption of goods. Akbar proclaimed himself *padshah,* or king of kings, a title that recalled ancient

> **service nobility** A privileged governing class whose members depended entirely on the state rather than on inherited property and titles for their status and income.

Gathering the almond crop. This painting from the *Baburnama*, the memoir of the Mughal conqueror Babur, is included in an illustrated edition published after the ruler's death. Peasants gather the nuts and load bags onto pack animals while more elaborately dressed men weigh the harvest. Why would a ruler's memoirs include a depiction of agricultural activity?

Persian and Hindu ideas of the ruler as a semidivine personality. Antonio Monserrate, a Catholic missionary who resided at the imperial palace in the 1580s, described the subservience of Akbar's courtiers:

> His court is always thronged with multitudes of men of every type, though especially with the nobles, whom he commands to come from their provinces and reside at court for a certain period each year. When he goes outside the palace, he is surrounded and followed by these nobles and a strong body-guard. They have to go on foot until he gives them a nod to indicate that they may mount. All this adds greatly to the wonderful majesty and greatness of the royal court.[2]

Among early modern rulers, Akbar championed peculiarly liberal views on religion. He came to the throne as a Muslim, but much to the dismay of orthodox clerics, he proclaimed a divine religion centered on a Sufi, or mystical, fraternity that taught that all faiths have spiritual insights to offer. He invited Muslim theologians, Sufis, Hindu sages, and even visiting Roman Catholic priests to debate questions of morality and doctrine. He also took a benevolent view of Sikhism, a new Indian religion whose founder Nanak (1469–1539) taught reconciliation of Hinduism and Islam through simple love of God, pacifism, and strict moral conduct. He gave the Sikhs land in the city of Amritsar to build their Golden Temple, which remains today the world headquarters of the Sikh faith. He also abolished a number of taxes that Hindus had to pay, and he allowed them to build new temples. Akbar's religious movement died with him, but his creative mix of political might and cultural tolerance almost certainly contributed to the social stability that characterized India for nearly a century after his reign.

Akbar had the fortune to come to power at a time of accelerating demographic and economic growth in South Asia. Its population approached 100 million, and the cities of Agra, Bijapur, and Ahmedabad were among the largest in the world. The subcontinent had immense resources in grain, cotton, silk, pepper, sugar, indigo, gems, and timber. Indian spinners and weavers had for centuries led the world in cotton textile production, and once European mariners opened the oceanic routes, global demand for Indian cottons swelled. Akbar obliged his subjects to pay taxes in copper, silver, or gold coins, a policy that pushed more rural farmers into the commercial market to earn money. The economy of Bengal, the rainforested region of the lower Ganges River, was particularly dynamic. Mughal armies conquered Bengal, then encouraged peasants from other parts of India, predominantly Muslims, to migrate there to clear forests, drain swamps, and transform the Ganges delta into endless tracts of rice paddy.

Akbar's successors. Akbar had three intelligent, strong-willed successors: Jahangir (r. 1605–1627), Shah Jahan (r. 1628–1658), and Aurangzeb (r. 1658–1707). These kings maintained Akbar's administrative system for the most part, and they continued to add territories to the empire. Jahangir, one of Akbar's sons, consolidated his father's achievements, though in fact his Iranian wife Nur Jahan had a huge influence on state affairs, promoting Persian styles in imperial art and craft, and for a time acting as the de facto ruler. Jahangir's son Shah Jahan also looked toward Muslim Persia for models of civilized art and letters, launching a splendid building program that included the glorious Taj Mahal.

Aurangzeb, the last of the great Mughals, waged wars of conquest throughout the central plateau and sent armies into India's far south. His campaigns, however, consumed twenty-six years of bloody, immensely expensive fighting. To keep revenue flowing in, he taxed rural populations more harshly, which in the later years of his reign provoked rural uprisings and banditry. In stark contrast to Akbar, he also rigorously enforced Muslim orthodoxy, forcing Hindus out of government service, pulling down Hindu temples, and making war on the pacifist Sikhs, who had to take up

arms to survive. His narrow view of religion clearly weakened social and cultural bonds within the empire. After he died, the empire deteriorated rapidly, making way for new power groups to carve out local bases of their own. As we will see in Chapter 18, these groups included armed merchants of the English East India Company.

Russia: From Principality to Empire

Russia joined the club of multiethnic empires near the end of the sixteenth century. This state encompassed a much smaller population than the Mughal or Ming Chinese states, but it expanded so rapidly over such great distances that by 1800 it was the world's largest monarchy, in square miles.

St. Basil's Cathedral, Moscow. Ivan the Terrible commissioned this Russian Orthodox cathedral following military victories along the Volga. The building, located on Moscow's Red Square, blends Byzantine arches, towers that resemble northern Russian churches, and features of Asian minarets. Why might the tsar build a monumental church in the center of Moscow after conquering territory in Inner Eurasia?

This was a striking phenomenon considering that Russia originated in the mid-fifteenth century as Moscovy, a small state centered on the city of Moscow.

The rise of Moscovy. Mongol conquerors had subjugated the Russian-speaking lands in the 1240s, but when their power waned two centuries later, the Moscovite princes Ivan III (r. 1462–1505) and his son Vasily III (r. 1505–1533) progressively eliminated rival regional rulers. Their conquests yielded extensive wheat and timber lands, plus key commercial towns, notably the northern fur trade emporium of Novgorod. The early Russian monarchs, or tsars (ZAHRS, from the word "caesar"), allied closely with the Russian Orthodox Church and represented themselves as agents of God and guardians of Christian truth. They also imposed their authority over the land-owning Russian aristocracy, known collectively as the boyars. They did this partly by creating a new governing class drawn largely from a pool of talented military and civil officers who received revenues from farm estates in return for unconditional loyalty. Like the Mughals in India, the tsars aimed to create a service nobility that had no large properties or aristocratic family attachments and could counterbalance the influence of the traditional boyar families.

Ivan IV, who ruled for fifty-two years (1533–1584), pursued the centralizing policies of his predecessors so pitilessly that

his subjects came to know him as "Ivan the Terrible." He founded new ministries of state, as well as a special group of imperial enforcers that dressed in menacing black uniforms and carried brooms as emblems of their mission to cleanse the land of treason. In 1550 he founded the *streltsy,* a professional force of musketeers. These soldiers resembled the janissaries in the Ottoman empire, though they were freemen rather than military slaves. Deeply suspicious of the Russian aristocracy, Ivan periodically terrorized nobles families and seized their lands.

Russia's Eurasian empire. Between 1552 and 1556 Ivan IV's armies seized the middle and lower Volga River valley from regional Muslim rulers. These victories had great significance. First, they gave Russia control of the strategic north-south trade route linking the Baltic Sea with Southwest Asia and India. Second, they pushed Russian power closer to the Black Sea and the political orbit of the Ottoman empire. In the later 1500s, the two empires entered into diplomatic and commercial exchanges, but relations also became increasingly tense, leading to wars in later centuries. To the east, cavalry in service to the tsar crossed over the Ural Mountains in the 1580s to penetrate western Siberia. These gun-toting horse soldiers, known as Cossacks, had diverse origins. Many were former Muslim herders, others landless Slavic peasants. They made their living by trading furs and plundering Siberian villages, but they also spearheaded the conquests that gave the tsars access to boundless resources in furs, timber, and potential wheat land.

To the west, the early tsars sought stronger political and cultural contacts with Europe's Catholic states. In the fifteenth century, Russian merchants, envoys, and scholars began traveling regularly to Germany, Italy, France, and England. Relations with western neighbors, however, were not all happy. Starting in 1558, Ivan IV engaged in a prolonged war with the kingdoms of Sweden and Poland-Lithuania over control of Baltic coastlands. He coveted a warm-water port on the west, but he failed to get it after a quarter-century of fighting.

The high cost of Ivan's wars put heavy pressure on Russian and other Slavic peasants to pay taxes and generate income for aristocratic estate lords. To escape their lot, many peasants fled to sparsely populated lands in the Ukraine or western Siberia. To prevent such flight and to meet rising demand in Europe for Russian wheat, the imperial government placed new

Yermak Timofeyevich, conqueror of Siberia. This lithograph depicts a Cossack leader responsible for key military victories that enabled Russian expansion into Siberia in the late sixteenth century. This picture, made 300 years later, combines military symbols and images from several regions and time periods. Why might a nineteenth-century artist depict a sixteenth-century soldier in Roman battle dress? What other elements in the lithograph suggest warriors from different places and eras?

restrictions on farm tenants, gradually reducing them from legally free rent-paying peasants to serfs. This status bound them to live on a particular estate and pay dues to its master. Ironically, serfdom spread widely in Russia at the same time it was disappearing in western Europe.

Ivan's political repression and exhausting wars contributed after his death to a severe "time of troubles." Between 1598 and 1613, central authority nearly collapsed amid civil war, famine, peasant rebellion, and Polish and Swedish border invasions. The state returned to stability, however, after Russian nobles elected Mikhail Romanov tsar (r. 1613–1645). The new Romanov dynasty initiated more conquests in Inner Eurasia and reigned over the empire for more than three hundred years.

Japan and the Tokugawa

Among relatively smaller Afroeurasian states, Japan advanced toward political unity and strong central government in the late 1500s. In the previous two and a half centuries, the Japanese island chain had been politically divided into territories of numerous self-governing estate lords, known as daimyo. Supported by paid knights, or samurai, the daimyo constituted Japan's aristocratic ruling class. The emperor, who resided in the city of Kyoto, had only ritual functions. He appointed a shogun, or "great general," who ideally ruled Japan as his agent. But under the Ashikaga shoguns (1336–1573), named for the noble family that controlled that office, local daimyo did largely as they pleased. After Portuguese merchants introduced firearms to Japan in 1543 and local gunsmiths learned how to make them, warfare among the most powerful daimyo grew in intensity.

Starting in the 1550s, however, Oda Nobunaga (1534–1582), a local warlord from the big island of Honshu, made effective use of both long pikes and muskets to defeat several rival lords. At his death by assassination, his forces controlled a large part of Honshu. Toyotomi Hideyoshi (1536–1598), a general who built his career in service to Nobunaga, assembled an army of 300,000 soldiers and within a few years emerged as military lord of three of the archipelago's four major islands. Flush with victories at home, he also launched an amphibious invasion of Korea in 1592, even boasting, "I shall take even China in hand, and have control of it during my lifetime."[3] By assaulting Korea, however, he overreached badly. The Korean navy, which included heavily timbered ships equipped with artillery, harassed Japanese military supply lines in the Korea Strait. After six years of intermittent fighting, the Chinese government, which had close ties with Korea's Choson dynasty, sent an army that helped expel the intruders.

Hideyoshi died a much weakened ruler. Nevertheless, Tokugawa Ieyasu (r. 1603–1616), a Hideyoshi ally, held the state together. He took the title of shogun (made legitimate by the endorsement of the ceremonial emperor) and inaugurated the long era of the Tokugawa (TOH-koo-GAH-wah) shogunate (1603–1867). Similarly to other centralizing

powers in Afroeurasia, this new regime required a strong army and a steady revenue flow to reduce the power of local magnates and provincial town leaders. Ieyasu and his successors accumulated immense tracts of taxable farm land, forbade ordinary people to own weapons, tore down many castles held by samurai knights, and obliged the 250 or so regional daimyo to contribute to the central treasury. To keep these aristocrats on a short political leash, the shoguns made them live in the capital city of Edo (modern Tokyo) every other year. The Tokugawa did not, however, try to govern the countryside in the direct way that imperial bureaucrats did in Ming China. Rather, they worked out a pragmatic

Tokugawa Ieyasu. The first Tokugawa shogun is depicted here as a ruler rather than a warrior. He is seated formally and framed by drapery displaying the Tokugawa family crest—three hollyhock leaves in a circle. In what ways does this silk hanging scroll symbolically legitimize the shogun's centralization of political power in Japan?

bargain with the daimyo that allowed these lords to run local administration and maintain small armies. This division between central and provincial power permitted the shogunate and the daimyo to work together to keep the peace and extract wealth from millions of farmers. From the perspective of ordinary men and women, all levels of government were authoritarian and demanding. On the other hand, Japan achieved greater political stability in the seventeenth century than it had enjoyed for several hundred years.

Strong Monarchies in Southeast Asia

In Indochina (mainland Southeast Asia), the tropical rice-growing lands south of China, trends toward political consolidation got seriously under way in the late fifteenth century. Three kingdoms—Burma (Myanmar), Thailand, and Vietnam—gained control of most of Indochina, which had a population in 1600 of perhaps ten million (see Map 17.2). These three Buddhist monarchies conquered and assimilated numerous smaller states and mountain chiefdoms, using some of the same state-strengthening techniques as other Afroeurasian monarchies. They acquired firearms, organized conscript armies, and adopted new governing strategies for wringing revenue from their subjects. In the sixteenth century they hired foreign advisors and mercenaries, mainly Europeans but also Japanese. All three kingdoms financed centralization with wealth from flourishing rice economies centered on the region's great river valleys.

The Burmese state launched a centralizing project shortly after 1500, conquering neighbors up and down the Irrawaddy

MAP 17.2 Major Southeast Asian states, sixteenth century.

In the premodern centuries, China and its Confucian values wielded great cultural influence in Vietnam. South Asia's Hindu and Buddhist traditions had comparable impact on Burma, Thailand, and Cambodia. What geographical factors might help account for this difference?

River valley. Similarly, Vietnam expanded from the state's core region in the Red River valley southward along the coast of the South China Sea. Near the end of the sixteenth century, two aristocratic families, one in the north and the other in the south, divided Vietnam into two autonomous power centers, though these leaders kept up a fiction of unity by paying allegiance to the same, politically feeble emperor. Thailand also had great military success. In the later fifteenth century the energetic King Trailok (r. 1448–1488) colonized Cambodia and the Mekong River valley, codified royal laws, and reduced independent noble strongholds to the status of tax-paying provinces. After several fierce wars with Burma in the later sixteenth century, Thailand emerged as the stronger power.

The European States

In the fifteenth century, Europe west of Russia was a jumble of sovereign kingdoms, principalities, city-states, and mountain chieftaincies. By the end of the sixteenth century,

however, a small number of regional powers extended their authority at the expense of weaker monarchs and princes. This centralization process took place in the larger context of Europe's expanding population, production, and trade. Agricultural and commercial wealth gave the strongest states the means to build armies and administrative bureaucracies.

Large states and small. In rough terms, the most successful experiments in state consolidation took place at the western and eastern extremes of Europe (see Map 17.3). In the west, France, England, Portugal, Spain, and, after 1600, the Netherlands emerged as larger and more tightly centralized states, though in all of them rulers had regularly to negotiate and compromise with rich noble families and other local power groups. If we recognize that the Strait of Gibraltar was a negligible barrier to communication between the Iberian Peninsula and North Africa, we may add Morocco to this list. That Muslim sultanate was involved deeply with both Spain and Portugal in trade, diplomacy,

MAP 17.3 Major European states, 1600.

Consolidation of royal power over larger territories characterized some parts of Europe in the sixteenth century. How would you account for differences in the size and number of states in Europe compared to South Asia, Southeast Asia, or East Asia in the sixteenth century?

St. Bartholomew's Night, August 24, 1572. Huguenot artist François Dubois painted this image after fleeing to Switzerland. It is not known whether Dubois witnessed this event in Paris, but the painting depicts two incidents described or illustrated in other sources. The French queen Catherine de Medici, dressed in black, stands outside the palace to inspect a pile of dead bodies. The slain Huguenot leader Gaspard de Coligny hangs out a window. Does the artist reveal a pro-Protestant bias in this painting? If so, in what ways?

and war. It lost coastal enclaves to Portugal, but from the 1570s the Saadian dynasty (1554–1659) emerged as a strong and economically prosperous monarchy. Moroccan forces repelled a Portuguese invasion in 1578, and under Sultan Ahmad al-Mansur undertook, as we saw in the chapter introduction, a bold campaign to control trade across the Sahara Desert.

In eastern Europe, Poland-Lithuania, a state created in 1569 by the merger of two dynasties, encompassed more territory than any other European polity west of Russia. But its rulers continued to share power with the leading noble families, which collectively dominated financial and military affairs. In Scandinavia, Sweden emerged as a strong monarchy and, for a time, a leading player in European diplomacy and war. Most of southeastern Europe, by contrast, was incorporated into the Ottoman empire.

Europe's middle zone remained politically splintered. The Italian peninsula was divided into the city-states of Genoa, Florence, Milan, Venice, and a few others, together with the papal states (lands ruled directly by the Catholic pope) and territorial dependencies of Spain. In Germany, as well as in the Netherlands before 1600, a conglomeration of more than 150 dukedoms and free cities blanketed the land. Most of these small states paid formal allegiance to the Holy Roman emperors of the Habsburg dynasty, whose core territory was Austria. But on the local level, German princes and city councils remained largely free of royal interference.

Wars of religion. Between 1500 and 1650 the states of Europe fought multiple wars with one another over territory, resources, and the future of the Christian church. In 1517 Martin Luther (1483–1546), a German monk and a native of the Duchy of Saxony in central Germany, touched off the movement later labeled the Protestant Reformation when he publicly accused the Catholic hierarchy of rampant corruption and false doctrines. Initially Luther wanted to spark Christian reform, not rebellion, but events escalated quickly. Within barely two decades of his first public statements, new Protestant churches, which renounced the pope's authority, began to spring up across Europe. Moreover, religious quarrels broke out not only between loyal Catholics and Protestants in general but also between one Protestant community and another. All of Europe's rulers chose sides in these clashes, at the cost of much bitterness and bloodshed.

In that era, Europeans, like societies in most of the world, took it for granted that rulers had the right to specify the religious allegiance of their subjects. When a ruler opted for one or another Protestant church, the entire population was expected to conform. Protestant princes typically persecuted or expelled men and women who remained loyal to the Catholic Church. Catholic rulers did the same to Protestants. (We return to doctrinal and organizational changes in sixteenth-century Europe later in the chapter.)

Even before the religious wars broke out, two alliances of states, one headed by the Habsburg empire and the other by France, fought to shape Europe's political future. In 1519 Charles V (r. 1519–1556) succeeded to the Habsburg throne, inheriting sovereignty over a large part of central Europe (German- and Slavic-speaking regions), most of the Netherlands, parts of Italy, Spain, and the young Spanish empire in America and the Philippines. A pious and resolute Catholic, he envisioned himself transforming Europe from a conglomeration of squabbling kingdoms into a unitary Christian empire under Habsburg family leadership. Once Europe's states were united, Charles predicted, they would drive the Ottoman Turks from southeastern Europe and the Mediterranean. In fact, Charles spent more time warring with other Christian states than with the Ottomans. The French kings Francis I (r. 1515–1547) and Henry II (r. 1547–1559) had no intention of being absorbed into Charles's Christian empire and violently resisted the idea. France even allied with the Turks against him. After fighting France, Ottomans, and several German Protestant princes for three decades, Charles finally exhausted himself and his treasury. When he abdicated his throne in 1555, his brother Ferdinand (r. 1558–1564) inherited the German lands and the office of emperor; his son Philip II (r. 1556–1598) took Spain and the Spanish empire. Thereafter, European rulers accepted the reality that multiple centers of power would have to coexist, at least for the time being.

France, the Netherlands, and England.

In the later sixteenth century the titanic struggle between the Habsburgs and French alliances yielded to a series of smaller conflicts, civil wars, and popular rebellions, many of them colored by religious hostility. In France, battles between Catholic and Protestant factions continued on and off from 1562 to 1598, punctuated by urban massacres and assassinations. In 1572, for example, Catholic officials and soldiers marked St. Bartholomew's Day on August 24 by conspiring with Parisian mobs to murder thousands of Protestants. The slaughter then spread to other cities. France's civil war finally ended in compromise. The monarchy remained Catholic, but French Protestants

(Huguenots) received limited religious rights. Under King Henry IV (r. 1589–1610), France returned to political stability, and the monarchy amassed more power.

Traditionally the French king took advice on taxation and other matters from the Estates-General. This was a council of delegates from the country's social hierarchy of three "estates": the high Catholic clergy, the nobility, and the common population. The third estate was represented by merchants, lawyers, and other members of the bourgeoisie, or urban middle class. Louis XIII (r. 1610–1643), however, never called the Estates-General in to session after 1614, putting forward the doctrine that the ruler had responsibilities to his subjects for law, order, and territorial defense but that he answered directly to God, not to the three estates. In fact, no French king called the Estates-General for another 175 years. Meanwhile, the monarchs continued to consolidate power as salaried officials whittled away at the customary rights and powers of provincial aristocrats and notables, much as rulers were striving to do in other parts of Afroeurasia.

In the Netherlands, which belonged to the Habsburgs, several commercially prosperous cities revolted against Philip II, who followed Charles V on the Habsburg throne. In 1579 the rebels proclaimed independence as the United Provinces of the Netherlands, or simply the United Netherlands. (This new state was also known as the Dutch Republic and the United Provinces.) Fighting with Habsburg armies, however, dragged on intermittently for eighty years.

The *Armada Portrait* of Queen Elizabeth I. This late sixteenth-century portrait of the English queen exists in at least three different versions, attesting to the monarch's popularity and the powerful symbolism of the image. The windows behind Elizabeth offer two views on the English victory over the Spanish invasion fleet. Note that she has her back to the nighttime storm and turns toward the calmer scene on the left. What other symbols of the monarch's power can you identify in this picture?

Though Catholics and Protestants fought on both sides, the United Netherlands emerged eventually as a thoroughly Protestant country, whereas the Spanish Netherlands, the region that gained independence centuries later as Belgium, remained predominantly Catholic.

England entered the sixteenth century a much smaller, militarily weaker monarchy than either France or the Habsburg empire. King Henry VIII (r. 1509–1547) tried to reconquer territory that the English crown had once held in France but with no success. Henry also provoked a major religious crisis when in the 1530s he repudiated papal authority, made himself head of what became the Church of England, and seized the extensive lands held by Catholic monasteries. He did this, not because of any heartfelt conversion to Protestantism, but because of a dispute with the pope over his marital affairs and a larger ambition to gain religious as well as political supremacy in his realm. Under Elizabeth I (r. 1558–1603), Henry's daughter and successor, England enjoyed political stability and stayed out of foreign wars until the 1580s when it supported the Dutch fight for freedom from Spain. Elizabeth invested energetically in naval ship building, and in 1588 the English fleet defeated the Spanish Armada, a force Philip II launched in a failed attempt to invade Britain.

Like France, England traditionally had a royal advisory council, but this parliament, as it was called, gained rather than lost power in the early modern era. Parliament's members were landed aristocrats, high churchmen, lesser nobles, and, on occasion, town leaders. Henry VIII and Elizabeth pressured Parliament to bend to their will, but they also depended on it for taxes and loans, especially if they wished to fund wars. Gradually, Parliament won the authority to approve new taxes before the ruler had the legal right to collect them. This assembly of notables thus emerged as a more effective counterweight to kingly power than such advisory groups managed to do in other centralizing monarchies of the era.

The Songhay Empire

Population growth, agricultural expansion, and the development of trade networks all encouraged the formation of more and larger centralized states in Africa south of the Sahara in the fifteenth and sixteenth centuries (see Chapter 16). Trans-Saharan caravan trade, which linked the Mediterranean world with tropical Africa, spurred the development of monarchies in the Sudan, that is, the agrarian and partially urbanized region of open or wooded savannas just south of the desert.

Named for the ethnolinguistic population that inhabited a region along the Niger River where it passes close to the Sahara, Songhay was the largest African empire in the sixteenth century. It began as a modest chieftaincy paying tribute to Mali, the giant Sudanic state that had flourished in the thirteenth and fourteenth centuries. Mali's gradual deterioration left a regional power vacuum that Sunni Ali

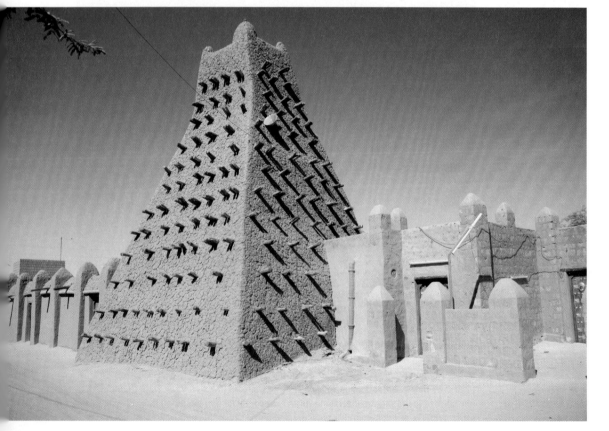

Sankore Mosque, Timbuktu. Like the structure in the city of Jenne (see Chapter 13, p. 382), this building combines the shape of a mosque—minaret and an interior courtyard—with Sudanic mud-brick architecture. The Sankore mosque was the focal point of Timbuktu's leading madrasa, or college of religion and law. It emerged as an important site of Muslim scholarship in the sixteenth century. What geographic and economic factors do you think contributed to Timbuktu's growth as a center of learning?

(r. 1464–1492) and Askiya Muhammad (r. 1493–1528), the two most energetic Songhay monarchs, rose to fill. Centered on Gao, a key commercial center on the Niger, Songhay at its height extended for more than seven hundred miles along the Niger and incorporated farming and herding peoples speaking numerous languages. The governing and commercial classes were largely Muslim, though the majority of the population adhered to traditional polytheistic beliefs and rituals.

Songhay exported gold, ivory, and slaves across the Sahara, but its economic foundation was farming and cattle herding. In Askiya Muhammad's time, Niger valley farmers constructed canals, dykes, and reservoirs, expanding irrigation to produce rice on a large scale. Around 1500 the region experienced the start of a climatic wet cycle. Over the ensuing decades, average annual rainfall increased, and summer rains extended farther into the fringes of the desert, opening up new areas for grain growing and cattle.

Askiya Muhammad undertook a pilgrimage to Mecca in 1495, and he funded mosques and patronized numerous Muslim scholars, both local intellectuals and visitors from North Africa. In the sixteenth century, Timbuktu gained a wide reputation as a center of Arabic learning. The Muslim scholar Leo Africanus, who crossed the Sahara from Morocco about 1510, described Timbuktu in his *History and Description of Africa:* "Here are many shops of artificers and merchants, and especially of such as weave linen and cotton cloth. And hither do the Barbarie [North African] merchants bring cloth of Europe. . . . Here are great store of doctors, judges, priests [Muslim clerics], and other learned men, that are bountifully maintained at the king's cost and charges. And hither are brought diverse manuscripts or written books out of Barbarie."[4]

Songhay had no firearms that we know of, but like the Ottomans and Safavids it recruited a standing army of military slaves to fight alongside local militias called up when needed. It fielded a massive cavalry force, its bowmen and lancers clothed in armor of thick cloth quilting. The king appointed royal kinsmen to provincial governorships, and scholars literate in Arabic constituted a central administration of secretaries and scribes organized in ministries.

As we described in the chapter introduction, Songhay's imperial history ended abruptly. The Moroccan musket and artillery troops that appeared suddenly from out of the desert in 1591 dispersed the Songhay cavalry in a single battle. In short order, chiefs and nobles who had paid tribute to the king rose in rebellion, and the central regime disintegrated. No monarchy of the scale of Mali or Songhay appeared again in the western Sudan until the nineteenth century.

The New Era of Guns

FOCUS In what ways did the wide adoption of gunpowder technology affect political, economic, and social patterns in Afroeurasia in the sixteenth century?

Among the instruments of centralizing power that Afroeurasian states deployed in the early modern era, none was more important than firearms. At the start of the thirteenth century, the world had no guns. In the sixteenth century it bristled with them, and they were beginning to transform the way humans waged war, organized governments, and kept public order.

In the two centuries from 1300 to 1500, artisans working in several lands progressively transformed primitive metal tubes that fired stone balls in wildly unpredictable directions into lethal artillery that could demolish castles, gouge gaping holes in the sides of ships, and kill many soldiers all at once. As technological and tactical innovations enhanced the power and accuracy of guns, wars became progressively more deadly. One scholar has estimated that in the first 1,500 years of the Common Era about 3.7 million men and women died from war-related causes, including famine and disease. But in the sixteenth century alone, about 1.6 million people died in wars. In the seventeenth century, the number jumped to 6.1 million.[5]

The Citadel of Turin, Italy, in 1644. Star forts, or *traces italienne*, replaced circular defensive walls in parts of Europe where rulers could afford these expensive strongholds. The triangular bastions, or projections, allowed soldiers on facing ramparts to give each other defensive cover. A deep moat or ditch and an outer defensive wall of loosely packed earth kept enemy artillery at a distance and forced advancing infantry into vulnerable positions before they could reach the inner stone walls. What other changes in military organization and tactics do you think the development of gunpowder weapons brought about?

New and Deadly Armies

By the later 1400s, rulers learned that gunpowder weapons worked best when manufactured in large numbers and issued to ranks of troops who fired volleys of shot at defensive fortifications or charging cavalry. Small states and stateless societies invariably lacked the material wealth to deploy such massed firepower. Even those states that could afford large arsenals had to solve numerous logistical and tactical problems that armies had never previously faced.

One key advance was recruitment of much larger infantry forces to fight alongside cavalry, which had traditionally enjoyed higher social status than foot soldiers. An infantry unit armed with muskets and marching in close order could devastate an advancing enemy with a wall of fire. Muskets, however, took longer to load than crossbows or longbows because the infantryman had to swab out the barrel and insert a powder charge and ball. Officers could speed up the firing rate, however, by organizing troops in ranks, or rows. In a battle, the front rank would fire, then move back to reload as the second row stepped forward. The earliest use of this tactic may have been in sixteenth-century Japan, where Oda Nobunaga taught soldiers to fire in multiple ranks. A short time later, Dutch officers refined this tactic by exhaustively drilling infantry to maneuver, load, and shoot in synchronized harmony. In the seventeenth century, massed infantry tactics spread to all armies in Europe, as well as to the Ottoman empire. Mounted warriors also got better at controlling handguns. Cavalry in sixteenth-century Morocco may have been the first in the world to master the art of firing guns from horseback.[6]

Rulers also had to recruit bigger armies to accommodate the complex technology of both artillery and the defenses against it. Bronze, brass, and cast iron artillery required large teams to transport and repair them. Sixteenth-century cannons did their most damage smashing holes in defensive walls. In response, Italian engineers made cities and castles less vulnerable by constructing earthen ramparts and ditches that kept enemy artillery from approaching too close and by placing defensive guns on high bastions. Consequently, rulers had to recruit even more soldiers to build and garrison massive fortifications.

After 1500 the size of armies catapulted upward. By 1595 France had 80,000 fighters on duty, and by 1710, around 360,000. Ming China maintained the largest military in the world, posting several hundred thousand soldiers along its frontier with Inner Eurasia. These figures would be even larger if they included the great numbers of noncombatants that almost always accompanied early modern armies on the march. Support personnel included supply contractors, mechanics, horse grooms, merchants, servants, and construction laborers. They also included many women, who went along as traders, cooks, laundresses, prostitutes, and caregivers to the sick and wounded. Wives and children frequently accompanied soldiers on the march, foraging for food not provided by the army. A Dutch document of 1622 describes

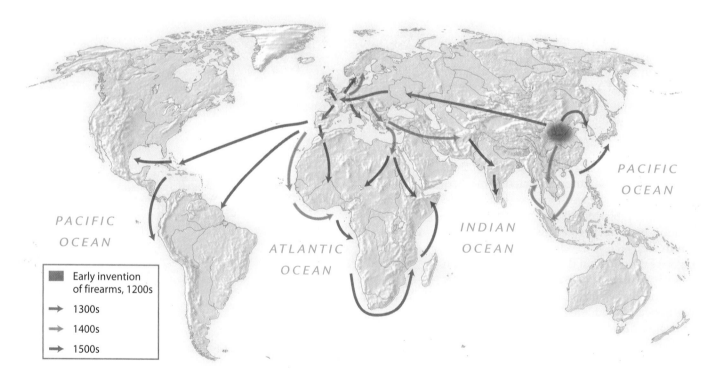

MAP 17.4 Spread of firearms, fourteenth through sixteenth centuries.

In the sixteenth century gunpowder weaponry reached every continent except Australia. What differences do you notice in the direction of the spread of firearms in the fourteenth century compared to the sixteenth? What might explain these differences?

Legend:
- Early invention of firearms, 1200s
- → 1300s
- → 1400s
- → 1500s

The Invention of Gunpowder and the First Casting of Bronze Cannon. This engraving by Dutch artist Philip Galle appeared in 1600 in a collection called *New Discoveries*. The image depicts many facets of arms production. Skilled craftsmen are at work while assistants stoke the fires and provide mechanical power—look carefully at the wheel on the left. Describe the action portrayed outside the foundry in the background on the right. Why might the engraver have included that detail?

"a small army of carts, baggage horses, nags, sutlers [traders], lackeys, women, children, and a rabble which numbered far more than the army itself."[7]

The Military Revolution

In the fourteenth and fifteenth centuries, gunpowder technology spread westward from China across Afroeurasia. After 1450, however, the patterns of innovation and diffusion became more complicated. The Ottoman Turks, for example, pioneered muskets with strong steel barrels. Indian metalsmiths excelled at making brass cannons, and French technicians led the way in designing light, mobile field artillery. Rulers aspiring to compete for wealth and territory had little choice but to join the stampede for guns.

The spread of firearms. States that lacked gunpowder weapons might face disaster, as the Songhay empire discovered in 1591 when Moroccan musketeers turned up. Firearms contributed, if much less decisively than disease epidemics, to Spain's rapid defeat of the Aztec and Inca empires. Ottoman forces seized Egypt and Syria in 1517 because musket and cannon units were not well integrated into the Mamluk army. Its aristocratic cavalry preferred to fight with bows, lances, and swords. The Ottoman army entered Egypt with guns booming and quickly overran the Mamluk horse regiments. Japan was something of an exception to the dominant pattern. The founders of the Tokugawa shogunate triumphed with the aid of cannons and musketry. In 1637, however, the shoguns had to put down a serious revolt led by musket-wielding Japanese

Christian converts. In the aftermath of that disturbance, the state gradually abolished the manufacture and sale of firearms and let its arsenal rust away. Since the shogunate enjoyed political stability and faced no imminent external threat, radical gun control worked well. Tokugawa Japan remained practically war free for more than 250 years.

After European sailors opened new transoceanic passages, knowledge of firearms spread faster, and heavy guns could be transported from one part of the world to another in a matter of months (see Map 17.4). Private gun merchants, mercenaries, and freelance technical advisors offered their services far and wide. German and Hungarian gunners advised the Ottoman army. Japanese musketeers fought for the king of Thailand. In China, the Ming government enlisted foreign advisors to strengthen firepower along its Inner Eurasian frontier. Ming commanders studied Turkish, Portuguese, and Dutch artillery designs and ordered Chinese metal founders to copy them. One observer described how Ming artillerymen in 1626 saved a northern city from an assault of Manchurian horse archers: "As the cannon went off, one could see in the light of the fires the barbarians and their horses being thrown up in the air; those who fell in the confusion were countless, and the villains, being badly defeated, ran away."[8] States also sent guns and military missions to allies. The Ottoman sultans shipped artillery to Southeast Asia to help Aceh, a Muslim kingdom on the island of Sumatra, fight off Portuguese assailants. In northeastern Africa, the Christian monarchy of Ethiopia bolstered its army with four hundred Portuguese musketeers, while neighboring Muslim states accepted help from Ottoman gunners.

Many Afroeurasian states with access to the sea supported navies of one size or another, and from the mid-sixteenth century, several rulers adopted the Iberian tactic of mounting cannons on ships (see Chapter 16). China, Korea, Japan, Vietnam, and Thailand, as well as Southeast Asian maritime kingdoms, built vessels to accommodate mortars or artillery, if only to defend ports and protect local sea trade. The Ottoman Turks built hundreds of armed galleys, which operated on all the seas from the Mediterranean to the Indian Ocean. Near the end of the sixteenth century, England, the United Netherlands, and France, the three richest states of northwestern Europe, began to deploy shipboard artillery to challenge Spanish and Portuguese dominance of the oceanic routes. These powers interloped on Portugal's lucrative spice trade in the Indian Ocean and negotiated their own deals with Asian sellers.

Paying for gunpowder armies. Historians have called the worldwide transition to gunpowder-based armies and navies a "military revolution" because of its far-reaching impact on economy and society. States aiming to make war on neighbors, subdue local aristocrats, and turn defiant peasants into submissive taxpayers had to recruit and pay fighters, expand chains of command, and procure guns, uniforms, horses, ships, and countless supplies. They had to ensure production of iron, copper, and other metals and build roads, bridges, and harbors to move troops and materiel. They had to employ metalsmiths, engineers, accountants, doctors, and commercial agents. In other words, no state could accumulate power without investing great sums of public money. Therefore, the military revolution also involved, as some historians have called it, a "fiscal revolution." That is, rulers

fisc The treasury of a sovereign state; a state department concerned with financial matters.

had to put heavy demands on the **fisc** if they hoped to achieve armed advantage over their rivals. The most powerful states sometimes dedicated 70 to 90 percent of their total annual budgets to military expenses, a much larger proportion of expenditure than any country allocates today.

European monarchs invented an array of new taxes to harvest revenue. In the seventeenth century, the tsars of Russia collected at least 280 different taxes, including levies on honey, salt, bathhouses, and the contracting of third marriages.[9] Some states strengthened direct rule in the provinces, sending officials from the capital to collect taxes, set up legal courts, and keep the peace in collaboration with local nobles, town magistrates, and religious leaders. Where they had the military backing to do it, royal agents bypassed these local authorities altogether. Many governments also borrowed from rich private families to get infusions of cash for wars. In Europe, bankers, such as the Fugger family of southern Germany, became immensely rich advancing funds to rulers. Big loans, however, pushed states deeper into debt, periodically destabilizing financial markets. The Spanish Habsburg emperor Philip II spent so much on his wars that, despite his access to American silver, he had to declare bankruptcy four different times.

The Limits of Central Power

We should not overemphasize the power of early modern regimes to monitor and regulate their subject populations. States learned how to do it on a much larger scale in later centuries. In the 1500s, communication technology, dependent as it was on animals, wagons, and boot leather, prevented micromanagement of far-flung provinces. Midsized states, such as France or Thailand, tended to have more success at direct rule than did giant ones like the Ottoman or Mughal empires. Central regimes also left economic improvements and education mostly to local communities and religious institutions. Some rulers undertook censuses and land surveys to maximize revenue collection, but early modern states had limited knowledge of the numbers, incomes, and whereabouts of the people they ruled, certainly compared to the databases that government agencies work with today.

Some monarchs strengthened their authority over local aristocrats and town authorities, though at the price of incessant negotiations over long-established rights, privileges, and legal jurisdictions. After dispatching soldiers to reduce a rural area to submission, rulers often found it less expensive and bothersome to let local leaders continue to run affairs and perhaps grant rights of **tax farming** to landed nobles or private contractors.

tax farming A system in which a government awards the right of tax collection to a private individual or group in return for a fee or a percentage of the taxes gathered.

State intrusions in local affairs rarely went uncontested. Revenue-hungry monarchs had to confront aristocratic resistance movements, urban uprisings, peasant rebellions, and banditry. Between 1514 and 1551, for example, the kings of France, fixated on raising money for wars, had to suppress tax revolts in ten different cities and six different regions.[10] The long Dutch revolt against the Spanish Habsburgs began as a violent tax protest in 1571. Rural men and women also slipped from the grasp of centralizing rulers simply by fleeing. In Mughal India, farmers frequently avoided burdensome taxes by running away to forests or sparsely populated frontiers where state agents would not venture. In Russia, tax-loathing peasants ran off to the Ukraine or Siberia to get beyond the tsar's reach.

Trends in Religion, Language, and Culture

FOCUS In what ways did political and economic changes in the sixteenth century affect patterns of cultural life in different parts of Afroeurasia?

The number of sovereign states in the world shrank in the sixteenth century because rulers with guns absorbed weaker states and societies into their own expanding territories. Similarly, and partly as a consequence of political centralization, consolidation also took place in religion, language, and styles of culture. By 1500, all of the major belief systems that exist today had already appeared in Afroeurasia. Three of them—Buddhism, Christianity, and Islam—reached out to millions of potential converts as missionaries, as well as merchants, soldiers, and scholars with religious messages to share, moved out along the global communication networks. These three universalist faiths progressively assimilated, modified, or displaced many purely local religious beliefs and practices, a phenomenon that had been occurring in earlier centuries. Global communication and interchange also sped up what linguists have labeled **language death**. Scholars have estimated that in the past one thousand years, the number of languages spoken in the world has fallen from between 10,000 and 15,000 to fewer than 7,000, and the process continues to accelerate. By one current estimate, one language goes extinct every two weeks.[11] In the early modern era, local tongues and the cultural ideas and practices that those tongues expressed lost ground to ascendant languages associated with expanding states, universalist religions, or merchant networks.

language death A process in which the number of native or fluent speakers of a particular language declines over time until no community of speakers remains.

Afroeurasia's religious landscape changed significantly in early modern times, not only because "big religions" spread more widely, but also because accelerating global change raised numerous new questions about humankind, nature, and the cosmos. Transoceanic communication confronted societies in both Afroeurasia and the Americas with ideas and things that seemed strange, unexplainable, and perhaps dangerous. Christians, for example, debated whether American Indians descended from Adam and Eve or, because the Bible does not account for them, represented an entirely separate divine creation. Chinese Confucian scholars who hosted European missionaries tried to wrap their minds around such novel ideas as the supreme being's taking a three-part form—Father, Son, and Holy Ghost. Practitioners of local polytheistic religions in Indonesia or West Africa met Muslims who urged them to renounce their nature spirits and household deities and submit to the One God.

The major universalist faiths had for many centuries experienced internal divisions or disagreements about belief and practice. The very fact that Buddhism, Christianity, and Islam spread so widely and crossed so many linguistic and ethnic frontiers made it inevitable that doctrinal differences and organizational splits would occur. The early modern era witnessed intense religious debates and ruptures, especially when popular movements to improve society or recharge moral energies gathered support.

Intellectual and Moral Ferment in China

In the last century and a half of the Ming dynasty, people in Beijing and several coastal cities began to debate the nature and proper direction of Chinese society. Rapid economic change, the growth of city populations, and new contacts with people and products from abroad stimulated their thinking. Roman Catholic missionaries were among the new influences, bringing Christian teachings, as well as astronomy, geometry, and clock making. These newcomers generated lively debate with Chinese intellectuals, though they had little impact on popular beliefs.

Millions of Chinese performed Buddhist and Daoist devotions, and the educated classes, especially the huge Ming bureaucracy, looked to the moral and ethical precepts of neo-Confucianism for guidance in social and public life. An amplification of the teachings of Confucius (551–479 B.C.E.) and other ancient sages, neo-Confucianism emphasized righteous moral behavior, daily ritual, respect for hierarchy, and dedication to family and local community. To encourage social harmony throughout the land, the Ming state made neo-Confucianism the imperial orthodoxy and closely regulated the activities of religious groups, including Muslims and Christians.

Chinese intellectuals nonetheless argued over neo-Confucian ideas during this period. Corruption and cronyism plagued the imperial government in the sixteenth century, and to some educated people, neo-Confucian doctrines appeared sterile and elitist. One response was a lively reform movement initiated by Wang Yangming (1472–1529), a Chinese military officer, public official, and philosopher. He argued that, contrary to neo-Confucian orthodoxy, all human beings possess innate moral knowledge and can therefore discern good from evil. Ordinary men and women may discover intuitively how to lead an honest life without mastering Confucian texts or performing complex rituals. Wang's proposition that neo-Confucian scholars had no corner on truth or virtue won him a large following among young literate people, including Buddhists and Daoists already inclined to personal introspection. After Wang died, some of his disciples expanded on his ideas to preach individual creativity, education for the poor, and respect for women's inherent intellectual abilities. Neo-Confucian officials who championed strict hierarchy and male authority struck back, and some of Wang's disciples ended up in prison or dead. Nevertheless, Wang's movement freed up and broadened the scope of Chinese intellectual life.

Tension between Sunni and Shi'a Muslims

Although Islam spread to more people than any other major faith in the early modern era, quarrels between Sunni Muslims and adherents of Shi'ism caused serious political and social distress. Sunni and Shi'a communities had shown for centuries that they could live near one another in mutual toleration. But when Shi'a doctrine became the "official" religion of the Safavid state, which occupied the geographical heart of the Muslim world, ill feelings were aggravated. The neighboring Ottomans, whose Sunni sultans claimed the title of caliph, doubted the loyalty of Shi'a communities within their empire. For their part, Shi'a clerical leaders rejected the legitimacy of the Ottoman caliph. Safavid and Ottoman armies fought each other mainly over territory, not doctrine, but mutually hostile religious rhetoric fueled this chronic conflict. Indeed, in the sixteenth and seventeenth centuries, the idea hardened that Sunni and Shi'a Islam constituted two distinct and mutually exclusive forms of the faith.

Religious Crisis in Europe

Religious organization in both Islam and Buddhism tended to be fluid, informal, and no more than loosely centralized. In Christianity, by contrast, churches formally supervised doctrine and practice. The Roman Catholic Church, the exclusive Christian organization in western and central Europe up to the sixteenth century, was a huge administrative, financial, and educational institution. When church leaders clashed over belief and worship, the crisis affected nearly everyone (see Map 17.5).

The Roman church had presided over western Europe's medieval cultural flowering. By 1400, however, the church's moral light was dimming. Its integrity depended on principled men and women occupying the highest offices—pope, cardinals, bishops, and the heads of monasteries and nunneries. In the 1300s the clergy's reputation plummeted. Many Christians faulted the church for failing to prevent or relieve the horrors of the Black Death, and they watched in bewilderment as two, and at one point three, rival popes struggled for supremacy for forty years (the Western Schism, 1378–1417). Across Europe, dismayed Christians told stories of corrupt and greedy bishops, priests with bastard children, and materialistic popes dedicated mainly to their family's fortunes. Higher-minded clerics bewailed this state of affairs but achieved little change.

The Protestant Reformation. Martin Luther reiterated the protests of earlier critics when in 1517 he published a scholarly disputation in the form of Ninety-Five Theses, directed mainly against the sale of indulgences. This was a church practice in which clerics took donations from people on the promise of offering special prayers to help deceased friends and relatives move up to heaven from purgatory (the place of temporary punishment for earthly sin). Luther denounced this "indulgences market," and he deplored priestly immorality and church wealth. He damned the pope as the antichrist and proposed bold new interpretations of biblical scripture. In 1520, to no one's surprise, the church excommunicated him. Resolute and brave, but also bad tempered and tactless, Luther might have died a martyr at the stake had not the Elector of Saxony and other German princes protected him from arrest. Those rulers had complex motives for supporting a religious rebel. In varying degrees they sympathized with Luther's religious ideas. But they also resented the flow of German wealth to the Vatican treasury, and they saw an opportunity to assert their rights of self-government against Charles V, the Holy Roman emperor and a staunch Catholic. Because mechanical printing presses were just then appearing across Europe, Luther's books, pamphlets, and hymns spread faster than they would have in any earlier age. He became something of a religious sensation, and within two decades, supportive Christians were organizing independent worship communities in Germany, Switzerland, and other countries.

All these protesters, or Protestants, rejected the pope's authority, but not all of them became "Lutherans." Other emerging leaders disagreed with Luther on various points of theology and church organization. For example, disputes arose among Protestants over the display of images of Jesus in church buildings, how churches should be governed, and what exactly Jesus meant at the Last Supper when he took a piece of bread and said, "This is my body." The most prominent early Protestant scholars and preachers included Ulrich Zwingli (1484–1531), who pioneered reform in Switzerland, and the French lawyer John Calvin (1509–1564), who set up a church in Geneva that became a model for Protestant organization across Europe. More radical groups, such as Anabaptists, Quakers, and Unitarians, variously advocated baptism for adults rather than infants, political pacifism, vows of poverty, and the principle that God's nature is singular rather than a separate but united trinity. In short, Protestant sects multiplied, and the Roman church permanently lost its monopoly over Christian doctrine and worship.

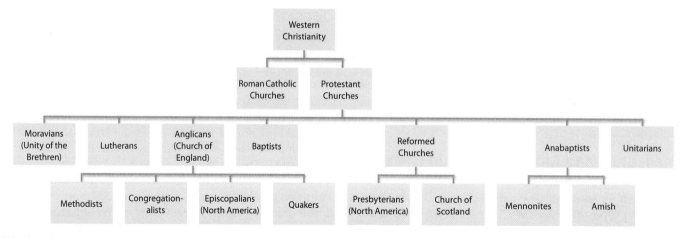

Principal divisions of western Christianity, sixteenth through eighteenth centuries.

MAP 17.5 Religions of Europe, 1560.

Where do religious boundaries match political borders on this map? Can you account for the places where religion and political rule coincide, and where they are different?

Map legend:
- Anglican
- Calvinist
- Calvinist-influenced
- Roman Catholic
- Lutheran
- Lutheran-influenced
- Boundary of the Holy Roman Empire

Protestant teachings. Despite their differences, Protestants shared certain precepts that generally distinguished them from Roman Catholics, and still do. One was the doctrine that the Holy Bible is the only valid Christian authority. Believers must seek divine truth through scripture alone. No bishop, priest, or saint has divine authority to intercede between an individual and God. This doctrine did much to encourage people to read their Bibles and stimulate literacy, but it also meant that Protestantism was sure to branch out in several directions.

Protestants also professed that human beings are justified, that is, redeemed or saved, exclusively by faith in God's love, not by anything they may do to overcome sin or to gain divine favor. The Catholic Church encouraged Christians to perform "good works" in expectation of realizing God's forgiveness and entry to heaven. These works included acts of kindness and charity but also obedience to church doctrines, laws, and sacraments. Protestant reformers countered that if people have heartfelt faith in God's grace, good works will follow naturally. In Luther's view, unconditional surrender to the divine will—without expectation that this devotion will guarantee any particular results—liberates Christians from the fear that they can never do enough good deeds or conquer enough of their sins to receive God's grace. Somewhat differently, John Calvin asserted that God predestined some to salvation and others to hell regardless of how many good works they might do. To Catholics, such a teaching suggested that God could be fickle and punitive.

Protestant churches also allowed members of the clergy to marry. The Catholic Church taught that priests and nuns must remain celibate, devoting themselves totally to God's service and remaining free of family cares and obligations. Protestant leaders argued to the contrary that wholesome family life would educate children in Christian virtue, help ministers avoid sexual sin, and provide pastors with female companions and helpmeets. In the early Protestant churches, women sometimes took on leadership roles as writers and organizers. Catholic and Protestant clerics mostly agreed, however, that although males and females are spiritually equal, women should keep silent in churches, submit themselves to the will of male relatives, and accept intellectual inferiority as part of the divine order of things. A few brave women retorted that Christians should challenge traditional gender roles inherited from the medieval

Religious differences in Germany, 1529. This woodcut depicting rival Christian services circulated in Europe in the new and inexpensive print medium aimed at popular audiences. On the right, a Catholic priest in elaborate robes preaches to a somewhat distracted congregation. On the left, a Protestant minister uses a Bible to preach to congregants, who are also reading Bibles. What other differences do you notice in the two scenes? What message do you think the creator of this woodcut aimed to convey?

church. As a German woman wrote in 1524, "Although St. Paul [in the New Testament] forbade women to preach in churches and instructed them to obey their husbands, what if the churches were full of liars?"[12] For the most part, however, these women's voices went unheard.

Europe became religiously plural after 1550, but no Protestant denomination advocated religious freedom. Rather, they all insisted on the correctness of their own particular version of Christian truth. Consequently, Lutherans, Calvinists, and members of other sects frequently persecuted (and sometimes murdered) one another. Catholic Spain convened special courts known as the Holy Inquisition to rid the country of all religious deviants—Muslims, Jews, and Protestants alike. Intolerance took a particularly abhorrent turn in the later sixteenth century, when trying, torturing, and executing people accused of witchcraft became a popular civic pastime in both Protestant and Catholic countries. The great majority of victims were women, often poor, elderly, socially isolated individuals who had few defenses against richer and more powerful people who accused them of conspiring with Satan.

The Catholic Reformation. Once a significant number of European rulers aligned themselves with Protestantism, the Roman church could not simply go on as before. Many Catholic clerics wanted reform as badly as Luther did but from within the existing church. Internal reform initiatives got under way in the 1540s, and they had two major aims: to frustrate Protestant success and to reinvigorate the church's

moral authority, tacitly recognizing that critics had made some legitimate points.

A Catholic reform council, which met intermittently between 1545 and 1563 in the Italian city of Trent, reaffirmed most of the church's fundamental doctrines but also took numerous actions to strengthen the clergy's moral and spiritual fiber. Church leaders insisted, for example, that priests and monks become literate. A series of devout church fathers, beginning with Pope Paul III (1534–1549), also worked for change. The Catholic Reformation, sometimes called the Counter Reformation, approved the creation of several new religious orders committed to restoring the church's integrity and energy. The Society of Jesus, or the Jesuits, founded in 1540 by the Spanish nobleman Ignatius Loyola (1491–1556), became most active on a world scale. Loyola argued that the spiritual weapons against Protestantism must include advanced education and missionary zeal. He established schools to train young priests, and he dispatched Jesuit missionaries to America, Africa, and Asia, where they often learned local languages and offered non-Christian rulers technical and scientific advice. In 1535 Angela Merici (1474–1540), an Italian aristocrat, founded the Company of St. Ursula. Members of this order, called Ursulines, took vows as nuns. But they resided with their families rather than in cloisters, and they dedicated themselves to Christian education of girls in both Europe and overseas colonies.

After 1650, following a century and a half of debilitating warfare among European states, the region's religious map generally stabilized. Most rulers agreed to accept one

A Mennonite minister and his wife. This oil painting by the celebrated Dutch artist Rembrandt van Rijn expresses the values of well-to-do Protestant elites in the Netherlands. Conelis Claesz Anslo, the clergyman, was the son of a successful merchant and leader of Amsterdam's Mennonite community. His wife Aeltje Gerritsdr Schoueten listens attentively to him. Although their dress is somber, the fur trim of his coat and the fine lace of Aeltje's cap display their wealth. The Asian tapestry used as a table covering and large books on the left signal Anslo's connections to the global market and his status as a man of learning. What do you think the image communicates about the status of women in Protestant households?

another's spiritual preferences. States sometimes persecuted minority sects, and Jewish or Muslim residents might be tolerated only as long as they accepted their legal and social inferiority. Northern Europe became predominantly Protestant, whereas the southern and eastern countries remained Catholic. Protestant movements budded early in Bohemia, Hungary, and Poland but then faltered owing to the energy of Catholic reform and the loyalty of rulers to Rome.

Vernacular Languages and the State

The centralization and expansion of states in the sixteenth century had important consequences for language and literate culture. When rulers deployed gunpowder armies to seize new territories or impose direct government on previously autonomous regions, they also often introduced the language and cultural preferences of the state's core area as the medium of administration and law. Moreover, local aristocrats and business leaders usually saw the political and social advantages of learning the language and imitating the fashions and public rituals of the central regime. Consequently, local languages and customs might gradually lose prestige and even disappear.

Across Afroeurasia, language consolidation accompanied nearly every state-centralizing project. In Europe, people babbled in many tongues, but in the early modern centuries a relatively small number of languages, all of them written, spread more widely. The most important of these **vernacular languages** were Italian, French, German, English,

vernacular language The native language commonly spoken by ordinary people in a region.

Individuals MATTER

Gracia Luna Mendes Nasi: A Sixteenth-Century Businesswoman

A bronze medal of Gracia Luna Mendes Nasi.

The Protestant and Catholic Reformations had grim consequences for European Jews. Rivaling one another to display their Christian piety, many clerical leaders fanned the always-smoldering fires of anti-Semitism, urging rulers to more ruthlessly restrict, segregate, or even expel their Jewish minorities. In response to intensifying legal discrimination and social pressures, tens of thousands of Jews left western Europe to resettle in Poland, North Africa, or the Ottoman empire. In those lands they found, not full social equality, but greater odds of living in peace and economic security.

The family of Gracia Luna Mendes Nasi (1510–1569) originated in Spain but moved to Portugal sometime after 1492, when King Ferdinand and Queen Isabella decreed that Jews must either become Catholics or leave the country. A few years later, the Portuguese crown made a similar decree. Not wanting to emigrate again, Gracia Nasi's parents accepted, or were forced to accept, conversion. Nasi therefore grew up a *converso*, or "New Christian," and when she was eighteen she married Francisco Mendes, also a *converso* and an immensely wealthy merchant banker.

Following her husband's untimely death in 1536, Nasi and her young daughter sailed to Antwerp, Europe's most thriving seaport. The Mendes family already had large mercantile interests there, and Gracia soon immersed herself in the business, which included the profitable Indian pepper trade between Lisbon and northern Europe. Plainly a woman of commercial talent, she took full charge of the Mendes fortune after her husband's brother died in 1542.

In the heat of the early Protestant movement, however, *conversos* were vulnerable to charges of being secret Jews bent on persuading other New Christians to renounce their faith. In this threatening climate, Nasi slipped out of Antwerp and made for Venice, where she arrived about 1546. The Mendes firm had commercial agents in several Italian cities, but Nasi found no permanent haven there. She even spent a short time in a Venetian prison and had to deposit part of the family fortune with the public treasury.

Consequently, in 1549, she moved again, this time to the Italian city of Ferrara. She and her fortune received a warmer welcome there, and she openly returned to her Jewish roots. The Roman church, however, demanded that the city enact stronger anti-Jewish legislation. Fortunately for Nasi, she had an invitation from the Ottoman emperor Suleyman to settle in Istanbul, much as a modern government might entice a major corporation to move in. In 1552 she left Christian Europe for good. Once established in the empire, where Jews enjoyed formal legal status, Nasi shed her *converso* identity and moved socially in the Jewish community. She lavishly patronized Jewish scholarship, synagogues, schools, and, some evidence suggests, new Jewish and *converso* immigrants arriving from western Europe.

Nasi never married again and died in 1569 at the age of fifty-nine. Running an international business empire of mammoth proportions, she was hardly typical of a sixteenth-century women, whatever her religion. But she does exemplify the remarkable migratory shift of western European Jews toward eastern Europe and the southern and eastern shores of the Mediterranean.

Thinking Critically

What political, social, cultural, or personal factors do you think were most important in explaining Gracia Mendes Nasi's success as a businesswoman?

Polish, Spanish, Portuguese, and Dutch. In France before the fourteenth century, for example, people spoke the language ancestral to modern French only in the Paris region. Elsewhere, twenty-two or so other tongues could be heard. French, however, was the language of the rising monarchy. Parisian French accompanied royal armies, administrators, and judges into the provinces, where local nobles and town merchants quickly concluded that they should learn it. In

1539 King Francis I decreed that all state documents must be produced "in the maternal French language," by which he meant Parisian French.[13] Today, only a few of the other old languages, notably Provençal, Breton, and Basque, are still spoken at all. In the British Isles, Henry VIII and other monarchs stipulated English as the state language and tried by various means to stifle use of Celtic tongues like Irish, Welsh, or Cornish in the royal domain. In 1536, for example,

Henry urged inhabitants of Galway, a part of Ireland under English rule, to endeavor "to speak English, and to use themselves after the English fashion; and specially that you, and every one of you, do put forth your child to school, to learn to speak English."[14]

In Asia, China had long had a standardized written language, but it also accommodated numerous Chinese dialects, as well as tongues of other linguistic families, notably Turkic. Confucian officials favored Mandarin Chinese, the dialect associated with the capital city of Beijing. Consequently, Mandarin evolved into the most prestigious medium of verbal communication throughout the empire. Urban presses generated thousands of books on innumerable subjects, and literacy expanded among both men and women. The Jesuit priest Matteo Ricci, who lived in Beijing from 1601 to 1611, remarked on "the exceedingly large number of books in circulation here and the ridiculously low prices at which they are sold."[15] In Southeast Asia, the rise of Burma, Thailand, and Vietnam as strong monarchies propelled the Burmese, Thai, and Vietnamese languages to regional primacy, thereby displacing in some measure local tongues that peoples of mountain and forest had traditionally spoken. Tokugawa Japan, by contrast, already had a single dominant vernacular. This circumstance, along with widespread literacy and a flourishing woodblock printing industry, promoted the archipelago's cultural unity.

Languages of Cultural Prestige

Whenever a language spread from one region to another, a full package of ideas and cultural behavior usually went with it because the elements of culture expressed through language, gesture, art, and ritual cannot be disentangled.

Arabic, Persian, and Turkish. Arabic and Persian shared high status as the principal carriers of Muslim theology, philosophy, literature, and science in the early modern centuries. Persian served as a medium of diplomacy and intellectual exchange from Bengal to the Mediterranean. Peoples of South Asia spoke many tongues, but Persian was the chief Mughal administrative language. Urdu, which is a Hindi language infused with Persian loan words, became an important literary medium in northern India. Muslims everywhere esteemed Arabic as the language of the Prophet Muhammad and the Holy Quran. It was the dominant language of all the western Muslim lands from Iraq to the Atlantic in early modern times, and it still is today. Arabic also served as the language of intellectual culture and political administration in Sudanic Africa.

In the Ottoman domains, Oghuz, the Turkic language that evolved into modern Turkish, competed successfully with Persian among government officials and the learned class. From the Topkapi Palace in Istanbul, the sultan dispensed patronage to poets, astronomers, geographers, and historians, who wrote in Arabic, as well as in Persian and Turkish, both of which used a modified Arabic script. By contrast, Greek, the language of the deceased Byzantine empire, went into permanent eclipse as a major carrier of new knowledge, though remaining the language of modern Greece and the Greek Orthodox Church.

Print languages of Europe. In Europe, mechanical printing presses began in the sixteenth century to pour out thousands of books and pamphlets in the leading vernacular languages. These "print languages" gradually standardized vocabularies and grammars. Partly because inexpensive books became available, more people learned to read vernaculars, especially in northern Europe. Literate women who had little access to classical Greek or Latin found at least narrow avenues for publishing essays, poetry, and religious pamphlets in the regional vernaculars. Novelists, playwrights, poets, and religious writers broadcast their works in vernaculars. Martin Luther produced floods of religious pamphlets in German. Miguel Cervantes's monumental novel titled *Don Quixote* was published in Spanish (in two parts in 1605 and 1615) and quickly translated into several other languages. The poet Anna Bijns (1494–1575) wrote satirical verse in Dutch. And the English writer William Shakespeare (1564–1616) produced much poetry and, we should note, thirty-two plays.

Languages of humanism. The European print languages carried the humanist movement from its base in northern Italy to all parts of the subcontinent. Humanism flowered in the later fourteenth century as an intellectual mission to recover the lost knowledge of the ancient Romans and Greeks (see Chapter 15). Its advocates prized education in grammar, rhetoric, history, and moral philosophy, which they believed gave students the disciplinary tools needed to understand classical texts. Humanist scholars also contended that the Bible should be as open to critical analysis as any other ancient document. In 1516 the Dutch intellectual Desiderius Erasmus (1469–1536), a loyal Roman Catholic but scathing critic of church vice and bigotry, published the first printed edition of the New Testament in Greek. The Oxford University cleric William Tyndale (1490–1536) later translated it from Greek into English—before being burned at the stake as a Protestant heretic. Educated men and women in Moscow read Latin scientific works and translated them into Russian. Tsar Ivan III married Sofia Palaiologina (1455–1503), a noblewoman raised in Italy who made a lifelong project of strengthening language and cultural ties between the Russian Orthodox and Roman Catholic worlds.

Conclusion

The start of the seventeenth century marked a significant transition in world history. By then, most states in Afroeurasia had access to firearms. The most successful ones acquired gunpowder armies, central bureaucracies, and law courts with increased powers to keep the peace, amass revenue, and safeguard commerce. Those states also exerted cultural influence on wider circles of population, persuading their subjects, especially the wealthy and educated classes, to accept greater homogeneity in religion, language, legal custom, and public taste. States had never wielded such power in any earlier era. Nevertheless, limitations on early modern systems of overland communication left plenty of room for subjects of centralizing rulers to protest, rebel, hide, run away, or keep local languages and cultural traditions alive.

As of the early seventeenth century, no single Afroeurasian state, no matter the size of its army, held a decided advantage over the others in commanding resources and labor or marshaling firepower. Because of the great global convergence of the same century, configurations of both regional and global power remained extremely fluid. The circulation of American silver, the spread of food crops to new places, rising population and productivity in many lands, and maritime innovations that made transoceanic travel routine all worked together to produce a genuinely global and increasingly complex system of commercial, cultural, and demographic exchange.

As a result, all but the most remote societies were forced to confront new ideas, products, and cultural challenges. Moreover, some states, social groups, and economic interests benefited from accelerating global change more than others did. Thus the largest centers of population, farm production, and manufacturing remained in Asia, and these resources supported a few mammoth and powerful states, plus numerous smaller ones. Even so, circumstances led western Europeans—not Poles, Russians, Ottoman Turks, or Ming Chinese—to take charge of maritime trade across the Atlantic and to exploit immense mineral and agricultural wealth in the Americas. We explore this emerging Atlantic system and other global developments of the later sixteenth and seventeenth centuries in Chapter 18.

• • •

Key Terms

capitulations 490	Jesuits 508	service nobility 492
Catholic Reformation (also, Counter Reformation) 508	language death 505	Sikhism 492
fisc 504	Moscovy 494	tax farming 504
gunpowder armies 491	Mughal empire 491	Tokugawa shogunate 495
Habsburg dynasty 498	Protestant Reformation 498	vernacular language 509
	Romanov dynasty 495	

Change over Time

1448–1488	King Trailok reigns in Thailand (Siam), creating a strong central state in Southeast Asia.
1453	Ottoman Turks capture Constantinople, strengthening the Ottoman sultanate's position as a major Afroeurasian power.
1469–1539	The sage Nanak lives in India and founds the Sikh religion.
1472–1529	The philosopher Wang Yangming lives in China and challenges the elitist principles of neo-Confucianism.
1493–1528	The Songhay empire in the Sudan region of Africa expands during the reign of Askiya Muhammad.
1516	The Dutch humanist Desiderius Erasmus publishes the first printed edition of the New Testament in Greek.
1517	Martin Luther publishes his Ninety-Five Theses critical of the Catholic Church, launching the movement that would become the Protestant Reformation.
1517	Ottoman forces armed with gunpowder weapons overthrow the Mamluks in Egypt and Syria.
1519–1556	Charles V reigns as Holy Roman emperor and head of the Habsburg dynasty, leading an unsuccessful attempt to unify Europe and drive out the Ottoman Turks.
1520–1566	Suleyman I "the Magnificent" rules the Ottoman empire during a period of expansion in southeastern Europe.
1533–1584	Central government is strengthened in Russia during the reign of Ivan IV ("Ivan the Terrible").
1540	Spanish nobleman Ignatius Loyola founds the Jesuits, a leading religious order of the Catholic Reformation.
1556–1605	Akbar the Great rules in South Asia, transforming the Mughal state into a powerful empire.
1564–1616	William Shakespeare lives in England as a playwright and poet.
1587–1629	The Safavid empire of Persia comes to full flower under the reign of Shah Abbas.
1600–1616	Tokugawa Ieyasu, founder of the Tokugawa shogunate, rules in Japan.

Please see end of book reference section for additional reading suggestions related to this chapter.

18 The Expanding Global Economy: Expectations and Inequalities

1550–1700

This map of the thriving port of Manila circa 1650, painted on the lid of a wooden chest, is centered on the fortified area reserved for Spaniards. Other foreigners and Filipinos lived outside the city walls.

very day, oil tankers and freighters pass through the channel that connects Manila Bay in the Philippines to the South China Sea. With thousands of stacked shipping containers sprawling over the waterfront, the city of Manila at the eastern end of the bay is one of the busiest ports in the world. It is also a culturally diverse city of more than twenty million people of Filipino, Chinese, Spanish, American, South Asian, and variously mixed ancestry. Four centuries ago, Manila was not so different, though much smaller. Founded by the Spanish explorer Miguel López de Legazpi in 1571, the town blossomed quickly into a major emporium. According to a seventeenth-century Italian traveler, it was "so equally situated between the wealthy kingdoms of the east and west, that it may be accounted one of the greatest places of trade in the world."[1]

Manila attracted merchants from many lands for one reason. Every year, a large vessel arrived from Acapulco, Mexico, loaded with silver from American mines. According to the official register, the cargo for 1602, 316,250 pounds of silver bars and coins. was valued at five million pesos.[2] Spanish merchants traded this specie for the silk garments, cotton cloths, gold, jewelry, porcelain, perfumes, and fine spices that both Asian and European sea traders brought to the port. Dockworkers packed the Acapulco ship with these wares, and it sailed back across the Pacific to Mexico. There, merchants came from New Spain (Mesoamerica), the Caribbean islands, and the Viceroyalty of Peru to buy the Asian cargo at a giant fair. Some of the goods were consumed in the Americas and some transshipped across the Atlantic to Europe. Meanwhile, other merchants carried silver from Manila to China and the lands around the Indian Ocean rim.

With the inauguration of the Manila galleons, which directly linked the Americas with Asia, the last big connection in the global chain of commerce was put in place. After 1572, shipping lanes joined all of the inhabited continents (except Australia) and all the major oceans to one another. By the end of the seventeenth century, it was no surprise to see French aristocrats donning beaver hats from Canada, West African farm women wearing Indian cottons, and Egyptian merchants dining on Chinese porcelain. Silver coins and ingots from American mines streamed across every sea, passed through every port, and lubricated the entire network of exchange. In the later sixteenth and the seventeenth centuries, as one historian has written, "Money went around the world and made the world go round."[3]

The first part of this chapter describes advances in shipping technology and mercantile organization that made possible the emergence of a globe-encircling network of exchange. It also investigates major economic and demographic consequences of the linkup between Afroeurasia and the Americas. In Chapter 16, we described the early and cataclysmic effects of that linkage on Native Americans, who perished by the millions from exposure to previously unknown Afroeurasian diseases. Here, we explore the continuing transoceanic exchange of plants and animals, a phenomenon whose biological and social effects worldwide dawned only gradually on human consciousness in the sixteenth and seventeenth centuries. Finally, we survey the early global exchange of American silver and its part in shaping a world economy.

The second section examines events in Afroeurasia in the later sixteenth and the seventeenth centuries in relation to the developing global exchange system. We first focus on Europe, a region that had occupied the far western edge of the Afroeurasian network but after 1492 was transformed into a hub of world trade. American silver poured into Europe, with

• • •

both beneficial and negative effects on the region's economy. We then move across the hemisphere to East Asia, looking at economic developments in both China and Japan, the first an importer and the second an exporter of tons of silver. Finally, we focus on Afroeurasia's long-distance trade, both the maritime routes of the Indian Ocean and China seas and the ancient silk roads. The advent of trade between Afroeurasia and the Americas strengthened rather than diminished Asia's already mature commercial economy.

In the third section we return to the Atlantic basin, where European entrepreneurs and trading companies acquired rights to land or commerce from their governments and then proceeded to exploit lucrative trade in furs and hides in North America and to set up commercial plantations in northeastern Brazil, the Caribbean, and other warm lowland areas. Plantations required great concentrations of labor, which depleted American Indian societies could not supply. We explore also in this section why New World capitalists turned to African slaves rather than Europeans to solve their labor problems. Finally, we investigate the circumstances under which Africans came to participate in the global economy in a way that enriched rulers and merchants but that inflicted misery on millions more.

A Panoramic View

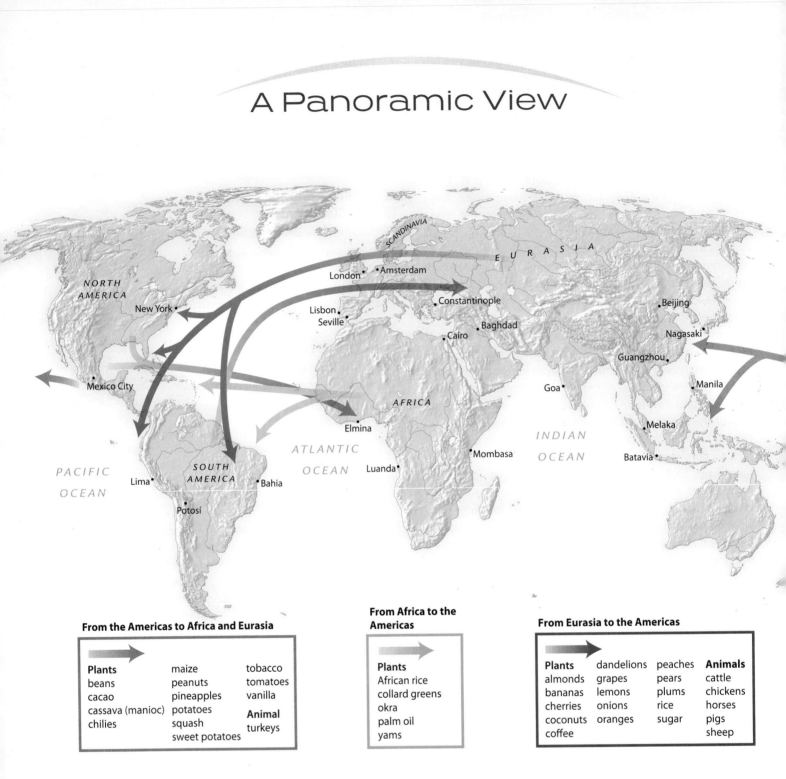

From the Americas to Africa and Eurasia

Plants
beans	maize	tobacco
cacao	peanuts	tomatoes
cassava (manioc)	pineapples	vanilla
chilies	potatoes	**Animal**
	squash	turkeys
	sweet potatoes	

From Africa to the Americas

Plants
African rice
collard greens
okra
palm oil
yams

From Eurasia to the Americas

Plants
			Animals
almonds	dandelions	peaches	cattle
bananas	grapes	pears	chickens
cherries	lemons	plums	horses
coconuts	onions	rice	pigs
coffee	oranges	sugar	sheep

MAP 18.1 The global diffusion of plants and animals, sixteenth to eighteenth centuries.
The Columbian Exchange had a profound effect on human diets. Can you locate the origins of the ingredients of one of your favorite meals?

The Global Network Takes Shape

FOCUS What historical evidence shows that a globe-encircling economy was emerging in the sixteenth and seventeenth centuries?

The great global convergence that started near the end of the fifteenth century proceeded gradually. Within a few decades of Columbus's voyages, sea captains discovered how to sail regularly back and forth between western Europe and both the Caribbean Sea and the Indian Ocean. But as of 1550, only two explorers, Giovanni Verrazano sailing for France and Esteban Gómez for Spain, had explored the length of North America's Atlantic seaboard. Spain and Portugal had barely started to organize their American empires or even to "discover" much of the land that they claimed for themselves. Only four Spanish expeditions had crossed the Pacific.

The era of blind probing from one island or stretch of sea to another, however, ended shortly. Shipwrights steadily improved vessel technology. Governments and merchants set up exploration and trading organizations. Infectious pathogens continued to kill American Indians, but by the early seventeenth century the transoceanic exchange of plants and animals began to have the opposite effect on Afroeurasia. There, new food crops increased supplies and improved nutrition, contributing to accelerating population growth. Shortly after 1550, Spanish entrepreneurs also began to extract silver from stupendously rich mines in Mexico and South America. This development, more than any other, jumpstarted the worldwide economy.

Technology and Organization for Global Exchange

In Chapter 16 we described the advances in ship design and navigation that allowed European sea captains to penetrate the Indian Ocean and cross the Atlantic. But before oceanic trade could become routinely profitable, shipwrights had to build vessels that efficiently combined size and strength with speed and maneuverability, while at the same time reducing production costs. Regular global commerce also required continuous advances in naval armament, navigational skills, geographical knowledge, provisioning methods for long voyages, and reliable sources of money to finance and insure complex and risky operations. In Europe, governments took the lead in organizing sea trade, but large international companies came to dominate exchange in the seventeenth century.

Ships. The type of ship known as the caravel, which carried the first generations of Atlantic explorers, was not adequate for repeated transoceanic voyages. But naval architects rose to the challenge, first in Spain and Portugal, then in northwestern Europe and along the coasts of Asia. Sharing design knowledge from port to port, shipwrights built vessels that were not only stronger but also more cost-efficient because they required smaller crews and therefore fewer provisions, which left more room for paying cargo. The multidecked carrack served as the workhorse of bulk transport between Europe and distant shores from about 1500 to 1630. Those vessels, however, were slow and difficult to maneuver in bad weather. The **galleon**, developed in the later sixteenth century, represented

> **galleon** A large, multidecked sailing vessel used for both war and commerce from the sixteenth to the eighteenth century.

a key advance. It combined the long, narrow hull of the medieval galley and the sails of the caravel with the imposing mass of the carrack. A strong frame allowed galleons to support both bulky cargos and heavy artillery mounted to fire from gun ports on each side of the hull.

Toward the end of the sixteenth century, shipbuilders in the Netherlands introduced the *fluyt*, or fly boat. Constructed of cheaper wood than galleons required, this vessel had a flat bottom, shorter masts, smaller sails, and fewer guns. It required half the crew of a galleon and half the money to build and operate. Though *fluyts* were slow, merchants used them profitably to haul high-volume commodities like timber, grain, fish, and salt. In the seventeenth century, they dominated the shipping lanes of northern Europe and, owing to their cargo capacity, typically returned large profits to their owners.

Trading companies. European governments and private capitalists collaborated in a variety of ways to expand seaborne commercial operations. Early in the sixteenth century, the Portuguese crown founded the House of India (*Casa da India*) to assert control over transoceanic trade. The Spanish government created the House of Trade (*Casa de Contratación*). These institutions compiled nautical information, trained pilots, registered cargo, inspected ships, collected duties, and enforced maritime laws. Through the House of India, Portugal exercised a monopoly on many spices and precious metals imported from Africa and Asia, selling these goods at a fixed price in Lisbon and reaping most of the profits. The Spanish House of Trade functioned more like a regulatory agency than a state-owned business, issuing licenses to private traders. A separate merchant guild settled disputes among traders and controlled access to commerce by restricting membership.

In the later sixteenth century, England experimented with a different form of commercial organization. The crown granted charters to companies that awarded them monopoly rights to trade or plant settlers in specific regions. Though having many of the same functions as the two Iberian institutions, the English entities were private firms that hired captains and crews. A strict division was maintained between managers, who ran the company, and investors,

A *fluyt* and other vessels in stormy seas. This seventeenth-century painting of Dutch coastal shipping shows the stern of a three-masted *fluyt*. The lateen-rigged third mast is not flying a sail. Other large ships are indistinctly visible in the distance, suggesting a busy shipping lane, where oceangoing vessels were provisioned and serviced by smaller craft, including the rowboat in the foreground. Why do you think so many different kinds of boats were used in seventeenth-century shipping?

chartered company A type of corporation in which the state granted specific rights and obligations to private investors to engage in exploration, commerce, or colonization.

who supplied capital and received dividends (shares of profit).

The English **chartered company** model soon spread to the Netherlands, France, Sweden, Denmark, Italy, and, eventually, even to Spain and Portugal. Stock markets that traded shares in chartered companies emerged in Amsterdam and London. In fact, a financial transformation began to take place in Europe as aristocrats and other affluent individuals redirected some of their capital from land, traditionally the principal source of wealth, to stocks, commodities, slaves, and other forms of investment associated with international trade.

The Continuing Columbian Exchange

When human beings began to cross the Atlantic to the Americas in the later fifteenth century, they brought all sorts of living organisms with them, from wheat and dandelions to horses, honeybees, brown rats, and, as we have seen, measles and smallpox. When people made the return trip, they introduced American organisms to Afroeurasia, including maize, potatoes, tomatoes, turkeys, rattlesnakes, and the bacterium that causes syphilis. In time the Columbian Exchange produced a worldwide biological revolution, though some organisms found niches in new environments much later than others. For example, European weeds began to crowd out native plants on Caribbean islands shortly after Columbus arrived. By contrast, the climbing vine called kudzu, native to Japan, did not begin to overrun the southeastern United States until the 1870s. North American raccoons made homes for themselves in Europe only in the mid-twentieth century.

Afroeurasian biota in the Americas. Columbus and the voyagers who followed him introduced many new plant and animal species to the Caribbean and Mesoamerica without thinking they were abetting a biological revolution (see Map 18.1). Ships had to carry enough food to sustain crews for months, so sailors kept live chickens, pigs, and cattle in their cargo holds, slaughtering them for meals as needed. Some of these animals survived the voyage and began immediately to multiply on land, frequently escaping their human owners, running into forests and swamps, and reverting to a feral, or wild, state. Within eight years of Columbus's first voyage, European pigs, which in that era looked more like wild boars than today's farm hogs, infested the island of Hispaniola and competed with indigenous animals for food.

Early colonizers also brought food plants on their ships in order to grow familiar homeland crops, wherever natural conditions permitted, rather than experiment with strange American ones. They understood how to cook Old World foods, preferred their taste, and knew they would not be poisoned by them. On his second voyage, Columbus introduced seeds or cuttings of chickpeas, melons, onions, radishes, lettuce, cabbage, and cauliflower, all of which eventually spread across the Western Hemisphere. Subsequent travelers imported bananas and rice, both of which became staples in tropical America. Grapevines and olive trees flourished in the coastal valleys of Peru and Chile. By the middle of the sixteenth century, Mexico grew so much wheat that it began exporting it to other regions. Old World cultural obligations might dictate the introduction of particular foods. For example, Europeans in America grew grapes and wheat partly because they needed wine and unleavened bread to celebrate the Catholic mass. Wherever Europeans established their dominance over Native Americans, they put them to work raising Afroeurasian crops and herds compatible with local climates. But Indians rarely added wheat or other foreign grains to their own diets, any more than early European colonizers wished to eat maize unless they had no alternative.

Livestock came to America with Europeans but then swarmed out ahead of them. Feral pigs made their homes on every island and coastal lowland they could reach. By the end of the sixteenth century, hundreds of thousands of cattle and sheep grazed in northern Mexico, and cattle herds doubled in size every year and a half. Cattle also accompanied Spanish conquistadors to Peru, then made their way through Andean mountain passes to the grasslands of Argentina. When Spanish settlers founded Buenos Aires in 1580, they found the surrounding area already teeming with cattle, perhaps forty-eight million of them by 1700. Horses followed a similar trajectory. Observing the herds near Tucumán in Argentina, one chronicler wrote, "They cover the face of the earth, and, when they cross the road, it is necessary for travelers to wait and let them pass, for a whole day or more."[4]

Europeans also brought species to America that neither they nor Native Americans wanted. These included various weeds—ferns, thistles, nettles, clover, and bluegrass—which invaded open spaces and stifled native vegetation. A most unwelcome import was various species of rats. These rodents multiplied faster than cattle and hogs and easily threatened village food supplies. By devouring grain, rats

Embarcadero de los Cavallos,

Loading horses for the voyage to the Americas. This engraving from about 1550 shows the precision required and risks involved in shipping livestock across the Atlantic. Given the difficulties, why would Spaniards have taken the trouble to transport large animals such as horses and cattle?

nearly forced early colonizers at both Buenos Aires and Jamestown, Virginia, to abandon their settlements. The chronicler Garcilaso de la Vega reported from Peru that they "bred in infinite numbers, overran the land, and destroyed the crops."[5]

American foods in Afroeurasia. Though initially reluctant to try American foods, Europeans brought many back to their homelands. These included plants that added variety, color, and spice to humdrum diets, including tomatoes, chilies, avocadoes, pineapples, and cacao beans. They also introduced plants that in time became nutritious and calorie-rich staples, notably maize, potatoes, sweet potatoes, and manioc (cassava). By the seventeenth century, these foods and others began to have profound effects on Afroeurasia's demography and dietary culture.

Columbus carried maize to Spain in 1493, and within another century, it became a major food crop for both humans and domestic animals throughout Iberia and in parts of France and Italy. Poor families in those regions gradually incorporated maize into their traditional porridge. Venetian merchants introduced maize to the Ottoman empire. It thrived in several parts of Southwest Asia, in Egypt, and in the Balkan Peninsula, where in the eighteenth century it became a staple crop.

European peasants resisted potatoes for more than a century, not knowing that these tubers produced more calories and a greater variety of nutrients per acre of land than the grains to which they were accustomed. By the 1600s, however, impoverished Irish farmers discovered that they could increase their health and extend their life on a daily diet of hardly anything other than potatoes and milk. In that century and the next, potato cultivation spread across the northern half of Europe, where climate and soils favored it. Even aristocrats served potatoes boiled, baked, or mashed at their lordly tables.

Iberian sailors introduced American food plants to parts of Afroeurasia besides Europe. Manioc, a root crop native to tropical America, has nutritional value mainly in vitamins, and the variety known as bitter manioc had to be specially processed to leech out poisons. But the plant is hardy and productive. From Brazil it encircled the globe, becoming an important food in tropical Africa, Southeast Asia, and southern China. Chinese farmers also began growing American maize, sweet potatoes, and peanuts early in the sixteenth century. Peasants planted sweet potatoes in northern and central highland regions of China where rice did not flourish, thereby enriching Chinese diets and sometimes cheating famine. Cultivators also learned how to rotate rice crops with peanuts, a nourishing legume, to improve soil fertility.

American staple crops added nutritional variety to Afroeurasian diets and bolstered immune systems. For example, in Ireland, where the mostly rural population began eating potatoes, the population rose by more than 450 percent, from about 1.5 to 8.5 million between 1600 and 1800. If a society could grow more than one staple, both potatoes and wheat for example, they might in years of bad weather lose one harvest but not the other, thereby averting hunger. Historians do not doubt that American foods contributed mightily to Afroeurasia's accelerating population growth after 1500.

Showers of silver. Ships returning from America to Europe also carried shiny metal. Europeans who went to the Americas found gold in several regions, but they discovered whole mountains of silver. This metal was a material commodity like any other, but rulers turned much of it into coins, which animated commercial transactions around the world. Between 1550 and 1800, Mexico and Peru produced 150,000 tons of the metal, more than 80 percent of the world's supply.[6]

Three factors were instrumental in launching the sixteenth-century silver boom. First, in 1545 prospectors uncovered an enormous deposit near Potosí, a site located in the highlands of Bolivia at an altitude of more than 13,000 feet. The following year, they found another lode near Zacatecas in north central Mexico. Second, miners initially used a German smelting process that worked only for high-grade ore. In the 1560s, however, Spanish technicians invented a new method that involved spreading crushed silver ore on flat areas, or "patios" and laboriously mixing it with mercury, water, salt, and copper sulfate. The silver metal and the mercury eventually formed an amalgam, which was then heated to drive off the mercury. Just as this process was being developed, prospectors discovered a large mercury source at Huancavelica in Peru. Transporting mercury to Potosí, mine owners sharply reduced costs and accelerated production. The third factor is that Francisco de Toledo, the Spanish viceroy of Peru, introduced a conscription labor system called the *mita* in order to exploit the mines to their full potential. Andean Indian villages had to supply a certain number of people each year to work at Huancavelica or Potosí. These people trekked long distances to the mines, where they worked in rotating shifts as excavators, carriers, millers, and refiners. Though legally free, they received little compensation and worked in harsh, life-threatening conditions. After visiting Huancavelica in 1616, the Catholic friar and missionary Antonio Vazquez de Espinosa reported:

The [mercury] ore was very rich black flint, and the excavation so extensive that it held more than 3,000 Indians working away hard with picks and hammers, breaking up that flint ore; and when they have filled their little sacks, the poor fellows, loaded down with ore, climb up those ladders or rigging. . . . Those who carry out the reduction of this ore have to be very careful and test cautiously; . . . otherwise they may easily get mercury poisoning and if they do, they are of no further use; their teeth fall out, and some die."[7]

Silver production involved a division of labor between government and private interests. Most silver mines and smelters were privately owned, but the Spanish crown controlled the mercury supply and impounded one-fifth of the processed silver in addition to taxes and duties. The imperial authorities also required all silver to pass through the official mints in Potosí or Mexico City to be cast into ingots or coins and stamped with the royal seal. This allowed officials to certify purity and collect the king's share. Not surprisingly, miners and merchants circumvented these regulations whenever possible. Illegal shipments may have surpassed the registered exports.

Silver flowed out of the mining regions by different routes (see Map 18.2). Pack animals hauled loads from Potosí to the coast of Peru, ships carried the cargo to Panama, and more animals lugged it across the isthmus to the Caribbean. From there, armed galleons transported it to Spain. Silver from the Zacatecas mines went overland to Mexico

Harsh labor in a Potosí silver mine. Potosí became one of the largest cities in the world in the seventeenth century. This 1602 image by Theodore de Bry, however, shows us not crowds in a booming city but Native American peasants working deep underground to extract silver for capitalist entrepreneurs. A prolific illustrator, de Bry's engravings provided many Europeans with their only glimpse of the Americas. How would you characterize his depiction of work in the mines?

City, and then from the port of Veracruz to Europe. The Manila galleon runs started in 1572. Meanwhile, smuggled silver poured out of both Mexico and South America. An estimated 15 to 30 percent of Potosí's metal left by an illegal "back door" that ran from Bolivia southeastward along the Rio de la Plata (River of Silver) to the Atlantic and the holds of waiting ships of various European origins.[8]

Afroeurasia and the Expanding World Economy

FOCUS What effects did global communication and exchange have on societies of Afroeurasia in the sixteenth and seventeenth centuries?

Many Afroeurasian societies experienced remarkable economic and demographic growth between 1500 and 1650. A factor in northern Eurasia may have been modest climatic

warming. The northern hemispheric cooling cycle called the Little Ice Age (see Chapter 15) lasted from the thirteenth to the nineteenth century, but within that phase weather patterns fluctuated from one decade to another. Northern temperatures rose two or three degrees Celsius in the later fifteenth and the sixteenth centuries. That trend brought more frequent years of warm, dry weather and improved farming conditions in northern latitudes, including China and Europe. Following the serious demographic decline of the fourteenth century, the populations of both regions surged in the sixteenth, China by around twenty-five million, Europe by five million. In all of Afroeurasia, numbers rose from around 418 to 545 million. Since the population of the Americas plunged in the same period, something close to 98 percent of all human beings lived in Afroeurasia as of 1600.[9]

In some regions, rising population meant potentially larger work forces and armies. In turn, generous state spending to build military assets and strategic industries

MAP 18.2 Global flows of silver in the seventeenth century.
Silver flowed both east and west from American mines. Can you think of finished goods or other commodities that circled the globe in both directions in the seventeenth century?

reinforced the upward economic trend. Indicators of this prosperity in densely populated regions included proliferation of rural market towns, increasing job specialization in manufacturing, more widespread use of money, and more sophisticated commercial institutions such as banks. The flow of silver from American mines also greatly stimulated money-based market exchanges.

Western Europe's Economic Surge

The first Portuguese ship laden with Indian pepper docked at Antwerp on the North Sea in 1501, and American silver began flowing into the Spanish port of Seville in the 1530s. But in fact Europe's remarkable economic expansion after 1450 had more to do with regional developments than with overseas trade. Population growth was a fundamental factor. Similarly to China, Europe began to recover from the huge epidemic-related mortality of the previous hundred years. The population plunge had made more farm land available, and that in turn allowed food production to grow faster than population, raising living standards again. Longer growing seasons associated with the temporary easing of the Little Ice Age also contributed to higher farm yields. In the sixteenth century, the population from the Atlantic to Russia surged from about 80 to 100 million. As in China, the growth rate slowed in the late 1500s, accelerating again after 1700.

In 1500, 90 to 95 percent of Europe's people lived in country villages and hamlets, but cities of twenty thousand or more began to multiply. By the end of the century, about 2.5 million people lived in the region's thirty-one largest cities, most of them located either in northwestern Europe or northern Italy. Antwerp, the most important northern center of commerce and banking until about 1570, reached a population of 100,000. Paris, the capital of the expanding French monarchy, grew from about 100,000 to 510,000 between 1500 and 1700, London from 40,000 to 575,000 in the same period.[10] The Netherlands, where Amsterdam replaced Antwerp as the chief financial center in the late 1500s, became the most densely urbanized part of Europe. Hundreds of miles of canals linked the region's towns with one another. Elegant homes and public buildings lined urban canals, and in the 1660s, street lights began to flicker on in the major centers.

Europe's growing markets. The sixteenth-century population surge magnified demand for food, fuel, clothing, and an array of manufactures. In response, entrepreneurs and commercial farmers put disposable wealth into many new capitalist ventures. Merchants moved goods from one part of Europe to another, taking advantage of the region's many navigable rivers for cheap inland transport. English and Spanish landlords raised sheep and exported wool. Scandinavian enterprisers mined copper and iron and

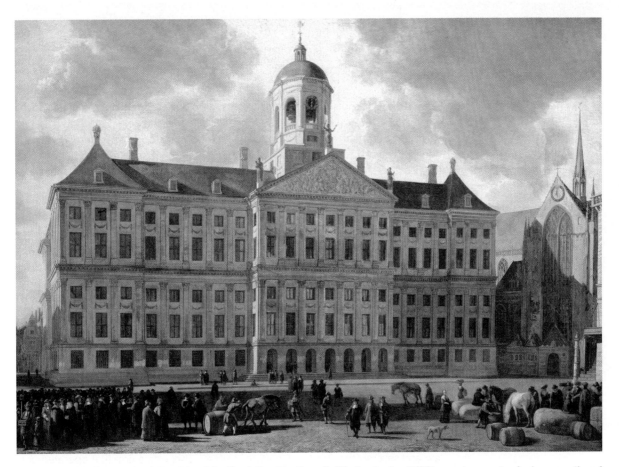

Urban revival in Europe. Gerrit Berckheyde's oil painting *The Town Hall in Amsterdam* (1673) reveals aspects of urban growth and concentrated wealth during the Dutch golden age. The size of the building, its imposing location on the city's main square, and the great cost of imported sandstone for the exterior walls and marble for the interior express the wealth and political clout of the merchant elite. The Town Hall casts a shadow on the Nieuwe Kerk (New Church), while market activity takes place in the square. What do you think the painting reveals about relationships among political, economic, and religious power in Dutch urban life?

felled trees for lumber and charcoal. Knitting, a technology developed centuries earlier in Muslim lands, became an important European industry, especially production of vividly colored stockings. Genoa and other northern Italian cities made fine silk fabrics. Dutch workshops turned out woolen and linen textiles, glassware, printed books, seagoing ships, and beer. Dutch *fluyts* moved bulk cargos of grain, timber, sugar, fish, and wine around the Baltic and the North Seas and into the Atlantic.

Europe needed to grow more grain, but in the western regions small farmers found it harder to acquire land, partly because of increasing population density and partly because many estate lords wanted to turn arable land into pasture to make money raising cattle and sheep for the market. One solution was to transform swamps and marshes into cropland. Ambitious drainage projects got under way, for example, in the Netherlands and in the low-lying area of southeastern England called the Fens. Farmers in northwestern Europe also had great success intensifying production, that is, coaxing greater yields out of a given

acreage. One key innovation was the four-field rotation system. One field was devoted to turnips or other crops to feed animals; a second one to alfalfa, clover, or other nitrogen-fixing plants to reinvigorate the soil; and the third and fourth to different grain crops. This strategy also involved more efficient ways of collecting domestic animal manure to fertilize crops. Raising productivity required hard work of all family members. Men and boys did most of the heavy labor, while women and girls gathered grain, looked after animals, and processed food. Waterwheels and windmills supplemented human or animal energy in much of Europe, though agricultural technology did not change radically in the early modern centuries. Meanwhile, in eastern Europe and Russia, aristocratic land-owners found new opportunity to grow grain specifically for export to western Europe, where new city dwellers and wage workers had to buy all their food.

The inflationary spiral. Despite Europe's remarkable economic growth, the gap between affluent minorities

Louis De Geer: A Capitalist Success Story

David Beck's 1649 portrait of Louis De Geer.

The career of Louis De Geer (1587–1652) nicely illustrates European economic dynamism in the early seventeenth century. Born in the Habsburg-ruled city of Liège in what is today Belgium, De Geer moved with his family to the young United Netherlands in 1595. Learning both business and copper making, he established himself as a merchant and financier before he was thirty. In 1615 he settled in Amsterdam, the energetic center of the Dutch economy. He also forged strong business ties with Elias Trip, his brother-in-law, and several other Trip relatives.

In 1618 the conflict known later as the Thirty Years' War broke out. This brutal struggle, which initially pitted Habsburg Catholics against Protestant princes, spread across central Europe, pulling in economically poor Sweden. The war generated huge demand for firearms. Sweden's king Gustavus Adolphus (reigned 1611–1632) needed badly to find ways to finance land and naval forces. Seizing an attractive opportunity, De Geer and Trip extended the king a series of loans, made payments on behalf of the Swedish government, and armed and equipped the royal army. Other private Dutch investors and manufacturers also fueled Sweden's economic expansion, as well as its emergence as an important European military power.

Gustavus Adolphus repaid loans from De Geer and Trip in a variety of ways but rarely directly. Rather, he awarded De Geer

monopolies on the copper and iron trades and allowed him to lease agricultural lands and set up a foundry in eastern Sweden. De Geer's complex business interests came to include gun sales, armament works, textile and paper mills, shipping wharves, a brewery, and metal foundries. In fact, De Geer and his Trip associates emerged as arguably the largest weapons traders in Europe, supplying Sweden, Venice, France, England, German states, and the United Netherlands with ships, artillery, muskets, bullets, grenades, and gunpowder.

Although De Geer kept a home in Amsterdam where his wife and children lived, he acquired Swedish citizenship in 1627. Thereafter, he continued moving between Amsterdam and Sweden, attending to his businesses in both locations and caring for his family after his wife died giving birth to their sixteenth child.

In 1640 he applied for recognition as a Swedish nobleman, another good strategic move. Only as a titled aristocrat could he legally own land and pass it to his children. Otherwise, his holdings would revert to the crown upon his death. His request was granted, and he soon became one of Sweden's biggest landholders. In addition to his many other business ventures, he organized and financed the Swedish African Company in 1647. This was a firm that operated under a royal charter. One of De Geer's last projects was sponsorship of a plan to found a joint Dutch-Swedish colony on the West African coast, though the scheme had little success.

De Geer died in 1652, a stupendously rich nobleman. He sired two aristocratic families, one in Sweden, the other in the Netherlands, and both lineages maintained their lucrative relations with the Swedish and Dutch governments for centuries. Political merchants like Louis de Geer personify an age in which power and profit, war and trade, government projects and private initiatives were intricately linked together.

Thinking Critically

In what ways do you think Louis De Geer's career illustrates the partnership between government and private capitalist interests in seventeenth-century Europe?

---

and the rest of the population yawned wider. Production of basic commodities like bread and firewood failed to keep pace with demand as the population rose. This drove prices relentlessly upward, a phenomenon of monetary **inflation** that historians call the **price revolution.** The continuing influx of silver into Europe also gradually reduced its value, along with that of gold and copper coins. From month to month, therefore, consumers had to spend more coins for a single loaf of bread. Some governments tried to cut military and administrative spending by debasing

inflation A rise in the general level of prices of goods and services in a society over time. Rising inflation means that the purchasing power of a given unit of currency declines.

price revolution A period of sustained inflation in Europe in the sixteenth and seventeenth centuries.

Agricultural life in rural Europe. *The Harvesters* (1565) by Pieter Bruegel the Elder was one of six large panels the celebrated artist painted to depict the seasons. The series originally hung in the home of a wealthy Antwerp merchant. The impression of abundance in this image comes not only from the lush wheat harvest but also from the scene of peasants resting for a meal, the agricultural activity in the background, and the view of commercial ships anchored in the distant bay. How would you compare the portrayal of people engaging in labor in this painting with the depiction on page 521?

coins, that is, by diluting their precious metal content without changing their value. This tactic worked only in the short term because devalued coins bought fewer loaves of bread than fully valued ones, pushing up prices even more.

Except in unusually prosperous regions around big cities, population growth coupled with rising prices made ordinary men and women poorer (see Figure 18.7). Since more people competed to sell their labor, estate lords and urban employers could keep down wages and also raise rents and fees on tenants. The ranks of day laborers and jobless folk consequently swelled. On family farms women often did almost all the work because husbands and sons went off to find wage jobs to bring in food. Although the practice of legally binding men and women to work on a particular estate (serfdom) nearly disappeared from western Europe by the sixteenth century, it actually grew in eastern Europe and Russia. There, the aristocratic class, which dominated government, got expanded legal rights to force peasants to stay put rather than freely sell their labor for wages or resettle on open land. That way, landlords retained the workers

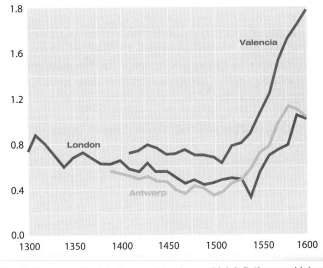

Consumer prices in grams of silver

The "price revolution" in Europe. Why do you think inflation was higher in Antwerp than in London or Valencia?

that brought them fortunes exporting grain. Throughout Europe, governments also raised taxes on ordinary people to finance increasingly expensive armies and bureaucracies. The masses, however, did not necessarily accept their growing impoverishment. Urban bread riots, peasant uprisings, and soldier rampages repeatedly jolted the ruling and moneymaking classes.

Shifting wealth and conflicts across Europe. During the sixteenth century, the geographical center of concentrated wealth in Europe moved gradually northward from Iberia to the Netherlands, France, and England. Spain became immensely rich early in the century, but its silver bonanza turned to stone. The Spanish Habsburg kings Charles V (r. 1519–1556) and Philip II (r. 1556–1598) disposed of huge amounts of silver to pay down debts incurred in European wars and to buy textiles, wine, guns, and other wares to ship to the American empire. "[Silver] falls on Spain as does rain on a roof," wrote a Venetian diplomat. "It pours on her and then flows away."[11] The Habsburg drive to dominate both Europe and America, including the ill-fated naval armada launched in 1588 to invade England, led the state into bottomless debt. Silver migrated steadily to England, the Netherlands, and northern Italy where entrepreneurs invested it in manufacturing, European trade, and commercial ventures abroad.

The Habsburg dynasty also became immersed in a particularly brutal struggle that engulfed much of Europe between 1618 and 1648. Called the Thirty Years' War, the conflict devastated large areas of Habsburg-ruled Germany. The conflict began as a Habsburg campaign to suppress German princes who had become Protestants. It ballooned, however, into a pan-European war that drew in France, Spain, the Netherlands, Poland, Sweden, and the Ottoman empire. The fighting degenerated into a vicious central European free-for-all as famines, epidemics, and roving mercenary bands stalked the region.

The war nearly wrecked Germany's agricultural and urban economy, and it so exhausted Europe's rulers that they finally agreed to a general settlement. In the Peace of Westphalia, a series of treaties signed in 1648, the Habsburgs gave up their ambition to dominate the German princes. More broadly, rulers agreed to stabilize their mutual frontiers, and they accepted the idea that sovereign states should determine the religion of their own realms. This accord reinforced the principle of territorial sovereignty that has guided international relations ever since: States should regard one another as equals in diplomatic dealings and should not interfere in one another's internal affairs. Following the war, religious passions also subsided, and Europeans generally accepted the reality of multiple Christian denominations rather than a single all-embracing church. Regional wars continued after 1648 but usually on a smaller scale. Only near the end of the century, however, did a new cycle of population and economic growth set in.

Centuries of Silver in East Asia

At the end of the sixteenth century, China, Korea, and Japan embraced something like 30 percent of the world's population. Most of East Asia experienced remarkable economic growth throughout that century. China expanded its market economy in conditions of general political stability. Japan also experienced steady growth, even though the Tokugawa government, which took power shortly after 1600, adopted policies that strictly limited the country's participation in world trade.

China the "silver sink." Like Europe, China moved into a new expansionary cycle in the later fifteenth century. In 1600 the Ming dynasty (1368–1644) ruled somewhere between 125 and 150 million people, and its demographic center continued to shift from the semiarid north toward the rainier rice-growing south. If an orbiting satellite could have produced a map of nighttime city lights in East Asia in the sixteenth century, it would have revealed a belt of illumination extending from Beijing in the north all the way to the southeastern coast. The light would have shone brightest in the densely urbanized lower Yangzi River valley. In the vast and dimly lit rural regions, industrious peasants, like their counterparts in northeastern Europe, coaxed high yields of grain from small plots of land using intensive labor methods. Silk and cotton production expanded in the Yangzi valley. Near the southern coast, sugar cane (an Afroeurasian crop) and tobacco (a new American one) boomed as commercial commodities.

The limited economic information we have suggests that China's population enjoyed life expectancies and living standards as high as people anywhere in the world. Most rural villagers and town dwellers wore warm clothing, consumed nutritious foods, and drank tea. Farm families routinely sold surplus crops in local markets. Nevertheless, even though Ming emperors abolished slave labor and made it harder for estate owners to evict tenants, the elite class lived far better than the masses. As in Europe, Chinese cities harbored large fluctuating populations of criminals, beggars, and underemployed refugees from rural famines or epidemics. Women toiled alongside men to grow and market crops, but few entered the urban labor force except in traditional roles as servants, entertainers, or prostitutes. Women of all classes remained firmly under male supervision.

In the first half of the sixteenth century, the Ming government enforced policies aimed at restricting Chinese participation in international trade. The regime was reluctant to divert public resources from defense of land frontiers. East Asian waters swarmed with Japanese, Malay, and private Chinese ships, plus European carracks, all of them seeking ways, legal or not, to trade for China's silk, tea, porcelain, and dozens of other products in demand across Afroeurasia. Starting in the 1520s, pirates and smugglers, many of them Japanese, repeatedly sacked Chinese ports

Rural life in Ming China. This detail from a Ming-era porcelain vase shows workers watering tea plants. Why might an affluent consumer of a decorative object have valued an image of agricultural work?

and interior towns, exploiting weak coastal security. Manufacturers and merchants who profited from China's robust commercialization appealed to the government to liberalize overseas mercantile policies. Ming forces finally counterattacked the coastal intruders, and in the 1560s agreed to relax trade restrictions on Chinese subjects. It continued, however, to limit the number of ports where foreigners, including Europeans, had permission to enter.

Japanese mines helped ease China's great demand for silver, and in the 1570s American coins and ingots began to flood in. Gomes Solis, a Portuguese merchant, wrote in 1621, "Silver wanders throughout the entire world in its peregrinations before flocking to China, where it remains, as if at its natural center."[12] Some observers referred to China as a "sink" into which the world's silver disappeared as into a black hole. But why did Chinese demand for silver soar? The simple answer is that the Ming regime needed a more reliable currency to oil its economy, the world's largest. The government tried to limit money use to paper bills and copper coins, but those currencies easily lost value, causing inflation. Merchants involved in foreign trade much preferred silver. Ming authorities at first bemoaned this metal hunger.

In 1551 one of them denounced "unscrupulous merchants who carry away to foreign lands precious commodities of the Middle Kingdom like silk yarn, brocades, damask, cotton, porcelain, and iron, which they exchange not for goods but only for gold and silver."[13]

Unable to find a workable alternative, the government finally adopted its own silver standard. Beginning in the 1570s it decreed laws, known collectively as the Single Whip Reforms, that converted all tax payments to fixed amounts of silver. In consequence, demand rose even faster. The timing was opportune for the Spanish, whose Pacific galleons were just starting to haul silver between Acapulco on the coast of Mexico and Manila in the Philippines. Some historians have argued that China's unquenchable silver demand allowed Spain to keep its huge American empire intact. If silver were not so cheap at the Potosí and Zacatecas mines and so expensive in China, the Spanish crown would not have reaped enough wealth to fight long wars in Europe and simultaneously pay for its New World colonies.

The silver influx profoundly affected the Chinese economy. The Ming reforms compelled people to pay taxes in silver, but its price kept rising. Consequently, millions of peasant families were hard put to meet their obligations. Many sold more crops and homespun silk or cotton in local markets to acquire coins, and this further stimulated the commercial economy. While the economy continued to expand, living standards for the great majority began to slip. Worse yet, so much metal streamed from American and Japanese mines that the world price began to fall. This meant that the Chinese government got less and less buying power from fixed tax revenues. Then in 1639–1640, silver imports nearly halted owing to political troubles in both Japan and the Philippines. This event sent China's commercial economy into a tailspin, shortly leading to the fall of the Ming and the rise of a new dynasty (see Chapter 19).

Japan and its silver boom. After the founding of the centralized Tokugawa shogunate in 1603 (see Chapter 17), Japan's economy accelerated briskly. Rural men and women converted woodland and dry plains into irrigated rice fields. Market towns multiplied, connected to one another by well-maintained gravel roads. Cargo ships tramped the islands' coasts, carrying rice, metals, and finished goods from one part of the archipelago to another. The Tokugawa encouraged market activity by issuing gold, silver, and copper coins. Japan's population more than doubled in the seventeenth century, from about twelve million to as many as thirty million. Cities also grew in number and size. The greatest were Osaka, a manufacturing and commercial center; Kyoto, the seat of the emperor's court; and Edo (Tokyo), the capital of the shogunate. By the early eighteenth century, Edo was one of the largest cities in the world, with a population of more than one million.

The Ming imperial government formally treated Japan as a subordinate, tributary kingdom like Korea or Vietnam.

Urban life in Kyoto. This early seventeenth-century decorative screen shows members of the Tokugawa family leaving the Nijo Castle. Tokugawa Ieyasu undertook construction of the castle as a residence for his family in the imperial capital. The fortified compound was situated in the center of the city.

In fact, the relationship between the two states turned mainly on mutually beneficial trade. When the Tokugawa came to power, that trade was doing well. Japanese prospectors discovered major new silver deposits in the early sixteenth century, and the shoguns consolidated their power partly by gaining control of the mines. Technicians began to produce large quantities of high-grade bullion, exporting between 165 and 206 tons of it in the early 1600s. Most of this silver went to China and in larger quantities than the American metal passing through Manila. In return, Japan's affluent classes acquired prestigious Chinese manufactures. Because of difficult political relations, the

Ming emperor formally banned direct trade with Japan, but Chinese merchants frequently ignored him.

Early in the sixteenth century, Portuguese and Spanish mariners also turned up in the China seas. They carried silk, sugar, deerskins, and medicines to Japan, exchanging those goods for silver, gold, and copper, which they sold in China or other Asian lands. Iberian Catholic missionaries also reached Japan, and they converted enough souls to establish a strong Christian minority on the southern island of Kyushu. The Tokugawa shoguns wanted to encourage foreign trade. But Catholic clerics, whose followers had plenty of imported guns, began to assert more political influence than the rulers were willing to. In 1613 the government clamped new regulations on foreign residents, prohibited Japanese from traveling abroad, tore down churches, and executed Christians. In 1637 a rural rebellion on Kyushu that displayed Christian symbols to protest famine and government mistreatment prompted closure of all remaining missions and most European trading posts. Legal overseas commerce continued only through a small number of carefully supervised ports. Dutch merchants retained permission to occupy just one entrepôt on a little island in Nagasaki Bay.

The Tokugawa had no desire to cut Japan off from the world economy but rather to ensure that Japanese merchants controlled external trade and that the government harvest its proper share of customs revenue. By the later seventeenth century, however, the silver mines began to give out, leading the shoguns to ban its export. That action reduced foreign trade in general, though the domestic economy continued to grow.

Asians and Europeans in the Southern Seas

European participation in global trade grew slowly for two centuries. Up to 1700 or later, the value of interregional exchange within Afroeurasia far exceeded the value of trans-Atlantic or trans-Pacific trade. Moreover, European captains carried costly spice cargos from Asia to Europe by way of the Cape of Good Hope. This trade, however, had much less value than the exchanges between one big Asian population center and another. In the southern seas, Asian and African sailors—Chinese, Malays, Indians, Persians, Arabs, Ethiopians, and Swahili East Africans—continued to move merchandise, both luxury wares and bulk commodities like rice, timber, and fish, from port to port.

American and Japanese silver pumped energy into the whole southern seas network. The increasing availability of silver stimulated commercial demand. Consequently, producers of agricultural commodities (rice, pepper, and cinnamon) and manufactures (cottons, silks, ceramics) ratcheted up their supply, employing larger numbers of men and women for wages as farm laborers, spinners, weavers, and potters. Silver, gold, and copper money fabricated in the mints of several states circulated as coins. Cowry shells, which came mainly from the Maldive Islands in the Indian Ocean, were also used as money

A Spanish doubloon. Gold coins such as this one were among the many currencies that facilitated seventeenth-century trade. The coin is inscribed with the name Philippus V (Philip V) and the date 1714. Philip was king of Spain when the coin was stamped.

in certain regions. Silver set the standard of value for other currencies, including Spanish coins such as "pieces of eight" and gold doubloons. Money coursed through the trade network like blood through veins, though clotting up in regions that ran large trade surpluses, including South Asia. In fact, South Asia, which had little silver, became a "silver sink" second only to China.

The Dutch move in. The Portuguese venturers who penetrated the Indian Ocean on carracks bristling with artillery gave Asian and African merchants an economic jolt (see Chapter 16). But the government in Lisbon never had nearly enough vessels or firepower to dominate Asian sea trade. The old circuits were not seriously interrupted, and Portuguese shippers eventually joined the "country trade," transporting goods from port to port in the southern seas without going back to Europe. They employed crews mainly of Asian, African, or mixed origin. Portuguese men who resided in coastal ports also became Asianized, marrying Asian women and producing male children who did the same. Portuguese became a *lingua franca,* or medium of trade and interethnic communication, all around the Indian Ocean rim.

In 1602, merchants in the Netherlands organized the Dutch East India Company, or VOC (Vereenigde Oost-Indische Compagnie), to trade in Asian waters. This joint-stock company operated under the authority of the States General, the governing assembly of the United Netherlands. The States General kept basic control but gave the company a monopoly on Dutch commerce in Asia, as well as the right to use force and negotiate treaties. The Netherlands had a population of less than two million, but, as we have seen, its merchants and manufacturers acquired great wealth and therefore capital for overseas investment.

In the first decade of the seventeenth century, VOC vessels sailed into the Indian Ocean with cannons blazing, as the Portuguese had done a century earlier. The United Netherlands was chronically at war with Spain, and in 1580 a royal succession crisis led to the unification of Spain and Portugal under the Spanish crown, a situation that lasted for sixty years. Consequently, the VOC aimed to destroy the bases of both those states and to seize control of the spice trade. In 1614 the company's governor-general told his board of directors: "You gentlemen ought to know from experience that trade in Asia should be conducted and maintained under the protection and with the aid of your own weapons, and that those weapons must be wielded with the profits gained by the trade. So trade cannot be maintained without war, nor war without trade."[14] In 1619 VOC troops invaded the port of Jakarta on the densely populated Indonesian island of Java. After killing or enslaving most of the population, the Dutch renamed the city Batavia (the Latin name for Holland) and from that base campaigned to monopolize the trade in nutmeg, mace, and cloves from the Moluccas Islands. In 1623 Dutch forces invaded the island of Taiwan, and in 1641 they evicted the Portuguese from the strategic port of Malacca. Eleven years later, the VOC established a way station on the South African coast. That settlement became Cape Town.

The English in South Asia. Founded in 1600, the English East India Company (EIC) was a joint-stock enterprise like the VOC. It spent its early decades in a power struggle with the Dutch over the Indonesian spice trade, and it seized some VOC bases. But soon it turned its attention to South Asia, most of which was part of the powerful Mughal empire (see Chapter 17). The Mughals permitted the EIC to set up a few trading posts on the South Asian coasts.

In 1639 the EIC founded a commercial station, or factory (supervised by an agent called the "factor"), at Madras (Chennai) on the Bay of Bengal to export Indian cotton textiles. Initially, European merchants acquired finished cloth in exchange for silver and other goods purchased elsewhere in Asia. Gradually, however, they became involved in production, depositing raw cotton and dyes with Indian spinners and weavers, then returning a few months later to collect the cloth. Thousands of rural households joined this production system, transforming the economy around Madras from agriculture to export-driven manufacturing. In the later seventeenth century, the EIC also carved out an enclave at Calcutta in Bengal west of the fertile Ganges River delta. Company officers encouraged local artisans to produce cotton and silk fabrics for export. In the same period, the Mughal state experienced growing political problems, prompting the EIC to fortify and extend its enclaves deeper inland.

A multicentered trading world. Neither the VOC nor the EIC had sufficient military power to dominate the southern seas from end to end or to keep out multiple competitors. The Portuguese held on to most of their Asian ports and kept on trafficking much as before. And several other European states—France, Denmark, Prussia, and Russia among them—formed companies that traded in the Indian Ocean with varying success. Muslim merchants from Gujarat in northwestern India maintained a far-flung trade network. The ports of Manila and Batavia attracted tens of thousands of Chinese merchants and craftworkers. As we have seen, the Tokugawa shogunate severely restricted the Dutch presence in Japan after 1637, and in 1662 the VOC abandoned its colony on Taiwan in the teeth of a Chinese invasion. Only in the Indonesian islands did the Dutch

entrench themselves solidly enough to lay the foundation of a territorial colony. Using brutal tactics such as blocking rice supplies from reaching island populations, the VOC tried to control spice production and trade. Even then, conflict with Indonesia maritime states continued on into the next century. For example, the sultanate of Aceh on the northwestern tip of Sumatra deployed a strong navy armed with cannon supplied by the Ottoman Turkish empire. Aceh repeatedly threatened both Portuguese and Dutch rule at Malacca. The Ming, Mughal, and Safavid empires, the giant Asian territorial monarchies, allowed Europeans to trade, not because they were too weak to prevent it, but because foreign commerce benefited their economies.

Overland Trade on the Silk Roads

Commerce along Inner Eurasia's silk roads continued to flourish in the early modern centuries, though on a much smaller scale than the sea trade. The routes and participants, however, changed significantly. First, long-distance movement of goods from China to the Mediterranean or Europe declined in importance relative to exchanges between neighboring regions. Ming China shipped silks, porcelain, paper, tea, and drugs overland to Central Asia in exchange for horses, sheep, and gems. Important routes also connected Central Asia to Mughal India, carrying foodstuffs like melons, apples, grapes, and almonds that did not grow well in South Asia. Central Asians also sent around 100,000 horses a year to the Mughal cavalry.

Second, trade swelled on Inner Eurasian north–south routes that linked the expanding Russian empire to China, India, Persia, and the Ottoman lands. Bukhara, Samarkand, and other Central Asian cities, loosely associated under the Turkic Uzbek dynasty, operated as key entrepôts. Sable and otter fur, which wealthy urban elites wanted nearly everywhere, led export trade from Russia and Siberia. As the Russian empire grew in population and territory, its rich estate lords and merchants desired more Indian textiles, pepper, and other warm-climate wares. Indian traders founded mercantile communities as far north as Astrakhan at the mouth of the Volga River to mediate this traffic.

The Atlantic Economy: Land, Capital, and Slave Labor

FOCUS What effects did the extensive use of African slave labor in the Americas have on economic and political developments in the lands rimming the Atlantic in the sixteenth and seventeenth centuries?

Before 1492 the Atlantic Ocean was a forbidding frontier. By the end of the seventeenth century, port towns lined its rim, nautical maps described its coastlines in detail, and people and goods moved routinely across it. In those two centuries, the demographic picture on the American side of the rim also changed dramatically. As American Indian populations plunged, Europeans crossed the ocean in growing numbers—soldiers, royal officials, missionaries, miners, trappers, artisans, plantation entrepreneurs, and workers. European fortune-seekers did not take long to realize the economic potential of not only silver mountains like Potosí, but also tropical lands where climate and soil offered great potential for commercial agriculture. The pace of European immigration, however, did not come close to meeting the demand for labor, and Native American populations could not fill it. Few Europeans without wealth, useful skills, or specific purpose were eager to migrate to America's tropical latitudes, where hard labor and several tropical diseases likely awaited them. Those who did migrate were mostly men, so in the early centuries the birthrate of Europeans in America remained low. Capitalist planters, however, found the solution to their worker problem by bringing in people from tropical Africa, the only dense pool of labor available on the Atlantic rim other than Europe.

In fact, more Africans than Europeans went to America on a yearly basis from the mid-1500s to the 1830s.[15] Tropical Africans did not wish to volunteer for grueling plantation labor in distant America any more than most European peasants did. European governments or private businesses had no moral or legal authority to enslave fellow Europeans in large numbers and ship them to America. But they could do this to Africans, as long as African elites with power or wealth agreed to cooperate in this enterprise. The Atlantic slave trade thus got under way.

The Atlantic Economy and African Slavery

Portuguese and other Europeans who sailed to Subsaharan Africa in the fifteenth and early sixteenth centuries soon discovered that if they wanted to acquire slaves they would not be able to do it by raiding or invading inland territory. African societies, some with armies, successfully fought back and soon acquired guns to help them do it. Also, tropical diseases, notably malaria and yellow fever, took a horrendous toll on Europeans who visited tropical African coasts. For example, British records show that among employees of the Royal African Company who arrived at West African trading ports between 1695 and 1722, six out of every ten died in the first year and only one ever returned home.[16] Until key medical breakthroughs in the later nineteenth century, Europeans died of diseases in Africa at almost the same rate that Native Americans died of Afroeurasian afflictions in the sixteenth century.

Nevertheless, European merchants ambitious or foolhardy enough to go to West or Central African coasts discovered that they could purchase slaves, along with gold, pepper, and other products, from local sellers in return for textiles and other manufactured goods. In the late fifteenth and early sixteenth centuries, Portuguese vessels carried

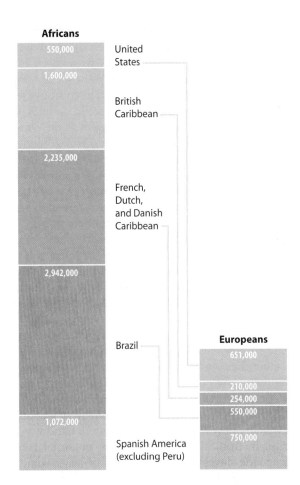

African and European immigration to the Americas, 1500–1820. Which region had the biggest difference between numbers of European and African migrants? Which regions had the greatest parity? What factors explain differences in the numbers of Africans and Europeans migrating to the Americas?

African slaves to the eastern Atlantic islands to perform plantation labor. They also took significant numbers to Europe. In 1550, for example, Lisbon had a population of about 10,000 captive Africans, most of them working as domestic servants, farm laborers, or artisan assistants. After 1520, when European economic exploitation of American territories got seriously under way and demand for labor there grew steadily, slave shippers found no serious technological obstacles to setting sail for Brazil or the Caribbean rather than for the Canary Islands or Portugal.

Why did Africans sell people? In premodern centuries, most agrarian societies in both Afroeurasia and the Americas practiced various forms of **social bondage,** meaning that certain individuals or groups held legal or customary rights to the labor of other people. Many

> **social bondage** A condition in which an individual or a group holds rights to a person's labor or services, whether for a limited period or for a lifetime. Social bondage may take a variety of forms, including slavery, serfdom, or indentured servitude.

societies practiced slavery, defined as the condition of individuals whose lives and labor were at the disposal of others without restriction. Serfdom, common in western Europe down to the fifteenth century, was a type of social bondage, but it had constraints. Masters could not, for example, legally sell serfs as movable property, as they could do with slaves. Also, tens of thousands of Europeans went to the Americas in the sixteenth and seventeenth centuries as bonded, or indentured, servants. Those men and women, typically impoverished or otherwise in desperate straits, agreed to contracts that obligated them to a period of service, often seven years. Their patron paid their passage and agreed to provide food and shelter. Because servants often worked in harsh and unhealthy conditions, many died before their term was up. Indentured servitude was one way for European entrepreneurs or rich families in America to acquire labor, but the numbers never met demand, especially on commercial plantations.

Historians have long debated the history and character of social bondage in Subsaharan Africa. Some scholars contend that slavery was widespread nearly everywhere. Individuals, families, or ruling groups having sufficient wealth accumulated slaves because of the absence of traditions of landed property. Powerful or rich individuals measured their status by how many men and women they controlled rather than by how much land they owned. Land was more abundant in tropical Africa than were potential laborers. Masters made slaves work in a variety of ways, sometimes doing hard farm labor, often serving as domestic servants, artisans, soldiers, or, in the case of women, concubines or wives. Masters also had the right to dispose of their slaves in trade. Because of this practice, Europeans who came to the African coast found they could tap an existing market in "disposable persons," acquiring them in return for manufactured goods.

Critics of this explanation argue that historical evidence for the existence of large numbers of slaves in West and Central Africa in, say, 1450, is limited and questionable. They contend that institutions of social bondage took several different forms and that not all people held in some type of "unfree" status should be categorized as slaves. These scholars also claim that if slavery was already extensive in tropical Africa when Europeans first appeared, how could it have expanded so much between the sixteenth and eighteenth centuries, which it clearly did? These historians, rather, see a process in which European merchants began to put great pressure on Africans to sell slaves by offering to buy them at prices that enterprising rulers, well-to-do merchants, and armed kidnappers could not refuse. In other words, if Africans having power and wealth wished to take part in the expanding Atlantic economy, they were going to have to do it partly by selling slaves.

The reign of sugar. From the early sixteenth century, Portuguese merchants contracted with the Spanish crown to supply slaves to its American colonies. By midcentury,

there were about 3,000 Africans in the Viceroyalty of Peru, and within another hundred years, at least 100,000. Another 35,000 lived in New Spain, that is, Spanish North America. In the early empire, African slaves and their descendants lived predominantly in towns, working at a variety of jobs, including service in colonial militias. Others toiled in mercury and silver mines.

By the mid-1500s, Europeans also began to open plantations to grow agricultural commodities for the global market, eventually to include sugar, tobacco, indigo, rice, wheat, cotton, cacao, and coffee. In the following two centuries, cane sugar became America's most valuable exportable crop (see Map 18.3). Sugar's journey to the Western Hemisphere was a long one. Farmers probably first domesticated cane in Southeast Asia as many as nine thousand years ago. From there it spread over the millennia to South Asia, where artisans invented processes for making crystalline sugar. From there, it progressed westward to Southwest Asia and from about 1000 C.E. to several Mediterranean islands. The rulers of Aragon in Iberia encouraged cultivation along the western Mediterranean coast, and Muslim land-owners founded a thriving industry in Morocco. By the fifteenth century, cane sugar rivaled honey as a popular sweetener and preservative throughout the Mediterranean basin.

Portuguese, Spanish, and Italian entrepreneurs also planted sugar in the rich volcanic soils of the eastern Atlantic islands. Those growers adopted a set of production methods that combined large capital investment, technically sophisticated mill machinery, tight management, and intensive labor performed increasingly by slaves working in closely supervised gangs. On the island of Madeira, technicians improved the process of extracting sugar juice by crushing cane between horizontal rollers. Workers transferred the sap to copper cauldrons and boiled it down to thick, dark syrup, or molasses. To refine the product further, they poured this liquid into clay vessels, where it dried out gradually, leaving behind solid "loaves" of tightly packed crystals, ready to be shipped.

In 1485, Portuguese capitalists started planting cane on São Tomé off the Central African coast (see Chapter 16). This successful experiment showed two things. First, planters could harvest and process sugar 1,300 miles from Europe and ship it there for sale at large profit. Second, they could do it entirely with African slave labor, which they obtained from the Kongo kingdom on the nearby mainland. A few decades later, other Portuguese entrepreneurs found that sugar also thrived in northeastern Brazil in conditions of high rainfall and dark rich soil. In a sense, the growing and processing of sugar as an integrated mode of production, including use of African slave labor, was extended from islands on the eastern side of the Atlantic to South America.

When American plantations proved successful, Portuguese shippers began to sail the Atlantic in a triangular pattern. Vessels debarked from Lisbon laden with textiles, metal ware, and other goods. They sailed to one or more African ports, exchanging their cargos for slaves and other

MAP 18.3 The global spread of sugar production.

The world's population developed a taste for this tropical crop. Why do you think it took so much longer for sugar growing to spread across Afroeurasia to the eastern Mediterranean than it took to spread from there to the Americas?

African products. Crossing the Atlantic, they sold their slaves in return for silver, gold, sugar, tobacco, indigo, hides, pearls, and other American merchandise, and then returned to Europe. Brazil seemed to offer endless square miles of fertile land, as well as abundant wood to feed the sugar boilers. As entrepreneurs increased production and improved mill technology, costs declined and profits rose. Trans-Atlantic transport costs also sank as ships came on line that went faster, required smaller crews, and had more cargo space. In 1571 Portugal founded a colony at Luanda on the coast of modern Angola, allying with local Africans to round up captives and bring them to port. From there, captains sailed on trade winds due west to Brazil. Angola soon became the principal source of labor for Portuguese plantations. By 1620, Brazilian mills produced an annual average of 15,000 to 22,000 tons of sugar. Simultaneously, European appetites for sugar began to grow. It provided quick energy to working men and women, and like tea and coffee it was a "drug food" with mildly addictive properties.

Dutch merchants witnessed the Brazilian bonanza and determined to cut themselves in. In 1621, investors founded the West Indies Company (WIC), a joint-stock firm paralleling the VOC. At first the WIC attacked Portuguese and Spanish ships, ports, and American territories, but this expensive strategy brought diminishing returns. The company therefore made a specialty of carrying the trade of others. Dutch technicians who learned about sugar mills in Brazil helped introduce them to developing English and French colonies in the Caribbean, where cane also flourished. The industry took off initially on the small English island of Barbados. By the 1670s this dot in the sea produced around 65 percent of the sugar England consumed. In the seventeenth and eighteenth centuries, plantation economies came to dominate several French and British islands, including Martinique, Haiti (the western half of Hispaniola), and Jamaica.

As the economic potential of sugar islands and other overseas colonial territories became apparent to western European states, each one formulated policies to try to ensure that it, rather than any rival country, would benefit, exclusively if possible, from the commerce that its dependencies generated. These policies and the ideas that inspired them became known as **mercantilism.**

> **mercantilism** An economic doctrine based on the idea that the world's exploitable wealth could not expand and that a state should therefore erect barriers to keep rival states out of its circuits of trade with its colonies.

Sugar production in the Caribbean. This seventeenth-century engraving shows African slaves driving oxen to power a crushing mill, which extracted juice from fresh sugar cane. The juice was boiled in vats like the two in the foreground to evaporate the water and reduce the juice to crystals. Sugar mill labor was intensive and dangerous. Why would European planters have preferred African slaves as laborers in this industry?

This economic doctrine was founded on the premise that the world's exploitable wealth was finite and on the whole not expandable. Rulers should therefore strive to accumulate more global riches than their rivals did, partly by acquiring productive colonies abroad and binding them to the home country in a closed system that walled off from competitors. A state's wealth was to be measured in reserves of gold and silver, accumulated by selling home manufactures abroad, by strictly regulating colonial imports, and by buying as little as possible from other countries. Central governments should take action to expand domestic manufacturing, encourage population growth, keep import tariffs high, cooperate with national trading firms, and spend generously on military forces to defend colonies and trade lines. As the Atlantic economy grew, mercantilist attitudes contributed to rising political tensions and outbreaks of war among the major European maritime powers. Britain, France, and the Netherlands generally implemented mercantilist strategies more successfully than did Spain or Portugal, which by the seventeenth century had weaker manufacturing economies and naval clout.

Commercial agriculture and slavery. Forced shipment of African slaves to America became a key element of mercantilist profit-seeking. In Portuguese Brazil, the African slave population rose from about three thousand in 1570 to fifteen thousand by the end of the century. Slave imports also accelerated in the Caribbean after 1640. There, Native American peoples had been all but wiped out. Both the British and the French tried to attract free immigrants from the homelands. That effort failed, largely because the islands gained a reputation in Europe as deadly hellholes. The only feasible alternative was African slave immigration, and by 1680 little Barbados had fifty thousand slaves. Within another twenty years, Africans and their offspring represented a demographic majority in northeastern Brazil and on several Caribbean islands.

Demand for slave labor in America continued to grow for two reasons. One was that the American plantation economy kept expanding, not only to grow sugar but also tobacco, indigo, cotton, and other exportable commodities. The other was that African slave populations in America did not on the whole reproduce themselves by natural increase. Planters

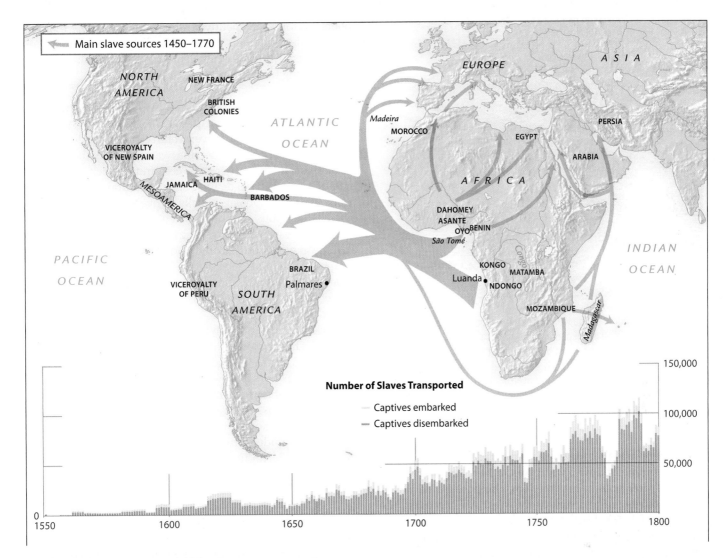

Number of Slaves Transported

— Captives embarked
— Captives disembarked

MAP 18.4 Trade of enslaved Africans, 1500–1800.

High mortality rates on the middle passage across the Atlantic meant that more slaves embarked from African ports than arrived on American shores. Why were the majority of African captives sold into Atlantic markets, despite the demand for slaves in several parts of Afroeurasia? Why were slaves taken in large numbers to some regions but not to others?

wanted to import mainly male slaves for hard field labor. Since enslaved men far outnumbered women, slave deaths consistently exceeded births. (Though women represented a small percentage of imports relative to males, they were not spared the ordeal of slavery. In fact, of all females who crossed the Atlantic to America before 1820, four out of every five were Africans.) Moreover, slaves on tropical plantations were unlikely to live more than about seven years. Consequently, planters made continuous demands on Atlantic merchants to bring more workers, even though slave prices climbed persistently over the long run.

The workings of the slave trade. African rulers and merchants began exporting enslaved men and women long before Europeans appeared on their coasts. Between the years 800 and 1600, for example, something like five thousand slaves, both men and women, crossed the Sahara Desert each year, along with gold and other goods, to serve

in wealthy households, workshops, or army units in Muslim lands. Indian Ocean traders also bought slaves in East Africa for shipment to Arabia, Egypt, Persia, or India. The Atlantic trade, therefore, represented not the advent of African forced migration but rather a major shift in its direction from Afroeurasian to American destinations (see Map 18.4). In the seventeenth century the trans-Saharan trade diminished, whereas more than 2.25 million Africans were taken to America. The Atlantic trade reached its zenith in the 1780s, a decade when about 866,000 Africans endured the ocean crossing, or "middle passage."[17]

These numbers do not account for the hundreds of thousands, if not millions, of slaves who died in transit. Historians have estimated that in the late seventeenth century as many as 10 percent of captive people perished on their way to the African coast or while waiting to be put on ships. Estimates from Angola suggest 40 percent.[18] Another 10 to 14 percent died at sea and countless more in wars, raids,

Cruelties of the middle passage. The death rate for captives crossing the Atlantic was as high as 15 percent. Slaves who caused trouble faced violent discipline, as we see in the background of this image. Dead and near-dead slaves were thrown to the sharks, but here sailors are casting apparently healthy and valuable slaves overboard. Why might that have happened? Can you speculate about the intended purpose of this mid-eighteenth century engraving?

and kidnappings that fueled the slave trade. Venture Smith, a West African child who was taken to New England in the 1730s but later bought his freedom, composed a narrative of his enslavement and trek to the West African coast, including his father's death at the hands of their captors: "The women and myself being pretty submissive, had tolerable treatment from the enemy, while my father was closely interrogated respecting his money which they knew he must have. But as he gave them no account of it, he was instantly cut and pounded on his body with great inhumanity. . . . I saw him while he was thus tortured to death. The shocking scene is to this day fresh in my mind, and I have often been overcome while thinking on it."[19]

From the point of debarkation, the misery of enslavement became progressively worse. The average trans-Atlantic voyage lasted between one and three months. On many ships, slaves spent most of the voyage shackled and confined to dark, stifling holds, where seasickness and other ills produced vomiting, diarrhea, severe dehydration, and sometimes death. In his eighteenth-century narrative, the former slave Olaudah Equiano wrote: "The stench of the hold . . . was so intolerably loathsome, that it was dangerous to remain there for any time. . . . The closeness of the place and the heat of the climate, added to the number in the ship, which was so crowded that each had scarcely room to turn himself, almost suffocated us."[20] Slaves who survived the middle passage went on to more trouble and usually an early grave, especially if they were consigned to sugar plantations. At harvest time, field slaves had to meet rigid daily quotas of cut cane. Workers who fed the cane into the mill's crushing

rollers performed repetitive, mind-numbing tasks that invited accidents, notably mangled hands or arms. Boiler tenders worked inside the equivalent of an oven, inhaling smoke and suffering burns.

Slave resistance. Africans frequently resisted their dismal fate. Portuguese sugar planters largely abandoned the island of São Tomé in the seventeenth century partly because escaped slaves waged guerrilla warfare from the interior mountains. In the Americas, men and women found numerous ways to rebel against their condition, ranging from subtle forms of sabotage, attacks on overseers and formation of secret religious or ethnic societies, to outright rebellion. Slaves also resisted by running away. South America and the Caribbean were dotted with remote, hidden communities of escaped slaves, called *macombos* in Portuguese and "maroon societies" in English. Some of these communities had no more than a dozen inhabitants; others had populations that rivaled European colonies. The most famous *macombo* was Palmares, a cluster of towns in northeastern Brazil's backcountry. This settlement may have had tens of thousands of residents in the second half of the seventeenth century. Palmares was effectively an African-style state, with a king, a council of nobles, an army equipped with guns, and defensive fortifications. Villagers grew a variety of crops, including sugar cane. Some of them owned their own slaves and occasionally raided European plantations to acquire more. In the 1670s, Portuguese militias launched a series of offensives, finally overrunning Palmares in 1694.

Change in Atlantic Africa

The expansion of the global economy after 1500 had transforming effects on Atlantic-facing tropical Africa. First, population generally declined between the sixteenth and the eighteenth centuries, a period when numbers elsewhere in Afroeurasia were trending rapidly upward. This happened partly because of violence and upheaval in particular regions associated with enslavement, partly because of slave exports, and partly because women of childbearing age who were put on slave ships, even though fewer in number than males, could no longer produce children in their homelands. Population loss might have been even worse, except that when slaving activity and associated warfare devastated a particular area, both African and European traders were obliged to move their operations elsewhere. This allowed the depopulated region time to recover at least some of its numbers.

African economic life also changed. Owing to their participation in international trade, both with slaves and other products, some regions experience significant economic growth. This prosperity, however, tended to benefit mainly small elites—rulers, warlords, merchants, and people who already used slaves for commercial farming or mining. These elites allied themselves, if only indirectly, with their European or American counterparts—company investors, bankers, shippers, planters, and political officials—in order to accumulate wealth. Also, African merchants had for centuries operated

Servants and Slaves on a Barbados Sugar Plantation

In 1647 Richard Ligon (ca. 1585–1662), an Englishman out of money and career options, saw a chance to make a fresh start somewhere in Britain's growing empire. He booked passage on a ship bound for Barbados, where English settlers had first arrived twenty years earlier. During three years in the Caribbean, however, Ligon's fortunes did not improve much. By 1652 he returned to England but then got himself locked up in a London debtors' prison. While behind bars, he wrote The True and Exact History of the Island of Barbadoes, *an account of his Caribbean adventure.*

The early English settlers on Barbados intended to found a predominantly white European society, but African slaves were also brought in from the start. When Ligon arrived there, sugar planters were using both white indentured servant and African slave labor. In this selection from his book, Ligon first describes the troubled lives of white workers and their reasons for plotting an uprising. He portrays African slaves as more contented with their situation than white servants. But he then contradicts this view by giving an account of slaves planning an act of sabotage. In the Caribbean, where potentially great sugar profits depended on relentless labor, such rebellion was far from uncommon.

The Island is divided into three sorts of men, viz. Masters, [white] Servants and [African] Slaves. The slaves and their posterity, being subject to their Masters for ever, are kept and preserv'd with greater care than the servants, who are theirs for but five years, according to the law of the Island. So that for the time, the servants have the worser lives, for they are put to very hard labor, ill lodging, and their diet very sleight. . . .

[S]ome cruel Masters will provoke their Servants so, by extreme ill usage, and often and cruel beating them, as they grow desperate, and so join together to revenge themselves upon them. . . .

A little before I came from thence, there was such a combination [plot] amongst them, as the like was never seen there before. Their sufferings being grown to a great height, and their daily complainings to one another (of the intolerable burdens they labour'd under) being spread throughout the Island; at the last, some amongst them, whose spirits were not able to endure such slavery, resolved to break through it, or die in the act; and so conspired with some others of their acquaintance; So that a day was appointed to fall upon their Masters, and cut all their throats, and by that means, to make themselves [not] only freemen, but Masters of the Island. And so closely [secretly] was this plot carried, as no discovery was made, till the day before they were to put it in act: And then one of them, either by the failing of his courage, or some new obligation from the love of his Master, revealed this long plotted conspiracy; and so by this timely advertisement [alert], the Masters were saved. . . . [W]hereof eighteen of the principal men in the conspiracy, and they the first leaders and contrivers of the plot, were put to death, for example to the rest. . . .

It has been accounted a strange thing, that the Negroes, being more than double the numbers of the Christians that are there, . . . that these should not commit some horrid massacre upon the Christians. . . . But there are three reasons that take away this wonder; the one is, They are not suffered to touch or handle any weapons: The other, That they are held in such awe [dread] and slavery, as they are fearful to appear in any daring act; and seeing the mustering of our men, and hearing their Gun-shot, (than which nothing is more terrible to them) their spirits are subjugated to so low a condition, as they dare not look up to any bold attempt. Besides these, there is a third reason, which stops all designs of that kind, and that is, They are fetch'd from several parts of Africa, who speak several languages, and by that means, one of them understands not another. . . .

I believe . . . that there are honest, faithful, and conscionable people amongst [the African slaves], as amongst those of Europe, or any other part of the world. . . .

A hint of this, I will give you in a lively example; and it was in a time when Victuals were scarce, and Plantins [plantains, which slaves consumed] were not then so frequently planted, as to afford them enough. So that some of the high spirited and turbulent amongst them, began to mutiny, and had a plot, secretly to be reveng'd on their Master. . . . These villains were resolved to make fire to such part of the boiling-house as they were sure would fire the rest, and so burn all, and yet seem ignorant of the fact, as a thing done by accident. But this plot was discovered, by some of the others who hated mischief; . . . and so traduc'd [accused] them to their Master, and brought in so many witnesses against them, as they were forc'd to confess, what they meant should have been put in act the next night.

Source: Richard Ligon, *The True and Exact History of the Island of Barbadoes,* 1657, ed. J. Edward Hutson (St. Michael, Barbados: Barbados National Trust, 2000), 64, 66–67, 75, 76.

Thinking Critically

Why, according to Ligon, did white indentured servants receive worse treatment than African slaves? Why were the indentured servants unable to go through with the plan to kill their masters? What three reasons does Ligon give for the lack of slave resistance on Barbados? According to him, when a group of slaves plotted sabotage, what motivated them and why did they fail?

Queen Nzinga negotiating with the Portuguese governor in Luanda, Angola, about 1620. Legend has it that when the governor refused to offer the queen a chair, a courtesy due to a political leader of equal rank, she refused to be slighted. Instead, she demonstrated both her power over her subjects and her keen negotiating tactics. Why do you think a seventeenth-century European engraving would commemorate this event?

financially sophisticated inland trade networks. Commercial routes, business customs, and credit systems simply became more elaborate in the centuries of the Atlantic trade. African rulers and merchants made rational business decisions to determine how many enslaved men and women should be put to work locally and how many might be sold to Europeans. Rulers hardly ever allowed peaceable and productive members of *their own societies* to be sold into the trade. But individuals having no place or standing in the community might be regarded as disposable, especially prisoners of war (often from wars having nothing directly to do with the slave trade), but also foreign refugees, criminals, outcasts, and kidnap victims.

A third sphere of change was political. The slave trade destabilized some African states but strengthened or helped give birth to others. International commerce offered rulers new economic opportunities, and this encouraged them to centralize political administration more tightly, extract revenue from their subjects more efficiently, and strengthen their control over production and commerce.

Central African states and Portuguese intruders.
The Kongo kingdom (see Chapter 16) centered south of the lower Congo River grew powerful in the later fifteenth century but fared poorly after Europeans arrived. Slave trading by both Portuguese and local Africans brought instability that the monarch was unable to prevent, and in the seventeenth century, the kingdom became enmeshed in a series of ruinous wars with the Portuguese in Angola. Internal political struggles followed those wars, generating large numbers of captives, which benefited no one except African and European slave merchants. The kingdom nearly disintegrated, though it managed to reconstitute itself in the next century.

Kingdoms lying south of Kongo connected themselves to the Atlantic economy as suppliers of slaves, ivory, and copper after 1575, when the Portuguese established a fortified post at Luanda, the core of a colony they named Angola. The neighboring Ndongo and Matamba states had to contend with growing Portuguese political and military influence aimed at expanding the supply of slaves for shipment to Brazil. When the king of Ndongo died in 1618, Nzinga (r. 1618–1663), a royal princess, seized power. A remarkable political strategist, she maneuvered among both the Portuguese and various Ndongo factions. But in the 1620s, Portuguese pressures grew too heavy to bear. Nzinga distanced herself from them by leading an army further inland to conquer the Matamba kingdom. She had little trouble establishing her authority because, whereas Ndongo had no tradition of rule by queens, Matamba did. For nearly four decades, Nzinga successfully defended Matamba against both the Portuguese and its African allies. At the same time, she made her own profitable arrangements with rulers and merchants of the Central African interior to direct caravans of slaves, ivory, and copper through Matamba to the Atlantic coast. For many Angolans today, Nzinga remains a mythic national heroine.

West African states. In the forest and savanna regions of West Africa, several states rose to regional power after 1600. One of these was the kingdom of Oyo, centered in wooded grasslands west of the Niger River. Oyo's rulers took part in slave trading, acquiring European textiles and other goods primarily to purchase horses brought south from the Sahara. Oyo fielded a formidable cavalry army, which pushed out the kingdom's frontiers and, in the process, acquired slaves for home labor or export. Southwest of Oyo, along the fringe between savanna and tropical rainforest, the kingdom of

Dahomey accumulated power in the seventeenth century by trading slaves for guns and building a large professional military. This force expanded to the coast in the early 1700s so that no competing power stood between it and European slave buyers. In the same period, Dahomey and Oyo battled each other, generating more slaves.

Farther west, the gold-producing region that is part of modern Ghana gave rise to a number of small states before 1500. In the late seventeenth century, one of these, the kingdom of Asante (Ashanti), rose under the leadership of Osei Tutu to dominate its neighbors. The common symbol of political authority in the region was a type of stool. According to Asante political legend, Anokye, the principal adviser to Osei Tutu, used magical power to conjure a stool of pure gold from out of the sky. Osei Tutu thereafter inspired intense political loyalty in the region, and several of his successors went on to conquer and incorporate much more territory. War and trade swept growing numbers of slaves into the kingdom. The rulers exported a calculated number of them every year but retained many more to work in fields, gold mines, and households. Slaves not sold off, or at least their children, might gain full integration into Asante society.

Asante royal stool. The golden stool of the Asantehene (king) is a sacred object that only the king himself may touch and few may see. Similarly shaped stools, however, serve ordinary people and are said to be the seat of the owner's soul. Each one is carved from a single block of wood, individually designed and symbolically decorated for the intended owner.

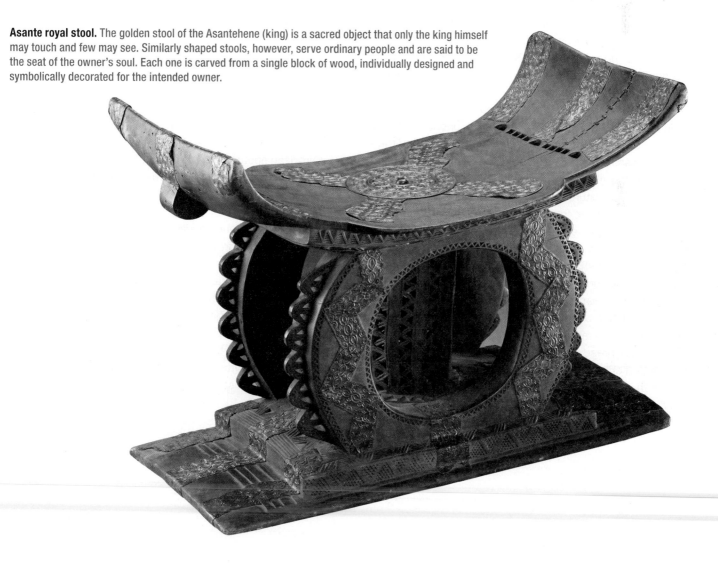

Conclusion

In Afroeurasia the middle decades of the seventeenth century marked a pause between a long period of remarkable demographic and economic growth, which started about 1400, and another, which got under way by 1700. The economic downturn that historians have described in the early and mid-1600s affected many societies, though not all. In both China and Europe, economic output faltered, income declined for many, and population growth slowed. Both the Ottoman and Safavid Persian empires also suffered rising inflation, a serious flight of silver and gold to pay for imports, and worsening poverty. The Atlantic slave trade began to take a significant toll in population and political stability in parts of West and Central Africa. On the other hand, economic growth appears to have characterized South Asia nearly throughout the century. In the West African savanna lands, a climatic wet phase set in around 1500, boosting population and farm production for two or three hundred years. In Europe the United Netherlands had its economic golden age in the mid-seventeenth century, whereas Germany, Spain, and several other states fared badly.

Scholars have linked seventeenth-century recession to a number of possible factors. Some point to declining production of American silver, which caused prices to drop and commerce to languish, notably in China and Europe. Others stress the economic effects of population growth rates leveling off or declining in some regions, a phenomenon that reduced demand for food and other commodities and therefore depressed both production and trade. More recently, historians and climatologists have investigated fluctuations in global temperatures attending the Little Ice Age, which extended altogether from the thirteenth to the nineteenth century (see Chapter 15). Temperatures in the Northern Hemisphere dropped significantly between the 1630s and 1650s. The cold snap was associated with severe winters, cold and rainy summers, floods, or droughts, depending on the region. Scholars have correlated these extreme conditions, including food shortages, with an upsurge of insurrections, revolutions, and wars from western Europe to Japan.[21]

The widespread economic slowdown, which appears to have lasted only a few decades, was a cyclical phenomenon and in the longer term had little effect on the world economy's continuing growth and commercialization. Between 1500 and 1700 the ships and overland transport that linked every part of Afroeurasia and the Americas with every other part spun a web of exchange far bigger and busier than in any previous era. The long-distance movement of commodities, manufactures, food crops, workers, and technical ideas produced new accumulations of wealth, especially in regions that already had large populations and complex agrarian economies. American silver mines, which European entrepreneurs seized from Native Americans, gave the global commercial system a huge dose of adrenaline, though ups and downs in silver supplies could also contribute to periodic or regional slumps.

The new global exchange net affected societies in different ways. As we have seen, it had disastrous consequences for indigenous Americans. In Africa, societies that faced the Atlantic eagerly joined the emerging global trade net but discovered that commerce in people benefited relatively few. Global trade poured great wealth into the agrarian societies of Asia because they had more commodities and manufactured goods to pump into world markets than other regions did. Western European states acquired possession of potentially monumental economic resources in the Americas, and they quickly fell to battling one another for those riches. They did not, however, have to fight Ottoman, Mughal, or Ming armies, which in the circumstances of the early modern era accumulated wealth in other ways than sending navies across the Atlantic or Pacific.

European economic exploitation of the Americas was, with the exception of silver and gold mining, getting under way in the second half of the seventeenth century. Commercial agriculture began to reach bonanza proportions, but only because Europeans found a way to bring in an unwilling African workforce. In Afroeurasia, on the other hand, Europeans were yet to exert much economic power relative to the big Asian states. And, in contrast to their American conquests, they controlled little African or Asian territory other than trading posts and coastal enclaves, almost always under agreements with local rulers. Europeans were to be seen just about everywhere in the world in the seventeenth century, but the circumstances that permitted their global domination two centuries later did not yet exist.

· · ·

Key Terms

Asante state 539
chartered company 518
Dutch East India Company
(VOC) 529

galleon 517
inflation 524
Manila galleon voyages 521
mercantilism 533

middle passage 535
price revolution 524
social bondage 531
Thirty Years' War 526

Change over Time

1545	Spanish prospectors discover enormous silver deposits near Potosí, Bolivia.
1570s	The Ming government in China requires tax payments in silver.
1572	Manila galleon voyages between America and the Philippines begin, creating the last major connection in the global chain of commerce.
1580s	The African slave population in Brazil starts to grow.
1600	The English East India Company is founded.
1602	The Dutch East India Company (VOC) is founded.
1607	The English found a settlement at Jamestown in North America.
1608	The French found a settlement at Quebec on the St. Lawrence River.
1618–1648	Much of central Europe is embroiled in the Thirty Years' War.
1619	Dutch forces seize the port of Jakarta (Batavia) on Java.
1630s–1650s	The Northern Hemisphere's temperature drops.
1637	The Tokugawa shogunate expels Europeans from Japan.
1650s	A sugar industry is established on the English island of Barbados.
1662	Chinese forces expel the Dutch from the island of Taiwan.
ca. 1680	The Asante state is founded in West Africa.

Please see end of book reference section for additional reading suggestions related to this chapter.

19 The Changing Balance of Wealth and Power

1650-1750

A storm in the Pacific shipwrecked Vitus Bering and his crew in 1741. Bering died on the Aleutian island that was later named in his honor.

welve thousand years ago, when the last Ice Age was just ending, a land bridge connected the eastern tip of Russia with Alaska. In 1728–1729, Vitus Bering, a Danish sea captain serving in the Russian navy, demonstrated to the world that this isthmus was long gone. Leading an expedition commissioned by Emperor Peter the Great, Bering sailed around the northeastern coastline of Eurasia and through the strait that now bears his name. Before entering the passage, he recorded in his ship's log an encounter with local Siberians. They told him what to expect: "August 8th, having arrived in north latitude 64°30′, eight men rowed to us from the shore in a skin boat, enquiring from whence we came and what was our business there. They said they were Chuikchi . . . and they told us that on the coast lived many of their nation; that the land not far from there takes a decided turn to the westward."[1] In other words, the land did not converge with the North American shore but veered away from it.

Bering did not find Alaska on that first trip, but in 1732 he set sail again, heading a much larger Russian mission. Lasting nearly a decade, the Great Northern Expedition, as it became known, involved more than three thousand people who charted northern Pacific waters and coastlines, collected scientific data, and looked for commercial opportunities. This time Bering reached the coast of North America, but he did not live to return home. His ship broke up on an island (later named Bering Island), and he died there of scurvy in 1741. Surviving crew members managed to build a small craft from the wreckage of their ship and sailed back to Siberia. They carried with them a load of valuable sea otter pelts, which helped inspire Russian trade settlement in Alaska a half-century later. A thread in the web of global connections now traversed the far North Pacific, and by the early 1800s the Russian empire extended from the northern coast of California to eastern Europe, a straight-line distance of more than 5,800 miles.

The integration of northern Pacific lands into global exchange networks is one aspect of the great world convergence that continued to intensify in the later seventeenth and the eighteenth centuries. This chapter focuses on three large-scale manifestations of that convergence: land-based empire building on a spectacular scale; encounters between indigenous peoples and new European settlers in lands distant from Europe; and a new intellectual movement centered in European cities to rethink long accepted explanations of the workings of nature as new knowledge of the world's geography, biology, and diverse human culture flowed in from all directions.

In the first part of the chapter we explore developments in politics and power relations in the century after 1650. The Qing (chihng) dynasty in China, the Romanov rulers in Russia, and the Spanish in America, using gunpowder technology and centralized systems of command, consolidated their power over immense territories. In 1750 these three states together sprawled across about 14,282,000 square miles of land, about 4.5 times more than the continental United States today.[2] By contrast, Europe remained an assemblage of competing states, some of them tiny, others large territorial monarchies that aimed to further centralize royal power. And as we described in Chapter 18, the Netherlands, Britain, France, and Portugal also projected naval and commercial power into Africa, Asia, and the Americas.

In the sixteenth century, Europeans went abroad as explorers, soldiers, merchants, missionaries, business entrepreneurs, and imperial officials. In the second part of the chapter we describe a new type of colonial activity that got under way in the seventeenth century. Increasing numbers of Europeans migrated across the seas or into the forests of Siberia as settlers intending to build farm communities

Chapter Outline

• • •

and to reshape land and society, to the extent they could, in the image of Europe. Indigenous peoples, who did not want their land and societies reshaped, naturally opposed these colonizing projects, though to no avail in the long run. By 1750, European settler colonies were well established in North America, Siberia, and South Africa.

Because western Europe began in the sixteenth century to play a new role as a hub of global maritime activity, new information about the world and its peoples poured in. This knowledge circulated widely among literate Europeans just at the time when the Renaissance study of human nature and behavior was reaching into every part of the subcontinent and when various Christian sects and denominations were proclaiming different, often conflicting versions of divine truth. In the final part of the chapter, we look at how these strands of thought converged in an intellectual movement that challenged the ancient wisdom handed down from Greek philosophers and church fathers and that presented radical new ways of describing reality. Yet even as European intellectuals questioned traditional certainties such as divine revelation and God's intervention in human affairs, the world's major belief systems continued to thrive and grow, notably Christianity and Islam.

A Panoramic View

MAP 19.1 Major states and colonial territories, 1700.

By 1700 five European powers had established significant overseas empires. How did these compare in territorial size to the large land empires in Afroeurasia?

Legend:
- England and territories
- France and territories
- United Netherlands and territories
- Portugal and territories
- Spain and territories

Empires and Big States

FOCUS In what ways may the aims and successes of Chinese, Russian, and Spanish land-based empire building in the seventeenth and eighteenth centuries be compared?

The period of world history from 1500 to 1650 saw the growth of two types of states (see Map 19.1). One type comprised the territorial monarchies that marshaled armies of both gun-carrying soldiers and tax-gathering bureaucrats to expand royal power (see Chapter 17). Several of these states, notably Ming China, Mughal India, Safavid Persia, the Ottoman Turkish sultanate, and the Habsburgs of central Europe, may be classed as empires because they incorporated extensive territories and culturally diverse populations. The other type included the European countries that acquired overseas territories in addition to building stronger central governments. Portugal and Spain did this first; Netherlands, England, and France then followed suit (see Chapter 18).

In the century after 1650, important shifts occurred in state power. Both China under the Qing dynasty (1644–1911) and Russia under the Romanov tsars (1613–1917) dispatched armies to conquer immense new areas of Inner Eurasia to exploit its resources and to tax its populations of farmers, herders, and hunters. Spain also emerged in that period as a super-sized imperial power as its soldiers, missionaries, and merchants intruded into new regions of both North and South America. The Ottoman, Habsburg, and French monarchies had all aspired in the sixteenth century to large-scale conquests within Europe. Amid the brutality and confusion of religious wars between Catholics and Protestants, however, none of these states achieved their ambitions. Rather, Europe remained divided among numerous states large and small, simultaneously trading, sharing ideas, making treaties, and fighting one another.

Chinese Prosperity and Imperialism

As we saw in Chapter 18, states in several parts of Afroeurasia experienced economic and political instability in the mid-seventeenth century. China was one of them. The Ming dynasty (1368–1644) became progressively destabilized after 1600. Courtiers, Confucian officials, and relatives of the emperor feuded continually for imperial favor and public influence. The court eunuchs, whose original job had been to guard the emperor, seized direct control of many government functions. Climatic conditions associated with the continuing Little Ice Age worsened across northern China in the 1620s, producing famines. Persistent decline in the price of silver reduced the value of tax receipts, and a sudden stoppage of silver imports in 1639–1640 precipitated an economic crisis. In those tumultuous conditions, peasant uprisings swept the northern and western provinces.

At the same time, the Manchus (also known as Jurchens), a people of the forests, mountains, and plains of Manchuria,

or Northeast China, pressed against the Ming imperial borders. Hung Taiji, the Manchu ruler in the mid-seventeenth century, created a strong central government modeled on the Chinese system. He named his dynasty the Qing, meaning "pure," and he pushed out the frontiers of his state to incorporate Mongols and Koreans. Ming frontier forces faced Manchu raids while simultaneously battling rural insurgents within China. In 1644 Chinese rebels captured Beijing, the imperial capital, and then Manchu cavalry seized the city from them. Manchu leaders claimed the Mandate of Heaven, or divine authority, to rule in the name of the five-year-old son of the deceased Hung Taiji. This boy reigned under the guidance of a **regent.** Meanwhile, the last Ming emperor committed suicide.

> **regent** An individual who administers the affairs of a state when the ruler is absent, disabled, or has not reached adulthood.

The Qing in power. Though Ming resistance held out in some regions for several years, the new regime made a fairly rapid transition from violent conquest to consolidation of power in both city and countryside. As foreign conquerors, the Qing endeavored to preserve their Manchu ethnic identity separate from the majority Han, or Chinese-speaking population they ruled. The Qing elite prohibited Manchu women from marrying Chinese men, though Manchu men could choose Chinese women as second wives or concubines. A system of parallel ranks characterized the high levels of Qing bureaucracy. That is, a Manchu and a Han Chinese official shared the same position. Each reported to the emperor, who encouraged them to spy on one another to ensure their loyalty to him alone.

Many Manchu-speaking officials learned to communicate in Mandarin Chinese, and government documents were issued in both languages. The Manchus adopted Confucian doctrines of good government, a strategy that achieved important political goals. The Qing emperor represented himself as the symbolic patriarch of a family constituted of all his subjects, and he proclaimed Confucian ideals of fair and just administration. The Ming imperial examination system, designed to train literate, competent, and dedicated public officials, was also retained. Confucianism provided a unifying framework for society but made room for religious toleration. In this respect the Qing carried on the Ming tradition of permitting Buddhists, Daoists, Muslims, and Christians to build places of worship and observe their rituals as long as they did not interfere in state business. The third Manchu emperor explained Qing ideas of religious diversity: "We Manchus have our own particular rites for honoring heaven; the Mongols, Chinese, Russians, and Europeans also have their own particular rites for honoring Heaven. . . . Everyone has his way of doing it."[3]

Qing expansion. Within a few decades of the Manchu victory, China's population and economy resumed the upward trend they had enjoyed in the sixteenth century. The

A display of imperial power. Qianlong, the sixth Qing emperor, used the Grand Canal to tour China's southern provinces in 1751. Such tours were a longstanding practice of Chinese rulers. This painting on silk by an imperial court artist is titled *The Qianlong Emperor's Southern Inspection Tour, Scroll Six: Entering Suzhou and the Grand Canal* (1770). What elements in this image suggest that the emperor's visit was an important event in Suzhou?

ruler named the Kangxi (kang-shee) emperor spent most of his sixty-one-year reign (1661–1722) enlarging the frontiers of China north, west, and east. To the north the Qing intended early on to bring the Amur River valley, a region of fertile land, timber, and fur-bearing animals, into the Chinese political orbit. Shortly before the Manchu victory, however, the Amur region began attracting some of the Russian trappers, traders, and army contingents that spearheaded imperial Russia's eastward advance into Siberia. Inevitably, Russian and Chinese troops came to blows. Fortunately, the two governments decided shortly that the valley might better serve as a middle ground for commerce rather than as a terrain of mutually debilitating war. In 1689 they agreed to the Treaty of Nerchinsk (a town near the Amur). By its terms, Russia relinquished claims to the valley, and the two powers marked out a border. They even erected markers written in Chinese, Russian, Manchu, Mongol, and Latin.

Settling this conflict with Russia freed Qing forces to move westward to deal with Zunghar, a Mongol state in the Inner Eurasian steppe that menaced China's western borders. A Qing army with gunpowder artillery defeated the Buddhist ruler Galdan Khan in 1696, and sixty-four years later Chinese forces fully annexed Zunghar territory. This

victory signaled that China no longer needed to make deals with Mongols or other steppe cavalry armies to secure the empire's western frontiers. Qing troops continued pushing west, subduing other Mongol and Turkic peoples, occupying oasis towns, bringing in Han Chinese immigrant settlers, and absorbing the huge region that is modern China's Xinjiang province. In 1720 a Qing army captured Lhasa, the principal city of Tibet and seat of the Buddhist Dalai Lama. Thereafter, Tibet became a Chinese dependency. These western conquests made the empire much more linguistically and culturally diverse, including absorption of millions more Muslims. In long-term perspective, the Qing and Russian advances together terminated a nearly four-thousand-year history of pastoral nomads forming powerful states in Inner Eurasia.

To the east, Qing seaborne forces captured the island of Taiwan from a Chinese merchant prince whose family ruled there after evicting the Dutch East India Company thirty-eight years earlier. After that victory in 1683, China adopted an "open seas" policy, encouraging active collaboration between government officials and Pacific merchants and opening six seaports in the south to shipping. Foreign commercial vessels were permitted to enter the port of

The Kangxi emperor in court dress. This silk scroll by an anonymous court painter depicts Kangxi, the longest-reigning Qing ruler. He was in power for sixty-one years.

Guangzhou. Qing officials enforced collection of port duties from visiting British, French, Danish, and (after 1789) American merchants. But when British traders asked to build a permanent station, the Qianlong emperor refused. As he wrote to Britain's King George III,

> "Your request for a small island near Chusan [Zhoushan], where your merchants may reside and goods be warehoused, arises from your desire to develop trade.... Consider, moreover, that England is not the only barbarian land which wishes to establish relations with our civilization and trade with our Empire: supposing that other nations were all to imitate your evil example and beseech me to present them each and all with a site for trading purposes, how could I possibly comply? This also is a flagrant infringement of the usage of my empire and cannot possibly be entertained."[4]

The ruler was not averse to commerce but insisted on the strict subordination of foreign visitors to imperial authority.

Russia from the Pacific to Poland

The reorganized and centralized Russian state that emerged in the fifteenth century suffered both fierce internal struggles and border invasions from Poland and Sweden in the early seventeenth century (see Chapter 17). After claiming the Russian throne, the teenaged tsar Mikhail Romanov (r. 1613–1645) managed to solidify his authority to the advantage of his successors. The early Romanov tsars made land grants to *boyars,* or members of the titled aristocracy, who supported the dynasty. Laws imposed in 1649 reduced free peasants to the status of serfs obligated to work on large estates, making these grants even more valuable. Political stability at the top also permitted Russian rulers to increase spending on territorial expansion, which brought the state more tax wealth, natural resources, and trade.

The ambitions of Peter the Great. Nearly paralleling the reign of the Kangxi emperor in Qing China, Peter I, known as Peter the Great (r. 1682–1725), transformed Russia, first into a regional power, then into both a trans-hemispheric empire and an important member of the European state system. Peter insisted on unlimited authority, an ideal of **absolutism** that Ottoman, Persian, and Mughal monarchs had refined in the previous century and

> **absolutism** A political doctrine asserting that in a monarchy the ruler holds sole and unquestionable power by divine authority.

that several European rulers also adopted. Like them, Peter claimed that God granted the monarch a "divine right" to govern and that opposition to the monarch constituted opposition to God. All subjects from noble lords on down therefore owed allegiance to the monarch above all other loyalties. For several millennia kings and queens around the world had associated themselves with godly power. But European rulers, including Peter, tried more forcefully than in the past to nullify the independent authority of aristocratic assemblies, town councils, religious authorities, and other groups that had traditionally claimed social or political privileges and responsibilities. Royal claims of absolutism implied that monarchs had the exclusive right to make decisions for the well-being of their subjects and to impose on them whatever religious practice they thought best.

Peter much admired the technology and administrative techniques that enabled western European states to amass power and establish overseas empires. In 1697–1698, he and an entourage made two trips west to study shipbuilding, sailing, military strategy, administration, and scientific ideas. He consulted with master naval architects in Dutch shipyards, even dressing himself in workers' clothes to labor alongside shipbuilders. He visited textile workshops and museums, conversed with Dutch and English scholars, and corresponded with French intellectuals.

Returning to Moscow, Peter introduced numerous changes, including a stronger central bureaucracy accountable to him and up-to-date armaments to strengthen the army, which by 1715 numbered about 215,000 conscripted soldiers. He further reduced the local power of the land-owning *boyars* by creating the Table of Ranks, which gave nobles precedence at court based on their meritorious service to the state rather than on their aristocratic family tree. He bolstered royal control of the Russian Orthodox Church, even replacing its patriarch with a council of priests that operated according to the tsar's rules. He initiated westward-looking cultural and education reforms, including a decree that all children of nobles and officials must learn mathematics. He founded a medical school, supported Russia's first newspaper, and set up a scientific academy. To make visible the drastic cultural reorientation he desired, he ordered men to cut off their traditional beards and forced his courtiers to wear western European–style hats, coats, and underwear. To the horror of Orthodox churchmen, he held salons in which men and women socialized together in one room. Not surprisingly, Peter's reforms encountered resistance from conservative leaders, but under his relentless pressure, coupled with Russian military successes, they gained elite support.

Tsar Peter I, imperial modernizer. Peter the Great stands in front of newly constructed St. Petersburg. What symbols of imperial power and of Peter's modernization efforts did artist Grigory Semyonovich Musikiysky incorporate into this miniature enamel portrait?

Empire building west, south, and east. Peter and his successors, especially the empress Catherine II (Catherine the Great, r. 1762–1796), pursued campaigns of overland expansion that tsars had initiated in the fifteenth century. The pace and scope of this expansion was staggering. Imperial territory tripled in the 1700s. Similarly to China in the same period, conquests transformed Russia into a complex multicultural state. The tsars generally tolerated ethnic and religious diversity but insisted on the primacy of Russian cultural and political leadership. They strengthened their historic alliance with the Cossacks, a polyglot collection of mounted fighters and merchants that originated mainly in the Ukraine. Armed Cossack bands, which included both Christians and Muslims and speakers of several different languages, spearheaded many of the emperor's expansionary campaigns.

Looking west, the tsars had long coveted warm water ports on the Baltic Sea, the passage to the wider maritime world. Peter realized this goal after defeating Sweden in the Great Northern War, a struggle that endured from 1700 to 1721. Deploying his newly modernized forces, he obliterated the Swedish army, effectively ending that country's role as a Baltic power and obliging all the major European states to recognize that Russia was going to join their club. In 1703 he set thousands of engineers, artisans, and peasants to work building St. Petersburg, an entirely new city

and imperial capital on marshland where the Neva River empties into the Baltic.

To the south and southeast, Peter's forces seized territory in the Ukraine from the kingdom of Poland-Lithuania, and they continued to fight Ottoman Turkish forces for access to the Black Sea. Catherine the Great made huge gains in those directions late in the century. She seized the eastern third of Poland in a coldblooded deal with the Austrian and Prussian monarchies to divide up and eradicate that country as a sovereign state. The army also expelled the Ottomans from the Black Sea's northern shores. To the east, Peter intensified Russian military advances into Siberia, seeking new agricultural lands and commerce. Cossacks subjugated local peoples in the name of the tsar and traded for furs and other forest products. By 1639 Russians reached the Pacific Ocean, then penetrated the Amur River valley. As we have seen, these forays led to the Treaty of Nerchinsk (1689), which calmed border conflict between Russia and China.

After Vitus Bering explored the sea passage between Siberia and North America, Russian trappers and traders began inching their way through the Aleutian Islands and along the Alaskan coast. In 1804 the Russian American Company occupied the little port of Sitka in southern Alaska. Eight years later, the company set up a trading and farming station at Fort Ross in northern California, building a stockade and an Orthodox chapel and making occasional contact with Spanish and later Mexican officers and missionaries advancing from the south. The company occupied this distant post until 1841. Russians interacted with native Siberians and Alaskans in a variety of ways. The newcomers, almost all of them males, frequently married or cohabited with local women, producing children that adapted themselves to two different cultural worlds. Russian merchants and trappers sought mutually beneficial trade with Siberians, offering rewards for collecting furs. But Russians also intimidated and attacked native communities that put up resistance, a portent of the "Russianizing" of Siberia that was to come.

The Spanish Empire in America

As of 1650, Spain and its colonial possessions constituted an empire second only to Russia in territorial extent. The Spanish monarchy's American lands far exceeded the size of Spain itself. In the mid-seventeenth century, the American empire already had several large Spanish-governed cities, busy trade networks, and control over extensive rural areas, all held together by shared laws, an evolving central governing structure, and the Roman Catholic Church.

Governing Spanish America. Despite persistent Native American resistance in remote areas and wars with rival European states for trade and land, the empire continued to grow as imperial forces conquered deep interior lands. At its territorial peak in the early 1800s, it stretched from northern California to the tip of South America, including several Caribbean islands. This realm was initially divided into two huge viceroyalties governed by appointees of the Spanish crown. Mexico City became the capital of New Spain, Lima the center of the Viceroyalty of Peru.

In contrast to Beijing and Moscow, Madrid, the imperial capital, was separated from its giant land empire by an ocean. Consequently, viceroys and other colonial officials tended to exercise more autonomous power than the crown would have preferred. The viceroys sometimes disagreed with royal proclamations and dragged their feet in implementing them. Since it could take up to two years to send a message to Spain and receive a reply, officials had plenty of time to do things their own way. The relationship between the crown and colonial elites evolved into a system in which Madrid secured the loyalty of colonial officials, landlords, and mine owners—a tiny percentage of the American population—by allowing them to buy and sell lucrative administrative offices, appropriate Indian land, and evade numerous laws intended to protect ordinary people from labor or tax abuse.

The daily lives of all Spanish American subjects centered on the pueblos (towns), haciendas (large landed estates), Catholic missions, and presidios (garrisons). Provincial governors and judges had legal oversight of Spanish town councils made up entirely of local white men of wealth. In towns distant from the viceroyal capitals, these councils usually had a good deal of freedom to make policies that served their interests. In the countryside, individual estate owners had wide latitude to discipline their families, black slaves, and Indian laborers as they saw fit, echoing the power of feudal lords in medieval Spain. In the huge rural expanses of both Mesoamerica and Peru, the Spanish authorities could only keep order, collect taxes, and recruit workers with the collaboration of local indigenous nobles and chiefs. These heads of villages and kinship groups walked a fine line between Spanish demands for revenue and labor and the pleas of commoners for protection against imperial exactions. As Spanish government and law became entrenched, however, many local leaders transformed themselves into oppressive and wealth-seeking agents of the colonial regime.

Paralleling the viceroy's bureaucracy, imperial judicial courts called *audiencias* judged civil and criminal cases. These tribunals were obligated to recognize the legal standing of people of all social statuses and ethnic backgrounds. The courts typically favored the interests of Europeans, though commoners occasionally won disputes over property ownership or labor abuse. Both the *audiencias* and the viceroys ideally took direction from the Council of the Indies, a body of nobles and court favorites that met in Madrid to advise the king on imperial policies.

The Spanish monarch had the authority to nominate all of the empire's church officials, collect tithes, and found new churches, missions, and monasteries. This tight meshing of church and state meant that Catholic institutions played a particularly prominent role in the Spanish colonies. Several religious orders, including Dominicans, Franciscans, and Jesuits, founded both urban churches, which people of European descent attended, and missions, which primarily served Indians. Missionaries converted Indians, ideally attended to their moral and material needs, and encouraged them to become "civilized" by learning Spanish and adopting European dress and diet. Mission friars also typically made heavy demands on Indians to grow food and pay a variety of fees.

The empire's social profile. Many Spaniards and other Europeans traveled to the American empire to serve as soldiers, missionaries, or government officials, but others migrated in search of trade, urban business, or plantation ownership. In 1650 the European population living in Spanish America numbered about 600,000, rising to 3.8 million by 1825. This group consisted of both *peninsulares* (pehn-INH-soo-LAH-rayz), the elite class of men and women born

Hacienda Xcanchakan. Many of the haciendas that colonists established in the seventeenth century gave their owners great wealth and endured as large agricultural enterprises for two centuries or more. This estate on Mexico's Yucatan Peninsula caught the eye of the nineteenth-century English artist Frederick Catherwood. How did a small Mexican elite succeed in controlling huge tracts of land and the large Indian and *mestizo* labor forces needed to make estates productive for so long?

creole A person of African or European descent born in the Americas.

in Europe, and **creoles,** that is, people of European descent born in America. Before the nineteenth century, these groups together remained a small minority of the total population. Despite the sixteenth century's catastrophic mortality, Indians continued to far outnumber Europeans throughout most of South America and Mesoamerica. After about 1620, the Indian population began gradually to recover. In some lowland regions and on Caribbean islands, African slaves outnumbered both European and Indian inhabitants. As in Russian Siberia, though with a much larger base population, unions between men and women of different ethnoracial identities became common throughout the Spanish empire. Some of these unions were formalized in marriage; often they were not. Either way, they produced children of mixed ancestry. Social conventions emerged to categorize these *castas,* or mixed "races," according to their various permutations: Spanish father–Indian mother, Spanish mother–African father, Indian father–African mother, and so on. Generally, people of mixed race occupied higher steps in the empire's rigid social hierarchy than Indians or African slaves. In Mexico the *mestizo* population, the group descended predominantly from unions between Indians and Europeans, came to constitute nearly 25 percent of the population by 1650 and about 40 percent by 1810.[5]

Imperial reforms. Changes in the Spanish monarchy had direct consequences for the American empire. Because of special dynastic circumstances, Philip V, a grandson of the French Bourbon ruler Louis (LOO-ee) XIV, mounted the Spanish throne. Philip and his two Bourbon successors implemented a series of reforms both at home and in the colonies to centralize and modernize economic and political structures. In Spain the king had limited success challenging the long-held power of nobles, town elites, and high church clergy. But across the Atlantic, political reforms to improve government efficiency met with less resistance. To strengthen regional administration, the crown created two new viceroyalties: New Granada (1739), with its capital at Bogotá in modern Colombia; and Rio de la Plata (1776), centered on Buenos Aires in the far south. The reforms also aimed to check the growing power of affluent creoles, who dominated the colonial economy. The crown tended to distrust American-born elites and moved to bar them from high-ranking offices. The main effect, however, was to alienate this economically vital class from the imperial government.

As demand in Europe for sugar, tobacco, hides, and other products continued to climb, the Bourbon government initiated other reforms to increase customs revenues on American exports. After 1770, coffee and cacao joined sugar on the roster of crops exported from the Spanish Caribbean colonies. Cattle ranching in the Rio de la Plata region and a revival of silver mining in Mexico and Peru also signaled higher economic growth. All of these operations depended on intensive use of low-paid manual labor. Even small colonial manufacturing relied on coercion. A German visitor to a Mexican textile factory in 1803 noted troubling conditions "not only with the great imperfection of the technical process . . . but . . . also with the unhealthiness of the situation, and the bad treatment to which the workers are exposed. Free men, Indians, and people of color are confounded with the criminals distributed . . . among the manufactories, in order to be compelled to work. All appear half naked, covered with rags, meager, and deformed."[6] Owing to conditions like these, miners and others who worked for low wages increasingly expressed their grievances in strikes and spontaneous uprisings.

Europe: Successes and Failures of Absolutism

In the first half of the sixteenth century, the Habsburg emperor Charles V imagined himself transforming Europe into a unitary empire under the moral leadership of the Roman Catholic Church. France, the Ottoman empire, and German princes who had converted to Protestantism—all Habsburg enemies—sabotaged this dream, and Europe remained a collection of diverse and competing states (see Map 19.2).

Colonial family life, ca. 1715. This representation of a mixed-race family is typical of a genre known as casta paintings. These works aimed to specify racial identities and depict social hierarchies based on birth, skin color, ethnicity, and place of origin. The painter, Juan Rodriguez Juarez, was a Spaniard who lived and worked in New Spain. What attitude toward interracial families does the painting seem to communicate?

MAP 19.2 European states in 1750.
Many competing states shared the European landscape. What geographical and political challenges were European rulers who sought to expand their territories in this period likely to face?

The religious passions that the Protestant Reformation triggered eventually played themselves out, and by the complex terms of the Peace of Westphalia of 1648, Europe's monarchs and princes resolved a number of troublesome territorial issues and stabilized religious divisions in central Europe between Catholic and Protestant areas. Subsequently, rulers generally resigned themselves, at least for the time being, to a politically segmented Europe, even though they continued as before to try to seize one another's territories and resources. In the century after 1648, wars continued in one part or another of Europe almost without interruption. Generally though, limited strategic objectives rather than religious hatred motivated fighting. European states also fielded more rigorously disciplined armies—professional forces that fought set battles, rather than running riot in the countryside or murdering large numbers of civilians.

In a sense, Europe's monarchs returned after 1648 to the business of strengthening and consolidating state power, a trend that had started back in the fifteenth century before religious and civil strife interrupted it. Not only in Europe but across Afroeurasia, states had undertaken centralizing projects using firearms technology and new approaches to top-down bureaucratic government to expand their borders and to rule their own populations more efficiently. These projects continued in the seventeenth and eighteenth centuries, in some places successfully, as in Qing China and Romanov Russia, and in other places unsuccessfully, as in South Asia, where the Mughal empire began to fragment not long after 1700.

Most Europeans no doubt yearned for social order after decades of violent religious discord and an economic depression in the mid-seventeenth century. Responding to this mood, rulers of several states reactivated projects to reduce the independent power of aristocratic landlords and strengthen the authority of royal officials. Like Peter and Catherine in Russia, western European rulers claimed absolute authority. Jean Domat (1625–1696), a French legal expert and eloquent proponent of absolutism, wrote: "Since government is necessary for the public good, and God Himself has established it, it is consequently also necessary for

Political resolution. As part of the general Peace of Westphalia in 1648, Dutch and Spanish officials concluded the Treaty of Münster, ending the long war between them and granting independence to the Dutch Republic. Gerard Ter Borch, a noted Dutch portrait painter, rendered both Dutch and Spanish delegates in detail in this work titled *The Swearing of the Oath of Ratification of the Treaty of Münster* (1648). Do you think a Spanish painter might have represented this event differently? Why or why not?

those who are subject to government, to be submissive and obedient. For otherwise they would resist God Himself."[7] Subjects must obey those who head the state, but rulers also have a duty to govern justly, in accordance with God's will. This doctrine contradicted the earlier European tradition of shared governance between the monarch and other influential groups within society. Nevertheless, if rulers improved law, order, and the economy, while winning battles abroad, their subjects tended to go along with absolutist pretensions.

Even the most successful divine right monarchs ruled less absolutely than they might have liked. Communication and transport remained dependent on animal muscle, sail, or oar, and it took about as much time to send troops or government instructions from one province to another in 1750 as it had three hundred years earlier. This meant that village peasants, town elders, and local nobles could often ignore, delay, or resist orders sent out from the capital. Furthermore, all absolutist rulers had greater success negotiating and

making deals with local power groups than in violently repressing them. Still, in every European country, provincial groups that did not want the central state nosing deeper into their lives periodically rioted, murdered state officials, or even tried to start civil wars.

French absolutism. Some European monarchs put absolutist ideals into practice more effectively than others. Reigning together for a total of 165 years (1610–1774), the French Bourbon monarchs Louis XIII, XIV, and XV had remarkable success shifting power from provincial aristocrats to themselves and their appointed ministers of state. Like sixteenth-century Russian tsars and Mughal emperors in South Asia, Louis XIII (r. 1610–1643) and his chief minister Cardinal Richelieu introduced a service nobility: an elite class of political administrators who owed their status and livelihoods entirely to the monarchy. These individuals, called "nobles of the robe," came largely from the rising urban bourgeois class of merchants and professionals.

Diplomatic splendor of Louis XIV's court. This painting, credited to the studio of the artist Antoine Coypel, depicts the French king receiving an ambassador from the Safavid empire of Persia. What symbolic role might art forms like this have played in legitimizing absolute monarchy?

Louis XIII also transferred provincial administration from local noble families to *intendants*. These were royal officers who held their positions temporarily and had no family or financial interests in the provinces where they served.

Louis XIV (r. 1643–1715) expended much creative energy transforming proud aristocrats into royal subordinates. He showered them with honors, gifts, and other symbols of status while simultaneously undermining their independent action. Jean Domat wrote that sovereigns should have the right "to make manifest the authority and dignity of such wide-ranging and lofty power." In line with that doctrine, Louis made himself an object of awe and reverence, building the extravagant palace of Versailles (vehr-SEYE) outside Paris, associating himself with the Greek sun god Apollo, and creating intricate court rituals to celebrate his grandeur. He enticed France's nobles to Versailles, offering them nonstop partying, sexual adventure, and chances to compete with one another, not for land and power, but for the king's personal notice. And he kept a close eye on them for any sign of defiance.

The Bourbon monarchs also wanted religious conformity. On one hand, they tolerated no interference from the pope in the administration of the French church; on the other hand, they had no interest in religious freedom. In 1598 King Henry IV (r. 1589–1610) had signed the Edict of Nantes, which award Huguenots, or French Protestants, limited rights to worship. Louis XIII, however, terminated Protestant control of certain towns. Louis XIV revoked the edict altogether in 1685, ordering churches to close and Huguenot clergy to leave the realm. Indeed, thousands of Protestants fled France, taking their literacy, skills, and successful businesses to places like the Netherlands, Germany, and England, where rulers welcomed them.

Absolutist monarchs across Afroeurasia discovered that political centralization, war making, and magnificent displays of power were hugely expensive; thus they were incessantly thinking up new ways to raise money. The French kings had rich resources to work with—a realm of twenty million people (twice the population of Russia), abundant and productive land, burgeoning commercial cities, and a growing overseas empire. They did not try to force the nobility and the clergy to pay direct taxes, but they chose competent financial advisers to help them impose levies on ordinary people more rationally and systematically. They also built canals and roads, subsidized textile and other industries, and promoted shipbuilding and overseas trade. Economic growth, they understood, generated imports, exports, and private money-making, all of which could be taxed.

Like so many other monarchies of the era, however, France continued to let spending far outrun revenue, especially outlays for wars in both Europe and abroad. Louis XIV, believing that absolutist success required military glory, attacked both the Dutch Republic and Habsburg territories and spent the last years of his reign fighting the debilitating War of the Spanish Succession (1701–1714). When he died, France was financially exhausted. Louis XV (r. 1715–1774) returned the country to relative peace, but only until 1740, when new fighting broke out among the European powers. This put even greater strains on the French economy and Bourbon absolutist hopes.

Prussian militarism. In the aftermath of the Thirty Years' War, Germany was divided into about three hundred princedoms, bishoprics, and free cities, most of which paid no more than ceremonial allegiance to the Habsburg emperor in Vienna. Nevertheless, in northern Germany a succession of three rulers of the Hohenzollern family built a formidable professional army and progressively gathered together several discontinuous territories that by the end of the eighteenth century emerged as an important European power. These territories included Brandenburg, location of the modest capital city of Berlin, and Prussia, which had earlier been a dependency of Poland. The Hohenzollern kings, whose state church was Lutheran, financed army and administration by collecting a variety of direct and indirect taxes, promoting industries, and squeezing revenue out of serfs who toiled on dynastic lands. Traditionally, diets, or assemblies of aristocrats and other notables, had local governing powers in Hohenzollern territories. But Frederick William, known as the Great Elector (r. 1640–1688), advanced an absolutist plan to centralize taxation, gutting the diets' taxing authority and making them irrelevant.

Frederick William I (r. 1713–1740), who made clear he answered only to God, organized the state mainly around the needs of the army, increasing its personnel to eighty thousand, including large numbers of draftees. Like the French, he moved to drain the noble class (*junkers*) of local autonomy. But instead of drawing them to a pleasure palace like Versailles, he assimilated them into the army officer corps, where the emphasis was on duty, honor, and loyalty to the crown. He also made the nobility pay direct taxes, which the Bourbons had not dared to do, and he replaced elected city councils with his own officials. Frederick II (Frederick the Great, r. 1740–1786) continued the absolutist policies of his predecessor but also deployed the army more aggressively, seizing important territories from both Austria and Poland. This enlarged state became the core of modern Germany.

Austrian multiculturalism. Although the rise of Prussia much weakened the Austrian Habsburg's already-

Frederick the Great inspects his troops. All of Europe's absolutist monarchs fielded strong armies. This painting portrays Frederick reviewing a regiment from Hesse, one of the component states in the centralized Prussian kingdom. Why did artists frequently depict Frederick as a military commander?

declining authority in Germany, the empire under Leopold I (r. 1657–1705) made dramatic territorial gains to the east. In 1683 Ottoman Turkish forces assaulted the walls of Vienna, the Habsburg capital, as they had done in 1529. The offensive fell short, however, and Austria counterattacked in the 1690s, driving the Ottoman government out of Hungary. This victory transformed the Habsburg state into a more culturally diverse collection of ethnic and religious groups than it had ever been. Leopold claimed absolute authority, but he did not succeed in imposing full centralization and certainly not cultural uniformity. German and Hungarian land magnates retained substantial power. Moreover, German, Hungarian, Serb, Romanian, and several other ethnolinguistic communities held more closely to their separate regional cultural identities than to any concept of a unitary society under the Habsburg crown.

British power sharing. In the Netherlands, Poland for a time, and Britain, political assemblies representing the elite classes of society successfully rejected divine-right absolutism and established governments of collective leadership. When Queen Elizabeth I died in 1603, England's Parliament had already firmly established its authority to debate and approve new taxes. James VI of Scotland, who succeeded Elizabeth as James I of England (r. 1603–1625), had eager hopes of absolutist rule and let his subjects know it: "It is atheism and blasphemy to dispute what God can do: . . . so it is presumptuous and high contempt in a subject to dispute what a king can do, or say that a king cannot do this or that."[8] James, who inaugurated the Stuart dynasty, thus put himself at loggerheads with Parliament as soon as he grasped the crown. His son and successor Charles I

King Charles I's last walk. This nineteenth-century painting by Ernest Crofts portrays Puritan soldiers marching Charles I, convicted of treason, to his beheading in January 1649. With this act, Parliament abolished the British monarchy, though its restoration came just eleven years later. Does the artist express sympathy for the king or for the soldiers, or neither?

(r. 1625–1649) took the same view of royal supremacy; consequently, a tug-of-war between king and Parliament continued for nearly four decades.

The Lords and the Commons constituted the two Houses of Parliament, and members of the Commons zealously guarded their right to approve taxes. The merchants, professionals, and members of the gentry (lower nobility) who dominated the Commons also turned England's wheels of industry and commerce. They wanted to expand their participation in government, especially to influence foreign policy. Parliament won some concessions from James because he needed money. The religious strife that engulfed the European continent in the early 1600s also roiled England. The Church of England, or Anglican church, had severed ties with Rome in the previous century. Nevertheless, strict Protestants in the tradition of the Reformation leader John Calvin believed the Anglican faith should replace excessive ceremony and the hierarchy of bishops with simple services, more preaching, lay (nonclerical) church governance, and stern policing of the public's moral behavior. Some of the righteous Puritans who wished to cleanse Christian practice of any vestiges of Catholicism went off to America to found the Massachusetts Bay Colony. Others, however, broadcast their grievances through Parliament.

Charles I tried for a decade to govern without convening Parliament and to force religious uniformity on both English and Scottish Christians. But facing both rebellion in Ireland (whose common people remained Catholic) and an invasion from Scotland, he was obliged to call Parliament into session in 1640 to raise money to deal with these crises. Consequently, the Commons acquired new leverage to make more demands. Charles responded by forming his own army without Parliament's funding. Members of the Commons did the same, and the country descended into civil war. Most European countries faced aristocratic or peasant uprisings in this period, but England had a revolution on its hands.

The British Isles experienced a whirlwind of changes between 1642, when the civil conflict started, and 1660, when Charles II took the throne. In 1645 the Puritan commander Oliver Cromwell assumed charge of the parliamentary army and within four years captured and executed Charles I, an event that stunned the crowned heads of Europe. Parliament declared its supremacy, abolished the monarchy, and wrote a constitution. In effect England became a republic, called the Commonwealth. Cromwell led an army into Ireland and suppressed the rebellion there, killing tens of thousands of Irish Catholics and transferring much land to rich English families. Historians have made the point that English overseas empire building really began in Ireland. Cromwell's forces also invaded and secured Commonwealth rule over Scotland. Despite Parliament, he awarded himself dictatorial powers, ran the country as a military state, and enforced a Calvinist moral code that, among other things, forbade dancing and theaters. He did, however, allow limited freedom of worship.

Cromwell died in 1658 and, amid popular weariness over two decades of turmoil, Parliament moved in 1660 to invite Charles II, son of the executed king, to restore the monarchy. Even so, king and Parliament continued to jockey for political dominance for another three decades. During the Restoration, as the period became known, religious antagonisms also continued between Anglicans, who once again dominated Parliament, and Calvinists and other dissenters who demanded religious toleration for themselves. Both groups feared that Charles II had Catholic sympathies, and his brother James II, who took the throne in 1685, was indeed a Catholic. Both Anglicans and other Protestants turned against him. In 1688 Parliament invited William of Orange—the Protestant *stadholder,* or chief administrator, of the United Netherlands—to take the English throne as coruler with his wife Mary, James II's Protestant daughter.

This sudden change, called afterward the Glorious Revolution, saw Parliament enact a Bill of Rights that established its full lawmaking authority and the principle that legislature and monarch must share sovereignty. Kings and queens would no longer rule by divine or even hereditary right but on the foundation of an unwritten contract with their subjects. Religious toleration was also extended, though restrictions remained on non-Anglicans, especially Catholics. We should not conclude, however, that the Glorious Revolution put Britain on the road to popular democracy. Voting was sharply restricted to property-owning adult males, and for another two centuries the House of Commons remained under the domination of the land-owning gentry together with professionals and wealthy businesspeople whose families frequently intermarried. Nevertheless, the absolutism that continued to loom over the European continent was gone for good in Britain.

European Settlement and the Fate of Indigenous Peoples

FOCUS In what ways may the political, social, and cultural characteristics of early European settler colonies in North America, Siberia, and South Africa be compared, including relations between settlers and indigenous populations?

As political and religious troubles gripped England, men and women began migrating in modest numbers to North America. This small trans-Atlantic stream represented the start of a globe-encircling movement of Europeans to regions thousands of miles from their homelands. This movement continued throughout the eighteenth century and surged mightily in the nineteenth and early twentieth centuries. Europeans migrated as permanent settlers mainly to the world's temperate latitudes both north and south of the equator, where they aimed to create societies founded on the languages, institutions, and cultural practices that they brought with them. Their success at planting settlements resulted in formation of a particular type of society, one in which Europeans living far from Europe came in time to constitute the great majority of the population. Historians have named this type of society a **neo-Europe.** Before 1800, neo-European societies emerged principally in eastern North America,

neo-Europe A region outside of Europe, predominantly in temperate latitudes, where people of European descent came to make up a large majority of the population.

Siberia, and the Cape region of South Africa. (Later they would form in Australia and the southern third of South America.) In terms of both demography and culture, this type of society differed from others where Europeans *ruled* but nonetheless remained a small fraction of the population relative either to indigenous people, as in Mexico or Peru, or African slaves, as in the Caribbean and northeastern Brazil. In Mexico the population of exclusively European ancestry remained small. The *mestizo* population of mixed European and Indian descent evolved into a large minority by the early nineteenth century, but in the neo-Europes mixed populations remained small as percentages of the total—and they became smaller as European settlers continued to arrive.

Most Europeans left home as settlers because of land shortage, poverty, religious persecution, or trouble with the law. Most of these emigrants did not intend to serve an imperial government, convert souls, or make a quick fortune and depart. Free settlers, rather, hoped to work the land, take up craft and commerce, and raise families. Settlers were drawn mainly to temperate zones because those regions were climatically and ecologically similar to western Europe. These destinations promised somewhat healthier disease environments than tropical latitudes did. And newcomers could grow crops (wheat, barley) and herd domestic animals (cattle, sheep) that they already knew about (see Table 19.1).

European settlers also enjoyed an advantage they did not fully understand. In most temperate lands where immigrants appeared, indigenous populations were already seriously declining or soon would be. This happened primarily because infectious diseases of Afroeurasian origin devastated native societies before significant numbers of Europeans even arrived, or else settlers introduced unknown pathogens that set in motion terrible epidemics. New diseases killed millions in Mesoamerica and Andean South America, but the native agrarian populations in those places were so large and dense that they continued to constitute large majorities relative to Europeans. This was not the case in eastern North

TABLE 19.1 Types of Colonial Societies in the Seventeenth and Eighteenth Centuries

Type	Political Organization	Population Profile	Examples
Imperial society	A small minority population of European officials and soldiers administers the imperial territory and rules a large majority of indigenous people.	Over time, a population of mixed European and indigenous descent becomes a significant minority.	Spanish Viceroyalty of Peru British India Russia (excluding Siberia)
Settler society	European officials, soldiers, and settlers administer the colony.	European settlers, most of them farmers and artisans, rise in numbers to constitute a large majority population. The indigenous population declines to a small minority.	British North America St. Lawrence River valley (Canada) Cape of Good Hope (South Africa) Siberia
Plantation society	A small minority of European officials and soldiers rules a large majority population of slaves imported from Africa.	A population of mixed European and African descent rises in numbers to constitute a significant minority. The indigenous population declines to a small minority or disappears.	Northeastern Brazil Caribbean islands Mauritius (Indian Ocean)

America, Siberia, or the South African Cape. In those places, local populations were relatively smaller, and, despite their determination to resist, their numbers dwindled rapidly under the persistent assault of lethal maladies and European settlers with guns.

Early European Settlers in North America

North America's temperate latitudes began to attract European migrants early in the seventeenth century (see Map 19.3). The first settlements were founded in the St. Lawrence River valley and along the Atlantic seaboard, though they remained small and scattered for several decades. Many Europeans crossed the ocean as free settlers, though others left home as indentured servants contracted to work for a master for a specified number of years. Still others traveled as exiled criminals or rebels. Migrants also brought in African slaves, though in far smaller numbers than were transported to the plantations of the Caribbean or Brazil.

Europeans, Indians, and beaver pelts. Attracted by the beavers, black foxes, and other furry creatures whose pelts commanded a market among affluent Europeans, French traders sailed up the St. Lawrence River to found settlements at Quebec (1608) and Montreal (1611). Indians who spoke Algonquian languages bartered with those strangers, offering furs and hides for textiles, liquor, metal ware, and sometimes guns. As the fur trade grew, both Europeans and Indians became locked into the world economy. The merchants, few in number relative to Indian populations, had no choice except to ally with local leaders, accept their trade customs, and employ them as hunters and guides. Conversely, Native Americans warmed quickly to European manufactured goods. As a Montagnais Indian remarked, "The beaver does everything perfectly well, it makes kettles, hatchets, swords, knives, bread; in short, it makes everything."[9]

Native American societies of upper North America had long fought one another for resources, but those conflicts tended to be short. The fur trade changed that, especially when some warrior groups acquired firearms, using them to prey more violently on gunless neighbors to seize their hunting lands. Algonquian groups who allied with French traders also battled Iroquois peoples who lived in what later became New York State. Iroquoians made their own alliances with the Dutch, who built forts along the Hudson River, founding New Amsterdam on Manhattan Island in 1625. Meanwhile, Europeans penetrated Indian lands farther west. French explorers, fur traders, and Jesuit missionaries advanced into the Great Lakes region after 1635, and English sea merchants began building posts on Hudson's Bay in the 1670s.

France's royal government encouraged French peasants to emigrate to the St. Lawrence valley, called New France, to open farms and keep out potential English aggressors. These communities grew slowly. Most settlers had no agricultural knowledge, and the sex ratio remained heavily weighted toward young men. To adjust this imbalance, the crown enlisted Parisian orphan girls to go to the colony. These "daughters of the king" were expected to marry a settler. Nevertheless, New France had only about three thousand European residents in 1663, and immigration all but dried up a decade later. Even so, the few that did come reproduced at a remarkable rate in the long term. Numbers reached about fifteen thousand by 1700 and continued to rise thereafter. Simultaneously, the Indian population of New France, pushed off their lands and suffering from repeated barrages of smallpox and other infections, shrank steadily. Today the French-speaking population of Canada numbers nearly 7.5 million.

English settler colonies. English men and women migrated to North America in the later seventeenth century in much larger numbers than French people did. They landed mainly on the coastlands extending from Massachusetts to Chesapeake Bay. Settler families and indentured servants began to arrive in New England in 1620, hoping to make livings from the land. They left home amid chronic

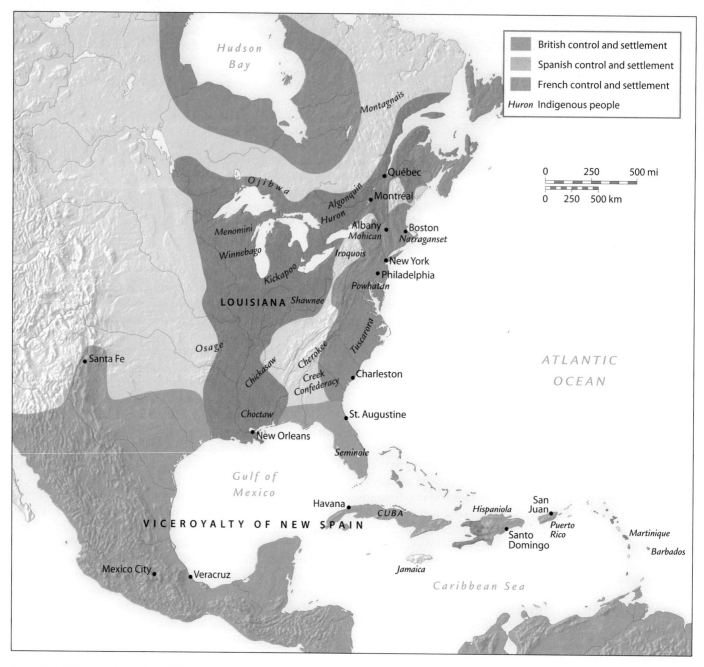

MAP 19.3 North America, 1750.

France claimed all the territory shaded in green. To what extent were its territorial claims supported by colonial occupation and settlement? How would you compare the extent of French and British claims with the reality of political occupation in each case?

political troubles, high population growth, and rising poverty. Large-scale commercial farming in England also pushed growing numbers of peasants off the land and into low-paying jobs or vagrancy. In those circumstances settlement in North America could look appealing.

A large portion of early migrants to New England and the mid-Atlantic region represented religious groups—Pilgrims, Puritans, Catholics—dissatisfied with prevailing trends at home. Puritans, who founded the Massachusetts Bay Colony,

intended to build a "New Jerusalem," a Christian utopia to serve as a beacon of Protestant virtue. Persecuted Catholics later settled in Maryland. Quakers, another dissenting Protestant group, founded Pennsylvania.

From an economic standpoint, Virginia was the most successful early English venture. The Virginia Company of London financed a settlement on the James River in 1607. After a rocky start, villages multiplied and population grew. Small land-owners produced food, while private entrepreneurs opened agricultural estates. Sugarcane did not grow well, but local tobacco did. In 1638, Virginia produced more than three million pounds of leaves. Before long, American tobacco became a popular European addiction.

Entrepreneurs also began to carve out tobacco, indigo, cotton, and rice plantations in the Carolinas and Georgia, at first employing indentured labor. By the late seventeenth century, however, planters realized what sugar growers in the Caribbean already understood. European immigrant labor was not going to meet the needs of expanding plantation economies. Consequently, land-owners adopted the Caribbean system of putting captured Africans to work in closely watched gangs. By 1750 African slaves accounted for about 40 percent of the population in Virginia and Maryland.

Native American resistance and retreat. Early cooperation and neighborly coexistence between Indians and Europeans gave way to increasing hostility. Small numbers of Indian converts to Protestantism learned to read and write. But prospects of social harmony based on shared education and religion faded quickly as Europeans pushed for more land and total social domination. In Massachusetts much of the Native American population had already succumbed to smallpox epidemics in 1617–1619 and 1633. Surviving Indian communities, colonial leaders argued, had no right to the land because they failed to cultivate it properly, or in any case they were guilty of "godless ignorance and blasphemous idolatry."[10] In 1675–1676, Wampanoag, Narragansett, and other New England Indians rose in rebellion against the spreading Massachusetts Bay Colony, briefly threatening its survival. The rising ultimately collapsed, however, and thereafter New England's Indian population steadily withered. In Virginia a violent three-way struggle broke out in 1675 between Powhatan Indians, rebellious land-hungry settlers, and the British governor. This disturbance cost many Powhatan lives. In the face of long-term settler plans "for extirpating all Indians without distinction of friends or enemies,"[11] Powhatan groups either retreated westward or resigned themselves to farming or servile jobs in the colonial economy.

In the eighteenth century the English colonies remained overwhelmingly rural. Nevertheless, the settler population swelled, rising between 1680 and 1750 from 150,000 to more than one million. Both agriculture and trade flourished. Boston, New York, Philadelphia, and Charleston grew into respectable cities. As this emerging neo-Europe became more important to the English economy, the imperial government sought to exercise more control. King James II (r. 1685–1688) tried to centralize royal authority in North America. But after the Glorious Revolution of 1688, all twelve of the colonies (Georgia, the thirteenth, was founded in 1732) reclaimed their separate political identities, including both royal governors and representative assemblies of land-owning European males.

Russian Settlement of Siberia

The Russians, Ukrainians, and other eastern Europeans who migrated to Siberia in the seventeenth and eighteenth centuries did not have to cross an ocean to begin building a neo-European society there. But similarly to French and English settlers in North America, they moved into temperate latitudes where wheat, cattle, and hogs could be raised. They had political and military support from the Russian state. They encountered relatively small populations of farmers, herders, and hunters. And they brought with them guns, plows, timber saws, and infectious diseases that would help clear these "small people," as Russians liked

Resistance to colonial settlement. Although Indians burned Brookfield, Massachusetts, and other villages during the 1675–1676 Narraganset War, they could not sustain their challenge to the expanding Massachusetts Bay Colony. How would you account for the deterioration of relations between Native Americans and settlers in New England?

to call them, out of the way. European settlement of Siberia, however, took a long time, and, like North America, the region did not achieve its full neo-European demographic character until well into the nineteenth century.

The territory that Russian settlers entered beginning in the seventeenth century had fundamental climatic and ecological similarities to northern Canada. In the far north, tundra supported low plant cover and reindeer herds. Farther south were boundless forests of fir, spruce, and pine. In both zones winter temperatures were extreme and rainfall unreliable. Consequently, the indigenous peoples who spoke Tangut, Samoyed, Yakut, and several other languages made their livings hunting, foraging, farming, fishing, and herding, depending generally on the ecological region they occupied. They lived in small, usually mobile groups, and coastal communities hunted seal, whale, and walrus.

Trade and tribute. The fur trade motivated early European colonization in Siberia as it did in upper North America. Russian trappers shipped sable, ermine, and sea otter pelts westward to be sold to affluent folk at huge price markups. As in North America, however, fur-bearing animals were a finite resource. Once traders depleted a region, they had to move on. The relentless search for fur brought Russians to the Pacific by the 1630s.

Encounters between Siberians and Russian settlers had mixed consequences. Compared to upper North American Indians, Siberians had modest defensive power and therefore less leverage to form trading partnerships with Europeans than Iroquois or Hurons did. Russian traders supplied Siberians with axes, cloth, tea, tobacco, and alcohol in return for pelts. But as representatives of the imperial state, Russians also demanded fur as formal tribute. Orders from Moscow declared: "The [Russian] serving and trading men should be ordered to bring under the sovereign's exalted hand the . . . diverse foreigners of various tongues who live . . . in new and hostile lands."[12] Though the government appealed for "kindness" in collecting tribute, officials and merchants often held women and children hostage until they received deliveries and conscripted local people to serve as porters, guides, interpreters, and laborers. Furthermore, Siberia was far enough away from the densely populated lands of Eurasia that infections like measles, smallpox, and various venereal diseases were unknown until Russians introduced them. The first smallpox epidemic raged through Siberian communities as early as 1630, and these scourges tended to recur every ten or twenty years.

Advancing farmers. Despite the harsh climate and vast distances, Russian and Ukrainian farmers followed the trappers and merchants into Siberia, especially to its southern, warmer zone. These migrants, who had started moving into western Siberia as early as the fifteenth century, included peasants looking for land, serfs escaping their lords, fugitive criminals, and religious dissenters. Indigenous people were

A sustained demand for furs. Siberian sable and other fur remained an important commodity in Russia's trade with western Europe for centuries after trappers first began to exploit this resource. The affluent woman in this late eighteenth-century drawing from a series on Paris fashions is bedecked in expensive fur. What other products illustrate connections between expanding empires and growing global commerce in the seventeenth and eighteenth centuries?

welcome to live in European settlements as long as they adopted Russian language and dress as well as Christianity.

Peter the Great regarded the "civilizing" of Siberians as an important modernizing project. Small cities like Irkutsk began to rise up. By 1760 Irkutsk was connected to Moscow by a muddy trail called the Siberian Road. New towns supported civic life, including local governing councils, churches, libraries, and theaters. Imperial officials, however, had a hard time persuading even the most adventurous Russians to migrate to Alaska or down the North American coast. Those "overseas" settlements depended for their survival mainly on residents of mixed European and Indian parentage.

Symbols of colonial power. This well-known painting, *The Landing of Jan van Riebeeck, 6 April 1652*, presents an idealized view of early contact between Dutch settlers and indigenous Khoisan peoples in South Africa. The artist, Charles Davidson Bell, was a British civil servant who worked in South Africa in the mid-nineteenth century. What features of clothing and posture did Bell choose to emphasize in portraying the two groups? How would you account for those choices?

Europeans and Khoisan in South Africa

In the temperate latitudes of the Southern Hemisphere, the first place where Europeans founded a society of farming settlers was in the Cape region at the southern tip of Africa. Like both upper North America and Siberia, this was a region of relatively small-scale human habitation, not dense, city-building populations. Local people spoke languages in the very ancient Khoisan (KOI-sahn) family. Twenty-nine of these languages, characterized by their distinctive clicking sounds, are spoken today, though by relatively few people. In the seventeenth century, Khoisan speakers lived in seasonally mobile foraging and hunting groups. Some Khoisan also herded cattle and sheep. These pastoralists placed great social value on their livestock. Large herds signaled both economic wealth and respectable community status.

The early Dutch outpost. In 1652 the directors of the Dutch East India Company (VOC) issued instructions to land a crew at the Cape of Good Hope to set up a refreshment station for ships making the arduous but profitable six-month passage between Amsterdam and Batavia (modern Jakarta), the principal Dutch enclave in Indonesia. The VOC planned to limit investment at the Cape to a small defensive fort, access to timber for ship repairs, and some farms to supply vessels with grain, vegetables, and meat. The little outpost succeeded, partly because the moderate climate supported food crops familiar to European farmers. VOC officials thought the Khoisan had plenty of surplus cattle to trade, but they did not understand the social significance of herd possession and got limited cooperation. Relations remained tense, and the two groups began rustling each other's cattle.

From outpost to colony. Within five years of its founding, the Cape settlement began to expand. Initially, a few soldiers received grants of land to raise crops and animals. The Dutch lacked sufficient military power to coerce local

The Journal of a Dutch Commander at the Cape of Good Hope

When Dutch East India Company (VOC) officials under Jan van Riebeeck decided to establish a refreshment station on the South African coast, they did not have to negotiate for space with well-armed kingdoms, as they did in Southeast Asia. But they did have to deal with multiple Khoisan groups that hunted, fished, and herded cattle. The early colonists gradually recognized the complexity of Khoisan alliances, animosities, and interests. They also realized that superior weapons did not translate smoothly into immediate political domination. A few Khoisan individuals worked with the colonists, though collaboration put them in the awkward position of not having the full trust of either Europeans or their own communities. After the company began importing slaves in 1658, relationships became even more complicated as runaway captives joined Khoisan groups, strengthening their ability to challenge VOC control.

Van Riebeeck brought his family from the Netherlands to the Cape, and Krotoa, the daughter of a Khoisan chief, joined the household as a servant. She learned Dutch, converted to Christianity, and served as a VOC interpreter. She eventually married a VOC official and had children. But when her husband died, both the Dutch and the Khoisan societies rejected her. She ended her life in prison, a pariah without social identity.

The following excerpts from the VOC journal reveal the company's attempts to understand and manage local conditions. Note the range of dates in these three entries.

February 25, 1652. Aboard the Diamant, *anchored in Table Bay.*

This evening we went ashore . . . to consider where the fort should be built. Also had 2 savages on board this evening, one of whom could speak a little English. We generously filled their bellies with food and drink. As far as we could gather cattle could not be obtained from them for—as they gave us to understand by means of broken English and signs—they were only fishermen and the cattle were always supplied by those from Saldania [farther up the coast].

April 10, 1652. At the site of the fort construction.

About noon a small band of 9 or 10 savages from Saldania arrived, against whom the [fishermen], who sit outside our tents with their wives and children every day, arranged themselves in battle order and advanced toward them with assegais [spears], bows and arrows with such courage and fury that we had sufficient to do to check them. . . . [We] succeeded in arranging a truce between them, so that for the rest of the day they remained at peace with one another in the vicinity of our tents. Those from Saldania, by means of signs and the use of broken English, as well as some Dutch words . . . gave us to understand that for copper and tobacco they would bring cattle and sheep within a few days. By good and liberal treatment we urged them to do so.

July 1, 1658. At the fort.

Today almost all the Hottentots . . . who had been searching for . . . fugitive slaves returned without any and reported that they could find none. Thereupon all the [Khoisan] prisoners and their wives [detained by the Company] began to weep and wail lustily, as they had been told that they would not be released until all the slaves had been brought back to us. They evidently saw little chance of that happening just yet. . . . The interpreter Doman maintains that they had never seen the fugitives, who had run away of their own accord. This we showed him that we did not believe. On the contrary, we feel that we are correct in presuming [the Khoisan are helping the fugitive slaves], for the Hottentot women were too familiar with the slaves in the beginning and gave them many things. The result is that they have to be satisfied to remain in captivity until we recover the slaves or know what has really become of them. This made the interpreter Doman hang his head and seem much depressed, as also Eva [as Krotoa was called by the Dutch], who said that the Hottentots would kill her if we did not release [high ranking Khoisan hostages]. She was told to keep within the fort, and that if anyone harmed her, the Commander would have him captured as well.

To set the minds of the hostages at rest, the Commander in person told them to have no fear for no harm would come to them, and said that everything was being done to recover the runaway slaves. They were given some tobacco, bread, and brandy, which seemed to cheer them up somewhat.

Source: Journal of Jan van Riebeeck, ed. H. B. Thom (Amsterdam and Cape Town: A. A. Balkema, 1952), 1:25, 30; 2:294–295.

Thinking Critically

What do you think may have constituted the colonists' hospitality, generosity, and "liberal treatment" of Khoisan in these passages? What evidence do you find of hostile attitudes? Why would the interpreters Doman and Krotoa feel threatened by the VOC's seizure of Khoisan hostages? What hints, if any, do you think this document offers regarding Khoisan attitudes toward the settlers?

Khoisan into servile labor, so they began bringing in slaves from the VOC's ports on the Indian Ocean. By 1658 the basic demographic profile of the colony was emerging. A minority of European settlers, overwhelmingly men, depended mainly on Asian slave labor to do farm work. In the following decades, the Dutch authorities issued land grants farther away from the Cape fort, and the population of both Europeans and Asians rose gradually, from about four hundred in 1662 to twenty thousand by 1780.[13]

The early Cape colony was culturally diverse. Sexual and marital unions crossed ethnic, linguistic, and religious lines. This happened chiefly because European men continued throughout the eighteenth century to outnumber settler women by three to two.[14] The top level of the VOC governing elite was Dutch and Calvinist Protestant. But new settlers came from across northwestern Europe, including Dutch, German, and Scandinavian farmers, as well as Huguenots escaping religious repression in France. The Afrikaans language, for example, is based on sixteenth-century spoken Dutch but also incorporates words and grammatical influences from French and Portuguese, as well as Southeast Asian languages introduced by slaves. The Cape diet was equally varied, combining European bread, meat, wine, and brandy with African game and Indian Ocean rice, coffee, tea and spices. By the end of the eighteenth century, the population also practiced Protestant Christianity in several forms.

The growth of the colony cost Khoisan hunters and herders dearly. Colonial records point to communities being pushed to the margins of their former hunting and grazing lands. And as Europeans and their slaves advanced along the coast and into the interior to plow land and graze their own herds, Khoisan men and women lost their options for independent life. Consequently, more of them resigned themselves to servile employment on settler farms. Like native Siberians, Cape Khoisan occupied a territorial extremity of Afroeurasia. They therefore lacked effective immunities to a number of infectious diseases. Smallpox, introduced at the Cape by either Europeans or Asians, took an appalling toll. An epidemic in 1713 hit Khoisan communities particularly hard, sparing scarcely one in ten individuals.

In the early eighteenth century, Khoisan society in the Cape region effectively collapsed. As this happened, the Southern Hemisphere's first Neo-Europe began to take shape. In contrast to Siberia, however, greater South Africa was not simply a land of mobile hunters and herders. Not far north and east of the Cape lived much larger, denser farming and cattle-keeping populations of Africans speaking Bantu languages, peoples more resistant to infectious Afroeurasian diseases than were the Khoisan. By the later eighteenth century, these populations met the moving frontier of European settlement with much stiffer economic competition and military resistance than the Khoisan had been able to mount. The South African neo-Europe remained territorially small and, in contrast to North America and Siberia, did not last long.

Alternative Visions of God, Nature, and the Universe

FOCUS How did the scientific revolution and the Enlightenment represent a new system of knowledge, and what factors help explain the continuing growth of Islam and Christianity in the seventeenth and eighteenth centuries?

In the hubs of European overseas empires, especially London, Amsterdam, and Paris, scientists, philosophers, and practical technicians sorted through cascades of new information from across the seas. Africans, Asians, and Native Americans offered much of this knowledge—from Iroquoian kinship relations to West African plant species to Confucian imperial court ceremonies—to European visitors, who returned home with it for study and interpretation. Moreover, the work of making sense of new knowledge took place in a post-Protestant Reformation religious environment in which novel ideas about the natural world no longer had to conform exclusively to the doctrines of the Catholic Church. Growing numbers of intellectuals felt free to challenge truths received from the Bible, the ancient Greeks, and church theologians. An intensive project to reexamine long-accepted explanations of the workings of nature, the cosmos, and human society, an endeavor whose two fundamental elements were the scientific revolution and the Enlightenment, got under way. Also, because peoples around the world participated in interpreting and transmitting this knowledge and because it circulated continuously from one region of the world to another, the project was a global one from the start.

As this rethinking of the nature of things proceeded, people in both Europe and other societies continued their religious quests to understand the operation of the divine in human affairs and come to grips with moral questions, the prospects of salvation, and responsibilities to family and community in a rapidly changing world The world's major religions of salvation and missionary outreach—Islam, Christianity, and Buddhism—all continued to grow, a phenomenon aided greatly by the new world-girdling routes of transport and travel.

The Scientific Revolution

Since the emergence of *Homo sapiens* more than 200,000 years ago, bright flashes of scientific and technical innovation have occurred periodically in one society or another. One of those moments of illumination took place in the seventeenth and eighteenth centuries, and it was centered in western Europe. This burst of scientific inquiry and invention was not inevitable. Rather, political, economic, and cultural circumstances of the time came together to set it in motion.

After the opening of the oceanic passages in the fifteenth and sixteenth centuries, Europeans had continuous and startling encounters with peoples, plants, animals, landscapes, and climates that they previously knew little or nothing about. This roused great curiosity and a yearning for fresh explanations of natural phenomena and of how the world got to be the way it is. As thinkers sought to make sense of the flood of new knowledge, they brought together three existing intellectual strands: ancient Greek philosophy, especially logic; the medieval European synthesis of this thought; and scientific and mathematical writings of South Asian, Greek, and Muslim thinkers. They also began to work out new methods to verify information to ensure that what people thought they knew about the world was true.

"Scientific revolution" may be too strong a term to describe these first steps toward a systematic rethinking of what philosophers then called the "laws of nature." But over the course of two centuries, this work produced a dramatic shift toward explanations of the world founded on empirical observation, controlled experimentation, careful recording, analytical reasoning, and sharing of knowledge among scholarly communities. By the 1700s European governments and church authorities, whether Catholic or Protestant, interfered less in the publication and circulation of new ideas than they had just a century earlier. New technical instruments such as telescopes and microscopes greatly magnified human powers to observe. Mathematics emerged as the fundamental language for describing phenomena and for communicating and testing scientific hypotheses among educated scholars. European universities, founded in earlier centuries as self-governing corporations, served well as incubators of new theories and speculations. As novel explanations of reality circulated widely, those founded on religious teachings, ancient philosophies, folklore, or other forms of wisdom handed down from earlier generations lost some, though not nearly all, of their power to guide human behavior.

Sun and earth. An early battle between empirical observation and traditional wisdom took place over the celestial relationship between the sun and our planet. Until the sixteenth century, astronomers in both Europe and the major Muslim centers of learning agreed that the earth occupied the center of the universe. This understanding was based on the work of Claudius Ptolemy, the second-century Greek-speaking scholar who lived in Alexandria in Egypt. In his book titled the *Almagest,* he proposed a geocentric, or earth-centered model of the universe in which all other heavenly bodies revolved around our world in nested spheres. Ptolemy remained the accepted authority on astronomy during the next 1,300 years.

Nicolaus Copernicus (1473–1543), a Polish scholar and Catholic cleric, put forth the first serious challenge to the Ptolemaic system in 1543 when he published *On the Revolutions of the Celestial Spheres.* The book tackled problems in Ptolemy's model by proposing that the earth orbited around the sun, along with other planets and stars. Copernicus founded his challenge to Ptolemaic astronomy on his own reading of ancient Greek texts but also on two

mathematical theorems formulated by Muslim scholars during the previous two centuries. Copernicus's heliocentric, or sun-centered theory had significant flaws and failed to attract widespread support. But in the following century, other scholars revised and refined the Copernican model, while theologians grappled with the implications of moving God's earthly creation out of the center of the cosmos. Johannes Kepler built on the work of the Danish astronomer Tycho Brahe to postulate that planetary orbits are elliptical, rather than round. The Catholic Church enlisted its own scholars to refute heliocentric claims as contrary to received truth. In 1633 the church's inquisition pronounced Galileo Galilei a heretic, sentencing him to house arrest for the rest of his life for publicly advocating a heliocentric universe. His *Dialogue Concerning the Two Chief World Systems* (1632) combined logical reasoning with evidence of telescopic observations to argue that the corrected Copernican system had greater explanatory power than the Ptolemaic model.

Sir Isaac Newton (1642–1727) analyzes light. An English physicist, mathematician, astronomer, natural philosopher, alchemist, and theologian, Newton carefully recorded his observations of the natural world, laying foundations for modern scientific knowledge. Here he uses a prism to investigate the constituent colors in a ray of light. What does this nineteenth-century engraving reveal about the tools and methods used in early scientific experiments?

A generation later the English scientist Isaac Newton published *Philosophiae Naturalis Principia Mathematica* (1687), which describes universal gravitation and the laws of motion, demonstrating a connection between gravity and Kepler's laws of planetary motion, thereby confirming the heliocentric theory. Newton's work defined specific laws of physics and set a standard for the next three centuries of scientific writing, combining accessible prose with detailed mathematical explanations of physical motion. Newton's work also had global scope.

Observation and experimentation in many fields. Remarkable advances took place in a number of fields besides astronomy and physics. Experiments in biology, chemistry, optics, and medicine changed not just what people knew about the world, but how they knew it. The English philosopher Francis Bacon articulated new scholarly methods that relied on personal observation, not just on libraries of ancient texts. He argued for a total reconstruction of science, the arts, and all human knowledge to found conclusions on the careful observation, cataloging, and analysis of natural phenomena. He also advocated inductive reasoning, that is, the method of arriving at a general hypothesis or theory regarding a phenomenon from careful observation of specific examples of that phenomenon. His effort to devise a systematic classification of human knowledge not based simply on received wisdom was instrumental to the development of modern thought.

The questioning of tradition spread outward from scientific inquiry, which at this time was little separated from philosophy and other branches of knowledge. In fact, scientists like Newton were known as "natural philosophers." Their work reinforced a growing conviction that much new knowledge was yet to be discovered, not simply dug up from the past. Governments began to look to science for potential contributions to economic progress and military advantage. By the mid-1600s, European states became more interested in promoting the spirit of inquiry than in punishing it. In 1660 Charles II of England granted a charter to the Royal Society of London for the Promotion of Natural Knowledge. It began publishing a scientific periodical to disseminate new developments. The French government approved a Royal Academy of Sciences in 1666.

The Enlightenment: Rethinking Human Nature and Society

The Enlightenment was a wide-ranging, many-sided intellectual movement among thinkers centered in Europe to put all inherited descriptions of nature and society to the test of reason. The movement emerged from several strands of thought. Most important was the work of scientists, especially Isaac Newton. He argued that universal physical laws governed all God's creation, that these laws could be expressed in mathematical equations applicable in all times and places, and that humans could understand the workings of the universe through their God-given powers of reason. John Locke, an English physician, politician, and colleague of Isaac Newton, was among the first to contend that if scientists like Newton could discover and articulate the laws of nature, then humans could also reason their way to clearer understanding of the operations of both the individual human mind and collective social behavior. Like the scientific revolution, the Enlightenment also aimed to make sense of the blizzard of knowledge arriving from other parts of the world. Finally, it built on the Renaissance commitment to humanistic education and creative thought, the Protestant Christian idea that individuals must discover God and their relation to him through private study and prayer, and reform efforts within the Catholic Church to rid it of ignorance, corruption, and superstitions that had no base in scripture.

Observing and recording the natural world. The German artist Maria Sibylla Merian worked for a time in the Dutch colony of Surinam in South America. Like many of her drawings, this illustration of a pair of common morpho butterflies (ca. 1719) shows the interconnected life cycles of plants and insects. Many Europeans of this period believed that insects spontaneously generated from mud or rotten meat. How does Merian's illustration exemplify modern scientific method?

TABLE 19.2 Innovative Thinkers of the Seventeenth and Eighteenth Centuries

Individual	Country	Achievements
Baha' al-Din ibn Ḥusayn al-Amili 1547–1621	Persia	Prominent mathematician, astronomer, poet, and Sufi mystic in Persia's Safavid empire; revived the study of mathematics in Persia.
Francis Bacon 1561–1623	England	Proposed a system of inquiry founded on empirical and inductive reasoning, later called the scientific method.
Galileo Galilei 1564–1642	Italy	Drawing on evidence from telescopic observations, supported Copernicus's heliocentric theory; discovered the moons of Jupiter.
Johannes Kepler 1571–1630	Germany	Proposed, following Copernicus, that the earth revolves around the sun (heliocentrism) and postulated three planetary laws of motion.
Yoshida Mitsuyoshi (Yoshida Kōyū) 1598–1672	Japan	Known along with two other scholars as the Three Arithmeticians; wrote the oldest surviving Japanese mathematical text.
Gadadhara Bhattacharya 1604–1709	India	Wrote prolific volumes on language, mind, law, and the concept of "meaning"; analyzed the emotive power of language and expression.
Margaret Cavendish 1623–1673	England	Wrote voluminously on power, manners, science, philosophy, and gender; an early writer of science fiction who also advocated for animal rights.
John Locke 1632–1704	England	Wrote extensively on theories of both knowledge (epistemology) and natural rights, postulating the idea of a social contract between ruler and subjects.
Isaac Newton 1642–1727	England	Set forth three laws of motion and described the operation of gravity; developed the calculus as a branch of mathematics.
Maria Sibylla Merian 1647–1717	Germany	Created observational drawings of numerous insect species that contributed to the discovery of insect metamorphosis; a founder of the scientific field of entomology.
Juana Inés de la Cruz 1651–1695	Mexico	Self-taught nun, poet, and scholar; wrote extensively on Christian philosophy and theology and defended the right of women to education and intellectual inquiry.
Baron de Montesquieu 1689–1755	France	Powerfully influenced liberal political theory, notably the concept of the separation of powers in government.
Voltaire 1694–1778	France	Historian, philosopher, and social critic; attacked the intolerance, superstition, oppression, and authoritarianism of the European old regime.
Benjamin Franklin 1706–1790	United States	Pursued research on electricity, sea currents, meteorology, and the nature of atoms; a revolutionary leader and diplomat who also founded the first lending library in the United States.
Carl Linnaeus 1707–1778	Sweden	Invented the modern system of naming and classifying organisms.
Jean-Jacques Rousseau 1712–1778	Switzerland	Wrote three major works that explored questions of morality, equality, freedom, government, and education; asserted that humans are good by nature but have been corrupted by society.
Dai Zhen 1724–1777	China	Neo-Confucian philosopher; wrote on human nature and metaphysics and incisively criticized earlier Confucian thinkers.
Immanuel Kant 1724–1804	Germany	Moral philosopher; proposed that humans have knowledge of reality only through the exercise of their rational faculties; had a large impact on modern philosophical speculation.
Ivan Shuvalov 1727–1797	Russia	Powerful figure in the Russian imperial court; championed the arts and humanities; first minister of education and overseer of Moscow University.
David Rittenhouse 1732–1796	United States	Astronomer, mathematician, and inventor; wrote an account of the transit of Venus and calculated to near accuracy the distance between the earth and the sun.
William Jones 1746–1794	England	Proposed structural relationships between South Asian and European languages, a hypothesis that launched the field of Indo-European studies.
Mary Wollstonecraft 1759–1797	England	Argued in *A Vindication of the Rights of Woman* that females are naturally equal to men but are deprived of education and the opportunity to develop fully their intellectual faculties.

Challenges to the Old Regime. Enlightenment figures, known in France as *philosophes,* explored humankind's relation to God, nature, and the universe from nearly every conceivable angle, sometimes making their arguments with mathematical equations and geometrical proofs (see Table 19.2). Many of them expressed faith that if scientific methods and enlightened reasoning guided human action, then continuous material well-being and progress could be ensured. Few of them advocated radical action to dismantle religious institutions, governments, or even absolutist

old regime The political and social system in France and other European monarchies between the sixteenth and eighteenth centuries; characterized by a rigid class hierarchy and rulers' claims to absolute authority.

monarchies, but most were highly critical of what they saw as the irrational, arbitrary, fanatical, or cruel aspects of what later was called the **old regime.** This term refers to the prevailing European social pyramid, the hierarchy of ranks from the monarch and the nobility on down based not on talent, education, occupation, or even wealth, but fundamentally on privilege either inherited or awarded by the state.

According to Locke, higher reasoning power distinguished humans from animals. This entitled people to certain **natural rights,** which no government should be allowed to take away without just cause, namely, "life, liberty, and property." Locke expressed his philosophy in many works, two of which particularly influenced political thought in England and eventually around the world. The first, *A Letter Concerning Toleration,* helped justify Parliament's passage of the English Toleration Act following the Glorious Revolution of 1688. That bill significantly lightened discrimination against religious dissenters. In 1690 Locke published *Two Treatises of Government* to justify England's emergence as a constitutional, limited monarchy. He attacked absolutism, contending that government must be a civil contract between citizens and government. Both parties operated under legal obligations that, if unfulfilled, released the other party from its obligations.

natural rights Universal and inherent rights of human beings bestowed by nature or divine power.

Innovative thinkers in France also spoke out against the excesses of the old regime. These *philosophes,* including mathematicians, poets, playwrights, novelists, and essayists—argued that rationality, not faith, custom, superstition, or revelation, should guide human affairs. Their debates collectively made a case for religious toleration, natural rights, eradication of cruel and unusual punishments, and even abolition of slavery. For some Enlightenment thinkers, such as the French poet and playwright Voltaire, the Christian church obstructed rationality and progress because of its rigidity and hypocrisy and the ignorance and dogmatism of its clergy. But even the skeptical Voltaire accepted the existence of a supreme being. Most Enlightenment philosophers, including Locke, Immanuel Kant, and Georg Wilhelm Friedrich Hegel, found no incompatibility between reason and faith, believing that human reason reflected God's wisdom and benevolence.

Some *philosophes* defined man's rationality in ways that excluded women. Jean-Jacques Rousseau, a creative thinker and a popularizer of Enlightenment ideas, argued that the male of the species in his natural state was fully equipped to solve the thorny problems of existence, many of which were the fault of civilization. But women, he believed, did not possess the ability to reason and thus the capacity to advance society except as nurturers of their families. A woman's physical functions overwhelmed her intellectual ones. "The male is male only at certain moments; the female is female her whole life," Rousseau wrote in *Emile* (1762), a treatise on education. Rousseau did not mean to degrade women by his statements but to exalt all that in his view was "natural" in them. Some women echoed his sentiments. In *Letters on the Female Mind* (1792), British author Laetitia Hawkins concurred that "the feminine intellect has less strength and more acuteness. . . . [W]e show less perseverance and more vivacity."[15] Writings of Hawkins and other women helped open a new debate about women's rights toward the end of the eighteenth century. In 1792 Mary Wollstonecraft, an English essayist, wrote history's first indisputably feminist tract, *A Vindication of the Rights of Woman.* She argued that the social training given to girls taught them to be frivolous, vain, and incapable. If educated equally, women would be the intellectual match of men.

Europe's new breed of natural philosophers filtered great amounts of data and used it to formulate new theories, both natural and social. One debate swirled around the idea that because people around the world looked and behaved so differently from one another, God must have created man and woman more than once, a theory that some said contradicted the Bible and therefore could not be true. Carl Linnaeus, the Swedish botanist who devised the modern system for classifying plants and animals, identified five races of humans having particular physical and mental tendencies. (He also believed some human groups had tails.) Enlightenment sages generated early theories of inherent racial qualities and differences that scientists demolished fully only in the late twentieth century. As information, whether accurate or not, regarding American Indians, Pacific Islanders, Chinese, and Africans reached Europe, Enlightenment writers ventured all sorts of social and cultural comparisons, sometimes to affirm European and Christian superiority but quite often to critique European habits and institutions. In 1721, for example, the Baron de Montesquieu published the *Persian Letters,* an imaginary account of two Persian gentlemen who visited France and commented critically on various aspects of society.

Several eighteenth-century European monarchs invited Enlightenment thinkers such as Voltaire to their courts or exchanged letters with them. These rulers, including Frederick II of Prussia, Catherine II of Russia, and the Habsburg emperor Joseph II (r. 1780–1790), saw no particular contradiction between their claims to absolute political authority and the thought of French *philosophes.* For them, Enlightenment rationality translated into programs to improve government efficiency, codify laws, eliminate senseless torture of prisoners, advance technical education, promote the arts, and reform agriculture and industry in ways that would improve the lives of peasants and workers at least marginally, thereby improving their productivity and raising their taxable incomes. These rulers could chat amiably about natural rights and enlightened government without thinking that such notions should in any way upset the existing old regime hierarchy.

Communicating the Enlightenment. Individuals engaged in scientific and philosophical inquiry collectively produced a huge body of writings. But the Enlightenment was not simply an elite phenomenon. Many outstanding contributors were individuals of modest origins and means. Diatribes against intolerance, bigotry, and the political status quo became commonplace in newspapers, novels, essays, and pamphlets, most of these contributions the work of authors now forgotten. The Enlightenment was in large part a middle-class phenomenon made possible by inexpensive printing technology, the spread of literacy, and the emergence of libraries and coffeehouses, all media of communication that reinforced one another. The educated class gathered in public literary societies, some of which admitted women, to read popular works of the day.

Encyclopedias and dictionaries became a pronounced expression of the Enlightenment, putting forth the doctrine that any person who aspired to self-improvement must have a comprehensive knowledge of science, technology, and the humanities. For people of relatively low social status, these volumes could be an entry into polite society. In England, Ephraim Chambers edited what is considered the first modern encyclopedia. It went through five editions between 1728 and 1744. A French publisher, recognizing good market potential, commissioned Denis Diderot and Jean le Rond d'Alembert to edit *Encyclopédie*, "a systematic dictionary of the sciences, arts, and crafts" that reached twenty-eight volumes. Scottish and German encyclopedias soon followed. The renowned British author Samuel Johnson published the first edition of a *Dictionary of the English Language* in 1755. The work contains 42,773 word entries, some of them laced with humor: "Lexicographer. writer of dictionaries; a harmless drudge that busies himself in tracing the original, and detailing the signification of words;" and "Politician. 1. One versed in the arts of government; one skilled in politicks. 2. A man of artifice; one of deep contrivance."[16]

Although the scientific revolution and the Enlightenment were predominantly western European movements, they diffused quickly to parts of the world where people spoke or read European languages. Eastern European states, notably Poland and Russia, had their own Enlightenment figures. In Moscow, Ivan Shuvalov, minister of education and Catherine II's lover, played a major role in founding both Moscow University and the Russian Academy of Arts. Far to the west in British North America, Benjamin Franklin's path-breaking experiments with electricity earned him admission to the French Royal Academy of Sciences. In Massachusetts, John Winthrop III at Harvard College measured the distance between the earth and the sun with near accuracy. The Enlightenment idea of the natural equality of all humans began in the mid-eighteenth century to inspire some colonial religious leaders and intellectuals to plead for the abolition of slavery. Simultaneously, the ideas that came

out of the English Civil War and Glorious Revolution, combined with Enlightenment political thought, stirred colonial leaders to protest British imperial injustices and, finally, to declare independence in defense of their "inalienable rights" (see Chapter 20).

The Continuing Growth of Islam and Christianity

Modern science emerged in the seventeenth and eighteenth centuries as a particular way of describing nature and the cosmos based on practical observation of material phenomena and, from that evidence, formulation of general theories and principles. In other words, science evolved as a specific system of knowledge. Other complex systems of knowledge, however, also existed, notably, the major world religions. They too sought to explain universal truths. The scientific revolution and the Christian system of knowledge challenged each other on numerous points. But they also influenced each other's development, and both remained intact. In the same period that modern scientific thought took root in Europe, the major religions, especially Islam and Christianity, attracted growing numbers of adherents. The success of these religions rested fundamentally on the ways they explained existence, roused hopes, and guided human conduct. They also benefited, however, from the great world convergence—the opportunities that worldwide communication and transport, as well as empire building, offered to introduce the faith to more people across greater distances.

Islam in Afroeurasia. Islam grew faster than any other major religion in the early modern centuries. Muslim merchants, artisans, and scholars carried the faith to new places, often taking passage on European ships. Muslim pilgrims traveled from all directions and in larger numbers to make the sacred pilgrimage to Mecca and Medina in Arabia. In the early modern period about fifteen thousand South Asians made the pilgrimage yearly, most of them by sea.[17] These devotees often returned home eager to share the message of the Quran with unbelievers.

Sufi saints and devotees contributed immensely to conversions in regions where Islam had previously been a minority faith or completely unknown. Sufism appealed to individuals seeking not only a community of fellow worshipers but also individual spiritual enlightenment. It represented the mystical side of Islam, the quest to achieve direct and personal communion with God. From the eleventh century, Sufi teachings and practices became progressively integrated into both Sunni and Shi'a Muslim life. Sufi practitioners typically followed a pious teacher, or "friend of God," who guided them along a spiritual path. The journey might involve a wide range of devotions, including study of mystical texts, visits to the shrines of deceased Sufi divines, and participation in sessions of chanting or dancing aimed at achieving a transcendent state. Most Sufi disciples also joined one or more religious associations, or orders, whose members pursued a distinctive path to enlightenment. For Muslim women, who did not typically occupy public or religious offices, Sufi devotions and affiliation offered an arena for religious expression and leadership. By the sixteenth century, Sufi organizations numbered in the hundreds, and some had branches in several regions.

When Sufi missionaries advanced into new regions, they often adapted to local, non-Muslim religious practices, contending that sincere commitment to God was more important than conformity to details of Muslim law. **Syncretism** was not uncommon on the frontiers where Islam met Hinduism, Buddhism, Christianity, and local religions. Examples of such compromise included symbolic linking of Hindu gods and goddesses with venerated Muslim saints; transforming sacred trees, rocks, or ponds into Muslim shrines; and wearing charms containing written phrases from the Quran to ward off evil spirits.

> **syncretism** In religion, the blending of beliefs or practices from two or more different belief systems; also the incorporation of beliefs or practices of one belief system by another.

From the sixteenth to the early eighteenth century, the Muslim Mughal dynasty ruled much of South Asia, but the majority population followed a variety of devotions that collectively we call the Hindu tradition. Sufi believers converted significant numbers of South Asians, notably in Bengal, the region of the lower Ganges River. The Mughal rulers encouraged Muslim farmers to migrate to the Ganges valley to cut forests and plant rice, cotton, and other crops, thereby extending agricultural lands that could be taxed. These pioneers assumed a leading role in the wave of economic expansion that benefited Bengal starting in the later seventeenth century. Sufism, together with the economic success of many Muslim entrepreneurs and merchants, firmly established Islam in the region, eventually as the majority faith.

Merchants, traveling scholars, and holy preachers, many from South Asia, introduced Islam to island Southeast Asia beginning in the fourteenth century. By the 1500s the religion was established across the Indonesian archipelago. Advancing northeastward from there, Muslim traders and Sufis founded communities in the southern Philippine Islands in the sixteenth century, even as Spanish priests introduced Catholic Christianity around Manila in the north.

Islam spread briskly in Subsaharan Africa from the later 1600s. Muslim populations had dominated the commercial towns along the East African coast for several centuries. Conversion intensified from the end of the seventeenth century, when the sultans of Oman, a maritime state located at the southeastern end of the Arabian Peninsula, built a formidable navy and began to dominate the major East African ports. From that time, Muslim merchants began to introduce their religion along the trade routes that led into the East African interior. In South Africa, the VOC brought in Muslim slaves and political prisoners. Islam's message also proved attractive to non-Muslim slaves, offering them a focus of social and devotional life separate from their Christian masters. In West Africa in the seventeenth century, Muslims both ruled and dominated trade in the savanna lands just south of the Sahara, and Sufi brotherhoods carried the faith to rural herders and farmers. The extensive conversion of peoples of Sudanic West Africa, however, did not take place until the nineteenth century (see Chapter 22). A significant percentage of the slaves transported to the Americas from the sixteenth to the nineteenth century were West African Muslims. Christian masters, however, prohibited Muslim slaves in America from open communal worship. Practice could be preserved only in fragmentary ways or in secret.

Christianity around the world. The Roman Catholic Church enjoyed global reach in the sixteenth century because Portuguese, Spanish, and Italian sea captains, virtually all of them Catholics, opened the global sea routes and

Christianity made local. Nahuatl artists decorated the church of Santa María de Tonantzintla starting in the early seventeenth century. This detail from an interior wall shows a Catholic bishop flanked by women wearing local headdresses. What other Native American influences do you see in this picture? What does this artwork suggest about local understandings of Christianity?

Individuals MATTER

Dona Beatriz Kimpa Vita: Visionary Christian of the Kongo

Dona Beatriz as portrayed in a letter written by Father Bernardo da Gallo, who interviewed her after her spirit possession in 1704.

In 1665, the once proud and powerful Kong kingdom, an African realm the size of England, descended into civil war, as rival lords fought over succession to the throne. This war was still raging four decades later, when Dona Beatriz Kimpa Vita (1684–1706), a twenty-year-old Christian woman, determined to intervene. As she lay wracked by illness, she dreamed that the Catholic saint Anthony of Padua had entered her body. When she recovered, she began traveling throughout Kongo, speaking out against both factional violence and enslavement and attracting followers to what became known as the Antonian Movement. St. Anthony instructed her, she preached, to heal the kingdom of civil strife.

She also preached a novel Christian theology, declaring the teachings of European clerics in the Kongo were incorrect in important particulars. Jesus Christ, she proclaimed, was not born in Bethlehem, but in São Salvador, the Kongo capital. Nazareth was a corruption of the name Nsundi, a northern province of Kongo where Christ had been baptized. Mary, his Kongolese mother, had been a slave when she and Joseph sought shelter on the night of the messiah's birth. Though Dona Beatriz and the Antonian Movement recognized the authority of the pope, they rejected the presence of Portuguese monks of the Capuchin order and wanted to spread their distinct Kongolese version of Christian truth.

Dona Beatriz's preaching exerted a powerful pull on the Kongolese population for both religious and political reasons. The Antonian Movement gained devoted adherents among both the nobility and the common people, many of them tired of civil conflict and rampant slave trading. Dona Beatriz and her followers, however, placed Pedro, the reigning king at the time, in an awkward and dangerous position. He resented the condescension of Capuchin missionaries, but he could not allow a charismatic young woman to undermine his authority. In 1706 the king ordered Dona Beatriz arrested and tried on charges of witchcraft and heresy. Convicted, she was burned on a flaming pyre.

Though the Antonian Movement continued after Dona Beatriz's death, thousands of her followers were rounded up and sold into slavery. Capuchin monks objected but only because these captives were shipped to Protestant countries. Many, in fact, may have ended up in South Carolina, which, after Haiti, had the second largest concentration of slaves from Kongo. In 1740, Catholic Kongolese slaves led a bloody though futile rebellion against their masters near the Stono River in South Carolina. Their battle cry was "*lukangu*," which in the Kongo language meant both "liberty" and "salvation."[19]

Thinking Critically

Would you characterize Dona Beatriz as an anti-European resistance leader? Why or why not?

---

began conquering the Americas. Missionaries who followed the conquistadors across the Atlantic began baptizing Indians. Priests and monks had the greatest initial success in Mesoamerica and Andean South America, where people had previously lived under Aztec or Inca rule and were therefore accustomed to an "official" religion and a priesthood associated with the state. In other words, the institution and hierarchy of the Catholic Church moved into the place of the Aztec and Inca religions.

Though one Spanish priest reported baptizing up to fourteen thousand Indians in a single day,[18] such mass conversions did not typically run deep. Syncretism flourished as many local religious practices became intermeshed with Christian ones. Since Spanish clergy usually spent little time in rural villages, they appointed local people to run churches. The Spanish called these native helpers "cantors" and "sacristans." In Mexico, however, Nahuatl speakers persisted in calling them "*teopantlaca*," the name given to workers in the old Aztec temples. Spanish priests granted villagers their own patron saints, but Indians routinely melded these Christian figures with local deities that they believed watched over their communities. The Spanish required Indians to accept one God and the Holy Trinity but also shared with their imperial subjects popular Christian beliefs in the power of magical and supernatural forces in various manifestations. In short, Spanish missionaries and Mexican Indians shared some common religious ground even though they often assigned different meanings to the same rituals and beliefs.

In China and other parts of Asia, Christian conversion proceeded slowly. In contrast to the situation in the Americas, wherever the Portuguese seized coastal enclaves or entered ports to trade, they had to deal with local authorities and urban populations who could limit or prohibit missionary activity. The Jesuit priest Francis Xavier (1506–1552) preached in Japan, ordering priests under him to observe Japanese etiquette and conduct themselves in the manner of Zen Buddhist dignitaries. By 1600 the church counted 300,000 Japanese believers, most on the southern island of Kyusu. But the Buddhist Tokugawa shoguns, who consolidated their power in the early seventeenth century, clamped down on Christian conversion and worship and Catholic communities withered away (see Chapter 18). In China, Matteo Ricci (1552–1610) and other Jesuit priests secured permission to preach and build churches, and they tried to show parallels between Catholic doctrine and Chinese Confucian philosophy. Both the Ming and the early Qing royal courts made use of Jesuit knowledge of cartography, astronomy, mathematics, clock making, and firearms technology. The Catholic missions, however, reached few ordinary Chinese. After 1704, when an envoy from the pope insolently announced that Chinese Christians must be prohibited from venerating their family ancestors, the emperor had missionaries expelled. The church's hopes of large-scale conversion evaporated after that.

Wherever Portuguese, Dutch, British, or French merchants founded stations along the West and Central African coasts, they introduced their own Catholic or Protestant religion. But Europeans operated in most places as the guests of African rulers and usually huddled close to their posts. Christianity did not therefore spread far before the eighteenth century, though the ancient Christian church in Ethiopia, whose teachings differed significantly from either Catholic or Protestant churches, continued to flourish. In tropical Africa, Europeans achieved the most conversions in the Central African Kongo kingdom, whose royal family became Catholic early in the sixteenth century. Subsequent monarchs vigorously promoted the Christian gospel, and the religion became deeply ingrained in Kongolese life.

Jesuit missionaries in China. Jesuits combined assimilation of Chinese cultural forms, European scientific knowledge, and Christian theology to persuade potential Asian converts. What evidence does this engraving provide of their blending Christian and Chinese symbols?

This involved, however, significant syncretism, as Catholic and older Kongolese religious practices intermingled.

• • •

Conclusion

In the sixteenth and early seventeenth centuries, rulers of a number of Afroeurasian states demonstrated that by fielding gunpowder armies and more effectively taxing their populations to pay for huge military expenditures, they could build stronger, more highly centralized states and even territorial or seaborne empires. Large-scale state building continued in the period from 1650 to 1800, a process assisted by the increasing sophistication and deadliness of firearms technology.

The world map of powerful states, however, changed significantly. The Muslim-ruled Mughal, Persian, and Ottoman empires reached the end of their long expansionary phases in the seventeenth century and either shrank or, in the case of Safavid Persia, disappeared. In the same era, however, Russian and Chinese armies advanced across the immense spaces of Inner Eurasia in opposite directions, while avoiding prolonged conflict with each other. In Europe, France, England, the Netherlands, Prussia, and (for a time) Sweden became both politically and economically stronger, while the Habsburg empire expanded deeper into southeastern Europe at the expense of the Ottoman state. By contrast, Portugal and Spain dropped to a lower rank in the hierarchy of European power.

European empire building overseas succeeded spectacularly in the Americas. The Spanish crown, despite economic troubles at home, continued to exploit its great Latin American viceroyalties, and Portugal progressively subjugated more of Brazil's Native American population. Britain, France, and the Netherlands seized territories in the Caribbean and eastern North America. All five of these powers deployed naval power to either acquire or hang on to coastal enclaves and islands in Asia and tropical Africa, but in those regions the balance of territorial power remained firmly in the hands of local rulers.

In the seventeenth century, Europeans also undertook a new kind of long-distance expansion, founding colonies of settlers in eastern North America, Siberia, and the Cape region of South Africa. In these regions, populations of mainly European descent not only made themselves politically dominant, but with the help of infectious diseases and armed aggression gradually succeeded in displacing native indigenous communities to create neo-Europes, societies whose populations and cultural form were of largely European origin. Across much of the world's temperate zones, these societies would grow much larger in the nineteenth century, to the grim detriment of indigenous peoples.

In the seventeenth and eighteenth centuries, networks of both transoceanic and long-distance overland communication became increasingly complex. As that happened, all but the most isolated societies had to confront immense amounts of new information arriving from afar. This avalanche of knowledge, circulating from one part of the world to another, provoked new questions about the universe, nature, and human society, as well as growing distrust of old answers. Peoples around the world took part in generating knowledge and posing fresh ideas , though the intellectual hub of this phenomenon was the globally connected ports and capitals of western Europe. The resulting scientific revolution and cultural Enlightenment changed forever the premises and methods for discovering and knowing truth. The new ways of thinking challenged time-honored religious doctrines on many points. Nevertheless, the great missionary religions, especially Christianity and Islam, continued to grow apace as monks, priests, ministers, pious scholars, and Sufi devotees fanned out along land and sea routes to share their own solutions to the problem of being.

• • •

Key Terms

absolutism 547	neo-Europe 556	Qing dynasty 545
creole 550	New Spain and the Viceroyalty of Peru 549	regent 545
English Civil War 568		scientific revolution 563
Enlightenment 563	old regime 567	syncretism 569
Glorious Revolution 556	Peace of Westphalia 551	Treaty of Nerchinsk 546
natural rights 567	*philosophes* 566	War of the Spanish Succession 554

Change over Time

1582	Confucian scholars encounter Catholic Christian missionaries in China.
1632	Galileo Galilei offers proof of heliocentric theory of planetary motion.
1639	Russian explorers advancing across Siberia reach the Pacific.
1642–1660	The English Civil War involves temporary abolition of monarchy.
1643–1715	Louis XIV rules France, promoting absolutist principles.
1644	The Qing dynasty comes to power in China, replacing the Ming dynasty.
1648	The Peace of Westphalia proposes principles to guide international relations in Europe.
1652	Khoisan peoples of South Africa encounter Dutch East India Company (VOC) colonizers.
1654–1722	The Kangxi emperor expands China's land frontiers.
1675–1676	Native Americans unsuccessfully rebel against settlers in Massachusetts Bay Colony.
1682–1725	Peter the Great transforms Russia into a major European power.
1687	Isaac Newton publishes *The Principia,* detailing laws of gravity and motion.
1688	The Glorious Revolution in Britain limits the monarchy's power.
1689	China and Russia settle land frontier disputes with the Treaty of Nerchinsk.
1690	John Locke publishes *Two Treatises of Government,* criticizing absolutist government.
1690s	The Austrian Habsburg empire drives Ottoman forces out of Hungary.
1701–1714	The War of the Spanish Succession drains economies of western European states, especially France.
1713–1740	Frederick William I consolidates power in Prussia.
1792	Mary Wollstonecraft publishes *A Vindication of the Rights of Woman,* arguing for equal education for women.
Early 1800s	The Spanish American empire reaches its greatest territorial extent.

Please see end of chapter reference section for additional reading suggestions related to this chapter.

part 6

The Modern World Takes Shape

1750–1914

In the middle decades of the eighteenth century, human life on earth began to change at an accelerating speed. The transformations of the past 250 years—in society, economy, and human interaction with the physical and natural environment—are comparable in their historical significance only with the invention of agriculture 12,000 years ago. In this book we associate these transformations, which are still under way, with the modern era or, simply, modernity. In Part 6 we survey the modern period from about 1750 to 1914, the year World War I broke out.

Scholars of history have long debated the factors that distinguish the modern age from all earlier times. In our view, the development on which all other transformations turned was the onset of what we call the "energy revolution." In the later 1700s, humans found ways to tap an immense stockpile of energy concentrated in fossil fuels—coal first, then petroleum and natural gas. Since then, exploitation of this underground energy bonanza has permitted levels of population growth, economic productivity, social complexity, military destructiveness, and human intervention in the environment inconceivable in any earlier era. Today the average individual uses something like 46,000 times more energy than our ancestors did 12,000 years ago, and most of that increase has occurred since 1750. The modern era, however, also has several other characteristics, all interrelated in complex ways with the energy revolution and with one another:

Thomas Edison's incandescent bulb, invented in the 1880s.

■ Humans have for the first time acquired the technical power not only to adapt successfully to the earth's environment but, for good or ill, to *transform* it. In other words, our own species, rather than physical and natural forces, has since sometime in the nineteenth century become the chief instrument of change in the earth's ecology, geology, and atmosphere.

■ The growth rate of world population began to accelerate in the mid-eighteenth century far faster than in any earlier time. The world had about 770 million people in 1750 and more than 7 billion by 2012. About 28 percent of all humans who were ever alive have lived since 1750. This growth has carried with it much greater social complexity, seen, for example, in the rise of giant cities. Between 1000 and 1700 C.E., the world had no more than three cities with populations in excess of 1 million. In 2000, there were 299 such cities.[1]

■ Rates of technological and scientific advance have accelerated greatly since the eighteenth century, and no slowdown appears in sight. This rush of novelties began in connection with the energy revolution and the accompanying industrial revolution with its countless transformations in manufacturing, farming, and communication. Today, innovations in science and technology proliferate at breathtaking speed. Material advances, together with huge inputs of fossil fuel and to some extent nuclear energy, account for the accelerating rate of long-term global economic growth since the late eighteenth century.

■ Networks of world-girdling commercial, cultural, biological, and migratory exchange have become much denser and more complicated in the past 250 years. Global exchanges, especially messages transmitted instantaneously through electronic networks, have made possible a great acceleration of "collective learning." This is the ability that humans, unlike any other living species, possess to amass, store up, and transmit information, much of it useful to human well-being, some of it harmful.[2]

■ States, that is, territories whose inhabitants live under the authority of a central government of one type or another, have come to exercise both military power and command over the lives of their own citizens on a scale unknown in premodern times.

■ A new kind of political thought emerged in the eighteenth century centered on the twin ideas that God and nature have bestowed on human beings certain indisputable rights and that the source of any government's authority is rightfully the "people," not kings or high priests. This ideology gradually captured the whole world's imagination, provoking wars and revolutions but also animating both private capitalist enterprise and the political experiment to organize the world in sovereign nation-states, nearly two hundred of them.

In exploring the period from 1750 to 1914, we should keep in mind that the meaning and direction of the modern age are unknown to us because it is still in progress. Revolutions in economy, social organization, microbiology, or electronics may already be happening, though we cannot yet see their shape or significance. We should remember, for example, that the computerized and digitized world we live in today would have been unimaginable to the nineteenth-century scientists who first harnessed electrical energy and unknowingly made possible smartphones, genetic decoding, and Facebook.

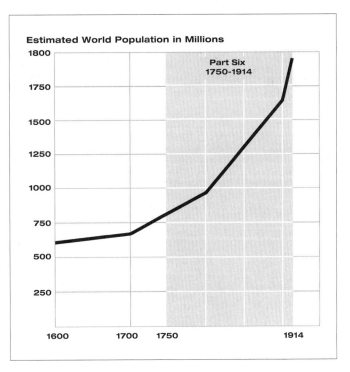

Estimated World Population in Millions

Part Six 1750–1914

20 Waves of Revolution
1720–1830

Coffeehouses were important sites of political conversations in the eighteenth century.

A free and lively newspaper culture has been a feature of democratic societies in modern times, but is this medium disappearing? Communication experts have been asking this question ever since the Internet emerged as a carrier of news, opinion, and advertising. In the United States, print editions of most major newspapers have been steadily losing circulation, and some have gone exclusively online. Futurists have predicted that newsprint will vanish entirely before the end of the current century.

If newspapers endure only in cyberspace, they will have had a relatively short history as a print medium. Daily or weekly broadsheets with small circulations first appeared in western Europe and British North America in the late 1600s and in other parts of the world barely two hundred years ago. Newspapers flourished in connection with the epic transformations that took place in human society in the eighteenth and nineteenth centuries. News writers could gather more information and put it in print faster as roads improved, ships got faster, postal services were set up, and, in the early nineteenth century, steamships, railroads, and the telegraph were invented. Newspapers helped meet the capitalist world's constant demand for quick information about political conditions, wars, prices, and the movement of commodities. The popular revolutions that erupted in North America and Europe in the late eighteenth century spawned many new broadsheets to inform the public of late-breaking events and to promote one political view or another. In the following century, steam-powered presses rolled out thousands of copies of news sheets. The handful of newspapers published worldwide in the 1700s grew to an estimated 3,168 by 1828 and to more than 31,000 by 1900.

The rise of the newspaper was one event in a large cluster of changes that we associate with modernity. This chapter spans the period from approximately 1720 to 1830 and focuses on the momentous political and social changes that occurred in the world in those 110 years. This was an era of accelerating global population growth, a nearly continuous surge in the volume and value of global commerce, a dramatic increase in the number of people using money to buy and sell goods in the market, and the creation of far more complex networks of transport and communication. These developments inspired radical new thinking about how to organize society and manage change, and they brought higher standards of living to millions in some parts of the world. They also, however, aggravated political and social stresses for many more millions and triggered conflict among classes, ethnic peoples, and rival states.

In the first part of the chapter we explore the relationship between rapid change in the world economy, especially the complex intermeshing of societies through commerce, and the mounting problems that the world's large states faced in financing bureaucracies, fielding armies, and keeping public order. In the middle decades of the eighteenth century, European states, especially Britain, France, Habsburg Austria, Prussia, and Russia, projected more military power relative to the large Asian empires than ever before. They also competed violently with one another for shares of accumulating global wealth. European states, North American Indians, and South Asians all clashed in the Seven Years' War from 1756 to 1763, a "world war" that helped set the stage for several popular revolts.

The second part of the chapter investigates the first wave of revolutionary movements that took place on both

Chapter Outline

WORLD ECONOMY AND POLITICS, 1720–1763
A Commercializing World
Troubled Empires in Asia
Global Sea Trade and the Eighteenth-Century "World War"

REVOLUTIONS ON THE NORTH ATLANTIC RIM
The Global Context of Popular Revolt
The War of Independence in North America
The French Revolution
The Idea of Nationalism
The Birth of Haiti

WEIGHING THE EVIDENCE Toussaint Louverture Writes to the French Directory

THE SECOND WAVE: REVOLUTIONS IN LATIN AMERICA
Colonial Society on the Eve of Rebellion
The Wars of Independence

INDIVIDUALS MATTER José de San Martín: Liberator of the Southern Andes

Many Young States

• • •

sides of the North Atlantic between 1775 and 1815. Political, economic, and cultural forces reverberating back and forth across the ocean intricately linked the rebellions that erupted in British North America, France, and Haiti. Those movements drew on new ideas about natural rights and the "sovereignty of the people" that had emerged from the Enlightenment (see Chapter 19), ideas that have shaped protest, revolution, and the organization of governments ever since.

The final part of the chapter explores the second wave of revolutions, which engulfed nearly all of Latin America. These insurgencies took place in social environments that differed greatly from British North America and Haiti, but as in the British colonies, they were led mainly by American-born, property-owning men of European descent. The wars of independence ended Portugal's rule of Brazil and nearly obliterated Spain's enormous American empire, replacing it with multiple states founded on modern patriotic ideas of self-government by and for the people.

A Panoramic View

MAP 20.1 Major states and colonial territories after the Seven Years' War (1756–1763).

Empires claimed huge swaths of territory—some in contiguous stretches of land and others overseas. Desire for even more territory and wealth fueled rivalries among empires. What aspects of this political map of states after the Seven Years' War might explain the global nature of that conflict among European powers?

World Economy and Politics, 1720–1763

FOCUS To what extent was the growth of the world economy connected to changes in the relative power of large states during the eighteenth century?

Scholars have conventionally dated the political and social upheavals that enveloped much of the world in the later eighteenth and early nineteenth centuries to the outbreak of rebellion in Britain's thirteen North American colonies in 1775. More recently, however, historians have offered evidence that beginning about 1720 several of Afroeurasia's large and prosperous states experienced growing economic problems, political turbulence, and social stresses. In several place these troubles led to regional rebellions and new wars.

Observers of the world scene would not likely have foreseen the impending instability. Its early signs appeared against a background of intense and accelerating global economic activity. The world was rapidly commercializing. The buying and selling of raw commodities, manufactured products, and labor in response to changing prices and market conditions was surging upward both locally and between regions. The later seventeenth and the eighteenth centuries also witnessed a phenomenon in which families with relatively modest incomes began to purchase more material goods on the market and to pay for them by working harder and for longer hours than they ever had before.

Global commercialization raised the stakes for all states determined to stay in the competitive game and to acquire greater wealth. It put added pressure on them to control more farm land and mines, dominate trade routes, protect markets against foreign merchants, and grab new colonies before their rivals moved in ahead of them. These objectives, however, required rulers continually to expand bureaucracies, recruit new troops, and upgrade expensive military technology. The costs of government therefore mounted at an accelerating rate, especially where armies had to defend long frontiers or overseas colonies. The expense of simply *maintaining* a state's status as a major regional player, regardless of further expansion, obliged governments to impose heavier taxes on their populations of peasants, town dwellers, and money-making merchants. Heavier fiscal burdens, however, triggered rural uprisings, urban riots, or colonial protests that cost the state even more treasure to suppress. Signs that powerful states were losing the struggle to pay for their own centralizing and military success appeared first in Asia and then in Europe.

A Commercializing World

By the early eighteenth century, nearly every state in Afroeurasia, whether giant empire or tiny kingdom, was connected in some degree to the global commercial system that moved commodities, manufactured goods, and laboring men and women from one place to another. A combination of private profit-seeking and commercial competition between states motivated the emerging modern commercial system. The merchants who ran it relied increasingly on gold, silver, and other forms of money to make their transactions. Commercialization depended on an assortment of capitalist institutions and practices—partnerships, joint-stock companies, banks, credit, currency conversion mechanisms, insurance policies, merchant information networks, and strategies to persuade consumers to buy new products.

The commercializing trend, however, was still at a primitive stage compared to today. Tens of millions of people lived by subsistence farming or herding and had no more than occasional contacts with the market. Others were shut out of the commercial system because their labor was controlled or owned by others. In eastern Europe and Russia, for example, millions of serfs had to turn over much of their farm production to estate-owning nobles, who then sold it for export to western Europe at profit only to themselves. The African slave trade was part of a highly commercialized system that benefited African rulers, American plantation owners, Atlantic merchants, and European manufacturers but not the slaves who brought in immensely profitable harvests of tropical sugar and tobacco.

Industrious revolutions. The demands and habits of consumers around the world began to change rapidly in the eighteenth century as many new and alluring products came on the market. For example, hardly any Europeans had ever tasted Chinese tea in 1664, when British East India Company officials presented two pounds of it to King Charles II. In the next few decades, however, tea caught on in Britain as an energy-supplying and mildly addictive beverage mixed with sugar. Imports from China rose from around 38,000 pounds in 1690 to 37.4 million by the 1750s.[6] As choices of new foods and other goods multiplied, consumers throughout the world became fussier about the wares they wanted to buy. In regions like southern China, Japan, India, western Europe, and the British North American colonies, where commercialization was proceeding fast, people who made money acquired more extravagant tastes for fine textiles, art, and home furnishings that only land-owning aristocrats had previously been able to afford. In West Africa, local merchants might refuse to sell captives to European slave shippers unless they could buy Indian calico cotton textiles with particular prints, not last year's outmoded fashions.

On a global scale, more rural farmers and artisans sold at market whatever surpluses they might manage to produce. More people abandoned their fields altogether and earned wages to buy food, clothing, and furnishings. In western Europe, for example, ordinary men and women purchased more goods from foreign places, including tobacco, sugar, tea, coffee, wine, Indian cottons, cheap porcelain tableware, and exotic furniture. Wherever people who were not goods. This persistent industriousness and the resulting rise in demand for goods stimulated international commerce and gave more incentive to people to master complicated specializations or make technical improvements in farming or manufacturing.

Asia's economic weight. The center of gravity of global production and commerce remained in Asia until after 1750. Between the sixteenth and eighteenth centuries, remarkable demographic and economic growth took place in East and South Asia. China, India, and Japan together accounted for about 55 percent of the world's total population, compared to western Europe's 12 percent. China's population more than doubled in the eighteenth century, from about 160 million to 350 million. One measure of comparison between Asian and western European economies is farming productivity, the agricultural output of an average worker in a given time period. In 1750, productivity in the Yangzi River valley, China's richest agricultural region, was about the same as it was in England and the Netherlands, the two most productive countries in Europe. **Real wages** of agricultural workers were approximately the same in southern China and west-

> **real wages** Wages estimated in the amount of goods those wages will buy rather than in the face value of money paid.

ern Europe, as was life expectancy, at about forty years. China put out more than 30 percent of the world's manufactures, whereas India and Europe produced about 23 percent each (see table: Shares of world manufacturing output[2]). Knowledgeable Europeans recognized China's economic muscle. Adam Smith, the Scottish economic thinker, observed in 1776 that "China is a much richer country than any part of Europe." As for India, it was by far the world's largest exporter of hand-woven cotton textiles. As of 1750, weavers in southern India may well have enjoyed higher standards of living than their counterparts in Britain.[3]

Japan's economy achieved stunning growth in the seventeenth century under the government of the Tokugawa shogunate, though it slowed after about 1700. This probably happened in large part because the archipelago's population could no longer find much new arable soil or forests to exploit. Industrious Japanese peasants continued to increase their output but mainly by making small technical improvements or working longer hours to raise their productivity. Commercial fishermen also exploited the seas around Japan more intensively, catching fish that enriched supplies of food protein and fertilizer. Unlike western European countries, Japan had no overseas colonies from which to draw resources. Even so, the country remained highly commercialized, and it continued to trade with China, Korea, and Southeast Asia until the later eighteenth century. As of 1750, a larger percentage of Japan's population—about twenty-six million in all—lived in cities than did the populations of southern China or Britain. Edo (Tokyo) swelled to more than one million inhabitants, making it one of the largest cities in the world.

Indian fabrics influenced British fashion. A young woman's jacket and matching petticoat exemplify eighteenth-century European fashion. The fabric, which is hand-painted cotton chintz, came from the Coromandel coast in southeastern India. The flowers are a typical Indian design. An English tailor made the outfit around 1780. What might account for the popularity of exotic fabrics in England in that period?

wealthy aspired to consume more goods, they became participants in what historians have called industrious revolutions. This means that laboring men and women bought more goods rather than making them at home. They did this chiefly by working harder and more productively. Younger family members might toil longer hours on the farm, and adults might spend more working days earning wages. Families might fabricate a single specialized product at home but purchase rather than make their own candles, tables, or chairs. We have good evidence from western Europe, China, and Japan that men worked longer hours and more days of the year and that more women and children took up wage labor to satisfy hankerings for a wider selection of consumer

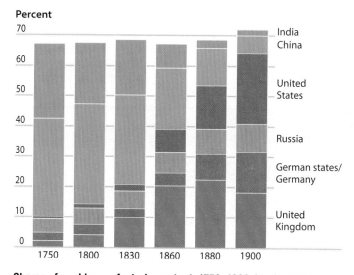

Percent

Shares of world manufacturing output, 1750–1900. In what countries did manufacturing increase during the late eighteenth and nineteenth centuries? Where did manufacturing stay relatively constant? Which regions lost significant shares of global production? What factors might help explain these changes?

Commercializing tropical Africa. In the early eighteenth century, peoples of Africa south of the Sahara Desert were already well entangled in the web of global commerce, though not in the same way that Chinese or South Asians were. The European capitalist entrepreneurs and merchants who developed the Atlantic economy bought gold, textiles, and numerous other commodities from African coastal merchants and the rulers of such monarchies as Ashanti, Dahomey, and Benin (see Chapter 18). Nevertheless, by the seventeenth century, Europeans visitors wanted slaves more than any material product, and as commercial plantations multiplied in the Americas, the demand for slave labor increased constantly. In the 1700s, more than six million men and women were forced to cross the Atlantic to work in bondage until they died. Traffic in captives also thrived from West Africa across the Sahara Desert to the Muslim Mediterranean and from the eastern side of the continent to the Arabian Peninsula, Persia, and India. In the mid-eighteenth century, the total number of Africans taken from their homelands may have numbered about seventy thousand annually.

The slave trade was not only a human tragedy but also a disaster for African economies. It deprived particular regions that were agriculturally rich of hundreds of thousands of productive farmers, artisans, and community leaders, as well as women of childbearing age. Just when the populations of China, Europe, and other parts of Eurasia were swelling, tropical Africa's population, which was about fifty million in the mid-eighteenth century, either held steady or declined slightly. Most regions from which slaves were taken would have gained economically from higher populations because arable land and pasture were

abundant. Furthermore, along the Atlantic coasts, European merchants sold shiploads of cotton cloth and iron goods in exchange for slaves. These imports gradually depressed once-flourishing African textile and iron-working industries. Rulers and merchants tried to meet the incessant demands European slave buyers made, and this led to more wars, population displacements, famines, and crime. In West and Central African coastal regions, slave trading significantly reduced male populations. This meant that the burden of agricultural labor fell more heavily on women than ever before. In short, in the mid-eighteenth century, economic output in East and South Asia remained strong and western Europe's economic star was rising. By contrast, violent trafficking in people weakened the commercial position many African societies may otherwise have had in the advancing wold economy.

Troubled Empires in Asia

Among the great Asian states, China under the Qing dynasty (1644–1911) remained prosperous and largely free of internal strife until nearly 1800. However, the three giant Muslim empires of the era experienced serious financial and governing problems in the early eighteenth century. The Safavid empire of Persia flourished under the talented ruler Shah Abbas (reigned 1587–1629) and for several decades thereafter (see Chapter 17). The costs of maintaining a larger gunpowder army continued to mount so relentlessly, however, that the government eventually allowed it to deteriorate. In 1722, a motley force of mounted rebels from Afghanistan overran Isfahan, the Safavid's fabled capital, and the dynasty collapsed. Until late in the century, Persia remained divided among competing military lords, none of whom managed to rebuild stable central authority.

To the east, the Mughal empire of South Asia, whose Muslim military elite ruled tens of millions of Hindu farmers and town dwellers, reached its greatest territorial extent under the rule of Aurangzeb (r. 1658–1707). The imperial regime had always negotiated the loyalty of locally powerful estate owners by generously awarding them rights to tax revenues from land. The government, however, found it increasingly difficult to make these grants as the costs of conquest and administration mounted. Aurangzeb kept restless local elites in line through great force of will, but his successors had few of his talents. After he died, local magnates and even provincial governors found they could defy central authority. Many of them also amassed wealth independently in South Asia's expanding commercial sphere, buying and selling crops of maize, tobacco, and chili peppers (all introduced earlier from the Americas) and doing business in cotton textiles.

As landlords accumulated new resources and the Mughal government creaked and sagged under its heavy financial burdens, regional rebellions multiplied. In 1739 the Persian warlord Nadir Shah invaded northern India and ferociously sacked Delhi before retreating. In the first half of

Sultan Selim III (r. 1789–1807) receiving dignitaries at the Topkapi Palace. The Ottoman court in Constantinople was the focal point of imperial administration. Here the Sultan is attended by courtiers, officials, and Janissaries.

the eighteenth century, the Mughal empire splintered into a number of regional power centers. Some of them offered ceremonial allegiance to the Mughal sultan in Delhi, others not even that. The Marathas, a confederation of Marathi-speaking clans based in central South Asia's Deccan Plateau, most vividly exposed Mughal weakness by creating a regional empire of their own that spanned nearly all of central India. In Mysore in the far southwest, Haider Ali and his son Tipu Sultan founded a state in the 1760s that fielded an army of sixty thousand and equipped it with artillery.

In contrast to the Safavids and the Mughals, the Ottoman empire, the third great Turkic-ruled state, remained a major Afroeurasian military power throughout the eighteenth century. After a long and losing war with Habsburg Austria, the empire had to cede several of its European provinces in 1699 (see Chapter 19). But it gained some of them back in the following decades and only began to suffer severe and permanent territorial losses in the war with Russia that ran from 1768 to 1774.

Nevertheless, growing fiscal difficulties and the rapidly changing world economy steadily wore down Ottoman resources. The sultans installed in their fabulous Topkapi Palace in Constantinople became increasingly isolated from administrative affairs. Ministers of state who tried to make reforms repeatedly lost out to entrenched political and religious groups. The Janissaries, the slave army that had led the empire to military glory in earlier times, deteriorated from a highly disciplined fighting corps to a bloated assemblage of competing factions, each with business and commercial interests and an inclination to riot in the streets at the slightest challenge to their privileges. As in the Mughal empire, weakness at the top allowed elite landholders in the rural lands of both Anatolia (modern Turkey) and southeastern Europe to collect rents and taxes on their own account, rather than on behalf of the state. European governments and trading firms clamored for lower tariffs on imports, which deprived the Turkish state of an important source of revenue. Chronic price inflation, caused partly by the flow of American silver into the Ottoman economy, made life more expensive for thousands of bureaucrats and soldiers on fixed salaries and pensions. In addition, the land-owning elite demanded larger rents from local peasants. Many rural men and women fled the countryside for Constantinople and other cities, where they swelled the ranks of the underemployed.

Despite these numerous problems, the Ottoman empire continued in many ways to function as before. Uprisings and urban disturbances occurred with growing frequency, but dissenters hardly ever questioned the legitimacy of the Ottoman government. All kinds of institutions bound subjects of the sultan together—guilds, Muslim Sufi organizations, and local kinship groups. The Muslim legal system worked efficiently, and the Muslim, Christian, and Jewish communities within the empire regulated their own affairs. The main development was a process of decentralization in which power became more diffused through the empire to the advantage of local elite groups, clans, and estate magnates.

Global Sea Trade and the Eighteenth-Century "World War"

The major European states expended huge sums periodically fighting one another in the seventeenth and early eighteenth centuries and, in the case of Britain, France, the Netherlands, and Spain, expanding and defending their commercial and strategic interests. In the 1600s the Atlantic and Indian Oceans became theaters of intense competition among the main European naval powers. In the Atlantic, rivalry over the trade connecting Europe, Africa, and the Americas involved almost exclusively the western European states. The scene in the Indian Ocean and the China seas, however, was quite different. There, the chartered trading companies of Britain, France, and the Netherlands had the biggest ships and marine artillery, but the great majority of merchants and sailors operating in the southern seas were Chinese, Malays, South Asians, Arabs, and East Africans, including people who worked as crew members on European-owned vessels. In the ports of Southeast Asia, Chinese merchant and business communities grew steadily throughout the eighteenth century. For example, by 1800 the Chinese residents of Batavia, the Dutch East India Company's big port on Java in Indonesia, numbered nearly 100,000, far more than the population of Dutch company employees.

European belligerence in the southern seas. European competition for southern seas trade in cotton, silk, spices, porcelain, and tea intensified as the century progressed, in part because trading firm profits slumped gradually. Since the sixteenth century, Europe failed to offer many products other than silver that Asians wanted to buy. European merchants pumped more specie from American mines into the Asian economy. But as they did that the value of silver relative to gold began to decline so that a given unit of silver coinage bought fewer Asian goods. Moreover, the European East Indies companies learned early that despite their shipboard firepower, they could not come close to controlling the southern sea routes or the multitude of local traders and vessels that crowded into the network.

Europeans could monopolize direct sea commerce between the Indian Ocean and Europe, but they had to compete with Asians for the lucrative "carrying trade" between one part of Asia or eastern Africa and another. And when it came to negotiating prices, Europeans had to depend on local rulers, entrepreneurs, and merchants who dominated the production of commodities and their transport from inland fields or mines to the ports where European ships awaited.

In response to shrinking profits, both the Dutch and British East India Companies took aggressive action. On Java, the Dutch sent armed bands from Batavia to the mountainous interior to seize direct control of more of the island's trade and to tax Javanese peasants. In 1725 they began to force highland farmers to grow coffee for export. In the same period the British firm strengthened the fortifications around its trading posts in South Asia, especially Bombay (Mumbai), which faced the Arabian Sea, and Madras (Chennai) and Calcutta (Kolkata) on the Bay of Bengal.

Calcutta emerged as the company's most profitable port, attracting a burgeoning trade in fine cotton and silk goods from the fertile and populous Ganges River delta. Local Indian merchants funneled textiles to the port, and Indian bankers supplied European traders with commercial capital. Calcutta and the company's other posts were formal dependencies of the Mughal emperor. But as imperial authority waned, the company began to defy the Delhi government, behaving much like Marathas and other rebellious South Asian power groups. In 1757, British East India Company accountant turned military leader Robert Clive took advantage of both Mughal weakness and divisions among local princes to seize Bengali territory using paid Indian troops supplied with British guns. This initiative gave the company control of inland markets, huge farm estates, and, more important for company finances, taxing rights. Clive himself became immensely rich.

In the following decades, company forces carrying up-to-date flintlock handguns advanced far up the Ganges valley. In 1799 troops invaded Mysore and killed Tipu Sultan after he tried and failed to get military help from France. The British Parliament fretted that by seizing territory rather than just trading from coastal stations the company was pulling the country into financial quicksand. But company shareholders were delighted, and company revenues helped pay for British naval operations around the world. Consequently, European colonization of India crept forward, partly by military action and partly by negotiations with local chiefs and princes who were badly outgunned.

The Seven Years' War. In its drive for territory and trade, the British East India Company faced opposition not only from South Asians but also from France, which had its own commercial stake in Indian Ocean commerce. Clashes between French and British naval vessels off the coast of India were among numerous episodes in a panoramic conflict among European states that lasted from 1756 to 1763. Because these states waged war in several far-flung places and because the combatants perceived it as a grim struggle for finite resources on a global scale, some historians have characterized it as the eighteenth century's "world war" (see Map 20.1).

The conflict had its prelude between 1754 and 1756 in the forests of the Ohio River valley, a region already under contention among France, Britain, Spain, and several Native American peoples. Fur traders operating from Britain's North American colonies wanted access to the Ohio and the Mississippi beyond. French troops began building forts to keep them out. When a British colonial militia under the leadership of an inexperienced, twenty-two-year-old colonel named George Washington marched into the Ohio country, a French force beat it badly, obliging the commander and his survivors to straggle back across the Appalachian Mountains. After a second French victory the following year, the exasperated British crown sent in a much larger force, setting off more fighting in North America, where the conflict became known as the French and Indian War.

In 1756, hostilities broke out in Europe, when Maria Theresa, the Empress of Austria, attacked Prussia to get back the rich province of Silesia, which Austria had lost fourteen years earlier. France and Russia joined the Austrian side, and in response England allied with Prussia. Under its king and brilliant military strategist Frederick the Great, Prussia held the advantage over Austria, though all the belligerents exhausted their war treasuries. The fighting stopped without significant change to Europe's political map.

Meanwhile, British and French forces clashed in North America, the Caribbean, the Mediterranean, West Africa, and South Asia. The British government spent lavish sums on the Royal Navy, which in the end outgunned and outlasted France, whose finances were in dire shape. By seizing Quebec City and Montreal on the St. Lawrence River in 1759–1760, Britain forced France to abandon Canada and to negotiate for peace. Under the terms of the Treaty of Paris of 1763, France ceded Canada and French Louisiana east of the Mississippi River to Britain. Britain's ally Spain was awarded the western part of Louisiana. In South Asia, France agreed to pull its warships back from the coast. It did not, however, lose its Caribbean island possessions. This outcome made a huge difference to France since the value of slave-grown sugar alone was much greater than all the wealth extracted from Canada. (The treaty also allowed France to retain sovereignty over St. Pierre and Miquelon, two tiny islands just off the coast of Canada's Newfoundland and Labrador province. These little fishing bases remain French overseas territories to this day.)

Both France and Britain emerged from the Seven Years' War strapped for cash, but Britain was now the world's top maritime power. The Royal Navy had sufficient ships and seaborne artillery to protect British merchants, plantation growers, and fur traders almost anywhere in the world these entrepreneurs cared to operate. Ships could also move raw commodities and manufactures in and out of British home ports with less risk than ever from foreign interlopers.

Revolutions on the North Atlantic Rim

FOCUS What major similarities and differences exist in the origins, development, and short-term consequences of revolutions in British North America, France, and Haiti?

In the four decades following the Seven Years' War, the political and social stresses attending global economic change exploded in violent popular uprisings. Britain's thirteen North American colonies revolted in 1775 and after six years of war achieved self-government as the Western Hemisphere's first **republic.** France burst into revolution in 1789, an event that not only turned French society inside out but also triggered war and political upheaval that gripped Europe for more than a quarter of a century. In the French Caribbean sugar island of Saint Domingue (Haiti), both slaves and free men and women of African descent banded together to fight colonial armies for thirteen years, finally achieving independence in 1804.

> **republic** A type of government in which sovereign power rests with a body of citizens possessing rights to vote to approve laws and to select public officials and representatives.

The Global Context of Popular Revolt

In the later decades of the eighteenth century, the world population, which had been rising since the fifteenth century, began to rise at a faster rate. But about the same time, economic growth appears to have ended a long upward cycle and leveled off. Wherever population advanced faster than food production, prices for the necessities of life spiraled upward. Squeezed financially more than ever, centralized states with armies and bureaucracies to support opted for the usual solution: They imposed heavier taxes on their populations and collected them more ruthlessly.

Faced with the twin burden of higher prices and heavier tax bills, rural farmers, urban workers, and enterprising businesspeople from North America to China expressed their discontent in petitions, demonstrations, riots, and insurrections. To suppress such unrest, states had to raise even more cash or risk loss of their authority. If they boosted tariffs and commercial fees, governments easily alienated entrepreneurs and merchants, whose importance to commerce gave them political influence. Literate and well-informed people were usually better positioned to protest state taxes and fees than peasants were. This was certainly the case in overseas colonies, where settlers of European descent gradually built their own power bases and distinctive cultural identities.

At the low end of the social scale, peasants, serfs, and slaves instigated numerous uprisings in the later eighteenth century against taxes and brutal labor. In Russia under the rule of Catherine II (r. 1762–1796), tax increases, relentless military conscription, and rising grain prices accompanied

Peasants attack nobles and clergy in the Battle of Kazan, 1774. Pugachev's Rebellion, like many other eighteenth-century uprisings, challenged political and social elites who exploited peasants. Russian artist Fyodor Antonovich painted this scene in 1847. He shows a priest trying to protect a nobleman from an armed crowd. How would you describe the artist's point of view regarding the rebellion?

her campaigns of imperial expansion. Consequently, thousands of Russian peasants in the Volga River region rebelled in 1773–1774 under the leadership of Emelian Pugachev, a onetime imperial army officer. Catherine crushed the insurgents, but only after they spent a year pillaging the countryside, burning towns, and killing estate lords. In China, late-eighteenth-century problems of rising population, faltering living standards, and imperial tax demands ignited several regional revolts. In 1796 the religious sect known as the White Lotus Society sparked a massive peasant rising north of the Yangzi River, preaching the imminent coming of a savior in the form of the Buddha. The rebellion endured for eight years, exposing unexpected frailty in the Qing dynasty's economic and political health.

The War of Independence in North America

The rebellion that broke out in Britain's thirteen North American colonies in 1775 followed directly on the Seven Years' War. France's withdrawal from almost its entire North American domain immediately affected relations between Britain and both Native Americans and white colonists. Indians living in the Ohio River region had preserved self-rule by astutely playing France and Britain off against each other. But this game ended in 1763. Fearing that France's retreat would encourage Britain to seize more land, the Ottawa chief Pontiac organized a multitribal military alliance, which attacked European settlers and captured several British forts. After British reinforcements and colonial militias intervened, the war ended in an uneasy truce. Not long after it started, the crown proclaimed that the lands west of the Appalachian mountain crest were to be off limits to colonial settlers. It did not want colonists starting new and expensive wars with Indians. Nor did it want them to trade or otherwise fraternize with the Spanish on the Mississippi or divert fur trade from licensed British companies.

Though the imperial army never seriously enforced this proclamation, its enactment nonetheless infuriated colonial leaders. They thought the whole point of victory over France had been to open trans-Appalachia to land-hungry farmers, including thousands of Europeans who migrated to North America every year. The colonial population of white settlers and their American-born offspring, plus African slaves and free blacks, swelled from about 150,000 in 1680 to more than one million by 1750. The colonies prospered from agriculture, craft and the export of timber, furs, fish, grain, and tobacco, and they all firmly supported Britain in its war with France. The rewards of loyalty, however, seemed meager. The economic boom that accompanied the war's early years dissipated, but colonial numbers continued to soar, causing serious price inflation and declining living standards for many ordinary men and women.

Cracking down on the colonies. The Seven Years' War left Britain saddled with twice as much debt as it had had in the 1750s. Consequently, the young and eager King George III (r. 1760–1820) cooperated with Parliament to impose tighter political control over North America in order to extract more revenue from colonial property owners. George argued, not without reason, that the colonists had traditionally paid much lower taxes than people did in Britain and that they ought to carry a larger share of imperial costs, including the costs of their own military protection. King and Parliament resolved to end this "benign neglect" and rule the thirteen colonies as they did their Caribbean possessions and Bengal, that is, as territorial dependencies existing to serve the economic and political interests of the British empire. Between 1763 and 1774, Parliament imposed a series of mercantilist laws on the North Americans—including the Sugar Act, the Stamp Act, and the Tea Act—intended to amass revenue and obstruct colonial merchants and manufacturers who competed with English businesses.

Until 1774 few colonists questioned Britain's political authority. But for a century and a half, they had been building neo-European colonies in North America, societies culturally derived from the Old World but possessing their own distinctive styles and much pride in managing their own local affairs. In the decades before the Seven Years' War, Britain had allowed colonial assemblies of elected, property-owning white males to initiate laws. Colonial leaders regarded these deliberative powers as consistent with the principles of limited monarchy that England's own civil conflict and Glorious Revolution in the previous century had affirmed (see Chapter 19). Like England, the colonies had lively public forums—newspapers, urban coffee houses, political discussion societies— that freely debated the issues of the day. After

1740 the ideas of the Enlightenment, the intellectual and cultural movement to replace irrational traditions and autocratic rulers with individual rights and reasoned government (see Chapter 19), became a popular subject of colonial debate. Consequently, political leaders nurtured deepening grievances over British "tyranny" and violation of both the rights of colonial Englishmen and the natural and universal "rights of man."

In 1774 the crown responded to growing public agitation by cracking down on the colonies harder than ever. As boycotts and street protests spiraled into armed clashes, some colonists began to think about the unthinkable—separation from Britain. Early in 1776, Thomas Paine, an English immigrant to Philadelphia, published *Common Sense,* a political pamphlet arguing brazenly that George III was a "royal brute" and that monarchy was a "ridiculous" form of government. The booklet sold 500,000 copies in a few months.

British customs official John Malcolm tarred and feathered, 1774. This political cartoon was published in Portsmouth, New Hampshire, with the caption, "The Bostonians paying the Excise Man, or tarring and feathering." The artist also depicts colonists dumping tea into Boston Harbor, though the Boston Tea Party had occurred earlier. Why do you think colonial protesters singled out a port official for such harsh treatment?

The storm finally broke when the Continental Congress, an assembly of colonial delegates, announced that the king had committed such a variety of "abuses and usurpations" that the territories had the right to detach themselves from royal authority altogether. This was the leading argument of the Declaration of Independence, a ringing statement of Enlightenment ideology: "We hold these truths to be self-evident, that all men are created equal, that they are endowed by their Creator with certain inalienable Rights, that among these are Life, Liberty, and the pursuit of Happiness." It was not inevitable that all thirteen colonies would join the rebellion. But they had many complaints in common, as well as postal systems and newspapers that helped weld them into a single domain of cultural and political communication. A fledgling sense of distinctly American **patriotism** had also been building slowly, especially among creoles, that is, colonists born in America.

> **patriotism** An emotional or sentimental attachment to a place, an ethnic people, or a way of life; in modern times often to one's national homeland.

Revolutionary war and a new kind of state. Under the command of George Washington, the rebels battled imperial forces for six bloody years. At the same time, they contended with thousands of fellow colonials who for various reasons sided with the crown, many of them ultimately fleeing to Ontario or other parts of Canada. Eager for revenge over its humiliation in the Seven Years' War, France allied with the insurgents in 1778. Spain and the Netherlands soon joined the pact, which effectively ignited another "world war," mainly on the sea, between Britain and several European powers. The Americans would likely have lost their struggle, at least in the short run, without generous European financial and military help. For example, at Yorktown, Virginia, where the war effectively ended in 1781, the British army surrendered to a rebel force whose ranks numbered more French and Spanish troops than colonists. Two years later, Britain agreed to a peace treaty that not only sealed the independence of the United States of America but also ceded to it crown territories as far west as the Mississippi.

After winning the war, the ex-colonies formed a loose union, but the central government first constituted under the Articles of Confederation had very limited authority. In 1787, delegates convened in Philadelphia to fashion a system that would yield one viable state on the world stage, rather than thirteen feeble ones. The result was a new constitution and its associated Bill of Rights. This document established a republic rather than a monarchy, defining the young state as a "social contract" between government and people. That made it radically different from the eighteenth-century global norm of autocratic kingship. Like the Declaration of Independence, the Constitution explicitly affirmed Enlightenment principles, including the idea that sovereignty is a possession of the "people" as citizens, not of a ruler commanding the obedience of subjects. The Constitution instituted three branches of government designed to check and balance one another. Also in stark contrast to European practice, the document's First Amendment stated simply that "Congress shall make no law respecting an establishment of religion, or prohibiting the free exercise thereof." The Constitution left much power to the thirteen former colonies, but it also erected a federal government with sufficient executive and lawmaking authority to convince the leading European states to take it seriously.

An astonishing global innovation in its time, the American governing charter announced that the new state aimed to "secure the Blessings of Liberty to ourselves and our Posterity." This admirable goal, however, sternly qualified the definition of "ourselves." The Constitution made no mention whatsoever of Native Americans as members of the new civic community, and the federal government encouraged settlers to move into Indian land west of the Appalachians. Nor did the Constitution's promise of liberty and prosperity extend to the enslaved. During the war, around eighty thousand African slaves fled to the British lines on the promise of freedom, though another five thousand, including free blacks, joined the rebellion. The founding fathers, however, put no restrictions on slavery in order to ensure that the southern states, whose economies depended on black labor, would accept the document. Colonial women were also excluded from civic life. They had contributed to the revolutionary cause in countless ways, boycotting British goods, making clothing for soldiers, and collecting money for the cause. But English political tradition, Enlightenment thought, and Christian teaching coalesced in support of the maxim that women belonged by the laws of God and nature in the "private sphere" of home and hearth. No state enfranchised women, with the remarkable exception of New Jersey. There, unmarried women and widows who met certain property restrictions could vote, though only from 1776 to 1807. The same social class of propertied males that had dominated political and economic life before the revolution emerged at the end of it still in charge.

In 1797 George Washington retired to his Virginia plantation after serving two terms as president of the United States. This voluntary departure, so uncharacteristic of power holders in the eighteenth century, signaled that the new nation was indeed functioning as a republic. Even though nonwhites and women were largely left out, moderate legal and political reforms favoring accountable government, individual rights, and legal equality continued to accumulate.

The French Revolution

France was another matter altogether. Its revolution and the American war shared the animating ideas of **popular sovereignty,** liberty, and equality that circulated on both sides of the Atlantic. In both cases, monarchies gave way to republics. But upheaval in France lasted for twenty-six years, counting the period under the rulership of

> **popular sovereignty** The doctrine that the sovereignty or independence of the state is vested in the people, and that the government is responsible to the will of the citizenry.

Napoleon Bonaparte, and it differed from the American experience in many ways. Fundamentally the North Americans sought to found a new sovereign state and a new government, separated from the one that had ruled it as a colony. French rebels aimed to keep the sovereign state of France but to change its government, initially attempting to reform it, then acting to replace it with a drastically different kind of regime. The American war was a harsh military struggle, but the French Revolution produced political and social mayhem, upending the established order of society and temporarily remodeling the map of Europe.

France and Europe on the eve of revolution. Europe in the middle decades of the eighteenth century was a region of multiple states whose royal dynasties claimed absolute authority over their subjects. Only in Britain and the United Netherlands did assemblies of elected, property-owning males formally participate in collective government. Nevertheless, the accelerating growth of capitalist enterprise and global trade, together with the spread of new ideas about sovereignty, rights, and government-by-reason, posed a challenge that hereditary rulers, land-owning aristocracies, and high officials of established Christian churches—the guardians of what historians call the European Old Regime—could hardly have foreseen.

France under the Bourbon dynasty had the largest population in Europe (about twenty-six million) and possessed great wealth in agriculture and manufacturing. Even after its territorial losses to England at the end of the Seven Years' War, it retained rich sugar colonies in the Caribbean, slave-buying ports in West Africa, and extensive international trade. But like so many other authoritarian states of that era, it faced deep debt, soaring public costs, and a population that continued to grow just as the global economy generally slowed. The monarchy hoped that by joining the rebellious North American colonies against Britain, it might reclaim at least some of the strategic influence it had exercised in the North Atlantic before 1763. The major consequence of the intervention, however, was a lot more debt.

France depended more than Britain did on millions of peasants to contribute to the state treasury. The central government, however, had no fair, uniform system for imposing taxes and collected them inefficiently nearly everywhere. Private entrepreneurs contracted with the government to collect public revenue but kept large percentages for themselves. Nobles and well-placed clergymen enjoyed

A faut esperer q'eu se jeu la Finira bentot

The burdens of the Third Estate. This satirical cartoon represents the three estates—clergy, nobles, and commoners—as women. The French caption reads, "Let's hope this game finishes soon." The artist included several details that signaled class differences to eighteenth-century viewers. For example, compare the aristocrat's dainty slippers to the peasant's wooden shoes. What message might the nun's hand gesture or the aristocrat's decorated hat suggest?

exemptions from almost all taxes. Royal officials repeatedly proposed fiscal reforms but had little success. About 30 percent of peasants owned their own crop or grazing land, but rising grain prices in the 1770s and 1780s fell hard on the rest, as well as on the poor of Paris and other cities. In bad harvest years, failed farmers and destitute laborers clogged the roads seeking jobs or charity. France's silk and cotton handloom industries generally flourished, but they expanded and contracted from year to year and suffered a serious downturn in 1786. Despite these volatile economic conditions, the two Bourbon kings Louis XV (r. 1715–1774) and Louis XVI (r. 1774–1792) tried to solve their debt problems by saddling the common population with additional taxes that even the most fortunate peasants could barely pay. Meanwhile, big land-owners complained bitterly that inflation cramped their deluxe lifestyles.

Peasants grumbled, rioted, and turned to banditry. But France's urban bourgeoisie, or middle class of merchants, entrepreneurs, bankers, lawyers, bureaucrats, and intellectuals, had more influence with the monarchy. This class benefited from global commercialization, and it grew about threefold in the eighteenth century. Across Europe, educated middle classes, together with sympathetic members of the aristocracy, had for several decades been fashioning a new public style of culture centered on sociable discussion and debate on the great issues of the day—science, social reform, religion, and the arts. In time, the public opinions of middle-class people who read popular newspapers and attended scientific and political meetings began to have an impact on the decisions of at least some of Europe's hereditary rulers. France had a knowledge-seeking, capitalist-minded middle class—indeed a much larger one than in North America— ready to speak out on questions of rights, liberties, and good government. The royal household, which dwelled in splendor in the Paris suburb of Versailles, tried intermittently and with little success to refute the Old Regime's fundamental contradiction—the denial of legitimate political voice to society's economically most productive sector. The educated public relentlessly pressured government ministers to face up to severe fiscal problems. There was even a spirited underground press that viciously lampooned the royal family, blaming France's troubles on its depravity and greed.

Ships sailed constantly back and forth across the North Atlantic, and the North American rebellion seized the French public's imagination as soon as it began. Here was a new country putting the "rights of man" into action. The Declaration of Independence circulated in French newspapers. Soldiers returning from the American war spread stories of patriotic heroism and the triumph of reason over despotism. Benjamin Franklin, who resided in Paris during part of the war, became a French celebrity. Moreover, French critics of autocratic government cheered Enlightenment-inspired uprisings in the United Netherlands, the Habsburg-ruled Netherlands, and Poland between 1787 and 1791, then watched in anger as royal armies crushed these movements. Poland, one of Europe's largest states in the seventeenth century, vanished from the political map as Russia, Prussia, and Austria violently partitioned it among them between 1772 and 1795. France had a tradition extending back to medieval times of royal consultation with the three main divisions of society, called the **three estates.** But no king had bothered to call a meeting of the Estates-General, as

three estates The principal social classes or orders constituting societies in premodern Europe: the Roman Catholic clergy, the titled nobility, and everyone else.

this advisory body was known, since 1614. When Louis XVI, a man more interested in the workings of mechanical locks than the political system, failed to halt the country's slide toward fiscal bankruptcy, public pressure from the middle class and some noble families finally persuaded him to summon the Estates-General into session.

Toward France's First Republic. By authorizing the Estates-General to elect deputies and convene in Paris, King Louis tacitly admitted its legitimacy as a representative body. Grasping this concession, leaders of the third estate, who were mainly professionals, intellectuals, and business-people, convened in June 1789 to form a National Assembly and to take the country's fate into their own hands. Some of the high clergy and nobility supported them. This upstart legislature proceeded to write the Declaration of the Rights of Man and the Citizen as preamble to a future constitution. Echoing the American Declaration of Independence, the document announced that the "nation," that is, the people of France, possessed sovereignty, not the king. Furthermore, all citizens had natural rights to "liberty, property, security, and resistance to oppression." This manifesto affirmed the principles of freedom of the press and religion and fair legal procedures. In the ensuing months, the National Assembly confiscated Catholic Church lands (to help pay down the public debt), made priests employees of the state (Civil Constitution of the Clergy), gave citizenship to Protestants and Jews, and thoroughly reorganized France's administrative and tax system. Millions of peasants were relieved of traditional customary fees, which landlords had collected for centuries. Buying and selling political offices was outlawed, and nearly all public officials, including judges and Catholic bishops, had to submit themselves to election. Under the Old Regime, France had 300,000 nobles with exclusive political and social privileges. The National Assembly abolished these privileges and in 1791 terminated noble titles altogether.

Meanwhile, French peasants and urban workers also mobilized themselves and entered the political fray. The country's common classes were bigger by many millions than they were in Britain's thirteen North American colonies, and they nursed profound social and economic grievances. Terrible harvests in 1788–1789 caused widespread hunger and more bitter complaints against the crown, while the meeting of the Estates-General excited zealous hopes. There, popular mobs pulled down the Bastille prison, a symbol of royal oppression, and in several cities mobs rioted over bread prices. In the countryside, farmers burned the chateaus of aristocrats. In October 1789 a small army of working-class women marched on the Palace of Versailles, compelling the king to move his court into the city.

Many women, however, came to the opinion that despite their political activism the revolution was quickly leaving them behind. In cities and towns across France, women expressed their dismay in newspaper articles and pamphlets, and some formed revolutionary associations that paralleled

Parisian women leading an armed crowd to Versailles, October 1789. Women's actions were important in many facets of the French Revolution, from mass protests like the march depicted here to publication of political treatises. The women pulling the cannon and others carrying pole weapons are wearing commoner's clothing. At the left of the scene, activists are encouraging an upper-class woman to join the march. What does this image suggest about the role of social class in the Revolution?

numerous male-dominated clubs. Olympe de Gouges, a writer and daughter of a butcher, railed against the failure of the Declaration of Rights to grant any to women explicitly. In 1791 she penned the Declaration of the Rights of Woman and the Female Citizen. This document emulated the language of the 1789 declaration but inserted women throughout. The first article of the National Assembly's pronouncement stated that "men are born and remain free and equal in rights." De Gouges wrote, "Woman is born free and lives equal to man in her rights." For holding seditious beliefs, De Gouges was eventually executed, and French women waited another 151 years to get the right to vote.

In 1792 the revolution turned more radical, violent, and politically polarized. Leaders of a newly elected Legislative Assembly (constituted in the fall of 1791 and later renamed the National Convention) attempted to guide events but felt increasingly threatened by adversaries both at home and abroad. Many pious peasants turned against the revolution because of new restrictions on the Catholic Church. Thousands of aristocrats and army officers fled abroad to plot counterrevolution in league with Europe's deeply conservative Old Regime monarchs. To preempt an attack by its

hostile neighbors, the revolutionary government declared war on Austria in the spring of 1792. By the following year, France was also at war with Prussia, Britain, Spain, and the United Netherlands. In response, the legislature drafted a citizen's army, a remarkable development in itself in a global era of professional soldiers, mercenaries, and slave regiments. The prolonged fighting energized millions of men and women to defend the revolutionary cause by forging guns, sewing uniforms, eating less bread, and volunteering for the army, which grew to more than 700,000 combatants by late 1793. War with so much of the rest of Europe gave life to the abstract concept that all people of France, jointly possessing sovereignty and inalienable rights, therefore possessed a shared identity. Still, solidarity remained far from universal. Many young men shunned military service, peasants protected antirevolutionary priests and nuns, and in the spring of 1793 a full-scale rebellion broke out in rural western France in the name of king and church.

In the revolution's early days, the great majority of French people took the monarchy for granted as the natural foundation of the social order. They could not imagine doing away with it. Revolutionary leaders, however, soon became

King Louis XVI's execution, January 1793. The National Convention convicted Louis of treason after he attempted to flee from France. This public spectacle inaugurated the Reign of Terror—a particularly violent period in the Revolution. Notice the contrast between the gruesome display of the king's severed head and the calm order that appears to prevail among the military onlookers. Why would contemporary observers have regarded Louis's execution as a turning point in the Revolution?

constitutional monarchy A type of government in which a monarch, usually a member of a family that enjoys hereditary succession, serves as head of state. Under the terms of a constitution or body of laws, however, the monarch surrenders part or all of his or her governing power to a legislature and judiciary.

divided between those advocating a **constitutional monarchy** in which the king's power would be limited (the British model) and those pressing for a republic (the United States model). Radical republicans formed the Jacobin Club (named after a Parisian spot where the association first met), and its branch groups spread across France. From 1789 to 1792 the national legislature moved deeper into uncharted political waters, finally eliminating the monarchy altogether in the fall of 1792, instituting a republican constitution, and, in the following January, decapitating the hapless Louis along with his Austrian queen Marie Antoinette. Monarchs in the rest of Europe reacted to this spectacle in horror.

The year of the Terror. Civil rebellion and foreign wars, made worse by spiraling shortages of money and bread,

deepened the mood of chronic crisis and helped push even more radical leaders to power. In 1793 the National Convention turned over much of its authority to a twelve-man Committee of Public Safety, which moved to eradicate all perceived opposition. Falling under the leadership of the lawyer Maximilien Robespierre (1758–1794), the committee set out to cleanse the nation of traitors and antirevolutionary opinions, replace Christianity with a Cult of Reason, and transform all citizens into eager republicans through cultural reeducation. To erect this "Republic of Virtue," Robespierre and his agents demanded distinctly republican songs, festivals, art, plays, names, and dress. "If the mainspring of popular government in peacetime is virtue," Robespierre declared, "amid revolution it is at the same time [both] virtue and terror."[4] To its credit, the National Convention also abolished slavery in early 1794, conferring rights of citizenship to all black males in the French colonies.

Over a period of seventeen months, the committee's agents arrested more than 300,000 people and executed 17,000 of them. Eventually, however, the Terror devoured its own and burned itself out. In July 1794, Robespierre himself climbed the steps to the guillotine along with many of his supporters.

France under the Directory. In the next phase of the revolution, the National Convention managed to write a new constitution, restoring a wobbly stability under an executive council called the Directory. Meanwhile, republican armies continued to advance victoriously across Europe, and in the Netherlands, Italy, and Switzerland the invaders set up revolutionary "sister republics." The Directory reversed the most radical enactments of the Republic of Virtue and returned to the fundamental principles of the First Republic. The "people" remained sovereign, the principle of civil equality remained intact, elections were held, and women were allowed to exert influence through political writings and activism. The Directory, however, was also corrupt and politically inept.

Napoleon's European empire. In 1799 France retreated measurably from the trend toward civil freedom and democracy when Napoleon Bonaparte took power and launched sixteen years of empire building. Napoleon followed in the tradition of rulers, notably Charlemagne in the eighth century and the Habsburg monarch Charles V in the sixteenth, who envisioned Europe as a unitary imperial state comparable to other giant Afroeurasian empires. He also yearned to restore to France the global power the last two Bourbon kings had squandered. Indeed, at the height of his authority, Napoleon liked seeing himself depicted in art as a Roman emperor.

Born on the Mediterranean island of Corsica, Napoleon rose to power through the ranks of the revolutionary army. In 1795 he took command of French forces in Italy and made himself a national hero by displaying military genius and overrunning a large part of the peninsula. In 1798 the Directory dispatched him with a huge force of forty thousand troops to invade Egypt, which was then a self-governing province of the Ottoman empire. The Directory had several strategic aims. Conquest of both Egypt and Syria would help counterbalance the loss of Canada to England and provide a valuable source of grain for the home population. By occupying the northern end of the Red Sea, France could also challenge Britain's lines of communication with South Asia and revive maritime power in the Indian Ocean.

Ruled by a Turkish-speaking military elite that prized cavalry warfare, Egypt fell quickly in a barrage of withering French musket and cannon fire. The conquerors set quickly to work to reorganize Egypt's administration and finance along lines they regarded as modern. Napoleon also brought with him a large contingent of engineers, scientists, doctors, architects, and language experts to study Egypt and prepare to transform it. The experiment, however, was short-lived. The British navy destroyed Napoleon's fleet, Egyptians organized popular resistance, and French soldiers died of infectious diseases in large numbers. In 1801 the occupiers left. Among Egyptian officials and intellectuals, however, France's shocking display of military might triggered a long debate over the merits of modernizing Egypt along these lines.

Returning to Paris at a moment of domestic unrest, Napoleon engineered a *coup d'état* (koo day-TAH), abolished the Directory, and in 1799 assumed sweeping powers under a new constitution. During the ensuing decade, he made himself master of much of Europe, even restoring the principle of monarchy by crowning himself hereditary emperor of France in 1804 (see Map 20.2). By keeping public order and winning battles, he continued to enjoy broad popular support. He absorbed some neighboring territories into the French

> *coup d'état* The sudden overthrow of an existing government by a small group. A "stroke of state" in French.

Napoleon I on his Imperial Throne. This portrait by the French artist Jean-Auguste-Dominique Ingres shows Napoleon in his coronation regalia, holding the scepter of Charlemagne in his right hand and the hand of justice in his left. He also wears a golden wreath of laurels, invoking the emperors of Rome. Why do you think the artist portrayed Napoleon displaying symbols of past imperial glory so soon after the Revolution abolished the monarchy?

MAP 20.2 The Napoleonic empire.
What might you conclude about Napoleon's territorial ambitions from the location of major battle sites on this map?

state and created several new republics as French clients. The Austrian and Prussian monarchies retained their sovereignty but gave up territory.

In creating this empire, Napoleon built the largest army that Europe had ever known, drafting a total of about 2.3 million young men and selecting officers more for their military competency than their aristocratic pedigrees. This force had remarkable morale, the first in modern history to conceive of itself less as a professional, paid, or unwillingly conscripted force than as an instrument of the sovereign French people. In the occupied lands, men and women with republican sentiments at first welcomed the intruders, and Napoleon ordered economic and civil reforms, for example, abolishing serfdom wherever it existed in occupied areas. He also imposed heavy taxes and military conscription on dependent countries, however, and in most conquered territories the local welcome soon wore thin.

Napoleon was of two minds about the revolution. On one hand, he admired enlightened rationality, the idea of civil equality, and the principle of popular sovereignty. He endorsed modern scientific research and created a state-supported

system of schools (*lycées*) for boys from well-to-do families. He had no reputation for Christian piety, but he made peace with the Roman Catholic Church, though insisting on freedom of worship. He declined to bring back the traditional French aristocracy but rather created a service nobility, that is, an elite of titled individuals whose status depended entirely on the pleasure of the state. In 1804 he instituted the Civil Code (Napoleonic Code), a rational, uniform legal system to replace a tangle of often inconsistent provincial laws. The Code embodied Enlightenment principles of private property and individual liberty, including equality before the law and freedom of contract. It also regulated numerous details of daily life, including the rights and responsibilities of employers, employees, husbands, wives, parents, and children. More generally, the Code contributed to France's social and cultural integration, and it eventually had a profound influence on European, French colonial, and Latin American legal systems.

Napoleon, however, was no radical republican. He loathed the idea of free speech if it permitted criticism of the state. He put stringent curbs on political expression, and his agents censored art, drama, and the press. The number of Parisian newspapers dropped from seventy-three in 1800 to four in 1811. He created a secret police and crushed all organized political opposition. The Civil Code reaffirmed the principle of men's intellectual and moral superiority over women, imposing new restrictions on divorce and prohibiting wives from bringing suits or disposing of property without their husbands' consent. For women of the revolution, this represented a discouraging backward step.

Napoleon's fall. In 1810 France loomed over Europe, but within six years the empire vanished. Napoleon conquered far and wide, but the imperial system was never stabilized. The emperor had no significant success against the British navy. Nor did his campaign to prohibit commerce between Britain and the rest of Europe, a policy called the Continental System, work well in the long run. As we shall see, Napoleon also lost control of Saint Domingue and its sugar exports. In 1800 he signed a treaty with Spain to recover the western part of the Louisiana Territory but then sold it to the United States three years later at a bargain price. And in Europe, people who turned against Napoleonic rule organized protest and resistance inspired by France's own revolutionary ideals. In Spain, for example, patriotic insurgents aided by Britain fought French occupying troops for six years. This was the first armed conflict to be called a *guerrilla* or "little war" owing to Spanish tactics of hit-and-run, sabotage, and assassination.

In 1812 Napoleon made the disastrous decision to invade Russia, enraged that Tsar Alexander I had broken an existing alliance. The invading force of 650,000, the largest field army in European history, fought its way to Moscow only to face an evacuated and burned city, a dearth of supplies, and a long winter retreat to Germany, which reduced the army to barely 10,000 men fit for combat. This debacle heartened France's enemies and triggered more wars of liberation. Losing the support of his own ministers and generals, Napoleon abdicated in 1814 and was exiled to the island of Elba off the Italian coast. The following year the Napoleonic era had its famous coda, when the general eluded his minders on Elba and raised a new army, only to suffer terminal defeat at the Battle of Waterloo in Belgium. Taking no more chances, the victorious powers sent him to St. Helena, a tiny island in the South Atlantic, where he died in 1821.

When Napoleon was confined on Elba, Klemens von Metternich, the prime minister of Austria, called a meeting of European states in Vienna to negotiate the region's postwar political order. The Congress of Vienna did not restore borders and sovereignties exactly as they had existed before the French Revolution, but the heads of the most important states agreed on two things: first, to collaborate to stop any of their number from behaving aggressively in the future and, second, to suppress radical republicans and other extremists wherever they reared their heads. Louis XVIII, brother of the executed king, was placed on the French throne, though under a constitution that constrained his power somewhat. The principles of popular sovereignty, however, had already sunk deep roots in France. The new Louis and his royal successors never regained full popular acceptance, and more revolutions were shortly to follow.

The Idea of Nationalism

The Napoleonic regime may have run roughshod over individual liberties, but the founding of the French republic, the country's wars with its neighbors, and Napoleon's program to centralize and integrate political and legal institutions helped bring about a new popular consciousness of national identity. Today, virtually all sovereign states share a fundamentally nationalist ideology. And most people reflexively accept the idea that a world of sovereign nation-states is "in the nature of things." But in fact, the concepts of **nation-state** and **nationalism** did not exist two and a half centuries ago, and they took on life only gradually beginning in the late 1700s.

Where and when did the inhabitants of particular territories first conceive of themselves as possessing a common national identity? Historians have vigorous debates about this question, though many agree that wherever it happened—England? the Spanish American empire? France?—literate political and cultural leaders were the first to acquire and consciously express the idea of the nation as a special kind of community. There is no doubt that the revolutions in both North America and France, and later in Latin America, activated the powerful Enlightenment principle that the legitimacy of the state, that is, its lawfulness, is derived from the will of the "people"—not from the monarch or any individual claiming to act as an agent of God. Eighteenth-century republicans, as well as advocates of limited monarchy, came to conceive of the "people" as a group of individuals sharing not only inalienable rights but also a common territory, historical experience, language, cultural distinctiveness, and hope for the future. This community constituted the "nation." National-*ism* took form as the doctrine that in order to preserve its rights and freedoms the national community is entitled to govern itself as a sovereign territory, to form a state. Corollary to that, the state and its government are legitimate only if they represent the nation's will.

Men and women naturally owed loyalty to a variety of different groups—family, village, artisan guild, religious community, and so on. But nationalism announced that individuals owed their *highest* allegiance to their nation-state. Indeed, they should be prepared to die to defend it. These ideas, that the national community has the right both to

> **nation-state** A sovereign territorial state whose inhabitants share, or are ideally expected to share, common language, cultural traditions, history, and aspirations for the future.

> **nationalism** An ideology centered on the natural rights of a people or "nation" to constitute a sovereign state.

govern itself and to claim citizens' ultimate allegiance, separated modern nationalism from older forms of patriotism, for example, popular displays of loyalty to a monarch or emotional attachment to an ethnic homeland.

In 1789 the population ruled by the king of France spoke several different languages and had strong regional identities. The revolution sometimes aggravated those differences, but it also planted the idea that citizens should take pride in their common "Frenchness." The mobilization of a citizen army, achieved by a combination of conscription and emotional appeals to the French nation, strengthened this new kind of identity. As one young soldier from eastern France wrote to his parents, "Either you will see me return bathed in glory, or you will have a son who is a worthy citizen of France who knows how to die for the defense of his country."[5]

Napoleon consistently represented himself as the supreme embodiment of the French nation. His conquests broadcast nationalist ideas across Europe, first by introducing revolutionary principles of citizen equality and access to justice, later by unintentionally rousing populations he had subjugated to put forward their own nationalist credos in opposition to French occupation. Guerrilla war in Spain, secret societies in occupied Italy, and dogged resistance in Russia were all incubators of nationalism, which in the nineteenth century gradually captured the imagination, not only of literate men and women, but also of urban workers, peasants, and colonized peoples.

A cockade from the French Revolution. Both men and women pinned ribbons like this one to their hats or lapels to show their support for the Revolution. The idea of a shared political commitment was an important building block of emerging nationalism. What symbols of shared identity have served to mobilize nationalist feeling in the United States or other countries?

The Birth of Haiti

While the French Revolution was playing itself out, another popular **insurgency,** intimately connected to events in France, took place between 1789 and 1804 in the colony of Saint Domingue, later renamed Haiti, in the Caribbean Sea (see Table 20.1). In contrast to the British North American colonies, Saint Domingue was not a European settler colony but a tropical plantation society whose inhabitants were overwhelmingly of African origin, most of them slaves. We may characterize the Haitian rebellion as the most revolutionary of all movements on the Atlantic

insurgency An organized, usually internal rebellion against a government or its policies, sometimes employing guerrilla or terror tactics.

rim because it abolished an entire social system founded on slavery. Nevertheless, the price of liberty ran high: thirteen years of brutal wars and a devastated economy.

Plantation society. In the eighteenth century, French planters exported sugar, coffee, tobacco, and cotton from Saint Domingue, which occupied the western third of the island Hispaniola. (The other two-thirds was the Spanish possession of Santo Domingo.) Together with Martinique and Guadalupe, France's two smaller Caribbean dependencies, Saint Domingue produced more exportable wealth in commercial crops than Spain's entire American empire. As in all plantation societies in the Americas, a small minority of Europeans and their descendants stood atop the political and social pyramid. But in 1790 this group numbered only about forty thousand, or around 7 percent of the colony's total numbers. It included plantation owners, colonial officers, and merchants, but also a larger group of relatively poor whites, who made their livings in farming, trade, or government. Beneath whites in rank order was the minority population of free people of African or mixed racial descent, known also as *affranchis* (freed people). This group embraced a range of economic statuses, from unskilled ex-slaves and female sex partners of white men to successful farmers with slaves of their own. The slave population, both people born on the island (creoles) and new arrivals from tropical Africa, occupied the society's bottom level. Living in a colony a little larger than Maryland, this population numbered close to 500,000—nearly twice as many slaves as in the entire United States in 1790. To meet world demand for sugar and coffee and to make up for the typically short lifespan of slaves, planters depended on steady labor imports. Between 1785 and 1790, for example, slave ships annually brought about thirty thousand slaves to the colony from West Africa.

Relations between and within these three broad social categories were tense in the late eighteenth century, the strains all related to Saint Domingue's prominent place in world trade. The poor white population included many people who had migrated from France to seek their fortunes but resented the planter elite, which controlled the bulk of wealth. The *affranchis,* despite their free status, suffered systematic social discrimination at the hands of all whites.

TABLE 20.1 Key Dates in the French and Haitian Revolutions

Year	France	Saint Domingue (Haiti)
1789	**May** Meeting of Estates-General **June** National Assembly formed **July** Fall of the Bastille **August** Declaration of the Right of Man	
1790	**July** National Assembly enacts Civil Constitution of the Clergy	
1791	**July** Louis XVI accepts constitutional monarchy but resists reforms **October** Legislative Assembly meets under Constitution of 1791	**May** French National Assembly grants full political rights to free blacks in Haiti **August** Slave uprising on Saint Domingue; Toussaint Louverture emerges as military leader
1792	**April** France declares war on Austria **September** France becomes a republic	
1793	**January** Louis XVI executed **April** Committee of Public Safety appointed and Terror begins	**September** British and Spanish troops invade Saint Domingue
1794	**February** Slavery abolished in French colonies **July** Radical leader Robespierre executed	
1795	**October** Directory government takes power	
1796	**March** Napoleon named commander of armies in Italy	
1798	**May** Napoleon invades Egypt	
1799	**December** Coup against Directory; Napoleon becomes First Consul	
1800		**August** Toussaint becomes commander-in-chief in Saint Domingue
1802		**February** French forces invade Saint Domingue to reestablish control **May** Napoleon reinstates slavery in French colonies **June** French forces arrest Toussaint and deport him to France
1803	**April** France cedes Louisiana to the United States	**November** French troops leave Saint Domingue
1804	**May** Napoleon crowned emperor of France	**January** Dessaline proclaims Haiti's independence
1805	**October** British navy defeats French at Battle of Trafalgar	
1812	**June** Napoleon invades Russia	
1814	**September** Congress of Vienna convenes	
1815	**June–October** Napoleon defeated and exiled to St. Helena	

They could not, for example, legally marry into white families. Talk in Europe of the rights of man resonated loudly with *affranchis* as soon as it reached the colony.

The grievances of the slave majority produced not merely resentment but dismay and fury. Planters and their henchmen struggled to contain those feelings by brutal repression. Creole slaves who caused no trouble might get jobs as household servants, work bosses, or petty enforcers. But most African-born slaves, who did not initially know Haitian Creole (the French-based, African-influenced language spoken in the colony), labored under the whip in the fields and mills. Slaves, however, did not lack for means of defiance. In the later eighteenth century, shippers brought in large numbers of captives from the lower Congo River region. Many of them, predominantly young males, had been soldiers in Africa and possessed military skills. Slaves on the plantations who spoke the same language or came from the same part of Africa created informal secret societies or "nations" and elected their own "kings" and "queens" following African practice. When rebellion broke out, these societies served as cells for organizing resistance.

The long revolution. Like the French Revolution, the movement on Saint Domingue passed through several distinct phases, all of them closely interlocked with events in France. In the first phase, from 1789 to 1791, both white colonists and *affranchis*, receiving news of the National Assembly, held high hopes of benefiting from the new regime in Paris. Both groups sent delegations to France to try to influence politics, and Haitian whites set up elected regional assemblies. Planters, poor whites, and *affranchis*, however, saw the revolution from different angles of vision. The richest landowners talked much about liberty, meaning greater colonial self-rule or even independence in imitation of the United States, though on terms that left slavery intact. Poor whites wanted full equality with the planter class. The *affranchis*

Revolution in Saint Domingue. Slaves and French forces alike had to contend with rugged terrain, tropical climate, and infectious diseases in order to survive and fight. Toussaint Louverture stands in the center of this painting, fending off a French assault. How might Toussaint have used the island's geography to his military advantage?

wanted equality with all whites. In May 1791, in fact, the National Assembly granted legal equality to free blacks whose parents were also free, an action most colonial whites furiously opposed. In the meantime, these three groups fell to fighting with one another on the island, each one claiming to represent the true spirit of the French Revolution.

A sudden and massive slave insurrection announced the second phase of the rebellion. In the summer and fall of 1791, slaves looted plantations, burned cane fields, and murdered planter families. Armed white militias retaliated quickly, killing slaves in much greater numbers. Slaves may have responded to rumors that the king of France had already emancipated them. Secret societies appear to have kept alive African political ideas that kings should have limited powers and rule justly. These groups, together with creole slaves who had good knowledge of colonial society, helped organize fighters and provided commanders.

Saint Domingue remained in near anarchy from 1791 to 1794. French troops arrived to try to calm the situation, but soldiers died of yellow fever and other tropical diseases at an alarming rate. The scene became even more complicated in 1793, when Spain and Britain, both at war with revolutionary France, invaded Saint Domingue to further their own strategic interests in the Caribbean.

Between 1794 and 1802, the third phase of the revolution, the ex-slave Toussaint Louverture (too-SAN loo-ver-CHURE) dominated the military and political scene. A creole slave who gained his freedom at the age of thirty, Toussaint rose to a commandership in the rebellion. A gifted guerrilla tactician who knew how to read, he successfully bridged the social divide between slaves and the other elements of society. When the French National Convention abolished slavery in all overseas colonies, Toussaint joined with French republican officials on the island to fight Spanish and British occupying forces. Yellow fever also served the resistance, killing 15,000 of 25,000 British soldiers. In 1800 the French government appointed Toussaint governor of Saint Domingue, though he founded no democratic regime. A newly written constitution concentrated nearly all power in his hands. Recognizing commodity exports as key to the island's economic viability, he also tried with mixed success to impose schemes of forced labor and sharecropping on liberated slaves to get them back to work on the plantations.

Toussaint Louverture Writes to the French Directory

After the French Revolution's most radical period ended and the more conservative Directory came to power, the Haitian revolutionary leader Toussaint Louverture feared that the government in Paris would reverse the National Convention's 1794 decree to abolish slavery in the colonies. Some political factions in Paris wanted to do exactly that. In November 1797, Toussaint wrote to the Directory, reassuring it of his loyalty to the republic and its high ideals but at the same time insisting that the freedom of his people must not be compromised.

The attempts on that liberty which the [French] colonists propose are all the more to be feared because it is with the veil of patriotism that they cover their detestable plans. We know that they seek to impose some of them on you by illusory and specious promises, in order to see renewed in this colony its former scenes of horror. Already perfidious emissaries have stepped in among us to ferment the destructive leaven prepared by the hand of liberticides. But they will not succeed. I swear by all that liberty holds most sacred. My attachment to France, my knowledge of the blacks, make it my duty not to leave you ignorant either of the crimes which they meditate or the oath that we renew, to bury ourselves under the ruins of a country revived by liberty rather than suffer the return of slavery.

It is for you, Citizens Directors, to turn from over our heads the storm which the eternal enemies of our liberty are preparing in the shades of silence. It is for you to enlighten the legislature, it is for you to prevent the enemies of the present system from spreading themselves on our unfortunate shores to sully it with new crimes. Do not allow our brothers, our friends, to be sacrificed to men who wish to reign over the ruins of the human species. . . .

I send you with this letter a declaration which will acquaint you with the unity that exists between the proprietors of Saint Domingue who are in France, those in the United States, and those who serve under the English banner. You will see there a resolution, unequivocal and carefully constructed, for the restoration of slavery; you will see there that their determination to succeed has led them to envelop themselves in the mantle of liberty in order to strike it more deadly blows. . . .

Do they think that men who have been able to enjoy the blessing of liberty will calmly see it snatched away? They supported their chains only so long as they did not know any condition of life more happy than that of slavery. But today when they have left it, if they had a thousand lives they would sacrifice them all rather than be forced into slavery again. But no, the same hand which has broken our chains will not enslave us anew. France will not revoke her principles, she will not withdraw from us the greatest of her benefits. . . . But if, to reestablish slavery in Saint Domingue, this was done, then I declare to you it would be to attempt the impossible; we have known how to face dangers to obtain our liberty, we shall know how to brave death to maintain it. . . .

It is sufficient to renew, my hand in yours, the oath that I have made, to cease to live before gratitude dies in my heart, before I cease to be faithful to France and to my duty, before the god of liberty is profaned and sullied by the liberticides, before they can snatch from my hands that sword, those arms, which France confided to me for the defense of its rights and those of humanity, for the triumph of liberty and equality.

Source: C. L. R. James, *The Black Jacobins: Toussaint L'Ouverture and the San Domingo Revolution,* 2nd ed. rev. (New York: Vintage Books, 1963), 195–197.

Thinking Critically

What evidence do you see in Toussaint's letter that he was familiar with ideas that inspired the American and French Revolutions? Along with appeals to the principles of the French republic, what argument does Toussaint make for not reinstating slavery? How would you interpret Toussaint's statement that the eagerness of some French factions to restore slavery "has led them to envelop themselves in the mantle of liberty in order to strike it more deadly blows"?

Saint Domingue fought its war of independence in the final revolutionary phase from 1802 to 1804. Napoleon, who wished to reinstate the slave regime, sent troops to invade the island. They seized all the ports and captured Toussaint, sending him to France, where he died in prison in 1803. Nevertheless, backcountry resistance continued, and French soldiers fell ill and died by the thousands. After France and Britain went to war in 1803, Napoleon decided to cut his losses and revise his priorities by selling Louisiana to the United States and pulling his army from Saint Domingue. The following year Haiti declared independence under the command of Jean-Jacques Dessalines, one of Toussaint's former officers. Unfortunately, the long revolution left both towns and plantations in desolation. The sovereign Haitian population, largely illiterate and abjectly poor, had to struggle on for decades in nearly total political isolation, its government a dictatorship in republican guise. France did not recognize Haiti's independence until 1825, the United States not until 1862.

Toussaint Louverture in command. This portrait presents the Haitian leader dressed as a European military officer. An aide waits with a saddled horse. Toussaint sits before a glass of wine. Behind him is a comfortable-looking house. How would you compare this scene with the depiction of the commander on page 597?

The Second Wave: Revolutions in Latin America

FOCUS What factors contributed to the success of revolutionary movements in overturning Spanish and Portuguese colonial rule in the Americas?

Independence movements started later and struggled for freedom longer in Spain's and Portugal's American colonies than in Britain's thirteen North American colonies or in Haiti. The prelude to Latin American revolutions was Napoleon's invasion of Spain and Portugal in 1807–1808, which forced the kings of both countries to flee. Lacking direction from Madrid, **juntas** took control of political affairs in several Spanish American

junta A committee or council that seizes control of a local or national government, especially following civil upheaval or revolution.

cities in defiance of local imperial officials. In 1810, armed rebellions broke out in Buenos Aires and Caracas. That same year Miguel Hidalgo, a Mexican parish priest, launched a peasant revolt against Spanish authority in the viceroyalty of New Spain (the imperial territories of North America and most of Central America).

After the Spanish king Ferdinand VII (r. 1808, 1814–1833) returned to his throne in Madrid, fifteen years of bloody fighting ensued between colonial rebels and Spanish troops. Only in 1828 did Spain finally abandon mainland America, leaving a cluster of new republics to replace the four colonial viceroyalties. The Spanish empire endured only on the islands of Cuba and Puerto Rico. As for Brazil, Napoleon's attack on Portugal in 1807 obliged the royal government to leave Lisbon, cross the Atlantic, and reconstitute itself in Rio de Janeiro. In 1822 Brazil achieved independence without a long revolutionary struggle, in large measure because the reform-minded Prince Dom Pedro refused to accompany his father King João VI (r. 1816–1826) back to Portugal at the end of the Napoleonic interlude. Instead, he cooperated with the Brazilian propertied elite to head a new constitutional monarchy.

Colonial Society on the Eve of Rebellion

In both Spanish America and the thirteen British colonies, revolts started when political and economic grievances against European imperial masters became intolerable. In both cases, property-owning white creoles led the movements after failing to gain relief from onerous taxes and mercantilist policies that choked business and trade. And in both cases, Enlightenment ideas about rights and liberties provided ideological fuel for insurgency. Latin American leaders also drew on the North American and French revolutions for models of resistance and republican government.

Nevertheless, the differences between the British and Spanish spheres of revolution were striking. First, the Spanish empire was much larger geographically and culturally more complex than Britain's thirteen colonies. Huge distances separated cities from one another, overland transport was rudimentary, and the empire's major regions, each with distinctive climate, ecology, and ethnolinguistic groups, maintained only irregular contacts with one another. The Spanish viceroyalties also differed from the British colonies in the makeup of their social hierarchy. In North America, people of European descent substantially outnumbered black slaves and Indians. In Spanish America as a whole it was the reverse. Of the seventeen million or so inhabitants, Indians accounted for about 44 percent, *castas* (people of mixed ancestry) 32 percent, whites 19 percent, and blacks 5 percent. These ratios varied from one part of the empire to another, but colonial law and cultural practice preserved a fairly uniform and inflexible social hierarchy: *Peninsulares* (whites born in Europe) stood at the apex of privilege and power, white creoles occupied the second level, and then *castas*, Indians, and blacks followed in descending order (see Chapter 18). Largely because of this combination of geographical and human factors, colonial rebels found themselves launching several uprisings rather than one.

The white creole property-owners at the forefront of the independence movements had distinctive aspirations. They harbored simmering resentments against *peninsulares,* who often lived in America temporarily but nonetheless cornered the high positions as officials, military men, and Catholic clerics. *Peninsulares* made up less than 5 percent of the white population, but they habitually touted their social superiority and sometimes accumulated great wealth before returning to Spain. The crown enacted political reforms in the eighteenth century, but like the British in North America, they did this, not to extend local liberties, but to keep order, control the flow of trade, and tax subjects more efficiently. In contrast to the thirteen colonies, Spanish America had never been allowed colonial legislatures where propertied creoles might exercise local authority or vent grievances. Creole leaders denounced these injustices, knowing that it was they, not *peninsulares,* who largely built the Spanish American economy—its haciendas, mines, plantations, and export trade.

Creoles and *peninsulares,* however, found common ground quickly enough when it came to complaints from the classes below *them* on the social scale. In most of Spanish America, the two white groups peered down on a mass of peasants, ranch hands, servants, and slaves whose numbers far exceeded theirs. They generally shared a determination to keep those classes in their "proper place" as compliant laborers and social inferiors. As much as creoles chafed under Spanish authoritarianism, hardly any of them wanted a social revolution "from the bottom." In the 1790s most creoles recoiled at news of the French terror and of slaves burning Haitian plantations. When the insurgent priest Hidalgo raised Mexican Indians and *mestizos* (people of mixed white and Indian descent) against Spanish oppression and failed to stop killings of white property owners, many creoles turned against him. Spanish troops caught and executed Hidalgo in 1811, though the rural rebellion continued.

The Wars of Independence

Despite creole fears of losing control of events, the pace of change accelerated rapidly after 1810. Many leaders hesitated at first to renounce allegiance to King Ferdinand VII but finally despaired of his ever agreeing to negotiate over the political liberties they thought they deserved. In 1814,

Father Miguel Hidalgo and the Declaration of the War of Independence. This large mural shows two aspects of Mexico's fight for independence from Spain. On the left, Father Hidalgo proclaims "The Cry of Dolores" on September 16, 1810, voicing the resistance of Indians and other commoners to the rule of a small minority. On the right, members of the elite debate the terms of independence. Mexican artist Juan O'Gorman painted the mural in Chapultepec Castle, a former royal residence converted to a national history museum in 1939. What political or social purpose might O'Gorman have intended this mural to serve more than a century after the revolution?

José de San Martín: Liberator of the Southern Andes

José de San Martín (1778–1850) was born in Argentina, the son of an imperial lieutenant-governor. His *peninsular* parents took him to Spain when he was a child, and there he joined the army as a cadet at the age of eleven. He first saw action in 1791 in a fight against Muslim forces for control of the North African port of Oran. Later he won distinction in the Spanish struggle against Napoleon. Attracted to the political reform ideas swirling through Europe, he left the army in 1811 and sailed for Buenos Aires, where creole rebels had declared independence. He organized an army of resistance in far western Argentina and in January 1817 led a force of five thousand soldiers, a majority of whom were blacks and mulattoes, across frigid, 12,000-foot passes of the southern Andes to Chile. The Andes crossing severely weakened his army, but he nonetheless achieved an extraordinary logistical feat. In February his forces ousted Spanish and loyalist troops from Santiago, Chile's main city.

The Chilean land-owning class offered San Martín the country's presidency, but, declining political office, he planned an attack to liberate the viceroyalty of Peru. Because a thousand miles and the stark Atacama Desert separated Santiago from Lima, capital of Peru, he collaborated with the British navy in 1820 to transport his army up the coast. A cautious commander, he landed north of Lima, then waited a year hoping that because he was nearby the urban population would rise up against their Spanish masters. This did not happen, but when he finally advanced on the city, the viceroy and his forces fled. He entered Lima in July 1821, though only after the local creole leaders declared independence. "I have no ambition to be the conqueror of Peru," he protested. "The country has now become sensible of its true interests, and it is right the inhabitants should have the means of expressing what they think."

San Martín reluctantly agreed, however, to take command as Protector of Peru. In this office he immediately started making liberal reforms. He liberated Indians from tribute payments and forced labor, and he proclaimed that children born of slaves after independence must be free. In a decree foreshadowing the new era of nationalism, he declared, "The aborigines [indigenous population] shall not be called Indians or natives; they are children *and* citizens of Peru and they shall be known as Peruvians." Lima's conservative creole class, however, largely opposed the Protector's reforms, and his honeymoon with them ended quickly.

In mid-1822 San Martín went to northern Peru to meet with Simón Bolívar, whose army was moving south through Ecuador. No one knows what the two generals said to each other, but according to an eyewitness they emerged from the meeting "frowning gravely." They had conflicting visions of the ex-empire's political future. In any case Bolívar held the stronger military hand and was eager for political power. He carried through Peru's liberation, effectively concluding the Spanish American wars of independence, then took office as president of both Peru and Gran Colombia. San Martín, meanwhile, returned to Lima, resigned his office two months later, and eventually made his way back to Europe. Bolívar, after struggling to hold Gran Colombia together, died of tuberculosis in 1830. San Martín passed away quietly in his daughter's house near Paris in 1850, outliving Bolívar by twenty years.

General José de San Martin.

Thinking Critically

What factors do you think might have motivated San Martín to leave South America after the Spanish defeat rather than remain to play a political role in one of the new republics?

---

after the French withdrew from Spain and Ferdinand returned to Madrid, he sent a large force to smash the American insurrections.

At first, Spanish troops, in collaboration with *peninsulares* and creoles who remained loyal to the crown, went on the offensive. The rural revolt in Mexico became fragmented, and the Spanish administration suppressed creole demands for free elections. After 1816, however, the military situation began to change. Rebel leaders from Mexico to Argentina doggedly continued to fight, and the government in Spain, battling both serious debt problems and urban protesters demanding limited monarchy, could not afford to send more soldiers to America. In the far south, José de San Martín ousted the Spanish from Chile and much of Peru. In the northern viceroyalty of New Granada, Simón Bolívar, a creole land-owner, welded together a rebel army of creoles, *castas,* cowboy cavalry from the Venezuelan plains, and even slaves, who were promised emancipation.

By 1821 this force seized the regions that are now Venezuela and Colombia and in the next four years defeated royalist armies in Ecuador and Peru.

Leaders of Spanish American independence movements had a variety of ideas about the precise form that new sovereign governments should take. Simón Bolívar was a republican, an advocate of governance by the propertied creole class, a relentless political infighter, and for nearly a decade the authoritarian president of the short-lived republic of Gran Colombia. José de San Martín, by contrast, was a constitutional monarchist, a liberal reformer, and a gifted general who had little stomach for politics.

Mexico achieved independence following a chain of events closely intertwined with political developments in Europe, where a revolt in 1820 persuaded Ferdinand VII to accept a constitution that would limit his authority and establish a legislature. This turn of events, which the Mexican viceroy supported, revived creole hopes and impelled both them and the *peninsulares* to try to achieve political change without violent revolution. Augustín de Iturbide, a creole and a royalist military commander, came to the fore to broker a compromise among all social groups, aiming to safeguard the interests of *peninsulares,* creoles, the Catholic Church, and the army, though he also promised legal equality for all Mexicans except slaves. In effect, a conservative leadership maneuvered a sort of counter-revolution against the radical populist rebels that Hidalgo had represented. Indeed, Iturbide took power in 1821 as "constitutional emperor" of Mexico. Ten years of fighting, however, left the country in bad economic straits. Iturbide proved to be an inept decision maker, and in 1823 disgruntled army officers forced him out, replacing the short-lived monarchy with a republic.

Many Young States

Some independence leaders, notably Bolívar, had visions of leading Spanish America quickly to prosperity and world influence as a single super-federation in imitation of the United States. Creole property-owners throughout the former empire shared commercial interests, spoke Spanish, read the newspapers that sprang to life in the major cities, and, for the most part, thought of themselves as "Americanos" with a common history of discrimination at the hands of *peninsulares.* But union was not to be. Spanish America extended about eight thousand miles from California to Cape Horn, and regional cultural identities and political interests had hardened over three centuries of imperial rule. Creole elites in different regions had little experience working together. In any case they aimed first to substitute themselves for royal officials in the *existing* administrative units. Even partial federation plans failed. Bolívar's Gran Colombia quickly fragmented into Venezuela, Colombia, Ecuador, and eventually Panama. The viceroyalty of Rio de

Independent Latin American states in 1830

MAP 20.3 The Americas in 1830.
What geographical factors might help explain why Spain's American empire broke initially into eleven sovereign states rather than remaining united as one?

La Plata fractured into Argentina, Paraguay, Uruguay, and Bolivia (see Map 20.3). The United Provinces of Central America lasted as a unitary state until 1840 and then broke into five small republics. By contrast, enormous Brazil, despite deeply embedded regionalisms, managed to hold together, partly because of the astute leadership of the young king Dom Pedro and partly because the slave population numbered in the millions, persuading white elites that they had better stick together.

In both Spanish America and Brazil, property-owning males of European descent occupied the pinnacle of the social hierarchy both before and after the wars of independence.

Revolutionary leader Manuela Sáenz (1797–1856). A military strategist, soldier, politician, and activist, Sáenz played an important role in Latin American independence. As with many other politically engaged women, postindependence histories downplayed her participation. Historians have only recently begun to investigate her political and cultural significance, instead of focusing on the relationship she had with Simón Bolívar. How would you account for the changing perceptions of women's contributions to Latin American independence movements?

As in the young United States, profound social and economic inequalities remained to be addressed. In the first decades of independence, all the new states except Brazil and the remaining Spanish colonies of Cuba and Puerto Rico abolished slavery. Even so, Indians and free blacks participated little in public life, and castas climbed social and political ladders at a discouraging pace. Women of all classes fought valiantly in the wars, and several gained fame as patriots. Juana Azurduy, a Bolivian casta, led a cavalry charge against Spanish troops in 1816. Gertrudis Bocanegra served as a courier for Mexican rebels, as many women did, until the Spanish caught and executed her. Manuela Sáenz, the illegitimate daughter of an affluent *peninsular* and the mistress of Simón Bolívar, served the revolutionary movement as intelligence agent, fighter, nurse, and postindependence politician. The freedom movements, however, left male patriarchy largely intact. Nowhere in Latin America did women achieve voting rights or liberalization of restrictive marriage laws. Rather, their men folk expected them to observe the new age of independence from home.

. . .

Conclusion

The violent and sometimes chaotic revolutions that took place in Europe and the Western Hemisphere between 1775 to 1830 firmly planted in the human imagination the novel idea that a community of people welded together by shared rights and responsibilities could form a sovereign state. This idea clashed head on with the principle—conceived thousands of years earlier—that the state existed of, by, and for its ruling elite of kings, queens, aristocrats, generals, and priests. We should not conclude, however, that the modern revolutions spelled the triumph of democracy around the Atlantic rim or anywhere else. When Britain lost its thirteen North American colonies, it did not then proceed to prevent trouble in colonized Ireland, South Asia, or the Caribbean by granting popular rights and freedoms. Rather, the crown did its utmost to shore up its authoritarian power. At home, the British government gave the vote to more adult males in 1832 but continued to respond to popular political protests with police repression and restrictions on speech and assembly. In France, radical democratic revolution shifted to Napoleonic despotism, then in 1815 to the restoration of yet another King Louis and a constitution that rigidly limited voting rights. The Congress of Vienna either restored royal autocrats to their thrones or endorsed conservative constitutional monarchies. Haiti went quickly from a democracy of liberated slaves to a politically isolated dictatorship. In the new Latin American republics, propertied elites or rural warlords took full charge of affairs, leaving Indians, blacks, and castas nearly as politically marginalized as they had been under Spanish or Portuguese rule. The young United States not only kept 10 percent of its population in slavery but also launched its own imperial adventure to conquer and subjugate Native Americans. As of 1830, a large majority of the world's population continued to live as subjects of monarchs who suffered no formal limits on their power.

Nevertheless, 1830 represented a transitional moment in the modern era. In the following decades, the complexities and uncertainties of the rapidly changing world economy impelled more communities to demand rights, liberties, and national self-determination. More urban workers and country peasants mobilized themselves to take part in public life, more males gained voting and officeholding rights in particular countries, opponents of slavery and the slave trade gained strength, and the ideas that fueled the Atlantic revolutions began to arouse literate men and women in cities across Asia and Africa.

• • •

Key Terms

American Revolution 599
British East India Company 579
constitutional monarchy 591
coup d'état 592
French Revolution 587
Haitian Revolution 595
insurgency 595

junta 599
Mysore state 582
nation-state 594
nationalism 594
patriotism 587
popular sovereignty 587
Pugachev's Rebellion 585

real wages 580
republic 584
Seven Years' War 583
three estates 589
trans-Atlantic slave trade 579
U.S. Constitution 587
White Lotus Rebellion 585

Change over Time

1722	The Safavid empire in Persia collapses after allowing its gunpowder army to deteriorate.
1756–1763	England, France, and their allies clash in Europe and abroad during the Seven Years' War.
1757	The British East India Company begins to seize territory in India.
1761–1799	South Asia's Mughal empire breaks apart; the Mysore state is established in southern India.
1768–1774	The Ottoman empire loses significant territory in war with Russia.
1773–1774	The Pugachev peasant rebellion erupts in Russia during the reign of Catherine II.
1775–1781	British colonists fight for independence in the American Revolution.
1780s	The trans-Atlantic slave trade reaches its numerical peak.
1787	The U.S. Constitution is signed by state delegates meeting in Philadelphia.
1789–1799	French government and society is transformed by the French Revolution and a series of revolutionary councils.
1789–1804	The plantation colony of Saint Domingue wins independence from France and an end to the slave regime in the Haitian Revolution.
1796–1814	The White Lotus peasant rebellion weakens Qing China.
1798	French forces led by Napoleon capture the Ottoman province of Egypt.
1799–1814	France embarks on empire building under Napoleon Bonaparte.
1810–1828	Wars of independence erupt across Latin America.

Please see end of book reference section for additional reading suggestions related to this chapter.

21 Energy and Industrialization
1750–1850

George and Robert Stephenson's *Rocket* locomotive.

anny Kemble, a young London stage actress, had an exciting experience in the summer of 1830. She received an invitation to ride on a test run of the *Rocket,* a steam-driven locomotive engine built to carry passengers and freight between Liverpool, England's busy west coast port, and the cotton-textile-producing city of Manchester thirty miles to the east. Designed by George and Robert Stephenson, a father and son team, the *Rocket* could pull coaches and flatcars at speeds in excess of thirty miles per hour. "You cannot conceive what that sensation of cutting the air was," Fanny later wrote. "The wind, which was strong, or perhaps the force of our thrusting against it, absolutely weighted my eyelids down. . . . When I closed my eyes this sensation of flying was quite delightful, and strange beyond description; yet strange as it was, I had a perfect sense of security, and not the slightest fear."[1] Though Kemble thrilled at the locomotive's power, her confidence in the safety of rail transport was not entirely warranted. When the Liverpool and Manchester Railway formally opened on September 15 with eight locomotives pulling passengers between the two cities on parallel tracks, William Huskisson, a member of Parliament, died of injuries suffered after he slipped and fell into the path of an oncoming train.

Despite this disaster, the Liverpool and Manchester line, the world's first fully operational intercity railroad, proved an immediate success. Not only did it move passengers at unheard of speeds, but it soon supplanted the local canal network by reducing from days to hours the time it took to transport cotton bales from the Liverpool docks to Manchester. By 1838, Britain had 743 miles of track; by 1850, it had 6,088. By then, rail lines were stretching out across continental Europe, the United States, Canada, Russia, and, a few years later, India.

Early locomotives could burn wood or charcoal in their fireboxes to heat water for steam, but they also used coal or its more efficient chemical derivative, called coke. At the time the coke-burning *Rocket* went into service, humans had long known the potential of coal as a source of useful energy. The nineteenth-century development we call the energy revolution, however, began to transform humankind's relationship to the whole material world. The marriage of coal and pressurized steam enabled our species to smash through limits on economic growth that had been in place for 200,000 years. This breakthrough was a key characteristic of the industrial revolution, an unprecedented surge in human capacity to organize production, manufacture goods, innovate technologically, and manipulate the planet's natural and physical environment.

The first section of the chapter introduces the energy revolution, the development that began barely two centuries ago and soon enabled humans to exploit immense stores of energy concentrated in underground hydrocarbon deposits. Our species also began to master the technical means to convert this treasury into useful mechanical power. These developments transformed the earlier ecological system under which human society had invented agriculture, built cities, forged empires, and created complex systems of commercial and cultural interchange.

The second part of the chapter examines how the exploitation of coal and steam led to an immense increase in the scale of industry early in the nineteenth century. This investigation requires a close look at Britain and the remarkable technological and social changes that took place there. That relatively small country, however, had complex economic and political connections with other parts of the world. Large-scale industrialization would not have occurred in Britain when it did if those connections had not existed. From the start, therefore, the industrial revolution was a

• • •

global development, an event inseparable from multifaceted changes in the wider world economy.

In the final section of the chapter we explore how quickly steam-powered industrial production became a global phenomenon. Technical innovation and factory building continued apace in Britain in the first half of the nineteenth century, and industrialization began to take hold in eastern North America and continental Europe. Egypt emerged as a site of early experimentation with steam power, though its particular experience revealed the great pressures peoples in many parts of the world came under to supply raw materials rather than develop their own industrial economies. Britain took a commanding lead in world commerce, a status made possible by its unrivaled production of textiles and other exportable products and by an immensely powerful navy deployed to advance the state's interests around the world. Industrialists and international merchants became advocates of free trade, arguing that if countries lowered their barriers to foreign imports, especially British ones, everyone would ultimately benefit. In the realm of ideas, the tenets of free trade were woven into the more complex ideology of liberalism, a body of political and economic thought that guided the expansion of the capitalist world economy throughout the nineteenth century.

A Panoramic View

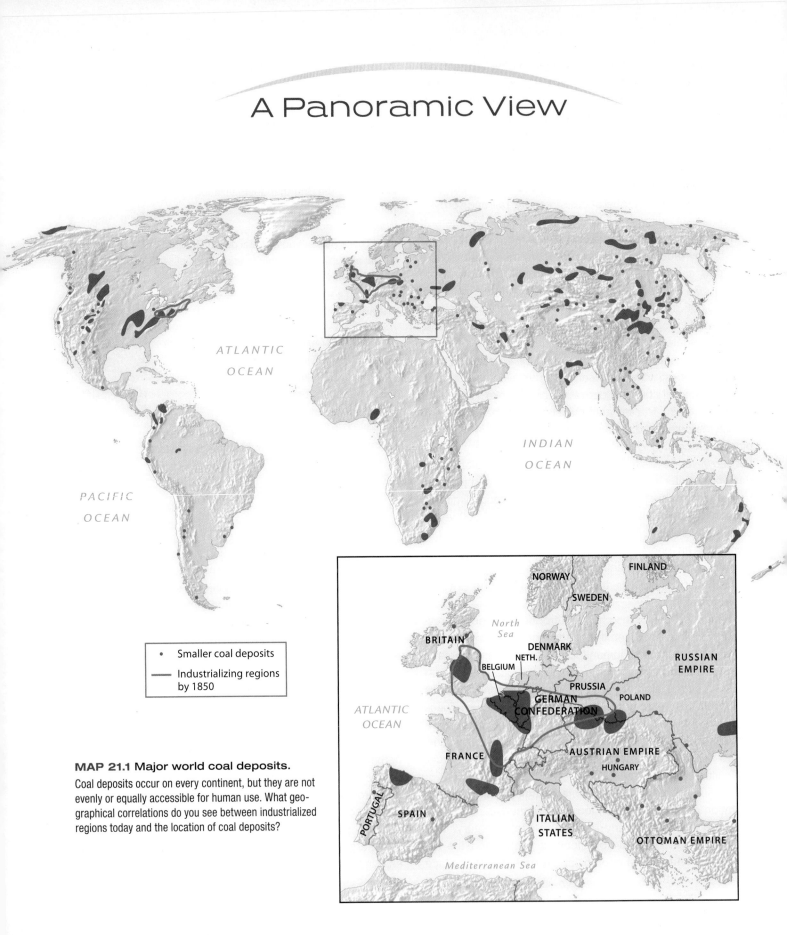

MAP 21.1 Major world coal deposits.

Coal deposits occur on every continent, but they are not evenly or equally accessible for human use. What geographical correlations do you see between industrialized regions today and the location of coal deposits?

Smaller coal deposits

Industrializing regions by 1850

The Energy Revolution

FOCUS What were the basic features of the energy revolution, and why did it represent a critical turning point in human history?

During most of our history, humans have had access only to sources of energy concentrated on the surface of the earth, or barely below it. Solar rays blanket the face of the planet, where plants convert that radiation into chemical energy through photosynthesis. A thin film of arable soil and the uppermost layer of the seas have throughout most of our history provided the food that we and our domesticated animals consume, then transform into muscle and brain energy required for useful work. The earth's outer membrane has also supplied the biomass (wood and other plant material) that humans have burned to release heat energy for light, warmth, cooking, pot making, and metal forging. Within the past few thousand years, inventors began to construct sailing ships, windmills, and waterwheels, which harnessed a little of the mechanical (kinetic) energy produced by surface winds and flowing water. But less than two hundred years ago, people and draft animals were still the chief "prime movers."

The Fuel That Lies Beneath

In some parts of the world, immense stocks of untapped energy lay deep below the earth's surface. From thousands to hundreds of millions of years ago, plant matter became submerged under layers of water, mud, and rock. Consequently, some of the energy stored in this matter did not dissipate but remained intact and, under relentless heat and pressure, became fossilized and densely concentrated, producing coal, crude oil, and natural gas, also known as **fossil fuels.** As one historian has put it, deep coal deposits are energy-rich "subterranean forests," biomass that once stood green and leafy in the sunshine (see Map 21.1).[2]

fossil fuels Hydrocarbon deposits, especially coal, crude oil, and natural gas, derived from the remains of once-living plant and animal organisms; these deposits are burned to produce heat energy.

Until the eighteenth century, people could get at deposits of burnable fossil matter only where they could find them quite near the ground. In China, Japan, Europe, and other regions, people have mined coal from surface outcrops, washouts, or open pits since ancient times, and they have known that coal burns hotter and slower than an equivalent weight of wood or charcoal. From at least the tenth century, artisans who built China's flourishing iron industry used large quantities of coal, along with wood and charcoal, to heat blast furnaces. This technology worked well in northern China for several hundred years because abundant deposits of iron ore and coal were close to each other. No premodern society, however, had the knowledge or skills to exploit coal's full potential. Coal gives off more harmful gases than wood does, and burning coal in an open fire or in an inefficient furnace captures little of its stored heat energy. Moreover, deep hard-rock coal mining was beyond any society's technical capacity before the eighteenth century. Extracting and concentrating the heat energy of petroleum or natural gas presented even bigger technical problems.

The **energy revolution** got under way only when people figured out how to mine coal on a much larger scale and then convert it more efficiently into heat energy and horsepower. This happened in connection with two nearly simultaneous developments. One was the invention of machines, initially driven by animals, windmills, or waterwheels, that could produce sustained, powerful repetitive motion in order to manufacture products in unprecedented quantities and at record speeds. These devices could replace muscle action, for example, to spin yarn or weave cloth. The use of mechanical devices for manufacturing or for lifting water has a long history. Individually operated machines for reeling and winding silk filaments came into use in China no later than the eleventh century. About the same time, innovators in Muslim Southwest Asia invented mechanical devices to twist silk thread. In other words, the pioneers of the **industrial revolution** did not invent mechanized manufacturing. Rather they invented more complex and efficient machines for performing repetitive tasks, and they put them into use on a much larger scale.

energy revolution The massive increase of useful heat energy made available to humans by extracting and burning fossil fuels.

industrial revolution The technological and economic processes whereby industrialization based on fossil-fuel energy, steam engines, and complex machines led to worldwide economic, social, and environmental transformations.

The second big development was the invention of the steam engine. Fundamentally, this is a mechanism that puts steam under pressure to drive a piston (or multiple pistons) up and down in a closed cylinder and to do it efficiently enough to generate repetitive force that humans, animals, or waterwheels could not match. Engineers first connected steam engines to pumps to lift groundwater from coal or other mines, but this innovation immediately suggested numerous other applications of pressurized steam. Thus, the power of steam engines and manufacturing machines became intertwined.

By the early nineteenth century, a process of self-sustaining innovation began to take hold. New energy sources, machines, production methods, technical ideas, and markets for goods interacted dynamically, stimulating more innovations, which fed back positively on one another. Economic thinkers began to talk of the possibility of unremitting, self-generating innovation, and with it continuous economic growth. "From west to east, and from north to south," an official of the Liverpool and Manchester Railway declared exuberantly in 1830, "the mechanical principle, the philosophy of the nineteenth century, will spread and extend itself. . . . The genius of the age, like a mighty river of the new world, flows onwards, full, rapid, and irresistible."[3]

The End of the Biological Old Regime

In Chapter 20 we described the European Old Regime as the socially rigid and politically authoritarian system that existed in Europe before the French Revolution. More recently, scholars have introduced the concept of the **biological old regime.** This is the idea that for all of history up to the late eighteenth century, plants,

biological old regime Human history before the nineteenth century, when economic production depended almost entirely on capturing flows of energy from the sun.

animals, and people all depended for survival on the day-to-day stream of energy from solar radiation. Humans cannot in any continuous way increase the amount of solar energy that reaches the surface of the earth and makes plants grow. Consequently, the resources of the land are finite. Exploiting them involves tradeoffs: Cutting forests to provide a source of heat means that less wood is available to build houses or ships; using land to pasture animals means that less is available for crops.

These constraints on land meant that not even the richest societies could break through thick ceilings on productive growth. In premodern times, if a society expanded its territories or achieved a burst of technical creativity, it might produce more food and manufactures for several decades or even centuries. The majority of its people might enjoy rising incomes and living standards. In such prosperous times, population typically increased. But that growth eventually outran the rate of economic advance. In other words, more people put pressure on the land's finite resources. Consequently, production of food and goods slowed down again, and living standards, except for the wealthiest and most powerful class, declined. Moreover, the biological old regime had a collection of pranks to play on a productive society. Droughts, floods, famines, epidemics, rebellions, or foreign invasions could easily sabotage growth. Agrarian abundance depended heavily on good harvests and reasonably stable social conditions. In the eighteenth century, scholars in both China and western Europe expressed vague fears that rapid population growth was putting too much strain on both crop and forest land and that economic crisis lay ahead.

Near the end of the century, however, humans began to challenge the biological old regime's limits on growth by exploiting not only solar energy available on the surface of the earth but also energy stored underground in the form of fossil fuels. *Input* of immense quantities of new energy to propel pistons, wheels, gears, lathes, and pulleys permitted *output* of far more goods than was possible when their manufacture depended on muscle, water, or wind. This development spelled the end of the biological old regime because the rate of world energy production, and with it the production of food and material goods, rose much faster than ever before. On a global scale, the world's gross domestic product (GDP) per capita (per person), or its total output of goods and services divided by total population, rose by nearly four times between 1500 (when the biological old regime was in full force) and 1900. On a global scale, this growth nearly kept up with the rate of population increase (see graph).[4]

Population in millions

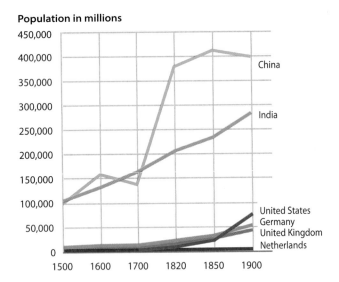

GDP per capita, 1990 international dollars

Population and GDP, 1500–1900. Which countries experienced the biggest change in population during these centuries? Which saw the largest per capita economic growth? Based on this data, what would you infer about regional differences in the relationship between population growth and change in per capita GDP?

Industry on a New Scale

FOCUS How did the interplay of events in England and other parts of the world in the late eighteenth and early nineteenth centuries contribute to industrialization?

Chinese traders in Malacca, Hindu bankers in Calcutta, and Swahili merchants in Zanzibar could recognize as easily as Europeans the potential wealth that might come from enlarging the scale of enterprises to produce and exchange goods. But in 1750, no one could have imagined any country's having the technology or capital to expand manufacturing output many times over and to continuously accelerate production in a range of industries. Over the next several decades, however, Britain, or more specifically the midlands and north of England, did accomplish this transformation. In 1815 Patrick Colquhoun, a Scottish merchant, marveled:

> It is impossible to contemplate the progress of manufactures in Great Britain within the last thirty years without wonder and astonishment. Its rapidity . . . exceeds all credibility. The improvement of the steam engines, but above all the facilities afforded to the great branches of the woolen and cotton manufactories by ingenious machinery, invigorated by capital and skill, are beyond all calculation.[5]

The "progress of manufactures" in Britain was indeed an extraordinary development in world history. Generations of historians have debated the question of how and why large-scale industrialization took off first in England. In investigating these events, we should keep two factors in mind. One is that once inventors and entrepreneurs in Britain began to understand the economic potential of steam-driven, fossil-fueled machines, the idea spread rapidly to other parts of the world. An industrial revolution was unlikely to happen independently some place else, because it became a global event in a very short time. Peoples all around the world rapidly became enmeshed in it in one way or another. The second factor is that Britain's early industrialization took place in a global frame. Its domestic economy was embedded in the world economy. We must therefore look beyond England itself for explanations of how fossil-fueled industry got started.

Cotton and the Drift to Industrialization

At the start of the eighteenth century, Britain had a productive agricultural economy, having in the previous two centuries followed northern France and the Low Countries (the region centered on modern Belgium, the Netherlands, and Luxembourg) in adopting a range of innovative farming techniques. Britain also produced and exported copious amounts of wool and woolen fabric. Cotton, however, would not grow in the northern European climate. Britain relied chiefly on South Asia, the world's largest cotton exporter, for expertly dyed and printed cotton goods. Lightweight, low-priced, brightly colored Indian "calicos" imported by the East India Company became so popular that wool, linen, and silk manufacturers feared their industries might collapse. In the words of one dismayed English commentator writing in the early 1700s, "[Cotton] crept into our houses, our

closets and bedchambers; curtains, cushions, chairs, and at last beds themselves were nothing but Callicoes or Indian stuffs. In short, almost everything that used to be made of wool or silk . . . was supplied by the Indian trade."[6] English businesspeople complained that South Asia exported tons of cheap cotton because spinners and weavers there labored in poverty. In fact, real wages were probably higher for Indian textile workers than they were for English laborers because food prices in South Asia were relatively lower.

Shortly after 1700 the British Parliament tried to plug the Indian calico stream by raising port tariffs, thereby protecting the fledgling English industry. It is not clear whether this action stimulated English business directly, but it helped inspire some entrepreneurs to investigate new methods of manufacturing textiles at home that would cut both labor costs and the price of finished goods. They did this knowing they would still have to depend on imports of raw cotton from South Asia or other places where farmers could grow it.

Textile spinning and weaving traditionally took place in farmers' homes and village workshops. Crafts workers' dexterous fingers, even though assisted by spinning wheels and handlooms, did most of the work. Capitalist merchants, however, learned to accelerate production by introducing variations of the **putting-out system.** This

> **putting-out system** A production method in which employers distributed raw materials to individuals or families, who then made finished goods, typically woolen or cotton yarn or cloth, and returned these goods to the employer for payment.

Four women engaged in cottage textile production. This 1791 print shows Irish women spinning, reeling, and boiling yarn, working in the putting-out system. Notice the child helping tend the fire and the pets in the foreground—details that emphasize the domestic location of the work. How might this work have compared to household production intended for family consumption, rather than to fulfill a contract with a textile merchant?

economic practice, first used in the woolen industry, involved wholesalers distributing, or "putting out" raw material to cottagers in a locality and paying them by the piece to spin yarn or weave cloth. The merchants then collected the finished work to be dyed, printed, sold domestically, or exported. This system was different from home handicraft industry because workers did not buy their own materials or sell their finished products at the local market.

About 1730, however, entrepreneurs began to introduce new machines. Here, the global network of knowledge exchange came into play. In small mills in central England, manufacturers produced silk thread from imported silkworm cocoons by drawing out the raw fiber and winding it evenly on reels using hand-operated machines. Designs for these devices came directly from Italy, though they almost certainly originated in China, where, as we have seen, the textile industry had invented various mechanical contrivances centuries earlier. When English reeling mills first opened, engineers studied the technology to see how it might apply to cotton spinning. In 1730 John Kay, the son of an English farmer, invented the flying shuttle, a device that significantly speeded up cotton handloom weaving.

A practical invention, however, may trigger the need for other inventions. Weavers using the flying shuttle could produce cloth faster, but workers who produced cotton yarn on traditional spinning wheels could not keep up with weavers' demand for it. James Hargreaves, a weaver with no formal education, solved the problem in 1765 by inventing the spinning jenny. According to the legend, his daughter, whose name was Jenny, accidentally knocked the family spinning wheel over one day, prompting Hargreaves to think about how he might design a machine that would draw out wool or cotton fiber and twist it into thread. The operator turned a crank that spun eight spindles at once, multiplying the work of a single spinning wheel by that many times.

Four years later, Richard Arkwright devised the water frame, a more efficient spinning machine powered by a waterwheel rather than a crank. Women and children with little technical skill managed water frames in return for humble wages. In 1779 Samuel Crompton invented the "spinning mule," a more complicated apparatus that produced yarn of South Asian quality. A power-assisted mule could spin one hundred pounds of cotton in about 300 hours, a feat that would have taken an Indian hand spinner about 50,000 hours, or five years and nine months of work! England had rivers and streams in abundance, and as the cloth industry grew, waterwheels became the chief source of power for the new machines.

These innovations in spinning now meant that yarn could be turned out *faster* than weaving machines could use it. In 1784, however, Edmund Cartwright, a minister of the Church of England, invented a power loom that could do the job of numerous handloom operators working manually. Other mechanisms and techniques came to England from the wider world. In 1785, for example, Claude Berthollet, a French chemist, demonstrated how to bleach

A worker using a Jacquard loom. The swags of punch cards at the top of the loom contained code that produced complicated woven patterns in cloth. These looms were among the many innovations that increased textile production in Britain and France. Emerging technology also meant that less-skilled workers could operate machinery that produced fine quality cloth. Why might workers have targeted these looms for destruction when they violently resisted changing working conditions?

textiles with chlorine. In 1804 Joseph Jacquard, also French, invented a loom that used punched cards to create a rudimentary binary coding technology for weaving complex patterns into cloth. Knowledge of dyes, notably a coveted bright red, passed from workshops in Ottoman Turkey to France, Switzerland, and England. Across the Atlantic, Eli Whitney invented the cotton gin in 1793. This startlingly simple cylindrical device drastically reduced the work hours required to clean green-seed cotton, triggering the opening of millions of acres in the American south to fiber production and African slave labor. In the early nineteenth century the United States surpassed the Caribbean and India as the largest supplier of raw cotton to the mills multiplying across England.

Mines and Machines

Wide, deep vaults of coal run underneath parts of England, Wales, and Scotland, and over the centuries people collected tons of it at the surface or from shallow mines (see Map 21.1). Coal consumption in Britain grew steadily in premodern times, mainly because the mineral was cheap relative to firewood and charcoal. In fact, as population grew and forests fell to the axe, wood became increasingly expensive. By the seventeenth century, coal substituted for wood in many urban homes and businesses in Britain and some parts of continental Europe. If British miners tried to dig deep for coal, however, groundwater inevitably flowed into shafts and tunnels. Mechanical pumps operated by workers or horses were too inefficient to keep up with seepage.

The union of steam and coal. English inventors, notably Thomas Newcomen, began in the early 1700s to tinker with "atmospheric engines," adapting ideas from scientific research on air pressure and vacuums. Miners put Newcomen's early steam machine to work both pumping water out of coal tunnels and forcing fresh air into them. This engine was not very efficient, but it suggested a new line of experimentation. Margaret Bryan, an English girls' school headmistress, explained in a science textbook she published in 1806: "But for this machine we could never have enjoyed the advantages of coal fuel in our time; as our forefathers had dug the pits as far as they could go: for the water rising in them from different fissures prevented working deeper;

but this machine enables us to drain all the water from the mine, as it rises to impede the miners in their progress."[7]

In the 1760s James Watt, a Scottish instrument maker and businessman, built a much more efficient engine that transferred a piston's thrust to a rotating shaft, producing a circular motion that could be applied to many new mechanical tasks. About two decades later, Samuel Crompton successfully attached steam engines to his power looms. This meant that cotton mills did not have to be located next to streams but could be built anywhere near a wood or coal source. Though a general shift from water to steam power in the textile industry took several more decades to accomplish, manufacturers in both Britain and continental Europe used Watt engines to power cotton, paper, flour, and iron mills, which numbered in all around 2,500 by 1800.

British entrepreneurs also recognized the mutually reinforcing uses of coal and steam. Coal cost less than wood or charcoal to drive steam engines; engines powered by coal permitted deep extraction of even more coal; and expansion of coal mining increased the demand for more and better engines for a widening range of industries. In the second half of the eighteenth century, British coal production multiplied more than three times. By 1800 the country was producing an astonishing 90 percent of the world's total supply.

Iron: The third component. Until late in the eighteenth century, coal had limited potential for smelting iron. Because of coal's chemical impurities, it produced pig iron, a

Children working in a British coal mine, 1844. Their small size meant they could fit into tight workspaces, so children worked in particularly brutal conditions underground. Children often labored as hurriers, dragging wagons of coal from the mining face to the surface in tunnels as small as 18 inches tall—depicted here in the middle horizontal tunnel. How does the work underground differ from work above ground in this lithograph?

substance that was too brittle to refine into usable wrought iron. In the 1780s, however, Abraham Darby, an ironware maker, found a way to use coal much more efficiently in iron smelting by first coking it, that is, by heating it in air-tight ovens to drive off chemical residues. The resulting coke had a high carbon content and did not contaminate iron ore in the blast furnace. Coke was also more suitable than coal for cooking and many new industrial processes. Two other key innovations of the late century were steam pumps designed to shoot air into industrial furnaces and mechanical rollers that forced impurities out of iron much faster than numerous blacksmiths could do it.

Iron ore was plentiful in Britain, and metal production grew five times between 1720 and 1804. In turn, many new iron products supplied the mining and textile industries. The British navy had an insatiable appetite for iron for guns and ship fittings. The farms that supplied the country's growing population required iron wagon wheels, plowshares, horseshoes, and shovels. Thus, agriculture also became increasingly dependent on steam, coal, and iron.

Steam engines on tracks. Industrialization was under way in Britain for several decades before railway lines began to compete with canals, roads, and coastal shipping lanes to move commodities and people more than short distances. Well before the eighteenth century, miners in Britain and on the continent moved loads of ore short distances by setting carts with grooved wheels on rails to reduce friction. Workers or animals then pushed or pulled the wagons. A steam engine on wheels could make a coal cart go, but only if it could generate enough horsepower to move itself, the engine carriage, and the loaded carts.

In 1800 Richard Trevithick, the son of a miner, invented the earliest working locomotive by designing a compact engine that pressurized steam much more efficiently than James Watt's engine did. Because of skepticism among miners, Trevithick had to introduce his engine to the public as an amusement ride. Doubts dissolved, however, especially after 1820, when foundries began to turn out wrought iron rails that could support heavy loads without breaking. In 1830, the same year that the *Rocket* began pulling amazed passengers between Liverpool and Manchester, a passenger line opened in the United States between Baltimore and Elliott, Maryland. The railroad-building race was on.

Iron used to make pumps, rails, locomotives, and other products to mine and transport coal

Steam engines attached to pumps to remove water from coal mines

Coal production soars

Iron production soars

Coal used to power more steam engines; coal transformed into coke

Steam engines and coke used to smelt iron

Steam, coal, and iron: a positive feedback loop. What conclusions can you draw from this diagram about the role of coal in the process of industrialization?

Working in Factories

Long before modern times and in several parts of the world, governments and private entrepreneurs learned the advantages of bringing groups of workers to central locations to manufacture weapons, build ships, or weave cloth under close supervision. The idea was to increase the scale and speed of production. Historians have also argued that tropical American sugar plantations were prototypes of the modern factory. Most of the African slaves on these plantations worked full time in the fields, but some operated the mills, which resembled modern factories in several respects. A sugar mill was a large central building that housed heavy crushing and boiling equipment. Managers imposed a division of labor, grouping workers by gradations of skill and dividing them into crews that performed different tasks. At harvest time, when the mills often operated around the clock, the sequence of cane cutting and milling had to be synchronized meticulously, requiring rigorous discipline and punctuality. Finally, workers toiled in conditions of continuous heat, noise, and danger. A planter on the Caribbean island of Barbados, writing in 1700, described mill operations: "'Tis to live in a perpetual Noise and Hurry; . . . since the climate is so hot and the labor so constant, that the Servants [slaves] night and day stand in the great Boyling Houses, where there are Six or Seven large Coppers or Furnaces kept perpetually Boyling."[8]

The spinning, weaving, and iron-smelting factories that began to rise up in Britain in the late eighteenth century had regimens similar to slave plantations. Manufacturing operations used heavy, complicated machines that could not be "put out" to workers' shops or cottages but had to be concentrated in central buildings. Mill workers did not perform every phase of production but learned to carry out specialized, repetitive tasks, chiefly feeding and tending the machines. Since idle factories generated no return on investment, supervisors had to make sure that all phases of production ran smoothly and perhaps day and night. Regular work shifts had to be scheduled, clocks and whistles had to be installed, and slack workers had to be penalized appropriately.

Workers in early English mills were wage earners, not slaves. But from the point of view of owners, who invested large, often borrowed sums in buildings and equipment, the pace of production required a strict hierarchy of authority. Profit margins were usually narrow, so owners kept wages as low as possible, though pay rose slowly as factories multiplied. Much like slave plantation owners, English industrialists preoccupied with efficiency could easily think of their workers as impersonal components of the system—units of muscle to be hired, fired, and disciplined as production schedules demanded. After 1820, when steam engines came into wider use in textile production, the pace and rigidity of work sped up even more.

Naturally enough, self-respecting farmers and artisans did not clamor for jobs in noisy, claustrophobic mills, and many complained bitterly about losing skilled occupations to machines. But despite the negatives of factory work, workers became available, notably owing to rapid population growth after 1750 and the steady transfer of farm land from smallholders and tenants to large agricultural estates. These big farmers paid even lower wages than workers might earn in industrial mills. Factory hands had little incentive to work hard, but the ever-looming threat of job or wage loss helped keep the machines humming. In central and northern England the population of urban workers rose spectacularly. For example, Manchester, a city at the center of the mill country, grew from 24,000 people in 1773 to 250,000 by 1850. Even so, factories did not appear everywhere in Britain, and in the early industrial decades the great majority of people continued to farm, do unskilled work, or make clothing, leather goods, nails, and many other products by hand.

Was There Something Special about Britain?

Britain cannot claim to be the birthplace of the factory, but it was the first country in the world where factories crammed with machines and powered by a new source of energy began to multiply on the landscape. It was also where factories became the central workplaces in a new economic system capable of turning out goods on scales previously unimaginable. It was in Britain that businesspeople began to see signs that human society might just be capable of self-sustaining, perpetually accelerating economic growth, an inconceivable notion under the biological old regime.

In the long perspective of history, large-scale industrialization might have gotten under way in some part of the world besides Britain. But it could not have happened just anywhere, because it required a location where society possessed a certain density and complexity of population, food production, knowledge, and skill, as well as access to wider networks of economic and cultural exchange. Between the fifteenth and eighteenth centuries, northern Italy, the Netherlands, southern China, and parts of South Asia all experienced periods of technical brilliance and economic flowering, only to fall back to more modest levels of growth. Britain might have met a comparable fate. Industrialization there advanced quite fitfully until about 1830, and the population continued to grow faster than domestic resources. In the world at large, the later eighteenth century was a period of economic slowing. In Britain both agricultural productivity and real wages slumped. Nevertheless, industrialization did not stall out, and sometime after 1830 Britain crossed the line from being an innovative society like others before it to one where steam power and fossil fuel set economic growth spiraling upward.

We also cannot explain early industrialization, as scholars used to do, by pointing to special cultural or social traits that British people, or Europeans in general, possessed. Historians have richly demonstrated that most types of values and attitudes—for example, individual desire to take initiative or to innovate to solve problems—are likely to be found in all complex societies. We need, rather, to pay attention to the attitudes and practices that appear to have had the strongest influence on the directions a society has taken at a particular historical moment. We must explain industrial development in England by a convergence of factors—food production, energy sources, technology, communication, government, social relations, intellectual tendencies, and interactions with other parts of the world. Also, we should recognize that Britain did not achieve a complete industrial revolution that only later spread to other parts of the world. Key processes got under way first in Britain, but many innovations in technology and the organization of industrial production and commerce originated in other parts of the world as the nineteenth century proceeded.

Food for workers. Industrialization could continue beyond a certain point only if the society could produce or import sufficient food to sustain growing numbers of men and women to work in industry rather than grow their own meals. In fact, England was an unusually productive agricultural society in the two centuries before industrialization began. Like farmers in southern China, South Asia, Japan, and the European Low Countries—all regions where population was increasing—English cultivators found ways to squeeze higher crop yields from given acreages of land. English farmers at first borrowed a number of ideas from the Netherlands. These included ingenious techniques for draining marshes, new crop rotation strategies to enrich soil, more efficient use of animal manure for fertilizer, and construction of more windmills and watermills. One distinctively English innovation was the expansion of commercial agriculture, that is, the concentration of more crop and pasture land in the hands of wealthy land-owners attuned to the capitalist market. Historians continue to debate whether this "enclosure movement," which involved transferring land from peasant producers to commercial estate lords by legal or extralegal means, improved agricultural output very much. It certainly changed the way millions of ordinary men and women made their livings. Big land-owners collected rents from tenant farmers and hired day laborers who worked for modest wages. In the eighteenth century, England's landholding peasantry nearly disappeared, whereas in France, for example, it represented the vast majority of the population. Ex-farmers moved in

A critique of parliamentary politics. England's local political officials did not escape criticism. The property qualification meant that only a minority of men were eligible to vote for members of Parliament, so politicians did not necessarily represent the interests of the majority of their constituents. This oil painting, *Chairing the Member* (1755), is the final installment in a four-part series called *The Humours of an Election*. The artist William Hogarth was an English painter, printmaker, satirist, cartoonist, and social critic. The scene depicts a victorious candidate being carried through the streets in celebration, but Hogarth's critique of an electoral system marred by bribery and intimidation would have been clear to eighteenth-century viewers. What elements of the image suggest Hogarth was poking fun at the election, and its result?

growing numbers to towns and cities, where they worked for wages if they could find work at all. Eventually, much of this growing urban population drifted into the waiting arms of factory owners.

Agricultural productivity in Britain leveled off around 1750, just when population started growing faster and industrialization was getting under way. However, like other European states that possessed overseas colonies (mainly Spain, Portugal, France, and the Netherlands), Britain had access to extensive food and fiber resources from beyond its own shores. North America and the Caribbean supplied Britain with grain, sugar, cotton, coffee, timber, fish, and numerous other products, and these resources became increasingly important as industrialization moved into high gear. In effect, the Americas provided productive land that Britain would have had to possess (but did not) in order to sustain the high rate of economic growth that it achieved.

For example, by the late eighteenth century, English sheep farmers would have had to expand pasture land by many millions of acres, which was not possible, in order to produce the equivalent yardage of textiles, produced from wool, that could instead be made from cotton grown in America or other overseas regions. By around 1800, England would have required somewhere between one and two million acres of farm land (which it did not have) to produce the food calories that the population consumed by eating imported American sugar. As industrialization continued in the nineteenth century, imports accounted for an increasing percentage of the British population's diet.[9]

British government and industrialization. After enduring nearly a half-century of civil war and political crisis, which finally ended with the Glorious Revolution of 1688 (see Chapter 19), Britain entered the eighteenth century as a limited monarchy. The king or queen remained head of state, but Parliament, a legislature elected by a minority population of male, property-owning citizens, had prime authority to govern. For example, in contrast to rulers in most of continental Europe, the British crown could not seize property arbitrarily, unilaterally impose taxes, or arrest and imprison people simply by ordering a judge or police officer to do it. British common law specified that people accused of crimes must face a jury of their peers, not a crown-appointed judge who rendered a verdict. All these laws and institutions served the interests—in fact they were *intended* to serve the interests—of people more likely to invest in technical innovation and industrial growth if they knew their property would remain secure. Compared to the continental monarchies, Britain was also a more decentralized state. That is, much of the country's day-to-day government rested with locally elected officials rather than with governors, commandants, and tax agents sent out from the capital. Typically, these local magistrates were members of the land-owning and business class and therefore mostly stayed out of the way of entrepreneurs and artisans who experimented with new machines and commercial strategies.

The founding of the Bank of England in 1694 illustrates Parliament's business-oriented disposition shortly after the Glorious Revolution. The bank functioned to support Britain's commercial growth and international trade. It issued bonds, that is, it borrowed money from British subjects, guaranteeing those loans with the capital the bank steadily accumulated. This borrowed capital was Britain's "national debt," but the bank made regular interest payments on that debt, thereby attracting more investment in it. A large part of the bank's assets went into expanding the Royal Navy, an investment that safeguarded Britain's catapulting income from global trade.

Parliamentary government, however, does not provide a sufficient explanation for industrialization. The Netherlands also had a collective government of capitalist-minded property owners but did not begin to build factories until well into the nineteenth century. Conversely, Germany after its unification in 1870 achieved spectacular industrial success under the direction, not of an elected legislature, but of a small authoritarian oligarchy. Nor did industry take root in Britain because Parliament kept taxes low. On the contrary, it taxed British subjects at a much higher rate than did France or other autocratic monarchies. Moreover, Parliament did not invest directly in industrialization. Early factory, canal, and railway builders had to depend on private startup capital, often from family and friends.

A final political factor is that Britain remained a relatively stable society throughout the early industrial decades. Although government and business achieved this tranquility partly by allying to repress sometimes adamant working-class protest over wages, factory conditions, and unemployment, Britain was a haven of peace compared to continental Europe. There, people who contributed new machines and technical processes had to carry on amid the turbulent conditions of the French Revolution, war between France and several other states, and Napoleon Bonaparte's imperial venture (see Chapter 20). Industrialization might have gotten under way on the continent somewhat earlier were it not for this protracted time of troubles.

Creative energy in science and technology.

One of the hallmarks of modernity has been continuous technical and scientific innovation, rather than the temporary surges of it in one part of the world or another that characterized the agrarian age. In the seventeenth and eighteenth centuries, Europe's scientific revolution generated a torrent of new ideas about nature and the universe, though it drew on the accumulated wisdom of all of Afroeurasia and on vast new knowledge that poured in from America following the sixteenth-century global convergence (see Chapters 16 and 19). In Europe, thinkers probed the heart of nature by subjecting it to rational, mathematical analysis and to careful observation, rather than by fitting it, one way or another, into principles and dogmas inherited from the Bible, early Christian texts, or ancient Greek philosophy. Careful observation of the physical and natural world required inventions that allowed investigators to peer deeper into phenomena (microscopes and telescopes), to create special environmental conditions (electrostatic machines, vacuum pumps, prisms), and to precisely measure observed phenomena (micrometers, thermometers, and sextants). These devices had themselves to be accurately designed and tooled, as well as standardized to ensure consistency.

To give one instance, John Harrison, an eighteenth-century clockmaker, spent decades holed up in a workshop in Yorkshire trying to build a special clock so delicately balanced that it would keep accurate time on a pitching ship. He finally succeeded, producing a chronometer, as it was called, that allowed sea captains to keep track of the time difference between a given location and the port from which they debarked. Mariners needed that knowledge in order to accurately calculate longitude, that is, a vessel's position east or west of the port of departure. In Britain, scientific work and material instrumentation supported each other. Precise and powerful devices led to new scientific discoveries, which demanded more and better contrivances to expand and compound those discoveries. John Harrison's chronometer, for example, was a crucial aid to Captain James Cook in mapping Pacific islands in the 1770s.

Researchers used scientific instruments throughout Europe, in the colonies of Europe, and to some extent in the Ottoman empire and China. In Britain, however, interest in mechanisms, engines, and gadgets, and in the knowledge they might reveal, reached the dimensions of a popular craze. Scientific societies hosted talks and demonstrations that attracted men and women from all levels of society. Mechanical demonstrations became a form of public entertainment. Aristocratic scholars, craftspeople, and machinists communicated with one another through meetings and associations to discuss connections between scientific principles

John Harrison's marine chronometer. The British Parliament established a prize in 1714 to reward the first person to devise a method to measure accurately a ship's longitude at sea. Harrison's H4, a bit bigger than a pocket-watch, proved successful at keeping accurate time during an Atlantic crossing in 1761, despite the rolling and pitching of the ship, which disrupted the mechanism of standard eighteenth-century timekeepers. Harrison's work laid the groundwork for modern watches. Why might the government have encouraged this scientific research with a significant financial prize?

and down-to-earth technical problems. From the 1750s British secondary schools taught not only the classical curriculum centered on Latin, but also algebra, physics, surveying, and other subjects considered of practical use to ambitious young men. By the 1780s academies for girls taught science and mechanics. Margaret Bryan's 1806 textbook titled *Lectures on Natural Philosophy* combined genteel religious moralizing with rich expositions of the writings of Isaac Newton.

The career of James Watt vividly illustrates these eighteenth-century trends. The son of a Scottish builder, he studied in both England and Scotland to master the arts of instrument making. In 1765 he applied this experience, as well as knowledge of Newton's energy theories and Joseph Black's work on the properties of latent heat, to improve on the Newcomen steam engine. He regarded himself as a hardheaded businessman, but he also participated in the Lunar Society, an association of intellectuals dedicated to

scientific achievement. "Geometry and algebra with the science of calculation in general," he advised his son, "are the foundation of all useful science, without a complete knowledge of them natural philosophy is but an amusement."[10] Watt's wife Annie collaborated with him in both science and business and undertook research of her own in chemistry to explore practical applications of chlorine bleach.

Britain's partiality for empirical science, that is, inquiry grounded in observation, experiment, and practical application, cannot be generalized for all of Europe. It contrasted markedly with the deductive logic favored in France, whereby scientific thinkers attempted to explain the workings of nature by rational, mathematical analysis founded on established principles. Though French technologists made several key contributions to mechanical industry, highly educated scholars in France and other continental countries showed little interest until the nineteenth century in the gears, pulleys, clocks, and pumps that engrossed British innovators.

Social and Environmental Consequences of Early Industrialization

When industrialization first got under way, no one could have foreseen how railroads, massive coal burning, and regimented factory work might transform daily life. Nor could anyone have perceived what became a fundamental feature of modernity: the continuous acceleration of change, not just in Britain but eventually everywhere in the world.

The rapid rise of global population that we associate with modernity preceded the industrial revolution but continued to accompany it. In Britain, population growth, urbanization, and industrialization positively reinforced one another earlier than in other societies. England's population grew by a little less than 1 million in the seventeenth century but by nearly 8.7 million by 1801.[11] More abundant food supplies, a wider variety of foods, more wage jobs, and improved public hygiene combined to generate this startling acceleration. A trend toward earlier marriage may have contributed as well. In Britain and other northern European countries, people traditionally delayed marriage later than in many other parts of the world. But the opportunities for wage labor, including factory employment, encouraged young women and men to start their own households earlier than if they had to wait to inherit a farm or other family property. In the eighteenth century, London's population grew from about 550,000 to 860,000, making it the largest city in Europe and perhaps the second biggest in the world, after Beijing. In the English midlands, cities like Birmingham, Liverpool, Manchester, and Leeds mushroomed as well. By 1800 about 28 percent of England's people lived in cities, a far higher proportion than in any continental European country (see Map 21.2).

Discontents of the new industrial working class. The multitudes who moved from countryside to city faced

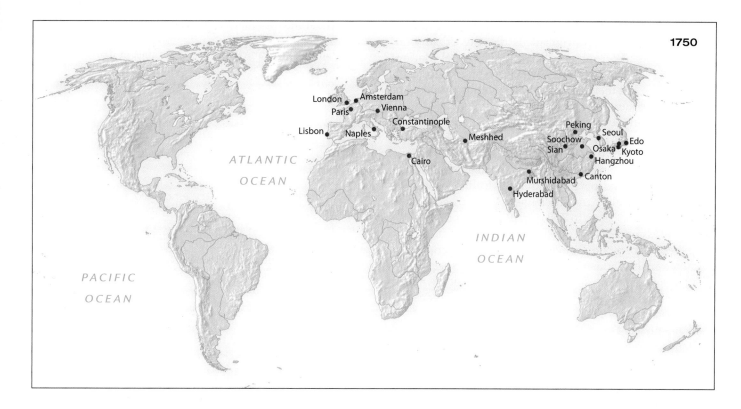

1750

London Amsterdam
Paris Vienna
Lisbon Naples Constantinople
Meshhed
Peking Seoul
Soochow Edo
Sian Osaka Kyoto
Hangzhou
Cairo Canton
Murshidabad
Hyderabad

ATLANTIC OCEAN

PACIFIC OCEAN

INDIAN OCEAN

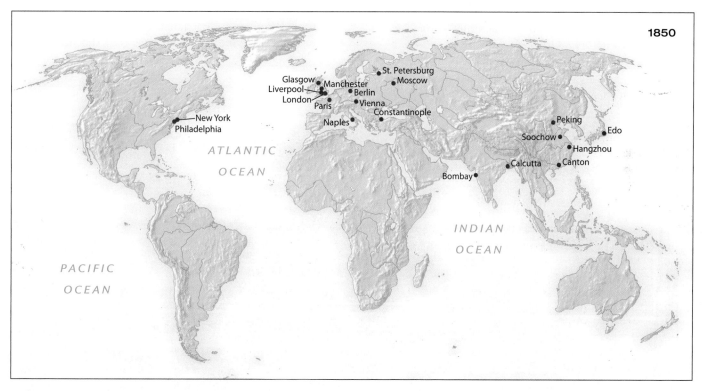

1850

St. Petersburg
Glasgow Manchester Moscow
Liverpool Berlin
London Paris Vienna
Naples Constantinople
Peking
New York Soochow Edo
Philadelphia Hangzhou
Canton
Calcutta
Bombay

ATLANTIC OCEAN

PACIFIC OCEAN

INDIAN OCEAN

MAP 21.2 The world's twenty largest cities, 1750 (top) and 1850.

Which regions of the world gained more large cities during this one-hundred-year period? Which regions lost cities in the top twenty? May a general change in the geographical distribution of cities be inferred during that century? What factors might explain increased urbanization?

sprawling slums, jammed apartments, filthy groundwater, wretched sanitation, and contagious disease. Urban working conditions also contrasted sharply with rural routines. Both adults and children typically labored on the farm from dawn to dusk, but they worked at home, setting the pace and relying on the family for support in bad times. The putting-out system allowed women and children to spin yarn and weave cloth under the supervision of a husband or parent, not an impatient shift boss. In the new factories, this way of life changed dramatically. In fact, mill managers looked to English prisons and penal workhouses for models of how to keep workers alert and disciplined. Work days typically stretched from 6:00 a.m. to 7:00 p.m. Illiterate employees had to learn to keep track of time on factory floor clocks. Physical strain, repetitive motion, and industrial accidents crippled or deformed many. Industrial workers had a life expectancy of about seventeen years shorter than the moneyed owners of the plants and machines. In the early industrial decades, neither trade unions nor labor protection laws existed.

Elizabeth Bentley, a women from Leeds in the English midlands, typified a young, female linen-mill worker. She entered the factory when she was six years old, in about 1809. In 1832 she answered questions before the Sadler Committee, a parliamentary commission called to investigate British labor conditions:

What were your hours of labor in that mill? — From 5 in the morning till 9 at night. . . .

What time was allowed for your meals? — Forty minutes at noon.

Had you any time to get your breakfast or drinking? — No, we got it as we could. . . .

Your labor is very excessive? — Yes; you have not time for any thing.

Suppose you flagged a little, or were too late, what would they do? — Strap [whip] us. . . . Girls as well as boys? — Yes.

Have you ever been strapped? — Yes.
Severely? — Yes.[12]

The British textile industry employed far more women and children than men until well into the nineteenth century. In London's silk industry in 1765, women and children outnumbered men fourteen to one. By contrast, males dominated occupations in mining, construction, and leather making. Business leaders appear to have assumed that women and girls were innately suited to work in industries incorporating new technologies. James Hargreaves, for example, configured the dimensions of his spinning jenny from the premise that a young girl would likely operate it.[13] In other words, machine textile manufacturing was "gendered" for women from the start. Entrepreneurs believed that females had superior motor skills for operating textile machines and naturally possessed the proper cooperative and submissive attitudes necessary for factory work. Women, industrialists argued, had ideal qualities for innovative industries because they did not have to

Women making pens. More than 50 women sit at individual grindstones finishing metal pen nibs at the Hank Wells & Co. factory in Birmingham, England. What differences in communal work do you notice between this image and the depiction of women engaged in cottage textile production on page 611?

Ned Ludd: Legendary Foe of Industry

The word *Luddite* is colloquial English for anyone who dislikes new technology or cannot get the hang of it. This expression originated with Ned Ludd, a character in the mold of Robin Hood, who robbed the rich to help the poor. In English tradition Ned Ludd rose through the ranks of the laboring poor to become a "general," and some of his followers wanted to make him king. In fact, he may have existed only in the imaginations of English workers. Perhaps a living person inspired his legendary personality, but as an actor of historical significance he was a composite individual, a symbolic embodiment of working-class anxieties brought on by bewildering economic change.

Political and economic developments combined in the early nineteenth century to spread misery among English workers. Britain had been fighting Napoleon since 1803, and the emperor impeded Britain's trade with the European continent. English warehouses were overstuffed with cloth intended for export. Excess supply led employers to cut their workforces, which were already reduced because of mechanization. One person operating a steam-powered loom could do the work of two hundred or three hundred people. Parliament supported speedy industrialization without much regard for the poorer classes, overturning legislation that limited the use of labor-saving devices. Although some wealthy landlords and factory barons sympathized with the plight of the poor, most agreed that economic progress came first.

In 1811, following a poor harvest season in parts of England, masked bands of laborers calling themselves Luddites began breaking into mills at night to demolish the newfangled machines that had taken over their jobs. In Nottinghamshire, insurgents sent threatening letters to factory owners ordering them to dismantle their equipment. When owners refused to comply, rioters took hammers to more than four hundred textile looms. The British government sent nearly two thousand soldiers to restore order, but saboteurs continued to destroy machines.

From Nottinghamshire, the insurgency spread rapidly to five other midlands counties. Numerous individuals invoked "General Ned" as their leader, signing his name to protest letters. In the spring and summer of 1812, food riots broke out. Some protesters claimed Lady Ludd, the legendary general's reputed wife, as their leader. At night, small bands roamed the countryside, stealing grain and demanding guns. Lead pipes, faucets, and fittings disappeared from churches and other buildings and were melted into bullets. The Luddites renounced violence toward persons, but at least one manufacturer was killed, and more than a dozen workers died in skirmishes with soldiers. Insurgents burned five factories and attacked dozens more. The movement had no coherent plan of action, but leaders demanded respect for skilled

Luddites wrecking carpet-weaving machinery.

craftsmanship, the valuing of workers as partners in production, and the outlawing of industrial machines. English authorities watched highways and taverns for Ned Ludd, but he never turned up. They tried until 1816 to arrest him for robbery, arson, and the destruction of private property, all offenses that carried the death penalty.

Mass arrests and harsh penalties finally brought the protests under control. Food rioters and machine breakers were convicted regardless of age. Twenty-four men, women, and children were hanged, one a sixteen-year-old whose crime was to stand guard outside a mill while his confederates attacked it. In addition to the people executed, eighteen Luddites were imprisoned in England, and fifty-one were transported in chains to Australia to serve terms of seven years or longer. Luddism withered away by 1816, and the general himself was never found. Nevertheless, the movement exposed worker discontent, and it foreshadowed the parliamentary worker reform and the organized labor movement that was shortly to come.

Thinking Critically

Do you think it would have made a difference to the temporary success of the Luddite movement if Ned Ludd had not existed as the primary leader or even as a real person?

shed traditions of craftsmanship that tied male artisans to old-fashioned ways of doing things.

Entrepreneurs also "sold" factory mechanization to the public as a fine way to create jobs for poor women and girls. Indeed, male artisans commonly lost work both to machines and to the unskilled employees who tended them. In 1786, for example, textile craftsmen in the midlands formally protested the coming of factories that used scribbling machines, which were mechanical devices for preparing wool for spinning: "One machine will do as much work in one day as would otherwise employ twenty men. How are those men, thus thrown out of employ to provide for their families?"[14]

As working conditions in mines and factories worsened, which they generally continued to do until the 1840s, shouts of protest became louder. In the early decades, workers expressed their discontent in petitions, walkouts, absenteeism, riots, and public rallies, but also in drunkenness, prostitution, mental collapse, and suicide. Since the new machines were the handiest targets of loathing, disgruntled workers sometimes destroyed them, or even attacked their inventors. In 1753, for example, workers assaulted the home of John Kay, the inventor of the flying shuttle, forcing him to flee to France, where he died in poverty. In 1806, workers in France organized a public "execution" of the Jacquard loom, ritually destroying one of the machines to protest job losses. In response to persistent protest and fear of disorder, the British Parliament voted in 1824 to permit workers to form trade unions to advocate for rights and better conditions and in certain circumstances to call strikes. The trade union movement, however, advanced slowly in Britain and got virtually nowhere in continental Europe until after midcentury.

"An evil and corrosive smoke." Since ancient times, cities were incubators of ill health because they put large numbers of people in close quarters with diseased animals, the smoke of burning biomass, and bodily waste. In the eighteenth century, cities throughout the world suffered from these curses. In Britain, however, industrialization and the shift to coal energy released new toxins and pollutants into the environment. Manufacturing waste poured into rivers and lakes, and water runoff from cities contaminated the surrounding countryside. Air quality declined as well, especially in London. That city's high concentration of people, houses, and workshops generated a significant differential in air temperature between the city and the surrounding countryside. When this differential became too large for normal wind movements to dissipate, it transformed the city into a more or less permanent "heat island" that trapped unhealthy gasses.

In the early industrial period, people had a poor grasp of the consequences of pollution. No one, for example, recognized the connection between urban typhus or cholera epidemics and contaminated water. But as early as the seventeenth century, Londoners complained bitterly about bad air and squarely blamed the growing use of coal for manufacturing and home heating. In 1664 John Evelyn, an English pamphleteer, deplored "with just Indignation" that "this Glorious and Ancient City . . . which commands the Proud Ocean to the Indies, and reaches to the farthest Antipodes, should wrap her stately head in Clowds of Smoake and Sulfur, so full of Stink and Darknesse." According to Evelyn, coal smoke fouled the water supply, ate away buildings, spoiled laundry, killed bees, and made people sick: "Is there under Heaven such Coughing and Snuffing to be heard, as in the London Churches and Assemblies of People, where the Barking and the Spitting is incessant and most importunate?" Those who profited from coal mining campaigned to muffle protest, arguing that coal fumes might even be beneficial because they cleansed the air of pests and poisonous humors. The physician Samuel Hahnemann wrote in 1787 that the high incidence of lung diseases in London had nothing to do with coal vapors but could to be attributed to "night life, excess of heating, drink and food, the enormous indulgence of tea . . . and the most horrifying and often unnatural passions."[15] By the early 1800s coal burning began to have a significant effect on air quality in German cities that were close to coal sources. According to an official who visited the United States in the late 1830s, the young industrial city of Pittsburgh was already enshrouded in "a dense, black smoke, which . . . falls in flakes of soot upon the dwellings and persons of the inhabitants."[16]

Industrialization and Global Trade in the Early Nineteenth Century

FOCUS What were the fundamental features of new doctrines of free trade and liberalism in the late eighteenth and early nineteenth centuries?

The foundational period of the industrial revolution overlapped in time with the popular revolutions that took place in Europe and the Americas. Few of the millions of people involved in the political upheavals of 1775–1815 knew anything about steam engines or power looms. The obscurity of these new contraptions, however, began to lift rapidly in the early 1800s, not only because machines and factories came into use beyond Britain, but also because producers around the globe needed to increase outputs of food and other commodities to supply the new manufacturing centers. Industrial growth also required that both rich and poor be induced to consume the merchandise that factories poured out. The industrial revolution evolved during the nineteenth century as a world event, occurring not only where steam engines, factories, and railroads appeared, but also where people produced raw commodities destined for mills and urban populations and where people consumed industrial goods. In other words, it occurred just about everywhere.

The Energy Revolution Takes Hold

In Britain, demand for wage workers in new factories and in all sorts of urban crafts and services accelerated rapidly after 1820. The real wages of workers, which had remained stagnant during the early decades of industrialization, began to rise. Between 1800 and 1850 the country's total population doubled from about nine to eighteen million. At midcentury half of Britain's population lived in cities, a far higher proportion than anywhere else in the world. London's population grew from about 860,000 in 1800 to about 4.2 million by 1875. Factories increased cotton production about elevenfold, a success that inspired entrepreneurs to apply steam power to many other types of manufacture. Industries that made bricks, pottery, paper, beer, and numerous other products became mechanized. In 1850 Britain's population was about 4.5 percent of China's, but Britain used fifty times more energy than China did, in large part because steam and coal drove so many machines.

The tentacles of transport reached out in all directions as private businesses undertook hundreds of road, canal, railroad, and iron bridge projects. Canal digging continued apace in the early nineteenth century because barges could move large tonnages of coal and iron ore from mine to factory. In the 1840s, however, steam locomotives proved they could pull heavy loads over long distances faster and at cheaper rates than barges, spelling the end of the canal boom. Rail lines, together with improved roads and coach routes, meant that people could exchange business and technical information more efficiently. The volume of letters and packages moving across Britain surged after 1840, when a talented modernizer named Rowland Hill inspired a project to standardize mail charges and introduce the adhesive postage stamp.

Industrialization on the European continent. After 1815, when the Napoleonic Wars ended, manufacturers on the continent cut back military-related production, triggering a serious economic slump that lasted nearly five years. In the four decades after 1820, however, steam industries spread rapidly in Belgium, France, the Netherlands, Germany, and the Austrian empire (see Map 21.3). In that period the major European powers stayed mostly at peace with one another, a condition that benefited industrialization, especially in areas well-endowed with raw materials, local labor, or natural transport corridors.

Large-scale industry advanced fastest in Belgium (which became a separate state from the Netherlands in 1831). Its

Open-cast mines at Blanzy, France. Industrialization transformed both cities and the countryside. This scene, painted in 1857 by Ignace François Bonhomme, shows the magnitude of changes to the landscape caused by large-scale resource extraction. Notice how small the human figures in the foreground are. What does this painting suggest about how people responded to these changes in the nineteenth century?

MAP 21.3 Urbanization and industrialization in Europe, 1850.

Urbanization accompanied industrial growth in the nineteenth century. What do you notice about railroads and industrial sites in Germany compared to France or Britain in 1850? What might account for Germany's less urbanized population?

plants specialized in producing coal, iron, textiles, glass, and armaments. German mine owners began to use steam engines in coal fields of the Ruhr Valley in the 1830s, though industrialization advanced slowly at first, in large part because Germany remained divided into numerous states and principalities until 1871. In France, novice industrialists drawing heavily on British technology made impressive headway in steam-driven textile and iron production in the 1830s and 1840s. French inventors also contributed numerous mechanical devices and processes, including looms, linen spinners, and gas lighting. Even so, the country did not come close to catching up with Britain in overall production, and it gradually fell behind Germany. France had a predominantly peasant population slow to consume manufactures or to move into cities to take mill and foundry jobs. In Portugal, Spain, Italy, and the Balkan lands, clusters of industry began to appear in later decades. For example, Milan, destined to become Italy's greatest manufacturing

The waterfront in Cincinnati, Ohio, 1848. Steamboats and other vessels are moored in front of a mix of commercial and residential buildings in an image captured by Charles Fontayne and William Porter applying an early photographic process called daguerreotype. They used this emerging technology to create a multiframe panorama that captured about two miles of Cincinnati's booming riverfront. Why might a growing industrial city have captured the attention of photographers experimenting with a new medium?

center in the twentieth century, had only two steam engines in 1841. Nevertheless, as industrialization in Britain and some continental regions became rooted, Europe's share of global GDP soared upward. According to one estimate, it grew from about 24 percent of total world GDP in 1820 to 34 percent in 1870.[17]

The United States. Close economic and cultural ties between Britain and the United States after the Napoleonic Wars increased the flow of industrial technology and financial capital westward across the Atlantic. British skill and investment helped build the textile mills that sprouted in New England in the 1820s. African slave laborers in the South spurred industrialization by supplying both northern mills and the much bigger British textile sector with cotton fiber. Raw cotton sales to Britain brought large infusions of foreign currency into the United States, capital that American banks then loaned to industrial, transport, and mining entrepreneurs to speed development.

The United States joined western Europe in developing a successful industrial sector before 1850. As in Britain, the first generation of textile mills in the northeastern states used flowing water to power spinning and weaving machines, and they also employed large numbers of girls and women. The workforce in factories in Lowell, Massachusetts, the leading U.S. textile town, was about 70 percent female. A surge of canal construction between 1820 and 1840 animated economic growth, reducing the transport

cost of bulk goods in and out of the deep American interior. By 1840, however, private companies had laid about three thousand miles of rail line in the Northeast. In the following decade the network spread west and south, bringing the canal boom to an end. Fossil-fuel energy also came to America in the 1840s, when abundant coal deposits were discovered in Pennsylvania. Industrialization moved into the Ohio River basin, and by 1840 Cincinnati, situated on the edge of the midwestern plains, was the country's third largest manufacturing city.

Egypt's early industrial experiment. Egypt was the first country outside of western Europe and the United States to introduce complex machines and house them in factories. It was the first place in the world where the state, rather than private individuals or firms, organized, directed, and chiefly profited from those enterprises, an approach to industrialization that other countries would later adopt. Egypt's program did not go well, however, owing in part to British efforts to undermine it.

Egypt was formally part of the Ottoman empire, but a small class of Turkish military men, or *mamluks* governed the country autonomously, extracting revenues from the Arabic-speaking masses. Four years after France's ill-fated invasion of the Nile valley, which ended in 1801 (see Chapter 20), Muhammad Ali, an Ottoman army officer of Albanian origin rose to power as Egypt's governor (r. 1805–1848). Impressed by the easy victory that Napoleon's forces achieved

Muhammad Ali. This 1840 portrait by a French artist depicts the Egyptian ruler as he presided over efforts to modernize the economy and expand territorially. How can you account for the British government's opposition to Egypt's industrialization?

over *mamluk* cavalry, he launched a crash program to modernize the army and government, revitalize the verdant Nile River valley's agrarian economy, and make Egypt a regional power to be reckoned with. He swept away the conservative *mamluk* elite, hired French and British military advisers, sent Egyptian officers to Europe for training, and opened institutes for future officers and bureaucrats to learn foreign languages, engineering, medicine, and chemistry. He reorganized government ministries and the tax system to channel more wealth to the state. He had no interest in constitutions or parliaments. Rather, he conceived of economic growth, as most contemporary autocrats did, as a strategy for transferring revenue from ordinary people to the state and its ruling class.

To finance these reforms, Muhammad Ali moved to increase the agrarian population's output of cotton, silk, wool, and flax (for linen). He drafted peasants into labor gangs to renovate the Nile valley's irrigation system. With European advice he introduced a new variety of long-staple cotton, which had strong fibers and held up well on mechanical looms. He also recognized the economic logic of manufacturing textiles at home in order to clothe both his army and the general population at direct benefit to the state, not to foreign importers. The first textile workshop opened in Cairo about 1818, and by the 1830s that city and others had about thirty factories producing cotton, silk, linen, and woolen fabrics. Carding machines (for disentangling and aligning fibers), spinning mules, and power looms were put into service. Animal traction powered most of these devices, but a few used imported steam engines. Muhammad Ali also built weapons factories to turn out muskets.

In the later 1830s, however, new political and economic problems plagued Egypt's fledgling industrialization. Military costs rose astronomically as Muhammad Ali embarked on wars of conquest. Between 1811 and 1831, he invaded western Arabia, the Sudan (Upper Nile valley), and the Ottoman provinces of Syria to find resources that Egypt needed and to magnify his international reputation. Scarce investment capital, lack of coal, and a chronic shortage of wood also restricted energy supplies.

Muhammad Ali's attack on Syria provoked the wrath of Britain, which regarded an ascendant Egypt as a potential threat to its lines of communication with colonial India. In 1838, Britain signed an agreement with the Ottoman state, to which Egypt still officially belonged, which lowered import tariffs on European textiles and prohibited the commercial monopolies that Muhammad Ali had imposed. Two years later, British and Ottoman troops drove Egyptian forces out of Syria and compelled Muhammad Ali to drastically reduce his army, his biggest domestic market for clothing and guns.

British action and a dearth of energy resources sentenced Egypt's budding textile industry to failure. Gradually, the workshops fell idle, and after Muhammad Ali died in 1849, Britain kept up pressure on the Egyptian government to export more raw cotton. That strategy enriched Egyptian officials, merchants, and land-owners but did not produce broad-based economic development. Consequently, Egypt took part in the industrial revolution after 1840 mainly as a supplier of farm commodities to industrializing countries.

The Threads of Commerce

In the nineteenth century the volume of world trade grew nearly twenty times, a spectacular acceleration compared to any earlier era. Global exchanges of raw materials, manufactures, and migrating workers reached nearly everyone on the planet, and the capitalist industries, labor systems, and institutions that we associate today with "economic globalization" largely took shape. This happened primarily because fossil-fuel industries in Britain, joined by new ones in continental Europe and the United States, churned out stupendous volumes of merchandise. This torrent, however, could have slowed if markets for these wares, raw materials for factories, and city populations had not grown as well.

Tracks, propellers, and copper wires. Commerce grew spectacularly because of continuing, multiple innovations

MAP 21.4 Railways in 1860.

In what regions of North America and Europe were the densest rail networks built by 1860? How would you account for relatively high density construction in those particular areas? Why do you think railway building started later in India than in Europe or the United States but earlier than, for example, in China or West Africa?

in steam-powered transport and electrical communication, which brought novel consumer goods to millions more people, opened up new sources of minerals and foodstuffs, and speeded the exchange of market information. Total world railway mileage grew nearly fifteenfold between 1840 and 1860, mainly in Europe and North America, though extensive track laying was shortly to follow in India, Latin America, and Australia (see Map 21.4). In 1807 the American entrepreneur Robert Fulton rigged a wood-fueled Watt engine to a paddlewheel on a river vessel, inventing the first commercially successful steamboat. In 1833 the *Royal William,* a vessel operating almost entirely under steam power, crossed the Atlantic from Canada to England. Three years later, John Ericcson, a Swedish inventor, patented the first successful screw propeller, a more efficient underwater drive mechanism than paddlewheels. Early steam vessels had advantages over sailing ships because they did not depend on changeable winds, though exquisitely engineered sail craft, notably clipper ships, made long oceanic voyages well into the second half of the century.

The telegraph, which transmitted a pattern of electrical impulses along a wire, was the first reliable, nearly instantaneous form of long-distance communication in history. In 1837, inventors in England and the United States separately built telegraph machines operated by inexpensive batteries. Samuel Morse, the American inventor, created the more efficient device. In 1844 he transmitted the phrase "What hath God wrought!" from Baltimore to Washington, D.C. Seven years later, a convention of European states adopted Morse's telegraphic code as the international standard for transmitting messages. In this way, the world adapted its first universal language. Railroad builders commonly erected telegraph lines alongside tracks, so the two communication systems grew together. As workers strung copper wires across continents, telegraphy had a growing impact on production and commerce: It allowed high-velocity transmission of the sort of information about political conditions, weather, harvests, prices, and currency rates that businesspeople needed to make rational and timely economic decisions.

Britain, the trade colossus. In the *Communist Manifesto,* published in 1848, Karl Marx (see Chapter 22) characterized the rising power of the capitalist money-making class, which he called the bourgeoisie, as a worldwide, and in his view fateful, development:

The need of a constantly expanding market for its products chases the bourgeoisie over the whole surface of the globe.

It must nestle everywhere, settle everywhere, establish connections everywhere. . . . In place of the old wants, satisfied by the production of the country, we find new wants, requiring for their satisfaction the products of distant lands and climes. In place of the old local and national seclusion and self-sufficiency, we have intercourse in every direction, universal interdependence of nations.[18]

Marx's model for this globe-trotting bourgeoisie was no doubt an Englishman. When he wrote those words, Britain loomed over world commerce, finance, and shipping. This happened fundamentally because that country sprinted far out ahead of the rest of the world in applying fossil-fuel energy to industry. Between 1820 and 1870 the value of British exports increased nearly 1,000 percent. Consequently, the country accumulated a vast store of surplus capital. Some of this wealth funded expansion of the Royal Navy, which patrolled the world. And much of it flowed into domestic and overseas investments in railroads, mines, shipyards, banks, insurance services, and numerous other enterprises.

Cotton textiles became the premier British export. English mills turned out hundreds of millions of yards of fabric, and consumer markets in the rest of the world could not get enough of it. By the late 1850s, plantations in the southern United States exported about 600 million pounds of cotton a year. Planters also bought back some of this cotton, as it were, by importing cheap English fabric to clothe their enslaved black workers.

The consequences of British textile production for South Asia were catastrophic. For many centuries India had been the world's leading cloth producer, but from about 1820, spinners and weavers started losing even their own domestic market to British machine-made cottons. Thereafter, the region underwent a drastic economic shift from cloth manufacturer to grower of raw fiber for European factories. Several million Bengalese weavers lost their livelihoods, and many families turned from manufacturing to farming, just when the British workforce was moving in the opposite direction. The British East India Company, which by 1850 ruled most of South Asia and profited handsomely from cloth imports, had no interest in permitting Indian entrepreneurs to build their own textile factories. Between 1750 and 1860, Britain's share of world manufacturing output rose steadily, from 2 percent to 20 percent, while India's dropped from 25 percent to 9 percent (see graph).[19]

Free Trade and the New Doctrine of Liberalism

Between the sixteenth and eighteenth centuries, European commercial states generally subscribed to the economic doctrine of mercantilism, which held that the world's exploitable wealth could not expand and that the home country and its colonies should erect high barriers to exclude rival states from intruding into its circuits of trade. A state's chief mercantilist weapon was customs taxes on foreign imports, which raised their price to consumers and presumably limited markets for them (see Chapter 18). States such as China, Japan, and the Ottoman empire also traditionally imposed high customs duties or tightly restricted foreign trade. Although these protective policies worked only part of the time, mercantilism dominated European economic thought for decades after the hum of British textile machines suggested that world wealth might be expandable after all.

The age of mercantilism faded after 1820, when continuous improvements in steam-powered manufacturing steadily drove down the price of cotton goods. British industrialists began to question the logic of blocking foreign imports with high tariffs if those goods would not in any case compete with cheaper home-produced items. For example, why should Britain keep out Indian textiles now that British cottons not only supplied the home market but were flooding into India as well? If Britain unilaterally dropped customs barriers in favor of **free trade,** would not other countries do the same and world commerce boom for all?

> **free trade** An economic doctrine contending that trade among states should be unrestricted, principally by lowering or eliminating tariffs or duties on imported goods; factors of supply and demand should mainly determine price.

Britain would also disproportionately benefit because it was the top industrial and naval power.

In the first half of the nineteenth century, the free-trade movement slowly gathered momentum. In the decade and a half after 1846, when Parliament rescinded the Corn Laws, which had restricted imports of foreign wheat and other grains, Britain eliminated virtually all protectionist tariffs. Its global commerce thrived under this new regime, and by the 1860s, all the industrializing countries of continental Europe, even largely rural Russia, were scrambling to sign

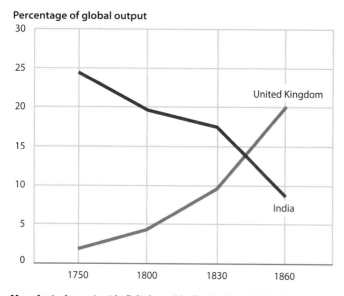

Percentage of global output

Manufacturing output in Britain and India, 1750 and 1860. How can you account for the relative change in British and Indian manufacturing output between 1750 and 1860?

tariff-busting treaties with one another in order to take advantage of new trade opportunities.

The high price of free trade. To dismantle protectionism everywhere, British free-traders saw no reason why the Royal Navy should not lend a hand. This flotilla, government leaders argued, must safeguard British commerce, especially the seaward approaches to colonial South Asia. The navy should not have to transport many ground troops but only capture key ports and coastal enclaves that could serve as operational and supply bases. Thus, in the early nineteenth century, British forces seized the formerly Dutch Cape Colony at the tip of South Africa (1806), the island of Malta in the Mediterranean (1814), Singapore on the Strait of Malacca (1819), and Aden at the entrance to the Red Sea (1839). Naval squadrons were then well positioned to pressure Asian and African states to lower trade barriers to British goods. Indeed, several states opted to negotiate what became known as "unequal treaties." In 1838, as we have seen, Britain persuaded the militarily weaker Ottoman empire to sign a free-trade pact, which worked overwhelmingly to the advantage of European importers.

Free trade by coercion played out dramatically in China. British textile producers wanted badly to split open the potentially huge East Asian market. The Qing imperial government, however, strictly regulated seaborne trade with foreigners and limited it exclusively to the port of Guangzhou (Canton). A hopeful British trade delegation visited the Qianlong emperor in Beijing in 1793 but failed to get restrictions loosened. Considering China's still healthy productivity, the emperor's rebuff was perfectly rational, if not very far-sighted regarding the direction of his country's economy: "There is nothing we lack. . . . We have never set much store on strange or ingenious objects, nor do we need any more of your country's manufactures."[20] British merchant capitalists found this response galling because their own compatriots were drinking millions of cups of imported Chinese tea. This habit grew steadily in the eighteenth century. Tea and sugar together made a marvelous and only mildly addictive "drug food," and it gave tired urban workers quick jolts of caloric energy. East India Company merchants, however, had to pay for tea chiefly with silver because Asian markets did not want much of anything else Europe had to offer.

As tea consumption soared, the company discovered that China offered a promising market for opium, a more expensive and addictive drug food than tea or sugar. It also discovered that Indian farmers in Bengal could be induced to grow the poppies from which opium was made. Company merchants purchased opium at low cost from Bengali middlemen, then sold it at a huge markup to Chinese buyers. The Qing government forbade importation of opium, so Chinese wholesalers had to take delivery of it off the south China coast and smuggle it in. The trade grew fast after 1800, as a cheaper, more powerful opium compound became available and as more affluent, urban Chinese acquired a taste for it, despite its debilitating effects on health and livelihood. By the mid-1830s, British merchants were

Customers in a Chinese opium den. This late nineteenth-century engraving is based on a drawing by Thomas Allom, a British artist and architect who traveled to East Asia. The detailed representation inside a Chinese building shows opium smokers in various states of intoxication. What reasons did British merchants and officials give for promoting the opium trade when there was evidence of the drug's harmful effects?

On Legalizing Opium in China

In 1800 the Qing imperial government banned the importation and domestic production of opium, but not all officials agreed with the decision. Opponents of the ban generally agreed that opium addiction represented a serious social problem, but they also believed the state should manage the substance rather than criminalize it. If opium imports were legal, they argued, the government would be able to impose tariffs on the drug. It could also require that opium be paid for with merchandise such as tea in order to stem the outflow of silver resulting from persistent opium smuggling.

Xu Naiji, a Beijing scholar-official, favored legalization and in 1836 made an argument for it in a "memorial," or formal written communication, to the emperor Daoguang. Xu denounced opium use, but he recognized that addicts would do anything to get it and that smugglers were happy to oblige them. By banning imports, China created an illegal narcotics trade that in turn fed violence, corruption, and economic stagnation. Legalizing and regulating opium would help eliminate those problems. The passage below is taken from Xu's memorial.

The emperor also received memorials from officials who wanted even stricter prohibitions on both importation and use. Zhu Zun, an imperial bureaucrat like Xu, predicted that if opium were legalized, it would no longer carry a social stigma and addicts would overrun the country. The emperor sided with this man, not Xu, and in 1838 he ordered a vigorous campaign against opium, a policy that led to war with Britain the following year.

I would humbly represent that opium was originally ranked among medicines; its qualities are stimulant; it also checks excessive secretions; and prevents the evil effects of noxious vapors. . . . When any one is long habituated to inhaling it, it becomes necessary to resort to it at regular intervals, and the habit of using it, being inveterate, is destructive of time, injurious to property, and yet dear to one even as life. Of those who use it to great excess, the breath becomes feeble, the body wasted, the face sallow, the teeth black; the individuals themselves clearly see the evil effects of it, yet cannot refrain from it. . . .

In Qianlong's reign [1735–1796], as well as previously, opium was inserted in the tariff of Canton as a medicine, subject to a duty. . . . After this, it was prohibited. In the first year of Jiaqing [1796], those found guilty of smoking opium were subject only to the punishment of the pillory and bamboo. Now they have, in the course of time, become liable to the severest penalties. . . . Yet the smokers of the drug have increased in number, and the practice has spread throughout almost the whole empire. . . . Formerly, the barbarian [European] merchants brought foreign money to China; which, being paid in exchange for goods, was a source of pecuniary advantage to the people of all the seaboard provinces. But latterly, the barbarian merchants have clandestinely sold opium for money; which has rendered it unnecessary for them to import foreign silver. Thus foreign money has been going out of the country, while none comes into it. . . .

It is proposed entirely to cut off the foreign trade, and thus to remove the root to dam up the source of the evil? . . . While the dealers in opium are the English alone; it would be wrong, for the sake of cutting off the English trade, to cut off that of all the other nations. Besides, the hundreds of thousands of people living on the seacoast depend wholly on trade for their livelihood, and how are they to be disposed of? Moreover, the barbarian ships, being on the high seas, can repair to any island that may be selected as an entrepôt, and the native sea-going vessels can meet them there; it is then impossible to cut off the trade. . . .

Since then, it will not answer to close our ports against [all trade], and since the laws issued against opium are quite inoperative, the only method left is to revert to the former system, to permit the barbarian merchants to import opium paying duty thereon as a medicine, and to require that, after having passed the custom-house, it shall be delivered to the [Chinese] merchants only in exchange for merchandise, and that no money be paid for it. . . . Offenders when caught should be punished by the entire destruction of the opium they have, and the confiscation of the money that be found with them. With regard to officers, civil and military, and to the scholars and common soldiers, the first are called on to fulfill the duties of their rank and attend to the public good; the others, to cultivate their talent and become fit for public usefulness. None of these, therefore, must be permitted to contract a practice so bad, or to walk in a path which will lead only to the utter waste of their time and destruction of their property. . . . It becomes my duty, then, to request that it be enacted, that any officer, scholar, or soldier, found guilty of secretly smoking opium, shall be immediately dismissed from public employ, without being made liable to any other penalty.

Source: John Slade, *A Narrative of the Late Proceedings and Events in China* (Canton: Canton Register, 1839), 1–5; reproduced in Pei-kai Cheng and Michael Lestz, with Jonathan D. Spence, *The Search for Modern China: A Documentary Collection* (New York: Norton, 1999), 111–114.

Thinking Critically

How had the punishments for smoking opium changed between the late eighteenth century and Xu's day? Why did Xu not want to ban all foreign trade with China? How did he think the legalization of opium would benefit both Chinese people and foreign merchants? If you were the emperor of China, would you have favored legalization or banning of opium imports? Why? How might you compare this controversy with debates about drug trade and use today?

selling more than 1,800 tons of opium in the Chinese market every year.

Because of this demand, the international flow of silver between Europe and East Asia went into reverse: British traders could buy tea with Indian opium rather than coins, while their Chinese counterparts now had to export not only tea and manufactures but also their own country's silver reserves to satisfy drug appetites. For the first time in the Common Era, China experienced a foreign trade deficit, while revenues from tea and opium sales piled up in London banks.

In 1838 the Qing government, facing not only a weakening economy but also high social costs of addiction and drug-fueled crime, launched a campaign to eradicate the trade. When Chinese authorities seized 20,000 chests of opium in Guangzhou, the East India Company recognized a golden chance to force China to join the free-trade era. In 1839 the firm dispatched a squad of battleships and steamers, including one ironclad gunboat, to the Chinese coast, triggering the First Anglo-Chinese War, or Opium War. Company ships bombarded imperial shore defenses and a Qing fleet, while several vessels mounted with heavy guns sailed up the Yangzi River. The emperor had no choice but to sue for peace.

By the punitive terms that ended the conflict in 1842, Britain annexed the island of Hong Kong, forced down import tariff rates, and acquired the right to trade any and all manufactures in five Chinese ports. Trade in opium remained illegal until 1860, but it continued anyway. Once Britain demonstrated that "gunboat diplomacy" was an effective way to open new markets to European goods, France, Russia, and the United States moved quickly to demand that the emperor grant them similar concessions. The industrial revolution thus reached China in a way that was distinctly detrimental to its own economy.

Liberalism: An ideology for the capitalist world economy. The First Anglo-Chinese War (a second one was fought between 1856 and 1860 to expand European privileges in China) was just one episode in the momentous transformations in global economic relations that took place in the nineteenth century. Political and economic leaders wanted to understand the meaning of these transformations and the social disturbances that seemed connected to them. Capitalist investors and governments also wanted to manage and forecast economic change in whatever measure they could.

liberalism A set of economic and political doctrines advocating individual freedom, unrestricted market competition, free trade, constitutional government, and confidence in human progress; sometimes called "classical liberalism."

Liberalism, which was both a political and an economic doctrine, emerged as a set of explanatory ideas that many leaders found persuasive.

Derived from the Latin word *liber,* meaning "free," liberalism initially evoked the principle of limited government, whether practiced in a republic or a constitutional monarchy. Rooted intellectually in the eighteenth-century Enlightenment and slowly elaborated during the Atlantic revolutions, liberalism championed legal protection of private property, representative government, an independent judiciary, scientific and technological progress, economic decision-making based on rational calculation rather than static tradition, and international commerce unfettered by state tariff barriers. Many liberals also advocated free public education, religious toleration, secular government (no state religion), and reforms to improve social conditions of the poor.

All these ideas rested on the premise that the liberty of individuals to think and act as they like, especially to accumulate and dispose of property, should be constrained only to protect the public good. In the words of the English political philosopher John Stuart Mill (1806–1873), "The sole end for which mankind are warranted, individually or collectively, in interfering with the liberty of action of any of their numbers, is self-protection. That the only purpose for which power can be rightfully exercised over any member of a civilized community, against his will, is to prevent harm to

Adam Smith portrayed as a man of letters and property in 1790. This engraving by fellow Scotsman John Kay presents the influential political-economist with books and writing material, formally posed for a portrait. What liberal ideas does this image of Smith reinforce?

others."[21] The Scottish philosopher Adam Smith (1723–1790) had argued earlier in the *Wealth of Nations* that buyers and sellers in the capitalist market advance the welfare of all by simply attending to their own private interests. Governments should practice *laissez faire,* a French term meaning, loosely, "non-intervention." They should allow individuals to buy and sell property freely, abolish tariffs on imports, and otherwise refrain from regulating or interfering in the marketplace except to ensure public safety.

Witnessing the wonders of industry, liberal writers and politicians professed great confidence in the world's material progress. They wished to promote sensible reforms to improve society and to blaze a trail of moderation between two extreme forces. On one side, liberals saw political conservatives, who clung to dead customs, upper-class privileges, church dogma, and the economic status quo. On the other side, they saw radical republicans and other zealots, who would give power to the illiterate, propertyless, sometimes irrational masses, thus risking upheaval in the social order. Liberals who experienced political revolution in France and the Americas had widely ranging views about democracy, or "rule by the people." Some greatly feared that if democracy meant rule by "interested and overbearing majorities," as the American statesman James Madison referred to it, then society might end up in the hands of the "mob"—common folk of the sort that perpetrated the worst excesses of the French Revolution. For other liberals, democracy should be society's goal, but with voting and officeholding rights extended to more citizens only by careful stages. Elected representatives and magistrates should be property-owning adult males. Such men would presumably guard legal rights and refrain from meddling in the operation of the free market.

Economic and political liberalism blended together, though some exponents accepted certain aspects of this ideology while rejecting others. For example, industrialists tended to stress the inviolability of private property and free trade, whereas the poor and unenfranchised warmed to the promise of political equality. Autocratic monarchs in Europe and dictatorial presidents of Latin American republics might also identify themselves as liberal in their dedication to rational economic policies, private wealth, and technological progress. But this type of liberal had no interest in redistributing wealth to ordinary men and women or allowing popularly elected legislatures free rein over the country's affairs. Though liberalism had many, sometimes conflicting tendencies, it emerged in the early nineteenth century as the creed that guided and informed the expansion of global capitalism. By the 1830s small circles of intellectuals and business leaders in places like India, Egypt, and the Ottoman empire were also discussing how liberal ideas might be applied in their own societies.

●   ●   ●

Conclusion

This book takes the view that the modern era, or modernity, got under way about 250 years ago and that it represented the sharpest turn in the human venture since the invention of farming 12,000 years earlier. At the top of our list of the characteristics of modernity (see the introduction to Part 6) is the human capacity for harvesting and using energy on a large enough scale to transform our species' fundamental relationship to the material world. This chapter has addressed the early decades of that transformation. According to one scholar, humans who lived about a thousand years ago used a per-capita average of about 26,000 calories of energy per day, mostly energy generated by human or animal muscle. Currently, the average individual uses at least 230,000 calories every day, thanks to a multitude of machines. The better part of that increase has taken place in the past 150 years.[22] Between 1750 and 1900, the efficiency of industrial labor grew about two hundred times. That is, a worker at the end of the nineteenth century could produce in a week's time what a worker in 1750 could produce in four years.[23]

The revolutionary scope of developments in Britain between 1750 and 1850 would not at the time have been noticed in most of the world. After all, in Europe as a whole in 1800, human and animal muscle still supplied about 80 percent of useful mechanical energy. Steam engines provided only about 4 percent.[24] As the midpoint of the nineteenth century approached, the highest levels of energy consumption for manufacturing were concentrated in Britain, parts of continental western Europe, and the United States. And in all those regions the consumption rate was soaring. By contrast, the relative share of energy use in China, South Asia, and the central Muslim lands was falling rapidly.

This development correlates to a large shift in the configuration of global power. For the first time in history, western Europeans and North Americans shot ahead of the rest of the world in their ability to mass-produce goods, develop new technologies and industrial processes, invent lethal weapons, create sophisticated commercial and banking systems, communicate across long distance, and move wage workers from countryside to city or from one part of the world to another. In the next few chapters we will see how humankind's success at breaking through the limits of the biological old regime served the economic and power interests of some societies and classes much more than others.

●   ●   ●

Key Terms

biological old regime 610
capitalism 632
energy revolution 609
First Anglo-Chinese War
(Opium War) 631

fossil fuels 609
free trade 628
industrial revolution 609
liberalism 631

Luddites 621
putting-out system 611

Change over Time

1694	Parliament founds the Bank of England to support Britain's commercial growth and international trade.
1765	James Hargreaves invents the spinning jenny.
1769	James Watt patents an improved steam engine.
1784	Edmund Cartwright designs the first power loom.
1793	Eli Whitney invents the cotton gin.
1804	Joseph Jacquard invents a loom for weaving patterns in cloth.
1805–1848	Muhammad Ali rules in Egypt, instituting industrializing reforms.
1811–1816	Luddites destroy industrial machinery in England.
1819	British forces seize Singapore in the Strait of Malacca.
1830	The Liverpool and Manchester Railway opens.
1833	A steamship crosses the Atlantic for the first time.
1838	The Ottoman empire signs a trade agreement with Britain.
1842	Britain annexes Hong Kong and secures trading rights as victors in the First Anglo-Chinese War (Opium War).
1844	Samuel Morse transmits telegraphic code from Baltimore to Washington, D.C.
1848	Karl Marx publishes the *Communist Manifesto.*

Please see end of book reference section for additional reading suggestions related to this chapter.

22 Coping with Change in the New Industrial Era

1830–1870

Queen Victoria and family (center left) admiring a display in the Crystal Palace.

In the spring of 1851, thousands of exhibitors from around the world gathered in Hyde Park, London, for the opening of the Great Exhibition of the Industry of All Nations. On display within the colossal Crystal Palace, so named for its dazzling glass walls and ceilings, were the latest machines and manufactures, as well as handicrafts, artworks, and exotic plants, animals, minerals. Six million visitors flocked to the exposition to marvel at the goods and cultural artifacts of many lands. Organized by the Royal Society for the Encouragement of Arts, Manufactures and Commerce, the Great Exhibition aimed to educate the public, spur technological progress, and illustrate the marvelous potential of unfettered world trade.

Exploring this array of products, wonders, and amazing inventions (including a primitive ancestor of the fax machine), attentive visitors must have thought about the dizzying speed of change in the world, though no one could have understood how compellingly the fair displayed the arrival of the modern age. London's population of about 2.3 million in 1850 was more than one-third of what the entire world's population had been in 8000 B.C.E. Between 1830 and 1870, global population grew by about 130 million, about three and a half times as much as in the entire first millennium B.C.E. Industrialization continued to spread across Europe and the United States, and global industrial output in those four decades increased by around 50 percent. In 1800 a steam engine could put out more than 100,000 watts of power, by 1870 about 1 million. Also by that year, rail locomotives could go more than sixty miles per hour, faster than any horse. Looking back, we can see that in the middle decades of the nineteenth century, the world of machines, communication networks, urban living, and governing systems became much more like the one we live in today.

The Crystal Palace housed exhibits from overseas regions where British people and numerous other Europeans were settling in large numbers between 1830 and 1870. The first section of the chapter explores the global conditions that prompted a rapid acceleration of human migration from one part of the world to another in the nineteenth century. Tens of millions of men and women from both Europe and Asia traveled far from home to seek work, opportunity, and refuge, even as the forced transfer of African slaves across the Atlantic to American plantations finally came to an end. Mass global migration was multidirectional and complex, and it had profound, often disastrous consequences for the indigenous populations on whose lands newcomers encroached.

In the second part of the chapter we consider how societies in Europe, the Americas, and the Muslim lands attempted to reimagine government and the social order in the

Chapter Outline

WAVES OF MIGRANTS
The End of the Atlantic Slave Trade
The Outpouring from Europe
Neo-Europes and the Fates
of Indigenous Populations
Migrations of Asians and Africans
Oceania Connected

GROUNDSWELLS OF POLITICAL AND SOCIAL REFORM
Nationalism and the Power of the People
Varieties of Socialism
Movements for Women's Rights
Movements for Political Reform
and Unification in Europe
Modernizing Reforms in Muslim Lands

WEIGHING THE EVIDENCE A Moroccan Diplomat in France

The Limits of Liberalism in Latin America

RELIGION AND REFORM
Global Trends and Religious Change
Christian Evangelism
Jewish Reform
Religious Reform and Revolution
in the Muslim World

INDIVIDUALS MATTER Ram Mohan Roy: Hindu Reformer

GLOBAL CHANGE AND THE CALAMITOUS WARS OF MIDCENTURY
The Crimean War and the Industrialization
of Violence
Paraguay: A War of Annihilation
The Taiping Rebellion in China
The Great Indian Rebellion
The American Civil War

• • •

face of perplexing demographic and economic change. The Great Exhibition trumpeted not only liberalism, the doctrine that extolled free trade, private property, and limited government, but also nationalism, the principle that human beings naturally cluster together in distinct cultural communities, or nations, and that every genuine nation has an inherent right to govern itself. The mid-nineteenth century was the period when nationalism and liberalism as intertwined ideologies began in some measure to shape human thought and action through much of the world. Also in this era, thinkers who witnessed the social injustices and inequalities that

A Panoramic View

MAP 22.1 Global migrations, 1820–1913.
Large scale migrations affected every inhabited region of the world in the nineteenth century. Which migration routes were part of networks that operated within empires? Which routes linked independent states with one another?

accompanied industrialization began to frame the principles of socialism as a critique of liberal capitalist economics and an alternative path to the future.

The Great Exhibition did not neglect the representation of religious faith. Indeed, in midcentury, most people in the world looked to their religions and traditional moral codes as guides to bewildering change in the conditions of life. The third section of the chapter explores connections between modern technology and religion, religious reform, and the activism of missionaries.

In the final part of the chapter, we survey the surge of wars and revolutions that agitated the world in the middle decades of the century. The Great Exhibition was on some level an affirmation that in 1851 peace reigned in most of Europe and that civilized and orderly progress lay ahead. But for humankind as a whole, the 1850s and 1860s were decades of war and revolution on an unprecedented scale of violence. These conflagrations were all linked to the disruptions that attended the great transition to fossil-fuel industry and globe-embracing capitalism.

Waves of Migrants

FOCUS Why did many millions of people undertake long-distance migrations in the nineteenth century?

In the nineteenth century, roughly 150 million people worldwide left their homes to seek wealth, work, or a better chance of survival in foreign places (see Map 22.1). This migration represented a spectacular acceleration of human movement compared to any earlier century. It happened because the industrial revolution created colossal demands for labor, not only in rapidly growing manufacturing centers but everywhere that capitalist entrepreneurs oversaw production of raw materials for industry and food for urban workers. Railways, clipper ships, and steamer networks met the physical challenge of moving millions of people across continents and oceans. The anxieties of migration also diminished somewhat because telegraph lines and faster mail services allowed friends and family members to keep in regular contact with one another over longer distances.

Rapid global population growth in the nineteenth century provided businesses with a much larger potential labor force to meet the multitude of new job demands. Nineteenth-century capitalists argued that this force should earn cash wages and be liberated both from government restrictions on travel and from customary labor obligations to chiefs and landlords. Consequently, the forms of migration changed dramatically in the nineteenth century. The number of people who migrated long distances as slaves to toil entirely for someone else's benefit declined sharply, though forced labor systems by no means disappeared. Conversely, the numbers who migrated voluntarily, if often under economic or political pressures, increased by many millions.

The End of the Atlantic Slave Trade

From the sixteenth century to the early nineteenth, about eight million enslaved African men and women were transported across the Atlantic to the Americas. The slave trade produced the largest and most sustained transoceanic flow of peoples in those centuries. The number of Africans arriving in American ports exceeded the number of free Europeans by four to one. The trade reached its numerical peak in the 1780s. It declined gradually thereafter until about 1840, then dropped fast, ending altogether around 1870. But why *did* the slave trade end, considering that in the nineteenth century many societies in the world accepted slavery as customary and normal? The answers lie in the growth of social movements to end the slave trade and to emancipate slaves, as well as economic changes in the Atlantic region.

Antislavery movements. In eighteenth-century Europe, several leading Enlightenment thinkers denounced slavery as incompatible with the natural rights of human beings. Between 1761 and 1800, Portugal, Britain, and several northern states in the United States made slavery illegal on home territory. In 1794 the French revolutionary government outlawed slavery both at home and in overseas possessions, though Napoleon restored the institution eight years later. An internationally linked antislavery movement was slow to develop, but abolitionist organizations, for example, the British Anti-Slavery Society, formed in countries on both sides of the Atlantic. In Britain evangelical Christians and small numbers of freed Africans agitated against both slavery and the slave trade, branding it manifestly inconsistent with both human rights and the moral responsibility to introduce Christian civilization to Africans. Economic liberals also joined the emancipation chorus, arguing for the benefits of a free and mobile work force.

Between 1803 and 1814 the pressure of antislavery movements pushed Britain, the United States, Denmark, and the Netherlands to outlaw slave trading, though abolition of the institution of slavery took decades longer. France, Spain, Portugal, and most of the new Latin American states outlawed the trade in the ensuing decades. However, it fell mainly to the British navy, with some help from French and American vessels, to enforce the new policy by intercepting slave ships when they left African ports. Beginning in the 1820s naval crews caught and arrested numerous shippers, releasing their human cargos mainly to the tiny British colony of Sierra Leone in West Africa. Owing to the immense length of the continental coast, however, the patrols seized only a fraction of outbound slave ships. Until 1850, plantation owners in Brazil continued to purchase an average of about thirty-seven thousand slaves a year, mainly from West Central Africa.

The changing economics of slave labor. On the American side, the demand for slave labor remained high in countries where the practice was legal and plantation agriculture profitable. Industries relying on slave labor—coffee in Brazil, sugar in Cuba, and cotton in the United States—continued to expand to meet world market demand. Although the United States outlawed slave imports in 1807, the American-born slave population reproduced itself, thereby making up for the loss of imported labor. In Brazil and Cuba, however, native-born slave numbers continued to show a net yearly decline, owing largely to the lethal conditions of work on tropical plantations. Consequently, both of those countries tried to keep the Atlantic trade going as long as they could.

Planters and merchants, however, had increasing trouble defending their labor system, which came under economic as well as social attack. The abolition of slavery in Haiti following the long revolutionary struggle there (see Chapter 20) inspired slave uprisings elsewhere, for example, the Nat Turner rebellion in Virginia in 1831 and a rising of Muslim slaves in Bahia, Brazil, in 1835. These and numerous other insurgencies forced planters and colonial governments to spend increasing sums on armed security. Liberal Britain eliminated tariffs on sugar imports in 1846, which slashed the world price and further reduced planters' profits. On the global scale, European capitalists found attractive new investment opportunities besides American sugar. Consequently, international capital shifted toward mechanical industries, railway building, mining, and commercial farming in places like South Asia, South Africa, Latin America, Canada, and the United States, using legally free if not necessarily well-treated wage laborers.

Once most European states abolished slavery, they mounted pressure on other countries to follow suit. Britain outlawed the institution in its colonies in 1833, France (for a second time) in 1848, and the United States in 1865, following its civil war. Thereafter, the United States joined the European democracies in urging Brazil and Cuba (still a Spanish colony) to enact full emancipation, though politically dominant sugar and coffee interests prevented that from happening until the late 1880s.

The Outpouring from Europe

The transition from predominantly African to heavily European and Asian transoceanic migration took place in the decades after 1820. Somewhere between fifty and fifty-five million men and women emigrated from Europe up to 1939. In the nineteenth century most Europeans emigrated voluntarily and sold their labor freely, though poverty or misfortune could impose their own forms of servitude on settlers. In contrast to African slaves, European migrants had legal freedom to move from place to place. A minority of them returned permanently to Europe for one reason or another. Others traveled regularly back and forth between Europe and points abroad to do seasonal agricultural work,

for example, laborers who made repeated trips between Italy and Argentina or Brazil.

Beachheads and neo-Europes. The great majority of migrants went to regions where other Europeans in much smaller numbers had already established what we have called neo-European societies, places where the newcomers put down roots, worked the land, and attempted to recreate as best they could the European cultural and social environments they had left behind. In those places the population of European ancestry came to far outnumber indigenous populations (see Chapter 19). In 1800 the largest frontier of permanent European migration was the young United States, which then had about 4.3 million people of European descent, plus another 1 million African slaves, free blacks, and American Indians. Other, demographically smaller regions of settlement before 1800 included eastern Canada, Siberia, the Cape region of South Africa, and Australia. All those regions attracted much greater settlement in the nineteenth century.

Why did so many people leave Europe? In a sense the scattering of millions of European migrants to faraway lands represented a global extension of the even more complicated journeys of people from one part of Europe to another. In the first century of industrialization, Europe was a whirl of human movement, some of it one way and permanent, much of it round trip and temporary.

Three developments underlay this mobility. First, the continuing growth of capitalist industry and commercial agriculture required movable labor, that is, workers who could be shifted to places where factories and mines were opening and who could be hired and fired at will. Second, new canal, rail, and steamship networks meant that people could travel both faster and more reliably from one worksite to another. For example, Europe's rail network grew from 1,700 miles in 1840 to 63,300 miles by 1870. Third, Europe's population doubled between 1820 and 1913, from about 170 million to more than 340 million. With that growth came increased competition for land and employment. Although industrialization created many new jobs and prosperity in parts of Europe, uneven economic development between one region and another, plus fluctuations in prices and wages forced multitudes in poorer and more rural countries to relocate to find work.

Rural people left their lands by the millions to take urban or agricultural wage jobs. Many had lost their plots to capitalist landlords or simply hoped to escape chronic poverty. The elimination of serfdom in Poland, Prussia, Austria, and Russia between 1807 and 1861 propelled growing numbers of eastern European and Russian peasants into the migratory stream of wage seekers. Most of those migrants were men and teenage boys. Married men often sought seasonal or temporary work away from home, while wives and daughters continued to work the family plots. By 1850 half the population of most European cities had been born elsewhere.

Fewer people might have left Europe for new shores if more farm land had been available or industry had developed faster in the east and south. But this was not the case. Consequently, population movement within Europe spilled out across the world to New York, Chicago, Toronto, Buenos Aires, and Sydney, then onward to farming frontiers. Many people also fled Europe in the extremity of famine, revolution, or persecution. The Irish famine of 1845–1852, a catastrophe caused by loss of potato crops to a devastating fungus, washed the poorest of the poor onto foreign shores,

about 1.8 million people by 1855. In the aftermath of revolutionary movements that briefly upended Europe in 1848, a wave of migrants headed to America in fear of political reprisals. Jews deserted their homes by the hundreds of thousands to escape anti-Semitic persecution or violence. In the 1880s pogroms in Russia, that is, organized massacres or ethnic cleansing of Jews, triggered mass flight.

In short, several forces combined to "push" people out of Europe. Other forces worked to pull them overseas. Emigrants usually had high expectations that in places where neo-Europes were emerging they would find cheap land and a cultural and social life not too different from the one they were leaving behind. Moreover, getting there was not prohibitively expensive, because transport costs dropped steadily as railway and steamship routes multiplied. Before 1870, emigrants came principally from the northern European lands stretching from Ireland and Britain to Germany and Scandinavia. After that date, millions of Italians, Poles, and Russians gravitated to the industrial core regions of western Europe, then out again to overseas destinations. The proportion of women in emigrant groups varied widely among different nationalities. Most women traveled with families or followed fathers, husbands, and fiancés who had preceded them to find employment.

Neo-Europes and Indigenous Populations

For several millennia before the nineteenth century, peoples who foraged, herded animals, or practiced subsistence farming on the margins of densely agrarian and citied lands had been gradually losing their livings and habitats to invaders or immigrants who possessed superior numbers, technologies, and armed power. This process sped up after 1800. Neo-Europes formed where indigenous societies retreated, shrank in size, or died, despite their attempts to fight back.

Russian Jewish immigrants arriving in New York City with their belongings. Pogroms prompted a thirty-year migration of Jews out of Russia and eastern Europe. Why might some U.S. citizens have responded to this illustration with sympathy but others with hostility?

North America. In the thirteen British colonies of North America, European colonizers battled and expelled Native Americans whose numbers had already been depleted by diseases that the first waves of Europeans or African slaves introduced two or three centuries earlier (see Chapter 16). Conversely, the descendants of Europeans multiplied. In 1820 the United States (twenty-two states at that point) already had a population of 9.6 million, 82 percent of it of European descent. As migrants poured into the Southeast and Midwest, government authorities collaborated with them to subjugate, kill, or expel Indians still living east of the Mississippi. The largest southern groups, including the Cherokee, Choctaw, and Creek, cultivated and hunted lands that immigrant farmers and cotton planters wanted. President Andrew Jackson (1829–1837) ensured the availability of land to white Americans and their black slaves by pushing the great majority of Indians across the Mississippi River to stark reservations in the Oklahoma territory.

Nevertheless, Native Americans contested the immigrant intrusion. Fighting between Indians and settlers marked every phase of the westward advance. In Florida, for example, Seminole Indians rebelled in 1835 rather than relocate to Oklahoma. Fighting alongside runaway African slaves from strongholds in the Everglades, the insurgents held off U.S. soldiers for seven years. The federal government ended the war in 1842 without ever forcing all the Seminoles out of their swamps and forests.

South America. The temperate southern cone of South America—Argentina, Uruguay, Chile, and southern Brazil—attracted a growing multitude of European migrants, especially in the later nineteenth century. Wheat, horses, cattle, and sheep flourished on the pampas, or prairies, west and south of the Plata River. Export of hides, wool, and grain grown on some of the richest soil in the world provided the economic foundation for the neo-European society that gradually took hold. Between 1870 and World War I, about six million Spanish, Italian, and other European workers moved to Argentina.

As for the native peoples, their numbers had been historically small compared to the societies of the Andean highlands. Alien diseases shrank them even more, and resistance that Indian cavalry put up on the southern pampas ultimately proved futile. Today the descendants of European immigrants make up 97 percent of Argentina's population of more than forty million.

Australia. Although Australia lies eight thousand miles from Europe, 92 percent of its current population claims European descent. Aborigines, the indigenous people who had Australia to themselves barely more than two hundred years ago, number just 1 percent. The settling of the continent by Europeans began in 1788, when a fleet of British naval vessels landed at Botany Bay in the far southeast to set up a penal settlement. Between 1788 and 1852 the British crown condemned more than 160,000 men, women, and children to "transportation" to the Australian colony of New South Wales. Women accounted for about one-sixth of these involuntary travelers, and, like many of the men, they were often poor people found guilty of minor crimes. Above this penal class, which labored in slave-like and unhealthy conditions, stood a small hierarchy of British officials, military officers, merchants, and land-owners. In the 1830s free European farmers began to export wool and beef, linking New South Wales to the global economy. The settler population, however, grew slowly until 1851, when gold prospectors hit pay dirt. After that, voluntary migrants scrambled in, swelling the population from about 400,000 in 1850 to 1.4 million just ten years later.

Meanwhile, Aboriginal hunting and foraging bands slowly retreated and withered. Like the Americas, Australia had for thousands of years remained isolated from the teeming pool of infectious diseases endemic to Afroeurasia. When the early European settlers introduced influenza, smallpox, and other virulent ills, epidemics raged through indigenous communities. By the 1820s European settlers began pushing inland. Aborigines regarded land as communal property, but Europeans saw individual ownership as the natural form of land use. Since no one presumably "owned" Aboriginal land, it was free for the taking. According to one British official, "It is in the order of nature that, as civilization advances, savage nations must be exterminated."[1] Carving out commercial farms and huge stock ranches, European immigrants pushed native communities toward the arid interior or massacred those who refused to fall back. After 1850 the balance of population shifted steadily in favor of the immigrants.

Siberia. The enormous Inner Eurasian land of Siberia was different from other emerging neo-Europes because it was within Afroeurasia, not separated from it by a span of ocean. However, the indigenous population, which included Yakuts, Evenks (Tungus), and numerous other hunting, fishing, and horse-herding groups, lived far enough away from Afroeurasia's denser population centers that they fell easily to the same noxious diseases that killed Australian Aborigines and Native Americans (see Chapter 19). In the late eighteenth century, for example, a pestilence on the Pacific peninsula of Kamchatka carried off as much as three-quarters of the local inhabitants.

Between 1830 and 1914, Siberia became overwhelmingly European. Similarly to Australia, the discovery of gold in the 1830s brought a fresh wave of immigrants. In 1858–1860, one-sided treaties between Russia and the weakened Chinese empire opened new lands to farm settlement in the Amur River valley north of Mongolia. The emancipation of Russian serfs in 1861 propelled hundreds of thousands of men and women over the following decades to migrate eastward. After 1880, new mine, rail, and commercial farm enterprises in southern Siberia drew in five million more.

Europeans and Aborigines exchange goods—at a distance. The French writer and artist Jacques Arago drew this scene about 1820 during a visit to Australia. What features of the picture suggest that the meeting was probably tense and might easily have turned violent?

Migrations of Asians and Africans

Next to Europe, India and China were the largest suppliers of migrant workers to plantations, mines, factories, and railroads in distant lands. Between 1820 and 1914, approximately twelve million men and women left those lands on the promise of work or opportunity abroad. This number represented about one-fifth of the European exodus, and more Asians than Europeans eventually returned home. Nevertheless, in Southeast Asia, the Indian Ocean rim lands, and the Americas, Chinese and Indian migrants planted permanent minority communities.

Nineteenth-century Chinese migrants perpetuated on a growing scale a long tradition of settlement in Southeast Asian cities from the Philippines to Burma. Indian neighborhoods sprang up in almost every part of the British empire where employers needed labor, for example, in Malaya, South Africa, and British Guiana in South America. The great majority of Asian migrants went to areas where commercial export agriculture was expanding. For example, as the African slave trade shrank, European investors opened new sugar plantations in South Africa, Southeast Asia, and Oceania, employing Indian and Chinese contract workers.

The meaning of "voluntary migration." Like Europeans, most Asians left home voluntarily, but that term had shades of meaning. Most traveled to ports and boarded ships because they had experienced economic stress or discontent. Beginning in the 1820s, for example, the British colonial authorities in India systematically organized labor

transport of poor people to other parts of the empire to do farm work. In China, land shortages arising from population growth, price inflation, rebellion, and periodic drought propelled tens of thousands out of the country every year, especially from the densely populated southern provinces. Labor recruiters, whether Europeans or Asians, often deceived illiterate men and women about the intended destination, the working conditions, or the promised wages. In Portuguese Macao, off China's coast, for example, unscrupulous recruiters sometimes snared poor Chinese into games of chance, then demanded that they or a family member pay losses by accepting an overseas labor contract requiring work over a specified period of time.

The great majority of emigrants from South and East Asia were boys and men, but women also left home, especially migrating to places where the labor importers wanted to encourage men to settle permanently. Also, the social conventions of Chinese and Indian societies restricted women from circulating in public as freely as European women could. For example, the midcentury gold rushes that happened in both California and Australia attracted tens of thousands of Chinese construction workers. Of the 65,000 Chinese in California in 1860, only 1,800 were women. Some single women went abroad voluntarily, but many were kidnapped or deceived and ended up as prostitutes or domestic servants.

Asian workers in tropical America. The decline and eventual end of slavery created a serious labor crisis for plantation owners in the Caribbean and South America.

with 12 lashes; if he persists, with 18 more, and if even thus he should not enter on his course of duty, he may be put in irons, and made to sleep in the stocks."[2]

Continuing slave trade. Even though the trans-Atlantic slave trade shrank to insignificance between 1840 and 1870, human trafficking continued, whether legally or not, wherever people could be held in bondage. Commercial planters from the southern United States continued to buy and sell slaves and move them from one state to another until 1865. Between 1820 and 1860, Brazilian merchants moved about one million slaves from depleted sugar plantations in the northeast to expanding coffee-growing lands in the south. Slavery and slave trading remained a customary practice in many Asian lands and most of Africa throughout the nineteenth century. Industrialization in Europe increased demand for African commodities such as lumber, peanut oil, and palm oil. Consequently, slavery actually expanded in some parts of West and Central Africa in the mid-nineteenth century as rulers and proprietors responded to new opportunities in the global economy.

In northeastern Africa, the Egyptian ruler Muhammad Ali (see Chapter 21) invaded the upper Nile River valley (today the republics of Sudan and South Sudan) in 1820 to capture boys and young men to serve as military slaves. Thereafter, Sudanese merchant expeditions armed with modern guns raided far to the south, enslaving villagers and selling them downriver to Egypt. To the west, slave traffic across the Sahara declined steadily in the nineteenth century, though in the middle decades around four thousand slaves a year may have entered Morocco, most of them women. Along the Indian Ocean coast of Africa, the sultanate of Oman and Zanzibar tapped East Africa for ivory and slaves in exchange for imported textiles. At midcentury, armed convoys drove as many as fifty thousand slaves a year from the interior to the Indian Ocean coast. Some of them, predominantly women, were then shipped to Arabia and other Muslim lands for domestic or sexual service. Others were taken to Zanzibar Island, where they harvested cloves, a popular spice in the international market. Under British pressure the Omani sultan abolished the export slave trade in 1873, though effective enforcement came slowly.

Oceania Connected

The peoples who inhabited the immense Pacific basin became permanently incorporated into the global network

Chinese immigrants working in a sugar factory in Cuba, 1872. Men and women from East and South Asia filled a labor void after the importation of African slaves declined. Working conditions, however, did not much improve for Asian laborers under contract. What factors might have motivated people to cross the Pacific to engage in ardous, dangerous work for little pay?

Many freed slaves stayed on plantations, but others left to plow their own farms or work in towns. Consequently, colonial governments and private planters devised new schemes to replace slaves with contract workers. Historians have asked whether contract labor work might typically have been as harsh as slave labor. Asian workers bound for the Caribbean or South America usually suffered dreadful shipboard conditions, and their employers sometimes housed them in barracks originally built for slaves. Between 1853 and 1874, about 125,000 Chinese workers debarked in Cuba, where slavery was still legal. There, they sweated in the cane fields alongside black slaves, and they suffered numerous restrictions and punishments set forth in Cuban law: "The colonist disobeying the voice of the superior, whether it be refusing to work, or any other obligation, may be corrected

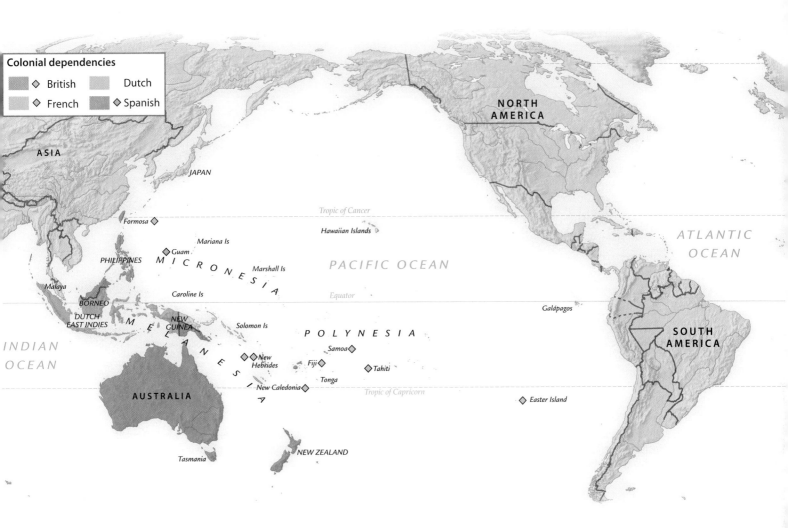

MAP 22.2 The Pacific basin, 1760–1880.
Considering that the Pacific is dotted with thousands of islands and the Atlantic is not, why did it take nearly three centuries longer to establish routine communications across the Pacific than it did across the Atlantic?

Within the map, the following labels appear:

Colonial dependencies
- ◇ British
- ◇ French
- Dutch
- ◇ Spanish

ASIA · NORTH AMERICA · SOUTH AMERICA · JAPAN · Formosa · Mariana Is · Guam · PHILIPPINES · MICRONESIA · Marshall Is · PACIFIC OCEAN · Malaya · BORNEO · Caroline Is · Equator · DUTCH EAST INDIES · MELANESIA · NEW GUINEA · Solomon Is · POLYNESIA · INDIAN OCEAN · New Hebrides · Fiji · Samoa · Tahiti · Tonga · New Caledonia · AUSTRALIA · Tropic of Capricorn · Easter Island · Galápagos · ATLANTIC OCEAN · Tropic of Cancer · Hawaiian Islands · Tasmania · NEW ZEALAND

of migration and trade in the later eighteenth century (see Map 22.2). Over a period of about 2,600 years, migrants who spoke Polynesian languages had sailed outrigger canoes to explore and settle many of the ocean's twenty-five thousand islands. Those colonizers adapted ingeniously to a variety of climates and natural environments, building societies that ranged from hunter-forager bands in southern New Zealand to small kingdoms on Tonga and the Hawaiian Islands. But they maintained no sustained contact with Afroeurasia, the Americas, or Australia. Then, beginning in the 1760s, European mariners, notably the English explorer James Cook, crisscrossed the Pacific in growing numbers, landing on many islands, introducing new crops and animals, opening mines and plantations, and founding Christian missions.

The perils of contact. In the early nineteenth century, Oceania became a new zone of world commerce and migration, though the cost in lives and environmental degradation ran high. The thousands of Europeans and Asians who sailed into the Pacific brought with them a "suitcase" of plants, domestic animals, pests, and microorganisms, many of them unknown to Polynesians. Like Australian Aborigines, Pacific Islanders initially suffered catastrophic die-off owing to exposure to unfamiliar infectious diseases, including smallpox, measles, and influenza. For example, when European settlers started arriving in New Zealand in 1840, the Maori population may have numbered 100,000 or more. By 1858 it declined to 56,000, owing mainly to imported infections.

Merchants and migrants swarmed into the Pacific to exploit resources of both land and sea. Russian, American, and Australian hunters profited handsomely from trade in seal fur, though by 1840 they nearly wiped out this species in the Pacific. Beginning in 1819 American and other whale hunters entered the ocean. Whale oil commanded a huge market for lighting, industrial lubrication, and cooking. The industry flourished at first, but hunters rapidly depleted several species, forcing this enterprise to shut down almost entirely for several decades after 1860.

Whalers in the port of Honolulu, Hawaii, 1849. Though ship owners were typically American or European, whaling crews included Pacific Islanders. Honolulu's buildings, too, reveal a blend of European and Hawaiian architecture. What elements of this nineteenth-century engraving might have seemed unusual or exotic to American viewers?

In the later century, thousands of Polynesians migrated from island to island to find jobs in commercial agriculture and shipping. A sugar industry in Fiji succeeded because planters attracted contract laborers from South Asia. Their descendants make up nearly 40 percent of the population today. Sometimes, however, migration was induced by brute force. In several parts of the Pacific, armed labor contractors made a business of kidnapping islanders, a practice called "blackbirding." In 1862–1863, Peruvian kidnappers carried off about 1,500 men and women from Rapa Nui (Easter Island) to work in South American mines and sugar fields.

The birth of the "Pacific world." As trade grew across the Pacific, port cities multiplied. Oceania offered a variety of exotic commodities that East Asians wanted to buy, including sealskins, otter pelts, pearls, and ambergris, which is an intestinal secretion of sperm whales used as a spice, in perfume, and as an aphrodisiac. Honolulu, today the capital of Hawaii, emerged after 1820 as the key mid-ocean trans-shipment center. Vessels converged there from Guangzhou (Canton), Manila, Sydney, and several Latin American ports, as well as from small havens along the coasts of California and Canada, where Native Americans and European settlers sold furs, skins, and timber.

Gold rushes in California (1849), Australia (1851), and British Columbia (1858) added yellow metal to the Pacific exchange web. The gold bonanzas did not last long, but they revved the Pacific economy chiefly because European populations in the mining regions became permanently much bigger. California grew from about 15,000 inhabitants in 1848 (not counting American Indians) to more than 250,000 in 1852. Southeastern Australia experienced similarly explosive immigration. Fast clipper ships and then steamers progressively shortened Pacific crossing times.

Groundswells of Political and Social Reform

FOCUS What historical factors account for the rise of a variety of reformist and revolutionary political movements in the nineteenth century?

In every era of world history over the past five thousand years, prophets, reformers, and revolutionaries have stepped forward in times of change to offer solutions to problems of instability, economic stress, or social injustice. Beginning in the eighteenth century, however, the pace of global population growth, industrialization, and human migration accelerated at such a rapid pace that movements proposing better ways to manage or restructure society multiplied around the globe. Newspapers, telegraph lines, railways, and urban coffeehouses all permitted would-be reformers to spread their ideas much faster and farther than ever before. The nineteenth century, we might say, was the first age of "isms"—liberalism, republicanism, conservatism, nationalism, socialism, and communism. All of these ideologies were imprecise, complicated, and prone to spin off in multiple directions. Nevertheless, they animated social movements that greatly affected the course of change as the century progressed.

Nationalism and the Power of the People

Public debates in Europe and the Americas over the ideas of nationalism and liberalism (see Chapters 20 and 21) were barely separable from each other. Both ideologies grew in the nineteenth century as political doctrines of great appeal to capitalists, governing elites, and affluent urbanites. But by midcentury, nationalism began to resonate deeply in the cultural and emotional lives of ordinary people, as liberalism did not. In the past hundred years, nationalism has been the most potent force in the world for mobilizing popular action.

According to nationalist thought, a group of people sharing a common language, cultural forms, history, and a sense of common destiny ought in the natural order of things to enjoy sovereign self-government. When the society achieved that aim, it constituted a nation-state. By appealing to such nationalist feeling, central governments could both shore up popular loyalty and organize citizens for public action more effectively than they had in any previous era. States could take advantage of new communication technologies to encourage people to "imagine themselves" as a single community, even though the sovereign territory embraced individuals, perhaps tens of millions of them, who were not culturally homogeneous and knew little or nothing about one another's daily lives.[3]

Modern states, especially the large ones, invariably included different social classes and political interest groups. Urban workers agitated for higher wages, ethnic communities demanded regional self-government, liberals pressed rulers for legal equality and economic freedoms, and radicals urged broader democracy. At the opposite end of the political spectrum, conservatives, including both aristocrats and many rural peasants, contended that traditional ways such as a strict social hierarchy and a state-sanctioned church should be preserved and honored as the social glue that held society together.

Because of these various pressures and conflicts, governments turned with growing enthusiasm to the idea of the national community as a way to soften social tensions. Governments also tended increasingly to claim legitimacy—their rightfulness and legality as managers of the state—in secular rather than religious terms, that is, as advocates of the welfare and rights of national citizens rather than as agents of God. To be sure, the ingredients of a national community in the making often included a dominant religious culture, though priests and other clerics tended steadily to lose political power in favor of secular rulers and officials. Elements of a national society also typically included history, literature, music, folklore, and legend. Governments supported public education that would instill patriotic love and selfless service to the state. They promoted civic ceremonies, stirring anthems, a single vernacular language, and a set of founding leaders and patriotic heroes that everyone should revere. In the United States and the Latin American republics, for example, the wars of independence provided a wealth of narratives (George Washington at Valley Forge and the liberation exploits of Simón Bolívar) to feed sentiments of common nationality. In Europe the first half of the nineteenth century was the era of the Romantic Movement, when folkways and fables served as sources of inspiration for modern poetry, novels, and music seeking to capture the nation's "soul."

French citizens defend the Republic. *The Departure of the Volunteers of 1792* by the sculptor François Rude adorns one of the four pillars of the Arc de Triomphe, which Napoleon erected in Paris in 1836 to celebrate the glory of France. A Winged Victory leads volunteers to battle in a scene so connected to French patriotism that the relief has become known as "The Marseillaise," after the revolutionary song that became the national anthem. How might an image like this one have served to galvanize shared national identity?

Varieties of Socialism

socialism A variety of ideologies that advocate social equality and justice and the community's collective control and management of economic institutions; in Marxist thought, socialism follows capitalism in society's transition to communism.

The word *socialism* originally evoked the idea of a society founded on cooperation and mutual concern rather than on individual self-interest. Among intellectuals and activists agitating for reform in the nineteenth century, socialists often championed the democratic and egalitarian ideals of nationalism, but they questioned liberalism's most cherished tenets. All socialists regarded liberalism as an inadequate and at least partially misguided response to the harsh realities of industrialization. Socialists did not share liberal confidence that the selfish pursuit of profit would benefit all levels of society. Rather, private ownership of industry, accumulation of capital in the hands of a few, and ruthless competition all made for appalling working conditions and nearly hopeless life prospects for wage earners and their families. Workers were "wage slaves"—men and women at the mercy of capitalist owners. Low pay, unsafe mills, and urban squalor not only created misery for workers but also led inevitably to social conflict and disintegration. Society must therefore be reformed and restructured to achieve fairer distribution of expanding riches. Socialists generally supported the struggles of artisans, factory hands, and miners to improve their lot by marching, striking, organizing trade unions, and agitating for government action. And many socialist leaders doubled as theoreticians and public activists.

One of the earliest socialist pioneers was Claude Henri de Saint-Simon (1760–1825), a French nobleman who nevertheless despised aristocratic privilege and wealth. He was one of the first writers to argue that free-market competition would in fact benefit relatively few and that industrialization should be linked to society's general welfare. He advocated planned industrial communities in which politicians would relinquish power to entrepreneurs, engineers, and bankers. Those experts would advance economic and technological progress while scientists and artists took charge of civic and moral affairs. Saint-Simon influenced other socialist innovators in Europe and the United States who set up, or at least sketched out, small-scale utopian communities, where workers would share equally in the fruits of production or at least receive fair treatment from employers. For example, Robert Owen (1771–1858), a Welsh factory manager, founded a textile-producing community in Scotland in 1810 that catered to the security and comfort of workers. But like other utopian projects, this one did not outlast its founder.

The most elaborate statement of socialist principles, and the most pungent critique of capitalist economics, came from the pen of the German philosopher and activist Karl Marx (1818–1883). He and Friedrich Engels (1820–1995), his

Karl Marx. Though he championed the rights of working people, Marx came from a prosperous family. He studied philosophy in German universities, where his social activism began to bloom. In 1845 he famously wrote, "The philosophers have only interpreted the world in various ways—the point however is to change it."

longtime collaborator, emerged at midcentury as the leading proponents of what they called "scientific socialism." In 1848 Marx published the *Communist Manifesto,* which set forth his fundamental idea that the laboring masses could achieve economic and social justice only through revolutionary struggle. Moving to England the following year, he spent the rest of his life there, much of it reading and thinking in the British Library and elaborating his ideas in *Das Kapital* ("Capital").

Marx drew on earlier socialist ideas but also scorned the utopians for thinking that programs of kindly cooperation among employers, governments, and workers would ever produce a just society. He also thought that class distinctions

bourgeoisie The urban middle class; in Marxist thought, the property-owning class that oppresses the working class.

proletariat The working class; in Marxist theory, the class that must overthrow the capitalist bourgeoisie to achieve control of the means of production.

were much more important than national ones. He contended that the industrial elite, or **bourgeoisie,** merely fooled workers into thinking that it shared with them a national bond. To the contrary, wage workers everywhere, whom he called the **proletariat,** must unite against their bourgeois oppressors. Marx argued from what he called a "materialist" standpoint that work, or "production," was central to all social organization and that history was fundamentally a class struggle between those who controlled the "means of production" and those who did not. In the modern era, industrial capitalists had replaced slave owners and estate lords as the dominant class. Now, Marx proclaimed, the proletariat must rise up to recover for itself the means of production, securing its interests by confiscating all productive property. Factories, farms, and businesses must be held in common for everyone's use and benefit.

For Marx, history was a process in which conflict over contrasting social systems would inevitably lead to a higher form of society. In the *Communist Manifesto,* he argued that the proletariat would ultimately triumph: "What the bourgeoisie therefore produces, above all, are its own grave-diggers. Its fall and the victory of the proletariat are equally inevitable."[4] Once workers overthrew the owners of capital, class struggle would end and **communism,** the existence of society without class or private property, would be established worldwide.

communism A dimension of socialist thought that advocates revolution to eradicate capitalism and establish the universal triumph of the proletariat.

Socialists founded political parties and labor unions in most European states in the second half of the century, though some of them rejected or modified Marx's radical program. Marxian socialists also struggled with two developments they did not expect. One was that legal reforms and continuing economic growth progressively lifted workers' standards of living in the industrializing countries without proletarian revolution. The other was that nationalism proved a powerful tool for persuading ordinary people to identify with even their richest fellow citizens. Nevertheless, the power of Marxist ideas grew as the century proceeded and the gap between rich and poor continued to widen on a global scale.

Movements for Women's Rights

For some thinkers, both liberals and socialists, the logic of their doctrines demanded radical change in the civic rights and responsibilities of women. Around the world, women had long fought to loosen the control of men over such institutions as marriage, divorce, property ownership, and religious

leadership. The new European ideologies, however, offered frameworks for thinking critically about the social relations between women and men. Several women, for example, rose to prominence in the socialist movement. The English activist Anna Wheeler campaigned tirelessly for women's rights and in 1825 coauthored the bluntly titled book *Appeal of One Half of the Human Race, Women, Against the Pretensions of the Other, Men.*

Many women educated in the United States and Britain saw a blatant inconsistency between slave emancipation and the web of legal inequalities that kept females out of public life. In 1840 the male organizers of the World Anti-Slavery Convention in London initially stopped female delegates at

Elizabeth Cady Stanton speaking at the first Woman's Rights Convention, 1848. Making bold political claims, Stanton addressed a mostly female audience in the Wesleyan Methodist Chapel in Seneca Falls, New York. What might you infer from this picture regarding the social class of Stanton's supporters?

the door, then compromised by allowing them to be seated behind a curtain. Eight years after she attended that conference, Elizabeth Cady Stanton joined with her fellow American Lucretia Mott to convene the first women's rights meeting in Seneca Falls, New York. The delegates' Declaration of Sentiments demanded women's enfranchisement. Slave abolitionism, however, tended to overshadow their budding movement. In 1870 the U.S. Congress passed the Fourteenth Amendment, which gave the vote to freed male slaves but not to the women of any race. In Britain, though bills introduced in Parliament to enfranchise women failed repeatedly throughout the nineteenth century, a movement for women's rights initiated in 1851 continued to grow. In that same decade, liberals in Mexico began to lobby for expanded female education, and the Argentine-born writer Paula Manso de Noronha launched a feminist magazine in Brazil.

Movements for Political Reform and Unification in Europe

Between 1815 and 1848, Europeans lived with a vexing and potentially explosive contradiction. An assortment of dynastic monarchies, their ruling houses almost all related to one another by blood, endeavored to limit as much as possible the effects of the French Revolution, especially any drift toward popular democracy or social revolution. Simultaneously, however, liberals, nationalists, and radical democrats—their ranks growing among the urban administrative and professional classes—pushed for reforms. In almost every European country, protest marches, strikes, or urban riots disturbed the relative peace that prevailed among the region's states.

Some of those popular actions succeeded in forcing change. In France, Parisian insurgents overthrew the deeply reactionary King Charles X (reigned 1824–1830) in the July Revolution of 1830, replacing him with Louis-Philippe (r. 1830–1848), a nobleman dubbed the "Citizen King" because he accepted his mandate from the French National Assembly, not from God. The same year, rebels succeeded in splitting the Netherlands to create the new constitutional monarchy of Belgium. Greece achieved independence in 1830 after an alliance of middle-class merchants and mountain chieftains, with help from the British navy, drove out their Ottoman Turkish rulers. Britain also experienced industrial walkouts, protest rallies, and, in Ireland, rural insurrections. Liberal members of Parliament slowly pushed through political reforms. In 1832 Parliament voted to lower property requirements for male voters. This doubled the size of the electorate, though only to about 217,000 out of a population of 27 million.

Revolutionary movements of 1848. Then, in 1848, popular uprisings burst forth across Europe, surprising not only liberals but also socialists and republicans who had longed for just such an event. Street fighting broke out in Paris, targeting King Louis-Philippe, whose liberalism did not go nearly far enough for many. When the army failed to quash the insurrection, the king abdicated. Telegraphs and trains carried the breaking news across Europe, triggering urban uprisings, first in several major German cities, then in the Habsburg empire and Italy. In several places, rural farmers rose up as well, seizing towns and burning down their landlords' stately houses. Within just a month, French insurgents proclaimed a republic, the Habsburg emperor lost control of several cities, and revolutionary leaders in some of the small states of Germany and Italy began to write new constitutions. In far-off Brazil, rebels briefly rose up against Emperor Pedro II.

Social and political discontent had clearly been building for three decades. Urban workers complained of bad wages and vile working conditions. Men objected to the loss of their jobs to wage-earning women. Peasants protested against chronic poverty and consolidation of land into big estates. Minority ethnic groups in the Austrian, Russian, and Ottoman empires began to hatch their own nationalist movements. In the three years before the uprisings, moreover, western Europe experienced two seasons of bad harvests, rising food prices, and a moderate drop-off in economic growth. Anxious governments either froze in panic or retaliated so ineptly that even more people joined the insurrections.

The revolutions of 1848, however, played themselves out within a year. Government forces regrouped, and the laborers and artisans who had taken to the streets did not succeed in coordinating their actions in different cities. In France, the army killed ten thousand street fighters. In Hungary, Russian troops helped the emperor crush a rising of Magyar (Hungarian) nationalists seeking independence from Austria. Reactionary governments returned to power, but the risings frightened them and caused them much expense. Not wanting to witness such a pan-European explosion again, most dynastic regimes moved gradually over the next two decades to concede at least moderate political reforms and to try to identify themselves more intimately with the national community.

European nation-building after 1848. Liberal and nationalist ideologies were powerful enough in the two decades after the uprisings to inspire three successful nationalist movements, which reshaped Europe's political geography. In Hungary, Magyar nationalists did not stop agitating for independence from Austria. In 1867 the emperor Franz-Joseph agreed to a power-sharing arrangement called the Dual Monarchy. It retained him as head of state of both Austria and Hungary but granted each region its own parliament and control of internal affairs.

In the Italian peninsula, a nationalist movement to weld together a unified Italy took concrete shape in the first half of the century. In 1848 the region was a patchwork of territories variously ruled by Austria, the kingdom of Piedmont-Sardinia, the Spanish Bourbon dynasty, the pope, and several minor princes. However, secret independence associations multiplied in most of those territories. In Piedmont-Sardinia, Camillo di Cavour, prime minister to King Victor

Wilhelm I of Prussia proclaimed Kaiser of Germany following its unification, 1871. Anton von Werner's 1885 oil painting, *The Proclamation of the German Empire*, depicts Kaiser Wilhelm flanked by nobles, including Crown Prince Friedrich on his right. Otto von Bismarck, wearing a white tunic, stands facing the king. The royal family commissioned this painting to commemorate Bismarck's 70th birthday.

Emmanuel II (r. 1849–1878), worked doggedly to construct economic foundations for unification by modernizing industry, building rail lines, and expanding the army. He also played a skillful political game, negotiating with France's Napoleon III for support against Austria.

Modern Italy came quickly together between 1859 and 1870. With the help of French troops, Piedmont expelled Austrian forces from most of the northern peninsula and unified it under the banner of Italian nationalism. Giuseppe Garibaldi, a passionate revolutionary who had fought for democracy in Brazil and Uruguay, launched a private and brilliantly successful expedition to bring Sicily and the south into the Italian union. In 1861 a newly constituted parliament proclaimed Victor Emmanuel king of Italy. In the following nine years, the new state seized Venice from Austria and all of the pope's territories except the Vatican. Italy thus emerged as an independent constitutional monarchy that embraced most of Europe's Italian speakers.

Like Italy, Germany in midcentury was a collection of loosely confederated states. Prince Otto von Bismarck (1815–1898), the premier of the kingdom of Prussia under Wilhelm I, cared more for aristocratic privileges than for liberal principles. But he worked ceaselessly to expand Prussia's territorial reach and economic power, regarding military victories and rapid industrialization as potent ways to stimulate unity.

In a series of deft political and military maneuvers starting in 1864, Bismarck provoked successive wars with Denmark, Austria, and France, winning them all after short campaigns and then annexing additional German-speaking territories to Prussia. Victory in the Franco-Prussian War (1870–1871) brought down Emperor Napoleon III, cost France

its provinces of Alsace and Lorraine, and generated enduring antagonism between Germany and the Third Republic, the new French parliamentary government created in 1871. In the triumphant aftermath of victory in France, all remaining German-speaking states, except for Austria with its multitude of ethnic minorities, joined Prussia to form a unitary monarchy that same year. The new Germany, however, was no democracy. "The great questions of the day," Bismarck declared, "will not be settled by speeches or majority votes—that was the great mistake of 1848 and 1849— but by blood and iron." Power remained concentrated in the hands of the emperor and his central ministries, though Bismarck placated liberals by agreeing to a parliament (Reichstag) elected by property-owning males.

Modernizing Reforms in Muslim Lands

Since the fifteenth or sixteenth century, several Muslim monarchies, similarly to China, Russia, and western European states, had been occupied with projects to strengthen and extend central power by adopting both firearms technology and new, more efficient ways of governing and taxing their populations. As global commercial relations became more complex and European states projected more military and economic might, the political elites of most Muslim states considered new policies, which historians have called "defensive modernization." These military, technical, and administrative reforms were intended to stave off European diplomatic and commercial pressures or even prevent foreign invasion.

In the early 1800s liberal and nationalist ideas began trickling into major Muslim cities, reaching small numbers of army officers, officials, and international traders, especially people with knowledge of European languages. Muslim rulers knew well that European states were outpacing them technologically. Austrian armies had overpowered Ottoman forces in southeastern Europe; the British were conquering South Asia; Napoleon had invaded Egypt in 1798; and Greece, with British help, successfully threw off Turkish rule in 1830. Urban intellectuals and educated officers speculated on possible connections between material power and new ideas and institutions like constitutions, legislatures, and civil rights. Many reform-minded Muslim leaders favored fundamental secular changes, or modernization unimpeded by established cultural ways and authority figures. The trick for Muslim governments was to select innovations from abroad without upsetting delicate agreements with various power groups—religious leaders, land magnates, rural tribes—on which the stability of the state depended.

Reforms in the Ottoman empire.

Among Muslim states, the Ottoman empire launched by far the most ambitious modernizing experiment, initiating military, administrative, educational, and political reforms. The Tanzimat, or "Reorganization," as these reforms became known, began with Sultan Mahmud II (r. 1808–1839) and continued through several of his successors. In the military sphere the government hired French and Prussian advisers, translated French army manuals into Turkish, and imported up-to-date European weaponry. In 1826 Mahmud deployed a well-trained force to eradicate, amid great bloodshed, the janissary corps, the conservatively minded class of soldiers and artisans that had maintained a semi-independent army (see Chapter 17). To modernize education, the government sent young men to Europe to study, and it opened new schools to train future officers and civil servants in European languages, administration, and science. Tanzimat reformers gradually reorganized the state bureaucracy along French lines and, much to the dismay of the religious establishment, laced the Muslim legal system (*shari'a*) with language taken from the French Civil Code. Appropriately characterized as the "French-Knowers," reformist officers donned European-style uniforms, and bureaucrats traded their robes for western frockcoats.

The most audacious modernizers also pushed for new laws founded on liberal and nationalist principles. Before the Tanzimat, the major Christian and Jewish groups in the empire enjoyed autonomy over their internal affairs but also lived under legal restrictions that did not apply to Muslims. Between 1839 and 1869 a series of imperial edicts made all religious and ethnic communities equal citizens and subject to the same laws and reforms. Like European nationalists, Turkish leaders tried to infuse the culturally diverse population of thirty million with feelings of patriotic attachment to the Ottoman state. Reforms based on this essentially secular Ottomanist ideology culminated in a constitution (1876) that instituted a national elected assembly and put mild restrictions on the sultan's power.

Unfortunately for the modernizers, the Tanzimat era ended shortly after the new constitution appeared. The reformers themselves tended to be out of touch with peasants and urban workers and therefore lacked mass support. Moreover, the plan to cultivate a united Ottoman cultural identity ran up against local nationalisms that were awakening among Serbs, Bulgarians, Romanians, and several other ethnic communities within the empire. Finally, the government continued to sign "unequal treaties" with European powers (see Chapter 21) and contracted large loans with European banks. These policies sank the state ever deeper into

Students of the Ottoman Military Medical School. Western education was an important aspect of the Tanzimat reforms. The students wear Western-style military uniforms along with the modern Turkish headgear, or fez. Notice the skeletons and other bones posed in the photograph. Why might a formal group portrait like this one have been important to the reform movement?

A Moroccan Diplomat in France

Several Muslim states besides the Ottoman empire experimented with modernizing reforms in the mid-nineteenth century, though on a much smaller scale. These states included Iran, Egypt, Tunisia, and Morocco. The kingdom of Morocco ventured only the most cautious steps toward military and administrative modernization, though some members of the official class centered in the capital city of Fez took a serious interest in European affairs.

In early 1845 Mulay Abd al-Rahman, the reigning sultan, assembled a diplomatic embassy to visit France and the government of King Louis-Philippe. The sultan instructed the delegation to negotiate a solution to violence along Morocco's border with Algeria, which France had invaded fifteen years earlier. He also advised the mission to learn as much as possible about French society and come back with insights that might help explain its apparent military prowess. Muhammad al-Saffar, a young legal scholar and secretary in the employ of the embassy's diplomatic leader, kept notes during the group's stay in France and wrote an account of the adventure upon his return. In this selection, Al-Saffar offers his views on French economic values, military power, and religion.

The people of Paris, men and women alike, are tireless in their pursuit of wealth. They are never idle or lazy. The women are like the men in that regard, or perhaps even more so. . . . Even though they have all kinds of amusements and spectacles of the most marvelous kinds, they are not distracted from their work, and give every moment its due. . . . Nor do they excuse someone for being poor, for indeed death is easier for them than poverty, and the poor man there is seen as vile and contemptible. . . .

Their Sultan [King] summoned us to attend a review of the troops as an extravagant expression of his high esteem for us, . . . We were blinded by the flashing of their swords, the gleam of the horses' trappings, the shine of their helmets, and the radiance of the armor they wore both front and back. . . .

So it went until all had passed, leaving our hearts consumed with fire from what we had seen of their overwhelming power and mastery, their preparations and good training, their putting everything in its proper place. In comparison with the weakness of Islam, the dissipation of its strength, and the disrupted condition of its people, how confident they are, how

impressive their state of readiness, how competent they are in matters of state, how firm their laws, how capable in war and successful in vanquishing their enemies—not because of their courage, bravery, or religious zeal, but because of their marvelous organization, their uncanny mastery over affairs, and their strict adherence to the law. . . .

In Aix [Aix-en-Provence] we saw a huge cross made of wood standing on one side of the town square. At its top was a smaller bit of wood made into the likeness of a crucified man, naked except for a cloth covering his maleness. What a sight it was! . . . They claim he is Jesus, that is to say, a likeness of him crucified. . . . May [God] preserve them from that, and may He be raised high above what the sinners say. The proof of our eyes only increased our insight into their unbelief, the falsity of their creed, and the stupidity of their reasoning. Thanks be to God who guided us to the true religion.

Source: Susan Gilson Miller, trans. and ed., *Disorienting Encounters: Travels of a Moroccan Scholar in France in 1845–46: The Voyage of Muhammad as-Saffar* (Berkeley: University of California Press, 1992), 108, 110, 153, 190, 193–194.

Thinking Critically

Which aspects of French society and culture impress Al-Saffar, and which do not? Why do you think his views are ambivalent? What inferences might you make about Moroccan society in the 1840s, based on Al-Saffar's observations about France?

---

debt. Sultan Abdul Hamid II, who came to power in 1876, had no sympathy for European-style reforms. He halted the Tanzimat, suspended the new constitution, and ruled in the old autocratic manner until 1909.

The fate of Muslim Algeria. In the territory that is today the Republic of Algeria, Muslims witnessed a demonstration of Europe's raw military power when in 1830 French forces crossed the Mediterranean to seize the port of Algiers. Before

then, an elite of Turkish military men owing formal loyalty to the Ottoman sultan ruled the cities and towns along Algeria's Mediterranean coast. Self-governing Arabic- and Berber-speaking tribes held sway in the interior plains and mountains. France's Charles X, motivated more by hunger for political prestige than by any clear strategic aim, exploited a minor diplomatic incident to occupy Algiers. When local resistance erupted, the intruders found themselves fighting for more territory than they had planned. The French quickly eliminated the Turkish regime, but rural populations led by Abd al-Qadir battled French forces for nearly fifteen years. An Arab cavalry warrior esteemed for his Muslim learning, Abd al-Qadir founded a centralized Algerian state in interior areas beyond French reach. He also modernized his struggle by acquiring up-to-date weaponry and arguing his cause to European newspaper reporters. In 1840, however, France unleashed a scorched-earth campaign to make Algeria's Mediterranean hinterlands safe for land-hungry European settlers, who were beginning to pour in. In 1847 Abd al-Qadir was caught and deported, though popular risings continued to shake the country for another quarter-century.

The Limits of Liberalism in Latin America

Liberal ideas spread widely among educated city dwellers in the Latin American states that gained independence from Spain in the 1820s. The sixteen states created in the aftermath of the liberation wars became constitutional republics. Only Brazil remained a monarchy after Portugal withdrew. Land-owners, professionals, and government functionaries who admired the European and North American models of popular sovereignty formed liberal blocs in almost every country to press for continuing reforms. Liberals had no desire to perpetuate the authoritarianism and restricted commerce that had characterized the Spanish and Portuguese colonial empires, and they yearned to reduce the power of the Roman Catholic Church over social life and education.

During the first few decades after independence, however, liberal hopes wilted. Activist political groups remained small, and liberals quarreled incessantly with conservatives; each group promoted its own political and economic agenda. Like their counterparts in Catholic European countries, conservatives argued for strict social ranking between land-owning elites and ordinary people, and they honored the church as the preserver of tradition. Liberals contended that a combination of modern technology, property rights, and free trade would push their countries along Europe's path of material progress. But in fact, most of Latin America remained economically stagnant until after 1850. The wars of independence had wrecked economic infrastructures, and most of the urban educated class, including liberals proclaiming universal equality, held deep cultural prejudices against the Indians, *mestizos,* and black workers that inhabited the rural backlands.

Dictators on horseback. When postindependence governments achieved little economic change, military officers seized power, sometimes in rural regions, sometimes in whole countries. Across Latin America, the period from 1830 to 1860 was the age of the **caudillos** (kahw-DEE-yohs), political strongmen who led their own Indian

caudillos Autocratic political bosses or dictators, especially in the postindependence period in Latin America.

and *mestizo* cavalry and who typically ruled with clenched fists. In several countries these warlords competed ruthlessly with one another for power and land, inflicting prolonged political and economic turmoil in the process. Those who fought their way to national ascendancy retained republican institutions and symbols but routinely stuffed ballot boxes and suspended representative assemblies.

Two larger-than-life caudillos were Juan Manuel de Rosas and Antonio López de Santa Anna. Rosas dominated Argentina from 1829 to 1852. He personified the caudillo ideal, galloping with gauchos (cowboys), proclaiming himself champion of the poor, and having his own portrait placed on church altars. Simultaneously, he protected the wealth of the land magnates. He finally fell to an enemy alliance of exiled liberals and rival caudillos.

In Mexico, Santa Anna served as caudillo-president of the republic nine different times between 1833 and 1855. Like Rosas, he had the support of rich patrons, who locked up huge acreages of land while the economy stagnated. As one midcentury liberal wrote, "There are Mexican landowners who occupy (if one can apply the word "occupation" to a purely imaginary thing) a greater extent of land . . . even than one or more European countries. Over this vast expanse of land, much of which lies idle, . . . live scattered four to five million Mexicans who have no other means of subsistence than agriculture yet are forbidden the use of the land."[5] Mexico's still rudimentary communication system made sustained central management of the state, which extended from tropical forests to northern California, nearly impossible. In the north, settlers from the United States penetrated Texas and in 1836 declared independence from Mexico. They also legalized slavery again. In the Yucatan Peninsula, a rebellion of Maya farmers simmered well into the second half of the century.

The Santa Anna era ended in the traumatic aftermath of war with the United States from 1846 to 1848, an episode that cost Mexico half its territory. The United States was industrializing, settlers were pouring across the Mississippi, and President James Polk aimed to annex territory all the way to the Pacific. The Mexican government lacked comparable economic resources and suffered from chronic political factionalism. U.S. forces occupied Mexico City briefly but did not pursue annexation south of the Rio Grande. The federal government was more interested in settling American and European migrants on western Indian lands than in ruling millions of Mexican farmers.

Liberal revival. After 1850, liberal elites took back the presidential palaces in several Latin American countries, including Mexico, Argentina, Colombia, and Chile. Those states wrote new constitutions, trimmed the power of the church, and dropped tariffs in order to export more minerals and farm commodities. In many countries, *mestizos* and Indians began to take a freer part in civic life. Liberal regimes abolished slavery in most countries by 1854, though

Mexican cavalry charge a U.S. artillery position. Mexican artist Julio Michaud y Thomas depicts the 1847 Battle of Sacramento near the city of Chihuahua. Mexican troops outnumbered the Americans three to one, but U.S. artillery power forced them to retreat with "great confusion in their ranks." How does Michaud's lithograph express a Mexican nationalist perspective on the Mexican-American War?

especially in the later nineteenth century, typically defined the national community partly in terms of its religious culture. For example, Polish nationalism identified with the Roman Catholic Church and Serbian nationalism with the Serbian Orthodox Church. Secular liberals critiqued conservative church hierarchies but religious beliefs not so often. Under liberal pressures, monarchs associated with an official state religion came slowly to accept wider religious liberties. The Protestant constitutional monarchies of northern Europe, for example, progressively abolished discriminatory laws against Roman Catholics.

For hundreds of millions of farmers and urban workers, who, like educated men and women, worried about the directions the world might be taking, religion provided a fundamental moral foundation for coping with rural impoverishment, job insecurities, price fluctuations, and taxes. Spiritual teachings provided ideological frameworks for thinking about the world, finding meaning in it, and perhaps making it better.

nowhere did women gain rights to active citizenship. In Mexico, liberal reformers under Benito Juárez, an Indian and two-time president, achieved stability and conditions for economic growth in the late 1860s.

Nationalism gelled slowly in Latin American countries. In the decades after independence, popular identification with Mexico, Venezuela, Chile, or any of the new republics as distinct national communities barely existed. Even so, newspapers and café talk in the larger towns helped broadcast economic and political news along with a rising national consciousness. Such sentiment took longer to spread to the countryside, but in the late nineteenth century, rising literacy rates together with patriotic expressions in art and literature broadened the base of the imagined community in all Latin American countries.

Religion and Reform

FOCUS How did established religions and new religious movements address popular concerns about rapid economic and social change in the nineteenth century?

Liberalism and nationalism were secular ideologies, but they did not disdain all religion. Emerging nationalist movements,

Global Trends and Religious Change

Two broad developments presented the world's religions with both dangers and opportunities. First, religious leaders saw their political power eroded in several parts of the world. This happened partly because republics in Europe and the Americas whittled away the independent authority of churches. Or they "disestablished" religious organization, as the United States Bill of Rights did in prohibiting Congress from making laws "respecting an establishment of religion." Clerics also lost power because some states, for example, the Ottoman empire in the Tanzimat period, gave government officials tighter management over religious affairs and protected freedom of worship for minority groups.

The second development was the revolution of steampowered travel and mechanical printing, which allowed religious ideas to circulate wider and faster. In the nineteenth century, pilgrims traveled in larger numbers than ever before to holy sites—Roman Catholics to Rome, Muslims to Mecca, Hindus to the banks of the Ganges—where they identified intellectually and emotionally with a larger community of co-believers. Modern transport carried missionaries to previously inaccessible countries. Printing presses cranked out Bibles, Qurans, Buddhist texts, and the literature of new sects and reform movements.

These two trends contributed in turn to important changes in religious life. The adherents of the major traditions, particularly Buddhism, Christianity, Islam, and Hinduism, became more acutely aware that they belonged to a "world religion." This happened as leaders disseminated authoritative versions of sacred texts and worked to standardize and purify doctrines. In 1864, for example, the Roman Catholic pope Pius IX published the "Syllabus of the Most Important Errors of Our Time," which clarified and reaffirmed the church's position on numerous issues ranging from state–church relations to marriage. In Muslim lands, the Ottomans and other rulers regularized the curriculum taught in universities and strengthened their supervision of religious law courts. In India, intellectual and moral leaders worked together to make Hindu belief and practice more coherent, knowing that from ancient times this tradition had embraced a multitude of ideas and devotions. The idea of Hinduism as a unitary tradition entered the popular imagination of millions of Indians only in the nineteenth century.

Christian Evangelism

evangelism The practice of propagating the Christian gospel by preaching, personal witnessing, and missionary work.

A new spirit of **evangelism** permeated both Protestant and Catholic communities. The term *evangelism*, derived from Greek, refers to the sharing of the Christian Gospels. Protestants had traditionally been less zealous than Roman Catholics about leading strangers to Christ. But this changed in the nineteenth century as Protestants realized the power of print to spread the holy word, as well as the urgency of ministering to those who endured urban poverty. Church organizations became more deeply engaged in modern social issues, taking up causes like slave abolition, alcohol addiction, education, and poor relief. For example, political groups broadly described as Christian socialists argued that social compassion and justice lay at the heart of the Gospels. In 1865 the English preacher William Booth founded the Salvation Army, a new denomination with military ranks and uniforms that waged war for Christ among the working classes of London.

In the middle decades of the century, Protestant migrants from northern Europe carried evangelical zeal to the growing neo-Europes, transforming Australia, New Zealand, and Canada into mainly Protestant lands (though French-speaking Canada remained predominantly Catholic). By 1870 the United States was the largest Protestant country in the world. Traveling pastors fanned out across the country, holding gospel meetings and saving souls. America was also fertile ground for new faiths. The Church of Jesus Christ of Latter-day Saints (Mormonism), which grew as migrants poured westward, established a powerful base among new settlers in Utah. In Massachusetts, Mary Baker Eddy (1821–1910) founded the Christian Science

Catherine Booth, mother of the Salvation Army. An impressive speaker, she partnered with her husband William to reach out to the urban poor. She also advocated eloquently for women's ministry in a time when females were excluded from speaking in most Christian churches. What might account for Catherine Booth's popularity as a preacher among middle-class British Christians, when the focus of her evangelical work was criminals, addicts, and other outcasts?

church, which taught that redemption and healing were to be found through self-surrender to rational spiritual laws. In Africa, Asia, and the Island Pacific, Protestant missionary organizations competed with Catholic priests and nuns who had been proselytizing abroad since the sixteenth century. Wherever British forces seized new territory, missionaries from the Church of England and other Protestant denominations invariably turned up. Catholic missions similarly followed the French flag. Wherever they went, Christian missions included teachers and medical personnel, many of them women.

Jewish Reform

Within the world's dispersed Jewish communities, new movements arose to adapt religious practice to ideals of

Ram Mohan Roy: Hindu Reformer

In the commercial ports of South Asia, European liberal ideas circulated among young Hindu and Muslim intellectuals, who fiercely debated the challenges of British East India Company rule and the rapid commercialization buffeting the subcontinent. Among these thinkers was Ram Mohan Roy (1772–1833), who rose to public prominence as an advocate of modernization and a tireless reformer of traditional Hindu beliefs and practices.

Roy belonged to a small elite of well-educated Hindus determined to fathom Europe's swelling economic and military power by grappling seriously with European ideas. These scholars learned English and studied the European Enlightenment alongside the classics of Indian religion and philosophy. A man of high caste from the region of Bengal, Roy received a thorough classical education, including studies in Bengali, Hindi, Sanskrit, Persian, and Arabic. A young man of boundless intellectual energy, he went on to master English and even learned some Greek, Latin, and Hebrew.

In his thirties Roy took a post with the East India Company, as other literate men did, and he rose as high in the giant British firm as a native Indian was allowed to go. In 1814, however, he left the company to join other Hindu intellectuals in Calcutta to talk and write about religion, philosophy, and politics. His studies led him to conclude that over the centuries layers of false belief, deadening ritual, and baneful superstition had concealed the original Hindu faith. The pure teachings of ancient India, he argued, attested to a universal monotheism; to a religion founded on reason, not on the personal authority of priests; to social equality, not caste hierarchy; and to egalitarian relations between men and women. Despite his own family's attachment to traditions that subordinated women to male relatives, he denounced polygamy, child marriage, and male exploitation of women's labor. He also denounced *sati*, the custom of high-caste women throwing themselves on their husband's funeral pyre as proof of their fidelity. This stance pleased English liberals, who looked down on most Hindu practices as antiquated and barbarous, even though there is little evidence of *sati* being widely practiced.

Roy believed that Indian spirituality, washed of unreasonable customs, was readily adaptable to the modern world and had much to give to it. Fundamentally a moral reformer, he also aimed to harmonize religious belief with the new doctrines of secular liberalism, which were just beginning to reach the elites of Asian cities. For example, as much as he loved Sanskrit learning, he advocated a modern system of education that would employ "European gentlemen of talent and education to instruct the natives of India in mathematics, natural philosophy, chemistry, anatomy, and other useful sciences."[6]

Ram Mohan Roy

Roy was well versed on the French Revolution, sympathized with popular uprisings in places like Ireland, and imagined the day when South Asians would again take charge of their own affairs. In his time, nationalist ideology was still in its formative phase. Nevertheless, he and his fellow activists were the first to express the idea of South Asia, not just as the land of Bengalis, Punjabis, Sikhs, and numerous other ethnic and religious groups, but as India, a distinct cultural community whose members deserved modern rights to equality and justice. On this idea Roy's intellectual successors founded the Indian nationalist movement in the decades after his passing. He died of meningitis in 1833 during a visit to England.

Thinking Critically

Why do you think that Ram Mohan Roy's proposals for change in South Asian society did not include a demand that Britain and its East India Company immediately restore the region's political independence?

---

modernity and national citizenship. The German thinker Moses Mendelssohn (1729–1786), a leader of the reform movement known as the Jewish Enlightenment, translated the Hebrew Bible (Old Testament) into German and urged Jews to strive for integration into the social and cultural mainstreams of the countries where they lived. In the early nineteenth century, German Jewish intellectuals established schools to teach modern subjects in addition to religious texts. Mendelssohn and others argued that Judaism must change with the times rather than cling to laws belonging to ancient Jewish kingdoms long vanished.

Pushed by liberal opinion, many European governments, though not all, gradually lifted limitations on Jewish civil and cultural rights. Where Jews became more successfully linked into national life, notably in Germany, Austria, Britain, and the United States, growing numbers embraced what became known as Reform Judaism. Its adherents simplified rituals, ended sexual segregation in worship, and introduced sermons in vernacular languages.

Religious Reform and Revolution in the Muslim World

Like Christians and Jews, devout Muslims responded to the acceleration of global change in a variety of ways. In urban intellectual circles, Muslims talked of ways to join Islamic beliefs and traditions with modern science and liberal ideology. The Iranian-born writer and activist Jamal al-Din al-Afghani (1839–1897) sparked the imagination of young Muslims in the early 1870s by insisting that Muslims must stand up to European material power. This would require reviving feelings of unity among all Muslims as members of the universal *umma*, or "community of believers." Al-Afghani was the first Muslim thinker to put forward the idea of pan-Islamic solidarity as a modern political ideology.

The Wahhabi movement. In the Arabian Peninsula, tarnished faith and gross materialism, though not anything that Europeans in particular were doing, troubled the pious scholar Muhammad ibn Abd al-Wahhab (1703–1792). He urged Muslims to renew their spiritual commitment by dedicating themselves to the Quran and to the authentic traditions of the Prophet Muhammad as the foundation of law and daily life. He rigorously criticized local popular beliefs that had seeped into Islamic culture, as well as Sufi

mystical practices, which included veneration of living or deceased holy men. His school of thought, which became known as Wahhabism, demanded reverence for God alone. He also argued that Muslims must fulfill the Quranic requirement to respect women and their legal rights, though later Wahhabi leaders largely failed him on this point.

Ibn Abd al-Wahhab allied with Muhammad ibn Sa'ud, an Arabian warrior chief, who in 1808 conquered Mecca and a large part of Arabia. That success ended the relatively loose rule that the Ottoman empire exercised in the region and replaced it with a new state based on Wahhabi teachings. This kingdom, however, flourished only a few years before an Egyptian army invaded the peninsula and reduced it (at least for the time being) to a small desert principality. Nevertheless, the Wahhabi call to return to belief and worship presumably as practiced in the early Muslim centuries continued to influence Islamic reform movements, especially in West Africa, India, and Indonesia. Wahhabism is the religious ideology of the modern kingdom of Saudi Arabia founded in 1932, and in the past few decades its precepts have inspired radical Muslim political movements, including al-Qaida.

Religious revolution in West Africa. The impulse to reform also inflamed popular uprisings in West Africa. Islam had been established for centuries in the Sudanic region, that is, the savanna lands south of the Sahara Desert, though mainly among urban merchants, scholars, and ruling families. In the eighteenth century Muslim reformers

Warriors of the Sokoto Caliphate. This American engraving from 1857 shows Sokoto horsemen and infantry raiding for slaves. Why might the artist have focused on slavery rather than depicting the Muslim religious reform that also contributed to Sokoto's imperial success?

THE SLAVE HUNT.

in the area that is today Senegal, Gambia, and Guinea over-threw chiefs and land-owning nobles that they believed violated the Muslim ideals of good governance. At the center of those movements were the Fula (or Fulani), a predominantly cattle-herding people who increasingly identified with Islam.

In the early nineteenth century Usuman dan Fodio (1754–1817), a town-dwelling Fula and respected Muslim scholar, led a rebellion that changed the political and religious map of West Africa. His targets were the rulers of the large and prosperous city-states that are today part of Nigeria and Niger. The rulers of those walled cities, the largest of which was Kano, spoke the Hausa language and identified themselves as Muslims, but they gave little attention to religious duties or law. Dan Fodio called upon Muslim Fula and non-Muslim Hausa peasants (the majority of the population) to join together to overthrow their tyrannical rulers, whom he accused of a multitude of transgressions, including the enslavement of fellow Muslims. Like Abd al-Wahhab in Arabia, dan Fodio aimed to strengthen the Muslim community by cleansing it of local folk beliefs. But in contrast to the Wahhabis, he embraced the Sufi tradition and indeed propagated his movement through the Qadiriyya, a large mystical fraternity. Among family members who helped lead the revolution, dan Fodio's daughter Nana Asma'u played a key part as an essayist and poet who called upon women to educate their children in orthodox Muslim practice.

Between 1803 and 1808 dan Fodio's force of mounted archers and spearmen swept several Hausa dynasties out of power. He united the city-states under his rule, taking the title of *khalifa* (caliph), a rank that combined religious and political authority. Under Muhammad Bello, his son and successor, the Sokoto caliphate continued to conquer territories east, west, and south until it eventually became one of the largest empires in Africa. The successors of dan Fodio, however, failed to sustain his reformist zeal. Within a short time, they came to resemble the Hausa princes they had replaced, amassing property, trading slaves, and imposing burdensome taxes. Nevertheless, dan Fodio's example inspired similar Muslim revolutions in other parts of West Africa. Because of those movements and the continuing work of the Sufi fraternities, Islam became the predominant religion across Sudanic Africa by the end of the century.

Global Change and the Calamitous Wars of Midcentury

FOCUS Why did so many wars break out in the middle decades of the nineteenth century, and why did these wars produce death and destruction on such a large scale?

On a world scale the 1850s and 1860s were decades of extraordinary violence. Each of the disastrous conflicts of the period had its distinctive causes, but all of them were bound up with the explosive growth of the capitalist world economy, advances in military technology linked to mass production, and the social stresses of rapid change. One historical estimate suggests that more people died in war and rebellion during those decades than in any comparable period earlier in history. Such mortality was not to be exceeded until the catastrophe of World War I.[7] Two of the most destructive clashes of the period, the Crimean War (1853–1856) in the Crimean Peninsula (today part of Ukraine) and the War of the Triple Alliance (1864–1870) in South America, pitted one sovereign state against others. Three of the conflicts, the Taiping Rebellion in China (1851–1864), the Great Indian Rebellion in South Asia (1857–1859), and the American Civil War (1861–1865), were internal revolts against central state authority (see Map 22.3).

The Crimean War and the Industrialization of Violence

Imperial Russia in the nineteenth century deployed its huge land army to expand its borders, pushing in the west against the Ottoman empire. Conflict between Russia and the Ottoman empire over territory in what is today Romania triggered the war in October 1853. The following year Britain and France joined with the Ottomans to blunt Russia's advance by invading the Crimean Peninsula, Russian-ruled territory on the northern rim of the Black Sea. The European powers had no urgent interest in the Crimea, but their political and commercial strategies required that Russia be prevented from controlling Black Sea shipping, invading southeastern Europe, or seizing Ottoman Constantinople, which guarded the vital Bosporus strait that gave access to the Mediterranean.

The war lasted barely more than two years, but it cost the lives of an estimated 264,000 soldiers in combat and an even greater number from diseases such as dysentery and cholera. Historians generally agree that generals on both sides hopelessly mismanaged the fighting, but the belligerents also introduced new technologies and tactics that foreshadowed the American Civil War and even World War I. These included field communication by telegraph, steam-powered supply vessels, massive artillery barrages, and, in the British and French forces, new rifles that could shoot accurately eight hundred yards farther than older muskets. This was the first modern war in which military machines of the industrial era wreaked serious havoc. It was also the first war recorded by photographers. Primarily because Britain and France could easily resupply their forces by sea, they eventually forced Russia to sue for peace. The struggle checked Russian ambitions in the region, at least for a time, though it also signaled growing volatility in relations among the European powers.

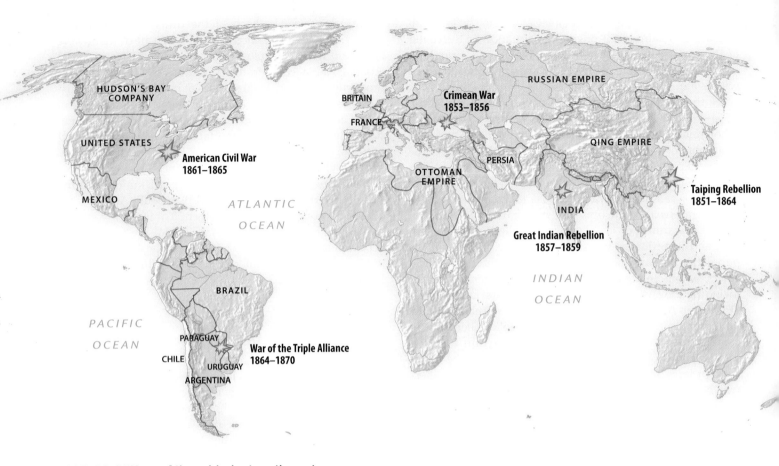

MAP 22.3 Wars of the mid-nineteenth century.
Which of these wars, if any, might be described as a colonial resistance movement?

Paraguay: A War of Annihilation

In South America the waning of the era of caudillo strongmen and the revival of liberal-minded governments restored political calm to most countries and spurred economic growth, especially in exports of raw commodities. Tensions grew, however, among countries over control of regional resources and the ports and transport routes that afforded access to world markets. Such pressures led the land-locked republic of Paraguay to war against its three neighbors.

In 1860 Paraguay had a remarkably prosperous economy based on crops that the Guaraní Indian population grew. Between 1840 and 1870 Carlos Antonio López, followed by his son Francisco Solano, ran Paraguay as a dictatorship with republican trappings. Still, they had a modernizing agenda that included abolishing slavery, promoting literacy, building industries on a small scale, and creating a well-equipped military. Francisco López even visited the Crimean War front to get military ideas, and he modeled his force on the French army.

The War of the Triple Alliance broke out in 1864, when Brazil invaded Uruguay, inciting López's fears that those two countries in collaboration with Argentina would restrict Paraguay's access to the Atlantic ports of Buenos Aires and Montevideo. When López declared war on Brazil, all three of his neighbors did indeed gang up on him. Though Paraguay had an army of seventy thousand soldiers, by far the largest in the region, the alliance gradually wore down the country amid ghastly carnage. In five years of fighting, more than 300,000 combatants died on both sides, and in Paraguay invading armies slaughtered people indiscriminately, reducing the population by 20 percent, including the great majority of adult males. In the peace that finally came in 1870, the country lost large chunks of territory to the victors, as well as most of the economic gains it had made earlier. Thereafter, the economy became increasingly tied to foreign merchants, land speculators, and banks.

The Taiping Rebellion in China

By far the bloodiest conflict of midcentury was not a war between states but a volcanic protest of a people against its own government. Historians have estimated that the Taiping (TEYE-pihng) Rebellion of 1851–1864 cost between ten and thirty million Chinese lives, either in combat or from the disease and hunger that accompanied the destruction.

The Taiping revolt was the biggest of several popular risings that challenged the authority of the Qing dynasty in the nineteenth century. All of these movements grew out of peasant grievances over land shortages linked to growing population, price inflation, government negligence, and, in some areas, floods and famines. China's humiliating defeat by Britain in the Anglo-Chinese wars of 1839–1842 and 1856–1860 (see Chapter 21) exposed the empire's military weakness. Chinese of all classes also saw weakness in the growing numbers of foreigners doing business in the ports, in the degrading unequal treaties the Qing government had to accept, and in the opium trade, which debilitated millions of men and women while enriching European merchants.

Hong Xiuquan (hoong shee-OH-chew-an, 1814–1864), the leader of the Taiping movement, was a poor schoolteacher from southern China who had failed the Confucian civil service exams and could not get a place in the imperial bureaucracy. After reading bits of Christian literature, he had a vision instructing him that he was the younger brother of Jesus sent by God to right the wrongs of the world. He had only minimal contact with European missionaries in China, but he preached to aggrieved peasants an austere doctrine that, vaguely echoing European socialism, proclaimed the equality of men and women and the eradication of private property. He denounced female foot-binding, opium use, prostitution, and gambling, and he promised to stock public granaries for famine relief, which the Qing government had neglected to do.

In 1851 Hong declared himself leader of the Kingdom of Heavenly Peace (Taiping), which would soon embrace the world. Amassing a following of hundreds of thousands of Chinese farmers and workers, he and his poorly equipped army overran several cities in southern and central China, flattened opposing militias, and executed rich land-owners. In 1853 the rebels captured the northern metropolis of Nanjing and killed most of its inhabitants. Although government forces repulsed an attack on Beijing, Hong's army grew to about a million men and women and took control of seventeen provinces.

Hong ruled from Nanjing for a decade, but his lieutenants frequently quarreled. Little came of his radical reform plans. In the meantime, wealthy families and bureaucrats gradually organized opposition. In 1864 a Qing army retook Nanjing,

Qing troops attack a rebel stronghold at Tientsin. This image conveys the magnitude of the Taiping Rebellion, which resulted in huge casualties on both sides of the civil war. What elements of the painting suggest it commemorates a Qing victory?

killing about 100,000 beleaguered rebels. Hong soon died in mysterious circumstances. The end of the rebellion left China economically depleted and more vulnerable than ever to European political pressures. The imperial government had to defer to regional lords and officers to quell the rebellion and try to revive farms and cities. Consequently, the regime lost more of its authority over provincial leaders, a process that worked to the benefit of foreign merchants, who wished to be regulated as little as possible. Nevertheless, the revolt roused small bands of Chinese modernizers to search for new ways to strengthen the empire's defenses against European power and the gales of economic change.

The Great Indian Rebellion

In contrast to China, most of South Asia in midcentury was already a European colonial possession. It was therefore bound more tightly to the capitalist world economy than China was, a fact visible to anyone who watched raw cotton, opium, and migrant labor flowing out of Indian Ocean ports in return for growing volumes of European manufactures.

In 1857 local soldiers in the pay of the East India Company mutinied against their European officers, triggering a popular revolt that within a few months engulfed northern and central India. Mutinies flared in several towns after Indian garrison troops, or *sepoys*, refused to load rifles that officers had issued them because the cartridges were smeared with either pig fat, which Muslim soldiers would not touch, or beef tallow, which repelled Hindus. Behind this cultural complaint, however, lay numerous grievances over inadequate salaries, bad living conditions, use of Indian troops to support British conquests in Burma, and racist policies that permitted only Europeans to hold officer ranks. More broadly, millions of South Asians seethed over the company's rapacious taxation and its refusal to seriously consult Indians on any aspect of colonial policy. The revolt had no central direction, but rebel forces marched on Delhi and several other large cities, amid much burning of villages, executions, and other horrific violence. The company spent a full year suppressing insurgencies in several different regions.

The rebellion had long-term consequences for both India and Britain. Parliament in London dissolved the East India Company and assumed direct control over the colony, henceforth known as the British Raj, or "Rule." The new British governors, or viceroys, initiated many reforms to strengthen colonial authority and internal communication, though not to widen Indian political participation. Reforms also encouraged more systematic exploitation of the country's resources for the benefit of European firms and a small sector of wealthy Indian land-owners and investors. The rebellion cost the British government millions of pounds and therefore hardened colonial resolve to crush any new insurgency.

The American Civil War

More blood ran in the American Civil War than in any other conflict of the era except for the Taiping catastrophe. Similarly to the situation in Germany and Italy before their unifications, the United States suffered tensions between those who believed concentrated power was the key to material progress and those who defended regional autonomy. In the first half of the nineteenth century the country had a relatively weak central government. The federal bureaucracy in Washington, D.C., was tiny, especially compared to those in countries like France or the Ottoman empire. The country had no integrated communication or transport system, not even a single national currency. Although Americans envisioned their land as a cultural community dedicated to republican principles, there were deep economic and political divisions. The most toxic of these centered on slavery.

On this issue the United States swam against the Atlantic current. All European states except Spain abolished slavery in their American colonies by midcentury, as did all Latin American countries except Brazil. In the southern United States, by contrast, slavery grew and spread. The plantation-owning class and its political allies played a key part in the industrial revolution—not by industrializing, but by making themselves the world's chief supplier of raw cotton to both Britain and the northern states. Although abolitionism gained strong support in the North, southern leaders insisted that slavery was essential to economic growth.

The dispute became aggravated every time the United States acquired new land. In the space of fifty years the country more than tripled in size, acquiring the huge Louisiana Territory from Napoleon in 1803, adding Florida and land in the Pacific Northwest in 1819, and seizing millions more square miles, including California, in the settlement of the Mexican War of 1848. All these acquisitions raised the thorny question of where slavery should be allowed. Capitalist and political interests in the North perceived the west as wide open space for the throngs of new settlers from Europe. The army would deal with obstinate Indians, and towns and railways would rise up everywhere. This vision had no room for planters bent on locking up huge tracts of land to produce crops with slave gangs. Southern slave owners also feared that their workers would try to run away to new free states with abundant land. Between 1820 and 1854, Congress enacted a series of compromises that treated each phase of westward expansion as a matter of balancing northern and southern interests—permitting slavery in one new state but not another. In the 1850s, political relations between North and South deteriorated steadily.

Opposing the extension of slavery, northern leaders founded the Republican Party. When its candidate, Abraham Lincoln, won the presidency in 1860, eleven southern states seceded from the union, joining together to form the Confederate States of America. In stark contrast to the 1848 revolutions in Europe or even the Taiping Rebellion, this revolt did not aim to broaden democracy or win social justice but to perpetuate black bondage.

To Lincoln, who had written that "that portion of the earth's surface which is owned and inhabited by the people of the United States, is well adapted to be the home of one national family," the secession was unacceptable.[8] The war that followed, mostly a protracted Union invasion of the South, lasted almost four years and caused nearly a million casualties, including about 620,000 combat deaths. At first, Lincoln justified the war as a mission to save the union, not end slavery, but in early 1863 he proclaimed the emancipation of slaves in all the rebellious states, though not in slave

Freed slaves travel north. Copies of Lincoln's Emancipation Proclamation decorate the coach and serve as flags. This illustration appeared in a French magazine, suggesting that the proclamation attracted international interest. What events in French history might this image have brought to mind?

states that remained in the union. The proclamation encouraged slaves to flee to the North, permitted blacks to join the Union army, and roused livelier sympathy in Europe, especially in Britain, for the northern cause.

The Civil War showed on a far larger scale than the Crimean conflict the power of mechanized industry to wear down an economically weaker enemy, if not win every battle. The Union pumped vast amounts of capital into factories in order to produce arms, ammunition, food, uniforms, locomotives, and steel rails. The accurate, long-range rifles introduced in the Crimea were further improved, and inventors made early experiments with machine guns. The war produced great butchery on both sides, but it eventually exhausted the Confederacy, which depended heavily on European imports to sustain its fight.

Near the end of the war, Congress passed the Thirteenth Amendment to the Constitution, which ended slavery everywhere in the United States. Subsequent amendments granted rights of citizenship to all African Americans and the vote to black males, though another century would pass before these rights were seriously enforced in the South. The war also propelled the United States to the rank of a major industrial state. By 1873 only Britain exceeded it in industrial output. Finally, the conflict shifted the balance of power in the United States in favor of the central government. For the first time, it became a proactive maker of national policy, sponsoring a national bank, a common currency, a homestead policy for the West, broader education for the young, and a transcontinental railway.

Conclusion

In the middle decades of the nineteenth century, the transition from the agrarian era in human history, which lasted 10,000 years, to the fossil-fuel age, in which we now live, went into full swing. In the half-century this chapter has explored, world population grew by more than 20 percent, global GDP increased by more than 60 percent, and the value of British exports alone grew by nearly 1,000 percent. Changes like these inevitably had a radical reordering effect on the way millions of people worked, thought, and organized themselves. This was the first period in which mass, long-distance migration took place to supply the global economy with infusions of wage labor for thousands of new enterprises around the world. Also in this period, reformers worked out elaborate new secular ideologies to try to explain and manage a world profoundly different from the one into which they were born. Religious leaders brought their spiritual and ethical systems to bear on the same problem.

Throughout those fifty years, western Europe, the first region to harness the energy of coal on a large scale, accumulated scientific knowledge, technical power, and disposable capital much faster than any other region of the world, with the exception of the United States. After 1870, as we will see in Chapter 23, European states deployed their armies, engineers, entrepreneurs, and migrant settlers to dominate by one means or another a large part of the planet.

• • •

Key Terms

American Civil War 638
bourgeoisie 647
British Raj 660
caudillos 652
communism 647
Crimean War 657
evangelism 654

Great Indian Rebellion 657
Mexican-American War 652
neo-Europe 638
pogrom 639
potato famine 639
proletariat 647
revolutions of 1848 639

secular 645
socialism 646
Taiping Rebellion 657
Tanzimat 650
War of the Triple Alliance 657

Change over Time

1788	First European settlers reach Australia.
1803	Usuman dan Fodio launches Muslim revolution in West African Sudan.
1808	Wahhabi forces seize Mecca in Arabia.
1829–1852	Caudillo Juan Manuel de Rosas rules in Argentina.
1830	French forces undertake invasion of Algeria. Greece wins independence from the Ottoman empire.
1832	The British political reform act expands voting rights.
1839–1876	The Ottoman state institutes modernizing reforms known as the Tanzimat.
1840s	The trans-Atlantic slave trade begins a rapid decline.
1846–1848	Mexico under Santa Anna loses half of its territory to the United States in the Mexican-American War.
1848	Insurrections rock Europe in the revolutions of 1848.
1845–1852	A potato famine propels massive migrations from Ireland.
1848	Karl Marx publishes the *Communist Manifesto*.
1851–1864	Millions die as a result of the Taiping Rebellion against Qing rule in China.
1854–1856	The French, British, and Ottomans ally to thwart Russian expansion in the Crimean War.
1857–1859	Indian Rebellion against the British East India Company spreads across South Asia; Parliament creates the British Raj.
1861–1865	North and South fight over slavery and secession in the American Civil War.
1864–1870	The War of the Triple Alliance pits Paraguay against its neighbors in South America.
1870–1871	Italy and also Germany complete the process of unification.

Please see end of book reference section for additional reading suggestions related to this chapter.

23 Capital, Technology, and the Changing Balance of Global Power

1860-1914

The Ueno railway station in Tokyo, Japan, 1885.

Satellite photo technology has given us striking images of the earth at night. On a world projection, we can see the brilliantly lighted megalopolis that runs from Boston to Washington, D.C., and the gas flares burning in Saudi Arabian oil fields. If we look carefully, we can also see a single thread of light running almost continuously from northeastern China westward across Eurasia to the bright star that represents the city of Moscow. This long filament traces the line of the trans-Siberian railroad. It is visible from space because of the numerous cities and industrial centers that have grown up along it since it opened in 1903.

Steam locomotives, majestic train stations, and steel tracks running across continents are vivid symbols of the capitalist world economy in the second half of the nineteenth century. Railroads connected factory cities to one another and opened the deepest interiors of Eurasia and the Americas to mining and commercial farming. They carried peasant families by the millions away from ancestral villages to jobs in cities and on tropical plantations. Locomotives and steamships transported European soldiers to new conquests in Africa, Asia, and the Pacific basin. Almost everywhere that railways were laid, Europeans or Americans arrived to invest capital, introduce steam technology, and provide engineering and scientific skill. For a period of about seventy years, western

Europe, together with Japan and the United States, dominated the globe—militarily and economically—to an extent no empire of the previous five thousand years had ever come close to doing. These decades were, we might say, the "European moment" in human history.

In the first section of the chapter we examine the pattern of events that transformed fossil-fueled industry into a world-scale phenomenon. Between 1860 and 1914, factories multiplied in western Europe and the United States, and new clusters of industry sprang up in Russia and Japan. In those same decades, entrepreneurs in many other countries experimented with steam-powered machinery, though on more limited scales. According to one estimate, per-capita gross domestic product (GDP), that is, the world's total output of goods and services divided by total population, rose by about 18 percent between 1500 and 1820 B.C.E. but by more than 100 percent between 1820 and the outbreak of World War I in 1914.[1] Population growth worldwide continued to soar, a phenomenon made possible by continuous innovations in medicine, public health, and agricultural technology. Simultaneously, however, humans and their machines continued to alter and degrade the globe's natural and physical environment at a quickening pace.

The second part of the chapter explores the increasingly complex global network of communication and exchange associated with modern industrialization. Manufacturers depended on constant in-flows of food, raw materials, and labor from other regions. In turn, they searched around the world for buyers of their finished goods. The gap between rich and poor regions opened wider, and radical changes occurred in the way both city dwellers and rural people lived and worked.

In the third section we recount the era's most dramatic story, the armed assaults by several European countries, as well as Japan and the United States, on technically weaker societies, mainly in the tropical latitudes of Africa and Asia. This wave of warfare resulted directly from power rivalries among European states themselves, a competitive imperialism that began to accelerate after the unification of Germany in 1871. As military aggressions mounted, African and Asian peoples devised various strategies to cope with the invaders, some organizing armed resistance movements, others negotiating terms of submission. A few states managed to preserve their independence, but tens of millions of people had to accept new colonial masters.

Chapter Outline

A Panoramic View

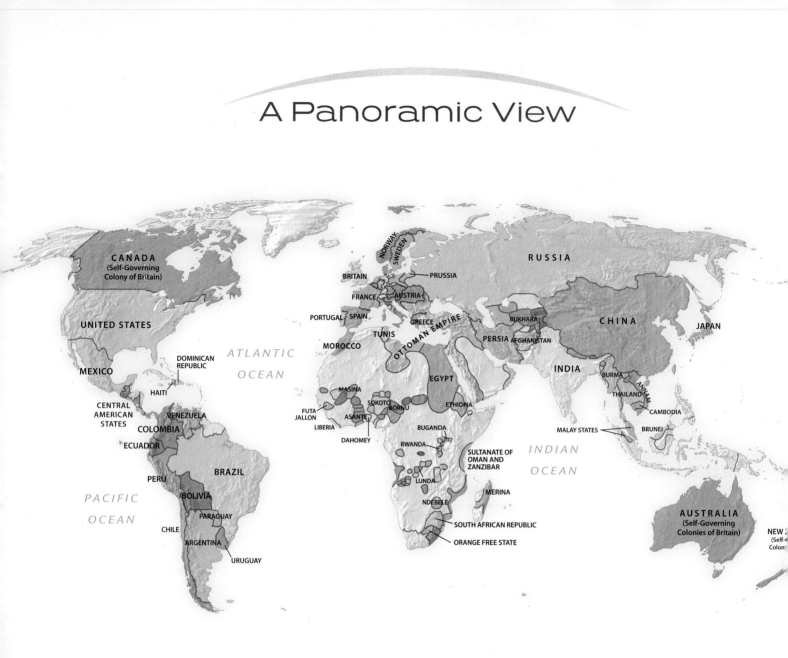

MAP 23.1 Major states, 1860.

From small kingdoms to huge empires, independent states provided the basis of political organization across most of the world in the mid-nineteenth century. What factors might help explain why in some regions several small states existed in clusters but in other regions single states spanned extensive territories?

The Spread of Steam-Powered Industry

FOCUS Why did industrialization projects have more success in some regions than in others?

Britain emerged in the early nineteenth century as the world's leader in steam engine technology. By midcentury the marriage of steam and coal transformed the country into an economic powerhouse. On the European continent, industrial hubs continued to grow and multiply. By the 1880s the United States became a major exporter of goods, and by the 1890s Russia and Japan joined the club of countries whose technical modernization produced strong economic growth. In fact in nearly every society with an agricultural economy and a relatively dense population, groups of merchants, officials, and intellectuals advocated for industrialization, even if circumstances prevented them from having much success anytime before World War I.

Wealthy Britain

By 1870 more than half the population of England worked in industry, though mainly in shops employing fewer than two dozen men or women, not in big factories. Late in the century, England remained the most densely industrialized region in the world, though its share of world GDP declined gradually relative to that of other, newer manufacturing countries. British business leaders, accustomed to the spectacular success of the century's first half, tended to resist risky new technologies. Consequently, the rate of growth slowed. Because of urbanization, the country also imported increasing amounts of food, which resulted in trade deficits with both continental Europe and big grain-growing countries like the United States.

British capitalists, however, did not worry too much about industrial productivity at home. Many of them made huge profits from worldwide banking and insurance services and from global investments in railroads, mines, shipbuilding, and other modernization projects. Industrialists also enjoyed special trade advantages. British factories exported massive quantities of cheap goods to India, an imperial possession. Like all conquering powers in history, Britain ran its colonies mainly to benefit itself. Official policies protected British manufacturers while inhibiting Indian entrepreneurs, of whom there were many, from building home industries that could compete with European products. After the first Anglo-Chinese War (1839–1842), British merchants also gained handsomely from the sale of Indian opium in China (see Chapter 21). Consequently, Britain enjoyed large trade surpluses with both India and China. This arrangement kept investors awash in capital and went far to compensate for the country's industrial lag relative to states like Germany or the United States.

Industrial Hubs in Europe and the United States

On the European continent, steam-powered industry developed mainly along an arc of coal- and iron-rich territory that extended from northeastern France through Belgium to Germany (see Map 23.2). Belgium was a densely industrialized country by 1850. France, which had a much larger peasant population and fewer coal resources than Britain, moved

The Krupp Steelworks, 1880.
Companies specializing in heavy industry flourished in Germany after 1871. Why do you think Germany was able to excel at steel production in the late nineteenth century?

MAP 23.2 Industrialized and industrializing regions, 1900.

How does this map show that industrialization was uncommon but not unknown in colonial dependencies by the end of the nineteenth century?

at a slower pace than its northern neighbors. In 1870 it took a serious economic blow when it lost the Franco-Prussian War and had to transfer its iron-rich Alsace-Lorraine region to Germany. Nevertheless, new manufacturing enterprises continued to multiply, including a profusion of workshops that made furniture for export and, in eastern France, thriving silk-weaving centers. By 1870 the country had a national steam railway network that expanded to 25,000 miles of track in the following forty years.

German industry advanced rapidly after 1870, when political unification transformed a region of competing monarchies and dukedoms into a single state with an integrated economy. Exploiting deep coal and iron reserves, German capitalists invested heavily in steel plants. Their innovative technology steadily reduced the cost to mass-produce high-quality metal for rails, industrial equipment, and armaments. Germans also pioneered chemical industries, which fabricated synthetic dyes, chemical fertilizers, and dynamite. And they innovated in electrical technology, inventing the first industrially useful electric generator, or dynamo, in 1870.

The Netherlands, the Scandinavian countries, and some areas within the Austro-Hungarian empire industrialized vigorously in the later nineteenth century. By the 1890s smokestacks also began to appear on the horizons of northern Italy and northeastern Spain. By contrast, western France, most of Spain, southern Italy, Poland, and the Balkan countries built few factories or rail lines. These were all regions having relatively few cities, small entrepreneurial classes, low levels of investment capital, and strong land-owning elites that depended on masses of rural peasant labor. Nevertheless, those areas participated in the world economy by continuing to produce primary commodities such as grain, wool, timber, and minerals for export to Europe's industrial core zones. They also contributed labor, sending millions of poor farmers and workers into the migrant streams to European cities or to points abroad.

More than twenty-five million able-bodied women and men streamed into the United States between 1865 and 1915, from China as well as from Europe, contributing to America's tremendous economic expansion in the decades following the Civil War. Northern manufacturers of textiles, steel products, and weapons rapidly expanded production during the war years. In 1860 the northeastern states provided jobs to more than 70 percent of manufacturing workers. But new railroads and river steamers carried job seekers west and south to Buffalo, Pittsburgh, Cincinnati, St. Louis, and Chicago, where workshops, factories, and processing plants turned out clothing, ironware, steel, furniture, lumber, meat, and hides (see Map 23.2). Fossil-fuel industry grew at an exhausting pace. For example, a huge plant that efficiently transformed iron into steel using the recently invented Bessemer process opened in Pittsburgh in 1881. It employed four hundred men working twelve-hour shifts without rest or meals. The owners of such mills maintained strong economic ties with European bankers and industrialists, who loaned them venture capital and helped keep them up to date on technology. The United States had plenty of coal and iron ore, and by the mid-1880s, it generated about 30 percent of total global industrial output, as much as Britain.

Smokestacks in Russia

Like the United States, Russia was a giant state that sprawled across a continental land mass. In 1870 its population, though overwhelmingly rural and mostly illiterate, was more than twice that of the United States. The government of the tsar (emperor) was rigidly authoritarian, permitting no national representative institutions. The small merchant class had industrial ambitions but remained politically weak. In these respects Russia resembled much of eastern Europe.

Russian rulers had long encouraged commercial ties with western Europe, and they supported military industries both to bolster the empire's international standing and to speed the conquest of Inner Eurasia. The government, however, kept a short leash on would-be industrialists, fearing that a strong private business class might challenge the aristocratic land-owners, who were the tsar's chief allies. Nor did the regime want a large urban labor force that might press for political rights or socialist labor unions, as workers were doing in western Europe.

In midcentury, however, Moscow's policies began to change. Russia's defeat at the hands of Britain, France, and the Ottoman Turks in the midcentury Crimean War (see Chapter 22) brought home the sad inadequacies of the empire's technology and internal communications. This realization triggered economic reforms. The government subsequently removed barriers to foreign investment, streamlined commercial laws, founded state banks, and began building railroads. Tsar Alexander II (reigned 1855–1881) abolished serfdom in 1861, but the state did little to help freed serfs acquire land of their own rather than work for low wages on large farm estates.

In the early 1890s the Russian government, not private entrepreneurs, initiated a comprehensive industrialization plan, imitating Egypt's state-directed though unsuccessful industrializing scheme earlier in the century. The tsar's economic architect was Sergei Witte, a man of merchant roots who took over the ministry of finance. Witte feared that Russia, an important grain exporter to western Europe, might slide into economic dependence on the big industrialized countries rather than imitate them. In 1899, he lamented, "The economic relations of Russia with Western Europe are fully comparable to the relations of colonial countries with their metropolises. . . ." Russia, he declared, must not be "the eternal handmaiden of states which are more developed economically."[2]

Under Witte's direction, Russia encouraged foreign investment and technical advice, and it poured tax revenues into steam power, mining, iron metallurgy, and mechanized farming. The trans-Siberian railway, Witte's favorite project, opened Siberia to large-scale farm and mineral exploitation. Russia's economic growth managed to keep pace with population, and by 1914, three million men and women worked in factories. Even so, the country could not easily catch up to western Europe or the United States because industrialization started later and from a lower economic baseline. In

Peasants in a Russian village. This photo from the later nineteenth century records the unpaved streets, rough-hewn timber houses, and poorly clothed residents of a rural settlement. Why might an image like this one have encouraged the Russian government to pursue industrialization?

1913 Russia's per-capita GDP was only a little more than a quarter that of the United States.[3]

The Meiji Restoration and Japanese Industry

As in Russia, Japan's governing elite looked warily at the economic power of western Europe and the United States. Its members fiercely debated the merits of a state-led industrialization campaign. The proponents squarely won the argument, but only after three decades of political struggle.

Since 1603 the Tokugawa shogunate (Chapter 20) had worked remarkably well as a semicentralized government carefully juggling the particular interests of several groups: the imperial court of the emperor (a ceremonial figure without governing power), the central administration headed by the shogun, the land-owning daimyo (aristocrats), the elite samurai warrior class, the town-based merchants, and the village authorities who spoke for the rural masses. By the early 1800s, however, the country faced grim financial problems. The remarkable expansion of farming that had characterized the seventeenth century leveled out in the eighteenth because the three big rice-producing islands had little virgin land left. The population of about twenty-seven million remained stable in numbers and highly productive, so living standards did not decline severely. Nevertheless, bad harvests occurred repeatedly, erosion and flooding took a toll, and silver mines and forests became depleted. The shoguns faced shrinking tax revenues, violent feuds among daimyo landlords, and recurring protests by land-hungry peasants. The Tokugawa also enforced a "closed country" policy to restrict foreign trade and cultural contact. This strategy deprived Japan of profitable commerce with other parts of Afroeurasia. But it also shielded Japanese producers from foreign competition, and it kept European merchants from selling guns to potentially rebellious daimyo or peasants.

Foreign merchants and the end of the Tokugawa. By the 1840s the shogunate could no longer disregard Europe's expanding power in East Asia. When British naval steamers defeated China in the Anglo-Chinese War, Japanese officialdom reacted in alarm. Would their island kingdom be the next target? Just as defeat in the Crimean War stunned Russia's rulers, so the Anglo-Chinese conflict jolted the Japanese elite into intense arguments over the meaning of European seaborne power. Debate turned into national crisis in 1853, when the American commander Matthew Perry barged uninvited into Tokyo (Edo) harbor at the head of eight heavily armed naval ships. The shogun had little choice but to accept a "convention of peace and amity," an agreement requiring Japan to open several ports to trade with Americans. Britain, France, Russia, and other European powers soon negotiated their own pacts.

The collapse of the closed country policy, coupled with continuing economic distress, exploded into civil war in the mid-1860s. A rebel coalition of daimyo and samurai warriors captured Tokyo, abolished the shogunate, and restored supreme executive authority to the young emperor, who had ascended the throne in 1867. This turning point became known as the Meiji (MAY-jee) Restoration after the emperor's reign name. However, the aristocratic faction that seized power, not the emperor alone, exercised political authority.

From 1868 to 1882 the Meiji rulers struggled to create an efficient centralized state. They terminated all independent authority of daimyo land-owners, and they sent legions of civil officials, many of them ex-samurai knights, to the provinces to regulate taxes and draft young men into a new national army. The leaders who favored adoption of European industrial technology and models of government gained full political control with the emperor's blessing. Japanese diplomats, engineers, and students began traveling to Europe and North America. As of 1875, more than five hundred foreigners, most of them Europeans, held advisory jobs in the Japanese government. By 1890 a large majority of young boys were enrolled in new public elementary schools, where they studied modern math and science. About 35 percent of girls went to school, too, raising female literacy rates much higher than in most countries outside of Europe and North America.

Factories and prime ministers. Meiji Japan soon joined the modern energy revolution (see Map 23.2). Engineers harnessed steam power to coal, iron, and copper mining. They built factories, mechanized the silk industry, laid rail lines, and churned out handguns, cannons, and naval vessels. As in Russia, the government invested in new technology, railroads, and iron manufacturing. However, private businesses, such as the rapidly growing Mitsubishi firm, also invested enormous sums in an array of industries. Agricultural production rose once again as the government streamlined land-use rights for peasants and introduced new machinery and fertilizers.

Japan went much further than Russia in experimenting with European-style governing institutions. In 1889 the emperor promulgated a national constitution that provided for a prime minister, a cabinet, and a two-house legislature comprised of an elective body called the Diet and an assembly of hereditary peers, like the House of Lords in Britain. The democratic base, however, was narrow. Only males who met strict property qualifications—about 2 percent of the population—could vote. Moreover, a tight oligarchy of wealthy men continued to dominate the Meiji regime. Even so, the government correctly guessed that a radical break with the past would encourage the European powers to respect Japanese sovereignty, rather than challenge it, as they were doing in China.

Between 1890 and World War I, Japan evolved an industrial economy that exported silks and other finished goods and that, like Britain and Germany, imported increasing amounts of foodstuffs and raw materials. Several factors encouraged Japan's sudden ascent into the fossil-fuel era.

Japanese school girls, 1905. Both girls and boys benefited from educational reforms begun during the Meiji Restoration. What conditions in Japan in the late nineteenth century might have convinced the government to invest in popular education?

First, in contrast to Russia or the Ottoman empire, Japan was nearly homogeneous in language and culture, free of the ethnic tensions that might have stalled popular support for change. Japanese people almost universally revered the emperor, who gave his royal blessing to the modernizing program. Second, the population remained quite stable straight through the Tokugawa and early Meiji periods. Numbers began to rise after 1875, but so did economic expansion, which kept living standards up during the early industrial decades. Third, the samurai warrior class played a special role. For the most part, these nobles, most of them literate, had a value system that encouraged loyal service to people above them on the social ladder. Many samurai moved easily into salaried managerial jobs in the Meiji administration, national army, and industry. Finally, the American and European intrusion happened so abruptly, in contrast to the more prolonged commercial penetration of China or the Ottoman empire, that Japanese leaders had to make drastic choices with little hesitation. Thanks to deft policy decisions and large helpings of luck, the country transformed itself in barely three decades into a new center of fossil-fuel industry.

Industrialization on Smaller Scales: Gains and Disappointments

Elsewhere in the world, entrepreneurs and political leaders launched new industrial experiments, at least on a modest scale. The worthy but limited successes of these initiatives revealed the problems that could thwart eager capitalists in countries with relatively weak technological bases.

Internal and external obstacles to industrialization. In some countries, those in power failed to see any special benefit in encouraging mechanical industries as long as peasants or slaves provided cheap labor and the land-owning elite made money exporting raw commodities and food. Also, potential capital for investment tended to pile up exponentially in the leading industrial countries but remained chronically scarce almost everywhere else. Another obstacle was unequal treaty signing: Militarily and economically strong states pressured weaker ones to open ports to trade, set low import duties, grant special privileges to foreign merchants, and in some places to give up territory, all without offering the disadvantaged partner much in return other than potential wealth for merchants and officials.

In this way strong states erected what historians have labeled **informal empires.** That is, Britain, France, Germany, the United States, and Japan used inequitable tariffs, large bank loans, and displays of naval power to compromise the independence of other states in order to serve their own strategic and commercial interests. By imposing such controls the industrial giants stood to dominate global commerce without having to take on the inevitably huge costs of invading and ruling countries whose economies they wished to manipulate. Although Britain conquered South Asia and France subjugated Algeria by stages, European governments generally preferred to exercise less expensive, informal influences on

informal empire A situation in which a powerful state protects its interests in a foreign society by exerting political and economic influence but without assuming the costs of territorial control.

Turkish carpet production, 1910. Despite the introduction of some steam-powered textile factories, artisanal carpet production on large hand looms remained important to the Turkish economy. In this scene, workers prepare wool and tie knots of colored fabric. The finished part of the carpet is rolled up at the base of the loom. What might you infer from this photograph about the division of labor by age and gender?

weaker countries, at least until the 1880s, as we see later in the chapter.

Despite relentless big-power pressures, several societies with largely agricultural economies created small islands of industry. In some cases these experiments provided models for later development. Experiments in the Ottoman empire and British-ruled South Asia are two examples.

Turkish carpets. Even though Egypt's ambitious industrialization program withered, hopeful capitalists in the Ottoman empire started up new textile enterprises after 1875. Economic and political conditions were not especially favorable. Between 80 percent and 90 percent of the empire's population of nearly twenty-six million lived by farming or craftwork. Surplus capital was meager, and unequal treaties with European states allowed mass imports of cheap fabrics and other goods that the empire's artisans had once produced themselves. The state also had to pay interest on growing debts to European banks, expenditure that forced higher taxes on people who might otherwise have put capital into new businesses.

Nevertheless, small groups of entrepreneurs—including Muslims, Christians, and Jews—imported European textile machinery, mainly to produce patterned, multicolored carpets that Europeans called "oriental rugs." These carpets had a large market in Muslim lands and a growing one among prosperous middle-class families in Europe

and the United States. Ottoman manufacturers combined traditional hand-weaving methods with small steam-powered factories to spin cotton, reel silk, and weave carpets. They introduced new synthetic dyes from Europe and supplied weavers with "cartoons," that is, preset templates of rug designs that merchants knew would sell. Shop owners kept wages down by employing mostly rural women of little education. But even though this industry flourished, it remained dependent on European merchants for machinery and for carpet sales abroad. Moreover, it did not generate nearly enough surplus capital to trigger industrial production of numerous other goods. Finally, no energy revolution could have taken off in that period without huge supplies of coal, which the Ottoman empire did not have. At the end of the nineteenth century the Turkish economy remained overwhelmingly agrarian.

South Asian industrialists. Entrepreneurs in South Asia undertook some remarkable factory-building projects despite major obstacles. Unlike the Ottoman empire or China, India was not a sovereign state in the later century but a British imperial possession. In the eyes of British industrialists, the subcontinent's population of more than 250 million (compared to about 31 million in Britain itself) offered a huge captive market. India's handloom weaving industry, which had exported cotton fabrics far and wide for centuries, declined steadily as European merchants bought raw fiber instead, shipped it to home factories, then sold machine-made cloth back to South Asians at prices lower than locally made cloth. In short, South Asia experienced serious **deindustrialization** in the nineteenth century, trending from high to much lower textile manufacturing.

deindustrialization An economic process in which a state or region loses at least part of the capability it previously had to manufacture goods, especially owing to foreign competition or intervention.

Even so, Indian businesspeople continued to finance internal trade, invest in commercial land, and explore industrial possibilities. In the late 1850s, groups of South Asian and European entrepreneurs collaborated to start up steam-powered mills to make products that did not compete with British textiles, notably bags, mats, rope, and other coarsely woven products fashioned from jute, a tropical fiber. J. N. Tata, a Bombay (Mumbai) merchant who first made money with a cotton mill, founded India's first modern iron and steel plants. He traveled to Europe and the United States to study metallurgy, and after he died his sons and other family members sold shares of stock, mainly to Indians, to build a steel complex near Calcutta. The enterprise succeeded, and at the start of World War I, the Tata company was supplying tons of rail stock to the colonial transport authority. Today, Tata is a conglomerate of corporations and one of the world's largest steel producers.

Capitalism's Global Reach

FOCUS In what ways was the global economy changing in the later nineteenth century?

Few countries built large factory complexes in the nineteenth century. Rather, people took part in the industrial revolution in many different ways, producing food and fiber, working for capitalist firms, and consuming imported manufactures. Millions of people worked in steel and textile mills, but many millions more harvested grain, picked cotton, cut timber, or tapped wild rubber.

The Worldwide Communication Grid

In the first half of the nineteenth century, some economic thinkers in Europe feared that industrialization could sputter out because markets for manufactures would not grow nearly fast enough to keep up with factory output. Industrial overproduction had already contributed to short-term economic downtowns. The problem did not, however, reach crisis proportions in the middle decades of the century in large part because producers were able to cultivate new markets farther from home. Modern rail and steamship lines allowed cargos to move on regular timetables. This gave merchants and manufacturers more confidence to plan operations and estimate prices. Long-distance telegraph lines hummed with orders for raw materials, price quotes, and money transfers.

The United States, Britain, Germany, France, and Russia led the world in railway construction (see Table 23.1). Canada, Australia, and Argentina also built impressive systems, benefiting from European capital and expertise. In the United States, rail engineers joined the Atlantic to the Pacific in 1869; Canada did it sixteen years later. Private companies developed India's rail network, partly to strengthen British military control over the subcontinent following the Great Indian Rebellion of 1857–1858 (see Chapter 22). Rails were also laid in Egypt, the Ottoman empire, Japan, Algeria, South Africa, and almost all Latin American countries. By 1880 a person could travel by rail directly from Mexico City to New York. The opening of the Suez Canal to steamships in 1869 slashed trade costs by shrinking the travel time between Asian and European ports. In 1800 it took two years to exchange a set of business letters between London and Calcutta. By 1914 it took four weeks.

The age of undersea cable communication opened in 1851 when technicians sent messages over a line strung across the English Channel. After engineers completed a cable line

TABLE 23.1 Lengths of Railway Networks in Seven Countries (in kilometers)[4]

| Year | Country | | | | | | |
	United States	Britain	Germany	Russia	India	Japan	Argentina
1860	49,286	14,603	11,089	1,626	1,542	—	9.8
1880	186,111	25,060	33,838	22,865	15,764	—	6,500 (1885)
1900	416,461	30,079	51,678	53,234	40,396	5,720 (1899)	8,138
1910	566,099	32,184	61,209	66,581	52,767	11,479 (1914)	28,574

Inauguration of the Suez Canal, November 17, 1869. Ships powered by a combination of sail and steam—along with a typical Egyptian felucca with white sails—traverse the canal as spectators watch. What causal connection might you make between the advent of steamships and the building of the canal?

between Britain and Canada in 1858, New Yorkers held a public celebration. One banner proclaimed:

> MARRIED,
> On Thursday, August 5, 1958,
> In the Church of Progress,
> At the altar of Commerce,
> The Old to the New World.
> May they never be divorced![5]

This marriage, however, had a rough start because the line quickly went dead. Nevertheless, workers tried again, pumping in more powerful electrical current and inventing materials that protected underwater lines from corrosion and breakage. A new trans-Atlantic line laid in 1866 kept working. Four years later, British technicians connected London to the west coast of India, making it possible for an English mill operator to telegraph a cotton order to India in minutes.

Feeding Industrial Societies

As millions of people poured into cities in the later nineteenth century to work in manufacturing, service, and export–import industries, other people had to supply them with nutriment, including foodstuffs that offered simply caloric energy or a bit of pleasure. Farmers who lived close to burgeoning cities could not come close to meeting the demand, so food had to be shipped in from afar. Fortunately for hungry workers, the new steam-powered transport systems increased the speed and lowered the cost of moving grain and other foods from one part of the world to another.

Food from the neo-Europes. Urban workers in industrialized Europe wanted to eat wheat, beef, pork, and mutton, but increasingly these staples had to come from other temperate regions of the world. In the 1880s the United States became a major exporter of wheat and other crops. The grassy plains that stretched 1,200 miles from the Appalachians to the Rockies invited experiments in super-scale farming. Once the army drove Native American peoples out of the way and private companies built railroads to haul grain and livestock from prairie to city, commercial farmers moved in with the McCormick reaper and other mechanical devices. Flush with British capital, Canada followed the United States in mechanizing farming, mining, and transport. In the late century, investors began to exploit the grain, timber, and mineral riches of Canada's western territories from Manitoba to British Columbia. In Australia, stock ranchers pushed deeper into the arid Outback, displacing Aboriginal hunter-foragers to make room for millions of sheep. Climates friendly to wheat, sheep, and cattle spurred economic growth in the southern cone of South America. Between 1871 and 1915 about 2.5 million Europeans settled permanently in Argentina, many of them making their livings exporting wheat and beef from the fertile pampas.

Tropical groceries and drug foods. Foods that flourished in tropical latitudes, including seed oils, nuts, fruits, and spices also commanded growing urban markets. Most desirable of all were the "drug foods," that is, pleasurable, in some cases addictive stimulants and narcotics, especially sugar, tea, coffee, cocoa, tobacco, and opium. Shipped in bulk from tropical plantations, these substances altered the dietary habits of men and women in every country where urban classes could afford them. A chronicler of nineteenth-century English cooking describes the popular new taste for sugar-loaded desserts: "Even the plainest dinner served above

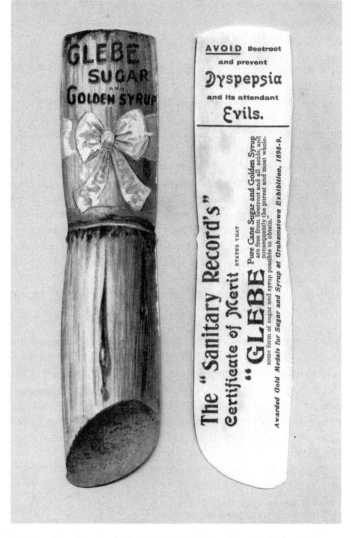

The benefits of sugar. In the late nineteenth century the Glebe refinery in Plaistow, a London suburb, manufactured golden syrup from imported cane sugar. How does this Glebe advertisement illustrate the importance of sugar as a product of mass consumption?

the poverty line was not complete without its pudding. Hot puddings, cold puddings, steamed puddings, baked puddings, pies, tarts, creams, . . . milk puddings, suet puddings."[6]

Tea and coffee mixed with sugar energized tired workers and helped restrain their thirst for rum or gin. Coffee houses and tea shops multiplied as gathering places for the middle and working classes. Consumption of tobacco and opium—to relax the body, sedate the mind, or relieve pain—also rose dramatically. British merchants gladly helped addict millions of Chinese to opium, a powerful morphine alkaloid that financed purchases of tea, Britain's favorite but much milder drug.

Capitalist farming. Merchants could meet soaring demand for tropical goods only because investors opened millions of acres of land to commercial farming. European and American entrepreneurs, often in collaboration with Asian, African, and Latin American rulers and landlords, cleared great swaths of tropical forest and grassland for cash-crop production. To consolidate small properties into big plantations, entrepreneurs, often in collaboration with governments, bought up or confiscated peasant plots and required cultivators to pay taxes in money rather than goods to force them into wage jobs. For example, the government in Argentina and other South American countries allowed wealthy investors to buy up large tracts of prairie to produce food and wool for overseas markets. In South Asia, British colonial authorities encouraged wealthy individuals to consolidate land into big estates, which paid scant wages to men and women who had previously owned their own spinning wheels and looms. In 1869 the British cotton commissioner explained in blunt terms the objective of colonial commercial policy in one part of India:

> Now it is not too much to hope, that, with a branch railway to this tract, European piece goods might be imported so as to undersell the native cloth. The effect would be, that, not only would a larger supply of the raw material be obtained—for what is now worked up into yarn would be exported—but the larger population now employed in spinning and weaving would be made available for agricultural labor.[7]

Commercial crop enterprises expanded in many regions in the later nineteenth century, including coffee in Brazil, sugar in Cuba, cocoa in the Gold Coast (Ghana), palm oil in Nigeria, rubber in Malaya, and rice in Southeast Asia. Large-scale cotton growing spread from the United States to India, Egypt, Brazil, and eastern Russia. Land-owners recruited local peasant workers at the lowest possible wages or brought in foreign contract labor, sometimes from great distances (see Chapter 22).

European and American capitalists, supervising unskilled work gangs, built rail lines in countries that produced tropical exports, though mainly to siphon commodities to seaports and waiting ships, not to help the countries integrate economically. Profits from these lines went to investors and local elites. This happened, for example, in Mexico, where the authoritarian president Porfirio Díaz (who ruled most of the time from 1876 to 1910) extended the country's rail network to 15,000 miles by 1911. Diaz talked of unifying the Mexican nation, but in league with foreign bankers and engineers, he aimed first to streamline the export of copper, lead, zinc, and a range of tropical crops to the benefit of investors, wealthy Mexican families, and the state.

Farmers in debt. The movement of once self-sufficient farmers into agricultural wage work often led to impoverishment. This happened notably in the world's cotton fields. The American Civil War (1861–1865) drastically disrupted the southern states' export of slave-grown cotton. This development drove raw cotton prices rapidly upward. In India, Egypt, Brazil, and a few other regions where landowning or rent-paying peasants grew cotton for the market, entrepreneurs with capital saw this price trend as an excellent business opportunity. They pressed independent farmers to grow less food for themselves and more cotton for the market. Indeed, millions of peasants took the plunge and initially enjoyed good returns. Between 1860 and 1866, cotton exports doubled in India and tripled in Brazil.

Families that grew less food, however, typically had to borrow from landlords or local moneylenders to pay taxes, buy seed and tools, and make ends meet while their cotton crops ripened. After the Civil War ended, American cotton production revived quickly and world prices plummeted. Small cotton farmers everywhere found themselves spiraling into debt. If they could not meet their obligations year after year, they became **debt peons,** men and women destined to perform agricultural or other wage work and make regular debt payments for the rest of their lives. In the later nineteenth century, millions of farmers in India, Egypt, Latin America, and the southern United States harvested cotton or other crops for the global market whether they wanted to or not.

> **debt peon** A laborer, usually on a farm or plantation, who works under obligation to repay a loan.

Rich Regions, Poor Regions

From the dawn of complex societies six thousand years ago to the industrial revolution, all agrarian societies had richer and poorer social classes. Typically, aristocratic classes enjoyed generous access to surplus riches, while farmers and workers had much humbler standards of living, whether they lived in China, West Africa, or Spain. By the late nineteenth century, however, disparities in living standards correlated with social rank not only *within* a society but also *between* societies in different parts of the world. Most notably, average individual incomes and life expectancies improved in the major industrializing regions faster than in countries producing only primary commodities. Near the end of the century, for example, an industrial worker in Berlin might expect to live around forty-two years, but a laborer in Bombay only twenty-eight years.[8] Farm families in India, China, and Peru were generally getting poorer, whereas farm families in France, Germany, and Canada were bettering their lot, at least a little. This widening gap between "have" and "have-not" societies has confounded humankind ever since. Several factors contributed to it, some of them local but others of global scope.

World population growth. First, the world's population grew from about 1.27 billion to nearly 1.8 billion between 1870 and 1914. On a global scale, cropland expanded greatly as well. However, in many predominantly rural regions, notably in Latin America, poverty intensified because population growth accelerated but neither new land nor many labor-saving technological improvements became available. Consequently, living standards declined. Even so, chronic impoverishment cannot be attributed simply to "overpopulation." In China, for example, living standards generally fell even though the country's overall population grew only moderately between 1870 and 1913.

An uneven playing field. The buildup of investment capital, technical skill, and military power in the industrializing countries gave them a powerful advantage over nonindustrialized countries. They could drive out local industries by importing their own cheap goods, depress local wages by introducing foreign migrant workers, or apply political pressure to force down tariffs—all of which hurt the weaker country's economy. These arrangements rigged the system, as it were, making it profoundly difficult for nonindustrializing states to diversify their economies, especially when their own affluent class colluded with Western capitalists to accumulate wealth. In Mexico, for example, the real wages of ordinary men and women fell throughout the thirty-four years that Díaz ruled, whereas foreign investors and two hundred elite families amassed about 50 percent of the land.

Ups and downs in the global economy. Under the biological old regime, that is, the world before the modern energy revolution, economic well-being in all agrarian lands depended on the quality of annual harvests, which depended on natural and social conditions—weather, natural disasters, social stability, foreign invasion, and so on. However, as countries industrialized and global trade surged, world economic conditions became more vulnerable to what economists began to call **business cycles.** These fluctuations in production, consumption, and trade were related to changing balances between industrial output of goods and consumer demand for them. They might last anywhere from a few months to several years. Also, the greater global economic integration ensured that a downturn in one part of the world might affect growth in other regions as well.

> **business cycle** A sequence of economic activity typically characterized by recession, recovery, growth, and repeated recession.

In 1873, for example, a severe depression spread around the world, and commodity prices plunged. Company financial shares plummeted, railroads went bankrupt, and iron mills shut down. To reduce costs, both factory owners and commodity producers cut wages. Landholding peasants lost income when prices fell. Indeed, prices for cotton, sugar, tea, and other tropical merchandise remained depressed for nearly a quarter-century. The world economy shifted into a new expansive phase only in 1896, but by then more of the world's population than ever had become locked into long-term poverty.

Deforestation and drought. A final factor in the growing gap between rich and poor regions was environmental change. In the nineteenth century, humans dramatically accelerated their efforts to burn and clear forests to supply

A family starving during an El Niño famine in India. In periods of drought, people suffered especially badly in regions where commercial crops had replaced local food production.

lumber and grow more food and fiber. In Brazil, coffee fields consumed immense tracts of tropical forest. In equatorial Indonesia, Dutch and other European planters and loggers eradicated millions of acres of natural growth. Deforestation profited some, but it also led quickly to soil erosion and exhaustion, which could mean diminishing returns on intense labor on both large plantations and small family farms. Governments and land-owners could have retarded deforestation if they had tried harder, and a few regimes, notably Japan, implemented serious conservation programs.

Global "weather events" were another matter. At three different periods in the later nineteenth century—1876–1877, 1889–1891, and 1896–1902—severe droughts followed by ghastly famines afflicted large areas of Asia, Africa, Latin America, and to some extent North America and Europe. These natural crises were associated with successive El Niño Southern Oscillations, the periodic atmospheric phenomenon related to a rise in surface temperatures in the South Pacific Ocean. A journalist described the consequences of the 1878 drought in Mogador (Essaouira), a city on the Atlantic coast of Morocco: "The pauper population of Mogador, always disproportionately large . . . is being rapidly increased by numerous famished Jewish and [Muslim] families from the adjacent districts. It is a fearful sight to see some of them— mere living skeletons. . . . They are selling their clothes and furniture to obtain food.[9]

El Niño episodes were nothing new in history, but these droughts happened to coincide with decades when capitalists extracted larger and larger amounts of foodstuffs from rural lands. In South Asia, for example, the British colonial regime took the view that help for the poor was admirable but that nothing should interfere with commodity exports. Indeed, rail cars and steamships continued to load wheat destined for England as starving Indians stood watching. In Asia alone, the death toll from the three El Niño events reached twenty to twenty-five million. The famines also debilitated sovereign states, especially in tropical Africa and Southeast Asia, making them more vulnerable to the European invasions that, as we shall see, came in the late century.

The Lot of the Urban Working Classes

Laboring men and women around the world devised numerous creative strategies to improve their economic conditions. The later nineteenth century, especially following the crash of 1873, witnessed a rising tide of protest against low wages, urban squalor, and limited rights. In the major industrializing countries, workers marched and rallied with some success. Men in skilled trades like carpentry or masonry formed unions, and sometimes skilled and unskilled laborers joined together in the same associations. These organizations engaged in strikes, demonstrations, and political lobbying to get pay raises, reduce the workday, abolish child labor, and protect product standards. Many unions adopted Marxist or other socialist ideologies and bonded with socialist political parties. Others, like the American Federation of Labor in the United States, sought to improve labor conditions within the liberal capitalist framework. In Germany, the conservative chancellor Otto von Bismarck repressed socialist unions but at the same time lured popular support by giving workers benefits such as disability insurance and old age allowances. Nevertheless, the Marxist

Domestic servants at Pembroke College, Oxford University. Both households and institutional employers hired servants to clean, cook, serve at table, wash laundry, and care for children. What would you infer about the gender, age, or racial profile of staff members of this Oxford residential college in the late nineteenth century?

labor and political movement grew larger in Germany than in any other European country.

Women in the labor force. The number of women worldwide who worked in the wage economy increased dramatically in the later nineteenth century. In places where indenture, share cropping, or debt peonage were common, women often toiled alongside men in the fields, while also keeping homes, cooking, and rearing children. Men and boys predominated in plantation and mine labor, especially when workers had to migrate long distances from their homes. Women remained in rural areas, often on poor land, to manage small farms.

In Japan in the late nineteenth century, large numbers of young, unmarried village women went to urban factories to work long hours for modest wages. At that time women constituted a larger percentage of the industrial workforce in Japan than in most industrializing countries. In western Europe, by contrast, the proportion of females in factory work actually declined in the later nineteenth century. Women who went to the mills, the patriarchal argument ran, drove down men's wages, tempted men to transgress their Christian morals, and loosened traditional male control over wives and daughters.

In western Europe, male cultural and social leaders formulated moral standards generally characterized as "Victorian," after Britain's Queen Victoria (r. 1837–1901). Advanced technical and scientific educations, as well as most skilled and managerial jobs, were considered inappropriate for

women, whom God presumably made intellectually and emotionally weaker than men. By contrast, nationalist ideology awarded high cultural status to motherhood because women had the sacred responsibility to produce and educate future citizens. Western employers who hired women in skilled jobs sometimes simply redefined those positions as "unskilled" in order to reduce wages. An array of occupations were socially "gendered" to permit women to take them: primary school teaching, domestic service, sewing machine operation, and retail work as "shop girls." Thousands of other jobs were gendered "men only" irrespective of the physical demands.

Outlines of a global middle class. In today's world, the vast majority of people in industrialized countries identify themselves as members of the "middle class." In general terms, this means that they have, or aspire to have, sufficient income to enjoy the basic benefits of consumer society—comfortable homes, automobiles, electronic gear, access to education, and so on. In less economically developed countries, the self-defining middle class may be much smaller but typically has similar expectations. This class has generally defined itself socially as occupying a rung *below* both the aristocratic land-owning class and the "high bourgeoisie" that made fortunes in commerce and industry. It ranked itself *above* those who worked with their hands, had little education, or occupied the margins of society. In Britain, one informal standard of middle-class membership was having the resources to employ servants rather than to be one. Typically, the middle class embraced lawyers, doctors, scientists, engineers, teachers, journalists, civil servants, midlevel managers, and business owners. In nonindustrialized countries, merchants, professionals, educators, intellectuals, and government employees defined relatively small middle classes.

Certain characteristics of the nineteenth-century global middle class stand out. First, the industrial revolution required many more people with specialized skills and advanced education, far more than the world had ever needed before relative to total population. Second, middle-class men and women lived mostly in cities because that is where the businesses, legal offices, schools, and newspapers were. This was as true of Bombay, Constantinople (Istanbul), and Mexico City as it was of London or New York. City-dwelling middle classes around the world began to think of themselves as "modern," that is, as the sector of society that aspired to particular standards of material ownership, dress, cuisine, and leisure activity. Third, the global balance of wealth and power tipped so far to the side of western Europe in the later nineteenth century that Europeans won the privilege, at least for a time, of setting the rules of how "modern" people should look, act, and think. Wherever Europeans traveled outside Europe, they took with them their Victorian values,

liberal or socialist ideas, and distinctive wardrobes. At the same time, more Japanese, Turks, Indians, and Mexicans from moneyed families journeyed to European or American cities, which showed them models for modern living.

Middle groups everywhere tended to accept the symbols and badges of modernity that Europeans set. Men in Buenos Aires, Alexandria, Tokyo, and Chicago all sported the same suits and top hats as Londoners and Parisians. Designed to express the wearer's industriousness and self-discipline, these were drab, functional garments. Middle-class men and women from Caracas to Hong Kong gathered in coffee houses and tea shops to talk art and politics; they took up sports like lawn tennis and cricket; and they made an effort to learn French or English, the languages of international prestige. Women of affluent modernizing families, notably in Japan and Latin America, hung European paintings on their walls, accompanied their husbands to the opera, and wedged themselves into whalebone corsets. Middle classes everywhere read newspapers to keep up with national and global events.

Urban middle classes around the world, though still a small minority of global population, acquired a certain uniformity of outlook and style. This cultural conversion, however, had limits. Witnessing Europe's mounting economic

Monkey-show.

屋　樂　の　居　芝　猿

All the monkeys dressed in European style, and in every respect trying to ape Foreigners.

The Monkey Show. The artist Kinkichiro Honda published cartoons in influential Japanese newspapers. This one is captioned, "All the monkeys dressed in European style, and in every respect trying to ape Foreigners." What broad developments in Japan might account for Honda's lampooning of the Japanese adoption of Western dress?

and military aggression in the world, many young modernizers sought a middle road between overt cultural "westernization" and reaffirmation of their native country's values and customs. In Japan, for example, young urban sophisticates indulged in a "Western craze" in the 1880s, reading European literature and sporting European waistcoats and hoop skirts. Within a decade, however, the cultural pendulum swung part way back toward traditional Japanese styles as people gained confidence in modifying Western ways to suit Japanese life. In the Ottoman empire, many modern-minded men adopted European dress, but they exchanged their traditional turbans for the conical, flat-topped North African fez, not the European top hat.

Globalizing Business, Technology, and Science

The global middle class rose in sync with both big business and highly organized scientific research. Modern industries required larger and more complex business organizations than the international trading firms of earlier centuries. Companies hoping to become major players had to structure themselves to handle complicated technologies, mass output, huge fixed expenses, and simultaneous manufacture of several different product lines. Investments, especially in heavy industries like steel or chemicals, also grew to unprecedented levels.

The managers of companies were less likely to be the owners along with their sons, brothers, and uncles than salaried executives directing a hierarchy of accountants, engineers, and laborers. Many successful family-owned businesses were incorporated and thereafter dominated by wealthy shareholders. Companies sometimes combined their businesses to form cartels or trusts, organizations that pooled huge amounts of capital and sometimes colluded to keep prices high and discourage newcomers from entering the competition. This trend toward greater economic concentration continued into the twentieth century, although some governments, such as the United States under President Theodore Roosevelt, took action to stop monopolistic abuses that artificially jacked up prices.

Some corporations moved to control all stages of production from extraction of raw materials through manufacturing to marketing. To do this, they had to control operations in multiple locations, sometimes in several different countries. For example, the firm founded by Friedrich Krupp in 1811 and passed on to his son Alfred (who started running it in 1826 at the tender age of fourteen) rose to loom over the German metallurgical industry, producing guns, naval ships, and numerous consumer products. At the time of Alfred Krupp's death in 1887, the company employed twenty-one thousand people and had sold military wares to forty-six countries.

Scientists in Europe and the United States made startling advances in both theoretical and applied fields in the later nineteenth century. Physics emerged as a distinct modern discipline in the 1840s with the discovery of the laws of thermodynamics, which describe the behavior of energy. In chemistry, scholars widely accepted the theory that atoms were primary chemical units and cells the basic building blocks of organic life. The Russian chemist Dmitri Mendeleev arranged the sixty-three known elements into the periodic table while also predicting that more elements would be discovered. In biology the germ theory of disease, associated notably with the French scientist Louis Pasteur, produced many beneficial applications to public health. In *The Origin of Species*, published in 1859, Charles Darwin proposed that life-forms are not fixed but evolving and that evolution occurs through the process of natural selection. Darwin argued that animal and plant species exhibit subtle

Darwin's theory of evolution sparked great controversy. This Parisian satirical magazine was not alone in depicting Charles Darwin as a monkey. What point do you think the artist intended to make by showing Darwin hanging from "the tree of science"?

differences and that competition for survival among species selects for any small genetic advantage. That advantage is then passed on to offspring. This revolutionary idea sent tremors through the scientific world and triggered intense public controversy over the notion that human beings share a common natural history with all animals, from apes to the simplest organisms.

More than ever, scientific discoveries depended not only on ingenious minds but also on systematic organization and partnership. In the early industrial era, technical entrepreneurs and scientists exchanged ideas, but their networks were informal and scattered. Practical inventors and engineers rarely had much formal education. Consequently, steam-powered machines were churning out finished goods decades before any theoretical scientist figured out why those contrivances actually worked. After 1850, however, scientists and practical technologists began to work together more methodically, setting up organizations dedicated to scientific research and its applications. German universities, which were government-supported institutions, took the lead in founding academic departments specifically for new scientific disciplines. Young scholars had to acquire formal Ph.D. degrees, and scientific knowledge was for the first time consolidated in textbooks. In Japan, modernizing educators founded the first universities in Tokyo in the 1880s, institutions that taught science, engineering, and medicine.

In countries where broad industrialization did not take place, modern-minded intellectuals nonetheless banded together to advance scientific and technical knowledge. In the Ottoman empire, for example, scholars translated hundreds of European scientific and technical works into Turkish or Arabic. New European-style schools and technical institutes adopted Turkish editions of textbooks in medicine, mathematics, chemistry, and other disciplines. In China, scholar-bureaucrats of the Confucian tradition resisted newfangled scientific theories, but independent Chinese thinkers collaborated with Protestant missionaries from Europe and the United States to translate scientific texts and promote modern curriculum in mission schools.

Starting about 1850, European governments and big businesses discovered the benefits of putting scientific minds to work in the service of economic growth. German universities were the first to collaborate with private industries to found research laboratories. Big companies also created their own research centers. In 1874, for example, the Friedrich Bayer Company, a German manufacturer of chemicals, dyes, and pharmaceuticals (including Bayer Aspirin), established a research division that eventually employed more than one hundred scientists. Two years later, Thomas Edison, a prodigious inventor, opened an industrial research laboratory in Menlo Park, New Jersey. Formal collaborative research also took root in Russia and Japan. In 1882 Russian scientists founded the world's first laboratory to improve the performance of railway locomotives.

European Imperialism and Popular Resistance

FOCUS Why did numerous societies in Africa, Asia, the Americas, and Oceania lose their political independence to European, Japanese, or American invaders in the late nineteenth and early twentieth centuries?

Over the course of four decades, beginning about 1870, the leading European powers undertook the conquest of most of tropical Africa, Southeast Asia, and the Island Pacific. Military forces under the command of European officers invaded and occupied about 18.6 million square miles, or 20 percent of the earth's total land area. The British empire alone grew from about 9.5 million square miles in 1860 to 12.7 million by 1909. On the eve of World War I, its colonial population numbered something like 444 million.[10] France, Germany, the Netherlands, Italy, and Portugal also waged wars abroad, either to build new empires or to enlarge colonies they already had. King Leopold II (r. 1865–1909) of Belgium carved out a private empire in the Congo River region. Near the end of the century, Japan seized Taiwan and other western Pacific islands; U.S. forces occupied the Philippines and Guam, as well as Cuba and Puerto Rico in the Caribbean (see Map 23.3).

Historians have conventionally labeled these aggressions the **new imperialism** to distinguish this late nineteenth-century surge of overseas conquests from those that took place sporadically in the 350 years after 1492. States that possessed the most advanced technologies and largest stores of capital assaulted and, in almost every case, overpowered societies that lacked comparable wealth or military tools. The states and ethnic peoples subjected to invasion, however, devised a variety of strategies to defend themselves and fight back. These ranged from pitched counterattacks and protracted guerrilla wars to mass flight and negotiated surrender. Whatever the indigenous response, the invading forces had by 1900 gained sufficient military control in Africa and Southeast Asia to start organizing colonial governments and extracting exportable resources.

new imperialism The campaigns of colonial empire building that several European powers plus Japan and the United States undertook in the late nineteenth and early twentieth centuries against other societies, especially in Africa and Southeast Asia.

The Road to Colonialism in Africa and Southeast Asia

Scholars have dubbed the European partition of most of Africa a "scramble" for new colonies. These assaults were indeed something of a free-for-all in the sense that seven different European states launched campaigns on multiple fronts in the space of five years (1879–1884). But the conquest

◇	British dependencies		Spanish dependencies			Dutch dependencies
◆	Portuguese dependencies	◆	German dependencies			Belgian dependencies
◇	French dependencies		Italian dependencies		◇	U.S. dependencies

MAP 23.3 Imperial states and their empires, 1913.
Which empires had the largest territorial claims on the eve of World War I? Which states in Africa and Asia did not become colonial dependencies in that period? What geographical elements might help account for their success at preserving their independence?

period lasted into the twentieth century. The invasions typically involved fitful military advances in the face of resistance, uncertainty over strategic objectives, shortages of soldiers and supplies, criticism from the European home front, and gross ignorance of the people and geography of the territories being seized.

Tensions in Europe. The multiple European invasions of immense territories in Africa and Southeast Asia had much more to do with international political relations than with well-organized plans to grab and exploit particular foreign lands. Those relations remained fluid and tense throughout the later century. The unifications of Italy and Germany in 1870–1871 put two large new centralized states on the chessboard of European power relations. Under Chancellor Bismarck, Germany expanded its industries faster than Britain, mass-producing armaments and building a steel-hulled navy. After losing coal-rich Alsace-Lorraine to Germany in the Franco-Prussian War of 1870, France under the regime known as the Third Republic (1871–1940) continued to industrialize and produce armaments in anticipation of taking back those territories. However, some French politicians, officials, journalists, and businesspeople, if not the public at large, thought new territorial acquisitions abroad might in the meantime shore up the country's prestige as a great power. As much as Britain contested Germany's armament, it also worried about French imperial ambitions. Britain and France remained suspicious of one another's intentions, and the absence of a formal alliance between them

served Bismarck's interests well. Britain also had strained relations with Russia owing to the tsar's expansionary drive up to the northern frontiers of Persia and Afghanistan. Britain regarded those countries as critical buffers against a possible Russian attack on India.

The economic depression that started in 1873 further aggravated European anxieties. It drove all the industrializing countries except Britain to raise tariffs, which helped domestic businesses but soured friendly international exchange. The economic slump also provoked the major powers to think about new outlets for capital investment, even though they had little idea what opportunities for it they might find in tropical Africa or Southeast Asia. Belgium's parliamentary government had no interest in overseas expansion, but Leopold II, the constitutional monarch, thought foreign conquest might be a good way to enrich himself and his royal house. He concocted the idea of identifying a vulnerable tropical territory, then sending a mercenary force to seize it and put the population to work to his profit. When he targeted the Congo River valley and its ivory and rubber resources without notifying the other powers of precisely what he was up to, he strained Europe's international relations even more.

Numerous individuals and private groups also complicated the political picture by launching their own projects in tropical lands and lobbying their governments to support them. These newcomers included trading companies, Christian missionaries, geographical expeditions, and a variety of adventurers looking for exotic encounters that might make for a best-selling book. For example, the Welsh-born American Henry Morton Stanley trekked through the central African rainforest with armed caravans paid for by European or American newspapers.

Annexation fever in Africa.

Political stresses in Europe probably made it inevitable that armies would be deployed. Between 1879 and 1884, the pace of events accelerated on several fronts. From enclaves founded in the time of the Atlantic slave trade on the West African coast near the mouth of the Senegal River, French marines advanced far up the Senegal valley, making commercial treaties with local African authorities as they went and without necessarily getting advance approval from the government in Paris. In North Africa, France invaded Tunisia in 1881, having already gained domination of that country's finances. Tunisia became a **protectorate,** that is, it remained a legally sovereign Muslim state but under French political control. In Egypt the government of Ismail Pasha (r. 1863–1879) tried to fend off European economic pressures by taking on modernization projects, notably the Suez Canal. But those expensive schemes resulted in huge debts to European banks. When Egypt went bankrupt in 1876, Britain and France took partial control of the state's fiscal affairs. Five years later, rebels under the command of Ahmad Urabi, an Egyptian army officer, tried to wrest power from Ismail Pasha's beleaguered government. In response, British forces moved in to restore order and defend the canal. As for Germany, its government had shown no interest in overseas colonies before France and Britain started making moves. In 1884, however, it sent armed expeditions to annex colonial beachheads in four different parts of Africa and in Oceania.

> **protectorate** A type of colonial relationship in which a foreign power takes control of the top levels of government in the colonized territory but permits it to retain formal, if largely fictional sovereignty.

Because the European powers threatened to clash with one another over their new tropical conquests and claims, Bismarck called an urgent international conference in Berlin in 1884. The conferees managed to resolve a tangle of disputes over rights to territory, especially in the Niger and Congo River valleys, and to set rules, not necessarily followed later, for parceling out territories not yet occupied. A key agreement recognized King Leopold's right to penetrate the Congo region, his piece of what he called the "magnificent African cake." No African rulers, however, were invited to the table. The conference mainly signaled to the world that the colonial starting gun had already sounded, though at that point Europeans ruled only a small part of the African land mass.

In hatching their invasion plans, the European powers had faint knowledge of the African interior or the commodities and markets they might find there. None of them, however, wanted any of their rivals to seize a disproportionate share of whatever riches might be discovered. Many European merchants and industrialists pressured their governments to undertake military campaigns, dreaming that precious metals and other bonanzas might turn up. Neither in tropical Africa nor in Southeast Asia, however, did much European businesses investment materialize relative to the huge ventures in Latin America or the United States.

After 1890, European military assaults on African societies intensified. None of the aggressors committed large numbers of their own troops to the campaigns. Rather, European officers usually led soldiers brought in from other colonies, fighters who had no fellow feelings for the people they were attacking. France dispatched Muslim Algerian contingents to fight in West Africa, and Britain sent Indian infantry to East Africa. In the Congo, mercenaries from several European states hired on as officers in King Leopold's private army. These soldiers-for-hire conscripted African men and boys into what was bizarrely called the Public Force, a virtual slave army charged with suppressing resistance and forcing Congolese to deliver quotas of ivory and wild rubber to the king's commercial agents. These operations involved sustained and horrifying violence.

Children mutilated by King Leopold II's employees in Congo. This photograph, taken about 1905, shows villagers who were brutally punished for not meeting their quotas collecting ivory or wild rubber. Mola (seated) lost both hands to gangrene after Leopold's henchmen bound them too tightly. Yoka's right hand was cut off to encourage others to work harder. Who do you think might have recorded these atrocities and for what reason?

Displaying unbounded hypocrisy, Leopold named his new colony the Congo Free State.

Conquests in Southeast Asia.

European-led armies advanced into the interior of mainland Southeast Asia by fits and starts. In 1852 British troops invaded part of the kingdom of Myanmar (Burma) in order to shield India's border on the east. In the following three decades, Indian columns under British command penetrated the fertile Irrawaddy River valley and the neighboring highlands, finally destroying the Myanmar state in 1886. As long as it had Myanmar as a buffer, Britain made no serious objection to France's advances against Annam (Vietnam) and Cambodia, where it had long-standing commercial interests. The attack on Annam got under way in 1859. Despite military help from Chinese troops, the Annamese Nguyen dynasty had to accept a French protectorate in 1885, though local resistance continued for another fifteen years. In island Southeast Asia, the Netherlands had ruled densely populated Java since the early seventeenth century but secured control over most of the Indonesian archipelago after 1860. By 1914, Thailand was the only large state in Southeast Asia not under European control.

Japan and the United States join in.

Japan confirmed its membership in the fraternity of industrial powers by seizing the island of Taiwan, a part of China, in the Sino-Japanese War of 1894–1895. In 1905 it fought a war with Russia, which we discuss in Chapter 24 in the context of events leading to World War I. In 1910 Japan invaded Korea. The United States joined the imperial club in East Asia because of the Spanish-American War of 1898. Rather like Germany, the United States seized territories abroad less to meet clear economic or security objectives than to enhance national prestige. It went to war with Spain in declared solidarity with Cuban nationalists, who had launched an insurrection against their Spanish rulers in 1895. The United States intervened, easily ejected Spain, then set up a military occupation and disbanded the rebel forces. Cuba became formally independent, but Washington exercised an informal protectorate over the country for several decades and permanently annexed Guantánamo Bay as a naval base. American forces seized most of the other territories that remained of Spain's five-hundred-year-old empire, including Puerto Rico, the Philippines, and the Pacific island of Guam. The war lasted just 123 days.

Imperialism in the Pacific.

Although an interconnected Pacific world of commerce, migration, and cultural exchange emerged early in the nineteenth century (see Chapter 22), European powers showed little interest in seizing islands. There were a few exceptions. New Zealand, a destination of European settlers since the early century, became a British crown colony in 1841. Thirty-three years later Britain occupied Fiji, though many observers back home failed to see what the benefit might be. Prodded by Catholic missionaries, France took Tahiti in 1842.

Wary of one another's potential strategic advantages, however, the major powers finally succumbed to annexation fever in the 1880s, hoping, as they did in tropical Africa, that the economic payoffs might be worth the great transport and administrative expense. Most Polynesian islanders lost their freedom sometime between 1870 and 1914 to invaders from Britain, France, Germany, or the United States. A few islands went to Chile, Australia, and New Zealand by international agreements, though no one asked Polynesians for their approval.

States that grew bigger.

Because the story of late-nineteenth-century imperialism usually focuses on encounters between Europeans and Africans or Asians, we may forget that some powers simply extended their land borders and subjugated neighboring societies. Between 1864 and 1880, Russian imperial forces terminated the last independent Muslim states in Central Asia, the region of steppes and mountains east of the Caspian Sea. Russian engineers followed with railway and irrigation projects, and by 1900 Muslim laborers under Russian rule were harvesting large volumes of cotton for the world market.

In South America, Brazil claimed sovereignty over most of the huge Amazon rainforest. But the government largely left its Indian hunters and farmers to themselves until the early 1880s, when global demand for rubber propelled thousands of European fortune-seekers, along with the Brazilian army, much deeper into the river basin to collect wild sap. Nine hundred miles up the Amazon, the city of Manaus became the center of a widening circle of Brazilian state power and trade, at little advantage to Amazonian Indians.

In North America, Indian societies of the Great Plains began to confront wagon trains of white settlers moving into the region or through it to reach California and Oregon. Some plains tribes, such as the Omaha and Pawnee, farmed the land; others, including the Cheyenne, Oglala Sioux, and Shoshone, had nomadic economies centered on hunting buffalo from horseback. As white immigrants occupied more land west of the Mississippi and joined the hunt for buffalo (sometimes for pure sport), Native American groups had to compete more ruthlessly with one another for diminishing resources. As buffalo herds dwindled, relations deteriorated and violence worsened both among Indian tribes and between them and intrusive white settlers. In 1851 the U.S. government, aspiring to extend neo-European settler society into the plains, persuaded Indian leaders to agree to the first of many treaties that restricted particular tribes to defined areas apart from where whites intended to settle. Herding and buffalo-hunting peoples regarded such confinement as economically disastrous.

Sioux, Apache, and other tribes, however, resented this confinement and fiercely resisted it. In the decade after the Civil War, fighting raged between U.S. Army cavalry and

Chief Geronimo and other Apache warriors. Geronimo fought the U.S. army for forcing Native Americans on to reservations. This photo was taken shortly before his surrender in 1886. How do you think non-Indian Americans might have responded to this picture?

Cheyenne, Sioux, and other mobile warrior bands sometimes armed with guns. The army, however, advanced relentlessly, much of the time driven by General William T. Sherman's dictum that "the more we can kill this year, the less will have to be killed the next war, for the more I see of these Indians the more convinced I am that they all have to be killed or maintained as a species of paupers."[11] By the late 1890s all but the most remote Native American societies submitted to the U.S. government and to life on reservations of marginal economic value.

Why Did European Invasions Succeed?

Whatever ambitions they might have had, European states would have had a hard struggle founding large empires in the world's tropical latitudes before about 1850. Dangerous disease environments were one obstacle. The lack of clear European military superiority over African or Asian societies was another. Both of these impediments were overcome in the second half of the century.

European health in tropical lands. Before the mid-nineteenth century, any European army that ventured into the tropics risked serious losses to malaria, yellow fever, or other diseases, as Napoleon Bonaparte's generals discovered when they tried to reconquer Haiti in 1802–1803 (see Chapter 20). Most Africans or Southeast Asians, on the other hand, did not suffer catastrophic mortality following contact with Europeans, as American Indians had in the sixteenth century. Over the millennia, most peoples of Afroeurasia had acquired the same biological defenses Europeans possessed for fighting major infections like measles, smallpox, and influenza. Only the most isolated groups, for example, hunters of eastern Siberia or Khoisan

herders of the South African Cape region, lacked those partial protections.

Starting in the 1840s, however, Europeans who went to the tropics began to live longer because of the availability of quinine. This medication, a substance extracted from the bark of the South American cinchona tree, offered significant defense against malaria. From that point, mortality from this parasite declined everywhere in the world where soldiers took quinine in proper doses. Also, tropical medicine emerged as a research field in Europe in the late 1800s, leading to advances that showed a link between certain species of mosquitoes and the microorganisms that cause both malaria and yellow fever. This discovery spurred campaigns to eradicate mosquitoes near military camps and garrisons, which drastically reduced troop death rates. Together, new drugs and public health measures permitted Europeans to penetrate and rule tropical lands without suffering disastrous disease mortality.

The military technology gap. European states dominated the world's sea lanes throughout the nineteenth century, but only after 1870 did they gain decisive technical superiority on land. Handheld guns of earlier generations had to be loaded through the barrel and fired one shot at a time. Tight discipline and synchronized firing maneuvers gave some advantage, but resisting populations had ploys of their own such as guerrilla tactics in forest or mountain terrain or skillful cavalry operations. For example, France invaded Algeria in 1830, but it took the army nearly fifteen years and tens of thousands of troops to break Muslim resistance.

In the late nineteenth century, however, advances in firearms technology multiplied. New handgun types had rifled, or grooved, barrels that made the bullet spin, a trick

The power of the Maxim gun.
British arms manufacturers demonstrate the destructive power of a machine gun to Chinese ambassador Li Hung Chang outside London in 1896. Why would gun makers want to give this demonstration, and why would the ambassador be interested in seeing it?

of physics that greatly increased range and accuracy. Rifles that fired cartridges loaded at the breech, that is, the rear part of the barrel, came into wide use in the American Civil War and in European colonial campaigns thereafter. Single-shot breech-loaders could be reloaded in seconds. In the 1870s gunsmiths reduced firing time even more by inventing repeating rifles, such as the American sixteen-shot Winchester, which accommodated magazines, or detachable containers loaded with bullets.

The Maxim gun, the first truly effective machine gun, arrived in the early 1880s and thereafter served as the decisive weapon in many colonial encounters. In 1893, for example, forces under the British South Africa Company destroyed the powerful Ndebele (uhn-duh-BEE-lee) kingdom in the territory that is today Zimbabwe. One eyewitness described the effect of the company's machine gun on African resisters: "The Maxim gun far exceeded all expectations and mowed them down literally like grass. . . . The natives told the king that they did not fear us or our rifles, but they could not kill the beast that went pooh! pooh! by which they mean the Maxim."[12] In 1898 British-led forces invaded the Muslim state known as the Mahdiyya in what is today the Sudan. Sailing up the Nile on steamboats, British and Egyptian troops leveled repeaters, Maxim guns, and field artillery against a huge but poorly armed defending force. At the end of the key battle, fewer than forty soldiers on the British side lay dead. The Mahdiyya army lost 11,000.

In many battles in both Africa and Southeast Asia, defending forces had guns, often bought from European traders or sometimes manufactured locally. The problem was technological lag: Resisting forces could rarely acquire the most advanced generation of weapons that European factories mass produced and supplied to colonial regiments. Consequently, the imperialist powers enjoyed a large comparative advantage in military technology from about 1870 until well into the twentieth century.

European confidence and ideas of race. European states had the technical power to violently seize other peoples' lands. But since they regarded themselves as modern, civilized nations, they had to invent intellectual and moral justifications for doing it. The rationale for late-nineteenth-century imperialism, elaborated by scholars, journalists, religious leaders, and politicians, centered on the idea that Europeans possessed not only cultural but also biological superiority to the societies they were subjugating. The colonized, so the argument ran, were both culturally backward, requiring a higher civilization to lead them forward, and mentally deficient, requiring wise and intelligent caretakers to help them struggle into the modern world.

Historically, most societies have indulged in ethnocentric arrogance, regarding themselves as smarter or morally better than the folk living over the mountain or across the river. European cultural conceit was fundamentally no different. In the later nineteenth century, however, the language and methods of science were invoked to validate a claim that Europeans were innately superior to people who looked physically different from them. In the mid-1800s, some European writers pursued the notion that humankind might be subdivided into different biological varieties. These distinct "races," they insisted, could be ranked on a scale of mental capability. Naturally enough, the people who proposed such a biological hierarchy placed themselves on the highest rung. Skin color, plus some other easily observable physical characteristic like nose width or head shape, became the primary determinant of a group's place on the spectrum—the darker the skin color, the lower the position on the chart of intellectual skill, moral responsibility, and cultural potential.

The intellectual movement to categorize human groups in this way is known historically as pseudo-scientific racism, that is, a view of human differences founded on misleading and phony applications of science. It was one aspect of social Darwinism, a wider European movement that played off, and distorted, Charles Darwin's theory of natural selection. Social Darwinists contended that dependent and debased elements of society—poor people, illiterates, criminals, women—occupy their inferior positions because over time they have exhibited less biological fitness than those who have had greater success in life, notably respectable, property-owning, white males. Pseudo-scientific racism thoroughly confused genetically inherited characteristics with culturally learned ones, contending, for example, that natural criminals could be identified by their low foreheads.

For European imperialists, dark-skinned peoples in places like tropical Africa had failed to create complex and dazzling technologies because their biological deficiencies trapped them at one level or another of barbarism. In the later nineteenth century, pseudo-scientific racist doctrine achieved nearly universal acceptance among educated people in Western societies. It enjoyed its widest acceptance in Europe just when the new imperialism was getting under way. In Africa and Southeast Asia, all victories reinforced European confidence in their biological qualifications for ruling the "lesser races." Only in the second half of the twentieth century did the absurdity of pseudo-scientific racism become fully exposed.

Resistance Movements and Their Consequences

Despite their lethal weaponry, European invaders tended to advance slowly enough to allow local African and Southeast Asian authorities time to organize armed resistance if they chose to do it. States that already had military forces and strong governing institutions stood the best chance of mobilizing resistance. Peoples having no central state organization, however, were also capable of rallying popular opposition to European intrusion. Even when combat failed, leaders could usually strike political bargains with their new rulers, who more often than not had fewer troops, weapons, supplies, and administrative personnel than they would have liked. African leaders sometimes negotiated political deals that allowed them to retain at least some of their traditional power and economic resources.

The East African empire of Tippu Tip. In the decades leading to the European conquests, many societies in Africa and Southeast Asia stepped up their involvement in international trade. This developments inevitably raised the stakes for political power. One manifestation of this competition was the emergence of new regional empires, states that used European technology, especially imported guns, to strengthen their rule and their access to commercial resources. In some places, therefore, fighting between regional rulers and Europeans took the form of rival empire building.

Hamid bin Muhammad, a Swahili-speaking ivory and slave merchant known popularly as Tippu Tip (ca. 1840–1905), carved out a large empire in the East African interior. Deploying soldiers, ivory hunters, and slave raiders armed with imported guns, he emerged as a potent political figure in the upper Congo River region in 1874. Swahili merchants and regional commanders reported to him in the framework of a loosely organized federation. From his capital at Kasongo, west of Lake Tanganyika, Tippu Tip fashioned a political administration, laid out roads and plantations, and monopolized the sale of ivory, which porters hauled to the Indian Ocean coast for export. He put thousands of captives to work as slave soldiers and farm laborers. Captive women grew food for his fighters. In 1887 King Leopold, whose mercenary army was just then penetrating the eastern Congo, tried to legitimize his Congo Free State by appointing Tippu Tip as a provincial governor, a position he held until 1891. He spent his last years in comfortable retirement in a coastal town.

Samori Ture and the French. In the West African savanna region, Samori Ture (ca. 1830–1900), built another sprawling empire. A member of the Muslim merchant class that dominated regional trade, he founded a state in the early 1870s in the region of modern Guinea near the headwaters of the Senegal and Niger Rivers. At first, this state was just one of several kingdoms that Muslim merchants organized to consolidate their domination of agriculture and trade. Samori, however, succeeded in seizing important gold fields and then used this mineral wealth to defeat competing rulers and incorporate tens of thousands of farming and herding peoples into his realm. He invoked Islam, still a minority religion in the region, as an ideology of imperial unity.

When Samori first emerged as a state builder, France controlled Atlantic coastal enclaves and a stretch of the Senegal valley. As French officers leading Senegalese troops pushed farther up the valley, military columns soon came face to face with Samori's cavalry. From 1882 to 1886 the two forces skirmished repeatedly. A master of mounted hit-and-run warfare, Samori harassed French troops and avoided head-on battles. Eventually, however, he diverted his army eastward away from the French to conquer new territory in what is today the northern Ivory Coast and Ghana, subjecting local rulers to tribute payments as he went.

Samori continually improved his arsenal of modern weapons, buying single-shot and repeating rifles from British

French troops capture Samori Ture, 1898. Samori (at the left of the photograph, facing the camera) resisted French colonial expansion in West Africa for more than a decade. After his capture, the French exiled him to Gabon, where he died within two years. Notice the presence of African soldiers serving in the French colonial forces. Compare the tone and character of this photograph with the one of Geronimo on page 685.

merchants based in Sierra Leone to the south. He also employed several hundred blacksmiths to make copies of French repeaters, while village women manufactured gunpowder. However, as French and British forces raced each other to seize more West African territory, Samori had to retreat even farther east. He had no time to consolidate a strong state, and his modern weaponry finally proved no match for French artillery and machine guns. His thirty-year imperial adventure ended in 1898 when he was captured and sent into exile. Where he had ruled, French administrators began to move in.

Resistance movements without states. In both Africa and Southeast Asia, societies that lacked central governments nonetheless found ways to organize popular resistance, often drawing on religious ideas. One example is the Maji Maji Rebellion in Tanganyika (modern Tanzania) in East Africa. There, German-led forces had barely established a colony when, in 1905, Africans representing diverse ethnic groups rose together in resistance. Priestly leaders of local religions inspired this mass movement by instructing people to drink sanctified water, which they claimed had the power to bind fighters together in unity and to make European bullets harmless. German commanders suppressed the rebellion with great brutality, but it took a year.

In Zimbabwe, known in the colonial era as Southern Rhodesia, an explosive revolt broke out in 1896. The Shona-speaking peoples were the largest language group in the region, but they were organized in numerous local chiefdoms,

not a centralized state. By contrast, the Ndebele, who spoke a different language, maintained a cohesive military kingdom in the west of the country. In 1890 Cecil Rhodes, the British mining magnate, founded the British South Africa Company to penetrate Zimbabwe. He aimed to search for gold and to keep that region out of the hands of Germany. Company troops defeated the Ndebele state, then levied taxes on the African population, recruited forced labor, and allowed European farm settlers to confiscate land and cattle.

Under those stresses, both the Ndebele and the Shona rose in rebellion. In a speech before Cecil Rhodes, a senior Ndebele chief offered his explanation of why this happened: "I myself once visited Bulawayo [the British South Africa Company's principal town], . . . and I sat down before the Court House, sending messages to the Chief Magistrate that I waited to pay my respects to him." The nobleman and his entourage waited throughout the day, finally sending word that his people were getting hungry. "The answer from the Chief Magistrate . . . was that the town was full of stray dogs; dog to dog; we might kill those and eat them if we could catch them. So I left Bulawayo that night; and when next I tried to visit the Chief Magistrate it was with my [warriors] behind me. . . . Who blames me?"[13]

Local prophets, who served as mediums for divine instruction from the high god known as Mwari, stepped forward to lead the uprising. These spirit mediums assured people that a new day of freedom would soon dawn. A network of mediums woven through both Ndebele and Shona

Contrasting Perspectives on War in East Africa

Between 1884 and 1907 the German invasion of Tanganyika in East Africa set off numerous violent encounters between the African population and the combined force of Europeans and conscripted local soldiers. Karl Peters, a fervent German imperialist, played a key part in the early conquering campaign, leading two armed expeditions to persuade African authorities, by whatever means necessary, to transfer their territories to German sovereignty. The first selection here is from a book titled New Light on Dark Africa, *which Peters published in 1890. He describes his dealings with the Wagogo people of central Tanzania and his methods for stifling their opposition.*

In some parts of East Africa, popular resistance to German rule continued for years. For example, the Yao, a people who specialized in long-distance ivory trade, fought for nearly a decade, village by village. In 1890 Machemba, a Yao leader, wrote a letter to the German commander who had demanded his surrender. The second passage is an English translation of part of the German version of the letter, which Machemba wrote in the Swahili language.

DOCUMENT 1 Karl Peters on the Wagogo

I had made up my mind to practice patience in this country to the utmost possible extent, to get through peacefully; but practically I could not help seeing how impossible it is to get on with natures like these negroes without recourse to corporal punishment. . . . For these people themselves it is much better, if they are made clearly to understand that lying, thieving, and cheating are not exactly the things that ought to be in this world, but that human society rests upon a certain reciprocity of responsibility and service. Beyond all question, that is the manner in which the way will be best and most safely prepared for the opening up of Africa. To make oneself the object of insolence of the natives is the very way to confirm the blacks in the lowest qualities of their characters, and especially to degrade our race in their eyes. . . . We were still sitting at breakfast, when some rascally Wagogo began to crowd round our tent, and one of them placed himself rudely in front of the entrance. On my requesting him to be off, he grinned impudently, but remained where he was. Hereupon Herr von Tiedemann, who sat nearest to the door, sprang from his seat, seized the fellow, and flung him on one side. I too jumped up, and called out to Hussein to lay hold of him, and to teach him a lesson with the hippopotamus-hide whip.

DOCUMENT 2 Machemba on the Germans

I have listened to your words but can find no reason why I should obey you—I would rather die first. I have no relations with you and cannot bring it to my mind that you have given me so much as a *pesa* [fraction of a rupee] or the quarter of a *pesa* or a needle or a thread. I look for some reason why I should obey you and find not the smallest. If it should be friendship that you desire, then I am ready for it, today and always; but to be your subject, that I cannot be. . . . If it should be war you desire, then I am ready but never to be your subject. . . . I do not fall at your feet, for you are God's creature just as I am. . . . I am sultan here in my land. You are sultan there in yours. Yet listen, I do not say to you that you should obey me; for I know that you are a free man. . . . As for me, I will not come to you, and if you are strong enough, then come and fetch me.

Sources: Karl Peters, *New Light on Dark Africa*, trans. H. W. Dulcken (London: Ward, Lock, and Co., 1891), 192, 215; "Macemba: Facing Invasion," in Basil Davidson, ed., *The African Past: Chronicles from Antiquity to Modern Times* (New York: Grosset and Dunlap, 1967), 357–358.

Thinking Critically

How do these two accounts differ in the way they represent hostilities between Europeans and Africans? How do they differ in the way the writer portrays his opponent? How might you explain these differences in attitude and choice of language?

---

society coordinated resistance. The rebellion shocked the company, which nearly went bankrupt putting it down. Reinforcements from South Africa and tons of weaponry finally exhausted the rebels, though fighting continued until 1903 at a cost of about 450 European and 8,000 African dead.

States That Survived

The major European states had the technical potential to take over any African or Asian country they liked. Pragmatically, however, they preferred in certain regions to exercise informal imperialism in order to restrain both colonial budgets and great power rivalries. China, whose internal

Chulalongkorn: Modernizing Monarch

King Chulalongkorn and the Thai royal family.

In 1868 King Mongkut of Thailand (r. 1851–1868), a man of broad scientific interests, traveled from the royal capital of Bangkok to the Malay Peninsula to witness a total eclipse of the sun. Among his entourage was Prince Chulalongkorn (Rama V, r. 1868–1910), his fifteen-year-old son and presumed heir to the throne. During the journey, both father and son contracted malaria, and shortly after returning to Bangkok, Mongkut fell ill and died. Chulalongkorn recovered, however, and the royal councilors ratified his accession to the throne.

During the first four years of his reign, Chulalongkorn deferred to his ministers for day-to-day government while he gradually recovered his health. He also continued his education in both traditional Buddhist learning and modern sciences, which his father had insisted he and his numerous royal brothers receive. The memoirs of Anna Leonowens, an Englishwoman who tutored the young princes in the 1860s, inspired the Broadway musical *The King and I,* plus three Hollywood movies.

In 1873 Chulalongkorn took direct command of his realm, determined, as Mongkut had been, to save Thailand from a European invasion. Mongkut had appeased Britain and France with commercial concessions and a cautious program to modernize administration and technology. Chulalongkorn understood as well as his father the political dilemmas the monarchy faced. If he moved too aggressively to modernize, he risked inciting entrenched elites and conservative Buddhist leaders to open rebellion. That might in turn provoke a British or French assault. On the other hand, if he did not modernize to the extent that those powers demanded, he might still come under attack.

For nearly a quarter of a century, the king and his ministers maneuvered the state through this political minefield. Gradually the king replaced the "old guard" among his officials with eager young modernizers, many of them members of the royal lineage. In 1897 he visited Europe. Observing that even industrialized England accommodated time-honored traditions, he gained confidence that Thailand could find a middle road between modern reform and its distinct Buddhist culture. "I am convinced," he declared in 1898, "that there exists no incompatibility between such acquisition [of European science] and the maintenance of our individuality as an independent Asiatic nation."[14]

In his final two decades, he stepped up the pace of reform, reorganizing finance, adopting a legal system based partly on French law, and strengthening central authority over vassal princes and provincial estate lords. He also built railroads, improved rice irrigation, abolished slavery, and organized a small but efficient army, all measures that stimulated the country's market economy. In addition, he used his diplomatic skills to play on the continuing colonial rivalry between France and Britain and to convince all the European powers that he ruled a progressive state worthy of international respect.

Chulalongkorn reigned until 1910, straight through the era of European colonial expansion in Southeast Asia. He avoided indebtedness to European financial interests, and at the start of the new century, Thailand had an economy strong enough to generate huge annual exports of rice, as well as an emerging national culture centered on reverence for the monarchy. Nevertheless, he achieved these successes at a price. Under British and French pressure, he agreed to transfer more than 175,000 square miles of border territories to colonized Vietnam, Laos, Malaya, and Burma. He also had to accept one-sided tariff agreements and privileges for European companies. In contrast to Japan, Thailand did not manage to ignite large-scale industrialization. Rather, it remained a commodity-producing country, its people's well-being dependent on fluctuations in the global market.

Thinking Critically

What factor do you think was most important in Thailand's success at remaining free of European colonial rule?

The Battle of Adwa, 1896. King Menelik II (bottom center, on horseback) is depicted leading well-armed Ethiopian troops, are firing both machine guns and rifles as Christian clergy look on. How are the Italians represented in this painting?

politics became increasingly tumultuous in the late nineteenth century, remained sovereign under the Qing dynasty as it had since 1644. However, the western European powers, plus Russia and Japan, held China in economic bondage through foreign-ruled "treaty ports" and outright annexations of Hong Kong and Taiwan. Similarly, the Ottoman empire preserved its membership in the European club of states through modernizing reforms and agile diplomatic footwork. Moreover, no European government wanted to see the monarchy that straddled the shipping lanes between the Mediterranean and the Black Seas become the possession of any single colonial power.

Ethiopia under the Solomonid dynasty was the only large African polity to keep its independence by defeating a European invader on the field of battle. King Menelik II (r. 1889–1913) ascended the throne determined to modernize his army and to expand the royal territory outward from the Ethiopian highlands, whose population was predominantly Christian. Acquiring breech-loading rifles, artillery, and machine guns from European merchants, Menelik built

a secondary empire, subordinating millions of previously autonomous farming and herding peoples to the status of Ethiopian taxpayers. But at the same time, Italy, anxious to join the "scramble" alongside the bigger European players, seized ports on the Red Sea and in 1896 sent an army ten thousand strong into the mountainous interior. Ignoring the fact that Italian traders had already sold Menelik thousands of guns, the invaders suffered defeat at the battle of Adwa (Adowa) at a cost of seven thousand dead, wounded, or captured. The Italians retreated to their coastal holdings, and Ethiopia, having proved its mettle to the other European powers, remained independent for another thirty-seven years.

In Southeast Asia, Thailand survived as a sovereign state by modernizing reforms and a series of commercial and territorial compromises with Britain and France. It also had the luck of being recognized by those two powers as a convenient cushion between Burma, a formal British possession after 1886, and Annam and Cambodia, which France made into colonial protectorates.

* * *

Conclusion

In 1800 the world supported at least several hundred sovereign empires, kingdoms, republics, and city-states. One hundred and ten years later, independent polities numbered fewer than sixty. This consolidation happened because so many states, both large and small, were enfolded into one European colonial empire or another. In 1914 Europeans or their descendants occupied, ruled, or economically dominated as much as 88 percent of the earth's inhabited land area. Moreover, Europeans continued to emigrate by the millions to temperate North and South America, Southern Africa, Siberia, Australia, and New Zealand, further marginalizing what remained of indigenous populations.

In contrast to states in Africa and Southeast Asia, three neo-European countries made strides toward political freedom rather than losing it. Canada, once a collection of British holdings, won its own constitution and full self-government in 1867. Australia devolved into an independent federated union of states in 1901, and New Zealand achieved self-rule in 1907. All three countries retained the British monarch as their head of state. In 1910 Britain granted South Africa self-governing dominion status, acceding power to a white minority population that progressively locked the African majority out of political participation.

The new tropical colonies, on the other hand, followed the pattern of India, where a small corps of alien administrators and military officers ruled millions with the help of European soldiers, technicians, civil servants, doctors, nurses, and missionaries. Once the conquerors quelled resistance, they governed, not through numbers, but through control of communications, cooperation from local leaders, and the abiding threat of violent repression.

On the eve of World War I, therefore, a thin layer of Europeans (plus lesser numbers of Japanese and Americans) claimed autocratic authority over more than 500 million Africans, Asians, and Pacific Islanders. In China, the Ottoman empire, Persia, and a few other places, Europeans did not rule but pulled the strings of international trade and finance. Even so, this global hegemony was more brittle than either colonizers or colonized could have seen in 1914. The acute tensions among the European powers, which colonial adventures abroad aggravated, burst into all-out war in the summer of 1914. World War I did not immediately bring down any overseas empire except Germany's. But it weakened colonial confidence and emboldened the colonized to mount new forms of resistance. In other words, not only was European world domination short lived, but it was never for a moment uncontested.

• • •

Key Terms

business cycle 676	Meiji Restoration 670	Spanish-American War 684
debt peon 676	new imperialism 681	Suez Canal 673
deindustrialization 673	*The Origin of Species* 680	trans-Siberian railway 669
informal empire 671	protectorate 683	
Maji Maji Rebellion 688	Social Darwinism 687	

Change over Time

1861	Tsar Alexander II abolishes serfdom in Russia.
1862–1890	Otto von Bismarck serves as chancellor of Germany.
1866	A trans-Atlantic cable line is successfully completed.
1867	Canada achieves self-government.
1868	Civil war in Japan ends under the Meiji Restoration.
1868–1910	Chulalongkorn (Rama V) reigns in Thailand, successfully maintaining independence from European powers.
1869	A transcontinental railroad is completed in the United States, connecting Atlantic to Pacific. The Suez Canal opens, shortening travel time between Asian and European ports.
ca. 1870–1898	Samori Ture builds an empire in West Africa, clashing with French forces.
1873	A global economic depression begins.
1874–1891	Tippu Tip rules in the East African interior.
1876–1910	Porfirio Díaz rules in Mexico, extending the rail network to boost exports.
1881	British military occupies Egypt.
1885	France imposes a protectorate on Vietnam.
1885–1908	Belgian king Leopold II controls the Congo Free State.
1895	Japan takes Taiwan from China in the Sino-Japanese War.
1896	Ethiopian troops defeat an invading Italian army.
1896–1903	The Shona and Ndebele rebel against British control in Zimbabwe (Southern Rhodesia).
1898	Mexico loses half of its territory to the United States in the Spanish-American War.
1903	The trans-Siberian railroad opens.
1905–1907	The Maji Maji Rebellion in East Africa pits a coalition of African groups against German-led forces.
1914	World War I begins.

Please see end of book reference section for additional reading suggestions related to this chapter.

part 7

The Promise and the Perils of Accelerating Change

1890-Present

Dubai's Burj Khalifa, completed in 2010, is the tallest building in the world.

We have taken the view in this book that human history is a story of growing complexity, both in the nature of interconnections among individuals and groups and in relations between people and their natural and physical environments. The pace at which humans have created and become enmeshed in new forms of complexity began accelerating faster with the fossil-fuel revolution of the eighteenth century. Today, the rapidity of global change sometimes astounds and bewilders us. The term *globalization* has entered the language to capture the idea that human society is continuously restructuring itself in all sorts of ways and that human interconnections are becoming continuously more elaborate and intense.

In the introduction to Part 6, we identified several complex historical trends that gave shape to the modern era and that have sharply distinguished it from the preceding twelve thousand years of the agrarian age. These trends of accelerating energy exploitation, population growth, technological innovation, human intercommunication, state power, popular political participation, and environmental change have continued into the twentieth and early twenty-first centuries. On the global scale these developments represent strong historical continuities—consistent patterns—from the eighteenth century to the present. At somewhat lower scales of change, turning points and indeed jarring breaks have been evident, especially in matters of political power, war, and economy. Among the globally dramatic *discontinuities,* we may count World War I, the Great Depression, World War II, the Cold War, the emergence of dozens of new sovereign states from former colonial empires, the collapse of the Soviet Union, and the Great Recession of 2007–2009.

Events like those turned the world in new directions and reverberated across the years. We should not, however, allow the momentous events and startling disruptions of the past 125 years to distract us too much from the deeper structural trends that have characterized the modern world so far and that shape our daily lives in ways that we may rarely think about.

■ Since the eighteenth century, humans have acquired an astonishing and growing capacity to control energy for useful work. The rate of energy consumption from fossil fuels and nuclear power soared in the twentieth century. According to one estimate, humans probably used more energy in that period than in all earlier history, and the rate of consumption continues to accelerate.[1]

■ The rate of world population growth accelerated in tandem with the energy revolution, reaching a historic peak rate between 1950 and 2000. In the new century, however, the growth rate has slowed, a change linked to declining birth rates in many parts of the world. In absolute numbers, population will continue to climb through at least the next century. However, if the growth rate keeps dropping, a major turning point in modern demographic history may be taking place, allowing humankind to remove population explosion, if nothing else, from the long list of ecological challenges it faces. The rate of global urbanization has dropped somewhat, as well, but people have continued to pour into cities. In the twentieth century the world's urban population rose from 14 percent to more than 50 percent.[2]

■ Technological and scientific innovations, including the new energy technologies, have continued to multiply in peace and war, good times and bad, since the 1700s. In the past century both scientific advances and useful inventions have come one after another. In the past thirty years the electronics revolution has reinforced and accelerated innovation in virtually all other technical and scientific fields. Human capacity to generate, transmit, analyze, and store information has been growing exponentially since the birth of the Internet in the 1970s. Is the world transforming itself into a single, immeasurably complex "brain" in which everyone and everything is networked together electronically?

■ Since the start of the modern era, the sovereign state has remained the primary structure for organizing and interlinking humans in large and permanent groups. Because of the power of nationalist ideology, people living together in states have, at least in some measure, come to think of themselves as sharing common cultural and social identity. The state system has remained fundamentally intact in the past century, but its character has been changing quickly since the end of World War II. The number of states in the world has grown by several dozen, and large overseas empires of earlier centuries have disappeared. Sovereign states continue to insist on freedom from external interference. But the international operations of corporations, banks, and nongovernmental organizations; the flow of information and money across borders; and the actions of ethnic nationalists, religious revolutionaries, and warlords within states have all contributed to erosion of sovereignty as people

a hundred years ago would no doubt have understood it. The number and variety of "political actors" on the world scene has swelled, and the state system is in great flux. In the past century, for example, states have taken on much greater legal responsibility for implementing and enforcing human rights.

■ Finally, the energy revolution, plus soaring population growth, economic productivity, and technical advance, have had the unintended consequence of seriously altering, in fact despoiling, the earth's geological, ecological, and atmospheric systems. The evidence of global environmental degradation became so apparent by the 1960s that people in a position to influence government policy and business practice began to sound alarms. An environmental movement took hold, and governments, corporations, and a variety of public interest organizations have taken steps to slow or reverse some forms of environmental damage to forest, soil, sea, atmosphere, and other living species. However, political and corporate resistance, as well as human tendencies to evade environmental challenges, have hindered progress. Furthermore, the world became environmentally conscious just when big developing states such as China, Brazil, India, and Nigeria started ramping up their energy use to compete economically with the older industrial powers of Europe and North America. Consequently, the natural and physical systems on which life depends have continued to deteriorate. Our species is faced with either restoring an ecological balance between human action and the earth's fundamental systems, primarily by developing new energy sources, or else retreating to lower levels of population and social complexity.

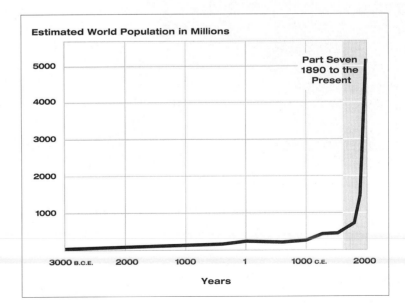

Estimated World Population in Millions

Part Seven 1890 to the Present

Years

24 Innovation, Revolution, and Global Crisis

1890–1920

Telephone operators work the switchboard at the American military headquarters in St.-Mihiel, France during World War I. Gas masks and helmets hang at the ready in case of a German attack.

M ost of us have become accustomed to communicating with disembodied computer voices on the telephone, often telling us to "hold." In the early decades of telephone communication, however, customers had to speak to a switchboard operator, who manually connected the lines between the caller and the other party. Operators wearing earphones sat at banks of switchboards plugging wires into jacks to connect calls.

When the first telephone exchanges were set up in the late 1870s, companies hired teenage boys as operators. Many of these lads, however, were not up to the job. They jostled each other, yelled into the receiver, insulted customers, and caused general havoc in the switchboard office. Firms then began to hire young, unmarried, reasonably educated women, and the job of telephonist soon became thoroughly gendered. Society came to define this occupation as naturally suited to women, or, more precisely, to middle-class white women without foreign accents. Females, or so late-nineteenth-century male managers argued, possessed certain "natural" traits that men were less likely to have: maternal patience, cooperative natures, devotion to details, and soft voices. Furthermore, phone companies, like most wage-paying firms, could get away with paying women lower salaries than men for comparable work. Switchboard skills became so closely identified with young women that the United States sent more than two hundred operators to Europe during World War I to handle military phone communications. Some of them worked near the front lines, where there were almost no other women except for nurses. In addition to the standard qualifications, these "hello girls," as they were known, had to speak both English and French.

The telephone contributed along with several other new machines to a huge advance in the speed and density of worldwide communication in the quarter-century before World War I. In the first part of this chapter, we situate this new communication and transport technology in the context of the sharp upswing that took place in the world economy in the mid-1890s, after more than twenty years of modest growth punctuated by recurrent recessions. Good times for well-employed and educated men and women, especially in industrializing countries and big commercial cities, inspired renewed faith in the power of science, technology, and capitalist enterprise to drive limitless material progress. On the whole, the gross domestic product of countries and regions worldwide grew spectacularly between 1896 and 1914, compared to any earlier era.

Chapter Outline

TURN-OF-THE-CENTURY PROSPERITY, 1890–1914
Commerce and Gold
Urbanization and Migration
Scientific and Technological Advances

GLOBAL INEQUITIES AND THEIR CONSEQUENCES
Drought and Plague
Africa and Southeast Asia under New Colonial Rulers
Worker Protest and Nationalist Ferment in Europe
Five Revolutions

INDIVIDUALS MATTER Qiu Jin: Social Reformer

THE GREAT WAR, 1914–1918
Lighting the Fuse
A World at War
Total War
Russia: From War to Revolution
Peace and Consequences

WEIGHING THE EVIDENCE Arab Independence That Was Not to Be

• • •

This boom, however, was severely lopsided. As growth *in general* ascended, the income gaps between the prosperous and the poor became wider. The second section of this chapter looks at the underside of prosperity and progress in the quarter-century before the global war broke out. Epidemics, famines, colonial exploitation, worker protest, and, in the first years of the twentieth century, armed popular rebellions counted among the distresses and upheavals of that period. Here, we survey revolutionary movements in Russia, Iran, Ottoman Turkey, China, and Mexico.

At the turn of the century, many educated observers predicted a long run of global progress and prosperity despite intense competition among Europe's Great Powers, plus Japan and the United States, to accumulate overseas territories and material resources. In fact, world economic growth aggravated rather than defused those rivalries, which after 1900 became increasingly toxic, rigid, and emotional. The last section of the chapter investigates the Great War, as people commonly called World War I. In the early summer of 1914, Europe's monarchs, prime ministers, and generals thought that if a general clash occurred it would be like wars of the previous half-century—localized, short, and not

A Panoramic View

MAP 24.1 States and colonial dependencies, 1910.
On the eve of World War I, western European countries, the United States, and Japan claimed or administered large parts of Africa, Asia, and the Island Pacific. Which countries claimed the largest overseas empires?

unbearably expensive. Instead, the struggle lasted more than four years, took close to sixteen million military and civilian lives, aborted global economic growth, and spilled from Europe into Africa, Asia, the Americas, and the Island Pacific. In this chapter, we focus on the conflict's global dimensions, its relationship to industry and technology, and its immediate, largely disastrous consequences.

Turn-of-the-Century Prosperity, 1890–1914

FOCUS What factors might have accounted for accelerating global economic growth in the period from 1890 to 1914?

One of the ironies of the Great War is that the twenty years leading up to it witnessed unprecedented economic growth and a better quality of life for many millions of people. Accelerating economic growth has been the very *long-term* global trend during the past thousand years. But this general upward drift has been uneven. Since fossil-fuel-powered industrialization got under way, fluctuations of growth and recession—what economists call "business cycles"—have followed one another every few decades. As we saw in Chapter 23, a severe recession in agricultural production and industry overtook the world in 1873 and lasted several years. In 1896, by contrast, a vigorous expansive phase commenced, and it continued without a significant break until 1914. Fossil-fuel industries in western Europe and the United States flourished and multiplied, corporate enterprises grew much bigger, and serious industrialization took root for the first time in the Netherlands, Scandinavia, Italy, Russia, and Japan (see Chapter 23). Urban workers in most industrializing countries enjoyed real wage increases and access to more consumer products from around the globe. In big cities from Chicago to Shanghai, new sanitation systems, wide boulevards, and mechanized transport improved urban living for many. Ornate railway terminals buzzed with activity, and affluent leisure-seekers escaped to distant spas and resorts. In Europe and North America the money-making classes fared so well that they came to think of the period as *la belle époque*, "the beautiful era" (see Map 24.1).

Commerce and Gold

The volume of world trade more than doubled between 1896 and 1913, increasing in value from about $8 billion to $18 billion. Western European investors moved mountains of capital overseas, some to tropical colonies but even more to Neo-European countries (the United States, Canada, Australia, and the southern cone of South America) to finance railways, harbors, mining operations, lumber mills, and factories. Companies could transport goods by ship and rail faster and at lower cost than ever before, partly because cheap coal fueled steam engines. Capitalist entrepreneurs and investors traveled the world seeking opportunities, and advances in telegraph, telephone, and undersea cable technology allowed them to transmit financial information from one continent to another almost instantaneously. The British economist John Maynard Keynes (1883–1946) recalled that in the years before World War I a well-off resident of London "could secure forthwith, if he wished it, cheap and comfortable means of transport to any country or climate without

passport or other formality, and then proceed abroad to foreign quarters . . . bearing coined wealth upon his person, and would consider himself greatly aggrieved and much surprised at the least interference—He regarded this state of affairs as normal, certain, and permanent."[1]

To smooth the flow of goods and money, the industrializing states took steps after 1870 to join Britain in pegging the value of their national currencies to a gold standard, that is, to a fixed price for an ounce of gold. Once the value of a currency was set relative to gold, it also became fixed relative to other currencies already on the gold standard. This system stabilized exchange rates among currencies. Consequently, prices for goods fluctuated less from one region to another, and businesspeople could conduct commercial transactions with fewer complications. The world's gold supply was ample owing to nineteenth-century mining rushes in California, Australia, Canada, Alaska, and especially South Africa. Britain, the dominant world financial power in the late century, largely set the gold standard rules, and other states wanting to carry weight in the international economy had to play by them. If a country subscribed to the gold standard, however, it could not unilaterally lower the value of its currency as a way to reduce the price of its exports and thereby increase their sale. This could present a disadvantage to poorer states dependent on exports of primary commodities.

Urbanization and Migration

Wherever populations became more involved in international exchange, towns and cities grew bigger. In 1900 the world had at least sixteen cities with more than one million people, compared to only four cities of that size a century earlier. Twelve of these cities were in western Europe or North America, the other four were Tokyo, Beijing, Calcutta, and St. Petersburg.[2] Cities that mainly channeled exports and imports through the markets and warehouses might grow as fast as industrial centers. Buenos Aires, which exported beef and wheat from Argentina and neighboring countries, attracted thousands of European immigrants annually. By 1909 it had 1.2 million inhabitants, a growth of 250 percent in twenty years. Some metropolises appeared out of nowhere. In South Africa, where prospectors discovered gold in 1886, the lonely prairie settlement of Johannesburg exploded into a city of 100,000 people—and five hundred saloons—in a single decade. In the 1880s rising demand in industrial countries for rubber for insulation and auto and bicycle tires triggered a rush in the Amazon River basin to collect and export wild rubber. This bonanza converted Manaus, a sleepy Brazilian provincial capital in the depths of the rainforest, into a thriving urban center with a river port complex and a grand opera house.

The number of people who migrated long distances from home grew throughout the 1800s, peaking on the eve of the Great War. In the late decades of the nineteenth century, the great majority of migrants started from southern and eastern

Teatro Amazonas in Manaus, Brazil. This elaborate opera house was built in the heart of Amazonia between 1884 and 1896. Financed in part by the rubber boom, the building includes French roof tiles, English steel, and Italian marble. Why do you think Brazilians constructed an extravagant theater in such an isolated town?

Chinese and Russians transplanted themselves to farm lands and mines in northeastern Asia (Siberia and Manchuria). An equal number of people, mostly Chinese and Indians, migrated to tropical Southeast Asia.

Scientific and Technological Advances

International collaboration among private firms, research labs, governments, and universities continued to get more complex and to raise the scale of business enterprises. Scientists made new discoveries whose theoretical significance and practical applications would become fully realized only decades later. These advances included the discovery of X-rays, scientific proof that matter consists of atoms, and the early formulation of quantum mechanics by the European researchers Max Planck, Albert Einstein, and Niels Bohr. In 1909–1910 the German scientists Fritz Haber and Carl Bosch made one of the twentieth century's most momentous breakthroughs in chemical engineering by synthesizing ammonia on an industrial scale. This allowed nitrogen from the air to be converted into liquid form and processed into solid nitrates. This compound was used to make gunpowder and dynamite but also the nitrate fertilizers that hugely enhanced crop production and eventually revolutionized agricultural output in much of the world.

In the immediate prewar decades, communication and transport systems—railways, scheduled steamship lines, telegraphy, and newspapers with mass readership—became steadily more efficient. The invention of refrigerated steamships in the 1870s allowed plantation capitalists to ship tropical fruits and vegetables by sea, which opened year-round markets for such exotic fare in regions of temperate climate. Australia and New Zealand offered employment opportunities to immigrants to raise sheep and ship refrigerated mutton to English tables eight thousand miles away. Between 1890 and 1910, for example, Britain, France, Germany, and the United States extended their combined rail systems by about 162,000 miles. Engineers laid an undersea cable from San Francisco to Sydney by way of Hawaii, spanning the Pacific with telegraphic communication. By 1911 Britain had a telegraph system that linked London with major colonial territories without having to use the wires of any rival states, thus ensuring the security of political and military signals. The Panama Canal, which opened under American authority in 1914 after ten years of continuous work, shortened steamship travel between the Pacific

Europe, Russia, India, and China. Steadily falling transportation rates helped persuade people to seek better paying jobs abroad or simply to escape prosecution for crimes, political harassment by repressive governments, or, especially in the case of eastern European Jews, religious persecution. The United States and other neo-European lands continued to attract large numbers to work in expanding manufacturing industries. In tropic latitudes, plantation and mine managers needed continuous inflows of workers. Between 1900 and 1911, fourteen million Europeans migrated to the Americas, Australia, and New Zealand. In 1913 alone, 1.1 million and the Atlantic by thousands of miles. Other technological innovations permitted both humans and their messages to transcend the limits of rails and copper wire and literally fly through the air.

Transmitting speech. The telephone that Alexander Graham Bell invented in 1876 carried the human voice over a wire by converting it into electrical impulses. Early telephone networks linked offices, businesses, and homes in a number of urban areas. Phone sets sold fast in the United States, partly because people who did not have these gadgets began to feel disconnected from friends and associates who did. In the late 1890s the Italian physicist Guglielmo Marconi freed electrical communication from any dependence on wire by broadcasting signals on radio waves, a form of electromagnetic radiation. Marconi's work represented a fruitful marriage between science and technology. In 1887 the German scientist Heinrich Hertz demonstrated the existence of radio waves. Marconi built on Hertz's research to invent a practical wireless technology. In 1901 he transmitted a radio signal, the letter *S* in Morse code, from England to the coast of Canada. Within a few years, radio operators were routinely transmitting signals from ship to shore. On April 14, 1912, the British luxury liner *Titanic* struck a massive iceberg in the North Atlantic, but as it sank, its crew radioed distress signals to nearby vessels, bringing rescuers to the scene and saving lives. By 1915 scientists devised a way for electromagnetic waves to carry human speech. European states with overseas territories began to supplement their telegraph networks with chains of transmitting towers to link their imperial capitals with their colonies.

Preserving sound and motion. While experimenting with telephone technology in 1877, Thomas Edison (1847–1931) inadvertently invented the first primitive phonograph, a machine that used a carbon stylus, or needle, to store replicas of sound waves in grooves on the surface of a rotating cylinder. Another stylus could then "play back" these tiny undulations by transmitting them through a sound box. A decade later, Emile Berliner (1851–1929), a German immigrant to the United States, invented a system for storing and reproducing sounds on flat discs, or "records." By 1915 the 78 revolution per minute (rpm) disc became the standard phonographic medium. It permitted complex and extended sound patterns—stories, lectures, political speeches, musical performances—to be recorded, saved, and sent from one listener to another.

Like phonograph records, photographs captured immediate reality—a pretty landscape, the portrait of a monarch, a dead soldier on a battlefield—and then preserved it for others to see. Photography was already a sophisticated technology in the 1880s when Étienne-Jules Marey (1830–1904), a French physician, invented a camera capable of taking multiple still photos at the rate of one per second. When these images were projected at the same speed, they created the illusion of reality in motion. Edison invented a similar camera

and soon thereafter the Kinetoscope, a projection box with a peephole that showed a short motion picture set to music. The first commercial Kinetoscope parlor opened in New York City in 1894.

The following year, the French inventors Auguste and Louis Lumière built the first lightweight movie camera and projector. The brothers recorded French daily life, filmed comedy shorts, made newsreels, and sent a team of camera operators around the world to show movies and shoot new material. In India, director-producer Dadasaheb Phalke made a full-length dramatic film in 1913, foreshadowing the "Bollywood" industry that was to come.

The new communication media, together with the telegraph and popular newspapers, made it possible for humans to mentally encompass their planet on a scale never known before. The volume of information available even to people having only marginal connections to communication networks grew exponentially. Dissemination of sounds, photos, and moving images made access to information more open and democratic, first in the wealthiest countries, but soon in parts of the world where low literacy rates did not prevent people from listening and watching. Filmmakers also learned that sequences of filmed images could be edited in a way that stirred emotions, aroused indignation, or sold products. Political leaders used the new media to connect with citizens but also doctored speech and imagery to amplify nationalist feeling or "spin" the news in their favor. In addition, governments had a harder time hiding wars, atrocities, and disasters from public view. In the late nineteenth century, for example, Christian missionaries

A scene from *Raja Harischandra*. Dadasaheb Phalke directed the first full-length Indian film in 1913, bringing to life a legendary Indian king whose story is recounted in the *Ramayana*, one of the great Indian epics.

Global influences in modern art. Pablo Picasso's large and daring oil painting, *Les Demoiselles d'Avignon* (1907), shows five prostitutes in intimidating poses not characteristically feminine for that period. Two of the women wear masks that evoke African art. Picasso's painting was controversial when he first unveiled it in Paris. Why might African imagery have contributed to emerging ideas of what was modern in the early twentieth century? © The Gallery Collection/Corbis © 2013 Estate of Pablo Picasso/Artists Rights Society (ARS), New York.

Motorcars and airplanes. Electrical communications permitted people to interact in real time over long distances without anyone having to go anywhere. The automobile and the airplane (along with the chain-driven bicycle invented in the 1880s), by contrast, allowed people to travel great distances even for work or leisure. Nineteenth-century coal-burning steam engines took up a lot of room on a locomotive or steamship. By contrast, the gas-powered internal combustion engine, developed mainly by German engineers beginning in the 1860s, could be made smaller, cheaper, and more efficient than conventional steam machines.

Just the names alone of technological pioneers like Gottlieb Daimler, Carl Benz, Rudolf Diesel, and Henry Ford signal their contributions to the manufacture of "horseless carriages" with internal combustion engines. Cars and trucks, which most adults could readily learn to drive, liberated overland transport from both rails and timetables. Advances in petroleum chemistry, plus large oil strikes in the United States, Latin America, and the Middle East, sent the price of gasoline plummeting early in the twentieth century, making automobiles more affordable. Starting in 1913, Henry Ford deftly combined two nineteenth-century industrial ideas, the assembly line and the use of interchangeable parts, to mass-produce black Model T automobiles. Proclaiming that he would "build a motorcar for the great multitudes," Ford raised his workers' wages to enable them to buy a Model T, thereby creating a mass consumer market. **Fordism,** as it became known, involved hiring workers to perform the same specialized task over and over again. These men and women traded job flexibility and satisfaction for higher pay and the means to buy more manufactured products. Critics disparaged Fordism for chaining men and women to boring, alienating work. Nevertheless, motorcar sales in the United States, by far the biggest market before World War I, grew from 4,000 in 1900 to 895,000 by 1915.

> **Fordism** A system of technology and organization, named after Henry Ford, which aims both to produce goods at minimal cost through standardization and mass production and to pay wage workers rates that allow them to consume the products they make.

Lightweight internal combustion engines also made mechanical flight possible. A petroleum distillate called benzine drove the propeller that lifted Orville and Wilbur Wright's heavier-than-air machine off the ground in North Carolina in 1903. It flew for twelve seconds the first time, then for longer intervals. Within six years of the Wright

serving in India used cheap Kodak cameras to photograph the ravages of famine, exposing the fact that the colonial government was doing little to relieve the suffering.

As speech, music, and imagery ricocheted around the world, people had increasingly to confront ideas and life ways different from their own. News photos, recordings, and movies amplified the trend toward cultural uniformity among the wealthy and middle classes, who adopted the fashions, music, and leisure activities they saw and heard about. New media tended to favor ideas emanating from Europe or North America because those regions led the technological advance. But cultural flows moved in all directions. West African sculpture informed the art of the young Pablo Picasso, for example, because he saw it at an exhibition in Paris, public museums being yet another growing medium of communication. In short, the cultural globalization that characterized the twentieth century got seriously under way when people thousands of miles apart could see, hear, and experience the same things nearly simultaneously.

Brothers' experiment, the French aviator Louis Blériot piloted an aircraft across the English Channel. By 1911 airmail services were established in North America, Britain, and India. Like wireless radio, the airplane eliminated an earthbound obstacle to communication.

Global Inequities and Their Consequences

FOCUS What social, economic, and environmental circumstances contributed to large protest and revolutionary movements at the dawn of the twentieth century?

The quarter-century before World War I was a period of global contradictions. The global economy became much larger and far more complex and integrated than it had ever been before. Tens of millions of people benefited from this growth, enjoying resurgent prosperity and new material wonders. But rapid economic growth and complexity also aggravated social stress and dislocation, and through these decades hundreds of millions remained poor or got poorer. The beneficiaries of good times lived disproportionately in the cities of industrializing regions in Europe, North America, and Japan. Elsewhere, the new affluence favored mainly elite property-owning classes who put themselves in positions to profit from commercial farming, import–export business, or compensation for services to European colonial masters. In some places, growing global trade benefited landholding peasants who sold surplus crops at prices higher than what they needed for food, rents, and taxes. More typically, however, farmers drawn into the world market found themselves prisoners to landlord exploitation, debt, price fluctuations, and cycles of bad weather.

Drought and Plague

An irony of late-nineteenth-century economic expansion is its correlation to natural disasters that took millions of lives and worsened poverty in many lands (see Map 24.2). The last of three major clusters of El Niño climatic disturbances took place between 1896 and 1902 (see Chapter 23). In several parts of the world, reduced rainfall caused successive years of bad harvests. When industrialized states suffered serious crop losses, as Britain did in 1895, they could reduce shortages by importing more grain from abroad. Most countries, however, did not have the global commercial power, railways, or government capital to keep subsistence farmers and wage earners fed during repeated food crises. European colonial officials consistently argued that famines, which hit dependent territories in Africa and in South and Southeast Asia, should not interfere with the operation of export markets, even for grain, because these shipments

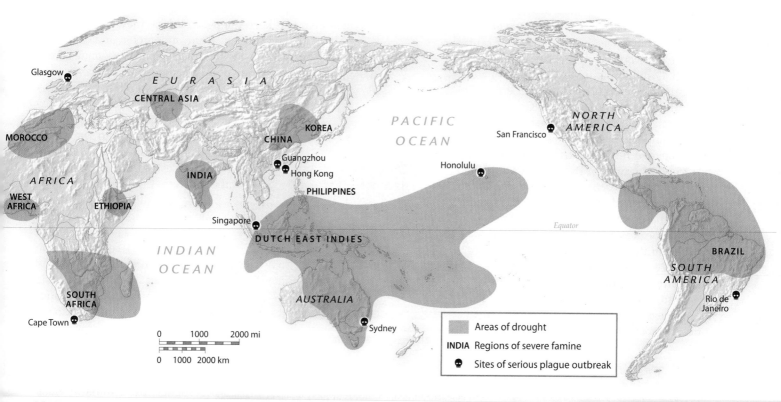

MAP 24.2 Regions of drought and plague in the late nineteenth century.
What geographical aspects did the sites of plague outbreak have in common? To what extent did regions of drought overlap with European colonial territories?

benefited the colonial homeland. For example, in northern India, which experienced terrible dearth in 1896, European merchants continued to export wheat to compensate for Britain's own crop deficits. Meanwhile, the Indian colonial government rejected vigorous famine relief as too expensive. Reporting from India in 1896, an American missionary described the desperation of people who had no money to buy grain at the soaring market price:

> Already grain riots are common. Grain merchants will not sell grain, largely because they know the price will greatly increase. . . . So people break open grain shops and granaries, and threaten to kill the merchants if they interfere. . . . These people say to the police and courts: "Arrest us for stealing and support us in jail. There we shall not die from starvation."[3]

In 1896–1897, perhaps as many as eighteen million Indians perished from malnutrition, starvation, or infectious diseases. Consequently, India entered the twentieth century in conditions of deteriorating economic conditions and falling standards of living for much of the population.

Hunger and malnutrition made people more susceptible to cholera, diphtheria, or other contagious diseases. In the late nineteenth century, famines worsened mortality from epidemics of bubonic plague. This disease, associated with the bacterium *Yersinia pestis*, had killed millions of people in several parts of Afroeurasia in the mid-fourteenth century, the great pandemic known as the Black Death. Humans could become infected by the bite of fleas that lived on rodents and that carried the plague bacterium.

Like the Black Death five and a half centuries earlier, plague spread in the 1800s along routes of travel. Originating in the highlands of western China about midcentury, an epidemic struck the ports of Guangzhou (Canton) and Hong Kong in 1894. Commercial steamships whose nonpaying passengers included infected rats and fleas then transmitted the disease to other seaports. By 1901 eruptions had occurred in cities as distant from one another as Singapore, Cape Town, Sydney, Glasgow, Rio de Janeiro, Honolulu, and San Francisco. In South Asia something like ten to twelve million people died of plague by the 1920s. The disease continued to attack urban populations here and there until about 1950, when mortality dropped off owing to effective antibiotic treatment.

Africa and Southeast Asia under New Colonial Rulers

Map 24.1, at the beginning of this chapter, shows either a European power or the United States claiming

Anticolonial heroine Yaa Asantewaa. The Queen Mother served a politically important role in the Asante kingdom, in which women held offices parallel to those of male chiefs. Yaa Asantewaa used her influential position to mobilize an uprising against British colonizers in 1900. When Asante chiefs hesitated to act, Yaa Asantewaa responded, "If you the chiefs of Asante are going to behave like cowards and not fight, you should exchange your loincloths for my undergarments."

authority over most of Africa and Southeast Asia. The invasions of the previous thirty years (see Chapter 23) awarded foreign conquerors the right to decide among themselves the boundary lines between those units. Of the thirty-nine territories superimposed on Africa, thirty-seven were new European dependencies; the remaining two were the sovereign states of Ethiopia and Liberia (the latter a country where the United States exerted strong diplomatic and economic influence). In Southeast Asia, Thailand retained its independence, but together five European powers and the United States claimed authority over the rest of the region.

As of 1914, however, invading forces still did not fully control, or even occupy, all the territories they had assigned themselves on the map. In several parts of Africa and Southeast Asia, guerrilla bands continued to fight, while local rebellions frequently interrupted development of colonial administrations. In maritime Southeast Asia, for example, the Dutch ruled Java and other islands in the late nineteenth century but continued to mount operations to control large areas of the vast Indonesian archipelago. In West Africa, British forces thought in 1896 that they had conquered the once powerful Asante empire, but four years later its leaders instigated a revolt that took colonial soldiers nine months to put down.

Colonial objectives. In the areas of Africa and Southeast Asia where imperial governors had firm control at the start of the new century, they typically aimed to achieve three principal goals. One was to create an administrative system and keep the peace, which inevitably required the cooperation of local monarchs and notables. The second was to collect enough revenues from the colonized population so that it, rather than taxpayers back in Europe, would pay the costs of government. The third was to encourage export of whatever valuable commodities might be funneled from the colony into the world market—rubber from Malaysia, palm oil from West Africa, copper from the Belgian Congo. These enterprises brought additional revenue to the colonial regime and business profits to European import–export companies. No early colonial administration in Africa or Southeast Asia made serious plans to offer mass education, advanced technical skills, or paths to political participation to subject populations.

Neither imperial governments nor foreign businesses invested much wealth in the economies of the new African or Southeast Asian dependencies, especially compared to European capital investments in North America, Australia, or Latin America. Mining and commercial agriculture offered low-wage employment in some regions, but these European-owned enterprises drained wealth from the colony rather than circulating it back into colonial development that would raise living standards for all. We look more closely at twentieth-century colonial systems in Chapter 25.

Gold and poverty in South Africa. South Africa illustrates how the economic lot of the majority population generally worsened in the late nineteenth century even as wealth grew at an astonishing rate. As of 1890, descendants of European settlers made up less than 10 percent of what is today the Republic of South Africa, but whites controlled all but small pockets of territory. Britain held the regions known as Cape Colony and Natal, while Afrikaners, the descendants of earlier Dutch and other European immigrants, ruled two republics—the Transvaal and the Orange Free State. Afrikaners governed both states as a racially superior social caste. For them, the idea of equality for Africans, the overwhelming majority, was "contrary to the laws of God and the natural distinction of race and religion."[4]

South Africa had exported diamonds since the 1860s, but after prospectors discovered gold in the Transvaal in 1886, the economic value of the region escalated. By the late nineteenth century, South Africa was supplying fully 25 percent of the world's gold, more Europeans were arriving to take skilled and semiskilled jobs, and men and women from greater southern Africa were streaming to mushrooming cities to seek low-wage work in the mines.

African hopes for greater rights rose during the South African War (Boer War), when Britain attacked the two Afrikaner republics in 1899, intending to annex them. British business magnates, notably Cecil Rhodes, despised the Afrikaner governments for heavily taxing the mining companies and refusing to grant full political rights even to English-speaking immigrants. To Britain's surprise, Afrikaner commandos mounted a tenacious guerrilla insurgency. In response, British troops burned Afrikaner farms, poisoned wells, and herded women and children into the twentieth century's first concentration camps, where thousands died of malnutrition and disease. Many Europeans reacted in dismay to these tactics, and when the Afrikaner leaders finally surrendered in 1902, the British moved quickly to reconcile with them. Both sides wanted to ensure that whites would continue to dominate society and have access to the subordinate African labor they needed to operate the mines and big farms. During the fighting, neither side wanted to recruit Africans for combat, fearing that if they contributed significantly to the outcome, they might feel justified in making social and economic demands. In fact, Africans materially supported both Afrikaner and British operations as construction and transport workers, couriers, scouts, and food producers. Military devastation also caused them much suffering. Nevertheless, the treaty

Miners travel to the rock face on a cable car, 1888. South Africa's nascent mining industry depended on both heavy machinery and intense manual labor. Higher-paid skilled work was reserved for white workers, many of whom were recent immigrants. What does this photo suggest about the hazards of mine work?

that ended the war omitted any mention of African rights. In 1910 Britain went further, awarding a unified South Africa self-rule under Afrikaner domination, leaving Africans subject to increasing repression and impoverishment.

Worker Protest and Nationalist Ferment in Europe

Even as economic growth accelerated in the first decade of the twentieth century, Europe seethed with protest and rebellion. In the western European democracies, socialists and other reformers kept up a steady barrage of strikes and marches to demand higher wages and better job conditions. Notably in Britain and the United States, urban women agitated for equal rights and enfranchisement, sometimes at risk of imprisonment. Also in the United States, the progressive movement, which bloomed in the aftermath of the economic

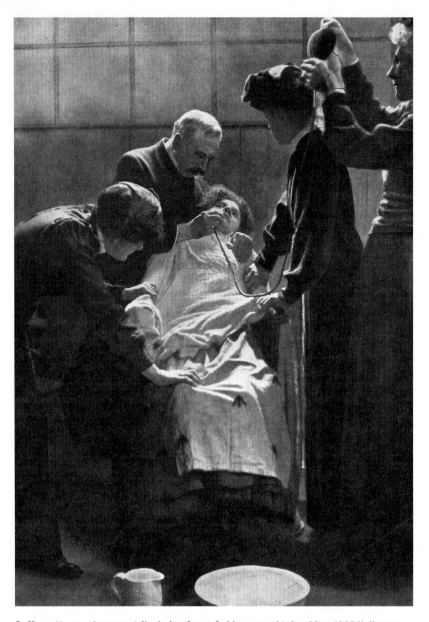

Suffragette on a hunger strike being force-fed by a nasal tube. After 1903 Holloway Prison in London housed many women arrested for political activism. What factors account for violent exchanges between police and women's rights advocates?

1878 the Great Powers of Europe responded to rising nationalist tensions by agreeing to support the independence of Serbia, Montenegro, Bulgaria, and Romania, though in fact none of those new states was ethnically homogeneous.

The pseudo-scientific racist ideas that emerged in the mid-nineteenth century (see Chapter 23) incited leaders advocating exclusive, us-versus-them forms of nationalism. Race theorists argued that people who shared the same language and cultural background also shared an exclusive biological inheritance that made them innately different from their neighbors and perhaps genetically superior to them as well. Self-styled "social psychologists," perverting Darwin's ideas about natural selection and recklessly confusing genetically inherited traits with culturally learned characteristics, claimed biological connections between the way people looked (skin color, skull shape) and their innate mental capacities. These caricatures of experimental science not only ranked all Europeans far above all Asians and Africans in the racial pecking order. Some theorists partitioned Europeans themselves into higher and lower races, arguing for example that the superior traits of northern Europeans included "being Protestant," whereas southern Europeans exposed their genetic shortcomings by being darker skinned and Roman Catholic.

Five Revolutions

In the first eleven years of the twentieth century, violent revolutionary movements erupted in Russia, Iran, Ottoman Turkey, China, and Mexico. In all of them, insurrectionists rose against their own governments, not foreign colonial overlords. But like Africans and Asians who resisted colonial rule, these rebels demanded democratic government, civil liberties, and greater economic security. In all five countries, ordinary men and women perceived themselves as benefiting little from the industrial and commercial boom of 1896–1914. Political activists regarded the existing regime as an unresponsive dynastic relic (Russia, Iran, Turkey, and China) or a republic-in-name-only that answered to wealthy elites and foreign companies (Mexico). In all cases except Russia, the rebels brought down the existing government, though without restoring political calm in the short run.

The 1905 Revolution in Russia. A colossal pan-Eurasian empire and, owing to its huge army, a European Great Power, Russia experienced energetic industrialization and rapid economic growth in the 1890s (see Chapter 23). Most Russians remained rural, poor, and ill-educated, but the

recession of 1893, brought together many reform societies to fight for labor legislation, universal education, improved housing, healthier cities, and corruption-free government.

Nationalism had been a potent public ideology in Europe through most of the nineteenth century. But Europeans increasingly venerated the nation, not so much as a community of citizens dedicated to sovereignty and universal rights, than as a defined ethnoracial group sharing a common language, culture, history, and destiny to the exclusion of outsiders. In southeastern Europe, where spiraling population growth in the nineteenth century aggravated unemployment and landlessness, radical young nationalists proclaimed their Serbian, Hungarian, Bulgarian, Albanian, or other ethnic identity in opposition to the oppression of the Austrian, Russian, or Ottoman Turkish regimes that ruled them. In urbanized and industrial worker population expanded fast, as did a money-making, reform-minded middle class of entrepreneurs, merchants, and intellectuals. On the other hand, Russia's manufacturing cities had unhealthy environments, workers suffered wretched working conditions, peasants paid crushing taxes, and the middle class fumed over its exclusion from the authoritarian government of Tsar Nicholas II (reigned 1894–1917).

In those conditions, urban laborers organized secret unions and staged regular strikes. Intellectual and business leaders in St. Petersburg, Moscow, and other industrial cities founded political associations and newspapers to demand reforms. They differed, however, on the best way to achieve change. Liberal democrats wanted a limited, constitutional monarchy. Many socialists thought the peasantry should lead a revolution. Communists, including the up-and-coming Marxist theoretician Vladimir Ilyich Lenin, contended that only the proletariat, that is, the urban working class, could overthrow the tsar's regime. The tsar responded to all talk of reform with more repression, dismissing the idea of a constitution for Russia as "senseless dreams."

A series of crises at the turn of the century, however, undermined the tsar's authority. In 1898–1899 bad harvests followed one another and industrial growth nearly stagnated. Then in February 1904 Russia and Japan, both countries coveting new territories in East Asia in conditions

of spreading political ferment in China, went to war over competing interests in Manchuria, Korea, and the Liaodong Peninsula (east of Beijing). The fighting went badly for Russia, and in May 1905 Japan's technically superior navy sank most of a Russian flotilla in the Tsushima Strait between Japan and Korea. This victory ended the war and ensured Japan's paramount interests in Korea and Manchuria.

Russia's successive military defeats in East Asia precipitated waves of popular protest in Moscow and other cities. In January 1905, 150,000 workers demonstrated in front of the tsar's Winter Palace in St. Petersburg, petitioning their sovereign to "break down the wall between yourself and your people."[5] In response, imperial troops killed several hundred men and women. This massacre triggered several months of strikes, peasant uprisings, assassinations, and military mutinies. In the industrial cities, workers organized their own elected political action councils known as **soviets,** an institution that would take on new meaning in the following decade. The tsar finally agreed to voting rights for adult males and an elected parliament (duma). But he refused to respect the new assembly's authority, and protests and insurgencies continued. The regime probably

> **soviet** Revolutionary workers' councils that served during the Russian Revolution as local units of government and civil order. The term was applied later to legislative bodies within the communist regime.

Russian crowds demand social reform, 1905. The first Russian Revolution brought thousands of demonstrators into the streets of St. Petersburg. The resulting massacre became known as Bloody Sunday. What might have prompted government troops to fire on this apparently peaceful crowd?

survived the 1905 revolt only because competing ideological factions could not unite and because most middle-class Russians could not bring themselves to identify with the interests of the rural masses.

Iran's fight for a constitution.

Throughout the nineteenth century, both Russia and Britain put heavy diplomatic and military pressure on the Qajar dynasty (1794–1925), which ruled Iran. Britain insisted that the governments of Afghanistan and Iran entertain no policy that might encourage Russia to threaten or attack India. For its part, Russia yearned for a warm-water naval port in the Persian Gulf, which bordered Iran on the southwest. Muzzafir al-Din Shah, Iran's autocratic monarch (r. 1896–1906) lacked an effective tax-gathering bureaucracy. Desperate for money to maintain his lavish court, he borrowed large sums from Russian, British, and French banks. In 1901 he sold oil-drilling rights in a large part of Iran to a British entrepreneur.

In response to such foreign intrusions, reform societies sprouted in several cities. In December 1905, demonstrators massed in the capital of Tehran to demand a constitutional monarchy. Muzzafir al-Din faced mounting protests from varied groups: artisans and merchants who chafed over cheap European imports, Shi'ite Muslim leaders who condemned foreign influence as an offense against Islam, and educated liberals who demanded a European-style constitution. The king finally called a constituent assembly, which enacted laws that transformed Iran into a limited monarchy.

Muzzafir al-Din died in late 1906, however, and his successor moved violently to restore autocracy. The country then descended into a civil war that dragged on for four years. In those chaotic conditions, Russia and Britain agreed to partition Iran into two spheres of influence. In 1911 they invaded the northern and southern provinces, respectively, not to create formal colonies but to ensure informal domination. The civil war ended with Iran a constitutional monarchy but its import–export economy in the hands of foreign companies and their wealthy Iranian collaborators.

Young Turks in revolt.

Japan's victory over Russia, the Russian Revolution of 1905, and the Iranian revolt all energized popular opposition to Sultan Abdul Hamid II, the Ottoman Turkish empire's ruler (r. 1876–1909). He believed in material modernization, including new military technology, advanced technical education, and telegraph and rail construction. But drawing support from the empire's most conservative land-owning families and Muslim leaders, he successfully suppressed a budding liberal reform movement early in his reign (see Chapter 22). He suspended a new liberal constitution within two years of its adoption and reinstated an autocratic and increasingly repressive government. Liberal opponents of this regime, mainly low-level officials, university students, and young military officers, continued to agitate for reform from underground or exile. As in

Iran, these activists formed secret societies. The Committee of Union and Progress (CUP), whose members became popularly known as Young Turks, emerged as the umbrella organization for groups demanding restoration of the constitution, military modernization, and an end to economic dependence on foreign companies and banks. In 1908 a band of officers, fed up with Abdul Hamid's neglect of the army, staged an uprising in league with the CUP. Alarmed by this turn of events, the sultan reinstituted the constitution and announced elections to a new parliament. When Abdul Hamid's conservative supporters tried to raise a counterrevolution, however, army units marched on Constantinople (modern Istanbul) and forced the sultan to abdicate in favor of a younger brother who had no power base.

This power seizure triggered five years of disruptive wrangling among political factions, though CUP leaders finally established their authority. This constitutional regime, however, became increasingly dictatorial. The Young Turks adopted an ideology that idealized the empire as a multicultural state in which all ethnic and religious communities should enjoy civil toleration and equality. But in fact the Turkish-speaking urban population moved toward a more exclusive ethnic nationalism similar to the trend across much of Europe.

The end of the Chinese empire.

The steep tilt of economic and military power toward Europe, the United States, and Japan in the later nineteenth century profoundly affected China. That state's political turmoil, moreover, was all the more dramatic because the country numbered nearly half a billion people, twenty-three times the population of the Ottoman empire. Relentless European pressures, a steady hemorrhage of silver to pay for imports, the catastrophic Taiping Rebellion, and recurring famines combined to undermine the Qing dynasty's political authority and financial solvency (see Chapter 22). As in Russia, Iran, and Turkey, young liberal modernizers railed against autocratic monarchy and its apparent helplessness in the face of foreign penetration and dizzying economic change. In 1894–1895, Japan's modern army readily defeated China's larger but poorly equipped forces in the Sino-Japanese War. The conflict started over rivalry for influence in Korea. It ended with Japan dominant there and in control of the big island of Taiwan, which had been part of the Chinese empire since the seventeenth century. In the aftermath of the Japanese victory, Britain, France, and Russia pressured the Qing government into approving their control over large chunks of Chinese territory where they would have preeminent trade rights and merchant exemptions from Chinese law. Consequently, the Qing gave up full political control of dozens of **treaty ports.** In those places, European merchants and their Chinese associates did business free of import taxes.

> **treaty ports** Sea or river ports in China where, as a consequence of diplomatic and military pressure, foreigners gained special privileges to engage in trade and enjoy exemptions from Chinese laws and courts.

The imperial court proved helpless to resist this informal empire building. The Empress Dowager Cixi (r. 1861–1908), a tenacious autocrat, had ruled China as regent, or guardian and substitute, for two emperors, first a young son and after 1875 Guangxu (wang-soo), a nephew. She and the Confucian scholar-bureaucrats who served her professed little interest in technical modernization and much contempt for both Europeans and reform-minded Chinese.

Simultaneously, the cluster of El Niño disturbances of 1896–1902 hit the northern provinces furiously, setting off popular rebellion. Severe droughts alternated with massive monsoon floods, causing the death or displacement of millions of peasants. Seeking a cosmic explanation for such disaster, the Harmonious Fists, or Boxers—a secret society devoted to martial arts and rituals believed to convey special powers—targeted foreigners as the source of China's misfortunes. The Boxers preached eradication of European and American missionaries, who were at that time founding many churches in China. In 1899–1900 the Boxers appealed to impoverished young men, as well as rural women known as Red Lanterns, to seize foreign property, pull down telegraph lines, demolish churches, and kill both missionaries and their Chinese converts. Some Qing governors tried to quell the insurrection, but the Empress Dowager urged it on.

In response to Boxer provocations, Japan, Russia, Germany, France, Britain, and the United States organized a multinational army in the summer of 1900. Armed with

Empress Dowager Cixi after her 1902 return to Beijing. The Qing court tried to improve foreign diplomatic relations after the Boxer uprising. The Empress reached out in particular to wives of diplomats, thinking they might be open to appeals of friendship. In this photograph the Empress holds hands with Sarah Pike Conger, the wife of the U.S. envoy. The child is the daughter of the photographer. How might an image like this have changed both Chinese and foreign perceptions of the Qing rulers?

Qiu Jin: Social Reformer

Poet Qin Jin in a man's attire.

Most Chinese reformers of the early twentieth century recognized that the country's modern self-strengthening must include drastic changes in the social status and public roles of women. Criticism was particularly leveled at female seclusion in the home, lack of educational opportunity, and the traditional custom of foot binding. If women were hobbled in so many ways, especially members of the best educated and most affluent families, how could they help modernize society and expel alien occupiers? Amid the deterioration of Qing authority, literate young women began to join the blooming nationalist movement and to speak out for the social emancipation of their sex.

After the foreign seizure of Beijing in 1900, Qiu Jin (1875–1907), a women raised in a moderately well-off family in the eastern coastal province of Zhejiang, vowed to devote herself to China's transformation. Her parents allowed her to get an education, but she nonetheless found herself trapped in an arranged marriage to an older man with typically conservative ideas about wifely behavior. In 1904, at the age of twenty-nine, she broke with her husband and boarded a ship for Japan. While at sea, she wrote "Preoccupation (Written while in Japan)," a poem that later became famous:

> A lusterless sun and a wan moon have cast heaven and earth
> in obscurity—
> Sinking with help,
> more imperiled than anyone else,
> are the women of my race.
> Searching for a remedy,

> I pawned my jewelry, left behind my children,
> And sailed across the ocean
> to this foreign land.
> Unbinding my feet, I washed away
> a thousand years of poison.
> My heart fired with excitement, I awoke
> one hundred slumbering flower-spirits.
> But pity my shagreen [leather] handkerchief—
> Half stained with tears
> and half with blood.[6]

In Japan, Qiu Jin entered a women's vocational school but also joined the Revolutionary Alliance, a coalition formed by Sun Zhongshan to unite fragmented anti-Qing organizations. She prepared herself for revolution by practicing marksmanship and bomb-making. Like many young Chinese, she witnessed Japan's military triumph over Russia in 1905 with a mixture of admiration and anxiety. The victory vindicated Japan's program of rapid modernization but also put into relief that state's continuing threat to China.

In 1906 Qiu Jin returned to China, where she took a job directing a girls' school in the coastal city of Shaoxing. There she developed a sports program that included martial arts and military drills, in effect, revolutionary military training. She also founded the *Chinese Women's Journal,* a feminist periodical that exposed the evils of foot binding, arranged marriages, female infanticide, and wife-beating. She became notorious for her eccentricities, leading her sports class in a man's long gown and black leather shoes and riding a horse astride rather than sidesaddle as a decent woman was expected to do.

In 1907, she joined a cousin in a plot to stage an anti-Qing uprising. Imperial police seized her at her school along with compromising documents. Her captors tortured her for information, and when she refused to cooperate, they led her to the school parade ground, where they decapitated her. News of her courage spread rapidly, and nationalists hailed her as a martyr, an icon of women's freedom, and a beacon to young revolutionaries, who, four years later, brought down the Qing regime.

Thinking Critically

What relationship, if any, do you see between Qiu Jin's family background and early life and her career as a social reformer?

up-to-date rifles, machine guns, and artillery, this force advanced inland, killing tens of thousands of Chinese peasants, whether they were Boxers or not. The invaders seized Beijing, forcing the Empress Dowager to flee. The suppression of the insurrection left China vulnerable to full-scale foreign invasion. But international quarreling and the enormous potential costs of conquering China persuaded the Great Powers to hold back.

Military humiliation helped convince the Qing government to initiate at least moderate reforms, including military and administrative modernization, improved communication networks, and investment in education. In 1908 both the Empress Dowager and Guangxu died, leaving the succession to Puyi, who climbed onto the throne at age two. The following year a small electorate of males chose provincial assemblies, which were to select members of a national parliament.

For the growing class of radicalized reformers, however, the modern "self-strengthening" that China required could not be left to traditional Confucian palace officials. Like Young Turks, many Chinese reformers operated from exile. They published radical magazines, wrote letters to compatriots in China, and raised money. Sun Zhongshan (Sun Yat-sen, 1866–1925), the most famous liberal reformer of the early twentieth century, studied medicine in British-ruled Hong Kong and became a Christian. He allied with secret societies opposed to Qing rule, advocated a constitutional republic, and traveled to Europe and the United States to find funds and political backers.

The 268-year-old Qing dynasty collapsed in 1911, faster than its revolutionary opponents expected. Rebellious army officers seized power in part of the Yangzi River valley and declared the region independent of imperial authority. The news spread by telegraph to other officers and to new provincial assemblies. Within several weeks, more than a dozen provinces seceded. The court guardians of the child emperor Puyi had no choice but to agree to a constitutional republic. Sun Zhongshan quickly returned from abroad, but the former Qing general who assumed the presidency had no tolerance for democracy. This left the revolutionary government in turmoil, and in 1913 military men took over most of China's provinces, reorganizing them into personal fiefdoms defended by private armies. The foreign concession holders trafficked directly with these warlords, and the new central government proved impotent. China's postrevolutionary fate was to be thirty-six more years of division and war.

The Mexican Revolution. In contrast to the four movements discussed so far, the Mexican Revolution, which broke out in 1910, aimed initially to replace not a dynastic monarch, but the government of a long-established republic. At the end of the nineteenth century, the Western Hemisphere was a world zone of republics—nineteen of them. There was also Canada, a constitutional monarchy, and an assortment of small colonial possessions. The republics ranged from popular though partially restricted democracies (the United States), to liberal regimes dominated by business and land-owning elites (Argentina), to dictatorships that made sure that elections were decided in advance. Mexico, headed by Porfirio Díaz from 1876 to 1911, falls into the last category.

The Porfiriato, as the Díaz regime was known, promoted liberal policies only in the material sphere. That is, he and a group of intellectual collaborators known as *cientificos* aimed to achieve modernization and progress, not by broadening rights and civic participation, but by strengthening the power and wealth of the state by expanding rail lines, mine operations, and textile production. The country's track network grew from about 400 miles in 1876 to nearly 12,000 miles by 1910. Its main functions, however, were to transport soldiers around the country and to channel minerals and commercial farm products out of Mexico in exchange for foreign manufactures. Díaz opened the country to European and U.S. investors, who formed a tightly knit capitalist fraternity with Mexican mine owners, land barons, and officeholders.

On the underside of economic growth were the Mexican masses whose labor produced everything the country exported. Only a small part of the overwhelmingly rural Indian and *mestizo* population owned land, and the Porfiriato aimed by legal means or otherwise to accelerate transfers of communal village lands to privately owned estates worked by low-wage tenants and day laborers. While agricultural exports boomed, harvests of maize, the country's basic food staple, languished. The elite class of mainly creole families (Mexicans of European descent) tended to regard *mestizos* and Indians through a racialist lens, dismissing them as genetically incapable of rising out of poverty.

Mexico's economic growth, however, also produced a new breed of urban, educated men and women—lawyers, engineers, teachers, merchants, and business owners—who abhorred the concentration of wealth in a few hundred families. These liberals founded associations pledged to individual rights, fair elections, freedom from foreign domination, and fairer distribution of the country's riches.

Grievance and protest exploded into revolution in 1910, when the octogenarian Díaz, after first proclaiming his retirement and a new era of free elections, presented himself for office once again. He also had Francisco Madero (1873–1913), a liberal reformer who ran against him, thrown into jail on the eve of the election. Madero subsequently fled to the United States, where he appealed to the Mexican people to rise up. Soon enough, local insurrections broke out in several regions. Emiliano Zapata, a former horse trainer who demanded restoration of expropriated peasant lands, led one uprising in the south. Pancho Villa, an ex-rustler, commanded another insurgency in the far north. Faced with rebellion on all sides, Díaz gave up and fled to Paris in 1911. Madero entered Mexico City in triumph.

During the next nine years, however, the country fragmented into rival and often warring ideological factions,

Rebel leader Emiliano Zapata (1879–1914). What features of this undated photo emphasize Zapata's role as a revolutionary general?

including middle-class liberals who wanted moderate changes, populist revolutionaries like Zapata, and counter-revolutionary peasants who supported the conservative Roman Catholic Church leadership. U.S. forces intervened in the revolution twice, once to pursue Pancho Villa south of the Rio Grande and once to occupy the port of Veracruz to blockade arms imports. Madero was assassinated in 1913, and though liberal leaders wrote a new constitution four years later, stable central authority was restored only in 1920 under the leadership of liberal property owners. In 1929, representatives of this group formed the National

Revolutionary Party (later the Party of Revolutionary Institutions, or PRI). The organization clothed itself in revolutionary and nationalist rhetoric, but Mexico nonetheless devolved into a rigid one-party state that restricted the operations of unions, the press, or rival political groups.

The Great War, 1914–1918

FOCUS Why did warfare between 1914 and 1918 reach such extreme levels of violence and destruction?

As grim as it was, revolutionary violence in the early twentieth century was restrained compared to World War I, in which something close to ten million military personnel died. Over four years the war's average *daily* death toll was 1,459 Russians, 1,303 Germans, 890 French, and 457 British combatants.[7] All but six European states were involved in the fighting. British soldiers warred against Germans in East Africa and against Turks in Iraq. Australians, New Zealanders, Canadians, South Asians, Africans, and eventually Americans fought in Europe. British and German ships and submarines pursued one another in the Baltic, the North Sea, and the South Atlantic. The struggle devastated large areas of Europe, sent world trade plummeting, and buried both winners and losers under mountains of debt.

In the perspective of any time after 1918, the war looks so irrational and horrifying that it nearly defies historical explanation. We cannot simply tote up a list of causes that made the catastrophe inevitable. There was no unstoppable march toward war in the previous years but rather a conjuncture of events in 1914 that, if rearranged even slightly, might have prevented the conflict, at least at that moment. Right up to that year, middle-class Europeans who gathered in opera houses and stylish cafés had stout hopes that peace and economic good times would continue indefinitely.

Nevertheless, political anxieties clouded Europe's splendid cityscapes of iron and glass. Competing nationalist, socialist, racist, and other provocative ideologies fueled social-class and ethnolinguistic tensions. The incessant rivalry among Britain, France, Germany, and Russia for shares of expanding world wealth gradually eroded the previously accepted rules for getting along together. In defiance of free-trade principles, all the major states except Britain raised tariff walls higher to protect home industries. International strains became so acute by the summer of 1914 that war, when it erupted, did not come as a great surprise to many European leaders. But they assured the public nonetheless that the conflict would be "over by Christmas." They did not imagine fifty-two months of savage, relentless fighting.

Lighting the Fuse

War broke out in 1914 under circumstances in which pacts and agreements that had once been fluid and pragmatic had become progressively unyielding. Europe hardened into two blocs of alliances in conditions of mounting suspicion and menace. Germany, Austria-Hungary, and the Ottoman empire joined forces as the Central Powers. France, Britain, and Russia formed the opposing Allied Powers.

Britain, France, and Germany.

These alliances involved two fundamentally different kinds of states. Britain, France, and Germany were Europe's richest industrial powers. They had the largest overseas empires and the biggest stakes in world trade. They were also established national states. In other words, their populations, especially the urban middle classes, had largely accepted the nationalist ideology that the state and the national cultural community were, or should ideally be, identical. Popular allegiance to the state must therefore take precedence over loyalties to local ethnic communities or religions. In those countries, nationalism expressed itself in representative assemblies (though in Germany the voting electorate was small) and in anthems, flags, a national language, and often zealously nationalistic newspapers. Public schools and army service were also crucial institutions for teaching patriotic love and duty.

On the chessboard of power in western Europe, Germany gradually crept ahead of its two rivals. In 1900 its population exceeded that of both Britain and France by many millions. It had higher production in key industries like coal and steel. It led the way in electrical and chemical technologies and fielded Europe's largest land army next to Russia. Kaiser Wilhelm II, Germany's militaristic head of state, clamored for more overseas colonies, ordered construction of a world-class navy, and competed with France for diplomatic influence in Morocco, a sovereign monarchy.

In response to these expansionist signals, France, which had already lost its eastern provinces to Germany in the Franco-Prussian War of 1870, stepped up arms production and strengthened the alliance it had made with Russia in 1892. Britain concluded that the kaiser could have no reason to build a sea force other than to challenge the Royal Navy. In 1904 Britain and France signed the Entente (ahn-TAHNT) Cordial, which settled outstanding colonial disputes. Three years later, Russia joined those two powers in the Triple Entente.

Germany, France, and Britain all poured national wealth into armaments, manufacturing far more guns, shells, and ships than what they would need if they remained at peace with one another. This feverish race suggested to the competitors that if war was on the way, it might be better to fight a short, conclusive one sooner rather than later. German leaders also perceived the Triple Entente as dangerous encirclement.

Already allied with the Austro-Hungarian empire, they nurtured close relations with Ottoman Turkey as preparation for a day of reckoning.

The three multiethnic empires.

The political and social profiles of Austria-Hungary, Russia, and the Ottoman empire were rather different from the western European powers. All three had autocratic imperial governments. None of the three could be described as a national state. Rather, they embraced diverse ethnolinguistic groups that in many cases formed their own nationalist movements to agitate for one measure or another of self-government. The populations of these empires were overwhelmingly rural, and though industries were growing in Russia and Austria, both states lagged far behind Germany and Britain.

THE BOILING POINT.

Imperial politics in the Balkans reach the boiling point. This 1912 cartoon from the British humor magazine *Punch* depicts France, Britain, Germany, Russia, and Austria-Hungary grappling with challenges to European stability. What problems were these great powers trying to contain?

The shatter zone for these empires was the Balkan Peninsula. As we have seen, Serbia, Montenegro, Romania, and Bulgaria broke free of Ottoman rule in the last quarter of the nineteenth century. Austria and Russia ratified the independence of these states but then competed fiercely with each other for influence over them. The Balkans thus remained a boiling political cauldron. Russia, a predominantly Slavic-speaking power, projected itself into the Balkans as the champion of Serbs, Bulgarians, Macedonians, and all other peoples who spoke Slavic languages. This patronage encouraged Serbian nationalists to dream of a "Greater Serbia" that would one day dominate southeastern Europe. Austria-Hungary, however, could not abide this prospect. In 1908 Austria annexed the Slavic region of Bosnia-Herzegovina, which poisoned its relations with Russia. In 1912 and 1913 two Balkan Wars involving several small regional powers resulted in the Turks losing nearly all their remaining European territory and Serbia doubling its own. In response to that development, Austrian officials talked of invading and dismantling Serbia altogether.

A World at War

In all of Europe's major rival states, generals made contingency plans for war because that was part of their job. In Germany the high command devised the Schlieffen (SHLEE-fn) Plan in 1905. This strategy projected a rapid and massive assault across Belgium to quickly overpower France. Quick success there would free troops to invade and defeat Russia before it had time to fully mobilize its presumably lumbering army. Austria-Hungary would force Russia to spread its forces by launching its own invasion. Kaiser Wilhelm assured himself with more hope than realism that Britain would stay out of the fight because "she will have to." After 1905 the Schlieffen strategy became so congealed in German military minds that once it was activated, political leaders with second thoughts about war would not be able to stop it.

Some historians have labeled World War I the "Third Balkan War" because it looked for a short time as if it might be just one more dreary but short-lived conflict in southeastern Europe. On June 28, 1914, Serbian nationalists assassinated Archduke Franz Ferdinand, the heir to the Austro-Hungarian throne, when he visited Bosnia-Herzegovina. Austria immediately made heavy demands on Serbia to atone for the murder, then, failing to receive satisfaction, declared war. Germany backed Austria to the full. This was perhaps the key moment. If the kaiser had restrained Austria, Russia would likely have held back as well. But the German government, fearing a large Slavic state to its south, let militarist sentiment have the upper hand. In a complicated sequence of events that historians have been interpreting ever since, the regional war escalated quickly. As Austria prepared to invade Serbia, the tsar commanded his army to mobilize to aid Russia's Slavic friend. When that happened, Germany declared war on both Russia and France without any immediate provocation from them. On August 3, German troops penetrated Belgium. The next day, Britain, which had earlier guaranteed that little country's neutrality and believed it had to aid France, declared war on Germany. German units got within thirty miles of Paris, but the Schlieffen Plan failed. French forces counterattacked. One general commandeered taxicabs to rush reinforcements from Paris train stations to the front. At that point, both sides started digging in to hold their ground, and rapid troop advances skidded to a halt. This meant that Germany and Austria-Hungary would have to fight a war on two fronts (see Map 24.3).

The Western Front. Along the battle lines that extended across Belgium and northeastern France, soldiers on both sides excavated labyrinthine networks of deep trenches and bunkers. Concrete fortifications and tangles of barbed wire protected the trench lines, and hundreds of thousands of troops burrowed in so well that massive artillery barrages consistently failed to prepare the ground for successful attacks. Rather, as European armies had already learned in colonial wars, the machine gun proved to be a marvelous apparatus for mowing down wave after wave of advancing infantry. In the Battle of Verdun in February 1916, 420,000 French and German soldiers died. At the Battle of the Somme River, fought between July and November of that year, the German, French, and British armies together sustained more than 1.1 million casualties, including 58,000 British losses on the first day of the fight.

For the generals on both sides, every murderous offensive was to be the "final push," but none of those drives went far until August 1918, when Allied forces started advancing against exhausted German soldiers. Four years of trench warfare caused indescribable suffering. The deep ditches and bunkers filled with water, mud, rats, excrement, and corpses. Soldiers became malnourished and contracted infections such as trench mouth. Others developed neurological disorders, including facial ticks and severe depression—a bundle of maladies that doctors summed up as "shellshock," or, in today's language, posttraumatic stress disorder. The English poet Siegfried Sassoon, who fought at the Battle of the Somme, caught the psychological terror of combat in his poem "Attack":

> Men jostle and climb to meet the bristling fire.
> Lines of grey, muttering faces, masked with fear,
> They leave their trenches, going over the top,
> While time ticks blank and busy on their wrists,
> And hope, with furtive eyes and grappling fists,
> Flounders in mud. O Jesus, make it stop![8]

The Eastern Front. Russian forces advanced fast enough at the start of the war to advance across Poland into northeastern Germany. But German divisions then forced them back. On the Eastern Front, fighting was somewhat more mobile than in the west owing to larger distances, wider dispersion of troops (from the Baltic Sea to Serbia), and shortages of guns. Nevertheless, neither side achieved a

German attack in the west, August 1914
→ Schlieffen plan invasion routes
→ Actual German invasion routes
→ Allied counteroffensives
— Armistice line, Nov. 11, 1918

- Triple Entente and colonial possessions
- Allies of Triple Entente and colonial possessions
- Central Powers
- Neutral states
→ Allies' thrust
→ Central Powers' thrust
····· War fronts

MAP 24.3 World War I.

In what ways might the great geographical extent of the war have complicated military operations for both the Central Powers and the Allies?

decisive advance. When the fighting on the Western Front bogged down, the Allies tried to open new offensive lines in southeastern Europe. One was an assault on the Gallipoli Peninsula on the Dardanelles Straits (1915–1916) to capture Constantinople, the Ottoman capital. This campaign failed at deadly cost. Italy remained neutral until 1915 but then entered the war on the Allied side to only minor effect.

The war's global scope. The conflict might have remained confined to Europe if France, Germany, and especially Britain had not had colonies and vital commercial interests around the world. The German alliance recruited Bulgaria to its side, but thirty-six states joined the Allies, if only near the war's end. These countries included the United States, Australia, New Zealand, Canada, and South Africa. Approximately 331,000 Australians and 365,000 Canadians served overseas, many of them on the Western Front. Japan joined the Allies at the outset of the war, though largely to advance its own expansionist aims in East Asia. Its forces attacked German shipping and seized both its territorial concession in China and several of its Pacific island colonies. Britain recruited soldiers from its African, Asian, and

Infantry troops from Senegal head toward the front. Colonial subjects made significant contributions during World War I as soldiers and laborers. How might the war have encouraged changes in the ways colonized peoples and their colonizers perceived each other?

Caribbean colonies. Indian troops made by far the largest contribution, with more than 825,000 of them fighting in the British army. Nearly 7 percent of France's army comprised volunteers or draftees from Algeria, Morocco, Senegal, Niger, and other dependencies. As many as 71,000 of them died in service. Britain and France also recruited hundreds of thousands of colonials to perform labor in war zones and behind the lines on railroads and in factories.

The war also extended to East Africa, a region divided into British, German, and Portuguese colonial territories. German commanders and their African conscripts advanced from Tanganyika (modern Tanzania) deep into neighboring British and Portuguese colonies. Nearly fifteen thousand African soldiers died in German service, and scorched-earth tactics caused food shortages that ravaged village populations. On the British side, losses of African soldiers and carriers exceeded 100,000, compared to a little over 3,000 Europeans and white South Africans. Germany's East African forces did not finally surrender until mid-November 1918, two weeks after the war ended in Europe.

In the Middle East, the Young Turk modernizers who ruled the Ottoman state in 1914 debated passionately whether to enter the war and on whose side. They finally joined the Central Powers, hoping to regain lost territory in the Balkans and to fend off a potential Russian invasion. This decision impelled the Allies to attack the empire's Arabic-speaking provinces. British forces operating from both Egypt and India gradually advanced into the Arabic-speaking lands under Turkish rule, encouraged by young Arab activists who were just then forming anti-Ottoman nationalist societies. In the summer of 1916, Prince Faysal, a son of Sharif Husayn ibn Ali, who governed the holy cities of Mecca and Medina under Ottoman authority, took charge of a revolt of western Arabian tribes against the Turks. In collaboration with a British army advancing from Egypt and the advice of British liaison officers such as T. E. Lawrence (Lawrence of Arabia), the Arab insurgents helped drive the Turkish army from Palestine, Syria, and Iraq.

The fight at sea and the entry of the United States. The economies of the opposing industrial powers relied on world trade for minerals, food, and other commodities to sustain both troops in the field and people at home. Britain depended on the Royal Navy to protect its shipping lanes to its colonies and to important trade partners like the United States. Germany, on the other hand, failed to break a British blockade of the North Sea, which prevented even neutral ships from moving between northern German ports and the Atlantic and causing appalling food shortages in German cities. To fight back on the seas, German engineers pioneered diesel-powered submarines, or U-boats, which torpedoed Allied ships. In April 1917, for example, U-boats sank about 25 percent of the ships leaving British ports. In effect, both sides aimed to use naval technology to weaken each other's civilian populations, if possible, by starvation.

The war at sea triggered the United States to enter the fight. Germany at first avoided submarine attacks on American vessels but decided early in 1917 that it could no longer

On patrol during the Arab Revolt. Arab rebels waged guerrilla warfare against Ottoman forces as British units advanced against the empire from Egypt. What geographical factors might have encouraged Arab nationalists to raise an insurrection during the war (see Map 24.3)?

afford such restraint. Though many Americans loathed the idea of plunging into Europe's incomprehensible "civil war," President Woodrow Wilson (in office, 1913–1921) concluded that German militarism represented a global threat. In April 1917 he persuaded Congress to join the Allies.

Largely because Russia pulled out of the war in the fall of that year amid revolution at home, Germany attempted to break through the Western Front before American troops could get there. The gambit did not work, and in 1918 U.S. soldiers and supplies poured into France. Those fresh forces tipped the balance in the Allies' favor, even though the fighting went on until November. About two million U.S. troops served in western Europe, 126,000 of them never to return home.

Total War

World War I differed from any earlier war, not only because of its global scope and enormous cost in lives, but also because entire societies, not just armies and governments, were mobilized to fight it. The major opposing states mustered numerous public institutions, private businesses, the entire economic infrastructure, and men and women of all classes and occupations to win the struggle, waging what historians call **total war**. Because the fighting dragged on and on, both the Western and Eastern Fronts became gaping "black holes" for soldiers, arms, and supplies. The adversaries thought they had no choice except to transform their societies into war-making machines, diverting their economies from consumer to military production and placing millions of civilians in war-related jobs. Governments began to stage-manage social and economic life on a far larger scale than ever before.

> **total war** Warfare, especially characteristic of World Wars I and II, in which the opposing states mobilize their civilian populations and all available resources to achieve victory; also a wartime policy intended to damage or destroy both the enemy's military forces and its economic infrastructure and social fabric.

Mobilizing the people. When hostilities broke out, hundreds of thousands of patriotic young people flocked to the flag. In the warring countries, peace activists became scarce, and the vast majority of rank-and-file socialist and communist party members suspended their international workers' struggle against capitalist subjugation in order

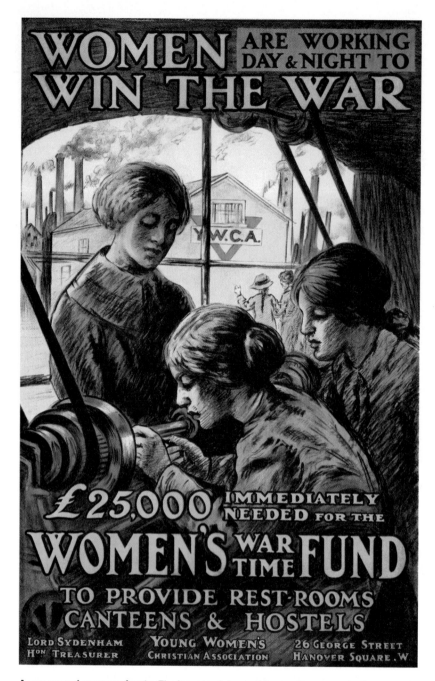

A war waged on many fronts. The increased demand for mostly young, single women to work in war industries strained available housing and support services. What strategies does this poster use to encourage public donations to funds for women workers?

nurses. Others served and sometimes gave up their lives as intelligence agents, reporting on enemy troop movements or spying in other ways. In Belgium, women served in the White Lady network, which spied on the German occupiers. On the home fronts, middle- and upper-class women formed various auxiliary organizations to recruit soldiers, patrol around army bases, sew uniforms, drive trucks, run public transport, and care for the wounded. In Britain, France, Germany, and the United States, millions of women took jobs in munitions factories and other industrial plants to replace men in service. In the Krupp armaments industry in one German city, for example, the female workforce went from zero in 1914 to thirty thousand in 1918. On both sides, rural women and their children managed farms in the absence of menfolk.

Pumping up production. When neither side achieved a quick knockout blow, both adopted strategies to deploy forces of destruction on a massive scale. This required rallying the society's total store of scientific, technological, and industrial skill. Indeed, Britain, France, and Germany generated new technologies and raised industrial output to levels that left the early industrial era in the dust. Because armies on both sides were so big, weapons manufacturers faced the critical challenge of devising machines that would kill large numbers of enemy combatants impersonally and fast. Machine guns were mass produced and continually improved, and munitions plants geared up to produce tens of thousands of artillery shells every day. German chemists pioneered different types of poison gas. Allied scientists made their own recipes in response, and both started firing gas canisters over enemy trenches. Engineers invented more effective masks and respirators, but even so, gas attacks caused great fear among troops and probably accounted for about 1.2 million total casualties.[9]

The warring powers also put new communication and transport technologies to effective use. The internal combustion engine powered supply trucks, troop vehicles, and ambulances. Early farm tractors with caterpillar tracks inspired the first battlefield tanks, which British generals put into service in 1916 to only limited effect. To combat German U-boats, the Allies grouped vessels in dense, destroyer-protected convoys, and their factories turned out ships faster than subs could sink them. Aircraft served in the war mainly for reconnaissance and modestly effective bombing and strafing. At war's end Britain had fifty thousand planes.

help the nation meet its emergency. Most of the adversaries already had large armies of conscripts when the war started. Britain did not, but 750,000 men volunteered for military service in the first two months of the fight.

Laws and deep-rooted traditions prevented women from volunteering for regular military service in any country. The one exception was Russia, where several thousand women served, notably in a unit called the Battalion of Death, which sent some female combatants to the front late in the war. Armies did, however, employ thousands of women as field

Total war and big government. Governments of the major opposing states amassed more authority than they had ever had in the nineteenth century. Central administrations were indeed the only bodies that could manage mobilization of whole societies. Government ministries, departments, and agencies proliferated to undertake specific war-related tasks. The number of people employed by government increased dramatically. Public officials took control of railroads, strategic industries, and research laboratories. Some states greatly expanded their roles in social welfare, supplementing or replacing activities that voluntary organizations had provided previously. These new activities included day nurseries, public housing, soup kitchens, refugee services, health clinics, food rationing, and workers' compensation plans.

All governments restricted civil liberties to one degree or another, suspending elections, curtailing press freedom, censoring mail, and sometimes either ignoring or encouraging persecution of citizens whose families originated in enemy countries. In the United States, laws in nearly half the states prohibited teaching and speaking German. Throughout the later nineteenth century, exclusive ethnic nationalisms had aggravated anti-Semitic prejudices. During the war, anti-Semites in eastern Europe and in some measure in the western European democracies harassed Jews as an imagined "enemy within." In 1915 the Ottoman government dealt with rising Christian Armenian nationalism in eastern Turkey by systematically massacring villagers and summarily evacuating hundreds of thousands more southward into the Syrian Desert. This proved to be a death march, and all told perhaps one million Armenians died in this horror of ethnic cleansing. When the war ended, democratically elected governments in Europe suspended many regulations and controls. But the model of vigorous state intervention was there to be applied again when the world faced new crises in the following decades.

Russia: From War to Revolution

Although the Russian imperial government enacted modest political and social reforms following the abortive 1905 revolution, Tsar Nicholas and his aristocratic inner circle remained blind to the need for far-reaching change. Even so, the Russian working and middle classes in the cities endorsed the national war cause as enthusiastically as their counterparts in western Europe. For the most part, labor unions and socialist parties, typically suspicious of tsarist appeals for popular unity, joined the march to battle.

The end of the Romanov empire. By 1917, however, extreme war weariness was setting in on both sides of the conflict. In western Europe, it was manifested in labor strikes, food riots, soldier mutinies, and covert diplomatic initiatives to end the carnage. For Russia, the fighting took 1.7 million lives by 1917, and German forces continued to advance across Poland. With no victories and little reform,

popular discontent transmuted into rage. On the Eastern Front, mutinies and mass surrenders multiplied. By 1917, Russians suffered grave food shortages, and peasants refused to sell grain to the government at fixed low prices. The army had to replace legions of dead and wounded soldiers with both urban middle-class men, who often had liberal or socialist sympathies, and poorly trained farmers, whose love for the tsar had long faded. In February 1917 bread rationing in St. Petersburg incited ten thousand women to march against the government. The violent repression that followed only incited more protests, labor strikes, and army disaffection.

As turmoil spread to more cities and into the countryside in the following month, pragmatic leaders finally persuaded Nicholas to abdicate. This act terminated the three-hundred-year-old Romanov dynasty and left the *duma,* the weak parliamentary assembly created in 1905, to form a new provisional government and restore public order. But as in Mexico and China about the same time, it proved easier to pull down the old system than to set up a new one. Dominated by moderate conservatives and constitutional liberals, the provisional regime watched helplessly as urban activists, many of them communists, organized soviets, or social workers' councils, in Moscow, St. Petersburg, and other cities. Meanwhile, peasants seized aristocratic estates, while non-Russian ethnic groups in places such as Ukraine and Latvia laid plans to secede from the empire. When tsarist authority collapsed, so did army discipline. Soldiers deserted en masse or assaulted officers who tried to force them to fight.

The October Revolution. The provisional government became mired in factionalism, while the most radical socialist and communist groups amassed popular support. Some socialist parties focused on rural land reform, but Marxist leaders like Lenin and Lev Trotsky looked to the urban working class, or proletariat, to foment revolution. After 1903 Lenin rose to leadership of the Bolsheviks (BOHL-shih-vehkz), or Majoritarians, a communist faction that demanded strict party discipline, dedicated activism, and unbending commitment to a proletarian government that would exclude the capitalist bourgeoisie, including constitutionalist liberals. In October 1917 Bolshevik militants, aided by army elements and good luck, seized power in St. Petersburg (renamed Petrograd) and disbanded the provisional regime. This audacious coup brought more socialist groups into Lenin's camp. The rapidly assembled Congress of Soviets under Bolshevik leadership claimed supreme political authority in the name of all workers' soviets. This sudden turnover of power amazed even Lenin himself: "You know, from persecution and a life underground," he remarked to Trotsky, " to come so suddenly into power, . . . it makes you giddy."[10]

In addition to abolishing private ownership of land, giving workers' committees management of factories, and replacing the tsarist legal system with "people's courts," the new Soviet government moved immediately to take Russia out of the war. By that time, German units were advancing

Lenin and Trotsky celebrate the second anniversary of the Bolshevik Revolution. This photograph from 1919 shows both revolutionary leaders at a ceremony in Red Square. Lenin stands at the top of the steps; Trotsky is next to him, wearing a military uniform, arm raised in a salute. Trotsky later lost a power struggle with Stalin and was assassinated in Mexico on Stalin's orders. When this photo was used in a 1967 Soviet book about Lenin, Trotsky was airbrushed out of it.

unchecked into Russian territory. Consequently, Lenin agreed to harsh terms. In the Treaty of Brest-Litovsk of March 1918, Russia ceded to Germany all the old empire's western borderlands, including Finland, the Baltic lands, Poland, and part of Ukraine. Though the new regime later retrieved some of that territory, it permanently lost authority over millions of people and much agricultural land. For their part, the Allied Powers, dismayed at both Russia's betrayal and the shocking communist takeover, now eyed their former partner with hostility.

Lenin's October Revolution led quickly to Soviet control over many Russian cities but only a small part of the boundless rural lands that stretched to the Pacific. At the end of 1917 the Bolsheviks had nothing close to majority popular support and no effective army of their own. Opponents of the new government recovered quickly, leading to two years of bloody civil war before the new communist ruling elite made itself secure.

Peace and Consequences

With Russia out of the war, Germany shifted forces to the Western Front for a big push. Britain and France, however, had access to global sources of food and materials, notably from the United States, that Germany and Austria did

THE GREAT WAR	
1914	Assassination of Archduke Franz Ferdinand in Sarajevo. German forces invade Belgium and France but fail to seize Paris. Western and Eastern Front lines form.
1915	Allied assault on Turkish peninsula of Gallipoli.
1916	Battle of Verdun and Battle of the Somme River.
1917	The United States declares war on Germany and sends troops to Europe. The Russian Revolution begins. Russia signs an armistice with Germany.
1918	Treaty of Brest-Litovsk. German forces fail to break through on the Western Front. Armistice ends hostilities.
1919	Paris Peace Conference.

not. By early 1918, Germany's economy was stretched thin and its population exhausted and malnourished. Worker strikes erupted and socialist parties gained strength, giving the kaiser good reason to fear a Russian-style revolution. When the western offensive met a wall of fresh American troops, an ordered retreat followed quickly. The armistice of November 11, 1918, ended the fighting, though the Allies achieved no crushing victory on the field; nor did they

Devastation on the Western Front. Human casualties were compounded by environmental damage during World War I. What does this photograph of soldiers posing in the charred remains of a forest tell us about the conditions and consequences of modern warfare?

invade and occupy Germany. Nevertheless, the kaiser abdicated amid a flurry of urban uprisings spearheaded by communists and other radicals. Russian Bolsheviks had high hopes of a German workers' revolution, but moderate socialists and anticommunists crushed the insurrections and proclaimed a new liberal republic.

The grim aftermath. The roughly sixteen million people who died as a result of the Great War numbered only about three million less those who died in all wars worldwide in the entire nineteenth century.[11] Those losses washed over countless more millions—the families, friends, and communities of the dead. France, for example, lost half its male population between the ages of fifteen and thirty. Another twenty-one million or so returned from the war blinded, crippled, or otherwise injured. The war zones produced countless refugees, 600,000 from Belgium alone. Surviving African and Asian soldiers who fought on one side or the other returned home to find jobs in short supply and the same thoroughly authoritarian imperial systems in place as before the war.

Most of the conflict's physical devastation afflicted Poland, Serbia, Belgium, and northeastern France, where the heaviest fighting took place. Trenches, shell craters, and fires turned hundreds of thousands of acres of farm and forest into smoking wilderness. Although much of this land was eventually restored, entire villages disappeared forever. There is no doubt that atmospheric pollution from soot, smoke, and sulfur dioxide increased hugely during the war, especially in industrial zones like the English midlands or Germany's Ruhr Valley, where factories operated day and night. Total costs of the war in public expenditure reached nearly $150 billion on the Allied side, and all the European states involved in it found themselves swamped in debt. Only the United States and Japan emerged as financial winners. Japan's wartime exports nearly tripled, and the United States became a creditor rather than a debtor state for the first time in its history.

The influenza pandemic. Amid the violence of the war's final year, an infectious disease pandemic visited nearly every part of the world, wreaking more misery and death. The war itself helped empower this particularly virulent strain of influenza, for which no vaccination existed. A severe outbreak occurred at an army base in Kansas in March 1918. Infected soldiers then transmitted the virus along the military transport network to other bases and from there to Britain and France. In 1918 and early 1919 the flu killed upwards of forty million people worldwide, that is, millions more than died in the fighting. Although the pathological explanation is unclear, this particular virus sickened or killed more men and women in their twenties than the older age groups typically at risk.

Like the plague outbreak of the 1890s, the flu pandemic spread around the world by steamship. In the port of Cape Town, South Africa, for example, 4 percent of the population perished within a month. From ports the virus moved inland. In the Americas the contagion ripped through

Arab Independence That Was Not to Be

Starting in July 1915, Sharif Husayn ibn Ali, the governor of Mecca and Medina, exchanged a series of letters with the British High Commissioner in Egypt regarding political independence for Arabic-speaking peoples. Husayn vowed to raise a revolt against Ottoman authority in return for assurances of British support for a sovereign Arab state following victory over Turkey. Britain appeared to make promises to that effect, despite several qualifications. Instead, Britain and France safeguarded their own alliance by settling in advance potential disputes over the postwar Middle East. France had long-standing interests in Syria but worried that Britain, which was leading the Allied campaign against the Turks, might move to dominate the entire region. Accordingly, in May 1916, Mark Sykes, a British civil servant, and François Picot, a French one, negotiated a secret treaty to partition the Middle East, betraying assurances of Arab self-determination. This partition, as shown in Document 3, took place in 1919.

DOCUMENT 1 Sharif Husayn to the British High Commissioner, July 1915

Whereas the whole of the Arab nation without any exception have decided in these last years to accomplish their freedom, and grasp the reins of their administration both in theory and practice; and whereas they have found and felt that it is in the interest of the Government of Great Britain to support them and aid them in the attainment of their firm and lawful intentions.

Firstly—England will acknowledge the independence of the Arab countries, bounded on the north by Mersina and Adana [in modern Turkey] up to the 37th degree of latitude, . . . up to the border of Persia [Iran]; on the east by the borders of Persia up to the Gulf of Basra; on the south by the Indian Ocean, with the exception of the position of Aden to remain as it is; on the west by the Red Sea, the Mediterranean Sea up to Mersina. England to approve the proclamation of an Arab Khalifate of Islam.

Secondly—The Arab Government of the Sharif will acknowledge that England shall have the preference in all economic enterprises in the Arab countries whenever conditions of enterprises are otherwise equal. . . .

Consequently, and as the whole of the Arab nation have (praise be to God) agreed and united for the attainment, at all costs and finally, of this noble object, they beg the Government of Great Britain to answer them positively or negatively in a period of thirty days after receiving this intimation.

DOCUMENT 2 British Foreign Office to French Embassy in London, May 1916

It is accordingly understood between the French and British governments:

That France and Great Britain are prepared to recognize and protect an independent Arab state or a confederation of Arab states (a) and (b) marked on the annexed map [see Document 3], under the suzerainty of an Arab chief. That in area (a) France, and in area (b) Great Britain, shall have priority of right of enterprise and local loans. That in area (a) France, and in area (b) Great Britain, shall alone supply advisers or foreign functionaries at the request of the Arab state or confederation of Arab states.

That in the blue area France, and in the red area Great Britain, shall be allowed to establish such direct or indirect administration or control as they desire and as they may think fit to arrange with the Arab state or confederation of Arab states.

That in the brown area [appears yellow on map] there shall be established an international administration, the form of which is to be decided upon after consultation with Russia, and subsequently in consultation with the other allies, and the representatives of the sheriff [Sharif] of Mecca.

Sources: Husayn Letter: Quoted in Marvin Gettleman and Stuart Schaar, eds., *The Middle East and Islamic World Reader* (New York: Grove Press, 2003), 114–115. Sykes-Picot Agreement: Mideast Gateway, http://www.mideastweb.org.

Thinking Critically

What specific words and phrases in these two texts indicate a divergence between Arab and European aims in the Middle East? The Sykes-Picot Agreement refers to recognition of "an independent Arab state or a confederation of Arab states." But what other language in that text qualifies the French and British understanding of Arab independence? According to Sharif Husayn's specifications, how would the Arab state he proposed look on a map of the Middle East? Has a state with those approximate boundaries ever existed since World War I? How did Husayn's expectations differ from the territorial division agreed upon by France and Great Britain shown in Document 3?

The map of the Sykes-Picot Agreement partitions a large swath of the Ottoman Empire into territory directly administered by France (in blue), France's region of exclusive influence (labeled A), territory directly controlled by Britain (in red), and Britain's sphere of exclusive influence (labeled B).

Mexico, Chile, Brazil, and Argentina. South Asian ports, important nodes in the British wartime shipping web, were hit hard, and the affliction then crossed the subcontinent, inflicting perhaps half the total of global deaths. In Australia, two epidemic waves killed about twelve thousand. In the United States no major city escaped, and about 675,000 Americans died.

The death toll dropped in the spring of 1919, and the particular virus that caused the pandemic disappeared eventually. Those who survived exposure acquired immunity to that particular strain. Nevertheless, the flu outbreak inflicted on the world great anxiety, tragedy, and loss of human productivity just as it was striving to pull itself from the muck of war.

The peace treaties. The monumental task of restoring political stability to a depleted world fell in the short term on the diplomats who met at a series of international conferences held between 1919 and 1924, starting with the Paris Peace Conference. The victorious powers dominated these meetings and took it upon themselves to deal with the wreckage of four huge monarchies—Germany, Austria-Hungary, Ottoman Turkey, and Russia. Three of those empires were the war's big losers. The forth was transforming itself into a communist state pledging global socialist revolution. The several conferences produced treaties that redrew political boundaries, created brand new states, and pronounced sentence on the defeated countries.

When leaders of the principal Allied powers—Britain, France, Italy, the United States, and Japan—initiated the treaty-making process at Versailles in January 1919, they first put forth high-minded visions of a safe, peaceful, and democratic world. Then, they got down to their hard-nosed plan to gather the spoils of victory, enfeeble Germany indefinitely, politically isolate the Russian communists, and get back to the business of ruling much of Africa and Asia. British and French leaders could not go along with Woodrow Wilson's ideal of "peace without victory," if they hoped to retain public support at home. The French prime minister Georges Clemenceau summed up European leaders' skepticism and wariness about Wilson: "Never before has any political assembly heard so fine a sermon on what humans might be capable of if only they weren't human."

Wilson brought to Versailles his Fourteen Points, a set of goals for a new world order that emphasized the commitment of sovereign states to collective security (as opposed to se-

> **self-determination** The idea put forth during and after World War I that a society sharing common language, history, and cultural traditions should have the right to decide its own political future and govern its own affairs.

cret bilateral deals) and the rights of ethnically based national communities to political **self-determination.** The European Allies, however, knew all too well that the war ended without seriously damaging Germany's future military and industrial potential. They insisted, therefore, that it be stripped of large chunks of territory,

prohibited from recovering its overseas colonies, permitted only a small defensive army, and obligated to accept responsibility for starting the war. This "war guilt clause" served as justification for imposing on Germany more than $330 billion in **reparations** to the victorious states. This punishment served the domestic interests of French and British leaders, who desperately needed money

> **reparations** The act of making amends or giving satisfaction for an injustice or injury; payment of compensation by a defeated state for presumed damages inflicted on another state as a result of war between them.

to repay their own war debts, principally to American banks. German diplomats were not allowed to take part in the Versailles conference but nonetheless had to sign the treaty. The kaiser's empire was transformed into a militarily frail republic, and Germans nearly universally felt humiliated and aggrieved. In the aftermath of Versailles, radical German parties on the left and right struggled to dominate the country and to undo the treaties.

The last of Wilson's Fourteen Points declared that "a general association of nations must be formed under specific covenants for the purpose of affording mutual guarantees of political independence and territorial integrity to great and small states alike." The Versailles treaty duly established the League of Nations, the first formal organization of sovereign states dedicated to worldwide collective security through open negotiations. The League started out providing an institutional forum for communication among states and for international humanitarian, educational, and statistical work. Germany, Russia, and the United States, however, were not charter members. The Allied victors refused to allow the first two countries to join, and the U.S. Senate, averse to further European entanglements, kept America out.

The complexities of self-determination. The postwar agreements made a shambles of Wilson's principle of self-determination, which would ideally have provided a democratic nation-state to every significant ethnolinguistic group that had formerly been enclosed in one of the four defunct empires. The proposal was hopelessly unworkable. On the ground, most of eastern and southern Europe's numerous ethnic peoples were jumbled together, not territorially separate. Consequently, a nation-state created for one group within the former Austro-Hungarian or Ottoman empire would almost inevitably have its own minorities clamoring for *their* nation-states. Insofar as self-determination became a reality, it favored groups that had supported the Allies, notably Poles, Romanians, Serbians, and Italians. By contrast, it penalized groups that had joined the other side—Germans, German-speaking Austrians, Hungarians, Bulgarians, and Turks.

In Russia in 1919, Lenin had not yet consolidated Communist Party authority, but that year his regime sponsored a congress of the Comintern, or Communist International, to support socialist revolutionary parties around the globe.

From the Allied perspective, such subversive provocation offered a persuasive rationale for quarantining the "disease" of Bolshevik communism behind a line of seven new sovereign states with governments guaranteed to be anti-Russian. Four of them—Lithuania, Poland, Hungary, and Romania—had historical precedents as sovereign states; the others—Finland, Latvia, and Estonia—were creations of the Allied treaty makers. Serbian nationalists got to dominate Yugoslavia, a new multiethnic state of Slavic-speaking peoples previously enfolded within the Austro-Hungarian or Turkish empires. Czechoslovakia was similarly set up as an assemblage of ethnolinguistic groups.

When Wilson proclaimed his Fourteen Points, nationalist groups throughout the colonized world experienced what historians have called the "Wilsonian Moment."[12] For a few brief months, they anticipated that the American leader would use his considerable moral authority to convince the European imperial powers to grant genuine democratic self-determination to all subjugated peoples, not just in Europe but throughout the world. Wilson, however, failed to challenge European colonial authority with any vigor on this point, and the Wilsonian Moment evaporated. The victorious powers, despite their massive postwar debts and the war's blatant exposure of the myth of innate European moral superiority, expected to return to business as usual in ruling most of Africa and a good part of Asia. In the peace accords, the populations of Germany's African colonies were not invited to discuss their future self-determination. Rather, these dependencies were arbitrarily transferred to Britain, France, or South Africa (and its white government) under League of Nations supervision. Britain and France took over the defeated Ottoman empire's former Arabic-speaking provinces under a similar arrangement, despite promises to the contrary to Arab leaders. Young nationalists in colonized territories profoundly resented these actions, prompting them in the postwar decades to organize political movements, first to petition for reforms in imperial regimes and, when that process moved too slowly, to demand their sovereign freedom, as we will see in the coming chapters.

• • •

Conclusion

We have no way of knowing how the world would have changed during the twentieth century's second decade if World War I had not happened. There is no doubt, however, that the conflict not only caused far more death and devastation than any previous war but that it begat numerous long-term problems. Despite capitalist hopes, the global economy did not bounce back to prewar levels. Britain and France slowed European recovery generally by refusing to help reintegrate industrialized, heavily populated Germany. Germans, knowing that the Allies never decisively crushed their army on the battlefield, fumed over their country's degradation and dishonor. In eastern and southeastern Europe, nationalists complained that the settlements gave other ethnic groups too much territory and power or their own not enough. In Europe's Asian and African colonial territories, nationalist leaders gained popular support as soon as people discovered that self-determination was meant to apply to Europeans, but not to them. The war aggravated problems of air pollution, water contamination, and deforestation already under way in industrialized countries. Wartime scientists and engineers made numerous useful discoveries and innovations, but these included weapons of unprecedented power. The bluntest assessment of how well diplomats in tailcoats and top hats restored global stability is that within twenty short years another great war broke, a calamity more brutal and destructive than the first.

• • •

Key Terms

Bolshevik 719	Great War (World War I) 699	Russian Revolution of 1905 708
Boxers 709	League of Nations 724	self-determination 724
Comintern 724	Mexican Revolution 711	soviet 707
Fordism 702	October Revolution (Bolshevik	total war 717
Fourteen Points 724	Revolution) 719	treaty ports 708
gold standard 699	reparations 724	Young Turks 708

Change over Time

1886	Gold is discovered in South Africa.
1896–1902	A series of El Niño–related floods and droughts affects harvests and triggers widespread famine.
1896–1914	The global economy experiences strong growth.
1899–1902	Britain makes war on Afrikaner governments in South Africa in the Boer War.
1901	The first trans-Atlantic wireless transmission strengthens the global communication network.
1905	Waves of popular protest challenge the tsar's authority in the Russian Revolution. Japan defeats Russia in the Russo-Japanese War.
1906	Iran adopts a constitution; civil war breaks out after the death of the shah.
1908	Young Turks force the sultan to abdicate in the Ottoman empire.
1910	The Mexican Revolution begins, with the goal of overthrowing the Díaz regime (Porfiriato). German scientists discover how to make solid nitrates, a key component of gunpowder, dynamite, and fertilizer.
1911	The Qing dynasty collapses in the wake of the Chinese Revolution.
1914	The Panama Canal opens, speeding steamship traffic between the Atlantic and Pacific.
1914–1918	The Allied and Central Powers and their colonies clash in World War I.
1916	The Arab Revolt against Ottoman rule begins.
1917	Russia withdrawals from World War I; the Russian Revolution begins.
1918–1919	An influenza pandemic strikes around the globe.
1919	Nationalist groups throughout the colonized world experience the "Wilsonian Moment." The Paris Peace Conference sets the terms of German reparations and ignores colonial requests for self-determination.

Please see end of book reference section for additional reading suggestions related to this chapter.

25 Turbulent Decades
1918-1935

The General Trans-Saharan Company connected North and West Africa with motor vehicle and air services, though unpaved tracks across the desert could not accommodate sleek busses like the one shown in this poster.

Bidon 5, or Gas Can 5 in English, is a spot in a particularly desolate part of the Sahara Desert where in 1926 employees of the General Trans-Saharan Company set up a refueling depot for automobiles and airplanes. During the previous quarter-century, French colonial forces had seized control of the central Sahara's major oases and their Berber and Arab populations. In the 1920s the company began building numerous gas and water stations like Bidon 5 to facilitate travel and eventual mining operations in landscapes friendly in earlier times only to camel caravans. In 1920 French military pilots made the first flight across the Sahara, though it included many fuel stops. Four planes started the journey. Two did not get far, and a third crashed in a waterless tract, where one of the three crew members died. The fourth plane made it to the Niger River in what is today Mali. In 1922–1923 a French team in Citroën automobiles drove from northern Algeria to Timbuktu on the Niger in twenty-two days. Four years later, another Frenchman crossed the great void on a motorcycle. Trans-Saharan airmail and trucking services soon followed. French visionaries laid plans to crisscross the desert with rail lines, though that project never came to reality.

To the world's entrepreneurs, engineers, and scientists, the internal combustion engine's conquest of the Sahara was just one sign that a new age of technological innovation was at hand. Perhaps World War I, they surmised, had been only a brief, unfortunate interruption of modernity's exhilarating progressive march. The first part of this chapter examines some key developments of the

1920s that on the whole bolstered faith in humankind's dynamism and progress. The Great War turned out to have no lasting negative effect on global population growth or urbanization. The war itself also stimulated new technical and scientific research, including revolutionary theories about the workings of the universe.

In the economic and political spheres, however, expectations of a new era of prosperity and calm gradually faded. The global economy did not resume a heady upward spiral. Rather, the gross domestic product of the major European industrialized countries grew at half the rate of the boom that had preceded the war.[1] Most countries continued to struggle with inflation, chronic unemployment, or both. The second section of the chapter connects the economic insecurities of the 1920s and early 1930s to the spread of ultranationalist and authoritarian political regimes. Liberal democratic governments survived in western Europe and the Americas, but authoritarian leaders having no patience for multiparty legislatures and individual rights seized power, sometimes to popular acclaim, in much of Europe and in some countries of Latin America and Asia.

As of 1920, about one-third of the world's population lived under governments imposed by foreign invaders from across the seas. In the chapter's third part we explore interwar developments in the colonial dependencies of several European powers, plus Japan and the United States. Postwar treaty-making led to national independence for some groups previously enclosed within the Russian, German, Austro-Hungarian, or Ottoman empires. But on the global scale, colonial empires got bigger after the war, not smaller. In the early 1920s, all the states that held colonies were republics or constitutional monarchies, but they ruled their possessions by force, not by the consent of the governed. The very condition of imperial repression, however, accelerated social and economic change in the colonies and strengthened nationalist movements for self-rule.

The final section of the chapter surveys the Great Depression. Striking just eleven years after World War I, it represented the twentieth century's second globe-encompassing crisis. If some economic thinkers saw a business downturn coming in 1929, no one expected it to mutate into a financial and commercial catastrophe for much of the world. The depression caused great misery. It also propelled many states to amass even more central power than they had during World War I in order to grapple with the economic crisis. The most economically developed states also initiated public programs aimed at protecting citizens from the worst effects of economic downswings. Unfortunately, popular frustration and despair also played into the hands of popular demagogues and dictators even more ruthless than the ones who had seized power in the 1920s.

Chapter Outline

POSTWAR TRENDS IN SOCIETY AND CULTURE
Population Trends
New Ways of Living in the Industrialized World
Scientific Challenges
to the Knowable Universe
Modernity and Modernism

INDIVIDUALS MATTER Diego Rivera:
Mexican Modernist

CLASHING IDEOLOGIES IN THE POLITICAL ARENA
Democratic Hopes
The Soviet Union: Communist Authoritarianism
Nationalists and Communists in China
New Governments on the Political Right

WEIGHING THE EVIDENCE Turkish Views
on Dress and National Identity
Left and Right in Latin America

COLONIAL RULE AND ITS OPPONENTS IN AFRICA AND ASIA
Economy and Society in the Colonial Empires
Ways of Ruling
Foreign Immigrants in Colonized Lands
Colonial Rule Contested

THE GREAT DEPRESSION AND ITS CONSEQUENCES
The Steep Descent
Depression and the Continuing Trend
toward Authoritarian Leaders

A Panoramic View

MAP 25.1 States, colonial dependencies, and League of Nations Mandates, 1925.

Which states had large territorial claims overseas in 1925? Where were most of those colonies located? What factors can explain changes in imperial land claims between 1910 and 1925 (see Map 24.1)?

Map legend:
- British dependencies
- French dependencies
- Spanish dependencies
- ◆ Portuguese dependencies
- Japanese dependencies
- Dutch dependencies
- Italian dependencies
- U.S. dependencies
- Belgian dependencies
- IRAQ League of Nations Mandate territory

Postwar Trends in Society and Culture

FOCUS What were key social, cultural, and scientific trends in the decade after World War I?

In the 1920s the pace of change in global population, urbanization, technology, and science continued at high speed. Unlike earlier generations, educated classes even warmed to the idea that the faster the world changed, the better off everyone would be. Philosophers, writers, and artists argued

modernism The movement in the arts and humanities that embraces innovation and experimentation and rejects adherence to traditional forms and values.

that continuous change is a fundamental condition of human life that should be embraced with enthusiasm, an idea summed up by the term **modernism.**

Population Trends

World War I and the influenza pandemic of 1918–1919 together took around fifty-six million lives, a number representing about 3.2 percent of the world's population in 1910. That many deaths from combat, bombs, hunger, and disease in just five years was ghastly, but it had no effect on the global population surge under way since the 1700s. Population worldwide *rose* by about 3 percent between 1910 and 1920, canceling the loss. Between 1920 and 1940, the earth accommodated about 410 million more people, a trend inseparable from issues of worldwide food production and economic inequality.

Demographic transition, or not. After the Great War, regional shares of world population began to shift decidedly away from Europe and toward other densely populated regions. In the early decades of the twentieth century, Europe

demographic transition The stabilization of population level in a society resulting from the decline of both fertility rates and death rates.

as a whole experienced what social scientists call **demographic transition.** Since the eighteenth century, accelerating population growth had been associated primarily with declining death rates, a phenomenon linked to improved food supplies and nutrition and to lower mortality from infectious diseases (despite recurrent epidemics of maladies such as influenza). But in Europe sometime after 1900, *both* the death rate and the fertility rate, the average number of children a woman bore in her lifetime, declined. Lower fertility rates partially counteracted growth spurred by lower death rates, thereby lowering the *rate* of annual population increase. Declining births were associated with a complex combination of factors, including rising living standards, relatively late marriage, and improved birth control methods.

By contrast, in Latin America, South Asia, Subsaharan Africa, and (after World War II) China, death rates declined

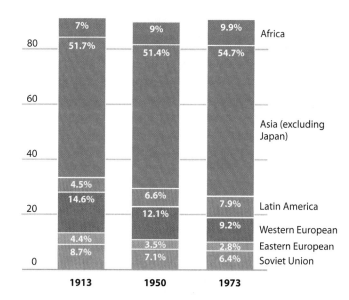

Percentage of world total

Changing shares of world population by region, 1913–1973. Shares of total world population increased in Africa, Asia, and Latin America during those sixty years because population growth rates remained relatively high. Regions with lower growth rates had declining shares.

but fertility rates remained high. In other words, people gained longer average life expectancies, as clean water, hygiene measures, and vaccinations against infectious diseases became more widely available. At the same time, however, women continued on average to bear the same number of children they had in the nineteenth century, or even more. This was a sure formula for swelling population growth rates.[2]

In regions of high growth rates, the long-term consequences included increased pressure on farm land, declining standards of living, stepped up migration from countryside to city, and accelerating deforestation owing to heavier demand for firewood, timber, and cleared fields. For example, the rate of forest depletion worldwide rose from an average of about 7.4 million acres per year between 1850 and 1919 to 28.4 million between 1920 and 1949.[3]

Postwar urbanization. In the first half of the twentieth century, the great majority of humans still tended crops or herded animals. As of 1930, only about 17 percent of the population of Latin America lived in cities. In South Asia it was 12 percent and in Africa, 7 percent. Nevertheless, cities became bigger and more numerous on every inhabited continent after World War I. By 1920 half the population of the United States lived in cities; Japan reached that benchmark about 1935.

Throughout most of history, cities had been incubators of infectious and lethal diseases. Populations grew only because in-migration exceeded the mortality rate. By World War I, however, cities were becoming safer places to live, especially in richer countries, owing to advances in public health and disease prevention. Higher, denser urban populations naturally generated more waste, air pollution, and the unhealthy microbes and particles that accompanied them. Wealthier cities, however, built complex sewer networks and shunted garbage to waterways or rural landfills. In the United States, for example, cities took to "reclaiming" neighboring wetlands by filling them with garbage and ash.

Postwar migration patterns. After World War I, Chinese and Indian migration to Southeast Asia surged to the annual levels of the prewar decades. But westward migration across the Atlantic, which had carried nearly fifteen million Europeans to the United States between 1900 and 1914, recovered only partially. In the 1920s the United States had imposed strict immigration quotas on certain European nationalities and on Asians, a policy that reflected narrowing nationalist views of who should and should not be invited in. Brazil also introduced restrictive immigration laws in the 1920s.

On the regional and national levels, numerous complex population shifts took place after World War I. In the war's immediate aftermath, millions of refugees and people seeking to leave one ethnic region for another crisscrossed Europe. Christian Armenians who faced persecution and death during the Ottoman state's wartime ethnic cleansing of 1915 (see Chapter 24) fled to Syria, Lebanon, and various other lands around the world. In 1922 Greece and Turkey, after years of hostilities, agreed to a compulsory exchange that sent about 1.2 million Eastern Orthodox Christians from Turkey to Greece and half a million Muslims from Greece to Turkey. In North America, where the United States exempted Latin Americans from immigration restrictions, almost 500,000 Mexicans moved to the southwestern states in the 1920s in search of work.

New Ways of Living in the Industrialized World

Numerous new inventions and mass production techniques materialized during the Great War because governments instructed scientists and engineers to find technical solutions to particular military and industrial problems. In the interwar years, both governments and corporations continued to support research on larger, more efficient scales by organizing teams of scientists, engineers, managers, government bureaucrats, and university professors to work collaboratively.

Research and development labs dedicated to deliberate innovation proliferated after the war. Professional teams either invented or greatly improved upon such marvels as

nylon, synthetic rubber, and the affordable fluorescent lamp. Of course, individuals continued to come up with bright ideas. Talented loners invented the helicopter, the ballpoint pen, the vacuum tube, insulin, penicillin, and cellophane. In 1907 Leo Baekeland, a Belgian scientist, invented Bakelite, one of the earliest plastic materials, by synthesizing large molecules of the type found in many natural vegetables. Following the lead of North Americans, western Europeans started laying out hard-earned cash for cars, record players, radios, and movie tickets. By 1927, assembly lines of the Ford Motor Company boosted production of Model Ts to fifteen million. In the same decade, Brazilian entrepreneurs began to import "automobile kits" from abroad for local assembly and sale.

The torrent of new things transformed work and family life in countless ways. First in the United States and by the 1920s in western Europe, radios and phonographs transmitted jazz and other popular music that celebrated personal and sexual freedom. Evenings at the local picture house increasingly crowded out family conversations and reading sessions. Hollywood films exalted urban glamour, enticing young men and women to escape the farm and head to the city. The automobile gave people more personal and occupational mobility, accelerating the spread of residential suburbs. Intercity roads, parking lots, and new suburbs altered, indeed scarred, physical and natural landscapes, displacing farms, villages, and wild habitats. In the United States the network of intercity highways grew from 387,000 miles in 1921 to 1.3 million by 1940. First in the industrialized countries and then around the world, cities and industries became electrified. Nighttime lighting allowed factories to run work shifts around the clock, and it pushed women's domestic work deeper into the evening.

Scientific Challenges to the Knowable Universe

The pace of scientific discovery, which quickened in the late nineteenth century, moved even faster after World War I. Progress in physical, chemical, and biological theories tended to be incremental—a small breakthrough here, another one there. In physics, however, scientists working in Europe between 1900 and 1930 made theoretical leaps that began to transform humankind's conception of reality. Isaac Newton and other geniuses of the seventeenth and eighteenth centuries had conceived of an orderly, stable, and predictable

Art Deco radio, 1930. The development of plastics made mass-produced decorative objects and useful goods more affordable for ordinary consumers. Art Deco used the same basic geometric shapes—circles and squares—and sharp angles of modern machines, arranged in attractive designs.

cosmos governed by laws expressible in exact mathematical terms. In the late nineteenth century, however, a small band of gifted thinkers, including the German physicist Albert Einstein, began to deconstruct this universe. In 1905 Einstein presented his theory of relativity, which demonstrated mathematically that there is no single spatial and chronological framework within the universe. Rather, time and space are relative to the individual or object measuring them. For example, gravity affects the passage of time so that clocks in space, distant from the planet's gravitational pull, would run faster than earthbound timekeepers. Einstein also helped redefine matter itself by showing that matter and energy are not distinct phenomena but instead are equivalent to each other, that is, $E = mc^2$. These ideas were bewilderingly at odds with both human sense perception and modern science up to that point. At first, most of the world rejected or ignored them.

Einstein believed that the new relativity would somehow be reconciled with the old physics. However, Werner Heisenberg, another German scientist, challenged even this premise. A pioneer in quantum mechanics, which describes the wave properties of submicroscopic particles, Heisenberg contended in 1927 that if one probes deeply enough into the tiniest elements that constitute matter, the "knowability" of the universe evaporates. According to his "uncertainty principle," it is not possible to determine simultaneously the exact position and speed of a particle such as an electron orbiting the nucleus of an atom. The more precisely we measure the position, the less we can know of the speed. If we look at where the particle is, we cannot know where it is going, and vice versa. The very act of measuring the particle alters its behavior. Or more broadly, the physical universe simply cannot be described fully. And if it cannot, its fundamental laws can never be entirely known. In the ensuing decades, scientists adjusted to the "uncertainty principle" as a working hypothesis, and the new physics stimulated many avenues of research that had long-term practical applications, such as radar, electronics, atom splitting, and the nuclear bomb.

Modernity and Modernism

In the late nineteenth century the reality of modernity—the rapid acceleration of change in nearly every sphere of life—began to impose itself on human consciousness, at least in industrialized and densely urbanized parts of the world. In the cities of western Europe, intellectuals argued that change should be understood as both continuous and invigorating and that no time-honored tradition of how to observe and interpret the world should be considered safe from challenge. A corps of writers, artists, scholars, and cultural critics took on the special mission of questioning conventional views of the world and prevailing standards of morality, taste, and respectability. To this end they experimented with fresh forms of literature, architecture, painting, dance, music, and film.

Very broadly, modernism as a cultural ideology signified an attitude of welcome and acclaim for the modern age and for any creative act that might evoke or illuminate modern life. Modernists zealously embraced the new, the here-and-now, rather than striving to resist and control change as entrenched political and religious elites tended to do. World War I strengthened the modernist critique. To unorthodox thinkers, the war's horrors and sheer mindlessness discredited traditional values, smug faith in rationality, and entrenched hierarchies (even in presumed democratic countries). Writers and artists expressed great cultural disillusionment but also resolved to reshape the world.

Heisenberg's uncertainty principle seemed to play into the modernist idea that rational thought cannot reveal the whole of reality. So did the ideas of the Austrian physician Sigmund Freud. He argued that the survival of organized society depended on people behaving rationally but that this required a mighty struggle against irrational and instinctual impulses. In 1900 he published *The Interpretation of Dreams*, which hypothesized that desire, self-delusion, and aggression ruled the deep structures of the brain, the "unconscious mind." People suffer guilt as a result of habitually repressing primal drives, especially sexual ones. This subconscious turmoil may then produce emotional disturbances, psychoses, or even physical illnesses. Freud contended that civilization's standards and laws serve to control base instincts. He also insisted, however, that the scientific method of therapy he called psychoanalysis could draw the mind's deepest, darkest operations to the surface

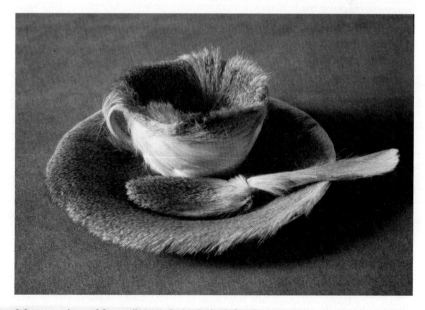

A famous piece of Surrealist art. Swiss artist Méret Oppenheim's teacup, saucer, and spoon are covered in the fur of a Chinese gazelle. She made the work in 1936. Why is this creation considered a statement of modernism? © UPPA/Photoshot © 2013 Artists Rights Society (ARS), New York/ProLitteris, Zurich.

Diego Rivera: Mexican Modernist

Diego Rivera and Frida Kahlo at an art exhibition in New York, 1930s.

The fact that modernism warmly embraced all things new practically ensured that its artistic movements would take off in many different directions. Early modernist painters like Picasso disputed the conventional idea that paintings should depict human figures and their world realistically. Diego Rivera (1886–1957), a graduate of a traditional art school in Mexico City, joined this modernist cause in his youth as an aspiring Cubist painter. But he soon followed other modernist impulses, painting murals in which naturalistically proportioned figures bore witness to Mexico's history and culture, including the Revolution of 1910. Rivera's modernism was expressed in his commitment to art that portrayed the lives of ordinary people, evoked Mexico's ethnic heritage, and served nationalist and revolutionary aims.

A son of urban middle-class parents, Rivera lived in Europe from 1911 to 1921, immersing himself in the heady art scene there and gradually refining his own vision. Distancing himself from Cubism, he left Paris for Italy in 1920, where he studied, among other things, fresco construction, that is, the labor-intensive art of painting on wet plaster. Rivera believed that art should be accessible to all, not just the affluent classes, and he came to regard the fresco technique, applied to enormous murals on the walls of public buildings, as an ideal form of public art.

In 1921 Rivera returned to Mexico to participate in a government-sponsored program to create public murals with national and revolutionary themes. A leading figure in the Mexican Muralism movement, Rivera painted colorful epic scenes that depicted the country's Aztec past, the suffering of its people under Spanish rule, and the stirring events of the revolution. Rivera's art also commented harshly on Mexico's vulnerability to foreign and particularly capitalist interference. Both a nationalist and a Marxist, Rivera joined the Mexican Communist Party in 1922 and spent time in the Soviet Union in 1927–1928. He was expelled from the party in 1929, however, for criticizing Joseph Stalin's iron-handed rule. Nevertheless, he remained dedicated to socialist revolutionary ideals.

Though he married multiple times and had a notorious reputation as a womanizer, Rivera formed an enduring if stormy partnership with the painter Frida Kahlo, a woman eventually recognized as one of the early twentieth century's great artists. Rivera and Kahlo married in 1929 and, except for a brief divorce in 1939–1940, remained together until her death in 1954. Rivera's Marxist politics did not stop him from accepting commissions from some of the world's leading capitalists. Accompanied by Kahlo, Rivera traveled to the United States in 1930. He first painted murals in San Francisco, then moved at the invitation of Henry Ford to the Detroit Institute, where he undertook *Detroit Industry,* a monumental series of twenty-seven panels depicting both people at work in the Ford Motor Company and general themes of scientific and technological progress. Owing to his left-wing sentiments, which showed frequently in his art, his work in the United States caused considerable public commotion. In 1933 he inserted an image of the Russian communist revolutionary V. I. Lenin into a mural he painted at Rockefeller Center in New York. After he refused requests to erase Lenin from the mural, Rivera's sponsors had it destroyed.

In 1933 Rivera returned to Mexico, where he continued to produce murals as well as more commercial paintings of scenes from Mexican culture. He made a last, brief trip to the United States in 1940 to paint a series of murals for San Francisco's Golden Gate Exposition. He continued to paint in his later years, adding art to public spaces nearly until his death in 1957.

Thinking Critically

In what ways do you think Diego Rivera's career exemplified modernist cultural trends?

and effectively treat mental disease. Although Freud quickly provoked innumerable criticisms and countertheories, he, more powerfully than any other scientist of the early century, revealed mind and personality as an immense inner universe.

First in Europe, but soon in other parts of the world, numerous modernist movements succeeded one another—

Impressionism, Post-Impressionism, Symbolism, Expressionism, Cubism, Futurism, Dadaism, Art Deco, Surrealism, Constructivism, and musical atonality. Claude Monet and other artists of the Impressionist school, already at work in the 1870s, contended that painters should probe the pure sensations of nature and daily life by experimenting with color, light, form, and motion. In 1890 the French artist Maurice

Denis wrote, "It is well to remember that a picture—before being a battle horse, a nude woman, or some anecdote—is essentially a flat surface covered with colors assembled in a certain order."[4] That observation evoked the modernist urge to demolish illusions and penetrate to the honest heart of things. In the first decade of the twentieth century, Pablo Picasso (1881–1973) and his fellow Cubists reveled in distorting objective reality, disassembling objects, including the human figure, then putting them back together on canvas in jumbled bits and pieces that might baffle the viewer but also uncover some deeper reality (see Picasso's *Les Demoiselles d'Avignon* in Chapter 24). The Surrealists drew on Freud's psychoanalytical technique to paint disturbing, illogical images of the sort we see in dreams. Writers such as James Joyce and Gertrude Stein produced novels and poems that recorded private "streams of consciousness" or that abandoned standard rules of grammar and word order. The Russian composer Igor Stravinsky wrote music that substituted ambiguous chords, clashing sounds, and haunting rhythms for the harmonic melodies of the European classical tradition. Audiences tended to react to modernist experimentation with confusion, if not ridicule and shock. For modernists, however, this was precisely the point. If too many people found what they created easy to digest, then they were not pursuing their mission radically enough.

Modernist movements found eager disciples in places like Buenos Aires, Shanghai, and Tokyo, and artists and writers merged Western materials and styles with local traditions. Chinese painters applied European techniques to traditional visual themes. In several Muslim countries, writers experimented with Western poetry and prose fiction, and musicians combined local with European composition and instrumentation. The Iranian artist Muhammad Ghaffari (1848–1940) exemplified the small number of Muslim artists who traveled to Europe to study modernist painting. He returned home to open an art school in Tehran in 1911 to teach European techniques and styles. Modernists prided themselves on openness to unfamiliar art forms. For example, Japanese woodblock prints, a long-established art in that country, attracted a booming European market. They profoundly influenced the work of Western artists such as Henri Toulouse-Lautrec and the American painter Mary Cassatt. According to the French art critic Theodore Duret, "As soon as people looked at Japanese pictures, where the most glaring, piercing colors were placed side by side, they finally understood that there were new methods for reproducing certain effects of nature."[5]

Clashing Ideologies in the Political Arena

FOCUS Why did a number of authoritarian states emerge in the interwar years?

By the close of World War I, the modern idea that governments ought to exercise authority only with the consent of the "people" achieved nearly universal acceptance among sovereign states as a political ideal. Autocracy, defined here as the doctrine that rulers acquire legitimacy through tradition and inheritance, and usually with the endorsement of God, nearly disappeared. This happened in the wake of events that destroyed deep-rooted imperial dynasties in China, Iran, Russia, Germany, Austria-Hungary, and Ottoman Turkey in the early twentieth century. All the governments that replaced those empires claimed legitimacy as the rightful agents of the "will of the people."

States presumably founded on this principle, however, did not necessarily subscribe to the ideals of liberal democracy, in other words, to a political system characterized by contested legislative elections, independent judicial institutions, guaranteed liberties, and few legal restrictions on capitalist enterprise. In the decade after the war, many political activists took the view that the world needed governments with stronger executive authority to fire up patriotic pride, unify the masses, and get things done. For them, parliamentary debates and private freedoms frustrated decisive action in uncertain and dangerous times. In numerous states, authoritarian leaders found they could woo mass support by promising to act for the "nation."

Democratic Hopes

The western European and American leaders who signed the treaties ending World War I hoped that liberal democracy would soon sweep the world whether in the form of republics (like France and the United States) or constitutional monarchies (like Britain, Sweden, and the Netherlands). The signs looked quite good. Within two years of the war, the number of republics in Europe multiplied from three to thirteen. In the nine new national states that replaced Russian, German, Austrian, or Ottoman territories in eastern and central Europe, elected officials governed under the terms of a constitution in which "the people" held supreme authority. The defunct German empire became the somewhat smaller Weimar Republic, named after the city where its constitution was enacted. The core area of the former Ottoman empire became the Republic of Turkey.

The number of voting citizens in the world also swelled, as states both new and old broadened the franchise to include women, as well as males formerly excluded because of low social status or income. The Great War, which mobilized women to serve their nations in unprecedented ways, roused feminists to step up their demands for full civic rights and responsibilities. Between 1915 and 1920, women gained voting rights in Iceland, Denmark, the Netherlands, England, Germany, Russia, the new eastern European states, all forty-eight of the United States, and six provinces of China. Many more states, including most of the Latin American republics, enfranchised women during the following thirty years. In the postwar decades, many new organizations and publications called for women's full legal, social, and sexual equality. In the United States, for example, Margaret Sanger wrote voluminously in support

Margaret Sanger, champion of birth control. Sanger and her supporters endured heckling when they advocated publicly for women having greater control over their reproductive function. When challenged by a passerby, "Have you never heard God's word to 'be fruitful and multiply and replenish the earth'?", one of Sanger's fellow activists replied, "They've already done that."

of birth control as essential to women's social liberation. In Egypt, Huda Sha'rawi, a dedicated nationalist, founded the Egyptian Feminist Union in 1923. Sha'rawi and her associates gained public attention by arguing that traditional practices such as veiling, arranged marriages, and male control over divorce were distortions of Islamic teaching.

By the mid-1920s, however, the champions of liberal democracy had to reassess their hopes. In none of the major industrialized countries did elected governments succeed in meeting popular expectations for economic growth, employment, and social welfare. Consequently, those states, including Britain, France, Germany, and the United States, faced recurrent strikes, walkouts, and street demonstrations. Urban working classes rightly perceived that despite

regular elections the same bureaucratic and business elites that had dominated national affairs before World War I, and that had disastrously failed to prevent it, largely remained at the top of the political heap. Victorious France, whose Third Republic featured weak executive authority and a National Assembly often immobilized by quarreling political parties, offered a poor model of progressive, efficient postwar democracy.

The Soviet Union: Communist Authoritarianism

In Russia the abdication of Tsar Nicholas II in 1917 led, not to a new liberal era, but to the triumph of Bolshevik revolutionaries under the leadership of V. I. Lenin (see Chapter 24). For two years, the "Whites," a shaky coalition of liberals, monarchists, moderate socialists, and peasants, fought the communist "Reds" and their mostly urban supporters for political dominance. The Bolshevik ascent horrified the capitalist leaders of Britain, France, the United States, and Japan. Hoping to prevent the communists from consolidating power, those states materially aided various White groups and between 1918 and 1920 sent military expeditions to occupy several points of Russian territory in the north, south, and east. Those foreign incursions were halfhearted, however, and served only to rouse Russian nationalist feeling to Lenin's advantage. By late 1920 the unity and discipline of the communist forces won out. Within another two years, the new regime founded the Union of Soviet Socialist Republics, "soviet" referring to communist workers' councils formed during the revolution. Against heavy odds, the Bolshevik regime effectively held together the greater part of the old tsarist empire.

The early communist state. The communist revolutionary leadership aimed to transform society primarily to the benefit of the urban working class, or proletariat, that is, to establish social democracy as opposed to capitalist-friendly liberal democracy. Guided by the writings of Karl Marx (see Chapter 22), leaders of the communist variant of socialism constituted a "vanguard" of professional revolutionaries to bring about worker supremacy. They intended to sweep away bourgeois capitalism, abolish private property, eliminate class divisions, and achieve social justice. In Lenin's view, however, this grand project required the party to take charge of the means of production and distribution—from factories and banks to apartments and retail stores. Under the Soviet constitution, men and women went to the polls to elect representatives to local and regional soviets. Even though the Communist Party selected all candidates in advance, many socialists and social democrats (members of the political "left") in western Europe and the United States admired the Bolshevik design for improving the lot and ensuring the dignity of laboring men and women.

In 1921 Lenin initiated the New Economic Policy (NEP), a plan to fulfill socialist goals by stages. It allowed Russian peasants to sell surplus crops privately at local markets, that is, to behave like rural capitalists, as long as they paid the Soviet government a fixed percentage of harvest yields. Under the NEP, farm production rose rapidly. However, after 1924, when Lenin died, Joseph Stalin, the son of a poor villager from Georgia in the Caucasus Mountains, came gradually to power promoting a different economic agenda. Stalin wished to transform Russia into a first-rank industrial power. In his mind, profit-minded peasants had to be suppressed in order to transfer more wealth from the land to the industrial proletariat. Fast industrialization would not only restore national purpose, he insisted, but also forestall any foreign state from invading Russian territory, as Germany had done in the Great War. Stalin infused communist ideology with Russian nationalism, declaring that "socialism in one country" rather than immediate international worker revolution must be the near-term goal.

Industrialization by decree. Stalin launched his industrializing drive by waging war against his own rural population. In 1928 he renounced the NEP and instituted a Five Year Plan, which involved creating huge, mechanized, state-run collective farms where peasants had to live communally to produce food for the growing industrial labor force. Peasants who resisted relocation to collectives typically found themselves being herded to factories, mines, Siberian concentration camps, or execution grounds. As one party official observed, "A ruthless struggle is going on between the peasantry and our regime. . . . It has cost millions of lives, but the collective farm system is here to stay."[6] By 1933, 83 percent of Soviet farm land was under state control.

Between 1928 and 1939 the country brought off an astonishing industrial expansion, especially in heavy industries, such as coal, oil, iron, electricity, and chemicals. Giant hydroelectric dams spanned rivers, factory cities arose out of nowhere, state-employed engineers and scientists labored feverishly to advance Russia's technological modernization, and factory managers competed to meet grueling production targets. The national literacy rate climbed rapidly, and the government offered advanced education to thousands of young Soviet men and women. Russia's gross domestic product nearly tripled, reaching a level second only to that of the United States.

Many intellectuals in Western countries continued to praise Soviet economic gains, not seeing, or not wishing to see, the terrible social costs of such spectacular growth.

By collectivizing, coercing, and terrorizing the rural population, the communist state procured bigger grain shipments to cities. But in the 1930s the great majority of peasants became profoundly disaffected and overall farm yields declined steadily. A horrendous famine in 1932–1933 took several million lives partly because of government ruthlessness and inefficiency. The Soviet state poured resources into heavy industries like steel and concrete, telling ordinary men and women that they would have to go without the automobiles, phonographs, and numerous imported goods that western Europeans and Americans were

Stalin promotes the Five Year Plan. This 1931 poster proclaims, "The Victory of the Five Year Plan Is a Strike Against Capitalism." Stalin was willing to kill millions of people to achieve the plan's vision of a modern, collective economy. Which social groups is the plan crushing in this poster?

autarky A country that aims to achieve economic independence and self-sufficiency, especially freedom from dependence on external trade or assistance; also autarkic.

coming to take for granted. Stalin aimed to make the Soviet state **autarkic,** free of all dependence on foreign commerce.

Nationalists and Communists in China

To Soviet Bolsheviks in the early 1920s, China, formally a republic since 1912, looked like a field where seeds of proletarian revolution might sprout. China, however, remained in political tumult throughout the interwar decades. Beijing, the formal capital, became the headquarters of a regional warlord who jockeyed for power with other strongmen, crime rings, and bandit gangs. In the far south, the revolutionary leader Sun Zhongshan organized the Nationalist People's Party (Guomindang) and laid plans to restore national unity. He advocated parliamentary government but also championed a social democratic program to improve workers' lives and redistribute land to impoverished peasants. He enjoyed keen support among China's young city dwellers, some of them schooled abroad or by Western missionaries. These youths demanded both material modernization and thorough renovation of the country's antimodern cultural identity. In 1919 *New Youth,* a radical magazine founded at Beijing University, proclaimed: "To promote social progress, we have to destroy prejudices camouflaged as 'law of Heaven and Earth' or 'eternal practice of all times.' We, on our part, have decided not only to discard all these traditional or conventional concepts but also to create new ideas that synthesize old and contemporary philosophies in addition to those of our own. We wish to cultivate a new spirit for our times."[7]

China had entered the war on the Allied side, but the victorious powers nonetheless clung to the territorial and commercial controls they had imposed on China in the previous century. The consequence in 1919 in several Chinese cities was the May Fourth Movement, an outburst of student protests and worker strikes that forced the hapless warlord government in Beijing to refuse to sign the Treaty of Versailles.

Needing support wherever he could find it, Sun Zhongshan accepted organizational aid from both the Soviet government and the Comintern, the international revolutionary arm of the communist movement. Some young Chinese took up the study of Marxism, and by 1925, the year Sun Zhongshan died, the new Chinese Communist Party was strong enough to convince the leaders of his Nationalist People's Party to accept a pragmatic alliance. The following year nationalist and communist military forces launched a combined expedition under the command of Jieshi (Chiang Kai-shek), a son of a wealthy land-owner, to overpower the northern warlords and reunify the country. Jiang proclaimed his support for a republic but fervently opposed any communist role in it. As the military operation proceeded, he abruptly terminated the pact with the Communist Party and ordered

Jiang Jieshi and Madam Jiang in Nanjing, 1930. In 1927, Jiang married Song Meiling, a member of a Chinese Christian business family and a graduate of Wellesley College in Massachusetts. As Madame Jiang, she threw herself into Chinese politics, partnering with her husband to strengthen his grip on power. She died in 2003 in New York at the age of 105.

mass arrests and summary executions of both communists and socialists. Between 1927 and 1930 Jiang hounded communists throughout the country and suppressed or won over most of the remaining warlords. Much preferring Jiang to the communists, the European powers and the United States recognized the nationalist government and gradually gave up their long-standing territorial privileges.

Fundamental economic and social troubles remained. Jiang made no move to limit the operations of industrialists, bankers, and estate owners, whether Chinese or foreign. The lot of the rural poor did not improve much. And despite the republican governing structure, Jiang and his army erected a transparently authoritarian regime. The common population became increasingly dissatisfied. In the southern interior, Mao Zedong (Tse-tung, 1893–1976), a communist leader who had eluded Jiang's roundup, began building a power base of his own (see Chapter 26).

New Governments on the Political Right

Jiang Jieshi's success in China was a victory for the ideological "right." Political groups of the left generally advocated change in society primarily to improve the lot of ordinary men and women, recognizing the injustices embedded in traditional social and economic class divisions. Parties of the right, by contrast, championed the maintenance of political order, respect for traditional authority, and the preservation of established national culture and moral values. On both the left and right sides of the political spectrum, ideals and programs varied from one political group to another. In predominantly rural countries, rightists typically endorsed a stable hierarchy of social classes, the leadership of land-owning magnates and conservative religious authorities, and government policies that kept urban worker activism under careful control. The more extreme right-wing parties almost always scorned liberal democratic institutions as faction ridden, indecisive, and poorly equipped to counteract communist or other left-wing subversion.

Right-wing sympathies in Europe. Rightist political groups gained strength in many European countries in the decade after World War I. Seventeen states that had liberal parliaments as of 1920 either abolished or hobbled those bodies sometime in the following twenty years. Instead, a mix of rightist one-party states, royal despots, and military dictators took power, notably in Italy, Spain, Hungary, Portugal, Poland, Yugoslavia, and Romania.

Right-wing authoritarianism appealed to citizens for a number of reasons. One was postwar fear among governing elites, urban middle classes, and many peasant farmers that communist revolution might spread beyond Russia. Worker uprisings in Germany, Hungary, and Austria amplified these anxieties. Another issue was the failure of liberal governments to address slow industrial recovery and chronic unemployment. A wave of monetary inflation swept central and eastern Europe between 1920 and 1923. Germany's currency fell one trillion times its value in 1913, wiping out people's saving and obliging them to buy loaves of bread with wheelbarrows of cash. This crisis discredited the government of the Weimar Republic and sparked demands for more forceful leadership. Rightist groups also benefited from popular discontent over the war settlements. Italians chafed at the meager territorial rewards they received for joining the winning side, whereas Germans charged that timid politicians had rushed their country into surrender.

Fascism in Italy. Forces of the right achieved an important victory in 1922, when Benito Mussolini, a journalist and leader of the new Fascist Party, became prime minister in Italy, a constitutional monarchy. Parliamentary wrangling among a host of parties, together with rising unemployment and inflation, led first to urban violence between partisans of the left and right, then to fascist ascendancy in the legislature. Mussolini, known later as Il Duce (The Leader), became prime minister by democratic procedures, but he imposed public order from the top. Millions of Italians applauded.

Benito Mussolini marching with a group of Blackshirts in Rome, 1922. A charismatic leader, Mussolini appealed to public sentiment and emotion. Once elected as prime minister, he gutted political opposition, used secret police against his enemies, and outlawed labor strikes, securing his status as dictator by 1926. What elements of this photograph depict Mussolini as a man of the people? What elements suggest his authoritarian view of how Italy should be governed?

Like most right-wing parties, Mussolini's Fascists promoted nationalism, antiliberalism, anticommunism, military strength, and government by decisive action. He also promoted state "corporatism," that is, the organizing of society into industrial and occupational interest groups that together would presumably form an organic, harmonious social whole. In fact, corporatism served mainly to undermine the influence of labor unions and protect industrial capitalists who backed Mussolini's dictatorship.

fascism A political ideology that advocates authoritarian leadership, intense national loyalty, cultural renewal, and rejection of both liberal democracy and socialism.

The term *fascism* derives from the Latin word *fasces*, an ancient Roman emblem symbolizing imperial authority. The key distinction between fascism and other forms of rightist politics was its drive to mobilize mass support. Radiating macho charisma, Mussolini deftly used newspapers, radio, and public rallies to appeal to popular longings for national unity, international respect, and a larger colonial empire. The Fascist regime kept King Victor Emmanuel III on his throne as ceremonial head of state, and the Roman Catholic Pope retained sovereignty over the 110 acres of Vatican City in the heart of Rome. But Mussolini repressed all political opposition and deployed gangs of supporters called Blackshirts to intimidate uncooperative citizens. He instructed

totalitarianism A political ideology and governing policies that mandate strong central control and regulation of both public and private thought and behavior.

Italian women to abandon their quest for equal rights and get busy producing fascist babies. Indeed, he intended the state to be **totalitarian,** organized to penetrate and manage all levels of society down to the nuclear family.

Nationalism and authoritarian power in Turkey. In the five years following World War I, Turkey emerged from the ruins of the Ottoman empire as a new sovereign republic. It had a parliament and popular elections, but as in Italy those liberal institutions masked the entrenchment of a highly centralized authoritarian government.

Mustafa Kemal Atatürk, a Turkish hero of World War I, emerged as the chief architect of the new republic. By the terms of the postwar settlement, the former empire was compressed into a small, semisovereign country in Anatolia, the heartland of ethnic Turkey. The rest of the realm, including the Arabic-speaking Middle East, was transferred by one political arrangement or another to Britain, France, Italy, or Greece. In those humiliating circumstances, Atatürk (meaning "Father of the Turks," as he later became known) joined with other military officers and several resistance groups to raise rebellion against the Ottoman sultan and to defy the war settlement. In the spring of 1920, these insurgents formed a republican government, choosing Atatürk as president. Their forces routed Greek troops from western Anatolia and seized Istanbul (Constantinople), the capital city. At that point, Britain and France thought it pragmatic to renegotiate the postwar treaty. By 1923 the major European powers recognized Turkey's full sovereignty as a republic.

Atatürk abandoned the old Ottoman ideal of a multiethnic state in favor of an exclusive Turkish nationalism. He also labored throughout his fifteen-year rule to transform Turkey into a modern secular (nonreligious) nation-state

Atatürk inspecting troops in Constantinople, 1926. The Turkish president, fedora in hand, is flanked by the prime minister and the minister of war.

Turkish Views on Dress and National Identity

Across Asia and Africa, nationalist reformers sought to explain why Western countries appeared to surge ahead in military and industrial power while their own countries lagged behind. The answer, some argued, lay in European cultural practices and behavior. If people in other countries adopted European habits, the argument went, they would help their nations advance faster.

From this perspective, clothing took on particular importance. Turkish nationalists urged citizens to abandon "native dress" and copy Western styles to help instill in people a modernizing spirit. Similarly, in China, republican leaders denounced the queue, or "pigtail" that men traditionally wore as a symbol of the decadent, antimodern Qing dynasty. A modern China must be a "queue-less" China, they proclaimed, and this hairstyle eventually disappeared.

Atatürk admonished men to throw off the fez, the conical-shaped headgear that Turks had worn before World War I (even though this headgear had come into fashion in the nineteenth century as a modern replacement for the traditional turban). Many Turks took off their fezzes voluntarily, but Atatürk was not content with gradual change. In 1925 he imposed a Hat Law ordering men to put on Western fedoras or other headgear. He viewed the fez as a visual emblem of Muslim identity not compatible with modern secular society. Those who ignored the Hat Law could be imprisoned. Atatürk campaigned energetically for the new policy. The first selection below is taken from a speech Atatürk gave in 1925, a few months after the Hat Law was passed. The second selection is from an article written in 1929 by Turkish novelist, feminist, and nationalist Halidé Edib. Writing while in exile from Turkey, she explained why she considered the law misguided.

DOCUMENT 1 Atatürk, August 1925

Gentlemen, the Turkish people who founded the Turkish republic are civilized; they are civilized in history and in reality. But I tell you . . . that the people of the Turkish Republic, who claim to be civilized, must show and prove that they are civilized, by their ideas and their mentality, by their family life and their way of living. In a word, the truly civilized people of Turkey . . . must prove in fact that they are civilized and advanced persons also in their outward aspect. I must make these last words clear to you, so that the whole country and the world may easily understand what I mean. I shall put my explanations to you in the form of a question.

Is our dress national? (Cries of no!)
Is it civilized and international? (Cries of no, no!)
I agree with you. This grotesque mixture of styles is neither national nor international. . . .

My friends, there is no need to seek and revive the costume of Turan [Central Asia]. A civilized, international dress is worthy and appropriate for our nation, and we will wear it. Boots or shoes on our feet, trousers on our legs, shirt and tie, jacket and waistcoat—and, of course, to complete these, a cover with a brim on our heads. I want to make this clear. This head-covering is called a "hat."

DOCUMENT 2 Halidé Edib, 1929

The first and most spectacular of these [reforms] was the so-called "hat law," passed in 1925. It was also the most futile and superficial in comparison with the others which followed. But it was the *only one* which accomplished a change overnight even in outside appearances. In a week it made the Turks don European hats (the only part of the city-dweller's outfit which was still un-Westernized) and made them look like Westerners, although the manner in which it was accomplished was utterly un-Western. The Westernization of Turkey is not and should not be a question of mere external imitation and gesture. It is a much deeper and more significant process. To tell the Turk to put on a certain headdress and "get civilized" or be hanged, or imprisoned, is absurd, to say the least. . . . Among all the recent measures, this was the most seriously opposed in the country itself. Any opposition to the hat law was labeled as reactionary. The interesting fact connected with the substitution of the hat for the Turkish fez

is that of all the changes of the last four years it attracted the greatest attention in the Western world. The many fundamental changes taking place in Turkey have been either unnoticed or criticized, or treated as unimportant items of foreign news in Western papers. But the moment the Turks put hats on their heads, the general cry in the West was, "at last the Turks are civilized; they wear hats." Hence those who enacted the hat law might say: "We have killed a few, and imprisoned a large number, but it was good psychology: has anything in the past brought Turkey so into the limelight? Has anything brought the Turk nearer to the European in the European mind?" . . .

In Turkey, the first substantial result of the law was that it enriched European hat factories at the expense of the already impoverished Turks.

Sources: Atatürk quoted in Bernard Lewis, *The Emergence of Modern Turkey*, 2nd ed. (New York: Oxford University Press, 1968), 268–269; Halidé Edib, "Dictatorship and Reforms in Turkey," *Yale Review*, 19 (Sept. 1929): 30–32.

Thinking Critically

What kind of clothing did Atatürk regard as "civilized"? Why do you think he believed Turks should adopt this style of dress? How did Edib's views on the Hat Law differ from those of Atatürk? What do you think she meant by noting that the law was implemented in an "utterly un-Western" way? Why did she think some Turks opposed the law? Think of some countries besides Turkey and China where particular dress has served as a symbol of national identity or patriotic commitment.

modeled on those of western Europe. Turkish men (and, after 1934, women) elected a legislative assembly, which periodically chose the national president. In 1926 he replaced Islamic law (*shari'a*), with a civil code based on the Swiss and other European systems. On another cultural front, he ordered scholars to create a Latin alphabet for writing Turkish to replace the traditional Arabic-derived script. He made primary education compulsory, and thereafter the populaton's literacy rate soared. Convinced that symbols of change must accompany substance, he instructed Turkish men to wear European-style clothing and encouraged women to discard their traditional Muslim veils.

Like Mussolini, Atatürk used modern media to rouse nationalist feeling, and he built an authoritarian apparatus capable of suppressing any serious challenge to his grand projects. Contrary to liberal democratic principles, he banned all political parties except for the Republican People's Party, which he headed. Minority populations, especially Armenians and Kurds, lost all rights to distinctive cultural recognition. The government centralized economic policy, collaborating with private business to develop industry and agriculture, though the results remained modest. By transforming Turkey into an internationally respected nation-state, Atatürk, as authoritarian as he was, inspired young nationalists in Asia and Africa to oppose European colonial rule.

Japan's shift to the right. After 1918, Japan gradually transformed itself from a liberal constitutional monarchy with very limited popular participation into an authoritarian regime commanded by a nationalist elite of right-wing civilians and military officers. Like the United States, Japan emerged from World War I economically stronger than it had been in 1914. It tripled its export trade during and after the war, which helped finance more industrialization at home and capital investments abroad. Japan's population grew from fifty-one to seventy million between 1914 and 1940, and Tokyo rivaled London and New York as a premier world city where young urbanites crowded into movie theaters and jazz clubs. At the Washington Conference of 1921–1922, Japan agreed with the other major powers to limit naval tonnage and to renounce aggressive action against China. The Pacific rim appeared to be entering a new era of international cooperation.

Despite spectacular industrial statistics, however, Japan did not enjoy social calm in the 1920s. Business conditions fluctuated, the agricultural economy remained depressed, and urban unemployment stayed high. Amid dizzying economic change (and a devastating earthquake in Tokyo in 1923), political parties multiplied along a scale from communist revolutionaries on the left to fascist-sympathizing ultranationalists on the right. Strikes, rallies, and student demonstrations punctuated city life. Parties of both left and right attacked the national parliament (Diet) as corrupt, apathetic, and beholden to affluent property owners and professional politicians. The Diet enacted some liberal reforms, such as universal male suffrage, but its harshest critics regarded all parliamentary institutions as bankrupt. In 1928 the government carried out mass arrests of communists, unionists, and other activists, an action that took the wind out of left-wing groups but energized the political right.

In the nationalist view, Japan also faced a crisis of economic survival among major powers. Throughout the 1920s the country became increasingly dependent on food, mineral, and timber imports because domestic production could not keep up with population growth and urban demand. Japan had nearly 130,000 automobiles by 1937, but domestic wells could not come close to filling gas tanks. Japan exploited its East Asian colonial possessions, Korea, Taiwan, and part of Manchuria (northeastern China), for rice and other commodities. Amid the early symptoms of the global depression in 1930, conspiracies, political assassinations, and an attempted army takeover left the legislature immobilized and popular sympathy shifting right.

Left and Right in Latin America

Like Japan and industrialized Europe, Latin America experienced renewed economic growth after World War I. But the trend was erratic, social tensions mounted, and political groups of all persuasions struggled for power in many of the seventeen republics stretching from Mexico to Argentina. At the start of the century, a wealthy top stratum of families owning large businesses, farms, and ranches dominated political and economic affairs nearly everywhere. However, an urban bourgeoisie of bureaucrats, lawyers, managers, teachers, merchants, and intellectuals gained steadily in numbers and, during economic upswings, personal income. This rising middle class resented the lock on power that the old land-owning elite continued to possess in most countries. Latin America's population growth rate was probably the highest in the world in the interwar decades. Hopes of employment attracted Indians and *mestizos* from countryside to city. Many of them were illiterate and poorly skilled for anything but farming, and they crowded into apartment buildings and new shantytowns. By 1930 Buenos Aires, Argentina's capital, ranked among the top ten largest cities in the world, with 2.2 million people.

In the 1920s almost all Latin American states had import-export economies, as they had had in the nineteenth century. They supplied foodstuffs, fiber, and minerals to the industrial centers of Europe and North America, earning currency that paid for imported manufactures. World prices for commodities such as copper, petroleum, sugar, coffee, and bananas fluctuated throughout the decade, but the system worked well enough from the perspective of foreign companies and the local elites, politicians, and trading firms allied with them. Capitalists in the United States, a country awash in surplus capital after World War I, gradually supplanted British banks and firms (except in Argentina) as the principal suppliers of loans and direct investments.

Urbanization in Buenos Aires. This scene on the Calle Congalio, a retail shopping street, shows some of the consequences of urban growth in Latin America. How might this photo be interpreted as presenting either a positive or a negative view of twentieth-century urban life?

Burgeoning cities progressively altered social and economic landscapes. Elite power groups could no longer easily ignore either the growing middle class or the crowds of new urbanites fresh from rural villages. Urban leaders could see that an export economy, one in which American and European trading companies exercised great political influence, would produce much less growth and fewer new jobs than an economy based on home industries. As Victor Raúl Haya de la Torre, the leader of the populist Aprista Party in Peru argued, "It is this middle group that is being pushed to ruination. . . . The great foreign firms extract our wealth and then sell it outside our country. Consequently, there is no opportunity for the middle class."[8] In cities like Buenos Aires, Santiago, Lima, and São Paulo, middle-class activists pressured wealth-dominated legislatures to broaden the democratic base. Labor unions attracted the unskilled and

underemployed. Urban feminist organizations pressed for women's voting rights, which no Latin American country offered before 1929.

In these troubled conditions, new leaders rose to power (and often fell again) in several states in the interwar period. Political parties exploited every nationalist phrase and symbol they could think of to mobilize mass support. As in Europe, voting publics warmed to the idea of stronger presidencies, having lost faith in corrupt, squabbling parliaments. In some states, notably Argentina, Uruguay, Chile, and Costa Rica, the urban middle class replaced the old land-owning families as the government's most important constituency. In Mexico, the only Latin American country to experience sweeping social revolution in the early twentieth century (see Chapter 24), political stability returned gradually after 1917. Under the constitution of that year, the presidency commanded much more power than the legislature, and after 1929 the National Revolutionary Party extinguished all significant opposition. In spite of one-party rule, the revolution left the great land-owning families politically weakened, the Roman Catholic Church expelled from politics, and both urban workers and country peasants with stronger voices in political affairs

Colonial Rule and Its Opponents in Africa and Asia

> **FOCUS** What political, economic, and social conditions in colonial empires contributed to the rise of nationalist resistance movements?

In 1920 close to six hundred million people lived under the rule of one or another of nine colonial states. The vast majority of dependent peoples inhabited Africa or Asia, though there were also relatively small colonial territories in the Pacific basin, the Caribbean, and South America.

Under the terms of the settlements ending World War I, the victorious Allies deprived Germany of all its foreign possessions. Those lands, however, did not gain freedom. Germany's four colonies in Africa went to Britain, France, or the Union of South Africa as League of Nations Mandates. The League authorized, or mandated, those powers to administer the former German territories until some unspecified time when they might be ready to govern themselves. To the dismay of Middle Eastern nationalists, the peace settlements also converted the former Ottoman empire's predominantly Arabic-speaking provinces into mandates run by France or Britain.

Britain gave up only one important imperial possession following the war, the southern counties of Ireland. After eight hundred years of English rule, the Irish Free State was born in 1923. Independence, however, came after more than two years of bitter fighting between British security forces and the nationalist Irish Republican Army, which wanted sovereignty for all of Ireland. More than three-quarters of the island was overwhelmingly Roman Catholic and pronationalist, but several northern counties, the region called Ulster, had Protestant majorities and were determined to remain within the United Kingdom. By the terms of the peace settlement, Ireland was partitioned.

Economy and Society in the Colonial Empires

In the interwar years the world's colonized peoples were overwhelmingly rural, earning their livings as farmers, herders, artisans, laborers, and traders. Nevertheless, these lands became increasingly entangled with the international economy. In Africa and Asia, colonial dependency mainly strengthened the kind of system that existed in Latin America: export of raw commodities and import of most finished goods.

All the colonial powers proclaimed the general principle that their rule should benefit both the subject population and the citizens of the **metropole**. Dependent peoples should labor for their own well-being but

metropole The colonizer's home country and seat of supreme imperial authority.

also advance the economic interests of the metropole's business firms, banks, and consumers. Lord Frederick Lugard, a British general who served as governor of the West African colony of Nigeria, contended that a "dual mandate" should motivate colonial economic activity. He described this philosophy in the culturally arrogant terms typical of the European imperial class: "Let it be admitted at the outset that European brains, capital, and energy have not been, and never will be expended in developing the resources of Africa from motives of pure philanthropy; that Europe is in Africa for the mutual benefit of her own industrial classes, and of the native races in their progress to a higher plane."[9]

In the decade after World War I, efforts to implement dual mandates produced substantial economic growth in some parts of colonial Africa and Asia, especially when food, fiber, and the products of mines—tin from Malaysia, oil from Iraq, copper from the Belgian Congo—commanded high international prices. But most colonial regimes discouraged local manufacturing because the products would likely compete with goods that capitalist firms wished to import. The colonizers built roads and railways, but with the partial exception of India, these transport lines served, not to internally integrate dependent economies, but to move commodities from interior regions to seaports for export, and foreign goods in the opposite direction (see Map 25.2).

Despite little industrial development in most colonies, import–export business kindled rapid economic and social change. People earned more income from wages, used money more widely, and migrated farther in search of jobs. Where foreign firms invested in plantations, mines, or railroads, they usually employed large numbers of laborers. In the early colonial decades, subsistence farmers often resisted wage labor. Consequently, imperial officers and private entrepreneurs sometimes coerced people into labor gangs or forced villages to meet quotas for saleable crops. They also pushed rural people into wage work by requiring them to pay taxes in money, not farm produce.

In several colonies, farmers who managed to stay on the land did well selling "cash crops" during the war and the early 1920s, when commodity prices were favorable. Coffee growers in Indonesia, rice farmers in Burma and Vietnam, cotton producers in Uganda, and peanut cultivators in Senegal saw their living standards rise in some years. In the British Gold Coast colony (later Ghana) in West Africa, farmers began planting cocoa trees in the 1890s. By 1917 they were exporting 118,000 tons of beans every year. For Ghanaians in the cocoa-producing regions, higher incomes meant better housing, more schools, and declining infant mortality.

During the interwar period, more people moved within and between colonies. Wage seekers tended to migrate from regions of limited economic opportunity to areas where colonial capitalists needed more workers than the local population could supply. Rubber plantations and coal mines in the southern part of French-ruled Vietnam attracted laborers from the poor but densely populated north. In Indonesia the Dutch government encouraged people, including large numbers of young women, to move from crowded Java to the less populated island of Sumatra, where they worked on tobacco plantations. Copper mines in the southern Belgian Congo and northern Rhodesia (Zambia) pulled in labor from all over central and southern Africa. A worker who traveled five hundred miles from the central Congo to the Ruashi Mine near the flourishing colonial city of Elizabethville (Lubumbashi), recorded his impressions of the harsh life in a migrant camp in the 1920s: "Yes, we lost many of our people at Ruashi, some died from work accidents, others, the majority, from diarrhea. The man who had diarrhea one day died in two or three days. All of us wanted only one thing: to terminate our contract and return to our country."[10]

In colonized lands, more men than women earned wages, though the picture was complex. When families grew cash crops, husbands typically controlled the earnings but still counted on wives to contribute labor in addition to caring for home, children, and household plots. In regions where polygyny was common, men sometimes acquired additional wives, if they could afford it, specifically to increase their cash crop output. During Ghana's cocoa boom, for example, male farmers did this so brazenly that young women launched a successful protest movement, refusing to work for their husbands, starting cocoa farms of their own, or declining to marry at all.

As in Latin America, rural men and women flocked to African and Asian towns to look for jobs as construction workers, artisans, domestic servants, clerks, or police. Rural women hoping to help the family or advance themselves found city employment as servants, food sellers, hoteliers, or sex workers. Burgeoning cities became arenas of social experimentation as newcomers sought security and new

MAP 25.2 European and African rail networks after World War I.
What geographical, political, or economic factors help explain the locations of railway construction in Africa in the 1920s and 1930s? How would you explain the differences between European and African rail networks in terms of their extent and density?

identity. Urban associations ranged from ethnic societies, sports clubs, dance groups, and military bands to labor unions and new religious denominations. In the first half of the twentieth century, both Roman Catholic and Protestant churches made large gains in tropical Africa and among Vietnamese- and Chinese-speaking populations in Southeast Asia. Islam also continued to grow in Subsaharan Africa, often because of the proselytizing energy of Sufi associations, which served both the social welfare and spiritual needs of converts. Dozens of towns in Africa and Asia more than doubled in population in the first half of the twentieth century. Casablanca on the Atlantic coast of French-ruled Morocco, for example, grew from 20,000 people in 1897 to 257,000 by 1936. Some towns flourished next to mining or commercial farming zones, others as ports or colonial administrative centers. In some places towns that had not existed before the nineteenth century appeared suddenly. These included Nairobi, the capital of colonial Kenya, and Kuala Lumpur, which sprang up in Malaysia near tin mines.

Ways of Ruling

Colonial powers whose home governments were democratic had to justify their autocratic rule of other peoples on racial and cultural grounds. The "modern and civilized" metropole, they argued, must shepherd "backward and primitive" colonial subjects to a better future. Dependent peoples might advance toward self-government but only at a measured pace, usually estimated in decades if not centuries.

Theories of rule. All the colonial powers aimed to ensure law and order in their dependencies, but beyond that the ideas and practices of imperial rule varied widely. France, Portugal, Belgium, and Japan favored the theory of direct rule, which specified that a single chain of bureaucratic command should extend from the metropole down to the local district in the colony. Direct rule should involve removal of established monarchs or chiefs because they could not be trusted with modern administration and would obstruct the colonial work of introducing civilization to backward subjects. French colonial ideology centered on the metropole's "civilizing mission" to teach dependent peoples the French language, through which they might advance step by step toward rational learning, material progress, and eventual assimilation with the French nation.

Britain, the Netherlands, and the United States (in the Philippines) leaned toward theories of **indirect rule,** allowing existing African or Asian political authorities to govern on local or regional levels as long as they pledged loyalty to the imperial state. In contrast to their French counterparts, British rulers saw no obligation to assimilate subject peoples to British culture. Africans and Asians, they declared, suffered from cultural and indeed racial disabilities that prevented them from such conversion.

indirect rule Theory and practice of colonial government favoring the appointment of local leaders as political intermediaries between the colonizer and the indigenous population.

Colonial realities. Despite these divergent ideas about colonial governance, relations between imperial masters and their subjects were much more complicated on the ground. Day-to-day administration depended mainly on local conditions, not on policies hatched in London or Paris. The French government, despite its ideal of culturally bonding colonial populations to the metropole, offered French-language education to very few. Every colonial territory produced a small class of *évolués*, or "evolved persons," who spoke and wrote in French and in a few places acquired the rights of citizens. But otherwise, colonial governors ruled by an authoritarian law code that excluded most men and women from many rights that French citizens took for granted.

For its part, Britain applied indirect rule partially and erratically. In India, the regime extended self-government to a group of traditional Indian princes and, after World War I, permitted limited decision-making power to provincial legislatures. But the Indian Civil Service, whose high officials were British, directly ruled about two-thirds of India's population. Indirect rule worked quite efficiently in a region like northern Nigeria, where the Sokoto caliphate, an important Muslim empire before British conquest in the early 1900s (see Chapter 22), had a well-organized civil service perfectly capable of managing local affairs. Nigerian princes retained much of their authoritarian power over millions of people, and the British administration saved money. By contrast, in places such as Tanganyika (Tanzania) in East Africa, colonial officials dealt with thousands of self-governing villages, kinship groups, and small chieftaincies rather than with functioning states. There, indirect rule operated mainly at the local level. In fact, all colonial governments employed thousands of local men and women as village heads, soldiers, clerks, secretaries, and maintenance workers. None of the empires could have functioned without them.

Foreign Immigrants in Colonized Lands

Some colonial dependencies took in migrants from other parts of the world in sufficient numbers to significantly alter the territory's political and social character. Every colonial regime needed skilled or educated people from the metropole or other countries to serve as administrators, engineers, business agents, and military officers. Most of those expatriates, however, stayed only long enough to do business or complete a tour of duty before returning home. As of 1920, for example, British-born men and women resident in India numbered less than 0.3 percent of the total population.

Settlers from overseas. In a few parts of Africa, however, European settlers had a large impact on colonial society and government. As in the neo-European societies that developed in earlier modern centuries in North America, the southern cone of South America, Siberia, and Australia, settlers migrated to African territories, not to work or serve temporarily, but to found permanent communities where they expected to live a fundamentally European way of life and enjoy a higher standard of living than they had had at home. They went almost exclusively to colonies, or regions within colonies, where the climate was reasonably temperate and the tropical disease environment not excessively threatening. They also acquired land in those places, routinely displacing African farmers by legal or extralegal means and with colonial government support.

In the early twentieth century, British citizens migrated to Southern Rhodesia (Zimbabwe) and the temperate highlands of Kenya. At the other end of Africa, France's conquest of Algeria, which started in 1830, opened that

Muslim princes from northern Nigeria. In that region the British asserted colonial rule indirectly through local leaders like these men: the Emir of Gwanda, the Sultan of Sokoto, and the Emir of Kano. This photograph was taken in 1934, when the three men visited London. How might such a journey have strengthened their authority in Nigeria?

Mediterranean country to land-hungry French, Spanish, Portuguese, Greek, and Maltese settlers (see Chapter 22). France dismissed any idea of Algerian self-determination by annexing the territory to the French state, as if it were a province like Normandy or Brittany. Most of the country's Arabic- and Berber-speaking Muslim majority was reduced to the status of a landless, dependent wage-earning class as large European agribusinesses appropriated peasant farm land. This majority population had scant access to education or skilled jobs. European migration to South Africa was distinctive because Europeans had been settling there since the mid-seventeenth century (see Chapter 19) and because that country was a self-governing state rather than a British colony after 1910. Predominantly English-speaking settlers moved there in growing numbers in the late nineteenth century, following the discovery of diamonds and gold. By 1920 the European population numbered nearly 15 percent. The Union of South Africa had a parliamentary form of government that progressively restricted participation to the white minority, which spoke either English or Afrikaans (the language of descendants of Dutch settlers). In 1913 the all-white parliament passed the Native Land Act, which prohibited Africans from owning more than 7 percent of the country's land (later changed to 14 percent). This repressive legislation benefited white farmers and effectively pushed more Africans off the land and into white-owned gold mines and other growing industries.

In every African colony that had significant numbers of European settlers, they remained a small minority of the total population (about 11 percent in Algeria but less than 1 percent in Kenya). Nevertheless, settlers expected the European colonial government to protect them and to grant them economic opportunities and social privileges that the great majority did not enjoy, as well as access to cheap local labor for their farms and households. Settlers also exercised political influence in the colony out of all proportion to their numbers, and, having adopted the colony as their homeland, most of them became fierce opponents of any reform that might lead toward majority rule.

Overseas settlement in the interwar period was not limited to Europeans. In the 1920s millions of Chinese and South Asian men and women moved to French, Dutch, and British colonies.[11] More than 150,000 South Asians went to South Africa between 1860 and 1911, mostly to work on sugar plantations. In the late nineteenth century, Indian soldiers played a major part in Britain's seizure of East African territories, and tens of thousands of civilians arrived to build a rail line from Mombasa on the coast of Kenya to Uganda in the deep interior. South Asians came to form a socially subordinate middle group in East Africa between the African majority and the small British administrative and settler class.

Jewish settlers in Palestine. Jewish migration from Europe to Palestine, a British-ruled mandate territory in the interwar period, seriously altered the political dynamics of the predominantly Arabic-speaking Middle East. From about 1880 to World War I, millions of Jews who suffered anti-Semitic persecutions in Russia and eastern Europe migrated to the United States and other distant lands. Long-established Jewish minorities already inhabited Middle Eastern cities under Ottoman rule, but small numbers of new migrants founded farm communities in Palestine, a region within the Ottoman province of Syria before the war.

Those settlements were creations of the Zionist movement, which Theodore Herzl and other European Jews initiated in the 1880s to advance Jewish political nationalism and the idea of a modern Jewish state in Palestine, whose inhabitants were largely Arabic-speaking Muslims or Christians. During World War I the Zionist movement in London nurtured contacts with sympathetic members of the British government. In late 1917 Arthur Balfour, the British foreign secretary, announced that the government looked with favor on "the establishment in Palestine of a National Home for the Jewish people, and will use their best endeavors to facilitate the achievement of this object, it being clearly understood that nothing shall be done which may prejudice the civil and religious rights of existing non-Jewish communities in Palestine."[12] When the League of Nations assigned Palestine to Britain as a postwar mandate, it also endorsed the Balfour Declaration. Zionists, arguing that Jews had a historic right to live in Palestine, worked to legitimize a national homeland there by promoting more settlement. Indeed, between 1922 and 1936, the Jewish population rose from about 93,000 to more than 382,000.

During the interwar years Arab farmers and immigrant Jews came into increasing conflict over control of Palestine's land and water. Jewish settlers, often aided by Zionist capital investment, purchased land from Arab owners, especially from wealthy notables willing to sell at advantageous prices. The British administration also urged Arab cultivators off the land by imposing steep taxes to be paid in cash. Those practices resulted in a growing class of landless Arab peasants. They partly blamed Arab landlords and the British regime for their troubles, but they also directed their anger at the growing Jewish minority.

Inept British policy made matters worse. The administration tried to walk a narrow line between Jewish and Arab interests, but the British high commissioners who governed Palestine did almost nothing to develop machinery for eventual self-government—no constitution, legislature, or elections above the local level. This meant that Jewish and Arab groups formed completely separate civic and labor organizations, which seldom communicated with each other. In 1929 and again in 1936, tensions between Arabs and Jews exploded in violence, and a large-scale Arab peasant revolt preoccupied British forces from 1937 to 1939. Both Zionists and Arab nationalists wanted the British to leave Palestine, but to completely contradictory ends: Zionists wished to clear the way for a sovereign Jewish state, the Arabs to achieve independence under majority rule. World War II provided only a momentary lull in this conflict.

Colonial Rule Contested

The imperial states liked to represent the interwar decades as a kind of colonial "golden age" when peace, order, and progress reigned in their dependencies. But it would be hard to find a single moment between the late nineteenth century and the end of World War II when there were not, in one colony or another, people who resisted, disputed, or rebelled against their subjugated condition.

Persistent rebellion. After the Great War's victorious powers made clear they had no intention of extending self-determination to their African or Asian subjects, they faced both sudden rebellions and the formation of new nationalist political organizations committed to colonial reforms and ultimately to independence. In 1920, for example, rural farmers in Iraq rose up against the newly proclaimed British mandate there. In quashing the revolt, British forces killed about ten thousand Iraqis. In Syria and Lebanon, diverse religious communities joined together in 1925 to revolt against the French mandate government. The insurgency continued for two years. In the mountains of northern Morocco, Muhammad ibn Abd al-Karim (Abdelkrim), a modernizing Muslim reformer, led a rebellion against the Spanish colonial protectorate. The rising persisted from 1921 to 1926, costing the Spanish army tens of thousands of casualties at the hands of greatly outnumbered Berber fighters. The insurrection ended only when Spain got help from French troops.

City-based nationalist movements. Leaders of postwar nationalist movements, which ranged from cultural clubs to political parties, came chiefly from urban middle-class groups that had at least modest education and financial means. Colonial regimes offered more than primary education to relatively few, and they expected their well-schooled dependents to loyally serve the colonial order. In

Muhammad ibn Abd al-Karim. The Berber leader left his career in the Spanish colonial government in Morocco to organize local resistance. He established the Republic of the Rif, serving as its president from 1921 to 1926, when Spanish and French forces crushed it. Why do you think Abd al-Karim is dressed differently from the people gathered around him?

fact, educated men and women experienced more acutely than any other colonized group the contradictions of imperial rule. They typically spoke the colonizer's language, possessed special skills, and held jobs carrying serious responsibilities. Nevertheless, their rulers routinely excluded them from the upper ranks of administration and business, denied them legal equality, segregated them socially, and sometimes mocked them for aspiring to a level of "civilization" that their inferior ethnoracial identity presumably made impossible.

In Egypt, for example, a group of nationalists led by Sa'd Zaghlul, an intellectual and lawyer from Cairo, asked the British imperial administration for permission to represent Egypt at the Paris Peace Conference. When the rulers responded by deporting Zaghlul and other nationalists, Egyptians of all classes poured into the streets to demand full independence. British forces took several months to crush the rising at the cost of about eight hundred Egyptian lives. The Egyptian Revolution of 1919, Zaghlul wrote, "turned the tables against the colonizing power and alerted the entire world to the fact that there is an oppressed nation calling out for justice."[13] In 1922 Britain agreed to restore Egypt's sovereignty, but the plan was so hedged with restrictions that opposition grew more insistent.

Many interwar nationalists envisioned freedom in the shape of liberal democracy, deftly using its ideals against European masters, who claimed to have invented it. But others admired the Soviet model of worker revolution and rapid material progress. The early career of Ho Chi Minh (1890–1969) illustrates the communist appeal. The son of a poor Vietnamese scholar and a kitchen assistant working in France, Ho (who used a different name at the time) tried to present a petition to U.S. president Woodrow Wilson in Paris to plead for self-rule for Vietnam, then a harshly ruled French colony. Ho got nowhere, and the following year he forsook Wilsonian liberalism for Marxism. In 1930 he helped found the Indochinese Communist Party to work against the French regime.

India and Gandhi. In South Asia, small groups of urban intellectuals had been petitioning their British masters for liberal reforms since the mid-nineteenth century. Those leaders took advantage of India's growing sense of national identity, which formed in connection with rapid urbanization and the colony's relatively sophisticated communication network. The Indian National Congress (INC), founded in 1885 by lawyers and other English-educated men, pressed continually for more political participation and better jobs. During World War I, when Britain needed to ensure India's

loyalty, the government announced its intention to guide the territory toward "realization of responsible government . . . as an integral part of the British empire."[14] In 1919 the Raj, as the British colonial regime was called, approved limited changes, including transfer of certain decision-making powers to Indian provincial legislatures. But almost simultaneously it undercut those initiatives by harshly repressing nationalist activity. In April 1919, in the northern city of Amritsar, a British general ordered troops to fire on peaceful demonstrators. The notorious Amritsar Massacre, which left about 370 men and women dead, radicalized many nationalists.

That same year Mohandas K. Gandhi (1869–1948), a member of an affluent Hindu family from the western region of Gujarat, rose to prominence in the INC. He had earned a law degree in London and subsequently spent twenty years in South Africa, where he advocated for the Indian community. While he was there, he formulated a strategy of resistance to British rule founded on nonviolence, self-sacrifice, and the principle of *satyagraha*, the moral precept that conflicts

Gandhi leading the Salt *Satyagraha*, 1930. Gandhi walked for twenty-four days from his home to the seaside, joined along the 240-mile route by thousands of Indians. The marchers protested the British colonial government's monopoly on salt production. By collecting salt without paying tax, Gandhi intentionally broke what he regarded as an unjust law. This movement provoked other acts of nonviolent civil disobedience, resulting in more than 80,000 arrests.

should be resolved through shared understanding of universal truths. In a pamphlet written in 1908, he explained what he meant by "passive resistance," though he later preferred the term *non-cooperation*: "[It] is a method of securing rights by personal suffering; it is the reverse of resistance by arms. . . . For instance, the Government of the day has passed a law which is applicable to me. I do not like it. If, by using violence, I force the government to repeal the law. I am employing what may be termed body-force. If I do not obey the law and accept the penalty for its breach, I use soul-force. It involves sacrifice of self."[15]

Between 1920 and the outbreak of World War II, Gandhi became the Indian nationalist movement's most influential leader. Removing the European-style suit and tie he had worn as a lawyer, he donned a loincloth of coarse white cotton, urging Indians to spin and weave their own cloth, a symbolic affirmation of *swadeshi*, or Indian economic self-sufficiency. To be sure, Gandhi had numerous Indian opponents and enemies, for example, nationalists who preferred armed resistance and the traditional princes whose local authority would disappear if South Asia achieved independence as a unified national state. For extended periods, especially 1920–1922 and 1930–1934, Gandhi and his supporters led boycotts, fasts, marches, and other acts of civil disobedience in protest against British rule, calmly submitting to police violence and jail sentences. In other years, the nationalist movement waned as the British made additional moderate concessions and some nationalists turned back to collaboration with the regime.

Gandhi strove to bring Hindus and Muslims, India's two giant religious groups, together in common alliance against Britain. But he also consistently argued that India should remain a society of distinct religious communities under one national umbrella. After 1922, Hindu and Muslim nationalists, the first concentrated in the INC, the second in the Muslim League, competed for political influence in particular provinces rather than working consistently together for independence. In 1935 the INC demonstrated its dominance by winning nearly half the seats in provincial legislatures. However, in the midst of global depression and looming threats to peace in Europe, Britain remained unwilling to schedule a definitive transfer of power.

The Great Depression and Its Consequences

FOCUS Why did the Great Depression occur, and what were its major social and political consequences?

The ups and downs that characterized the world economy in the 1920s did not deeply distress most economists and business leaders. In the modern world, they had learned, economic ups and downs were in the nature of things. In October 1929, however, the New York Stock Exchange crashed, and by 1933, production, consumption, trade, and employment worldwide plunged to such depths that some feared the worst. Was the modern economy disintegrating and humankind returning to the preindustrial age? The answer turned out to be no. But the Great Depression, which dragged on nearly to the end of the decade, had an enormous impact on social and political life from the industrial heartlands to the most rural colonial dependencies.

The Steep Descent

Since the 1930s economic historians have been arguing over the balance of factors that led to the Great Depression. Most scholars agree that the slump had multiple causes. They also agree that global interconnectivity had by that time become so fluid and complex that a serious recession in any industrialized region was bound to affect the rest of the world in one way or another.

An unbalanced boom. The resurgence of manufacturing and trade that took place in the mid-1920s radiated mainly from the United States. Emerging from World War I without material damage at home and with its European allies owing it more than $7 billion, the United States had abundant investment capital and a population of eager middle-class consumers. This was America's Roaring Twenties. The U.S. Congress, not persuaded that involvement in the world war had been necessary, remained in a mood of **isolationism.** Private bankers, on the other hand, pumped billions in loans into Europe and Japan, recharging industry and commerce in those places. U.S. banks, under the 1924 program called the Dawes Plan, loaned the Weimar Republic hundreds of millions of dollars both to help stabilize the German economy after three years of raging inflation and to allow the regime to meet scheduled war reparation demands from France and Britain. Those two states, in turn, used reparation payments partly to reduce their war debts to the United States. This financial turnstile could work, however, only if American banks continued to grease it.

isolationism The national policy or political doctrine of avoiding complex political or economic relations with foreign countries.

Speculation and debt in lethal combination. In 1928 the American money that financed postwar recovery in western Europe, as well as business projects all over the world, started drying up. This happened chiefly because continuing prosperity in the United States (except for farmers, who faced declining food and fiber prices) fueled a hot stock market. Millions of middle-class Americans withdrew their savings or borrowed money to join the action, and big investors started calling in loans from Europe and elsewhere in order to shift their money to Wall Street. Market speculation rose to a frenzy. When the U.S. government tried to calm it by raising interest rates, foreign capitalists and governments lost access to cheap American loans and had to pay more to service existing ones. At the same time,

Congress, still sour on economic internationalism, raised tariffs on imported manufactures, a policy that impeded industrialized Europe from earning dollars to pay down debt.

In the fall of 1929, Wall Street stocks became so overvalued that investors began selling them off. On October 24, the day called Black Thursday, the market bubble exploded. During the following two years, stock prices, banks, and industry sank together. Investors of all economic classes could no longer pay on bank loans they had taken to buy into the market. Worrying that banks might go under, depositors withdrew savings *en masse*, which produced the very results feared. In that era, no mechanisms existed for quickly moving dollars from one bank to another, there was no federal deposit insurance, and Washington politicians had no inclination to rescue private lending institutions. Thousands of banks closed their doors, deposits vanished, foreclosures multiplied, and millions of Americans suddenly had no money to spend. Because investment capital evaporated, industrial production in the United States dropped by about a third between 1929 and 1931 and employers laid off workers in record numbers. The number of automobiles produced in the United States decreased by half. One of the few industries that continued to prosper was movies. Tickets were cheap, and the unemployed had something to do in the long afternoons.

On the eve of the market crash, the United States produced more than 40 percent of world economic output. When its economy began to tumble, the crisis quickly reverberated around the world. In 1931 the banking crisis spread across Europe. That year Germany's entire financial system virtually fell apart. As factories shut down on both sides of the Atlantic, unemployment soared. By 1932, 44 percent of German workers were jobless. Similar crises struck countries like Argentina, Brazil, and Turkey, whose industrial sectors had been growing in the 1920s. In Japan the freeze on American investments and a drastic drop in the price of exported silk sent the economy into shock. In the United States and Canada a severe drought in western areas in 1932–1934 aggravated the depression. This disaster turned nearly ten million acres of fragile wheat land into a howling "dust bowl," forcing tens of thousands of farmers off the land and into chronic unemployment.

Keynesian economics. The magnitude of the depression, which reduced the value of world commerce from $36 billion to $12 billion in less than four years, sent most governments scrambling to salvage their own national economies as best they could. Autarky—national economic self-sufficiency—became the dominant credo. The major industrial states followed conventional procedures to try to halt the slide: let wages fall, raise tariffs on foreign imports, balance the budget, and wait for the crisis to pass. One after another, states defected from the international gold standard. When a country did that, the value of its national currency (no longer pegged to gold) typically declined, but this devaluation also made exports cheaper and stimulated

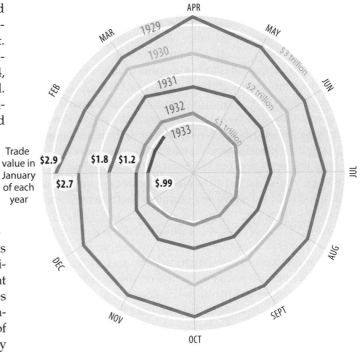

Trade value in January of each year

$2.9 $1.8 $1.2
$2.7 $.99

Value of Trade Imports (Trillions of Dollars)

Declining world trade, 1929–1933. What factors contributed to the decline in world trade shown on this chart? Source: Charles P. Kindleberger, *World in Depression, 1929–1939* (Berkeley: University of California Press, 1986), 170.

price increases. Britain, the architect of the gold standard, left it in 1931; the United States followed two years later.

The depression, however, did not reach bottom nearly as soon as the capitalist world expected, and the standard remedies did not work. The British economist John Maynard Keynes, whose philosophy achieved renown as **Keynesianism**, proposed a different and unorthodox approach. He observed that entrepreneurs and investors remained immobile out of fear that if they pumped new money into the deflated economy, others would fail to join in. Since this was a self-reinforcing trap, Keynes argued, governments had to get business moving again because they were the only institutions with the cash resources to do it, even though this meant heavy borrowing for public investment.

> **Keynesianism** Economic theories of John Maynard Keynes that promote government monetary and financial policies aimed at increasing employment and stimulating economic growth.

Leaders in the liberal democracies generally questioned Keynes's approach because it meant concentrating more power in the government and upsetting the natural functioning of the capitalist market. Nevertheless, a shift began to take place. In 1933 Sweden set the pace by introducing public works projects and unemployment assistance programs financed by government borrowing. In France the socialist government known as the Popular Front (1936–1938) enacted a barrage of new laws, including ambitious public works and the forty-hour work week. In the United States, President Franklin D. Roosevelt (in office, 1933–1945) introduced the New Deal in 1935, which gave employment to almost nine million men and women to build dams, roads, bridges, airports, parks, and public edifices and to fund arts and cultural projects. All of these programs pumped dollars into the sputtering economy. The New Deal also created a national minimum wage, federal deposit insurance for individual savings, and, later than most European states, a social security system. In short, the big slump pushed most industrialized countries further in the direction of social democracy—government committed to broad social and economic welfare for citizens.

The depression beyond the major industrialized regions.
The effects of the big slump on the predominantly rural populations of Latin America, Asia, and Africa varied widely. Farm families that subsisted on the food they grew often managed to get through the depression years without suffering lower living standards than they already had. Nevertheless, states and colonies that produced just one or two commodities for export, such as tea, cotton, or palm oil, faced severe price drops and unemployment. In West Africa the price of cash crops overall plunged by nearly 70 percent. In Brazil the government burned coffee beans or used them to fuel rail locomotives to reduce the unsold glut. In Southeast Asia, plantations, mines, and city commerce stagnated, prompting millions of Chinese and Indian immigrants to return to their homelands. Colonial administrations had

smaller budgets during the depression, so they cut back on already modest education and development spending.

Most countries whose economies relied heavily on commodity exports suffered badly when prices plummeted. In the Latin American countries of Argentina, Brazil, Chile, El Salvador, Guatemala, Honduras, and Peru, groups of military officers who thought their elected governments were incompetent to handle the crisis seized power, all within one year of the 1929 market crash. Those states and most others in the region endeavored to rouse nationalist sentiment in favor of recovery policies that included new home industries, state control of foreign trade, and long-range economic planning. In Mexico President Lázaro Cárdenas put the government at the forefront of economic development and in 1934 introduced serious reforms to give peasants more land. Four years later he nationalized Mexico's oil industry, an action that infuriated U.S. oil companies but received popular acclaim at home. In India the British regime had such great need of tax revenues during the hard times that it encouraged Indian industrialists to expand their operations. By the late 1930s India was producing enough steel to fill 70 percent of its needs.

The depression skips Russia.
As we saw, Joseph Stalin put the Soviet Union on the path to extreme autarky in the mid-1920s. He shunned international economic agreements and poured massive state resources into technological modernization and heavy industry. This process started before the depression and continued straight through it. While the

Crowds celebrate the Mexican expropriation of oil, March 18, 1938. President Cárdenas used property rights established in the 1917 constitution to claim petroleum reserves beneath Mexican soil on behalf of the nation. Why might this action have prompted people to take to the streets?

United States and western Europe remained bogged in unemployment, Russia kept people working, increasing its industrial output by 500 percent between 1928 and 1937. But Stalin's rigorous Five Year Plans had harsh consequences. Rural populations suffered severe food shortages, and industrial workers had little access to consumer goods beyond the necessities. Millions of Soviet citizens performed slave labor in Siberia. Between 1928 and 1934 the Soviet prison population rose from 30,000 to 500,000.

Depression and the Continuing Trend toward Authoritarian Leaders

The United States, Britain, France, and several other states showed that liberal democratic governments could muddle through the depression intact. Nevertheless, the global trend toward authoritarianism continued without interruption in the 1930s as aspiring political leaders promised tough action and autarkic policies to save their nations. Nine more European states veered sharply to the authoritarian right, abandoning legislatures and party politics for top-down governments that were anticommunist, antiliberal, and fervently nationalist. Right-wing political groups in both Europe and Latin America emulated the style and tactics of the Italian Fascist Party. In their view, "democracy" was not a matter of multiparty elections but perpetual public theater—parades, flags, fiery speeches, militarized youth groups, fancy uniforms—to acclaim authoritarian leaders as guardians of their nations' cultural and political purity.

The political right takes charge in Japan. The onrush of depression in 1930 boosted public support in Japan for nationalist parties and military men clamoring for more imperial conquests to secure vital resources. The following year, army elements fabricated an excuse to invade and seize the whole of Manchuria. Jiang Jieshi, president of China, protested the invasion to the League of Nations, but it had no mechanism for military intervention. Also in 1931 a coalition of officers, industrialists, and high bureaucrats attained control of the Japanese legislature, adopting an ultranationalist ideology. Japan pulled itself gradually out of the depression after 1932 partly by massive state expenditure on the army and navy. In 1937 the country launched a full-scale invasion of China (see Chapter 26).

The rise of the Nazi Party in Germany. The Great Depression struck Germany harder than any other European country. Unemployment there soared from about three million in 1930 to six million in 1932. Working Germans, already devastated by astronomical inflation from 1920 to 1923, watched in dismay as their incomes and savings

Adolf Hitler at the time of the Munich Beer Hall Putsch. This 1924 photograph shows Hitler (on the left) with collaborators Emil Maurice, Hermann Kriebel, Rudolf Hess, and Friedrich Weber. Compare Hitler's appearance in traditional Tyrolean clothing to Atatürk's decision around the same time to enforce the adoption of Western business attire in Turkey. In what ways did the two men's political use of symbols of national identity differ?

disappeared once again. By this time, popular support for the postwar Weimar Republic had badly corroded. In the national legislature (Reichstag), effective decision making depended on alliances among numerous parties that invariably proved unstable.

Throughout the 1920s the Reichstag coalitions gradually shifted to the right, though not nearly fast enough in the view of groups like the National Socialist German Workers' Party, later known simply as the Nazi Party. After World War I this upstart group attracted disgruntled war veterans, among them Adolph Hitler (1889–1945), a one-time artist and street vendor from a working-class family in Austria. Demonstrating a flair for impassioned speech-making, Hitler rose to party leadership. After a bungled uprising against the Weimar government in Munich in 1923 known as the Beer Hall Putsch, Hitler spent several months in jail. The Nazi Party was banned, but it continued to campaign illegally on a platform of zealous nationalism, revenge for the Treaty of Versailles, territorial expansion, and hatred of liberals, communists, and Jews. Hitler much admired Mussolini's style of paramilitary theatrics, founding, for example, a league of fervently loyal "storm troopers" to bully or terrorize opponents.

When the depression hit Germany, politics became more deeply polarized than ever. In 1930 the Nazi Party took the second largest number of seats in Reichstag elections. Two years later, Nazis and communists (the far right and the far left) gained between them a majority of support among German voters. Like ultranationalist parties in other countries, the Nazis appealed especially to middle-class clerks, civil servants, storekeepers, military veterans, unskilled laborers, and farmers. These were Germans who suffered badly in the depression but also felt alienated from the industrial and financial elite on one side and powerful socialist and communist labor unions on the other.

Like Mussolini, Hitler achieved power by constitutional means. Following the election of 1932 he persuaded Paul von Hindenburg, the aging and largely powerless president of the German republic, to appoint him chancellor, that is, prime minister. Germany's traditionally conservative business elite accepted this decision, assuming that they would easily control the Austrian demagogue and his party once he took office. In short order, however, the Reichstag awarded Hitler emergency powers, which he deployed to suspend the Weimar constitution and all parliamentary institutions, effectively appointing himself dictator. Between 1933 and 1936 he gained total command of the German state and, always claiming to represent the will of the nation, moved to destroy all political opposition. In Chapter 26 we return to Nazi-ruled Germany and its part in the outbreak of World War II.

• • •

Conclusion

In the two decades after World War I, a shrewd observer of the global scene might have thought that humankind was moving simultaneously in two directions. On the one hand, interrelationships among peoples inhabiting different parts of the world continued to move along the path of greater complexity. Communication and transport technologies became ever more powerful. Professional news agencies such as Reuters, Havas, and the Associated Press made news a commodity, devoting themselves solely to gathering and disseminating information—the current cotton price in Uganda, the Tokyo earthquake, the latest Hollywood scandal. Diplomats and politicians continued to gather in capital cities to grapple with international disputes. Educated men and women traveled to international congresses to work for social and civic betterment and scientific advances. The League of Nations did commendable work around the world in cultural, health, and social welfare fields. The Olympic Games convened every four years throughout the interwar period, with four of the meets in European cities and one in Los Angeles. Uruguay hosted the first World Cup Soccer tournament in 1930.

On the other hand, the pace of global economic integration fluctuated erratically and then ground to a halt. In the depression years, industrial employment declined more than in any earlier recorded period. Middle-class incomes plunged, and the global gap between rich and poor got wider. Collectively, the world's sovereign states responded to the depression, not by doubling efforts toward economic cooperation, but by seeking more perfect autarky—freedom from economic dependence on fellow states. In the process of finding solutions to dire economic problems, dozens of governments rose and fell, often through violence.

By pulling economic and financial levers, whether big military spending (Japan and Germany) or huge new government investment programs (western Europe and the United States), states slowly pulled themselves out of the pit. These efforts did not, however, lead in the short term to a new era of growth but to another global war, this one longer and more destructive than the first.

• • •

Key Terms

autarky 738
Black Thursday 751
demographic transition 731
fascism 740
Great Depression 750
Guomindang 738

indirect rule 746
isolationism 750
Keynesianism 751
League of Nations Mandates 743
metropole 744
modernism 731

Nazi Party 753
New Deal 752
New Economic Policy (NEP) 736
totalitarianism 740

Change over Time

1900	Sigmund Freud's *The Interpretation of Dreams* is published.
1905	Albert Einstein announces theory of relativity.
1910	South Africa becomes a self-governing state under Afrikaner domination.
1919	German colonies and Ottoman provinces are turned over to Britain, France, or South Africa according to the League of Nations Mandate system. Egyptians demand independence from Britain in the Egyptian Revolution of 1919. Mohandas Gandhi begins activist career in India.
1920	Iraqis revolt against British rule. Turks fight for an independent Turkish Republic; Atatürk becomes president.
1921–1926	Abd al-Karim leads a rebellion against Spanish rule in Morocco.
1922	Benito Mussolini takes power in Italy. The USSR is formed.
1923	The Irish Free State is established; Northern Ireland (Ulster) removes itself from the new state.
1924	The Dawes Plan for German reparation payments goes into effect.
1927	Werner Heisenberg theorizes the "uncertainty principle."
1928	Stalin's first Five Year Plan goes into effect in the Soviet Union.
1929–1938	Economies around the world tumble in the Great Depression.
1931	Japan invades Manchuria.
1933	Hitler becomes chancellor of Germany.
1935	U.S. president Franklin Roosevelt announces New Deal.
1938	Mexico nationalizes its oil industry.

Please see end of book reference section for additional reading suggestions related to this chapter.

26 World War II and Its Aftermath

1933–1950

A shot from Leni Riefenstahl's 1934 film *Triumph of the Will* documenting a Nazi Party rally in Nuremberg.

I n the first half of the twentieth century, the movie became a tool of war. Dozens of countries established national film industries, and governments took an early interest in cinema for its propaganda value. Political leaders recognized the power of moving pictures not only to report and preserve visual representations of the world but also to alter and manipulate them. During the 1930s and World War II, both democratic and authoritarian states sponsored entertainment films intended to inspire national unity, boost military morale, and report current events in ways that accentuated the good news and downplayed the bad. In Germany under Nazi Party rule, filmmakers made numerous documentaries depicting Adolf Hitler as a nationally revered superhero. In 1934 the gifted director Leni Riefenstahl made *Triumph of the Will,* a record of Hitler's appearance at a gigantic Nazi political rally in the city of Nuremberg. In this ingenious feat of propaganda, Hitler's airplane descends to Nuremberg through billowing clouds, as if from heaven, and, stepping from the plane, the Führer is engulfed in a sea of drums, trumpets, and rapturous faces. In the United States the federal government commissioned a series of seven wartime movies titled *Why We Fight.* Brilliantly editing stock newsreel footage and charging the soundtrack with patriotic rhetoric and stirring music, the films roused both troops and civilians to the necessity of total victory over the German and Japanese aggressors.

Mass persuasion through film and other modern media is just one gauge of the growing power that states acquired in the twentieth century to rally citizens behind government action. In the 1930s Japan, Germany, and, on a more modest scale, Italy marshaled their populations and national resources to build territorial empires. Britain, the United States, and other democratic countries also knew how to mobilize citizens for war and sacrifice. But the Great Depression left them wary of risking a second global conflict in order to stop this new imperialist surge.

As the world struggled out of the depression, its most powerful states did little to rebuild an international system of open trade and shared security. Rather, they flocked into competing and increasingly antagonistic regional blocs (see Map 26.1). One of these crystallized around Germany, a second around Japan, and a third around the Union of Soviet Socialist Republics. Britain and France looked to their respective overseas colonial empires for economic support. The United States dominated the business and trade of the Western Hemisphere. In 1939, tensions and antagonisms among these power groups exploded into war, first in central and western Europe and then in the North Atlantic, North Africa, Russia, the western Pacific, and Southeast Asia. The

Chapter Outline

EMPIRE BUILDING AND GLOBAL CRISIS
Empire of the Sun
The Nazi State
Italy's Foreign Aggressions
Fascist Dictatorship in Spain

THE GREATEST WAR
The Years of Axis Victory, 1939–1942
The Years of Counteroffensive, 1942–1945
The Second Total War

INDIVIDUALS MATTER Olga Lisikova:
Soviet Combat Pilot

The War beyond the Theaters of War
The War and the Global Environment

WEIGHING THE EVIDENCE Propaganda for Wartime Conservation

IN THE WAKE OF WAR, 1945–1950
Restoring Stability, Enforcing Justice
The Two New Empires
World War II and the Challenge
to Colonial Empires
Communist Victory in China

• • •

regional blocs rearranged themselves into two giant military alliances that pitted the world's mightiest industrial states against each other. Something similar had happened in World War I, but now the opposing countries possessed far greater destructive power than they had had in 1914.

The first part of this chapter investigates the run-up to World War II in the context of Japanese, German, and Italian empire building, adventures that emerged out of the dire conditions of the Great Depression. Germany under Nazi rule, moreover, deviated from nineteenth-century imperialism because it aspired to carve its empire, not out of pieces of Africa or Asia, but from the very heart of Europe. Until 1939 the major democracies trusted that some combination of negotiations and enlightened reason would persuade Nazis, Italian fascists, and Japanese militarists to moderate their belligerent behavior. These hopes proved futile. The second part of the chapter surveys the world war from September 1939, when Germany invaded Poland, to August 1945, when American planes dropped atomic bombs on Hiroshima and Nagasaki, driving Japan to unconditional surrender. We also explore key social, technological, and environmental developments that attended the war.

A Panoramic View

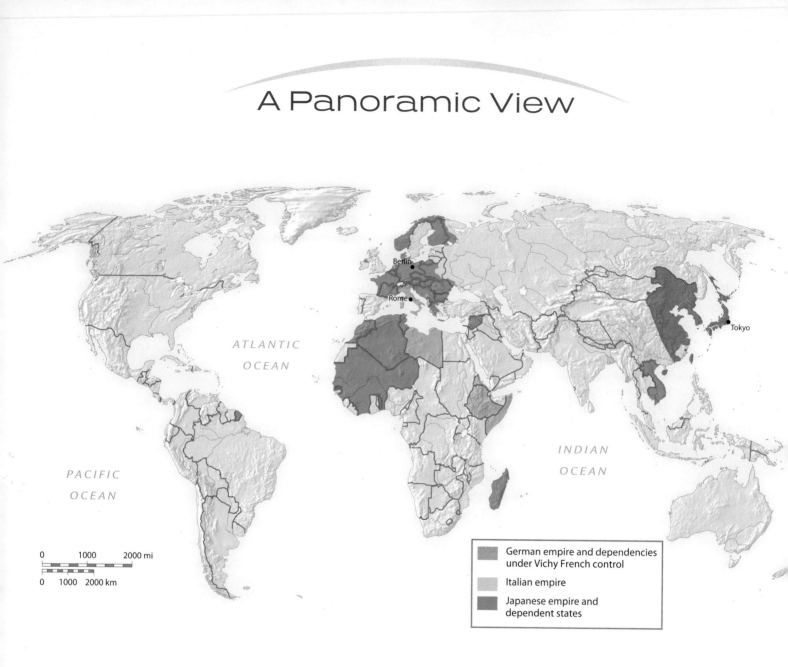

MAP 26.1 German, Japanese, and Italian empires and dependent states, early 1941.
What resources and strategic advantages did the Axis powers gain through territorial expansion? What logistical challenges did these wartime empires face?

The chapter's final section addresses events that took place in the immediate aftermath of the war, five years in which the world haltingly recovered from the conflagration. Even as the war wound down, relations between the United States and the Soviet Union degenerated into mutual recrimination and distrust. Nor could the European powers with colonial empires expect to return to business as usual. In Africa and Asia the end of the war triggered demands for new governments that would serve the popular will and end foreign exploitation.

Empire Building and Global Crisis

FOCUS How did authoritarian, ultranationalist states succeed in amassing power in the 1930s?

Some historians have lumped World Wars I and II together and called them the twentieth century's "Thirty Years' War," playing on the conflict of that name that took place in Europe in the 1600s. From this perspective, the so-called interwar years were nothing but a partial lull in a long global struggle that reached its zenith of death and destruction between 1939 and 1945.

This interpretation has something to commend it, but the perpetrators of war in 1914 and 1939 had very different intentions. The World War I adversaries had aimed to alter the balance of power in Europe but not to drastically rewrite its map. In the decade leading to World War II, by contrast, Germany and Japan instigated violent imperial exploits far exceeding in scope and ambition the imaginings of any of the combatants in World War I. Like so many other countries in the interwar decades, Germany, Japan, and Italy exchanged liberal elective governments for authoritarian ones. They moved to the far right of the political spectrum, displaying intense nationalism, militarism, and contempt in equal measure for both communism and multiparty democracy. All three countries justified conquest as essential to the survival of the nation and aimed to achieve economic self-sufficiency partly by exploiting the labor and resources of subjugated peoples. In the late 1930s they entered into a series of accords with one another, culminating in 1940 with the tripartite alliance known thereafter as the Axis.

Empire of the Sun

In the two decades after World War I, the brilliant red disk at the center of the Japanese flag flew over a country growing impressively in population and industrial might. This power, however, depended on a continuous search for overseas resources, notably oil, which the islands did not have. For committed nationalists, Japan had either to extend its sphere of economic domination beyond Taiwan, Korea, southern Manchuria, and some Pacific islands—territories it had seized between 1895 and 1910—or resign itself to diminishing influence among the world's industrial states.

Demands for military action, particularly against China, became more strident during the Great Depression, which hit Japan hard from 1930 to 1932 (see Chapter 25). Amid social stress, public assassinations, and attempted coups, political factions led principally by ultranationalist army officers strengthened their grip on the national legislature (Diet). In September 1931, army units already in control of part of southern Manchuria launched a full-scale invasion of that region, sweeping aside nationalist Chinese forces. Japan erected a puppet Manchurian state called Manchukuo and began to extract the region's abundant coal, iron, gold, and other chemical resources. Back in Europe, the League of Nations noisily protested the invasion but did nothing.

After 1932 Japan pulled out of the depression by spending massive public sums on industry and armaments, while leaders proclaiming an ultranationalist creed—unquestioning loyalty to emperor and state, renunciation of Western liberalism, and assertion of Japanese racial superiority—took full control of the government. This regime improved social services, but it smothered socialist, communist, and feminist groups and suppressed nearly all democratic institutions. Expressing warm admiration for European fascism, the new leaders idealized women as patriotic mothers and homemakers who had no need for voting rights. They also envisioned Japan dominating a huge economic zone embracing all of East and Southeast Asia. According to a booklet produced by the ministry of education, that whole region was destined to be Japan's "paddy field."[1]

Easy victory in Manchuria encouraged Japan to seize more territory. In 1937, land and air forces moved out from Manchuria to invade northern China on a broad front.

The Battle of Shanghai. Japanese soldiers fought their way through the city in 1937. The invasion compounded the disruption China was already suffering owing to civil war between nationalist and communist forces. What factors motivated the Japanese army to seize more Chinese territory after it captured Manchuria?

President Jiang Jieshi and the nationalist Chinese army fought tenaciously but were doubtless weakened by having spent the previous six years battling communists and other internal enemies. The invasion's ferocity drew global outrage, especially the assault on Nanjing, the nationalist capital, where Japanese troops slaughtered tens of thousands of people and indiscriminately raped women. By 1939 a million Japanese soldiers controlled most of the cities of northern and central China. However, they still did not rule about 60 percent of the country's rural population. Both nationalist and communist forces, though at odds with each other, continued to resist.

The Nazi State

While Japan pursued its dream of empire in Asia, Adolf Hitler and the Nazi Party moved to make Germany the preeminent power in Europe. Hitler became chancellor of Germany in January 1933 in conditions of alarming economic crisis, a situation that allowed him to dismiss the parliament and assume emergency powers (see Chapter 25). During his twelve years of rule, he never called the legislature back. In August 1934 he assumed the title of Führer, or Supreme Leader, effectively abolishing the German republic that had existed since 1919. Germany became informally known as the Third Reich, or the Third Empire, succeeding earlier manifestations of German imperial grandeur. Like other authoritarian rulers of the era but with special talent for commanding hero worship, Hitler represented himself as the embodiment of the nation's spirit and destiny.

An admirer of Italian fascism, Hitler took less than three years to set up a totalitarian regime more intrusive and despotic than Benito Mussolini's. For all his hatred of communism, he in fact imitated Joseph Stalin in the Soviet Union by building an apparatus of state bureaucrats, informers, secret police (the Gestapo), and elite military units (the *Schutzstaffel,* or SS). During its first six months alone, the Nazi regime imprisoned thirty thousand political opponents and other perceived troublemakers. Hitler also ordered Gestapo and SS agents to jail or execute army officers, politicians, old rivals, and even Nazi Party members he wanted out of the way.

Nazi racial dreams. Hitler set forth his peculiar world view in *Mein Kampf* (My Struggle), a rambling, hate-filled, partly autobiographical work that he compiled while in prison in 1924. For Marxists, history turned on social class struggle. For Hitler the key to past and future was the clash of races. This conflict would end when the "Aryans," a mythical racial group of superior intelligence and hardihood, achieved dominance over all lesser forms of humanity. As Aryans, Hitler declared, the German people, or *volk,* must defend themselves at all cost against contamination by racially defective peoples. For him, racial mixing would inevitably lead to "physical and intellectual regression."[2] He

excluded the majority of Europeans from Aryan membership, especially Jews, Roma (Gypsies), Poles, Czechs, Russians, and all other Slavs. He most emphatically excluded Africans and Asians. At one point, he expressed admiration for Britain's subjugation of millions of dark-skinned peoples but ridiculed the idea of their ever gaining self-rule. The way to deal with Indian nationalists, he is reported to have said, should be clear enough: "Shoot Gandhi, and if that does not suffice to reduce them to submission, shoot a dozen leading members of [the Indian National] Congress; and if that does not suffice, shoot 200 and so on until order is established."[3]

Anti-Semitic prejudice was commonplace in interwar Europe, but to Hitler the Jews represented the single greatest threat to the German nation. Jews, he declared, had no homeland or nation of their own but worked their way into the societies of others and fed off them. Their intellectual and psychological defects were legion—greed, cunning, dishonesty. According to this Nazi delusion, wherever one looked for socialists, liberals, grasping capitalists, or communists, there one would find Jews.

As early as 1933 the Nazi Party took steps to cleanse the nation of the unwanted and unfit, subjecting them to imprisonment, banishment, sterilization, medical neglect, euthanasia, or execution. Alcoholics, feminists, gay people, the mentally infirm, or anyone who failed to show avid enthusiasm for the Nazi regime became targets of persecution. The project to isolate Jews got under way systematically in 1935 with proclamation of the Nuremberg Laws. These acts dispossessed Jews of German citizenship, prohibited them from marrying non-Jews, and harassed them in numerous other humiliating ways. Such zealous interference in the lives of certain groups meant that the Nazi state had in fact to watch and regulate *everyone.* Gradually, all public institutions from schools and churches to newspapers and social clubs came under strict Nazi control. "The right of personal freedom," Hitler wrote, "recedes before the duty to preserve the race."[4] Like Italian fascists, Nazi leaders defined the emancipation of women as freedom to serve the state and to bear as many young Aryans as possible.

Despite its extreme authoritarianism, the Nazi government commanded growing popular support, especially among urban middle classes. By massive public spending, it pulled Germany out of the depression faster than any liberal democratic state managed to do. By 1938 Germany's jobless rate fell to less than 1 percent. The state also offered citizens generous social benefits, including housing, childcare, and medical services. Hitler revitalized heavy industry, publicly financing metallurgical, chemical, and weapons factories, even though arms manufacture violated the World War I settlement. He generally followed fascist Italy's example of collaborating with conservative business leaders and big corporations. One of his pet public projects was the autobahn, the world's first superhighway network. He also worked with Ferdinand Porsche, the German automotive

An ideal Aryan family. This Nazi-era image idealizes family life and a connection to nature through agricultural toil. This poster shares with other Nazi propaganda a celebration of motherhood and hard work. Notice the mother's tan line where her dress is open to nurse the baby. How might the Nazi government have intended Germans to respond to this poster?

that would ensure supplies of farm goods and minerals on terms favorable to Germans.

Nazi empire building. From the start of his political career, Hitler preached that Germany's salvation depended on territorial conquest. "Only an adequately large space on this earth," he argued, "assures a nation of freedom of existence."[5] The idea that the German nation must either enlarge its "living space" (*lebensraum* in German) or end up as a slave to other, racially polluted groups became a fundamental tenet of Nazi ideology. The regime's immediate project was to gather all German-speaking peoples, including the millions who over the centuries had migrated to various parts of central and eastern Europe, into a unitary German state. But more than that, Hitler set his sights on all of eastern Europe and Russia as "the necessary soil for our German people"—a great frontier of conquest and settlement extending all the way to the Ural Mountains.[6] Once under the authority of the Third Reich, the existing, mainly Slavic populations would be transformed into a gigantic pool of forced labor. The weak and undesirable, including all Jews, would have to be either driven deep into Inner Eurasia or liquidated. Along the way to victory in the east, the Reich would naturally terminate the Russian communist state, ensuring that never again would Germany be surrounded by hostile powers, as it had been in World War I.

Until the late 1930s neither the Soviet Union nor the Western democracies took Hitler's imperial dream nearly seriously enough. The Western powers failed to intervene decisively partly because Hitler built his empire by incremental steps. They protested each act of aggression, but then reluctantly accepted it, hoping that Germany would ask for nothing more. In 1936 Hitler sent troops into the Rhineland, the industrially rich western area of Germany that had been demilitarized since 1919. In March 1938 he intimidated Austria, a predominantly German-speaking state, into accepting annexation to the "Greater German Reich." About the same time, he demanded that Czechoslovakia cede substantial parts of its territory to Germany, charging that German minorities there were being oppressed. In September 1938 he met with European leaders in Munich, where France and Britain agreed to the takeover, neither of them wanting to start a war over a small Slavic state. Neville Chamberlain, the British prime minister, declared that the Munich conference had achieved "peace in our time." Six months later, however, Nazis collaborated with local fascist

designer, to build a small, fuel-efficient automobile priced, like the Ford Model T, for working citizens. Porsche produced a prototype of the Volkswagen, or "people's car" in 1935, though few Germans acquired these Beetles until after the war.

Like both Mussolini and Stalin, Hitler believed that national strength and independence must be achieved through autarky—economic self-reliance—not membership in an international system of trade and cooperation. He pulled Germany out of the League of Nations and stopped making World War I reparations to France and Britain. Envisioning Germany at the center of a great economic power bloc, he directed his agents to persuade or bully weaker states of central and eastern Europe to sign commercial agreements

Emperor Haile Selassie addressing the League of Nations, 1936. The Ethiopian emperor's appeals to the international community to help resist the Italian invasion went unanswered. Why do you think none of the major powers were willing to come to Ethiopia's aid?

leaders to seize control of the rest of Czechoslovakia, as well as part of Lithuania in northeastern Europe.

Italy's Foreign Aggressions

Benito Mussolini, who took power in Italy in 1922, proclaimed that national solidarity required foreign conquest, imagining himself the heir of ancient Roman emperors. Italy had played a modest part in Europe's late-nineteenth-century imperialist surge, seizing Libya across the Mediterranean, as well as Eritrea and Somaliland in northeastern Africa. An Italian army had invaded Ethiopia in 1896 but suffered ignominious defeat (see Chapter 23). Mussolini spent the early years of his rule strengthening the Italian economy and army. Then in 1935 he dispatched 100,000 troops to invade Ethiopia again, equipping them with motorized transport, tanks, aircraft, and, contrary to international law, poison gas. The Ethiopian army fought resolutely but lost to carpet bombing, unbridled attacks on civilians, and mass executions. Haile Selassie (r. 1930–1974), Ethiopia's emperor, appealed to the League of Nations for help: "On many occasions I have asked for financial assistance for the purchase of arms. That assistance has been constantly refused me. What, then, in practice, is the meaning of . . . collective security?"[7] The League denounced the invasion but proved no more willing to help Ethiopia than it had Manchuria in 1931. In 1939 and under cover of Hitler's assault on Czechoslovakia, Mussolini also invaded Albania, a small Balkan monarchy that he knew he could beat. Neither Britain nor France tried to stop him.

Fascist Dictatorship in Spain

Between 1936 and 1939 Spain fell into a ferocious civil war that produced between 400,000 and 1 million casualties. Spain in the 1930s was a microcosm of European ideological struggles between the political right and left. In 1931 a republican government assumed power but made little progress in solving Spain's acute problems of rural poverty and industrial exploitation of low-paid urban workers. In 1936 a shaky coalition of liberals, socialists, communists, and regional separatists, constituting a Popular Front of the political left, won parliamentary elections. Within months, however, General Francisco Franco (in office, 1938-1973) and other right-wing military officers attempted a *coup d'état* that triggered the civil struggle. The Spanish Civil War also had a colonial dimension because Franco initially based his movement in the part of northern Morocco that Spain had ruled since 1912.

The three-year war pitted the communist-dominated coalition of the left against an ultranationalist alliance of military men, land-owners, fascist paramilitary groups, and the deeply conservative hierarchy of the Spanish Catholic Church. Even though Franco was less a doctrinaire fascist than a pragmatic nationalist, the wider world perceived the war as a titanic struggle between political right and left. Stalin sent Soviet aid to the republican side. Forty thousand leftist foreign volunteers, including the Abraham Lincoln Brigade from the United States, joined the cause, many of them dying in combat. On the nationalist side, Franco got help from German air squadrons, which bombed republican-held areas. Wary that a republican victory might lead to a communist takeover, Britain and France refused to help neutralize the German intervention. But Franco's victory in 1939, together with Czechoslovakia's calamity, persuaded Britain and France to oppose further Nazi expansion.

The Greatest War

FOCUS What factors explain why a second global war occurred in the first half of the twentieth century?

The Wehrmacht, or German army, invaded Poland in early September 1939, precipitating European war. Between then and mid-1942 the Nazi empire grew to colossal size, extending from Arctic tundra to the North African Sahara and from the Atlantic coast of France to the Black Sea. Parallel to this expansion, Japanese forces overran a large part of China, almost all of Southeast Asia, and numerous Pacific islands. Only in 1942 did a large coalition of countries led by the United States, Russia, and Britain begin to confront the Axis powers. From then until 1945, battles raged on land and sea, and casualties of both soldiers and civilians soared into the tens of millions. In this chapter we survey the war's broad outline, including changes it brought in the social, economic, and environmental spheres.

The Years of Axis Victory, 1939–1942

At certain points between 1940 and early 1942, many well-informed observers thought the war was about to end in Axis victory. Germany, its allies, and its client states achieved control of more than three-quarters of Europe. Sweden, Switzerland, Spain, Portugal, and Ireland remained neutral, but all of those states except Ireland endured persistent Nazi intimidation. After German forces overran France, they created the Vichy (vee-SHEE) puppet regime, which permitted Axis collaborators to take control of France's colonies in North and West Africa and in Southeast Asia. In western Europe, only Great Britain continued fight. To the east, Japan forged an empire even bigger than Germany's, by 1942 the largest the world had ever seen, if one counts the seas that the Japanese navy patrolled.

War in East Asia and Poland. Fighting in Europe and on China's northwestern frontier announced the start of general war. In August 1939, and much to the dismay of Britain and France, Germany signed a nonaggression pact with the Soviet Union. This accord included an arrangement to divide Poland and other eastern European states between the two powers in the event of war. Here was Stalin, the leader of the international communist movement, making common cause with the rabidly anticommunist Hitler. How did this deal come about? Stalin knew perfectly well Hitler's designs on Russian territory, but he needed to buy time. He could call up millions of soldiers, but they were poorly equipped compared to the German Wehrmacht (armed forces) divisions facing eastern Europe. Furthermore, in the late 1930s Stalin conducted a brutal purge of both army officers and Communist Party officials in order to root out political enemies, real or imagined. The purges devastated the upper ranks of the officer corps and left the entire chain of command in shambles. By pragmatically allying with Germany, Stalin aimed to rebuild the Red Army with a new generation of loyal subordinates, regain eastern European territory lost in World War I, and encourage Germany to exhaust itself fighting a war with Britain

SOMEONE IS TAKING SOMEONE FOR A WALK

The Nazi–Soviet Pact, 1939. This cartoon published in London's *Evening Standard* shows Stalin and Hitler strolling along the border they established after dividing Poland between them. How did the cartoonist portray this alliance between the Soviet Union and Germany? What details suggest that this arrangement was not stable?

and France rather than with him. The pact also bought time for Hitler. He had long believed that German conquest to the east first required eliminating France and Britain as viable enemies. He expected to perform that task in short order and then, nonaggression pact or no pact, invade Russia.

In Japan the Nazi–Soviet pact caused serious rethinking of imperial priorities. Japan and Russia had fought a war in 1905 (see Chapter 24), and they remained rivals for influence in northeast Asia. Since early 1939 the two states had been fighting an undeclared war intermittently along the border between Manchuria and Mongolia, a Soviet client state. In late August the Russian army won a decisive victory, prompting the leaders in Tokyo to cut their losses, patch up relations with Russia, and redirect military operations from northeastern Asia to the British, French, and Dutch colonies in Southeast Asia. This is exactly what Hitler hoped Japan would do.

The Wehrmacht invaded Poland in September 1939, knowing that state had to be secured before they could launch an invasion of western Europe. Despite fierce Polish resistance, Nazi forces quickly overran the western third of the country, while Russian divisions seized the eastern provinces, all according to plan. When the fighting ended, Joseph Goebbels, Hitler's propaganda chief, made clear Nazi intentions for the Polish people. They are, he wrote, "completely primitive, stupid, and amorphous. . . . The Führer has no intention of assimilating the Poles. . . . This nation's civilization is not worth consideration."[8] Operating with this mindset, the invaders indiscriminately killed Polish civilians, burned villages, executed intellectuals, machine-gunned the disabled, and herded several hundred thousand Jews and others to ghettos in central Poland to make space for German settlers. In the eastern region, the Soviet occupiers killed or imprisoned even more people in the months after the invasion, for example, massacring about twenty-two thousand army officers and other Poles in the Katyn Forest in March 1940.

The fall of western Europe. When the Wehrmacht assaulted Poland, Britain and France declared war, though neither had sufficient land forces to stop Hitler from driving west. Between April and the end of June 1940, German mechanized divisions supported by the Luftwaffe (air force) invaded Denmark, Norway, the Netherlands, Luxembourg, Belgium, and France one after the other. By mid-June, the Nazi swastika flew over Paris. Retreating on two fronts, British and French troops converged on Dunkirk on the northern coast of France, where a hastily arranged swarm of seacraft gathered to ferry 338,000 soldiers across the English Channel to safety. Cloudy skies limited German air attacks. "The bad weather has grounded the Luftwaffe," the army chief of staff complained, "and we must now stand by and watch countless thousands of the enemy get away to England right under our noses."[9] Once in Britain, surviving French troops formed the Free French organization under the leadership of Charles de Gaulle (1990–1970).

Meanwhile, German forces fanned out across western Europe as far as the Mediterranean coast and the Spanish frontier. Hitler intended to absorb most conquered territory directly into the Third Reich. However, he allowed a **collaborationist** government led by Marshall Philippe Pétain, an elderly World War I hero, to administer the southern provinces of France from the small city of Vichy. The war in western Europe seemed to be over. Millions of Europeans, relieved that it had ended quickly, were quite prepared to wait and see what Hitler's victory might bring. Rosie Waldeck, a German-born correspondent living in Romania in the summer of 1940, captured the resigned public mood: "The fall of France formed the climax to twenty years of failure of the promises of democracy to handle unemployment, inflation, deflations, labor unrest, party egoism, and what not. . . . Hitler, Europe felt, was a smart guy—disagreeable but smart. . . . Why not try his way."[10] Other millions, however, wanted no part of Hitler's way, and in every defeated country resistance movements of noncooperation, sabotage, and guerrilla warfare gradually took shape, though these activities tended to be scattered and out of communication with one another.

> **collaborationist** A government, a group, or an individual that cooperates with foreign enemies, usually an occupying power.

In Britain, Prime Minister Winston Churchill (1874–1965) refused to accept German domination of continental Europe in return for peace. Not yet prepared to invade England, Hitler ordered massive aerial bombing to bring the country to its knees. Royal Air Force (RAF) fighter planes fought back, however, and British scientists developed superior radar technology to track and intercept enemy aircraft. The airborne Battle of Britain raged during the fall and winter of 1940–1941, with the Luftwaffe dropping tens of thousands of explosive and incendiary bombs on British factories, cities, harbors, and ships. The RAF shot down attacking planes faster than German factories could replace them. Consequently, Hitler shelved his invasion plans, confident that he could deal with Britain once he defeated Russia. The bombing eased up, leaving Britain economically exhausted but with some breathing space to rebuild.

War in the Atlantic. As soon as Britain and Germany went to war, their navies began to engage each other from the North Sea to the South Atlantic. By conquering France, Germany gained access to new ocean-facing ports. Its surface navy was much smaller than Britain's, but its submarines, or U-boats, roamed the Atlantic. Between October and December 1940 alone, German naval craft sank more than 700,000 tons of British shipping. The sea war brought Europe's crisis closer to the United States. Britain desperately needed North American food and war materiel, but the United States had neutrality laws prohibiting it from helping either side. The U.S. Congress was not eager for another great war twenty-three years after the first. The Franklin Roosevelt administration, however, became persuaded that if Britain fell, the U.S. navy would have to defend the North Atlantic against Germany while facing Japanese aggression in the Pacific at the same time. Public opinion also shifted in Roosevelt's favor, and in March 1941, Congress enacted the Lend-Lease program, which effectively freed the president to offer Britain, and later Russia, billions of dollars in military aid. The following summer, the navy began escorting convoys as far across the Atlantic as Iceland. By October, American and German vessels were attacking each other, even though no state of war yet existed between the two countries.

The "war of annihilation" in Russia. The Nazi–Soviet nonaggression pact collapsed abruptly on June 22, 1941, when three German army groups invaded the Soviet Union simultaneously. Stalin received the news in shock. In the following seventeen months, the Wehrmacht penetrated hundreds of miles into Russia. Hitler was confident of victory because his army had already invaded Yugoslavia and Greece and pressured Hungary, Romania, and Bulgaria into joining the Axis. Moreover, Nazi race theory made no room for effective Russian resistance, a German military handbook declaring that Slavic soldiers, being "slow-witted," were "incapable of decisive resistance against a well-commanded, well-equipped force."[11] Hitler told his high command that the invasion of Russia would be a "war of annihilation."

Between June and December 1941, German troops overran western Soviet defenses, destroyed the Soviet air force, and captured hundreds of thousands of prisoners. As the armies advanced, they also got busy clearing living space for the racially pure. The Wehrmacht burned thousands of villages, shot or hanged Communist Party leaders and numerous other civilians, and sent thousands of men and women to slave labor camps in Germany. The Nazi regime let upward of two million Russian war prisoners starve or freeze to death. The invaders rounded up and murdered Jews, often in village squares, and these atrocities grew rapidly in scope and ferocity. Some Ukrainians and other non-Russian minorities at first welcomed the Germans as liberators from Stalinist despotism. But instead of cooperating with these groups, Nazi officers followed Hitler's orders to "spread such terror as to crush every will to resist among the population."[12]

Within six months of the assault, however, it became clear that Germany would not replicate its triumphant march across western Europe. In July 1941 Stalin proclaimed that Russia would fight a "Great Patriotic War" of defense. Fired by this nationalist appeal, the Red Army recovered its footing and partisan guerrillas began to operate behind German lines. In December, Soviet forces stopped the Wehrmacht before it reached Moscow. Early in 1942 Hitler ordered a

For Motherland, honor, and freedom! Soviet posters during World War II urged citizens to support the "Great Patriotic War." What features of this poster might have inspired popular support for the war effort?

major offensive in southern Russia to seize Soviet oil wells in the Caucasus region. But this advance stretched German supply lines dangerously thin.

Japan at its imperial zenith. War engulfed Southeast Asia and the Pacific in late 1941, when Japan nearly simultaneously attacked Hong Kong, Malaya, Singapore, Indonesia, the Philippines, and the American naval base at Pearl Harbor in Hawaii. Germany's spectacular successes in western Europe gave Japan a golden opportunity to move against the French, Dutch, and British colonies in Southeast Asia, territories that offered rich resources in oil, rubber, tin, rice, and other critical commodities. Leaders in Tokyo proclaimed that these territories were now part of the Greater East Asia Co-Prosperity Sphere, an economic and political bloc whose conquered populations would presumably work with Japanese overlords in a spirit of Asian brotherhood. Japan's wartime needs for resources and labor, however, meant that harsh repression quickly eclipsed all schemes for "co-prosperity."

The Japanese strategy for unqualified victory assumed a free hand in both China and Southeast Asia. That meant preventing the United States from intervening. Tojo Hideki, the Japanese prime minister, assessed the situation in 1941: "Two years from now we will have no petroleum for military use; ships will stop moving. . . . I fear that we would become a third-class nation after two or three years if we merely sat tight."[13] The U.S. government balked at war with Japan while its own naval buildup was in progress, but in July 1941 President Franklin D. Roosevelt imposed an **embargo** on trade in oil and other strategic commodities. Consequently, Tokyo resolved to attack Pearl Harbor from the air, knocking the American Pacific fleet out of action long enough to secure Southeast Asia, including the American-ruled Philippines.

> **embargo** A legal restriction or prohibition imposed on trade.

In the first six months after Pearl Harbor, Japan's multiple amphibious and air assaults succeeded spectacularly. About 130,000 British, Australian, and Indian troops surrendered in Hong Kong, Malaya, and Singapore. In Indonesia, Dutch resistance collapsed quickly, and thereafter the archipelago's oil and rubber flowed exclusively to Japan's war industries. The U.S. public overwhelmingly supported Roosevelt's mobilization for war, even though damage to the Pacific Fleet prevented a quick military response. In support of his Asian ally, Hitler ordered that war be declared on the United States, which ensured that in due course the United States would enter the European conflict alongside Britain. Winston Churchill later reminisced that when the United States went to war with Germany, he "went to bed and slept the sleep of the saved and thankful."[14]

Italy's early setbacks. Mussolini, Hitler's ally, declared war on Britain and France when he was convinced the Nazis had western Europe in hand. As the Battle of Britain raged, he launched his own offensive campaigns, attacking Greece through Albania and western Egypt through Libya. His generals botched both campaigns, however, and had to fall back. Italy also quickly lost its Ethiopian colony. In early 1941 a coalition of Ethiopian fighters, units from British African colonies, Congolese troops, and both black and white South Africans drove the Italian army out of Ethiopia, Eritrea, and Somaliland. Emperor Haile Selassie returned to his throne after an exile of less than seven years.

The Years of Counteroffensive, 1942–1945

Both Germany and Japan understood that a prolonged war would pit them against states having greater long-term access to global resources. The Soviet Union had to be destroyed, Britain humbled, and the United States persuaded to let Germany and Japan have their regional empires without a fight. After three violent years, however, the Axis achieved none of those objectives.

Hitler announced a "New Order" for Europe, which some interpreted as a plan for shared economic development. But he had no thought, as it turned out, of a "family of nations" under German leadership. Nazi officers proceeded ruthlessly to extract Europe's resources and labor to support the fighting elsewhere. Any expectation that Nazi rule might at least mean political calm and economic reconstruction dissipated rapidly. Japanese forces similarly squandered opportunities for good will in Southeast Asia, killing or imprisoning large numbers of civilians and cruelly exploiting labor, in other words, behaving worse than the European colonial rulers they had replaced.

Hitler's failure to knock the Soviet Union quickly out of the war also allowed Stalin time to mobilize the labor and resources of the Russian heartland. The Red Army and millions of workers moved whole industrial plants eastward by truck and rail to locations in Inner Eurasia that German bombers could not reach. Stalin successfully rallied the population to fight a national war, though he was no less authoritarian than Hitler. Stalin tapped Russia's deep interior for millions of draftees, including gulag prisoners herded to the front as cannon fodder. The German army simply could not kill Russian conscripts nearly as fast as they were marched to the battle lines.

Stalin scorned capitalist democracy as much as Churchill and Roosevelt disliked communism, but the three leaders transcended their deep suspicions to form a "Grand Alliance" against the common aggressor. From 1942 the United States channeled huge shipments of supplies to the Red Army, mostly through northern Russian ports or Iran, which British and Russian forces jointly occupied in mid-1941. Fourteen states joined the Allied coalition early on, nine of them, including Belgium, Poland, and the Netherlands, represented by governments-in-exile. In short, Germany and Japan faced a growing coalition of enemies (see Map 26.2).

THE YEARS OF AXIS VICTORY	
1939	Nazi–Soviet nonaggression pact. German invasion of Poland.
1940	German conquest of continental western Europe. Aerial bombing of Britain.
1941	German invasion of the Soviet Union. Japanese expansion in Southeast Asia and the Pacific; attack on Pearl Harbor. Failed Italian campaigns.

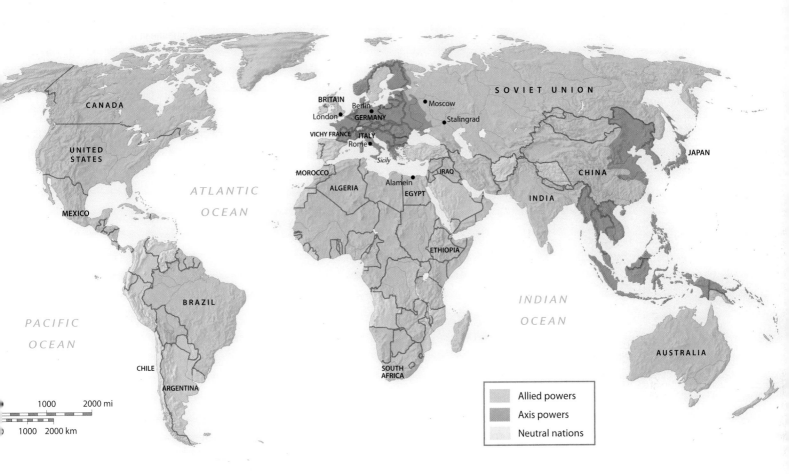

MAP 26.2 Allied and Axis states, mid-1943.

Describe the changes in territory claimed by the Axis states from early 1941 (Map 26.1) to mid-1943. Why do you think there were so few neutral states by this point in the war?

A war running on oil. The Allies moved into Iran (despite the anger of Iranian nationalists) partly to protect British-controlled oil fields there. In fact, the search for fuel energy illustrates the widening resource gap between the Allies and the Axis as the conflict dragged on. Factories, ships, tanks, and airplanes consumed colossal amounts of fossil fuel. Far more than World War I, this was a war of internal combustion engines. The United States had abundant coal and oil reserves for making numerous hydrocarbon products, including synthetic rubber. U.S. oil companies laid the Big Inch and the Little Big Inch, two pipelines that by the summer of 1943 pumped crude and refined petroleum overland from Texas to East Coast ports. Those projects reduced dependence on oil tankers, which were vulnerable to U-boat attacks. British companies rapidly expanded oil production in the Middle East. In Iraq, which devolved from a British-ruled mandate to a sovereign constitutional monarchy in 1932, pro-German nationalists seized power in April 1941. British and Indian troops, however, immediately toppled this regime and kept the Iraqi fields pumping oil to the Allies.

The oil problems of the Axis powers went from bad to worse as the war stretched on. The Wehrmacht thirsted for fuel, but Germany had almost no domestic oil. The oil fields of Romania, a Nazi client state, became the army's main source of crude. In mid-1943, however, Allied planes started bombing Romanian refineries, and the German advance in Russia lost its momentum well short of the Caucasus petroleum reserves. Japan was also an oil-poor country. It captured the wells and refineries of Indonesia, but from 1944 Allied naval attacks increasingly disrupted the long tanker routes to Japanese ports.

The turning tide of battle. Between mid-1942 and June 1944, when the Allies invaded France, the balance of fire power gradually shifted. New American aircraft carriers and battle cruisers regrouped in the central Pacific. U.S. and Japanese carrier-based planes fought their first major engagement in the Coral Sea northeast of Australia in April 1942. At the Battle of Midway the following month, an American fleet stopped Japan's Pacific advance, destroying four carriers. From that point, Japanese commanders had to shift to defending the huge Pacific perimeter they had secured only months earlier. Ferocious fighting for control of one island after another continued for more than three years.

British soldiers guarding an oil pipeline in Palestine, 1941. This pipeline brought oil from Iraq to the port of Haifa on Palestine's Mediterranean coast. Why was Haifa a port of great strategic importance during World War II?

North Africa was a theater of war from 1940 until mid-1943. After the fall of France, the entire southern shore of the Mediterranean west of Egypt became Axis territory. Italy ruled Libya, and pro-Vichy officials took charge of the French colonial governments in Tunisia, Algeria, and Morocco. Early in 1941 a German army under the command of General Erwin Rommel arrived in North Africa determined to overrun both Egypt and the Middle Eastern oil fields that lay beyond. Egypt had become a constitutional monarchy in 1922 following four decades of British rule, but Britain nevertheless retained rights to garrison the Suez Canal Zone. Consequently, British, Australian, and New Zealander troops poured into the country. Seesaw battles raged in the Libyan and western Egyptian deserts for nearly two years. But after victory at Alamein in October 1942, the Allies took the offensive, and fuel-starved Axis forces retreated to Tunisia. The following month, American, British, and Free French armies landed in Morocco and Algeria, removed the Vichy governments, and pushed eastward. Fighting in North Africa ended in May 1943, when a quarter-million Axis troops surrendered in northern Tunisia. From there, Allied divisions organized an invasion of Italy.

Just as the North African war wound down, the Red Army halted the German advance into Russia. In the deep winter of 1942–1943, more than two million German and Russian combatants clashed for control of the city of Stalingrad, an industrial and communication center that controlled the flow of oil from the Caucasus to the Russian heartland. The German Sixth Army took most of the city in November 1942 but had to rely on long supply lines from the west. The invaders suffered both body-numbing cold and vicious hand-to hand combat in the bombed-out city center. "My hands are done for," a German soldier wrote. "The little finger of my left hand is missing and—what's even worse—the three middle fingers of my right one are frozen. . . . The best thing I can do with the little finger is to shoot with it."[15] Russian tank and infantry forces under General Georgi Zhukov gradually massed around the city, finally surrounding the German army and, in February 1943, forcing its surrender. The Red Army prevailed at the cost of about 110,000 dead, wounded, missing, or captured and 40,000 civilian lives. Axis casualties may have exceeded 800,000.

Stalingrad turned out to be the eastern limit of the Nazi empire, which after that defeat had no hope of capturing the Caucasus oil fields. Fighting shifted into central Russia, but at Kursk in July, the Russians smashed a German offensive in the biggest tank battle in world history, throwing the invaders permanently on the defensive. That same month an Allied army crossed the hundred-mile-wide strait between Tunisia and Sicily, launching the liberation of Italy. These gains also heartened partisan resistance movements throughout Nazi-ruled Europe. In Yugoslavia, for example, the communist leader Tito organized a guerrilla army to strike back at the German occupiers. By 1944 his commanders controlled much of the country.

China's three-cornered war. The people of China fought a civil war and a national liberation struggle simultaneously. Between 1937 and 1939 the Japanese seized most of the

Red Army soldiers marching victoriously after the Battle of Stalingrad. Soviet forces stopped German eastward expansion with this victory. What elements of this photograph from February 1943 suggest a celebration? What elements document the high price the Soviets paid for victory?

cities, industries, and transport networks of eastern China. Jiang Jieshi moved the nationalist army and government deep into the interior, safe for the time being from Japanese land forces. The Allies could help the nationalists only by airborne deliveries of arms, materiel, and advisors over the Himalayan "hump" from India. Nationalist leaders, however, also made problems for themselves. They allied with landlords to exploit peasants, bought and sold army conscripts as if they were slaves, and winked at clandestine trade with the Japanese.

Meanwhile, communist forces under the leadership of Mao Zedong fought Japan from their own strongholds. In 1927 Jiang had launched a campaign to eradicate the Chinese Communist Party and nearly succeeded (see Chapter 25). But in 1934–1935 Mao Zedong led about twenty thousand soldiers on a six-thousand-mile journey, a legendary trek known as the Long March, from southeastern China to a safe base in the northwest. Mao had taken part in founding the Chinese Communist Party in 1921, but in contrast to most of his comrades, he abandoned urban worker organization in order to mobilize peasants for revolution. Recasting Marxist-Leninist teaching, he argued that communist cadres should both lead and learn from hardworking peasants, not just the city proletariat. In 1927 he wrote: "If we allot ten points to the accomplishments of the democratic revolution, then the achievements of the urban dwellers and the military units rate only three points,

while the remaining seven points should go to the peasants in their rural revolution. . . . There must be a revolutionary tidal wave in the countryside."[16] Mao and his lieutenants proved much more effective than the nationalists in redistributing land, building schools, and opening leadership positions to women. They also outmatched the nationalists in mustering peasants to fight the Japanese.

Indeed, World War II became a three-way struggle in which nationalists, communists, and Japanese all fought each other. In 1941 Jiang ordered an attack on a communist army, and after that, cooperation between these two sides collapsed. Much to the annoyance of Allied advisors, Jiang kept his best-trained divisions from fighting the Japanese, expecting that the communists would in the longer run prove the greater threat. A 1944 intelligence memo reported Jiang as saying: "You Americans are going to beat the Japanese some day. . . . On the other hand, if I let Mao Zedong push his propaganda across Free China, we run the risk—and so do you Americans—of winning for nothing."[17] For their part, communist partisans seized control of extensive rural areas, which the Japanese could not effectively garrison for lack of personnel. In fact, Chinese nationalists and communists together tied down about 40 percent of the entire Japanese army.

The Axis empires under siege. From the spring of 1943 to late summer 1945, the Allied powers ground down and finally terminated the Axis empires. Italy's fascist regime was the first to go. By the time the Allies invaded Sicily in mid-1943, the great majority of Italians wanted out of the war. But because Hitler sent troops into Italy, combat continued there for another two years. Allied forces fought their way to Rome, then toward the Alps. In April 1945 Italian partisans captured Mussolini and executed him.

In the sea and air war, the Allies gradually gained supremacy. In the North Atlantic, German U-boat attacks diminished early in 1943, thwarted by a number of innovations in maritime warfare. Radar detected enemy craft on the surface, sonar used sound waves to find submarines, and electrical HF/DF equipment, known colloquially as "huff-duff," was used to pinpoint the source of U-boat radio transmissions. Allied aircraft operating mainly from England began bombing Germany on a large scale in the spring of 1942, not only to destroy material targets but also to terrorize and demoralize the enemy population, just as the Luftwaffe had done over Britain. German airplane factories could not keep pace with losses to their own squadrons, and by April 1944 the Allies had full air superiority.

From the summer of 1943, the Red Army advanced westward toward Germany in a series of victorious surges. In the west, Allied commanders waited until they had amassed a colossal armada in southern England before launching an amphibious invasion of France, which took place on June 6, 1944. The landing and the ensuing Battle of Normandy between June and late August cost both sides approximately

THE YEARS OF COUNTEROFFENSIVE	
1942	U.S. entry into war. Battle of Midway in the Pacific.
1943	Allies win North Africa, invade Italy. Soviet victory in Battle of Stalingrad; westward advance of Red Army.
1944	Allied victory in Battle of Normandy. Liberation of Paris. Allies stop German advance in the Ardennes Forest, Belgium.
1945	Battle of Iwo Jima in the Pacific. Execution of Mussolini. Churchill, Roosevelt, and Stalin meet at Yalta in the Soviet Union. Germany surrenders. Allies liberate the Philippines from the Japanese. Atomic bombing of Hiroshima and Nagasaki. Japan surrenders.

425,000 dead, wounded, and missing. Nevertheless, the Allies liberated Paris on August 25. The drive into western Germany, however, took nearly another year. Consequently, Russian forces had time to penetrate most of Nazi-ruled central Europe well ahead of American or British divisions. The last big air assaults on Germany took place in the winter of 1945. Finding that strategic bombing of German military and industrial targets failed to do adequate damage, the U.S. and British air forces turned to carpet bombing of several major German cities. These attacks supported the Soviet advance, and by April the Red Army had Berlin surrounded. Hitler committed suicide in his Berlin bunker on April 30, and a week later the German high command surrendered, ending the Third Reich twelve years after its founding.

In Asia, Allied submarines wreaked havoc on Japanese shipping throughout 1944. By the end of the year, Japan's petroleum supplies were running out. Beginning in June, newly developed B-29 long-range bombers attacked Japan's industrial and population centers. In October, U.S. forces, aided by local guerrillas, started the grueling campaign to take back the Philippines. As the war in Europe drew to an end, Allied forces blockaded Japan's sea routes and dropped thousands of incendiary bombs on Tokyo and other cities. When the Japanese government still refused to negotiate peace terms, Harry S. Truman (in office, 1945–1953), who became president in April 1945 on the death of Roosevelt, ordered an atomic bomb attack, first on Hiroshima on August 6 and another on Nagasaki three days later. On August 15, Emperor Hirohito, contradicting the wishes of his most diehard commanders, ordered Japan's surrender, thereby preempting the planned Allied invasion of the islands.

A mother adjusts her son's bandages in Hiroshima, October 1945. Both mother and son were injured in the atomic bomb blast. They are lying on the floor of a bank building that was converted to a makeshift hospital. The extensive damage to buildings complicated efforts to tend to survivors, many of whose wounds proved fatal. Why did images such as this one especially shock viewers around the world, even though civilian casualties were common throughout the war?

The Second Total War

The twentieth century's second great conflict mobilized populations for total war on an even larger scale than the first one. Central governments organized and regulated society and economy more rigorously. Opposing states rained many more tons of bombs and shells down on one another to destroy infrastructure and demoralize civilians. And the war provoked greater extremes of repression, persecution, and brutality than any earlier struggle in history. In World War I, military deaths totaled 8 to 10 million, but in World War II the total was 22 to 25 million.

The continuing growth of state power. Many governments accrued more power between 1930 and 1945 as leaders endeavored first to pull national economies out of depression and second to fight another global war. Germany, Italy, Japan, and Russia had authoritarian governments, which regulated national economies however they liked without much question. The Nazi regime created numerous state-owned manufacturing and financial enterprises. To control inflation it routinely intervened in the market to regulate prices and wages, even by the crudest means. According to Hitler, "Inflation is lack of discipline. . . . I'll see to it that prices remain stable. That's what my storm troopers are for. Woe to those who raise prices. . . . You'll see."[18]

On the Allied side the British government took charge of industrial production and agriculture, gave scientists and engineers deadlines for new military inventions, told people to plant "victory gardens," and put the entire population on rations. In the United States, full mobilization got under way after Pearl Harbor. Roosevelt set up the War Production Board and numerous other public agencies, the federal payroll swelled, and most Americans started paying income taxes for the first time. Government and business cooperated extensively, market forces continued to operate, and companies profited.

The war affected state attitudes toward human rights differently depending on the country. Germany, Italy, and Japan sharply curtailed private freedoms several years before the war, and Stalin consistently ignored them. In Britain and the United States, most democratic institutions continued to function, though the governments restricted the press and other forms of public expression in the interest of unity and security. The Roosevelt administration blatantly discriminated against Japanese Americans shortly after Pearl Harbor by ordering them to leave their homes in the western states for detention camps in remote places, arguing that these people, about 110,000 men, women, and children, might sympathize with the enemy. The government manifestly violated civil rights laws, pandered to anti-Asian racist sentiment, and failed to restore lost property and businesses to the detainees after the war.

Women mobilized. In all warring states, armies occupied only the top level of a sprawling pyramid of civilian and auxiliary support. In every country, the mass conscription, disablement, and deaths of adult men meant that everyone else, especially women, had to accept wartime duties. Millions of British and American women took wage and volunteer jobs or enlisted in the military. More than two million women joined the British wartime labor force; another million signed on for military or civilian defense service. In the United States the Roosevelt administration urged women to go to work as a patriotic duty, though they consistently received lower wages than men for comparable jobs. By 1944 the U.S. labor force included about nineteen million women, many of them working to make tanks, ships, airplanes, and uniforms. Rosie the Riveter emblemized national fortitude and sacrifice in image and song:

> All the day long,
> Whether rain or shine,
> She's a part of the assembly line.
> She's making history,
> Working for victory,
> Rosie the Riveter.
> Keeps a sharp lookout for sabotage,
> Sitting up there on the fuselage.

The German, Italian, and Japanese regimes were slow to send more women into wage work owing to ultranationalist ideology that idealized motherhood and family duty as anchors of the nation. Nazi leaders preferred to exploit low-paid foreign conscripts, prisoners of war (POWs), or slaves to meet German industrial demands, though many of those workers were in fact women. Japanese officials urged women to stay home and reproduce at a faster rate, though females eventually had to make up for extreme industrial labor shortages. In the Soviet Union, by contrast, the state mobilized women for war work in great numbers, partly because Communist Party ideology extolled equal opportunities for members of the proletariat, whether male or female. By 1943, women comprised more than 55 percent of the Russian industrial workforce.

Social conventions kept women out of uniformed combat in most of the belligerent states except for Russia. In Japan, women organized and managed thousands of "neighborhood associations," which distributed food, sold war bonds, and collected taxes. In the United States, about 350,000 women joined the armed services, mainly in the Women's Army Corps (WAC) and the Navy's WAVES. Thousands of military nurses served in war theaters, and women also flew new combat aircraft from U.S. factories to airfields in Britain. In countries under Nazi or Japanese occupation, women played vital roles in local resistance movements as fighters, nurses, couriers, and spies. In the Soviet Union, several hundred thousand women served at the war front as infantry, fighter pilots, snipers, and tank drivers.

If the war emancipated women in some respects, it caused terrible suffering for millions more. Prostitution, sometimes voluntary but often coerced, flourished around military bases of all countries. The Japanese conscripted about 200,000 Korean, Chinese, and Filipino girls and

Individuals MATTER

Olga Lisikova: Soviet Combat Pilot

Combat pilot Olga Lisikova

In October 1941 the Soviet Union became the first country in the world to allow women pilots to fly in combat. By the end of the war approximately 12 percent of Soviet pilots were women. The air force formed three all-female regiments, which flew a combined thirty thousand war missions. Women were also attached to mixed-sex regiments and flew alongside men.

Olga Lisikova distinguished herself as the only woman pilot in an otherwise all-male division. Trained in the late 1930s, she flew for Aeroflot, the civil aviation agency. During the 1939–1940 war between the Soviet Union and Finland, she transported injured soldiers to medical facilities, continuing to fly into her eighth month of pregnancy. When her daughter was less than a year old, Germany invaded the Soviet Union. Lisikova and her husband, also a pilot, left their child with a relative and reported for military service. She performed medical evacuations and transported cargo, in addition to ferrying officials around the country.

On one occasion in August 1941, Lisikova was flying two severely wounded soldiers to a hospital, when a German fighter plane spotted her:

When I saw that a German fighter was on my tail, I still thought that he would see the red crosses and leave me alone. . . . But the fighter closed up on me. I had several seconds before my life would end. . . . In such extreme circumstances, a person's brain works in an unusual manner: I saw an overhang, and I literally thrust my airplane under this overhang. The burst that was launched by the fighter passed over my aircraft and cut into the other bank of the [Msta] river. . . . In these places it flowed between steep banks. I pressed the stick and flew lower and lower, flying directly over the water, darting back and forth with the river. . . . Then I came upon an airfield—Verebye, and set my aircraft down without an approach. When my aircraft stopped, I looked around. People were running up to me from all sides, shouting something and waving. I did not understand. I climbed down from the cabin, looked around, and saw that the Messerschmitt [German fighter] was burning. It had dived on my airplane and began to pull out, but the aircraft had bottomed out.[19]

Following this episode, the Soviet government awarded Lisikova the Order of the Red Banner for heroism in combat.

Surrounded by male pilots, Lisikova tried to ensure that her sex would never be held against her. Reflecting on her war service many decades later, she remembered that her division commander had warned that "where the failure of a male pilot could pass unnoticed, mine would always be under surveillance." Consequently, she resolved that "I would do everything better than the men."[20] She flew 280 combat missions during the war, eventually earning a spot in the Intelligence Directorate of the General Staff of the Red Army. In that assignment, she flew paratroopers behind enemy lines and also carried out supply drops. Like most other female pilots in the Soviet military, however, her service ended not long after the war's conclusion. She flew her last mission in 1946.

Thinking Critically

What factors do you think motivated the Soviet Union to recruit women for air combat missions in World War II, when most of the countries at war barred women from this role?

---

women to prostitute themselves as "comfort women" to male soldiers. The Germans put about ten thousand French women in concentration camps on charges of resistance activity. Only about 5 percent of them returned home. The Nazis also targeted Jewish, Slavic, and other "undesirable" women of reproductive age for imprisonment or execution on the grounds that if they married or had sex with Germans, they would produce racially contaminated children.

Genocidal war. If the majority of civilians killed in the war died randomly, from bombs, shells, diseases, or lack of food, many millions were deliberately murdered. Ethnic cleansing, our contemporary term for the mass killing or expulsion of one group by another, has accompanied wars and social conflicts for many centuries. In World War II, however, premeditated brutality reached epic proportion. Systematic killing on a large scale included the Japanese army's butchery of civilians in Nanjing, China, in 1938; Stalin's deadly deportation of non-Russian ethnic groups before and during the war; and the Croatian fascist party's murder of more than 330,000 Orthodox Christian Serbs.

The Nazis, however, elevated methodical murder of particular classes of people to the level of a ghastly industrial enterprise. Implementing Hitler's grand plan to dispose of all who threatened Aryan racial destiny, the Third Reich systematically killed approximately six million Jews and about an equal number of Poles, Russians, Ukrainians, Roma, gays, and the physically or mentally disabled. During the first six weeks of the invasion of Poland, SS and other Nazi units shot or hanged more than sixteen thousand people, about five thousand of them Jews.

genocide The premeditated, purposeful killing of large numbers of members of a particular national, racial, ethnic, or religious group.

By 1942 the Nazi state marked Jews and Roma for **genocide,** while murdering Slavs, POWs, and other prisoners more haphazardly or keeping them barely alive for forced labor. To carry out their Final Solution of the "Jewish problem," Nazi officials built new concentration camps and refitted existing ones, including Auschwitz, Treblinka, Belzec, Sobibor, and Bergen-Belsen. At some of these camps, prison guards killed men, women, and children in large gas chambers, then either buried the corpses or cremated them in ovens. Nazi officials puzzled over ways to make this complicated task run more efficiently. At the Treblinka extermination center in Poland, for example, camp technicians introduced "time and motion" innovations to move large numbers of the condemned from train arrival platform to gas chamber in less than forty-five minutes.[21] The language of extermination became bureaucratic and abstract. Victims were "items for transportation" to be "processed," "resettled," or given "special treatment." As the Wehrmacht began to retreat, Nazi officers worked even more zealously to round up Jews and other disposable persons from conquered territories. The Nazis killed something like 65 percent of Europe's Jews before Germany surrendered, the genocidal machinery grinding to a halt only when Allied troops approached the death camps and the staffs fled.

The spectrum of human response to the Holocaust ranged from enthusiastic participation to heroic resistance. Many captives walked into the gas chambers as they were told. But others incited riots, prison outbreaks, and insurrections, for example, the furious but hopeless uprising of the Warsaw ghetto population in April 1943. In Germany, millions of citizens blandly accepted the government's violent anti-Semitism, but others hid Jews throughout the war. Fascist governments in Romania and Hungary organized their own mass killings of Jews, but in Bulgaria more than 80 percent of the Jewish community survived because King Boris III, though allied with Germany, stopped cooperating with Nazi deportation. The documentary evidence shows that the British and American governments responded unhurriedly to a growing stream of intelligence information about Nazi death camps. Only when the Allies came face to face with emaciated inmates and piles of corpses did they proclaim the extent of the horror.

The dimensions of death. World War II lasted about a year and a half longer than World War I, and it killed twice as many people partly because of the power of its weaponry—automatic rifles, long-range bombers, explosive rockets, and atomic bombs. Together, combat, disease, hunger, and organized murder claimed about 2.6 percent of the 1940 global population of around 2.27 billion. In the Soviet Union, 25 million people died, about two-thirds of them civilians. In early 1945 the U.S. and British air forces, having found that strategic bombing of German military and industrial targets did insufficient damage, launched carpet bombing raids on several German cities. The firebombing of Dresden flattened the city center and killed between 120,000 and 150,000 people, mostly civilians. The nuclear attacks on Hiroshima and Nagasaki killed about 220,000. War conditions combined with poor harvests could also set

Survivors of the Buchenwald concentration camp. Emaciated slaves greeted U.S. troops who entered this camp in central Germany in April 1945. Many other prisoners died of malnutrition or starvation during the war. Notice how little bunk space each prisoner had. Some are using metal food bowls as pillows. How do you think images like this one affected the postwar settlement?

off famine. In India, for example, two million people died in Bengal in 1943 because the Japanese invasion of neighboring Burma cut off rice imports. Nevertheless, British authorities refused to divert food intended for big cities or armies. As in the case of World War I, however, massive war deaths did not produce a net global population decline because average life expectancies continued to rise (excepting frightful mortality in particular war-torn places) along with birth rates. Between 1940 and 1950, world population grew by around 11 percent.

The War beyond the Theaters of War

Before the war ended, fifty-one countries or governments-in-exile joined the Allies, though significant fighting took place in only eighteen countries. In other words, the conflict pulled in many states, not because they were attacked or contributed troops, but because the war seriously affected their political and economic interests. Profoundly disrupting the world economy and interstate relations, the war left no society completely untouched.

Latin America and the war. Except for naval battles in the western Atlantic, fighting remained as far from Latin America as it did from the United States. Nevertheless, every Latin American state joined the Allies before the struggle ended. Brazil sent an infantry force to Italy, and Mexico contributed a Pacific fighter squadron. Some countries, Argentina and Chile, for example, entered the war near its end to ensure good relations with the victorious United States and to qualify for charter membership in the United Nations.

In general, World War II served Latin American economies well. The Great Depression pushed many states to intervene more forcefully in economic affairs, and this trend continued during the war. Prices for exports rose, the United States having a huge wartime need for Latin American food and minerals. Brazilian rubber, Cuban sugar, and Venezuelan and Mexican oil were all immensely important to the Allied war effort. Latin American industries also profited by expanding manufacturing to help meet the rising middle-class demand for radios, refrigerators, and other trappings of modern urban life. This wartime growth, however, benefited mainly the middle and wealthy classes.

Colonized peoples and the war. The populations of African and Asian dependencies were invariably drawn into the conflict by their colonial masters. British colonies made vital contributions of resources, labor, and fighting skill to the struggle against the Axis. After the Germans marched into Paris, much of the French overseas empire, including North and West Africa, fell under the control of the Vichy collaborationist regime for at least part of the war. In France's central African colonies, by contrast, administrators led by Félix Éboué, the governor of Chad and a man of African descent from French Guiana in South America, declared their loyalty to the Free French. Consequently, from late 1940, Charles de Gaulle had not only an office in London but also a territorial base in Brazzaville in the French Congo. Belgium fell to the Nazis, but its gigantic Congo colony remained out of Axis reach. Congolese farmers and miners supplied the Allies with strategic materials, including uranium that American scientists used to build the atomic bomb.

Soldiers from Allied colonies fought in all the major theaters of war. Thousands of Indians put on uniforms to defend South Asia against a potential Japanese invasion through Burma. Thousands more fought under British command in the Middle East and Southeast Asia, and for the first time Indian officers were permitted to rise to high ranks. After the Allies invaded North Africa, fighters from French-ruled Morocco, Algeria, and Tunisia took part in the campaign to liberate Italy and Germany. At times, forces under Free French command were more than 50 percent African.

Even before Southeast Asians realized the fraudulence of Japan's "co-prosperity sphere," they began to organize resistance. In Malaya, communists and other insurgents, principally from the large Chinese minority, organized rural bases for launching guerrilla attacks against the occupiers. Filipinos set up similar operations in mountain forests. In Vietnam the nationalist leader Ho Chi Minh led the communist Viet Minh's resistance against both the Japanese and the French colonial government, which was under Vichy control. As Japanese power waned, Ho's forces seized much of northern and central Vietnam.

The War and the Global Environment

A hypothetical chart of global environmental change in the twentieth century would undoubtedly show sharp spikes during the two great wars. In those years, humans exploited, manipulated, and damaged the biosphere at an especially frenzied pace in order to achieve urgent military and economic objectives. Both the warring states and the countries they traded with accelerated economic production, thereby consuming global resources and generating waste at unprecedented levels.

Combat, including aerial bombardment, caused enormous environmental harm, if only in the short term. In places of intense fighting, such as the western Soviet Union or certain Pacific islands, flora, fauna, and soils were devastated, though they tended to recover gradually after the armies went away. Explosive and incendiary bombs nearly leveled cities like Dresden, Hamburg, Berlin, Warsaw, and Tokyo, but rebuilding commenced soon after the war. In China, nationalist forces tried to slow the Japanese advance by dynamiting levees on the Yellow River, an act of sabotage that drowned hundreds of thousands of Chinese and inundated millions of acres of farm land. Nevertheless, the dikes were rebuilt shortly after 1945.

Not all military destruction, however, was so easily set right. DDT, a chemical insecticide developed in the late 1930s, saved soldiers from typhus, malaria, and other diseases in

UNDER EBOUE, FIGHTING FRENCH AFRICA HAS BECOME AN IMPORTANT SOURCE OF MANPOWER FOR THE UNITED NATIONS.

FIGHTING FRENCH AFRICA

HIS COURAGEOUS ACTION IN CHAD PROVINCE PREVENTED A JUNCTION BETWEEN GENERAL GRAZIANI AND HIS LIBYAN ARMY, AND THE DUKE OF AOSTA'S FASCIST ARMY IN ETHIOPIA.

Felix Eboué
GOVERNOR GENERAL FIGHTING FRENCH AFRICA
SCHOLAR STATESMAN SOLDIER —

THE FACT THAT HIS DECISION ENDANGERED THE LIVES OF HIS THREE SONS AND DAUGHTER IN OCCUPIED FRANCE DID NOT DETER HIM FROM CASTING HIS LOT WITH THE UNITED NATIONS

Alston for OWI

Governor Félix Eboué and the war effort in Africa. This poster by Harlem-based artist Charles Alston chronicles Eboué's contributions to the Allies in French Equatorial Africa during and after World War II. What aspects of Eboué's career did Alston choose to emphasize? What might account for those choices?

both Europe and the South Pacific. This compound, however, also permeated soils and poisoned marine and bird life, a fact not well understood until the 1960s. Toxic nuclear radiation continued to kill Japanese long after the war ended, about fifty thousand of them by 1975.

The war forced the belligerent states to initiate agricultural and industrial crash programs to feed and supply their military services. Many countries extended production of commercial food and fiber crops to steep hillsides, which in regions such as tropical Southeast Asia worsened soil erosion. More intensive farming, plus voracious consumption of timber for wartime construction, also accelerated the rate of global deforestation. In Britain the war used up about half

the country's remaining forests.[22] The Germans clear-cut huge areas of Poland and Norway to get lumber. In Japan, where woodland conservation had long been government policy, the war compelled destruction of forest stands that in some cases had been nurtured for centuries. When the conflict ended, pressure on forests worldwide only increased because so much rebuilding had to be done.

Ironically, warfare eased environmental degradation in some circumstances. All the combatant states introduced measures to conserve fuel, electricity, and food. Atlantic fish stocks recovered significantly during the war because commercial fishing boats had to stay in port. After the Allies bombed places like the Ruhr Valley and the Berlin region,

Propaganda for Wartime Conservation

During World War II, governments on both sides of the conflict rallied their citizens by commissioning propaganda posters. These posters, which typically went on display in public spaces such as courthouses and post offices, broadcast a variety of messages. The German and Japanese governments put up posters to spread their ideology of racial superiority, depicting minority ethnic or religious groups as subhuman or sinister. American and British posters portrayed Japan and Germany as dire threats to democracy and freedom. Posters exhorted citizens to mobilize for victory by joining the army or taking on extra employment.

Posters, as well as movies, radio messages, and newspaper announcements, urged citizens to support wartime production and supply by conserving resources. By deferring purchases of cars or clothing and by consuming less meat or gasoline, citizens would speed factory production of tanks, jeeps, airplanes, ammunition, and uniforms. Wartime posters reminded citizens to grow "victory gardens" to free up food supplies for soldiers. The two posters shown here promote communal sharing and conserving of resources as acts of patriotic cooperation and vigilance. After the war ended, however, such broadsides soon disappeared, superseded, especially in the United States, by private advertisements urging consumers to buy more consumer products.

British wartime poster

U.S. wartime poster

Thinking Critically

What message do you think each poster intends to deliver? How do the posters use the figure of Hitler to make their point? What does "humble pie" mean in the text of the British poster? Why do you think that conservation posters like these disappeared right after the war? Would you characterize these posters as elements of a wartime environmental movement? Why or why not? Do the messages of these posters have relevance today? If so, how?

smoke-belching factories fell silent and skies cleared. After the war, however, the factories fired up again, and a new surge of global economic growth only sped human intervention in the workings of the biosphere.

In the Wake of War, 1945–1950

FOCUS What were major consequences of World War II, and how did global political and economic conditions change in the five years after the war?

Big wars cause all sorts of trouble even after they have ended. Populations are left displaced and wandering, economies and communication systems are shattered, food and fuel are in short supply, and social disorder threatens. States that were strong are suddenly weak; others bristle with new power. Because of want, insecurity, and cravings for revenge, killing continues. All of these things happened in the half-decade following World War II. Restabilizing and rebuilding the world presented an immense task. Indeed, many leaders feared that the world might quickly plunge back into deep economic depression. Nevertheless, governments, businesses, and charitable organizations immediately took up the tasks of reconstruction and revival.

The European colonial empires that had existed before the war could not, however, be put back the way they were. The global conflict created new conditions that made imperial systems dating back to the nineteenth century or earlier much more difficult to sustain. Consequently, between 1945 and 1950 the British, French, and Dutch empires shrank significantly, and ten new sovereign states appeared in Asia. Korea regained its independence from Japan, though it shortly split into two separate states. In China, communist forces drove the nationalist government to Taiwan and proclaimed a new Chinese people's republic.

Restoring Stability, Enforcing Justice

Victory celebrations took place against a backdrop of continuing misery and violence. Across Europe, partisans and angry citizens executed hundreds of Nazi collaborators, and they stripped women accused of sleeping with Axis soldiers and then shaved their heads. Reports of Poles killing Jews even after the Nazis had left helped persuade 200,000 Holocaust survivors to leave eastern Europe forever. In the heavy

combat zones, postwar food shortages left millions malnourished or dead. About two million Russians and Ukrainians died in 1946 because of bad harvests. In Poland, Czechoslovakia, and other eastern European countries, liberated subjects of the Third Reich expelled several million German residents, both long-established minorities and those who had settled during wartime to escape the Soviet army.

The Geneva Conventions, which were rules of war that sovereign states had been drawing up since the nineteenth century, provided the legal basis for prosecuting individuals for war crimes. The Allies convened an international military tribunal in the German city of Nuremberg in 1945 and a similar tribunal in Tokyo the following year. These

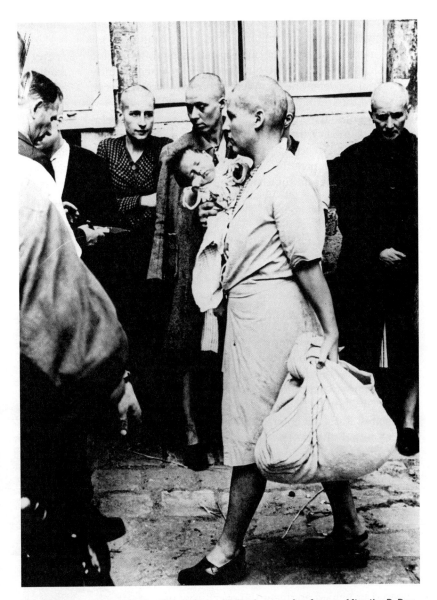

French women accused of collaborating with Nazi occupying forces. After the D-Day invasion and the liberation of French cities, Resistance partisans shaved the heads of women who socialized with German soldiers, had sexual relationships with them, or were suspected of passing information to the enemy. This photograph, taken in August 1944 in Chartres, shows women walking past jeering onlookers. The baby's father was a German. Why might citizens have shaved women's heads as a form of community punishment?

courts pronounced a few dozen Nazi or Japanese leaders guilty of crimes against humanity and hanged or imprisoned the convicted. But many more Axis officers and officials escaped or were never charged. To prevent highly skilled German scientists and engineers from falling into Soviet hands, the U.S. government office known as the Joint Intelligence Objectives Agency initiated a postwar program called Operation Paperclip to bring as many of them as possible to America to work. These individuals included many former members of the Nazi Party, including war criminals. The agency, however, deliberately doctored, disguised, or hid the biographies of many of these individuals and gave them American security clearances.

The war ended with American, British, and Soviet troops in control of different parts of Germany. Those states agreed to occupy three separate military zones, plus a fourth one for France. Berlin, the bombed-out German capital, lay inside the designated Soviet zone but was to be governed jointly by the four powers. The occupiers outlawed the Nazi Party, disbanded the German army, and arrested and interrogated thousands of Nazi officials, though some escaped by joining the stream of civilian refugees. After Japan surrendered, 300,000 mostly American troops fanned out across the Pacific islands to enforce the authority of the new occupation government under its supreme commander General Douglas MacArthur.

The Two New Empires

The pattern of global power changed drastically in the five years after the war. The German, Japanese, and Italian empires vanished, and the United States and the Soviet Union emerged as the big imperial winners. American global influence in some ways echoed the "informal empires" of Britain and France in the nineteenth century. The United States did not directly take charge of large foreign territories, except for its temporary occupations in Germany, Japan, and other former Axis states. Rather, it entered into accords and treaties to aid and defend friendly countries, and it rose to dominate the postwar international trade and financial system. It also projected armed might—a navy and air force that ranged around the world, a large concentration of troops in western Europe, and numerous foreign military bases. By the mid-1950s the United States had 450 bases in more than thirty-five countries. Within less than a decade of the war, the Central Intelligence Agency engineered or helped engineer the overthrow of elected governments in Iran (1953) and Guatemala (1954) as perceived threats to American political and corporate interests.

Despite Russia's immense wartime losses, Stalin drove the Soviet industrial economy to rapid postwar recovery. Like the United States,

Russia asserted influence abroad informally, though with particularly heavy-handed tactics in eastern Europe. Moscow made sure that friendly and cooperative Communist Party officials ruled the eastern third of Germany and, by 1948, Poland, Czechoslovakia, Hungary, Romania, Bulgaria, and Albania. (Stalin had absorbed the Baltic states of Estonia, Latvia, and Lithuania into the Soviet Union in 1940.) Finland, Yugoslavia, and Austria remained politically neutral, whereas Greece and Turkey eventually became allies of the United States. In Asia the Soviets established close, if sometimes rocky relations with the communist regimes that took control in China, North Korea, and Vietnam in the decade following the war. In the rest of the world the two new superpowers began to compete intensely for political and economic sway.

American power in action. The United States emerged from the war with much greater industrial capacity than any other country. It had abundant cheap energy, mammoth stores of foreign currency, and a banking system to which other countries owed billions. Even though at that point the country depended little on the rest of the world, the American public favored continued international engagement in much greater numbers than after World War I. Many Americans feared a replay of the catastrophic economic crisis that had fed Nazi success. If the wealthiest state in the world did little to assist the damaged economies of Europe and East Asia, social discontent might breed new versions of Hitler. The United States, internationalists argued, had much to gain by helping war-torn countries, both allies and foes, get back on the road to recovery. This would presumably strengthen

Delegates at the Bretton Woods conference, 1944. Representatives from all forty-four Allied nations signed international monetary and trade agreements intended to revive the global economy.

democratic and capitalist institutions. Most Americans also favored new international bodies that would terminate the era of protectionism and lackluster trade that had generally prevailed since 1914. The Atlantic Charter, which Roosevelt and Churchill had signed in August 1941, envisioned a postwar world in which all states would have "access, on equal terms, to the trade and to the raw materials of the world."[23]

In July 1944, less than a month after the Allied invasion of France, representatives from more than forty countries met in Bretton Woods, New Hampshire. There, they established the International Monetary Fund (IMF) and the International Bank for Reconstruction and Development (World Bank). They also formulated new rules and procedures designed to liberalize trade, prime the pump of capital investment in war-damaged countries, and stabilize the global currency exchange system.

The United States loomed over the Bretton Woods conference and the numerous international meetings that followed. In 1947 President Truman announced the Marshall Plan, named after George C. Marshall, the secretary of state, to flood Europe with reconstruction aid, eventually about $14 billion in direct grants. Truman contended that revival of international commerce and cooperation depended on Europe's robust recovery, including Germany's. Lavish aid would also presumably check the influence of Soviet-backed communist parties. For similar reasons, the United States awarded Japan an aid package of $500 million to rekindle its civilian economy.

The United Nations. The American vision of a world of sovereign states trading freely and committed to one another's security in the framework of a capitalist world economy included support of the United Nations organization. Founded just before the end of the war, this new club of states aimed to promote international cooperation in numerous spheres, including economic development and human rights. Unlike the League of Nations, its troubled predecessor, the UN Charter assigned peacekeeping responsibilities to a fifteen-member Security Council with power to deploy troops, if necessary, to resolve international conflicts before they got out of hand. The five permanent members of the council—the United States, the Soviet Union, Britain, France, and China (represented by the nationalist government)—retained the power to veto resolutions. In 1945 the world had high hopes that these five victorious allies would work together constructively to prevent new conflicts. Instead, the Soviet Union and the other four permanent members became immediately engaged in disputes and rivalries, even though numerous economic and cultural projects got under way.

Allies to adversaries: The early Cold War. After the war, one event after another aggravated relations between the United States and the Soviet Union. On both sides, every tactical military move, every initiative to make new allies, and every hard-line political announcement tended to compound the antagonism until it hardened into a permanent state of affairs, a **Cold War** that stopped short of any disastrous military clash.

Even before the war ended, American and Soviet leaders viewed world prospects through different geopolitical prisms. The United States and Britain agreed that Russia deserved special influence in postwar Eastern Europe considering that victory over Germany in 1945 depended on the Soviet advance to Berlin. They also knew that during the three years of fighting leading to the Allied landing at Normandy in June 1944, the Red Army had been responsible for more than 90 percent of Germany's military casualties. Shortly after the war, however, the Soviets took actions the Western powers regarded as uncooperative and intimidating. It made claims to special influence over Turkey. It took its time pulling troops out of Iran. It kept three million soldiers under arms compared to half that number in the U.S. services. Stalin positioned most of these troops between Russia and Western Europe. To him, this deployment had a compelling logic, considering that his country had been invaded from that direction just a few years earlier. When the Western European democracies looked east, however, they saw Soviet tank and infantry divisions facing them.

Moscow also saw U.S. political and economic influence growing in nearly every country in the world that Soviet troops did not actually occupy. They watched as pro-American politicians in France and Italy tried to subvert strong communist parties by denying them participation in governing cabinets. And they regarded the Bretton Woods plan for a new era of international capitalism as a threat to the Soviet socialist experiment. Stalin continued to strive for economic self-sufficiency apart from the global capitalist system. At the same time, the United States did nothing to negotiate compromises that might have led to greater Russian participation.

The two powers may indeed have come closer to violent confrontation in the immediate postwar years than at any later time. In 1946 Stalin proclaimed that armed conflict between communism and capitalism was inevitable. The following year President Truman announced that "it must be the policy of the United States to support free peoples who are resisting attempted subjugation by armed minorities or by outside pressures."[24] From this statement came the Truman Doctrine, a policy inspired by Secretary of State George Kennan to "contain" the Soviet Union within the zone of power it held at the end of the war. In the first test of this policy, Truman persuaded Congress to vote $400 million in economic and military assistance to Turkey, where Stalin wanted territorial concessions and military bases. In Greece, communist rebels who had led resistance against the German occupation continued their armed struggle against a postwar right-wing government. This regime, however, was pro-Western, and the United States gave it millions in aid to successfully suppress the communist insurgency. Stalin protested vigorously but did not intervene. Meanwhile, the Soviet Union

Cold War The state of antagonism, distrust, and rivalry that existed between the United States and the Soviet Union and their respective allies from the end of World War II to the late 1980s.

achieved important victories. Communist parties under Russian protection seized power in Poland, Hungary, and Czechoslovakia between 1945 and 1948, despite Stalin's promises to allow multiparty elections in all three countries.

Ground zero of the early Cold War was Germany. The Soviet Union could not agree with the United States, Britain, and France on a postwar plan to create a united Germany that would remain militarily harmless. By 1948 the three Western powers started to set up a new German administration and to rebuild industry in the two-thirds of the country they occupied, as well as in their sectors of Berlin, which was surrounded by the Soviet zone. Stalin feared a strong new German state in alliance with the United States, and in April 1948 he tried to obstruct this development by blockading land access to Berlin. American, British, and

French cargo pilots checked this move by dropping food and other supplies to the two million Berliners who did not live in the Soviet sector. This airlift continued for nearly a year, with planes arriving over the city at an average of three-minute intervals. Stalin condemned this operation, but both sides played out the crisis with restraint, and in May 1949 the Soviets withdrew the blockade.

Within a few months of the standoff, however, Germany was formally divided into two hostile states, the Federal Republic in the west and the Democratic Republic in the east (see Map 26.3). The Berlin blockade also impelled the United States to join with nine Western European countries and Canada to form the North Atlantic Treaty Organization (NATO), a military and political alliance to ensure the security of Western Europe. (In 1955, the Soviet Union

MAP 26.3 Central Europe, 1948.

The immediate post-World War II settlement divided Germany into four occupied zones, each administered by one of the victorious powers. Since Berlin lay entirely within the Soviet zone, why do you think the Soviets agreed to an American, French, and British military presence there?

and its Eastern European allies created the Warsaw Pact as a counteralliance.) Relations between the two sides entered an ice age of mutual suspicion and recrimination that never more than partially thawed during the following forty years.

World War II and the Challenge to Colonial Empires

National independence movements in most Asian and African colonies gained momentum in the postwar years for a number of reasons. First, colonial soldiers who had fought for the Allied cause in Europe or Asia often returned home to unemployment and almost always to continuing social discrimination. These veterans blamed colonial administrations for these conditions, and with good reason. Second, the European imperial powers wanted to keep their colonies, but they faced a dilemma. They had to address such huge rebuilding demands at home that they could afford neither to placate nationalist organizations with generous development aid nor mobilize enough armed force to try to eradicate them. Third, both the United States and the Soviet Union generally encouraged nationalist independence movements. Most Americans cared more about advancing U.S. commercial interests abroad than in shoring up old colonial systems that restricted trade with outsiders. The Russian leadership, declaring that Marxist-Leninist principles would not tolerate capitalist exploitation of conquered peoples, sided with nationalists—as long as they did not raise their heads in Russia's own empire.

Finally, the war effectively destroyed the intellectual and moral rationales for European colonial rule, based as they were on an ideology of innate biological and cultural differences between "civilized" and "uncivilized" peoples. Nazi genocidal horror exposed the folly of such theories of political domination. At the end of the war, these notions were a standing embarrassment to imperial states that called themselves democracies. Jawaharlal Nehru (1889–1964), the Indian nationalist leader, wrote in 1943: "Biologists tell us that racialism is a myth and there is no such thing as a master race. But we in India have known racialism in all its forms ever since the commencement of British rule. The whole ideology of this rule was that of the . . . Master race, and the structure of government was based upon it."[25]

New states and a new war in the Middle East. With German and Italian forces out of the Middle East and North Africa, Britain and France sought to reassert their influence in the region's affairs. The independent states of Iraq and Egypt held to a pro-British line after the war. So did Transjordan (later Jordan) after 1946, when Britain gave up its League of Nations Mandate to rule this desert monarchy. France aimed to preserve its economic and cultural clout in Syria and Lebanon while also agreeing to relinquish its mandates there.

Political circumstances in Palestine, the coastal land facing the eastern Mediterranean, were different from those in the rest of the Arabic-speaking world. Also a British-ruled mandate, Palestine had a mostly Arabic-speaking population, the majority Muslim and an important minority Christian. However, with the support of the international Zionist movement to create a national Jewish state, Jews began to migrate there in the late nineteenth century (see Chapter 25). About 300,000 arrived in the 1930s as Nazi persecutions worsened in Europe. By 1940 about 30 percent of Palestine's population of 1.53 million was Jewish.

Since World War I the British government had supported the idea of a Jewish "homeland" in Palestine but did almost nothing to help build national institutions through which all elements of the population might work together. Rather, Arab and Jewish political groups increasingly isolated themselves from each another, while acts of intercommunal violence proliferated. Wishing to muster Arab support for the Allies, Britain announced in 1939 that it had no policy to transform Palestine into a Jewish state. Rather, it scheduled the territory for independence in ten years, presumably with a politically dominant Arab majority.

The war suspended this plan for six years, but even before the Axis surrendered, the struggle for Palestine resumed. Under the leadership of David Ben-Gurion, Jews mobilized to drive out the British and proclaim a Jewish state. The Haganah, or Jewish defense force, launched an insurgency that included sabotage, assaults on British personnel, and, in collaboration with the Irgun and Stern Gang guerrilla organizations, staged terrorist attacks, including partial destruction of the King David Hotel in Jerusalem. World War II left Britain financially bankrupt and therefore incapable of forceful action in Palestine. Consequently, it invited the United Nations to find a solution. In November 1947 the UN General Assembly voted by a substantial majority, including the votes of both the United States and the Soviet Union, to **partition** Palestine into separate Jewish and Arab states and to internationalize the city of Jerusalem. The "no" votes included all the members of the Arab League, a newly formed coalition of countries that vehemently opposed a Jewish polity in a region whose majority population was Arab.

partition The division of a political entity into two or more separate, autonomous territories.

When the British government announced imminent withdrawal, civil war broke out. Haganah forces moved to seize the territory that the UN partition resolution assigned to the proposed Jewish state, including plans to clear villages or urban neighborhoods that resisted. Arab residents, who still occupied much of that territory, fought back. Bombings, ambushes, and street battles multiplied. In April 1948, for example, Jewish partisans massacred 250 Arab villagers, including women and children. Arabs retaliated by killing seventy Jewish medical personnel. In the wake of this violence, hundreds of thousands of Arabs, both villagers and the urban educated classes, fled into neighboring countries. British security forces departed formally in May 1948 without transferring political authority to anyone. The

MAP 26.4 The Middle East and Egypt, 1950.

How might a look at this 1950 map have aroused fear or antagonism on the part of both Israelis and Arabs in the neighboring countries regarding the future of the region?

civil struggle ballooned immediately into regional war. Ben-Gurion declared the independence of Israel, but the armies of Egypt, Syria, Iraq, and Jordan advanced into Palestine to abort it. Over the seven months of the first Arab–Israeli War, Haganah fighters pushed back the invaders, who coordinated their operations poorly, and took control of parts of Palestine that had not in fact been allotted to Israel under the UN partition plan. The single Arab strategic success was the Jordanian army's seizure of the eastern part of Jerusalem.

Finally, in January 1949 the American UN representative, Ralph Bunche, got the warring parties to negotiate an armistice. In the months that followed, individual Arab states worked out their own cease-fire agreements with Israel, even though none of them recognized the new state. In effect, the war produced partition, but not between a Jewish state and an Arab Palestinian one. Rather, Israel took one part of the territory, Jordan occupied Jerusalem and land west of the Jordan River (known from then on as the West Bank), and Egypt held the Gaza Strip along the Mediterranean coast.

The fighting produced a massive exchange of populations. More than 700,000 Arabs fled Palestine, nearly 500,000 of them moving into refugee camps in Jordan and the Gaza Strip. Israel's Arab population fell to about 20 percent, where it remains today. The Israelis had no master plan to expel Arabs from conquered territory. Nevertheless, the Haganah instigated forced evacuations, used tactics to scare away Arabs, and attacked Arab villages that appeared hostile. The neighboring Arab states proved unwilling, mainly for domestic political reasons, to take in large numbers of Palestinians, and the Israeli government refused to allow Arabs to return home without a comprehensive peace settlement. Meanwhile, many more Jews arrived in Israel, raising the population to about one million by 1950.

Thus, the European colonial era ended in the Middle East with the region in a state of profound tension. Israel, enjoying strong American backing, insisted that the Arab states accept the new international map. Their rulers, however, knew that their own popular legitimacy depended on adamant refusal to do this. Thus, the Middle East suffered its own Cold War until 1956, when hostilities broke out again (see Chapter 26).

India: Independence and division. South Asia's wartime hardships, the great strains on colonial resources, and the bankruptcy of race-based imperial ideology worked

Palestinian refugees leave their homes. This news photograph from November 4, 1948, shows Palestinians walking to Lebanon. Israeli Jews date the founding of their independent state to 1948, while Palestinians and Israel's Arab citizens mourn the year of their defeat, which they call "al-naqba," the catastrophe. Does this photo have political relevance today? If so, in what way?

together to speed the withdrawal of Britain from India within two years of the war's end. This event marked a monumental transfer of political power from colonizer to colonized: India was nearly eighteen times larger than Britain and had more than eight times more people. Its independence also inspired comparable movements across Asia and Africa. Almost immediately, however, colonial India split into two states, India and Pakistan. This event signaled the sort of ethnic and religious strife that would trouble numerous new nations in the second half of the century.

In the interwar decades, the Indian National Congress, the colony's leading nationalist movement under the guidance of Mohandas K. Gandhi had lobbied its British overlords incessantly to share power and indeed gained expanded authority over provincial legislatures. Jawaharlal Nehru, an English-educated lawyer and committed socialist, emerged as an astute Congress leader. The outbreak of the war radicalized nationalist demands, especially after August 1942, when nationalist strikes and insurgent attacks broke out, and the British responded with armed repression and imprisonment of Congress leaders. Late in the war, however, Britain realized that it lacked the financial resources to continue to rule nearly 450 million people against their will. Consequently, the British viceroy, or governor, reopened negotiations with Congress leaders.

During the war, however, India's passage to independence became extremely complicated. In the late 1930s the Muslim League, a party dedicated to the political interests of India's large Muslim minority (about a quarter of the population), charged that Hindu political and economic interests would be favored over those of Muslims in a British-style parliamentary system. In the late 1930s Muhammad Ali Jinnah (1876–1948), the rising star of the Muslim League, advanced the idea, until then foreign to the vast majority of Indians of any religion, that the country consisted of *two* "nations." Hinduism and Islam, Jinnah proclaimed, constituted "two different civilizations which are based mainly on conflicting ideas and concepts. . . . To yoke together two such nations under a single state, one as a numerical minority and the other as a majority, must lead to growing discontent and final destruction."[26] If India were to remain whole, the Muslim nation must govern provinces with Muslims majorities, especially the Punjab in the northwest and Bengal in the northeast. Muslim nationalists named these territories "Pakistan," meaning "land of the pure" in the Urdu language. By no means did all Muslim leaders share Jinnah's two-nations vision, but more of them joined him as fears of Hindu domination grew.

Three-cornered negotiations among the Congress, the Muslim League, and the British authority resumed right after the war. But the parties could not reach agreement, and tensions mounted. In August 1946, violence broke out in Calcutta, triggering a year of sporadic Hindu–Muslim clashes across northern India. As the strife worsened, Muslims in predominantly Hindu areas fled by the millions to the northwest or to Bengal. Millions of Hindus escaped in the opposite direction.

Gandhi, Nehru, Jinnah, and Lord Mountbatten, the last English viceroy, all pleaded for restraint, but to little avail. Despairing of any other solution, Nehru and Jinnah declared the independence of India and Pakistan as separate states in August 1947. When the partition became reality, the two-way ethnic cleansing became even more violent, with mobs halting refugee trains and massacring passengers who did not share their religion. In late 1947 alone, about five million Hindus, as well as adherents of the Sikh religion, fled from the northwest into independent India; an even greater number of Muslims headed into Pakistan. The culminating irony of this calamity was the assassination of Gandhi, the apostle of nonviolence, at the hands of a Hindu extremist in January 1948. At the dawn of independence, then, both India and Pakistan faced immense problems of building stable political institutions.

Decolonization in Southeast Asia. Within a decade of Indian and Pakistani independence, most of the colonized territories of Southeast Asia became sovereign as well. When World War II broke out, strong nationalist movements already existed in Burma, Vietnam, Indonesia, and the Philippines. Weaker ones struggled to gain traction in overwhelmingly rural Cambodia and Laos, as well as in Malaya, where ethnic tensions between native Malays and large Chinese and Indian minorities hindered nationalist unity. As in India, Southeast Asian nationalist leaders were mostly professionals, intellectuals, students, and members of affluent families. These elites typically spoke the colonizer's language and favored strategies that combined Western political ideas with local cultural and religious traditions. Most leaders drew inspiration from Gandhi. Nationalist visions of independence, however, varied widely. Many advocated European-style parliamentary governments, others wanted nations founded on Buddhist or Muslim values, and still others urged Marxist-Leninist revolution.

In some places independence came rapidly. Once the British resolved to pull out of India, they also agreed to transfer power to nationalist governments in Burma and Ceylon (later Sri Lanka) in 1948. The United States restored sovereignty to the Philippines less than a year after Japan's surrender. However, U.S. authorities largely dismissed the rural Filipino guerrillas who had helped fight the Japanese and instead turned power over to the established professional and land-owning class. This elite cooperated readily with American business interests and accepted ninety-nine-year leases for twenty-three U.S. military bases. "Our safest course," gushed Manuel Roxas, the Philippines' first president, "is in the glittering wake of America."[27]

By contrast, in the Dutch colony of Indonesia a colonial war had to be fought. The Japanese had occupied Indonesia

President Sukarno addressing a crowd, 1946. Sukarno led Indonesia's fight for independence. The Netherlands did not relinquish control until 1949, but in 2005 the Dutch government recognized Indonesia's original 1945 declaration of independence. The placard in the crowd proclaims support for the nationalist PBI, the Labor Party of Indonesia.

Postwar Hanoi under Viet Minh rule. Viet Minh soldiers stand guard as a military parade rumbles through the streets of Hanoi in northern Vietnam. Ho Chi Minh's nationalist regime controlled the city throughout the anti-colonial struggle against France, which endured from 1946 to 1954.

during the war, and the Germans had seized the Netherlands. Once the Axis powers surrendered, the Dutch wanted their colony back. Harsh Japanese rule, however, had roused both nationalist feeling and a new sense of common Indonesian identity among ethnically diverse people strung out across 13,670 islands. Ahmed Sukarno, a university graduate from a poor Muslim family, rose to the forefront of the freedom movement, preaching a loose national ideology founded on democracy, social justice, and belief in God. When nationalists declared independence, Dutch forces moved in to crush the insurgency. Both the United States and the Soviet Union pressured the Netherlands, whose postwar economy was in shambles, to follow the British example in India. Finally yielding in 1949, the Netherlands transferred sovereignty to an independent state dominated by Sukarno and Indonesia's educated and affluent class.

France also wanted its Southeast Asian possessions restored after the war. In Vietnam, however, nationalists under the leadership of Ho Chi Minh and the Communist Party already had control of much of the northern region. A founder of the Indochinese Communist Party in 1930, Ho and his comrades launched peasant resistance in northern Vietnam. After 1941 they fought both Japan and its French puppet regime. In August 1945 Ho led the communist Viet Minh (Vietnamese Independence League) into Hanoi, the French colonial capital in the north.

That success marked the start of a brutal conflict that continued for nearly a decade. The United States had aided

and advised Ho in his fight against the Axis. But as the Cold War settled in, the Americans abandoned him, throwing massive aid to the French side in order to prevent a communist victory. Colonial forces, however, failed to suppress Viet Minh guerrillas, and in 1954, after a humiliating defeat at the Battle of Dien Bien Phu, France agreed to leave Vietnam. Thereafter, the country remained divided between a communist-ruled north, and an American-supported, anti-communist regime in the south, a situation that would persist for another twenty-one years.

Communist Victory in China

When Japan surrendered, China faced the resumption of a festering civil war between nationalist and communist partisans. Anxious to see Jiang Jieshi's Nationalist Party in full control, the United States helped airlift his troops into most of China's major cities. It also urged him to parley with Mao Zedong to allow the Communist Party to take part in a postwar democratic government. Jiang refused, negotiations collapsed by the end of 1946, and war broke out again in full force.

Within three years, the communists won the war after Mao's forces encircled numerous cities, bottling up nationalist troops. As communist units captured Beijing and swept into southern China, Jiang and about two million nationalist soldiers fled to Taiwan. Mao then announced the birth of the People's Republic of China, the first major communist triumph since the Russian Revolution of 1917. Meanwhile, the Soviet Union, having declared war on Japan just a week before it surrendered, sent forces into the northern half of Korea. U.S. troops occupied the southern half, and the United Nations sanctioned a provisional division of Korea at the thirty-eighth parallel of latitude.

• • •

Conclusion

From prelude to aftermath, World War II riveted humankind's attention. It cost about sixty million lives and left several of the world's important industrial centers knocked flat. It severely disrupted international trade, migration, and cultural exchange. The end of the conflict presented new and intractable problems—smoldering cities that had to be rebuilt, tens of millions of refugees to be resettled, and massive debts to be paid. Furthermore, the victorious Grand Alliance between the Western liberal democracies and the Soviet Union collapsed in bitter suspicion and rivalry.

Yet, as tumultuous as the war was, it interrupted modernity's long-term trends only briefly. On the global scale, population continued to rise at an accelerating rate. Human energy consumption continued to soar. Scientific and technological innovation surged, and many wartime novelties—radar, nuclear fission, antibiotics—found socially beneficial uses after 1945. The war set off a race between the belligerents to boost the speed and range of communication and transport. (The American test pilot Charles Yeager broke the sound barrier in a rocket-powered aircraft just two years after the war ended.) The destruction of the Axis empires had no significant impact on the continuing accumulation of power in the hands of states. The ideologies of liberal democracy and several variants of socialism, which spread around the world in the nineteenth century, found new appeal after the war. At least for a time, overtly fascist political movements were discredited. Finally, the brisk global economic growth that had characterized long stretches of the eighteenth and nineteenth centuries resumed about 1950. Before long, as we see in Chapter 27, economists were convincing themselves that the whole calamitous period from 1914 to 1945 was just a brief and unfortunate deviation from modernity's long and upward economic spiral.

• • •

Key Terms

Cold War 779
collaborationist 764
embargo 766
genocide 773
Greater East Asia Co-Prosperity Sphere 766
Hiroshima and Nagasaki 770

Holocaust 773
International Monetary Fund (IMF) 779
Marshall Plan 779
North Atlantic Treaty Organization (NATO) 780
partition 781

Third Reich 760
United Nations 774
Warsaw Pact 781
World Bank 780
World War II 760

Change over Time

1934–1935	Mao Zedong leads communist soldiers across China in the Long March.
1935	Italy invades Ethiopia.
1936–1939	Nationalists defeat a leftist coalition in the Spanish Civil War.
1937	Japan invades China.
1938	Germany annexes Austria. Munich agreement endorses German occupation of Czechoslovakia.
1939–1945	Allied and Axis powers clash in World War II.
1944	The United States hosts a global gathering known as the Bretton Woods conference, which establishes the International Monetary Fund and the World Bank.
1945	The United Nations Charter is signed. Ho Chi Minh leads the communist Viet Minh into Hanoi.
1945–1948	Communists seize power in several Eastern European countries.
1946	Jordan, Lebanon, and Syria win independence.
1947	India and Pakistan win independence.
1948–1949	Israel declares independence; the First Arab–Israeli War engulfs the Middle East. Stalin sets up Berlin blockade; Western allies airlift supplies and food.
1949	North Atlantic Treaty Organization (NATO) is founded to ensure the security of Western Europe. Indonesia wins independence. Communist forces achieve victory in China.

Please see end of chapter reference section for additional reading suggestions related to this chapter.

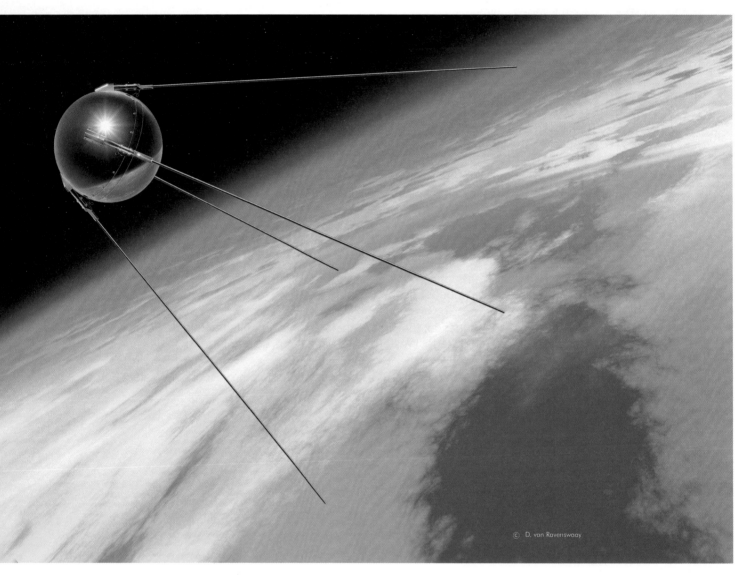

© D. van Ravenswaay

Sputnik I, the first artificial satellite in Earth's orbit.

In February 1945 Arthur C. Clarke, the British science writer later celebrated for such books as *2001: A Space Odyssey,* wrote to the editor of *Wireless World* magazine. He argued in his letter that World War II rocket technology had advanced to the point where "artificial satellites" could be launched into orbit around the earth. The transmitters on these devices would broadcast research data about the upper atmosphere. Almost as an afterthought, Clarke also proposed that if a satellite were placed at the correct height above the equator to make one revolution every twenty-four hours, it would remain in a stationary position relative to the ground. "Three repeater stations, 120 degrees apart in the correct orbit," he wrote, "could give television and microwave coverage to the entire planet." In other words, these satellites could hypothetically relay signals instantly from any point on earth to any other point, a feat not possible at ground level. Clarke mused that the technical hurdles to satellite broadcasting might be overcome "perhaps half a century ahead."

In fact, the Soviet Union put Sputnik, a transmitting satellite the size of a beach ball, into orbit in October 1957, just twelve years after Clarke wrote his visionary letter. The United States shot Explorer I into space the following year, and in 1962 the AT&T corporation, working with the National Aeronautics and Space Administration (NASA) launched Telstar, the first orbital satellite to relay TV signals. By 1964, governments and corporations were firing satellites into orbit at a rate of about ten a month. In 1969 three Americans landed on the moon.

The remarkable pace of satellite communication and space exploration was one expression of the extraordinary economic and technological surge that characterized the three decades after World War II. In the immediate aftermath of that devastating conflict, world leaders could not have foreseen that by 1950 both global population and economic production would veer sharply upward. The first part of this chapter explores this phenomenon, its causes, and its implications for both human social development and the planet's physical and natural health.

Scientific research animated the space age but so did the intense rivalry that developed between the United States and the Soviet Union, the subject of the second section of the chapter. The wartime Grand Alliance sealed in 1941 between the Western democracies and the Soviet Union deteriorated into acrimony even before the struggle ended (see Chapter 26). The United States and Russia never hurled

Chapter Outline

POPULATION AND ECONOMY: AN ERA OF SPECTACULAR GROWTH
Global Population at Its Crest
The Postwar Economic Boom
Economic Growth in Communist States
The Worldwide Lure of Industrialization
Cities, Suburbs, and Shantytowns
Postwar Consumer Society
The Biosphere in Distress

THE COLD WAR WEARS ON
The Era of Mutually Assured Destruction
The Cold War Goes Global

FIGHTS FOR FREEDOM AND JUSTICE
Paths to Independence:
Protest and Negotiation
Paths to Independence:
Insurgency and Revolution

WEIGHING THE EVIDENCE Frantz Fanon on the Shortcomings of the National Bourgeoisie

Struggles for Stability in Young States
High Expectations and Social Protest

INDIVIDUALS MATTER Alexander Dubček: Leader of the Prague Spring

• • •

armored divisions or nuclear missiles at each other, so in that sense the conflict remained a "cold" war. But the venomous rhetoric and brinksmanship of the two political blocs, plus their strategic interventions in the affairs of numerous other states in Latin America, Africa, and Asia, kept the world in a state of chronic anxiety for nearly forty years.

The third part of the chapter investigates the relationship between expanding global growth and accelerating demands around the world for political freedom and social justice. These rising expectations among the colonized and the poor, as well as among well-fed but discontented middle classes, produced political tensions, indeed several civil wars and revolutionary movements. Between 1950 and 1975 the world as a whole advanced to unparalleled material prosperity, but the chasm between the richest and the poorest social groups and world regions continued to widen.

A Panoramic View

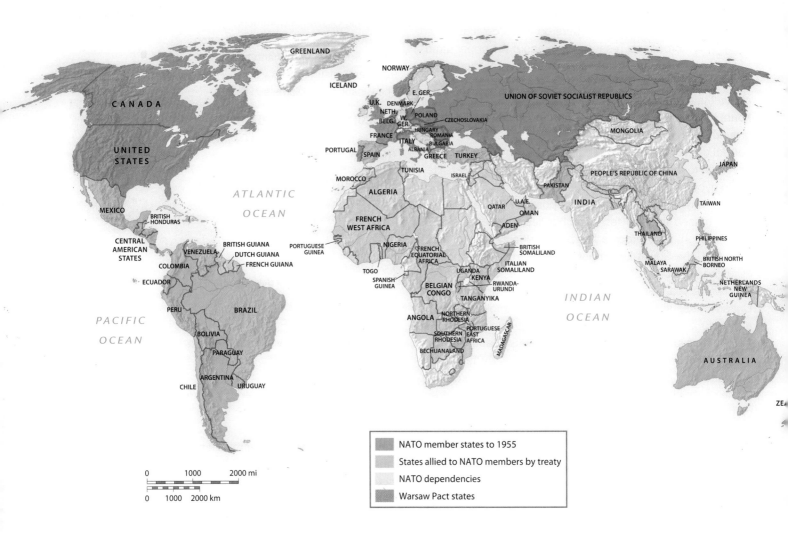

MAP 27.1 Political and military alliances, 1955.

The Cold War produced a politically bipolar global landscape. Which states remained outside the Warsaw Pact or NATO alliances? What factors might have encouraged certain states to maintain neutrality?

Population and Economy: An Era of Spectacular Growth

FOCUS Why did the world economy grow at such a rapidly accelerating rate in the three decades following World War II, and what were major social consequences of that growth?

The mid-twentieth century was a significant turning point for the global economy and the world's population. In the three decades after World War II, production of material wealth worldwide advanced at a much faster rate than it had during the previous thirty years. In some countries people consumed goods on a scale their grandparents would have thought unimaginable. Also about midcentury, the population growth rate, which had been accelerating since the eighteenth century, shot up even faster.

These two trends reinforced each other. Economic growth and new technology allowed the planet to accommodate more people, and more people meant an expanding supply of labor in places where economic success required it. In countries where population grew faster than the economy, however, living standards for peasants and workers typically declined. Stunning economic growth on the world scale proved compatible with both worsening poverty and environmental degradation in many places.

Global Population at Its Crest

In the third quarter of the twentieth century, the world's population growth rate ran higher than in any previous historical era; it also ran higher than after 1975. During those twenty-five years, some societies moved through a demographic transition (see Chapter 25). This meant that people lived longer on average (the mortality rate declined), but women had fewer children (the fertility rate also declined). The population growth rate therefore slowed. This happened in Europe and North America (north of Mexico) and a little later in Eastern Europe, Russia, Japan, and some Latin American states. In several regions, however, fertility rates remained high but mortality rates dropped faster than ever; consequently, growth rates went up. In much of Africa, Asia, and Latin America, populations grew at a rate of about 2.5 percent per year, much higher than, for example, in Western Europe. India's population grew from about 360 million in 1950 to 580 million by 1973, a number only slightly less than the world's entire population in 1600.

Several factors contributed to spiraling population after World War II. One of these was the post–World War II **baby boom**. Despite the general trend of slowing growth rates in many

baby boom A period of increased birthrates, especially in Western countries, from the end of World War II to about 1957.

Western industrialized countries, a spike occurred just after the war, as more young people, released from military service or war-related work, started families amid improving economic conditions. In the United States and Britain, for example, millions of women lost wartime jobs. Consequently, they returned in large numbers to domestic life, and new offspring soon arrived. The baby boom lasted until about 1957, when fertility rates declined again.

On the global scale, the population surge may be linked to an array of new drugs and pesticides, which pushed down mortality rates, especially in tropical and subtropical regions. Vaccination campaigns combated lethal diseases such as cholera, typhus, diphtheria, and polio, raising the survival rate of small children. Smallpox was exterminated, the last known case occurring in East Africa in 1977. DDT, the chemical pesticide first used in World War II, killed insects that transmitted typhus and malaria. Gradual postwar improvements in nutrition and water treatment, especially in large cities, also helped lower annual mortality.

The Postwar Economic Boom

Extraordinary global economic growth after World War II manifested itself in several ways: a huge expansion of capitalist industry, a resurgence of international trade and investment, continuous quickening of scientific and technical innovation, rising incomes for hundreds of millions of people, and much greater consumption of both fossil fuels and material goods. Remarkable rises in gross domestic product per capita occurred not only in the large capitalist economies but also in the communist states and at least some of the new nations that emerged from colonial dependency.

Evidence of boom times. The United States primed the growth pump worldwide. In 1945 it controlled nearly two-thirds of the globe's industrial output. However, once the Western European states and Japan dug themselves out of physical ruin, they began to register even higher growth rates than the United States. In the Soviet Union, communist economic planners showed they could also perform postwar miracles. That country's industrial output doubled between 1945 and 1950 alone and kept on growing into the 1960s. On the global scale, manufacturing grew fourfold between 1950 and 1975, and world trade doubled every ten years (see graph: Change in GDP per capita from 1914 to 1975[1]). In the major capitalist states, unemployment plunged, and workers enjoyed rising real wages. Both inflation and cyclical business downturns remained mild.

Integrating the capitalist economies. At the international Bretton Woods conference in New Hampshire in 1944 (see Chapter 26), the leading capitalist states vowed to advance global peace and prosperity by setting up postwar institutions for international cooperation, collective security, stabilization of currencies, low-tariff trade, and new investment in war-ravaged countries. When the war ended,

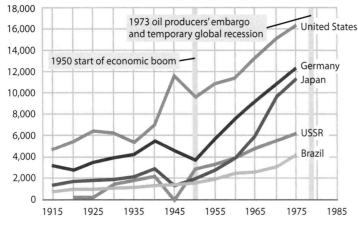

1990 International dollars

- 1973 oil producers' embargo and temporary global recession
- United States
- Germany
- Japan
- 1950 start of economic boom
- USSR
- Brazil

Change in GDP per capita from 1914 to 1975. Which countries experienced the greatest growth in GDP in this period? How would you characterize overall change in GDP in this period? What factors can account for the spike in U.S. GDP just after the sharp decline in Soviet GDP in 1945?

Italy, Japan, and the two-thirds of Germany that became the capitalist Federal Republic (West Germany) subscribed to the Bretton Woods plan. The countries that collaborated to promote economic integration formalized their association in 1961 as the Organization for Economic Cooperation and Development (OECD), a group that included seventeen European states, the United States, Canada, Turkey, and (within three years) Japan.

In the 1950s the United States presided firmly over this club of capitalist states and the "Bretton Woods system," a set of rules that states were expected to follow in doing business with one another. Economic leaders agreed to make the U.S. dollar the world's anchor currency, pegging its value to gold at a fixed rate of $35 an ounce. Other countries then pegged their currencies to the dollar, though provision was made for states to alter the value of their currency to deal with economic or financial crises. The system worked well for nearly two decades. It discouraged disruptive currency fluctuations and stimulated international commerce and investment. Twenty-three countries established the General Agreement on Tariffs and Trade (GATT) in 1947 to sponsor successive "rounds" of negotiations to lower customs duties on manufactured goods. The United States, Japan, and Western Europe all experienced huge export booms in consequence. Until the 1970s they produced together more than 80 percent of the world's manufactured exports, trading the greater part of those goods with one another.

In the postwar years, American corporations, flush with new consumer products, technologies, and disposable capital, dominated international investment. These firms put money in foreign countries by building factories and opening marketing offices. Between 1950 and 1973, U.S. corporate investment in Western Europe and Japan grew from $2 billion to $41 billion. Companies that mass-produced technologically complex products like automobiles ballooned in size. For example, Chrysler, Ford, and General Motors, the

three major American automakers, all opened plants in Western Europe. By the late 1960s they commanded more than 25 percent of that region's consumer market for cars and trucks. Eventually, European and Japanese companies penetrated foreign markets as well.

The European Economic Community. The ruin of war convinced many Western European leaders that the region must exchange autarky—enclosed national self-sufficiency—for economic integration, even political federation. These leaders knew that the German Federal Republic would not be held back economically for long, and they wanted it to direct its energies toward the region's economic resurgence and not into a new military buildup. The United States encouraged a pan-European partnership. John Foster Dulles, secretary of state during the Dwight D. Eisenhower presidency (1953–1960), had argued back in 1941 that when the war was over the "reestablishment of some twenty-five wholly independent sovereign states in Europe would be political folly."[2] European integration would presumably serve the objectives of Bretton Woods, enlarge markets for American goods, and counteract communist subversion.

Several states were ready to advance in that direction. In 1952 the German Federal Republic, France, Belgium, the Netherlands, Luxembourg, and Italy joined together to launch the European Coal and Steel Community (ECSC), an international regulatory authority that created a common market for those two resources among the member states. This was a remarkable achievement, considering that Germany and Italy had been mortal enemies of the other four members just a few years earlier. In fact, the agency worked so well that these six states negotiated a much broader common market for goods, founding the European Economic Community (EEC) in 1957 under the terms of the Treaty of Rome. By the 1960s free trade and commercial cooperation among an expanding list of members were transforming Western Europe into a global economic powerhouse.

Capitalism and the welfare state. The idea that the state has a responsibility to guarantee at least minimal economic safety nets for all citizens gained nearly universal acceptance during the twentieth century, at least as a social principle. Leaders committed to the Bretton Woods system generally understood that wage-earning citizens, including labor union members and democratic socialists, would buy into plans for greater global economic integration only if the state continued to guarantee people basic security against company failures, wage losses, layoffs, and sudden business downturns.

Consequently, the **welfare state** grew along with the global economy, though disproportionately faster in Western Europe than in the

> **welfare state** An approach to government in which the state uses public funds to protect and promote the health and social well-being of all citizens.

United States, where public opinion remained divided about federal government activism. Owing to postwar prosperity, governments accumulated revenue to expand services such as health care, disability insurance, low-cost housing, pensions, public education, and grants to college students. In the third quarter of the century, this partnership between capitalist enterprise and social democracy worked quite well. In all the leading industrial states, poverty generally declined, worker wages rose, and leaders of the moderate left and right cooperated.

Economic Growth in Communist States

Between 1945 and 1955 the number of countries dedicated to the Marxist-Leninist brand of socialist ideology grew from one—the Soviet Union—to twelve, including eight in Eastern Europe, plus China, Mongolia, North Korea, and North Vietnam (see Map 27.1). The number of people living under communist governments increased by hundreds of millions. Many of these states experienced impressive economic growth in the 1950s. The Soviet economy grew faster than that of any Western capitalist country, though from a lower starting point. China enjoyed unprecedented growth from 1952 and 1957. All of these states shunned the Bretton Woods club, which, as they well knew, functioned in large measure to advance the global political and economic interests of the United States. Rather, they adopted highly centralized state planning and control generally modeled on Soviet-style socialism.

Soviet successes. Under Joseph Stalin's long rule, the Soviet economy moved to the rhythm of successive Five Year Plans, sets of government-mandated economic goals. The state, not private enterprises, owned the country's industrial plants, transport systems, and commercial institutions, as well as most of its farming. The state, not the market, determined prices and wages. After World War II, Stalin continued to mobilize the Soviet population for industrial development as if the fighting had not stopped. Living standards remained modest, and most consumer goods were available to only the *nomenklatura*—the upper levels of the communist civil and military bureaucracy.

The Soviet economy continued to grow under the guidance of Nikita Khrushchev (1894–1971), the brash and boisterous coal miner's son who rose to the top of the Soviet political hierarchy within two years of Stalin's death. He denounced his predecessor's harsh domestic repression and global isolation, but he had full faith in socialism to improve life for ordinary citizens. During Khrushchev's

years in command (1953–1964), he shifted some state investment from heavy industry to consumer products like shoes, clothing, and radios. He expanded low-cost housing, public services, and higher education, notably for young women. He revived Soviet farming with new machinery, fertilizers, and irrigation projects for collective farms. Gradually, rural living standards improved. Khrushchev also caught the capitalist world off guard in October 1957, when Soviet engineers launched Sputnik into earth orbit on a ballistic missile. This event sent the American public into an uproar over the country's failure to stay ahead of its communist rival in science and technology.

Khrushchev announced that within twenty years the Soviet economy would leave the capitalist states far behind. "When we catch you up . . . , in passing you up, we will wave to you," he told then–U.S. vice president Richard Nixon in 1959.[3] These confident proclamations, however, masked serious weaknesses. Many party bureaucrats despised Khrushchev's reforms and did all they could to sabotage them. State controls, though relaxed slightly, continued to stifle broad technical innovation. Despite the initial Soviet breakthrough in ballistic missile testing, Russia had only 4 operational missiles by 1962; the United States had 224.

Nikita Khrushchev and Richard Nixon discuss consumer economics. In 1959 the U.S. government opened an exhibit in Moscow featuring a typical American suburban house complete with labor-saving appliances. Touring the exhibition together, the Soviet premier and the American vice president engaged in an impromptu conversation (through interpreters) about their respective national economies. The exchange, known as the Kitchen Debate, was captured with new color videotape technology and broadcast in both countries. Why might Khrushchev and Nixon have debated household consumption as part of a larger conversation about economic ideology?

Khrushchev's political opponents forced him from office in 1964, though he had "de-Stalinized" the political culture enough that his successors sent him into obscure retirement, not to Siberia. Leonid Brezhnev and Alexei Kosygin then rose to leadership. They continued to make modest social reforms and greatly increased Soviet foreign trade. But they also invested heavily once again in state planning, heavy industry, and the military. During the rest of the decade, economic growth slowed steadily; by the early 1970s, the Soviet economy was close to stagnant.

China leaps forward and back. Like Stalin in Russia, Mao Zedong aimed to make the People's Republic of China a self-sufficient industrial power. The country experienced periods of impressive economic growth between 1949 and 1976, the year Mao died. During those twenty-seven years, however, the economy oscillated wildly, in large part because of deep policy disagreements within the ruling Communist Party. Mao was determined to industrialize China at breakneck speed without compromising the Marxist-Leninist vision of radical social equality—no rich and poor peasants, no landlords, no capitalist bourgeoisie. Generally, when the state tried to orchestrate the economy from the top, growth waned. When it backed off, for example, permitting rural farmers to buy and sell privately in local markets, growth accelerated but income inequalities also widened.

For a few years after its 1949 victory, the communist government left petty capitalism in the countryside mostly alone, and with generous aid from the Soviet Union the Chinese economy grew rapidly. Between 1950 and 1957, life expectancy rose by twenty-one years. The number of children in school soared, and new laws alleviated the exploitation of rural women by abolishing child marriage and permitting divorce by mutual consent.

In the mid-1950s, however, Mao and his inner circle decided that the country must ramp up farm output to sustain industrial expansion and the rapidly growing urban workforce. He therefore ordered wholesale collectivization of agriculture. Peasants were to labor for the state, not for themselves. When village-size collectives proved insufficiently productive, the regime hatched grander plans, dispatching tens of millions of rural men and women to giant irrigation projects and to huge communes where they shared dormitories, dining halls, communal nurseries, and "happy homes" for the elderly. To increase iron and steel production, the state also instructed peasants to build and operate miniature blast furnaces. China, Mao proclaimed, would make a "Great Leap Forward" into socialist utopia.

Instead, from 1958 to 1961 the country descended into famine. Farm output on the big but inefficient communes plummeted. Backyard mills produced inferior metal and prevented peasants from tending crops. A succession of disastrous harvests left vast rural areas with no food at all. Upwards of thirty million people, unable to survive on grass, bark, and shoe leather, died of starvation and disease, probably more than perished in World War II. Soviet help also shrank because relations between the two countries soured over a range of issues, including simmering territorial disputes along their mutual border. Economic conditions became so bad that leaders who favored smaller collectives and private plots for peasants recovered political influence. For a few years, growth returned—along with greater income differences.

In 1966, however, China descended again into turmoil. Mao, reacting to critics within the party and opposing any resurgence of capitalism, proclaimed the Great Proletarian Cultural Revolution. This mass popular mobilization aimed to cleanse party and society of bourgeois values, foreign influences, and ideological impurities. In effect, Mao and his hard-core supporters, including his radical wife Jiang Qing, unleashed young intellectuals, students, and workers against the very government establishment that he headed. More than two years of political tumult and economic stagnation

A worker stokes a backyard blast furnace. Chinese peasants set up over one million smelters in the "battle for steel," an attempt to make steel on an industrial scale through the collective efforts of many rural communities. Why did localized steel manufacturing not produce the results Mao expected, in spite of a long history of impressive peasant productivity?

followed. Maoist Red Guards intimidated and even murdered people even faintly suspected of bourgeois "wrong thinking," including ownership of Western pop records. Millions of educated men and women were exiled to villages where peasants instructed them in proper revolutionary attitudes. Red Guard enthusiasm began to wane in the late 1960s, and the economy revived quickly. Meanwhile, high party officials devoted themselves to vicious infighting over succession to the elderly and failing Mao. This state of affairs continued until his death in 1976.

The Worldwide Lure of Industrialization

As the postwar world economy blossomed, the idea that industrialization was the key to prosperity spread rapidly from the big capitalist and socialist economies to dozens of other states. In most of these smaller countries, leaders tried to follow a middle road between private investment and centralized planning and control. They remained leery of the Bretton Woods system, arguing that economic progress required high tariffs to protect new industries, not closer ties with foreign corporations and banks.

Economies in Latin America. During the Great Depression and World War II, when global trade shrank, several Latin American republics experimented with **import substitution industrialization, or ISI.** These programs aimed to reduce both commercial dependence on more economically developed countries and vulnerability to global economic swings. Through ISI, a country could slow the export of natural resources and reduce somewhat its reliance on foreign capital. The state, however, had to prime the development pump by investing in and managing industries and transport networks. In the 1950s ISI produced some good results. Mexico quadrupled its manufacturing output between 1945 and 1973. By the mid-1960s Brazil, which occupies nearly half the land area of South America, produced nearly all its own consumer goods. Even so, foreign investment did not wither. Between 1950 and 1965, for example, American companies invested $3.8 billion in Latin American enterprises, reaping in return profits of $7.5 billion.

During and right after World War II, several Latin American states worked to strengthen democratic institutions, including voting rights for women. This trend, however, did not last. With the notable exceptions of Chile and Uruguay, authoritarian governments of one type or another, some of them military regimes, seized power, most in close alliance with the U.S. government. Typically, those governments represented pragmatic alliances among the army, business leaders, professionals, urban middle classes, and industrial workers, all groups that wanted technical modernization and industrial self-sufficiency. Between 1962 and 1966

> **import substitution industrialization (ISI)** Government economic policies to encourage national industries to produce finished goods that would otherwise be imported.

alone, military coups took place in nine Latin American countries, including Brazil.

Even the most dictatorial governments, however, adopted nationalist and sometimes even socialist rhetoric, rallying city populations with promises of welfare services and better living standards. In Argentina, for example, President Juan Perón (in office 1946–1955, 1973–1974) kept a tight rein on power but also appealed to the urban masses and labor unions for support. Eva Duarte, the president's wife, rose from soap opera actress to brilliant advocate of the poor against the traditional land-owning class. Known affectionately as "Evita," she helped women get the vote in 1947, though also arguing that women best served the nation by staying home. Nonetheless, except in Mexico, reforms to transfer land from estate lords to peasants made little progress. In the late 1960s about 17 percent of Latin American proprietors owned about 90 percent of the land. Population also rose faster than national economies, producing inflation, rural joblessness, and swelling urban poverty in many countries.

Economic challenges in new states. In all the territories that achieved independence from colonial rule in the decade after World War II, new leaders aimed to modernize their economies by building national industries. The largest and most technically advanced of these new states was India, which in 1950 had about 372 million people, more than twice as many as in all of Latin America. In pointed contrast to most states in Asia, India achieved growth while simultaneously building a vivacious, if disorderly, democracy. Jawaharlal Nehru, who led India and the Congress Party from 1947 to 1964, was a socialist and radical modernizer devoted to rapid industrialization. He emulated the Soviet Union in launching ambitious five-year development plans, but he also collaborated with Indian capitalists, of which there were many. Huge state investment produced impressive results. In the 1950s, iron, steel, textile, and automobile industries all advanced. In the 1960s, however, the economy slowed. Like several Latin American states, India shifted too much public investment from agriculture to heavy industry when population was rising fast. Irrigating more land, using more chemical fertilizers, and planting hybrid seeds helped produce more food, but rural poverty remained pervasive, propelling millions to migrate to cities like Bombay (Mumbai), Calcutta (Kolkata), and New Delhi.

Growth varied widely in other Asia territories, though four of them began to show remarkable success in the early 1960s. South Korea, the Republic of China on Taiwan, the largely self-governing British colony of Hong Kong, and Singapore, which gained independence from Britain in 1965, rejected the Latin American model of manufacturing mainly to supply home consumers. Instead, they favored new enterprises to make finished products to export to the rest of the world. None of these countries had abundant natural resources, but by making high-quality goods and keeping costs down, they became the "Asian tigers," competing vigorously in global markets.

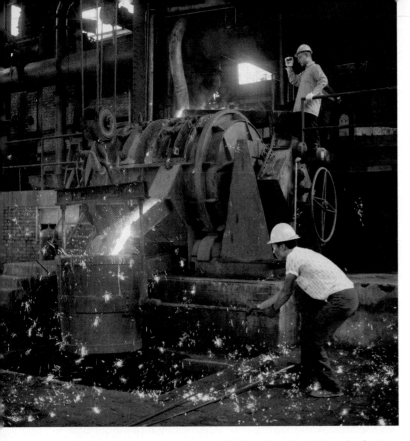

Steel workers operate a forge at the Hsin Yee Metal Industries factory in Taiwan. Like other Asian tiger economies, Taiwan increased its output of both heavy industry and consumer goods starting in the 1960s. How did this economic strategy compare to efforts to industrialize in mainland China during the same period?

Cities, Suburbs, and Shantytowns

Population and economic growth together boosted the world's city dwellers from about 25 percent in 1950 to 40 percent by 1980. At midcentury there were 67 cities with populations in excess of one million; by 1975 there were 172.[4] The distribution of big cities on the world map also changed, with Asia taking the lead from Europe and North America (see Map 27.2).

In the boom years, cities in both industrialized and developing countries became more complex and more densely populated as centers of interdependent economic activity—manufacturing, processing, transport, research, higher education, government administration, and a multitude of services. Cars, new roads, and public transport systems also allowed people to live farther from historic centers, transforming some cities into sprawling metropolitan regions. For example, in the Kanto area of Japan after World War II, Tokyo and several other cities fused into one giant **megalopolis,** which today has a population in excess of thirty-six million. In North America and Europe, families with sufficient income to buy houses and cars spilled out from city centers into leafy suburbs, and businesses soon followed them. In less industrialized countries,

megalopolis An extensive and densely urbanized region or chain of urbanized regions.

urban sprawl resulted much less from outward suburbanization than from inward movement of poor rural people, who erected shantytowns in widening rings around city cores. In urbanizing regions like South Asia and tropical Africa, the first generation or two of city newcomers were predominantly men; women remained in villages to carry on with farm work. Family and ethnic networks, however, continued to tie urban settlements with ancestral villages. Also, clusters of urban huts and shacks often evolved into communities made stable by more balanced sex ratios, new families, and civic and religious organizations.

Postwar Consumer Society

The continuing fossil-fuel revolution made it possible for industry to produce more consumer goods than ever before. This torrent of new products inevitably produced cultural and psychological transformations. More men and women, first in the booming industrial economies, subscribed to a "culture of consumption." This way of living, which centered on desires to acquire and display "things," profoundly influenced economic decisions, social relations, and expectations of individual fulfillment. In fact, modern middle classes around the world came to define themselves partly by their ability to consume goods and enjoy pleasures that the lower classes—the great majority—could not afford.

The United States exited World War II as a rich society ready to shop. Refrigerators, kitchen ranges, TVs, automobiles, and single-family homes were among the most coveted "big-ticket" items. In the 1950s consumer spending also rose exponentially in Western Europe, Canada, and Australia. In France, for example, the proportion of homes with indoor toilets rose from 25 percent in 1954 to 75 percent in 1975. In the 1960s **consumerism** hit Japan. In the Soviet Union and communist Eastern Europe young men and women persistently clamored for more goods than their governments were willing or able to supply. The regimes in Poland, Hungary, Czechoslovakia, and East Germany raised consumer production somewhat in the late 1950s, but mostly they promised full employment rather than generous wages and mountains of merchandise.

consumerism Social and cultural values and practices centered on the accumulation and consumption of material goods.

After World War II, private businesses spent much larger portions of their budgets on advertising, product testing, and customer relations strategies. The Burton's men's clothing chain in Britain exemplifies consumerist tactics. The 1953 edition of its "Manager's Guide" declared that salesmanship was the "art of making people want what you have to sell.... Create desire to possess strong enough to overcome a natural antipathy to parting with money, and you will make sale after sale."[5] Consumer capitalists also invented new credit mechanisms, notably home mortgage loans, installment buying, and store credit cards, so that customers with average

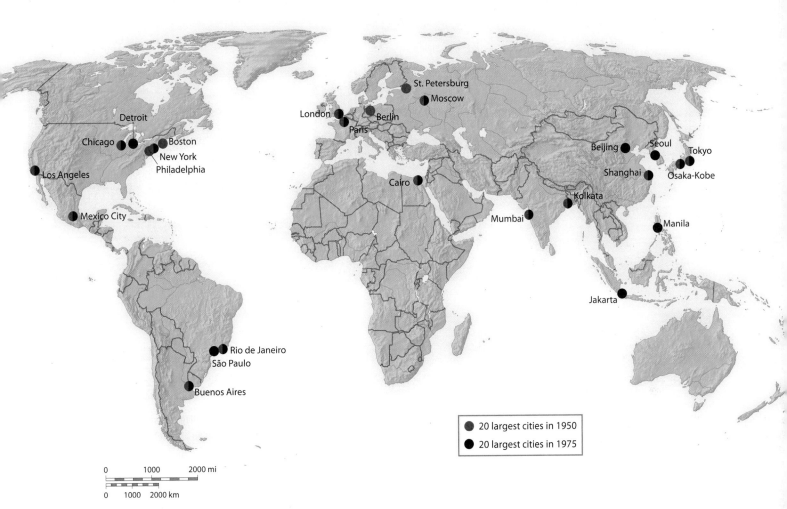

MAP 27.2 The world's twenty largest cities in 1950 and 1975.

Which of the largest cities in 1950 were no longer among the top twenty in 1975? What factors account for the shifting locations of the largest cities between 1950 and 1975?

incomes might enjoy instant gratification. Moreover, corporations devoted more research and development to inventing products designed specifically to make last year's goods seem outdated and unfashionable, a strategy known as planned obsolescence. Auto makers, for example, introduced new vehicle designs every year, hoping the Smiths would trade in their old model in order to climb a rung above the Joneses on the ladder of social prestige.

Consumption and social change. Consumerism had profound social effects in the richest societies. People could travel more freely, get better health care, and cut drudgery with work-saving technology. Economists worried at first that if the consumer economy fulfilled most desires and the welfare state kept everyone above water, then people would work less, thereby reducing productivity. In fact, the opposite happened. People tended to work harder and longer as their incomes rose, persuaded that more purchasing power would make them happier.

Economic growth and consumerism significantly changed the lives of middle- and working-class women. After a slump in female employment after the war, both married and single women poured back into wage work, squeezing homemaking into fewer available hours. Manufacturers relentlessly pursed female buyers, recognizing that they often made major domestic buying decisions. Ironically, dishwashers, ovens, and steam irons helped push women into the labor market but convinced few men that they might also master those machines. On the whole, employed women continued to earn less than men and to hit "glass ceilings" when promotions came around.

Postwar consumer culture had many critics. Social observers, especially in Europe, complained that popular yearning for material goods replaced community values with self-absorbed individualism. In the 1950s, European intellectuals saw the United States as a gigantic material culture pump, flooding the world with its movies, comic books, plastic doodads, and other spirit-numbing wares. In the 1960s, however,

Consumer advertising proliferated in the 1960s. A scene at a London train station illustrates the opportunities a diverse range of advertisers had to reach future customers, both women and men. What income levels and demographic groups do you think the advertisers in this picture were hoping to reach?

fears of an American cultural invasion largely evaporated in Western Europe, as people there adopted their own distinctive consumer cultures. They drove smaller cars to navigate the narrow streets of ancient European cities. Their filmmakers competed energetically with Hollywood, the Italian director Sergio Leone, for example, making idiosyncratic American "westerns" on location in Spain. The cultural invasion in fact reversed direction when British music and fashion hit American shores, and European corporations sold American consumers on the glamour of European goods.

The Biosphere in Distress

Humans altered and exploited the earthly biosphere at a rapidly accelerating rate in the postwar decades. Energy from fossil fuels—coal, petroleum, and natural gas—drove a threefold jump in global gross domestic product between 1950 and 1973. A parade of technological innovations—better chemical refining processes, high-pressure pipelines, larger tanker ships—allowed for the massive exploitation of fossil-fuel reserves. By 1975 humankind was consuming 2.3 billion tons of oil per year—up from 10 million in 1890. The Middle East joined Russia, Romania, Mexico, Venezuela, and the United States as a major oil-producing region. Fossil-fuel combustion, along with turbo-generating dams,

fed most of the world's insatiable appetite for electricity. In the mid-1950s the Soviet Union, the United States, and Britain began to tap nuclear power for everyday use. From then until the 1980s, nuclear power plants multiplied in several other countries, notably France.

In the postwar decades, rapid economic and demographic growth had a much greater impact on the planet's physical and natural environment than anyone seems to have understood at the time. There is no doubt that degradation of the planet's soils, water systems, and atmosphere advanced steadily.

Manipulating soil, water, and seed. History's earliest farmers began to deplete the planet's thin soil layer by disturbing it with sticks and hoes. By the twentieth century, mechanized farming, lumbering, mining, and building caused billions of tons of soil to wash or blow away every year. Serious erosion could be checked to some extent by reforestation or other expensive measures that peasants could seldom afford. In mountainous Rwanda in East Africa, for example, population density increased from 80 to 180 people per square kilometer between 1948 and 1978. Farmers there waged a constant struggle to slow hillside soil loss. In postwar Brazil, commercial growers clear-cut millions of acres of forest to expand coffee production, causing massive soil runoff.

Expanding metallurgical and chemical production after the war generated mountains and rivers of toxic waste from mines, factories, smelters, and refineries. By 1950 most cities in developed countries had safe drinking water, but in much of the world urbanization far outpaced construction of enclosed sewers and water treatment plants. Consequently, water-borne diseases like cholera and typhoid continued to kill millions, especially small children. Even in places with good water treatment, businesses, governments, and private citizens tended to regard lakes and rivers as convenient cesspits. In the 1950s, for example, heavy industry made a fast recovery in northern Europe's Rhineland, but this also transformed the lower Rhine River into a chemical and metallurgical gutter largely devoid of aquatic life. Serious cleanup efforts began only in the late 1970s.

Soil and water degradation was also an unintended consequence of immense dam and irrigation projects. Between 1950 and 1980, irrigated land worldwide increased by close to 200 million acres.[6] Irrigation could vastly increase crop yields and therefore raise peasant incomes and promote exports. But it also presented long-term problems. Chemical fertilizers seeped from irrigated land back into canals and rivers, stimulating the buildup of algae and other nutrient-devouring plants, which clogged channels and starved aquatic life.

One example is particularly poignant. In Egypt, Gamal Abdel Nasser, the military ruler from 1952 to 1970, ordered construction of a high dam at Aswan on the middle Nile River, an enormous project that started in 1960 and took a decade to complete. The dam stopped the Nile's annual summer flood, which had sustained Egypt's agrarian civilization for five thousand years. Instead, downstream flow was regulated to allow crop irrigation all year round. Presumably, Egypt would then be able to feed its rapidly growing population and to export large surpluses of cotton and other commodities. Signs of trouble, however, soon appeared. The millions of tons of silt that for millennia had flowed across the lower valley and the Nile delta every summer accumulated instead in Lake Nasser, the huge reservoir behind the dam. Consequently, farming downstream depended on massive annual infusions of chemical fertilizer, much of which had to be purchased abroad. Riotous blooms of algae and water hyacinths clogged irrigation canals and even water delivery to Cairo. In the absence of annual silt flow, Mediterranean sea water pushed deeper inland, threatening the farm-rich Nile delta. Nasser had hoped for agricultural self-sufficiency, but today Egypt imports as much as 60 percent of its annual food supply.

Global population could not have increased at the rate it did after the war without an accompanying rise in food production. In the postwar decades, scientists and engineers applied modern technology to ramp up farm yields, in some places by a factor of ten. Bioengineers developed new strains of wheat, rice, and maize (corn) bred specifically

Building the Aswan High Dam. A worker pauses to change his shoes at the site of this ambitious project, which involved both massive manual labor and heavy machinery. Partly funded by the USSR, the dam was to be a big step toward Egypt's food and energy self-sufficiency. What role might nationalist appeals have played in arousing popular support for the project?

Green Revolution Acceleration of world agricultural production, especially from the 1960s, resulting from use of high-yielding varieties of food crops, synthetic fertilizers, pesticides, and expanded irrigation systems.

to produce luxuriant crop yields, but only in the presence of chemical fertilizers, pesticides, and immense volumes of irrigation water. This **Green Revolution**, which got under way slowly in the 1930s, spread from the United States to Mexico, where wheat harvests tripled between 1944 and 1960. In the following two decades, many populous countries, including Turkey, India, Pakistan, Indonesia, China, South Korea, and the Philippines produced enough wheat or rice to keep up with the pace of population growth.

Yet unintended consequences multiplied. In much of Asia, Africa, and Latin America, technology that raised farm productivity tended to benefit large-scale landlords and companies disproportionately relative to individual farm families. Gasoline-powered machinery, fertilizers, and irrigation water represented enormous inputs of energy and capital that only big land-owners could usually afford. Hybridized seeds produced high-yield food plants, but the seeds of those plants were sterile. Consequently, farmers had to buy new seeds every year from firms that owned patents to them. This state of affairs hugely benefited biotechnology corporations but not small farmers in developing countries. Nor could family farmers compete easily with big growers capable of producing crops in volume and therefore keeping

market prices down. In the 1970s millions of farmers, especially in Asia, left the land to find subsistence wage work.

Air pollution. Early in the twentieth century, a London physician coined the term *smog* to describe the "smoky fog" that hung over large cities. The word came to mean the atmospheric haze that forms when sunlight chemically reacts with the nitrogen oxides and hydrocarbons emitted by internal combustion engines. Smog causes eye and respiratory maladies, and it harms many types of flora. During the postwar boom, factories, mines, farms, and motor vehicles spewed record tonnages of chemical contaminants into the atmosphere. Only in the 1960s, however, did scientists begin systematically to measure air contamination in big cities and industrial regions. By then, the richer countries were taking steps to bring urban air pollution under at least partial control. London roused itself to action after December 1952, when a combination of weather conditions shrouded the city in a weeklong toxic fog. The Great Smog caused nearly four thousand deaths from respiratory diseases. In the 1950s and 1960s, contamination affecting whole regions reached appalling levels in places like the São Paulo area in Brazil and the Ruhr valley in northwestern Europe.

Even the most technologically innovative countries were slow to address pollution from motor vehicles, whose numbers in the world grew from 50 million in 1930 to 500 million by 1985. Some metropolitan areas, for example, Mexico City, Los Angeles, Athens, and Tehran, began to suffer acutely

Daytime traffic during the Great Smog. A bus navigates the streets of London in December 1952, as commuters brave foul conditions caused by hydrocarbon emissions. Why did air quality deteriorate so much before residents of industrialized countries began to take measures to counteract pollution?

because cars became so numerous, the sun shines many days a year, and surrounding mountains prevent smog dispersion. Also, beginning in the 1920s, oil corporations improved gasoline efficiency by adding lead, which caused toxic elevations in human blood streams. Concerted efforts to reduce tailpipe contamination got under way in the late 1960s, but urban pollution worldwide was still getting worse as of 1975.

In 1962 Rachel Carson, an American zoologist, published *Silent Spring,* an indictment of the chemical industry for selling DDT and other pesticides that killed animal life. Despite intense corporate opposition, her work roused scientific and public consciousness about the environment. Not until the following decade, however, did governments and public interest groups begin to make commitments to retard and if possible reverse numerous forms of environmental degradation (see Chapter 28).

The Cold War Wears On

FOCUS How did the Cold War affect political and economic relations among the world's peoples in the three decades following World War II?

The Cold War, whose early years we described in the context of World War II's aftermath (see Chapter 26), may be conceived as a struggle between two contrasting political and economic visions. The United States aspired to lead the world to economic prosperity through democracy and capitalism. The Soviet Union, China, and other communist states were equally determined to shun capitalist internationalism. The communist regimes, rather, aimed to demonstrate that Marxist-Leninist teachings, together with central planning, economic self-sufficiency, and subordination of private interests to the state, would produce material well-being and social equality for all. On the ground, Europe remained divided at what Winston Churchill called the iron curtain: The armies of the United States and its Western European NATO stood nose to nose with divisions of the Warsaw Pact, the military alliance that the Soviet Union formed with its Eastern European junior partners in 1955 (see Map 27.1).

The Era of Mutually Assured Destruction

The existence of nuclear weapons shaped all international relations after 1945. The world's most powerful states had gone to war in both 1914 and 1939 on the assumption that whatever the cost, winners would eventually emerge from the wreckage and start to rebuild. A war fought with atomic bombs, however, threatened to snuff out the human species altogether. Who would rebuild after that? The United States, which showed what even small fission bombs could do to two Japanese cities, held a monopoly on atomic technology for four years. But Stalin ordered a nuclear crash program

that yielded a successful atomic test on the Inner Eurasian steppes in 1949.

The Korean War as test case. The war that erupted in Korea in 1950 might have provoked a nuclear confrontation, but it did not. Like Germany, Korea found itself divided at the end of the world war, a Soviet-allied communist government installed in the north, and a U.S.-backed republic in the south, the two states separated by an arbitrary border at the thirty-eighth parallel of latitude. But as soon as both major powers withdrew their troops from the Korean peninsula in 1948–1949, north and south threatened to attack each other.

The Soviet Union, having signed a mutual defense pact with Mao Zedong and perhaps hoping to discourage postwar Japan from drawing too close to the United States, gave Kim Il-Sung, the leader of North Korea, a green light to invade the south and reunify the peninsula under communist rule. He thought the United States would not interfere. Instead, the U.S. government convinced the United Nations Security Council (on a day when the Soviet delegation was absent) to authorize military intervention. The ensuing war lasted just over three years. At the start, North Korean forces nearly overran the peninsula, but a counterassault under General Douglas MacArthur drove close to North Korea's border with China at the Yalu River. Believing such provocation could compromise his own hold on power, Mao ordered 300,000 Chinese troops to cross the Yalu in October 1950. That onslaught pushed American and allied divisions back, but then the war degenerated into grinding stalemate. Neither Stalin nor U.S. president Harry Truman wanted to

Troops of the People's Liberation Army, North Korea, October 1950. Chinese forces sent to support the communist North Korean government were unequally equipped to battle United Nations forces led by the United States. Notice the ragtag uniforms and the soldiers in the front row wearing only sandals. Nevertheless, these troops managed to halt UN advances and bring the war to a stalemate. Why might Mao have risked sending poorly equipped soldiers to war?

drop atomic bombs to decide the future of Korea, and in July 1953 the adversaries signed an armistice, leaving the peninsula still divided. Something like 2.8 million Koreans died in the war. The conflict aggravated mistrust between the United States and Russia and sent American relations with China into deep freeze for more than two decades.

Cold War fears and hopes. The Korean War also intensified the nuclear arms race. In 1952 the United States tested the first hydrogen bomb, which worked on the principle of nuclear fusion. The detonation in the South Pacific produced a 10.4 million ton explosion, five hundred times larger than the blast over Nagasaki. The Soviets evened that playing field the following year. Between 1952 and 1974, Britain, France, China, Israel, and India all joined the nuclear club, though their arsenals remained relatively small. By the mid-1960s both Russia and the United States had submarine fleets armed with enough nuclear missiles to kill hundreds of millions of people in a single afternoon.

Leaders in both Washington and Moscow could imagine the likely consequence of an all-out missile exchange, and it scared them from the start. When Mao Zedong remarked in 1957 that China could lose three hundred million people in a nuclear strike and still recover nicely, Soviet and Americans leaders were equally appalled. In 1959 President Dwight Eisenhower mused darkly that if missiles started flying "you might as well go out and shoot everyone you see and then shoot yourself."[7] In the early 1960s the United States openly proclaimed a policy of **mutually assured destruction,** or **MAD,** the dubious theory that if no one expected to come out of a nuclear war alive, then no one would start one.

mutually assured destruction (MAD) The doctrine aimed at preventing nuclear war between the United States and the Soviet Union by shared knowledge that, if either side attacked, both would suffer mass destruction.

The Cold War in the 1950s and 1960s had a strange inconsistency. On the one hand, the adversaries continued to expand their military arsenals and spy networks. Each side warned the other that it would answer an attack with a rain of nuclear fire. In the 1950s, however, American intelligence revealed that the United States had far greater nuclear and long-range missile capability than Russia did. The Soviets knew this, too, which drove them to turn up the volume of threats. The U.S. propaganda machines responded in kind. On the other hand, both powers proclaimed their commitment to peaceful coexistence. They held periodic summit meetings and organized cultural exchanges. Trade between the Soviet bloc and the Western industrial states grew rapidly in the 1960s. In 1963 the United States and the Soviet Union signed the Limited Test Ban Treaty, which prohibited nuclear testing in the atmosphere. Additional agreements followed, culminating in the 1972 Anti-Ballistic Missile Treaty, which banned nuclear states from developing defenses against incoming rockets.

The European stalemate. After Stalin lifted the land blockade of West Berlin (see Chapter 26), the Cold War adversaries moved toward a cautious understanding that neither would attack or otherwise destabilize the other's half of Europe, barring the most extreme provocation. For example, in 1956, Hungarian citizens, angered over repression and poor progress in living standards, revolted against their communist government, demanding withdrawal from the Soviet bloc. Within a few days, however, the Red Army moved in to suppress the insurgency, at a cost of some twenty thousand Hungarian lives. The United States and its allies denounced the aggression but did nothing more, confirming, to the dismay of street fighters in Budapest, their policy of nonintervention in the affairs of Soviet satellites.

Then, in 1961, the Soviet Union collaborated with the communist-ruled German Democratic Republic (GDR) to build a wall, first of barbed wire, then of concrete, to seal East Berlin and the rest of the GDR from West Berlin. Unable to stop citizens, especially skilled and educated ones, from fleeing to booming West Berlin, the GDR put up the barrier as a measure of desperation. The Western allies protested but also knew that the wall just might reduce tensions in central Europe. John F. Kennedy, recently inaugurated as U.S. president (in office 1961–1963), conceded that "it's not a very nice solution, but a wall is a hell of a lot better than a war."[8]

The Cold War Goes Global

An irony of the Cold War is that even though American and Soviet missiles remained on their launch pads, something like fifty-five wars of varying scope, both civil and international, either started or were already in progress between 1950 and 1975. Both superpowers intervened in several of these conflicts, hoping to cultivate new allies and advance their own strategic and ideological interests. The Cold War therefore played out across Asia, Africa, and Latin America, often with unforeseen consequences.

In Iran, for example, the government of Prime Minister Muhammad Mosaddiq tried in the early 1950s to build a constitutional democracy that limited the powers of the hitherto authoritarian monarchy of Muhammad Reza Shah (reigned, 1941–1979). To reduce foreign control over the economy, Mosaddiq nationalized the Anglo-Iranian Oil Company. Fearing both disruption of oil deliveries to Europe and Mosaddiq's tolerance for communist political activity, the U.S. Central Intelligence Agency (CIA) conspired with British operatives and conservative Iranian military officers in 1953 to overthrow the regime. Reza Shah returned to full power, and the United States gained a close ally. But the people of Iran got twenty-seven more years of royal despotism. Similarly, in 1954 the United States collaborated with right-wing army officers in Guatemala to oust President Jacobo Arbenz (in office 1951–1954). He had not only enacted land reforms that offended the United Fruit Company, an American corporation, but also cultivated friendly ties with communist governments. Following the coup, Guatemala descended into decades of military dictatorship and civil war.

On the Soviet side, Khrushchev and his successors also saw opportunities to project Soviet imperial power in informal ways. He energized Russian foreign policy, offering economic and military aid to friendly or neutral countries and exploiting unstable situations. The Cold War reached a critical turning point in 1962, when the Soviets installed intermediate range missiles in Cuba. Three years earlier, Fidel Castro (in office 1959–2008) and a guerrilla army dedicated to radical, Marxist-inspired social reform had emerged from mountain hideouts to overthrow the oppressive government of Fulgencio Batista, a close ally of American business. When Castro confiscated $1 billion worth of American property, the United States broke diplomatic relations. Having nowhere else to turn, Castro asked the Soviet Union to buy Cuban sugar, its main export, and to provide technical and military aid. In response, President Kennedy authorized the CIA and Cuban exiles to invade the island at the Bay of Pigs, a wretchedly planned operation that ended in disaster. Nevertheless, Kennedy continued to try to destabilize Castro's regime, including a trade embargo.

The Cuban revolution surprised Soviet leaders because a Marxist-Leninist regime had come to power in the Western Hemisphere without them having done anything to make it happen. Khrushchev apparently thought that by placing missiles in Cuba he would simultaneously protect his new client and encourage communist revolutionaries elsewhere in Latin America. "It was clear to me," he later wrote, "that we might very well lose Cuba if we didn't take some decisive steps in her defense."[9] When Kennedy learned that Soviet rockets were to be installed ninety miles from Florida, he saw no choice but confrontation. In October 1962 he announced to jittery television audiences around the world that a Soviet missile launch on any target in the Western Hemisphere would provoke immediate retaliation. But rather than ordering air strikes on the rocket sites, he dispatched a naval flotilla to block Soviet supply ships from reaching Cuba. Knowing well that the United States far outgunned him in numbers of intercontinental missiles, Khrushchev backed down. The crisis did not end, however, in American triumph. Khrushchev negotiated removal of the missiles already in Cuba for withdrawal of U.S. nuclear weapons from Turkey and Kennedy's promise not to invade the island again.

The Cuban missile crisis had important political consequences. Both superpowers grasped more urgently the need to keep lines of communication open between them to prevent mutual misunderstandings, however loud the public rhetoric. Though the Soviets agreed to tread lightly in Latin America, the two powers ratcheted up their rivalry in the young states of Asia and Africa. Meanwhile, Castro's light shone brighter than ever among leftist and communist leaders around the world because he had stood up to his mighty capitalist neighbor.

Fights for Freedom and Justice

FOCUS In what ways did global economic and political change in the three decades after World War II affect the development of movements for colonial independence and social reform?

The fact that some societies in the postwar world enjoyed rising living standards and reasonably responsible governments roused yearnings for similar life benefits nearly everywhere else. In colonial dependencies and in states with relatively small economies, disappointed economic hopes among middle and poorer classes aggravated social tensions and helped stir popular revolutions, civil struggles, and violent protests. After a cluster of newly independent states joined the United Nations between 1946 and 1950, there was a five-year lull. The second wave of colonial flag-lowering started in 1955, continuing steadily, especially in Africa, during the following two decades. In 1950 the United Nations had 50 members; by 1975 it had 144 (see Map 27.3). In addition to movements against colonial rule,

Khrushchev pulls his rockets out of Cuba. This cartoon, originally published in the *Hartford Times*, parodies the Soviet Union's decision to withdraw its ballistic missiles from Castro's Cuba. Edmund Valtman, the artist, won the Pulitzer Prize for editorial cartoons in 1962. How does this image portray the relationship between Cuba and the USSR?

1945–1950
1951–1955
1956–1980
✦ Violent anticolonial conflicts

MALTA 1964
CYPRUS 1960
TUNISIA 1956
MOROCCO 1956
ISRAEL 1948
SYRIA 1946
WESTERN SAHARA 1975
ALGERIA 1962
LIBYA 1951
JORDAN 1946
KUWAIT 1961
PAKISTAN 1947
MAURITANIA 1960
MALI 1960
NIGER 1960
BAHRAIN 1971
QATAR 1971
U.A.E 1971
INDIA 1947
LAOS 1954
NORTH VIETNAM 1954
SENEGAL 1960
CHAD 1960
OMAN 1971
PAKISTAN 1947
BANGLADESH 1973
MYANMAR (BURMA) 1948
Vietnam unified 1975
GAMBIA 1965
GUINEA 1958
BURKINA FASO 1960
BENIN 1960
NIGERIA 1960
SUDAN 1956
YEMEN 1967
SOUTH YEMEN 1967
SRI LANKA (CEYLON) 1948
SOUTH VIETNAM 1954
PHILIPPINES 1946
CÔTE D'IVOIRE 1960
CENTRAL AFRICAN REP. 1960
CAMBODIA 1953
GUINEA-BISSAU 1974
SIERRE LEONE 1961
GHANA 1957
TOGO 1960
CAMEROON 1960
SOMALIA 1960
MALDIVES 1965
MALAYSIA 1963
SÃO TOMÉ AND PRÍNCIPE
GABON 1960
CONGO 1960
UGANDA 1962
KENYA 1963
EQUATORIAL GUINEA 1968
RWANDA 1962
REP. OF CONGO 1960
BURUNDI 1962
TANZANIA 1966
INDONESIA 1949
PAPUA NEW GUINEA 1975
ANGOLA 1975
COMOROS 1975
ZAMBIA 1964
MALAWI 1964
MAURITIUS 1968
ZIMBABWE 1980
MOZAMBIQUE 1975
BOTSWANA 1966
MADAGASCAR 1960
SWAZILAND 1968
LESOTHO 1966
AUSTRALIA

0   1000   2000 mi
0   1000   2000 km

MAP 27.3 New sovereign states in Afroeurasia, 1945–1980.
Why did many Asian dependencies achieve independence between 1945 and 1956 and so many African ones only after 1956? What political or cultural similarities and differences do you notice among the dependencies that had violent struggles before achieving independence?

millions of people in sovereign states, including the richest countries in the world, took to the streets to register dissent over inequality and oppression. Popular protest around the world reached a crescendo in 1968.

Paths to Independence: Protest and Negotiation

Between 1956 and 1980 forty new states emerged in Africa. In most cases the decolonization process took place without battlefield violence. Nationalist parties waged their struggles with petitions, marches, strikes, boycotts, and short urban uprisings, tactics that produced death and injury, but not on a grand scale. In no African colony did nationalist leaders wish to break up the territory or wreck its governing apparatus. Rather, nationalists aimed initially to assume full control of the same administrative organs and the same territorial boundaries that European invaders had created earlier.

None of the imperial powers in Africa—Britain, France, Belgium, Portugal, and Spain—expected to leave as soon as they did. After World War II, Britain and France proclaimed new economic and political development programs, expecting that small minorities of men and women with Western educations would willingly collaborate to improve, at a gradual pace, the living standards of poor majorities. Most nationalists, on the contrary, regarded every useful economic project and every small political reform as an argument for full independence sooner rather than later. Moreover, between 1950 and 1975, one imperial power after another (the last being Portugal) conceded that they could no longer afford their empires, neither the expense of relentless suppression of nationalist opposition nor the costs of serious economic development.

To politicians in London and Paris, the alternative of letting leaders of new nations largely finance their own development, while at the same time cultivating friendly business relations with them, looked increasingly attractive.

Britain, moreover, was willing to defer to the United States in formulating strategies to keep communists or other anti-capitalist radicals from getting control of nationalist movements or seizing power in new states.

New states in British Africa. Great Britain had fifteen dependencies in Africa, the largest of them Nigeria, which had a population in 1960 of nearly forty million, eight times more people than in Scotland. Since the interwar decades, British administrators had been working with small educated elites to expand, without any sense of hurry, indigenous participation in political institutions like advisory councils, local governments, or civil services. But after 1945, independence movements gained momentum. In the British Gold Coast, renamed Ghana after independence, Kwame Nkrumah (1909–1972) emerged in the late 1940s as tropical Africa's first larger-than-life nationalist hero and mass organizer. Educated in the United States and inspired by Gandhi's nonviolent resistance strategies in India, he formed the Convention People's Party (CPP), which coordinated rallies, marches, strikes, and boycotts to push relentlessly against the British regime.

In 1951 Britain agreed to a general election, hoping that the radical CPP would lose it. That did not happen, and colonial officials had no choice but to appoint Nkrumah, who was in jail at the time, "leader of government business." In 1954, African American writer Richard Wright visited Ghana. Attending a CPP rally, he bore witness to Nkrumah's remarkable ability to rouse urban crowds and personify the nationalist cause.

> The speaker [one of Nkrumah's supporters] threw a challenging question in English requiring a yes or no answer, for he wanted the audience to participate in the meeting . . .

> "Nkrumah has led you this far and he will lead you on! . . . You must believe that he'll never let you down! He went to prison for you; he suffered for you; he'll lay down his life for you! . . .
> "Will *he* fight for you?
> "Yes!
> "Will *you* fight for him?
> "Yes!
> "And what are we fighting for?
> "FREE—DOOOOM! FREE—DOOOOM!"[10]

Three years later, Ghana achieved independence under Nkrumah's presidency. Between then and 1965, Britain dispossessed itself of ten other dependencies in Africa, including enormous Nigeria, without prolonged violence.

New states in French Africa. Shortly after World War II the newly constituted French Fourth Republic declared that it had no intention of shedding its Asian and African empire. By the end of 1954, however, the Viet Minh nationalist army had forced France to leave Vietnam (see Chapter 26), and Muslim nationalists had started an insurrection in Algeria. Those developments inspired educated elites, trade unions, and urban youth in France's immense tropical African territories to press for self-rule. The people of those colonies also watched nationalists in Morocco and Tunisia win independence from France in 1956 with warm support from the United States.

As in the British case, France's postwar government announced plans to develop its tropical African dependencies and to expand the number of *évolués*—Africans considered culturally "evolved" because they had French-style educations—to be permitted to stand for election to the French National Assembly. As in the British colonies, however, nationalists, with some encouragement from French

Voters cast their ballots in Senegal, 1956. Africans in French colonies voted for representatives to the French National Assembly, but this limited civic participation did not quell nationalist resistance to colonial rule. Some Africans tore up their ballots to protest the lack of African control of local government, arguing that representation in Paris was no substitute for independence. How did the timing of voting rights for women in French-ruled Africa compare with that of women's enfranchisement in France (see the section called "Feminist movements").

Frantz Fanon on the Shortcomings of the National Bourgeoisie

One of the most influential texts to emerge from colonial independence movements is Frantz Fanon's The Wretched of the Earth. *Fanon (1925–1961) came from a middle-class family on the French Caribbean island of Martinique. During World War II he went to North Africa to join the Free French resistance against the Germans. He was wounded in battle and awarded the Croix de Guerre. After the war he studied medicine and psychiatry in France. There, he became starkly aware of the limits of social assimilation. Though he had grown up in a thoroughly French environment and fought for the country, whites never viewed him as an equal. His interest in the psychological effects of colonialism resulted in his first book,* Black Skin, White Masks *(1952).*

In 1953 Fanon accepted a position at an Algerian psychiatric hospital and gave support to FLN revolutionaries. He became acutely aware, through experiences of his patients, of the violent foundations of French colonial rule. In 1956 the French government expelled him from Algeria. He then moved to Tunisia where he continued his work on behalf of Algerian independence.

Suffering from terminal leukemia, Fanon wrote The Wretched of the Earth *in 1961. The book attracted notoriety for its apparent approval of violence as a means to end colonial rule. Fanon recognized, however, that both perpetrators and victims of violence can never escape its psychological effects. In subsequent essays he explained that revolutionary violence must be short lived, or it will destroy all whom it touches.*

In the excerpt below, he discusses how the nation (here referring to a body of people with shared political goals) must negotiate the transition from colonialism to independence. Within a general Marxist framework of class struggle, Fanon argues that the indigenous colonial bourgeoisie are ill equipped to lead the nation because they have identified with the values of their capitalist colonial oppressors and lost touch with the masses.

The national middle class which takes over power at the end of the colonial regime is an under-developed middle class. It has practically no economic power, and in any case it is in no way commensurate with the bourgeoisie of the mother country which it hopes to replace. . . .

Seen through its eyes, its mission has nothing to do with transforming the nation; it consists, prosaically, of being the transmission line between the nation and a capitalism, rampant though camouflaged, which today puts on the masque of neocolonialism. The national bourgeoisie will be quite content with the role of the Western bourgeoisie's business agent, and it will play its part without any complexes in a most dignified manner. But this same lucrative role, this cheap-jack's function, this meanness of outlook and this absence of all ambition symbolize the incapability of the national middle class to fulfill its historic role of bourgeoisie. Here, the dynamic, pioneer aspect, the characteristics of the inventor and of the discoverer of new worlds which are found in all national bourgeoisies are lamentably absent. In the colonial countries, the spirit of indulgence is dominant at the core of the bourgeoisie; and this is because the national bourgeoisie identifies itself with the Western bourgeoisie, from whom it has learnt its lessons. It follows the Western bourgeoisie along its path of negation and decadence without ever having emulated it in its first stages of exploration and invention, stages which are an acquisition of that Western bourgeoisie whatever the circumstances. . . . The national bourgeoisie will be greatly helped on its way towards decadence by the Western bourgeoisies, who come to

it as tourists avid for the exotic, for big-game hunting and for casinos. . . . Because it is bereft of ideas, because it lives to itself and cuts itself off from the people, undermined by its hereditary incapacity to think in terms of all the problems of the nation as seen from the point of view of the whole of that nation, the national middle class will have nothing better to do than to take on the role of manager for Western enterprise, and it will in practice set up its country as the brothel of Europe. . . .

If you really wish your country to avoid regression, or at best halts and uncertainties, a rapid step must be taken from national consciousness to political and social consciousness. . . . The battle-line against hunger, against ignorance, against poverty and against unawareness ought to be ever present in the muscles and the intelligences of men and women. . . . There must be an economic program; there must also be a doctrine concerning the division of wealth and social relations. . . . It is only when men and women are included on a vast scale in enlightened and fruitful work that form and body are given to that consciousness. . . . The living expression of the nation is the moving consciousness of the whole of the people; it is the coherent, enlightened action of men and women. . . . No leader, however valuable he may be, can substitute himself for the popular will; and the national government, before concerning itself about international prestige, ought first to give back their dignity to all citizens.

Source: Frantz Fanon, *The Wretched of the Earth,* trans. Constance Farrington (New York: Grove Press, 1965), 149, 152–154, 203–205.

Thinking Critically

Why, in Fanon's view, does the national middle class feel a stronger relationship to the colonizer than it does to others in its own country? What do you think Fanon means by saying that the middle class will turn its country into the "brothel of Europe"? What do you think he means by the term "neocolonialism"? What problems must a new nation first address to ensure its viability? From this selection, what can you infer about Fanon's views of those taking power in newly independent countries? In what ways, if any, does the selection reveal the influence of Marxism on Fanon's thought?

communists and socialists, agitated for one reform and compromise after another. Urban laborers, dissatisfied with pay, working conditions, and social discrimination, continued to organize strikes, and a stream of young men and women in big cities like Dakar and Abidjan joined nationalist political groups. In 1956 the government in Paris responded by dividing French West Africa and French Equatorial Africa, its two big colonial federations, into smaller political units, hoping to fragment and weaken nationalist elites. This scheme had little effect, and in any case revolutionary violence in Algeria spread to France, bringing the Fourth Republic to its knees in 1958. Charles De Gaulle, leader of the Free French in World War II, came out of retirement to proclaim the Fifth Republic and preside over a new constitution. He made one last effort to keep the African colonies within the French fold but by then had run out of persuasive arguments. In 1960 fourteen new republics in West and Equatorial Africa, plus the island of Madagascar, achieved full sovereignty.

Paths to Independence: Insurgency and Revolution

Among the dozens of territories that sought and won independence in the third quarter of the century, only a few witnessed prolonged fighting between colonizer and colonized. One example is the British East African colony of Kenya, where a small but politically powerful European settler population adamantly opposed African independence. There, violence broke out in 1952. African guerrillas, mainly Kikuyu-speaking peasants and urban poor frustrated over landlessness, unemployment, and low-wage labor on European-owned coffee and tea estates, set up rebel bases in central Kenya's forests. Colonial forces, which gave the uprising the derogatory name Mau Mau, launched counterinsurgency operations and imprisoned tens of thousands of men and women. The fighting ended in 1955, after 95 Europeans and at least 11,500 Africans lost their lives. Shortly afterward, however, London decided to negotiate decolonization before another violent outbreak occurred. Kenya became independent in 1963 under the presidency of Jomo Kenyatta.

The Algerian Revolution. Algeria was different from all other French overseas colonies because its inhabitants included about one million people of European origin. They constituted a minority of about 15 percent of the population, which was predominantly Arabic- or Berber-speaking Muslims. Most European settlers fiercely opposed Algerian self-rule under any authority except its own, and the Fourth Republic regarded the territory, not as a dependent colony, but as a permanent part of France. The economic and social gulf between the privileged, mostly city-dwelling European minority and the Muslim population of peasants, urban workers, and small entrepreneurs was immense. Under great settler pressure, successive French governments refused to make any significant moves toward majority rule.

The consequence was eight years of bitter war. In November 1954, just a few months after France withdrew from Vietnam in defeat, Algerian insurgents instigated a countrywide rebellion. The National Liberation Front (FLN), which orchestrated the rising, demanded a sovereign, democratic, and socialist Algeria guided by Islamic ideals. The French authorities responded with brutal repression, which only spread the revolutionary fire. By mid-1957 the colonial army appeared to be winning the war, but the FLN continued to operate from havens in neighboring Morocco and Tunisia. Facing both colossal costs and nothing but intransigence on the part of settler leaders, De Gaulle opened negotiations with the FLN in 1960. Independence came two years later. About 85 percent of the European population refused Algerian citizenship and fled the country in near panic during the final months of the war. The new nationalist regime took over a country in a state of physical and economic collapse.

Southern Africa. Armed struggles broke out in three southern African colonies in the 1960s. The British dependency of Southern Rhodesia (Zimbabwe after independence) had a European settler population of only about 5 percent, but this minority dominated politics and the export economy. Watching Britain give up one African possession after another and counting on support from white-ruled South Africa, Southern Rhodesia's white leaders made a Unilateral Declaration of Independence in 1965 to perpetuate their authority. Britain protested but did not send troops. Zimbabwe's African nationalist parties stepped up guerrilla operations. Meanwhile, armed resistance also intensified in the two big Portuguese colonies of Angola and Mozambique. In those cases the metropolitan government, itself an authoritarian dictatorship under António Salazar, refused all negotiation with nationalist leaders. In 1974, Portuguese officers, weary of protracted African wars of no discernible benefit to tiny Portugal, overthrew Salazar, paving the way for democracy at home and independence for the colonies in 1975. In consequence, Zimbabwe's guerrilla fighters were able to take advantage of sanctuaries in Angola and Mozambique, which led to negotiated independence under majority rule in 1980.

Struggles for Stability in Young States

In the 1950s and 1960s new states celebrated independence flush with hope for rapid economic development. Few of these states had much industry. Rather, they exported food and mineral commodities, as they had during the colonial era. During the postwar global boom, however, world prices for many commodities rose higher, which translated into at least modest growth for many new countries. In Ghana, the Ivory Coast, and Kenya, among other states, society made impressive gains in health care, life expectancy, and education.

Yet rising gross domestic product seldom produced long-term political calm. Few of the states that started out as presidential republics or constitutional monarchies followed India's path to democracy. In the 1950s and 1960s military officers seized power in many states. Eighteen coups took place in Africa alone. In several countries, elected presidents transformed themselves into dictators, banning all political parties except their own. In a few states, debilitating civil wars broke out.

Upon gaining independence, nationalist leaders took over the civil services, police, and communication networks that the colonial regimes had left behind. Most new governments also put themselves in control of economic resources with the goal of creating a more equitable society. In most of these countries, however, development plans lost steam. Highly skilled workers, up-to-date technology, and investment capital were usually in short supply. Railway, telephone, and electrical networks did not improve nearly fast enough after decades of colonial neglect. Government-paid jobs mushroomed, but industrialization projects did not. By the mid-1960s the global boom had passed its peak. Revenue from export commodities, typically a young state's biggest income source, began to drop. Where top leaders had failed to secure their own power, disgruntled political groups, often military men (the army being the only organization with plenty of guns) threw the old nationalist leaders out.

In Ghana, for example, Kwame Nkrumah, the founding president, lost power to a military faction in 1966 after the price of cocoa, the country's leading export, began to plummet. That same year, Nigeria, suffering from severe tensions among regional political groups, experienced the first of a long series of military takeovers. Competition for control of newly discovered oil made matters worse and led directly to a three-year civil war (1967–1970) in which the southeastern region tried unsuccessfully to form a separate state named Biafra.

The Congo fell into civil turmoil just two weeks after it celebrated independence from Belgium in June 1960. In contrast to Britain and France, Belgium not only banned all nationalist political activity in its enormous colony until the mid-1950s, but also permitted only a handful of Africans to get responsible government jobs or even high school educations. When popular riots broke out in the capital city of Leopoldville (Kinshasa), the Belgian regime organized slapdash elections to a new Congolese legislature, then abruptly abandoned the colony.

Independent Congo unraveled almost immediately. More riots broke out, army units mutinied, and in the copper-rich southern province of Katanga rebels in alliance with European mining interests declared a separate state. Just before independence, Patrice Lumumba (1925–1961), a former postal clerk, founded a national political party dedicated to transcending the country's complex ethnic and linguistic divisions. But as the Congo's first prime minister, he faced an agonizing task of restoring order. There is no evidence that Lumumba was a communist, but his radical denunciation of Belgium and a plea to the Soviet Union to send aid moved the United States to support a UN peacekeeping force.

Patrice Lumumba, Congo's first prime minister, leaving the National Senate, 1960. The first democratically elected leader of Congo faced huge challenges during his twelve-week term in office. In this photo Lumumba celebrates the 41–2 vote of confidence, called in response to his handling of the Katanga succession. In 2002, Belgium issued an apology to Congo for Lumumba's murder in 1961.

Lumumba agreed to this plan, but in 1961, Joseph Mobutu, a rising Congolese military star, conspired with Belgian operatives and the U.S. CIA to have the prime minister murdered. UN troops extinguished the Katanga rebellion in 1963, and two years later, after about a million Congolese had died in violent upheaval, Mobutu seized full power. There he remained for more than thirty years, keeping the country unified, cooperating with capitalist mining enterprise, and adamantly opposing the slightest democratic reform.

The turbulent Middle East. The era of formal European colonial rule ended in most of the Arabic-speaking Middle East shortly after World War II. Even so, continuing hostility between the Jewish state of Israel and its neighbors, concentrations of hundreds of thousands of Palestinian refugees in camps in Egypt and Jordan, and the rising international stakes for access to Middle Eastern oil made for volatile postcolonial conditions. Popular opinion in the Arab states overwhelmingly regarded Israel as a foreign intruder and proxy for continuing Western imperial domination. Israel gained international credibility by winning the 1948 war with its Arab neighbors and believed it deserved regional acceptance. But tensions remained high, including chronic fighting along the border between Israel and Egypt. Arab leaders dealing with pressing economic problems at home had no wish to undermine their own authority by moving to normalize relations with Israel.

Arab national governments, some ideologically socialist, others pro-Western and conservative, quarreled intensely with each other, but they also joined together to fight three more wars with Israel, in 1956, 1967, and 1973. In Egypt, President Gamal Abdel Nasser put himself forward as champion of regional unification, promising to absorb Israel into a large pan-Arab state. In 1956 he negotiated with the British to end their occupation of the Suez Canal Zone, but shortly thereafter he suddenly nationalized the canal's operation. Two-thirds of Western Europe's oil supplies passed through the waterway, and in October, Britain, France, and Israel devised a secret plan to take back the canal and overthrow Nasser. When the military operation got under way, the United States, seeing the situation from a wider regional perspective, refused to back its allies. "How could we possibly support Britain and France," President Eisenhower protested, "if in doing so we lose the whole Arab world?"[11] The Soviet Union, which had good relations with Nasser, threatened nuclear retaliation if the attack did not stop. Neither Britain nor France could afford to defy U.S. opinion. Within a few weeks they and the Israelis pulled out of Egyptian territory, ending the Suez Crisis. The war made Nasser a regional hero. On its side, Israel demonstrated once again its military strength but also reinforced the Arab conviction that Israel had no genuine desire for peace with its neighbors.

Shaky calm prevailed for eleven years, but in the spring of 1967 tensions reached a boiling point once again. Nasser continued to seek Arab unity by vowing to extinguish Israel, while the Soviet Union sent both Egypt and Syria cargos of weapons. The United States proclaimed its commitment to Israel's defense while tending carefully to its oil interests elsewhere in the region. Following a succession of miscues between Israel and its neighbors over who intended to do what, Israeli jets simultaneously attacked Egypt, Syria, and Jordan on June 5, destroying the air forces of all three countries. Israeli forces then invaded the Sinai Peninsula, Gaza, the Golan Heights in Syria, and the West Bank (Jordanian territory west of the Jordan River). Israel's victory in this Six Day War (or June War) discredited all the Arab regimes, especially Nasser, whose army lost twelve thousand soldiers, the Sinai oil fields, and revenue from the Suez Canal, which remained closed to shipping until 1975. Israel occupied 28,000 square miles of new territory, which included 300,000 Arabs, many of them impoverished refugees from the 1948 conflict (see Map 27.4). The war compounded regional hostilities and strengthened the hand of Palestinians determined to wage guerrilla warfare against Israel. The

MAP 27.4 Israel and its occupied territories.

What aspects of physical geography might have affected the course and outcome of the 1967 Arab–Israeli War?

Legend:
- Israel after UN partition of Palestine, 1947
- Territory occupied by Israel in 1948–1949
- Territory occupied by Israel in 1967

fourth war of the era broke out in 1973, an event associated with the economic crises to be described in Chapter 28.

Vietnam between civil war and Cold War.
Vietnam achieved independence in 1954, several years sooner than most of France's colonies, because communist Viet Minh forces under the leadership of Ho Chi Minh humbled the French army in battle. Vietnam, however, did not achieve unification. Ho's Indochinese Communist Party controlled the north but not the south, where anticommunist sentiment remained strong, especially among the land-owning elite and the politically influential Roman Catholic minority population. Terms of Vietnam's independence (the Geneva Accords) projected reunification in 1956, following an election. But no vote took place because the United States, replacing France as patron of pro-Western political groups throughout Southeast Asia, engineered the installation of Ngo Dinh Diem, a staunch anticommunist, as president of South Vietnam.

In the north, Ho's regime, with aid from both the Soviet Union and China, adopted socialist prescriptions of one-party control, state-led industrialization, and land reforms to give private estate lands to peasants. In the south, by contrast, the Diem government allied itself with the land-owning class and made policies that favored Catholics over the Buddhist majority. Despite injections of American money, Diem steadily lost popular support, while pro-communist elements in the countryside organized the National Liberation Front (NLF), or Viet Cong, to incite revolution. Vowing to reunite Vietnam, Ho supported the NLF, provoking all-out war between north and south by the early 1960s. Both the United States and the Soviet Union came to see this struggle as a microcosm of their own global contest. The U.S. government declared that it would not stomach any more communist regimes in Asia, while the Soviets intensified their strategy to support not only communist but radical leftist governments wherever they could.

In 1963 the United States allowed South Vietnamese officers to overthrow and kill Diem, although political leadership continued to deteriorate. The Saigon government moved rapidly into the informal American imperial orbit, depending on the United States for as much as 80 percent of its economy. When NLF forces seized control of about half of South Vietnam, U.S. military forces took on more of the fighting. U.S. president Lyndon Johnson (in office 1963–1969) saw the war as a test of U.S. credibility. "If we are driven from the field in Viet-Nam, then no nation can ever again have the same confidence in American promise, or in American protection."[12] From 1965 to 1973 Presidents Johnson and Richard Nixon (in office 1969–1974) tried successively to achieve victory by military escalation, including deployment of more than 500,000 troops and strategic bombing of both North and South Vietnam, plus NLF and North Vietnamese sanctuaries in Cambodia.

These tactics stopped neither Viet Cong operations nor the movements of North Vietnamese troops into the south. In 1968 the NLF launched the Tet Offensive, a militarily unsuccessful but nonetheless shocking series of urban guerrilla assaults that reached the gates of the U.S. embassy in Saigon. After that, American public opinion shifted steadily against the war as a waste of life and resources. Nixon attempted to get out of Vietnam with honor by dropping more bombs while at the same time withdrawing troops and opening negotiations with the North Vietnamese. The adversaries finally concluded a ceasefire agreement in 1973. But two years later, the South Vietnamese army collapsed, as northern forces overran the country, finally reuniting it. More than fifty-eight thousand Americans and about four million Vietnamese died in the war.

A refugee runs with her possessions during the Tet Offensive. Vietcong and North Vietnamese fighters launched urban assaults in January 1968, destabilizing Saigon and several other cities. Although the U.S. and South Vietnamese armies regained control of Saigon by March, the battle signaled a turning point in American opinion of the war. How might photos like this one have affected American attitudes?

High Expectations and Social Protest

Peoples who were subjects of neither foreign colonial masters nor rapacious dictators but nonetheless suffered discrimination, powerlessness, or poverty found new voice in the 1960s. Young people, many of them college students, added to the wave of social discontent with protests against the war in Vietnam, stifling conformism in education, and the failure of parents and other authority figures to understand the anxieties and aspirations of a generation that grew up enveloped in material plenty. If a single thread ran through the social protest movements of this period, it was the conviction that societies that congratulated themselves for being prosperous and democratic failed too often to guarantee the social equality and individual freedom that a world without fascist empires was supposed to offer. The movements that sprang up in the 1960s generally adopted the symbols and rhetoric of the political left, though the ideological spectrum ran from moderate democratic socialism to the radical revolutionism inspired by Mao Zedong.

Discrimination and racism in the post-Nazi decades. To the global majority, systems of social inequality founded on a hierarchy of superior and inferior races looked especially antiquated and hateful in the post-Nazi era. In a few places, however, such systems held on after the war. In the United States, Martin Luther King, Jr., and others led the nonviolent, Gandhi-inspired civil rights movement to end legalized racism in the southern states. The movement set in motion a series of legislative and court actions culminating in the Civil Rights Act of 1964, which guaranteed all adult Americans the right to vote. These new laws were partial victories, and in the later 1960s, social dissenters focused on economic discrimination against blacks and other minorities, especially in the inner cities of the North and West.

The most notorious case of institutionalized racism was South Africa, where the dominant population of European descent represented, not the majority as in the American South, but a minority of about 20 percent of a total 1950 population of 12.4 million. Africans, the group subject to the most drastic repression and discrimination, numbered about 68 percent. Minorities of "Coloreds" (people of mixed race) and Asians had only slightly better legal status. Like the European minority in Algeria, South African whites, who spoke Afrikaans or English, regarded themselves as home-grown citizens of their country, not as foreign colonial rulers. The great majority of them believed white domination to be rooted in the natural order of things.

Nevertheless, South Africa was changing fast after World War II. The mineral and farm export economy boomed, and Africans poured into the cities and mining areas, seeking wage work and relief from life on parched and unfertile rural land. As their numbers grew, these urban dwellers became increasingly impatient with pervasive racism. In 1948, however, the ultraconservative National Party won a majority in the parliamentary government, an election in which blacks could not vote. The new government responded to rapid social transformations by fortifying the existing system with new laws known collectively as **apartheid,** or "separation." These measures aimed to deny Africans any rights to live permanently in cities. Rather, the state required them to have legal residence in designated rural "homelands," or Bantustans, where they constituted giant pools of labor to be moved temporarily in and out of cities or mines as needed. Apartheid laws also included strict social segregation, bans on interracial marriage, and requirements that African men and women carry "pass books" authorizing them to travel from one place to another. In the 1950s the government spent twelve times more per capita on the education of white children than on Africans, a large percentage of whom did not attend school at all.

In a resource-rich country whose continuing industrialization required increasing economic flexibility and integration, apartheid was utterly irrational. It was founded ultimately on well-justified white fears that Africans despised the racist order. From the late 1940s onward, in fact, South Africa descended into festering civil conflict punctuated by strikes, boycotts, and marches. State authorities responded harshly, for example, shooting sixty-nine Africans at an anti–pass law rally at Sharpeville in 1960. After that incident, the African National Congress (ANC) and the more radical Pan-African Congress, the two major African nationalist parties, organized armed units that carried out acts of sabotage. The white government banned the ANC and in 1964 sent Nelson Mandela (1918-) and other nationalist leaders to serve life sentences on desolate Robben Island in the South Atlantic. At his trial on charges of sabotage, Mandela explained why he had taken recourse to violence: "We were placed in a position in which we had either to accept a permanent state of inferiority, or to defy the government. We chose to defy the law. . . . When . . . the government resorted to a show of force to crush opposition to its policies, only then did we decide to answer violence with violence."[13]

The imprisonment of ANC leaders seriously hurt the resistance movement, but in the meantime more Africans managed to gain literacy and even attend universities, though within the framework of segregated "Bantu education." This group became increasingly politicized and internationally connected. In 1976, radicalized students spearheaded a new and ultimately successful mass movement for freedom (see Chapter 28).

In other parts of the world, efforts to fight oppression had mixed results. In Northern Ireland, which remained part of the United Kingdom after the Republic of Ireland achieved independence in 1922, Roman Catholics organized mass demonstrations in 1968 to protest economic inequality and the political domination of the Protestant majority. This initially peaceful action degenerated into fighting between

apartheid The political and legal system in force in South Africa from 1948 to 1994 designed to ensure the domination of the white minority over the majority population.

Protesters flee from police gunfire in Sharpeville, South Africa. Police used live ammunition to disperse participants in a peaceful demonstration organized by the Pan-Africanist Congress to protest race-based pass laws. Many of the sixty-nine dead were shot in the back. How might this event have radicalized both black South Africans and international opposition to the white minority government?

Catholic and Protestant paramilitary bands, which provoked British military intervention. Peace was not achieved until 1998. In Latin America, left-leaning Roman Catholic clergy came to the defense of poor Indian and *mestizo* majorities, proclaiming a new "liberation theology" dedicated to alleviating poverty, hunger, disease, and class discrimination. Most activists in this movement assisted poor neighborhoods and villages, but religious and political conservatives branded them as disguised Marxists. The movement faded in the 1970s when Pope John Paul II, a fierce anticommunist, turned against it.

Radicalism in the 1960s. Between 1964 and 1970, young activists representing the most advantaged populations in the world took to the streets, mobilizing an assortment of radical movements for equality and justice. Underlying this radical turn was the coming of age of the baby-boom generation, the relatively large demographic group born in Europe and North America in the decade after World War II. Responding to the postwar economic upswing, baby boomers flooded into colleges and universities. The rising incomes of working parents, the declining demand for youthful farm labor, and the opening of many new public universities propelled this development. The United States led the way in mass higher education, but Western European student enrollments also rose, depending on the country, anywhere from 300 to 900 percent between 1960 and 1980.

Middle-class students of the postwar decades tended to have high expectations of both satisfying careers and the world's material and moral progress. By the 1960s, however,

disappointment and skepticism began to set in. Political and cultural leaders appeared to endorse spirit-sapping consumerism rather than creativity, "establishment politics" rather than participatory democracy, capitalist profits rather than social justice, and threats of nuclear annihilation rather than global peace. Universities as semi-enclosed intellectual and social communities proved to be warm incubators for radicalism, the more so when educational authorities tried to contain free expression. Student activists trended to the political left ideologically, specifically to the New Left, a movement for social justice that was as wary of doctrinaire, state-controlled communism as it was of capitalist materialism.

Radical organizations and spontaneous protests sprouted across the industrialized world and among urban middle-class youth nearly everywhere. Television broadcasts of demonstrations, marches, and confrontations between protesters and police reinforced the impression of a worldwide community of young people who shared a common fight for justice, a global cohort that, according to a slogan of the times, "did not trust anyone over thirty." In the United States, the civil rights movement fueled broader-based radicalism that targeted the Vietnam War, the draft, and corporations that built weapons. Students in Europe, Japan, Mexico, and many other places took up similar causes but also protested the failure of governments to expand university access nearly fast enough to meet demand.

Student and, in some countries, worker protests reached a crescendo in the spring and summer of 1968. In the United States, public opinion turned against the Vietnam quagmire,

A May Day rally in Paris, 1968. Thousands of workers and students marched across the city. Their banners demand peace in Vietnam, higher wages, and an end to the state of emergency the French government imposed in an attempt to quell protests.

Protesters arrested in Mexico City. Demonstrations turned violent on October 3, 1968, as university students clashed with police. The event, known as the "Massacre of Tlatelolco" after the urban plaza where it occurred, killed as many as three hundred people, though Mexican media reported only 27 dead at the time. How would you characterize the range of government responses to popular protests in the 1960s in different countries?

Alexander Dubček: Leader of the Prague Spring

Alexander Dubček addresses factory workers in Prague, August 1968.

Shortly after Alexander Dubček (DOOB-chehk, 1921–1992) assumed the office of secretary of the Czechoslovakian Communist Party in January 1968, he promised reforms to establish "socialism with a human face." In the following months, he announced new social and economic freedoms. But on August 21 he watched in alarm as Soviet army forces invaded his country, abruptly ending what became known as the Prague Spring.

Dubček was born in Czechoslovakia's eastern Slovak ethnic region in 1921, but he spent his early years with his family in the Soviet Union. There he enjoyed a quiet childhood and, despite Joseph Stalin's repressive rule, acquired a strong faith in Soviet communist leadership. He returned to Czechoslovakia in the late 1930s and during World War II took part in anti-German resistance. After the war he became a leader in the Slovak wing of the Czechoslovakian Communist Party and in the 1950s was selected to study at a political institute in Moscow. His time there coincided with Nikita Khrushchev's de-Stalinization campaign, a strategy that in Dubček's view showed the party could relax controls on economic and political life without jeopardizing its authority. He returned to Czechoslovakia in the late 1950s determined to work for similar reforms at home.

A retiring individual without notable speaking skill, Dubček nonetheless rose in 1963 to leadership of the Slovak Communist Party. During the next several years, Slovakians enjoyed more freedom of expression than their ethnic Czech counterparts, who lived under the hardline leadership of Antonín Novotný. Resisting all economic or social reforms and charged with corruption, Novotný yielded his party leadership to Dubček in January 1968. The new secretary moved quickly to loosen authoritarian controls on Czech citizens, authorizing new workers' councils and relaxing laws governing public speech and foreign travel. He pursued a program to implement "democratic socialism" within ten years, but he also insisted on firm party control and solid allegiance to the Soviet Union. Consequently, Dubček had to perform an intricate balancing act between popular pressure for liberalizing reforms and Russian wariness that Czechoslovakia could gradually slip out of the Soviet bloc. Dubček also faced rising criticism from other Eastern European communist leaders, who feared their own citizens' attraction to Czech-style reforms.

Dubček held talks with the Soviets in the summer of 1968 but refused to call off a planned conference to reform the party structure or agree to garrison Soviet troops on Czechoslovakian territory. This was too much for Leonid Brezhnev, general secretary of the Soviet Communist Party. On the night of August 20, Russian tanks, supported by small units from other Soviet bloc states, rolled across the Czech frontier and occupied Prague without encountering armed resistance. In the following months, Dubček tried to salvage some reforms, and Czechs launched a campaign of passive resistance. But in April 1969, he was stripped of party membership and the following year was sent to an obscure job in the forestry service, where he remained for nineteen years.

By suppressing the Prague Spring, the Soviet Union baldly reasserted its hegemony over Eastern Europe. But it severely damaged Soviet claims to leadership of the global communist movement. Romanian, Yugoslavian, and Chinese communist leaders all deplored the invasion. So did the communist parties of Western Europe and the leaders of student protest movements worldwide. As for Dubček, he returned to public life during Czechoslovakia's 1989 Velvet Revolution, when communist rule ended. He was elected chairman of the Czecho-Slovak parliament, a position he held until his death in 1992.

Thinking Critically

How do you think Dubček reconciled his commitment to the exclusive authority of the Communist Party in Czechoslovakia with his conviction that the country needed political and economic reforms?

and countrywide campus demonstrations helped persuade President Johnson to renounce a bid for reelection that year. In Paris students barricaded streets and took over parts of the city, while workers staged wildcat strikes. In the aftermath of these disturbances, President Charles De Gaulle retired to his country home, where he died a few months later. In Czechoslovakia, student demonstrations played a part in the "Prague Spring," a brief period of political liberalization that ended when Soviet and Eastern European armies sent in tanks to restore full subservience to Moscow. Student activism, along with the accompanying counterculture of rock music, flamboyant dress, long hair, drug taking, communal living, and declarations of sexual freedom, continued at a high pitch until 1970, when it lost steam quite rapidly, owing less to repression than to general exhaustion and bitter splits and conflict among various protesting groups.

Feminist movements. In the aftermath of World War II, people yearned for social stability. For the great majority of male leaders, return to normalcy meant restoring conventional family life: Women should step down from the wage jobs they had during the war and partner with breadwinning husbands to bring up young citizens and make wise consumer choices. As Cold War tensions worsened, Western leaders also contended that families in the care of modest and morally upright women offered the country's best defense against communist agents of class warfare. In the socialist countries, postwar normalcy generally meant that women should continue to work at factory and farm jobs as they had before the war, while performing the same domestic duties they always had. In most newly emerging states, male elites insisted that women who had served nationalist movements as political organizers or guerrilla fighters help build the nation on a bedrock of strong families. In Algeria, for example, the image of women as revolutionary fighters, bomb makers, and spies gave way after

independence to the ideal of the Muslim woman at home teaching children proper nationalist and Islamic values.

In the industrialized countries, however, the ideal of stay-at-home wife and mother flew in the face of facts. Throughout the 1950s and 1960s the number of females, including married women, in the paid workforce grew steadily. So also did the number of women seeking higher education. Women sought greater sexual freedom as courts and legislatures became more tolerant of birth control and family planning, notably in Europe and Japan, where wartime fears of population decline receded. Women also gained full voting rights shortly after the war in France, several Latin American countries, and most new postcolonial states.

Social and economic progress, however, did not keep pace with legal changes. In the environment of universities and competitive workplaces, women increasingly challenged the hypothesis, relentlessly urged by consumer business, that women who were not content with family care, home beautification, and personal appearance somehow suffered from psychic or emotional deficiencies. In the United States and Europe, feminist writers, including Betty Friedan, Simone de Beauvoir, and Gloria Steinem, persuaded more women that they had permission to seek opportunity and satisfaction beyond house and neighborhood. "We can no longer ignore," Friedan wrote in *The Feminine Mystique* in 1963, "that voice within women that says: 'I want something more than my husband and my children and my home.'"[14]

In the 1960s, women began to organize on a number of fronts to advocate fairness at work, reproductive choice, and attention to prostitution as a social affliction. These associations, for example, the National Organization for Women (NOW) founded in the United States in 1966, proliferated first in Western countries. They appeared shortly thereafter in Asian and African cities. This feminist wave was just gathering force in 1975, when the United Nations proclaimed "International Women's Year" and sponsored the first major international conference on women's rights in Mexico City.

· · ·

Conclusion

The third quarter of the twentieth century is still so recent that any estimation of its most important developments for the world's history must remain tentative. Consider just three factors—population, economy, and environment. The global population growth rate reached its all-time peak during those twenty-five years. It might conceivably soar again in the future, but many demographers believe that it is likely to fall in the coming century owing to the continuing decline of both mortality and birthrates.

The global economic growth rate also reached its highest historic level during that quarter-century, a feat that increased living standards in much of the world but did not prevent a widening breach between the richest and poorest populations. Since the early 1970s, global economic growth has been more volatile (see Chapter 28).

Regarding the environment, humans consumed nonrenewable energy and manipulated the biosphere on an unprecedented scale between 1950 and 1975. Human action greatly sped up ecological degradation in several different physical and natural systems. After 1975, however, humans for the first time became acutely aware of the potential damage they were causing. Consequently, some political, business, and civic leaders took action to slow environmental deterioration, though at a far more leisurely pace than seems justified from our present vantage point.

• • •

Key Terms

apartheid 811
Asian tigers 795
baby boom 791
Bretton Woods system 792
consumerism 796
Cuban missile crisis 803
feminist movement 815
Great Leap Forward 794

Great Proletarian Cultural Revolution 794
Green Revolution 800
import substitution industrialization (ISI) 795
iron curtain 801
Korean War 801
megalopolis 796

mutually assured destruction (MAD) 802
Prague Spring 815
Six Day War 809
Suez Crisis 809
Vietnam War 812
welfare state 792

Please see end of book reference section for additional reading suggestions related to this chapter.

Change over Time

Year	Event
1948	The South African government institutes apartheid.
1950–1953	The Korean War pits the Soviet-backed north against U.S.-backed south.
1952	The United States tests the first hydrogen bomb. London's Great Smog raises awareness of air pollution.
1952–1955	Kenyan guerrillas fight British colonial forces in the Mau Mau rebellion.
1953	With help from U.S. and British operatives, military officers in Iran overthrow the Mosaddiq government and reinstate the king, Reza Shah.
1954	France withdraws in defeat from Vietnam.
1954–1962	Algerian insurgents battle French authorities in the Algerian Revolution.
1955	Soviet-allied states form the Warsaw Pact.
1955–1975	Vietnam becomes the theater of a civil war and Cold War conflict.
1957	Ghana achieves independence from Britain under Kwame Nkrumah. The Soviet Union launches Sputnik, the first artificial satellite to orbit the globe. The European Economic Community is founded.
1958–1961	Mao Zedong initiates the "Great Leap Forward" to speed China's industrialization.
1960	Fourteen former French colonies in Africa win independence.
1961	A number of capitalist states form the Organization for Economic Cooperation and Development (OECD). The German Democratic Republic attempts to stop emigration with the Berlin Wall.
1962	Rachel Carson's *Silent Spring* raises awareness of the environmental toll of pesticides. The United States and Soviet Union face off in the Cuban missile crisis.
1963	The United States and the Soviet Union sign the Limited Test Ban Treaty.
1965	Britain, France, and Israel's plan to take back the Suez Canal from Egypt leads to the Suez Crisis.
1967	Israel defeats its Arab neighbors in the Six Day War.
1967–1970	Competition for control of oil leads to civil war in Nigeria.
1968	Worldwide student demonstrations coalesce around social justice issues. Soviet and Eastern European armies put an end to the Prague Spring in Czechoslovakia.
1970	The Aswan High Dam in Egypt begins operation.
1975	Portuguese African colonies gain independence. The United Nations proclaims International Women's Year.

28 Countercurrents of Change

1970 to the Present

A representation of global Internet traffic, in which each line is a data path.

Tim Berners-Lee thought about calling the software he created for sharing scientific documents between different computers the "Mine of Information" or the "Information Mesh." He finally decided on the "World Wide Web." Electronic communication had preoccupied him since childhood. Growing up in England, he built make-believe computers out of cardboard boxes, and while he was studying physics at Oxford University, he constructed a real computer using an old TV set and a soldering iron. In 1989 he went to work as a consultant at CERN, the renowned nuclear physics research center in Geneva, Switzerland.

There, he discovered that collaborating scientists had no efficient way to locate and study particular documents or data sets on one another's computers. "I found it frustrating," he later wrote, "that in those days, there was different information on different computers, but you had to log on to different computers to get at it. . . . Often it was just easier to go and ask people when they were having coffee."[1] The Internet was already available to researchers as a system for connecting computers, but scientists lacked convenient ways to share information while they sat at their individual machines.

In 1990 Berners-Lee set out to develop a relatively uncomplicated coding system for hypertext, that is, text on a computer that has embedded in it links to other text residing on the same or other computers.

His design had three fundamental elements. One was code for creating hypertext that could be used on different types of computers. He named that system HyperText Markup Language, or HTML. The second was a standard code for identifying and viewing a body of content, or "page" displayed on a computer screen. He called a page's "address" its Uniform Resource Locator (URL). Third, he worked out code for moving around the Internet from one URL to another. This was the HyperText Transfer Protocol (HTTP).

When Berners-Lee's colleagues saw that this World Wide Web (www) worked well, some of them argued that people should pay CERN a fee to use it. Berners-Lee adamantly opposed this option, insisting that the system be free because science would likely benefit in direct proportion to the number of professional users. The web was to have no central database or manager but rather to exist as an imaginary place in cyberspace where anyone who accepted the coding rules could read other people's web sites or put their own site "online."

Berners-Lee created the first World Wide Web site (http://info.cern.ch) in 1991, and thereafter web pages multiplied rapidly. The application passed quickly beyond the confines of science to the wider public. In 1992 he uploaded the first photo, a color image of Les Horribles Cernettes, a women's rock band that CERN employees started. The topic of that site suggested the web's immense possibilities beyond the networks of scientific exchange. And so it has come to pass. By mid-2012 the world had more than 4.2 billion Internet users and about 190 million active web sites.

Electronic innovations and their applications to science, energy production, manufacturing, human health, social organizations, and many other things continue to multiply at hyperspeed. In this book we have taken the view that human history is a story of growing complexity, both in the nature of interconnections among individuals and groups and in relations between people and their natural and physical environments. The pace at which humans have created and become enmeshed in new forms of complexity began accelerating faster with the fossil-fuel revolution of the eighteenth century. The rapidity of global change in the past few decades sometimes astounds and bewilders us. The term *globalization* has entered the language to encapsulate the idea that, first, human society is continuously restructuring itself in all sorts of ways and, second, human interconnections are becoming continuously more elaborate and intense.

Among animal species, humans possess a uniquely powerful aptitude for creating complexity because of what world historian David Christian has called "collective learning," the capacity to accumulate, share, organize, preserve, and transmit larger and larger amounts of information—so far without any limit in sight. In the past forty years the process of collective learning has sped up primarily owing to

• • •

the invention of complex electronic systems. These systems underlie or influence almost all other forms of change in the past few decades. The first part of this chapter therefore explores the revolution in electronic technology and its transforming effect on the ways people broadcast, analyze, and store information on a planet whose population has nearly doubled in the past forty years.

More than any other material factor, electronic innovation has powered the accelerating trends in the world toward integration and connectedness, and these trends have benefited humankind in countless ways. At the same time, however, innovation has not prevented, indeed it has contributed to, severe inequities in the way people live, as well as social anxieties, international rivalries, political violence, criminal behavior, and environmental degradation. To flourish as a species, humankind has created—appears to need

A Panoramic View

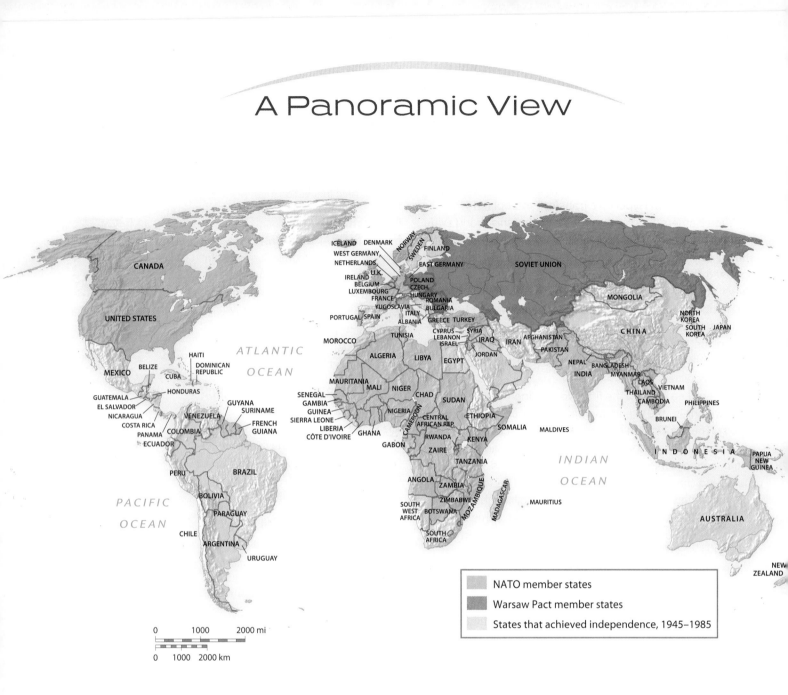

MAP 28.1 The geopolitical world, 1985.
The Cold War was often characterized as an east–west conflict. How does a global perspective encourage you to also think about north–south differences?

to create—increasingly complex systems, networks, and institutions. But as these structures become denser and more tangled, the more prone they become to instability, malfunction, or breakdown. (Indeed, scientists argue that the coherence and stability of all physical and natural systems, not just human ones, require constant inputs of energy to keep them from falling apart.) In the remaining parts of this chapter we explore human experience in the past forty years in the economic, political, and environmental realms, examining both trends of global integration and the countercurrents that have produced fragmentation, conflict, and dysfunction.

An Electrified World

FOCUS How has electronic technology transformed human communication systems and scientific and medical knowledge in the past four decades?

Electricity became a servant of human communication in the nineteenth century, when inventors discovered how to convert electrical impulses transmitted through copper wires into coded language that individuals at each end of the wire could understand. The first useful application was the telegraph. Since its advent in the 1830s, humans have put electrical charges to work energizing thousands of kinds of machines, especially those that transmit and store information.

The Era of the Integrated Circuit

In the 1950s engineers began replacing the vacuum tubes that had previously controlled electrical current in computers and other electronic appliances with much smaller solid state transistors that had semiconducting properties—the potential to conduct electricity under certain conditions. A transistor is fundamentally an electronic device that controls the flow of an electrical current and is used principally as an amplifier or a switch. Transistor technology formed a happy marriage with the binary number system, which involves only *ones* (switch on) and *zeros* (switch off) sequenced precisely to carry programmed instructions. In the 1960s scientists discovered ways to link transistors together in integrated circuits, channeling electrical energy to perform complex operations. Invention of the microchip, a wafer of silicon inscribed with numerous transistors and other electronic components, set off a contest among engineers to reduce the size of integrated circuits. The more components a chip could carry, the more data it could process. The Intel company produced a chip in 1971 that held 2,300 transistors. Today, engineers using a sophisticated technology called photolithography can place more than two billion transistors on a single chip. Integrated circuitry has become essential to nearly every type of technological advance of the past half-century that uses electricity.

The shrinking computer. During World War II, British and American scientists devised an electronic calculator to break German war codes. In the following two decades, computer research expanded in scope to take on problems of electronically processing, storing, and transmitting large quantities of data for many purposes. At first, mostly scientists, governments, and big companies used computers. The United States and the Soviet Union deployed them to fight the Cold War. The U.S. government, for example, contracted with International Business Machines (IBM) to develop early warning defenses against a Soviet air attack. Early computers were huge. The SAGE system for detecting Soviet bombers involved forty-eight computers in different locations, each one taking up about an acre of space. In the 1970s microchip circuitry solved the problem of making much smaller and more powerful computers that could perform many new tasks. The Apollo space program, including six manned moon landings between 1969 and 1972, depended on small computers. All these missions together, however, used about as much computational power as it takes today to carry out a single Internet search on a search engine like Google.

In the later 1970s young electronics experts around San Jose, California—the Silicon Valley—launched the personal computer industry. Knowing that millions of Americans already had televisions and typewriters, these inventors built user-friendly machines that incorporated screens and keyboards instead of complex programming cards and tapes. In 1976 Steven Jobs and Stephen Wozniak introduced the Apple II, a personal machine housed in a plastic case. In 1980 IBM entered the personal computer market, adopting the MS-DOS operating system (the software to perform the computer's fundamental tasks) created by Bill Gates and Paul Allen, founders of the Microsoft Corporation. In 1985 MS-DOS gave way to Windows. Laptops became available in the mid-1980s, and personal computer sales soared. About one billion of them came into use worldwide between 1980 and 2008.[2]

In the early 1970s the U.S. Department of Defense initiated a project to link computers at different locations to facilitate collaborative research. The result was the **Internet,** a "network of networks" that allowed scientists and military personnel to communicate with one another's

> **Internet** A global computer network connecting smaller networks, all of which use the same set of communication formats and rules.

machines. As this technology advanced, public pressure grew to make it available to all. Among the scientists who helped build the system, Radia Perlman began work in the 1980s to improve the way messages were routed from one computer to another, winning her the title "Mother of the Internet." As we saw in the chapter introduction, Tim Berners-Lee invented the World Wide Web, which greatly simplified data sharing. In 1993, engineers at the University of Illinois introduced Mosaic, a program that nonspecialists could easily use to "browse" for information on the Internet. Mosaic provided the primary model for later generations of browsers, including Netscape Navigator, Internet Explorer, Firefox, and Google Chrome. By 1996 forty million people were using the Internet to access the web and connect their own sites to it.

Streams of data. In the 1970s technical barriers to moving information nearly instantaneously from one part of the world to another fell in rapid order. Satellite technology, first demonstrated in 1957 when the Soviet Union launched Sputnik (see Chapter 27), advanced quickly. Between that year and 1989, the Soviet Union, the United States, and a few other countries launched 3,196 satellites. Engineers invented increasingly ingenious ways for satellite transmitters connected to earthbound computers to process telephone calls and television signals and to monitor weather, map the earth's surface, and detect the locations of weapons and troop movements. In 1993 twenty-four satellites linked together activated the first Global Positioning System (GPS). Within several years, personal navigation devices became available to millions of consumers at relatively low cost.

In the 1980s engineers began laying networks of fiber optic cable. Constructed of thin strands of refined glass bundled together, these lines could transmit pulses of light that were converted into electrical signals carrying messages and images at near light speed. As of 2013 a single cable could transmit thirty million phone calls across the Atlantic Ocean in one second. In the 1970s scientists first devised machines that connected telephones through localized radio "cells" rather than wires. The city of Tokyo built the first cellular phone network in 1979. Since then, many rural and relatively poor regions in the world have skipped directly from no telephone service at all to cellular technology. Powerful handheld computers dubbed "smartphones" appeared on the market early in the new century. Their Internet connections and applications (apps) can perform thousands of functions. Some owners even use them to make telephone calls! As communication technology has become more sophisticated, its cost has also fallen rapidly. Consequently, the webs of world communication have become much more efficient and incalculably dense. In 1945 a three-minute phone call from Britain to the United States cost about $75. Today, a software application like Skype allows voice and video communication between computer users anywhere in the world at no direct charge.

The Electronics of Transport

Although humans can transmit information at lightning speed, they cannot move themselves from place to place much faster than they could in 1960. (Rocket travel in space is much speedier, but so far fewer than six hundred men and women have experienced it.) Electronic systems, however, have greatly advanced both the reliability and efficiency of

Satellites orbiting the earth perform many tasks. Among numerous other functions, satellite communication helps auto commuters avoid traffic congestion and shows scientists trends in urban air pollution. How have you recently benefited from satellite technology to communicate with someone or retrieve information?

A digital representation of the human genome. A museum displays a complete map of our genetic code. A team of scientists from six countries collaborated on the project. They announced this significant breakthrough fifty years after Watson and Crick first documented the double helix structure of DNA molecules.

transportation. In the late 1960s engineers invented metal containers of standard size to move cargo between ships, rail cars, and truck trailers without unpacking and repacking. Container shipping has reduced costs significantly, but the system works only because computers keep accurate track of the locations of millions of boxes. When the 1967 Arab–Israeli War closed the Suez Canal for eight years, supertankers were built to ship crude oil from the Middle East. These enormous vessels, which typically carry two million barrels of oil, depend on such sophisticated electronic navigation, meteorological, and monitoring systems that they sail with crews of as few as twenty people.

Computers have become fundamental to the design and operation of trains, automobiles, and airplanes. Auto companies began installing onboard computers in cars in the early 1980s, mainly because high oil prices and rising pollution demanded greater attention to fuel efficiency. By the 1990s computers controlled ignition, timing, fuel injection, and exhaust emissions. Auto mechanics also learned to analyze computer data to improve performance and diagnose malfunctions. The fuel-efficient hybrid vehicles that appeared on the roads after 2000 depended on computers to smoothly transfer the propulsion source back and forth between the electric motor and the gasoline engine. More recently, automotive engineers have experimented with vehicles that virtually drive themselves, transforming cars into wheeled robots. The airplane industry tells a similar story. In 2011 the Boeing company began delivering the 787 Dreamliner, an intricately computerized plane designed for high fuel efficiency. Partly owing to aeronautic advances, as well as electronic reservation and boarding systems, the

number of daily air travelers worldwide quadrupled between 1975 and 2009 to about 7.7 million.

Computers and the Body

Electronic technology has largely driven advances in science and engineering in recent decades, remarkably so in medical research and practice. Magnetic resonance imaging and other visualizing devices can peer into the deep recesses of the human body, discovering cancers in their early stages. Scientists can better understand the structure of molecules linked to diseases by modeling them on computers in three dimensions. In the 1980s researchers began to theorize the potential of nanotechnology, including ways to manipulate individual atoms or molecules to build miniscule "chips" of extraordinary precision. This field will have practical medical applications in the near future. Computers have already revolutionized health care systems in industrialized countries. People can get instant access to their medical records, hospital personnel can more accurately diagnose and monitor patients, and health professionals having different kinds of expertise can share information no matter where they are in the world.

Ever since the scientists James Watson and Francis Crick produced a model of the structure of deoxyribonucleic acid (DNA) at Cambridge University in 1953, advances in the study of the genes resident in human cells have come one after another. In the 1970s molecular biologists in the United States invented techniques for splicing strands of DNA, typically from different organisms, then recombining them to produce DNA that can alleviate genetically related diseases. In 1990 the U.S. government formally launched the Human Genome Project, an international endeavor to sequence the human body's approximately 100,000 genes, as well as the three billion or so base pairs, that is, strands of DNA that are bonded together in the shape of a double helix. The Human Genome Project was completed in 2003, a task that would have been impossible without immense computational power. Since then, the genome "map" has provided researchers with remarkable tools for understanding genetic factors in disease. The new field of pharmacogenomics, for example, aims to demonstrate how an individual's precise genetic constitution may affect the body's reaction to particular drugs, leading the way to drug designs customized for particular individuals.

Unintended Consequences of Electronic Innovation

The electronic revolution has generated not only amazement but also a host of worries. Like all systems in the universe, electronic ones tend to become more fragile and unpredictable as they advance in complexity. By the 1990s it became apparent that electronic networks held the world together in vital ways but that society also had to expend great mental and physical energy to keep networks functioning and to meet global demand for even more complex systems. Fears that computer glitches could set off false attack alarms haunted the Cold War. Near the end of the twentieth century, software engineers theorized that global communication systems might collapse because computer clocks had not been designed to switch from "19" to "20" years. In the few years leading up to New Year 2000, businesses and governments spent billions of dollars correcting code to solve the "Y2K" problem. A media barrage predicting that a general computer collapse might take place anyway caused a serious global cyber panic. The crisis was short-lived, however, because no major electronic meltdown took place.

The Internet developed in the 1990s into an enormous public space with no rules to determine who may enter it and for what purpose. Personal computers connected to the Internet became windows on the world but also receptacles for floods of unwanted messages from advertisers, interest groups, and pornographers, as well as targets for electronic vandals, fraudsters, identity thieves, and clandestine corporate intelligence gatherers. The term "computer virus" to describe programs that self-replicate, often for malevolent purposes, came into use after 1984. Electronic communications have vastly enlarged humankind's capacity for collective deception and propaganda. National armies have become thoroughly dependent on computer systems. Indeed, military personnel have distanced themselves more successfully than ever from war's death and destruction with the help of surveillance satellites, smart bombs, and attack drones piloted from thousands of miles away. Cyber warfare has become a reality. For example, Stuxnet, a set

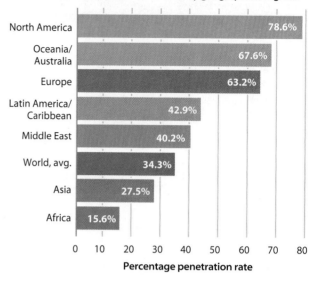

World internet penetration rates by geographical regions

Region	Percentage penetration rate
North America	78.6%
Oceania/Australia	67.6%
Europe	63.2%
Latin America/Caribbean	42.9%
Middle East	40.2%
World, avg.	34.3%
Asia	27.5%
Africa	15.6%

Percentage penetration rate

World Internet penetration rates, 2012. This bar graph shows the estimated number of Internet users as a percentage of the total population. What economic and social factors might account for the regional differences in Internet penetration indicated on this graph?

of variant computer codes designed to infect and disable Iran's uranium enrichment centrifuges, was deployed by the United States and Israel as early as 2007. Corporations, governments, and home computer users alike continue to spend billions of dollars every year defending electronic systems against data theft, malicious control, and sabotage.

Global access to electronic networks has, like standards of living, also suffered from severe regional imbalance. Some governments, including China, North Korea, and Iran, have deliberately blocked citizen access to particular Internet sites to try to limit political dissent and control public opinion. A larger problem is that many people around the world, especially poor people, still have little access to electronic resources other than radio and television. The number of Internet users in the world grew from a little more than 360 million in 2000 to 2.4 billion by 2012. That still left about 66 percent of humankind without it. In 2012 nearly 80 percent of North Americans had access but less than 16 percent of Africans did. The potential economic, cultural, and health benefits of personal computers and Internet access to poor farmers, for example, far outweigh the risks and aggravations of going online.

Countercurrents in the Global Economy

FOCUS Why have some regions of the world developed economically and raised standards of living more successfully than others in recent decades?

In the modern era, humans have commanded far more energy, material wealth, and knowledge than in any earlier time. Today, our species has access to about one hundred times more useful energy than it did before the fossil-fuel energy surge. The global trend of the past century has been a spectacular rise in gross domestic product (GDP) from about $2.7 trillion in 1913, the eve of World War I, to $75 trillion by 2013. To be sure, growth has followed a bumpy course. GDP plunged during the Great Depression of the 1930s, then rose again. During the long economic boom after World War II, GDP growth followed a nearly steady upward trajectory (see Chapter 27). Since the 1970s, however, the track has become more jagged. Business cycles—short-term phases of growth and stagnation—have followed one another at intervals of usually less than a decade. A severe drop occurred between late 2007 and 2009, and global recovery proceeded slowly thereafter. Serious economic fluctuations in recent years have invariably had global impact, in large part because electronic systems have linked national economies tightly together, a phenomenon that has vastly sped up financial transactions but also enhanced the risks of instability and loss of managerial control. Nonetheless, many economists argue that the global economy will continue its long-term upward trend because human society has the technical capacity and creative ingenuity to generate increasing amounts of energy and wealth for at least another century.

The fundamental countercurrent to this narrative of growth has been the widening gap between rich and poor. Despite numerous technological miracles and many worthy plans to advance economic justice, the *distribution* of global wealth has become increasingly lopsided. In the past forty years, the world's population *as a whole* has by the measures of income and life expectancy become better off. But economic growth has benefited some people and some countries far more than others. Hundreds of millions of people continue to suffer unemployment, malnutrition, illiteracy, social oppression, and early death.

The 1970s: An Economic Turning Point

The financial system that the United States and its wartime allies set up at the Bretton Woods conference in New Hampshire in the waning months of World War II began to run into trouble by 1970 (see Chapter 27). The mechanisms that pegged the currencies of capitalist countries to the U.S. dollar at a fixed rate of $35 to an ounce of gold stabilized international monetary transactions. But as war-damaged economies recovered, currency exchange rates needed more flexibility. Recuperating states like Britain, France, the German Federal Republic, and Japan could better serve their own national economic goals by uncoupling their currencies from the dollar. For example, a country could decrease the value of its currency relative to the dollar and thereby make its exports cheaper on the world market. In the late 1960s, the real value of the dollar declined relative to other currencies despite the fixed gold price. Foreign banks and investors began selling dollars and buying gold, draining American gold reserves. In response, the United States took steps in 1971 to leave the gold standard; more countries soon followed. This development gave states greater economic

Consumers adapt to the 1973 oil shock. This horse-drawn Volkswagen was a creative German response to a nationwide vehicle ban on Sundays. Rationing at gas pumps encouraged more people in the United States and Western Europe to walk, ride bicycles, and take public transportation. To what extent did the crisis change consumers' fuel consumption behavior in the long term?

freedom. But it also ushered in an era when global finance became more complicated, exchange rates more unstable, and monetary coordination among countries more difficult.

The end of Bretton Woods freed states to print more money and pump it into their economies, but these policies aggravated **inflation,** and consumer purchasing power subsequently fell. A military crisis in late 1973 worsened the inflationary spiral and sparked a serious global recession. In October, Egypt and Syria launched an attack on Israel. They aimed to recover national territory that had been under Israeli occupation since 1967 and persuade the United States to force a settlement of the long-running Arab–Israeli conflict. The war lasted less than three weeks, though at a cost of nearly fourteen thousand lives on both sides. In support of Egypt and Syria, the Arab members of the Organization of Petroleum Exporting Countries (OPEC), an association to coordinate petroleum policies, declared an oil embargo against states that supported Israel, vowing to enforce it until Israeli forces withdrew from all occupied territories. As the embargo took hold, international demand for petroleum rose far beyond available supplies, prices for all sorts of goods rocketed up, world trade slumped, and the global

> **inflation** An upward trend in the prices of goods and services.

economy stagnated. In 1978–1979 a second "oil shock" struck when a popular revolution in Iran replaced the autocratic king Muhammad Reza Shah with a government dominated by Shi'a Muslim clerics. The accompanying social upheaval disrupted Iranian oil production, and world oil prices soared again, triggering another worldwide economic slide.

After the first oil crisis, most major capitalist economies—the United States, Japan, and the Western European states—contracted the economic disease called "stagflation," an alarming combination of inflation, sluggish business activity, and falling employment. Near the end of the decade, however, the United States introduced monetary policies that pushed short-term interest rates from near zero to 10 percent and higher. This "tight money" strategy obliged companies to cut borrowing and hold down both prices and wages. Inflation eased, and several European states followed the American lead. The new policies set off another recession, but the major capitalist states recovered gradually without inciting another inflationary surge. Nevertheless, inflation continued to plague particular countries and regions, for example, Latin America throughout the 1980s.

Conflicting Capitalist Doctrines

The economic troubles resulting from oil shocks and rampant inflation ignited furious debates among economists and politicians over the benefits of the modern welfare state. After World War II, Western political leaders broadly agreed that capitalism could thrive even though governments spent heavily on social programs such as pension security and health care to protect citizens from jarring economic ups and downs. John Maynard Keynes, the most influential economist of the mid-twentieth century, argued that in times of recession governments should spend more to counteract the depressive effects of low private investment and high unemployment. Beginning in the late 1970s, however, economically conservative leaders, notably Prime Minister Margaret Thatcher in Britain (in office 1979–1990) and President Ronald Reagan in the United States (in office 1981–1989), contended that the welfare state had become bloated and that too much public spending dampened business confidence in long-term economic growth. The private sector, so the argument ran, would by itself generate healthy revenue and raise employment. These **neoliberals,** as they came to be called, claimed the heritage of nineteenth-century economic liberalism, which urged limited government and the sanctity of private property (see Chapter 21). They championed policies to reduce taxes, trim regulations, lower tariffs, privatize certain services, and encourage individual self-sufficiency.

> **neoliberalism** An economic and political ideology advocating reduced government intervention in economic matters, privatization of state-owned enterprises, free trade, open markets, and deregulation of business.

Since the 1980s capitalist economies around the world have tended to swing from Keynesian to neoliberal policies erratically and inconsistently. For example, neoliberal

Ronald Reagan and Margaret Thatcher speak to reporters, 1982.
The U.S. president and the British prime minister forged a formidable political alliance. Their terms in office overlapped for eight years. The two largely agreed on neoliberal domestic agendas and assertive foreign policies.

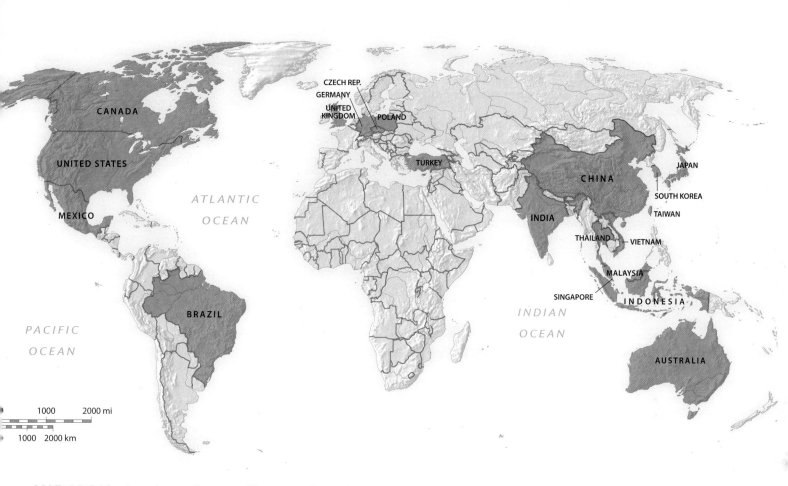

MAP 28.2 The twenty most competitive manufacturing countries, 2013.
Which countries would not have been on this map in 1975? What factors help explain the global shift in manufacturing?

leaders advised big public spending cuts, but most industrialized states nonetheless accrued unprecedented deficits in the 1980s. Under Reagan the U.S. deficit rose from $60 to $220 billion between 1980 and 1986, owing mostly to military spending. The Great Recession of 2007–2009 and the slow recovery that followed in most capitalist states called forth contradictory solutions. Neoliberals demanded draconian cuts in both government budgets and taxes to restore business confidence and spur investment. Keynesian economists advocated large infusions of borrowed public money into economies to stimulate employment, consumer demand, and therefore growth, leaving the issue of deficit reduction until good times returned.

Shifting Centers of Economic Power

After the Bretton Woods system was dismantled, international capital flow sped up as countries exported more goods. Neoliberal strategies gained more public support in many industrialized countries, and governments took steps to free up market activity by trimming regulations on banks, airlines, and multinational corporations. More developing states abandoned quests for economic self-sufficiency and waded into the global market, cutting import tariffs, privatizing industries, and generally deregulating economic activity. Since the 1990s nearly every state in the world (the few exceptions include North Korea and Cuba) has sought integration into the capitalist world system. International financial markets, which deal in currency exchange, investment, and borrowing, grew spectacularly from about $160 billion in 1973 to $140 *trillion* by 2012.

In fact, loan transactions have climbed to unprecedented levels of volume and complexity. In the past few decades, corporations have borrowed immense sums to expand operations or acquire other companies, and governments have paid for armies and public services by borrowing many billions more than they collect in revenue. For example, the United States borrowed heavily after 2001 in connection with the Afghanistan and Iraq wars, rising social service costs, and the recession of 2007–2009. From 2007 to 2012, U.S. debt rose on average $3.93 billion a day.

This advance toward global financial complexity inevitably altered the lineup of major economic players. In the 1950s and 1960s the states of North America and Europe, plus Japan, produced about 90 percent of the world's manufactured goods and sold them mainly to each other (see Map 28.2). Most of Asia, Africa, and Latin America remained solidly agrarian, marketing food, fiber, minerals, and the labor of their own citizens as foreign workers. Since the 1970s, however, new manufacturing centers have emerged and international exchange has become much more elaborate.[3] Corporations have more routinely opened and closed manufacturing plants depending on the comparative costs of materials and wages in particular countries. Manufacture of product components has become globalized, so that, for example, the laptop a student buys in an American electronics store may be the product of research undertaken in Japan, investment secured in Germany, rare metals mined in Congo, and skilled assembly performed in Taiwan.

Asian tigers and tiger cubs. Beginning in the late 1960s, Taiwan, South Korea, Hong Kong, and Singapore, all of them places short on exportable raw commodities, followed Japan's lead in building export-oriented manufacturing industries (see Chapter 27). These four "Asian tigers" invested generously in new electronic technology and education, and they benefited from women's economic productivity. By the 1980s women constituted more than 30 percent of the labor forces in these countries, though generally earning lower wages than men for comparable work. South Korea achieved the most impressive economic miracle, transforming itself from an impoverished, mostly rural state in 1960 to a builder of automobiles and the wealthy host of the 1988 Olympic Games. The tigers also sponsored new industries in other states where they could employ workers at lower wages than they could at home. In the 1990s those investments helped several "tiger cubs," notably Indonesia, Malaysia, the Philippines, and Thailand, jumpstart export industries. Vietnam made its first market reforms in 1986, barely a decade after the end of the Vietnam War and the country's unification under Communist Party rule. Owing primarily to looser trade controls, the value of Vietnam's exports rose from $14.3 billion in 2000 to $114.6 billion 2012.[4]

China in the global market. Economic transformations began to take place in China in 1978, when Deng Xiaoping (1904–1997), the leader of the Chinese Communist Party, vowed to revive and modernize the economy, after nearly three decades of central planning and wildly oscillating economic performance under Mao Zedong. He and his political allies initiated market reforms that allowed Chinese farmers, local businesses, and, after about a decade, large industries to buy and sell goods privately. In 1980 China opened fourteen coastal cities to foreign capital investment, which poured in. This influx triggered successive surges of economic growth and exploding urbanization. Both the government and private entrepreneurs began investing surplus earnings abroad, notably in Subsaharan Africa and Latin America. Before the mid-eighteenth century, China had the largest manufacturing output in the world. By

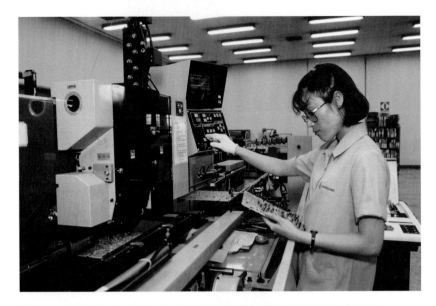

A Korean worker tests electronic components. This 1987 photograph shows a Samsung computer and television factory in Seoul. What social or cultural factors in Korea might have encouraged or permitted women to take factory jobs?

2010 it claimed that status again by slightly surpassing the United States. The Chinese Communist Party, however, eagerly joined the capitalist world economy while refusing to enact significant democratic and civil rights reforms. Mass demonstrations against party intransigence in April 1989 ended in the People's Liberation Army massacring about 1,300 citizens in Beijing's Tiananmen Square. The country has since remained an authoritarian state, though the ruling party's Marxist-Leninist ideology has lost all meaning.

India and its Silicon Valley. Ironically, India, a democratic state with a large private sector, tried to keep its economy sheltered from the gales of international commerce and finance longer than its giant communist neighbor did. For forty years after independence from Britain (1947), the social democratic approach of the Indian National Congress— self-sufficiency, strong central government controls, food subsidies—guided the economy. However, faced with soaring national debt and anemic exports, the government gradually adopted more market-oriented policies starting in 1991. By the end of that decade, foreign investors were arriving in force, including people of South Asian origin who had earlier emigrated to the United States and founded successful companies there, including Sun Microsystems and Hotmail. Business innovators found a special market niche producing and exporting information technology. At first, they profited from **outsourcing** operations such as data processing or call-in support services. In the new century, however, Indian firms have expanded research and development into a variety of electronic fields. The city of Bangalore has been labeled India's Silicon Valley. Among the top manufacturing countries in the world in 2009, India

> **outsourcing** The business practice of reducing costs by transferring work to outside contractors, including foreign companies.

An Artist's Comment on Capitalism in China

Under Mao Zedong, chairman of the Communist Party of China from 1949 to 1976, party leaders tightly controlled artistic expression. During the height of the Great Proletarian Cultural Revolution in 1966–1968, when Mao roused Chinese youth to cleanse the country of all signs of "capitalist revisionism," visual artists mass produced graphically striking posters that celebrated socialist solidarity and sacrifice. The image on the left is one example. Young revolutionaries, however, forbade all art that hinted of "bourgeois values."

After Mao's death in 1976, the new party leaders who gradually opened China to the world economy allowed artists and writers wider creative scope. In the 1980s Chinese visual artists began to attract international attention as they explored numerous new themes and media and founded new creative movements. One of these was Political Pop, a movement that drew on the aesthetic style of American Pop Art of the 1960s and 1970s to comment on the stark political and social contrasts between Mao's China and the era of capitalist enterprise and consumption that has followed. Wang Guangyi, a native of northeastern China who witnessed the most radical phase of the Cultural Revolution as a boy, emerged in the 1990s as a leading Political Pop artist. In a series of paintings he called the Great Criticism, *he combined Cultural Revolution poster imagery with references to the Western consumer products that newly affluent Chinese were eager to buy.*

In the Great Criticism *image on the right, Wang depicts two figures similar to those on the Cultural Revolution poster—forward-looking, radiant, and happy workers. In both images the red-covered book* Quotations from Chairman Mao Zedong *appears. Wang appropriates the dominant red color in the Cultural Revolution work, but he paints in a style reminiscent of the work of Artists like Andy Warhol. The numbers scattered across the painting represent serial numbers that workers stamp on manufactured products. Wang's image evokes both the old China and the new, but as in other paintings in this series, he leaves the viewer with questions about his intentions.*

Thinking Critically

In terms of subject matter and artistic style, what similarities and differences do you find in the two images? Why do you think Wang chose to reference Coca-Cola in this image? Do you think he is criticizing China's embrace of capitalism? Or might he be ridiculing the Cultural Revolution and its propaganda? Do you think Wang's image throws light on the China of the late 1990s? In what way?

A political poster from the Cultural Revolution. It says, "Strive to collect scrap metal and other waste materials!"

Wang Guangyi's *Great Criticism: Coca-Cola*, 1993.

New Year's celebrations on the remains of the Berlin Wall, 1990. Crowds began to breach the wall and demolish it with sledge hammers in November 1989. In the distance revelers stand atop the Brandenburg Gate, a nineteenth-century peace monument located in East Germany. Why do you think pieces of the wall remain potent symbols of protest even today?

came in twelfth, just four ranks below Britain, its former colonial master.[5]

The end of central planning in Russia and Eastern Europe. Like China before 1978, the Soviet Union and its Eastern European allies pursued a socialist model of economic development and self-sufficiency. Government employees—planners, managers, and technicians—determined prices, wages, and the distribution of economic resources. Directed by this bureaucracy, the Soviet economy slowed in the 1970s and became increasingly dependent on trade with Western countries for food and finished goods. The Soviet GDP in 1980 was more than 80 percent smaller than that of the United States, though oil exports permitted Moscow to fund a gigantic army. In 1981 President Reagan ramped up U.S. military spending, eventually including a Strategic Defense Initiative, popularly called "star wars," to build a complex missile defense system. The Soviet Union could not keep pace and indeed headed toward economic exhaustion. In 1985 Mikhail Gorbachev (in office 1985–1991), named general secretary of the Soviet Communist Party, launched a campaign of bold political reforms (*glasnost)* and economic liberalization (*perestroika*).

In the socialist states of Eastern Europe, popular demands for economic and political reform rapidly intensified after Gorbachev announced that the Soviet Union would no longer send in tanks to suppress public protests, as it had done in Czechoslovakia in 1968. In the German Democratic Republic (East Germany), government confusion and paralysis over citizen demands for uninhibited international travel led border guards to open gates in the wall that divided the eastern and western sectors of Berlin. In November 1989, jubilant crowds started pulling down the wall. In the following months, Germany was reunified and elections across Eastern Europe ended the communist party monopolies that had prevailed since the end of World War II.

The fifteen federated republics that made up the Soviet Union answered to Moscow, but in several of them, the nationalist sentiments of peoples speaking languages and cherishing ethnic traditions other than Russian lay just beneath the surface. Watching the dissolution of the communist regimes in Eastern Europe, those nationalists questioned the advantages of remaining part of the economically anemic Soviet Union. Early in 1991, Lithuania, a Soviet republic that had once been a sovereign Baltic state, declared its independence. In the ensuing months all fifteen republics formally separated from one another without great violence. Gorbachev had planned to introduce limited Western-style reforms, not to dismantle the Soviet Union. Nevertheless, it ceased to exist on December 25, 1991.

MAP 28.3 Geopolitical change in Eastern Europe and Inner Eurasia, 1985 and 2013.

What historical developments account for major changes on the political map of this region between 1985 and 2013?

Those tumultuous events led to a decade of disarray in both the former Soviet Union and Eastern Europe, as new political regimes attempted to reinvent their societies and economies. In the new Russia (the Russian Federation), upstart capitalist entrepreneurs, many of them former Soviet bureaucrats and industrial managers, bought up state-owned property at fire-sale prices and, often in league with Western business interests, got immensely rich. By contrast, the standard of living plunged for the great majority. In the new century, however, most Eastern European states built stable, mostly democratic governments, and several of them achieved impressive growth as Western investors flocked into Hungary, Poland, and Czechoslovakia to exploit new markets and cheap labor. Russia associated itself with capitalist Europe more tentatively, and since 2000 has not proceeded far in broadening its export economy beyond oil, natural gas, and other primary commodities. Under Vladimir Putin's presidency and prime ministership

(2000–present), it has continued to struggle for balance between forces favoring multiparty democracy and the country's long tradition of authoritarian rule.

The European Union as an economic power. Economic integration in the world's oldest center of fossil-fuel industrialization has proceeded gradually but persistently since six Western European states formed the European Economic Community in 1957 (see Chapter 27). The organization's membership grew to twelve between 1973 and 1986. The scale of economic cooperation rose after 1992 when, by the terms of the Maastricht Treaty, the federation changed its name to the European Union (EU) and formulated complex rules and institutions for moving goods, capital, and workers freely among member states. The treaty also strengthened the authority of the European Parliament headquartered in Brussels. In 1998 eleven member states agreed to adopt the euro as a common currency issued by the European Central

MAP 28.4 The European Union and the Eurozone, 2013.

This map of treaty agreements represents the greatest extent of interstate cooperation achieved in this region. How would you account for differences in the policies of particular states regarding EU membership and euro use?

Bank. Formation of the Eurozone, which currently has seventeen members, demolished more impediments to the rapid flow of goods and money from one state to another. Between 2004 and 2007 most Eastern European states joined the European Union, taking membership to twenty-eight by 2013 (see Map 28.4).

Nevertheless, the union is still a work in progress. The question of national sovereignty remains at the heart of debates over its future. Some leaders have long argued for full economic and even political integration leading to a United States of Europe, though an initiative to create an EU constitution failed in 2004. Every member country has *euroskeptics,* political parties and individuals that fear the loss of national independence and identity. Some parties argue for less EU interference in members' internal affairs (regulation of food safety or genetic engineering, for example), others for total withdrawal from the organization. British governments have remained consistently ambivalent about their country's economic marriage to continental Europe. Britain is a member of the EU, but it has not joined the Eurozone and has a vocal euroskeptic minority.

The seventeen members that adopted the euro did not at the same time thoroughly integrate their financial and banking systems. Because euro members have no national currency, they cannot alter monetary policy or print money to address problems of high debt or weak economic performance. Yet the economically healthiest members have no formal obligation to redistribute part of their national wealth to troubled members. The viability of the Eurozone came under threat starting with the 2007–2009 recession, which worsened economic imbalances between the richest members (especially Germany and France) and several struggling ones (Greece, Ireland, Italy, Spain, Cyprus). As one informed observer remarked, "The basic problem is that the EU is not a true union but more a collection of states that have not in any real sense ceded decision-making power to a central authority. The result is chaos fed by conflicting national objectives. . . . Instead of preserving sovereignty and nurturing democracy, it has created a situation where paymaster nations like Germany seek to impose the policy preferences of German voters on other states without regard to economic circumstances."[6] Despite these serious problems, the European Union remains a colossus on the world stage. It represents the largest economy in the world, and it unites nearly 504 million people in a unified market and a single domain of social and cultural exchange.

The Persistence of Poverty

The global economy has grown in most years since the end of World War II but so has the gap between the richest and poorest segments of the world's population. This is the fundamental economic contradiction of the recent past. In 2011, 42 percent of total global income went to the richest 10 percent of the world's population, and 1 percent went to the poorest 10 percent.[7] Within many individual countries, income gaps have also continued to widen. A country may achieve impressive economic growth over several years and still show widening income inequality if the growth benefits predominantly upper-income citizens. This condition has existed not only in very poor countries like Mozambique and Cambodia but also in the United States, Russia, and China. In 2011 the income gap between rich and poor was wider in the United States than in any European country.[8] If the middle sector in relatively wealthy countries cannot afford equal access to education, health care, or career mobility, productivity is certain to erode and social welfare costs will go up. The capitalist world economy cannot

Demonstrations against Greek austerity measures. Protesters in Athens' Syntagma Square threw stones at police in October 2011 as lawmakers imposed job, pay, and pension cuts on civil service workers, as well as imposing higher taxes, in an effort to keep the Greek government solvent. What factors may have led initially peaceful protests to turn violent?

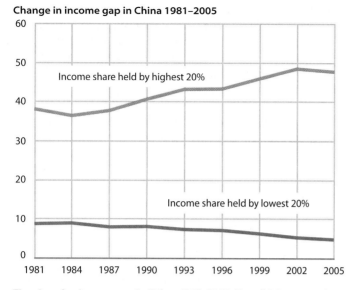

Change in income gap in China 1981–2005

Income share held by highest 20%

Income share held by lowest 20%

The changing income gap in China, 1981–2005. How did the proportion of income taken home by the highest 20 percent of Chinese wage earners change in this period? How did this figure change for those in the bottom 20 percent of wage earners? How would you account for the widening income gap after 1984?

sustain growth if billions of people are too poor to consume more than a small part of what it produces.

Because of recent economic successes in some countries, notably China, the percentage of the world's population living on less than $1.25 a day has declined somewhat since 1990. But at present nearly 1.3 billion people live on that amount or less, and most of them, especially in Africa, suffer from "multidimensional poverty." This means that they have little access to many things that affect the quality of living—healthful nutrition, clean water, sanitation, medical services, cooking fuel, education, or expectation of reasonably long life. Women living in such poverty also typically lack access to contraception, prenatal consultations, or professional help during birth.

Foreign invasions, civil wars, famines, floods, earthquakes, refugee displacement, and global or regional recessions all impoverish people, at least temporarily. The world economy, however, remains potentially productive enough to feed everyone. Multidimensional poverty, rather, is mainly a consequence of institutional and political factors that perpetuate grossly unequal *distribution* of global wealth.

Prospects for demographic transition. If the population of a country grows at a faster rate than its economy, living standards are likely to fall or remain stagnant. Since the early twentieth century, a growing number of states have moved through a significant demographic transition, in which people live longer but women have fewer children. That causes the population growth rate to level off (see Chapter 27). Unfortunately, quite a few states, especially in Africa and the Middle East, have remained in the early stages of that transition. Consequently, population has continued to grow at higher rates than economic expansion.

Reversing this condition requires strategies both to reduce fertility rates and to achieve real economic development, which means growth that benefits the great majority.

Perils of the market economy. In the 1970s, states that faced soaring fuel costs sought large international loans to finance development. Oil riches impelled Middle East states—Saudi Arabia premier among them—to put billions of "petrodollars" in the hands of big banks to loan out to developing countries, which spent part of that money to buy even more oil. The International Monetary Fund (IMF) and the World Bank, two institutions created as part of the Bretton Woods system, became important lenders. The IMF loans money to countries in particularly difficult straits, while insisting on economic and financial reforms. The World Bank provides funds to jumpstart development projects and attract private investors.

By the early 1980s many developing states began to experience severe debt crises. International lenders, fearful of never being repaid, turned off the money spigot. In Latin America, for example, prices for many exports began to fall in the 1980s. This reduced funds available for interest payments on loans. When lenders backed off, growth decelerated, food prices soared, and poverty worsened in much of the region. Mexico discovered rich oil deposits in 1978, prompting President José López Portillo to boast, "There are two kinds of countries in the world today—those that don't have oil and those that do. We have it."[9] Foreign investors eagerly rushed in with huge loans to feed the fossil-fuel bonanza. But after 1980, oil prices declined rapidly, plunging Mexico into deeper debt, recession, and worsening impoverishment. In the 1990s the countries of Africa as a whole used 40 percent of their earnings from exports simply to service loans.[10] Even though quite a few states reduced their debt burdens in that decade or later, massive borrowing has remained a key part of the global economy.

In the face of rising public debt, many states began in the 1980s to move from centrally planned systems to market economies and exchanged state welfare doctrines for neoliberal ones that encouraged corporate investment from abroad, reduced public spending, economic privatization, and export growth. The results have been mixed. Even in countries that have achieved impressive growth rates, poverty has worsened in connection with cutbacks in public employment and services and the diversion of national income to political elites and international corporations. Foreign investors have tended to favor projects in developing countries that bring short-term profits rather than to commit to long-term development of infrastructure—roads, rail lines, Internet connections, education, brand new industries—on which solid economic development must rest. In addition, rich states have given poorer ones much less aid as a percentage of their GDP than they promised back in the early 1970s. In 2008 the United States offered more economic aid than any other country in absolute dollars but gave only 0.19 percent of its GDP, about five times less than Sweden contributed.

Barriers to trade. Big industrialized states have had a habit of lecturing developing countries on the benefits of open markets. At the same time, they have imposed high tariffs on imports or awarded cash subsidies to their own farmers or manufacturers to help them keep costs and prices down. These policies have prevented producers in developing countries, especially farmers, from selling commodities to rich countries at competitive prices. For example, African farmers are expert producers of rice, wheat, cocoa, and textiles, but trade walls and subsidies have kept these goods out of potentially huge overseas markets.

Wealth and political power. In too many states, political leaders have regarded public wealth not as development capital but as the means to sustain a hierarchy of power in which a small group at the top redistributes public funds or private income to loyal followers, often members of their own extended families or ethnic communities. Conversely, citizens having economic grievances have sometimes abandoned civic activism for strategies to connect themselves to powerful patrons who might send bits and

pieces of wealth their way. Such systems are inevitably corrupt, and foreign governments and firms have too willingly rewarded elites in return for access to the official cooperation they need to run profitable enterprises. Countries with great economic potential have suffered from the "curse of oil," a vice that leads powerful people to use profits from fossil fuel or other extractive industries to lubricate the wheels of patron-client relationships rather than economic transformation. This has happened in Nigeria, for example, where vast offshore oil revenues have so far done little to benefit the population as a whole.

Women in the economy. Nearly half of the adult women in the world do not participate in the paid labor market. On the global scale, women earn about 75 percent of what men receive for comparable work. Low literacy levels and lack of job or entrepreneurial opportunities for women are less a consequence of formal religious teachings than of traditional practices that rigidly perpetuate male social and cultural domination. Many developing countries have only recently begun to mobilize the productive capacities of

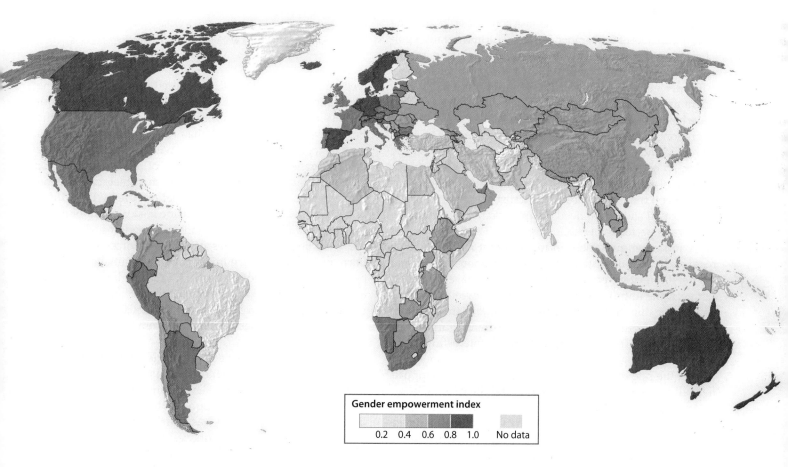

MAP 28.5 UN gender empowerment index, 2012.

Based on data from the UN Development Program, this index focuses on economic empowerment measured in terms of women's shares of legislative seats, shares of senior management positions, and income levels compared to men. The higher the score, the greater the level of women's empowerment. What economic and political characteristics might countries with high levels of empowerment have in common? What different characteristics might countries with lower levels of empowerment share?

women more effectively (see Map 28.5). More leaders may be recognizing that, as Hillary Clinton said in 2011, "There is a stimulative and ripple effect that kicks in when women have greater access to jobs and the economic lives of our countries. . . . By harnessing the economic potential of all women, we boost opportunity for all people."[11]

Migration and the Global Economy

Migration of large numbers of people from one part of the world to another has been a prominent feature of the modern centuries. The numbers have grown spectacularly—from about 2 million migrants in 1850 to 214 million in 2012. This trend faltered significantly only during the Great Depression and the two world wars. In the past forty years, mass migration has continued to accelerate despite the actions of most major receiving countries to restrict and manage immigration. These border controls aim generally to protect national sovereignty and the economic security of citizens. More specifically, they aim to select immigrants for their potential social and economic worth, prevent tourists from taking up permanent residence, and block migrants who have no economic resources or who pose criminal or political threats. The United States, for example, imposed much more stringent border and visa controls following the terrorist attacks of September 11, 2001. The immigration policies of some governments also cater to popular prejudices against immigrants as cultural aliens and troublemakers.

Border monitoring, however, has not been nearly as efficient as governments would like nor has it seriously impeded population mobility worldwide. Since 1970, mass migration has been an inevitable accompaniment to rapid economic and political change. Several developments have helped to accelerate population movement: the steady expansion of new industries and the rise of new manufacturing centers; the acceptance of capitalist market economics in almost all states; the need for immigrants or temporary workers to perform low-skill jobs; the fall of Eastern European and other authoritarian regimes that had previously restricted emigration; the steady flow of poor farmers and laborers into cities; political upheavals that have generated refugees; the improving efficiency of both travel and mechanisms for migrants to transmit money; and the development of electronic media that allow far-flung families and friends to stay in close communication. Interestingly, the *rate* of global migration in recent decades has not much exceeded the rate in the 1920s. The planet, however, supports five billion more people today than it did then.[12]

As in earlier decades of the twentieth century, the great majority of recent migrants have moved from less developed to more developed countries and to states rich in oil. And since 1970 many more countries have been sending citizens abroad, including China (since the 1980s), Southeast and South Asia, Eastern Europe (since the 1990s), Latin America, and both North and Subsaharan Africa. In many source countries, rising population, rapid urbanization, underemployment, and lack of opportunity even for

Syrian children in a refugee camp near the Turkish border. Syrians displaced by the civil war that began in 2011 wait in camps like this one to cross into Turkey or other neighboring countries. Hundreds of thousands of people in improvised settlements like this one have struggled for adequate sanitation, clean water, and medical care. What other recent conflicts in the world have bred large refugee camps?

well-educated people have driven emigration. In fact, the populations of relatively rich receiving states would decline if immigrants did not arrive. The fertility rate in the European Union as a whole has for several decades been too low to keep the population growing by natural increase (the difference between the number of births and number of deaths per year). Population growth, rather, depends on immigration. In 2005 the EU population rose by 1.9 million, but the inflow of people born outside it accounted for about 84 percent of that number.[13] In the oil kingdoms of the Middle East, large percentages of the workforces are foreign born, mainly temporary migrants. In Kuwait about 47 percent of the current population of 2.7 million is non-Kuwaiti, and foreigners hold 60 percent of the jobs.[14] In 2013 Qatar, a country smaller than New Jersey, had 250,000 citizens and 1.2 million foreign workers, mostly from South and Southeast Asia.[15]

Female migrants, especially single women and girls, have been subjected to labor exploitation and abuse in many countries. In an age when slavery and slave trading have been legally abolished throughout the world, human trafficking in women and girls has flourished. Illicit traffickers operating either within countries or across international borders deceive women into leaving home on the promise of a good job, persuade impoverished families to sell daughters, or simply kidnap vulnerable victims. According to a 2009 UN report, sexual exploitation, predominantly of women and girls, accounts for 79 percent of trafficking. Forced labor accounts for most of the remaining 21 percent.

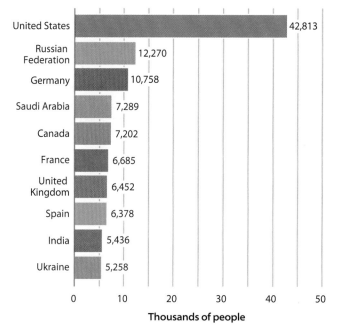

Countries with the largest number of international migrants, 2010. These ten countries received 52 percent of the world's migrants. What geographical, political, and economic factors might account for migration to these particular states?

In recent years, migrant women in several countries have become more politically active, publicly protesting discrimination or exploitation. These include Filipino women employed in domestic service jobs in the Middle East.[16]

Countercurrents in the Search for Global Order

FOCUS In what ways have systems for keeping order in the world changed since the 1970s?

In the past four decades, world population has grown by about 3.1 billion, humans have consumed finite energy resources on a colossal scale, and change has accelerated in virtually every sphere of life. These circumstances have put great pressure on societies to create more effective systems of global order. In one direction, human economic and technical structures have become larger and more complex. And keeping those structures going has required more complex and global-scale systems of cooperation and management. In the opposite direction, and in response to the very conditions we call **globalization,** humans continue, as they always have, to gather together in relatively small groups to

globalization The process by which peoples around the world have become increasingly interconnected through rapid communication and transport, resulting in both general acceleration of change and endeavors to strengthen the bonds of local community and identity.

seek security, well-being, and social identity. The communities that people form range from nuclear families, neighborhood societies, and local religious groups to nation-states and large international organizations. Cooperating communities also compete with one another, again as they always have, for material resources, sometimes in violent and irrational ways. Our species has good reason to want to perpetuate the immensely complex global systems it has created, especially institutions and networks that make life better. Yet these systems have not so far engendered world peace, environmental health, or anything close to global economic equality or justice. Consequently, there continues to be great tension between globalizing, integrating forces on the one hand and human urges to huddle together in communities to resist these forces, protect finite resources, and preserve shared rights and identity, on the other hand.

In the modern era, sovereign states have served as the primary institutions for maintaining social and political order. In the nineteenth century, nationalism proved to be a powerful new ideology for building states that not only exercised power but also sheltered a community bound together by shared language, culture, history, and destiny. Also in that century, states took the first shaky steps to create or encourage organizations dedicated to resolving conflicts, improving international communication, and promoting the world's economic, social, and cultural welfare. In the twentieth century, and especially since World War II, these organizations have multiplied and flourished in response to the colossal challenges of managing complex systems and addressing countless global problems.

The World State System since 1970

In the thirty years after World War II, the major colonial powers dismantled their empires. Consequently, the number of sovereign states in the world rose dramatically (see Chapter 27). Since 1975, dozens more colonial territories, mostly small ones, have achieved independence. In 1991, as we have seen, the Soviet Union broke into fifteen states. As of 2013 the United Nations had 193 sovereign members. These states range vastly in population, form of government, ethnic diversity, domestic resources, military power, and territorial size. (Russia is 813,000 times bigger than the sovereign state of Nauru in the Pacific Ocean.) Nevertheless, all of them claim the privilege of diplomatic equality with one another in accord with principles of sovereignty first worked out in Europe back in the seventeenth century. They also claim the right to govern and defend themselves without external interference.

Some political analysts argue that organizing the world in nearly two hundred separate states inhibits beneficial global integration and makes an already complicated world more unstable and dangerous. Other observers, however, claim that because states form, or aspire to form, national communities founded on cooperation and shared identity, they are still the most stable platforms on which to build democracy, advance human welfare, and protect individual rights.

Nelson Mandela addresses supporters in a Soweto soccer stadium.
This rally occurred shortly after his release from prison in 1990. He was incarcerated for twenty-seven years for opposing the minority apartheid government. In 1994 he led the once-banned African National Congress to electoral victory in South Africa's first nonracial election. How might different segments of South African society have reacted to seeing Mandela, once branded as a terrorist, speak in public?

In fact, several organizations have in recent years published annual reports evaluating every state in the world in terms of its success at democratic governance and commitment to citizens' rights.[17] These surveys have found that over the past forty years the number of states that may be characterized as partially if not fully democratic has grown significantly, while the number of authoritarian states has declined. This trend has been moderate, not spectacular. Some states have not improved their flawed records very much. Others have in recent years allowed democratic institutions to deteriorate, for example, Russia, Hungary, and Mali. But in still others, governments that not many years ago tyrannized their citizens have since mended their ways. In Eastern Europe most of the states that had one-party communist regimes before 1990 have made transitions to authentic parliamentary systems and free elections. The great majority of South American countries have transformed themselves from military or civilian dictatorships into societies where people vote in contested elections and enjoy more secure civil rights than they previously did. South Africa achieved majority rule in 1994 under the presidency of Nelson Mandela after a long winter, stretching back to the seventeenth century, when a white minority dominated society in every respect.

The end of bipolar politics. The possibility of nuclear annihilation loomed over the Cold War era, but some historians have suggested that international relations were more stable than after the freeze ended. The two superpowers and their allies, so the argument runs, had straightforward geopolitical aims: The future of the world rested on the triumph of either of two ideological visions. One was liberal democracy and free-market capitalism; the other was socialist society under the direct management of the state. The international politics of both alliances turned primarily on the objective of winning and holding the friendship of so-called third-world or nonaligned states.

The Cold War's bipolar politics were dangerous nonetheless. In the mid-1960s the United States and the Soviet Union entered into a period of improved relations known as *détente* (relaxation). Through the Helsinki Accords of 1975 they resolved outstanding issues over post–World War II frontiers in Europe, and they made progress limiting long-range missiles and nuclear warheads. The United States also normalized relations with the People's Republic of China following President Richard Nixon's decision, despite his avowed anticommunism, to visit Beijing in 1972. After 1975, however, Soviet–American relations worsened again over rivalry for influence in developing countries, nuclear disarmament failures, and tit-for-tat missile emplacements in Europe. The political temperature dropped further in June 1979, when Soviet forces invaded Afghanistan, an intrusion aimed at saving a friendly socialist regime there. In 1981 Ronald Reagan became U.S. president, vowing to increase military spending. Superpower relations reached bottom between 1982 and 1984, years in which strategic arms talks broke down and the Soviet Air Force shot down a Korean commercial airliner, claiming it was an American spy plane.

The Soviet economy generated little growth in those years, and Mikhail Gorbachev came to power in 1985 intent on reviving *détente* and implementing economic and political reforms. In the following two years, he pulled Soviet forces out of Afghanistan, where guerrilla fighters aided by the United States had kept up a war of resistance for eight years. In the rush of events leading to the dissolution of the Soviet Union, he was sidelined by Boris Yeltsin, who favored the breakup and who emerged as president of the newly declared Russian Federation. The Cold War ended abruptly by default as the Communist Party regime in Moscow crumbled (see Map 28.3).

The American giant. Some observers expected that bipolar politics (free world vs. communist world) would give way to a multipolar system in which several large states—the United States, Russia, China, Japan, and the EU countries—would share global leadership, and military power would be more diffused. In fact, the United States remained top dog not only in military might but also in its armed presence on land and sea around the world. Russia struggled economically to the end of the twentieth century and cut back its armed forces. The European Union moved toward commercial and monetary integration in the 1990s but proved reluctant to deploy military forces to deal with a crisis in its own backyard, the collapse of the multiethnic republic of Yugoslavia. That event in 1991–1992 led to three years of vicious interethnic warfare mainly among Serbs, Croats, and Bosnian Muslims. When Bosnian Serbs threatened wholesale ethnic cleansing of the Muslim population and UN peacekeepers proved ineffective, the United States intervened, coaxing its European NATO allies to launch air strikes to stop the carnage. In 1995 U.S. president Bill Clinton (in office 1993–2001) presided over an accord among the several states that by then had partitioned Yugoslavia. As for China, its new market economy grew spectacularly after 1978, but its military power remained technologically far behind that of the United States.

In the first decade of the new century, the United States faced no serious challenges to its global military supremacy. The attacks on New York and Washington, D.C., on September 11, 2001, raised popular fears that the country was nonetheless vulnerable to terrorist assaults. The administration of president George W. Bush (in office 2001–2009) consequently announced a "war on terror," particularly on al-Qaida, an international, though uncentralized revolutionary organization. Osama bin Laden, a wealthy Saudi who established a base in Afghanistan, emerged as al-Qaida's leader. American and other NATO contingents invaded Afghanistan in the fall of 2001, joining with Afghan rebels there to overthrow the Taliban regime, which sheltered al-Qaida. The mission succeeded quickly, but more NATO troops arrived to help secure a new, presumably pro-Western government. Progress on that front moved slowly, and thirteen years after the 2001 military campaign, there were still more than 87,000 NATO-led troops in Afghanistan, 60,000 of them Americans.

In 2003 the United States invaded Iraq, gathering a coalition of allies but also acting without securing the approval of the UN Security Council. The U.S. government's announced objective was to preempt the regime of President Saddam Hussein from collaborating with al-Qaida and from using chemical or other weapons of mass destruction. In fact, Hussein had not previously had friendly relations with al-Qaida, and weapons of mass destruction were never found. The invaders overthrew the Hussein regime in a matter of weeks, but the war quickly mutated into a combination civil conflict and anticoalition resistance movement that dragged on for eight years. When American troops finally departed in late 2011, Iraq's attempt to build multiparty democracy was in a fragile state and its economy operating far below its potential.

American actions in both Afghanistan and Iraq aggravated relations with the Russian Federation. Under the leadership of Vladimir Putin, Russia initiated a more assertive foreign policy, especially in opposition to the expansion of NATO to include most of the former Soviet Union's Eastern European allies. Putin fiercely objected to NATO membership for Ukraine and Georgia, both former Soviet republics, and to American plans to place ballistic missile defense hardware in the Czech Republic and Poland. U.S. president Barack Obama (in office 2009–) suspended both of those initiatives, but in 2008 Russia fought a brief war with Georgia to protect two pro-Russian breakaway provinces of that country. The status of these provinces has remained unresolved and a continuing source of Russian–American strain.

A World of Organizations

Political scientists have characterized the sovereign state system as fundamentally a condition of *anarchy*—a word of Greek origin meaning "absence of rulers"—in the sense that no overarching central authority, no world government, imposes laws on states that they must obey. Global complexity, however, has impelled states to cooperate with one another more effectively and on larger scales. They must do this partly to manage rapid change and partly to prevent the institutions and organizations that world order requires from falling apart. Since World War II, international organizations have multiplied by the hundreds. Through these institutions, sovereign governments work together under agreed sets of rules and procedures to achieve goals of mutual interest, whether collective security, tariff reduction, or improved communications nets. Global complexity, however, has also demanded more **transnational organizations** that promote order, stability, and well-being in the world. Their work often involves exerting pressure on sovereign states to change their policies or account for their actions.

> **transnational organization**
> An association of individual citizens or private groups that collaborates across national frontiers to carry out particular activities or programs.

In the nineteenth century, states in Europe began to collaborate more systematically to manage their complex interrelations, founding, for example, the international Red Cross (1863); the Universal Postal Union (1878); and the Hague Conference (1899), which formulated procedures for resolving international conflicts. Such organizations proliferated in the twentieth century, as the two world wars demonstrating plainly the urgency of building institutions that bound states together in dense networks of cooperation and mutual dependence.

Red Cross workers unload a boat in Katanga province, Congo. Food and medical supplies supported families returning to the region in 2006 after being displaced by civil war. Why have transnational organizations such as the Red Cross taken on increasingly visible roles in the world in the past half-century?

The United Nations. Since 1945 the United Nations has served as the world's preeminent institution for guiding and harmonizing international relations. Member states, which today include every sovereign polity in the world except Taiwan and Vatican City, must agree to abide by the articles of the UN Charter. That treaty set forth the fundamental purposes of the United Nations to uphold international peace and security, address international problems of all kinds, encourage amicable relations among states, and foster respect for human rights. The charter refers to both the relations among states and the rights and welfare of "peoples." Advocates of a strong United Nations have contended therefore that the organization has authority to intervene in the internal affairs of member states if they grossly oppress or abuse their citizens. In that sense the institution has challenged one of the principles of national sovereignty, freedom from external interference.

From its inception the UN Security Council, currently comprised of five permanent and ten rotating members, has had the authority to undertake military missions. In contrast to the League of Nations, its pre–World War II predecessor, the United Nations gives special powers to the Security Council's permanent members (today the United States, Britain, France, Russia, and China) and a majority of the full council membership to "take such action by air, sea, or land forces as may be necessary to maintain or restore international peace and security."[18] In the Cold War years, however, incessant rivalry among the United States,

the Soviet Union, and their respective allies drastically limited UN military action. The five permanent members had power to veto resolutions that came before them, and one or another member did so on substantive issues 193 times between 1945 and 1990. The council authorized armed intervention in Korea in 1950 only because the Soviet Union temporarily boycotted the proceedings. UN forces, made up of volunteers from member states, also undertook a number of peacekeeping operations, for example, creating a line of separation between Egyptian and Israeli troops following the Suez Crisis of 1956 (see Chapter 27).

After the cold war ended and the world's two biggest military powers stopped butting heads over nearly every proposed UN military operation, many more peacekeeping missions were launched. These operations included the dispatch of UN forces to try to end or contain calamitous civil wars. The Security Council also authorized the large coalition that drove Iraq out of Kuwait in 1991. This campaign boosted the United Nations' prestige and suggested an expanding role in preventing or repelling state aggression. Soldiers wearing the organization's signature blue helmets have had several peacekeeping, indeed peacemaking, successes, notably overseeing the resolution of long-running civil wars in Cambodia (1970–1991) and El Salvador (1979–1992). Attempted interventions in wars in Rwanda, Bosnia, Somalia, and Angola, however, had little success. In 1999 NATO deployed airpower to prevent Serbia from attacking its own Albanian-speaking citizens in the Kosovo region because

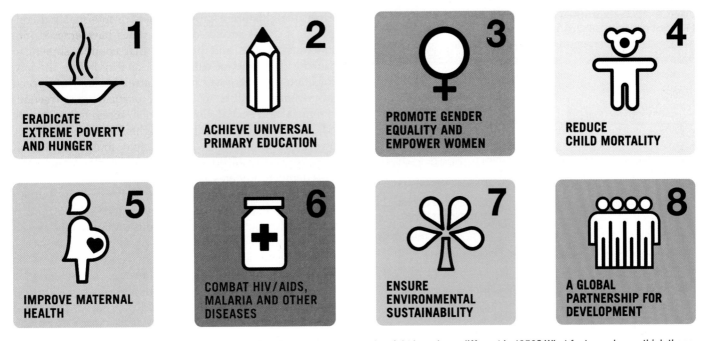

The UN Millennium Development Goals. How do you think UN development goals might have been different in 1950? What features do you think these goals have in common?

1 ERADICATE EXTREME POVERTY AND HUNGER

2 ACHIEVE UNIVERSAL PRIMARY EDUCATION

3 PROMOTE GENDER EQUALITY AND EMPOWER WOMEN

4 REDUCE CHILD MORTALITY

5 IMPROVE MATERNAL HEALTH

6 COMBAT HIV/AIDS, MALARIA AND OTHER DISEASES

7 ENSURE ENVIRONMENTAL SUSTAINABILITY

8 A GLOBAL PARTNERSHIP FOR DEVELOPMENT

Russian opposition prevented the Security Council from approving intervention. UN prestige as a peacekeeper dropped again in 2003 after the United States invaded Iraq without Security Council authorization.

The UN Charter (Article 1.3) enjoins members "to achieve international cooperation in solving international problems of an economic, social, cultural or humanitarian character." The number of UN agencies and projects dedicated to human rights and welfare has increased steadily since 1945, though member states have on the whole substantially reduced their contributions to these institutions. Nevertheless, UN organizations have carried on their benevolent work without receiving the media notoriety that armed missions have attracted. The organization has been a party to the striking progress made in nuclear and strategic arms control since 1990. It has sponsored numerous conferences of member states to address issues of human rights, population growth, the status and opportunities of women, and environmental degradation. In 2000 the United Nations outlined eight Millennium Development Goals that include cutting extreme poverty rates in half and providing primary education to the children of all member states. Progress has been made toward many of these goals, but it has slowed in the past few years owing to the complexity of the challenges and the inadequacy of funds from donor states.

International organizations on the regional scale. States in particular regions of the world have also grouped themselves into organizations to address a range of issues. During the Cold War, regional initiatives tended to be linked to one superpower bloc or the other. Since 1990, more regional organizations have formed, sometimes to strengthen collective security but also to take on social and economic problems having a particular regional character, for example, cooperation among African states to reduce high levels of HIV infection. Nearly every state in the world has become party to one or more regional organizations to reduce tariffs. These include the South American Common Market (Mecosur, 1991) and the North American Free Trade Agreement (NAFTA, 1992). No regional organization, however, has advanced as far as the European Union toward political and economic integration.

Transnational organizations. After World War II, more world leaders accepted the fact that national governments, even acting in close partnership with one another, could not address many complex global problems as effectively as more flexible, task-oriented, private organizations could. Transnational associations aim to serve human welfare apart from the interests of states or governing elites. The scholar Akira Iriye has written of the gradual emergence in the past century or so of an "international civil society" in which individuals and private groups band together to better the human condition in a variety of ways. He refers to networks "that are based upon a global consciousness, the idea that there is a wider world over and above separate states and national societies, and that individuals and groups, no matter where they are, share certain interests and concerns in that wider world."[19]

Many transnational associations may be categorized as international nongovernmental organizations (INGOs). These institutions have multiplied into the thousands to serve human welfare in areas such as conflict resolution, disarmament, humanitarian assistance, economic development,

TABLE 28.1. Examples of International Nongovernmental Organizations

Organization	Location	Mission
Acumen Fund	United States	Economic development
APOPO	Tanzania	Humanitarian services, landmine clearance
Ashoka	United States	Economic development, social entrepreneurship
Barefoot College	India	Education, skills training
BRAC	Bangladesh	Economic development
CARE International	Switzerland	Economic development, humanitarian services
Ceres	United States	Environmental sustainability
Clinton Health Access Initiative	United States	Public health
Cure Violence	United States	Antiviolence intervention
Danish Refugee Council	Denmark	Humanitarian services
Doctors without Borders	Switzerland	Public health services
Handicap International	France	Humanitarian services
Heifer International	United States	Economic development
International Rescue Committee	United States	Humanitarian services, refugee services
Landesa	United States	Land tenure rights
Mercy Corps	United States	Humanitarian services
One Acre Fund	Kenya	Economic development
Partners in Health	United States	Public health services
Root Capital	United States	Economic development
Wikimedia Foundation	United States	Education, knowledge dissemination

Source: *The Global Journal*, "The Top 100 NGOs 2013," http://theglobaljournal.net/top100NGOs/.

cultural exchange, environmental protection, and human rights (see Table 28.1). Many influential INGOS, such as international labor unions and faith-based groups, have memberships numbering in the millions, that is, more than the populations of many sovereign states. Electronic media also permit INGOs to disseminate information rapidly, archive millions of documents, and lobby governments and corporations to take action or modify policies. Dozens of INGOs have formal affiliation with the United Nations. For example, the delegations to the Kyoto conference on climate change in 1997 included 161 states and 236 transnational entities. In short, there are many public "actors" on the world stage today besides states.

Transnational groups have made especially important contributions to human rights. Since the United Nations adopted the Universal Declaration of Human Rights (1948) in response to the revelation of atrocities committed during World War II, sovereign states have come to accept that universal rights are a proper subject of international concern. In the past several decades, states have entered into numerous treaties and protocols that commit signers to ensuring the rights of citizens to equality before the law, protection against government abuse, freedom of speech and assembly, rights to political participation, freedom from racial and sexual discrimination, access to health care and education, and several other rights and liberties. States, however, have also been the principal abusers of human rights, especially authoritarian or weak regimes but sometimes democratic states as well.

The international mechanisms for enforcing human rights *inside* states are meager. Governments have tended to pick and choose the human rights violations they wish to protest, depending on their own political self-interests. This was especially true during the Cold War, when the United States and Russia looked the other way when their ideological and strategic allies committed serious abuses. INGOs unaligned with the political interests of particular states have worked effectively using persuasion and publicity to pressure governments to improve their human rights records. For example, Amnesty International, which grew rapidly in the 1970s and today has more than two million members, identifies and draws public attention to individuals imprisoned for political reasons. Other major INGOs include Human Rights Watch, the International Federation for Human Rights, and MADRE, a network of women's rights organizations.

Disorder and Breakdown in an Era of Global Integration

The demise of the Cold War brought a rush of hope for a new era of international peace and cooperation. Indeed, in the past quarter-century the world's strongest military powers have remained at peace with one another. And far fewer people have died in wars than in the mere six years of World War II. According to one study, the number of war deaths (both military and civilian) in the first ten years of the twenty-first century averaged about 55,000 people a year, compared to 180,000 a year between 1950 and 1989.[20] In those decades the Korean and Vietnam conflicts raged, and Iraq and Iran fought a border war, partly for control of oil fields, that dragged on for eight and a half years (1980–1988) and cost about 650,000 lives. Since then, no wars have reached that scale of violence, though 160,000 people died in Iraq during the American occupation of 2003–2011, nearly 80 percent of them Iraqi civilians.[21]

Wars after the Cold War. Nevertheless, more than one hundred relatively small wars have erupted since 1990, a few of them between states but mostly internal struggles for control of resources and power. Paradoxically, processes of global integration have themselves bred conflicts that have resulted in political and social disintegration. World demand for oil, rare minerals, illicit drugs, and many other commodities; the thriving international arms trade;

explosive growth rates of the urban poor; and the disproportionate flow of wealth to a minority of the world's population have made wars an inevitable corollary of globalization. If wars since 1990 have been less deadly than in previous years, they have nonetheless killed hundreds of thousands of men, women, and children and generated millions of refugees. Their horrors have included genocidal campaigns and civilian massacres, conscription of child soldiers, torture and execution of prisoners, and the rape, murder, and displacement of millions of women.

Most wars since 1990 have happened in relatively small or poor states where political disorder—marked by rebellions, interethnic clashes, rivalries between local warlords, and in some cases the intervention of foreign powers or hired mercenaries—has involved appalling violence (see Map 28.6). Several factors, always varying from one case to another, have operated to undermine central state authority. These have included chronic rural poverty, high unemployment rates of urban youth, rivalry for resources that command high world market demand (diamonds, rare earths, timber, cocaine), pervasive political corruption, and

oppressive governments that have sometimes endured only with the support of foreign patrons. Also, long-simmering social tensions rose to the surface in a number of states after the Cold War ended. That happened in part because oppressive or weak governments could no longer count on economic and military support from a Cold War patron to guarantee their power. Moreover, rulers who tried to build national unity on a platform of either anticommunism or anticapitalism discovered that these ideologies lost much of their popular appeal. In some countries, discontented political groups have had greater success than their own national governments in drawing on local ethnic or religious sentiments to foment rebellion.

Political identity and violence: Two cases. In the former Yugoslavia, regional ethnic and religious identities proved stronger than national allegiance when the country descended into crisis. A large majority of Yugoslavia's population shared a common secular culture and the Serbo-Croatian language. But the country was part Serbian Orthodox Christian, part Roman Catholic, and part

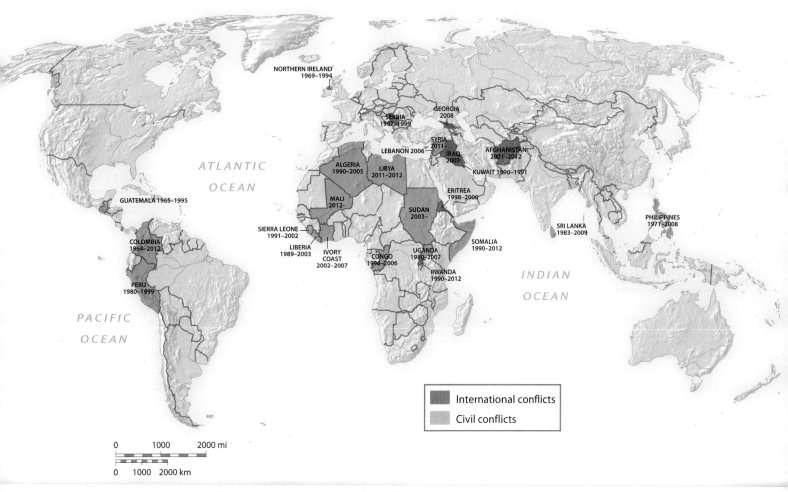

MAP 28.6 Twenty-five international and civil conflicts since 1990.
Which regions have largely escaped armed conflict since 1990? What factors might account for the proliferation of war in some regions and relative peace in others?

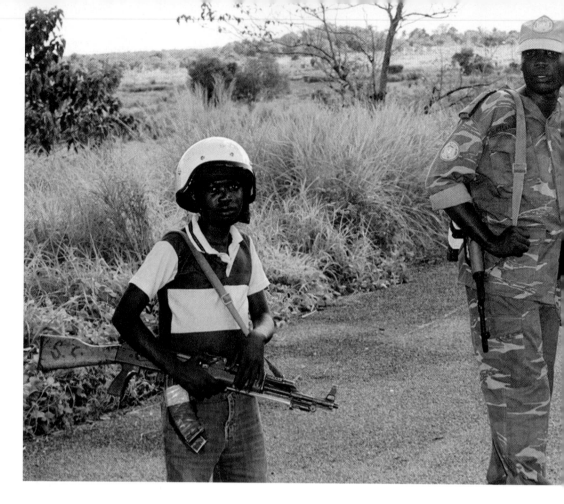

As local conflicts proliferated after the Cold War, rival factions fighting to control their country's resources or government increasingly used young boys and girls as armed combatants, cooks, porters, messengers, and sex slaves. What aspects of this boy's appearance do you find remarkable?

Muslim. In 1991–1992, shortly after the breakup of the Soviet Union, Yugoslavia fragmented, mainly over differences between leaders of the large Serbian minority, who insisted on dominating the state, and the other ethno-religious groups. After the breakup, regional cultural identities became much more politically useful than Yugoslav nationalism as leaders sought to build and defend several new republics from the wreckage of the old one. In the region of Bosnia, rivalry for land and power led to three years of war in which Bosnian Serb and Muslim communities revived ancient justifications for despising each other's cultural and historical identities and for clinging more fervently to their respective religious traditions than many of them had done when they were citizens of multiethnic Yugoslavia.

In the small East African state of Rwanda, the Belgian colonial administrators who ruled there until 1962 favored the aspirations of the Tutsi minority population, which traditionally herded cattle, over the majority of Hutu farmers. Even though both groups spoke the same language and shared much of their culture, tensions between them festered following national independence. Competition for land in conditions of rapidly rising population aggravated social friction, and the assassination of the Hutu president Juvénal Habyarimana in the spring of 1994 triggered Hutu armed attacks on Tutsis. Those assaults exploded quickly into a genocidal rampage that in the short span of three months took between 800,000 and 1 million lives. The victims also included many Hutu who opposed the genocide or who had marriage or other connections to their Tutsi neighbors. Neither the United Nations, the Organization of African Unity, nor any major world power took decisive action to stop the killing, which ended only when a Tutsi force seized the capital. After 1994 Tutsi and Hutu leaders achieved an uneasy reconciliation at home, though the Rwandan army and a variety of armed militias became involved in chronic and ongoing fighting in the neighboring Congo Democratic Republic.

Terrorism. The world had no trouble branding the September 11 attacks on the World Trade Center in New York and the Pentagon in Washington, D.C., as terrorism. The perpetrators carried out these airborne assaults to broadcast *political* grievances, not just to commit crimes. They aimed their strikes on civilians and on prominent symbols of power—bastions of global capitalism and American military might. They intended to instill fear and confusion, demoralize their adversary, or provoke a disproportionate militaristic response, probably all of those things. They professed an extreme ideology of change through violence, in their case a vision of Islam having little relationship to what millions of Muslims believe and practice. Finally, the aggressors demonstrated that the weak could inflict pain on the strong without their necessarily having any more ambitious strategic goal than that.

Terrorism is by no means a new tool of war. It was an element in both world wars and in anticolonial resistance movements. From the 1960s to the 1980s, extremists of various ideological persuasions hijacked airplanes, set off bombs, took hostages, and carried out assassinations and suicide missions. In the past two decades, however, terrorist violence has taken some new directions. First, more terrorist operations have transnational dimensions. Even if perpetrators planned attacks on single targets, they frequently have built networks that recruit, plan, raise money, and procure weapons in several countries simultaneously. Al-Qaida emerged as a guerrilla organization fighting Afghanistan's Soviet occupiers, but after 1989 it morphed into an international network of cells to combat Western military and cultural intrusions in the Muslim world.

Terrorist attack on New York's World Trade Center towers. The south tower erupts in flames after a hijacked commercial passenger plane crashed into it on September 11, 2001. Another commandeered plane had already struck the smoking north tower. A total of 2,937 people died in the attacks on the world trade towers and the Pentagon. Another forty passengers and crew members were killed in the crash of a fourth hijacked plane near Shanksville, Pennsylvania.

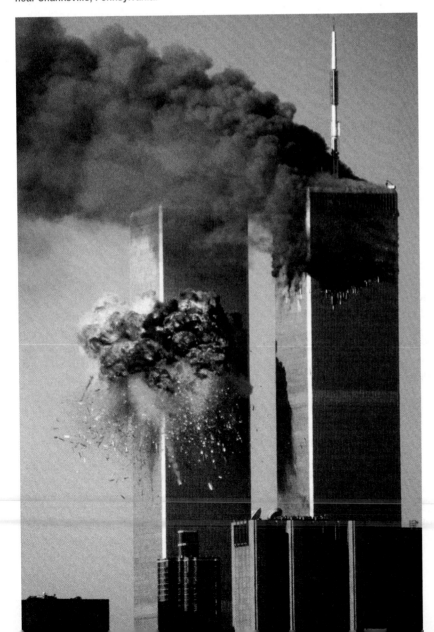

Second, terrorist groups have benefited immensely from the electronic revolution, using mobile phones, computers, and web sites to communicate plans, coordinate activities, and disseminate their messages. Third, at least a few sovereign states have given sanctuary and material support to terrorist groups at one time or another, notably Iran, Libya, and Syria. Fourth, throughout most of the twentieth century, anti-imperialist or Marxist-Leninist opposition to bourgeois capitalist oppression motivated many terrorist acts. Since 1990, however, terrorism has become a specialized weapon of underemployed, politically alienated young males in Asia and Africa, notably radicals who profess an "Islamist" religion characterized by rigid, puritanical ideology and a rhetoric of apocalypse and martyrdom. Fifth, terrorism has by definition represented a tactic of war wielded by a few against many. Consequently, terrorist conspiracies have frequently come to nothing, operations have failed regularly, and successful attacks have more often than not achieved little of benefit to the perpetrators. Nevertheless, the world has come to fear that terrorists may acquire portable weapons of mass destruction capable of killing tens or hundreds of thousands of people. The Japanese Aleph cult demonstrated the possibilities when in March 1995 its operatives released toxic sarin gas on five trains in the Tokyo subway system, killing thirteen and injuring hundreds more. Thus, global anxiety remains high that, despite vigorous police and military campaigns to root out extremists before they strike, civilian populations remain acutely vulnerable to terrorist violence on unprecedented scales.

Finally, terrorism, like other forms of warfare in the contemporary world, is a complex phenomenon requiring explanation. As reprehensible as it is, politically motivated violence springs from real social grievances and injustices—economic frustration or destitution, government oppression, lack of opportunity for political participation, spiritual or moral disquiet over an increasingly decadent and materialist world, and sheer anxiety over the complexity and speed of change. Political analysts continue to debate the relative importance of the cultural, economic, and social conditions that turn men and women to careers of political violence. In the case of the September 11 attacks, Osama bin Laden and other al-Qaida leaders offered precise rational explanations for plotting mayhem: American failure to address the aspirations of Palestinians in their conflict with Israel, Western economic sanctions against Iraq and their grim consequences for the Iraqi people, Western support for corrupt Middle Eastern regimes, and the posting of American troops in Saudi Arabia, an affront to Muslims who worship in the holy cities of Mecca and Medina.

Palestinians and Israelis

Terrorist acts have figured prominently in the long-running and agonizing conflict between the state of Israel and the Arabic-speaking peoples of Palestine. Israel has fought four wars with neighboring Arab states (1948, 1956, 1967, 1973), and to date it has established full diplomatic relations with only two of them, Egypt (1979) and Jordan (1994). In the aftermath of its victory in the 1967 war, Israeli forces occupied Egyptian, Jordanian, and Syrian territories. Israel returned the Sinai to Egypt (1980–1982) but continued to occupy the West Bank (lands west of the Jordan River that had been part of Jordan) and the Gaza Strip (formerly within Egypt). These lands already had large populations of Palestinian Arabs, most Muslim but also a significant Christian minority. Since the war of 1973, the region has seen two Israeli invasions of Lebanon to root out Palestinian and other Arab fighters (1982–1984 and 2006), two major Palestinian uprisings (1987–1991, 2000–2002), Iraqi missile attacks on Israel during the Gulf War (1991), a violent split between the two major Palestinian political parties (2006–2007), extensive fighting in Gaza (2008), and throughout those years a nearly steady drum beat of Arab terrorist attacks and violent Israeli military reprisals

The fundamental issues perpetuating this conflict have not changed greatly in the past sixty-some years. Jewish immigrant settlers founded Israel in a land where Arab farmers and townspeople had made their homes for many centuries. Following the 1967 war, Israel imposed its rule on millions more Palestinians in the West Bank and Gaza. Today, there are about 4.4 million Palestinians in the occupied territories (another 1.4 in Israel). But no sovereign Palestinian state exists. There is only the Palestinian Authority, created in 1994 under terms of the Oslo Accords between Israel and the Palestinian Liberation Organization (PLO), to administer Gaza and parts of the West Bank. In addition, successive Israeli governments have also allowed Jewish Israelis to settle in the West Bank in increasing numbers, even though that territory lies outside the state of Israel. (The government dismantled Jewish settlements in Gaza in 2005.) Thus, 4.4 million Palestinians continue to live in a state of political limbo. Several million more Palestinians have status as refugees in Jordan, Lebanon, and Syria but do not hold citizenship in those countries.

The past forty years have also seen intermittent peace talks between the Israeli government and Palestinian representatives, usually under the sponsorship of the United States. None of these parlays has solved several seemingly intractable problems: Who should govern and under what conditions the city of Jerusalem, a place holy to Muslims, Jews, and Christians alike? How should the borders between Israel and a new Palestinian state be drawn? Under whose authority should Jewish settlers in the West Bank live? Should Palestinians ever be permitted to return to homes they left behind in Israel more than sixty-five years ago? Who will support a Palestinian state's much-needed economic development?

To complicate matters further, elections in 2006 for a legislature under the Palestinian Authority put members of Hamas, a radical party, in control of Gaza, which Israeli troops have not occupied since 2005. Hamas does not formally recognize Israel's right to exist and has broken ties with the more moderate PLO in the West Bank. In the past few years, the contending parties have made no significant progress toward a "two state solution." And looming over the fluctuating political scene are three trends that will have to be addressed. One is unsettled conditions in the region following the so-called Arab Spring of 2011, which triggered the overthrow of existing authoritarian regimes in Tunisia, Egypt, Yemen, and Libya and the outbreak of civil war in Syria. No observer, however well informed, can confidently predict the long-term political complexion of new governments in those countries or how their relations with Israel and the Palestinian people will play out. A second issue is the near certainty that in Israel and the Palestinian territories combined, the Arabic-speaking Muslim population will soon outnumber Israeli Jews, leading to a condition in which a Jewish minority politically dominates and denies full citizenship rights to a Palestinian majority—a serious predicament for Israelis committed to democratic government. A third problem is worsening environmental stresses in the whole region, especially declining supplies of water, which Israeli industry and agriculture use in great quantities. A dropping water table threatens future economic growth in both Israel and a prospective Palestinian state.

Into the Anthropocene

FOCUS In what circumstances did the global environmental movement emerge, and how much success has it had slowing or reversing environmental degradation?

In recent years a number of environmental scientists have endorsed a startling idea: Sometime in the nineteenth century, the world entered a new age in which human beings, rather than slow-moving geological and climatic forces, became the primary agents of change in the earth's biosphere. In 2000 Paul Crutzen, a chemist and Nobel Prize winner, popularized the term **Anthropocene**—a word from the Greek *anthropo* referring to "human" and *cene,* meaning "new"—to describe this era. In his view

> **Anthropocene** The era beginning in the nineteenth century in which human beings have become the primary agents of change in the earth's biosphere.

the Anthropocene is superseding the Holocene, the post–Ice Age epoch in which we have been living for the past twelve thousand years. Crutzen and two colleagues have written, "Human activities have become so pervasive and profound that they rival the great forces of Nature. . . . The Earth is rapidly moving into a less biologically diverse, less forested, much warmer, and probably wetter and stormier state."[22]

Environmentalists have predicted that human society has reached such a level of complexity that it will soon lose the capacity to manage and control the vast material waste that complexity inevitably generates—carbon dioxide emissions, pesticide residue, stored radioactive plutonium, plastic bottles, and obsolete electronic devices. Humans will then have either to discover much better technological solutions to the problem of unhealthful, nature-destroying waste or else dismantle at least some complex systems—an unlikely prospect on a planet of seven billion people and counting. As we pointed out at the beginning of the chapter, if humans lose the ability to hold complex structures together through constant effort, those structures will inevitably break down of their own accord. One writer has observed that in the past two centuries humans have by their actions already undermined the complexity of animal life on the planet. They have done this by forcing thousands of species into extinction while vastly increasing the populations of a few species—cattle, sheep, pigs, chickens—that they want for their use.[23] Could our species eventually manipulate and alter natural and physical processes so much that its own existence as a complex organism becomes untenable?

Environment and Environmentalism

Humans have been modifying the planetary environment since our species emerged 200,000 years ago. As society became more complex, this intervention intensified. In Chapter 27 we described the connection between unprecedented economic growth in the thirty years after World War II and accelerating environmental change, much of it harmful. As a consequence of human economic activity, forest lands shrank, soil washed away, rivers and lakes turned poisonous, pollutants thickened the air, fresh water tables dropped, and more animal and plant species disappeared. Some types of environmental degradation had immediate and harsh effects on human well-being. But others altered landscapes and natural systems in ways that most of the world largely ignored. In the past four decades environmental change has become far more evident, in part because a drastic shift in public attitudes began to take place in the 1970s.

In the post–World War II years, political and economic leaders nearly everywhere, whether they were communists, capitalists, or nationalists in new developing countries, believed that sustained and accelerating economic growth would ultimately make life better for all. Consequently, those leaders ignored, either willfully or not, mounting scientific evidence of the serious and long-term environmental damage that unfettered economic growth might inflict. Or, if they recognized that human industry, agriculture, and

A solar array in Spain harvests the sun's energy. At this solar plant, mirrors follow the sun's track, reflecting light onto the central tower, which generates steam to power an electrical turbine. Spain was home to 40 percent of the world's solar installations in 2008.

urban crowding could injure the earth, they assumed either that nature would heal its own wounds or ingenious technologists would find ways to limit the destruction without getting in the way of growth.

The environmental movement. Public awareness of agricultural and industrial contamination grew moderately in the 1960s following publication of Rachel Carson's best-selling book *Silent Spring,* which exposed the lethal effects of widespread pesticide use (see Chapter 27). The year 1970 marked a watershed in environmental awareness in the United States. That year Democratic and Republican party leaders joined together to organize the first Earth Day, an event that mobilized about twenty thousand Americans to demand solutions to worsening environmental ills.

The Earth Day movement inspired many more public interest initiatives and helped awaken world consciousness to the problems and complexities of the emerging Anthropocene. The oil crisis of 1973 generated global anxiety over chronic fossil-fuel shortages and the lack of alternative or cleaner sources of energy. Under public pressure, governments in the Western democracies began to organize agencies and enact legislation to address environmental degradation. The United States offered a model for other countries by establishing the Environmental Protection Agency in 1970 and subsequently passing laws to clean up air and water. By the 1980s the governments of many other states, including young developing countries, began to organize environmental ministries and take action on some level to restrain forest cutting, protect wildlife, and reduce pollution. Also in that decade, politically minded environmentalists organized Green Parties in several Western countries.

Once the new earth consciousness became rooted, major disasters could no longer occur without massive public reaction. In December 1984, for example, the accidental release of methyl isocyanate gas and other toxic chemicals from a pesticide factory in Bhopal, India, killed about fifteen thousand people. The Bhopal disaster and its aftermath cast a long shadow over the Union Carbide Corporation, whose subsidiary owned the factory. Two years later, a disastrous explosion at the Chernobyl nuclear plant in the Soviet Ukraine contaminated to one degree or another most of Europe and caused the illness or deaths of thousands of people exposed to radioactive fallout. This calamity also exposed the communist state's bureaucratic incompetence and probably hastened the Soviet Union's collapse in 1990. An environmental movement bloomed in the new Russia, and it helped expose the appalling environmental damage wrought by Joseph Stalin and his Soviet successors. That movement has continued to grow despite scant encouragement from the central government, which has continued to pin the country's future on massive production of fossil fuels and minerals.

As early as the 1960s, governments negotiated bilateral and multilateral agreements on pollution reduction and other environmental issues. The United Nations held its first major conference on the human environment in Stockholm in 1972, producing a declaration of twenty-six principles on economic development and defense of the biosphere. Other international meetings followed, for example, the Copenhagen climate summit in 2009. In the past forty years, hundreds of INGOs have been founded to advance environmentalist agendas. These organizations, including Friends of the Earth, Greenpeace, and the Sierra Club, have persistently taken both governments and corporations to task for environmental mismanagement, including rampant deforestation and waste dumping. They have also monitored deficiencies in safety technologies and regulations that have caused such disasters as the Deepwater Horizon oil rig blowout in 2010, which killed eleven people and disgorged two hundred million gallons of crude oil into the Gulf of Mexico.

China's spectacular economic growth curve since the 1980s has coincided with the rise of global environmentalism. The timing here has been bad. Chinese leaders are perfectly aware of multiple environmental degradation crises, but they do not want to slow China's climb to the top rank of economic powers. Rapid reform of industrial practices will

Humans and wildlife suffer the consequences of environmental disasters. A local government official rescues a contaminated bird along the Louisiana coast after an explosion on BP's Deepwater Horizon drilling rig caused a massive oil spill. How might this 2010 event have set back or benefited the environmentalist movement?

be difficult. Lung-destroying air pollution hit record levels in northern China in 2013, and growing quantities of dust, mercury, and carbon monoxide have been wafting eastward over the Pacific to fall back to earth in North America.

Environmentalist success. Nevertheless, environmental activism has made impressive achievements. In many countries, especially the wealthiest, cleanup projects have partially cleared skies over big cities and brought dead waterways back to life. Some wild animal species have returned from the brink of extinction. Europe has recovered forest land to the extent it had a century and a half ago when the industrial revolution was going full speed.[24] Some industrialized countries have significantly reduced sulfur dioxide and lead emissions into the atmosphere. Many large corporations have begun, after years of resistance, to introduce more environmentally responsible policies and procedures; almost all of them have launched campaigns to refashion their public images as friends of the earth. In the 1980s and 1990s a remarkable international effort persuaded many states to reduce production of chlorofluorocarbons (CFCs), an organic compound used as a refrigerant, spray propellant, and solvent. When released into the atmosphere, CFCs disrupt and pierce holes in the ozone layer, the thin chemical blanket in the stratosphere that absorbs most of the sun's ultraviolet radiation. If that radiation reaches the planet's surface in significant amounts, it damages oceanic plankton essential to the health of the biosphere. It also afflicts humans with eye diseases and skin cancers. Fortunately, international cooperation has reduced CFC contamination so much that the ozone layer appears to be on the mend, though its full restoration will take decades.

The quest for energy sources to supplement fossil fuels has also advanced. Nuclear power has remained highly controversial in the aftermath of Chernobyl and, more recently, the 2011 earthquake and tsunami that severely damaged the nuclear plant in Fukushima, Japan. Nevertheless, about 11 percent of total energy production came from nuclear power in 2009, and today nearly 450 plants are in operation, the greatest number in the United States, France, and Japan. In the 1970s the potential of geothermal, solar, and wind power was known but hardly developed. In recent years science and engineering have raised the efficiency and lowered the cost of these energy producers, resulting, for example, in a fivefold increase in available solar power. Electric automobiles, which proved too costly and cumbersome to compete with internal combustion engine vehicles throughout the twentieth century, are now appearing on the road.

The Perils of Climate Change

The Holocene is an interglacial geological era, a period when the earth's surface temperature warms slightly in the interval between one ice age and another. But compared to the small temperature fluctuations that have accompanied most of the Holocene, the increase of about one degree Fahrenheit in the course of the twentieth century is ominous.

Wangari Maathai: Environmental Activist and Nobel Laureate

Kenya is one of those African countries whose population has grown stupendously since the early twentieth century. In the 1920s Kenya had about 2.7 million people. By 2013 numbers had risen to more than 44 million. This growth has put great pressure on land and water resources. The country has suffered extensive deforestation as Kenyans have cut down trees for fuel and lumber.

By the 1970s the negative effects of this deforestation were becoming apparent. Wangari Maathai (1940–2011), a professor of veterinary anatomy at the University of Nairobi and an advocate for women's rights at the institution, became concerned about the environmental destruction she was witnessing in her country. She began to combine her feminist activism with environmental advocacy, using her position in the National Council of Women of Kenya to launch a community-based tree planting program. Maathai encouraged women to plant and nurture tree seedlings in exchange for a small stipend, seeing this project as a way to steward the environment and create jobs for women at the same time. "It's the little things citizens do," she observed. "That's what will make the difference. My little thing is planting trees."[25] In 1977 she established the Green Belt Movement (GBM), a nongovernmental organization dedicated to planting trees on a much larger scale. Though the GBM received some financial and logistical support from Kenya's Ministry of Forestry, it got crucial assistance from international organizations like the UN Environment Program. Backed by international groups, the GBM did not have to depend on the Kenyan government's good graces for its survival.

The government indeed proved to be an unreliable partner. In the late 1980s Maathai began to speak out against the increasingly repressive single-party regime of President Daniel arap Moi. She first confronted Moi in 1989 when she campaigned to block the construction of a sixty-story business tower on the grounds of Uhuru Park in central Nairobi. Moi and his government repudiated her efforts and subjected her and the GBM to harassment. Nevertheless, Maathai and her supporters successfully lobbied international investors to withdraw their funding from the project, and Moi had to cancel it.

Throughout the 1990s Maathai and the GBM worked to enact democratic change in Kenya by registering voters and calling for constitutional reform. Maathai also protested multiple government attempts to transfer public land to commercial developers, often drawing international attention to these schemes and shaming the government into abandoning them. She was arrested numerous times and publicly criticized by Moi for not playing her part in society as an obliging and submissive woman.

Moi retired from office in 2002. He also saw his party lose the presidential election to a candidate from the National Rainbow Coalition, an alliance of parties that counted Maathai among its members. In the same election she stood as a candidate for parliament, winning

Wangari Maathai addresses the UN summit on climate change, 2009.

98 percent of the vote in her constituency. The following year, she took office as assistant minister for environment, natural resources and wildlife. In 2004 Maathai became the first African woman to win the Nobel Peace Prize, awarded to her for her impact on sustainable development, peace, and democracy. When she died of cancer in September 2011, she left behind a multidimensional legacy of service to democracy, feminism, human rights, and environmental conservation. "You cannot protect the environment," Maathai wrote, "unless you empower people, you inform them, and you help them understand that these resources are their own, that they must protect them."[26]

Thinking Critically

Wangari Maathai's activism addressed environmental degradation, women's empowerment, and democratic governance. Why do you think this combination of issues gave Maathai great public influence?

The world's scientific community is nearly unanimous in ascribing this remarkable surge to human action. If our species can significantly and for a long time alter planetary temperature, then we have clearly left the Holocene behind and entered the Anthropocene.

The heat the earth receives from the sun is radiated back toward space, but greenhouse gases, mainly water vapor but also carbon dioxide, methane, ozone, and nitrous oxide, trap most of the heat there. It then radiates back to the earth to warm its surface to a temperature that sustains life (59°F, on average). This greenhouse effect is therefore essential to life. Human intervention, however, has resulted in greater quantities of greenhouse gases rising into the lower atmosphere. The carbon dioxide concentration there has increased by

TABLE 28.2. Future Impacts of Global Warming in Three Regions

Africa	Australia and New Zealand	North America
Increased water stress for 75–250 million people by 2020	Intensified water security problems in southern and eastern Australia and parts of New Zealand, by 2030	Western mountains: decreased snowpack, more winter flooding, and reduced summer flows
Loss of arable land, reduced growing seasons, and reduced yields in some areas	Further loss of biodiversity in ecologically rich sites, by 2020	Increasing impacts on forests due to pests, diseases, and fire, with an extended period of high fire risk and large increases in area burned
Threats to low-lying coastal areas posed by sea-level rise	Increased risk from sea-level rise, more severe and more frequent storms, and coastal flooding in the Cairns region and southeast Queensland (Australia), Northland to Bay of Plenty (New Zealand), and other coastal communities, by 2050	In early decades of the century, during moderate climate change, 5 to 20 percent increase in total agricultural yields, with important regional variations; major challenges for crops with limited access to water or those near the warm end of their suitable range
Further degradation of mangroves and coral reefs	Some initial benefits in western and southern New Zealand, such as longer growing seasons, less frost, and increased rainfall	Increased intensity, duration, and number of heat waves in cities historically prone to them
Decreased fish stocks in large lakes	Decreased yields from agriculture and forestry by 2030, due to increased drought and fire, in much of southern and eastern Australia and parts of eastern New Zealand	Coastal areas: increased stress on people and property, due to climate change impacts interacting with development and pollution

Source: Adapted from University Corporation for Atmospheric Research, "Future Global Warming Impacts, by Region," http://www.ucar.edu/news/features/ climatechange/regionalimpacts-text.jsp; interactive map based on M. L. Parry, O. F. Canziani, J. P. Palutikof, P. J. van der Linden, and C. E. Hanson, eds. *Contribution of Working Group II to the Fourth Assessment Report of the Intergovernmental Panel on Climate Change, 2007* (New York: Cambridge University Press, 2007). © University Corporation for Atmospheric Research.

about one-third in the past two centuries. The chief cause of buildup has been fossil-fuel burning in factories and vehicle engines. Between 1990 and 2012 world petroleum production rose from nearly 66,500 to more than 89,000 barrels per day. The number of cars on the world's roads jumped from about 170 million to more than 1 billion between 1970 and 2012. Other important sources of gases that float into the atmosphere are wood burning, rice cultivation, chemical fertilizers, and livestock manure. Global deforestation also reduces the amount of carbon dioxide that living plant matter absorbs.

The effects of rising global temperature are not simply hotter weather but climatic instability—more rain in some places, worse drought in others, more frequent cyclone activity, loss of polar ice caps and glaciers, and a rise in sea levels. The Intergovernmental Panel on Climate Change has predicted a global temperature increase of anywhere from 2.5 to 10 degrees Fahrenheit in the next century. As the temperature climbs, the consequences will become more extreme, including rising seas that inundate low-lying islands and densely populated continental coasts (see Table 28.2).

Most of the world's political leaders remain fundamentally committed to the philosophy of continuous growth that has dominated economic thought since the industrial revolution. For example, in 2001 the administration of U.S. president George W. Bush, a champion of neoliberal economics, repudiated the 1997 Kyoto protocol to reduce greenhouse gas emissions on the grounds that it would interfere with American business growth. Even leaders who advocate strong environmental protection laws find it much easier to convince citizens to support short-term remedies rather than address long-term restructuring. Proper stewardship of the earth is also complicated by global commercial integration, which has intensified humankind's demand for more material goods, which must be grown or manufactured. We can hope that human ingenuity, coupled with serious if not drastic readjustments in the way we live, may prove sufficient to slow the pace of change, thereby avoiding massive social disruption and a forced return to simpler times.

•   •   •

Conclusion

This book has to have an ending, but the stories we have told in this final chapter have no conclusions. We cannot see

the full shape of the world-scale developments that have taken place in the past four decades because they are still in progress. We have identified what we think are important developments in the technological, economic, political, and environmental spheres. But we cannot know whether people living a hundred, fifty, or even just ten years in the future will think those developments are as important as we do now.

Scholars who study "big history," a relatively new field of inquiry that situates the human story in the much longer narrative of cosmic history from the Big Bang to the present, have demonstrated that we can predict the future of human society in the very long term with greater confidence than we can forecast, say, the next five years. Drawing on the evidence of astrophysics, for example, these "big historians" assure us that within probably less than two billion years, the sun will begin to expand, bombarding the earth with so much radiation that all living organisms will be extinguished. Our own species will almost certainly have already disappeared by then, probably within no more than a few million years from now. If the longevity of most other species is a valid measure, our extinction is likely to happen even if we tread far more lightly on the earth than we do now. In short, on very large scales of time, our fate is quite easy to foresee.

Let us drop down to the tiny scale of just the coming one hundred years and focus on human beings and their complex activities, relationships, and networks. We can predict from the experience of the previous century that the pace of change will continue to accelerate at a fast clip and that our numerous, intermeshed systems will become even more complex. We cannot, however, forecast with much precision the directions change will take. Will the acceleration of global population growth continue to slow down as much as demographers think? Will the income gap between the ultra-rich and the very poor get wider, or will it close at least a little? Will sovereign states matter even more in the twenty-second century than they do now? Or will regional and global associations that group people together for many different purposes replace states? Will the ideology of nationalism die away, or will it fuel even more conflicts between communities? Will the number of war deaths go up or down? How much will the earth's surface temperature rise, and in what ways will society have to restructure itself as that happens? No one can answer these questions with much assurance.

One change is almost certain to occur in the next century, or two at most: Our species will use up most of what remains of the fossil-fuel-energy jackpot it has enjoyed since the nineteenth century. If we as a species continue to consume nonrenewable energy at anything close to the current rate, the underground supplies of it, as well as the uranium that powers nuclear plants, will decline precipitously. Back in Chapter 21 we introduced the idea of the biological old regime, the long span of human history before the nineteenth century, when most of the energy humans used came from the shining sun, the renewable energy source that animates living things. When the fossil-fuel bonanza ends—the only major nonrenewable energy source capable of sustaining a human population in the billions—our species will be obliged to rely once again on the sun's renewable energy. A return to the biological old regime does not necessarily mean we will have to dismantle the complex systems we have been erecting at a frantic pace over the past two centuries. But we will have to achieve two objectives: First, we must develop technology to harvest energy from solar radiation on a far larger scale and at more manageable costs than we have done so far. Second, we must drastically reduce the rate at which we pollute and scar the earth, plunder its resources, and destroy its life-forms. Doing that will not require us to lower the global population by billions or abandon all complexity. We will not all have to be foragers, hunters, or subsistence farmers. But we will almost certainly have to retreat in some measure from the computer-driven, car-loving, and product-consuming way of life that so far remains a global aspiration.

• • •

Key Terms

al-Qaida 839	greenhouse effect 849	outsourcing 828
Anthropocene 846	inflation 825	*perestroika* 830
détente 838	international nongovernmental organization (INGO) 841	stagflation 825
European Union (EU) 832		terrorism 844
Eurozone 833	Internet 821	transnational organization 839
glasnost 830	neoliberalism 826	UN Security Council 839
globalization 837	Organization of Petroleum Exporting Countries (OPEC) 825	
Green Belt Movement (GBM) 849		

Change over Time

1972	The United Nations holds its first major conference on the environment in Stockholm.
1973	The OPEC oil embargo precipitates first global "oil shock."
1978	China initiates changes to modernize its economy.
1979	Tokyo activates the first cellular phone network.
1989	Crowds dismantle the Berlin Wall.
1991	The Soviet Union is officially dissolved. India begins to adopt more market-oriented policies. Tim Berners-Lee creates the first World Wide Web site.
1992–1995	Civil war rages in Bosnia after the breakup of Yugoslavia.
1993	The first Global Positioning System (GPS) is activated.
1994	Apartheid ends in South Africa. Hutu groups in Rwanda target Tutsis and sympathizers for genocidal mass slaughter.
1998	Eleven members of the European Union adopt the euro as a common currency.
2001	Al-Qaida terrorists hijack planes and strike the U.S. Pentagon and World Trade Center towers.
2003	The Human Genome Project identifies and maps genes and DNA sequences.
2003–2011	United States and coalition forces occupy Iraq.
2007–2009	Many countries experience an economic recession.
2011	An earthquake and tsunami severely damage the nuclear plant in Fukushima, Japan. Authoritarian regimes in Tunisia, Egypt, Yemen, and Libya are overthrown in the Arab Spring.

Please see end of book reference section for additional reading suggestions related to this chapter.

Glossary

absolutism A political doctrine asserting that in a monarchy the ruler holds sole and unquestionable power by divine authority.

Afroeurasia The land masses of Africa and Eurasia, together with adjacent islands, as a single spatial entity.

agrarian society A society in which agriculture, including both crop production and animal breeding, is the foundation of both subsistence and surplus wealth.

agricultural revolution The transition from collecting food in the wild to domesticating and producing particular plants and animals for human consumption.

Anthropocene The era beginning in the nineteenth century in which human beings have become the primary agents of change in the earth's biosphere.

apartheid The political and legal system in force in South Africa from 1948 to 1994; designed to ensure the domination of the white minority over the majority population.

asceticism The principle and practice of renouncing material comforts and pleasures in pursuit of an elevated moral or spiritual state.

australopithecines Several species of the earliest bipedal hominins, now extinct, whose remains have been found in eastern Africa.

autarky A country that aims to achieve economic independence and self-sufficiency, especially freedom from dependence on external trade or assistance; also autarkic.

authoritarian monarchy A state, headed by a king, a queen, or an emperor, whose ruling class demands strict authority over the rest of the population.

B

baby boom A period of increased birth rates, especially in Western countries, from the end of World War II to about 1957.

biological old regime Human history before the nineteenth century, when economic production depended almost entirely on capturing flows of energy from the sun.

biomass Plant matter, including wood, brush, straw, and animal waste, used especially as a source of fuel.

biosphere The zone of the earth that can support life.

bipedal Walking upright on two legs, one skill among others that distinguishes hominins from apes.

bishopric In the Catholic Church organization, a district (diocese) under the authority of a bishop.

Black Death An infectious disease, probably plague, that caused significant population decline in parts of Afroeurasia in the mid-fourteenth century.

bourgeoisie The social category of town-dwelling artisans, merchants, and bankers who occupied a position between rural peasants and the aristocratic class; in modern usage, the "middle class"; in Marxist thought, the property-owning class that oppresses the working class.

bronze age The era centered on the third and second millennia B.C.E. when bronze making was the most advanced metallurgical technology in the world.

bureaucracy A hierarchy of officials within a government that carries out the laws, decrees, and functions of the state.

business cycle A sequence of economic activity typically characterized by recession, fiscal recovery, growth, and fiscal decline.

C

caliph In Sunni Islam, the deputy or successor of the Prophet Muhammad as leader of the Muslim community.

canon law A code of laws and regulations governing a Christian church or denomination, especially in matters of faith, worship, moral behavior, and church administration.

capitulations International agreements in which one state awarded special privileges within its borders to subjects or citizens of another state.

caravel A type of light, highly maneuverable sailing vessel used by Iberian sailors in the Atlantic in the fifteenth and sixteenth centuries.

carrack An oceangoing ship, larger than a caravel, used extensively by Iberian mariners in the Atlantic and Indian Oceans in the fifteenth and sixteenth centuries.

caste A social class more or less rigidly separated from other classes by distinctions of heredity, occupation, wealth, or degree of ritual purity.

cathedral A church that serves as the seat, or headquarters, of a Christian bishop; typically, a large church that attracts worshipers and pilgrims from a wide surrounding region.

caudillos Autocratic political bosses or dictators, especially in the post-independence period in Latin America.

cavalry The part of a military force trained to fight mounted on horses or camels.

charter A document in which a state or other political authority granted specific rights or privileges to an individual, town, guild, or other organization to carry out particular functions.

chartered company A type of corporation in which the state granted specific rights and obligations to private investors to engage in exploration, commerce, or colonization.

chattel slavery A type of slavery in which the bonded individual has the social and sometimes legal status of a unit of property and therefore no formal rights or privileges in law.

city-state A politically sovereign urban center with adjacent agricultural land.

clan A type of social organization in which a group of people claim shared identity as descendants of a single, usually distant ancestor. Clan organization is common among pastoral nomadic societies.

clergy In Christianity, people ordained for religious vocations, as distinguished from ordinary worshipers.

codex A set of pages of parchment or other material stacked together and bound along one edge or, alternatively, a continuous strip of material folded accordion-style to form pages; a codex is to be distinguished from a scroll.

Cold War The state of antagonism, distrust, and rivalry that existed between the United States and the Soviet Union and their respective allies from the end of World War II to the late 1980s.

collaborationist A government, a group, or an individual who cooperates with foreign enemies, usually an occupying power.

collective learning The process whereby humans accumulate and share complex knowledge and transmit it from one generation to the next.

Columbian Exchange The transfer of living organisms, including plants, animals, microorganisms, and humans, between Afroeurasia and the Americas starting in 1492.

commercial diaspora Merchants who share cultural identity but who live among alien communities to operate networks of trade.

communism A dimension of socialist thought that advocates revolution to eradicate capitalism and establish the universal triumph of the proletariat.

complex society A type of society, also called a "civilization," possessing most of the following features: dense population, an agricultural economy, cities, a complex social hierarchy, complex occupational specialization, a centralized state, monumental building, a writing system, and a dominant belief system.

constitutional monarchy A type of government in which a monarch, usually a member of a family that enjoys hereditary succession, serves as head of state. Under the terms of a constitution or body of laws, however, the monarch surrenders part or all of his or her governing power to a legislature and a judiciary.

consumerism Social and cultural values and practices centered on the continuous accumulation and consumption of material goods.

corvée labor Unpaid labor required by a ruler, an estate lord, or another authority, usually for road work or other construction.

cosmopolitan Characteristic of a place where people of diverse origins come together or of an individual who travels widely.

coup d'état The sudden overthrow of an existing government by a small group. A "stroke of state" in French.

creole A person of African or European descent born in the Americas.

D

debt peon A laborer, usually on a farm or plantation, who works under obligation to repay a loan.

deindustrialization An economic process in which a state or region loses at least part of the capability it previously had to manufacture goods, especially owing to foreign competition or intervention.

demographic transition The stabilization of population level in a society resulting from the decline of both fertility rates and death rates.

deurbanization A social process in which cities in a particular region decline or disappear.

dynasty A sequence of rulers from a single family.

E

ecosystem A biological system in which living organisms—plants, animals, microorganisms, humans—interact with one another and with nonliving elements such as air, sunlight, soil, and water.

El Niño Southern Oscillation (ENSO) A warming of ocean surface temperatures that occurs about every five years in the equatorial Pacific Ocean. An El Niño episode produces unusual, sometimes extreme weather in various parts of the world. A Pacific cooling cycle is called La Niña.

embargo A legal restriction or prohibition imposed on trade.

empire A type of state in which a single political authority, often identified with a particular kinship, linguistic, or ethnic group, rules over peoples of different ethnic or linguistic identities.

encomienda A grant from the Spanish crown to its conquistadors or other Spanish settlers in the Americas, giving them the rights to the labor services and tribute payments of the indigenous people in a particular area.

energy revolution The massive increase of useful heat energy made available to humans by extracting and burning fossil fuels.

entrepôt A port or other urban center where merchants of different origins exchange goods and ship them onward.

equal-field system The Chinese system for state distribution of land; the state assigned fixed acreages of crop land to families on the basis of labor, both adult males and animals, available to work it.

eunuch A castrated male who typically served as a functionary in a royal court, especially as an attendant in the female quarters (harem).

evangelism The practice of propagating the Christian gospel by preaching, personal witnessing, and missionary work.

F

fascism A political ideology that advocates authoritarian leadership, intense national loyalty, cultural renewal, and rejection of both liberal democracy and socialism.

feudalism A hierarchical system of social and political organization in which an individual gives grants of land to other individuals in return for allegiance and service.

fief An estate of land an individual holds on condition of allegiance and service to the grantor.

filial piety The quality in children of showing respect and care for their parents and all ancestors.

fisc The treasury of a sovereign state; a state department concerned with financial matters; also fiscal.

flagellants In Christian Europe in the thirteenth and fourteenth centuries, individuals who whipped, or flagellated, themselves as an act of public penance for sin.

Fordism A system of technology and organization, named after Henry Ford, that aims both to produce goods at minimal cost through standardization and mass production and to pay wage workers rates that allow them to consume the products they make.

fossil fuels Hydrocarbon deposits, especially coal, crude oil, and natural gas, derived from the remains of once-living plant and animal organisms; these deposits are burned to produce heat energy.

free trade An economic doctrine contending that trade among states should be unrestricted, principally by lowering or eliminating tariffs or duties on imported goods; factors of supply and demand should mainly determine price.

freeholders Farmers who own the land they cultivate.

G

galleon A large, multidecked sailing vessel used for both war and commerce from the sixteenth to the eighteenth century.

genocide The premeditated, purposeful killing of large numbers of members of a particular national, racial, ethnic, or religious group.

geoglyph An image, a character, or a set of lines imprinted on a landscape, usually on a large scale, by moving rocks or soil or by cutting into the ground surface.

globalization The process by which peoples around the world have become increasingly interconnected through rapid communication and transport, resulting in both general acceleration of change and endeavors to strengthen the bonds of local community and identity.

glyph A graphic figure or character that conveys information, often a symbol carved or incised in relief.

Great Arid Zone The belt of arid and semiarid land that extends across Afroeurasia from the Sahara Desert in the west to the Gobi Desert in the east. It has been home both to pastoral nomadic communities and to farming societies where sufficient water is available.

Green Revolution Acceleration of world agricultural production, especially from the 1960s, resulting from use of high-yielding varieties of food crops, synthetic fertilizers, pesticides, and expanded irrigation systems.

H

Hellenistic Relating to the interaction between Greek language and culture and the languages and cultural forms of peoples of Southwest Asia, the Nile valley, the western Mediterranean, and the Black Sea region.

heresy In Christianity, beliefs or practices that contradict the church's official doctrine.

hominin The primate subfamily that includes all species of the genus *Homo*. Scientists commonly use "hominid" to refer to the family that includes both the *Homo* and the large ape species.

humanism European movement of the fourteenth to sixteenth centuries dedicated to rediscovering, investigating, and reinterpreting ancient Greek and Roman civilization.

I

ice age Any geological epoch, most recently the **Pleistocene** era (1.6 million to 12,000 years ago), when glaciers covered a large part of the world's surface.

imam In Islam in general, the individual who leads congregational worship and carries out other duties such as officiating at marriages.

import substitution industrialization (ISI) Government economic policies to encourage national industries to produce finished goods that would otherwise be imported.

indirect rule Theory and practice of colonial government favoring the appointment of local leaders as political intermediaries between the colonizer and the indigenous population.

industrial revolution The technological and economic processes whereby industrialization based on fossil-fuel energy, steam engines, and complex machines led to worldwide economic, social, and environmental transformations.

inflation A rise in the level of prices of goods and services over time. Rising inflation means that the purchasing power of a given unit of currency declines.

informal empire A situation in which a powerful state protects its interests in a foreign society by exerting political and economic influence but without assuming the costs of territorial control.

Inner Eurasia The interior land mass of Eurasia, whose dominant features are flat or rolling regions of grassy steppe or forest, interrupted by deserts and highland areas.

insurgency An organized, usually internal rebellion against a government or its policies, sometimes employing guerrilla or terror tactics.

interglacial A period of global warming and retreating glaciers between ice ages. Our current geological epoch, the **Holocene,** is an interglacial.

Internet A global computer network connecting smaller networks, all of which use the same set of communication formats and rules.

Isolationism The national policy or political doctrine of avoiding complex political or economic relations with foreign countries.

J

janissaries An elite infantry corps in the Ottoman Turkish state whose members were conscripted as boys from Christian families in southeastern Europe.

junta A committee or council that seizes control of a local or national government, especially following civil upheaval or revolution.

K

Keynesianism Economic theories of John Maynard Keynes that promote government monetary and financial policies aimed at increasing employment and stimulating economic growth.

khanate A state ruled by a khan; a Turkic or Mongol monarchy.

kinship The quality or state of being related by shared genealogical descent or by marriage. Kinship may also be claimed among a group of people for social or cultural reasons even though no biological relationship exists.

L

language death A process in which the number of native or fluent speakers of a particular language declines over time until no community of speakers remains.

latitude The imaginary east–west lines that circle the earth and that indicate distance in degrees north and south of the equator, which has the value of 0 degrees.

liberalism A set of economic and political doctrines advocating individual freedom, unrestricted market competition, free trade, constitutional government, and confidence in human progress; sometimes called "classical liberalism."

lingua franca A spoken or written language that facilitates commercial or diplomatic communication across cultural frontiers.

Little Ice Age A trend of climatic cooling that affected weather conditions chiefly in the Northern Hemisphere approximately from the late thirteenth to the mid-nineteenth century.

liturgy The established forms of public worship, especially the order of services, including rituals, prayers, readings, and hymns.

longitude The imaginary north–south lines that extend between the North Pole and the South Pole and that run perpendicular to lines of latitude. By international agreement the line with a value of 0 degrees, called the Prime Meridian, passes through Greenwich, England.

M

madrasa A center of higher learning dedicated mainly to the study of Islamic religious and legal subjects.

mamluk In Muslim states, a slave or freedman having primarily military or administrative duties.

manor In medieval Europe, a landed estate; also the main house or castle on the estate.

matrilineal succession The practice of tracing descent or the transmission of property or authority primarily through female relatives.

megalith A large stone sometimes roughly carved and used to build a structure often having religious significance.

megalopolis An extensive and densely urbanized region or chain of urbanized regions.

mercantilism An economic doctrine based on the idea that the world's exploitable wealth could not expand and that a state should therefore erect barriers to keep rival states out of its circuits of trade with its colonies.

meritocracy A government or other institution in which individuals are awarded office and responsibility based on their merit—intelligence, talents, or education—rather than merely on their social status or circumstances of birth.

Mesoamerica The region comprising southern Mexico plus the seven small Central American states.

metropole The colonizer's home country and seat of supreme imperial authority.

microlith A small blade of flaked stone used as a tool.

military slavery The personal bondage of an individual to a ruler or other authority with an obligation to provide military service.

milpa In Mesoamerica a farm plot created by cutting or burning forest and planted with maize, squash, beans, and other crops.

modernism The movement in the arts and humanities that embraces innovation and experimentation and rejects adherence to traditional forms and values.

monotheism The doctrine or belief that there is one supreme and universal deity.

monsoon winds The seasonally reversing winds that governed long-distance sailing in the Indian Ocean and China seas.

movable type printing A technology in which characters, especially alphabetic letters and punctuation, are individually carved or cast on pieces of wood, ceramic, or metal and then assembled into a text, inked, and printed on paper or other material.

mutually assured destruction (MAD) The doctrine aimed at preventing nuclear war between the United States and the Soviet Union by shared knowledge that, if either side attacked, both would suffer mass destruction.

mysticism The individual pursuit of knowledge or consciousness of spiritual truth or divine reality, through meditation, prayer, study, or ecstatic experience; also, mystical religion, teaching, or practice.

N

nation-state A sovereign territorial state whose inhabitants share, or are ideally expected to share, common language, cultural traditions, history, and aspirations for the future.

nationalism An ideology centered on the natural rights of a people or "nation" to constitute a sovereign state.

natural philosophy A method of scientific and moral inquiry founded on the idea that fundamental laws governing nature, including human behavior, may be discovered through the exercise of logic, reason, or careful observation.

natural rights Universal and inherent rights of human beings bestowed by nature or divine power.

neo-Europe A region outside of Europe, predominantly in temperate latitudes, where people of European descent came to make up a large majority of the population.

neoliberalism An economic and political ideology advocating reduced government intervention in economic matters, privatization of state-owned enterprises, free trade, open markets, and deregulation of business.

neolithic era The "new stone age" extending from about 10,000 to 4000 B.C.E. and characterized by refined stone toolmaking and the development of agriculture.

new imperialism The campaigns of colonial empire building that several European powers plus Japan and the United States undertook in the late nineteenth and early twentieth centuries against other societies, especially in Africa and Southeast Asia.

O

Oceania (also, the Island Pacific) The enormous region centered on the tropical Pacific Ocean and its islands. This definition of the region excludes Australia, though not New Zealand.

old regime The political and social system in France and other European monarchies between the sixteenth and eighteenth centuries; characterized by a rigid class hierarchy and rulers' claims to absolute authority.

oligarchy A political system in which a relatively small number of individuals or families control the government.

outsourcing The business practice of reducing costs by transferring work to outside contractors, including foreign companies.

P

paleoanthropologist A scientist concerned with the study of human evolution and the physical and behavioral characteristics of early humans and their biological ancestors.

paleolithic Meaning "old stone age," this period dates from approximately 2.5 million years ago, when hominin species first devised stone tools, to about 12,000 years ago, when humans started experimenting with agriculture.

pandemic An infectious disease that moves quickly from one region to another, affecting large numbers of people.

partition The division of a political entity into two or more separate, autonomous territories.

pastoral nomadism A type of economic and social organization in which livestock raising is the principal means of subsistence. Pastoral nomadic communities typically migrate seasonally in search of pasture and water.

pastoralism A type of economic and social organization involving the breeding and raising of domesticated hoofed animals, or livestock.

patriarch In the early Christian centuries, the title of the bishops of Rome, Constantinople, Jerusalem, Antioch, and Alexandria; in later centuries, the title of the highest official of the Greek Orthodox Church, as well as other Asian or African Christian churches.

patriarchy A society in which males dominate social, political, and cultural life.

patriotism An emotional or sentimental attachment to a place, an ethnic people, or a way of life; in modern times, the attachment is often to one's national homeland.

patron–client system A vertical social and political system in which individuals possessing relative degrees of power, wealth, or social status offer protection or economic benefits to other individuals in return for personal loyalty and services.

peasants The social and economic class of farmers or herders who hold relatively small amounts of productive land as owners, rent-paying tenants, or serfs bound to a particular estate.

phalanx A military formation in which soldiers march and fight in closely packed, disciplined ranks.

pogrom A violent attack on a minority community characterized by massacre and destruction of property; most commonly refers to assaults on Jews.

polis (plural, poleis) The ancient Greek term for a sovereign state centered on a single city; a city-state.

polytheism A belief system that incorporates multiple deities or spirits.

pope The title used from about the ninth century to designate the head of the Christian church in western and central Europe.

popular sovereignty The doctrine that the sovereignty or independence of the state is vested in the people, and that the government is responsible to the will of the citizenry.

price revolution A period of sustained inflation in Europe in the sixteenth and seventeenth centuries.

primogeniture The legal or customary right of the firstborn child, usually the firstborn male, to inherit a family's entire estate, sometimes including a noble title or office, to the exclusion of younger children.

principality A sovereign state or dependent territory, usually relatively small, ruled by a person with a noble title of high rank, for example, prince, princess, duke, or duchess.

proletariat The working class; in Marxist theory, the class that must overthrow the capitalist bourgeoisie to achieve control of the means of production.

proselytize To convert or attempt to convert an individual or group to one's religion.

protectorate A type of colonial relationship in which a foreign power takes control of the top levels of government in the colonized territory but permits it to retain formal, if largely fictional sovereignty.

pueblo A Spanish word meaning "village" or "small town." Spanish colonizers used this term to describe multistory stone or brick compounds that the Ancestral Puebloans (Anasazi) built in the American Southwest.

putting-out system A production method in which employers distributed raw materials to individuals or families, who then made finished goods, typically woolen or cotton yarn or cloth, and returned these goods to the employer for payment.

R

real wages Wages estimated in the amount of goods those wages will buy rather than in the face value of money paid.

regent An individual who administers the affairs of a state when the ruler is absent, is disabled, or has not reached adulthood.

reparations The act of making amends or giving satisfaction for an injustice or injury; payment of compensation by a defeated state for presumed damages inflicted on another state as a result of war between them.

republic A type of government in which supreme power rests with a body of citizens possessing rights to vote to approve laws and to select public officials and representatives.

Romanization The spread within the Roman empire, especially among elite classes, of a style of social and cultural life founded on practice in Roman Italy.

S

satrapy An administrative unit of the Persian empire under the authority of a satrap, or provincial governor.

scholastic theology In medieval Europe, systematic investigation of the relations between the authority of spiritual revelation and the claims of human reason; a method of disputation drawing on philosophy, particularly the works of the ancient Greek thinker Aristotle; also, scholasticism.

secular ruler In the Christian tradition, a monarch or other ruler who is not an ordained priest and does not formally represent the authority of the church; a temporal, as opposed to spiritual, leader.

self-determination The idea put forth during and after World War I that a society sharing common language, history, and cultural traditions should have the right to decide its own political future and govern its own affairs.

serfdom A system of labor in which farmers were legally bound to work for and pay fees to a particular landlord in return for protection.

service nobility A privileged governing class whose members depended entirely on the state rather than on inherited property and titles for their status and income.

shaman A man or woman who the community believes has access to supernatural forces or beings and who can appeal to the spirit world to discern the future, bring good fortune, or perform physical healing.

shari'a The body of Islamic laws and moral precepts principally the Quran and the sayings and actions of the Prophet Muhammad.

shifting agriculture A method of crop production in which a farmer clears and cultivates a plot of land until the soil loses its nutrient value, and then moves on to clear and plant a new field, allowing the first one to lie fallow and recover.

Sinification The spread within East Asia, especially among elite classes, of a style of social and cultural life founded on practice in China.

slavery The social institution in which an individual is held by law, custom, or simply coercion in servitude to another individual, a group, or the state.

social bondage A condition in which an individual or a group holds rights to a person's labor or services, whether for a limited period or for a lifetime. Social bondage may take a variety of forms, including slavery, serfdom, or indentured servitude.

socialism A variety of ideologies that advocate social equality and justice and the community's collective control and management of economic institutions; in Marxist thought, socialism follows capitalism in society's transition to communism.

southern seas The China seas and the Indian Ocean, including the Arabian Sea and the Bay of Bengal.

soviet Revolutionary workers' councils that served during the Russian Revolution as local units of government and civil order. The term was applied later to legislative bodies within the communist regime.

split inheritance The practice of dividing the estate of a person among different heirs.

syncretism In religion, the blending of beliefs or practices from two or more different belief systems; also the incorporation of beliefs or practices of one belief system by another.

T

tax farming A system in which a government awards the right of tax collection to a private individual or group in return for a fee or a percentage of the taxes gathered.

tectonic plates Irregular blocks of solid rock that make up the earth's lithosphere and that constantly shift and change shape.

terra preta A type of nutritionally rich soil that farmers of Amazonia produced by mixing charcoal, organic matter, and pottery shards. Literally, "black earth" in Portuguese.

three estates The principal social classes or orders constituting societies in premodern Europe: the Roman Catholic clergy, the titled nobility, and everyone else.

tribute Wealth in money or material goods paid by one group to another, often a conquered group to its conquerors, as an obligation of submission or allegiance.

total war Warfare, especially characteristic of World Wars I and II, in which the opposing states mobilize their civilian populations and all available resources to achieve victory; also a wartime policy intended to damage or destroy both the enemy's military forces and its economic infrastructure and social fabric.

totalitarianism A political ideology and governing policies that mandate strong central control and regulation of both public and private thought and behavior.

transnational organization An association of individual citizens or private groups that collaborates across national frontiers to carry out particular activities or programs.

treaty ports Sea or river ports in China where, as a consequence of diplomatic and military pressure, foreigners gained special privileges to engage in trade and enjoy exemptions from Chinese laws and courts.

tribe The largest social group in a region whose members claim shared descent.

U

ulama Muslim religious scholars, judges, teachers, and mosque officials.

universal empire A multiethnic state whose ruler claims a right to authority over all of humankind.

universalist religion A religion whose doctrines and practices aim to appeal to all people irrespective of their language, ethnicity, social class, or political affiliation.

V

vassal An individual who is subordinate to or dependent on another individual; in feudalism, an individual who holds land given by a lord in return for loyal service.

vernacular language The native language commonly spoken by ordinary people in a region.

viceroy An official appointed by a monarch to govern a colonial dependency as the sovereign's representative. *Vice* is a Latin prefix meaning "in place of" and *roy* means king. The territory administered by a viceroy is called a viceroyalty.

W

welfare state An approach to government in which the state uses public funds to protect and promote the health and social well-being of all citizens.

Recommended Reading

General Works on World History

Jerry H. Bentley. *Old World Encounters: Cross-Cultural Contacts and Exchanges in Pre-Modern Times.* New York: Oxford University Press, 1993.

Jerry H. Bentley, ed. *The Oxford Handbook of World History.* New York: Oxford University Press, 2011.

Jerry H. Bentley, Renate Bridenthal, and Anand A. Yang, eds. *Interactions: Transregional Perspectives on World History.* Honolulu: University of Hawai'i Press, 2005.

J. M. Blaut. *The Colonizer's Model of the World: Geographical Diffusionism and Eurocentric History.* New York: Guilford Press, 1993.

Cynthia Stokes Brown. *Big History: From the Big Bang to the Present.* New York: New Press, 2007.

Edmund Burke III, David Christian, and Ross E. Dunn. *World History: The Big Eras, A Compact History of Humankind for Teachers and Students.* Los Angeles: National Center for History in the Schools, 2012.

Tertius Chandler. *Four Thousand Years of Urban Growth: An Historical Census.* Lewiston/Queenston, ON: St. David's University Press, 1987.

David Christian. *Maps of Time: An Introduction to Big History.* Berkeley: University of California Press, 2004.

David Christian. *This Fleeting World: A Short History of Humanity.* Great Barrington, VT: Berkshire Publishing, 2007.

Pamela Kyle Crossley. *What Is Global History?* Malden, MA: Polity, 2008.

Ross E. Dunn, ed. *The New World History: A Teacher's Companion.* Boston: Bedford St. Martin's, 2000.

Marnie Hughes-Warrington, ed. *World Histories.* New York: Palgrave Macmillan, 2005.

Neil MacGregor. *A History of the World in 100 Objects.* New York: Viking, 2011.

Angus Maddison. *The World Economy: A Millennial Perspective.* Paris: Organization for Economic Co-operation and Development, 2001.

Patrick Manning. *Navigating World History: Historians Create a Global Past.* New York: Palgrave Macmillan, 2003.

John R. McNeill and William H. McNeill. *The Human Web: A Bird's-Eye View of World History.* New York: Norton, 2003.

William H. McNeill. *The Rise of the West: A History of the Human Community; with a Retrospective Essay.* Chicago: University of Chicago Press, 1992.

Douglas Northrup, ed. *A Companion to World History.* Hoboken, NJ: Wiley-Blackwell, 2012.

Introduction. The Earth: World History's Theater

Jared Diamond. *Guns, Germs, and Steel: The Fates of Human Societies.* New York: Norton, 1993.

Ross E. Dunn. "Afro-Eurasia," in William H. McNeill, ed. *Berkshire Encyclopedia of World History,* 5 vols. Great Barrington, MA: Berkshire Publishing, 2005. 1:44–50.

Marshall G. S. Hodgson. *Rethinking World History: Essays on Europe, Islam, and World History,* ed. Edmund Burke III. Cambridge: Cambridge University Press, 1993.

Martin W. Lewis and Kären E. Wigen. *The Myth of Continents: A Critique of Metageography.* Berkeley: University of California Press, 1997.

Mark Monmonier. *How to Lie with Maps,* 2nd ed. Chicago: Chicago University Press, 1996.

William J. Moseley, David A. Lanegran, and Kavita Pandit, eds. *The Introductory Reader in Human Geography: Contemporary Debates and Classic Writings.* Hoboken, NJ: Wiley-Blackwell, 2007.

John P. Snyder. *Flattening the Earth: Two Thousand Years of Map Projections.* Chicago: Chicago University Press, 1997.

Chapter 1. The Peopling of the World

Elizabeth Wayland Barber. *Women's Work: The First 20,000 Years: Women, Cloth, and Society in Early Times.* New York: Norton, 1994.

L. L. Cavalli-Sforza. *Genes, Peoples, and Languages,* trans. Mark Seielstad. New York: North Point Press, 2000.

Richard Dawkins. *The Greatest Show on Earth: The Evidence for Evolution.* New York: Free Press, 2009.

Margaret Ehrenberg. *Women in Prehistory.* Norman: University of Oklahoma Press, 1989.

Brian Fagan. *Cro-Magnon: How the Ice Age Gave Birth to the First Modern Humans.* London: Bloomsbury Press, 2010.

Clive Gamble. *Timewalkers: The Prehistory of Global Colonization.* Cambridge, MA: Harvard University Press, 1994.

Renée Heatherington. *Living in a Dangerous Climate: Climate Change and Human Evolution.* New York: Cambridge University Press, 2012.

Richard G. Klein. *The Dawn of Human Culture.* New York: Wiley, 2002.

David J. Meltzer. *First Peoples in a New World: Colonizing Ice Age America.* Berkeley: University of California Press, 2010.

Steve Olson. *Mapping Human History: Genes, Race, and Our Common Origins.* Boston: Mariner Books, 2003.

Lauren Ristvet. *In the Beginning: World History from Human Evolution to the First States.* Boston: McGraw-Hill, 2007.

Chris Stringer. *Lone Survivors: How We Came to Be the Only Humans on Earth.* New York: Times Book, 2012.

Chris Stringer and Peter Andrews. *The Complete World of Human Evolution,* 2nd ed. London: Thames & Hudson, 2012.

Ian Tattersall. *Masters of the Planet: The Search for Our Human Origins.* New York: Palgrave Macmillan, 2012.

Bernard A. Wood. *Human Evolution: A Very Short Introduction.* Oxford: Oxford University Press, 2005.

Thomas Wynn and Frederick L. Coolidge. *How to Think Like a Neanderthal.* New York: Oxford University Press, 2011.

Chapter 2. Farms, Cities, and the New Agrarian Age

Guillermo Algaze. *The Uruk World System: The Dynamics of Expansion of Early Mesopotamian Civilization,* 2nd ed. Chicago: University of Chicago Press, 2005.

Peter Bellwood. *First Farmers: The Origins of Agricultural Societies.* Malden, MA: Blackwell, 2005.

Richard W. Bulliet. *Hunters, Herders, and Hamburgers: The Past and Future of Human-Animal Relationships.* New York: Columbia University Press, 2005.

Harriet Crawford. *Sumer and the Sumerians,* 2nd ed. Cambridge: Cambridge University Press, 2004.

Christopher Ehret. *The Civilizations of Africa: A History to 1800.* Charlottesville: University of Virginia Press, 2002.

Barry J. Kemp. *Ancient Egypt: Anatomy of a Civilization,* 2nd ed. New York: Routledge, 2006.

Jonathan Mark Kenoyer. *Ancient Cities of the Indus Valley Civilization.* Oxford: Oxford University Press, 1998.

Jane R. McIntosh. *A Peaceful Realm: The Rise and Fall of the Indus Civilization.* Boulder, CO: Westview Press, 2002.

Steven Mithen. *After the Ice: A Global Human History, 20,000–5000 BC.* Cambridge, MA: Harvard University Press, 2003.

Gregory L. Possehl. *The Indus Civilization: A Contemporary Perspective.* Lanham, MD: AltaMira Press, 2003.

J. N. Postgate. *Early Mesopotamia: Society and Economy at the Dawn of History.* New York: Routledge, 1994.

William F. Ruddiman. *Plows, Plagues, and Petroleum: How Humans Took Control of Climate.* Princeton, NJ: Princeton University Press, 2005.

Ian Shaw. *Exploring Ancient Egypt.* New York: Oxford University Press, 2003.

Ian Tattersall. *The World from Beginnings to 4000 BCE.* Oxford: Oxford University Press, 2008.

Marc Van De Mieroop. *A History of the Ancient Near East ca. 3000–323 BC,* 2nd ed. Malden, MA: Wiley-Blackwell, 2006.

Nicholas Wade. *Before the Dawn: Recovering the Lost History of Our Ancestors.* New York: Penguin Press, 2006.

Chapter 3. Afroeurasia's Moving Frontiers: Farmers, Herders, and Charioteers

David W. Anthony. *The Horse, the Wheel and Language: How Bronze-Age Riders from the Eurasian Steppes Shaped the Modern World.* Princeton, NJ: Princeton University Press, 2007.

Edwin Bryant. *The Quest for the Origins of Vedic Culture: The Indo-Aryan Migration Debate.* Oxford: Oxford University Press, 2001.

Billie Jean Collins. *The Hittites and Their World.* Atlanta, GA: Society of Biblical Literature, 2007.

Barry Cunliffe. *The Ancient Celts.* New York: Oxford University Press, 1997.

Robert Drews. *The Coming of the Greeks: Indo-European Conquests in the Aegean and the Near East.* Princeton, NJ: Princeton University Press, 1988.

Robert Drews. *Early Riders: The Beginnings of Mounted Warfare in Asia and Europe.* New York: Routledge, 2008.

Kairn A. Klieman. *The Pygmies Were Our Compass: Bantu and Batwa in the History of West-Central Africa, Early Times to 1900.* Portsmouth, NH: Heinemann, 2003.

Philip L. Kohl. *The Making of Bronze Age Eurasia.* Cambridge: Cambridge University Press, 2009.

J. P. Mallory. *In Search of the Indo-Europeans: Language, Archaeology and Myth.* London: Thames & Hudson, 1989.

J. P. Mallory and Victor H. Mair. *The Tarim Mummies: Ancient China and the Mystery of the Earliest Peoples from the West.* London: Thames & Hudson, 2008.

James L. Newman. *The Peopling of Africa: A Geographic Interpretation.* New Haven, CT: Yale University Press, 1995.

Amanda H. Podany. *Brotherhood of Kings: How International Relations Shaped the Ancient Near East.* Oxford: Oxford University Press, 2010.

Alicia Sanchez-Mazas et al., eds. *Past Human Migrations in East Asia: Matching Archaeology, Linguistics and Genetics.* New York: Routledge, 2008.

Cynthia W. Shelmerdine, ed. *The Cambridge Companion to the Aegean Bronze Age.* New York: Cambridge University Press, 2008.

Robert L. Thorp. *China in the Early Bronze Age.* Philadelphia: University of Pennsylvania Press, 2006.

Marc Van De Mieroop. *King Hammurabi of Babylon: A Biography.* Hoboken, NJ: Wiley-Blackwell, 2004.

Chapter 4. Early Odysseys in the Americas, Australia, and Oceania

Richard E. W. Adams. *Prehistoric Mesoamerica,* 3rd ed. Norman: University of Oklahoma Press, 2005.

Peter S. Bellwood. *The Polynesians: Prehistory of an Island People,* rev. ed. London: Thames & Hudson, 1987.

I. C. Campbell. *Worlds Apart: A History of the Pacific Islands.* Christchurch, New Zealand: Canterbury University Press, 2011.

Donald Denoon, ed. *The Cambridge History of the Pacific Islanders.* Cambridge: Cambridge University Press, 1997.

Richard A. Diehl. *The Olmecs: America's First Civilization.* London: Thames & Hudson, 2004.

Tim Flannery. *The Eternal Frontier: An Ecological History of North America and Its Peoples.* New York: Grove Press, 2001.

Tim Flannery. *The Future Eaters. An Ecological History of the Australasian Lands and People.* New York: G. Braziller, 1995.

Valerie Hansen. *The Open Empire: A History of China to 1600.* New York: Norton, 2000.

Alice Beck Kehoe. *America Before the European Invasion.* New York: Longman, 2002.

Patrick V. Kirch. *On the Road of the Winds: An Archaeological History of the Pacific Islands before European Contact.* Berkeley: University of California Press, 2000.

Danièle Lavallée. *The First South Americans. The Peopling of a Continent from the Earliest Evidence to High Culture,* trans. Paul G. Bahn. Salt Lake City: University of Utah Press, 1995.

Harry Lourandos. *Continent of Hunter-Gatherers: New Perspectives in Australian Prehistory.* Cambridge: Cambridge University Press, 1997.

Charles C. Mann. *1491: New Revelations of the Americas before Columbus.* New York: Alfred A. Knopf, 2005.

Michael E. Moseley. *The Incas and Their Ancestors: The Archaeology of Peru,* rev. ed. London: Thames & Hudson, 2001.

Christopher A. Pool. *Olmec Archaeology and Early Mesoamerica.* Cambridge: Cambridge University Press, 2007.

Paul S. Ropp. *China in World History.* New York: Oxford University Press, 2010.

Helaine Silverman and William H. Isbell, eds. *Handbook of South American Archaeology.* New York: Springer, 2008.

Chapter 5. Afroeurasia: Centers of Power, Trade, and New Ideas

David Abulafia, ed. *The Mediterranean in History.* Los Angeles: J. Paul Getty Museum, 2003.

María Eugenia Aubet. *The Phoenicians and the West: Politics, Colonies, and Trade,* trans. Mary Turton. New York: Cambridge University Press, 1993.

Barry Cunliffe. *Europe between the Oceans, 9000 BC–AD 1000.* New Haven, CT: Yale University Press, 2008.

Oliver Dickinson. *The Aegean from Bronze Age to Iron Age: Continuity and Change between the Twelfth and Eighth Centuries.* New York: Routledge, 2007.

Robert Drews. *The End of the Bronze Age: Changes in Warfare and the Catastrophe ca. 1200 B.C.* Princeton, NJ: Princeton University Press, 1993.

David N. Edwards. *The Nubian Past: An Archaeology of the Sudan.* New York: Routledge, 2004.

Christopher Ehret. *An African Classical Age: Eastern and Southern Africa in World History, 1000 B.C. to A.D. 400.* Charlottesville: University Press of Virginia, 1998.

A. F. Harding. *European Societies in the Bronze Age.* New York: Cambridge University Press, 2000.

Sybille Haynes. *Etruscan Civilization. A Cultural History.* Los Angeles: J. Paul Getty Museum, 2000.

Cho-yun Hsü and Katheryn M. Linduff. *Western Chou Civilization.* New Haven, CT: Yale University Press, 1988.

Michael Loewe and Edward L. Shaughnessy, eds. *The Cambridge History of Ancient China: From the Origins of Civilization to 221 B.C.* New York: Cambridge University Press, 1999.

Howard N. Lupovitch. *Jews and Judaism in World History.* New York: Routledge, 2010.

Ian Shaw, ed. *The Oxford History of Ancient Egypt.* New York: Oxford University Press, 2004.

Burton Stein. *A History of India.* Malden, MA: Blackwell, 1998.

Romila Thapar. *Early India: From the Origins to AD 1300.* Berkeley: University of California Press, 2003.

Chapter 6. Empire Building and Cultural Exchange from India to the Mediterranean

Karen Armstrong. *Buddha.* New York: Viking, 2001.

Pierre Briant. *Alexander the Great and His Empire: A Short Introduction,* trans. Amélie Kuhrt. Princeton, NJ: Princeton University Press, 2010.

Maria Brosius. *The Persians: An Introduction.* New York: Routledge, 2006.

Glenn R. Bugh, ed. *The Cambridge Companion to the Hellenistic World.* New York: Cambridge University Press, 2006.

Barry W. Cunliffe. *The Extraordinary Voyage of Pytheas the Greek.* New York: Penguin, 2003.

R. Malcolm Errington. *A History of the Hellenistic World.* Malden, MA: Blackwell, 2008.

Richard C. Foltz. *Spirituality in the Land of the Noble: How Iran Shaped the World's Religions.* Oxford: Oneworld, 2004.

Richard N. Frye. *The Heritage of Central Asia: From Antiquity to the Turkish Empire.* Princeton, NJ: Markus Wiener, 1996.

Peter Green. *The Hellenistic Age: A History.* New York: Modern Library, 2007.

Herodotus. *The Histories,* trans. Robin Waterfield, with an introduction and notes by Carolyn Dewald. New York: Oxford University Press, 1998.

Sarah Pomeroy, Stanley M. Burstein, Walter Donlan, and Jennifer Tolbert Roberts. *Brief History of Ancient Greece: Politics, Society, and Culture.* New York: Oxford University Press, 2004.

Joyce E. Salisbury. *Encyclopedia of Women in the Ancient World.* Santa Barbara, CA: ABC-Clio, 2001.

Jean W. Sedlar. *India and the Greek World: A Study in the Transmission of Culture.* Totowa, NJ: Rowman & Littlefield, 1980.

Susan M. Sherwin-White and Amélie Kuhrt. *From Samarkhand to Sardis: A New Approach to the Seleucid Empire.* Berkeley: University of California Press, 1993.

Stanley A. Wolpert. *A New History of India,* 8th ed. New York: Oxford University Press, 2008.

Chapter 7. An Age of Giant Empires

Mary T. Boatwright, Daniel J. Gargola, and Richard J. A. Talbert. *The Romans: From Village to Empire.* New York: Oxford University Press, 2004.

Stanley Burstein, ed. *Ancient African Civilizations: Kush and Axum.* Princeton, NJ: Markus Wiener, 1998.

Nicola Di Cosmo. *Ancient China and Its Enemies: The Rise of Nomadic Power in East Asian History.* New York: Cambridge University Press, 2002.

Patricia Buckley Ebrey. *The Cambridge Illustrated History of China.* New York: Cambridge University Press, 1996.

Richard C. Foltz. *Religions of the Silk Roads: Overland Trade and Cultural Exchange from Antiquity to the Fifteenth Century.* New York: St. Martin's Griffin, 1999.

Peter Garnsey and Richard Saller. *The Roman Empire: Economy, Society and Culture.* London: Duckworth, 1987.

Thomas Harrison, ed. *The Great Empires of the Ancient World.* Los Angeles: J. Paul Getty Museum, 2009.

Donald Johnson and Jean Elliot Johnson. *Universal Religions in World History: The Spread of Buddhism, Christianity, and Islam to 1500.* New York: McGraw-Hill, 2007.

Mark Edward Lewis. *The Early Chinese Empires: Qin and Han.* Cambridge, MA: Harvard University Press, 2007.

Xinru Liu and Lynda Norene Shaffer. *Connections across Eurasia: Transportation, Communication, and Cultural Exchange on the Silk Roads.* New York: McGraw-Hill, 2007.

Victor H. Mair, ed. *Contact and Exchange in the Ancient World.* Honolulu: University of Hawai'i Press, 2006.

Stuart C. Munro-Hay. *Aksum: An African Civilization of Late Antiquity.* Edinburgh: Edinburgh University Press, 1991.

Walter Scheidel, ed. *Rome and China: Comparative Perspectives on Ancient World Empires.* New York: Oxford University Press, 2009.

Tansen Sen and Victor H. Mair. *Traditional China in Asian and World History.* Ann Arbor, MI: Association for Asian Studies, 2012.

Manoj K. Thakur. *India in the Age of Kanishka.* Delhi: Oriental Book Centre, 1998.

Roberta Tomber. *Indo-Roman Trade: From Pots to Pepper.* London: Duckworth, 2008.

Derek A. Welsby. *The Kingdom of Kush: The Napatan and Meroitic Empires.* Princeton, NJ: Markus Wiener, 1998.

Greg Woolf, ed. *Cambridge Illustrated History of the Roman World.* New York: Cambridge University Press, 2003.

Chapter 8. American Complexities

Richard E. W. Adams. *Prehistoric Mesoamerica,* 3rd ed. Norman: University of Oklahoma Press, 2005.

Garth Bawden. *The Moche.* Malden, MA: Blackwell, 1996.

William J. Conklin and Jeffrey Quilter, eds. *Chavín: Art, Architecture, and Culture.* Los Angeles: Cotsen Institute of Archaeology, 2008.

Arthur Demarest. *Ancient Maya: The Rise and Fall of a Rainforest Civilization.* Cambridge: Cambridge University Press, 2004.

Alice Beck Kehoe. *America before the European Invasion.* New York: Longman, 2002.

George R. Milner. *The Moundbuilders: Ancient Peoples of Eastern North America.* London: Thames & Hudson, 2004.

Prudence Rice. *Maya Political Science: Time, Astronomy, and the Cosmos.* Austin: University of Texas Press, 2004.

Frank Salomon and Stuart B. Schwartz, eds. *The Cambridge History of the Native Peoples of the Americas.* Vol. 3: *South America.* New York: Cambridge University Press, 1999.

Linda Schele and David Freidel. *A Forest of Kings: The Untold Story of the Ancient Maya.* New York: William Morrow, 1990.

Lynda Norene Shaffer. *Native Americans before 1492: The Moundbuilding Centers of the Eastern Woodlands.* Armonk, NY: M. E. Sharpe, 1992.

Robert J. Sharer. *Daily Life in Maya Civilization,* 2nd ed. Westport, CT: Greenwood Press, 2009.

Robert J. Sharer with Loa P. Traxler. *The Ancient Maya,* 6th ed. Stanford, CA: Stanford University Press, 2008.

Helaine Silverman and William H. Isbell, eds. *Handbook of South American Archaeology.* New York: Springer, 2008.

Bruce G. Trigger and Wilcomb E. Washburn, eds. *The Cambridge History of the Native Peoples of the Americas.* Vol. 1: *North America, Part I.* New York: Cambridge University Press, 1996.

Chapter 9. Turbulent Centuries

Thomas J. Barfield. *The Perilous Frontier: Nomadic Empires and China.* Malden, MA: Blackwell, 1989.

Peter Brown. *The Rise of Western Christendom: Triumph and Diversity, A.D. 200–1000,* 2nd ed. Malden, MA: Blackwell, 2003.

Averil Cameron. *The Byzantines.* Malden, MA: Blackwell, 2006.

Gert Chesi and Gerhard Merzeder, eds. *The Nok Culture: Art in Nigeria 2,500 Years Ago.* New York: Prestel, 2006.

Peter Christensen. *The Decline of Iranshahr: Irrigation and Environments in the History of the Middle East 500 B.C.E. to A.D. 1500.* Copenhagen: Museum Tusculanum Press, 1993.

David Christian. *A History of Russia, Central Asia and Mongolia.* Vol. 1: *Inner Eurasia from Prehistory to the Mongol Empire.* Malden, MA: Blackwell, 1998.

Graham Connah. *Forgotten Africa: An Introduction to Its Archaeology.* New York: Routledge, 2004.

Joe Cribb and Georgina Hermann, eds. *After Alexander: Central Asia before Islam.* New York: Oxford University Press, 2007.

Touraj Daryaee. *Sasanian Iran (224–651 CE): Portrait of a Late Antique Empire.* Costa Mesa, CA: Mazda Publishers, 2008.

Peter Heather. *The Fall of the Roman Empire: A New History of Rome and the Barbarians.* Oxford: Oxford University Press, 2006.

John Philip Jenkins. *The Lost History of Christianity: The Thousand-Year Golden Age of the Church in the Middle East, Africa, and Asia—and How It Died.* New York: HarperOne, 2008.

Roderick J. McIntosh. *Ancient Middle Niger: Urbanism and the Self-Organizing Landscape.* Cambridge: Cambridge University Press, 2005.

John Moorehead. *The Roman Empire Divided, 400–700.* London: Longman, 2001.

Scott Pearce, Audrey Spiro, and Patricia Ebrey, eds. *Culture and Power in the Reconstitution of the Chinese Realm, 200–600.* Cambridge, MA: Harvard University Press, 2001.

William Rosen. *Justinian's Flea: Plague, Empire, and the Birth of Europe.* New York: Viking, 2007.

Bryan Ward-Perkins. *The Fall of Rome and the End of Civilization.* Oxford: Oxford University Press, 2005.

Chapter 10. Afroeurasia in the Era of Arab Empire

Karen Armstrong. *Islam: A Short History.* New York: Modern Library, 2000.

Christopher I. Beckwith. *The Tibetan Empire in Central Asia.* Princeton, NJ: Princeton University Press, 1993.

Jonathan P. Berkey. *The Formation of Islam: Religion and Society in the Near East, 600–1800.* Cambridge: Cambridge University Press, 2003.

Fred M. Donner. *The Early Islamic Conquests.* Princeton, NJ: Princeton University Press, 1981.

Fred M. Donner. *Narrative of Islamic Origins: The Beginnings of Islamic Historical Writing.* Princeton, NJ: Darwin Press, 1998.

John Esposito. *Islam: The Straight Path,* 4th ed. New York: Oxford University Press, 2010.

Jacques Gernet. *Buddhism in Chinese Society: An Economic History from the Fifth to the Tenth Centuries,* trans. Franciscus Verellen. New York: Columbia University Press, 1995.

Peter B. Golden. *Central Asia in World History.* Oxford: Oxford University Press, 2011.

Albert Hourani. *A History of the Arab Peoples.* Cambridge: Belknap Press of Harvard University Press, 1991.

Mark Edward Lewis. *China's Cosmopolitan Empire: The Tang Dynasty.* Cambridge, MA: Belknap Press of Harvard University Press, 2009.

Michael McCormick. *Origins of the European Economy: Communications and Commerce, A.D. 300–900.* Cambridge: Cambridge University Press, 2001.

Thomas Sizgorich. *Violence and Belief in Late Antiquity: Militant Devotion in Christianity and Islam.* Philadelphia: University of Pennsylvania Press, 2008.

Chris Wickham. *Framing the Early Middle Ages: Europe and the Mediterranean, 400–800.* Oxford: Oxford University Press, 2005.

Irving M. Zeitlin. *The Historical Muhammad.* Malden, MA: Polity Press, 2007.

Chapter 11. State Power and Expanding Networks of Exchange

Jonathan M. Bloom. *Paper before Print: The History and Impact of Paper in the Islamic World.* New Haven, CT: Yale University Press, 2001.

Philip D. Curtin. *Cross-Cultural Trade in World History.* New York: Cambridge University Press, 1984.

Thomas F. Glick. *Islamic and Christian Spain in the Early Middle Ages.* Boston: Brill, 2005.

Kenneth R. Hall. *Maritime Trade and State Development in Early Southeast Asia.* Honolulu: University of Hawai'i Press, 1985.

Ahmed Y. al-Hassan and Donald R. Hill. *Islamic Technology: An Illustrated History.* Cambridge: Cambridge University Press, 1986.

Mark Horton and John Middleton. *The Swahili: The Social Landscape of a Mercantile Society.* Malden, MA: Blackwell, 2000.

Hugh Kennedy. *When Baghdad Ruled the Muslim World: The Rise and Fall of Islam's Greatest Dynasty.* Cambridge, MA: Da Capo Press, 2005.

Donald F. Logan, *The Vikings in History.* London: Routledge, 2005.

Seyyed Hossein Nasr. *Islamic Science: An Illustrated Study.* London: World Festival of Islam Publishing, 1976.

Joan R. Piggott. *The Emergence of Japanese Kingship.* Stanford, CA: Stanford University Press, 1997.

Alexandre Popovic. *The Revolt of African Slaves in Iraq in the 3rd/9th Century,* trans. Léon King, with a new introduction by Henry Louis Gates, Jr. Princeton, NJ: Markus Wiener, 1999.

David Robinson. *Muslim Societies in African History.* Cambridge: Cambridge University Press, 2004.

Edward H. Schafer. *The Golden Peaches of Samarkand: A Study of Tang Exotics.* Berkeley: University of California Press, 1963.

Lynda Norene Shaffer. *Maritime Southeast Asia to 1500.* Armonk, NY: M. E. Sharpe, 1996.

J. M. Wallace-Hadrill. *The Barbarian West, 400–1000,* rev. ed. Malden, MA: Blackwell, 1997.

Andrew Watson. *Agricultural Innovation in the Early Islamic World: The Diffusion of Crops and Farming Techniques, 700–1100.* Cambridge: Cambridge University Press, 1983.

Chapter 12. Dynamic Centuries across Afroeurasia

Thomas S. Asbridge. *The Crusades: The Authoritative History of the War for the Holy Land.* New York: Ecco Press, 2010.

Robert Bartlett. *The Making of Europe: Conquest, Colonization and Cultural Change, 950–1350.* Princeton, NJ: Princeton University Press, 1993.

Aziz Basan. *The Great Suljuqs: A History.* New York: Routledge, 2010.

Beverly J. Bossler. *Powerful Relations: Kinship, Status, and the State in Sung China (960–1279).* Cambridge, MA: Council on East Asian Studies, Harvard University, 1998.

Anne-Marie Eddé. *Saladin,* trans. Jane Marie Todd. Cambridge, MA: Belknap Press, 2011.

Carter Vaughn Findley. *The Turks in World History.* Oxford: Oxford University Press, 2005.

Robert Finlay. *The Pilgrim Art: The Culture of Porcelain in World History.* Berkeley: University of California Press, 2010.

Jacques Gernet. *Daily Life in China on the Eve of the Mongol Invasion, 1250–76,* trans. H. M. Wright. Stanford, CA: Stanford University Press, 1962.

Thomas F. Glick, Steven J. Livesey, and Faith Wallis, eds. *Medieval Science, Technology and Medicine: An Encyclopedia.* New York: Routledge, 2005.

C. Warren Hollister and Judith M. Bennett. *Medieval Europe: A Short History,* 10th ed. Boston: McGraw-Hill, 2005.

Dieter Kuhn. *The Age of Confucian Rule: The Song Transformation of China.* Cambridge, MA: Belknap Press of Harvard University Press, 2009.

Angeliki E. Laiou and Roy Parviz Mottahedeh, eds. *The Crusades from the Perspective of Byzantium and the Muslim World.* Washington, DC: Dumbarton Oaks Research Library and Collection, 2001.

J. R. S. Phillips. *The Medieval Expansion of Europe,* 2nd ed. Oxford: Oxford University Press, 1998.

Pierre Souyri. *The World Turned Upside Down: Medieval Japanese Society.* New York: Columbia University Press, 2001.

Richard von Glahn. *Fountain of Fortune: Money and Monetary Policy in China, 1000–1700.* Berkeley: University of California Press, 1996.

Chapter 13. Afroeurasia in the Era of Mongol Power

Ralph A. Austen. *Trans-Saharan Africa in World History.* Oxford: Oxford University Press, 2010.

David C. Conrad, trans. and ed. *Sunjata: A West African Epic of the Mande People,* narrated by Djanka Tassey Condé. Indianapolis: Hackett Publishing, 2004.

Ross E. Dunn. *The Adventures of Ibn Battuta, A Muslim Traveler of the 14th Century,* rev. ed. Berkeley: University of California Press, 2012.

Steven A. Epstein. *An Economic and Social History of Later Medieval Europe, 1000–1500.* New York: Cambridge University Press, 2009.

William W. Fitzhugh, Morris Rossabi, and William Honeychurch, eds. *Genghis Khan and the Mongol Empire.* Media, PA: Dino Don: Mongolian Preservation Foundation; Washington, DC: Arctic Studies Center, Smithsonian Institution; Seattle: Distributed by University of Washington Press, 2009.

Peter B. Golden. *Central Asia in World History.* Oxford: Oxford University Press, 2011.

Charles J. Halperin. *Russia and the Golden Horde: The Mongol Impact on Medieval Russian History.* Indianapolis: Indiana University Press, 1985.

Mark Horton and John Middleton. *The Swahili: The Social Landscape of a Mercantile Society.* Malden, MA: Blackwell, 2000.

Peter Jackson. *The Mongols and the West, 1221–1410.* New York: Pearson Longman, 2005.

Nehemiah Levtzion. *Ancient Ghana and Mali.* London: Methuen, 1973.

George Makdisi. *The Rise of Colleges: Institutions of Learning in Islam and the West.* Edinburgh: Edinburgh University Press, 1981.

Timothy May. *The Mongol Art of War: Chinggis Khan and the Mongol Military System.* Yardley, PA: Westholme Publishing, 2007.

David Morgan. *The Mongols,* 2nd ed. Malden, MA: Wiley-Blackwell, 2007.

Barbara H. Rosenwein. *A Short History of the Middle Ages.* Toronto: University of Toronto Press, 2009.

Morris Rossabi. *Voyager from Xanadu: Rabban Sauma and the First Journey from China to the West.* New York: Kodansha International, 1992.

Chapter 14. Cities and Empires in the Americas

Richard E. W. Adams. *Ancient Civilizations of the New World.* Boulder, CO: Westview Press, 1997.

Richard E. W. Adams and Murdo J. MacLeod, eds. *The Cambridge History of the Native Peoples of the Americas.* Vol. 2: *Mesoamerica.* New York: Cambridge University Press, 1996.

John Bierhorst. *The Hungry Woman: Myths and Legends of the Aztecs.* New York: Quill/William Morrow, 1993.

Inga Clendinnen. *Aztecs: An Interpretation.* Cambridge: Cambridge University Press, 1991.

Thomas E. Emerson. *Cahokia and the Archaeology of Power.* Tuscaloosa: University of Alabama Press, 1997.

John Hyslop. *The Inka Road System.* Orlando, FL: Academic Press, 1984.

James Lockhart. *The Nahuas after the Conquest: A Social and Cultural History of the Indians of Central Mexico, Sixteenth through Eighteenth Centuries.* Stanford, CA: Stanford University Press, 1992.

George R. Milner. *The Moundbuilders: Ancient Peoples of Eastern North America.* London: Thames & Hudson, 2004.

Michael E. Moseley. *The Incas and Their Ancestors: The Archaeology of Peru,* 2nd rev. ed. London: Thames & Hudson, 2001.

Stephen Plog. *Ancient Peoples of the American Southwest.* New York: Thames & Hudson, 2008.

María Rostworowski de Diez Canseco. *History of the Inca Realm.* New York: Cambridge University Press, 1999.

Frank Salomon and Stuart B. Schwartz, eds. *The Cambridge History of the Native Peoples of the Americas.* Vol. 3: *South America.* New York: Cambridge University Press, 1996.

Michael E. Smith. *The Aztecs,* 2nd ed. Malden, MA: Blackwell, 2003.

Dirk R. Van Tuerenhout. *The Aztecs: New Perspectives.* Santa Barbara, CA: ABC-CLIO, 2005.

Chapter 15. Calamities and Recoveries across Afroeurasia

John Aberth. *The First Horseman: Disease in Human History.* Upper Saddle River, NJ: Pearson Prentice Hall, 2007.

Timothy Brook. *The Troubled Empire: China in the Yuan and Ming Dynasties.* Cambridge, MA: Belknap Press of Harvard University Press, 2010.

Peter Burke, *The Renaissance,* 2nd ed. New York: St. Martin's Press, 1997.

Norman F. Cantor. *In the Wake of the Plague: The Black Death and the World It Made.* New York: Free Press, 2001.

Kenneth Chase. *Firearms: A Global History to 1700.* New York: Cambridge, 2003.

Samuel K. Cohn, Jr. *The Black Death Transformed: Disease and Culture in Early Renaissance Europe.* London: Arnold, 2002.

John W. Dardess. *Ming China, 1368–1644: A Concise History of a Resilient Empire.* Lanham, MD: Rowman & Littlefield, 2012.

Brian Fagan. *The Little Ice Age: How Climate Made History, 1300–1850.* New York: Basic Books, 2000.

George Holmes. *Europe: Hierarchy and Revolt, 1320–1450,* 2nd ed. Medford, MA: Blackwell, 2000.

Lisa Jardine. *Worldly Goods: A New History of the Renaissance.* New York: Norton, 1996.

William Chester Jordan. *The Great Famine: Northern Europe in the Early Fourteenth Century.* Princeton, NJ: Princeton University Press, 1996.

H. H. Lamb. *Climate, History and the Modern World,* 2nd ed. New York: Routledge, 1995.

Heath W. Lowry. *The Nature of the Early Ottoman State.* Albany: State University of New York Press, 2003.

Beatrice Forbes Manz. *The Rise and Rule of Tamerlane.* Cambridge: Cambridge University Press, 1989.

D. R. SarDesai. *India: The Definitive History.* Boulder, CO: Westview Press, 2008.

Chapter 16. Oceans Crossed, Worlds Connected

Leonard Y. Andaya. *Leaves of the Same Tree: Trade and Ethnicity in the Straits of Melaka.* Honolulu: University of Hawai'i Press, 2008.

Giancarlo Casale. *The Ottoman Age of Exploration.* New York: Oxford University Press, 2010.

Noble David Cook. *Born to Die: Disease and New World Conquest, 1492–1650.* New York: Cambridge University Press, 1998.

Alfred W. Crosby. *The Columbian Exchange: Biological and Cultural Consequences of 1492.* Westport, CT: Greenwood Press, 1972.

Jared Diamond. *Guns, Germs, and Steel: The Fates of Human Societies.* New York: Norton, 2005.

Felipe Fernández-Armesto. *Before Columbus: Exploration and Colonization from the Mediterranean to the Atlantic, 1229–1492.* Philadelphia: University of Pennsylvania Press, 1987.

Charles C. Mann. *1493: Uncovering the New World Columbus Created.* New York: Alfred A. Knopf, 2011.

Michael Pearson. *The Indian Ocean.* New York: Routledge, 2003.

William D. Phillips, Jr., and Carla Rahn Phillips. *The Worlds of Christopher Columbus.* New York: Cambridge University Press, 1992.

Kenneth Pomeranz and Steven Topik, eds. *The World That Trade Created: Society, Culture, and the World Economy, 1400 to the Present,* 3rd ed. Armonk, NY: M. E. Sharpe, 2013.

Matthew Restall. *Seven Myths of the Spanish Conquest.* New York: Oxford University Press, 2003.

Matthew Restall and Felipe Fernández-Armesto. *The Conquistadors: A Very Short Introduction.* New York: Oxford University Press, 2012.

A. J. R. Russell-Wood. *The Portuguese Empire, 1415–1808: A World on the Move.* Baltimore: Johns Hopkins University Press, 1998.

Sanjay Subrahmanyam. *The Portuguese Empire in Asia.* New York: Longman, 1993.

John. K. Thornton. *Africa and Africans in the Making of the Atlantic World, 1400–1800,* 2nd ed. New York: Cambridge University Press, 1998.

James D. Tracy, ed. *The Rise of Merchant Empires: Long-Distance Trade in the Early Modern World, 1350–1750.* Cambridge: Cambridge University Press, 1990.

Chapter 17. Afroeurasia and Its Powerful States

Jeremy Black. *War in the Early Modern World.* Boulder, CO: Westview Press, 1999.

Fernand Braudel. *Civilization and Capitalism, 15th–18th Century.* New York: Harper & Row, 1981–84.

Kenneth Chase. *Firearms: A Global History to 1700.* Cambridge: Cambridge University Press, 2003.

Stephen Frederic Dale. *The Muslim Empires of the Ottomans, Safavids, and Mughals.* New York: Cambridge University Press, 2010.

Natalie Zemon Davis. *Trickster Travels: A Sixteenth-Century Muslim between Worlds.* New York: Hill and Wang, 2006.

David Eltis. *The Military Revolution in Sixteenth-Century Europe.* New York: I. B. Tauris, 1995.

Jack A. Goldstone. *Revolution and Rebellion in the Early Modern World.* Berkeley: University of California Press, 1991.

Victor Lieberman. *Strange Parallels: Southeast Asia in Global Context, c 800–1830.* New York: Cambridge University Press, 2003.

William H. McNeill. *The Pursuit of Power: Technology, Armed Force, and Society since A.D. 1000.* Chicago: University of Chicago Press, 1982.

Harbans Mukhia. *The Mughals of India.* Malden, MA: Blackwell, 2004.

Geoffrey Parker. *Europe in Crisis, 1598–1648,* 2nd ed. Malden, MA: Blackwell, 2001.

Richard L. Smith. *Almad al-Mansur: Islamic Visionary.* New York: Pearson, 2006.

James D. Tracy. *Europe's Reformation, 1450–1650.* Lanham, MD: Rowman & Littlefield, 1999.

Merry E. Wiesner-Hanks. *Early Modern Europe, 1450–1789.* New York: Cambridge, 2006.

Merry E. Wiesner-Hanks. *Religious Transformations in the Early Modern World: A Brief History with Documents.* Boston: Bedford St. Martin's, 2009.

Chapter 18. The Expanding Global Economy: Expectations and Inequalities

Timothy Brook. *Vermeer's Hat: The Seventeenth Century and the Dawn of the Global World.* New York: Bloomsbury Press, 2008.

Alfred W. Crosby. *Ecological Imperialism: The Biological Expansion of Europe, 900–1900,* 2nd ed. New York: Cambridge University Press, 2004.

Philip D. Curtin. *The Rise and Fall of the Plantation Complex: Essays in Atlantic History*, 2nd ed. Cambridge: Cambridge University Press, 1998.

Jan De Vries. *Economy of Europe in an Age of Crisis, 1600–1750.* New York: Cambridge University Press, 1976.

Dennis O. Flynn and Arturo Giráldez, eds. *Metals and Monies in an Emerging Global Economy.* Aldershot: Variorum, 1997.

Andre Gunder Frank. *ReOrient: Global Economy in the Asian Age.* Berkeley: University of California Press, 1998.

Trevor R. Getz and Liz Clarke. *Abina and the Important Men: A Graphic History.* New York: Oxford University Press, 2011.

Jack P. Greene and Philip D. Morgan, eds. *Atlantic History: A Critical Reappraisal.* New York: Oxford University Press, 2009.

Karen Ordahl Kupperman. *The Atlantic in World History.* New York: Oxford University Press, 2012.

Patrick Manning. *The African Diaspora: A History through Culture.* New York: Columbia University Press, 2009.

Patrick Manning. *Slavery and African Life: Occidental, Oriental, and African Slave Trades.* New York: Cambridge University Press, 1990.

Kenneth Pomeranz. *The Great Divergence: China, Europe, and the Making of the Modern World Economy.* Princeton, NJ: Princeton University Press, 2000.

Marcus Rediker. *The Slave Ship: A Human History.* New York: Viking, 2007.

John F. Richards. *The Unending Frontier: An Environmental History of the Early Modern World.* Berkeley: University of California Press, 2003.

Stuart B. Schwartz, ed. *In Tropical Babylons: Sugar and the Making of the Atlantic World, 1450–1680.* Chapel Hill: University of North Carolina Press, 2004.

James Sweet. *Domingos Álvarez, African Healing, and the Intellectual History of the Atlantic World.* Chapel Hill: University of North Carolina Press, 2011.

John K. Thornton. *A Cultural History of the Atlantic World, 1250–1820.* Cambridge: Cambridge University Press, 2012.

Chapter 19. The Changing Balance of Wealth and Power

William Beik. *Louis XIV and Absolutism: A Brief History with Documents.* Boston: Bedford St. Martin's, 2000.

Jane Burbank and Frederick Cooper. *Empires in World History: Power and the Politics of Difference.* Princeton, NJ: Princeton University Press, 2010.

Luke Clossey. *Salvation and Globalization in the Early Jesuit Missions.* New York: Cambridge University Press, 2008.

Pamela Kyle Crossley. *The Manchus.* Malden, MA: Blackwell, 2002.

Richard Maxwell Eaton. *The Rise of Islam and the Bengal Frontier, 1204–1760.* Berkeley: University of California Press, 1993.

J. H. Elliott. *Empires of the Atlantic World: Britain and Spain in America, 1492–1830.* New Haven, CT: Yale University Press, 2006.

Richard Elphick. *Kraal and Castle: Khoikhoi and the founding of White South Africa.* New Haven, CT: Yale University Press, 1977.

John Henry. *The Scientific Revolution and the Origins of Modern Science,* 3rd ed. New York: Palgrave Macmillan, 2008.

David Igler. *The Great Ocean: Pacific Worlds from Captain Cook to the Gold Rush.* Oxford: Oxford University Press, 2013.

Margaret C. C. Jacob. *The Scientific Revolution: A Brief History with Documents.* Boston: Bedford St. Martin's Press, 2009.

Daniel R. Mandell. *King Philip's War: Colonial Expansion, Native Resistance, and the End of Indian Sovereignty.* Baltimore: Johns Hopkins University Press, 2010.

Peter C. Perdue. *China Marches West: The Qing Conquest of Central Eurasia.* Cambridge, MA: Belknap Press of Harvard University Press, 2005.

George Saliba. *Islamic Science and the Making of the European Renaissance.* Cambridge, MA: MIT Press, 2011.

Yuri Slezkine. *Arctic Mirrors: Russia and the Small Peoples of the North.* Ithaca, NY: Cornell University Press, 1994.

Alan Taylor. *American Colonies.* New York: Viking, 2001.

John K. Thornton. *The Kongolese Saint Anthony: Dona Beatriz Kimpa Vita and the Antonian Movement, 1684–1706.* New York: Cambridge University Press, 1998.

Kerry Ward. *Networks of Empire: Forced Migration in the Dutch East India Company.* Cambridge: Cambridge University Press, 2009.

Chapter 20. Waves of Revolution

Benedict Anderson. *Imagined Communities: Reflections on the Origin and Spread of Nationalism.* New York: Verso, 1991.

Nigel Aston. *The French Revolution, 1789–1804: Authority, Liberty and the Search for Stability.* New York: Palgrave Macmillan, 2004.

Daniel A. Baugh. *The Global Seven Years War, 1754–1763: Britain and France in a Great Power Contest.* New York: Longman, 2011.

C. A. Bayly. *The Birth of the Modern World, 1780–1914.* Malden, MA: Blackwell, 2004.

Thomas Bender. *A Nation among Nations: America's Place in World History.* New York: Hill and Wang, 2006.

Jack R. Censer and Lynn Hunt. *Liberty, Equality, Fraternity: The French Revolution.* University Park: Pennsylvania State University Press, 2001.

John Charles Chasteen. *Americanos: Latin America's Struggle for Independence.* New York: Oxford University Press, 2008.

Laurent Dubois. *Avengers of the New World: The Story of the Haitian Revolution.* Cambridge, MA: Belknap Press of Harvard University Press, 2004.

Susan Dunn. *Sister Revolutions: French Lightning, American Light.* New York: Faber and Faber, 1999.

Geoffrey Ellis. *The Napoleonic Empire.* New York: Palgrave Macmillan, 2003.

David Patrick Geggus. *Haitian Revolutionary Studies.* Bloomington: Indiana University Press, 2002.

Eric J. Hobsbawm. *The Age of Revolution, 1789–1848.* New York: Vintage, 1996.

Gary B. Nash. *The Unknown American Revolution: The Unruly Birth of Democracy and the Struggle to Create America.* New York: Viking, 2005.

Simon Schama. *Citizens: A Chronicle of the French Revolution.* New York: Alfred A. Knopf, 1989.

James D. Tracy, ed. *The Rise of Merchant Empires: Long-Distance Trade in the Early Modern World, 1, 350–1750.* Cambridge: Cambridge University Press, 1990.

Chapter 21. Energy and Industrialization

John Bezis-Selfa. *Forging America: Ironworkers, Adventurers, and the Industrial Revolution.* Ithaca, NY: Cornell University Press, 2003.

Alfred W. Crosby. *Children of the Sun: A History of Humanity's Unappeasable Appetite for Energy.* New York: Norton, 2006.

Harry Gregor Gelber. *Opium, Soldiers and Evangelicals: Britain's 1840–42 War with China, and Its Aftermath*. New York: Palgrave Macmillan, 2004.

Jack Goldstone. *Why Europe? The Rise of the West in World History, 1500–1850*. New York: McGraw-Hill, 2009.

Eric J. Hobsbawm. *Industry and Empire: The Birth of the Industrial Revolution*, new ed. New York: New Press, 1999.

J. E. Inikori. *Africans and the Industrial Revolution in England: A Study in International Trade and Economic Development*. New York: Cambridge University Press, 2002.

Margaret C. Jacob. *Scientific Culture and the Making of the Industrial West*. Oxford: Oxford University Press, 1997.

Penelope Lane, Neil Raven, and K. D. M. Snell, eds. *Women, Work and Wages in England, 1600–1850*. Rochester, NY: Boydell Press, 2004.

Robert B. Marks. *The Origins of the Modern World: A Global and Ecological Narrative from the Fifteenth to the Twenty-first Century*, 2nd ed. Lanham, MD: Rowman & Littlefield, 2007.

Sidney W. Mintz. *Sweetness and Power: The Place of Sugar in Modern History*. New York: Penguin, 1985.

Joel Mokyr. *The Gifts of Athena: Historical Origins of the Knowledge Economy*. Princeton, NJ: Princeton, University Press, 2002.

Ian Morris. *Why the West Rules—for Now: The Patterns of History, and What They Reveal about the Future*. New York: Farrar, Straus & Giroux, 2010.

Giorgio Riello. *Cotton: The Fabric That Made the Modern World*. New York: Cambridge University Press, 2013.

Vaclav Smil. *Energy in World History*. Boulder, CO: Westview Press, 1994.

Dava Sobel. *Longitude: The True Story of a Lone Genius Who Solved the Greatest Scientific Problem of His Time*. New York: Penguin Books, 1995.

Peter N. Stearns. *The Industrial Revolution in World History*, 2nd ed. Boulder, CO: Westview Press, 1998.

Chapter 22. Coping with Change in the New Industrial Era

Joyce Appleby. *The Relentless Revolution: A History of Capitalism*. New York: Norton, 2010.

Jeffrey Auerbach and Peter H. Hoffenberg, eds. *Britain, the Empire and the World at the Great Exhibition of 1851*. Burlington, VT: Ashgate, 2008.

Sven Beckert. *The Empire of Cotton*. New York: Macmillan, 2007.

John Charles Chasteen. *Born in Blood and Fire: A Concise History of Latin America*. New York: Norton, 2001.

Emma Christopher, Cassandra Pybus, and Marcus Rediker, eds. *Many Middle Passages: Forced Migration and the Making of the Modern World*. Berkeley: University of California Press, 2007.

Carter V. Findley. *Turkey, Islam, Nationalism, and Modernity: A History, 1789–2007*. New Haven, CT: Yale University Press, 2010.

Steven R. Fischer. *A History of the Pacific Islands*. New York: Palgrave, 2002.

Mervyn Hiskett. *The Sword of Truth: The Life and Times of the Shehu Usuman dan Fodio*. New York: Oxford University Press, 1973.

Adam Hochschild. *Bury the Chains: Prophets and Rebels in the Fight to Free an Empire's Slaves*. Boston: Houghton Mifflin, 2005.

Dirk Hoerder. *Cultures in Contact: World Migrations in the Second Millennium*. Durham, NC: Duke University Press, 2002.

Howard N. Lupovitch. *Jews and Judaism in World History*. New York: Routledge, 2010.

James M. McPherson. *Battle Cry of Freedom: The Civil War Era*. New York: Oxford University Press, 1988.

Jonathan D. Spence. *God's Chinese Son: The Taiping Heavenly Kingdom of Hong Xiuquan*. New York: Norton, 1996.

Jonathan Sperber. *The European Revolutions, 1848–1851*, 2nd ed. New York: Cambridge University Press, 2005.

Peter N. Stearns and Herrick Chapman. *European Society in Upheaval: Social History since 1750*, 3rd ed. New York: Prentice Hall, 1992.

Barbara Taylor. *Eve and the New Jerusalem: Socialism and Feminism in the Nineteenth Century*. New York: Pantheon Books, 1983.

Steven Topik, Carlos Marichal, and Zephry Frank, eds. *From Silver to Cocaine: Latin American Commodity Chains and the Building of the World Economy, 1500–2000*. Durham, NC: Duke University Press, 2006.

Chapter 23. Capital, Technology, and the Changing Balance of Global Power

A. Adu Boahen. *African Perspectives on Colonialism*. Baltimore: Johns Hopkins University Press, 1989.

Edmund Burke III. *Prelude to Protectorate in Morocco: Precolonial Protest and Resistance, 1860–1912*. Chicago: University of Chicago Press, 1976.

Philip D. Curtin. *Death by Migration: Europe's Encounters with the Tropical World in the Nineteenth Century*. New York: Cambridge University Press, 1989.

Philip D. Curtin. *The World and the West: The European Challenge and the Overseas Response in the Age of Empire*. New York: Cambridge University Press, 2000.

Dennis O. Flynn, Lionel Frost, and A. J. H. Latham. *Pacific Centuries: Pacific and Pacific Rim History since the Sixteenth Century*. New York: Routledge, 1999.

Daniel R. Headrick. *The Tools of Empire: Technology and European Imperialism in the Nineteenth Century*. New York: Oxford University Press, 1981.

Eric Hobsbawm. *The Age of Empire, 1875–1914*. New York: Vintage Books, 1989.

Adam Hochschild. *King Leopold's Ghost: A Story of Greed, Terror and Heroism in Colonial Africa*. Boston: Houghton Mifflin, 1999.

Peter J. Hugill. *Global Communications since 1844: Geopolitics and Technology*. Baltimore: Johns Hopkins University Press, 1999.

Marius B. Jansen. *The Making of Modern Japan*. Cambridge, MA: Belknap Press of Harvard University Press, 2002.

Harold G. Marcus. *The Life and Times of Menelik II: Ethiopia, 1844–1913*. Lawrence, NJ: Red Sea Press, 1995.

David A. Northrup. *Indentured Labor in the Age of Imperialism, 1838–1914*. New York: Cambridge University Press, 1995.

Timothy Parsons. *The British Imperial Century, 1815–1914: A World History Perspective*. Lanham, MD: Rowman & Littlefield, 1999.

Emily S. Rosenberg, ed. *A World Connecting, 1870–1945*. Cambridge, MA: Harvard University Press, 2012.

Nicholas Tarling. *Imperialism in Southeast Asia: "A Fleeting, Passing Phase."* New York: Routledge, 2001.

Theodore R. Weeks. *Across the Revolutionary Divide: Russia and the USSR, 1861–1945*. Malden, MA: Wiley-Blackwell, 2011.

H. L. Wesseling. *The European Colonial Empires, 1815–1919.* New York, Pearson/Longman, 2004.

Chapter 24. Innovation, Revolution, and Global Crisis

John M. Barry. *The Great Influenza: The Epic Story of the Deadliest Plague in History.* New York: Viking, 2004.

Ian F. W. Beckett. *The Great War, 1914–1918,* 2nd ed. New York: Pearson Longman, 2007.

Myron Echenberg. *Plague Ports: The Global Urban Impact of Bubonic Plague, 1894–1901.* New York: New York University Press, 2007.

Daniel R. Headrick. *The Tentacles of Progress: Technology Transfer in the Age of Imperialism, 1860–1940.* Oxford: Oxford University Press, 1988.

Peter J. Hugill. *Global Communications since 1844: Geopolitics and Technology.* Baltimore: Johns Hopkins University Press, 1999.

Nikki R. Keddie. *Modern Iran: Roots and Results of Revolution.* New Haven, CT: Yale University Press, 2006.

John Keegan. *The First World War.* New York: Alfred A. Knopf, 1999.

Alan Knight. *The Mexican Revolution.* Cambridge: Cambridge University Press, 1986.

John H. Morrow. *The Great War: An Imperial History.* New York: Routledge, 2004.

Michael S. Nieberg. *Fighting the Great War: A Global History.* Cambridge, MA: Harvard University Press, 2006.

Richard Pipes. *A Concise History of the Russian Revolution.* New York: Alfred A. Knopf, 1995.

Hew Strachan. *The First World War in Africa.* New York: Oxford University Press, 2004.

Robert Strayer. *The Communist Experiment: Revolution, Socialism, and Global Conflict in the Twentieth Century.* New York: McGraw-Hill, 2007.

Peter Zarrow. *China in War and Revolution, 1895–1949.* New York: Routledge, 2005.

Chapter 25. Turbulent Decades

A. Adu Boahen. *African Perspectives on Colonialism.* Baltimore: Johns Hopkins University Press, 1987.

Richard Evans. *The Coming of the Third Reich.* New York: Penguin Books, 2005.

Jeffry A. Frieden. *Global Capitalism: Its Rise and Fall in the Twentieth Century.* New York: Norton, 2006.

Daniel R. Headrick. *The Invisible Weapon: Telecommunications and International Politics, 1851–1945.* New York: Oxford University Press, 1991.

Richard L. Johnson, ed. *Gandhi's Experiments with Truth: Essential Writings by and about Mahatma Gandhi.* Lanham, MD: Lexington Books, 2006.

Ian Kershaw. *Hitler.* New York: Longman, 2001.

Pericles Lewis. *The Cambridge Introduction to Modernism.* New York: Cambridge University Press, 2007.

David Lindley. *Uncertainty: Einstein, Heisenberg, Bohr, and the Struggle for the Soul of Science.* New York: Doubleday, 2007.

Erez Manela. *The Wilsonian Moment: Self-Determination and the International Origins of Anticolonial Nationalism.* Oxford: Oxford University Press, 2007.

Mark Mazower. *Dark Continent: Europe's Twentieth Century.* New York: Viking, 2000.

Michael S. Neiberg. *Fighting the Great War: A Global History.* Cambridge, MA: Harvard University Press, 2005.

Robert Paxton. *The Anatomy of Fascism.* New York: Alfred A. Knopf, 2004.

C. R. Pennell. *A Country with a Government and a Flag: The Rif War in Morocco, 1921–1926.* Boulder, CO: Middle East and North African Studies Press, 1986.

Dietmar Rothermund. *The Global Impact of the Great Depression, 1929–1939.* New York: Routledge, 1996.

Thomas E. Skidmore, Peter H. Smith, and James N. Green. *Modern Latin America,* 7th ed. New York: Oxford University Press, 2010.

Chapter 26. World War II and Its Aftermath

Franz Ansprenger. *The Dissolution of the Colonial Empires.* London: Routledge, 1989.

Christopher Bayly and Tim Harper. *Forgotten Armies: The Fall of British Asia, 1941–1945.* Cambridge: Cambridge University Press, 2005.

Martha Byrd. *A World in Flames: A Concise History of World War II.* Tuscaloosa: University of Alabama Press, 2007.

Richard Evans. *The Third Reich at War.* New York: Penguin Press, 2009.

Richard Evans. *The Third Reich in Power, 1933–1939.* New York: Penguin Press, 2005.

John Lewis Gaddis. *The Cold War: A New History.* New York: Penguin Books, 2007.

John Keegan. *The Second World War.* New York: Penguin, 2005.

Peter Longerich. *Holocaust: The Nazi Persecution and Murder of the Jews.* New York: Oxford University Press, 2010.

Mark Mazower. *Hitler's Empire: How the Nazis Ruled Europe.* New York: Penguin Press, 2008.

William Murray and Allan R. Millett. *A War to Be Won: Fighting the Second World War.* Cambridge, MA: Harvard University Press, 2000.

Andrew Roberts. *The Storm of War: A New History of the Second World War.* New York: Harper, 2011.

Martin Shipway. *Decolonization and Its Impact: A Comparative Approach to the End of Colonial Empires.* Malden, MA: Blackwell, 2008.

Charles D. Smith. *Palestine and the Arab-Israeli Conflict: A History with Documents,* 7th ed. Boston: Bedford St. Martin's, 2010.

Anders Stephanson, *Manifest Destiny: American Expansion and the Empire of Right.* New York: Hill and Wang, 1996.

Jill Stephenson. *Women in Nazi Germany.* New York: Longman, 2001.

Chapter 27. The Global Boom and Its Contradictions

Michael Adas, ed. *Essays on Twentieth-Century History.* Philadelphia: Temple University Press, 2010.

David Birmingham. *The Decolonization of Africa.* Athens: Ohio University Press, 1995.

Matthew Connelly. *A Diplomatic Revolution: Algeria's Fight for Independence and the Origins of the Post-Cold War World.* New York: Oxford University Press, 2002.

Gerard J. De Groot. *The Sixties Unplugged: A Kaleidoscopic History of a Disorderly Decade.* Cambridge, MA: Harvard University Press, 2008.

Eric Hobsbawm. *The Age of Extremes: A History of the World, 1914–1991.* New York: Pantheon Books, 1995.

Tony Judt. *Postwar: A History of Europe since 1945.* New York: Penguin Books, 2005.

Walter LaFeber. *America, Russia, and the Cold War, 1945–2006,* 10th ed. Boston: McGraw-Hill, 2008.

Mark Atwood Lawrence. *The Vietnam War: A Concise International History.* New York: Oxford University Press, 2008.

John R. McNeill. *Something New under the Sun: An Environmental History of the Twentieth Century.* New York: Norton, 2000.

David Reynolds. *One World Divisible. A Global History since 1945.* New York: Norton, 2000.

Edward Roux. *Time Longer Than Rope: A History of the Black Man's Struggle for Freedom in South Africa.* Madison: University of Wisconsin Press, 1964.

Bonnie G. Smith, ed. *Global Feminisms since 1945.* New York: Routledge, 2000.

John Springhall. *Decolonization since 1945: The Collapse of European Overseas Empires.* New York: Palgrave, 2001.

Anders Stephanson. *Manifest Destiny: American Expansionism and the Empire of the Right.* New York: Hill and Wang, 1995.

Odd Arne Westad. *The Global Cold War: Third World Intervention and the Making of Our Times.* Cambridge: Cambridge University Press, 2005.

Chapter 28. Countercurrents of Change

Daron Acemoglu and James A. Robinson. *Why Nations Fail: The Origins of Power, Prosperity, Poverty.* New York: Crown Business, 2012.

F. Gerard Adams. *Globalization, Today and Tomorrow.* New York: Routledge, 2011.

Andrew J. Bacevich, *The American Empire: The Realities and Consequences of U.S. Diplomacy.* New York: Holt, 2008.

John Baylis, Steve Smith, and Patricia Owens. *The Globalization of World Politics: An Introduction to International Relations,* 5th ed. New York: Oxford University Press, 2011.

Edmund Burke III and Kenneth Pomeranz. *The Environment and World History.* Berkeley: University of California Press, 2009.

Peter Calvocoressi. *World Politics since 1945,* 9th ed. New York: Pearson Longman, 2009.

Stephen Castles and Mark J. Miller. *The Age of Migration: International Population Movements in the Modern World,* 4th ed. New York: Guilford Press, 1993.

Paul E. Ceruzzi. *Computing: A Concise History.* Cambridge, MA: MIT Press, 2012.

Akira Iriye. *Global Community: The Role of International Organizations in the Making of the Contemporary World.* Berkeley: University of California Press, 2002.

Victor K. McElheny. *Drawing the Map of Life: Inside the Human Genome Project.* New York: Basic Books, 2010.

Steven Pinker. *The Better Angels of Our Nature: Why Violence Has Declined.* New York: Penguin, 2012.

Joachim Radkau. *Nature and Power: A Global History of the Environment,* trans. Thomas Dunlap. New York: Cambridge University Press, 2008.

William L. Cleveland and Martin Bunton. *A History of the Modern Middle East.* 5th ed. Boulder, CO: Westview Press, 2013.

Fred Spier. *Big History and the Future of Humanity.* Malden, MA: Wiley-Blackwell, 2011.

Peter N. Stearns. *Globalization in World History.* New York: Routledge, 2010.

References

introduction

1. Martin W. Lewis and Kären E. Wigen, *The Myth of Continents: A Critique of Metageography* (Berkeley: University of California Press, 1997), 27.

chapter 1

1. Robert J. Wenke, *Patterns in Prehistory: Humankind's First Three Million Years,* 5th ed. (New York: Oxford University Press, 1990), 103.
2. Richard Leakey, *The Making of Mankind* (New York: Dutton, 1981), 117.
3. David Christian, *Maps of Time: An Introduction to Big History* (Berkeley: University of California Press, 2004), 146–148.
4. Christopher Stringer and Robin McKie, *African Exodus: The Origins of Modern Humanity* (New York: Holt, 1996), 117.
5. Elizabeth Wayland Barber, *Women's Work: The First 20,000 Years: Women, Cloth, and Society in Early Times* (New York: Norton, 1994).

chapter 2

1. Richard W. Bulliet, *Hunters, Herders, and Hamburgers: The Past and Future of Human-Animal Relationships* (New York: Columbia University Press, 2005).
2. Miriam Lichtheim, ed., *Ancient Egyptian Literature,* 3 vols. (Berkeley: University of California Press, 1973), 1:25–27.
3. Cyril Aldred, *The Egyptians,* rev. ed. (London: Thames and Hudson, 1984), 102.

chapter 3

1. David Christian, *Maps of Time: An Introduction to Big History* (Berkeley: University of California Press, 2004), 143.
2. Robert Hughes, *The Fatal Shore: The Epic of Australia's Founding* (New York: Alfred A. Knopf, 1987), 9.
3. David W. Anthony, *The Horse, the Wheel, and Language: How Bronze-Age Riders from the Eurasian Steppes Shaped the Modern World* (Princeton, NJ: Princeton University Press, 2007), 197–200.
4. Andrew Sherratt, *Economy and Society in Prehistoric Europe: Changing Perspectives* (Princeton, NJ: Princeton University Press, 1997).
5. Ibid.
6. Anthony, *The Horse, the Wheel, and Language,* 222.
7. Quoted in Billie Jean Collins, *The Hittites and Their World* (Atlanta, GA: Society of Biblical Literature, 2007), 93.
8. Quoted in J. P Mallory, *In Search of the Indo-Europeans: Language, Archaeology and Myth* (London: Thames and Hudson, 1989), 38.

chapter 4

1. Quoted in Colin M. MacLachlan and James E. Rodriguez O., *The Forging of the Cosmic Race: A Reinterpretation of Colonial Mexico* (Berkeley: University of California Press, 1980), 22–23.
2. Andrew Lawler, "Beyond the Family Feud: After Decades of Debate Are Younger Scholars Finally Asking the Right Questions about the Olmecs?" *Archaeology* 60 (Mar/April 2007): 20–25.

3. Terrence Kaufman, Running translation of La Mojarra Stele. Accessed September 19, 2012. http://anthropology.pitt.edu/faculty/kaufman.html.

chapter 5

1. Theodore A. Wertime, "The Pyrotechnologic Industries and Mediterranean Deforestation in Antiquity," *Journal of Field Archaeology* 10 (Winter 1983): 452.
2. Plato, *Critias,* trans. Benjamin Jowett. The Internet Classic Archive, http://classics.mit.edu/Plato/critias.html.
3. Both letters quoted in Marc Van de Mieroop, *A History of the Ancient Near East, ca. 3000–323 BC,* 2nd ed. (Malden, MA: Blackwell, 2007), 194.
4. Mark W. Chavalas, ed., *The Ancient Near East: Historical Sources in Translation* (Malden, MA: Blackwell, 2006), 288.
5. Holy Bible: New International Version, Genesis 12:1–5, BibleGateway .com.
6. Isaiah 37:10 (King James Version).
7. James Henry Breasted, trans., *Ancient Records of Egypt,* Part 4 (Chicago: University of Chicago Press, 1906), 861–883.
8. Population estimate compiled by David Christian in *Maps of Time: An Introduction to Big History* (Berkeley: University of California Press, 2004), 143.
9. Ibid., 326.

chapter 6

1. Herbert Cushing Tolman, *Ancient Persian Lexicon* (Nashville, TN: Vanderbilt University Press, 1908), 51.
2. Ibid., 51.
3. Roland G. Kent, *Old Persian,* 2nd ed. rev. (New Haven, CT: American Oriental Society, 1953), 140.
4. Quoted in Amélie Kuhrt, *The Ancient Near East, c. 3000–330 BC,* Vol. 2 (London: Routledge, 1995), 602.
5. Quoted in Ibid., 670.
6. Aristotle, *Politics,* trans. Benjamin Jowett (New York: Modern Library, 1943), 57.
7. Aristotle, *Metaphysics,* trans. Hippocrates G. Apostle (Bloomington: Indiana University Press, 1966), 14.
8. Margaret C. Miller, *Athens and Persia in the Fifth Century BC: A Study in Cultural Receptivity* (Cambridge: Cambridge University Press, 1997).
9. Rock Edict 13, *The Edicts of King Ashoka,* an English rendering by Ven. S. Dhammika (Kandy, Sri Lanka: Buddhist Publication Society, 1993), DharmaNet Edition, *Access to Insight,* June 5, 2010, http://www.accesstoinsight.org/lib/authors/dhammika/wheel386.html.
10. Pillar Edict 7, *The Edicts of King Ashoka.*
11. Herodotus, *The Histories,* trans. Robin Waterfield, with an introduction and notes by Carolyn Dewald (New York: Oxford University Press, 1998), 256.
12. Hippocrates, *Hippocratic Writings,* edited with an introduction by G.E.R. Lloyd, translated by J. Chadwick and W.N. Mann (New York: Penguin, 1983), 162.

chapter 7

1. Flavius Josephus, *The Great Roman-Jewish War: A.D. 66–70*, trans. William Whiston as revised by D. S. Margoliouth, ed., with an introduction by William R. Farmer (Gloucester, MA: Peter Smith, 1970), 248.

2. Cassius Dio Cocceianus, *Dio's Roman History*, trans. Earnest Cary (New York: Macmillan, 1914–27), 8:85.

3. Quoted in Richard Hingley and Christina Unwin, *Boudica: Iron Age Warrior Queen* (New York: Hambledon Continuum, 2005), 47.

4. Peter Garnsey and Richard Saller, *The Roman Empire: Economy, Society and Culture* (London: Duckworth, 1987), 20.

5. Confucius, *The Analects*, trans. Burton Watson (New York: Columbia University Press, 2007), 34.

6. Laozi, *Daodejing: The Book of the Way*, trans. Moss Roberts (Berkeley: University of California Press, 2001), 91.

7. Quoted in Stanley Burstein, ed., *Ancient African Civilizations: Kush and Axum* (Princeton, NJ: Markus Wiener, 1998), 99–100.

8. Wilfred H. Schoff, ed. and trans., *The Periplus of the Erythraean Sea: Travel and Trade in the Indian Ocean by a Merchant of the First Century* (New York: Longman, Green, 1912), 37–38.

9. Gary Keith Young, *Rome's Eastern Trade: International Commerce and Imperial Policy, 31 BC–AD 305* (London: Routledge, 2001), 181–189.

chapter 8

1. Diego de Landa, *Landa's Relación de las cosas de Yucatán: A translation*, ed. Alfred M. Tozzer (Cambridge, MA: Peabody Museum, 1941). Quoted in Robert J. Sharer with Loa P. Traxler, *The Ancient Maya*, 6th ed. (Palo Alto, CA: Stanford University Press, 2006), 126.

2. Richard E. W. Adams, *Prehistoric Mesoamerica*, 3rd ed. (Norman: University of Oklahoma Press, 2005), 290.

chapter 9

1. "Royal inscription found on the Kabah of Zartusht," Avesta—Zoroastrian Archives, http://www.avesta.org/mp/kz.html.

2. Lactantius, *Of the Manner in Which the Persecutors Died* (Whitefish, MT: Kessinger Publishing, 2004), 6.

3. Peter Heather, *The Fall of the Roman Empire: A New History of Rome and the Barbarians* (Oxford: Oxford University Press, 2006), 28.

4. "Edict of Milan (313 A.D.)," quoted in Paul Halsall, Internet Medieval Sourcebook, http://www.fordham.edu/halsall/sbook.html.

5. Heather, *Fall of the Roman Empire*, 126.

6. Quoted in ibid., 190.

7. Marcellinus Ammianus, *Marcellinus Ammianus*, with an English translation by John C. Rolfe (Cambridge, MA: Harvard University Press, 1958–1963), Book 31: 383–385.

8. Possidius, *Life of St. Augustine*, trans. and with an introduction by Herbert T. Weiskotten (Merchantville, NJ: Evolution Publishing, 2008), 40–41.

9. Jordanes, quoted in Heather, *Fall of the Roman Empire*, 319.

10. Hydatius, *The Chronicle of Hydatius and the Consularia Constantinopolitana*, trans. and ed. R. W. Burgess (New York: Oxford University Press, 1993), 103.

11. Procopius, *Procopius Works*, trans. Henry B. Dewing, Vol. 2 (Cambridge, MA: Harvard University Press, 1936), 329.

12. Peter Christensen, *The Decline of Iranshahr: Irrigation and Environments in the History of the Middle East, 500 B.C. to A.D. 1500* (Copenhagen: Museum Tusculanum Press, 1993), 81.

13. Brahmagupta, *Brahmasphutasiddhanta*, quoted in Ronald Green, *Nothing Matters: A Book about Nothing* (Arlesford, UK: John Hunt, 2011), 7.

14. Quoted in Burton Stein, *A History of India* (Malden, MA: Blackwell, 1998), 93.

15. I-Tsing (Yijing), *A Record of the Buddhist Religion as Practised in India and the Malay Archipelago (A.D. 671–695)*, trans. J. Takakusu (Oxford: Clarendon Press, 1896), xxxiv.

16. Indicopleustes Cosmas, *The Christian Topography of Cosmas, an Egyptian Monk*, trans. and ed. J. W. McCrindle (London: Hakluyt Society, 1897).

17. Tyrannius Rufinus (ca. 344–410), quoted in Stanley Burstein, ed., *Ancient African Civilizations: Kush and Axum* (Princeton, NJ: Markus Wiener, 1998), 94–96.

18. Data adapted from David Christian, *Maps of Time: An Introduction to Big History* (Berkeley: University of California Press, 2004), 344–345.

19. Stephen K. Sanderson, "Expanding World Commercialization: The Link between World-Systems and Civilizations," in Stephen K. Sanderson, ed., *Civilizations and World Systems: Studying World-Historical Change* (Walnut Creek, CA: AltaMira Press, 1995), 267.

chapter 10

1. Samuel Beal, trans. and ed., *The Life of Hiuen-Tsiang*, 2nd ed. (Delhi: Manshiram Manoharlal, 1973), 41, quoted in Sally Hovey Wriggins, *The Silk Road Journey with Xuanzang* (Boulder, CO: Westview Press, 2004), 32.

2. Richard W. Bulliet, *Islam: The View from the Edge* (New York: Columbia University Press, 1994), 40.

3. Edward F. Schafer, *The Golden Peaches of Samarkand: A Study of Tang Exotics* (Berkeley: University of California Press, 1963), 28.

4. Population estimates for the first millennium C.E. adapted from David Christian, *Maps of Time: An Introduction to Big History* (Berkeley: University of California Press, 2004), 344–345; Massimo Live-Bacci, *A Concise History of World Population* (Cambridge, MA: Blackwell, 1992), 31; Colin McEvedy and Richard Jones, *Atlas of World Population History* (New York: Penguin, 1978), 345–347.

chapter 11

1. Patricia Crone, *Slaves on Horses, the Evolution of the Islamic Polity* (Cambridge: Cambridge University Press, 1980).

2. Jahiz, *The Life and Works of Jahiz: Translations of Selected Texts by Charles Pellat*, trans. D. M. Hawke (Berkeley: University of California Press, 1969), quoted in Francis Robinson, ed., *The Cambridge Illustrated History of the Islamic World* (Cambridge: Cambridge University Press, 1996), 38.

3. Richard W. Bulliet, *Islam: The View from the Edge* (New York: Columbia University Press, 1994), 38–39.

4. Conrad Totman, *A History of Japan* (Oxford: Blackwell, 2000), 110; Akira Hayami, *The Historical Demography of Pre-modern Japan* (Toronto: University of Toronto Press, 1997), 41–42.

5. Ibid., 84.

6. Al-Bakri, *The Book of Routes and Realms*, quoted in N. Levtzion and J. F. P. Hopkins, *Corpus of Early Arabic Sources for West African History* (Cambridge: Cambridge University Press, 1981), 79–81.

7. Ibid., 79–81.

8. Lynda Shaffer, "Southernization," *Journal of World History* 5 (Spring 1994): 1–21.

part 4

1. I. G. Simmons, *Changing the Face of the Earth: Culture, Environment, History* (Hoboken, NJ: Wiley-Blackwell, 1996), 27.

chapter 12

1. Zhibin Zhang et al., "Periodic Climate Cooling Enhanced National Disasters and Wars in China during AD 10–1900," *Proceedings of*

the *Royal Society* 277 (2010): 3745–3753; Pingzhong Zhang et al., "A Test of Climate, Sun, and Culture Relationships from an 1810-Year Chinese Cave Record," *Science* 322 (Nov. 2008): 940–942.

2. Tu Cheng, quoted in Yoshinobu Shiba, *Commerce and Society in Song China,* Michigan Abstracts of Chinese and Japanese Works in Chinese History, no. 2 (Ann Arbor: Center for Chinese Studies, University of Michigan, 1970), 162–163.

3. Quoted in Charles O. Hucker, *China's Imperial Past: An Introduction to Chinese History and Culture* (Stanford, CA: Stanford University Press, 1975), 324.

4. Zhu Xi, quoted in Hucker, *China's Imperial Past,* 371. See also Allen Wittenborn translation of *Further Reflections on Things at Hand* (Lanham, MD: University Press of America, 2002).

5. Quoted in Robert Finlay, "The Pilgrim Art: The Culture of Porcelain in World History," *Journal of World History* 9 (Fall 1998): 152.

6. Al-Ghazali, *The Faith and Practice of al-Ghazali* by W. Montgomery Watt (London: Allen and Unwin, 1953), 56.

7. Sa'id al-Andalusi, *Science in the Medieval World: Book of the Categories of Nations,* trans. and ed. Sema'an I. Salem and Alok Kumar (Austin: University of Texas Press, 1991), 7.

8. Robert Bartlett, *The Making of Europe: Conquest, Colonization and Cultural Change, 950–1350* (Princeton, NJ: Princeton University Press, 1993), 144. [Citing here work of Walter Kuhn.]

9. Zakariya ibn Muhammad al-Qazwini, *Athar al-Bilad wa-Akhbar al-'Ibad* (Beirut, n.d.). Translated and quoted in Tim Mackintosh-Smith, *Travels with a Tangerine: A Journey in the Footnotes of Ibn Battutah* (London: John Murray, 2001), 126.

10. Quoted in Vern L. Bullough, Brenda Shelton, and Sarah Slavin, *The Subordinated Sex: A History of Attitudes toward Women* (Athens: University of Georgia Press, 1988), 126.

chapter 13

1. Rein Taagepera, "Size and Duration of Empires: Systematics of Size," *Social Science Research* 7 (1978): 108–127.

2. Thomas T. Allsen, *Culture and Conquest in Mongol Eurasia* (Cambridge: Cambridge University Press, 2001), 5.

3. John of Plano Carpini, "History of the Mongols," in *The Mongol Mission,* ed. and with an introduction by Christopher Dawson (London: Sheed and Ward, 1955), 18.

4. Igor de Rachewiltz, trans. and ed., *The Secret History of the Mongols: A Mongolian Epic Chronicle of the Thirteenth Century,* 2 vols. (Leiden: Brill, 2004), 1:23.

5. Ata Malik Juvaini, *The History of the World Conqueror,* trans. J. A. Boyle, 2 vols. (Cambridge, MA: Harvard University Press, 1958), 1:152.

6. S. A. M. Adshead, *Central Asia in World History* (New York: St. Martin's Press, 1993), 61.

7. Rashid al-Din, *The Successors of Genghis Khan,* trans. John Andrew Boyle (New York: Columbia University Press, 1971), 169.

8. Ibid., 199–200.

9. Ibid., 168, 199.

10. Quoted in John Andrew Boyle, *The Mongol World Empire, 1206–1370* (London: Variorum Reprints, 1977), 6–7.

11. David Morgan, *The Mongols* (New York: Blackwell, 1986), 151.

12. Quoted in Boyle, *Mongol World Empire,* 6.

13. F. W. Mote, *Imperial China, 900–1800* (Cambridge, MA: Harvard University Press, 1999), 504.

14. Hamd-Allah Mustawfi, *The Geographical Part of the Nuzhat al-Qulub,* trans. G. Le Strange (Leiden: Brill, 1919), 34.

15. Rashid al-Din, *Ta'rikh-i mubarak-i Ghazani,* ed. Karl Jahn (London: Luzac, 1940). Quoted in Allsen, *Culture and Conquest,* 121.

16. Ronald Latham, trans. and ed., *The Travels of Marco Polo* (New York: Penguin Books, 1958), 237.

17. Ibid., 290.

18. Ibn Battuta, quoted in Said Hamdun and Noël King, eds., *Ibn Battuta in Black Africa* (Princeton, NJ: Markus Wiener, 2005), 16.

19. Roger Bacon, *Opus Majus,* trans. Robert Belle Burke (Philadelphia: University of Pennsylvania Press, 1928), 2:583.

20. Nehemia Levtzion, *Ancient Ghana and Mali* (London: Methuen 1973), 131–133.

chapter 14

1. Richard E. W. Adams, *Prehistoric Mesoamerica,* 3rd ed. (Norman: University of Oklahoma Press, 2005), 299, 304.

2. Dirk R. Van Tuerenhout, *The Aztecs: New Perspectives* (Santa Barbara, CA: ABC-CLIO, 2005), 147.

3. Hernán Cortés, From Second Letter to Charles V, 1520, Modern History Sourcebook, http://www.fordham.edu/halsall/mod/1520cortes.asp.

4. Quoted in Michael E. Smith, *The Aztecs,* 2nd ed. (Malden, MA: Blackwell, 2003), 195.

5. Quoted in John Bierhorst, ed., *The Hungry Woman: Myths and Legends of the Aztecs* (New York: Morrow, 1984), 38, 99–111.

6. Juan de Betanzos, *Narrative of the Incas,* trans. and ed. Roland Hamilton and Dana Buchanan (Austin: University of Texas Press, 1996), 28–29.

7. Pedro Cieza de Leon, *Crónica del Perú,* quoted in María Rostworowski and Craig Morris, "The Fourfold Domain: Inka Power and Its Social Foundations," in *The Cambridge History of the Native Peoples of the Americas,* ed. Frank Salomon and Stuart Schwartz. Vol. 3, Part 1 (Cambridge: Cambridge University Press, 1999), 787.

chapter 15

1. Henry S. Lucas, "The Great European Famine of 1315, 1316, and 1317," *Speculum* 5 (1930): 365–366.

2. Ibn Khaldun, *The Muqaddimah: An Introduction to History,* trans. Franz Rosenthal, 3 vols. (Princeton, NJ: Princeton University Press, 1958), 1:64.

3. Giovanna Morelli et al., "*Yersinia Pestis* Genome Sequencing Identifies Patterns of Global Phylogenetic Diversity," *Nature Genetics* 42 (Dec. 2010): 1140–1145.

4. Ewen Callaway, "Plague Genome: The Black Death Decoded," *Nature* 478 (2011). Retrieved from http://www.nature.com/news/2011/111025/full/478444a.html.

5. Michael Dols, *The Black Death in the Middle East* (Princeton, NJ: Princeton University Press, 1977), 69.

6. Giovanni Boccaccio, *Decameron,* trans. John Payne, revised and annotated by Charles S. Singleton (Berkeley: University of California Press, 1982), 1:14–15.

7. Ibn Abi Hajalah, quoted in Dols, *Black Death in the Middle East,* 238.

8. Dols, *Black Death in the Middle East,* 265.

9. *The Chronicles of Jean Froissart,* trans. Lord Berners, selected, edited, and introduced by Gillian and William Anderson (Carbondale: Southern Illinois University Press, 1963), 138.

10. F. W. Mote, *Imperial China, 900–1800* (Cambridge, MA: Harvard University Press, 1999), 744–745.

11. Sally K. Church, "Zheng He: An Investigation into the Plausibility of 450-Ft Treasure Ships," *Monumenta Serica* 53 (2005): 1–43.

12. H. A. R. Gibb, trans. and ed., *The Travels of Ibn Battuta, A.D. 1325–1354,* Vol. 4, translation completed with annotations by C. F. Beckingham (London: Hakluyt Society, 1994), 814.

13. Kritovoulos, *History of Mehmed the Conqueror*, trans. Charles T. Riggs (Princeton, NJ: Princeton University Press, 1954), 25.

14. Kritovoulos, *History of Mehmed the Conqueror*, 66–67.

chapter 16

1. Al-Umari, quoted in D. T. Niane, ed., *General History of Africa*, Vol. 4: *Africa from the Twelfth to the Sixteenth Century* (Paris: UNESCO, 1984), 664–665.

2. Tertius Chandler, *Four Thousand Years of Urban Growth: An Historical Census* (Lewiston, NY: St. David's University Press, 1987), 477.

3. Antonio Galvão, *A Treatise on the Moluccas*, quoted in Anthony Reid, *Southeast Asia in the Age of Commerce, 1450–1680* (New Haven, CT: Yale University Press, 1988), 146

4. Tomé Pires, *The Suma Oriental*, trans. Armando Cortesão, 2 vols. (London: Hakluyt Society, 1944), 2:286.

5. Tomé Pires, *Suma Oriental*, 1:41–42.

6. Duarte Barbosa, *Livro* (London: Hakluyt Society, 1918–1921), 76–77.

7. Duarte Pacheco Pereira, *Esmeraldo de Situ Orbis*, trans. and ed. George H. T. Kimble (London: Hakluyt Society, 1937), 144.

8. Pedro Cieza de Leon, *The Second Part of the Chronicle of Peru*, trans. and ed. Clements R. Markham (London: Hakluyt Society, 1883), 57.

9. Quoted in Basil Davidson, *The African Past: Chronicles from Antiquity to Modern Times* (New York: Grosset & Dunlap, 1964), 192.

10. Michele de Cuneo, quoted in Noble David Cook, *Born to Die: Disease and New World Conquest, 1492–1630* (New York: Cambridge University Press, 1998), 28.

11. Luis de Figueroa and Alonso de Santo Domingo, quoted in Cook, *Born to Die*, 61.

12. Cook, *Born to Die*, 61.

13. *The Broken Spears: The Aztec Account of the Conquest of Mexico*, edited and with an introduction and new postscript by Miguel León-Portilla, expanded and updated edition (Boston: Beacon Press, 1992), 30.

14. Quoted in Robert McCaa, "Spanish and Nahuatl Views on Smallpox and Demographic Catastrophe in Mexico," *Journal of Interdisciplinary History* 25 (1995): 428–430.

15. Bernal Díaz del Castillo, *The True History of the Conquest of New Spain*, trans. Alfred Percival Maudslay (London: Hakluyt Society, 1908), 244.

16. *Reports on the Discovery of Peru*, trans. and ed. Clements R. Markham (New York: Burt Franklin, 1872), 56.

17. Quoted in Sanjay Subrahmanyam, "The Connected Histories of the Iberian Overseas Empires, 1500–1640," *American Historical Review* 112, no. 5 (Dec. 2007): 1368.

18. Quoted in Glenn J. Ames, *Vasco da Gama: Renaissance Crusader* (New York: Pearson Longman, 2005), 74.

19. Hans Mayr, *The Voyage and Acts of Dom Francisco*, quoted in G. S. P. Freeman-Grenville, *The East African Coast: Selected Documents* (London: Rex Collings, 1974), 111–112.

20. Dom João de Castro, quoted in Subrahmanyam, "Connected Histories," 1373.

chapter 17

1. Al-Ifrani, *Histoire de la dynastie saadienne au Maroc, 1511–1670*, trans. and ed. O. Houdas (Paris, 1886), 160–162, quoted in E. W. Bovill, *The Golden Trade of the Moors* (London: Oxford University Press, 1968), 165–166.

2. Antonio Monserrate, *The Commentary of Father Monserrate, S. J., on His Journey to the Court of Akbar*, trans. from Latin by J. S. Hoyland and annotated by S. N. Banerjee (London: Oxford University Press, 1922), 198.

3. Toyotomi Hideyoshi, *101 Letters of Hideyoshi: The Private Correspondence of Toyotomi Hideyoshi*, ed. and trans. Adriana Boscaro (Tokyo: Sophia University, 1975), 31.

4. Quoted in Edward William Bovill, *The Golden Trade of the Moors: West African Kingdoms in the Fourteenth century*, with a new introduction by Robert O. Collins (Princeton, NJ: Markus Wiener, 1995), 147–148.

5. William Eckhardt, "War-Related Deaths since 3,000 BC," *Bulletin of Peace Proposals* 22 (Dec. 1991): 437–443.

6. Weston F. Cook, *The Hundred Years War for Morocco: Gunpowder and the Military Revolution in the Early Modern Muslim World* (Boulder, CO: Westview Press, 1994).

7. Quoted in Barton C. Hacker, "Women and Military Institutions in Early Modern Europe: A Reconnaissance," *Signs* 6, no. 4 (1981): 648.

8. Quoted in Nicola Di Cosmo, "Did Guns Matter? Firearms and the Qing Formation," in *The Qing Formation in World-Historical Time*, ed. Lynn A. Struve (Cambridge, MA: Harvard University Press, 2004), 142.

9. Richard Hellie, "Russia, 1200–1850," in *The Rise of the Fiscal State in Europe, c. 1200–1850*, ed. Richard Bonney (Oxford: Oxford University Press, 1999), 493.

10. Charles Tilly, *European Revolutions, 1492–1992* (Oxford: Blackwell, 1993), 156.

11. Russ Rymer, "Vanishing Voices," *National Geographic* (July 2012), http://ngm.nationalgeographic.com/2012/07/vanishing-languages/rymer-text.

12. Quoted in Paul A. Russell, *Lay Theology in the Reformation: Popular Pamphleteers in Southwest Germany 1521–1525* (Cambridge: Cambridge University Press, 1986), 203.

13. Quoted in Nicholas Ostler, *Empires of the Word: A Language History of the World* (New York: HarperCollins, 2005), 404–405.

14. Quoted in ibid., 465.

15. Matteo Ricci, *China in the Sixteenth Century: The Journals of Matthew Ricci: 1583–1610*, trans. Louis J. Gallagher (New York: Random House, 1953), 21.

chapter 18

1. Gemelli Careri, quoted in Henry Kamen, *Empire: How Spain Became a World Power, 1492–1763* (New York: HarperCollins, 2003), 205.

2. William S. Atwell, "International Bullion Flows and the Chinese Economy, circa 1530–1650," in *Metals and Monies in an Emerging Global Economy*, ed. Dennis O. Flynn and Arturo Giráldez (Aldershot: Variorum, 1997), 147.

3. Andre Gunder Frank, *ReOrient: Global Economy in the Asian Age* (Berkeley: University of California Press, 1998), 131.

4. Vazquez de Espinosa, "Compendium and Description of the West Indies," quoted in Alfred W. Crosby, Jr., *The Columbian Exchange: Biological and Cultural Consequences of 1492* (Westport, CT: Praeger, 2003), 84.

5. Garciliaso de la Vega, quoted in Charles C. Mann, *1491: New Revelations of the Americas before Columbus* (New York: Alfred A. Knopf, 2005), 314.

6. Dennis O. Flynn and Arturo Giráldez, "Born with a 'Silver Spoon': The Origin of World Trade in 1571," *Journal of World History* 6, no. 2 (Fall 1995): 201–221.

7. Antonio Vázquez de Espinosa, *Compendium and Description of the West Indies*, trans. Charles Upson Clark (Washington, D.C.: Smithsonian Institution, 1942), 542–543.

8. Dennis O. Flynn and Arturo Giráldez, eds., *Metals and Monies in an Emerging Global Economy* (Aldershot: Variorum, 1997), xxiii.

9. Angus Maddison, *The World Economy: A Millennial Perspective* (Paris: Organization for Economic Co-operation and Development, 2001), 241, 243.

10. Ibid., 54.

11. Quoted in Carlo M. Cipolla, *Before the Industrial Revolution: European Society and Economy, 1000–1700*, 3rd ed. (New York: Norton, 1993), 239.

12. Quoted in Richard Von Glahn, *Fountain of Fortune: Money and Monetary Policy in China, 1000–1700* (Berkeley: University of California Press, 1996), 128–129.

13. Von Glahn, *Fountain of Fortune,* 126.

14. Quoted in Geoffrey Parker, "Europe and the Wider World, 1500–1700: The Military Balance," in James D. Tracy, ed., *The Political Economy of Merchant Empires* (Cambridge: Cambridge University Press, 1991), 179–180.

15. David Eltis, "Free and Coerced Transatlantic Migrations: Some Comparisons," *American Historical Review* 88, no. 2 (April 1983), 255.

16. Philip D. Curtin, *The Rise and Fall of the Plantation Complex* (Cambridge: Cambridge University Press, 1990), 39–40.

17. Paul E. Lovejoy, *Transformations in Slavery: A History of Slavery in Africa,* 2nd ed. (New York: Cambridge University Press, 2000), 47.

18. Ibid., 63.

19. Venture Smith, *A Narrative of the Life and Adventures of Venture, a Native of Africa* (New London, CT: C. Holt, 1798), 10–11.

20. G. I. Jones, ed., "Olaudah Equiano of the Niger Ibo," in Philip D. Curtin, ed. *Africa Remembered: Narratives of West Africans from the Era of the Slave Trade* (Madison: University of Wisconsin Press, 1968), 95.

21. Geoffrey Parker, "Crisis and Catastrophy: The Global Crisis of the Seventeenth Century Reconsidered," *American Historical Review* 113, no. 4 (Oct. 2008): 1053–1079.

chapter 19

1. William H. Dall, "A Critical Review of Bering's First Expedition, 1725–30, Together with a Translation of His Original Report upon It," *National Geographic Magazine* 2, no. 2 (1890): 141.

2. Rein Taagepera, "Size and Duration of Empires: Systematics of Size," *Social Science Research* 7 (1978): 108–127.

3. Emperor Yongzheng, quoted in Mark C. Elliott, *The Manchu Way: The Eight Banners and Ethnic Identity in Late Imperial China* (Stanford, CA: Stanford University Press, 2001), 241.

4. Emperor Qianlong, letter to King George III of Great Britain, 1793, in E. Backhouse and J. O. P. Bland, *Annals and Memoirs of the Court of Peking* (Boston: Houghton Mifflin, 1914), 328.

5. Richard Steckel and Michael Haines, eds., *The Population History of North America* (New York: Cambridge University Press, 1997).

6. Alexander von Humboldt, *Political Essays on the Kingdom of New Spain,* 4 vols. (London: Longman, Hurst, Rees, Orme, and Brown, 1811), 3:463–464.

7. Jean Domat, "On Social Order and Absolute Monarchy," Modern History Sourcebook, http://www.fordham.edu/Halsall/mod/modsbook.asp.

8. James I, Speech in the Star-Chamber, 1616, quoted in G. W. Prothero, ed., *Select Statutes and other Constitutional Documents Illustrative of the Reigns of Elizabeth and James I* (Oxford: Clarendon Press, 1898), 400.

9. Quoted in Alan Taylor, *American Colonies: The Settling of North America* (New York: Penguin, 2002), 98.

10. *The Harvard Charter of 1650,* Harvard University Archives, http://hollis.harvard.edu/?itemid=|misc/via|olvwork368905.

11. Robert Gray, *A Good Speed to Virginia* (London, 1609), quoted in Kate Aughterson, ed., *The English Renaissance: An Anthology of Sources and Documents* (New York: Routledge, 1998), 529.

12. N. S. Orlova, cited in Yuri Slezkine, *Arctic Mirrors: Russia and the Small Peoples of the North* (Ithaca, NY: Cornell University Press, 1994), 14.

13. James C. Armstrong and Nigel Anthony Worden, "The Slaves," in *The Shaping of South African Society, 1652–1840,* 2nd ed., ed. Richard Elphick and Hermann Giliomee (London: Maskew Miller Longman, 1989), 129.

14. Leonard Guelke, "Freehold Farmers and Frontier Settlers, 1657–1780," in Elphick and Giliomee, *Shaping of South Africa,* 66.

15. Laetitia Matilda Hawkins, "Letters on the Female Mind, Its Powers and Pursuits. Addressed to Miss H. M. Williams, with Particular Reference to Her Letters from France, 1793." Reprinted in Vivien Jones, *Women in the Eighteenth Century: Constructions of Femininity* (New York: Routledge, 1990), 118.

16. Samuel Johnson, *A Dictionary of the English Language,* 1st ed. (London: Times, 1983).

17. Michael Pearson, *The Indian Ocean* (New York: Routledge, 2003), 173.

18. John McManners, *The Oxford Illustrated History of Christianity* (Oxford: Oxford University, 2001), 310.

19. John K. Thornton, *The Kongolese Saint Anthony: Dona Beatriz Kimpa Vita and the Antonian Movement, 1684–1706* (New York: Cambridge University Press, 1998), 211–213.

part 6

1. George Modelski, *World Cities, –3000 to 2000* (Washington, D.C.: Faros2000, 2003), 63, 69–72.

2. David Christian, *Maps of Time: An Introduction to Big History* (Berkeley: University of California Press, 2004), 146–148.

chapter 20

1. Ronald Findlay and Kevin H. O'Rourke, *Power and Plenty: Trade, War, and the World Economy in the Second Millennium* (Princeton, NJ: Princeton University Press, 2007), 292.

2. Paul Kennedy, *The Rise and Fall of the Great Powers* (New York: Vintage Press, 1989), 149.

3. Prasannan Parthasarathi, *Why Europe Grew Rich and Asia Did Not: Global Economic Divergence, 1600–1850* (New York: Cambridge University Press, 2011), 37–46.

4. Quoted in Jack R. Censer and Lynn Hunt, *Liberty, Equality, Fraternity: The French Revolution* (University Park: Pennsylvania State University Press, 2001), 88.

5. Quoted in Alan I. Forrest, *Soldiers of the French Revolution (Bicentennial Reflections on the French Revolution)* (Durham, NC: Duke University Press, 1990), 157.

chapter 21

1. Frances Ann Kemble, *Records of a Girlhood* (New York: Henry Holt, 1879), 283.

2. Rolf Peter Sieferle, *The Subterranean Forest: Energy Systems and the Industrial Revolution* (Cambridge, UK: White Horse Press, 2001).

3. Henry Booth, *An Account of the Liverpool and Manchester Railway* (Philadelphia: Carey & Lea, 1831), 197, 198.

4. Angus Maddison, *The World Economy: A Millennial Perspective* (Paris: Organization for Economic Co-operation and Development, 2001), 241, 264.

5. Patrick Colquhoun, *A Treatise on the Wealth, Power, and Resources of the British Empire,* 2nd ed. (New York: Johnson Reprint Corp., 1965 [1815]), 68–69.

6. Quoted in Prasannan Parthasarathi, "Rethinking Wages and Competitiveness in the Eighteenth Century: Britain and South India," *Past and Present* 158 (Feb. 1998): 79.

7. Margaret Bryan, *Lectures on Natural Philosophy* (Cambridge: Cambridge University Press, 2011), 16.

8. Thomas Tryon quoted in Sydney W. Mintz, *Sweetness and Power: The Place of Sugar in Modern History* (New York: Penguin Books, 1985), 47–48.

9. Kenneth Pomeranz, *The Great Divergence: China, Europe, and the Making of the Modern World Economy* (Princeton, NJ: Princeton University Press, 2000), 274–276.

10. Quoted in Margaret C. Jacob, *Scientific Culture and the Making of the Industrial West* (New York: Oxford University Press, 1997), 110.

11. E. A. Wrigley and R. S. Schofield, *The Population of England, 1541–1871: A Reconstruction* (Cambridge, MA: Harvard University Press, 1981), 208–209.

12. Elizabeth Bentley, "Evidence Given before the Sadler Committee," *Parliamentary Papers*, 1831–1832, Vol. XV, 44, 95–97, 115, 195, 197, 339, 341–342.

13. Maxine Berg, "What Difference Did Women's Work Make to the Industrial Revolution," in *Women's Work: The English Experience, 1650–1914*, ed. Pamela Sharpe (London: Arnold, 1998), 161.

14. J. F. C. Harrison, *Society and Politics in England, 1780–1960* (New York: Harper & Row, 1965), 71–72.

15. Quoted in Sieferle, *Subterranean Forest*, 170.

16. Michael Chevalier, *United States: Being a Series of Letters on North America* (Boston: Weeks, Jordan and Co., 1839), 169.

17. Maddison, *World Economy*, 263.

18. Karl Marx and Frederick Engels, *The Communist Manifesto* (New York: Verso, 2012), 39.

19. Kennedy, *The Rise and Fall of the Great Powers*, 140.

20. Ssu-yü Teng and John K. Fairbank, *China's Response to the West: A Documentary Survey, 1839–1923* (Cambridge, MA: Harvard University Press, 1982), 19.

21. John Stuart Mill, *On Liberty* (New York: Penguin Books, 1986), 13.

22. David Christian, *Maps of Time: An Introduction to Big History* (Berkeley: University of California Press, 2004), 141; I. G. Simmons, *Changing the Face of the Earth: Culture, Environment, History*, 2nd ed. (Cambridge, MA: Blackwell, 1996), 27.

23. J. R. McNeill, *Something New under the Sun: An Environmental History of the Twentieth-Century World* (New York: Norton, 2000), 315.

24. Vaclav Smil, *Energy in World History* (Boulder, CO: Westview Press, 1994), 226.

chapter 22

1. Quoted in Robert Hughes, *The Fatal Shore: The Epic of Australia's Founding* (New York: Alfred A. Knopf, 1987), 278.

2. Quoted in Walton Look Lai, "Asian Contract and Free Migrations to the Americas," in David Eltis, ed., *Coerced and Free Labor Migrations: Global Perspectives* (Stanford, CA: Stanford University Press, 2002), 246.

3. Benedict Anderson presented the idea of the nation as "imagined community" in *Imagined Communities: Reflections on the Origin and Spread of Nationalism* (New York: Verso, 1983).

4. Karl Marx, *Manifesto of the Communist Party*, authorized English translation edited and annotated by Frederick Engels (London: W. Reeves, 1888).

5. Ponciano Arriaga, quoted in E. Bradford Burns, ed., *Latin America: Conflict and Creation, A Historical Reader* (Englewood Cliffs, NJ: Prentice Hall, 1993), 96.

6. Raja Rammohun Roy, "A Letter on English Education," in *English Works*, Part IV (Calcutta: Sadharan Brahmo Samaj, 1945), 33–36.

7. Michael Geyer and Charles Bright, "Global Violence and Nationalizing Wars in Eurasia and America: The Geopolitics of War in the Mid-Nineteenth Century," *Comparative Studies in Society and History* 38 (Oct. 1996): 619–657.

8. Abraham Lincoln, *Speeches and Writings*, ed. Don E. Fehrenbacher, 2 vols. (New York: Viking, 1989), 2:403.

chapter 23

1. Angus Maddison, *The World Economy: A Millennial Perspective* (Paris: Organization for Economic Co-operation and Development, 2001), 264.

2. T. H. Von Laue, "A Secret Memorandum of Sergei Witte on the Industrialization of Imperial Russia," *Journal of Modern History* 26 (March 1954): 66.

3. Maddison, *The World Economy*, 185.

4. Daniel R. Headrick, *Tentacles of Progress: Technology Transfers in the Age of Imperialism, 1850–1940* (New York: Oxford University Press, 1988), 55; W. Dean Kinzley, "Merging Lines: Organizing Japan's National Railroad, 1906–1914," *Journal of Transport History* 27, no. 2 (Sept. 2006): 48–49; Andrew M. Regalsky, "Foreign Capital, Local Interests and Railway Development in Argentina: French Investments in Railways, 1900–1914," *Journal of Latin American Studies*, 21, no. 3 (Oct. 1989): 427; A. G. Ford, "Capital Exports for Argentina," *Economic Journal* 68, 271 (Sept. 1958): 592.

5. C. T. McClenachan, *Detailed Report of the Proceedings Had in Commemoration of the Successful Laying of the Atlantic Telegraph Cable* (New York: Edmund Jones and Company, 1863), 48.

6. Elisabeth Aryton, *The Cookery of England* (Harmondsworth, UK: Penguin, 1974), 429–430, quoted in Sidney W. Mintz, *Sweetness and Power: The Place of Sugar in Modern History* (New York: Viking, 1985), 120.

7. Quoted in Sven Beckert, "Emancipation and Empire: Reconstructing the Worldwide Web of Cotton Production in the Age of the American Civil War," *American Historical Review* 109 (Dec. 2004): 1405–1438.

8. C. A. Bayly, *The Birth of the Modern World, 1780–1914* (Malden, MA: Blackwell, 2004), 189; Eric Hobsbawm, *The Age of Empire, 1875–1914* (New York: Vintage Books, 1989), 29.

9. Quoted in Mike Davis, *Late Victorian Holocausts: El Niño Famines and the Making of the Third World* (London: Verso, 2001), 107.

10. Niall Ferguson, *Empire: The Rise and Demise of the British World Order and the Lessons of Global Power* (New York: Basic Books, 2002), 201–202.

11. Quoted in Robert G. Athearn, *William Tecumseh Sherman and the Settlement of the West* (Norman: University of Oklahoma Press, 1956), 223.

12. Quoted in Ferguson, *Empire*, 188.

13. Oration of the Ndebele leader Somabulana, quoted in T. O. Ranger, *Revolt in Southern Rhodesia, 1896–97* (Evanston, IL: Northwestern University Press, 1967), 122.

14. Quoted in David K. Wyatt, *Thailand: A Short History*, 2nd ed. (New Haven, CT: Yale University Press, 2003), 197.

part 7

1. J. R. McNeill, *Something New under the Sun: An Environmental History of the Twentieth Century* (New York: Norton, 2000), 15.

2. *World Urbanization Prospects: The 2011 Revision* (New York: United Nations, 2012).

chapter 24

1. John Maynard Keynes, *The Economic Consequences of the Peace* (London: Macmillan, 1919), 101.

2. George Modelski, *World Cities: -3000 to 2000* (Washington, D.C.: Faros2000, 2003), 63.

3. R. Hume, "From Ahmednagar," *New York Times*, November 22, 1896, quoted in Mike Davis, *Late Victorian Holocausts: El Niño Famines and the Making of the Third World* (New York: Verso, 2001), 144.

4. Hermann Buhr Gillomee, *The Afrikaners: Biography of a People* (Charlottesville: University of Virginia Press, 2003), 152.

5. Lionel Kochan, *Russia in Revolution, 1890–1918* (New York: New American Library, 1967), 99.

6. Qiu Jin, "Preoccupation (Written while in Japan)," *Women Writers of Traditional China: An Anthology of Poetry and Criticism*, ed. Kang-I Sun Chang and Haun Saussy (Stanford, CA: Stanford University Press, 1999), 642–643.

7. Ian F. W. Beckett, *The Great War, 1914–1918*, 2nd ed. (London: Pearson Longman, 2007), 438.

8. Siegfried Sassoon, *Counter-Attack and Other Poems* (London: William Heinemann, 1918), 18.

9. Beckett, *The Great War*, 237.

10. Lev Trotsky, *My Life* (Harmondsworth, UK: Penguin, 1975), 351.

11. William Eckhardt, "Water-Related Deaths since 3000 BC," *Bulletin of Peace Proposals*, 22, no. 4 (1991): 437–443.

12. Erez Manela, *The Wilsonian Moment: Self-Determination and the International Origins of Anticolonial Nationalism* (Oxford: Oxford University Press, 2007).

chapter 25

1. Gross domestic product estimates are based on Angus Maddison, Historical Statistics, http://www.ggdc.net/maddison.

2. Angus Maddison, *The World Economy: A Millennial Perspective* (Paris: Organization for Economic Co-operation and Development, 2001), 243.

3. Michael Williams, *Deforesting the Earth: From Prehistory to Global Crisis* (Chicago: University of Chicago Press, 2003), 396.

4. Quoted in Pericles Lewis, *The Cambridge Introduction to Modernism* (Cambridge: Cambridge University Press, 2007), 1.

5. Quoted in Linda Nochin, *Impressionism and Post-Impressionism, 1874–1904* (Englewood Cliffs, NJ: Prentice-Hall, 1966), 8–9.

6. M. M. Khatayevich, quoted in Robert Conquest, *Harvest of Sorrow: Soviet Collectivization and the Terror-Famine* (New York: Oxford University Press, 1986), 261.

7. "A Declaration of Beliefs by the New Youth," in Dun J. Li, ed., *The Road to Communism: China since 1912* (New York: Van Nostrand Reinhold, 1969), 40.

8. Victor Raúl Haya de la Torre, quoted in Thomas E. Skidmore and Peter H. Smith, *Modern Latin America*, 6th ed. (New York: Oxford University Press, 2005), 219.

9. Frederick J. D. Lugard, *The Dual Mandate in British Tropical Africa*, quoted in Philip D. Curtin, ed., *Imperialism* (New York: Harper & Row, 1971), 317.

10. Yogolelo Tambwe ya Kasimba, "*Mission de recrutement des travailleurs de lU.M.H.K. au Kivu-Maniema (1926–1928)*," M.A. thesis, National University of Zaire, quoted in Bruce Fetter, ed., *Colonial Rule in Africa: Readings from Primary Sources* (Madison: University of Wisconsin Press, 1979), 117.

11. Adam McKeown, "Global Migration, 1846–1940," *Journal of World History* 15, no. 2 (June 2004): 167.

12. "Balfour Declaration," quoted in Charles D. Smith, *Palestine and the Arab-Israeli Conflict: A History with Documents*, 8th ed. (Boston: Bedford St. Martin's Press, 2013), 93–94.

13. Quoted in Erez Manela, *The Wilsonian Moment: Self-Determination and the International Origins of Anticolonial Nationalism* (Oxford: Oxford University Press, 2007), 142.

14. Edwin Montagu, Secretary of State for India, quoted in D. George Boyce, *Decolonization and the British Empire* (New York: St. Martin's Press, 1999), 89.

15. M. K. Gandhi, *Indian Home Rule*, 5th ed. (Madras: Ganesh, 1922), 87.

chapter 26

1. "The Way of Subjects," reprinted in Otto D. Tolischus, *Tokyo Record* (New York: Reynal & Hitchcock, 1943), 409, 427.

2. Adolf Hitler, *Mein Kampf*, trans. Ralph Manheim (Boston: Houghton Mifflin 1943), 286.

3. Quoted in Niall Ferguson, *Empire: The Rise and Demise of the British World Order and the Lessons for Global Power* (New York: Basic Books, 2004), 279–280.

4. Hitler, *Mein Kampf*, 255.

5. Ibid., 643.

6. Ibid., 666.

7. Quoted in Haile Selassi, "Address to the League of Nations," in Molefi Kete Asante and Abu S. Abarry, *African Intellectual Heritage: A Book of Sources* (Philadelphia: Temple University Press, 1996), 668.

8. Fred Taylor, trans. and ed., *The Goebbels Diaries, 1939–1941* (New York: G. P. Putnam, 1983), 16, 20.

9. Quoted in William L. Shirer, *The Rise and Fall of the Third Reich* (New York: Simon & Schuster, 1960), 736.

10. R. G. Waldeck, *Athene Palace* (New York: Robert M. McBride, 1942), 124.

11. Quoted in Mark Mazower, *Hitler's Empire: How the Nazis Ruled Europe* (New York: Penguin Press, 2008), 140–141.

12. Quoted in ibid., 144.

13. Quoted in Alvin D. Coox, "The Pacific War," in Peter Duus, *The Cambridge History of Japan*, Vol. 6: *The Twentieth Century* (Cambridge: Cambridge University Press, 1988), 336.

14. Winston Churchill, *The Second World War*, Vol. 3 (Boston: Houghton Mifflin, 1948–1953), 539.

15. "The Battle of Stalingrad," The History Learning Site, http://www.historylearningsite.co.uk/battle_of_stalingrad.htm.

16. Conrad Brandt, Benjamin Schwartz, and John K. Fairbank, eds., *A Documentary History of Chinese Communism* (Cambridge, MA: Harvard University Press, 1952), 83, 84.

17. Quoted in Gabriel Kolko, *The Politics of War: The World and United States Foreign Policy, 1943–1945* (New York: Random House, 1968), 205.

18. Quoted in Gerald D. Feldman, *The Great Disorder: Politics, Economics, and Society in the German Inflation, 1914–1924* (New York: Oxford University Press, 1993), 855.

19. Interview with Olga Mikhaylovna Lisikova, conducted by Oleg Korytov and Konstantin Chirkin, English translation by James F. Gebhardt, St. Petersburg, Dec. 11, 2007, http://lend-lease.airforce.ru/english/index.htm.

20. Quoted in Anne Noggle, *A Dance with Death: Soviet Airwomen in World War II* (College Station: Texas A&M University Press, 1994), 241.

21. Jean-Francois Steiner, *Treblinka* (New York: Simon & Schuster, 1979).

22. J. R. McNeill, *Something New under the Sun: An Environmental History of the Twentieth-Century World* (New York: Norton, 2000), 346.

23. "The Atlantic Charter," August 14, 1941, North Atlantic Treaty Organization (NATO), http://www.nato.int/cps/en/natolive/official_texts_16912.htm.

24. Edmund Jan Ozmanczyk, *Encyclopedia of the United Nations and International Agreements*, 3rd ed., Vol. 4 (New York: Routledge, 2004), 2379.

25. Jawaharlal Nehru, "Reveries in Jail," in *Nehru: The First Sixty Years*, ed. Dorothy Norman, Vol. 2 (New York: John Day, 1965), 142.

26. Quoted in Stephen Ha, ed., *Sources of Indian Tradition*, 2nd ed., Vol. 2, *Modern India and Pakistan* (New York: Columbia University Press, 1988), 230.

27. Quoted in Alfred W. McCoy, "Independence without Decolonization," in Robin Jeffrey, ed., *Asia—The Winning of Independence* (New York: St. Martin's Press, 1981), 26.

chapter 27

1. J. Bolt and J. L. van Zanden. "The First Update of the Maddison Project; Re-Estimating Growth Before 1820." Maddison Project Working Paper 4, 2013.

2. Ronald Pruessen, *John Foster Dulles: The Road to Power* (New York: Free Press, 1982), 309.

3. Richard M. Nixon, *The Challenges We Face: Edited and Compiled from the Speeches and Papers of Richard M. Nixon* (New York: McGraw-Hill, 1960), 220.

4. Tertius Chandler, *Four Thousand Years of Urban Growth: An Historical Census* (Lewiston, NY: St. David's University Press, 1987), 507, 511, 512.

5. Quoted in Frank Mort and Peter Thompson, "Retailing, Commercial Culture and Masculinity in 1950s Britain; The Case of Montague Burton, the 'Tailor of Taste,'" *History Workshop Journal* 38 (1994): 113.

6. Clive Ponting, *A New Green History of the World: The Environment and the Collapse of Great Civilizations* (New York: Penguin, 2007), 258.

7. Andrew P. N. Erdmann, "'War No Longer Has Any Logic Whatever': Dwight D. Eisenhower and the Thermonuclear War," in John Lewis Gaddis et al., eds., *Cold War Statesmen Confront the Bomb: Nuclear Diplomacy since 1945* (Oxford: Oxford University Press, 1999), 113.

8. Michael R. Beschloss, *The Crisis Years: Kennedy and Khrushchev, 1960–1963* (New York: Edward Burlingame, 1991), 278.

9. Nikita S. Khrushchev, *Khrushchev Remembers*, ed. and trans. Strobe Talbot (Boston: Little, Brown, 1970), 493.

10. Richard Wright, *Black Power: A Record of Reactions in a Land of Pathos* (New York: Harper & Brothers, 1954), 75–76.

11. Douglas Little, *American Orientalism: The United States and the Middle East since 1945*, 3rd ed. (Chapel Hill: University of North Carolina Press, 2008), 179.

12. John T. Woolley and Gerhard Peters, The American Presidency Project [online], Santa Barbara, CA, http://www.presidency.ucsb.edu/ws/?pid=27116.

13. Nelson Mandela, *In His Own Words* (New York: Little, Brown, 2003), 28.

14. Betty Friedan, *The Feminine Mystique* (New York: Norton, 1963), 32.

chapter 28

1. Tim Berners-Lee website, http://www.w3.org/People/Berners-Lee/.

2. Worldometers, Real Time World Statistics, http://www.worldometers.info/computers.

3. *2013 Global Manufacturing Competitiveness Index*, Deloitte LLP and U.S. Council on Competitiveness.

4. Index Mundi, Historical Data Graphs per Year, http://www.indexmundi.com; U.S. Central Intelligence Agency, World Factbook, Vietnam, https://www.cia.gov/library/publications/the-world-factbook.

5. Greyhill Advisors, "Manufacturing Output by Country," http://greyhill.com/manufacturing-by-country/.

6. David C. Unger, "Who Can Bring the E.U. to Its Senses?" *New York Times*, March 30, 2013.

7. The Conference Board of Canada, "World Income Inequality," September 2011, http://www.conferenceboard.ca/hcp/hot-topics/worldinequality.aspx.

8. Organization for Economic Cooperation and Development, StatExtracts, Income Distribution-Inequality, http://stats.oecd.org/Index.aspx?DataSetCode=INEQUALITY.

9. Quoted in Thomas E. Skidmore, Peter H. Smith, and James N. Green, *Modern Latin America*, 7th ed. (New York: Oxford University Press, 2010), 69.

10. United Nations, Office of the Special Adviser on Africa, "External Debt in Africa," Policy Brief No. 3 (October 2010).

11. Quoted in "Where Women Are Winning," *Newsweek Magazine*, Sept. 18, 2011.

12. Jose C. Moya and Adam McKeown, "World Migration in the Long Twentieth Century," in *Essays on Twentieth-Century History*, ed. Michael Adas for the American Historical Association (Philadelphia: Temple University Press, 2010), 34.

13. Stephen Castles and Mark J. Miller, *The Age of Migration: International Population Movements in the Modern World*, 4th ed. (New York: Guilford Press, 1993), 119–120.

14. U.S. Central Intelligence Agency, World Factbook, Qatar, https://www.cia.gov/library/publications/the-world-factbook.

15. Richard Morin, "Indentured Servitude in the Persian Gulf," *New York Times*, April 14, 2013.

16. United Nations Office on Drugs and Crime, *Global Report on Trafficking in Persons*, Feb. 2009, http://www.unodc.org/documents/Global_Report_on_TIP.pdf.

17. *The Economist*, Economist Intelligence Unit, "Democracy Index 2012," http://www.eiu.com; Freedom House, "Freedom in the World 2013," www.freedomhouse.org; World Democracy Audit, worldaudit.org.

18. United Nations Charter, Article 42.

19. Akira Iriya, *Global Community: The Role of International Organizations in the Making of the Contemporary World* (Berkeley: University of California Press, 2002), 8.

20. Joshua S. Goldstein, "Think Again: War," *Foreign Policy*, Sept.–Oct. 2011, http://www.foreignpolicy.com/articles/2011/08/15/think_again_war?page=0,0.

21. "Iraqi Deaths from Violence, 2003–2011," Iraq Body Count, http://www.iraqbodycount.org/.

22. Will Steffen, Paul J. Crutzen, and John R. McNeill, "The Anthropocene: Are Humans Now Overwhelming the Great Forces of Nature?" *Ambio* 36, no. 8 (Dec. 2007): 614–621.

23. Fred Spier, *Big History and the Future of Humanity* (Malden, MA: Wiley-Blackwell, 2011), 187–88.

24. John Richards, "Land Transformation," in *The Earth as Transformed by Human Action*, ed. B. L. Turner et al. (Cambridge: Cambridge University Press, 1990), 164.

25. Wangari Maathai, quoted in Nobel Women's Initiative, "Meet the Laureates," http://nobelwomensinitiative.org/meet-the-laureates/wangari-maathai/.

26. Wangari Maathai, quoted in *Los Angeles Times*, September 27, 2011.

Credits

LINE ART/TEXT

Chapter 2

p. 68: Miriam Lichtheim, *Ancient Egyptian Literature*, Volume I: *The Old and Middle Kingdoms*, pp. 118–120. © 1973, 2006 by the Regents of the University of California. Reprinted by permission of the University of California Press.

Chapter 3

p. 98: *Letters from Mesopotamia,* trans. A. Leo Oppenheim, pp. 122ff. Copyright © 1967 by The University of Chicago. Reprinted by permission of The University of Chicago Press.

Chapter 6

pp. 184, 185: "The Edicts of King Ashoka," an English rendering by Ven. S. Dhammika (Kandy, Sri Lanka: Buddhist Publication Society, 1993). © 1993 Buddhist Publication Society. Reprinted with permission.

Chapter 7

p. 204: Laozi, *Dao De Jing: The Book of the Way,* trans. Moss Roberts, p. 90. © 2001 by the Regents of the University of California. Reprinted by permission of the University of California Press.

Chapter 8

p. 234: Reprinted with the permission of Simon & Schuster, Inc. and The Ward & Balkin Agency, Inc. from *Popol Vuh* translated by Dennis Tedlock. Copyright © 1985, 1996 Dennis Tedlock; p. 240: Gordon R. Willey, *Introduction to American Archaeology,* vol. 2: *South America* (Englewood Cliffs, NJ: Prentice-Hall, 1971), Figure 3-38. © 1971 Gordon R. Willey.

Chapter 11

p. 330: *The Vinland Sagas: The Icelandic Sagas about the First Documented Voyages across the North Atlantic,* trans. Keneva Kunz (London and New York: Penguin, 2008), pp. 3–5. Translation copyright © Leifur Eiriksson, 1997. Reprinted by permission of Leifur Eiriksson Publishing Ltd.

Chapter 12

p. 342: Tu Cheng, quoted in Yoshinobu Shiba, *Commerce and Society in Sung China,* trans. Mark Elvin. Michigan Abstracts of Chinese and Japanese Works in Chinese History, no. 2 (Ann Arbor: Center for Chinese Studies, University of Michigan, 1970), pp. 162–163. Reprinted by permission of Center for Chinese Studies, University of Michigan; p. 352: *Letters of Medieval Jewish Traders,* trans. from the Arabic by S. D. Goitein, pp. 222–225. © 1973 Princeton University Press, copyright renewed 2001 by Princeton University Press. Reprinted by permission of Princeton University Press.

Chapter 13

pp. 385 ("When a ship . . ."), 394: Said Hamdun and Noël King, ed. and trans., *Ibn Battuta in Black Africa,* pp. 16, 58–59. Copyright © 1975 by Said Hamdun and Noël King. Reprinted by permission of Markus Wiener Publishers, Princeton, NJ.

Chapter 14

p. 415: Nezahualcoyotl, "The Flower Tree" in *Ancient American Poets,* trans. John Curl. Bilingual Press, 2005; p. 419: Garcilaso de la Vega, *Royal Commentaries of the Incas and General History of Peru,* Part One, trans. Harold V. Livermore (Austin, TX: University of Texas Press, 1966), pp. 204–206. Copyright © 1966 by The University of Texas Press.

Chapter 15

p. 431: M. J. Müller, "Ibnulkhatib's Bericht über die Pest," Sitzungsberichte der Königl. Bayerischen Akademie der Wissenschaften, 2 (1863): pp. 2–12. Translated from the Arabic with assistance from Dr. Walid Saleh. In John Aberth, *The First Horseman: Disease in Human History,* 1st Edition, pp. 44–46, © 2007. Reprinted by permission of Pearson Education, Inc., Upper Saddle River, New Jersey.

Chapter 18

p. 537: Richard Ligon, *The True and Exact History of the Island of Barbadoes, 1657,* ed. J. Edward Hutson (St. Michael, Barbados: Barbados National Trust, 2000), pp. 64, 66–67, 75, 76. Reprinted by permission of the Barbados National Trust.

Chapter 20

p. 598: C. L. R. James, *The Black Jacobins: Toussaint L'Ouverture and the San Domingo Revolution,* 2nd ed. Rev. (New York: Vintage Books, 1963), pp. 195–197. Reprinted by permission of Curtis Brown Group Ltd. (London).

Chapter 22

p. 651: Susan Gilson Miller, trans. and ed., *Disorienting Encounters: Travels of a Moroccan Scholar in France in 1845–46: The Voyage of Muhammad As-Saffar,* pp. 108, 110, 153, 190, 193–194. Copyright © 1992 by The Regents of the University of California. Reprinted by permission of the University of California Press.

Chapter 24

p. 710: Qiu Jin, "Preoccupation (Written while in Japan)" from *Women Writers of Traditional China,* edited by Kang-i Sun Chang and Haun Saussy. Copyright © 2000 by the Board of Trustees of the Leland Stanford Jr. University. With the permission of Stanford University Press, www.sup.org; p. 714: Extracted from ATTACK by Siegfried Sassoon by kind permission of the Estate of George Sassoon.

Chapter 25

p. 751: Charles P. Kindleberger, *World in Depression, 1929–1939,* p. 170 (Figure 10). © 1973, 1986 Deutscher Taschenbuch Verlag. © 1986 Charles P. Kindleberger. Reprinted by permission of the University of California Press.

Chapter 26

p. 771: *Rosie the Riveter*: Words and Music by Redd Evans and John Jacob Loeb. Copyright © 1942 (Renewed 1970, 1998) by Fred Ahlert Music Corporation and John Jacob Loeb Music Company/Administered by BMG Rights Management (US) LLC and Music Sales Corporation (ASCAP). International Copyright Secured. All Rights Reserved. Used by Permission. Reprinted

Michaud/akg-images; p. 382: © dbimages/Alamy; p. 384: © Digital Vision/Punchstock RF; p. 386: © Georg Gerster/Science Source; p. 388: © Sonia Halliday and Laura Lushington/Sonia Halliday Photographs; p. 389: © Prisma Bildagentur AG/Alamy; p. 390: © Kharbine-Tapabor/The Art Archive at Art Resource, NY; p. 393: © Michel Uyttebrioeck/Age Fotostock RF; p. 395: © Dirk Bakker/The Bridgeman Art Library.

Chapter 14

Opener: Photograph © Justin Kerr, K 4440; p. 399(1): © De Agostini/Getty Images; p. 399(2): © Photo Researchers/Photoshot; p. 402: © William R. Iseminger/Cahokia Mounds State Historic Site; p. 402(inset): © Ira Block/National Geographic Creative/Corbis; p. 404: © Walter Rawlings/Robert Harding World Imagery/Corbis; p. 406: © De Agostini/Getty Images; p. 407(top): © Ogphoto/Getty Images RF; p. 407(bottom): © Steve Allen/Getty Images RF; p. 408: © National Geographic Creative/Alamy; p. 409(top): © The Metropolitan Museum of Art. Image source: Art Resource, NY; pp. 409(bottom), 410: © The Trustees of the British Museum/Art Resource, NY; p. 411: © Nigel Pavitt/JAI/Corbis; p. 412: © UIG via Getty Images; p. 415: © David R. Frazier Photolibrary, Inc./Alamy; p. 416: © Spanish School/The Bridgeman Art Library/Getty Images; p. 417: © CarverMostardi/Alamy; p. 421(top): © The Granger Collection, New York; p. 421(bottom): © Photo Researchers/Photoshot.

Chapter 15

Opener: © Erich Lessing/Art Resource, NY; p. 425(1): ©Werner Forman/HIP/The Image Works; p. 425(2): © British Library Board/Robana/Art Resource, NY; p. 425(3): © ullstein bild/The Image Works; p. 429(top): John Montenieri/CDC; p. 429(bottom): © Getty Images/Digital Vision RF; p. 430: © Werner Forman/HIP/The Image Works; p. 432: © British Library Board/Robana/Art Resource, NY; p. 435: © Michael Klinec/Alamy; p. 436: © British Library Board/Robana/Art Resource, NY; p. 437: © The Art Archive at Art Resource, NY; p. 438: © Interfoto/Alamy; p. 440: © Robert Harding Picture Library/SuperStock; p. 441: © Imaginechina/Corbis; p. 442: © Dinodia Stock Connection Worldwide/Newscom; p. 443: © Roland and Sabrina Michaud/akg/The Image Works; p. 444: © ullstein bild/The Image Works; p. 445: © Fogg Art Museum, Harvard University Art Museums, USA/Gift of Sir Joseph Duveen/The Bridgeman Art Library; p. 447: © Italian School, (15th century)/Museo de Firenze Com'era, Florence, Italy/The Bridgeman Art Library; p. 449: © National Gallery, London, UK/The Bridgeman Art Library.

Chapter 16

Part Opener: © The Trustees of the British Museum/Art Resource, NY; p. 454: With permission of the Royal Ontario Museum © ROM; p. 455(1): © The Power of Forever Photography/Getty Images; p. 455(2): © Sofia Pereira/Lusoimages—Palaces/Alamy; p. 455(3): © Mireille Vautier/Alamy; p. 455(4): © Werner Forman/UIG/Age Fotostock; p. 458: © J E Bulloz/DEA/Age Fotostock; p. 460: © Album/Kurwenal/Prisma/Newscom; p. 461: © The Trustees of the British Museum/Art Resource, NY; p. 462: © The Granger Collection, New York; p. 463: © The Power of Forever Photography/Getty Images; p. 465: © Sofia Pereira/Lusoimages—Palaces/Alamy; p. 467: © Everett Collection/Newscom; p. 468(top): © Bridgeman-Giraudon/Art Resource, NY; p. 468(bottom): © North Wind Picture Archives/Alamy; p. 473: © The Granger Collection, New York; p. 474: © Mireille Vautier/Alamy; p. 475: © The Granger Collection, New York; p. 476: © De Agostini/A. Dagli Orti/Getty Images; p. 480: © Werner Forman/UIG/Age Fotostock; p. 481: © Werner Forman/Art Resource, NY.

Chapter 17

Opener: © De Agostini Picture Library/Getty Images; p. 485(1): © TopFoto/The Image Works; p. 485(2): © Historical Archive, Turin, Italy/Index/The Bridgeman Art Library; p. 485(3): © bpk, Berlin/Kupferstichkabinett, Staatliche Museen/Jorg P. Anders/Art Resource, NY; p. 488: © Giulio Veggi/Science Source; p. 490: © The British Library Board/The Image Works; p. 491: © dbimages/Alamy; p. 492: © The Granger Collection, New York; p. 493: © Digital Vision/Punchstock RF; p. 494: © Interfoto/Alamy; p. 495: © TopFoto/The Image Works; p. 498: © De Agostini Picture Library/akg-images; p. 499: © Archivart/Alamy; p. 500: © Ian Nellist/Alamy RF; p. 501: © Historical Archive, Turin, Italy/Index/The Bridgeman Art Library; p. 503: © Private Collection/The Stapleton Collection/The Bridgeman Art Library; p. 508: © bpk, Berlin/Kupferstichkabinett, Staatliche Museen/Jorg P. Anders/Art Resource, NY; p. 509: © Album/Prisma/Newscom; p. 510: © The Jewish Museum, New York/Art Resource, NY.

Chapter 18

Opener: © National Geographic/Getty Images; p. 515(1): © Fotosearch/Getty Images; p. 515(2): © Peter Newark Pictures/The Bridgeman Art Library; p. 515(3): © The Granger Collection, New York; p. 518: © National Maritime Museum, London/The Image Works; p. 519: © Fotosearch/Getty Images; p. 521: © Photo12/UIG/Getty Images; p. 523: © akg-images; p. 524: David Beck, Louis De Geer Photo © Nationalmuseum, Stockholm; p. 525: © The Metropolitan Museum of Art. Image source: Art Resource, NY. Detail; p. 527: © BeBa/Iberfoto/The Image Works; p. 528: © Werner Forman/Art Resource, NY; p. 529: © Peter Newark Pictures/The Bridgeman Art Library; p. 534: © The Granger Collection, New York; p. 536: © Corbis; p. 538: © Art Resource, NY; p. 539: © The Trustees of the British Museum/Art Resource, NY.

Chapter 19

Opener: © North Wind Picture Archives/Alamy; p. 543(1): © Universal History Archive/Getty Images; p. 543(2): © North Wind Picture Archives/Alamy; p. 543(3): © Academy of Natural Sciences of Philadelphia/Corbis; p. 546: © The Metropolitan Museum of Art. Image source: Art Resource, NY; p. 547: © Universal History Archive/Getty Images; p. 548: © Hermitage, St. Petersburg, Russia/The Bridgeman Art Library; p. 549: © The New York Public Library/Art Resource, NY; p. 550: © Breamore House, Hampshire, UK/The Bridgeman Art Library; p. 552: © National Gallery, London/Art Resource, NY; p. 553: © RMN-Grand Palais/Art Resource, NY; p. 554: © Museumslandschaft Hessen Kassel/The Bridgeman Art Library; p. 555: © Mansell/Time Life Pictures/Getty Images; p. 559: © North Wind Picture Archives/Alamy; p. 560: © akg-images/Laurent Lecat/Newscom; p. 561: © The Gallery Collection/Corbis; p. 564: © North Wind Picture Archives/Alamy; p. 565: © Academy of Natural Sciences of Philadelphia/Corbis; p. 569: © akg-images/Gilles Mermet/Newscom; p. 570: © Archivio Storico di Propaganda Fide; p. 571: © Dutch School/Getty Images.

Chapter 20

Part Opener: © SSPL/Science Museum/Art Resource, NY; p. 576: © The Trustees of the British Museum/Art Resource, NY; p. 577(1): © V&A Images, London/Art Resource, NY; p. 577(2): © akg-images/Newscom; p. 577(3): © The Granger Collection, New York; p. 580: © V&A Images, London/Art Resource, NY; p. 582: © De Agostini/Getty Images; p. 585: © Fine Art Images/Age Fotostock; p. 586: © Fotosearch/Getty Images; p. 588: © RMN-Grand Palais/Art Resource, NY; p. 590: © Photo12/UIG/Getty Images; p. 591: © akg-images/Newscom; p. 592: © John Parrot/Stocktrek Images/Getty Images RF; p. 595: © akg-images/Newscom; p. 597: © Bettmann/Corbis; p. 599: © Stock Montage/Getty Images; p. 600: © The Granger Collection, New York; p. 601: © Gianni Dagli Orti/The Art

Archive at Art Resource, NY; p. 603: © Jose Caruci/AP Photo.

Chapter 21

Opener: © Gianni Dagli Orti/The Art Archive at Art Resource, NY; p. 607(1): © Universal History Archive/Getty Images; p. 607(2): © Giraudon/The Bridgeman Art Library; p. 611: Library of Congress, Prints and Photographs Division [LC-USZC4-11219]; p. 612: © Universal History Archive/Getty Images; p. 613: © akg-images/Newscom; p. 616: © Erich Lessing/Art Resource, NY; p. 618: © National Maritime Museum, London/The Image Works; p. 620: © Image Asset Management Ltd./Alamy; p. 621: © Pictorial Press Ltd/Alamy; p. 623: © Archives Charmet/The Bridgeman Art Library; p. 625: © Fotosearch/Getty Images; p. 626: © Giraudon/The Bridgeman Art Library; p. 629: © Hulton Archive/Getty Images; p. 631: Library of Congress, Prints and Photographs Division [LC-USZ62-101759].

Chapter 22

Opener: © SSPL/Getty Images; p. 635(1): Library of Congress, Prints and Photographs Division [LC-USZ62-105116]; p. 635(2): © Hulton Archive/Getty Images; p. 635(3): © Roger-Viollet/The Image Works; p. 635(4): © The Granger Collection, New York; p. 638: © Culver Pictures/The Art Archive at Art Resource, NY; p. 639: Library of Congress, Prints and Photographs Division [LC-USZ62-105116]; p. 641: © Stapleton Collection/Corbis; p. 642: © North Wind Picture Archives/AP Photo; p. 644: © The Granger Collection, New York; p. 645: © Francois Rude/The Bridgeman Art Library/Getty Images; p. 646: © Hulton Archive/Getty Images; p. 647: © Bettmann/Corbis; p. 649: © Interfoto/Alamy; p. 650: Library of Congress, Prints and Photographs Division [LC-USZ62-77267]; p. 653: Yale Collection of Western Americana, Beinecke Rare Book and Manuscript Library; p. 654: © Roger-Viollet/The Image Works; p. 655: © BL/Robana/Age Fotostock; p. 656: © ullstein bild/The Granger Collection, New York; p. 659: © The Granger Collection, New York; p. 661: © Mary Evans Picture Library/The Image Works.

Chapter 23

Opener: © akg-images/Newscom; p. 665(1): © ullstein bild/The Granger Collection, New York; p. 665(2): © Amoret Tanner/Alamy; p. 665(3): © Silvio Fiore/TopFoto/The Image Works; p. 667: © ullstein bild/The Granger Collection, New York; p. 669: © The Granger Collection, New York; p. 671: © ullstein bild/The Granger Collection, New York; p. 672: © Mary Evans/ Grenville Collins/The Image Works; p. 674: © DeAgostini/Getty Images; p. 675: © Amoret Tanner/Alamy; p. 677: © Bettmann/Corbis; p. 678: © HIP/The Image Works; p. 679: Image from Honda, Kinkichiro, Kiyochika Kobayashi, Ai Maeda, and Isao Shimizu. 1985. *Jiyu minkenki no manga.* Tokyo: Chikuma Shobo: p. 35. Photo: Library of Congress [JC599.J3 J58 1985 Japan]; p. 680: © adoc-photos/Corbis; p. 683: © Cultural Heritage Images/Universal Images Group/Newscom; p. 685: © Corbis; p. 686: © Lordprice Collection/Alamy; p. 688: © Albert Harlingue/Roger Viollet/Getty Images; p. 690: © Hulton Archive/Getty Images; p. 691: © Silvio Fiore/TopFoto/The Image Works.

Chapter 24

Part Opener: © eye35.pix/Alamy; p. 696: © Corbis; p. 697(1): © Corbis/Age Fotostock RF; p. 697(2): © Bettmann/Corbis; p. 697(3): Library of Congress, Prints and Photographs Division [LC-USZC4-11161]; p. 700: © Corbis/Age Fotostock RF; p. 701: © Image Asset Management Ltd./Alamy; p. 702: © The Gallery Collection/Corbis © 2013 Estate of Pablo Picasso/Artists Rights Society (ARS), New York; p. 704: © Ariadne Van Zandbergen/Alamy; p. 705: © Gardiner F. Williams/National Geographic Creative/Corbis; p. 706: © Ingram Publishing RF; p. 707: © akg-images/RIA Nowosti/Newscom; p. 709: © The Granger Collection, New York; p. 710: © Xia Gongran Xinhua News Agency/Newscom; p. 712: © Bettmann/Corbis; p. 713: © Bettmann/Corbis; p. 716: © Roger Viollet/Getty Images; p. 717: © Robert Hunt Library/Mary Evans/The Image Works; p. 718: Library of Congress Prints, and Photographs Division [LC-USZC4-11161]; p. 720: © Mary Evans/Meledin Collection/The Image Works; p. 721: © akg-images/Alamy; p. 723: © The National Archives UK.

Chapter 25

Opener: © The Art Archive/Kharbine-Tapabor/Coll. Perrin; p. 729(1): John Gordon Rideout (American, 1898–1951). Radio, 1930–1933. Plaskon (plastic), metal, glass, 11¾ × 8⅞ × 7½ in. (29.8 × 22.5 × 19.1 cm). Brooklyn Museum, Purchased with funds given by The Walter Foundation, 85.9; p. 729(2): © Corbis; p. 729(3): © akg-images/The Image Works; p. 732: John Gordon Rideout (American, 1898–1951). Radio, 1930–1933. Plaskon (plastic), metal, glass, 11¾ × 8⅞ × 7½ in. (29.8 × 22.5 × 19.1 cm). Brooklyn Museum, Purchased with funds given by The Walter Foundation, 85.9; p. 733: © UPPA/Photoshot © 2013 Artists Rights Society (ARS), New York/ProLitteris, Zurich; p. 734: © Keystone-France/Gamma-Keystone via Getty Images; p. 736: © Bettmann/Corbis; p. 737: © Corbis; p. 738: © Bettmann/Corbis; p. 739: © Underwood & Underwood/Corbis; pp. 740, 743: © Bettmann/Corbis; p. 747: © Robert Sennecke/ullstein bild/The Image Works; p. 748: © Bettmann/Corbis; p. 749: © akg-images/The Image Works; p. 752: © Keystone-France/Gamma-Keystone via Getty Images; p. 753: © Popperfoto/Getty Images.

Chapter 26

Opener: © ullstein bild/akg-images; p. 757(1): © DIZ Muenchen GmbH, Sueddeutsche Zeitung Photo/Alamy; p. 757(2): © Laski Diffusion/Getty Images; p. 757(3): © Bettmann/Corbis; p. 759: © ullstein bild/The Granger Collection, New York; p. 761: © bpk, Berlin/Art Resource, NY; p. 762: © DIZ Muenchen GmbH, Sueddeutsche Zeitung Photo/Alamy; p. 763: © TopFoto/The Image Works; p. 765: © Laski Diffusion/Getty Images; p. 768: © SZ Photo/Scherl/The Image Works; p. 769: © Sovfoto/UIG via Getty Images; p. 770: © Hulton-Deutsch Collection/Corbis; p. 772: © Oleg Korytov Collection via Ilya Grinberg; p. 773: National Archives and Records Administration [NWDNS-208-AA-206K(31)]; p. 775: National Archives and Records Administration [NWDNS-208-COM-189]; p. 776(left): © Eileen Tweedy/The Art Archive at Art Resource, NY; p. 776(right): © Peter Newark Military Pictures/The Bridgeman Art Library; pp. 777, 778: © Bettmann/Corbis; p. 783: © AP Photo; p. 784: © John Florea/Time & Life Pictures/Getty Images; p. 785: © Bettmann/Corbis.

Chapter 27

Opener: © Detlev van Ravenswaay/Science Source; p. 789(1): © National Railway Museum/SSPL/The Image Works; p. 789(2): Library of Congress, Prints & Photographs Division, drawing by Edmund S. Valtman [LC-DIG-ppmsc-07978]; p. 789(3): © Keystone-France/Gamma-Keystone via Getty Images; pp. 793, 794: © Everett Collection/Age Fotostock; p. 796: © Paul Almasy/Corbis; p. 798: © National Railway Museum/SSPL/The Image Works; p. 799: © National Geographic/Getty Images; p. 800: © TopFoto/The Image Works; p. 801: © Bettmann/Corbis; p. 803: Library of Congress, Prints & Photographs Division, drawing by Edmund S. Valtman [LC-DIG-ppmsc-07978]; p. 805: © Keystone-France/Gamma-Keystone via Getty Images; p. 808: © Bettmann/Corbis; p. 810: © Nik Wheeler/Corbis; p. 812: © Africa Media Online/The Image Works; p. 813(top, bottom): © AP Photo; p. 814: © CTK/Alamy.

Chapter 28

Index

Justinian (Byzantine emperor), 249, 260
Juvaini, Ata Malik, 373

K

Ka'ba, 285, *285*, 287, *287*
Kahlo, Frida, *734*
Kaifeng, *338*, 343
Kamakura shogunate (Japan), 345–346, 377
Kaminaljuyú, 226–227
Kanem, 324
Kanem empire, 395
Kangxi (Chinese emperor), 546, *547*
Kanishka (Kushana king), 208
Kano, 657
Kant, Immanuel, 566, 567
Das Kapital (Marx), 646
Karakorum, 374
karma, 155, 181
Kassites, 96, 99
Kay, John, 612, 631
Kemble, Fanny, 606–607
Kennan, George, 779
Kennedy, John F., 802, 803
Kennewick Man, *35*, 36
Kenya, 807, 849
Kenyatta, Jomo, 807
Kepler, Johannes, 564, 565, 566
Kerma, 97
Keynes, John Maynard, 699, 751, 826
Keynesianism, 751–752, 826, 827
khagan, 283
Khazaria, 283, *283*, 329
Khmer state, 384, *384*
Khoikhoi people, 274
Khoisan people, 104–105, 561, 562, 563
Khosrow I (Sasanid emperor), 261
Khosrow II (Sasanid emperor), 253
Khrushchev, Nikita, 793, *793*, 803, 815
Khurasan, 290, 312
Khwarizm, 373, 380
al-Khwarizmi, Muhammad ibn, 317–318
Kiev, 329, 331, 377
Kikkuli, 95
Kilwa, 385
Kim Il-Sung, 801
King, Martin Luther, Jr., 811
The King and I, 690
kinship groups, 89, 292–293, 373–374
Kipchak khanate (Golden Horde), 374, 377, 379, 429, 433
Kitans, 341
Kitchen Debate, *793*
Kiuic, 233, 235, *235*
Knights Hospitaller, 362
Knights Templar, 362
Knossos, 82
Knutsson, Bengt, 431
Koine Greek, 179, 181
Kolkata (Calcutta), 530, 583
Kongo, 461–462, 466–467, *467*, 532, 539, 570, 571
Koran. *See* Quran
Korea
    Choson dynasty, 439, 495
    independence (1945), 777
    Japanese invasion (1910), 684
    Korean War, 801–802, *801*, 840
    Koryo dynasty, 345, 375
    post–World War II period, 786
    printing, *345*, 438
    Silla dynasty, 321, 322, *322*, 345
Korean War, 801–802, *801*, 840
Koryo dynasty (Korea), 345, 375
Kosovo, 840–841
Kosygin, Alexei, 794
Krak des Chevaliers, *362*
Kritovoulos, 444–445
Krupp, Alfred, 680
Krupp, Friedrich, 680

Kshatriya class, 153, 181
Kuala Lumpur, 746
Kubilai Khan (Mongol leader), 374–375, 376, 379, 380, 381, 384
Kunlun Mountains, 9
Kush, 151–152, 191, 208–209, *209*, 211
Kushana empire, 191, 207–208, *207*, 215, 251, 253–254, 264, 271
Kuwait, 836, 840
Kyoto (Heian), 321, 345, *528*

L

labor movements, 620, 621, 677–678, 706–707, 717–718, 743. *See also* socialism; working classes
Labors of the Months, *293*
Lady Dai, 203
Lady Hao, 87
Lady Xoc, 231, *231*
Laetoli, 20
Laguna de los Cerros site, 120
laissez faire, 632
Lake Chad, 324
Lake Titicaca, 117, 410, 417
La Mojarra Stele, 121, *121*
The Landing of Jan van Riebeeck (Bell), *561*
land masses, 4–6
language
    origins of, 30–33, *31*
    as root of culture, 31, 40–41
    See also languages
language death, 505
languages
    Achaemenid empire, 168
    Arabic, 279, 289, 292, 316, 326, 385, 511
    Australia, 125
    Austronesian, 105
    Axum, 211
    Celtic, 150
    Dravidian, 101, 152, 318
    Eskimo-Aleut language, 121
    extinction of, 505
    Farsi, 101, 161, 168, 316, 511
    Finno-Ugric, 328
    Germanic, 292
    Greek, 169, 179, 181, 199–200, 213, 511
    Indic, 100–101
    Indo-European, 92–93, *92*, 150, 152, 186
    Italic, 193
    Kush, 209
    Latin, 193, 200, 292, 364
    Linear A, 82
    Linear B, 99
    lingua fraca, 99, 179, 213, 529
    Mande, 272
    Mesoamerica, 229
    Na-Dene, 121
    Niger-Congo, 105, 324
    Oceania, 126, 128
    Papuan, 126
    Parthian empire, 207
    Romance languages, 292
    Roman empire, 193, 199–200
    Semitic, 95, 150, 168, 211
    Slavic, 292
    South Asia, 150, 152
    Turkish, 348, 349, 511, 742
    upper Paleolithic, 44
    vernacular, 388, 509–511
    See also writing
Lanzón stele, 240, *240*
Lápida de Bazán, *229*
lapis lazuli, 48–49, *48*
Lapita style, 127, *127*, 128
lateen sails, 213, 464
latifundia, 196
Latin America
    abolition of slavery, 652–653, 660
    debt crisis, 834

Great Depression, 752
    immigration, 732
    industrialization, 795
    influenza pandemic (1918–1919), 724
    interwar period, 742–743
    maps, *602*
    middle class, 679
    nationalism, 645, 653, 743
    revolutionary movements (1720–1830 C.E.), 577, 599–603, *600*, *602*
    social protest, 812
    U.S. role, 742, 778, 802–803
    War of the Triple Alliance, 658
    women, 603, 653, 743, 795
    and World War II, 774
Latin language, 193, 200, 292, 364
latitude, 6
La Venta site, 120
law
    Babylonian empire, *95*, 96
    Byzantine empire, 260
    China, 299
    Christian, 358
    Islamic, 310, *310*, 354, 488, 583
    Napoleonic Code, 593, 594, 650
    Roman empire, 198
    Spanish colonies in the Americas, 549
    Turkey, 742
law code of Hammurabi, *95*, 96
Lawrence, T. E., 716
League of Nations, 724, 743, 748, 759, 761, 762, *762*
Lebanon, 748, 781, 846
lebensraum, 761
Lectures on Natural Philosophy (Bryan), 618
Legalism, 201, 202
legal systems. *See* law
Lend-Lease Program, 765
Lenin, V. I., 707, 719, 720, 724, 736
Leo Africanus, 501
Leo III (Byzantine emperor), 291
Leo III (pope), 295, *297*
Leonardo da Vinci, 449
Leone, Sergio, 798
Leonowens, Anna, 690
Leopold I (Austro-Hungarian emperor), 554
Leopold II (king of Belgium), 681, 682, 683–684, 687
A Letter Concerning Toleration (Locke), 567
Letters on the Female Mind (Hawkins), 567
Levant, 73, 82, 137. *See also* Mediterranean basin; Middle East; Southwest Asia
Liao state, 341, 345
liberalism, 631–632
    and abolitionism, 637
    China, 711
    Latin America, 652–653, 711
    Muslim lands, 649–650
    Ottoman empire, 650, 708
liberation theology, 812
Libya, 768, 845, 846
life expectancy, 580, 731. *See also* population growth/decline
Ligon, Richard, 537
Li Hung Chang, *686*
Lima, 549
Limited Test Ban Treaty, 802
Lincoln, Abraham, 660–661
Lindisfarne, 327–328
lineage groups, 89, 186
Linear A, 82
Linear B, 99
lingua fraca, 99, 179, 213, 529
Linnaeus, Carl, 566, 567
Lion Gate (Hattusa), *93*
lion pillar (Vaishali), *183*
Lisikova, Olga, 772, *772*
literature
    ancient Greece, 99, 169
    China, 157